Handbook of Research in Mobile Business:
Technical, Methodological, and Social Perspectives

Second Edition

Bhuvan Unhelkar
MethodScience.com
University of Western Sydney, Australia

INFORMATION SCIENCE REFERENCE

Hershey · New York

Director of Editorial Content: Kristin Klinger
Director of Production: Jennifer Neidig
Managing Editor: Jamie Snavely
Assistant Managing Editor: Carole Coulson
Typesetter: Larissa Vinci
Cover Design: Lisa Tosheff
Printed at: Yurchak Printing Inc.

Published in the United States of America by
        Information Science Reference (an imprint of IGI Global)
        701 E. Chocolate Avenue, Suite 200
        Hershey PA 17033
        Tel: 717-533-8845
        Fax: 717-533-8661
        E-mail: cust@igi-global.com
        Web site: http://www.igi-global.com

and in the United Kingdom by
        Information Science Reference (an imprint of IGI Global)
        3 Henrietta Street
        Covent Garden
        London WC2E 8LU
        Tel: 44 20 7240 0856
        Fax: 44 20 7379 0609
        Web site: http://www.eurospanbookstore.com

Library of Congress Cataloging-in-Publication Data

Handbook of research in mobile business : technical, methodological and social perspectives / Bhuvan Unhelkar, editor. -- 2nd ed.

    p. cm.

Includes bibliographical references and index.

Summary: "This book collects the latest research advances in the rapidly evolving field of mobile business"--Provided by publisher.

ISBN 978-1-60566-156-8 (hardcover) -- ISBN 978-1-60566-157-5 (ebooki)

1. Mobile commerce. 2. Mobile communication systems--Economic aspects. I. Unhelkar, Bhuvan.

HF5548.34.H36 2009

658'.05--dc22

                        2008028573

British Cataloguing in Publication Data
A Cataloguing in Publication record for this book is available from the British Library.

All work contributed to this book is original material. The views expressed in this book are those of the authors, but not necessarily of the publisher.

Dedication

Keshav Raja

Editorial Advisory Board

List of Contributors

Table of Contents

Section III: Technology, Networks and Security

Detailed Table of Contents

Section I: Strategies and Methods

This opening chapter of the handbook approximately highlights the most important aspect of any technology to business – and that is "value". Value of mobile technologies in business accrues when the technology is applied in the economic as well as social dimension of the business. Younessi, through his unique style that combines theory, research, and practice, highlights this importance of mobile technology and its relevance in creating sustainability in business. The long-term strategic approach of all modern businesses needs to incorporate location and time independence as a fundamental that is provided by mobility. This chapter will provide the reader with an excellent understanding of what is implied by the term "value" in the context of mobile business, its variations such as utility value, exchange value and essential value, and a mathematical background for calculation of value. The chapter finally concludes with identification and optimization of organizational goals in the context of mobility.

The fundamentals of business economics and decision making are quite close to the theory of games. Therefore, it is only appropriate that game theory is used in providing tools, technologies, and applications that deal with business decision making. Mobile technologies and the resultant location-independence have immense potential to improve business decision making. The reason for the importance of game theory in the context of mobile business and technologies is the fact the game theory deals primarily with distributed optimization. This distributed optimization implies the opportunity for an individual user to make his or her decision in their own time and space. This chapter is an excellent introduction to strategic utilization of mobility as it considers the fundamentals of game theory and its demonstration in mobile business and technologies.

Collaboration between businesses is the key to the future of the economic environment of the future. Mobile technology provides and enhances the ability of businesses to collaborate with each other. However, this collaboration becomes unique and challenging when there are numerous small and medium enterprises (SMEs) involved in that collaboration. While collaborations hold the promise for global reach in a connected economy, there is a need to have a formal approach to transforming those organizations to mobile collaborative organizations. Mobile transformation was proposed by the author in the previous edition of this book. In this chapter, Marmaridis does an excellent job of presenting a research-based methodology for mobile collaboration (M-Collaboration). This chapter examines the challenges of mobile collaborations including trust, engagement, and interaction. This chapter provides the reader with a comprehensive understanding of mobile collaboration in the SME space and a field-tested mobile collaboration methodology for SME transformations.

Chapter IV

Jhoanna Rhodette Pedrasa, University of New South Wales, Australia
Eranga Perera, National ICT Australia, Australia
Aruna Seneviratne, National ICT Australia, Australia

The authors in this chapter, discuss one of the most significant aspect of mobile technologies – that of "context". While mobility is touted as the key technology that enables location-independence, this value of this location-independence to a user is based on his or her context. It is the context that makes a mobile application relevant to the user. This chapter takes the reader through a definition and discussion on what is implied by context and how context can be used in mobile systems. The challenges to context-aware mobility management are discussed next and the existing solutions to those challenges are surveyed. However, the authors then present their own architecture for handling context in mobile solutions.

Chapter V

Robert Harmon, Portland State University, USA
Tugrul Daim, Portland State University, USA

Location-based services (LBS) through the use of mobile technologies in business are based on the ability of mobile technologies to be able to provide value at a specific location of the user. The popularity and utility of LBS has lead to phenomenal technological infrastructure including networks, applications, and processes. However, at the same time, there are increasing challenges emerging due to the operational models of cellular network operators. These operational models provide competition between the operators, service providers, and enablers. Therefore, even though the customers are increasingly interested in location services, their uptake is stunted due to the competitive operational models of the network operators and service providers. Harmon and Daim do an excellent job, in this chapter, of evaluating the future of location-based services through a discussion and critical assessment of mobile technologies, service provision, mobile applications, the current market trends, and the issues related to strategic approaches in application of mobility in business.

Chapter VI

Bhuvan Unhelkar, MethodScience.com & University of Western Sydney, Australia

Mobile enterprises adopt mobile technologies in a strategic manner. This adoption of mobility by enterprises, however, needs to follow a process. A mobile enterprise transition framework provides this process for transition that is based on the meticulous consideration of the factors that affect transition. This chapter outlines a Mobile Enterprise Transition (MET) framework, for transitioning an organization to a mobile organization that is based on the dimensions of economic, technology, process, and sociology. These four dimensions for MET have been identified based on an understanding of people, processes, and technologies, and developed further as a comprehensive framework based on a detailed research project undertaken by the author. The purpose of this MET framework is to provide guidance and support that increases the chances of the transition's success as well as ameliorate associated risks.

Mobile collaboration is of ever increasing importance to business. Web Services (WS) technologies create the potential for an organization to collaborate with partners and customers by enabling its software applications to transact over the Internet. Mobile Web Services (MWS) take this collaborative ability of businesses a step further by making it location-independent. A vital element of this transition of organizations to collaborative organizations is a mobile process. A mobile process makes use of MWS as well as a mobile-enabled Service Oriented Architecture (SOA) for the enterprise. This chapter describes how the existing business processes of an organization are transitioned in to collaborative business processes that would result in a mobile Collaborative Web Based System (CWBS). This incorporation of MWS in a collaborative system happens at three interrelated yet distinct layers: policies, activities, and standards. This chapter develops these ideas and also presents the validation of these ideas through an action-research carried out by the authors in a large energy supplier organization in Melbourne, Australia.

Chapter VIII

Mobile technologies result in a collaborative business environment in which the businesses are able to interact with each other in a location-independent manner. The business processes based on mobile technologies need to be modelled, studied, and optimized in order to create value to the collaborative businesses. This chapter describes an action research study in a security organization wherein the impact of mobile technology is studied and validated for collaborative business processes in a security business. The chapter, thus, describes a Collaborative Web Based System (CWBS) that is specific to the security organization. Furthermore, this chapter also highlights the shortcomings of the existing security related processes and how they can be improved with mobility.

Chapter IX

The Internet wave that swept through business is likely to be seen as a ripple in a pond compared to the changes that are predicted from the adoption of mobility into business. Irrespective of industry sector, the mobile enablement (wrapping business around mobility) of business is expected to bring many opportunities and rewards; and like the Web enablement (wrapping business around the Internet) of business, a few challenges as well. Across all business areas, mobile business will need to support a mobile workforce, the operation of call (service) centres, and transaction processing and collaboration of virtual teams. Mobile business will also impact product offerings, the management of consumer choice and the focusing of communications with a sticky message. Mobile business will drive changes in management, revisions of business operations and the alignment of Information Communication Technology (ICT). This chapter discusses some of the common but important strategic elements to the successful mobile enablement of business.

Chapter X

Mobile business strategies help businesses make optimum use of mobile technologies as the prevent over spending or under utilization of the potential of mobile applications. A mobile strategic framework, as described in this chapter, provides the businesses with the necessary guidance in terms of approach, adoption, and operation of mobile applications. This chapter also discusses examples of mobile solutions which have been implemented in hospitals, retail Supply Chain Management (SCM) and in Customer Relationship Management (CRM). The mobile framework discussed here by Pg Hj Ali and Atkins is an extension of existing Intranet, Extranet, and Internet e-business application with mobility.

Chapter XI

Mobile computing is getting more and more attention these days, but the fact that there is still inadequate source of methodology to support mobile development, triggers the interest in this study to explore issues related to mobile development methodologies. The mobile developers are facing formidable challenges in the development of mobile application due to the specific demand and technical constraints of mobile environment. Selecting a suitable development methodology is believed to be the key answer to all these issues. Thus, this study aimed to propose a solution to resolve the issues. A decision matrix based on Pugh method was constructed to assist mobile developers especially the novices, to choose the methodology that suits the requirements of their mobile development projects. In order to rate the usefulness of the constructed matrix, an electronic version of the matrix was designed and developed, called md-Matrix. Detail descriptions of the processes involved in constructing the matrix and designing the electronic version of the constructed matrix are also described. Analysis of data gathered from a questionnaire given after the test of md-Matrix shows that participants fairly agreed that md-Matrix is useful in helping them to develop a mobile application.

Chapter XII

Studies on the use of mobile payment (m-payment) method for buying electronic book (e-book) are very scarce, possibly not yet available. Consequently, a study was undertaken to accomplish the main aim of proposing an m-payment model for marketing and purchasing e-books. A number of process flow models are proposed to serve as diagrammatic representations of the process models that are of concerned. The models clearly specify all the entities involved, such as Telco, merchants, buyers, and e-book providers, and how the data and transactions, are flowing from one entity to another. The processes of browsing, buying, and downloading e-books are also documented. In validating the process flow models, two prototypes, a WAP and WEB environments, were developed and tested to assess the model and system acceptance rating. Key findings indicate that m-payment is the most preferred payment method for buying e-book in higher learning institutions and the acceptance factors of such technology were found to be on the high and positive side.

Dilupa Ranatunga, University of Colombo, Sri Lanka
Rasika Withanage, University of Wales, UK
Dinesh Arunatileka, Freelance, Sri Lanka

This chapter describes marketing strategies in concept for wireless broadband services in the Sri Lankan market. It also emphasizes different technologies offering fixed and mobile broadband services. Wi-Fi services which are mentioned here has been on offer for few years but actual marketing of such services are not actively done in Sri Lanka. Various marketing strategies that could be used to market this technology are also analyzed to gain an insight to all readers. In addition, a grid is provided to help readers to choose between different available technologies.

Amit Lingarchani, University of Technology, Sydney, Australia

Mobility has a major impact on the collaborative abilities of business processes. This chapter discusses an approach to extending the collaborative business process model with mobility. Furthermore, this chapter also demonstrates how the mobile collaborative approach works in the "Medical Tourism" industry. Specifically, this chapter considers the booming Medical Tourism industry in India, which combines the travel of a person from a typical western nation (such as United States, United Kingdom, or Australia) to India to carry out a medical procedure (such as a heart operation) which would otherwise take a long waiting time and/or cost in multiples. There is a corresponding need and opportunities for collaboration between various available services like lodging, transport, pharmacies, insurance, and hospital organizations. This collaboration is important for the business and also for the consumer – the patient and the caregivers associated with the patient.

Rok Rupnik, University of Ljubljana, Slovenia

Mobile application development needs to handle the nuances of mobility as the process for development can be different. The mobile applications development methodology therefore needs to focus on the uniqueness of mobile applications, which is context-based computing. The mobile applications development methodology in this chapter is based on the research of the author that results in appropriate development phases and tasks which are carried out in order to produce a robust mobile application.

Keith Sherringham, IMS Corp, Australia
Bhuvan Unhelkar, MethodScience.com & University of Western Sydney, Australia

Value of business decision making depends on the availability of the required data and information at the right place and right time. This availability of information results in what is understood as knowledge to the business. Information Communication Technology (ICT) has been used to discern knowledge from data which can then be effectively converted to wisdom by the decision makers. This chapter goes into the details of how mobility is ideally positioned to provide knowledge and wisdom to the business decision makers through the location-independent correlation between variously located data and information.

Mobile Sales Force Automation can enhance the ability of sales teams to streamline their sales, supply chain and distribution networks. The ability of mobility to optimize the sales processes is further capitalized, as discussed in this chapter, by integrating sales-related software applications on a common mobile platform for business software. This integrated mobile platform and its relevance to sales is the core theme of this chapter.

Chapter XVIII

Mobile application development can succeed only when it is supported by corresponding software development processes. The authors have discovered that no one particular type of software process (such as waterfall, iterative, rapid, or agile) is suitable exclusively for a development project. This chapter presents the use of Composite Application Software Development Process Framework (CASDPF) that brings together the best of each of these types of processes for Mobile Applications Development.

Chapter XIX

This chapter is based on the need to have a strategic approach to incorporate mobile devices and their corresponding software and applications in an organization-wide strategy. The literature in this chapter deals with the common mobile devices, their operating systems and their critical applications. This literature study provides further basis for how to balance budgets and goals with the available mobile technologies in a strategic manner.

Chapter XX

Mobile technologies provide enormous opportunities for globalization. Mobile enables location-independent connectivity that forms the core of the globalization strategy of any organization. This chapter discusses the importance of strategic approach to the globalization with mobile business that results in sustainable competitive advantage.

Chapter XXI

The Model Driven Architecture (MDA) is an initiative of the Object Management Group (OMG) that considers visual modelling as crucial basis for future application development. This same MDA provides opportunity to deliver user driven solutions that unify solutions architecture, information management and business integration. MDA-based approach to mobile development is presented in this chapter together with some of the challenges and opportunities in using a business driven Model Driven Architecture approach.

Section II: Sociology and Culture

While Web services provide the opportunity to integrate various processes, mobile technologies create the opportunities to personalize them. This composite process-personalization (CPP) is nicely discussed in this chapter by Sadashivam and Tanik. In addition to the technical challenges, the CPP also addresses the need to model and integrate the interaction workers who drive the business processes. The chapter here outlines an agent-based approach to composite services development and demonstrates that approach in practice through a case study.

The "disruptive" nature of mobile technologies implies significant impact on the cultural aspects of a society. Conversely, the culture that is made up of the needs, beliefs and norms of a society also impact the usage of mobility. This chapter by Wagner and Klaus studies this significant cultural aspect of mobility by highlighting cultures' differences and their consequences for the diffusion of mobile technologies in business and society, as well as its acceptance in mobile direct marketing and mobile commerce.

The usability aspects of mobile gadgets play a crucial role in their acceptance by the users. Furthermore, this challenge of usability is exacerbated by the ongoing integration and convergence between mobile and wired networks and services. For example, the available bandwidth of a wireless connection, Web navigation on a wireless application and the various input-output methods for such applications are all part of the usability challenges of mobility – especially if the mobile applications are being offered on a common integrated platform. This chapter by Gurau takes a research-based approach in studying the challenges in terms of usability faced by mobile gadget users. The survey conducted for this chapter is based in the city of Montpellier in France.

Personalization of mobile devices opens up the gates for direct and focused marketing for businesses. Promotion of products and services has, thus, undergone a major revolution – with the mobile technologies providing appealing interfaces and presentations based on timing and location of the user. However, there is also a need to balance these advantages with the potential rejection and backlash by the customers if they consider this as an intrusion of their privacy. Wagner and Klaus discuss and demonstrate, with examples, this interesting aspect of direct marketing by businesses based on the mobile device usage in this chapter.

The chapter presents an excellent analysis of the influence of mobile user experience, ICT ownership, Mobile affinity, and Mobile Commerce compatibility in the Mobile-Commerce adoption processes. This chapter is based on an empirical study of 470 mobile users in the context of the Spanish market.

Mobility and the Internet have revolutionized the tourism industry leading to novice ways of utilizing these communications medium, such as medical tourism discussed elsewhere in this handbook. This particular chapter by Guzzo, Ferri, and Grifoni outlines the use of mobile and Web technologies in coordinating a travel plan. For example, through a combination of mobile Web, the potential traveler can search for various options for his or her travel, plan the travel, buy the tickets, and actually undertake the travel with the potential for dynamically changing the travel plan. This chapter is thus an excellent addition to the discussion on the social implications of Web applications and mobile devices and how they positively impact the attitude of the customers that can result in sustainable tourism.

Trust is, by far, the most important social aspect in adoption of mobility. This chapter by Karjaluoto and Kautonen goes deeper into this issue of trust that affects the consumers' desire to offer their personal data in mobile marketing. This discussion in this research-based chapter is based on a sampled survey of 200 young Finnish consumers of mobility that lead the authors to conclude that the main source of trust affecting the consumers' decision to participate in mobile marketing is the company's media presence, rather than personal experiences or social influence.

Chapter XXIX

Mobile virtual communities affect all dimensions of life including education, travel, governance, and healthcare. This chapter is based on the impact of mobile virtual communities in the healthcare arena. Mobile virtual healthcare communities are the hub of information exchange amongst patients and physicians. This information sharing is helping in providing pre- and post-event support for the patients as well as exchange of relevant information amongst doctors and other healthcare professionals – as discussed here.

Chapter XXX

Amongst the wide-ranging impacts of mobility on society, adolescents form a special and significant part. The authors in this chapter discuss this impact of mobility on the adolescent social structure including the parents, the teachers, peers/friends, and the young adolescents themselves. This chapter is based on a small research project to ascertain the views of the adolescents and the teachers of young adolescents within the Indian context.

Chapter XXXI

Heikki Karjaluoto, University of Oulu, Finland
Matti Leppäniemi, University of Oulu, Finland
Jari Sall, University of Oulu, Finland
Jaako Sinisalo, University of Oulu, Finland
Feng Li, University of Newcastle upon Tyne, UK

This chapter discusses the mobile network as a new medium for marketing communications. It illustrates that the mobile medium, defined as two-way communications via mobile handsets, can be utilized in a company's promotion mix by initiating and maintaining relationships. First, by using the mobile medium companies can attract new customers by organizing SMS (short message service) -based competitions and lotteries. Second, the mobile medium can be used as a relationship building tool as companies can send information and discount coupons to existing customers' mobile devices or collect marketing research data. The authors explore these scenarios by presenting and analyzing a mobile marketing case from Finland. The chapter concludes by pondering different future avenues for the mobile medium in promotion mix.

Chapter XXXII

Keyurkumar J. Patel, Box Hill Institute, Australia

Wireless Technology is growing at a phenomenal rate. Of the many present challenges highlighted by the author, increased security is one of the main challenges for both developers and end users. This chapter presents this important security aspect of implementing a mobile solution in the context of Sydney International airport. After tackling initial challenges and issues faced during the implementation of wireless technology, this chapter demonstrates how security issues and wireless application were implemented at this mobile-intense airport organization. The decision to deploy and manage the wireless spectrum throughout the Airport campus meant that the wireless LAN had to share the medium with public users, tenants and aircraft communications on the same bandwidth. Therefore, this case study also demonstrates invaluable approach to protect unintended users from breach of existing security policies adopted by their corporate network. Authentication and data privacy challenges, as well as complete WLAN connectivity for tenants, public and corporate usage is presented in this case study.

Section III: Technology, Networks and Security

Chapter XXXIII

Kumar Priyatam, BVB Collage of Engineering and Technology, India
R. M. Banakar, BVB Collage of Engineering and Technology, India
B. Shankaranand, National Institute of Technology, India

Channel estimation is a technique to understand and optimize the behaviour of a communications channel. Identifying and improving on the accuracy of channel estimation can improve system performance in a wireless environment that can result and fast and reliable communications. This chapter discusses the critical and limiting challenges of communication channels and approaches to addressing them, such as the SISO estimation.

The supply chains have become increasingly complex and interdependent in the globalization era. Regulatory authorities are demanding stricter customer compliance, and customers are demanding real-time data for better decision making. At the same time, customer demand is becoming more erratic thus the need for enhanced supply chain coordination with an objective to enhance overall customer value. Radio Frequency Identification RFID, an enabler of supply chain visibility, has the potential to provide customers with large amounts of information at any point in the movement of goods through the supply chain. This technology complements the barcode technology. However, with the acceptance of RFID technology, several managerial and technical issues arise. The focus of this chapter is to thus discuss the relevance of the RFID technology for enabling supply chain visibility and adoption related issues.

Cell Broadcasting (CB) is a cellular-based public notification system that has immense potential usage mainly in emergency warning facilities, at the global level, CB can broadcast a text alert or message to a large number of people (independently of their network operators) specific to a geographical area, covered either by a single cell or by the entire (regional or national) network. The CB feature of modern mobile networks creates opportunities for management of natural and manmade disasters. This chapter analyzes options for further evolution in several sectors including political, technical, and regulatory perspectives.

Chapter XXXVI

This chapter deals with the all important security aspect of mobility. Wireless transmissions include highly sensitive data that can lead itself to financial fraud. This chapter identifies and describes the issues surrounding the secure authentication of individuals attempting to access or transact with organizations using "wireless" online networks. This chapter then explains how to secure access to sensitive data with the use of multi-factor "out of band" authentication. Using CLEW, a mobile security product developed by the author's company.

This chapter describes mobile agents and their frameworks. While issues like latency factor, abrupt disconnection in service and minimal processing power appear to have been solved in the mobile agent paradigm, there is still a need to handle mobile transaction capabilities. This chapter deals with the use of mobile agent framework to incorporate transaction capabilities. An example Customer Relationship Management (CRM) is shown in use of the framework.

Chapter XXXVIII

R. B. Patel, M. M. Engineering College, India
Vijay Athavale, JIET, Jind, Haryana, India

One of the biggest challenges in future application development is device heterogeneity on varying mobile networks. This chapter presents a prototype for secure and reliable computing that addresses the issues and challenges in building multi-platform mobile applications that can run on heterogeneous devices. Furthermore, this chapter also describes how to allow a user to move/migrate a running application among heterogeneous devices that might be operating among different networks.

Chapter XXXIX

Sanjay Jasola, Wawasan Open University, Malaysia
Ramesh C. Sharma, Indira Gandhi National Open University, India

Next generation telecom networks will be having convergence of the so called "Quad" functions voice, data, TU, and streamity on IP based mobility solutions. Mobile IP is a TCP/IP-based protocol that has been standardized by the IETF (Internet Engineering Task Force) for supporting mobility. Mobile IP is part of both IPv4 and IPv6 standards. Mobile IP works at network layer (layer 3), influencing the routing of packets and can easily handle mobility among different media. This chapter discusses different technical operations involved in Mobile IPv4 and Mobile IPv6 and compares them.

Chapter XL

Bharti Trivedi, DDU Nadiad, India
Bhuvan Unhelkar, MethodScience.com & University of Western Sydney, Australia

This chapter aims to investigate and expand the role of mobile technologies in an Environmentally Responsible Business Strategy (ERBS). An ERBS with mobile technologies has the potential to help organizations achieve socially responsible goals of reducing green house emissions, reducing physical movement of men and materials, and recycling materials. This chapter delves deeper into the role of mobile technologies in creating and enhancing what can be considered as Environmental Intelligence (EI) – extending business intelligence with mobility for a Green enterprise.

Chapter XLI

Dirk Werth, Institute for Information Systems at German Research Centre for Artificial
Intelligence, Germany
Paul Makuch, Institute for Information Systems at German Research Centre for Artificial
Intelligence, Germany

The majority of enterprises use Enterprise Resource Planning (ERP) software to improve their business processes. Simultaneously, mobile technologies which can be used within ERP have gained further importance. This is so because ERP, together with mobile technologies, offers a wide spectrum of synergies and have a significant impact on enterprise efficiency. The improvement possibilities in ERP due to mobility range from sales activities, over logistic processes, up to effects on the human resource management.

Chapter XLII

A sensor network consists of tiny, low-powered, and multifunctional sensor devices and is able to perform complex tasks through the collaborative efforts of a large number of sensor nodes that are densely deployed within the sensing field. Maintaining connectivity and maximizing the network lifetime are among the critical considerations in designing sensor networks and its protocols. Conservation of limited energy reserves at each sensor node is one of the greatest challenges in a sensor network. It has been suggested that mobility of some nodes/entities in a sensor network can be exploited to improve network performance in a number of areas, including coverage, lifetime, connectivity and fault-tolerance. In this context, techniques for effectively utilizing the unique capabilities of mobile nodes have been attracting increasing research attention in the past few years. In this chapter, the authors will focus on some of the new and innovative techniques that have been recently proposed to handle a number of important problems in this field. They will also present a number of open problems and some developing trends and directions for future work in this emerging research area.

Chapter XLIII

In commercial cellular networks, like the systems based on direct sequence code division multiple access (DSCD-MA), many types of interferences can appear, starting from multi-user interference inside each sector in a cell to interoperator interference. Also unintentional jamming can be present due to co-existing systems at the same band, whereas intentional jamming arises mainly in military applications. Independent Component Analysis (ICA) use as an advanced pre-processing tool for blind suppression of interfering signals in direct sequence spread spectrum communication systems utilizing antenna arrays. The role of ICA is to provide an interference-mitigated signal to the conventional detection. Several ICA algorithms exist for performing Blind Source Separation (BSS). ICA has been used to extract interference signals, but very less literature is available on the performance, that is, how does it behave in communication environment. This needs an evaluation of its performance in communication environment. This chapter evaluates the performance of some major ICA algorithms like Bell and Sejnowski's infomax algorithm, Cardoso's Joint Approximate Diagonalization of Eigen matrices (JADE), Pearson-ICA and Comon's algorithm in a communication blind source separation problem. Independent signals representing Sub-Gaussian, Super-Gaussian and mix users are generated and then mixed linearly to simulate communication signals. Separation performance of ICA algorithms measure by performance index.

Chapter XLIV

This chapter describes a case study on installation of a Wi-Fi network in a chemical manufacturing company in India in order to connect its various dispersed manufacturing units, as well as the administrative offices. Initial studies indicated that a physical network was not appropriate due to the local corrosive chemical environment; the author's company was invited to install Wi-Fi network within the complex. This chapter reports on how the project progressed, the lessons learnt and the way to approach this kind of work in future in terms of wireless networking.

The purpose of this chapter is to explore and suggest how perceptions of the social context of an organization moderate the usage of an innovative technology. We propose a research model that is strongly grounded in theory and offer a number of associated propositions that can be used to investigate adoption and diffusion of mobile computing devices for business-to-business (B2B) interactions (including transactions and other informational exchanges). Mobile computing devices for B2B are treated as a technological innovation. An extension of existing adoption and diffusion models by considering the social contextual factors is necessary and appropriate in light of the fact that various aspects of the social context have been generally cited to be important in the introduction of new technologies. In particular, a micro-level analysis of this phenomenon for the introduction of new technologies is not common. Since the technological innovation that is considered here is very much in its nascent stages there may not as yet be a large body of users in a B2B context. Therefore, this provides a rich opportunity to conduct academic research. We expect this chapter to sow the seeds for extensive empirical research in the future.

Chapter XLVI

This chapter describes the extension of EA with mobility so as to facilitate easier implementation of applications that overcome the boundaries of time and location. This extension of EA with mobility results in a comprehensive Mobility Enterprise Architecture (M-EA) that provides the business with advantages of real-time business processes, reduced costs, increased client satisfaction, and better control. This chapter outlines the M-EA framework, which is based on the literature review, initial modeling and a case study carried out by the lead authors. Later, the framework is validated by another case study carried out at international software development organization. Further validation of the model is envisaged through action research in multinational organizations.

Chapter XLVII

Mobile Web Services (MWS) technologies, generally built around the ubiquitous Extensible Markup Language (XML), has provided many opportunities for integrating enterprise applications. Currently, the WS paradigm is driven through parameters however; the paradigm shift that can result in true collaborative business requires us to consider the business paradigm in terms of policies-processes-standards. This chapter based on experimental research carried out by the authors, demonstrates how the technologies of WS open up the doors to collaborative Enterprise Architecture Integration (EAI) and Service Oriented Architecture (SOA) resulting in developing mobile applications.

Chapter XLVIII

Wireless Web services need to handle the additional challenges of limited computing power, limited network bandwidth, limited battery life, and unpredictable online time, that come with mobility. This chapter discusses the challenges and solutions of wireless Web services. The issues worked on are: optimization of the wireless Web services messaging protocol, caching, and fault tolerance. This chapter also points out the limitations of the current approaches and outlines the future research directions on wireless Web services.

Chapter XLIX

David Curtis, MethodScience, Australia
Ming-Chien (Mindy) Wu, University of Western Sydney, Australia

The Mobile Enterprise Architecture (M-EA) model provides the organization with advantages of real-time business processing, better customer, and end-user services, and the addition of increased control across the entire organisation. The MEA function focuses on the collection and analysis of information including software applications, business processes, business information (data), technology, and governance (people). The chapter presents an overview of EA and M-EA models and also includes investigations of the advantages; limitations and blueprint overcome those challenges of M-EA implementation.

Chapter L

Ekata Mehul, Gujarat University, India
Vikram Limaye, India

Accessibility of "Wireless Ad Hoc Network" (WAHN) is an advantage as well as a challenge, particularly from a security viewpoint. Wireless security solutions include encryption, secure routing, quality of service, and so forth. However, each of these solutions is designed to operate in a particular situation; and it may fail to work successfully in other scenarios. This chapter offers an alternate to improving the trustworthiness of the neighbourhood and securing the routing procedure. This security is achieved by dynamically computing the trust in neighbours and selecting the most secure route from the available ones for the data transfer. There is also a provision to detect the compromised node and virtually removing it from the network.

Chapter LI

Barin N. Nag, Department of Management, Towson University, USA
Mark Siegal, National Library of Medicine, USA

Patient care has undergone dramatic improvement due to mobility. However, the volume of patient monitoring data mandates the use of Decision Support Systems (DSS) that provide clinical diagnoses and treatment methodology consistent with the urgency. This chapter describes clinical DSS that helps healthcare professionals, reduces workload, and providing better care for patients.

Section IV: Case Studies

Chapter LII

Marco Garito, Digital Business, Italy

This chapter describes mobile business applications and initiatives in companies who successfully implemented their go-to-market strategy in the wireless world. This chapter starts by describing the current market situation for mobile environment. This is followed by discussion on the Lateral Marketing approach and then some examples of mobile applications and services related to the approach.

Mobile commerce offers consumers the convenience and flexibility of mobile services anytime and at any place. Secured and private mobile business processes using a mobile gadget for payments are essential for the success of mobile commerce. Mobile payment is the process of two parties exchanging financial value using a mobile device in return for goods and services. This chapter is an analysis of the secure mobile payment services for real automated point of sale (PoS), which are frequently used in terminals such as vending machines.

Convergence of mobile technologies as discussed in this chapter includes RFID technology, Bar code and services. Thus the Service Oriented Architecture (SOA) in this convergence is the mainstay of the discussion in this chapter.

The concept of virtual organization requires a fine balance between business and technology. Globalized virtual organizations need to share common resources for communications, computing power, and data. Grid and mobile computing concepts also needs to be integrated in such global scenario, as discussed in this chapter.

This chapter introduces the use of mobile medical informatics as a means for improving clinical practice in Sudan. Mobility, together with medical informatics, provides opportunities for discovering patterns in complex clinical situations. Furthermore, the author brings together the Chaos Theory with mobile medical informatics to provide sound basis for information systems, that is based on understanding of intricate relationships between different factors influencing medical informatics.

Chapter LVII

This chapter describes Mobile WiMAX and demonstrates how it can be combined with GPS (Global Positioning System) for Traffic Management, solve traffic related offences and help in providing a clear way for PSV's (Public safety vehicles) like fire brigades and ambulances. Mobile WiMAX has increasingly gained extensive support in the industry. Demand on wireless internet bandwidth is increasing. Mobile WiMAX, also called WirelessMAN (Wireless Metropolitan Area Networks.), is Wi-Fi (Wireless Fidelity) of the Metro. Mobile WiMAX offers wireless Internet experience within the city as Wi-Fi offers within your office or home. This capability of Mobile WiMAX is presented here by Bhalla and Chaudhary, and applied for traffic management problem.

This chapter explains the results of an action research carried out at ImpexDocs in Sydney, Australia. The purpose of this action research is to investigate the business processes of the Export Companies that collaborate with the organizations involved in customs in Australia. The chapter provides an insight into applications of Collaborative Business Process Engineering (CBPE) in terms of improving the effectiveness and efficiency for all organizations involved in custom (especially export). The study demonstrates an understanding of the depth analyses of existing business processes under development investigates the collaboration between the export companies system with other enterprises involved, investigates the existing channels of collaboration and the common business processes threads that run thru multiple applications.

Foreword

Mobile technologies, mobile business and the relevance of mobility, overall, to our society have been a core area of my work over the past few years. As an active researcher and the organizer and past chair of the International Conference on Mobile Business series, I have been privileged to observe the advances in research and the practice of mobility in business and society. This handbook is an excellent representation globally of the mobility movement. Mobility includes the study of mobile devices, the capacities and security of wireless networks, the various ways to source contents for mobile service providers, the usability issues of small screen devices, mobile enterprise architectures, and the entertainment and educational value of mobility – to name but a few. These areas of mobility in business and society are highlighted in this second edition, edited. by Dr Unhelkar.

While I had the privilege of reviewing and writing the foreword to the previous edition of this handbook (which still remains a significant contribution to the field of mobility) this second edition has provided new and unique discussions from contributing authors in the areas of strategic use of mobility, context awareness in mobile computing, transitioning to mobile business, mobile networks and the ever increasing importance of the application of any technology (mobile technology in this case) to the environment. My own philosophy of research in the mobile domain is that industry practitioners and academics *must* collaborate to understand, document and provide practical solutions to the challenges of adopting mobility. Therefore, it is pleasing to once again note the inclusion of numerous industry case studies in this book.

As with the previous edition, this handbook provides a judicious combination of reporting research as well as sharing industrial expertise. These contributed chapters bring to the reader a sensible and practical combination of the theory and practice of mobility in business. The wide coverage of topics and the variety of contributors to this handbook make this book an excellent addition to the literature on mobile business.

The chapters in this book are of excellent quality and well referenced. They provide avid researchers with further links to extend and expand their research. The contributions to this handbook are from authors with varying backgrounds from a number of countries. The sharing of practical experiences from authors from around the globe y has been achieved in this edited work.

I highly recommend this handbook, and its previous edition, to both researchers and practitioners in the industry as an invaluable desktop reference. This book will not only aid practitioners in what they are currently doing with mobile business, but will also open up numerous directions for further investigative research work.

Associate Professor Dr. Elaine Lawrence
Head: School of Computing and Communications, Faculty of Engineering and Information Technology
University of Technology, Sydney
ICMB 2005 Conference General Co Chair
Sept. 2008, Sydney

Preface

Communication is the Key!

A VERY FAST MOVING WORLD

The person who can predict what is going to happen next in the field of mobile technologies and business might as well be gazing at a crystal ball. The difficulties that arise in predicting the next steps in the field of mobility are related to the rapid changes in all dimensions of mobility. The networks and contents related to mobile business are changing; the networks to transmit those contents are undergoing major change on their own, and the expectations of user experiences from a wide cross section of users are climbing beyond reach. This Second edition of the "Handbook of Research in Mobile Business" is in your hands precisely because of the aforementioned difficulty. The world of mobile technologies and business is undergoing a revolution of such mammoth proportions that no aspect of technology, business, or society remains untouched by it. While the discussion in the precursor to this edition still remain valid, and covers a wide area of this rapidly expanding domain, the current discussions cover many new thoughts and case studies, including mobile strategies application, gadgets, networks, contents, and myriad related elements. In fact, mobile technologies and their corresponding application to business is changing so fast that an acute need was felt to extend and augment to what was so rigorously edited and published a little more than a couple of years ago. While the discussions in the first edition of this handbook are still relevant to business, the world of mobile business has changed so rapidly that it now demands further discussions on how to incorporate mobility in business and what are its repercussions. The thinkers, researchers, scholars, consultants, and other practitioners who have contributed to the first edition had also felt the need for adding to and updating to what they had to say earlier, to share newer experiences, advantages and pitfalls; and finally, the publisher could also see this need and decided to produce this second edition of the handbook.

VALUE OF MOBILITY IS IN BUSINESS

Most of these topics and chapters in this handbook are new contributions from the participating authors. This second edition of the Handbook of Research in Mobile Business covers a wide gamut of topics relevant to use of mobile technologies in business such as mobile networks, applications, contents, security, processes, and social acceptability. Furthermore, again like the previous edition, this book is a judicious combination of research and practice. *That* forms the precise value of this book – the value it provides to business in enabling it to incorporate mobility in its business operations in a *strategic* manner. While there are some pure technical chapters in this work that include topics like networking, security, and applications, there are other chapters that bring a totally different perspective to mobility – such as privacy and legal issues, application to the environment, changes to the organizational structures and the effect of mobility on telecommuting.

As such, the mission of this second edition is the same as the first one:

"To make a substantial contribution to the literature on "mobility" encompassing excellence in research and innovation as well as demonstrated application of mobile technologies to mobile business"

CORE CONTENTS OF THIS HANDBOOK

Methods and applications, strategies, technical, networks , social and core studies.

Audience

Following are the major categories of readers for this book:

- **Strategic Management / Senior Management / CxOs /** will find the earlier discussions on strategic use of mobile technologies in business extremely relevant to what they are doing. That section of the book will be immense help to the readers in setting the strategic directions of their organizations with respect to mobility– especially because these chapters have been contributed by practicing senior managers.
- **Researchers** and **academics** will find numerous hooks in the research-based chapters of this book in terms of identifying areas of research, as well as following research methods when dealing with "mobility". Thus, the strong research focus of this book – especially the detailed and relevant references at the end of each contributed chapter, the research methodologies followed and the discussions on research results (especially some excellent "action research" based case studies) make this book an ideal reference point for active researchers in this area.
- **Programmers and architects** of mobile-enabled software systems will find the discussions on technologies, networks, and security directly applicable to their work.
- **Business process modellers** and **information architects** will find the chapters dealing with incorporation of mobile technologies in business processes quite relevant.
- **Methodologists** and **Change Managers** will be interested in the chapters that describe the transition processes from existing to mobile businesses.
- **Sociologists** and **legal experts** will find the discussions on cross-border socio-cultural issues in applications of mobile technologies and the resultant globalization of businesses a fascinating read.

Critiques

Readers are invited to submit criticism of this work. It will be an honour to receive genuine criticisms and comments on the chapters and their organization in this edited book. I am more than convinced that your criticisms will not only enrich the knowledge and understanding of the contributory authors and myself, but will also add to the general wealth of knowledge available to the ICT and Mobile community. Therefore, I give you, readers and critiques, a sincere *thank you* in advance.

Bhuvan Unhelkar
www.methodscience.com

Acknowledgment

The editor gratefully acknowledges all contributing authors of the chapters appearing in this book. Furthermore, I would specifically also like to thank the following individuals who put in varied effort to make this edition of value.

Warren Adkins
Ramesh Balachandran
Abbass Ghanbary
Vijay Khandelwal
Anand Kuppuswami
Amit Lingarchani
Javed Matin
Mohammed Maharmeh
San Murugesan
Christopher Payne
Prince Soundararajan
Ketan Vanjara
Mindy "Ming-Chein" Wu
Houman Younessi

My thanks also to my wife Asha, daughter Sonki Priyadarashani and son Keshav Raja as well as my extended family, Chinar & Girish Mamdapur. This second edition of the book also remains dedicated to my teenage son, Keshav Raja, who along with millions of teenagers, continue to amaze their parents, teachers and elders, in terms of their creative and sometimes morbid fascination with mobile technologies and gadgets.

About the Editor

Dr. **Bhuvan Unhelkar** (BE, MDBA, MSc, PhD; FACS) has 26+ years of strategic as well as hands-on professional experience in Information and Communication Technologies (ICT) and their application to business and management. He has notable international consulting and training expertise in software engineering (modelling, processes and quality), information architecture, service-oriented architecture, enterprise globalisation, web services and mobile business. His domain expertise includes Telecommunications, Governance, Finance and Banking. He earned his Doctorate in the area of "object orientation" from the University of Technology, Sydney. He leads the mobile research group at the University of Western Sydney, where he is also an adjunct Associate Professor. He has practised and trained business executives and ICT professionals around the world, taught in universities and authored 12 books (+currently completing 2) in the areas of Global Information Systems, Mobile Business, Software Excellence and Business Process Re-engineering. He is Fellow of the Australian Computer Society, Life member of the Computer Society of India and a Rotarian at St. Ives in Sydney.

Section I
Strategies and Methods

Chapter I
Strategic View on Creating Business Value through Mobile Technologies

Houman Younessi
Rensselaer Polytechnic Institute, USA

ABSTRACT

Business value from any technology comes when it is applied, in practice, by the business to earn economic as well as social advantage. This is particularly true of mobile technologies, wherein their ability to provide location and time independence is a significant advantage to business. Such an advantage, however, can only be derived when mobile technologies are carefully incorporated, with a long-term strategic view in mind. This chapter describes and discusses such strategic view of mobile technologies in order to create business value.

INTRODUCTION

This chapter deals with how mobile technologies might create business value. The main arguments revolve around an analysis of the concept of value and the idea of strategic incorporation of technology – in our case mobile technologies – in the business process. These arguments are developed by recognizing that the concept of business value subsumes the concept of profit. Profit oriented economic viability is a necessary but not sufficient condition for creation of value (Freeman et al., 2007-2008; Figge and Hahn, 2005). A distinction needs to be made between *utility value*, assessed subjectively by customers, which is related

to the concept of product quality, *exchange value*, which is realized in the form of revenue and economic profits and *essential value*, realized in the fundamental improvement of the societal condition. There is – in other words – a rising tide of informed opinion that sees ethical, moral, cultural and ecological sustainability of the firm and of the society as fundamental in any analysis of the purpose and goals of organizations and their approach to creation of value. The discussion herein applies these otherwise subjective concepts to value creation in a mobile business.

In line with such considerations, value creation and ultimately value maximization have as much to do with what product is available, as they do with where to sell it, to whom, when and at what price, but also – and unfortunately much ignored – why? Consider, for example, the offering of a mobile service to a sales force. Value maximization, has a lot to do with demand and how one navigates or manipulates this concept to one's advantage. Value maximization also has to do with the amount of supply and competing products that can satisfy the same demand. Simply put, values are maximized when each item to be sold is sold at the highest return possible for that particular item to be sold. From there on, it is all about figuring out the right mix. By this we mean: determining which item should be sold where and when. We will see shortly however, that such maximization produces potentially only a local maximum. A strategic plan that aims to create, reconfigure or improve an enterprise model or process must be cognizant of such distinctions relative to the concept of value. We will discuss this in some great detail later in the chapter.

Mobile technologies, as a part of an enterprise process remodeling option, offer some unique characteristics that are not available from other communications technologies. The powerful dual feature afforded by mobility of 'time and location' independence provides for immense potentials in enhancing the capabilities of the enterprise comparable only to earlier technological revolutions such as the original introduction of computing or electronic communication to the business world (Greenfield, 2006; Hansmann, 2003). Use of mobile technologies enables businesses to create and manage business processes that are not tied to a particular user location. This ability to handle business transactions at any place and time opens up opportunities for businesses to do a much better job of customizing, personalizing and altering their offerings to suit the customers -as time imperatives demand it. Furthermore, the relative low costs and abundant availability of mobile gadgets such as mobile phones, PDAs (Personal Digital Assistants) and integrated devices such as iPhones (latest release from Apple, in mid-2007) has brought the potential of mobility within the grasp of many organizations. It should be however stressed that the ready availability of a plethora of such low cost devices can be a potential trap for organizations contemplating making a move towards becoming a mobile business. Becoming a mobile business takes much more than just equipping the sales force with handheld devices.

Using mobile gadgets to carry out the same business processes that would otherwise have been conducted in a physical manner is not a true strategic use of mobility. This is so because, as with some previous revolutionary technologies, such usage would only be automation of the existing processes, a move that although at times economically efficacious, is often sub-optimal in its scope. Strategic use of mobility must benefit from a 'ground-up' holistic thinking, consideration of all internal as well as external factors of a business whether they might be, or are deemed to be, influenced by mobility or not! The greatest benefits always hide in corners into which one does not think of looking. Consideration of the human element, relative to customers' employees and other stakeholders must feature paramount in our considerations. The objective of introducing mobile technologies in short is to "re-"optimize the enterprise in terms of its ability to create value, using the new potential available in terms NOT of *mobile technologies per se* but in terms of *time and space independence*. It is the *concept* that is the enabler not the technology.

STRATEGIC BUSINESS VIEW

Today's business exists in a tetherless world. The next stage of the communication revolution is wireless/mobile communication. The potential for the elimination of physical connectivity between communicating devices results in profound changes in the nature of the relationship between people and processes. For example, the impact of mobility on the organization of the business and its relationship with customers can be potentially significant (Greenfield, 2006). The ability of businesses and customers to connect to each other – independent of time and location – is of course the core driver of this change. There is, thus, a corresponding social and behavioral revolution that is taking place hand-in-hand with the technological one mentioned earlier. However there is sufficient evidence extant, anecdotal and otherwise, pointing to the profound social and organizational changes that will be inevitable as a consequence of the (m-) revolution.

What is important to recognize is that, in general, technology is neither a necessary nor a sufficient precursor for productivity or progress. In fact, without due strategic considerations as are discussed in this chapter, technology can occasionally be detrimental to both! Consider, for example, the fact that the average time spent on a "computer" at work has increased by more than 60% compared only to a decade ago. Yet almost twice as many people feel that they are less productive in their jobs than workers did ten years ago.

The "paperless office" is consuming almost four times the paper the − I guess we can call it the "papered" office - consumed. There are many technical, process and social issues that have emerged as a consequence of introduction of information and communication technologies. The emergence of such issues has proven inevitable and universal; in the sense that they are not necessarily unique to the interaction of ICT and the work environment. With the advent of mobile technologies and the infusion of such technologies into business, social and behavioral re-orientation will be a certainty.

The challenge, as mentioned earlier, is not so much with the technology but rather with the way in which it is applied. More specifically, these challenges are as follows:

1. Recognizing and understanding the mobile technology that is available and its limitations as well as its potentials. We often expect too much, too soon,

2. Recognizing that it is not the mobile device or even the currently available technology that is the central issue but the process transformation, the new enabling concept, that is the core transformer. In our case, as I had mentioned before, it is not the PDA, it is the concept of time and location independence that is central.

3. Understanding that each new concept, each new technology including in the case of our discussion, each new advance in mobile technologies is a potential avenue for re-optimization of the enterprise. No optimization however is meaningful, productive or even possible without first identifying the objective, the goal towards which we optimize. I briefly stated earlier that we must not take our eyes off the objective of value creation and value maximization. This is the goal and not for example to have a sales force that can submit orders within 30 seconds of having taken them. Such capability may not be necessary, it may even be detrimental to business.

4. The process of introduction of the technology concerned and the management of the change that ensues. We must have a very definite and capable process of change management, a process of transition.

Nowhere are the four above observations more valid than when we discuss the potential of technologies that have been called "disruptive". This is a natural and obvious consequence. The more revolutionizing the technology, the more paramount the four issues above would loom. A long-term, well balanced, strategic view that is aimed at re-aligning (re-optimizing) the enterprise with our value creation objectives using the newly extant technology is therefore essential.

WHY IS VALUE AND VALUE CREATION SO IMPORTANT

Value creation, we said, subsumes the concept of profit and that profit oriented economic viability is a necessary but not sufficient condition for creation of value. Let us discuss this further and then see how we can apply value creation to mobile business. We distinguished between *utility value, exchange value* and *essential value,* We also spoke of value maximization and that the pursuit of maximizing only exchange value would be potentially only a local maximization.

The concept of elasticity of demand plays an important role here (Keat and Young; 2005). Elasticity of demand means to what degree can/would demand for a product change given changes in the economic environment, such as price? Profit maximization is partially based on the use of elasticity information to the benefit of the firm. Would it not be valuable to know demand levels and the elasticity's of demand and price before hand when we decide on a marketing strategy?

Demand and price estimation and forecasting would help indicate to us the required levels of production and is invaluable information for businesses who wish to thrive. Information must be gathered on prices, competing products, incomes and wealth, and many other factors in order to set correct policy. This is all however elementary!

Value maximization has also to do with cost of production and supply. If we could lower our costs − all other things the same − we can make a higher profit. At the simple level, costs are best managed when we make a lot of the same product and do not waste resources making them and they are good enough that all can be sold at the best obtainable price. We can do this by improving the efficiency of the process of production; by ensuing that we build high quality products; and that we are producing in high volume. Technology employed and innovation is a major factor in achieving these aims. Knowing how much to produce and how to produce high quality products requires the acquisition, retention, processing and dissemination of a lot of information. In this treatment we will deal with the fundamental building blocks of such required information and the means of using it to the advantage of the enterprise.

But value creation goes beyond this and we must ask ourselves: How long can one continue to engage in this enterprise?

Unless there is a logically more compelling reason, people in successful businesses wish to remain in the same business. In fact the secret lies in the phrase "unless there is a logically more compelling reason". These logically compelling reasons may be classified under two broad categories

a. Better opportunity. As an astute businessperson one may end a profit making enterprise in order to invest its resources into another enterprise that is even more profitable. I may stop selling domestic cars and turn to selling imported ones because imported cars would make more money for the same effort and investment. This is in line with the concept of opportunity cost

b. Growing danger to life or limb. All business entails risk, but there may come a time when the reward that ensues would not justify the risk. As I sell my Toledo swords to my Bedouin wholesaler in the middle of the dessert, I would be loath to sell the last sword, even if he pays an excellent price for it. British Petroleum and Siemens spend a lot of money that otherwise would be turned to profit on environmental and ecological programs. In other words, they consciously trade exchange value for essential value. They do not do so from an altruistic standpoint. To them, such "sacrifices" are the sword they keep for themselves. They consider doing so an investment in their own futures, in the form of an investment in the future of their resources and their customers. They realize that unless they did so, their business would not be sustainable. It is fundamentally important to avail ourselves of the relevant information accessible to determine how long one can continue the business in which one is engaged and when to stop or change approach – before it is too late. Would you have wished to have known about the stock market crash a week before it actually happened? The information requirement of business sustainability constitutes one of the central tenets here and we shall deal with the fundamental elements of what information is needed and how it is acquired and retained.

Let us now formalize the above discussions a little bit. Let us bring together some of the concepts discussed above in order to create a basis for future discussion.

It is safe to assume that we all wish to be involved with successful businesses and given the considerations and caveats above, we are interested in businesses that create value. We wish these to be as large as possible, and for us to be able to continue to enjoy making these levels of value. We have been talking about buying and selling so let us apply the same concept to the discussion at hand. Let us assume that you wish to purchase a business. What type of business would you wish to buy? Answer: one that is profitable and remains profitable for the long-term. In other words one would like to maximize the total dollar value one can get out of this venture. We need to determine the value of the firm as the present value of all expected future values which of course depends on three things:

a) Value levels, b) sustainability and longevity of the business, and c) risk that future (normalized) value may not be as large as current value (Hornigen, 2007).

Here, we employ the economic concept of value pricing. This year, value earned would be annual value estimated as annual value revenue minus annual value cost.

$$VR_0 - VC_0$$

We now consider that value revenue (VR) is the sum of the utility revenue (UR) and exchange revenue recognized (XR), measured as reified market opportunity gain and normal revenue respectively, plus the converted essential revenue recognized (ER).

$$VR = UR + XR + ER$$

Also, value cost (VC) is the sum of utility cost (UC) and exchange costs incurred (XC), measured as reified market opportunity loss and normal cost and the converted essential cost incurred (EC).

$$VC = UC + XC + EC$$

Now we know that value is the difference of utility revenue and utility cost or:

$$V = VR - VC$$

Substituting, we will have:

$$V = VR - VC = (UR + XR + ER) - (UC + XC + EC)$$

Rearranging, we get:

$$V = (XR - XC) + (UR - UC) + (ER - EC)$$

or,

$$V = XV + UV + EV$$

where XV and UV are exchange value and utility value respectively and EV is the extents of essential values.

In the special case of restricting ourselves to exchange value, this would be of course approximated as pure exchange revenue less pure exchange costs or:

$$V \approx XR - XC$$

There is a chance that next year the value may be higher or lower. In a complex way that we will not discuss here, the financial market determines the interest rate or the extent of that risk as a number between zero and unity (or a percentage rate). Assessing risk and projecting for next year, next year's value will be:

$$V_P = \frac{V_1}{1+i}$$

Where $V_1 = XV_1 + UV_1 + EV_1$ is next year's value figure and i is the interest rate. So, the value of the firm over two years would be

$$V_P = V_0 + \frac{V_1}{1+i}$$

Over n years, the value of the firm will be:

$$TV_P = \sum_{t=0}^{n} \frac{V_t}{(1+i)^t}$$

where V_t is expected profit in year t.
Substituting, we get:

$$TV_P = \sum_{t=0}^{n} \frac{VR_t - VC_t}{(1+i)^t} = \sum_{t=0}^{n} \frac{(XR_t - XC_t) + (UR_t - UC_t) + (ER_t - EC_t)}{(1+i)^t}$$

As such, the value of VR_t depends not only on the exchange realized profits, but also on the inter-related concepts of utility, demand, price, new product development, product quality and ecological, social, legal and technological impacts.

To bring this all back to the discussion of mobile technologies, we continue with our running example of "enabling" a sales force. Providing each member of an existing sales force with a mobile device may or may not have an impact in exchange revenue. The question will be whether the new device would in any way enhance the *revenue* generation process and if so do we understand exactly how? If so, there may very well be exchange revenue enhancement. But what about other types of revenue? How about utility revenue or essential revenue? Has the introduction of the device done anything positively for the quality of the sales experience for our customers? For our sales force? Has it helped attract better or more qualified salespeople? Has the introduction of the new mobile device helped attract new *potential* customers? In other words has it been instrumental in market development?

In general, firms would have or increase revenue if there was demand (or increased demand) for their products. There will be demand only if the product:

1. Satisfies a need or want
2. Represents an adequate level of quality
3. The required quality is offered at an acceptable price, and
4. Adds social, ecological and otherwise *essential* revenue

On the Cost Side, the Value of VC_t Depends on the Process, and Process Capability and Efficiency and Ecological, Social, Legal and Technological Impacts

The more wisely firms use their available resources for production, the greater their capacity to produce – all else being the same; or they can produce a set quantity for less cost. By production we do not simply mean making or fabricating a good. Although this is a common interpretation of the word, production in economic terms means not only the development of a good such as an automobile but also the provision of services such as fire insurance, catering services or stockbrokerage. In addition, production includes and production costs embrace the cost of making the product available in the market. So inventory, transportation and marketing and sales costs are part of production expenses. The production cost of a product, say a safety harness your firm sells is not just in the cost of fabrics, straps and other materials, but it is also in the cost of transporting it, marketing it, selling it, etc . So think of the term "production" not as a synonym to "making" but as "offering", or "making available" as in "produce that calculator so I may borrow it". This is where much of the argument for – and occasionally against – introduction of new technology and in our case, mobile ICT technologies, resides.

The argument for introduction of mobility may usually revolve around cost savings. However, given the arguments presented above with respect to value and different types of value considerations, we do need to pay a finer attention to the concept of cost. Let us say that it was determined that the introduction of mobile laptops to a sales force would in fact increase revenue, including revenue types beyond just the exchange revenue (as one might hope). Would this excess revenue be sufficient to cover the cost of the introduction of the technology? Let us say that the projections are that at a 60% cost point, production cost will increase by 5% (cost of purchase and maintenance of the equipment) and revenue will increase by 7%. This represents a 4% increase in value. Sounds great but have we considered all the costs? Cost of training, cost of transportation and loss (replacement) of the devices? Any financial cost analyst worth his or her salary would think of all of these costs (again one hopes), but what about the cost of loss of established and productive but "inflexible" salespeople who would leave the company because they do not wish to use these "new-fangled" contraptions? How about the image in the market? The potential negative marketing message? Not to mention the cost of disruption to business flow while the new system is being implemented. By implemented I do not mean simply acquired and installed. I mean established so that it operates at a desired and reasonable level of efficiency. How about the lost opportunity cost of investing the time, resources and energy into a project other than the one to equip the sales force with mobile ICT?

How wisely firms use their production resources has to do with their process capability. Processes that are wasteful of materials, energy, space or labor may be improved to have higher capability. Information on labor usage, lot sizes, process flow, set up times and similar concepts may be obtained and used to this end.

Processes that produce low quality products or have high "reject" rates may be likewise improved. Information on the root cause of defects, their distribution and their impact would help to this end.

Processes may also improve in efficiency and capability in the pure sense by improvements in the technology employed. Robots may be able to weld more accurately, faster and improve employee safety compared with a manual welding operation. Camera-controlled assembly lines can identify and reject defective units faster and more cost-effectively than through visual inspection. In the case of our discussion, mobile technologies may well be able to improve the process of acquisition, retention, processing and dissemination of information and to significantly improve the way we deal with the challenges, issues and processes stated above. However, not purely exchange revenues and costs but rather total value must be considered. The reader might consult (Whitten et al.; 2008) for a very interesting case of the impact of introducing ICT and mobile technologies in the healthcare industry.

Of significant import here is that *utility* costs and *essential* costs of business must not be ignored. That is, *that production does not threaten longer-term, higher levels of value creation.*

The Value of i Depends on Risk and Uncertainty about the Future

Interest rates are usually perceived or described as "the cost of money", and they vary. What is important to realize is why should money cost? And why should that cost be variable? Money costs because opportunity costs. Money that does not fund project A may fund project B. Project B may make more profit than project A. Note however that we said "may". There is an element of uncertainty. There is uncertainty about the future, about the health of the economy for instance or supply of money. There is uncertainty about future government policy, international trade, natural and man-made events such as climatic events or war, and many other factors. The level of such uncertainty does not remain constant, as such; the interest rate is usually a positive number that varies from time to time. It represents the risk about the future. Interest rates commonly used measure the uncertainty of general markets and money supply. But all those who have applied for mortgages know that interest rates offered are also a function of the creditworthiness of the applicant: in other words the risk level inherent in the deal. Same applies to firms. Ratings by international rating agencies measure the inherent risk of dealing with a particular entity want it to be a corporation, a government agency, or even countries. Interest rates these entities can negotiate when they borrow depend on these ratings.

Firms therefore need information on the health of their own operation. They also need information in order to forecast the behavior of the business environment in the future. Most internal financial systems are there to fulfill the first of these two requirements. Forecasting, market analysis and macro-economic modeling tools and/or services used by some firms are to fulfill the needs for the latter. In doing so, it is vital to consider *that production does not threaten longer-term, higher levels of value creation in the future.* Such circumstances would lead to less stable production and consumption (economic as well as social and ecological) environments which would in turn lead to higher risk and therefore higher interest rates.

In terms of mobile business and introduction of mobile technologies, the concept of risk and risk management is paramount. The first type of risk that comes to mind of course is that of increased information security risk. Mobile devices are "out there". They are by their very essence small, transportable, and as easily, mislaid, lost or stolen. However, many of these devices are gateways into your business. To say the least therefore, the physical layer of protection provided by walls, doors and security gates generally found in offices are no longer a protection for the mobile business. The issue of physical information security however is only one such security consideration when dealing with mobile technologies. These concerns and some means of identifying points of risk and vulnerability and also methods of dealing with such risks are being researched and about which work is being published (e.g. Adams and Katos, 2005;; Godbole, 2003; Javeenpaa et al., 2003; Phu and Jamieson, 2005). However, as discussed above, the issue of risk goes well beyond just security risks, physical or otherwise, but encompass legal, social, cultural, and risk of human error (Arthur et al., 2007). The important factor to consider here is that we must be vigilant so that the introduc-

tion of new technologies – such as mobile computing and communication devices, do not compromise our ability to create value in the future.

The Value of n Depends on the Sustainability and Longevity of the Business

The general attitude regarding enterprises has been that they will continue to produce indefinitely (Keat and Young, 2005). As far as it is known, major corporations do not develop "end-game" plans, unless the end is inevitable and in sight. Despite the fact that demise remains the only certainty – taxation not being as universal – most enterprises are of the attitude that they will continue forever. This is an incorrect attitude. The oldest continuing enterprises are only several hundred years old. Most organizations do not make it beyond a century and very few make it to 200. The question that becomes critical in this respect relative to the economic value of enterprises is to what extent does longevity matter?

MOBILE BUSINESS STRATEGY

In building a strategic framework for re-optimization of the enterprise processes to gainfully incorporate mobility, there are a number of concerns that we have to keep in mind:

1. Identification of enterprise goals and optimizing with respect to them clearly are the most important steps of all. Goals must align with value and value creation which is the business of all enterprise (actually by definition).

2. Optimization must always be towards a defined and meaningful goal. This in turn implies measurement. As such, all decisions and actions, as much as possible and at whatever level have to be on a measured basis. Metrication is the gateway to meaning. By this I mean that any business decision as to effecting changes with respect to the introduction of mobile technologies must be based on one or a set of measurable effects and the actions taken must be informed by one or a set of measurable and measured actions. Ad hoc introduction of process elements and technologies may succeed by chance but this is purely so; by chance. We also must note that measurement

Table 1. Major elements of valuation of firms

Element	Concept	Information Category	Information System
Revenue	Demand	Market trends and marketing Product quality Pricing	Data Acquisition Data Analysis Control Forecasting Optimization
Cost	Production	Process capability Technology	Forecasting Estimating Optimization Control
Risk	Uncertainty	Economic Environment Internal control	Forecasting Control
Longevity	Sustainability	Environment Integration and systemicity	Forecasting Optimization

is for two purposes: 1) assessment and steering, 2) Goal setting. We must be careful that when assessment is used in the former spirit that it is not punitive or stifling.

3. Correct reconciliation of stakeholder views would be paramount. To identify the correct goals, we need to focus on stakeholders and their wishes and perceptions. Stakeholders may be classified in three categories of clients, actors and owners.

4. Structures and interactions are the foci of concern. Structures define the environment and interactions define systems. Enterprises are systems. They are in fact a specific kind of system, they are a Human Activity System (HAS). Like other systems, they may be abstracted in terms of their inherent structural, transformational and temporal dimensions. By this I mean that they must be viewed in terms of their structures (what they consist of), their processes and functions (what they do and how change comes about within them and how they bring about change), and when things happen and in what sequence. Detailed models of all three dimensions are essential for comprehensive understanding of an enterprise model and how mobility might improve such an enterprise.

5. Systems are multi-layered and each layer has (is defined by) a focus. Within our contexts system layers might be defined as:

• **Layer 1:** Product: Demand side: Product Quality

• **Layer 2:** Production Process: Supply side: Process Efficiency

• **Layer 3:** Business/Organizational: Both Demand and Supply side: Organizational Effectiveness

• **Layer 4:** Enterprise/Ecological: Aggregate Demand and Supply: Ecological/Social Efficacy-Sustainability

6. On the demand side we can look at metrication of the marketing effort: For example, at the margin, what would be the impact f an extra $ spend on marketing activity X, once baselines are assumed. Would the idea of introducing mobile technologies or enhancing or upgrading the current level of use be productive?, how can time and space independence afforded by the use of mobile technologies assist in realizing a lean marketing approach? Within this context why would mobile technologies be introduced?, when? and how?

7. On the supply side we can start – again - with the concept of LEAN, and particularly lean production at Layer 2, and lean production plus lean service at layer 3. Process quality and process improvement methodologies might be applied here and such programs without question can utilize information source and time independence to their advantage. The challenge would be how to do it in YOUR business. Specifically we could look at the impact of individual decisions (production, service, marketing, etc) to invest and/or institute new strategies or activities on the competence, agility or health of the firm. For example if you are lean, are you healthy? In other words do things like lean (etc.) add to the bottom line or any other important attribute for which initially they were instituted? Again metrication is the essential element here. In order to determine if specific approaches work (e.g. some specific mobile strategy) one needs to determine a measure for say "efficacy", determine how much more efficacious the organization will be upon the introduction of such technology and the trends towards leanness AND a relation model that connects this measure to a measure of the attribute that was important and was the target of improvement (e.g. bottom-line). Again here, integration is the essence. Whatever enabling technology we employ, mobile ICT technologies being one instance, such technologies must integrate throughout the layers. In 6 above we discussed the impact and how to deal with the introduction of enabling technologies at layer 1 of the pyramid, that is on the demand side. But such introduction must integrate with the supply side at both the production layer (layer 2) and the layer above it which itself is an integrating layer.

8. Such a model of how such enabling technologies such as mobile ICT might be identified, justified and implemented may be produced through the development of a framework. We start with the general concept, we then determine the essential characteristics of the concept (five or six such characteristics), we then determine the attributes that represent these characteristics, if they are already measured, fine, if not, we propose a set of key concepts or processes that are central in that area and establish an ordinal measure of performance of that particular attribute. We do this kind of identification of characteristics

and their measures across the board. The result would be a spectrum of performance indicators (as many as 100 or more, but should aim to keep them between 15 and 50) each measured on an ordinal scale say from 0 to 5 (0 it is not done, 5 it is best practice).

9. Once all this is done one can use the instrument in two ways: a) to assess and measure the extent of a concept (e.g. leanness or effectiveness of mobile ICT introduction project) within a specific level of an organization or a particular process or project and; b) to do a gap analysis based on a comparison between status quo as determine though an assessment and an optimal scenario which often times one can be logically defined. At the very least a comparison to best practice is always possible.

It is implied also that in order to succeed, an enterprise must consider itself a part of and indeed be integrated into a larger system. Such an enterprise can obtain and use information at the meta-level that would otherwise be denied it if not thus integrated. Lack of access to this level of information is an important ingredient towards early demise. Enterprises that wish to continue to succeed must integrate. Much of this book is about how to achieve this integration.

As you can see, to acquire, manage, grow and most importantly re-optimize a successful enterprise one needs information. Information is obtained, manipulated, used, disseminated and retained. In the preceding sections we set the scene, using an economic basis for the identification of the type of information required to acquire, manage and grow a business. It should be now clear that success is contingent upon concentrating on the basic requirements of a firm in terms of systems of information acquisition, manipulation, dissemination and retention and the forms such systems may take and the technologies used to support such systems. Mobile ICT technologies should be an integral part of this larger "justified" system.

We also talked about the four major elements of valuation of firms. They were: revenue, cost, risk and time or longevity and the concepts that are critical in estimating each of these measures. These were: demand, production, uncertainty, and sustainability. We also briefly talked about the kind of information needed to conduct such measurements. The table below summarizes our findings so far.

Any strategy to incorporate mobile technologies – any strategy that provides a path to transitioning

9

into a mobile enterprise – must therefore at a minimum pay heed to these elements, concepts, categories and information systems. One way to keep on track therefore would be – in our planning – to start from the right hand side column of the table above and work our way backwards to the left-most column at all times asking ourselves, "does this decision support the spirit of the system, category, concept or finally element under question?" In one's strategic plans towards mobility, one must ensure that each level is underpinned reasonably, measurably and logically by the level below.

CONCLUSION

In this chapter we dealt with how mobile technologies might create business value. The presentation centered around an analysis of the concept of value and the idea of strategic incorporation of technology –in our case mobile technologies - in the business process.

We put forth that business value from any technology comes when it is applied, in practice, by the business to earn economic as well as social advantage. We showed that such value was also the true – in fact particularly true - of mobile technologies, wherein their ability to provide location and time independence is a significant advantage to business. However, such advantage can only be derived when mobile technologies are carefully incorporated, with a long-term strategic view in mind. The chapter described and discusses such strategic view of mobile technologies.

REFERENCES

Arthur, J., Bazaz, A., Nance, R., & Balci, O. (2007, July). Mitigating Security Risks in Systems that Support Pervasive Services and Computing: Access-Driven Verification, Validation and Testing. *Proceedings of the 2007 IEEE International Conference on Pervasive Services*, Istanbul, Turkey; IEEE Computer Society Press. pp. 109-117

Figge, F., & Hahn, T. (2005). The Cost of Sustainability Capital and the Creation of Sustainable Value by Companies. *Journal of Industrial Ecology, 9*(4).

Freeman, R., Hart, S., & Wheeler, D. (eds.) (2007-2008). *Business Value Creation and Society.* Cambridge, UK: Cambridge University Press.

Greenfield, A. (2006). *Everyware: The dawning age of ubiquitous computing. Indianapolis, IN: New Riders.*

Hansmann, U. (2003). *Pervasive Computing: The Mobile Word.* New York, NY: Springer.

Hornigen, C., Sundem, G., Stratton, W., Burgstahler, D., & Schatzberg, J. (2007). *Introduction to Management Accounting. 14th Edition; Upper Saddle River, NJ: Prentice-Hall.*

Keat, P., & Young, P. (2005). *Managerial Economics: Economic Tools for Today's Decision Makers. 5th Edition. Upper Saddle River, NJ: Prentice-Hall.*

Jarvenpaa, S., Lang, K., Takeda, Y., & Tuunainen, V. (2003). *Mobile commerce at crossroads. Communications of the ACM, 46*(12).

Phu, D., & Jamieson, R. (2005, July). Security Risks in Mobile Business. *Proceedings of the 2005 International Conference on Mobile Business (ICMB'05),* Sydney, Australia, IEEE Computer Society Press. pp. 121-127

Whitten, P., Mylod, D., Gavran, G., & Sypher, H. (2008). Most Wired Hospitals rate patient satisfaction *Communications of the ACM, 51*(4).

KEY TERMS

Business Sustainability: The extent to which a business is able or is likely to continue to perform its operations.

Essential Value: Value realized through fundamental improvement of the societal condition.

Exchange Value: Value realized through production of monetary revenue and measured by economic profits.

Mobile Technology(ies): ICT technologies used to provide the ability to compute and communicate electronically without restriction imposed by transmission wires and cables.

Utility Value: Value realized through ascribing usefulness to a good or service by the customer of that good or service.

Value: A measure of loss experienced in giving up a good or service.

Chapter II
Game Theory as a Tool in Mobile Technologies and Applications

Rajeev Agrawal
Kumaon Engineering College, India

ABSTRACT

Game theory is a tool used in the context of conflict interest among interacting decision makers. Game theory may be considered as a generalization of the decision theory that includes multiple players or decision makers. This chapter provides an introduction and overview of the game theory and demonstrates its potential applications in mobile business & technologies. Thus, the chapter provides a global outlook of game and economic theory and provides a comprehensive introduction to the more general subject of mathematical economics again in the context of mobile business. The reason for the importance of game theory in the context of mobile business & technologies is the fact that game theory deals primarily with distributed optimization. This distribution and optimization is individual user trade-users who are involved in making their own decisions in their own time and space. The chapter covers the role of game theory in different aspects of mobile applications, technologies and business.

INTRODUCTION

In the world of mobile business there are conflicting interests between two or more providers. To better understand the phenomenon, let A and B be two service providers in mobile communication field. There will be conflict of interest regarding business issues such as spectrum, tariff, region etc. In mathematical modeling A and B are called players and business is a game. The game should have minimum of two players and as the number of players increases the modeling complexity increases.

Sequential and simultaneous are two fundamental type of games. There are alternative moves in sequential gaming, which follow the rule "Look ahead and reason back". Where as in simultaneous game there is not necessarily any last move. One has to consider all possible combination and search for dominant strategy.

Game Theory can be classified into two categories (i) cooperative game theory (ii) non co-operative game theory. The non co-operative game can be zero sum game or non zero sum game. In zero sum game the gain of one player is equal to the loss of other player. In non-zero sum game the gain of one player is not equal to the loss of other player. The non-zero sum game was first introduce by John Nash .It is also called Nash equilibrium. Nash equilibrium is the universally used solution concept. However, co-operative game theory is totally different from non co-operative game theory. Co operative game theory is applied to solve different problem as this theory deals with the solution that are equitable. Further, the game can be modeled/played using certain strategies taken by a player in terms of pure or mixed strategies. In general if A takes m pure strategy and B takes n pure strategy than the game is called two person game or mxn rectangular game. A matrix is generated in terms of gain/loss (payoff matrix) if the player payoff functions are common to the players, a game is treated as game of complete information. Where as in the game of incomplete information at least to one player the payoff function is not known. To find the value of game $m \times n$ maxmin minmax principle is applied. The analytical condition of pure strategy of two-person sum game can be expressed as

$$\max_{x \varepsilon A} \min_{y \varepsilon B} f(x,y) \leq \min_{y \varepsilon B} \max_{x \varepsilon A} f(x,y)$$

In case of mixed strategies the analytical conclusion is given as

$$E(p,q) = \sum_{i=1}^{m} \sum_{j=1}^{n} a_{ij} p_i q_j;$$

where p and q are the mixed strategies of A and B respectively [a_{ij}], payoff matrix of order $m \times n$. The game can further be classified in terms of static or dynamic game. In the formal game the players do not have any information about the move/choices of other players i.e. the players have their own choices(bidding). In the later case the games have multiple move/stages (in case of chess, bargaining). To conclude the role of game theory which is " the study of multi person decision problem" can be used in different areas of study such as business, Engineering, Intelligence, biology, Social beliefs, Trade and so many other related areas.

The chapter is organized in five sections. In section 1 we provide the basic introduction of game theory, followed by the role of game theory in business, the application of game theoretic approach in different mobile technologies in section 2 and 3. The other aspect related to social perspective is discussed in section 4. We conclude the chapter in the last section.

ROLE OF GAME THEORY IN BUSINESS

Due to advances in information technology and e-commerce the decision and its consequences in business are affected by the interactions.(with customers, suppliers other business partners …) . Any business decision or action taken by a group or organization has multiple impacts due to the interacting group/member inside or outside the firm. In such scenario where the outcome of one depends on other and there is interactive decision making in such condition the role of game theory is interesting. The obvious question one can ask is the why to use game theory than other tools?. However, any approach such as decision tree or optimization infers/optimizes results from the perspective of one player only. It could not incorporate the strategic behaviour of other players. In previous section it was clearly established that game theory is a collection of tools for predicting outcomes of a players/group, which interacts, and an action of individual affects the payoff of other players/group in the game.

In Market Power

In business the companies often compete on prices and are involved in price war in order to control of the market share. In such cases the behaviour of the company can well be understood or analyzed using the game theory framework, which generally referred to as "Prisoner Dilemma". Assuming the business as a long time process the concept of repetition of interaction are captured for which organizations used different strategical move with the person/group/organization involved in the chain/interactions giving two widely used approaches based on vertical integration and virtual integration. In the initial phases the vertical integration was used and later due to globalization and information advancement concept of virtual integration came into existence. Game theory is being widely used in business and economic field due to its capability to add inputs to the process involving self interested agent, multiple interaction yielding improved strategic decision making.

Auction and Bid

The role of game theory for auction mechanism is also reported. A non-cooperative theory is used to find an appropriate order for the auction from different types of buyers. The buyers may be categorized in terms of risk neutral, risk averse and risk seeking (based on Von-Neumann Morgenstern utility function). Further, this non-cooperative game framework is resolved using Nash equilibrium. The problem with such type of approach is that the equation, which defines the game, might be intractable. To overcome this problem different types of approaches are used in the literature such as playing game several times with random selection using different strategy for optimizing the equations/sets. Game theoretic and other tools associated, plays an important role in the field of auction mechanism, which is a much studied area of interest in the field of Economics. Internet auction has added a new dimension to this field and is generally referred as combinatorial auction. Internet has created a larger interest in auction with advent of new auction forms/players. This includes group- buying, reverse auction and online auctions, which uses a new way to sell the items using buyout price. This can be permanent or temporary, formal is effective during entire period of auction, in contrast the buyout option disappears as soon as first bidder select the buyout price in temporary buyout.

Many researchers have analyzed different model using game theoretic approach. Such as with two bidders and two value model with risk averse bidder leading to a buyout price with high-value and bidders with low value waiting. This results in high yield for seller in comparison to ascending bid auction without any buyout price. Additional information on frequency of buyout price was also provided by some researchers; model using two risk neutral bidders, risk averse seller, role of impatience in buy now auction were also studied and reported in the literature.

The closing rule, hard and soft with bidding behaviour and their auction outcome is also reported.

Different Models Used in Auction Mechanism

In such online auction the bidder join or engaged in the auction process randomly obeying the Poisson process with parameter λ. Here the bidder is risk neutral and the expression in terms of utility (u), valuation (v), Price (P), time (τ, t) and discounting factor $\delta \epsilon (0,1)$ is give by the

$$U(v-p, \tau-t) = \delta^{z-1}(v-p)$$

Resulting in two choices i.e. buyout or bid. To conclude in the Internet world, the auction plays an important role in online business.

Further, the general auction (not through Internet) the problem is to "determine the winner from different bidders, taking into consideration to maximize the income of auctioneer". This is a problem for a given set of weighted parameters/variables. Other issues which are significant in Internet auctions are transmission cost, distributed computation interfere and the on-line problems. For better understanding of the reader a game theoretic framework based on Second- Price Auction is drawn.

- There is only one indivisible unit to bid
- There can be n potential bidders. The cost/value can be expressed as

$$0 \le v_1 \le v_2 \le v_i$$

Now considering that there are two bidder i.e. i=2
- The bids are submitted simultaneously i.e. $S_i \in [0, \infty]$
- The highest bid wins but he only pays the second bid ($\max_{j \ne i} = S_j$)
- The utility can be expressed as $v_i - \max_{j \ne i} s_j$

Let v_1, v_2 are the valuations and s_1, s_2 are bids than one can have the Pay-offs as

$$u_1 \equiv if \ s_1 \rangle s_2 \ then \ v_1 - s_2 \ else \ 0$$

$$u_2 \equiv if \ s_2 \rangle s_1 \ then \ v_2 - s_1 \ else \ 0$$

Now from Player's 1 view

Case 1

If $S_1 \le S_2$; the payoff is zero, if $S_2 \le V_1$ the payoff is $V_1 - S_2$ and if $V_1 < S_2 < S_1$ the payoff is negative. All theses condition reflects the Overbidding.

Figure 1. Fix-price mechanism [Source: Hanappi & Hanappi-Egger, 2001]

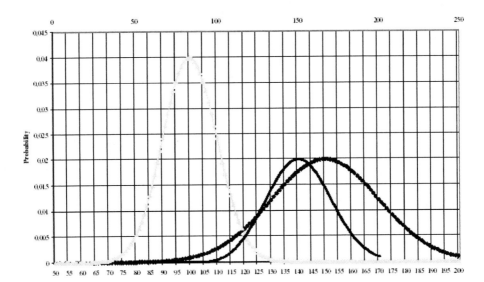

Figure 2. Negotiable mechanism source

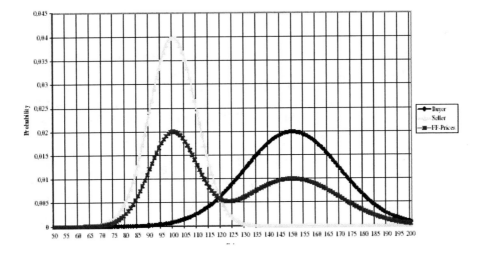

Case 2

If $S_1 \leq S_2$; the payoff is zero, if $S_2 \leq V_1$ the payoff is $V_1 - S_2$ and if $V_1 < S_2 < S_1$ the payoff is negative. This results in Underbidding.

Based on the above the best strategy for Player1 will be for the s1=v1 and for player 2 is to bid for s2=v2.

Software as Service Pricing

Any service, which has service provider and user are treated as multiparty. Software nowadays is treated as service and is an emerging business model in terms of its sale and distribution. The fundamental of such multiparty service becomes an optimization problem. However, its behaviour can be captured by game theory.

Figure 3. Game tree for general market

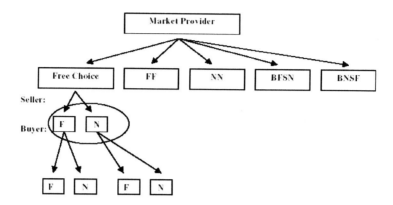

Game theoretic approach is applied for information pricing using a principle-agent game framework. In such type of framework information service provider (ISP) proposes a price for its services and user responds. This can be modeled using non-cooperative game, where service provider and users are treated as game leader and follower respectively.

ISP task is to maximize its profit through optimum price for this he requires to draw a desirable demand from user. The result of the game is the set of equilibrium equation, where both players (service provider, user) try to choose such strategy, which maximize their utility. The general expression for the service provider's optimization problem can be expressed as

$$R = \max_{P,E} [\int_{\theta_0}^{\theta} \{(P-C)q(P,\theta) + E\} f(\theta) d\theta]$$

where P=price, C=cost, E=entry fees, $q(P,\theta)$= demand function and $F(\theta)$=probability density function of type variable θ, with θ as consumer type

Electronic Commerce Market Mechanism

This discussion present a simple game theoretic approach to show that how one can model a 3-person game of a simple market with seller and a buyer. In general there are two basic market mechanism i.e. a fix price mechanism and negotiation mechanism. The fix price and Negotiable price mechanism can be best understood using a Normal-Normal model in which the fix price of seller and buyer have different mean and variance. For eg: in the given figures seller have mean=100 and variance = 10, buyer mean=150 and variance=20 respectively.

From Figure 1 it is clear that in case fix price mechanism there is no strategy and one should know its price only where as in case of negotiation mechanism a hyper rationale model is used. Accordingly, the player having high negotiation cost has to accept more unfavorable price. The above model is expressed in terms of price reached P_N as:

$$P_N = P_s + (P_B - P_S) * \frac{\delta_S (1-\delta_B)}{1-\delta_S \cdot \delta_B}$$

With P_S and P_B is reservation price of seller and buyer and δ_S and δ_B discount factor.

Based on these two mechanism one can have four different possibilities viz BFSF(buyer fix seller fix), BNFN (buyer negotiable seller negotiable), BFSN (buyer fix seller negotiable) and BNSF (buyer negotiable and seller fix). The game tree of this game is as shown below.

From the above it is clear that for successful economic behaviour the rules of the game are important any organization/group/individual/company who

Figure 4. Two player network

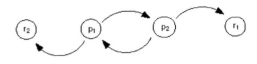

Figure 5. Network with intermediate players

can able to modify or give new set of rules using any method will be in advantage in long run. These can be through some freedom of choice to other player, knowledge of probability distribution, uncertainty or any additional knowledge, which gives new information to play the game.

GAME THEORY IN MOBILE TECHNOLOGIES

Game theory (GT) has been primarily used in Economics, other major field of application areas include politics and biology. In economics GT is used to model the competition of different groups/organization/companies. The Role of game theory has been taken in the area of mobile technologies which uses wireless communication network standard and concept. The area of networking where one finds the role of GT are mainly in context of routing, resource allocation, congestion control, traffic grooming. Due to proliferation of wireless communication, the role of game theory was also found useful in analyzing the Location of mobile user, Ad-hoc networks, QoS (quality of service) aware bandwidth allocation, admission control security of wireless sensor network, power control in CDMA. The field and areas are so numerous the same cannot be listed. This section gives insight into some of the basic problem of computer network (wired/wireless) where GT is successfully applied and used for further analysis of system design.

In the field of communication are there are two basic fundamental limitation bandwidth and noise. Limited radio spectrum/bandwidth leads to conflicts

of interest. To resolve this conflict one has to resort to certain methods/ways which are treated as "moves" in game theory. These moves affect the other players in the game. In most of the situation in wireless/mobile communication co-operation of the player requires synchronization and other additional signals which are often more difficult to incorporate, so the players agrees to provide a common platform of sharing the resources in distributed manner. In such game (non-cooperative) the players will be decision makers having conflict interest. As these players are actually users of mobile communication/technology, which are represented by their portable device called as mobile unit. These mobile units are rational and try to maximize the payoff or try to minimize their cost.

Finally, in case of mobile networks application rationality can be used to capture, generally all the interactions. However, there should be a reasonable adjustment of the payoff functions. For better understanding some of the problems where the GT framework is used are given below.

i.   **Forwarding of packets:** In any network the main objective of the sender (transmitter) is to send the packet/data to the destination (receiver) see Fig. In such situation one player acts to send its packet to its destination i.e. receiver and the other players acts as a forwarder. If any player forward/sends the packet of other player it cost a fixed cost $0<C<<1$. Here the payoff is difference of reward and cost. This is also called Forwarder's Dilemma in networks.

ii. **Joint packet forwarding game:** In joint packet the source (Se) wants to sends its packet to destination r however, there are two intermediate nodes (Players) between source and destination (see fig.). Player p_1 and p_2 has to forward the packet. This result in the game called joint packet forwarding game.

iii. **Multiple access game:** In multiple access game the player p_1 and p_2 wants to send their packets to their respective receivers using shared medium. In such situation mutual interfere will occur. The transmission cost of the packet is similar as in previous cases.

iv. **Jamming game:** In this case the player p_2 / p_1 prevent other player p_1 / p_2 from successfully transmitting his packet in the same channel in a given time. This game is referred as Jamming game. The player gets a payoff of $+1$ if attacker/ Jammer cannot jam his transmission and -1 if he is jammed.

Table 1. Application of game theory in relation to network Layer

NETWORK LAYER	APPLICATION OF GT
Upper Layers	Not yet explored (active field)
Network Layer	Forwarding Game (Forwarder's Dilemma, Joint Packet)
Medium Access Layer	Multiple access game
Physical Layer	Jamming game

Table 2. Equilibrium conditions for different network problems

Game	Nash Equilibrium state	Pareto-optimal state
Forwarder's Dilemma game.	(D,D)	(F,F)
Joint Packet Forwarding game.	(F, F) and (D, D)	(F,F)
Multiple Access Game.	(T, Q) and (Q, T)	(T, Q) and (Q, T)
Jamming game	NO	ALL

The table given below sketches the role of GT in terms of different layers used in OSI reference model.(used for any type of networking).

Further, these problems can also be extended/analyzed in terms of static or dynamic game framework with different strategies. The table below gives the equilibrium condition applicable to above problems using Nash and Pareto equilibrium.

Point Selection of Mobile User

In case of mobile communication users in a particular geographical area are non-uniformly distributed. Further, distribution of users in a network may be dynamic and often unpredictable. A user in a congested area could able to establish a link if he moves to a new area, which is less, loaded. In worst case scenario the user may require to move repeatedly resulting in instability of the system. However, there is tradeoff between the signal gained and the effort in moving additional distance to establish a link by the user by changing is location. Further, each user makes its own decision to change its location resulting in optimizing its benefit rather than other users or a system. The users are supposed to be selfish and

their moves affect the interest of the other users or in other term system as a whole.

A game theoretic approach is used to model the above mentioned system characteristic where on entering the system the user gets the information based on its requirements and preferences than user select a point evaluating the tradeoff. The result of such game theoretic framework is an assignment of user to access points.

Traffic Grooming in Optical Network

In optical network traffic grooming is a technique for considering low bandwidth traffics into higher bandwidth traffics. This can be analyzed using two node network with each node has two wavelengths (λ_0, λ_1) with two time slots (t_{s0}, t_{s1}) to cater the user coming into the system. A game theoretic approach can be used based on two different approaches i.e. co-operative and non-cooperative. Elementary cost can be defined based on different possible outcomes such as cost when new wavelength is used(a), cost of time-slot(b), cost of traffic exchange with same wavelength in time-slot(c) and wavelength conversion cost(d). A can also choose different strategies for the nodes. Table given below shows such payoff for two nodes n0 and n1.

18

Table 3. Payoff table for traffic grooming

	(ts_0, λ_0)	(ts_1, λ_0)	(ts_0, λ_1)	(ts_1, λ_1)
(ts_0, λ_0)	*	bc,bc	bd,abd	bcd,abcd
(ts_1, λ_0)	*	*	*	*
(ts_0, λ_1)	*	abcd,bcd	ab,ab	abc,abc
(ts_1, λ_1)	*	abd,bd	abc,abc	ab,ab

Congestion Control in Networking

Congestion is treated as one of the most fundamental problem in the networks. Game theoretic model is used to capture " how the users adapt their rates" in particular, relationship between user requirement and system performance is established represented by an equilibrium based on Nash or Pareto-optimal. As user are competing for the shared resources and move made by a particular user can affect the utility of other. In such scenario game theoretic is best-suited framework to model and for the evaluation of performance modeling. The system in such cases is given in the figure.

The systematic strategic game is formed as S = (N, A, U), where is n is number of users, A = shared link/channel and U is utility. The payoff in terms of utility function is drawn to obtain the required equilibrium. Here it is to be noted that one can use different hypothesis such as Darwinian, Myopia, Perturbation and self-regarding.

Ad-Hoc Networks

The problem of selfishness on the Internet which consists of ports connected together but they do not have any centralized control leads to a type of an Ad-hoc network. In such cases every node/player acts as self controlled node. The player may act as cooperative, adversant, selfish (maximize on utility affecting the utility of other) and may also refuse to forward packets. In such situation one should take into account the selfish behaviour on parts of the nodes/players. Game theory can describe interaction of selfish and rational individuals in terms of two person prisoner's dilemma with strategy as cooperative Vs defect, payoff/utility as reward/punishment with dominance. Using the above framework one can have the Nash equilibrium, cost of anarchy and can design a system for such selfish user.

Wireless Sensor Network

The cooperative game is very useful for security in wireless sensor network. In this game one has to formulate a cooperative game between sensor nodes and propose a novel framework for forming cluster in wireless sensor network. In this framework each cluster is in cooperative environment. We define a game strategy set that gives the guarantee to reach an equilibrium point. We also define a payoff function for it. The advantage of the framework comes from the

Figure 6. System with multiple inputs with shared link

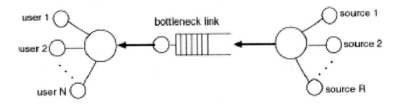

19

fact that we can apply and accumulate the cooperation and reputation in the utility function, while aggregating the quality of security. The payoff function between two sensor node should be dependent on their distance, and every nodes transmitter signal strength. When the transmitter signal strength is increased the node strongly cooperate with its neighbour A good security design for sensor network must be able to secure node to node communication for secure wireless network the cooperative game is defined as T=(I,S,U), I is the set of sensor nodes ,S is the set of strategies ,U is the payoff function for nodes. Our aim is to find the largest payoff function this function consist three main factor that are cooperation, reputation and quality of security.

In a Peer to Peer Network

Game theory is an ideal tool to model a system with selfish nodes. In a peer to peer network we use Nash equilibrium strategies. In peer to peer network system, nodes act as a client and server, they provide a service to each other node. One can use a game theory principal to determine when they should or should not serve other node. Node gain utility by obtaining service, loose utility while serving other node. A system designer can use Nash equilibrium to analyze the strategic choice made by different nodes.

Bit Rate Control in Video Coding Using Service Game Concept

In service game we suppose that the network lifetime to be infinitely large. We divide the total time into individual time period .The time period is represented by t and t = 1,2,3... In every time period each node gets a request for service. A request is assume to be fulfilled when any of the request service providers agree to serve. One node request only one service in each time period, and a node can receive multiple requests at the same time period. The service game can be defined as all the nodes acts as players with action associated with them. Since the propose mechanism is based on the player's reputation link, the benefit that a player draw from the system to its contribution. The benefit is a monotonically increasing function of a player's contribution, so this is a non-cooperative game among the player's. Where, each player wants to maximize its utility. Thus, we conclude that the only pure strategy Nash equilibrium of players select the

action such that action selected in each time period does not appear to be a likely convergence state for any useful peer to peer system. This shows the applicability of game theory to optimize the bit rate control in video coding.

Software Designed Radio Networks

Game Theory is used in Software Designed Radio Networks. In order to model the spectrum usage, radio frequency interference avoidance, and distributed radio resource management, the behavior of Software Defined Radios are predicted using game theory in an analytic mathematical framework.. The radios are the players in the game; the strategies in the game are based on the transmitter choosing, the value of the adaptive link characteristic that maximizes the spectral efficiency, while meeting a BER constraint. The goal of the game is to maximize the winnings. Here the winnings would be for a radio to accrue the most bandwidth, to achieve a particular performance target. Additionally, these approaches rest upon the assumption of higher-order rationality, i.e. the ability of a node to independently and recursively analyze a best response to other network nodes.

Modelling Imperfect Competition in Electricity/Mobile Tariffs

Game theory has been used to study imperfect competition in electricity markets. Two basic approaches are described in the literature. However, simulations show that the two approaches converge to the same outcome when unique Nash equilibrium exists and assumptions in the game theory approach are realistic.

Two main approaches have been used to study imperfect competition in electricity markets. These approaches are game theory and agent-based economics (ABE). The most common and more visited approach has been the game theory. Because the "conventional" economic modeling approach presented some shortcomings and limited ability to model all the intrinsic characteristics of electricity markets, the second approach, ABE approach is becoming more and more interesting in the recent years. Classical Game theory finds a market equilibrium. In a power market, a market equilibrium is defined as a set of prices, generator outputs, transmission flows, and consumptions that simultaneously satisfy each market participant's first order conditions for maximization of its profit while clearing the market. Such equilibrium is obtained by deriving first order and market clearing conditions and solving them simultaneously. A solution satisfying those conditions possesses the property that no participant will want to alter its decisions unilaterally: in game theoretic terms it is a well known Nash equilibrium. Further, this model can best be suited to explain the tariffs of mobile calls.

Game Theory as a Tool for Multiple Antenna

Various types of multiple antenna systems show how the lack of co-operation among the different entities is used by game theory. Game theory and multiple antennas can be classified based on the payoff received by each player in the game or by the configuration of users in the problem solved. Payoff based classes for example, the instantaneous, average or outage mutual information or the Signal to Interference and Noise ratio while user configuration based classes include the single-user Multiple-Input-Multiple-Output (MIMO) channel the vector interference channel the vector multiple access channel the vector broadcast channel problems and MIMO ad-hoc network. All these problems have a level of uncertainty or non-coordination that makes it difficult to use conventional analytic techniques and lends itself to analysis using non-cooperative game theory. In general, the solutions reached by these techniques are rarely fair and some level of cooperation can be introduced.

GAME THEORY AND INTERNET COMMERCE

Many decisions by humans, businesses, and automated agents in Internet transactions can be modeled in traditional game-theoretic terms. Examples include B-to-B price negotiation, B-to-C competition for customers, and C-to-C online auctions. If multiple viewpoints, uncertainty, and interval values are considered the use of fuzzy logic is inevitable. Game theory provides guidance for many of the trades in strategic competition. Games of two or more players can be modeled for fixed size market places or growing exchanges multiple step games such as repeated trials with or without stepwise memory can help an analyst to understand this phenomenon. Several web business areas have received game theoretic attention,

including software agents that compete or cooperate for their owner-consumers.

More sophisticated behavior is under investigation, including learning that accounts for competitor models and belief, bargaining, vagueness, common knowledge, and possible-state considerations. Coalitions of agents can cooperate economically, in partnership formation, contract negotiation, and delivery date negotiation. Reverse bid auction agents can account for cost and lead time, but also for less precise metrics like quality, capacity, inventory levels, reliability, variability, company stability, security, and secrecy. The area of e-commerce is still developing in unforeseeable ways. There are often several conflicting models and explanations for consumer behavior, with the resultant range of differing prescriptions for selling and buying strategies. Multiple conflicting model memberships like these are a well- explored area of fuzzy set logic.

The other areas where game theory has been used are to analyze routing and flow control in communication networks link adaptation in cellular radio networks power control, and throughput or rate maximization using iterative water-filling.

SOCIAL PERSPECTIVE OF GAME THEORY

Liberalization process has been changing the market of every industry through out the world. A major advantage of such liberalization is to give a better and efficient market and reasonable price, this introduces competition in the open market and the companies having major market shares opposes such type of moves and may slow the process. For this they adapt different strategies. To study these characteristics one has to resort to game theory approaches as this has direct social impact when the entity is related to a common man such as oil prices, electricity tariffs, Taxations etc.

International Relations and Projects

Game theory has been successful used in analyzing the trade relation between two countries. In such case the countries are treated as players and every player of the game wants to maximize its utility/gain. To optimize his gain each counties adopt different strategy, which affects the moves of other countries. This is well formulated in International relations using game theory. However, if countries are looking toward the national perspective and a long term relation with other player, the equilibrium results in zero sum game of two players. In case International projects where there are more than two countries involve such as Iran-Pakistan-India gas pipe line project the role of co-operative game theory is important to set strategical move/bid to maximize its gain.

In Socio-Mechanism for Belief Change

The application of game theory has been used in explaining socio-cognitive pertaining to belief revision. To formalize a game social relationship, composition rule based on social factors are considered. As each human has to play a different role in the society, the role can be categorized in terms of formal role and informal role or relationship. Suppose the person i has several role to play at a point of time t. These all role constitute a space S. For a particular instant of time if a person is playing a role as a friend in his group where he and his friends are players this situation can well be analyzed using GT framework where the goal of the players is not to maximize their gains but to result in a zero sum game or in favour of other player. On contrast to this the same person in his profession life wants to maximize his gain for which he uses different strategies. This change in the belief can be best modeled using game theory.

CONCLUSION

In this contribution it is demonstrated how the concept of game theory can be used and applied to different perspectives. Using problems /study from different fields such as business, technology (mobile) social it was established that the behaviour of the players can be analyzed using this framework. Furthermore, due to the page restriction much of the other aspects/detailed of the problem are not elaborated, specially in terms of mathematical modeling. However, the purpose of this chapter is to guide the interested reader to make familiar the basics of game theory and its application areas and to help them to take their own studies using game theory as a tool. For further studies readers are advice to follow the references given at the end of the chapter.

REFERENCES

Burns, T. R., & Gomolinska, A. (2001). Socio-cognitive mechanism of belief. *Journal of Cognitive system Research, 2*, 39-54.

Agah, A., Basu, K., & Das, S. K.(2006). Security enforcement in wireless sensor networks: A framework based on non-cooperative games. *Journal of pervasive and mobile computing, 2*, 137-158.

Agah, A., Das, S. K., & Basu, K. (2004). A game theory based approach for security in wireless sensor network. In proceeding of *IEEE, Performance, Computing and communication conference*, 259-263.

Ahmad, I., & Luo, J. (2006). On using game theory to optimize the rate control in video coding. *IEEE, Trans. on circuits and systems for video tech, 16*(2), 209-218.

Andreoiu, A., Bhattacharaya, K., & Canizares, C. (2005). Pricing power system stabilizers using game theory. *IEE proc. Gener. Trans. Distrb, 152*(6), 780-786.

Byde, A. (2003). Applying evolutionary game theory to auction mechanism design. *In proceeding of the IEEE, International conference on E-commerce CEC'03.*

Eidenbenz, S., Anilkumar, V. S., & Zust, S. (2003). Equilibrium in topology control games for ad-hoc networks. *In proceeding of International conference on mobile computing and networking*, 2-11.

Erhun, F., & Keskinocak, P. (2003). *Game theory in Business application.* (Tech. rep). School of Industrial and system engineering, Georgia Inst. of tech. Atlanta, GA.

Fan, X., Alpcan, T., Arcak, M., & et.al.(2006). A passivity approach to game-theoretic CDMA power control. *Automatica, 42*, 1837-1847.

Felegyhazi, M., & Haubaux, J. P. (2006). *Game theory in wireless networks: A tutorial.* (EPFL Tech. rpt. LCA-REPORT-2006-002). EPFL-Switzerland.

Fragnelli, V., & Moretti, S. (2007). *A game theoretic approach to the classification problem in gene expression data analysis.* Computer and mathematics with applications.doi:10.1016/j.camwa.2006.12.088.

Gunturi, S. & Paganinni, F. (2003). Game theoretic approach to power control in Cellular CDMA. *In proceeding of* IEEE, *Vehicular Tech, Conference VTC 2003-fall, 4,* 2362- 2366.

Gupta, R., & Somani, A. K. (2005). Game theory as a tool to strategize as well as predict nodes behaviour in peer-to-peer networks. *In proceeding of 11ᵗʰ International conference on parallel and distributed systems, ICPADS'05.* (pp. 244-249).

Hanappi, H., & Hanappi-Egger, E. (2001). Electronic commerce and market mechanism A game-theoretic approach. *In Proceeding of 34ᵗʰ Hawaii International conference on system sciences.* (p. 1039).

Krishna, V., & Rameh, V. C. (1998). Intelligent agents negotiation in market games part 1: Model. *IEEE, Trans. On power systems, 13*(3), 1103-1108.

MacKenzie, A. B., & Wicker, S. B. (2001). Game theory in communications: Motivation, Explanation and application to power control. *In Proceeding of IEEE, Global Telecommunication Conference GLOB-COM'01,* 821-826.

Menasche, D. S., Figueiredo, & Silva, E. (2005). An evolutionary game theoretic approach to congestion control. *Journal of performance Evaluation, 62,* 295-312.

Nhat, V., Obaid, A., & Poirier, P. (2005). Application of Game theory in Traffic grooming. *In Proceeding of Second IFIP International Conference in wireless and optical communications, WOCN 2005,* 383-387.
Mittal, K., Belding, E., & Suri, S. (2005). *A game theoretic analysis of wireless access point selection by mobile users.* (Tech. rep). Dept. of computer science, Univ. of California, Santa Barbara, U. S.

Niyato, D., & Hossain, E. (2007). A game theoretic approach to competitive spectrum sharing in cognitive radio network. *In proceeding of IEEE wireless communications and networking conference WCNC'07,* 16-20.

Niyato, N., & Hossain, E. (2007). QoS aware bandwidth allocation and admission control in IEEE 802.16 broadband wireless access networks: A non-cooperative game theoretic approach. *Journal of computer Networks, 51,* 3305-3321.

Oteri, O.(2007). Multiple antennas and game theory. *IEEE Radio and wireless symposium,* 87-90.

Padimitriou, C. H. (2001). Game theory and mathematical Economics: A theoretical computer scientist's introduction. *In proceeding of IEEE 42ⁿᵈ Symposium on foundation of computer science FOCS'01.*

Shu, X. N. & Feng, X. J. (2006). The analyses of international trade relationship between china and other Southeast Asian countries based on evolutionary game theory. *In Proceeding of International conference on Management Science and Engineering ICMSE 2006,* 1095-1100.

Silva, E. L., Morales, J. C., & Melo, A. C.(2001). Allocating congestion cost using game theory. *In proceeding of IEEE porto power tech conference.*

Silverman, S. J. (2006). Game theory and software defined radios. *In the proceeding of Military communications conference MILCOM'06,* 1-7.

Singh, H. (1999). Introduction to game theory and its application in electric power market. *IEEE computer application in power, 12*(4), 18-22.

Tian, C., Zheng, Y., Jiang, Z., & et.al.(2006). Software as service pricing: A game theory perspective. *In proceeding of IEEE International conference on service operations and logistics and informatics SOLI'06,* 215-218.

Xingli, Y., & Tingjie, L. (2007). Analysis of bid strategy with game theory in auction with buyout price. In proceeding of International conference on service systems and service management, 1-4.

Zakiuddin, I., Hawkins, T., & Moffat, N. (2005). Toward a game theoretic understanding of ad-hoc routing. *Electronics notes in theoretical computer science, 119,* 67-92.

KEY TERMS

Auction: Sale where article sold to a highest bidder, bidding process.

Business: Activity, profession, action demanding time and labour.

Combinatorial: Mathematical combination.

Congestion: Blocking, no space to move

Game Theory: A field to study the recognize sequences of moves, decision rule.

Internet Commerce: Transaction through computers.

Mobile: Portable device, device on move.

Multiple Access: Sharing of a channel, many user on a link.

Social: Related to society, large group of people.

Chapter III
A Methodology and Framework for Extending Mobile Transformations to Mobile Collaborations for SMEs

Ioakim (Makis) Marmaridis
IMTG Pty Ltd and University of Western Sydney, Australia

ABSTRACT

Enabling interorganizational collaboration for SMEs holds a lot of promise for increased competitiveness and global reach in a connected economy (Ripeanu, 2008; Marmaridis, 2004; Ginige 2004). An earlier book (Marmaridis & Unhelkar, 2005) examined the unique constraints that SME organizations have in embracing new technology – such as mobile technology. The solution proposed for overcoming these constraints is a methodology that is referred to as m-transformation (Marmaridis, 2006). Building on this work, this chapter now presents the next step in SME evolution, mobile collaboration (m-collaboration). The chapter details the concerns that must be overcome for SMEs to start collaborating rapidly with each other. It examines the role of trust in collaboration and provides a methodology suitable for handling the variation of trust throughout each collaborative engagement. It also presents a conceptual framework that can be used to implement the methodology and empower SMEs into embracing collaboration and realizing tangible benefits from it. Aspects of the methodology and conceptual framework have been presented in a number of international conferences already (Marmaridis, 2005); this chapter, however, puts the pieces together and presents the methodology and framework in their entirety. Upon completing this chapter, the reader will have a very good understanding of the landscape of collaboration in the SME space. Furthermore, the reader will be familiarized with the field-tested mobile collaboration methodology for SMEs and the conceptual framework for implementing it in real life.

INTRODUCTION

Mobile collaboration for SMEs has proved to be an elusive goal. Even though the term has been in the foreground of research circles (Marmaridis & Unhelkar, 2005; Looney, 2004) and commercial vendors (Spellman, 1997) for long time, actual tangible benefits are yet to be seen. The promises for operational efficiencies and streamlined processes that mobile collaboration advocates have been offering to organizations of all sizes are yet to be delivered for SMEs.

Mobile collaboration is defined as the intersection area of three key variables, mobile technology, mobility in the workforce and changing collaborative processes (Looney, 2004, Litiu, 2004; Arbab, 2002). Figure 1 below graphically represents this definition:

This chapter builds upon previous work on a methodology for M-Transformation for SMEs (Marmaridis & Unhelkar, 2005). This previous work explored the need and obstacles that SMEs face in adopting mobility as a practice for their internal operations. This chapter expands upon this area and provides insights into how SMEs can expand their use of mobile technology into achieving mobile collaboration in practice. The chapter first presents a brief overview of collaboration from traditional to electronic collaboration and mobile collaboration. Then it examines the barriers to enter mobile collaboration and analyses each of those offering mitigation strategies in the form of a methodology. The methodology covers not only technical issues

in regards to mobile technologies, it also takes into account organizational change and people issues to provide a holistic approach in dealing with the adoption of mobile collaboration for SMEs. Finally the chapter closes with the presentation of conceptual framework for the adoption of mobile collaboration by SMEs. This framework incorporates suggestions and steps from the methodology and enriches those with additional considerations about openness, security, accessibility, maintainability and other key factors that affect the rate of successful adoption of mobile collaboration (Marmaridis, 2005) in the SME space.

BACKGROUND TO MOBILE COLLABORATION FOR SMES

The author's experience both academically and professionally in the field of inter-organisational collaboration has shown that there is a very different rate of adoption between collaboration strategies for larger enterprises and SMEs. In the related field of mobile collaboration, the situation is very similar as well. Large organizations with distributed workforce spread across large geographic distances are investing heavily on mobile collaboration. The author's observations, reflection and analysis of real life projects suggest that mobile collaboration for SMEs is constrained by issues that exist in the research sphere as well as at the operational technology sphere. The research related questions that remain inadequately answered, if at all can be summed in the following statements:

- Whilst there is abundance of technology (Arbab, 2002; Dustdar, 2004), mobile collaboration is not realizing its full potential in the SME space
- Why are SMEs in particular finding it very hard to adopt such innovative technical solutions facilitating mobile collaboration
- What are the necessary pre-requisite steps an SME must take before they can successfully tackle the mobile collaboration opportunity.

At the technology level, some of the current issues include:

- Lack of benchmarks for comparing technologies that otherwise claim to fulfill the same organisational needs
- Lack of metrics for demonstrating return on investment (ROI) to SMEs that consider mobile collaboration

Figure 1. Defining mobile collaboration in terms of people, processes and technology

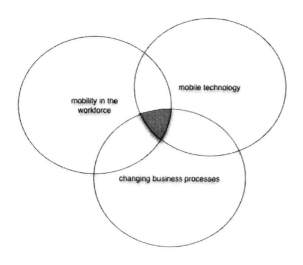

- Integration issues between point solutions that do not provide overall security and data confidentiality and non-repudiation in a collaborative setting across organizations.

EXTENDING MOBILE TRANSFORMATION TO MOBILE COLLABORATION FOR SMEs

Considerable amount of current research is taking place to provide the necessary concepts and technologies that SME and other organizations can easily employ to progress from a state of e-transformation (Kazanis, 2003) to that of Dynamic eCollaboration (Marmaridis, 2004, Marmaridis 2005). From the late 70s until the late 90s, technology penetration at all levels of business has soared. Nowadays, there are hardly any businesses that do not use information and communication technology (ICT) in some capacity either at their front or back office. Adoption of technology and mainly the personal computer (PC) saw that information has gradually become digital and with the Internet explosion connectivity became cheap and relatively easy. As a result interconnected systems are now something very commonly used across most businesses. Turning the vast number of interconnected computers though to a platform for collaboration is quite challenging. Dynamic eCollaboration promises to deliver on the ability for project-based, nearly ad-hoc collaboration for organizations of all sizes. While a lot of active work is happening in the area of Dynamic eCollaboration we are seeing in recent times another explosion in technology that many compare it to the PC revolution. This is the mobile device revolution, manifested in mobile phones and other personal, portable devices that are gaining penetration and capabilities at a rapid pace. Similarly to e-transformation, mobile devices become cheap and ubiquitous leading to the formation of yet another network of devices that are inter-connected and can be used as a platform for collaboration. Many consider mobile collaboration to be the next logical step in the evolutionary chain for SMEs where mobile technologies can be integrated as a cohesive whole in the operation of the business to further leverage existing infrastructure and enable adopting to change at increased speeds.

MOBILE COLLABORATION PREREQUISITES FOR SMEs

One of the biggest obstacles for SMEs to adopt mobile collaboration is that they lack a complete understanding of the prerequisites that must exist before such a goal is even considered. Mobile collaboration is defined in terms of people, processes and technology and there are prerequisites for each of these three elements that must be met before mobile collaboration can be targeted as an organization-wide practice.

People Prerequisites

People-related prerequisites can be further subdivided into two categories, external and internal in reference to the organization. External prerequisites relate to people across organizations that want to collaborate, potential collaborating partners. Internal relate to staff of the same organization that is looking to adopt mobile collaboration practices.

The most common and often overlooked external people prerequisite for mobile collaboration is the need for strong, continuous trust between all involved parties. Where this is not possible the collaborating people must share at least a basic level of trust for each other and also towards the systems they use to augment their collaboration. The need for trust between humans in a collaborative setting is already well understood (Coppola, 2004; Corbit, 2004). Trust towards systems is necessary, as they will play the role of information gatekeepers. If people are not able to trust that their information is going to be kept secure and confidential and therefore only accessible to intended recipients they are unlikely to embark on collaboration with others even if they trust the other parties (Ellison, 2004).

Internally, people must also be open to collaborating with others not only from within their organization but across numerous organizations as well. Whilst at the enterprise level the need for a receptive user population has been shown as paramount (Bennett 1998) and numerous texts exist explaining change management and methods for integrating new systems, process and business practices at existing organizations (Cohen, 2000; Conti, 2004) this is not the case for the SME space. There everyone assumes that because the organization is smaller it is enough for the general manager to decree that they will now be collaborating with other organizations for this to take place and for all staff to be cooperative. The author's experience strongly suggests that this is not the case at all. Most staff working for an SME hold a lot of pride in their job, they see themselves as necessary and important for the role they fulfill. Opening up collaboration may appear to some of these people as a threat either towards their status within their own organization or towards their long-term job security. Even though executive buy-in towards mobile collaboration is essential in an SME, it is also essential to have staff that sees benefits in mobile collaboration and who is willing to trust the systems and their business partners while embarking on it.

Process Prerequisites

A large organization has support processes in place that ensure it will strive for continuous process improvement, streamlining of operations and simplification of procedures wherever possible. Large organizations have permanently setup divisions whose purpose is to monitor and report on the operations aspects of other divisions. Even though bureaucracy and rigid structures do not allow the results of such established support processes to be as optimal as they could, they nevertheless exist. SMEs on the other hand are very much focused at the tactical level and their "modus operandi" is to put out fires on a daily basis leaving very little room for introspection and process improvement or refinement. Subsequently, many SMEs continue to operate using the same techniques and processes for many years.

This fact presents a problem for the adoption of mobile collaboration. Previous research work on business collaboration (Clements, 1995; Dustdar, 2003) has shown that business processes must be flexible enough so that they can be adapted to a collaborative project-based mode of operation when necessary (Marmaridis, 2006; Liang, 2007). Mobile collaboration has the potential of increasing the pace in getting things done between each party in the collaboration and therefore requires even more flexible processes that can be changed rapidly. An SME must therefore be prepared to quickly examine and re-configure their processes or at least a subset of those to fit within and take advantage of the benefits of speed that stem from mobile collaboration. Mobile technology alone is not panacea; it is not the solution for increased business competitiveness and gaining of strategic advantage. In fact when the relevant processes cannot be changed to suit the new mode of operation introduction of

technology will only result in slowing the entire organization down and potentially setting up the entire mobile collaboration effort for failure.

Technology Prerequisites

Technology is the third supporting pillar of mobile collaboration and it must be treated equally to the other two, people and processes. SMEs tend to either overlook the technology aspect of mobile collaboration or at best gloss over it without paying enough attention to the underlying technical solutions they employ for their mobility requirements. A lot of the times this is not strictly a problem with mobile collaboration, it is in fact a flow-on effect of poor choices made in the earlier phase of the organization's life, the mobile transformation phase in particular. By the time an organization feels enabled to proceed with mobile collaboration, they more than likely have already got some infrastructure in place that enabled them to experience the speed and convenience mobile technology has to offer. The issue however is that working mobile technology is not the same as open, standards-compliant, interoperable mobile technology. There is previously documented evidence to suggest that SMEs do not typically have the IT expertise or resources necessary to carry out exhaustive product comparisons before they embark on their purchases of technology for mobility (Marmaridis, 2005). Instead, SMEs rely on word of mouth, sales staff from various vendors and other informal or biased channels of information about technology. Compounding this with limited budgets for IT – and therefore price sensitive behavior - and ever-shrinking deadlines, one can see why in many cases sub-optimal technology changes are made at the earlier stage of m-transformation that prove road blocks for mobile collaboration in the future.

METHODOLOGY FOR EXPANDING FROM MOBILE TRANSFORMATION TO MOBILE COLLABORATION

The transition from mobile transformation to mobile collaboration must be a gradual one, following a step-by-step approach for mitigating risk and identifying bottlenecks before they present themselves as stumbling blocks to the process of adopting mobile collaboration. The high level methodology for SME mobile collaboration presented below can serve as a

Table 1. Summary steps for methodology for SME mobile collaboration adoption

Step taken	People	Processes	**Technology**
Identify current level of readiness	Are people ready to accept working with others? Is there sufficient internal trust?	How well understood and flexible current processes are?	Is the organization at the mobile transformation level yet? If not is it before or after?
Identify candidate areas of work for mobile collaboration enablement	Your staff that will be involved must be receptive of the upcoming changes	The process must be well documented and flexible enough	What existing systems and sources of information can you immediately leverage via mobile collaboration?
Assess the impact (positive or negative) from the introduction of mobile collaboration for the selected area(s) above	Can you afford to tie staff with mobile collaboration and have them be less productive at their current work?	The process should be non-core to your business	What levels of additional IT investment are necessary and can you afford those?
Introduce mobile collaboration in the organization	Ensure that people are happy to be involved and do not see it as a threat	Do not let mobile collaboration upset core business processes that may stop you from operating	Survey and implement IT support systems (evaluate both open source or proprietary). May want to engage expert consultants to assist with the evaluation
Look for potential collaboration partners	They should have receptive people who are open to sharing knowledge and work practices	Should employ flexible processes that are comparable to yours	Should employ open, standards-based technology wherever possible to minimize interoperability risks
Pilot collaborative project	Use only a small group of your staff and do not tie too many resources to this pilot project	Use one or more processes that will deliver the best value at the shortest time possible (low hanging fruit)	Use existing technology as much as possible and do not export mission critical systems or data
Embrace mobile collaboration as a standard business practice	Make mobility-enhanced collaboration part of your people's culture	Look for candidates for future collaborative projects	Permanently setup the hardware and software necessary to enable mobile collaboration on demand in the future
Collect operational measurements from the collaborative work and use them as feedback	Regularly poll your staff on the front line and listen to their suggestions for improvement, praises and problems while collaborating	Define, record and measure process improvement metrics for your key collaborative processes	Regularly check the performance of your technical solution, keep abreast of large changes in technology and access their usefulness in your situation
Re-iterate and refine the mobile collaboration practice at all levels	Augment your staff capability with external skills via mobile collaboration	Refine your processes and adopt or co-develop best practice with your collaborating parties	Invest time and money to keep technology a strategic tool; do not let it turn into a necessary evil

guide to this transition. The methodology is aligned with the three fundamental elements of support for mobile collaboration, people, processes, and technology and addresses the limitations that were previously discussed at all three areas. The table below summarizes the steps involved and a more detailed discussion follows soon after:

The entire methodology is structured around a core that support small, iterative steps towards assessing, experimenting, piloting and rolling out mobile collaboration in the organization. The approach offers maximum protection against risk and ensures that this initiative will not starve the rest of the organization from necessary resources in terms of people, technology or funds. Core feature of the methodology is that it is technology agnostic and can scale from small 5 people operations all the way up to the enterprise level. The scalability of the methodology serves as a future proofing measure against growth of the organisation. Finally, all the steps prescribed must be taken in the given order however not all are mandatory. There is inherent flexibility in which steps should be taken and which should be skipped, to better match the size of the organisation and the breadth of mobile collaboration that is required.

CONCEPTUAL FRAMEWORK TO SUPPORT MOBILE COLLABORATION

To help organizations avoid the pitfall of selecting and using technology that is suboptimal and even at times inadequate to carry them into the mobile collaboration phase of their growth a conceptual framework is presented below.

There are five core elements that the framework identifies and suggests as key indicators of the adequacy of the technical solution employed to power mobile collaboration. These indicators are:

Figure 2. Conceptual framework for mobile collaboration for SMEs

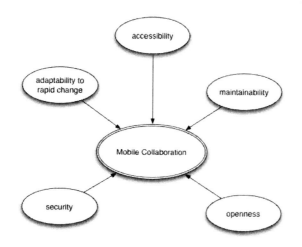

- **Accessibility:** Refers to the ability relevant staff from all collaborating organizations have to access information and system via mobile technology with ease. Any organisation that is looking to adopt mobile collaboration should settle for nothing less than anytime, anywhere access.
- **Maintainability:** Like all other IT systems, collaborative or not, technology must be maintained for performance and stability. Typically the more open the solution the better; with open source solutions preferred over closed, monolithic solutions.
- **Openness:** Refers to the degree of freedom each organization has to access the collaboration data and its meta-data via external tools for reporting, mining and other value-adding activities. Vendor lock-in through data encapsulation should be a sign of the past, no new solutions should be tolerated unless data is stored in an open format that can be queried freely using existing tools.
- **Security:** Including both on transit while in storage for data. As it was mentioned previously there may be trust between the parties involved but there are always others that may try and would certainly wish to gain access to information that is exchanged during a collaborative project.
- **Adaptability to rapid change:** Cost and complexity of the technical solution are key determining factors of whether it can be rapidly adopted to change, which is a given when dealing with multiple party collaboration between organizations. Rigid or inflexible technology can quickly turn from competitive advantage to the proverbial ball and chain that hinders progress in the organization.

Between the methodology and conceptual framework presented above you should now have all that is needed to sensibly identify whether mobile collaboration is a possible next step for your organization to take and if so you are well equipped to avoid most of the common pitfalls in the technology, process management and people issues.

FUTURE DIRECTION

Mobility allows for ubiquitous access to information and it can enhance our personal and professional lives. A lot of research is going into mobility and collaboration for personal and business use both at the SME and enterprise spheres. SMEs in particular stand to gain a lot from adopting mobile collaboration. This chapter should serve as a solid base for other researchers and practitioners in the field to see the immense possibilities in this area through the discussion of the issue surrounding the adoption of mobile collaboration by SMEs. A lot more work remains to be done and several interesting questions are still unanswered. Some of those include a method for calculating ROI for mobile collaboration that takes into account not only the technology but also changes that will benefit the organization from process improvement and people adoption to collaborative practices. Another promising area of research is in establishing metrics that can accurately measure productivity gains from embracing mobile collaboration and later develop into a toolset for decision-making on which collaborative project to engage with.

Mobile collaboration is still a relatively young area where a lot more work is needed to turn it into a mainstream business practice for SMEs. On the other hand, the future for it is bright and with no doubt be established over time given the ever-increasing pressure for SMEs to be competitive at a global level, operating against enterprises and other corporate giants.

CONCLUSION

This chapter has described what mobile collaboration is and how it presents itself as a natural next step in the evolution of SME organizations that have already previously embraced mobile technologies in their internal operations – therefore have become mobile transformed.

Along with the barriers of entry for SMEs embracing mobile collaboration this chapter also provided insights into the key areas of people, processes and technology and the role each plays in the adoption of mobile collaboration. The observations are based on the author's personal involvement in a range of collaboration-related projects at both the SME and enterprise sphere and on his deep research interest in business collaboration.

Finally the chapter provides two practical tools to the reader in the form of a methodology for adopting mobile collaboration within an SME and a conceptual framework that points key criteria the technical infrastructure must meet to offer optimum chances of success to the mobile collaboration adoption effort of the organization.

REFERENCES

Arbab, F., de Boer, F., Scholten, J., & Bonsangue, M. (2002, Jul 31). MoCha: A middleware based on mobile channels. *Computer Software and Applications Conference, 2002. COMPSAC 2002. Proceedings 26th Annual International* , 667 - 673.

Bennett, J., & Karat, J. (1998). *Working through Collaboration: A Framework for Designing Technology Support.* (p. 429).

Clements, P., Jones, R., Weston, R., & Edmonds, E. (1995). A framework for the realization of cooperative systems. *SIGOIS Bull. , 15*(3), 9-10.

Cohen, A., Cash, D., & Muller, M. (2000). Designing to support adversarial collaboration, 31-39.

Conti, M., Gregori, E., & Maselli, G. (2004). Cooperation issues in mobile ad hoc networks, 803-808.

Coppola, N., Hiltz, S., & Rotter, N. (2004). Building trust in virtual teams. *Professional Communication, IEEE Transactions on , 47*, 95-104.

Corbitt, G., Gardiner, L., & Wright, L. (2004). A comparison of team developmental stages, trust and performance for virtual versus face-to-face teams, 42-49.

Dustdar, S., & Gall, H. (2003). Architectural concerns in distributed and mobile collaborative systems., 475-483.

Dustdar, S., Gall, H., & Schmidt, R. (2004). Web services for groupware in distributed and mobile collaboration., 241-247.

Ellison, C., & Schneier, B. (2004, Jan 1). Ten risks of pki: what you are not being told about public key infrastructure. *Public Key Infrastructure: Building Trusted Applications and ... .*

Ginige, A. (2004). *Collaborating to Win - Creating an Effective Virtual Organisation.*

Kazanis, P. (2003). *Methodologies and Tools for E-Transformaing Small to Medium size Enterprises.*

Liang, X., Marmaridis, I., & Ginige, A. (2007). Facilitating Agile Model Driven Development and End-User Development for Evolving Web-based Workflow Applications. *e-Business Engineering, 2007. ICEBE 2007. IEEE International Conference*, 231 - 238.

Litiu, R., & Zeitoun, A. (2004). Infrastructure support for mobile collaboration, 31-40.

Looney, C., & Valacich, J. (2004). Mobile technologies and collaboration, 30.

Marmaridis, I., & Ginige, A. (2005). Framework for collaborative web applications. *Lecture notes in computer science* , 539-544.

Marmaridis, I., & Unhelkar, B. (2005). Challenges in Mobile Transformations: A Requirements Modeling Perspective for Small and Medium Enterprises. *Proceedings of the International Conference on Mobile Business (ICMB'05), 00*, 16-22.

Marmaridis, I., Ginige, J., & Ginige, A. (2004). Web-based architecture for Dynamic eCollaborative work. *International Conference on Software Engineering and Knowledge Engineering* .

Marmaridis, I., Ginige, J., Ginige, A., & Arunatilaka, S. (2004). *Architecture for Evolving and Maintainable Web Information Systems.*

Ripeanu, M., Singh, M., & Vazhkudai, S. (2008). Virtual Organizations [Guest Editors' Introduction]. *Internet Computing, IEEE , 12*(2), 10 - 12.

Spellman, P., Mosier, J., Deus, L., & Carlson, J. (1997). *Collaborative virtual workspace*, 197-203.

KEY TERMS

Collaborative Partners: Organizations that wish to undertake joint collaborative work with other like-minded organizations.

eCollaboration: ICT assisted collaborative work.

Mobile Collaboration: Collaborative work assisted by mobile technologies.

Mobile Transformation: An organization's embrace of mobile technologies and their use internally.

SME: Small and medium enterprises.

Chapter IV
Context Aware Mobility Management

Jhoanna Rhodette Pedrasa
University of New South Wales, Australia

Eranga Perera
National ICT Australia, Australia

Aruna Seneviratne
National ICT Australia, Australia

ABSTRACT

Context is any information that can enhance a computing system's relevance, timeliness, and usefulness to the user. Recent research has been devoted to the use of context in a mobile environment, particularly in handling the mobility itself. This chapter will start with defining what context is, how it is represented, and present a generalized system architecture. The authors then look at the problem of mobility in general and discuss existing solutions. Next they show how context can be leveraged to achieve more intelligent mobility management decisions. The authors highlight some of the research issues particular to context-aware mobility management and survey existing solutions. Last, they argue that these solutions have not truly addressed these issues and present their own architecture for handling mobility.

INTRODUCTION

In this section we attempt to define what context is and discuss some ways of modelling it. We also discuss the generalized framework for context-aware systems.

What is Context?

The term context has been defined in many ways and in many forms, but up to the time of this writing no single definition of context has been put forth that sufficiently captures all the various aspects of this term. Perhaps this reflects the existing "paradox" in context-aware computing. Understanding the concept of context is in itself one of the fundamental research challenges in this field (Schmidt, 2002).

The most widely accepted definition is by Dey (2001), defining context as "any information that can be used to characterize the situation of an entity" (p. 5). This very general definition of context by Dey has been formally extended by Zimmerman, et al (2007) to include a description of context using five fundamental categories, namely individuality, activity, location, time, and relations. In an attempt to better understand context, Henricksen, et al (2002) described it using the following characteristics:

- Context information can be static or dynamic. This implies that context exhibit temporal characteristics, as frequently we are not just interested of present context values but past and future (predicted) context as well.
- Context is imperfect – it can present contradicting, incomplete or even incorrect information. This imperfection stems from a number of reasons, such as sensors becoming faulty or information getting quickly out of date.
- Context can be represented in many ways. A significant gap exists between data captured from sensor outputs and the level of context needed by applications. A context model must be flexible enough to handle the different levels of granularity demanded by various applications.
- Relationships exist between context information. This relationship can be as simple as ownership, and can be exploited to infer that presence of a device mean presence of a person. A person's location also pinpoints his activity, if he is at a gym he is most probably engaging in some sort of exercise.

Context Models

A number of models have been proposed for representing context information. Strang & Linhofff-Popien (2004) categorized the most relevant context modelling approaches based on their representation of data for information exchange and we describe some of the more relevant ones here.

The *key-value model* assigns values to a key and uses a searching algorithm to look-up matching values. An example is the Context Toolkit (Dey, et al, 2001), the first system to define a software abstraction for context-aware applications. Although simple and easy to implement, it is difficult to share data among different entities using this model. An attempt to address this issue is the *mark-up scheme model*, which employs a hierarchical data structure consisting of tags and content. A number of these models are extensions of the Composite Capabilities / Preferences

Profile (CC/PP) standard (Klyne, et al, 2004), such as the one proposed by Indulska, et al (2003). This is the right step forward but by itself is insufficient to address more complex needs such as overriding and merging mechanisms. A totally different approach is the use of graphical models, which relies heavily on visual representation to ease development and understanding by designers. The context extension to Object-Role Modeling (ORM) by Henricksen, et al (2005) is an excellent example of this.

The most promising approach at present is the use of *ontology-based models*. They are the most expressive, extensible, flexible, and can easily support validation (Strang & Linhofff-Popien, 2004). Additionally, the World Wide Web consortium has put forth standards for the semantic web such as the Resource Description Framework (RDF) and the Web Ontology Language (OWL) which can easily be used for modelling context. Ontology-based context management systems have already been proposed, such as the Context Broker Architecture (Chen, et al, 2003), Context Management Framework (Floreen, et al, 2005) and Service-Oriented Context-Aware Middleware (Gu, et al, 2004). These architectures rely on one or more centralized components to manage the context information on behalf of the resource-deprived devices. Our proposed architecture minimizes this dependence on central servers by delegating most of the functions to the mobile nodes themselves.

Generalized Architecture of Context-Aware Systems

Baldauf, et al (2007) presented a general layered conceptual framework for context-aware systems, shown in Figure 1. This common architecture is identifiable to most context-aware management systems, though

Figure 1. General layered conceptual framework for context-aware systems (Baldauf et al, 2007)

Application
Storage / Management
Pre-processing
Raw Data Retrieval
Sensors

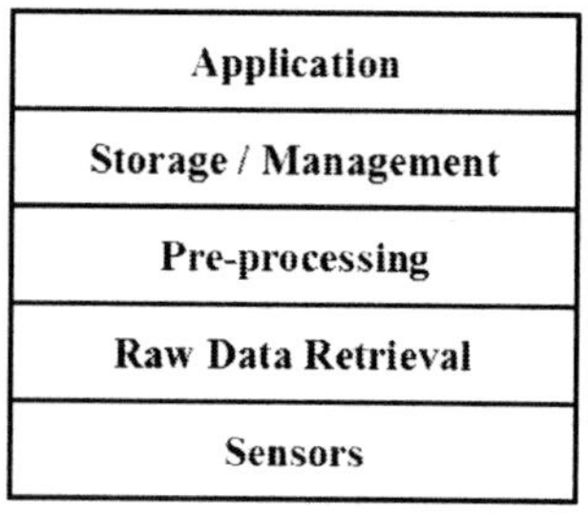

they might differ in name, location and functional range.

The lowest layer is a collection of *sensors*, which could be physical, logical or virtual. Physical sensors are hardware sensors deployed for capturing any physical data. Virtual sensors source context data from software applications or services. For instance, a person's location can be found by browsing the user's electronic diary or calendar. Logical sensors combine physical and virtual sensors in order to solve higher tasks.

On top of these sensors is a layer responsible for the *retrieval of raw context data*. These are drivers for physical sensors and APIs for virtual and logical sensors. The *pre-processing* layer is not implemented in every context aware system but may offer useful information if the raw data are too coarse-grained. This layer is responsible for reasoning and interpreting context information and may involve the aggregation of context data to infer higher level context. If multiple data sources are available, this layer will be tasked with resolving conflicts in sensor data.

The *storage and management layer* organizes the gathered data and offers them via a public interface to the client. Context can be distributed synchronously, with the client polling a central server at regular intervals, or in an asynchronous manner via subscriptions. Finally at the topmost layer is the *application*. Some frameworks use an additional layer between pre-processing and the applications that is tasked of making centralized decisions in behalf of all applications, resolving any conflicts that may arise.

The paper by Baldauf, et al (2007) presents a survey of context-aware systems and frameworks compares them according to various design criteria such as architecture, context model, processing of historical context data, security and privacy. The most common design approach for distributed context-aware frameworks use the layered infrastructure in Figure 1 with one or many centralized components. A centralized architecture potentially suffers the problem of scalability and reliability. Pervasive environments incorporate a large number of heterogeneous devices, which places a huge computational burden on central servers and can be a cause of bottleneck. We therefore propose a hierarchical architecture to circumvent these problems and additionally distribute most of the functionality to the mobile nodes themselves, thus minimizing their dependence on the centralized components.

THE MOBILITY PROBLEM

In this section we look at the problem of mobility in general. We first discuss the different types of mobility then move on to fundamental challenges of mobility management. We then examine existing mobility solutions and consider how context can be used to enhance management decisions.

Mobility Types

IMT 2000 has summarized mobility of multimedia services into the following four aspects:

- *Terminal (device) mobility* refers to a user's ability to move his terminal or device across different networks and access technologies while still maintaining communication.
- *User (personal) mobility* refers to the user's ability to access services using any terminal, anytime, anywhere. The user's identity remains the same irrespective of the device used and its network point of attachment.
- *Session mobility* refers to the seamless transfer of media of an ongoing communication session from one device to another.
- *Service mobility* refers to the network's ability to offer personalized services regardless of the end user's point of attachment. This implies that the network maintains the Quality of Service of ongoing sessions as the user roams. The network must also ensure that the user has access to all of its subscribed network services and features (e.g., pre-paid services) regardless of his point of attachment.

Existing Mobility Solutions

It is obvious that different types of mobility are best addressed at different layers of the networking stack. For instance, terminal mobility can be achieved at the network layer using the Mobile Internet Protocol (MIP) while session mobility can only be handled above the transport layer. In this section we briefly discuss some of the existing mobility solutions at each layer of the OSI stack.

Data Link Layer: The cellular GSM network essentially operates at the data link layer and was developed to handle mobile nodes from the start. Mobility can be managed by different entities: by a Base

Station Controller (BSC) when transferring between Base Transceiver Stations, within a Mobile Switching Centre (MSC) when changing BSCs, or between MSCs when moving to a different MSC. Another example is the IEEE 802.11 set of protocols which handle station mobility in a fashion that is transparent to the upper layers of the 802 LAN stack.

Network Layer: MIPv4 (Perkins C., et al, 2002) is the oldest and one of the most well known mobility protocols at the IP layer designed to handle terminal mobility. This protocol works by allowing a Mobile Host (MH) to retain its home address regardless of its location. When the Mobile Host visits a foreign network, it obtains a Care-of Address (CoA), which is an IP address specific to the Mobile Host's current point of attachment. The association between the permanent home address and the CoA is referred to as a 'binding'. MIPv6 (Johnson, et al, 2004), similar to its counterpart MIPv4, allows an IPv6 host to continue using its "permanent" home address as it moves around the Internet. However, due to the later design of the IPv6 protocol, provision for mobility support have been integrated into IPv6, and as result compared to MIPv4, MIPv6 is more efficient. These two protocols need the support of the network infrastructure and support from the end devices. Proxy Mobile IPv6 (Gundavelli, et al, 2007) is a network layer mobility management protocol which does not require any support from the end devices. However the mobility that this protocol can support is limited to within a single domain.

In order to provide mobility support for groups of nodes moving as a unit (referred to as a moving network) the network layer mobility protocol NEMO (Devarapalli, et al, 2005) has been proposed. This protocol relies on a Mobile Router to provide connectivity to all the nodes within the moving network and it is an extension to the host mobility protocol MIPv6.

Transport Layer: Host mobility protocols which leave the network infrastructure untouched and implements the whole functionality at the end devices mainly belongs to the transport layer. Migrate TCP (Snoeren & Balakrishnan, 2000) is one such host mobility management protocol which leaves the TCP semantics intact while requiring only minimal changes to the TCP state machine at the end hosts. This protocol works by the Mobile Host and Correspondent Node exchanging tokens to identify particular connections. When the Mobile Host moves it is able to re-establish the connection with the use of the token. Migrate TCP scheme proposes the use of DNS for location

management. Another connection migration method for mobility is Freeze TCP (Goff, et al, 2000). A connection is 'frozen' by advertising a zero window size to the Correspondent Node and is unfrozen after the handover. Packet loss is minimal with this scheme at the expense of higher delays.

MSocks (Maltz & Bhagwat, 1998) proposes the use of proxies to divide a host to host TCP connection into host-proxy and proxy-host communication. When the Mobile Host moves only the host-proxy connection needs to be re-established and the mobility is transparent to the Correspondent Node. The proxy is responsible for the location management of the Mobile Host and this has the drawback of the mobility support been restricted to the coverage of the proxy.

Application Layer: The Session Initiation Protocol (SIP) (Rosenburg, et al, 2002) is an application layer protocol which relies on a registrar server and location services server to keep track of all terminals associated with a given user. Regardless of the network location or terminals used with the SIP protocol a single personal identifier would support name mapping and redirection services. It has an inherent capability to support personal mobility due to its use of email style addresses to identify users.

Fundamental Challenges of Mobility Management

The mobility protocols however have not completely solved the problem of mobility management. Although they are certainly an integral component, they only address one aspect of mobility: locating the user or service. Snoeren, et al (2001) argues that a complete solution must address the following fundamental problems as well:

Consistent communication performance. Users should be able to enjoy predictable performance at an acceptable level in the face of changing network conditions and changing location of end-points.

Disconnecting gracefully and reconnecting timely. When communication is unexpectedly disrupted at the lower layers, applications must be allowed the chance to gracefully disconnect from the network instead of abruptly terminating the connection. Similarly, when service is restored, resumption of network connectivity has to be reported and the user or application should be able to re-establish the session with minimal effort (even automatically).

Hibernating efficiently. Re-establishment of disrupted sessions can only be achieved if relevant application state information is saved before suspending the affected communication.

Clearly much still needs to be done and context will play a significant role in addressing these challenges.

ENHANCING MOBILITY USING CONTEXT

In this section we discuss how context can be leveraged to achieve more intelligent mobility management decisions.

Interface to Connect to at Start-Up

When a device is booted up, at least one network interface must be turned on so that the device can be available for connection to the outside world. This raises the question of which interface should ideally be used by default. Different radio interfaces consume power at different levels. For instance, a Bluetooth device needs about 1–35 mA on average, while a Wi-Fi device typically requires between 100–350 mA (Ferro & Potorti, 2005). Additionally, these values change depending on whether the interface is on stand-by or transmitting. Wi-Fi and cellular networks have complementary energy profiles, with the GSM network consuming lesser energy than WiFi to stay connected but incurring much higher energy cost per MB of data transferred. Rahmati & Zhong (2007) showed that battery lifetime can be improved by as much as 35% by using cellular networks as the default network and switching to WiFi to transfer data. Thus, if minimizing battery consumption is the user's priority, the device should stay connected to a network which requires the least power and power on the other interfaces as needed. Aside from energy and cost concerns however, we also need to take into account other factors such as minimizing switching interfaces given the user's mobility state while keeping him connected at all times.

Operator

Users are currently limited in their choice of networks to connect to by contracts they have with their operator. Although global roaming agreements are fairly common, no such agreements exist for operators within the same domain. Thus it is possible in remote areas to be within radio vicinity but still unable to connect to the network because the user does not have an account with the operator. Additionally, operators for the most part operate on a tightly vertical environment. This is especially true for the cellular network, wherein a single operator owns the physical network, manages the day-to-day operations, and performs AAA services.

An attempt is being made to move away from this monolithic approach to a service composition framework, allowing for the full realization of the vision for "any" user to connect to "any" network as long as a service is available. A key component of this framework is the concept of dynamic roaming, whereby composition agreements are done on the fly at a micro level, down to the base station serving the user (Pöyhönen, et al, 2006).

Thus the network landscape of the future will be very different from what we have today. Users will have a large number of access networks to select from. With a service composition framework allowing users to connect to networks even when they do not have existing contracts, decisions become even more complex. It will be very important to consider the user's preferences and assist him given the myriad of choices available to him.

Handover

Handoff, also known as handover, is the transfer from one network point of attachment to another and is associated with device mobility. A *horizontal handover* is a handover on the same type of mobile network interface while a *vertical handover* is a handover between different mobile network technologies, ie switching from WiFi to GSM. Much work has been done to achieve seamless, optimal handovers but the problem has not been fully solved. An elegant make-before-break method for handling disconnections and delay tolerant networks must be explored to allow for graceful degradation of communications.

Prediction

Tagging and storing context information allows us to find patterns in the user as well as the network. Data mining and machine learning techniques can be employed to learn about these patterns in the hope of predicting future context information. Predictions can range from assessing the occurrence and length of network disconnections to approximating expected

Quality of Service on a given link. For instance, if we can predict that a 10-minute network disruption is imminent on a WiFi link, data can be pre-cached to avoid costly handovers to a UMTS interface during this short internal. However, if the predicted outage is much longer, we can scan the network for handover targets and set-up the connection before disconnecting gracefully from the old one.

Patterns in the user's behaviour is also an interesting aspect. Taheri and Romaya (2006) studied mobile users' past movement patterns and used clustering techniques to aid future paging decisions by the GSM network. They were able to show that their technique reduced the location updates by up to 65%, a huge reduction on network load.

A more challenging problem lies in the fact that although we can design sophisticated techniques, prediction still remains estimates of the future. Thus, just as with present context, there needs to be a "quality factor" which takes into account the probability values of predictions.

System

A systems approach to the mobility management problem must be used instead of attempting to handle everything at specific layers. As we have previously pointed out, different types of mobility is best handled at different layers of the protocol stack. Determining the mobility type, which layer and which protocol(s) to employ is a difficult task in itself, given that existing protocols where designed to address different aspects of the mobility problem and expert knowledge is needed to properly assess which ones to use. Writing out non-trivial rules governing the usage of these protocols in a generic way will not be easy, since we cannot aim to map out all possible user scenarios. Additionally, applications have various, sometimes conflicting, requirements which need to be reconciled with other system demands such as battery consumption and processing power.

User

Modelling user preferences and incorporating them into decision making would be easy if users knew what they want and can articulate these wishes. It is not always as straightforward however. For example, a user might say he prefers the cheapest connection that meets the minimum quality of service. This minimum

QoS varies from one application to another and even within an application – QoS requirements for a video call to the user's boss will probably be higher than a similar call to his wife. The user's preferences must also be reconciled with requirements or policies set by the system (device) and network operator. The problem is to determine which component ultimately has the final authority among the three and how to resolve the unavoidable conflicts which arise.

EXISTING CONTEXT-AWARE MOBILITY SOLUTIONS

In this section we discuss some existing systems which have been proposed for context-aware mobility management. There is quite a number of solutions and we do not attempt to provide and exhaustive listing here.

Context Transfer During Hand-off

Context transfer is the movement of context from one router to another as a means of re-establishing specific service (Kempf, et al, 2002). The Context Transfer Protocol (Loughney , et al, 2007) is proposed by the IETF Seamoby Working Group to facilitate fast handoff between Access Routers (AR) by transferring protocol state information in advance over the wired network. Using the wired network reduces traffic on the wireless link with the additional advantage of providing better security. Examples of context information transferred are Authorization, Authentication and Accounting (AAA), header compression, and Quality of Service (QoS). Context transfer allows the node to quickly re-establish the service at the new AR. New ARs are discovered using another protocol, the Candidate Access Router Discovery (CARD) Protocol (Liebsch, et al, 2005). CARD provides two basic functionalities: mapping between a Candidate Access Router's (CAR) layer 2 addresses and IP address, and discovery of capabilities of access routers. In the case when the mobile node has a number of CARs, CARD provides a means for the mobile node to choose the AR which best matches its data flow requirements. However, it does not specify how the node is to evaluate the various choices at hand.

The Context Transfer Protocol is a layer 3 solution to facilitate fast hand-off simply by transferring context information. Although the CARD protocol provides the means to disseminate information about access routers, we believe that a mobile node can make more intelligent decisions by processing these context information instead of just passing them around. Our proposed architecture transcends all the layers as well and can be used to influence decisions in layer 2 and layer 4.

Context-Aware Vertical Handover

Although context can be used for horizontal handovers, vertical handover is a more interesting problem due to the wide diversity in the characteristics of wireless access networks. Context information is crucial in making decisions on when to initiate the hand-off and which access technology to connect.

Balasubramaniam and Indulska (2004) used context to maintain the quality of service of multimedia applications during vertical handover between WiFi and GPRS networks. In their proposed scheme, context information is divided into a static profile and a dynamic profile. The static profile holds the context information that changes rarely while the dynamic profile provides the information about the current user and their network.

The handover scheme relies on components on the network to manage the context information and make corresponding decisions. A *Context Repository* holds the static context information and gathers and evaluates the dynamic context. An *Adaptability Manager* makes decisions about the context and determines whether adaptation is needed and a vertical handover must be performed. *Proxies* help maintain the QoS by double casting data on both networks and buffering packets.

Balasubramaniam extended their work and proposed a hierarchical architecture similar to ours based on active nodes (Balasubramaniam, et al, 2006). These *active nodes* perform context gathering and evaluation for the user based on active network technologies. Although the hierarchical solution solved the problem of scalability, all of the intelligence is still on the network components. We argue that mobile nodes of the future can have enough processing power and memory that some of the intelligence can be placed on the mobile node itself. Their work is unique however as it has the most extensive context model we have encountered so far.

Another example of a system for context-aware vertical handover is *Proton* (Vidales, et al 2005).

Proton is a policy-based system that uses a new kind of finite-state automata, a finite state transducer with tautness function and identities (TFFST), to model policies and resolve conflicts. These policies are stored and evaluated at the network and are deployed to the mobile nodes to drive its decisions.

Proton's architecture is divided into network-side and host-side components. Modules that involve high computational cost are located in the network. Policies are written in a high-level policy specification language and translated into evaluation models based on finite state transducers. The models are used by the conflict resolution module to build a finite state machine for each policy. These policies are then combined and evaluated to resolve all possible static and dynamic conflicts that may arise. Having resolved conflicts, the deterministic finite-state machines are then deployed to the mobile nodes. Hosts store these finite-state machines in their policy manager and use these to drive their mobility decisions.

The host has a context management layer responsible for collecting networking context information. Context data gathered is the device location, velocity, direction and angle of movement. User can also set their preferences for cost, QoS and security. Events from the context management layer serve as inputs to the policy management layer, which in turn decides the possible actions to execute using the TFFST. Certain special events can also trigger a specific finite state machine to be loaded. An enforcement layer is then responsible for performing the actions that result from the policy manager.

The Proton architecture is similar to our proposed architecture, which will be presented in the following sections, in the sense that context is managed by the mobile hosts themselves. However, although decisions in Proton are made by the host (using the finite state machines), evaluation of policies and conflict resolution are performed at the network. The use of finite-state machines makes decision-making an easy task for the mobile node. In contrast, our architecture splits the decision-making into high level and low level mobility decisions. Low level decisions are evaluated and made by the mobile host, while high-level mobility decisions are achieved by network/server components. Additionally, in our proposed architecture context information does not stay with the mobile node, but is stored by network components. This allows context history to be retrieved by the user using any device, even those which he accesses for the first time.

A PROPOSED DISTRIBUTED CONTEXT-AWARE MOBILITY SOLUTION

Assumptions

The following assumptions were used as *guidelines* when designing our proposed architecture.

- Mobile nodes of the future will have significant processing power and memory capacity. Even today, it is not uncommon to have notebooks and tablet PCs with a Pentium Dual Core processor, 80GB of hard disk space and 512MB of RAM. PDAs and cellular phones come with memory expansion modules, and 1GB of MMC or SD cards are available. Thus we can assume the devices in the future have enough capabilities to support some degree of context-management and decision-making at the node and not rely entirely on servers or network components.
- Mobile nodes of the future will have multiple radio interfaces and access networks: Bluetooth, WiFI (with all its variants), WiMAX, and UMTS/GPRS are just some of the access technologies available today, and devices of the future will support at least two of these technologies. With software defined radios, the possibilities become endless.
- Devices will have multiple mobility protocols coexisting in their stack: MIP and SIP are examples of two such protocols which have mature implementations and a wide installed user base. Both of these protocols have working groups in the IETF actively working to enhance their performance and increase their functionality. For instance, many extensions for MIP is available such as hierarchical MIP (HMIP) and Network Mobility (NeMO).
- Mobility protocols in the future will have implementations available which allows them to be downloaded by the device and installed upon reboot similar to application software: This implies that mobility modules can be run in user space instead of kernel space, thus eliminating the tight coupling that exists today between the TCP/IP stack and operating system. Although performance may be degraded, it allows for greater flexibility for devices to integrate mobility modules as needed.

Proposed Architecture

Figure 2 shows the hierarchical architecture of our context management system. The architecture supporting mobility management includes a Global Context Server, a number of Local Proxy and Adaptation Servers, and the Mobile Nodes themselves. Figure 3 shows the context information handled by these components.

The Global Context Server is essentially a static context repository and is the first point of contact of mobile nodes when invoking an application. Local Servers store the user's dynamic context repository and provide adaptation services such as transcoding and mobility modules. The Mobile Nodes are devices which the user has available around him and which have some sort of network connectivity.

The **Global Context Server** is a static context repository. Context models for all applications and services are stored here as well as system policies, which are general rules that apply to all users and default values in case user preferences are not specified. These policies are essentially {event-condition-actions}, specifying what actions are to be taken when a context event occurs and certain conditions are met. These context models and system policies are duplicated in all of the Local Servers, such that when a model or policy needs to be changed, only the Global Central Server is updated and it pushes the information to the Local Servers.

The Global Context Server also holds information about individual users, their preferences, what devices they have (which implies their authority to use them), the characteristics and capabilities of the device, and their context history. User-specific policies which override system policies are also stored here. The Global Context Server essentially holds the static profiles for each user.

The **Local Proxy and Adaptation Server** holds the dynamic context profile of each user it has been assigned. The Global Server sends the user's static profile to the Local Server and it uses this information, plus the information supplied by the user's devices, to start the dynamic profile. The main functions of the Local Server are to (a) aid the mobile node in making higher level mobility management decisions; (b) offer a variety of adaptation services; and (c) tag events in the user's run-time context profile for later storage.

High level mobility management decisions are decisions which a mobile device can not make alone as it involves other components. Session mobility is such

Figure 2. Architecture of our context management system

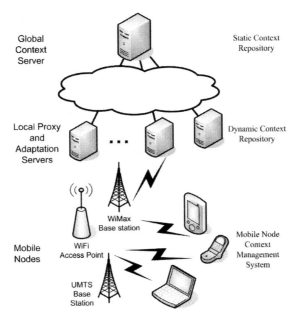

Figure 3. Context information

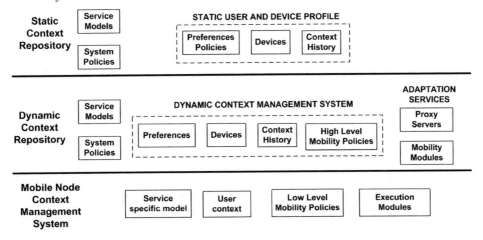

an example. Session mobility involves the coordination of at least two devices, the current device and the new device to which the session is to be transferred. If a number of candidate devices are available, these must be evaluated by the Local Server to determine the best device(s) to move the session. It may be possible that the session media has to be split among devices as well as the video stream need to be directed to a monitor and the voice stream is on a mobile phone. The Local Server will need to evaluate these decisions using the dynamic profile and the user's preferences (from the static context profile).

Session mobility may also involve reconciling differences in device capabilities. If a common codec does not exist, a transcoder need to be invoked. Providing adaptation services is another function of the Local Server, and transcoding is one such service. The transcoder may reside on the Local Server itself, or it may be on a separate machine. Rather than establishing a direct media session between the remote node and the Mobile Node, separate sessions are established between the transcoder and each of them, with the transcoder translating between the streams.

Other adaptation services offered by the Local Server is buffering of packets and double casting when the Mobile Node performs a vertical handover. As the Mobile Node migrates from the previous network to the new one, packets for the Mobile Node are sent on both connections to minimize packet loss and delay. Another adaptation service is to dispatch mobility modules, which are software codes for specific mobility protocols, to the Mobile Nodes. For instance, if a device has a Mobile IP module but its implementation does not support route optimization, the new code can be downloaded by the Mobile Node from the Local Server.

In order to make intelligent decisions, the Local Server must thus be kept updated of the Mobile Node's current context. Although querying of sensor information, pre-processing and aggregation of context data is performed by the Mobile Node, some information must be sent by the Mobile Node to the Local Server so it can have an accurate picture of the present context of the devices. This implies that context details have certain levels of granularity, which allows for the amount of traffic between the Mobile Node and Local Server to be reduced. Only information of the required granularity is passed on to the Local Server. This high level context should still be sufficient for the Local Server to make high level mobility decisions.

The last function of the Local Server is to tag certain context data for storage in the user's context history. Example context information that may prove useful in the future is the user's location, the current network, and the quality of service of his connection. If the user returns to the same location a few weeks later, this information can be retrieved to influence the decision on which access network to use. At the end of the session, the tagged context information is sent to the Global Server for updating and storage of the user's context history.

The **Mobile Node** middleware consists of a context management layer, a policy manager, and execution modules. The context manager retrieves the application specific model for the current service from the Local Server. It uses these models to determine which context information is relevant to the application and subscribes to appropriate available sensors for such information. Additional processing is performed to raise the level of abstraction of the gathered context data, a copy of which is sent to the Local Server.

The policy manager evaluates context triggers and makes low level mobility management decisions such as determining if a hand-over is necessary and to which access network to connect to. The execution modules carry out the decisions made by the policy manager, such as performing handovers when necessary. It also coordinates with the Local Server in executing high level decisions, such as terminating sessions or installing the software modules downloaded from the Local Server.

CONCLUSION

We have presented our proposed architecture for a context management system for mobility management. Our architecture consists of a Global Context Server acting as a static context repository. A number of Local Proxy and Adaptation Servers help manage the Mobile Node's dynamic context and make high level mobility decisions. The Mobile Nodes implement a context management middleware for gathering context data and inferencing higher level information. Low level mobility decisions are also made and executed at the node.

REFERENCES

Balasubramaniam, S., & Indulska, J. (2004). Vertical handover supporting pervasive computing in future wireless networks. *Computer Communications, 27*(8), 708-719.

Balasubramaniam, S., Pfeifer, T., & Indulska, J. (2006). Active node supporting context-aware vertical handover in pervasive computing environment with redundant positioning. In Proceedings of 1st International Symposium on Wireless Pervasive Computing, 1-6.

Baldauf, M., Dustdar, S., & Rosenberg, F. (2007). A Survey on context-aware systems. *International Journal of Ad Hoc and Ubiquitous Computing, 2*(4), 263-277.

Chen, H., Finin, T., & Joshi, A. (2003). An ontology for context-aware pervasive computing environments. *Knowledge Engineering Review, 18*(3), 197-207.

Context Aware Mobility Management

Devarapalli, V., Wakikawa, R., Petrescu, A., & Thubert, P. (2005). RFC 3963: NEtwork MObility (NEMO) Basic support protocol. Retrieved 4 November 2007 from http://www.rfc-editor.org/rfc/rfc3963.txt.

Dey, A. K. (2001). Understanding and using context. *Personal and Ubiquitous Computing*, 5(1), 4-7.

Dey, A. K., Abowd, G., & Salber, D. (2001). A conceptual framework and a toolkit for supporting the rapid prototyping of context-aware applications. *Human-Computer Interaction*, 16(2-4), 97-166.

Ferro, E. & Potorti, F. (2005). Bluetooth and Wi-Fi wireless protocols: a survey and a comparison. *IEEE Wireless Communications*, 12(1) 12 – 26.

Floreen, P., Przybilski, M., Nurmi, P., Koolwaaij, J.W., Tarlano, A., Wagner, M., Luther, M., Bataille, F., Boussard, M., Mrohs, B., & Lau, S. (2005). Towards a context management framework for MobiLife. In *Proceedings of 14th IST Mobile and Wireless Communications Summit. Retrieved 29 October 2007 from* http://www.cs.helsinki.fi/u/ptnurmi/publications.html.

Goff, T., Moronski, J., Phatak, D., & Gupta, V. (2000). Freeze-TCP: a true end-to-end TCP enhancement mechanism for mobile environments. In *Proceedings of 19th Annual Joint Conference of the IEEE Computer and Communications Societies: IEEE INFOCOM 2000*, 3, 1537 – 1545.

Gu, T., Pung, H., & Zhang, D. (2004). A middleware for building context-aware mobile services, In *Proceedings of IEEE 59th Vehicular Technology Conference, VTC Spring 2004*, 5, 2656- 2660.

Gundavelli, S., Leung, K., Devarapalli, V., Chowdury, K., & Patil, B. (2007). Proxy Mobile IPv6 (Work in Progress). Retrieved 4 November 2007 from http://tools.ietf.org/html/draft-ietf-netlmm-proxymip6-01.

Henricksen, K., Indulska, J., & Rakotonirainy, A. (2002). Modeling context information in pervasive computing systems. *In Proceedings of 1st International Conference on Pervasive Computing, Pervasive 2002: Lecture Notes in Computer Science*, 2414, 167-180).

Henricksen, K., Indulska, J., & McFadden, T. (2005) Modelling context information with ORM. In *International Workshop on Object-Role Modeling* (ORM*): Lecture Notes in Computer Science*, 3762, 626-635).

Indulska, J., Robinsona, R., Rakotonirainy, A., & Henricksen, K. (2003). Experiences in using CC/PP in context-aware systems. In *Proceedings Of The 4th International Conference On Mobile Data Management, MDM2003: Lecture Notes in Computer Science*, 2574, 247-261.

Johnson, D., Perkins, C., & Arkko, J. (2004). *RFC 3775: Mobility Support in IPv6*. Retrieved 4 November 2007 from http://www.rfc-editor.org/rfc/rfc3775.txt.

Kempf, J. (Ed.) (2006). RFC 3374: Reasons for performing context transfers between nodes in an IP access network. Retrieved 29 October 2007 from http://www.ietf.org/rfc/rfc3374.txt.

Klyne, G., Reynolds, F., Woodrow, C., Ohto, H., Hjelm, J., Butler, M., & Tran, L. (Eds) (2004). Composite Capability / Preference Profiles (CC/PP): Structure and Vocabularies 1.0. W3C Recommendation. Retrieved 29 October 2007 from http://www.w3.org/TR/CCPP-struct-vocab/.

Loughney, J. (Editor) (2005). RFC4067: Context Transfer Protocol (CXTP). Retrieved 29 October 2007 from http://www.ietf.org/rfc/rfc4067.txt

Liebsch, M., & Singh, A. (Editor) (2005). RFC 4066: Candidate Access Router Discovery. Retrieved 29 October 2007 from http://www.ietf.org/rfc/rfc4066.txt

Maltz, D., & Bhagwat, P. (1998). MSOCKS: An architecture for transport layer mobility. In *Proceedings of 17th Annual Joint Conference of the IEEE Computer and Communications Societies: IEEE INFOCOM 1998*, 3, 1037-1045.

Perkins, C., (Editor) (2002). RFC 3220: IP Mobility support for IPv4. Retrieved 4 November 2007 from http://www.rfc-editor.org/rfc/rfc3220.txt.

Pöyhönen, P., Strandberg, O., Markendahl, J., & Laganier, J. (2006). Business implications of composition framework in ambient networks. In *Helsinki Mobility Roundtable 2006*. Retrieved 29 October 2007 from http://project.hkkk.fi/helsinkimobility/submissions.htm.

Rahmati, A., & Zhong, L. (2007). Context for Wireless: Context-sensitive energy-efficient wireless data transfer. On *Proceedings of ACM/USENIX International Conference on Mobile Systems, Applications, and Services: MobiSys 2007*.

Rosenburg, J., Schulzrinne, H., Camarillo, G., Johnston, A., Peterson, J., Sparks, R., Handley, M., & Schooler, E. (2002). RFC 3261: Session Initiation

Protocol. Retrieved 4 November 2007 from http://www.rfc-editor.org/rfc/rfc3261.txt

Schmidt, A. (2002). *Ubiquitous computing – computing in context*. Unpublished doctoral dissertation. Lancaster University, United Kingdom.

Snoeren, A., & Balakrishnan, H. (2000). An end-to-end approach to host mobility. In *Proceedings of the Sixth Annual International Conference on Mobile Computing and Networking: MobiCom 2000*. (pp. 155-166).

Snoeren, A., Balakrishnan, H., & Kaashoek, M.F. (2001). Reconsidering Internet Mobility. In *Proceedings of the 8th Workshop on Hot Topics in Operating Systems, HotOS-VIII*.

Strang, T., & Linnhoff-Popien, C. (2004). A Context Modeling Survey. In *Workshop on Advanced Context Modelling, Reasoning and Management as part of the 6th International Conference on Ubiquitous Computing, UbiComp 2004*, Nottingham/England.

Taheri, J., & Zomaya, A. (2006). Clustering techniques for dynamic mobility management. In *MobiWac '06: Proceedings of the 4th ACM International Workshop on Mobility Management and Wireless Access* (pp 10 – 17).

Vidales, P., Baliosian, J., Serrat, J., Mapp, G., Stajano, F., & Hopper, A. (2006). Autonomic system for mobility support in 4G networks. *IEEE Journal on Selected Areas in Communications, 23*(12) 2288-2304.

Zimmermann, A., Lorenz, A., & Oppermann, R. (2007). An Operational Definition of Context. In *Proceedings of 6th International and Interdisciplinary Conference, CONTEXT 2007: Lecture Notes in Computer Science, 4635*. Modelling and Using Context (pp. 558-571).

KEY TERMS

Context: Any information that can be used to characterize the situation of an entity. Typical examples are location, identity, and state of people and computational objects.

Context Aware System: Computing system that provides relevant services and information to users based on their situational conditions.

Handoff (also known as handover): The process wherein a device transfers from one network point of attachment to another.

Horizontal Handover: Handover on the same type of mobile network interface.

Mobility Management: Management of the communications aspect as an entity (user or device) moves from one location to another so that network Quality of Service is maintained.

Ontology: A formal definition of a common set of terms that are used to describe and represent a domain.

Protocol: Special set of rules that end points in a telecommunications network use when they communicate.

Vertical Handover: A handover between different mobile network technologies, ie switching from WiFi to GSM.

Chapter V
Assessing the Future of Location–Based Services:
Technologies, Applications, and Strategies

Robert Harmon
Portland State University, USA

Tugrul Daim
Portland State University, USA

ABSTRACT

Location-based services (LBS) are approaching an inflection point. The continued rollout of the technological infrastructure, the availability of LBS applications, and the market's increasing awareness of their potential value should lead to increasing business opportunities. However, there is still a high degree of uncertainty in the LBS space. Challenges are emerging to the cellular network operator-centric LBS model. Hardware companies, application providers, competing infrastructure technologies (such as Wi-Fi, WiMAX, and satellite networks), and new competitors from the computer and Internet industries are all vying for market position. Customers are becoming interested in location services, but the uptake has been slow. New LBS business models and new strategies need to be considered. This chapter evaluates the future of location-based services through a critical assessment of the technology, service applications, market trends, and strategic issues.

INTRODUCTION

Are location-based services (LBS) finally ready to take off? For almost ten years LBS has been heralded as the next killer application in the wireless space. Yet the uptake for LBS has been very slow. Potential customers, both business and consumer, have a poor understanding of what LBS is. They perceive LBS to be complex, costly, and offering insufficient value to warrant adoption. Mobile operators may be mostly to blame for this. They have been slow to roll out services, targeted niche markets, offered poor service quality, charged high subscription fees, and limited the access of innovative third-party application providers to their closed networks. In a very real sense the operators' "walled gardens" have choked off promising paths for innovation. Joe Astroth, VP of the LBS division of Autodesk sums it up well: "LBS is the killer application that got killed on the way to the mainstream" (Baig, 2006).

However, this disappointing situation may be about to change. ABI Research projects worldwide subscribers of GPS-enabled LBS will grow from 12 million in 2007 to reach 315 million in 2011 (Morse, 2006). International Data Corporation (IDC) projects the location-based advertising (LBA) market alone to be a $2 billion market opportunity by 2011 (Boulton, 2007). North America and Western Europe will likely see the greatest growth. In North America, operators such as Verizon Wireless and Sprint with 3G networks have embraced GPS. European LBS has been limited by the lack of GPS capability. However, the continuing rollout of W-CDMA enabled smartphones with GPS chipsets will enable the growth of LBS there.

The extended gestational period for LBS has engendered reevaluation regarding its potential and its role as a standalone class of mobile services. Three key issues will determine the future of LBS:

1. Will LBS be a service category unto itself or will it be an added feature to existing services--adding value by increasing usability and enhancing the user's experience?
2. How will changes in customer expectations of the mobile Internet experience impact LBS?
3. What changes in LBS business models will occur as the mobile operators are challenged by Internet-based business models from competitors such as Google, Nokia, and Apple?

As the Internet and mobile worlds converge and LBS starts to look more promising, competitive issues will abound. The industry dynamics are already in flux as key players in the mobile ecosystem vie for power. Handset manufacturers are including GPS, Wi-Fi, VoIP, and soon WiMAX capabilities on their smartphone platforms that will enable users to bypass cellular networks. Google, with a regulatory boost from the Federal Communications Commission, is pushing to disrupt the market with the potential for a network-neutral open cellular system in the 700 MHz band (Gapper, 2007). LBS application providers are leveraging new handset and network technologies and partnering with other members of the operators' value chain to create innovative applications and to

challenge the operators' channel power. They are also developing applications that enable customers to "free ride" on cellular networks. The basic questions here are: What LBS services do users want, where will that value be generated in the LBS ecosystem, and who will capture it?

The Internet is by its very nature an open system. Anyone can launch a website or an e-commerce service. This is anathema for mobile operators who limit choice and competition with their walled-garden networks. The operators are coming under increasing pressure from customers, regulators, partners, and competitors to open their networks to innovation. With or without the operators' acquiescence, this opening is starting to happen with Wi-Fi and VoIP-capable smartphones. WiMAX, which recently became a 3G standard, will further challenge the operators' closed networks (Allison, 2007). Apple's Wi-Fi-enabled iPhone is the first major breach of AT&T's network and brand dominance. More openness and disruption is on the way which should favorably impact the growth of LBS.

Location-based services (LBS) provide location-specific information, often in context with other mobile applications, which is relevant to the mobile user's real-time choice behavior. These services determine the exact location of the user and can use push and/or pull information methods to respond to queries or suggest possible decision options to the mobile user. Knowledge of the user's location can be used to deliver context-relevant information to customers where and when they are most likely to buy. For mobile network operators, LBS has been viewed as a vehicle to improve average revenues per user (ARPU). This goal is increasingly important to operators as competition continues to erode voice-only ARPU.

The LBS application category emerged in the late 1990s in anticipation of the rollout of 3G cellular networks. However, it was government regulation mandating cellular operators to provide accurate cell phone location data for emergency calls that forced the development and deployment of location technologies. Although E911 in the U.S. and E112 in the EU were intended to increase public safety, they enabled the deployment of the technological infrastructure that is the basis for LBS (Rao and Minakakis, 2004; Unni & Harmon, 2006).

In the U.S., the FCC mandated specific performance requirements for E911 but did not require the mobile network operators to use a specific technology. Verizon Wireless and Sprint were early adopters of GPS capability with other carriers initially adopting less accurate triangulation, cell ID, angle of arrival methods, or ignoring the mandate because it was more cost effective to pay the fines. The North American LBS market will get a boost as AT&T and T-Mobile implement GPS capabilities in conjunction with their 3G network rollouts (Baig, 2006).

TECHNOLOGY DRIVERS OF LOCATION-ENABLEMENT

Location-based services are evolving into advanced multimedia information services that are delivered directly to users of mobile devices dependent upon their location. The media can be delivered to, or selected within any portable wireless device that is GPS or otherwise location-enabled and has the capacity to display multimedia content. The four primary technological drivers of advanced LBS are: location technology, data networks, smartphone handsets, and location-based software applications. The recent convergence of handset-based GPS, 3G data networks, smartphones and innovative integrated LBS applications has provided a favorable environment for the future development of LBS.

Location Technology

The commercial rollout of more accurate location technologies is a key enabler of higher value and more customer-relevant LBS. Table 1 provides a summary of most accurate advanced technologies to determine the location of a mobile handheld device. *Network based technologies* use the cellular network to determine the user's location. They are capable of locating any handset connected to the network, which is important since most Global System for Mobile (GSM) handsets are currently not GPS-capable. Uplink Time Difference of Arrival (U-TDOA) technology uses the network and location measuring units in the base stations to enable accurate (50-150m) location determination which works indoors and in urban canyons and does not require a GPS handset (Is LBS about to find an audience?, 2007).

The primary *handset-based technology* is the satellite based Global Positioning System (GPS). This Radio Frequency (RF) technology triangulates with three satellites to determine handset location. GPS-based LBS can operate independently of the cellular network on GPS-enabled smartphones with mapping and location applications. Overall, it is the most accurate location technology. However, GPS suffers from a line-of-sight requirement. It does not work well indoors, near tall buildings, or in other poor signal situations which has encouraged many LBS providers to prefer a hybrid location solution.

Hybrid technologies such as A-GPS attempt to minimize the line-of-sight drawbacks from pure GPS handset solutions. It incorporates the accuracy of a GPS solution for outside open areas and is network-assisted for poor GPS signal locations such as indoors. Accurate network location technologies such as U-TDOA maybe used for the hybrid assist. A-GPS technology appears to be the leading driver for highly accurate mobile location-based services (Is LBS about to find an audience?, 2007).

Short-range *local positioning technologies* such as Wi-Fi, Bluetooth, and Radio Frequency Identification (RFID) that may be built into the handset can provide accurate location data since the access point location is known. These technologies will become increasingly important for LBS providers which desire to avoid the cellular network operators' walled gardens or desire short-range assists where GPS or cellular network signals are weak.

Mobile Data Networks

Although the mobile industry is still in the process of completing the rollout of 3G wireless networks, operators are planning the migration to fourth-generation (4G) technology (Schenker, 2007, October 29). The International Telecommunications Union (ITU) will not release a standard definition for 4G until 2008 or 2009. 4G deployments are expected to start in the 2010-2012 timeframe. However, as depicted in Table 2, the primary 4G technologies are expected to be Long Term Evolution (LTE), Ultra Mobile Broadband (UMB), and IEEE 802.16m WiMAX (Mohney, 2007). All of the candidates would enable easy access for multimedia LBS applications from a wide variety of portable devices.

LTE is being promoted by Ericsson and Nokia for GSM networks. The GSM standard is used by over 80% of the world's wireless subscribers and may have the advantage overall in the cellular space (Schenker, 2007, October 29). Alternatively, Qualcomm is promoting UMB as the natural migration path for CDMA networks. Intel, Cisco, and Samsung are supporting mobile WiMAX which already has a 3G designation (Allison, 2007). Two widely-discussed requirements

Table 1. Location technology

	Technology	Description	Advantages	Disadvantages
Network-Based	**Uplink Time Difference of Arrival (U-TDOA)**	Compares the times at which a cell signal reaches multiple location measurement units installed at the operator's base stations. Accuracy is determined by the network layout and deployment density of base stations	RF technology Promoted as a position solution for indoors and urban canyons. Network-based, supports legacy handsets. Accuracy is 50m-150m. May be used with A-GPS for hybrid location solution	Significant upgrades to network base stations.
Handset-Based	**Global Positioning System (GPS)**	Radio-navigation system w/ 24 low-orbit satellites, triangulates with three satellites	RF technology Outdoor precision within 5m range Not dependent on network.	Line-of-sight issues Does not work well in urban canyons or indoors.
Hybrid Technology	**Assisted Global Positioning System (A-GPS)**	Satellite location with network assist. Enables location to be precisely determined over a global range. Facilitates location positioning inside buildings or in forests.	RF technology Most precise method for determining location over wide range of situations. Method of the future, accuracy falls in the range of 10m–50m.	Significant changes to network. Power consumption Does not work well for indoor positioning or in urban canyons. Expensive
Local Position	**W-LAN: Wi-Fi, Blue tooth, RFID**	Short range technologies	Highly accurate, 5m-50m. Most portable computing devices and many wireless handsets have, or will have some of these capabilities.	Limited geographical coverage.

are Orthogonal Frequency Division Multiple Access (OFDMA) and support for at least 100Mbps wide-area mobile applications (4G Technology, 2007).

With 4G on the horizon, some operators are using the opportunity to evaluate new options. Sprint opted out of UMB to build a WiMAX network covering 100 million potential customers by the end of 2008 (Edwards, 2007). Verizon Wireless is thought to be testing UMB and WiMAX, but strongly considering LTE. If Verizon does not adopt UMB that would greatly damage the CDMA roadmap and ecosystem which includes Qualcomm, Alcatel-Lucent, Nortel, LG, and Samsung (Schenker, 2007, October 29). AT&T has committed to LTE and T-Mobile is likely to as well.

Handset Technology

Mobile phones are rapidly becoming the primary portal for people to enter the world of information (Boulton, 2007). Science-fiction writer Bruce Sterling famously called the smartphone "the remote control for life"

(The phone of the future, 2006). The key observation is mobile phones of the future will have much more computing power and better displays and be able to do similar things that laptops do now (The phone of the future, 2006). With the price of memory falling rapidly, smartphones will have much more memory capacity. The desire to download music or video over the air (OTA) will be minimized since users could simply download an entire entertainment catalog from the Internet and store it as long as they wanted. Users will be able to purchase software applications that will run on any phone. They will have GPS and other location capability with maps and location services preloaded (Niccolai, 2007).

Future phones will double as fixed and mobile devices using Wi-Fi, WiMAX, or cellular networks depending on the situation. Voice over IP (VoIP) capability will be standard. With 4G networks, distance and voice-based pricing will go away with users paying one price for unlimited phone calls and data services. Phones will regularly be used for purchases and as

Table 2. Wireless network evolution

Wireless Technology Generation				
Network	1G	2G	3G	4G
Switching	Circuit-switched	Circuit-switched	Circuit and packet-switched	Packet-switched OFDMA-based
Applications	Voice telephony	Voice and basic data applications	Data and multimedia applications	IP based, advanced multimedia and streaming applications
Standards	NMT, AMPS, TACS, c-450, Radiocom 2000, JTACS	GSM, CDMAOne, D-AMPS, PDC, GPRS, EDGE, HSCSD	W-CDMA/UMTS, CDMA2000/EV-DO, TD-SCDMA WiMAX (OFDM)	Long Term Evolution (LTE)-GSM networks. Ultra Mobile Broadband (UMB)—CDMA networks. Mobile WiMAX, up to 30-mile range
Performance	Low, voice only	Downlink speeds up to 14.4Kbps or 64Kbps	Downlink speeds up to 46.7 Mbps, Uplink to 27 Mbps	Downlink up to 280 Mbps, uplink 68 Mbps
Openness	Operator dominant	Operator dominant—walled garden	Operator dominant—walled garden, some user choice	Application focus More openness More user choice

home and car keys. There will be a need for strong authentication for legitimate users.

Improved mobile phone displays are a key factor. They are becoming larger and brighter with higher resolutions that will enable detailed LBS mapping and augmented reality (AR) applications (Bolter & MacIntyre, 2007). AR augments the user's view of the world with digital creations in order to enhance education and entertainment experiences. For example, Nokia's mobile AR system includes a mobile phone, camera, GPS, accelerometers, and a compass that digitally accompanies a user on a sightseeing tour of a city. The system identifies and shows images of nearby attractions as the user approaches. The user can download additional information.

Screen technology currently is dominated by liquid crystal displays (LCDs). They are bright, high-resolution and can accurately display text and graphics. The iPhone with its touch screen has started to change expectations about smartphone displays. Other technologies include electronic paper which relies on ambient light rather than a backlight. A roll-up version is being planned for mobile applications (Displays to keep an eye on, 2007). Perhaps the most disruptive display technology is organic light emitting diodes (OLEDs). These displays are lighter, thinner, and offer wider viewing angles than LCDs. They do not need a backlight. OLED displays have appeared on

music players, cell phones and laptops. The primary drawback is the relatively short display lifetime which is less than half the life of an LCD. This drawback will improve as the technology matures.

Evolving LBS Applications

The last of our four classes of location-enablement technologies are the location-based services that utilize the handsets, location determination technologies, and high-speed mobile networks to bring the location-relevant solutions to users. Table 3 shows a summary of the LBS applications, in existence or planned, for business/government markets and consumer markets. The business/government applications such as asset tracking, logistics planning, and workforce management have had the best uptake so far since there is a direct economic model associated with them for the user (Cox, 2007). These services often involve some combination of GPS, Wi-Fi, and cellular technology. Interest is building for telemedicine (Maglogiannis & Hadjiefthymiades, 2006) and location-based advertising (Bruner & Kumar, 2007). The location-based advertising category is gaining real traction with the entry of Google into the mobile space (Gapper, 2007).

Customer management is a new business category for LBS. Insurance companies are offering location-

Table 3. Location-based services

CUSTOMER	LBS CATEGORY	LOCATION-BASED SERVICES
Business/Government	Navigation	Routing/dynamic navigational guidance Traffic status by location, Weather warnings Essential services
	Asset Tracking Logistics Planning	Tracking transportation equipment Real time monitoring of freight & equipment Location-sensitive contents Tracking stolen vehicles
	Workforce Management Employee Security	Tracking mobile employees Sales force management Travel information services Personal security
	Customer Management	Telematics-assisted car insurance, rate setting Vehicle usage, monitor teenage drivers
	Emergency Services	Police, Fire, Medical (E911, E112) Roadside assistance
	Law Enforcement Electronic Fencing	Prisoner monitoring and tracking Traffic enforcement—speed cameras Subpoena serving, jury tracking Homeland security—terrorist tracking
	Telemedicine	Acute patient care Patient monitoring
	Location-based advertising and promotions	Location and behaviorally-relevant coupon presentation, targeted ads, and promotional messages
	Mobile Commerce	Customer identification in a store or a neighborhood. E-wallet/Mobile POS, Dynamic pricing Promotional opportunity on sale of target product.
Consumer End-Users	Navigation	Turn-by-turn navigation Routing assistance, traffic status, speed trap location Weather-related traffic warnings Points of interest, essential services
	Family Tracking Monitoring Geo Fencing	Child tracking/monitoring/locating Monitoring elderly Medical monitoring Locating lost pets.
	Emergency services	Police, fire, medical (E911, E112) Roadside assistance Search and rescue missions Telemedicine—medical monitoring Stolen vehicle tracking
	Local search	Locates nearest restaurants, shows, dinner reservations, concierge services, transportation schedules, points of interest.
	Social Networking	Friend finder, mobile dating, mobile location experience sharing, user-generated content Geo-blogging, geo-tagged photos and videos
	Interactive mobile gaming	Uses communications, cameras, GPS, and RFID sensors to connect players, digital, and physical worlds to enable new experiences. Helps gamers interact with other gamers.

based services such as Safeco's "Teensurance" that features in-vehicle GPS that enables real-time tracking and monitoring of a teen's vehicle's location and speed by parents, and presumably provides usage data to the insurance company (Safeco, 2007). In the UK, Norwich Union offers a GPS service to set monthly insurance premiums by distance driven, time of day, and type of road driven (Reed, 2007). Initiatives are underway to enable cars to talk to roadside infrastructure and vehicle-to-vehicle. Roadside technology can be used to prevent accidents, locate stolen vehicles, and beam location-based ads into a passing vehicle (Reed, 2007).

On the consumer side, navigation, family tracking and monitoring, and emergency services are getting the most traction (LBS: lost and found, 2007). Consumers became familiar with navigation services through their use in vehicles. The after-market personal navigation devices category has been dominated by Tom Tom and Garmin (Hesseldahl, 2007, September 14). Nokia, with navigation ready GPS phones and its purchase of Navteq, will likely become a major player in this space (Hesseldahl, 2007, November 2).

Future consumer LBS applications include local search, social networking, and interactive mobile gaming. Recent research from IDC indicates that over 60% of consumers would be willing to accept a free ad-based usage model for local search (LBS finding favour, 2007). The huge success of social networking appears to be making the migration to the mobile web. LBS applications will include location-relevant features such as friends and events finding and user-generated content such as videos (Norton, 2007). Location-assisted collaborative mobile gaming leverages the trends of personalization, social networking, and entertainment as well (Kapko, 2007).

EMERGING INDUSTRY DYNAMICS

The competitive situation in the mobile wireless industry is in flux. We are beginning to see a new wave of change as Internet-based innovations wash over the industry (Malykhina & Martin, 2007; Martin, 2007, October 15). Disruption is coming and it will be driven by forces that emanate from both within the industry value chain and by new players from adjacent industries that already know how to succeed in the Internet space. The key drivers of industry change are: increased customer expectations, entry of new competitors and technologies from the Internet and computer indus-

tries, and the desire of the mobile operators' value chain members to gain a greater share of revenues by directly targeting end-users. Mobile industry handset manufacturers and software application providers are being joined by a host of new competitors from the adjacent computing industry that already successfully compete in the Internet space. Players such as Nokia, Apple, Motorola, Samsung, Intel, Microsoft, Google, Yahoo, Skype, and Cisco have market power with end-users that in most cases exceeds that of the wireless carriers (Kharif, 2007). New technologies such as WiMAX have mobile capabilities and performance that can threaten the cellular model.

The deployment of 3G technology is driving the mobile wireless industry to adopt an Internet-based, service-oriented model. Voice and data services in a packet-switched world are artificial distinctions that will be difficult to maintain. Consumers are coming to expect that the mobile wireless Internet experience should duplicate the one they already have at work, school, and home. From the operators' perspective it is not whether to adopt an Internet-oriented services model, but how to deploy it (Porter, 2001). An open Internet-based model is what operators fear most (Fry, 2006). They would become purveyors of commodity wireless ISP services. That is why they have fought to preserve the walled garden where they tightly control what services are offered, to whom, and at what price. Between these extremes are strategic options that harness the innovation of partners to develop new technologies and services. However, the operators will have to give up some power and control to stay viable or risk becoming disrupted. The walled garden business model of the wireless network operators is beginning to crack open. The end-users will benefit from increased competition. The operators have the most to lose. Competitors that understand the Internet value drivers of better, faster, and cheaper will likely be the big winners.

The LBS Industry Food Chain

An industry food chain is a hierarchical business ecosystem where the identity, roles, and relative power of the industry's participants define their market position (Harmon & Day, 2006; Iansiti & Levien, 2004; Moore, 1996). Industry food chain participants exist in an economic, political, and physical environment where the dynamics of their relationships affect strategic choices and outcomes and are characterized by uncertainty. Studying an industry's food chain can

Figure 1. The LBS industry food chain

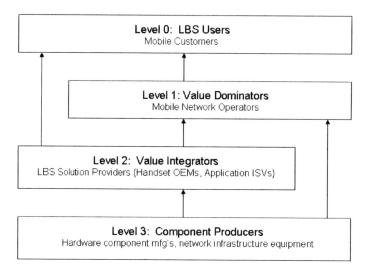

identify roles and strategic options of the participants and help to foresee competitive disruptions that may be on the horizon.

As represented in Figure 1, the LBS industry food chain participants are end-user mobile customers, network operator value dominators, hardware and application value integrators, and component hardware and network equipment producers.

LBS Customers

The mobile customer is at the top of the LBS industry food chain. It is at this level where all customer value is perceived, demand created, and profits realized. If the mobile customer does not see sufficient value (defined as delivered benefits) from the LBS service at the right price, no transactions will take place. The relative lack of perceived value as a result of high prices and low quality services is the reason for slow adoption of LBS. In a recent study by *Measuredup. com* over 80 per cent of mobile customers surveyed indicated that they were not pleased with their mobile operator's service (Caplan, 2007).

Emerging value drivers for LBS appear to be personal navigation and family monitoring such as child and elderly tracking (Baig 2006). Mobile Web2.0

applications such as social networking and interactive gaming are a nascent, but growing category. Potential LBS customers have become increasingly aware of in-vehicle and portable GPS-based navigation systems such as Garmin and Tom Tom as well as Internet-based mapping and satellite imagery from Google Maps and MapQuest (Martin, 2007, October 1). The advent of GPS-enabled mobile phones has set the stage for a new range of location-based services that may finally kick-start the category

A primary barrier to adoption is the privacy issue. Most customers will need to gain trust in the service provider with regard to how their information is used and safeguarded. (Schoenbachler & Gordon, 2002). Privacy policies are an important step as is the development of a permission-based relationship that is pull-oriented in nature. Few customers will want their phone to serve up an advertisement every time they pass a retail establishment unless there is a compelling value proposition associated with it. In addition, as the mobile Internet has become a reality, mobile services users are becoming impatient with the lack of choice and quality available from the mobile operators' closed networks. Pressure is building for the Mobile Web to offer an experience that builds on the openness and choice available on the fixed broadband Web (Segan, 2007).

Value Dominators

Since the industry's inception, the mobile operators have been the value dominators in the mobile industry food chain. They are the original brand managers (OBMs) of the industry. Operators such as Verizon, Sprint, AT&T Mobility, T-Mobile, and Vodafone have spent years to build the power of their networks' brands, primarily at the expense of the other members of the food chain (Malykhina and Martin, 2007).

These cellular operator OBMs have had the power over their partners to dictate the style, features, and usability of handsets, force private label or co-branding relationships, and to economically dominate infrastructure, handset, and application providers by limiting market access and dictating operator-favorable revenue-sharing requirements. Daren Tsui, CEO of mobile application developer and operator partner *mSpot,* sums up the situation: "The ecosystem is not healthy. You've got the developing community basically starving." (Kharif, 2007).

On the subscriber side the dominance continues. The operators can force multi-year contracts with high termination fees, and limit consumer choice options through their walled gardens where Web access and service selection is controlled by the carriers (Kharif, 2007). The poor-value story for consumers continues with handsets with disabled features, locked phones, lack of affordable international roaming plans, and inflexible subscription fees with extra, and sometimes hidden, charges (Caplan, 2007).

This position of dominance is ripe for disruption. Handset companies such as Apple and Nokia, with brand power that is superior to the operators, are not content to be weak players in the operators' food chain. New smartphones that can access the Internet with Wi-Fi connections and have VoIP capability are starting to crack the walled garden. Google, another major consumer brand, may be the biggest threat of all as it plans to enter the wireless arena with an open Internet-based business model that is likely to include free advertising-based mobile service and LBS offerings (Crocket, 2007).

Value Integrators

In the LBS food chain, the value integrators are the original equipment manufacturers (OEMs), mostly from Europe, U.S. and Asia, and the original design manufacturers (ODMs) from Asia. These companies design, develop, and manufacture the handsets and mobile devices for the mobile operators. OEM handset companies include Nokia, Motorola, Samsung, SonyEricsson, LG, and Apple.

In the software space, the value integrators are the independent software vendor (ISV) creators of geocoding and geoinformation software, operating systems, and LBS applications. They partner with or sell their applications to the mobile operators who control the end-user customer interface. The ISV category includes Autodesk, ESRI, Genasys, Microsoft MapPoint, DeCarta, Webraska, GeoVector, Wavemarket, SnapTrack, Trackwell Software, Yahoo, Microsoft, and Google. Several of these players also operate Internet portals.

Component Producers

Component producers are the electronic manufacturing services (EMS), semiconductor firms, and component, module, and subassembly manufacturers that serve the handset and hardware OEMs. These food chain members include Global Locate, SiRF GPS, Qualcomm, Broadcom, Intel, Freescale, Texas Instruments, and Samsung. Network equipment and infrastructure companies such as Alcatel, Ericsson, Nokia, and Cisco are also at this level. Although these food chain members are at the bottom of the food chain, their products are key ingredients to the mobile wireless and LBS solutions. Considerable economic value can be generated at this level. Prices generally tend to fall as volume production is achieved.

Disrupting the Food Chain

There is a shift underway in how the mobile industry will be organized. The impending disintermediation of the operators' value-dominator position in the LBS food chain is being driven by a services-centric strategy by the OEM handset makers and the ISV application providers as they attempt to move up and establish direct relationships with the end-user customers (See Figure 1). The end game of this strategy, if successful, would be the relegation of the network operator to the status of providing a "dumb pipe" similar to that of the fixed broadband ISPs.

It is interesting to note that several of the major LBS value integrators have significant brand power with end-users. In terms of brand rankings, Microsoft (#2), Nokia (#5), Google (#20), Samsung (#21), Apple (#33), Motorola (#77), and LG (#97) are among the top 100 global brands (Special Report, 2007). Conversely, in terms of advertising spending, cellular operators AT&T (#1), Verizon (#2), Sprint (#3), and T-Mobile (#13), are top spenders for media (100 leading national advertisers, 2007), but do not show up in the top-100 rankings of brand power. It would appear that the value integrators already have the end-user brand equity position that could be leveraged to move up the food chain to challenge the operators' value-dominator role. For example, some observers believe it was Apple's brand power and the introduction of the iPhone that may have saved AT&T flagging rebranding efforts after it acquired Cingular. But, AT&T had to grant Apple concessions in terms of revenue sharing and phone design, especially the Wi-Fi handset capability (Cuneo, 2007).

The most significant new mobile wireless competitors are Apple and Google which have entered the wireless industry with business models developed in the Internet-driven computer industry. Both companies will either introduce disruptive LBS solutions or enable their use in ways the operators will not favor. But, the company with the most advanced strategy in the short-run already dominates at the value integrator level of the food chain. That company is Nokia and it has decided that it needs to become a services company. In order to be successful with this strategy, value integrators need to open their platforms to encourage software companies to create innovative services applications. The operators have been very slow to do this. Apple, Google, and Nokia appear to be much faster to innovate.

Apple iPhone

On June 29, 2007, Apple launched the iPhone and became a major disruptor of the mobile wireless food chain. The phone features Wi-Fi access which enables its users to side load content from iTunes and the open Internet independent of AT&T's network. Now Apple has announced that it will release a software developer's kit that will open up the iPhone to independent software companies to create applications for the iPhone (Kharif, 2007). The power of Apple's brand, its growing iTunes multimedia services, and its strength in computers and the Internet provide Apple with a great opportunity to move up the mobile services food chain.

Nokia

Nokia commands approximately 40% of the handset market. It is starting to disrupt the mobile food chain in a big way. The handset maker is embracing a services-oriented strategy which includes a major thrust into LBS. In October 2007, they acquired Navteq, a U.S. mapping and LBS firm (Nokia plots services, 2007). In August, Nokia launched Ovi ("door" in Finnish) Internet and multimedia platform. Ovi will be that gateway to Nokia's Internet services, including a music store, games, Web communities, maps, and location services. Nokia has an installed base of over 200 million music capable handsets. Nokia's 6110 Navigator phone comes with GPS capability. Users can view their current location on a map, search for destinations, plot specific routes, and locate services such shops, hotels, gas stations, and restaurants (Reardon, 2007). Users can download maps directly to the handset. The navigation software and maps are free. Nokia will charge a fee for other services such as voice directions and live traffic updates. Like Apple, Nokia has opened its services platform to third-party developers. It has over 75,000 registered developers (Kharif, 2007). The major goals of the services strategy initiative are to develop closer relationships to end-users and capture a higher share of mobile services market (Schenker, 2007, September 10).

Google

Google, with its search-based advertising model, has been a major disruptor in the Internet space. Google's vision is to organize the world's information and to make it available to all. It now figures to extend this vision to the wireless world. Its goal is to make software and services as accessible on mobile networks as they are on the Internet (Sharma, 2007). Its plans include a "free" ad-based open wireless network, the gPhone, mapping, payment platform, and location-based services. It would be able to target real-time mobile ads to individual behavior—what you are doing, and where you are (Crocket 2007). The 2.5 billion phones in use exceed the number of personal computers and televisions combined and represent a huge growth market for location-targeted ads.

Google estimates that the location dimension will provide a 50% premium for mobile ads (Crockett,

2007). Google plans to connect advertisers with end-users through its mobile search engine, maps, YouTube, Gmail, and other applications. It is not difficult to imagine what combinations of Google's Global Positioning System, Google Maps, contact lists, and Web-browsing behavior would do for contextual targeting and the growth of new LBS applications (Sharma, 2007)

Google has the financial resources to bid on new wireless spectrum in the 700Mhz band, purchase struggling Sprint Nextel, or partner with a lower-tier carrier such as T-Mobile to launch the first free ad-supported nationwide wireless phone service. Google, along with Skype, is also lobbying the FCC for mobile "net neutrality" and "open access" where any handset could be used on any mobile network with any application (Jenkins 2007). Google intends to make the phone "open" as well. This will stimulate software developers to create new features and applications (Babcock, 2007). Google has recently announced the formation of its "Open Handset Alliance," to promote its platform called "Android." The alliance includes mobile operators, handset makers, service providers, software firms, and semiconductor firms (Delaney and Sharma, 2007). Sprint and T-Mobile are members of the alliance. Nokia and Apple are not.

Of course, Google wants to free-ride on others' broadband subscriptions just like it does in the fixed-broadband world. They want to make sure it does not share its search ad revenues with the operators. For the next several years, Google will have to work with operators to push its vision of the open wireless Internet. If it wins this battle between open and closed systems, the operators will have to work harder to avoid becoming commodity mobile ISP providers. Applications providers and customers would probably benefit. Whatever the outcome, Google's entry into the mobile services will have profound impact on the future shape of the mobile industry.

STRATEGIC TRENDS

Location-Relevant Services

One of the arguments about LBS is that it is not really a class of services, but an enabler of services. If location is an enabler, then it should be easily added to existing major services as an enhancement or upgrade. Location, in essence, would be a building block

for creating interactive services where contextual awareness is a key attribute. Context means enabling marketers to reach customers at the right location with the right solution at the precise time they are ready to buy (Kenny & Marshall, 2000). When contrasted with the standard Internet business model that uses banner and search-related ads to drive users to a website, location-based contextual marketing brings the site to the user, personalizing relevant information to fit the customer's real-time requirements at the point of need.

For instance, if a user wants to search "what's near me" on their GPS-enabled mobile phone in terms of a store, restaurant, or movie theater; location context would enable the marketer to suggest options near their position. They may even wish to determine if friends or family members are nearby. This information could be displayed on Google Maps with geo-spatial and satellite imagery of the location. Context would provide information on menus, what's playing, and pricing. Suggestions and promotions could be pushed to the wireless device to influence consumption choice. Restaurant and movie ratings, blog commentaries, and menus could be displayed to better inform the user. Tickets for events could be purchased with the mobile device. Context integrates the user's past behavior and preferences with the options provided by location and time (Kenny & Marshall 2000). Eventually, smart mobile location-enabled services will be able to sense and respond in real time to who the customer is, where they are, what they are doing, and what information they likely require (Mobile advertising, 2007).

From a marketing point of view, the rise of consumer use of wireless devices to access the Internet, shop online, and consume mobile services, provides a unique opportunity to real-time targeting of customers in virtual space (Luo, 2003). The convergence of location enablement, mobile services, and database marketing has generated excitement about potential for interactive marketing strategies. Contextual marketing (CM), which some call location-based marketing (LBM), will revolutionize direct marketing. These ideas are not new. Rayport and Sviokla (1994) identified content, context, and infrastructure as the key elements for creating customer value in an electronic "marketspace." Content is the essence of the information service offered to the mobile user. Infrastructure refers to the location-enabled mobile wireless network and associated devices. Context refers to the how, where, when, and under what conditions information is offered to mobile users.

The primary goal of CM is to increase the service provider's competitive advantage by delivering superior customer value as measured by increased customer satisfaction, loyalty, and service revenues (Luo and Seyedian, 2004). Mobile location-based advertising (LBA) is one type of CM that is more narrowly focused on advertising strategy and communication (Bruner & Kumar, 2007). LBA is more effective if it is "pull" rather than "push" oriented (Unni & Harmon, 2007). Pull-based LBA presents an ad only after the user requests particular information or a coupon on a one-time basis. Push-based LBA is sent to the wireless device without a specific request from the user. LBA is may provide a mass market opportunity if it is permission-based, personalized, and presented in the context of the activity the user is participating in and pull-oriented.

Open Business Models

The closed nature of the mobile wireless networks has undoubtedly led to the lack of innovation in mobile applications, especially LBS. The strategic entry of Apple and Google into the wireless industry will change how the industry is organized. Handset manufacturers are adding GPS capability and are opening up their platforms to mobile application developers. The handset makers are using their superior brand power to build relationships with end-user customers. Google is presenting the greatest challenge to the mobile operators. They are developing mobile search, advertising-based, location-relevant applications that at the very least will challenge the business models of the networks they run on. When Google rolls out the gPhone, and possibly its own free wireless network, it will be very difficult for the operators to do business as usual (Sharma, 2007).

Open business models from the fixed broadband world are coming to the wireless Web. The widespread existence of Wi-Fi networks and the commercialization of WiMAX will provide consumers and the new competitor alternatives to the cellular networks. It remains to be seen how long it will take for Apple, Google, Yahoo, Microsoft, and other companies from the Internet world to rearrange the mobile wireless and LBS market space, but it will likely happen.

Mobile Web 2.0

A shift in how information is generated, captured, organized, and shared is underway. Indeed, it is a shift in how the Web itself will be organized. At the core of this disruptive change is the personal information and social connections that people share to form social networks (Waters & Allison, 2007). Mobile Web 2.0 refers to Web 2.0 principals applied to the Mobile Web as accessed from cell phones, PDAs, and other mobile devices. It is based on the IP Multimedia Subsystem (IMS) that provides the framework for delivering Internet protocol (IP) multimedia to mobile users. IMS integrates the Internet with the mobile world. It uses cellular technologies to enable access to Internet technologies for the creation of high value services (Jaokar & Fish, 2006). The seven core principles of the Mobile Web 2.0 identified by Joakar and Fish are:

1. The Mobile Web is a Platform. Software as a Service (SaaS) is the combination of software and data. Therefore, it is important to create an ecosystem of software developers to create high value services. The more data the service can harness, such as location data, the more valuable the service is. Mobile Web 2.0 applications are able to harness the knowledge power of a large number of users.

2. Harnessing Collective Intelligence. This principle leverages user-generated content. This principle involves understanding of peer production, the wisdom of crowds, and network effects from user contributions.

3. Data is the Next "Intel Inside." Data is the key differentiator. The company that serves the data usually owns the data. This is particularly critical for LBS. Which company owns the data: the cellular operator, NavTech, Digital Globe, Google, or Nokia? There is likely a "chain of data" that is generated from different sources. Data that is easy to collect is not as valuable as data that is very complex and difficult to collect.

4. No Software Release Cycle. Mobile Web 2.0 services do not have a software release cycle. These applications are software plus data and need to re-index the data daily to maintain its value. Operations that generate the data are essential to Mobile Web 2.0 companies and users are treated as co-developers.

5. Lightweight Programming Models. Simpler technologies such as RSS and AJAX are the driving force behind Web 2.0 services. These technologies are designed to syndicate rather than orchestrate. They are opposite to the mobile operators' mindset of controlling access to data.

The services are designed for reuse. Innovation occurs from the combination of existing services.

6. Software Above the Level of a Single Device. The whole of the Web should be transparent and accessible by any device through a common browser. Devices should be a reporter of data as well as a consumer of data.

7. Rich User Experience. Services should be able to span content from many different sites. Users should have a seamless experience across various services. Instead of the user going to each site, the content from each site is going to the user as in the case of RSS.

Mobile Social Networking

Wireless social networking may be the killer application that disrupts the mobile world and the LBS space (Norton, 2007). Social networking sites claim well over 100 million members that share personal information, social connections, and, increasingly, location information. Sites such as MySpace and Facebook are growing fast. Social networking embodies the seven core principles of Mobile Web 2.0. Mobile operators are trying to embrace this trend by creating their own portals centered on their walled gardens, without much success. In the fixed broadband world, Web 2.0 applications are mostly ad-supported and free to "subscribers" whose social network behavior has skyrocketed accordingly. Even with a similar advertising model and interactive multimedia service quality, which are years away, mobile operators may not reap much revenue. They would likely have to bundle wireless data access at much lower rates to attract significant social networking volume (Norton, 2007).

Social networking portals are not open worlds; they are isolated islands unto themselves (Stross, 2007). Google, with its ownership of video-sharing site You-Tube, sees opportunity but its search crawler is not allowed on most social networking sites. Orkut, Google's multimedia social networking site, lags behind leaders MySpace and Facebook in terms of monthly visitors and page views (Stross, 2007). Google has changed its vision to "Social Will Be Everywhere" to attempt to break down yet another of the Web's walled gardens (Stross, 2007). Google is promoting a new open standard called "OpenSocial" for social networking. They have formed a consortium of social networking sites that includes number one site MySpace. By adopting a single set of standards, Google is betting the large

audience will draw the best software application developers (Waters & Allison, 2007). Developers will be able to write code that work on all sites. Facebook, which is partnering with Microsoft, has not yet joined the open consortium.

Google is also pushing for open interfaces between the social networking sites. This would ensure that personal data is no longer proprietary to just one site. Users would have more control over their personal information and the ability to take it anywhere on the Web (Waters & Allison, 2007). This would be very useful for determining whether anyone in a user's Web network is selling anything, in a nearby location, or wanting to communicate or show the user something in real time. It would also be beneficial for Google since it would open both the fixed and Mobile Web to its free services advertising-based business model.

Privacy, Security, and Safety

LBS provides unique opportunities for the wireless industry. It also brings with it responsibility to protect the user's identity, data security in use, storage, and transmission, and perhaps most importantly for the personal safety of the users themselves. It is a matter of trust between the user and the provider. Increasingly, this is becoming a legal requirement as well. News media stories of data breaches, misuse of data by marketers, stolen identities, online and location-based sexual predation, and spouses tracking cheating partners are becoming commonplace (Williams, 2006). Indeed, the growth of child-tracking LBS is likely a consequence of the ease of predators to target children online.

However, the wireless industry has some work to do in protecting customers and their data. A recent study by the Customer Respect Group found that the telecoms industry was worst for consumer privacy (Telecoms industry worst, 2007). It was judged worst for collecting excessive amounts of personal data and using the data for ongoing marketing campaigns. As mobile operators search for more customers and to sell more services to existing customers they are likely to collect and rely more heavily on personal data. With increasing LBS capability, that data will be more context-rich than ever. Nowhere is the need more critical than determining privacy requirements for LBS (Williams, 2006).

There are tradeoffs to be considered. If a provider locks down a service too tightly, usability will be diminished and costs may increase for the provider.

Customers may become frustrated if they are prompted too many times for authentication. Protection levels depend on the type of service. Applications that only involve a one-to-one interaction with a site are least complex. Interactions between family members and other trustworthy individuals are less complex than those between complete strangers. There is a need for a core set of privacy, security, and safety for LBS applications. This should not be left to the end of the application development cycle or viewed as a separate functionality. It should be integrated in to the application with appropriate levels of protection, unobtrusiveness, and convenience build in. (Williams 2006).

Perusco and Michael (2007) explored the impact of LBS technology on control, trust, privacy, and security and their impact on LBS users. The authors conclude that these four issues are interrelated, can have a demonstrable impact, and involve tradeoffs for LBS users and providers. Increased control can destroy trust, but, increased trust would lead to more privacy. Privacy, in turn, requires security as well as trust. If a person's location data is accessed by unauthorized individuals, privacy is breached; and possibly personal safety as well. Security refers to not only secure data, but secure LBS system components. If tracking devices cannot be removed by the user, then control is increased. The authors warn of unintended consequences of LBS and recommend that researchers and practitioners consider both the benefits and the possible unfavorable side effects of LBS.

For LBS developers and marketers, there is a lesson in this. LBS may be a key enabler for the next generation of applications for the Mobile Web. However, the requirements for privacy, security, and safety may be more than just a matter of trust. They may become the foundation of a successful new wireless business model or, if ignored or unsuccessfully managed, a barrier that will not be moved.

CONCLUSION

Web 2.0 and its wireless offspring Mobile Web 2.0, will truly reengineer how information is organized. Walled gardens and isolated islands will eventually give way to this open approach. The advent of 3G wireless networks and the impending development of faster, higher capacity 4G technologies will facilitate the convergence of the wired and wireless worlds. Users will use their smartphones and other devices in a wide variety of ways to access the Internet. Consumers are moving from making calls to accessing the Internet. With regards to function, it will matter little that one access route is wired and fixed, one is mobile and wireless, and another is wireless but short range. The real differentiator is contextual ability that only location information can bring.

The location-enablement potential for a wide variety of software applications would seemingly provide an overwhelming competitive advantage for mobile network operators. Their reliance on the closed-system business model has limited the ability of computer manufacturers, software companies, and even handset companies to participate in a marketspace that has eclipsed the computer industry in terms of users. For companies such as Google, Apple, Microsoft, Yahoo, MySpace, Facebook, and virtually all the Internet software developers this is an opportunity too big to ignore. If the mobile operators do not open up the market, it will likely be done for them. The operators' risk moving down the industry food chain to become commodity wireless ISP providers if they cannot find ways to preserve their competitive advantage in a newly opening world.

Google is by far the most disruptive force faced by the operators. Google will use the power of its open platform, its Open Handset Alliance partners, Mobile Web2.0 principles, and the customers' desire for choice to open the mobile operators' networks to innovation. Open systems solve the interoperability problem. Free services solve the pricing problem and generate lots of new users and usage. Bringing in handset makers, applications developers, and other partners opens up the ecosystem to innovation which further drives the market. A free advertising-driven location-based services model may prove to be a very compelling value proposition indeed.

REFERENCES

Allison, K. (2007, October 24). Cisco to purchase WiMAX supplier. *Financial Times, 19.*

Babcock, C. (2007, May 28). Software ecosystems: Can Salesforce, Google, and Facebook be fertile grounds for third-party development? We are about to find out, *Information Week,* 31-33.

Baig, E. C. (2006, June 2). Where in the world am I? Your phone might know; more consumer call on location-based services. *USA Today,* 1B.

Bolter, J. D. & MacIntyre, B. (2007, August). Is it alive or is it AR?. *IEEE Spectrum*, 31-35.

Boulton, C. (2007, October 10). Meet your new partner and rival. *Google, eWeek.com*, Retrieved November 1, 2007 from http://www.eweek.com/article2/0, 1895,2193951,00.asp.

Bruner, G. C., & Kumar A. (2007, Spring). Attitude toward location-based advertising. *Journal of Interactive Advertising*.

Caplan, J. (2007, June 27). The iPhone's carrier problem. *Time.com*, Retrieved July 2, 2007 from http://www.time.com/time/specials/2007/article/0,28804,1638782 _1638789_1637763,00.html.

Crockett, R. O. (2007, October 8). Will a Google phone change the game? Mobile biggies are quaking at the idea of competition from a free, ad-based service. *Business Week*, 38-39.

Cox, J. (2007, March 5). Vendors adding to wireless location-tracking products. *Network World, Retrieved* July 25, 2007 from http://www.networkworld.com/news/2007/030507-wireless-location-tracking.html.

Cuneo, A. (2007, October 22). AT&T's rebranding effort 'a failure of epic proportions? *Advertising Age, 1*, 58.

Delaney, K. J., & Sharma, A. (2007, November 6). Google, bidding for phone ads, lures partners. *The Wall Street Journal*, A1.

Displays to keep an eye on (2007, March 10). *The Economist Technology Quarterly*, 4-6.

Edwards, C. (2007, September 3). The Road to WiMax. *Businessweek.com*. Retrieved September 25, 2007 from http://businessweek.com/magazine/content/07_b4048401. htm?chan=mz.

4G technology shaping up ahead of time, (2007, August 21). *Telecoms.com*. Retrieved October 26, 2007 from http://telecoms.com/itmgcontent/tcoms/news/articles/200117453085.html.

Fry, J. (2006, July 3). Dreams of a truly mobile web: Net needs to escape its computer cage, but best of luck freeing it in the U.S. *The Wall Street Journal Online*. Retrieved August 8, 2007 from http://online.wsj.com/article/SB115144210174092228.html.

Gapper, J. (2007, November 1). Mighty Google rings in the changes. *Financial Times, 11*.

Hesseldahl, A. (2007, September 14). Mapping a wireless trend. *Businessweek.com*. Retrieved September 20, 2007 from http://businessweek.com/technology/content/sep2007/tc20070913_187668.htm.

Hesseldahl, A. (2007, September 14). Garmin and Tom Tom vie for TeleAtlas. *Businessweek.com*. Retrieved September 20, 2007 from http://businessweek.com/technology/content/nov2007/tc2007112_187668.htm.

Harmon, R. R., & Day, L. B. (2006). The dynamics of the corporate food chain: Strategy, power, and position in the age of outsourcing. In Kocaoglu, D. et al. (Eds.) *Technology Management for a Global Future*, Portland, OR: PICMET/IEEE, 256-263.

Iansiti, M., & Levien, R. (2004, March). Strategy as ecology. *Harvard Business Review, 82*(3), 68-78.

Is LBS about to find an audience? (2007, March 7). *Telecoms.com*. Retrieved September 7, 2007 from http://www.telecoms.com/itmgcontent/tcoms/new/articles/20017409731. html.

Jaokar, A., & Fish, T. (2006). *Mobile Web 2.0: The innovator's guide to developing and marketing next generation wireless/mobile applications*. London: futuretext, Ltd.

Jenkins, H. W. (2007, July 18), Sort of evil. *The Wall Street Journal*, A14.

Kapko, M. (2007, March 28). Maps, games lead location-based service applications. *RCR Wireless News, 30*.

Kharif, O. (2007, October 29), Apple, Google vs. big wireless. *Businessweek.com*. Retrieved October 29, 2007 from http://www.businessweek.com/technology/content/oct2007/tc20071029_749114.htm.

Kenny, D., & Marshall, J. F. (2000, November-December). Contextual marketing: the real business of the Internet. *Harvard Business Review, 78*(6), 119-125.

LBS finding favour (2007, September 26). *Telecoms. com*. Retrieved October 24, 2007 from http://telecoms.com/itmgcontent/tcoms/news/articles/20017464009.html.

LBS: Lost and found (2007, March 21). *Telecoms.com*. Retrieved October 26, 2007 from http://www.telecoms.com/itmgcontent/tcoms/news/articles/20017412775.html.

Luo, X. (2003). The performance implications of contextual marketing for electronic commerce. *Journal of Database Marketing, 10*(3), 231-239.

Luo, X., & Seyedian M. (2004). Contextual marketing and customer orientation strategy for E-Commerce: An empirical analysis. *International Journal of Electronic Commerce, 8*(2), 95-118.

Maglogiannis, I., & Hadjiefthymiades, S. (2006). Emerloc: Location-based services for emergency medical incidents. *International Journal of Medical Informatics, 7*(1), 1-13.

Malykhina, E., & Martin, R. (2007, May 14). Message to Cell Carriers. *Information Week*, 29-32.

Martin, R. (2007, October 1). Google unplugged: gPhone or not, Google's going mobile. *Information Week*, 19-20.

Martin, R. (2007, October 15). Big carriers confront change. *Information Week*, 32-33.

Mobile advertising: The next big thing (2007, October 6). *The Economist*, 73-74.

Mohney, D. (2007, October). The business case for enterprise WiMAX. *Von Magazine, 5*(3), 26-31.

Moore, J. F. (1996). *The death of competition: Leadership and strategy in the age of business ecosystems*, New York: Harper Business.

Morse, J. (2006, October 2). Separate studies come to same conclusion: LBS set for growth. *RCR Wireless News, 26*.

Niccolai, J. (2007, March 22). Update: Nokia ships N95 phone with GPS, *InfoWorld.com*. Retrieved October 23, 2007 from http://www.infoworld.com/article/07/03/22/HNnokiaphonewithgps_1.html.

Nokia plots services route with Navteq buy (2007, October 1). *Telecoms.com*. Retrieved October 26, 2007 from http://www.telecoms.com/itmgcontent/tcoms/news/ articles/20017465155.htm.

Norton, K. (2007, April 2). Mobile telcos rush to social networking. *Businessweek.com*, Retrieved November 3, 2007 from http://businessweek.com/globalbiz/content/apr2007/gb20070402_972976.htm.

One hundred leading national advertisers, (2007, June 25). *Advertising Age*. Retrieved October 29th, 2007 from http://adage.com/datacenter/article?article_id=118672.

Perusco, L., & Michael. K. (2007). Control, trust, privacy, and security: evaluating location-based services. *IEEE Technology and Society Magazine, 26*(1), 4-16.

Porter, M. E. (2001, March). Strategy and the Internet. *Harvard Business Review, 79*(3), 63-78.

Rao, B., & Minakakis, L. (2004). Assessing the business impact of location-based services. *Proceedings of the 37th Hawaii International Conference on System Sciences*, IEEE.

Rayport, J., & Sviokla, J. (1994, November-December). Managing in the marketspace. *Harvard Business Review, 72*(6), 141-150.

Reardon, M. (2007, February 15). Handset makers get in on location services. *C/net News.com*. Retrieved October 19, 2007, from http://www.news.com/Handset-makers-get-in-on-location-services/2100-1039_3-6159778.html.

Reed, J. (2007, August 2). Rewards for lack of drive. *Financial Times*, 8.

Safeco Insurance launches Teensurance program (2007, July 10). *Financetech.com*. Retrieved October 30, 2007, from http://www.finacetech.com/showArticle.jhtml? articleID= 201001385.

Sagan, S. (2007, September 4). Let wireless freedom ring. *PC Magazine, 54*.

Schenker, J. L. (2007, September 10). Nokia aims way beyond handsets. *Business Week, 38*.

Schenker, J. L. (2007, October 29). A 4G standards war is brewing. *Businessweek.com*. Retrieved October 29, 2007 from http://www.businessweek.com/technology/content/ oct2007/ tc20071027_900612.htm?chan=search.

Schoenbachler, D. D., & Gordon, G. L. (2002). Trust and customer willingness to provide information in data-base driven relationship marketing. *Journal of Interactive Marketing, 16*(3), 2-16.

Sharma, A. (2007, October 30). Can a Google phone connect with carriers? *The Wall Street Journal*, B1.

Special report: The 100 top brands (2007, August 6). *Business Week*, 59-64.

Stross, R. (2007, November 4). Why Google turned into a social butterfly. *New York Times*. Retrieved November 4, 2007 from http://nytimes.com/2007/11/04/technology/04digi.hml?_r=1&oref=slogin.

Telecoms industry worst for consumer privacy. (2007, March 6). *telecoms.com*, Retrieved November 4, 2007 from http://telecoms.com/itmgcontent/tcoms/news/articles/20017409490.html.

The Phone of the Future. (2006, December 2). *The Economist, Technology Quarterly*, 18-20.

Unni, R., & Harmon, R. R. (2006). Location-based services: Opportunities and challenges. In Unhelkar Bhuvan (Ed.) *Handbook of Research in Mobile Business: Technical, Methodological and Social Perspectives*, Hershey, PA: Idea Group Publishing, 18-34.

Unni, R., & Harmon, R. R. (2007, Spring). Perceived effectiveness of push vs. pull mobile location-based advertising. *Journal of Interactive Advertising*, 48-71.

Waters, R., & Allison, K. (2007, November 1). Google shapes up to social networking. *Financial Times*, 16.

Willams, D. H. (2006, October 25). LBS Development – Determining Privacy Requirements. *Directions Magazine*, Retrieved October 14, 2007 from http://www.directionsmag.com/article_id=2323.

KEY TERMS

Industry Food Chain: A hierarchical business ecosystem where the identity, roles, and relative power of the industry's participants define their market position. Industry food chain participants exist in an economic, political, and physical environment where the dynamics of their relationships affect strategic choices and outcomes and are characterized by uncertainty. Studying an industry's food chain can identify roles and strategic options of the participants and help to foresee competitive disruptions that may be on the horizon.

LBS Applications: Location-enabled services such as navigation, family tracking, emergency services, asset tracking, logistics planning, workforce management, customer management, location-based advertising, and social networking that are delivered over a mobile network to a location-ready multimedia handset.

Location-Based Services (LBS): Location-based services (LBS) provide location-specific information, often in context with other mobile applications, which is relevant to the mobile user's real-time choice behavior. These services determine the exact location of the user and can use push and/or pull information methods to respond to queries or suggest possible decision options to the mobile user. Knowledge of the user's location can be used to deliver context-relevant information to customers where and when they are most likely to buy.

Location Enablement: The use of GPS or other location technology, handsets, networks, applications, and infrastructure to deliver location-relevant information to any portable wireless device that has the capacity to display multimedia content.

Location-Relevant Services: Location determination is a building block for creating interactive services where contextual awareness is a key attribute. Context means enabling marketers to reach customers at the right location with the right solution at the precise time they are ready to buy. Location-relevant services bring the Internet site to the user, personalizing relevant information to fit the customer's real-time requirements at the point of need.

Location Technology: Advanced technologies that determine the location of a mobile handset device. *Network based technologies* use the cellular network to determine the user's location. The primary *handset-based technology* is the satellite based Global Positioning System (GPS). *Hybrid technologies* such as A-GPS attempt to minimize the line-of-sight drawbacks from pure GPS handset solutions. It incorporates the accuracy of a GPS solution for outside open areas and is network-assisted for poor GPS signal locations such as indoors. Short-range *local positioning technologies* such as Wi-Fi, Bluetooth, and Radio Frequency Identification (RFID) that may be built into the handset can provide accurate location data since the access point location is known.

Mobile Data Networks: 3G and 4G high-speed mobile networks that enable Internet access on mobile devices. 3G networks are circuit and packet switched and 4G is packet switched. Such networks use W-CDMA, CDMA2000, and WiMAX technology for 3G networks. OFDMA technologies such as Long Term Evolution (LTE) for GSM networks and Ultra Mobile Broadband (UMB) for CDMA networks and Mobile WiMAX are standards being proposed for 4G networks.

Mobile Social Network: A mobile location-enabled social structure made of nodes of individuals or organizations that are linked by values, visions, ideas, or friendship. The mobile social network is a map of all of the relevant ties between the nodes being studied leveraged by knowledge of each member's location. The network determines and leverages the social capital of individual actors to enhance each user's experience and the collective value of the network.

Mobile Web2.0: The foundation of Mobile Web 2.0 consists of personal information and social connections that people share to form social networks. The Mobile Web as accessed from cell phones, PDAs, and other mobile devices deliver Internet protocol (IP) multimedia to mobile users. It essentially harnesses user-generated content as the means for creating a rich user experiences capable of creating superior customer value.

Chapter VI
Creation of a Process Framework for Transitioning to a Mobile Enterprise

Bhuvan, Unhelkar
MethodScience.com & University of Western Sydney, Australia

ABSTRACT

This chapter presents the creation of a process framework that can be used by enterprises in order to transition to mobile enterprises. This framework facilitates adoption of mobile technologies by organizations in a strategic manner. A mobile enterprise transition framework provides a process for transition that is based on the factors that influence such transition. The Mobile Enterprise Transition (MET) framework, outlined in this chapter, is based on the four dimensions of economy, technology, methodology, and sociology. These four dimensions for MET have been identified based on an understanding of people, processes, and technologies. A research project undertaken by the author validates these four dimensions.

INTRODUCTION

This chapter presents an approach to transitioning to mobile enterprises. The earlier outline of this approach was published by Unhelkar (2005) and it contained three dimensions of a mobile enterprise transition framework. Later, based on the research undertaken by the author, this transition framework was modified and extended to result in a four dimensional framework. This framework is the core discussion topic of this chapter. A complete and in-depth discussion of this process framework also appears in Unhelkar (2008).

Mobile technologies form the basis of the communications revolution that has resulted in elimination of physical connectivity for people, processes and things. This wireless connectivity has resulted in significant impact on the organization of the business and its relationship with the customers. The ability of businesses and customers to connect to each other ubiquitously -independent of time and location – using mobile technologies is the core driver of this change. However, successful changes in terms of adoption of mobile technologies and applications in an organization depend on a process framework. This chapter discusses a Mobile Enterprise Transitions framework

for *transitioning* an organization to a mobile organization. The purpose of this MET framework is to
provide guidance in terms of people, processes and
technologies involved in successful transitioning of
the enterprises.

A MET can be defined by extending and refining
an earlier definition of mobile transformation given
by Marmaridis and Unhelkar (2005) as "evolution of
business practices through the adoption of suitable
mobile technologies and processes resulting in per-
vasiveness." This definition suggests that the MET
will facilitate incorporation of mobile technologies
in business processes that will result in pervasive
business activities independent of location and time.
The understanding of MET, however, needs to be
based on a firm understanding of how mobility is
unique and how it is different to land-based Internet
connectivity.

CONSIDERING THE NATURE OF
MOBILITY IN THE "MET"
FRAMEWORK

Electronic business transitions have been studied,
amongst others, by Ginige et al (2001), Lan and
Unhelkar (2005). However, the uniqueness of mobile
technologies in terms of their impact on business
has been discussed by Marmaridis and Unhelkar
(2005), Arunatileka and Unhelkar (2003), Godbole

and Unhelkar (2003), Lan and Unhelkar (2005), and
Unhelkar (2008). These authors have focussed on
the specific nature of mobility as depicted in Figure
1. The inner square in Figure 1 indicates land-based
connectivity between enterprises, functional units and
other fixed devices. This connectivity evolved from
the initial centralized connectivity of the mainframe,
followed by the client-server connectivity and finally
resulting in the Internet connectivity (business to
business - B2B and business to customer - B2C). The
Internet-based connectivity is further augmented by
the XML (eXtensible Markup Language) to facilitate
the Internet as a medium of computing, rather than
merely as a means of communication. However, as
depicted by the outer square in Figure 1, the external
wireless connectivity, by its very nature, is between
an individual and the business or between two individuals. As correctly stressed by Elliott and Phillips
(2004), a mobile phone is a far more personal device
that is carried by an individual as compared with a
desktop personal computer.

This nature of wireless connectivity needs to be
understood and incorporated in all dimensions of MET
(this could be based on discussions such as Thai et.al
(2003); the four dimensions are discussed next). For
example, economically, the cost of a mobile device has
dropped and continues to drop significantly making
is obligatory for businesses to consider mobility in
order to access and serve the customer. Technically,
it is essential to consider the "individuality" of the
mobile gadgets and their ability to be location-aware

Figure 1. Mobility is personal in nature (based on Unhelkar, 2005)

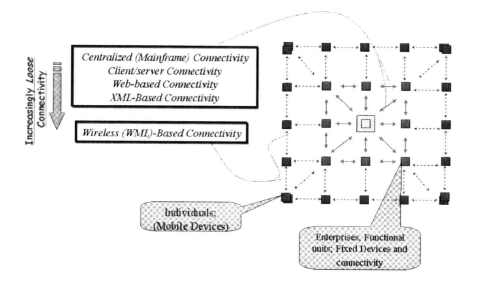

(see Adam and Katos (2005) for the resultant challenges of security and privacy of individuals that is different to the challenges in corresponding land-based connections). The activities and tasks of the methodological dimension should be created in a way that properly exploits the hand-held gadgets; and socially, mobile transitions need to consider the impact of mobility on the socio-cultural fabric of the society and the corresponding changing value systems like work ethics and social protocols. Thus, when businesses transitions from the land-based connectivity paradigm and incorporate wireless connectivity in their business practices, they have to ensure that an individual is considered in all their process dimensions as compared to when the business was organized only around land-based workstations.

THE FOUR DIMENSIONS OF A MOBILE ENTERPRISE TRANSITION FRAMEWORK

When an organization decides to incorporate mobility in its business, it is a strategic decision that is based on the primary question of "why" to "mobilize". This strategic decision is followed by investigations into the technical, methodological and social dimensions dealing respectively with the "what", "how" and "who" of the process. The transition process framework thus reveals itself into four major dimensions as shown in Figure 2 (based on Unhelkar (2003a) and (2008)). These dimensions of mobile transitions are, however, not exclusive to each other. When applied in practice,

they tend to overlap each other, resulting in a cohesive transition process. However, separate understanding of each of these dimensions is helpful in creating the MET framework in the first place. Thus, this discussion starts with the theoretical framework and then discusses its application in practice. The four process dimensions for a mobile enterprise transition, as shown in Figure 2, can be understood as follows:

- The Economic dimension deals with the core business driver of "why" to undertake the transition. Costs and competition have been the core business drivers for most business decisions and they are also true in this case. Reduction in costs and increase in competition encourage the business to undertake formal MET.
- The Technical dimension of the mobile transformation process considers "what" technologies are used in the transformation, and "what" deliverables are produced at the end of the process. Examples of issues discussed in this dimension include devices/gadgets, programming, databases, networking, security and architecture of mobile technologies participating in the MET.
- The Methodological dimension of the process deals primarily with the question of "how" to – amongst other things- model and design business processes, approach methodologies and quality in software processes and re-organize business structure and its relationship with customers and employees.
- The Social dimension of the transformation process focuses on "who" is involved in and influenced by the process. Typically these are

Figure 2. Four dimensions of a mobile enterprise transition framework (based on Unhelkar, 2008)

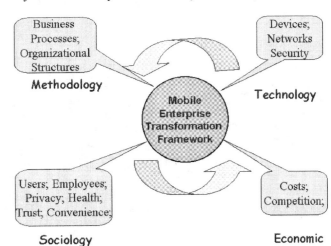

the users of the business (e.g. customers and employees) The discussion in this dimension deals with the effect of mobile technologies on the socio-cultural aspects of people's lives -especially the changing working formats and work ethics– and organizational and social structures.

The aforementioned four dimensions of MET are now discussed in greater detail.

ECONOMIC DIMENSION IN M-TRANSFORMATION

The question of "why" to "mobilize" provides the strategic reason for a business undertaking MET. The economic dimension considers the costs of running the business and maps it with the cost of acquiring mobility. Furthermore, the economic dimension is also concerned with the competition and how they are putting pressure on the business. Furthermore, the economic dimension also investigates the potential effect of mobility on customers as well as employees of the organization in terms of providing efficient service to the customers by conducting the business efficiently. Thus, "why" to "mobilize" is a strategic decision undertaken by the business decision makers of the organization. This decision to transition using the MET process framework can take the business to a global mobile playing field and therefore it has to be taken carefully and seriously.

TECHNICAL DIMENSION IN M-TRANSFORMATION

This technical dimension of the MET framework is concerned with the question of "what" technology to use, and "what" deliverables are produced at the end of the process. Thus, the technical dimension primarily includes the understanding and the application of the various mobile hardware devices and gadgets, issues of GPS enabled gadgets (3G) and wireless networking and security. The types of devices, their capacity and costs, and their usability are of utmost importance in this dimension. Mobile devices have developed well beyond the ubiquitous mobile phone, and now include a wide range of devices like Personal Digital Assistants (PDA) and wireless computers (typically laptops with

inbuilt wireless processors). Each device can have numerous features that need to be considered when they are incorporated in the business processes. For example, the ability of Wi-Fi enabled mobile gadgets to take photographs onsite and to instantly transmit them to the business centre has an invaluable application in processes that are related; for example to insurance claims, medical emergencies and sports. Additional device related issues include the ability of the devices to function alone -standalone-, or with other wireless components; for example, some wireless PCMCIA cards cannot be connected to the Internet and receive SMS messages simultaneously.

Functionality of mobile devices are further augmented by mobile networks, which play a significant role in terms of the device's abilities to browse, locate and transmit information. Some examples of technological challenges in networking include the incorporation of wireless broadband services, creation of local hotspots for services, integration of devices and their software with the existing organizational infrastructure, combination of WLAN (Wireless Local Area Network) and WWAN (Wireless Wide Area Network), satellite communications and even simple issues like user access through VPN or dialup connections. Mobile networking influences the breadth of coverage (i.e. area being covered) and the depth of coverage (the amount of information being transmitted/received) based on the available bandwidth, speed of transmission, as well as its reliability. At the individual level, the ability of infrared and Bluetooth enabled devices and the potentials offered by Radio Frequency Identification tags (RFID) are also increasingly playing an important role in mobile enterprise transitions.

Wireless connectivity has further provided opportunities for handheld devices to use computing power of other handheld and stationery devices, leading to the creation of wireless Grids (McKnight and Howison (2004), and Unhelkar (2004). Wireless grids facilitate creation of virtual processors that can be used to deliver far more functionalities than is evident today. For example, wireless grids can provide sufficient computing power for Mobile Internet Agents (as discussed by Subramanium et. al (2004)), enabling them to perform advanced functions like searching and comparing different products and services on handheld devices.

Security (as discussed by Godbole (2003) in the context of the Internet) is the next important part of the technical dimension. Mobility provides greater opportunity for unscrupulous 'tapping' into the networks, siphoning off data, information and even identities of the users as compared with land-based network. And because many mobile-enabled business processes (e.g. in healthcare domain with ambulances) depend heavily on the security of the mobile networks, protection of sensitive corporate data during transmission to and from a mobile devices (channel security and content security) is a vital issue in the technical dimension of MET.

Databases have evolved to content management systems (CMS) that are capable of storing audios, videos, photos, graphs and charts and many other content formats that could not be stored in a standard relational database. Technical dimension of MET has to, therefore, consider issues like the type and nature of content, location of contents influencing the speed and security of downloads, duration of content before they are replaced or upgraded, synchronization of contents between the mobile devices and back-end servers, and so on.

A mobile process is made up of a diverse range of heterogeneous mobile infrastructures including the hardware, operating system, messaging systems and databases –which all need to be integrated to provide mobile functionalities. Although most business applications today are web-enabled, they also need to be integrated further with mobile applications in order to make them mobile-web-enabled applications. Using SMS and MMS, creation of WiFi hotspots and incorporation of seamless wireless broadband through a single ISP are some practical options in such integrations. Some of the integration challenges for mobile infrastructures include issues such as the movement of the users, mobile nodes, fluctuating demands on the infrastructure (notably networks and databases), changing security needs (depending on the type of information required) and reliability (ability to restart transaction from any point in time).

Finally, usability can also be considered as an important technical issue (in addition to being a sociological issue) in MET–especially as more and more functionality is being provided on small screen mobile devices. Usability considerations, so vividly depicted by Constantine and Lockwood (1999), need to be extended further when it comes to mobile devices to ensure information is provided succinctly to the users. Wireless Markup Language (WML) can play an important part in removing unnecessary elements from the display of information on mobile devices.

METHODOLOGICAL DIMENSION IN M-TRANSFORMATION

The methodological dimension of MET primarily deals with the business processes, which can be understood as the "manner in which a business carries out its activities and tasks". These activities and tasks deal with both external parties and internally with its employees and management. The modelling of these business processes is complicated by the fact that the users (especially customers) have an expanding array of different types and models of mobile gadgets available to them. Not only do organizations making the transition doesn't have much control on these devices, but they are also faced with the ever increasing expectations by the users that the m-businesses will support their specific gadgets.

Whenever a business transitions to a mobile business, three possibilities emerge with respect to its business processes:

- Firstly, existing business processes are re-engineered to incorporate mobility; the re-engineered processes will be impacted by mobility in terms of location and time independence for the users
- Secondly, totally new business processes are brought in; as a result to the introduction of a mobile technology, and would otherwise have not existed and
- Thirdly, some redundant and/or irrelevant business processes are dropped and they do not make sense with the incorporation of mobility.

Each of the aforementioned process changes impact the individual user, as well as the organization and even the business sector as a whole. For example, the manner in which an employee would fill out his/her time sheets would change with the advent of mobility in the organization. Or the way in which a customer enquires about her balance in a banking environment will change depending on mobility in the process. Organizational processes, primarily dealing with other businesses, but also related to organizational structure and internal management, undergo change when mobility is incorporated in the business. Finally, as discussed by S'duk and Unhelkar (2005), an entire business sector made up of a group or collaboration of businesses could start interacting with each other through wireless applications and networks, resulting in a need to reengineer processes that criss-cross an industrial sector. This may result in the need for industrial process reengineering (IPR). For example, with mobile connectivity, an airline and a car hire company may need to change their business processes together to inform an individual of changes to flight timings on her hired mobile car dashboard; or a hospital, an insurance company and a company providing road side assistance may introduce new business processes that facilitates their collaboration to provide immediate care and support to a mobile subscriber who may have met with an accident. Similarly, advances in wireless grids further increase the opportunities for an industrial segment (or a dynamic group) to create entirely new business processes. For example, the creation of on-the-spot dynamic customer groups at shopping malls and sports venues was not feasible without the mobile connectivity; with this mobile connectivity businesses are able to target a group of customers dynamically. Extending Kanter's (2003) argument further, for future service growth mobile business processes need to continuously keep the user's context in mind to be able to fully exploit the dynamicity offered by mobility.

Deshpande *et.al* (2004), in the *Device Independent Web Engineering* workshop, describe how, with continuing advances in mobile communication capabilities, and dramatic reduction in costs of mobile devices, the demand for Web access from many different types of mobile devices has now gone up substantially. Incorporation of mobile Internet access has resulted in a paradigm shift in the way businesses and individuals tend to use the Internet. For example, customers, instead of making a call using a mobile phone may use its Internet capabilities to locate good consumer deals or find convenient service locations for their needs. Mobile Internet has also resulted in evolution of the customer relationship management (CRM) systems into what can be called mobile CRM (m-CRM) systems (Arunatileka and Unhelkar, 2003).

Reengineering of processes also needs to consider the devices that will facilitate the business processes. For example, for corporate solutions, we need to consider whether there are devices already deployed? And if so, can they be reused or are new devices required to be provided for the business processes? Finally, there is also a need to keep the software development methodologies in mind when the MET results in changes to the information systems of the transitioning organization. These methodologies can help in standardization, formal modelling of requirements, user-centered designs, understanding the technology of mobile network architectures, and issues in integrating mobile software with the existing software (Godbole, 2003). These technical process considerations will result in the implementation of good quality mobile applications and, as a result, would improve the overall quality of service offered by the business to its customers and users.

SOCIAL DIMENSION IN M-TRANSFORMATION

Mobility has had a significant impact on the quality of life of individuals and the society in which they live. While the location-aware mobile connectivity has dramatically increased the ability of individuals to communicate, it has also produced challenges in terms of privacy and new social protocols. The effect of globalization, as discussed by Devereaus and Johansen (1994), now needs to be further considered in the context of a global-mobile society. This is so because when a business enterprise undergoes a MET, it affects the socio-cultural aspects of both individuals and the groups they are part of. For example, should an individual answer the mobile phone provided by the company during his or her private time? Or should the mobile service provider be allowed to send unsolicited promotional messages to its subscribers? While mobility enables people to be productive anytime and anywhere, the need to separate personal from official work and responsibilities are far greater in today's mobile society. These social issues related to work ethics and behaviour in an Internet-based society, already studied by Ranjbar and Unhelkar (2003), need to be further extended and applied in the context of mobility in an MET.

The social advantages resulting from mobile technology infrastructures that may impact MET. For example, in developing nations (and even otherwise), the infrastructure costs associated with land-based Internet connectivity are far higher than corresponding costs of setting up wireless computing infrastructure. This results in an opportunity to reach people *en masse* through the relatively cheap mobile devices, and conducting business activities with them. The resulting change in the social landscape of a country is an extremely interesting phenomena that needs to be studied under this third dimension of MET.

Table 1. Mobility considerations in mobile Internet usage by business (based on Unhelkar, 2008)

	M-Informative	M-Transactive	M-Operative	M-Collaborative
Economic (Why)	Costs; Nuisance;	Profit Sharing; Alliance formation;	Costs; Inventory;	Trust; Legal mandates
Technology (What)	Device Availability and Access	Networking – Internet connectivity; Reliability; Security;	Intranet; Extranet; Groupware; Reliability	Portals; Groupware; Standards and inter-operability;
Methodology (How)	Personal Process	Business Process Engineering (BPR)	Organizational Policies; BPR	Industrial Process Reengineering; Business Collaboration
Sociology (Who)	Privacy; Access	Security, Confidence; Convenience;	Security, Trust, Workplace Regulations; Ethics;	Security, Trust, socio-cultural issues

CONSIDERING MOBILE BUSINESS INTERNET USAGE AND LEVELS IN THE "MET" FRAMEWORK

Mobile Internet usage has been discussed by Unhelkar (2003b). This usage describes the increasingly complex application of mobile internet by businesses in informative, transactive, operative and collaborative manners. The mapping of this usage with the four dimensions of the MET framework is summarised in Table 1. The subsequent sections describe that usage further from the point of view of understanding the MET.

Mobile Informative Layer

This is the usage of the Internet to merely provide information. As such, this is a one-way transfer of information requiring no security. Example of mobile informative usage include broadcasting of schedules, information of products, services or places, and capitalizing on the common Short Messaging Service (SMS) feature of mobile gadgets. Technically availability and access to a mobile device is important to enable provision of information. However, methodologically, it is the individual's process (or mode of usage of the device) that influences how the information is received. Socially, the information layer of mobile Internet usage has the potential for degenerating into mobile SPAM and other unsolicited messaging that is a part of MET challenge.

Mobile Transactive Layer

During this stage of Internet usage, businesses are more serious in conducting business on the Internet than they are during the informative usage. The transactive usage implies a "two-way" (or more) communication between the business and the user, resulting in sales of products and services as well as dealing with the third-party credit/debit card organizations that facilitate online payments. Technically, devices such as a wireless enabled PDA or laptop with necessary access and security on the mobile network are required to conduct these transactions. Methodologically, it will usually be a transaction with a user "known" to the business (for example, a registered bank user conducting account transactions), requiring businesses to incorporate upfront registration processes in dealing with their customers. Socially, the convenience of conducting two-way transactions will affect the individuals, but so will their confidence in the systems being used for such transactions.

Mobile Operative Layer

This layer deals with moving the core internal business processes (that are typically operational in nature) on to the mobile internet. Common examples of operative business processes that transition to the mobile internet include timesheets and inventory. Thus, mobile technologies may enable a manager using a simple mobile-enabled gadget (phone, pager of PDA) to keep track of employees; or may enable her to keep a tab on the inventory and place a re-order at the right time.

Mobile Collaborative Layer

This layer will result in numerous individuals as well as businesses all collaborating to satisfy the needs and demands of numerous other businesses. Groupware and portals are the technical starting points for collaborations. However, methodologically, with the collaborative usage of the mobile Internet, the MET will have to consider reengineering a group of collaborating businesses as against reengineering only a single business. Creation of collaborating business clusters can be an interesting study on its own, as discussed by Unhelkar (2003b), and may be considered in greater detail in MET. Socially, though, collaborative usage introduces challenges in terms of ability of business partners to communicate, trust and work together to satisfy common goals. Sociology, rather than technology, and all the associated socio-cultural issues is at the crux of the collaborative usage of the mobile Internet.

ENACTING MET

Describing a framework is not enough in practice. There is also a need to work out the details of enacting the framework. Thus, enactment of MET is its practical implementation that would bring about mobile transition in a real enterprise. During enactment, elements within the four dimensions of the MET discussed here need to be worked out in greater detail and carried out step-by-step. This execution of MET requires practical project planning and project management. Detailed discussion of the project management aspect of MET is out of scope for this discussion. However, there is a need to manage and contain the exposure to risks to the project as well as to the business itself as a result of MET. A well known approach to reducing risks in MET enactment is to apply it to a pilot project. This pilot project can be created and enacted over a relatively small part of the business. Based on suggestions by Brans (2003) and the practical experiences of the author, enactment of MET pilot should consider at least the following:

- Planning the pilot over an entire end-to-end chain of a small section of the business
- Identifying the champions within the organization who can demonstrate and use the output of MET in their activities
- Creating a suite of performance metrics and evaluating the results of the pilot for mobile enterprise transition through a suite of metrics
- Ensuring proper starting and completion of the pilot by announcement and information to stakeholders
- Properly time the transition to derive maximum benefit and cause minimum disruption to normal functioning of the business

CONCLUSION AND FUTURE DIRECTIONS

This chapter provides the outline of a framework for transitioning an enterprise to a mobile enterprise. This chapter outlines an orderly approach to mobile transformation make up of the four dimensions. The MET discussed here needs to be further augmented with appropriate people and tools to enable successful enactment of a mobile transition. However, this current outline of an MET framework is laid down with an intention to give directions to businesses incorporating mobility in provision of information, conducting of transactions with external businesses and customers, and also internally in its operations.

REFERENCES

Adam, C., & Katos, V. (2005, June) . The ubiquitous mobile and location-awareness time bomb", *Cutter IT Journal, 18*(6), 20-26

Arunatileka, D., & Unhelkar, B. (2003). Mobile Technologies, providing new possibilities in Customer Relationship Management. *Proceedings of 5th International Information Technology Conference,* Colombo, Sri Lanka, December.

Brans, P., (2003). *Mobilize Your Enterprise: Achieving Competitive Advantage through Wireless Technology,* © Hewlett-Packard, Pearson Education as Prentice Hall PTR, Upper Saddle River, NJ.

Constantine L., & Lockwood, L. (1999). *Software for Use: a Practical Guide to Models and Methods of Usage-centered Design,* Addison-Wesley. Also see www.foruse.com;

Deshpande, Y., Murugesan, S., Unhelkar, B., & Arunatileka, D. (2004). Workshop on Device Independent Web Engineering: Methodological Considerations and Challenges in Moving Web Applications from Desk-top to Diverse Mobile Devices. *Proceedings of the Device Independent Web Engineering Workshop,* Munich.

Devereaus M., & Johansen, R. (1994, *Global Work: Bridging Distance, Culture and Time,* Jossey-Bass, 38-39

Elliott, G., & Phillips, N. (2004). *Mobile Commerce and Wireless Computing Systems,* Pearson/Addison-Wesley, Harlow, England.

Ginige, A., Murugesan, S., & Kazanis, P. (2001). A Road Map for Successfully Transforming SMEs into E-Businesses. *Cutter IT Journal, 14.*

Godbole N. (2003). Mobile Computing: Security Issues in Hand-held Devices. *Paper presented at NASONES 2003 National Seminar on Networking and e-Security by Computer Society of India.*

Godbole, N., & Unhelkar, B. (2003). Enhancing Quality of Mobile Applications through Modeling.

Proceedings of Computer Society of India's 35th Convention, December, Indian Institute of Technology, Delhi, India

Kanter, T. (2003, February). Going wireless, enabling an adaptive and extensible environment. *Mobile Networks and Applications,* ACM Press New York, NY, USA, *8*(1), 37-50.

Lan, Y., & Unhelkar, B. (2005). *Global Enterprise Transitions.* Idea Group Publication (IGI press), Hershey, PA.

Marmaridis, I. (Makis), & Unhelkar, B. (2005). Challenges in Mobile Transformations: A Requirements modeling perspective for Small and Medium Enterprises. *Proceedings of International Conference on Mobile Business,* ICMB, Sydney,

McKnight L., & Howison, J. (2004). Wireless Grids: Distributed Resource Sharing by Mobile, Nomadic, and Fixed Devices. *IEEE Internet Computing,* Jul/Aug 2004 issue, http://dsonline.computer.org/0407/f/w4gei. htm (last accessed 19th July, 2004)

Ranjbar. M., & Unhelkar, B. (2003). Globalisation and Its Impact on Telecommuting: An Australian Perspective. *Presented at IBIM03 - International Business Information Management Conference (www.ibima. org),* Cairo, Egypt.

S'duk, R., & Unhelkar, B. (2005). Web Services Extending BPR to Industrial Process Reengineering. *Proceedings of International Resource Management Association (IRMA) Conference;* http://www.irma-international.org, San Diego, USA. 15th to 18th May.

Subramanium, C., Kuppuswami, A., & Unhelkar, B. (2004). Relevance of State, Nature, Scale and Location of Business E-Transformation in Web Services. *Proceedings of the 2004 International Symposium on Web Services and Applications (*ISWS'04: June 21-24, 2004, Las Vegas, Nevada, USA; http://www.world-academy-of-science.org)

Thai, B., Wan, Seneviratne, A., & Rakotoarivelo, T. (2003). Integrated personal mobility architecture: a complete personal mobility solution. *Mobile Networks and Applications,* 8(1), 27-36. ACM Press New York, NY, USA.

Unhelkar, B. (2003a). *Process Quality Assurance for UML-based Projects.* Boston, MA: Addison-Wesley.

Unhelkar, B. (2003b) Understanding Collaborations and Clusters in the e-Business World. We-B Conference, (www.we-bcentre.com; with Edith Cowan University), Perth, 23-24 Nov.

Unhelkar, B. (2004). Globalization with Mobility. *Presented at ADCOM 2004, 12th International Conference on Advanced Computing and Communications*, Ahmedabad, India.

Unhelkar, B. (2005). Transitioning to a Mobile Enterprise: A Three-Dimensional Framework. *Cutter IT Journal, 18*(8).

Unhelkar, B. (2008). *Mobile Enterprise Transition and Management.* New York, USA: Taylor and Francis (Auerbach) Publications.

KEY TERMS

Mobile Technologies: Are made up of wireless network, devices and contents. Mobile technologies are at the crux of the communications revolution.

Economic Dimension of MET: Describes the business reasons for undertaking transformation and includes discussions on costs and competition.

Technical Dimension of MET: Describes the technologies for transformation and include devices/gadgets, programming, databases, networking, security and architecture.

Methodological Dimension of MET: Deals primarily with the question of "how" to – amongst other things- model and design business processes, approach methodologies and quality in software processes.

Social Dimension of MET: Deals with "who" is involved in and influenced by the transformation and typically it includes the users, customers and employees of the business.

Chapter VII
Transitioning Business Processes to a Collaborative Business Environment with Mobility:
An Action Research Based on a Service Organization

Bhuvan Unhelkar
MethodScience.com & University of Western Sydney, Australia

Amit Tiwary
Origin Energy, Australia

Abbass Ghanbary
MethodScience.com & University of Western Sydney, Australia

ABSTRACT

Web Services (WS) technologies create the potential for an organization to collaborate with partners and customers by enabling its software applications to transact over the Internet. This collaboration is achieved by carefully incorporating Web Services in the organization's software applications, resulting in comprehensive Service-Oriented Architecture (SOA) for the enterprise. This incorporation of WS-enabled applications and components in the organization's overall enterprise architecture requires understanding of the service at three interrelated yet distinct layers: policies, activities, and standards. This chapter describes how the existing business processes of an organization are transitioned in to collaborative business processes that would result in a Collaborative Web-Based System (CWBS). The ideas presented in this chapter have been validated through an action-research carried out by the authors in a large energy supplier organization in Melbourne, Australia.

INTRODUCTION

This chapter reports the outcome of a study conducted in order to study and introduce collaborative business environment to the business processes of the organization. Furthermore, this study also observed the impact of such changes resulting from collaborative business processes to the overall organization. The theoretical background used for the collaborative business model is based on earlier work carried out by Ghanbary (2006a). This chapter also reports the validation of the collaborative business model through an action research project carried out in a large organization dealing with energy supplies of a large city in Australia.

According to Ghanbary (2006a), at present when business applications collaborate with each other, pre-qualification between the collaborating parties is mandatory. However by making use of the technologies of web services and formalizing the right channels of collaboration, it is possible for business applications to interact with each other without any pre-qualifications (This has been explained in detail later in the investigation section of this chapter). These interactions amongst business applications can result in wider opportunities for business to interact with their partners and clients that can provide better service for their customers and have a positive impact on their profit. This study understands and presents how business processes of multiple organizations could interact with each other in a free or open market, where pre-qualification or knowledge about each other's applications is not mandatory.

This chapter present the use of the model of CWBS proposed in Ghanbary and Unhelkar (2007) to present how it will help the real organization to use the technologies in order to achieve their collaborative objectives. Ghanbary (2006b) as well as Unhelkar (2006) have discussed the impact of mobility as an important element of the mobile transition process that is felt at both business and personal levels.

Based on (, 2006) a mobile business process is one that consists of one or more activities being performed at an uncertain location and requiring the worker to be mobile. Such a process can be supported by mobile systems to increase process efficiency. For processes that are supported by mobile systems, the term mobile enabled business process is more appropriate, to differentiate from a mobile business process.

This chapter is using the Business Process Modelling Notation (BPMN) to present the proposed model of CWBS. BPMN is the new standard for modelling business processes and web service processes, as put forth by the Business Process Management Initiative (BPMI - bpmi.org). BPMN is a core enabler of Business Process Management (BPM), a new initiative in enterprise architecture, which is concerned with managing change to improve business processes (http://www.telelogic.com).

The digital revolution has dramatically changed the business world to an extent wherein place and time are no longer barriers for business transactions (Weill & Vitale, 2001). The growth of the Internet and the World Wide Web has had a significant impact on business, commerce and industry (Murugesan, Deshpande, Hansen & Ginige, 2001).

Ghanbary and Arunataileka (2006) clearly state that the concepts of mobile communication, digital networks and service providers have advanced very rapidly in the last few years. This has lead to consideration of mobile communications and corresponding network providers' way beyond the well known data and voice transmissions and into the realm of mobile web services. Mobile commerce first emerged as an extension to e-commerce, by introducing wireless devices (Schwiderski-Grosche & Knospe, 2002). Mobile commerce is described as a discipline that involves mobile devices, applications, middleware and wireless networks (Varshney, 2002) all of which can be classified as mobile technologies. Based on (Gan, 2006) besides improving the user experience, mobile applications can also affect the work environment. In particular, the collaborations of disparate teams stand to benefit from presence awareness.

To achieve our aim of research, we have classified this chapter in the following sections: a) abstract b) introduction c) discussion on collaborative environment d) description of the action research organization e) validation of the proposed model of CWBS and f) conclusions & future directions.

DESCRIPTION OF THE ACTION RESEARCH ORGANIZATION

The organization is a leading Australian energy supplier which provides gas and electricity to over two million Australian homes and businesses. Currently, the service design supports the requirements developed in Arrange Fieldwork service contract. It proposes to either create new service or cancel an existing service contract.

Provide a service to a new customer requires the organization to identify the model of the *counter* used to identify the usage of the energy in the households. The organization under study needs to collaborate with other organizations such as gas, electricity, meter readers, electricians, plumbers and the people who will check the meter to identify what kind of services could be delivered to the specific customers. The common Government body already exists for the communications across the organization and gas and electricity companies. Multiple ombudsman agencies such as Victorian Energy Network Corporation "VEN-Corp" and National Electricity Markey Management company "NEMMCO" are the Government body to facilitate central component of gas and electricity industries B2B hub, in Australia. These hubs are used by various retailers and commodity distribution companies to exchange tasks and information. The proposed collaborative environments register these companies to extend their provided services to the organizations who seek their services.

The organization deployment of a reengineering process on Arrange Fieldwork provide an opportunity with the business agility they need to compete more effectively to consult, design, build and manage enterprise solutions spanning all core businesses and IT management processes in regards to provide a better service to their customers.

Improving the process by delivering an extensive portfolio ensure successful outcomes through a combination of professional expertise, successful track records and capabilities, which lower risk and ensure a return on investment.

In general the innovative product could be classified as followings:

- **Servers:** high performance, reliability and cutting-edge functionality.
- **Storage:** cost-effective enterprise-level performance, flexible capacity and world-class reliability.
- **Peripherals:** capacity-demanding, performance-intensive applications.

COLLABORATIVE ENVIRONMENT

Web Services technology enables applications to talk with each other that may be in separate technical environment. This leads to opportunities to collaborate electronically across the globe. On the other hand,

Service Oriented Architecture (SOA) is a platform, a backbone, in which the actual services can rest. Therefore, SOA is a strategic development of technology within an organization to enable it talk/deal with the rest of the world. The authors concentrate on the implementation of SOA in a suite of a business enabling multiple businesses to get together.

The Web Services technology has given the opportunity to application to 'talk" on disparate platforms. According to Marjanovic (2006) Web services are another important example of business process support technology. Web Services is self-contained, modular, Internet based applications, offered by different providers that have standard interface to enable efficient integration and implementation of complex business applications.

Composite web services enable flexible, on-demand integration of individual services offered by different providers to meet a specific business objective. This integration is made possible by the fact that web services are platform neutral so as long as they comply with the common standard they can be integrated into a more complex structure.

The organizations have adopted a closed architecture and SOA will be enabler of the open architecture talked about in academic world. Any major change requires well planned change strategies and here is where our concepts of policies, standards and activities are important. The organizations need to agree on the middle out approach of changes. The agreed process must be that if the changes to activities are making current policies unworkable, instead of some how fitting the activities with the outdated policies a review and policies change should be done. Similarly if the standards make activities obsolete, then activities must be modified. This requires a paradigm shift from top down or bottom up approach of processes, systems developments currently followed by most of the organizations.

The information technology investment over last thirty years has resulted in distributed and dispirited solutions and infrastructures. In any given fortune 500 organizations,, IT solutions will be a mix of systems that are using mainframes, midrange and other solution. The implementation of collaborative environment between organizations with distributed and legacy systems with closed architecture will require agreed standards to define web services.

Every organization based on their need to collaborate should define clearly collaboration policies. These collaboration policies should define the intended use the registered web service. The policies definition should be based on the internal process that should be encapsulated within the web service policies. For example if the web service should provide registration of a customer with the organization, internal registration business rules must be grouped to define the registration policy and in turn each policy could be defined as a web service. Each policy will have alternatives and exception business rules, these should be defined as activities with the policies. For example registration of a customer with an organization may have multiple activities such as credit validation of the customer, address validation or skills validation. Each logical group of these rules will be defined as activities and will be an operation of the web services. The data exchange and attributes should be defined as standards. These standards must be based on business information models, developed in the organization and pursue the business rules. The attributes of each entity that will patriciate in policies should be defined as standards.

The effective collaboration will require the rules of engagement for any modification to policies, activities and standards agreed and published before the web services are created.

The recommended rules are that the **policy change** should only happen when external factors such as legislations or business process changes will impact the collaboration model. The impact of the policy change may require activities and standards changes. It is anticipated that many a time the fine tuning of the activities will present opportunities to the business process changes or re-engineering. For example, if the current policy requires getting full customer details to create a quote, we need to enhance the policy where quotes could be provided based on generic information as well. The policy should cater for the "hot prospect" or the people who are ready to buy and should be given an accurate quote. The information collected in this case will be different from "may be" or "just browsing" prospects. The change of the information causes the activities to alter from "provide a quote" to provide a "indicative quote", "provide full quote" and the standards and information required will be different in each case. The activities and standards

Figure 1. The policy, activities and standards

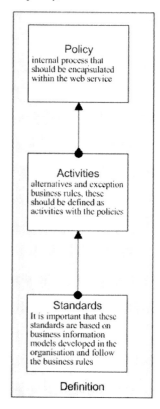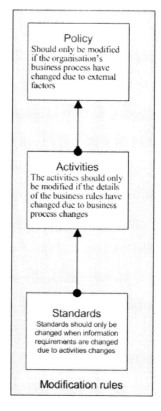

changes could be initiated by rules of engagement and information requirements changes.

Service Oriented Architecture gives an opportunity to architect new processes enabling multi organizational collaboration. Based on Yildiz, Marjanovic and Godart (2006) Service Oriented Architectures (SOA), especially Web Services, are emerging as middleware to implement cross-organizational processes.

The very recent advances in this domain such as WS-Coordination, WS-Agreement, WS-Policy are the actual agreements among involved Web Services. These technologies aim to specify the protocols supported by collaborating services such as the order in which individual services can be invoked or how the relevant message should be exchanged while they interact. According to (Gan, 2006) smart clients that enable presence, context sensitivity, location awareness, and real-time collaboration promise a new paradigm for mobile communications, delivering far richer, dynamic user experiences.

THE INVESTIGATION

The investigation was mainly in the way of organized interviews with the organization's managerial and technical staff and also studying some of the confidential documents of the business processes currently being used. The organization's clients include all sectors. A project could be classified as the provision of the organization's expertise to a client, organization and other related mentioned entities.

Modelling of Existing Processes of the Organization

The following Figure presents the genuine model of the organization. As demonstrated in the Figure 5, those services are available to internal as well as external parties. The core offering is also responsible for marketing, usability and the maintenance of the offered products and services.

The study identified that in under re-engineering existing processes, the other external parties such as electrician, plumbers, meter checker and reader can also find the required service by the organization. The organization submits a request for a specific service and the proposed Collaborative Web Based System (CWBS) will use any technology such as the Internet or any Mobile Internet devices to deliver the published application to the interested parties. The ticket will be logged, evaluated, allocated and the consultants

will find the suitable package. After delivery of the package and testing the task is completed.

Publishing the Service Required by the Organization

Publishing the consumable product/services on the proposed Collaborative Web Based System (CWBS) directory makes them available to the people who are capable of performing the requirement of the application (electrician, plumbers or meter reader and checker) but does not necessarily know the organization. By submitting a request to the directory they will be able to consume the request already published by the organization in the directory. Hence, these people are not necessarily in their office, the mobile applications could be included to the portal to deliver the request to the nearest tradesman to the location by the aid of GPS. This is a very important activity since this process leads to generation of more funds for the organization.

Proposed BPMN

The Business process Modeling Notation (BPMN) clearly demonstrates the interaction amongst all parties involved in a step by step process. These descriptions will be further used to draw BPMN diagrams which will graphically present the chain of activities.

Figure 2. Model of the studied organization's complex processes

The characteristic of the BPMN could be classified in the followings:

- Be constrained to support only the concepts of modeling that are applicable to business processes.
- Be useful in illuminating a complex executable process.
- The BPMN notation of a business process must be unambiguous. There should be a mapping from one or more BPMN notation instances to an execution level instance (www.omg.org/docs/pm/05-12-06.pp).

BPMN also offers clear technical business process diagram which represents the activities of the business process and the flow controls exactly the way they are performed. The mentioned advantages make the BPMN great tool for the test and validation of the proposed model.

A standard BPMN will provide businesses with the capability of understanding their internal business procedures in a graphical notation and will give organizations the ability to communicate these procedures in a standard manner. Furthermore, the graphical notation will facilitate the understanding of the performance collaborations and business transactions between the organizations. The following figures present the proposed model of the CWBS as far as the business processes of the organizations are concerned.

The Figure 3, present the process of the registering the organization in the proposed model of the collaborative environment. The system submits the form and after the data validation, registers the organization as a member. The organization is not recognized as a full member until the full validation/registration in the CWBS. The organization is only classified as the prospective member before the full registration.

Figure 4 presents how the CWBS place the registered organization (member) in the right place in the right directory. This will help the system to be able to locate the industry when they are needed. This will avoid the pollution in the directory as the

Figure 3. Proposed BPMN for the registration in CWBS

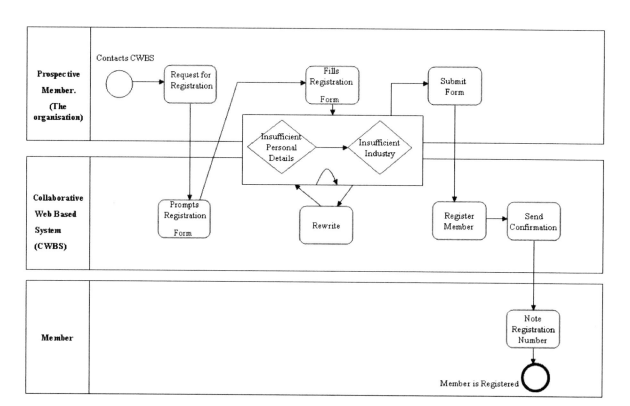

organization are categorised and placed under their desired industry.

Figure 5 presents how the proposed system will allow the organization to publish their request in the system and how the system will publish their request to find a suitable part capable of handling the request. The CWBS accept the request and identify the industry capable of handling it. Then check for the validity of the industry by identifying if any suitable party is registered in the system. The application will be forwarded in the level one directory to go to the right industry. The level 2 releases the name of the actual organisaions that are providing the service/product.

The mobile technology enables the trades people that are closest to the site receive the job to aid the organization proceed with the desired customer or-

der. These trades people might not be known to the organization but as long as they are registered in the system the job will be forwarded to them with the aid of Location Based System technology and Global Positioning Satellite.

Location Based Services (LBS) are engendering new passion in mobile services utilizing users' location information. Such spatio-temporal information processing entails the need for a dynamic middleware that accurately identifies changing user location and attaches dependent content in real-time without putting extra burden on users (Vyas and Yoon, 2006). Most fieldwork applications rely on GPS-based positioning, as positional accuracy is important and the cost of the device is not usually a deterrent. In these applications the mobile device establishes its own position. In

Figure 4. Proposed BPMN for placing the registration in the directory

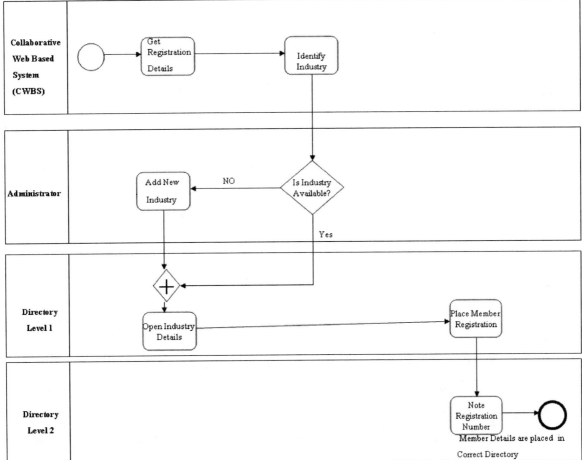

contrast, for LBS the position is usually fixed by the network (Shrrma & Nugent, 2006).

In Figure 6, the party that provides the service/product receives the application. After the evaluation of the application will informs the CWBS of their full capability or their partial capabilities to supply the product/service required. The CWBS will inform the requester of the additional date before the finalization.

CONCLUSION

This chapter explained how business processes of an energy supplier organization could collaborate with other organizations through CWBS which facilitates to improve their potential of their business activities. The business processes were engineered in the area of the collaboration and reengineered in the area of

mobility by the illustration of the BPMN diagrams by careful guideline and the principles to validate the proposed model of CWBS.

The confidentiality of the participated organization was respected while the business processes were fully validated in a collaborative environment.

In the process of this action research many issues were identified that could be classified as shortcomings or drawback of using the developed engineered and re-engineered processes. These issues could be classified as following:

- **Incompatible technology:** When some organizations (especially in security industry) are not updated in using the technology.
- **Competition:** When different organization prefer not to share in order to cause the competition out of the market. As an example, why would you allow your competitor to use your

Figure 5. Proposed BPMN for publishing the request

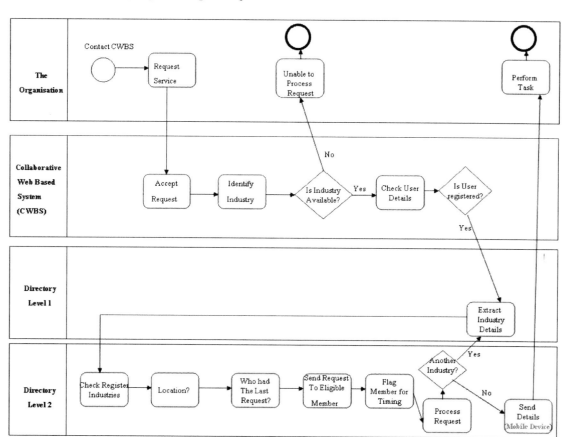

Figure 6. Proposed BPMN for consumption of the published request

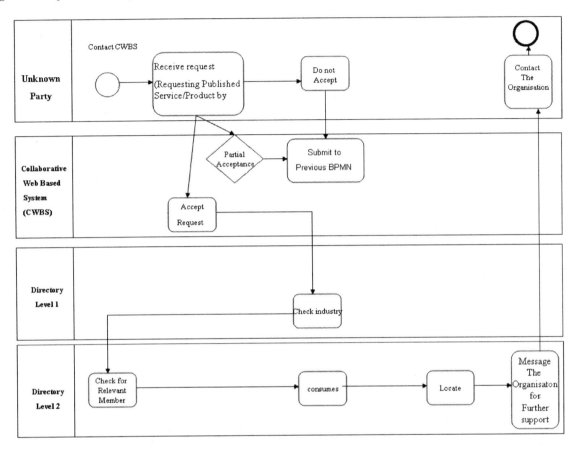

staff while you prefer him to lose the contract? This will give an opportunity to submit a new tender.

- **Legal issues:** Such as licensing agreement. The roles and regulations obliged to you by the government
- **Mistrust:** How could you trust your competitor? Or your employee to give you the right times?

Currently, there is an ambiguity involved in the collaboration since there are so many methodological and social drawbacks. However, by the aid of this study, when the true collaboration occurs, the organization will be ready for the collaborative environment.

Using ICT for collaboration amongst organizations is technically not complicated but can be difficult to achieve, especially when organizations involved have very different objectives and motivations. The key to the success is to really understand the various goals and drivers of the organizations that will be involved

in a collaborative network and create a system that not just aids collaborations but helps the individual organizations to achieve greater results (http://www.ncvo-networks.org.uk).

REFERENCES

Alag, H., (2006). Business Process Mobility. In B. Unhelkar (Ed.), Mobile Business : Technological, Methodological and Social Perspectives. New York: IDEA Gruop Publishing. ISBN: 1591408172

Gan, J. (2006). Developing Smart Clients to Mobile Applications. In B. Unhelkar (Ed.), Mobile Business : Technological, Methodological and Social Perspectives. New York: IDEA Gruop Publishing. ISBN: 1591408172

Ghanbary, A. (2006a). Collaborative Business Process Engineering Across Multiple Organizations.

A Doctoral Consortium. Proceedings of ACIS 2006 Conference. Adelaide, Australia.

Ghanbary, A. (2006b). Evaluation of Mobile Technologies in the Context of their Applications, Limitations and Transformation. In B. Unhelkar (Ed.), Mobile Business : Technological, Methodological and Social Perspectives. New York: IDEA Gruop Publishing. ISBN: 1591408172

Ghanbary, A., & Unhelkar, B. (2007). Technical and Logical Issues Arising from Collaboration across Multiple Organizations. Proceedings of IRMA Conference. IRMA 2007. Vancouver, Canada. 19-23 May.

Ghanbary, A., & Arunataileka, D. (2006). Investigating the Factors Impacting Personal Use of Mobile Technologies. Proceedings of the 2nd International Conference on Information Management and Business (IMB2006), Sydney, Australia. ISBN: 1 74108 122 X

Marjanovic, O. (2006). BPM - Bridging the gap between Business Processes and technologies for Process Management. Full Proceedings of the 2nd International Conference on Information Management and Business (IMB2006), Sydney, Australia. ISBN: 1 74108 122 X

Murugesan, S., Deshpande, Y., Hansen, S., & Ginige, A. (2001). Web Engineering: A New Discipline for Development of Web-Based Systems. In Murugesan, S. and Deshpande, Y. (Eds.), Web Engineering: Managing Diversity and Complexity of Web Application Development. Berlin, Germany: Springer-Verlag.

Schwiderski-Grosche, S., & Knospe, H. (2002). Secure mobile commerce. Electronics & Communication Engineering Journal, 14, 228–238).

Shrama, P., & Nugent, D. (2006). Mobile GIS-Challenges and Solutions. In B. Unhelkar (Ed.), Mobile Business : Technological, Methodological and Social Perspectives. New York: IDEA Group Publishing. ISBN: 1591408172

Unhelkar, B. (2006). Mobile Business: Technological, Methodological and Social Perspectives. New York: IDEA Gruop Publishing. ISBN: 1591408172

Varshney, U. (2002b). Multicast support in mobile commerce applications. Computer, 35 (2), 115–117.

Vyas, A., & Yoon, V. (2006). Information Management in Mobile Environments Using a Location-Aware Intelligent Agent System. In B. Unhelkar (Ed.), Mobile Business : Technological, Methodological and Social Perspectives. New York: IDEA Gruop Publishing. ISBN: 1591408172

Weill, P., & Vitale, M. R. (2001). Place to Space: Migrating to E-Business Models. Boston, MA, USA: Harvard Business School Press.

Yildiz, U., Marjanovic, O., & Godart, C. (2006). Contract-Driven Cross-Organizational Business Processes. Full Proceedings of the 2nd International Conference on Information Management and Business (IMB2006), Sydney, Australia. ISBN: 1 74108 122 X

NSW Vocational Education and Training Accreditation Board's www.vetab.nsw.gov.au. Accessed 19th October 2006

Food and Agriculture Organization of the United Nations http://www.fao.org/docrep/X5301E/x5301e03.htm. Accessed 19th October 2006

Prepare Mind Consultancy http://www.prepared-mind.be/collaborationC.html. Accessed 19th October 2006

NCVO ICT Foresight http://www.ncvo-networks.org.uk/blogs/ictforesight/2006/02/15/using-ict-for-collaboration/feed/. Accessed 19th October 2006

Telelogic Enterprise Life Cycle Management http://www.telelogic.com/standards/bpmn.cfm. Accessed 16th January 2007

The Object Management Group www.omg.org/docs/pm/05-12-06.ppt. Accessed 16th January 2007

Chapter VIII
Transitioning of Existing Business Processes to Collaborative and Mobile Business Processes:
An Action Research Based on a Security Service Organization

Abbass Ghanbary
MethodScience.com & University of Western Sydney, Australia

Bhuvan Unhelkar
MethodScience.com & University of Western Sydney, Australia

ABSTRACT

This chapter is based on a study at a selected organization to evaluate the impact of mobile technology and collaborative environment on its business processes. The existing business processes of the organization are placed within the proposed model of mobility. Also, additional collaborative business processes are engineered to operate on Collaborative Web-Based System (CWBS) in order to examine how an organization can benefit from the model. This chapter will also explain the shortcomings of the proposed re-engineered and engineered processes enabling better understanding of them. This study will help the organization under study to understand and experience the importance and value of the two important technologies of mobility and WS and the need to adapt them in order to remain competitive.

INTRODUCTION

This chapter reports the outcome of an action research project carried out in a security business named MAS Venue Services. The main objective of the study was to introduce mobile technologies and collaborative business environment to the business processes of the organization and observe the impact of such introduction. The theoretical background used was the m-transformation model described by (Arunatileka, 2006) and the collaborative business model presented by Ghanbary (2006a). As per (Unhelkar, 2005b) mobile technologies are at the crux of this communication revolution. These new mobile technologies have contributed to the elimination of physical connectivity for people, resulting in a significant impact of how organizations carry out their business processes. Therefore, mobile technologies and collaborative environment were considered important to MAS Venue Services business processes and was specifically studied here.

There has been many discussion on mobile transformation and a framework for such transformation is provided by Basole (2005b), Kalakota and Robinson (2002), Marmaridis and Unhelkar (2005) and Tsai and Gururajan (2005). Mobility is becoming increasingly important in business. This is so because mobility provides businesses with the unique ability to communicate independent, of their location. The importance of mobility is further underscored in its application to the business processes (Hawryszkiewycz & Steele, 2005). According to Arunataileka (2007) a mobile organisation has its internal and external business processes fully integrated with mobile technologies. This integration produces "location-independent" business processes that aim to improve productivity and efficiency, as compared with "non-mobile-enabled" business processes. Based on Ghanbary and Arunataileka (2006) the concepts of mobile communication, digital networks and service providers have advanced very rapidly in the last few years. This impact of mobile technology on the business processes has lead to consideration of mobile communications and corresponding network providers way beyond the well known data and voice transmissions and into the realm of mobile web services.

Based on (Barjis, 2006) a well-engineered, well-designed, and well-integrated m-business supports not only conducting business, but also adds collaboration, coordination, instant communication, and management features in the business.

The environment in which e-business systems operate is also changing. Businesses are no longer likely to have total control over the systems and networks upon which their e-business applications depend. E-business is the carrying out of business activities that lead to an exchange of value, where the parties interact electronically, using network or telecommunications technologies (Jones, Wilikens, Morris and Masera, 2000).

To achieve our aim of research, we have classified this chapter in the following sections: a) abstract b) introduction c) description of the action research organization d) re-engineered and engineered processes and e) conclusions.

DESCRIPTION OF THE ACTION RESEARCH ORGANIZATION

MAS Venue Services has 230 plus regular employees in their security and training operations. 99% of them have mobile phones (only 2 out of 230 do not have a mobile). Since the training arm is a regular operation and does not need mobility as a requisite. Our action research was focused upon the security operations arm.

The security operation of MAS Venue Services is two fold.

1. Operations with regular on-going services
2. Ad-hoc operations with sports/entertainment venues

The operations with regular on going services provide security services to organizations in various industries. Their regular customers are in the hospitality industry, business and education. They provide security personnel to cover regular shifts in these locations. The ad-hoc operations are services provided to events such as sports events and concerts. These services differ from one another and always had to be organized at the last few days since the actual requirements are received only in that period.

The operations manager at MAS Venue Services wanted the researchers to concentrate on the mentioned business processes namely;

Reengineered Processes:

- Creating the employees rosters
- Time sheet operations

Engineered Processes:

- Requesting staff from other venues
- Advertisement for the performed services by MAS Venue Services
- Recruiting staff

These business processes were looked at for re-engineering and engineering in order to introduce mobility and identify how the engineered processes will function in a collaborative environment across multiple organizations.

CREATING EMPLOYEE ROSTERS

The creating of rosters for regular shifts and the creation of rosters for the special event shifts are the main fold of the rosters. The regular shifts are known in advance therefore doing those rosters is a monthly routine job. The operations manager has the calendar of all the security personnel entered in the existing software in operation called Powerforce. The security personnel are given the roster about one month in advance by the operations manager. Any absence has to be notified one week in advance. Any sudden absence could only be due to a sickness.

Making rosters for special and ad hoc events is more difficult. The required number of security personnel at the event venue is only notified to the company days prior to the actual event. This requirement also could change at the last moment if the client wants more or less people. Therefore the operations manager has to allocate some people at the last moment and inform them via mobile phone. This process is already happening. When the researcher asked whether the message of informing the personnel about the event coming up using SMS services, the operations manager's answer was in the negative.

Operations manager's argument was that, some security personnel will not feed back and might not turn up for work and pretends that they did not receive the message. However if there was a voice call by the operations manager, then the confirmation is taken at the time of the call. Since MAS Venue Services is in the business of training, the training of security personnel to send back an acknowledgement for an SMS should not be difficult. Therefore if the operations manager could send a group SMS to everyone that are supposed to be working in the special event roster, it will save a lot of time. However the employees have to be trained to reply back. Apart from that, the creating of rosters did not have much usability for mobile technology.

TIME SHEET OPERATION

Time sheets are prepared weekly in the case of regular operations and per event in the case of special events. It is anyway important to get them in as soon as possible, so that the employees can be paid the week after the work has been performed. However there is a concern of trust to get the timings from the ground security personnel. The operations manager needs a confirmation from the site manager on the client site to make the payments. A timing mistake could be adjusted in the regular sites by adjusting from the next payment period. In a special event, this could not be done due to the fact that the payments are made case by case and thus an over payment has to be borne by the company. Therefore the existing process is to get the time sheets on chapter and get the site manager from the client site to sign for it. Once he has agreed that the times are correct, the payment has to get through to the company. At present, operations manager or one of his people visits all the different sites once a week to collect the signed time sheets. The site visits to two regular sites of MAS Venue Services revealed that the company has very cordial relationship with its regular clients. Therefore doing an adjustment in the next time period is not a problem. For special event time sheets, there will not be any changes proposed at this point of time due to trust issues with the employees.

PROPOSED TIME SHEET OPERATION

The researcher's propose to get the times of work to be sent to the operations manager through a mobile device. This proposal has three objectives.

- This will be a good start now, so that when MAS Venue Services is expanded in the future, the work will still be manageable to the operations manager.
- When the MAS Venue Services perform jobs in other states, this will be a good way to get their immediate time sheets which could be followed by an emailed work sheet for control and filing purposes.
- Once this process is fully in place, the same process could be expanded to special event time sheets. In this case, the times would be messaged to operations manager and site manager at the same time. Thereafter the site manager would be requested to inform the operations manager for any discrepancies or just acknowledge the times if there are discrepancies. The researchers do not want to propose this right now since this would be very drastic as an immediate change. But a staggered processes such as the one proposed would be easier without upsetting the stake holders.

Figure 1. The proposed time sheet operation activity

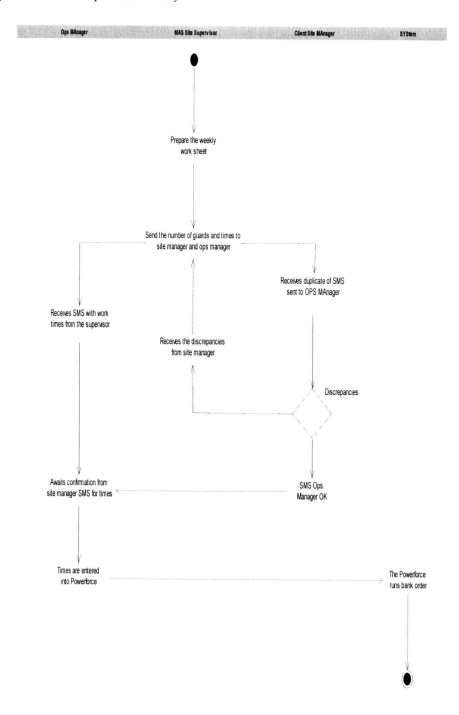

Table 1. Comparison of existing with the proposed time sheet activity

Event	Current Activity	Proposed Activity
Generation of time sheets	Generate chapter based time sheets and event reports	Generate chapter based sheets but the actual time with the guard identification is SMS via a mobile device
Feed back	Site manager physically signs off	Site Manager SMS the agreement to Ops Manager and also Physically sign off
Time taken to reach head office	Could take time due to physically collected from the sites	SMS is sent to Site Manager and Ops Manager which is much faster
Confirmation	Site Manager signs off	SMS from Site manager for confirmation. Signing of the physical sheet could be done later
Discrepancies	No discrepancies once the site manager signs and agrees	No discrepancies once the site manager sends SMS
Issues	Could be time consuming since each sheet is physically collected. Not manageable if the company has many sites.	Could be very fast once the site manager agrees with the process. Ideal for faraway sites.
Future activities	Has to be improved so that the process could be speeded up.	Process would be good if the site manager agrees and the supervisor could be properly trained.

The following diagrams are drawn using Unified Modeling Language (UML) notation activity diagrams (Unhelkar, 2005a).

The site manager signs the time sheet for verification. The time sheet is collected by the operations manager or his agent. Only some sites sends emails as the time sheet which in turn has to be entered into the Powerforce manually by the office staff. The other drawback of this method is the limitations it might have once the company starts expanding. The actual time sheet could be mailed for filing purposes later while an electronic transfer on the actual times which could be sent to the head office earlier for payroll purposes. Due to space constraints the existing activity diagram is not presented.

Figure 1 below suggests the proposed time sheet activity. The main difference here is that the supervisor is using a mobile device to send the initial data to the operations manager and the Client Site Manager. Client site manager either sends discrepancies back to the supervisor or sends an SMS to operations manager agreeing with the times. Once Operations manager receives the SMS with the times, from the site manager he straightaway enters the times in the Powerforce. In this case the delays are minimized and the salaries are paid in time.

The actual physical time sheet could be sent via snail mail later for filing purposes.

Once the mobile technology is introduced it could be used for further functionality. Based on (Alag, 2006) Businesses that aim to support mobile workers and enhance process effectiveness will need to consider extending their process and systems beyond the workplace.

The study identified how the proposed model of the Collaborative Web Based System (CWBS) could be applied to engineer additional processes for the organization. The study will discuss the current state of the processes in the organization and will demonstrate how the engineered Web Based processes will improve the functionality of the organization in a collaborative environment. The following reference presents the importance of the collaboration between organizations.

According to (Claret-Tournier & Lei & Chatwin and Young, 2006) the main goal of producing a new system is to provide the stakeholders involved in manufacturing, distributing, selling, servicing, and buying with the ability to authenticate the product.

Collaboration between development organizations is essential, to avoid confusing the local people, and to ensure better planning and a more efficient use of resources. http://www.fao.org/docrep/X5301E/x5301e03.htm

The competitive advantages achieved through electronic collaboration, encourage many organizations

Table 2. The proposed electronic collaborative processes and their existing occurrence

Proposed Electronic Collaborative Processes	Existing Occurrence of the proposed Processes
Requesting Staff (from other venues)	• Collaborating with two selected venues (Not online
Offer performed services	• Yellow pages directory • Advertised on MAS webpage • Word of mouth
Job Advertisement and Recruiting	• News chapters • Advertised on MAS webpage • Word of mouth • Send resume (Fax or post) • Calling them back for appointment

to share part of their internal data and information. http://www.preparedmind.be/collaborationC.html

A culture of collaboration and partnership between organizations in today's environment will need to further develop to realise the benefits. It is recognised by this research that organizations have sensitive information, collaboration does not necessarily mean that the organization have to share all their information. The technology will give us the opportunity to share the desired data. For this data to be used effectively, more than once, people are going to have to collaborate.

COLLABORATIVE ENVIRONMENT OF MAS VENUE SERVICES

The study was initiated by identifying the gap in the literature with regard to the collaboration across multiple organizations. In this chapter, a model for the collaboration across the unknown organization is presented. The Web Services technology will give the opportunity to application to 'talk" on disparate platforms. According to Marjanovic (2006) Web services are another important example of business process support technology. They are self-contained, modular, Internet based applications, offered by different providers that have standard interface to enable efficient integration and implementation of complex business applications.

Composite web services enable flexible, on-demand integration of individual services offered by different providers to meet a specific business objective. This integration is made possible by the fact that web services are platform neutral so as long as they comply with the common standard they can be integrated into a more complex structure.

On the other hand Service Oriented Architecture gives an opportunity to architect new processes enabling multi organizational collaboration. Based on Yildiz, Marjanovic and Godart (2006) Service Oriented Architectures (SOA), especially Web Services, are emerging as middleware to implement cross-organizational processes.

The very recent advances in this domain such as WS-Coordination, WS-Agreement, WS-Policy are the actual agreements among involved Web Services. These technologies aim to specify the protocols supported by collaborating services such as the order in which individual services can be invoked or how the relevant message should be exchanged while they interact.

MAS Venue Services only collaborate with two other selected security venues to roster their staff for the venues that requires big number of staff. If they can not fill the positions due to the shortage of the staff, they start losing money and eventually losing the contract. It was identified that Collaborative Business Process Engineering (CBPE) could engineer four additional processes for the organization to improve the outcome of their daily activities.

Table 2 present the proposed engineered collaborative processes and demonstrate how these activities occur in the existing daily activities.

Figure 2. The recommended solution for staff shortage

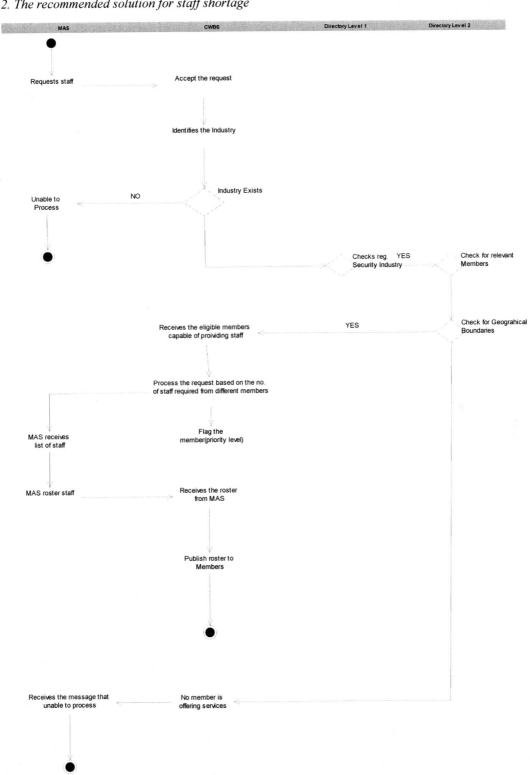

Figure 3. The process of registering the MAS performed services on CWBS

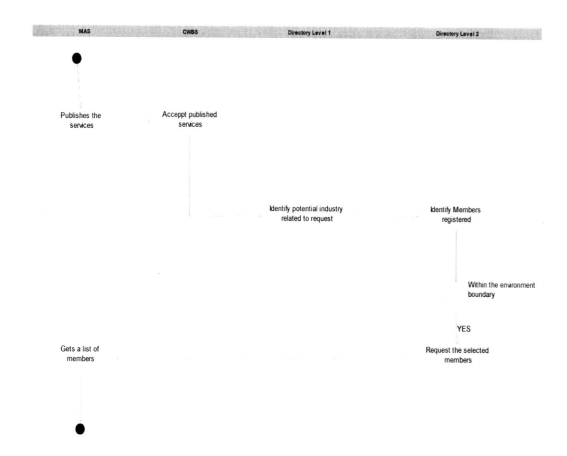

REQUESTING STAFF FROM OTHER VENUES

It was identified that MAS Venue Services needs to improve the staff list on regular basis since these people are employed on casual basis and they only work on the desired events. It was also mentioned that currently there are over 230 people exist on the list.

The operation manager has placed 50% of these people in active list. The remaining 50% are placed in inactive list of the Powerforce since these people are very uncommitted for accepting the allocated roster.

On a busy day, 70% of the staff in active list and 10% of the staff from inactive list participate to accept their allocated roster. The remaining 20% currently is being filled by two other selected venues as sub-contractor. The most important concern for the organization is how to fill the staff shortage on busy occasions especially if another venue requires more staff.

The investigation was initiated to identify how the technology could aid and rectify the mentioned problem. Figure 2 present the recommended solution in an activity diagram.

As it is demonstrated, the organization will submit a request on the proposed Collaborative Web Based System (CWBS). The request will go the UUDI directory level 1 to identify the desired industry. The level one directory submits the request to the relevant level 2 directory. The system will search all the venues registered in the level 2 directory to detect which of them has additional staff to hire. The benefit remains for

Figure 4. Recruitment request submitted on CWBS

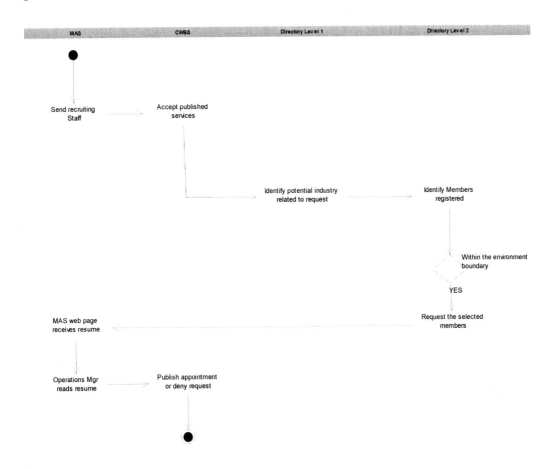

both parties as the organization will fill the gap of staff shortage and the other part gain a sub-contract.

ADEVERTISE FOR THE PERFORMED SERVICES BY MAS VENUE SERVICES

Currently the organization advertises on yellow pages, the organization website and word of mouth. The proposed CWBS help the organizations to register their offered service on the system for people who need their services. The proposed system is an electronic yellow pages directory that directs the request to a relevant industry and party for the further processes. In this action research, the organization under study already has their own web page and the system could submit the request direct to their webpage. Figure 3 present the process of registering the organization's services on the proposed system.

As illustrated, the organization can submit a request by offering their services on the proposed system and when the request is submitted by parties in need of the services that are offered by the organization, the request would go to them. Alternatively, if other venues need staff and the organization has additional staff on the mentioned date, they could sub contract their staff to the other venues if desired.

RECRUITING STAFF

The organization has to advertise for the recruitment on a monthly basis. As it was mentioned previously, the security guards are employed on casual basis and if they have not worked on a full financial year the operation manager of the organization will pull them out of the inactive list. The information of these people is registered in the Powerforce system however the system will never allocate them for a roster work.

During the action research, it was also identified that the organization can place their recruitment advertisement on CWBS. Figure 4 shows how the recruitment advertisement is posted on the proposed collaborative system.

In the existing system, the operation manager will place advertisement on news chapters, the organization webpage and constant word of mouth. After contacting the organization, they have to submit their resume by fax and post. Operation manager will read the resume and after the approval will call them back for an interview time for the final stages of the recruitment. It was mentioned by the operation manager that they desire to advertise on monthly basis however due to the busy schedule they are unable to attempt it.

In the proposed model, after submitting the request, people submit their resume on line and based on the approval of the operation manager the system will allocate an interview time for them. The busy schedule of the organization will have no impact on recruitment since by clicking a button they can advertise for the recruitment.

CONCLUSION

This chapter explained how m-enabling of business processes and CWBS facilitate the organization to improve their potential of their business activities. The business processes were engineered in the area of the collaboration and reengineered in the area of mobility by the illustration of the UML activity diagrams by careful guideline and the principles of the UML 2.0.

In the chapter, the confidentiality of the participated organization was respected while the business processes were mobile enabled in a fully collaborative environment.

REFERENCES

Alag, H. (2006). Business Process Mobility. In B. Unhelkar (Ed.), Mobile Business: Technological, Methodological and Social Perspectives. New York: IDEA Gruop Publishing.

Arunatileka, D. (2006). Applying Mobile Technologies to Banking Business Processes. In B. Unhelkar (Ed.), *Mobile Business: Technological, Methodological and Social Perspectives*. New York: Idea Group Publishing.

Arunatileka, D. (2007). *Mobile Transformation of Business Processes to Enhance Competitive Delivery of Services in Organisations*. PhD Thesis. University of Western Sydney.

Basole, R. C. (2005b). Transforming Enterprises through Mobile Applications : A Multi-Phase Framework. *Paper presented at the 11th America's Conference on Information Systems*, Omaha, USA.

Barjis, J. (2006). Overview and Understanding of Mobile Business in the Age of Communication. In B. Unhelkar (Ed.), *Mobile Business: Technological, Methodological and Social Perspectives*. New York: Idea Group Publishing.

Claret-Tournier, F., Lei, P., \Chatwin, C., & Young, R. (2006). Tracking Counterfeit with a secure online Track-and-Trace System. In B. Unhelkar (Ed.), Mobile Business: Technological, Methodological and Social Perspectives. New York: IDEA Gruop Publishing.

Ghanbary, A. (2006a). Collaborative Business Process Engineering Across Multiple Organizations. A Doctoral Consortium. *Proceedings of ACIS 2006 Conference*. Adelaide, Australia.

Ghanbary, A. (2006b). Evaluation of Mobile Technologies in the Context of their Applications, Limitations and Transformation. In B. Unhelkar (Ed.), Mobile Business: Technological, Methodological and Social Perspectives. New York: IDEA Gruop Publishing.

Ghanbary, A., & Arunataileka, D. (2006). Investigating the Factors Impacting Personal Use of Mobile Technologies. *Full Proceedings of the 2nd International Conference on Information Management and Business (IMB2006)*, Sydney, Australia. ISBN: 1 74108 122 X

Hawryszkiewycz, I., & Steele, R. (2005). A Framework for Integrating Mobility into Collaborative Business Processes. *Paper presented at the International Conference on Mobile Business*. ICMB 2005.

Jones, S., & Wilikens, M., & Morris, P., & Masera, M. (2000). A conceptual framework for understanding the needs and concerns of different stakeholders. *Communications of the ACM , 43(12)* 80-87.

Kalakota, R., & Robinson, M. (2002). *M-Business: The Race to Mobility*. New York, USA: McGraw Hill Professional

Marjanovic, O. (2006). BPM - Bridging the gap between Business Processes and technologies for Process Management. *Full Proceedings of the 2nd International Conference on Information Management and Business (IMB2006)*, Sydney, Australia. ISBN: 1 74108 122 X

Sanjay, G., Malhotra, A., & ElSawy, O. A., (2005). Coordinating for Flexibility in E-Business Supply Chains. *Journal of Management Information Systems*, pp. 7 - 46

Tsai, H. A. B., & Gururajan, R. (2005). Mobile Business: An exploratory study to define a framework for the transformation process. *Paper presented at the 10th Asia Pacific Decision Sciences Institution (APDSI) Conference*, Taipei, Taiwan.

Unhelkar, B. (2005a). *Practical Object Oriented Analysis*. Melbourne: Thomson Social Science Press.

Unhelkar, B. (2005b). Transitioning to a Mobile Enterprise: A three dimensional Framework. *Cutter IT Journal, 18*(8), 5-11.

Yildiz, U., & Marjanovic, O., & Godart, C. (2006). Contract-Driven Cross-Organizational Business Processes. *Full Proceedings of the 2nd International Conference on Information Management and Business (IMB2006)*, Sydney, Australia. ISBN: 1 74108 122 X

Powerforce User Manual Version – © OrYx Technology Pty Limited 1999, 2000, 2001. Publication of WexTech Systems, Inc.

NSW Vocational Education and Training Accreditation Board's: www.vetab.nsw.gov.au accessed 19th October 2006

Food and Agriculture Organization of the United Nations: http://www.fao.org/docrep/X5301E/x5301e03.htm accessed 19th October 2006

Prepare Mind Consultancy: http://www.preparedmind.be/collaborationC.html accessed 19th October 2006

NCVO ICT Foresight: http://www.ncvo-networks.org.uk/blogs/ictforesight/2006/02/15/using-ict-for-collaboration/feed/ accessed 19th October 2006

Telelogic Enterprise Life Cycle Management: http://www.telelogic.com/standards/bpmn.cfm accessed 16th January 2007

The Object Management Group: www.omg.org/docs/pm/05-12-06.ppt accessed 16th January 2007

Chapter IX
Strategic Elements for the Mobile Enablement of Business

Keith Sherringham
IMS Corp, Australia

Bhuvan Unhelkar
MethodScience.com & University of Western Sydney, Australia

ABSTRACT

The Internet wave that swept through business is likely to be seen as a ripple in a pond compared to the changes that are predicted from the adoption of mobility into business. Irrespective of industry sector, the mobile enablement (wrapping business around mobility) of business is expected to bring many opportunities and rewards; and like the Web enablement (wrapping business around the Internet) of business, a few challenges as well. Across all business areas, mobile business will need to support a mobile workforce, the operation of call (service) centres, and transaction processing and collaboration of virtual teams. Mobile business will also impact product offerings, the management of consumer choice and the focusing of communications with a sticky message. Mobile business will drive changes in management, revisions of business operations and the alignment of Information Communication Technology (ICT). This chapter discusses some of the common but important strategic elements to the successful mobile enablement of business.

INTRODUCTION

Although some businesses are starting to offer mobile services and others are preparing for mobile business, many organisations are still formulating the strategies and plans necessary for the mobile enablement of business. Mobile enablement of business can be understood as wrapping of the business around the core of mobile technologies. Organizations are also identifying the necessary processes and infrastructure changes to support mobile business. Like the Web enablement of business (wrapping business around the Internet) and the integration of the Internet and Web sites into business, common issues exist across all business areas and industry sectors in the mobile enablement of business. Excluding the industry specific market and consumer trends, some of the common and critical strategic business considerations upon mobile business are reviewed in this chapter. The ability of current Information Communication Technology (ICT) operations to support and deliver mobile business (Sherringham 2008) are of particular significance in this discussion.

BUSINESS CONSIDERATIONS IN MOBILE ENABLEMENT

Across industry sectors and many areas of business there are common elements that are required for the effective and efficient mobile enablement of business. Similar to the initiation of any other services and business changes, an effective strategy with a clear business case and well-defined expectations and outcomes are required for the mobile enablement of business.

Resembling the adoption of the Internet, the integration of mobile business will probably follow a phased implementation according to pragmatic business need with a proven business case to lower costs or grow revenue. Other considerations like the ability of the business to manage the change and the time it takes to optimise ICT necessary to support mobility would also drive a pragmatic phased approach.

The mobile enablement of business, including the delivery of services to mobile devices, is a business operation and not an ICT activity and unlike the initial adoption of the Internet that was often driven by ICT, businesses are driving the adoption of mobility by the business for the business. The fact that changes in ICT may be required is a consequence of the process (Unhelkar 2008a). ICT is not the driver of the mobile enablement process; changing market forces is the driver. The business is responding and ICT is the enabler of mobile business.

The extent and range of services in need of mobile enablement are expected to be approximately the same as those that were in need of Web enabling. Mobile enablement will be used to provide services on behalf of the business, to external parties, as well as optimising operations within a business.

For external customers a phased approach can be adopted with the alerts and messaging services being the first to be provided. Additional services for simple transaction processing and validation can be made available next. A focus on the provision of business critical information may also be a priority. As the capability of the business to provide and support mobile business grows, more complex processes can be progressively supplied. Customer interaction

will be a major driver in mobile business and as call centres transition to centres of service excellence, the ability to service mobile business will become a key plank of successful customer service operations (Unhelkar 2008b).

For internal needs, access to contact details on any device anywhere anytime may be the initial requirement; followed by the capabilities of ordering, purchasing and invoicing. Messaging, alerts and information access may come next, with support for advanced transaction processing provided subsequently. The need for collaboration and the power of the mobile device in business collaboration whether it is between employees and/or with channel partners will also come to the fore.

The key to the success of mobile business initiatives will be the business integration, change and the ability to guarantee service delivery. Common elements of the change required include:

- **Optimisation of process:** Resolution of the new processes and how business will operate.
- **Business logic:** Resolution of the business logic required to ensure the functioning of mobile business.
- **Data management:** Addressing the data management issues necessary.
- **Training:** Training of all relevant parties.
- **Support:** The support infrastructure provided to staff and customers to support mobile business.
- **Performance:** Realising the promised cost savings or revenue opportunities.
- **Communication:** Communication to all relevant parties on what is happening, how it is happening, the benefits and how to do things.

SIGNIFICANCE OF THE MOBILE DEVICE IN MOBILE BUSINESS ENABLEMENT

The significance of the mobile device within mobile business lies not only in the ability deliver innovative services to new markets but in the ability of the mobile device to drive out significant operational efficiencies. Any mobile business strategy and mobile enablement plan leverages the two key considerations of the mobile device: screen size and location.

Screen Size - When compared with the more palatial desktop presence, the smaller screen size of a mobile device is often seen as a barrier to the provision of mobile business services. Actually, the smaller screen of the mobile device drives a competitive advantage because of the elimination of the need for advanced information management skills (versions, locations, formats and applications) that are often currently required of users when completing even the most rudimentary of tasks. The small screen size of the mobile device makes it difficult for people to juggle information on the device screen, thus driving an organisation of and an alignment of information to context before delivery to the mobile device. Conversely, the large screens of the desktop perpetuate the information management inefficiency with a resulting higher cost of operation and un-assured service delivery.

The small screen of the mobile device also benefits business through a greater adoption of standardised process. By presenting the right information at the right stage in the process to achieve an outcome, users on mobile devices are delivering results and not spending their time searching and trying to define and remember processes - as often occurs at the desktop. Again, the large screens of the desktop often perpetuate inefficiency. For a user to work effectively on a mobile device, the rendering of data needs to be in the context and tightly integrated with work-flow (Sherringham and Unhelkar 2008a).

The small screen of the mobile device is expected to realise the operational efficiency for business - that of effective design in applications and user interfaces. For mobile business to work, the interface on the mobile device has to be accepted by users. Through the use of mobile devices, innovation and rationalisation in applications and user interfaces will be seen with a cascading impact upon the desktop. Ultimately one common interface shall exist across both the mobile device and desktop application with all of the advantages that such a standardisation would bring.

Realising the changes necessary to conduct mobile business on mobile devices may take some time and some innovation and thinking, but overall, the need to support a small screen is likely to drive significant business improvement as well as creating mobile business opportunities.

Location - The power and convenience of mobile business is often see to lie in the absence of a dependency upon location, i.e. people do not have to be physically in the office or at a specific physical location in order to conduct business. When it comes to the provision of information, however, location is very important because location is part of the information and service context. Offering people in one city a discount on products in another city is often counter productive. The location context is not just a matter of personal preference but also of device location.

The significance of location in the provision of service and context for the service needs to be included within mobile business strategies and implementation plans.

MOBILE ENABLEMENT IMPACTING BUSINESS PROCESS

Aligned with the change of processes brought about the screen size of the mobile device are the changes to processes necessary to support mobile business. The mobile enablement of business will see changes in how the business operates, variations in the processes required to support mobile business and modification in the detail of the business processes and in the transaction operations itself, i.e. mobile business redefines the knowledge worker assembly line (Sherringham 2005).

The Web enablement of business operations often highlighted inefficiencies within current business processes and mobile enablement is expected to realise further efficiencies. Much of the benefit is expected to come from clearly defining the steps of a process, how errors and exceptions are handled and in organising the information necessary to support these processes. An established process that guarantees service delivery can be optimised to work on mobile devices but processes that are not optimal within a desktop environment will not effectively transition to the mobile device.

For operation on mobile devices, business processes need to span multiple mobile devices. Issues to be resolved include:

- How will this process work on a stand alone device?
- How will this process continue if connection to the network is lost?
- How will this process resume when connection to the network is established?

Proven business experience shows that if mobile business is to be effective, these process issues need to be addressed from a business, a process and a technological perspective. Resolution of the required changes to business processes is an integral element of any mobile business strategy and mobile enablement because of its significant impact upon cost, time to market and expected return on investment.

An inevitability of mobile business will be the new requirements for audit, risk management, governance and compliance. Whilst any requirements are still to be defined and are likely to vary with industry sector, the need to keep records, to store messages and to track authentications from mobile devices will be common. Any audit, risk management and compliance considerations would impact upon both the demands for disk space storage as well as design considerations for mobile business solutions.

Within audit and compliance, lies the consideration of privacy requirements. With mobile business, privacy issues around employees, channel partners and customers becomes much more complicated. The simple act of knowing the location of a device and storing that data has privacy implications, particularly if the data are used outside of an organisation and for uses other than what it was collected for. As with other areas of mobile business, the legislation around privacy is still evolving but it will feature prominently within business operations.

The mobile enablement of business also brings alteration to business continuity management and disaster recovery management. Mobile business adds another dimension by adding complexity, whilst simultaneously providing tools to facilitate business continuity management. During a major incident, however, mobile devices may be rendered useless because of a loss of network connectivity.

One other element in business process necessary to support mobile business is that of authentication. The definition of mobile business services to be provided is significantly impacted by the authentication solution used. Authentication at the transaction level, the application level, the device level and the network level may all be required.

For financial transactions and payments, a higher level of authentication and security is often required. Effective authentication may include:

- User entering a user name and password for a service, e.g. banking.
- User is then called on the listed mobile device to advise that access is required (IVR solutions).
- User is then prompted to key in a PIN in real time that is validated before approval is provided.

The PIN is known only to the user and is NOT sent as an SMS message at time of login.

As well as mitigating risk (need user name and password, the listed mobile device and a PIN), this approach provides a level of security not achieved through SMS. SMS is suitable for alerts and messaging but is not preferred for transaction authentication. Resolution of authentication is key to solution design with an impact upon cost, offering and time to market.

ICT ALIGNMENT WITHIN MOBILE ENABLEMENT

The ability of ICT to deliver the requested services in an effective and efficient manner is a critical element of any mobile business strategy and mobile enablement (Wu and Unhelkar, 2008). Similar to Web enablement, those defining mobile enablement strategies should not under estimate the time it will take ICT to be ready to deliver the services required of ICT.

Many current ICT operations are already rising to the challenge of providing standardised environments and the capability to guarantee service delivery. The demands of mobile business will only serve as an additional driver for standardisation. The major areas to consider within ICT when setting mobile business strategy include: mobile device management, data management, the messaging environment, applications used, security and enterprise architecture including the network capabilities[a].

Mobile Device Management – The management of mobile devices has several business impacts. When providing services to external customers, a business has little control over the mobile devices used and supporting legacy devices, multiple devices, multiple systems and multiple applications is just the cost of doing business.

For services within an organisation, all of the advantages from a standardisation of the mobile device can be realised. Such a standardisation lowers the costs of deployment, maintenance, support and administration of the device; the services provided; the applications used and the support provided around the mobile business services. Any effective mobile business strategy would include a standardisation of the mobile device and where required, a standardisation of the desktop environment with all of the resulting impacts upon ICT (Kamogawa and Hitoshi 2004).

Realising mobile business shall see the deployment of effective solutions (technology and processes) for:

- **Asset management:** The mobile device is an asset of an organisation and like any other asset, its existence, occurrence and value need to be tracked and managed.
- **Device tracking:** Mobile devices are by nature prone to being lost and/or taken out of an organisation. Some form of device tracking solution is required[b].
- **Device administration:** Solutions are needed for the administration of the mobile device including its initial and ongoing configuration, operating system and application deployments, and upgrades and updates.
- **Stand alone operation:** Issues around a mobile device working as a stand alone as well as getting updates when the device is connected to the network need to be addressed.
- **Data synchronisation:** Solutions for the synchronisation of data between the mobile device and the original data source are required. This is to include versioning, shared access and concurrent usage.

Data Management - Other aspects of data management that impact directly on any mobile business implementation include:

- **Device storage:** Current mobile devices are less than suitable for long term data storage. Whilst the capacity to store data on a mobile device is likely to increase, any good mobile business strategy and implementation should assume that extended data storage on the mobile device shall NOT occur. Some short-term storage is obviously needed but a "no data storage on mobile device" strategy is the preferred approach. The business importance of "no data storage on mobile device" is further seen when all of the issues of trapping and the isolation of data on the desktop and the resulting business issues are considered.
- **Consolidated repositories:** Effective and efficient mobile business requires that data are single sourced from virtual consolidated repositories. The use of "virtual consolidated data repositories" compliments the "no data storage on mobile device" solution. These two

aforementioned fundamental principles are key to any mobile business strategy with subsequent impacts upon processes, services, deployment times and costs.

- **Storage demand:** The demands of mobile business will further drive the ever-increasing demand for disk space storage. The use of virtual consolidated repositories for single sourcing data and the need to record many of the transactions and messages being sent to and from any device anywhere anytime are key elements of the demand. Other significant demand will come from data streaming, video conferencing and messaging, and images and file sharing - all driven by the needs of mobile business.
- **Data synchronisation:** The synchronisation of data between mobile devices and consolidated repositories poses several issues in conducting mobile business and a resolution of synchronisation is important to services that require a "write element". Since data synchronisation is less of an issue for broadcast and query services (read only), many mobile business strategies and implementations would probably see broadcast and query type services provided first.

All of these data management issues impact upon the decisions of market offering and mobile enablement strategies.

Messaging Environment – As increasing demands are made from mobile business, the need for a consolidated messaging environment that guarantees service delivery across the channels comes to the fore. The model for this environment is the FedEx model. FedEx guarantees the delivery of parcels (packages) and mail (messages) as follows:

- There is a quality of hand-off to FedEx and without this quality of hand-off, the parcel is not taken, i.e. responsibility is at source and exception processing returns the package to source.
- FedEx has a scalable, reliable, industrial strength solution for the transfer of packets between defined points.
- There is a quality of hand-off from FedEx back to the customer for acceptance of the package.
- FedEx separates the acceptance, moving, storage and hand-off of the package. FedEx then has systems for error handling, reporting and archive of information.

- The environment and operations are standardised.

Whilst the parallel between the FedEx model and what is required of a consolidated messaging environment is self-evident, it is often the absence of a consolidated messaging environment that impacts upon mobile business and the offerings that can be taken to market.

Applications – Even though many core business applications have now been successfully Web enabled, mobile enablement will bring some additional challenges. In addition to the issues discussed previously on mobile device screen size, many business applications have been written from a features perspective assuming the palatial screen size of the desktop and not from a process perspective needed on a mobile device. The mobile enablement of business will drive a transition from feature rich applications to process orientated applications (Ghanbary 2006).

Security - The security issues around mobile business and mobile devices just add to the already complex security needs seen within business. Mobile business services can only be provided when the customer has the confidence to their security. A number of approaches to mobile transactions security have emerged, including multi-channel authentication that treat the channel for validation of security and the channel for delivery of transactions as separate from each other.

Enterprise Architecture - From all of the ICT considerations (screen size, process, authentication, device management, data management, messaging, security and applications) comes an assessment of the ability of an enterprise, its architecture and its ICT infrastructure to deliver mobile business. This assessment will in turn impact upon the business decisions for mobile business offerings (Unhelkar 2005).

If the infrastructure and solutions provided by ICT is highly standardised and is currently an effective assembly line for knowledge workers (Sherringham and Unhelkar 2008b), then a business has a competitive advantage and can readily adopt mobile business. The inability of ICT to deliver the knowledge worker assembly line may be a significant barrier to mobile business achievements.

PROVISIONING AND BUSINESS ALIGNMENT

Even though mobile business is still evolving and many of the market opportunities and product offerings are still to be defined, mobile enablement will need to include a provision for some of the trends identified in Table I and discussed in this section.

Mobile workers - The image of wandering knowledge workers creating a mobile office wherever needs dictate, completing tasks and then returning occasionally from the field all frazzled back to the office may be a bit simplistic but this will be close to the mark for many knowledge workers. Supporting mobile knowledge workers is a major plank of mobile enablement.

From call centres to centres of service excellence – Mobile business will drive further change within call centres. Call centres will be about having conversations with customers to meet needs, to problem solve and to manage expectation. Call centres will be centres of service excellence to value-add knowledge and to solve problems. These service centres will operate across geographical boundaries, seamlessly integrating globally to deliver valued services. Service centres will utilise and respond to the unified messaging environment, including mobile devices. This will increase the need for more skilled resources, fluent in communication across channels and who are proactive problem solvers. The management structures and business processes of the service centres will need to change accordingly.

Transaction processing - As more transactions are processed by ICT and less manual intervention is required; the skill set changes from routine transaction processing to pro-active problem solving when things go wrong. Resources are freed to focus on advanced and high value transaction processing, which cannot be done by ICT alone, and to manage customer expectation. All of these require more highly skilled workers with advanced problem solving, superior communication skills and the ability to leverage mobile business.

To operate and manage each part of the process, ever increasing specialisation is required, but when it comes to end-to-end problem solving and ownership of problems, generalists who can work with each of the areas of business are required. A balance of specialists and generalists is required in the workforce. Mobile

Table I. Summary of ICT trends in mobile business

Trend	Description	Business impact
Mobile workers	Knowledge workers using multiple devices and operating in diverse environments to meet customer needs.	The ICT infrastructure necessary needs to be implemented as part of any mobile business strategy. Complimented by necessary changes in process and management frameworks.
From call centres to centres of service excellence	Call centres change to centres of service excellence interacting with customers across all channels of communication, having conversation with customers to solve problems.	The need is for more skilled resources, fluent in communication across channels and who are proactive problem solvers.
Transaction processing	More transaction processing done by ICT. Need problem solvers to intervene when it goes wrong and staff freed up to focus on high value transactions that cannot be done by ICT.	Need to skill up the workforce and nurture proactive problem solving.
Virtual teams	Work becomes more project based with participants from many areas of business working collaboratively in virtual teams to deliver outcomes.	Mobile business strategies are needed to provide the necessary integrated communication, processes and information sharing to allow teams to work. A greater focus on soft skills is also required.
Planning	As the mobile business environment drives increased flexibility, there becomes a greater need to plan. The planning is about a framework that empowers delivery and providing infrastructure that allows people to adapt to meet customer needs.	Planning needs to provide clarity, the destination and the framework so that people are empowered to deliver. Revisions of planning processes, skilling of people and changes in performance measurement will all be required.
Management framework	Mobile business will pose new challenges for managers driving the emergence of new methods of management, new operational frameworks and new levels of accountability.	New management frameworks and skilling of management to manage a mobile and highly skilled workforce are required.
Product offering	Products and services come to market faster, have a shorter life expectancy in the market and need to be targeted to ever more specific market segments.	Supporting innovation and creativity and implementing organisational structures and culture to support innovation and creativity becomes part of a mobile business strategy.
Consumer choice	Customers increasingly look to the trusted adviser to lead them through the ocean of choice and complexity and to bring them safely to the wise outcome.	Changes in sales model are required, together with re-skilling of the sales team and a focusing of the message across channels.
Increasing expectation	Customers are requiring ever increasing levels of gratification and want them faster.	Re-skilling of staff and change of processes and management to ensure effective service delivery.
Getting the message across	Need to get a message across different channels in an environment of information overload where people tune out to cope and have shorter retention spans.	Need to communicate sticky messages with a requirement for skilling in effective communication across channels.

enablement requires change in the human resource skill set and expertise mix.

Virtual teams - With liberation from routine transaction processing, roles will have a greater customer engagement, a focus on improving service and contain more business optimisation activities. Much of this work will be project or piece specific, with teams coming together to achieve an outcome and then disbanding to work on the next one. The teams will often be virtual teams, collaborating globally across the time zones, with colleagues from diverse areas of business at various levels all drawn together to deliver outcomes. Mobile devices and supporting mobile business play a critical role in such collaboration.

Business will be about pulling together the resources from out-sourcers, off-shorers, in-house and others; bringing them together and ensuring delivery. For business it means new management strategies and innovative approaches to human resource management, hiring and career management. This will mean changes in the way out-sourcers and off-shorers have been engaged to-date and it will mean that many careers and multiple jobs will be the norm. Core staff will be retained in-house to drive innovation, to set strategy and framework, and to manage outcomes. Ownership and pro-active management of issues will be pivotal to performance and success. For out-sourcers and off-shorers all of this means many new and exciting opportunities for the provision of value-added services.

Planning – Mobile business requires that the flexibility necessary for operation in collaborative teams and centres of service excellence be provided. A flexible environment requires rapid communication, expeditious dissemination and management of information and working from diverse environments (home, office, coffee shop). Paradoxically, working in such vibrant and dynamic environments will require greater planning and NOT less. The planning is about clarity of vision, the destination and the framework. The planning is about providing infrastructure that can be readily used to meet customer needs. Management is then about empowering professionals to deliver the required outcomes as they see best, allowing decision making at source to meet customer needs. The planning process and implementation will leverage the power and capability of mobile devices and mobile business.

Management framework – To ensure success in the diverse mobile business environment, management needs to become more effective. Risk aversion, problem passing, lack of ownership and poor accountability are not sustainable in a mobile business environment. Management requires clarity of vision, setting the framework and managing to outcomes. Management will become more facilitative and management requires effective communication and skilling of the workforce across the communication channels. New management practices will be developed and implemented, with a revision of management framework and management skills.

Product offerings – In the mobile business environment, products and services come to market faster, have a shorter life expectancy in the market and need to be targeted to ever more specific market segments. Since competitors can now more readily copy and imitate products and quickly modify them to present new offerings, the need to differentiate and innovate will drive a greater use of mobile devices and collaboration. Supporting innovation and creativity and implementing organisational structures and culture to support innovation and creativity becomes part of a mobile business strategy.

Consumer choice – Consumers like choice and consumer demand drives market diversification. Paradoxically, consumers do not handle choice well. For all but the simplest of consumer decisions, customers can often feel overwhelmed from all of the choices available and often fear making a decision. Customers increasingly look to the trusted adviser to lead them through the ocean of choice and complexity and to bring them safely to the wise outcome.

Mobile business strategies are not about providing ever-increasing amounts of information and bombarding customers with choice. The effective mobile business strategies are about supporting customers to make wise decisions. This means focusing the message, a greater focus on soft skills as well as skilling of and changing the role of the sales team. The small screen size of the mobile device is very conducive to the "guiding to wise outcomes" approach.

Increasing expectation – The consumer cycle of product diversification, speed to market, and customer choice is serving to increase customer expectation. Customers are expecting more for less, expecting instant availability and an ever need for greater gratification. Access from mobile devices and instant communication will further drive the cycle. Mobile business strategies are integral meeting the increasing customer expectation and gratification spiral. Mobile business strategies that align to consumer need and that service customer expectation are likely to be effective.

Getting the message across – Customers are increasingly operating in an environment of information overload and are saturated with irrelevancies. The audience retention span is diminishing and more channels need to be supported (phone, storefront, mail-order, e-mail, electronic messaging, Web sites, home service, mobile device and set top box) in an integrated way. To get the message through, the message will need to be consistently and persistently communicated and above all, it must be sticky[c].

Getting a message across is not a matter of appealing to the lowest common denominator, it is about clarity of message and respecting the recipient. Mobile business strategies that increase the quality of message and focus the message for audience and channel of delivery are likely to be more effective.

CONCLUSION

Like the Web enabling of business, mobile enablement will provide business with many challenges and significant rewards. Just as the Internet is now integral to business, so will it be with mobile business. The main driver in the adoption of mobile business is likely to be the benefits derived from routine transaction processing accompanied by the need to support an ever increasingly mobile workforce collaborating in virtual teams.

The adoption of mobile business depends upon a clear strategy driven by the business for the business. Deploying mobile business solutions will probably use an incremental approach that drives out the issues associated with mobile business and laying down key infrastructure that other projects can leverage. This will then drive a greater adoption of mobile business and the provision of more services in a self-sustaining process.

REFERENCES

Ghanbary, A. (2006). Evaluation of Mobile Technologies in the Context of their Applications, Limitations and Transformations. *In Handbook of Research in Mobile Business.* Edited by Bhuvan U. IGL Global.

Kamogawa T., & Hitoshi O. (2004). Issues of E-Business implementation from Enterprise Architecture Viewpoint. *Proceedings of the 2004 International Symposium on Applications and the Internet Workshops (SAINT 2004 Workshops).*

Sherringham, K. (2005). Cookbook *for Market Dominance and Shareholder Value: Standardising the Roles of Knowledge Workers.* London: Athena Press (pp. 90).

Sherringham, K. (2008). Catching the Mobility Wave Information Age. April-May 2008. (p. 5).

Sherringham, K., & Unhelkar, B. (2008a). Real Time Decision Making and Mobile Technologies. In (Unhelkar et al. 2008) *Handbook of Research in Mobile Business: Technical, Methodological and Social Perspectives* – 2nd edition, IGI Global.

Sherringham, K., & Unhelkar, B. (2008b). Business Driven Enterprise Architecture and Applications to Support Mobile Business. In (Unhelkar et al. 2008) *Handbook of Research in Mobile Business: Technical, Methodological and Social Perspectives* – 2nd edition, IGI Global

Unhelkar, B. (2005). Transitioning to a Mobile Enterprise: A Three-Dimensional Framework Cutter. *IT Journa, 18*(8); Enterprise Architecture, *11*(3).

Unhelkar, B. (2008a). Mobile Enterprise Architecture. *Cutter Executive Report, 11*(3).

Unhelkar, B. (2008b). *Mobile Enterprise Transition and Management.* Auerbach (Taylor and Francis), New York, USA.

Wu, M., & Unhelkar, B. (2008). Extending Enterprise Architecture with Mobility. *2008 IEEE 67th Vehicular Technology Conference,* Singapore.

KEY TERMS

Centres of Service Excellence: Call centres will operate across geographical boundaries, seamlessly integrating globally having conversations with customers to meet needs, to problem solve and to manage expectation irrespective of the device used – become centres of service excellence.

FedEx Model: A model for the operation of a consolidated messaging environment based on the proven principles to move messages (parcels) around the world by leading logistics companies.

Knowledge Worker Assembly Line: Knowledge workers take information and value-add to it to provide services. ICT needs to provide the right information at the right time in the right way for knowledge workers to effectively operate, i.e. ICT is the assembly line for knowledge workers.

Mobile Enablement: The process of adapting a business to support mobile business with all of the cultural change, management structures, business process optimisation and ICT issues that are required.

Sticky Message: A message that stands out and is remembered because it is simple, unexpected, concrete, credible, emotional and often tells a story.

ENDNOTES

[1]   The network capabilities are not discussed extensively in this document due to their technical nature and because of the obvious issue of: if the network cannot support mobile business then this has to be addressed first.

[2]   This is not the same as tracking the user of the device with all of the privacy issues involved.

[3]   Sticky messages are simple, unexpected, concrete, credible, emotional and often tell a story.

Chapter X
Mobile Strategy for E-Business Solution

Anthony S. Atkins
Staffordshire University, UK

A. K. Hairul Nizam Pengiran Haji Ali
Staffordshire University, UK

ABSTRACT

It is becoming evident that mobile technology can enhance a current e-business system to provide competitive advantage in business activities. These enhancements in mobile device applications such as in mobile hotel check-in system, m-payment system for parking tickets, and mobile donor transplant system are evolving with usage of wireless technology such as Wi-Fi, Bluetooth, and WiMax (Worldwide Interoperability for Microwave Access). Other examples include wearable mobile technologies used in military observation tactics and civilian clothing accessories for entertainment purposes. The lack of current mobile strategies, can cause some businesses to over spend or under utilize potential mobile applications. The use of a mobile strategic framework will help provide the insights to improving companies in their commercial operations and examples of these mobile solutions are outlined in relation to commercial applications which have been implemented in hospitals, retail Supply Chain Management (SCM), and in Customer Relationship Management (CRM). These types of systems are known to improve quality of service and provide competitive advantage. A mobile framework is presented to introduce the application of user mobility to mobile usage as an extension of existing Intranet, Extranet, and Internet e-business application. This Mobile Business Application Framework could assist practitioners in identifying the financial and competitive aspects in relation to mobile technology applications into their business infrastructure.

INTRODUCTION

Mobility has become a key factor in Information Technology (IT) strategy (Savvas, 2007). The literature indicates that the use of mobile devices can assist the communication networks in business activities, such as Supply Chain Management (SCM), parcel tracking and Customer Relation Management (CRM) (UPS, 2005). Mobile Commerce (m-Commerce) operates where mobile devices facilitate business operations that enhance and improve commercial activities (Varshney and Vetter, 2002). In commercial organisations, mobile devices such as Personal Digital Assistant (PDA) phones can help business users to organise their daily activities such as taking notes, arranging appointments, storing contacts phones numbers, receiving emails and surfing the internet, from a single mobile device (Jervanpaa, 2006). Stockbrokers can receive critical information on their PDAs such as changes in financial stocks and shares at anytime and also access financial documents and make amendments with the use of built in word processing applications.

Short Messaging Services (SMS) is another mobile solution making mobile payments or m-Payments (Serbedzija et al, 2005). In Croatia, parking in the city can be difficult as parking areas can be on either side of the road, or one large central lot located far from the drivers destination, the hassle of walking to 'top up' a parking meter and then walking back to the destination can be tedious. The driver receives an SMS acknowledgement text to indicate the expiration time of the parking meter and can then choose to return to the vehicle or extend the parking meter by replying to the SMS text (Serbedzija, 2005).

Addenbrooke's Hospital in Cambridge, highly regarded for the success of kidney operations in the last few years is utilising Blackberry's mobile phone application to wirelessly connect to the hospital's centralised database to keep track of available organ donors. The use of mobile devices allows surgeons and doctors to make on the spot decisions as they track available donors that match with the patient's profile. An indirect application of using these mobile phones in this situation can also be used to assist emergency crews in applying first aid. In the event of an accident, by taking images of any unusual wounds and forwarding them to a specialists, a remote doctor can advise the ambulance crew to apply appropriate first aid to the victim (British Red Cross, 2004). The agility and mobility of using these mobile devices can prove advantageous to commercial operations (Harrington, 2006), especially e-commerce applications. The increased demand of mobile devices is due to the improvements of wireless technology that has allowed managers to select from a wide variety of mobile technology to apply to their business. The use of m-commerce can provide both competitive advantage and modern image to the business. However, there are risks associated with it, such as the cost of development, security issues relating to viruses and privacy policies. It is imperative that the business should analyse the type of mobile devices which can best enhance their business activity (Varshney and Vetter, 2002). The use of strategic IT frameworks could be used for assessing mobile business application to aid business practitioners in decision making.

A combination in the use of mobile applications and e-business can offer competitive advantage by creating new platforms to reach global markets (Farhoomand, 2003). The e-business services allow business companies to reduce costs and increase revenue from distribution. Increased online sales and the use of mobile devices can enhance mobile business activities. Mobile applications are currently being used in warehousing, Small and Medium Enterprise (SME) and Customer Relationship Management (CRM) systems that allow tracking of parcels etc. These types of mobile devices suit the business needs and activities of the companies concerned. This principle of distribution and transaction can be adapted for e-government or e-society applications. In these cases information can be distributed electronically similar to the e-society i2010, which the European Commission is developing for a European Information Society that promotes growth and jobs in the EU (Hines, 2007). John Hopkins Hospitals has implemented mobile applications to assists in their medical activities, such as e-prescriptions. This implementation saves the hospitals $1,000 per day by providing the pharmaceutical information and the medicine that the patient needs (Brian, 2006). The use of data retrieval through a mobile device can be similarly used in warehousing; Wal-Mart stocks can be identified using Radio Frequency Identification (RFID) tags read from a special mobile RFID reader (Sliwa, 2006). Nissan automobiles have a similar approach with CRM activities that allow the salesperson to answer customer queries on the spot (Greengard, 2006).

There are two types of mobile data retrieval technologies, which are classified as web-enabled and standalone. The Web-enabled architecture involves mobile devices to send and retrieve information from a centralised database. With the standalone database, the data are distributed and stored on the mobile devices. The database can share the data among mobile devices, but the original data remain in the mobile device for example using PDAs for collecting questionnaire data. The type of wireless technology used, such as Wireless Local Area Network (WLAN), Wifi, Bluetooth and WiMax, will also affect the type of mobile application that a company can apply in their business activities. The most popular ones are Bluetooth and Wi-fi connections which are simple and less expensive to use. Japanese Wagamama restaurant chains in the UK (Terry, 2006) apply this type of mobile devices. Wi-fi applications are more technically diverse as they can support both Personal Digital Assistants (PDA) and computer laptops. The evolution of mobile technology has provided new opportunities by extending mobile infrastructure into the business, which enables the business to gain competitive advantage. Although there are many strategic tools and techniques available such as Porter's competitive analysis and Value Chain (Porter, 2001), strategic tools for mobile applications appear to be limited (Varshney and Vetter, 2002; Chen and Nath, 2004), with little financial appraisal. A framework to assess strategic applications of mobile technology and pertinent infrastructure is outlined to assist business managers in making financial and technological decisions in mobile business environments.

EXTENTION TO M-COMMERCE

Improved computing infrastructure has provided e-business with an advantage, because it allows global accessibility from any access points either wired or wirelessly. The e-business serves its purpose by providing the capability to achieve revenue from low costs distribution and increased sales from the global market. Customers are able to access these websites not only from their homes, but also in cyber cafes, public hotspots where the users can access the internet using wireless LANs and even on a mobile phone. The development of 3G mobile phones and PDAs now have the ability to capture pictures and send them through MMS (Multimedia Messaging Service). The 3G phones also allow video calls, video clips, and surfing of the internet via GPRS (General Packet Radio Service) or CDMA (Code-Division Multiple Access), rather than through the classic WAP (Wireless Access Protocol). Users are now able to view web pages via their mobile devices depending whether their phones support Hyper-Text Mark-Up Language (HTML) or WAP capabilities. The increasing amount of mobile phone users within the next decade (Roto, 2007), would enable businesses to sell products electronically over the mobile platform, similar to earlier e-business concepts. One example of this is Ring tones, which has generated over $600 million in sales via consumers mobile phones (Mobile Youth, 2006). An example of a mobile application that assists in improving business activities is the PDA insurance quota service (Serbedzija, 2005). This application has been implemented in Germany where young adults find the idea of using a PDA device to electronically search insurance quotations for their automobiles very

useful, particularly as they are able to electronically enter their details via the mobile device. As a result, insurance companies in Germany have used these PDA's as their after sales activities to improve their Customer Relationship Management (CRM) performance with their customers. Unfortunately not all mobile technology can be applied to every business activities. Therefore, strategic tools and techniques are needed to assist companies in applying mobile applications into their business activities (Atkins, et al., 2006). The literature indicates that most mobile business applications are an extension of e-business rather than a separate technology (Sliwa, 2004; UPS, 2007; Hadfield, 2006; www.e-health-insider.com, 2004; Cyber-Lab, 2005).

HEALTH, SAFETY, AND PRIVACY ISSUES

This advancement of mobile devices has also brought about health and safety concerns of the intense usage and associated radiation could lead to cancer problems in the future (www.who.int, 2006). The radio frequency that mobile phones produce when they are on standby is very small, but during call times the type of wavelength it can emit is around 2 GHz during active transmission. The constant exposure to these mobile phones can cause 'heating' or 'thermal' effect to the ear when the user makes the call. This thermal effect has made the general public perceive that mobile phones could cause cancer (www.who.int, 2006). The effect on the brain when exposed to using this mobile technology is obviously a concern by the general public. The World Health Organisation (WHO) has indicated general health awareness and the possible dangers of mobile devices and of excessive use (www.who.int, 2006). The development of 3G technologies and the introduction of WiMax can involve around 47,000 base stations in the UK of which two thirds of these installations are on existing buildings. Another concern in the usage of mobile phones by the public is the location awareness that traces the user's mobile location anywhere in the world by satellite or cellular location awareness. This technology is similar to the use of locating GPS (Global Positioning System) which can be exploited by the military or police authorities with mobile users having no knowledge of being monitored.

MOBILE APPLICATIONS FRAMEWORK

Strategic planning is often used in starting a new product or in improving business activities in a competitive environment. Managers often use strategic tools for forward planning, or to propose a new solution to increase business profits. The planning usually involves identifying weaknesses, or opportunities in the business environment. The use of strategic management tools can provide helpful insights in competing against competitors (Ghalayini and Noble, 1996). Some business strategic tools involve applying new technology or merging with other business services to cut costs (Shaffer and Srinivasan, 2005). Other strategies suggest concentrating on the source of income, such as ensuring customer satisfaction, or improving relations with the suppliers and buyers. Some strategic ideas are ineffective because of the inability to predict environmental changes, coordination, and communication with the suppliers and the customers. Identifying a strategic tool that can be used in specific business tends to be difficult because of the array of tools available. Business tools such as the SWOT (Strength, Weaknesses, Opportunities and Threats) and PEST (Political, Economical, Socio-Cultural and Technological) are commonly used for marketing and in IT for business strategy. Strategic tools and techniques, such as the Strategic Grid (McFarlan et al, 1984), Porter's Five Forces (Porter, 2001), Value Chain (Porter, 2001), IT Business Alignment tool (Henderson, 1993), can improve business activities and assist in providing competitive advantage. The proposed Mobile Business Application Framework, in Figure 1, is an aid to business management in decision making within the three regions of user mobility. The framework consists of two sections, firstly the Financial Scorecard, as shown in Section A of Figure 1. The Financial Scorecard is used to assess the business process; activities and financial standing, similar to a cost benefit analysis, and can identify the weaknesses and opportunity of the company (Lorsh, 1993). The Financial Scorecard helps the business to measure performance and resolve customer relations and strategy issues. Figure 1 illustrates that the financial scorecard has four types of perspective as shown in Section A: the Financial, Customer, Learning, and Growth, and Internal Business Process respectively. Each of these perspectives evaluates the strength and weaknesses of the business by assessing the previous records of its activities. An example of the use of the scorecard is when a company is considering implementing a mobile technology to improve the inventory system using Radio Frequency Identification (RFID) technology. The company could evaluate the expected benefits by using the process cycle of the Financial Scorecard.

- In Part 1 of Figure 1, the process cycle of the Financial Scorecard starts with the Financial Perspective. Management assess Financial Perspective, looking at previous records or accounts of the business activities, to set objectives, measures and operational goals. At the end of the business process, the management can view the record and comment on the Management Initiatives. This feedback checks if the business has reached their intended goals or requires additional procedures to enhance their business.
- These Scorecard procedures are repeated for the Customer, Learning and Growth, and the Internal Business Perspective.
- The Internal Business Process uses the Mobile RFID Technology to enhance stock location processes in the warehouse. The Management Initiatives column indicated in Part 2 of Figure 1 will be used to record the success factor at the end of the implementation.
- As the cycle repeats, the Management Initiatives for the Financial Perspective are assessed and recorded, to monitor the effects of implementing a mobile technology in the business. This iterative process is repeated for the Customer, and the Learning and Growth Perspective.
- After completing the cycle (anti-clockwise in Part 1 of Figure 1) the Internal Business Process for implementing the mobile technology is assessed against the target goals as shown in Part 3.

In Figure 1, Section B illustrates the strategic framework and identifies the type of mobile device that would be suitable to the business. The framework indicated in Part 1 illustrates a radial wave, or a ripple, which depicts the mobility range for mobile applications involving the Internet, Extranet, and Intranet (Mobile Application Region). These three regions are shown on the horizontal axis of the Framework. The implementation of the mobile RFID technology is contained within the warehouse, consequently this is an Intranet region. In each region, there are also circular bands of

Figure 1. Mobile business application framework

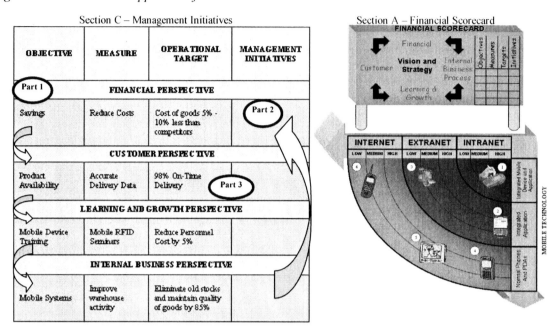

Section C – Management Initiatives

Section A – Financial Scorecard

Section B – Mobile Technology Application

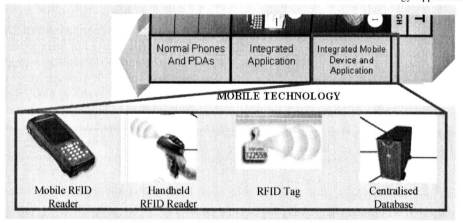

mobile usage. These bands are colour coded to signify 'critical data transfer,' which indicates the importance of data transmission to the business applications. The three different regions differentiate the types of mobile device and determine how the software application can be implemented in relation to business operations. The type of mobile device, or application, used in the business is shown by the vertical axis of the diagram. The Intranet and Extranet region of the framework,

illustrated in Figure 1, can apply a fully integrated mobile device or customised application using normal mobile phones, such as Wal-Mart Wireless Inventory Checking (Sliwa, 2004). Also users within the Internet region can use normal mobile devices but they will link or visit a web-enabled e-commerce database, to connect to an application, for example an SMS vending machine (SAFECOM, 2007).

MOBILE BUSINESS APPLICATION FRAMEWORK ON WAL-MART

Wal-Mart stores provide a range of goods including grocery goods, clothing, to electronics and frozen goods all in affordable prices (Sliwa, 2004). The current IT infrastructure of Wal-Mart is based on the provision of the efficient 'upstream' supply chain system. Their main intent is to support its strategy by providing support for the most efficient stock control, warehousing and distribution systems in the business (Cyber-Lab, 2005). The application of RFID technology has significantly improved their upstream supply chain. They are able to keep costs to a minimum by keeping track of Point-Of-Sales (POS) system and delivery times of the suppliers. Radio Frequency Identifiers (RFID) or identity tags, are small devices that look like label tags. They function by emitting small radio signals, which can be read by an RFID reader that can display a considerable amount of data tagged on them. Such devices are commonly used for locating and identifying stock crates and inventories in warehouses. Wal-Mart is well known for applying such technology in their business activities, particularly since they receive daily crates of perishable goods. Active and Passive tags are the two main types of RFID technologies that both function different according to supply chain

management in the warehouse. Active RFID tags have a built in battery which powers it continuously to emit constant Radio Frequency (RF) signals for the reader to detect. While Passive RFID relies on radio frequency energy from the reader in order to power that tag temporarily and then responds to the reader (Savi, 2007; Sensitech, 2007). In a warehouse where crates are not moved constantly, then the use of Passive RFID will suffice. Applying an Active RFID in a low activity warehouse will under-utilise the RFID technology. Therefore they are best suited when there is high activity of moving crates and materials. The constant process is very dynamic and unconstrained, thus having the ability to detect multi-tag Active RFID is the best option for this situation (Savi, 2007).

RELATION WITH MOBILE BUSINESS FRAMEWORK

In terms of comparing the proposed framework against the current inventory system in Wal-Mart, its implementation follows correspondingly to the framework and fits into the Intranet Region. This indicates that the use of the mobile devices in the warehouse is to track and identify the crates that arrive from deliveries and update accordingly into the inventory stock.

Figure 2. Integrated mobile/device and application

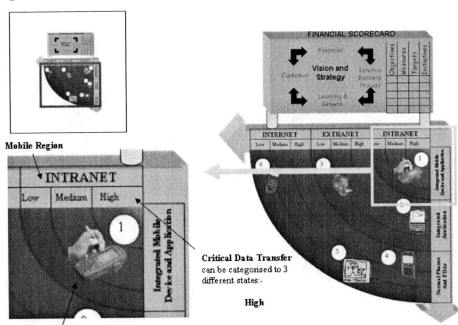

This business strategy analyses the business operations, identifies the weaknesses and indicates access for improving business activities. Figure 1 Section C outlines the improvements needed to commence in the new procurement year. In the Internal Business Process Perspective, Figure 1 Section C highlights the need for the use of mobile application systems. In the next stage, the framework will illustrate to the business managers what mobile devices can be applied in this situation. Figure 2 illustrates the type of mobile devices that can be used in the Integrated Mobile Device and Application for this region of the business area. Mobile devices will include the use of RFID tag, mobile RFID readers and a database system that tracks the tagged items.

- The use of these RFID tags is to identify crates incoming and outgoing crates of the Wal-mart warehouses.
- The overall goal of the implementation is to improve the business activity by reducing costs and time taken to locate specific supplier and inventories.

At the "Integrated Mobile/Device and Application" stage shown in Figure 2 of the framework will determine the type of critical data transfer. The data transferred between the centralised database and mobile devices will include type of stock, date, content and location of the crates.

The following includes additional features into the system:-

- Contingency arrangements include a barcode or serial no. which the user can key in manually in the event that the RFID tag is damaged.
- In this instance, the original data transfer is likely to be of the 'High' classification, because a delayed delivery may result in a severe chain reaction (i.e. compound shipment delays) due to their use of a just in time system.

CONCLUSION

The strategic framework tool presented here is designed to help managers identify where mobile technology can enhance their strategic business operations. The business strategy should align with IT strategy, organisational infrastructure and information system infrastructure, in order to provide competitive advan-

tage. Wi-fi and Bluetooth technologies are popular in businesses because of the effective wireless range. The short wireless range allows a more secure system, as the data transmission signal may be contained within the business area. Japanese restaurant Wagamama (Terry, 2006) has implemented Bluetooth technology within their business for order taking. WiMax, can be normally used to overcome geographical boundaries or avoid the problem of implementing cables. The proposed mobile strategic framework has been applied to several mobile commercial applicants is outlined (Pg Haji Ali, 2007; Pg Haji Ali and Atkins, 2007). It demonstrates the use of a Financial Scorecard to evaluate how the business cost effectiveness and departmental goals within the company can be assessed, allowing managers to identify and align strategic initiatives to the business (Lorsch, 1993). In the case of mobile technology, the strategic framework assesses the suitability of mobile devices for the business and considers the type of security and applications appropriate for a particular mobile device. The mobile strategic framework is designed to assist mangers to make informed decisions and increase competitive advantage in mobile infrastructure enhancements.

REFERENCES

Alexander, L. (2007). *Are Wireless Networks Safe?'* Retrieved 15 February 2007:-http://blogs.cio.com/node/656

Atkins, A. S., Pengiran Haji Ali, A. K. Hairul Nizam, & Shah, H. (October, 2006) Extending e-business applications using mobile technology. In *proceedings* of *International Conference on Mobile Technology, Applications and Systems, IEE Mobility Conference.* Bangkok Thailand. Retrieved from http://doi.acm.org/10.1145/1292331.1292381

Brian, K. (2006). *Lowering Health Care Costs Out-of-the-Box.* Retrieved 27 September 2006:-http://wireless.sys-con.com/read/40975.htm

British Red Cross (2004). *First aid at your fingertips.* Retrieved 6 July 2007:-http://www.redcross.org.uk/news.asp?id=41091

Chen, L., & Nath, R. (2004). A Framework for Mobile Business Application. *Int. J. Mobile Communications, 2*(4), 368-381

Cyber-Lab (2005). *A Supermarket uses RFID to Control Stock Inventory.* Retrieved 12 April 2006:-http://www2.cpttm.org.mo/cyberlab/rfid/wal-mart.html.en

E-Health Insider (2005). *Addebrooke's installs SMS Patient reminder system.* Retrieved at 1 March 2006:-http://www.e-health-insider.com/news/item.cfm?ID=1236

Farhoomand, A., & Ng, S. P. (2003). Creating Sustainable Competitive Advantage Through Internetworked Communities. *Communication of the ACM, 46*(9), 83-88.

Ghalayini, A. M., & Noble, J. S. (1996). The Changing Basis of Performance Measurement. *International Journal of Operations and Production Management, 16*(8), 63-80.

Greengard, S. (2001). Customer Services Goes Wireless. *Business Finance*, 35.

Hadfield, W. (2006). Police get Streetwyse to mobile ID checks. *Computer Weekly, 4,* 6

Harrington, (2006). *Standard and Guidelines WHO.* Retrieved 15 February 2007:-http://http://www.who.int/peh-emf/standards/en/

Haines, L.: Digital divide is self-repairing, says UK gov (2005). Retrieved 5 February 2007:-http://www.theregister.co.uk/2005/09/06/digital-divide/

Henderson, J. C, & Venkatraman, N. (1993). Strategic Alignment: Leveraging Information Technology for Transforming Organisations. *IBM Systems Journal, 32*(1), 4-16.

Jarvenpaa, S. L. (2006). Internet Goes Mobile: How Will Wireless Computing Affect Your Firm's Internet Strategy? Retrieved at May 2006:-http://web.hhs.se/cic/about/blkcoffee/Internet_Mobile_6-19_sj.pdf

Lorsch, J. W. (1993). Smelling Smoke: Why Boards of Directors Need the Balanced Scorecard. *Balanced Scorecard Report*, September-October, pp. 9.

McFarlan, F. W, James L. M, & Philip P. (1983). The Information Archipelago – Plotting a Course. *Harvard Business Review, 61,* 145-155.

Mobile Youth (2005). Retrieved 3 April 2006:-http://www.mobileyouth.org/my_item/ringtone_sales_build_600_mn_2005_revenues

Pg Hj Ali, A. H. N., & Atkins, A. S. (2007, June). A Strategic Business Tool For Mobile Infrastructure. *Wireless Ubiquitous Computing, International Conference on Enterprise Information Systems*, Funchal, Portugal. (pp.23-32).

Pg Hj Ali, A. H. N. (2007). *Mobile Business Application.* Masters by Research, Computing Science, Faculty of Computing, Engineering and Technology, Staffordshire University, United Kingdom – unpublished thesis.

Porter, M. E. (2001, March). Strategy and the Internet. *Harvard Business Review,* 63-78.

Roto, V. (2007). *Browsing on Mobile Phones.* Retrieved at 6 June 2007:-http://www.research.att.com/~rjana/WF12_Paper1.pdf

Savi Technologies (2007). Savi's RFID Solutions. Retrieved 6 June 2007:-http://www.savi.com/index.shtml

Savvas, A. (2007, February). Mobility is increasingly key to strategy. *Computer Weekly, 13,* 12

Serbedzija N, Fabiunke M., Schön F., & Beyer G. (2006). Multi-Client Car Insurance. *Proceedings of the IADIS International Conference WWW/Internet (ICWI) 2005, 2,* 30-34. 19-22 October, Lisbon, Portugal, ISBN: 972-8924-02-X

Shaffer, D., & Srinivasan, M. (2005). *Agile IT through SOA Requires New Technologies: How Not to Fall Into the Trap of Applying Archaic Integration Technologies!* Retrieved at 6 June 2007:-http://www.alignjournal.com/index.cfm?section=article&aid=310

Sliwa, C. (2004). *Wal-Mart CEO promises 'tough love' approach to RFID use.* Retrieved at 5 April 2006:-http://www.computerworld.com/mobiletopics/mobile/technology/story/0,10801,89011,00.html

Terry, L. (2006). Wireless Business and Technology. *Serving up wireless.* Retrieved 10 January 2006 from:-http://wbt.sys-con.com/read/40916.htm

UPS (2005). *Embracing Technology.* Retrieved 19 September 2005 from:-http://www.ups.com/content/corp/about/history/1999.html

Varshney, U., & Vetter, R. (2002). Mobile Commerce: Framework, Application and Networking Support. *Mobile Networks and Applications, 7,* 185-198.

KEY TERMS

Bluetooth Technology: Short-range wireless radio technology for connecting small devices, such as wireless PDAs and laptops, to each other and connect them in a wireless network.

E-Business: Electronic Business is any business process that relies on an automated information system.

M-Payment: Mobile Payment is the process for payment of goods or services with a mobile device such as a mobile phone, Personal Digital Assistant (PDA), or other wireless devices.

Mobile Business Application: Commercial usage of mobile electronic transaction in business operations.

Mobile Technology: Use of mobile telephony, mobile computing, and miscellaneous portable electronic devices, systems, and networks.

Strategic Framework: A framework to provide a focused solution for assisting in business decision-making.

Wi-Fi: Wireless Fidelity commonly used to broaden wireless interface of mobile computing devices, such as laptops in Local Area Network (LAN).

Chapter XI
Construction of Matrix and eMatrix for Mobile Development Methodologies

Norshuhada Shiratuddin
Universiti Utara Malaysia, Malaysia

Siti Mahfuzah Sarif
Universiti Utara Malaysia, Malaysia

ABSTRACT

Mobile computing is getting more and more attention these days, but the fact that there is still inadequate source of development methodologies to support mobile development, triggers the interest in this study to explore issues related to mobile development methodologies. The mobile developers are facing formidable challenges in the development of mobile application due to the specific demand and technical constraints of mobile environment. Selecting a suitable development methodology is believed to be the key answer to all these issues. Thus, this study aimed to propose a solution to resolve the issues. A decision matrix based on Pugh method was constructed to assist mobile developers especially the novices, to choose the methodology that suits the requirements of their mobile development projects. In order to rate the usefulness of the constructed matrix, an electronic version of the matrix was designed and developed, called m^d-Matrix. Detail descriptions of the processes involved in constructing the matrix and designing the electronic version of the constructed matrix are also described. Analysis of data gathered from a questionnaire given after the test of md-Matrix shows that participants fairly agreed that m^d-Matrix is useful in helping them to develop a mobile application.

INTRODUCTION

Charaf *et al.* (2006) described the mobile developer platform as still 'green'; with the developer culture as still budding. More over, the issue of comparing the performance quality of mobile applications to the wired applications is inevitable, which add to the complexity of mobile computing environment. Thus, there is always an urge to produce high quality mobile applications, which almost is impossible to achieve without patterns and methods proven in the applications of the desktop developments. Under this perspective, a good methodology is believed to address the issues of producing a completely defined result in any development process.

During the development of a system the use of a methodology is important as a project can be structured into small, well defined activities where the sequence and interaction of these activities can be specified. The use of diagrammatic and other modeling techniques gives a more precise or structured definition that is understandable by both users and developers. The use of structured analysis requires a clear "requirements statement" that all parties can comprehend, and it provides firm foundation for subsequent design and implementation. Moreover, methodology also improves project planning and control, and provides a better quality system resulting in a better end product, a better development process and a standardized process (Avison & Fitzgerald, 1990).

Pastor and Whiddett (1996) agreed that the key challenge among system developers is during selection of suitable development methodology. The chosen methodology will have a huge impact on different aspects of development; for instance the cost, time, resources needed and etc. Development methodologies vary according to many areas such as the type of applications developed, the end users, the approach taken, the issues addressed and the diagram used. Thus, to select an appropriate methodology which perfectly fits the required purpose and field would be tough, especially to the novice developers. In order to address this issue, this research has taken a detail approach to construct a decision matrix by referring selected mobile development methodologies (MDM) against a number of development methodology properties. The selected development methodologies are meant to be representative but not exhaustive, and each has been identified to be mobile environment specific methodology. The findings of how this decision matrix really helps the novice developers are based on the testing of users' perceived usefulness of the electronic version of the constructed decision matrix that is named as **m^d-Matrix**.

BACKGROUND

In this section we first present a discussion on the multimedia design approaches as they are closely related to the pertinent problem presented in this study. Then reviews of Mobile Multimedia Development and Pugh's Decision Matrix are outlined.

Multimedia Design Approaches

According to a study by Augusteyn *et al.* (1998), a number of multimedia design approaches are available to designers; however, a completely integrated approach to multimedia design does not seem to be available. Current approaches generally relate to components of multimedia design, such as graphical design, rather than guiding the entire design process. The lack of fully integrated multimedia design methodologies can be attributed to a number of factors.

Firstly, multimedia designers are still independently working out how to do things, so they are not at the stage where they can document processes thoroughly (Augusteyn *et al.*, 1998). Secondly, multimedia is a multidisciplinary field that must incorporate aspects of methodologies from all of the contributing fields, such as graphical design, instructional design, sound production, software development, human factors and so on. Thirdly, multimedia design approaches are developed in either university environments or by commercial organizations. Communication between these two groups is generally very poor. Most industry-based multimedia developers are also not involved with universities, as a consequence, they do not hear about the latest findings, theories, and approaches. Finally, most commercial organizations do not publicize their methodologies. This means that less experienced multimedia designers cannot learn from the more experienced ones.

All these issues are now also faced by those who want to develop mobile applications (Bertini *et al.*, 2006; Heikkinen & Still, 2005; Atkinson & Olla, 2004; Heyes, 2002; Afonso *et al.*, 1998). Even though, mobile computing have gained a lot of attention both in research and industry over the last decade, but there is still inadequate research aimed to assist systems developers, particularly in the mobile environment., to select the most appropriate methodology for their development project (GI Dagstuhl Research Seminar, 2006).

Mobile Development Methodology

Presently, the mobile environment is offering only a handful source of methodology to support the development process of mobile application (GI Dagstuhl Research Seminar, 2006). Many developers claimed that developing for mobile devices is more challenging than traditional software development but the question of how big are the differences between development of mobile applications and traditional software development is still fuzzy.

Heyes (2002) stated that developing mobile application is currently a very challenging task due to the specific demands and technical constraints of the mobile environment, such as limited capabilities and rapid evolution of terminal devices; various standards, protocols and network technologies; the needs to operate on a variety of different platforms; the specific needs of mobile terminal users; and strict time to meet market requirements. The main focus of this study is to find the ideal software development methodologies that have been designed or modified to suit the development of mobile applications. In this study we used mobile application development to refer to four major groups of mobile applications, namely mobile entertainment, mobile commerce, mobile learning and location based information systems. The aforementioned groups are used as to map with the MDM found during literature the search.

Pugh's Decision Matrix

A decision matrix allows the decision makers to structure, and then solves their problem by; specifying and prioritizing their needs with a list of criteria,

then evaluating, rating and comparing the different solutions, and finally selecting the best matching solution. Among one of the most popular decision matrices is based on Pugh method. The method evidently has proven it capability to avoid the mathematically proven drawbacks (Mullur *et al.*, 2003b) associated with the typical construction of the matrix such as weighted decision matrix method. Use of the Pugh's method begins with choosing the evaluation criteria for the concepts. The concept variants are then evaluated by comparing the other concepts to a so-called *datum* concept.

When considering each concept in each individual criterion against the datum concept, the following markings are used: plus (+) sign is entered in the respective cell of the evaluation matrix if the concept is considered better in the particular criterion than the datum concept, minus (-) sign is used if the concept is considered worse than the datum concept, and zero (0) if the concept is considered same to that of the datum concept. A score pattern for each concept is calculated as the number of plusses, minuses, and zero's.

The Pugh method could has the same formulation as in weighted decision matrix based method, with the added requirement that all weights must be equal to one. That is, no one selection criterion has more or less importance than any other criterion. In this respect, the Pugh method deliberately avoids the use of weights. In fact, Pugh himself argues that weights

Table 1. Demonstrative example of using Pugh's matrix to select an electric bicycle concept from three concepts

	CONCEPTS			
CRITERIA	**A**	**B**	**C**	**D**
Rider Stability	*D*	-	-	0
Use of Standard Parts	*A*	0	-	-
Complexity: Transmission	*T*	0	-	-
Manufacturing Cost	*U*	+	-	-
Maintenance Cost	*M*	-	0	0
Sum of (+)		1	0	0
Sum of (-)		2	4	3
Sum of 0's		2	1	2

Table 2. Examples of mobile development methodologies

Mobile Development Methodology	Mobile Application	Approach
Mobile-D (Abrahamsson *et al.* 2004)	Mobile Entertainment	Agile
Mobile RAD (Blue Dot Solutions, 2006)	Mobile Commerce	RAD
Dynamic Channel Model (Afonso et al., 1998)	Location Based Information Systems	Object Oriented
Mobile Engineering (MobE) (Papanikolaou & Mavromoustakos, 2006)	Mobile Learning	Process Driven

are misleading in nature (Mullur *et al.*, 2003b). This method is used to support judgments about qualitative information. It results in an abstract satisfaction calculation for each alternative. Pugh's method supports an individual's decision making and also uses consistent information. Table 1 shows a descriptive example of utilizing Pugh's method for a selection of an electric bicycle concept from three candidates (concepts).

The example demonstrated in Table 1 shows a Pugh-method based decision matrix used to select an electric bicycle concept from three concepts. In the example Concept A was taken as the datum. Each of other concepts were compared to the datum and given a + (i.e. better than), - (i.e. less than) or 0 (i.e. equivalent to) evaluation. Concept B appeared to be the strongest candidate since the total number of + sign is greater than other concepts. Thus, Concept B is the winning concept in this evaluation. The datum should be changed to re-evaluate all the concepts evenly. If one or more concepts remain strong through out the iterations then the concept will be the most likely candidate to move onto the detailed design stage.

METHODOLOGY FOR CONSTRUCTING THE DECISION MATRIX

In order to construct a reliable decision matrix, a better understanding of the main issue of this study is important. Thus, an in-depth literature search was employed. The use of data collection method like Internet browsing and archival research has leaded the way to important findings in this study. During the first

six weeks of the research period, ideas, information, issues and problems related to MDM and its development properties were gathered. Four mobile specific methodologies for development of specified mobile applications have been identified from the literature search. The number is meant to be representative but not exhaustive. We selected only those with mobile specific development criteria and those that have been tested with real development projects. All four MDM used in this study are identified as using different approaches in their development activities; one agile approach, one rapid application development approach, one object oriented approach and one process-driven approach. Table 2 lists four MDM used in the construction of the decision matrix.

The selected MDM are then closely analyzed with the help of two mobile experts who have practically been involved in many mobile development projects before and both come from two different backgrounds, one from higher learning institute and the other from private agency. A comparative analysis has been carried out against a set of existing software development method (SDM) properties proposed by Karam and Casselman (1993) in a study to catalog a framework for SDM. The list consists of twenty one properties which are categorized into three major groups, namely technical properties, managerial properties and usage properties. Some modifications have been made to some of the properties to suit the criteria of mobile development requirements and these are described below:

I. Technical Properties

- *Method Philosophy:* The methodology considers the importance of scenario-related, interaction related, user-related dimensions of mobile application development.

- *Life-cycle coverage:* Development phases covered by the methodology and the application development paradigm advocated for the method (e.g. conventional, prototyping, or transformational.

- *Work products & notations:* Method's work products (e.g. concept document, requirements documents, software designs, and test plans) and the notations (e.g. pseudo code, Petri nets, and English text) for documenting them.

- *Problem domain analysis:* Method's techniques and tools for analyzing and understanding the problem domain.

- *Procedure:* The sequence of steps suggested by the method for each phase. The sequence of steps is a framework for guiding the creative process in a manner that supports the method's philosophy.

- *Guidelines/Criteria/Measures:* Major design rules of each phase in the method. A precise design rule is the one that sufficiently detailed for any reasonably trained practitioner to apply under the same circumstances and obtain the same result.

- *Verification:* Processes used to determine the degree to which method's work products fulfill requirements.

- *Degree of formality:* Measures the extent to which the method's technical aspects are formal. The formality of a method depends on the formality of (1) the notations, (2) the relationships between phases and (3) verification of the relationships between phases.

- *Maintainability/Flexibility:* The ability to accommodate change during development and during evolution. Flexibility can be increased by information hiding (abstraction), and concise documentation.

- *Reusability:* Concerns degree to which project's work products can be reused on another. Example of reuse items are requirement specifications, architectural designs and test cases.

- *Concurrent processing:* Refer to support of concurrency during design phases (i.e. architectural design and detailed design, taken together.

- *Performance engineering:* Techniques used to shape the design at an early stage when the cost of change is still low. The techniques involve (1) ad hoc methods such as prototyping of criti-

cal sections of the application or time budget estimates; (2) formal performance estimation through analytic models or simulations.

- *Traceability:* Elements of method's traceability involve records of decisions, detailed rules for transitioning between development stages and work products and a record of coverage between work products.

- *Method specialization:* Considers the degree to which a method can be extended and/or specialized to a particular application domain.

II. Usage Properties

- *Application areas:* Application domains for which the method is well suited.

- *Reliability:* The application size for which a method is believed to be suitable for both development and maintenance. The most reliable source is documented project experience by similar development teams and for similar applications.

- *Automated support:* Concerns with the availability and usefulness of software tools to support the method's techniques.

- *Ease of instruction:* Simplicity of method's techniques, notations and instructional mechanisms.

- *Method maturity:* A mature method should show multiple uses (at least two) by the same development team.

III. Managerial Properties

- *Development organization:* Concerns with (1) methods of cost estimation, project planning and staffing, and (2) methods to determine progress of development or well-defined milestones from which progress can be inferred.

- *Ease of integration:* A method must be usable with the installed base and with existing tools and techniques within the organizations.

Table 3 illustrates the findings of the comparative analysis.

In order to construct the matrix, this study has decided upon implementation of Pugh method but with few modifications to suit with the objective of the matrix. In Pugh matrix, the matrix is prepared with columns to represent options (the methodologies) and the rows to represent criteria (the properties of

Table 3. Result of comparative analysis of four MDM against modified SDM properties

CRITERION	METHODOLOGY			
	Mobile-D	**Mobile RAD**	**Dynamic Channel**	**MobE**
Technical Properties				
Method Philosophy	Yes	Yes	Yes	Yes
Life-cycle coverage	Yes	Yes	Yes	Yes
Work products & notations	Yes	Yes	Yes	Yes
Problem domain analysis	Yes	Yes	Yes	Yes
Procedure	Yes	Yes	Yes	Yes
Guidelines/ Criteria/ Measures	Yes	Yes	Yes	Yes
Verification	Yes	Yes	Yes	Yes
Degree of formality	Yes	Yes	Yes	Yes
Maintainability/ Flexibility	Yes	Yes	Yes	No
Reusability	Yes	Yes	Yes	Yes
Concurrent Processing	Yes	Yes	Not Applicable	Yes
Performance Engineering	Yes	Yes	Yes	Yes
Traceability	Yes	Yes	Yes	Yes
Method specialization	Yes	Yes	Yes	Yes
Usage Properties				
Application areas	All	All	Information Dissemination	Mobile Learning
Reliability	Yes	Not Applicable	Yes	Not Applicable
Automated support	Yes	Yes	Yes	Yes
Ease of instruction	No	Yes	No	Yes
Method Maturity	Yes	Not Applicable	Yes	Not Applicable
Managerial Properties				
Development organization	Yes	Yes	Not Applicable	Yes
Ease of integration	No	Yes	Yes	Yes

the methodology). In this study, each of the MDM is set to be the *datum* (best fit methodology) of their respective applications. Table 4 illustrates the correct pair of application and its *datum*.

Before the options (the MDM) and the criteria (the SDM properties) and are included in the matrix, a further investigation on the significance of each items are conducted to correctly position the items in the matrix. Consequently, the position in the matrix can suggest a course of action for the selection. Since, all four MDM used in this study are identified as using different approaches in their development activities. Hence, the chronological factor of when these methodologies first been used in system development environment is the determining factor to position the methodologies in the horizontal axis of the matrix.

To complete the functions of matrix, each methodology has to be rated against the *datum* for every SDM properties with the help of the experts. As mentioned earlier, the *datum* for this decision matrix is pre-set and each type of mobile applications will have their respective *datum*. A plus (+), zero (0) and minus (-) sign is used to indicate whether the methodology is better, equivalent or less than that of the *datum,* respectively. Table 5 illustrates the result of this rating process.

In the constructed matrix, users are allowed to change the combination of criteria that they would like to consider in order to choose the most suitable methodology. All the selected criteria will be used as a basis to compare each methodology with the favorite methodology (i.e. *datum*). The decision matrix will determine the winning methodology by looking at the score pattern of + (i.e. better then the *datum*), - (i.e. less than the *datum*) and 0 (i.e. equivalent to the *datum*) sign for each methodology. Normally, the matrix will suggest to choose the methodology with

the highest score of "Sum of +". If the score for "Sum of +" is similar for at least two of the compared methodologies, the matrix will look for the lowest score of "Sum of -". If the score of "Sum of -" is similar between the compared methodologies which have the highest score of "Sum of +", the matrix will look for the highest score of "Sum of 0" to determine the winning methodology. In cases where the score of "Sum of +" for all compared methodologies is zero, the matrix will suggest to choose the favorite methodology (i.e. *datum*).

DESIGNING ELECTRONIC MATRIX

The electronic version of the constructed matrix is named as m^d-Matrix. The rationale behind the name came as in brief description of the whole function of the matrix, which is to help selecting suitable MDM using decision matrix approach. The m^d stands for mobile development and Matrix is the approach used in the decision making process. m^d-Matrix is designed and developed using the iterative approach in Boehm's Spiral Model. The approach emphasizes on the development of prototype and verified it at each end of the iterative cycles, until the fully functional integrated end product is presented. The code and development part of the m^d-Matrix were entirely done using Visual Basic 6.0 and the end product of the application is packaged in executable formats.

The flow design of the eMatrix is as displayed in Figure 1. The application start by prompting input from users to select the type of mobile applications to develop. The input will be used to decide which mobile application screen is to be displayed. Each mobile application has its respective decision matrix

Table 4. Mobile applications and their respective datum

MOBILE APPLICATION	DATUM
Mobile Entertainment	Mobile-D (Abrahamsson *et al.* 2004)
Mobile Commerce	Mobile RAD (Blue Dot Solutions, 2006)
Location Based Information	Dynamic Channel Model (Afonso et al., 1998)
Mobile Learning Systems	Mobile Engineering (MobE) (Papanikolaou & Mavromoustakos, 2006)

Table 5. Rating result of MDM against the datum of respective mobile applications

CRITERION	METHODOLOGY															
	Mobile-D				Mobile RAD				Dynamic Channel				MobE			
Technical Properties																
Method Philosophy	D	-	-	-	+	D	-	-	+	0	D	0	+	0	0	D
Life-cycle coverage	A	0	+	0	0	A	+	0	-	-	A	-	0	0	+	A
Work products & notations	T	0	-	-	0	T	-	-	+	+	T	+	+	+	-	T
Problem domain analysis	U	0	0	0	0	U	0	0	0	0	U	0	0	0	0	U
Procedure	M	+	0	0	-	M	-	-	0	+	M	0	0	+	0	M
Guidelines/Criteria/Measures	D	0	-	-	0	D	-	-	+	+	D	0	+	+	0	D
Verification	A	0	0	0	0	A	0	0	0	0	A	0	0	0	0	A
Degree of formality	T	+	0	-	0	T	-	-	+	+	T	0	+	+	0	T
Maintainability/Flexibility	U	+	0	+	-	U	-	+	0	+	U	+	-	-	-	U
Reusability	M	0	0	0	0	M	0	0	0	0	M	0	0	0	0	M
Concurrent Processing	D	0	+	+	0	D	+	+	-	-	D	0	-	-	-	D
Performance Engineering	A	0	0	+	0	A	0	+	0	0	A	+	-	-	-	A
Traceability	T	0	-	0	0	T	-	+	+	+	T	+	0	0	-	T
Method specialization	U	0	+	+	0	U	+	+	-	-	U	-	-	-	0	U
Usage Properties																
Application areas	M	+	+	+	0	M	-	-	-	-	M	-	-	-	0	M
Reliability	D	+	+	+	-	D	-	0	0	+	D	+	-	0	-	D
Automated support	A	-	-	0	+	A	0	+	+	0	A	0	0	-	-	A
Ease of instruction	T	-	-	-	+	T	+	0	0	-	T	-	+	0	+	T
Method Maturity	U	+	+	+	-	U	-	0	0	+	U	+	-	0	-	U
Managerial Properties																
Development organization	M	0	+	+	0	M	+	+	-	-	M	0	-	-	0	M
Ease of integration	D	-	-	-	+	D	+	+	+	-	D	-	+	0	+	D

page with respective pre-selected *datum*. If users need help with the electronic matrix, they can opt for help screen or else they can proceed with the decision making process. To start the process, users need to select their set of criteria and then the input will be used to computer the decision and later the result is presented as the output. After completing the first round, users have options either to reset the matrix for another round of decision making process or stop there and quit the application. If users choose to reset the matrix, the screen will be reset and users can repeat the same process of selecting criteria and getting result based on the selected criteria. This process can be iterative until users have decided on the set of criteria.

Interface Design of m^d-Matrix

The interface design of the m^d-Matrix emphasizes on minimum steps required to operate the matrix. As the matter of fact, the required steps to use the electronic matrix are reduced to only three steps.

i. Step 1: users need to choose the type of mobile applications to develop

ii. Step 2: users need to select set of criteria that they would like to consider for the development methodology

iii. Step 3: users obtain result by clicking on a Result button

The interface design of the electronic matrix also focuses on the method of input in order to increase the interactivity between users and application. The input mechanisms in the electronic matrix mainly include single click hyperlinks (all hypertexts are in blue color), radio buttons, check boxes and single click buttons. Clear instructions are also included and made noticeable with the use of standardized color which is red. Figure 2 illustrates the print screen of the electronic matrix interface.

Figure 1. Activities involved in the eMatrix

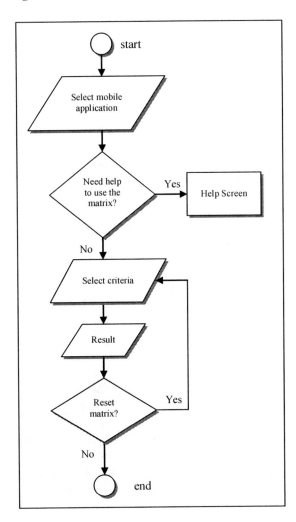

ASSESSING USEFULNESS OF M^D-MATRIX

To investigate the potential usefulness of applying our electronic matrix for selecting appropriate development methodologies for mobile applications, we conducted a users' perceived usefulness test which involved selected target groups. Testing with potential users of targeted group could raise the possibility of getting as efficient feedback as possible in a short period of time and with the all the available resources. The test involved users experimenting with the electronic matrix and then answering a satisfaction questionnaire which is inclusive of users' perceived usefulness questions based on the most referred Davis' (1989) Perceived Usefulness and Ease of Use (PUEU) questionnaire.

Test Design

Users' Perceived Usefulness Test

The test was conducted under a lab environment where eleven PCs were installed with m^d-Matrix application. After completing the test, the participants were asked to fill in the satisfaction questionnaire which consists of three parts to rate their level of perceived usefulness towards m^d-Matrix. The first part of the questionnaire asks about the users' background, the second part includes six structured questions based on Davis' (1989) Perceived Usefulness questionnaire that were scaled from one (unlikely) to seven (likely). In the third part of the questionnaire users were asked to give general evaluation on the use of m^d-Matrix.

User Involvement

Users who participated in this test should ideally represent those who have fair knowledge on mobile computing but have very little or no experience in actual development of mobile applications. As the matter of fact, this study is using the same definition aforementioned to describe the term novice developers as the target group for this study. For convenience, the participants are selected from group of post graduate students who were taking the mobile programming class in Universiti Utara Malaysia. This group fit the definition of novice developers since majority of them have either involved in limited number of development project or never involve in any actual development

Figure 2. Screen display of result from m^d-Matrix process

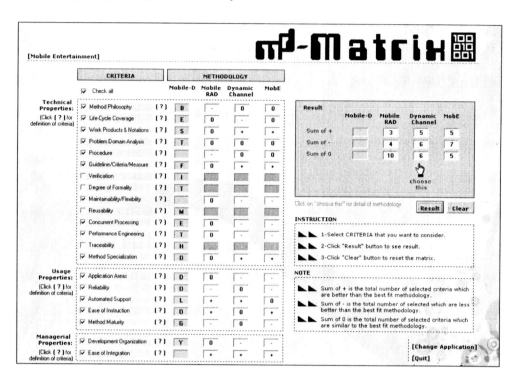

project but have the knowledge of mobile computing from theory lesson or readings.

A survey form was used to collect the post graduate students' background; name, email, course and a declaration of if they have experience in developing any mobile applications before. From sixty students registered under the mobile programming course, only twelve were selected and invited to participate in the test and from twelve invited students only eleven actually agreed to participate.

Out of the eleven participants, 54.6% of them have less than two years of experience in developing computer application. Whereas 36.3% of the participants have two to five years of experience in developing computer application and only 9.1% of the participants claimed that they have more than five years of experience in developing computer application (see Table 6). Also results show that 81.8% of the participants have the required knowledge in mobile computing. Whereas others (18.2%) claimed not having knowledge in mobile computing.

Conducting the Test

At the beginning of the test session participants were briefly introduced to functions of the application and they were also further informed about the aim of the test and their rights. During the test, the participants were let to operate the application at their own pace. Each participant was given a questionnaire to be completed once they have finished using the application.

The duration of the test ranged from two minutes to fifteen minutes where the mean to complete the test was 6.45 minutes (see Table 7). The table shows inconsistency in the time taken by all participants to complete the test.

Data Analysis

Users' Perceived Usefulness Questions

In Table 8 the analysis of score collected from the users' perceived usefulness testing is displayed. Question 1 recorded the highest average point of 5.36, which deliberately implies that the participants fairly agreed

Table 6. Years of experience in developing computer application

Experience in developing computer application	Frequency (F)	Percentage (%)
Less than 2 years	6	54.6
Between 2 to 5 years	4	36.3
More than 5 years	1	9.1
Total	11	100

that using the matrix before they start developing a mobile application would enable them to accomplish tasks more quickly. The test also came out with the same average point for question 3, where participants were asked whether the matrix is able to increase their productivity in development environment or not. This shows that the users sufficiently agreed with the idea that the matrix could help increasing their productivity in development environment. With the lowest average point of 4.73 for question 2, it shows that participants moderately agreed that the matrix would improve their development performance. Perhaps, the fact that the duration of this study did not cover until the development process actually finished, might cause the resulted score. After considering the average point of 4.91 for question 5, it can be implied that the participants found the matrix moderately help in making it easier for them to develop a mobile application. The average score of 5.27 point recorded for question 4 shows that most of the participants agreed that the matrix is sufficient enough to enhance their effectiveness in developing a mobile application. The same average score obtained from question 6, which shows that the electronic matrix is closer to very useful in helping them to develop a mobile application.

The result obtained from the users' perceived usefulness testing, witnessed a fairly high group average point of 5.15. This shows that the group of novice participants in this study perceived the matrix as sufficiently useful in helping them choosing the most suitable methodology for the development process of mobile applications.

Using the Electronic Decision Matrix

Overall, 90.9% (10 out of 11) of the participants thought the format of the decision matrix in m^d-Matrix was easy to understand. Another 9.1% (1 out of 11) thought that it was not easy to comprehend the format used for the decision matrix. Participants were also asked if m^d-Matrix was easy to use. All of them agreed that it was easy to use the application.

When asked whether they would use the application (m^d-Matrix) again to make decision on choosing the right methodology for their mobile development project, 36.4% (4 out of 11) of the participants said that they would do so. Another 63.6% (7 out of 11, which made up the majority) of the participants said they would not use it again. Perhaps, the nature of the test which did not cover the consequences of the execution of the suggested methodology, affect the resulted percentage. Users might not be motivated to use the application again since they have not been convinced by the result of implementing the suggested methodology into their development project. Eight participants (72.7%) said they would recommend the application to others who are about to make the same decision on suitable mobile methodology. Another 27.3% (3 out of 11) would not recommend the application probably because they were expecting m^d-Matrix to help them with more technical decisions of the development of mobile applications. Participants were also asked whether they found m^d-Matrix helpful in making decisions for choosing the most suitable development methodology for mobile applications. Eight of eleven participants (72.7%) thought it was helpful while another 27.3% (3 out of 11) participants did not think the application was helpful to them.

Table 7. Test completion times

Participant	Completion Time (nearest minutes)
1	5
2	5
3	3
4	3
5	3
6	2
7	5
8	15
9	15
10	10
11	5
Mean	**6.45**

Recommendations

In addition to the quantitative results discussed in the previous section, there were a number of comments and recommendations made by the participants. A list of the comments was compiled and separated into the following topic categories (major themes of each category are discussed below):

- **Clarity of the method used to make comparisons of methodologies against the favorite methodology (i.e. datum):** The comments in this category fell into two major groups; some said the method is reliable and made easy for the decision makers, whereas the other groups made comments that the method used should be clearer and more understandable.
- **Terminology Issues:** Two participants commented that the list of criteria included in m^d-Matrix need to use more understandable terminologies and they should not sound too jargon. It is understandable, that these selected users were considered as novice, hence there is a need to closely consider making the presentation of the application effectively understood.

- **Usefulness of the Application:** Participants thought that the application was useful for certain level of decision making that they have to deal with before developing a mobile application. Two of eleven participants also commented that m^d-Matrix should be made more dynamic in way that the application could accept changes or modifications. For instance, adding new criteria or options dynamically to the application.
- **Amount of Information in the Application:** Two of eleven participants commented that the application should also include additional information on other technical issues related to development of mobile applications, for instance the technology options for specific platform of mobile device.

FUTURE DIRECTION

This study has yet to explore other technical dependencies that exist across the mobile development environment that a functional application must content with. Among the typical restriction of developing mobile applications are its dependencies on particular combination of platform, operating system, device and network (Tarnacha & Maitland, 2006). Also included in the future works are selection of appropriate approaches and techniques to the mobile application development, and to improve the electronic matrix to become more dynamic by making the function to add on new criteria or new options available in the application.

CONCLUSION

As a conclusion, the constructed matrix together with its electronic version can be considered as practically reliable and useful in helping mobile developers, especially the novice to choose the most suitable development methodology before they start with the development process. It is believed that the challenges that will be faced by the new developers in developing mobile applications can be eased if they are appropriately educated about the importance of adopting a suitable methodology in their development process. Perhaps, changes need to be made to the curriculum of mobile computing courses so that it will emphasize more on choosing the right development methodology instead of jumping straight to the development process blindly.

Table 8. Analysis of users' perceived usefulness test

	1	2	3	4	5	6	7	8	9	10	11	Average
Question 1: Using the m^d-**Matrix** when I want to start developing a mobile application would enable me to accomplish tasks more quickly.	5	6	7	7	5	5	3	7	3	7	4	**5.36**
Question 2: Using the m^d-**Matrix** would improve my development performance.	5	7	3	5	4	6	3	6	4	4	5	**4.73**
Question 3: Using the m^d-**Matrix** in developing a mobile application would increase my productivity.	5	6	5	5	6	5	3	7	6	7	4	**5.36**
Question 4: Using the m^d-**Matrix** would enhance my effectiveness on developing a mobile application.	6	7	4	6	5	5	3	5	6	5	6	**5.27**
Question 5: Using the m^d-**Matrix** would make it easier to develop a mobile application.	6	7	6	4	3	6	3	7	4	3	5	**4.91**
Question 6: I would find the m^d-**Matrix** useful in developing a mobile application.	5	7	6	5	5	6	3	7	2	7	5	**5.27**
Group Mean Average												**5.15**

As the matter of fact, having the right methodology will indeed help to spearhead the delivery process of the product and avoid unnecessary mistake.

REFERENCES

Abrahamsson, P., Hanhineva, A., Hulkko, H., Ihme, T., Jaalinoja, J., Korkala, M., Koskela, J., Kyllonen, P., & Salo, O. (2004). Mobile-D: An Agile Approach for Mobile Application Development. *Proceedings of OOPSLA'04*, Vancouver, British Columbia, Canada. 174-175.

Afonso, A. P., Regateiro, F. S., & Silva, M. J. (1998). *Dynamic Channels: A New Development Methodology for Mobile Computing Applications.* Retrieved, December 18, 2006, from http://www.di.fc.ul.pt/biblioteca/tech-reports.

Atkinson, C., & Olla, P. (2004). Developing a wireless reference model for interpreting complexity in wireless projects. *Industrial Management & Data Systems, 104*, 262-272.

Augusteyn, D., Gunn, K., & Leung, Y.K. (1998). Formalized approaches for multimedia design-are they used by Australian designers? *Proceedings of 3rd Asia Pacific, Computer Human Interaction.*

Avison, D. E., & Fitzgerald, G. (1990). *Information Systems Development: Methodologies, Techniques and Tools.* New York: Blackwell.

Bertini, E., Gabrielli, S., & Kimani, S. (2006). Appropriating and Assessing Heuristics for Mobile Computing. *Proceedings of the working Conference on Advanced Visual Interfaces AVI'06*, Venezia, Italy. 119-126.

Blue Dot Solutions (2006). *Mobile RAD Methodology.* Retrieved March 28, 2007, from http://www.sneller.com/rad.htm .

Bryce, T. (2006). *Methodologies versus Techniques and Tools.* Retrieved March 28, 2007, from http://www.forteach.net/personaltech/software/43086.html .

Charaf, H., Kereskényi, R., & Forstner, B. (2006). Using Design Patterns in Mobile Communication Development. *Proceedings of IASTED Conference on Software Engineering 2006*, Innsbruck, Austria.

Davis, F.D. (1989). Perceived Usefulness, Perceived Ease of Use, and User Acceptance of Information Technology. *MIS Quarterly, 13*(3), 319-340.

GI Dagstuhl Research Seminar (2006). *Software Development Methodologies for Mobile Applications.* Retrieved March 26, 2007, from http://mobiapp.informatik.uni-stuttgart.de/mobiapp/CallForPaper?action=print .

Hansson, S.O. (2005). *Decision Theory, A Brief Introduction, 4, 24-25.* Retrieved, December 20, 2006, from http://www.infra.kth.se/~soh/decisiontheory.pdf .

Heikkinen, M. T., & Still, J. (2005). Business Networks and New Mobile Service Development. *Proceedings of the International Conference on Mobile Business (ICMB'05).*

Heyes, I. S. (2002). *Just Enough Wireless Computing.* Upper Saddle River, NI: Prentice Hall.

Horton, S. (2006). Designing Beneath the Surface of the Web. *Proceedings of WWW2006*, Edinburgh, UK.

Karam, G. M., & Casselman, R. S. (1993). A Cataloging Framework for Software Development Methods. *Computer, 26*(2), 35-39.

Mullur, A. A., Mattson, C. A., & Messac, A. (2003). New Decision Matrix Based Approach for Concept Selection Using Linear Physical Programming. *Proceedings of 44th AIAA/ASME/ASCE/AHS Structures, Structural Dynamics, and Material Conference*, Norfolk, Virginia.

Mullur, A. A., Mattson, C. A., & Messac, A. (2003b). Pitfalls of the Typical Construction of Decision Matrices for Concept Selection. *Proceedings of 41st Aerospace Sciences Meeting and Exhibit*, January 06-09, 2003, Reno, NV. 3-4.

Mavromoustakos, S., & Papanikolaou, K. (2006). Critical Success Factor for the Development of Mobile Learning Applications. *Proceedings of IASTED Conference on Internet and Multimedia Systems and Applications*, Innsbruck, Austria.

Pastor, J., & Whiddett, R. J. (1996). The Relationship between Systems Development Methodologies and Organizational Demographics: A Survey of New Zealand Organizations. *Proceedings of Information Systems Conference of New Zealand 1996.* 179.

Tarnacha, A., & Maitland, C. F. (2006). Entrepreneurship in Mobile Application Development. *Proceedings of ICEC'06*, Fredericton, Canada. (p. 590).

KEY TERMS

Decision Making Tool: A tool either electronic or not that is used to assist in decision making.

Decision Matrix: A matrix used to assist in decision making.

Electronic Matrix: An electronic version of a decision matrix.

Mobile Application: System application operating in mobile devices.

Mobile Development Methodology: Methodology used to develop mobile applications.

Mobile Novice Developer: Application developers that have limited experience in mobile development.

Perceived Usefulness: A measure of usefulness as perceived by potential application users.

Chapter XII
eBook Mobile Payment Process Model

Norshuhada Shiratuddin
Universiti Utara Malaysia, Malaysia

Shahizan Hassan
Universiti Utara Malaysia, Malaysia

Syamsul Bahrin Zaibon
Universiti Utara Malaysia, Malaysia

Sobihatun Nur Ab Salam
Universiti Utara Malaysia, Malaysia

ABSTRACT

Studies on the use of mobile payment (m-payment) method for buying electronic book (e-book) are very scarce, possibly not yet available. Consequently, a study was undertaken to accomplish the main aim of proposing an m-payment model for marketing and purchasing e-books. A number of process flow models are proposed to serve as diagrammatic representations of the process models that are of concerned. The models clearly specify all the entities involved, such as Telco, merchants, buyers, and e-book providers, and how the data and transactions, are flowing from one entity to another. The processes of browsing, buying, and downloading e-books are also documented. In validating the process flow models, two prototypes, a WAP and Web environments, were developed and tested to assess the model and system acceptance rating. Key findings indicate that m-payment is the most preferred payment method for buying e-book in higher learning institutions and the acceptance factors of such technology were found to be on the high and positive side.

INTRODUCTION

The project discussed in this article was motivated by a previous study titled Electronic Information Centre (eInfoC). eInfoC aims of providing academics a platform to publish and market their publications electronically was successfully implemented. Indeed, it was a pioneer project for publishing, promoting and marketing of electronic books (eBooks) in Malaysia particularly the higher learning institutions (HLIs). The project was initiated by several lecturers from the Universiti Utara Malaysia (UUM). The current payment practices in eInfoC are "forwarded by lecturer", credit cards, cash and cheque. However, due to buyers demands for a payment system that is accessible by the mass of students (especially HLIs), easy to use, convenient, and requires no major investment in the infrastructure and technologies, mobile payment (mPayment) was found through a survey in UUM as the most preferred solution.

mPayment can be defined as the use of mobile devices such as mobile phone, PDA (Personal Digital Assistance), tablet PC or mobile computer to make payment for purchasing goods and services. mPayment is popular among users for purchasing ring tones, games and music (Cellularnews.com, 2005), however the use of mPayment for buying eBook is scarce, possibly unavailable (Norshuhada, 2005; Norshuhada et al., 2006). Also, using mPayment method for buying eBook is seen as the most suitable method since majority of the higher learning institutions students own mobile phones. This is confirmed by a survey conducted in UUM (Norshuhada & Shahizan, 2005).

Therefore, to start implementing mPayment as the payment method for buying eBook, process flow models have to be proposed and developed, where the models serve as diagramatic representations of the processes that are involved. A study was undertaken to accomplish the objectives of proposing eBook mobile payment process flow models and assessing the acceptance of the technology. Next sections introduce mPayment concept and detail the proposed process flow. To validate the process flow models, a prototype was developed and this is discussed in the last section.

mPAYMENT CONCEPT

The emergence of mobile commerce (mCommerce) services and demand for these services is affected by the current mobile networks such as 2.5G, 3G and 4G. This provides an ideal environment for payment of content (digital and physical goods) and services. An interesting aspect about mPayment is that the mobile devices can be used as payment device for all types of payment situations, either electronic commerce (eCommerce) or standard commerce (Malte, 2001; Dahlstrom, 2001). McKitterick and Dowling (2003) stress that mPayment is nowadays gaining significant attraction and many users are already using mobile devices for mobile purchase (Adrian, 2002).

mPayment can be defined as any payment transactions involving the purchase of goods or services completed with wireless device such as a mobile phone, personal computer (wireless), or personal digital assistant (PDA). It is also defined as payments transactions carried out wirelessly via a mobile device; the process of two parties exchanging financial value using a mobile device in return for goods or services; and payment method, which is based on the mobile phone (Ondrus, 2003; Malte, 2001; Rabussier, 2001; Lussanet, 2001; Mobile Payment Forum, 2002; Gross, et al., 2004).

Based on the above definition, a fundamental demand for the mobile device is that it must be able to connect to a network to initiate a payment. The network could be GSM or Internet and the clearing and settlement instance could be a bank or mobile operator (Cervera, 2002). The most popular concept of mPayment is users are paying from mobile phones using either prepaid or post paid methods. In prepaid method, consumers pay in advance to obtain the content they desire with prepaid accounts that are deducted after each payment session. Voice prepaid cards and electronic purse are examples of these kinds of payment methods. In post paid method, payment is made through mobile phone bill (Ruengprat, 2003). Consumers receive the content and consume it before paying. In this article, we classify prepaid and post paid method as an mPayment, which is the basis of our proposed process flow models, discussed in the next section.

mPAYMENT PROCESS FLOW FOR BUYING EBOOKS

Here, we propose a comprehensive process flow for mobile payment system for buying eBook. Before we discuss the flow, which is in Process Flow Diagram (PFD), an overview of the used of Premium SMS (P-SMS) as the payment scheme for buying eBook and Receipt System as the method for collecting purchased eBook are discussed.

Premium SMS (P-SMS)

P-SMS is a profit sharing based system; a telecommunication company (Telco) and eBook Provider (eP) will share the profit from the transaction on the agreed ratio per successful SMS replied back to the buyer.

Telco as the network provider will deliver the SMS message and charge the buyer for the transaction while the eP will store, list, market, promote and provide the eBook. For example:

- Buyer A sends an SMS message to eInfoC short-code number (for example 36525) with request to purchase eBook A that is worth USD 4.95.
- The eInfoC will reply with a receipt to the corresponding buyer via Telco.
- Telco will forward the receipt to the buyer and charge the buyer with USD 4.95.
- Telco will share the revenue (USD 4.95) with eInfoC on the agreed ratio, for example 30 % to Telco and 70 % to eInfoC. Thus, Telco will receive USD 1.485 and eInfoC will receive USD 3.465 for the transaction.

Receipt System

Receipt is an SMS message sent out to the buyers from the eP that contains acknowledgement of successful transaction, password for the eBook purchased, and instructions on how to download (collect) the eBook. Buyers can use the receipt to collect the purchased eBook by visiting the eP's web site and entering the supplied password.

Process Flow

Figure 1 shows all the entities in the system, which consists of:

- **Buyers:** Buyers with mobile phones that support WAP and SMS function.
- **Merchant:** Merchant has the infrastructure to enable the P-SMS system and also has deal with several Telcos, thus eliminating the need for eP to negotiate with each individual Telco. Therefore, Merchant can act as the intermediary between eP and Telco.
- **Telco:** Telco as the wireless network provider will deliver the SMS message and charge the buyer according to the eBook price. The revenue from the transaction will be shared between Telco and eP.
- **Message Centre (MC):** All SMS messages that are transmitted to or from a mobile phone will be transmitted first to the MC. MC will process the message, store it and determine the destination address of the receiver.

- **eP:** The eP provides the eBook for sale. eP also pays fee to merchant to handle the mPayment system.
- **WAP site:** WAP site is the online eBook store that can be accessed from a mobile phone. Buyers can view lists of eBook product for sale and instruction on how to purchase the product.
- **Web site:** Buyers who purchased the eBook through P-SMS can download their eBooks from this web site by entering their mobile phone numbers and eBook passwords.

Using the PFD diagram in Figure 1 as the framework, the process flow can be further classified into three phases, which are:

- **Phase 1:** Browsing eBook Provider WAP site and making purchase.
- **Phase 2:** Payment scheme using P-SMS.
- **Phase 3:** Collecting purchased eBook using the receipt system.

All these three phases made up a system, which is called **mPSMS**.

Before proceeding to the next sections, readers should be familiarized with these terminologies:

- **MO:** Mobile Originated, an SMS message sent from a mobile phone, contains a product's keyword for an item to be purchased.
- **MT (Receipt):** Mobile Terminated, an SMS message sent to a mobile phone, contains a message acknowledging the successfulness of transaction, password, and instruction to download the eBook.
- **MC:** Message Center, when a user sends out an SMS message, the message will be transmitted first to the MC. MC will process the message, store it and determine the destination address of the receiver.
- **eBook Code:** A code used to identify an eBook, for example EB001.
- **Short-code number:** A special 5 digits number used for P-SMS scheme, for example 36652.

Phase 1: Browsing eP WAP Site and Making Purchase

In this phase, buyers browse the eP WAP site via his mobile phone, view description about eBook and make a purchase by sending an SMS message to the provided

Figure 1. Entities in mPSMS system

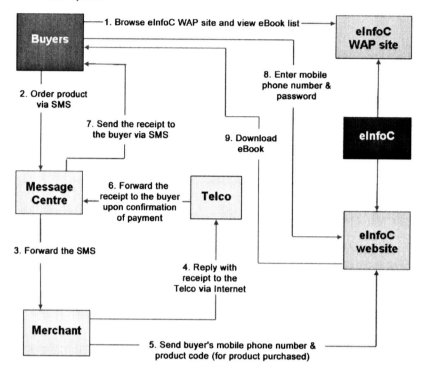

Short-code number. The processes of browsing eP WAP site and making purchase as depicted in Figure 2 contains of the following steps:

i.   A buyer browses the eP WAP site via micro browser embedded in the buyer's mobile phone.
ii. The buyer views a list of eBook items for sale and selects the item to view its descriptions.
iii. A brief description about the items will be displayed along with the eBook Code and the Short-code number.
iv. To buy an item, the buyer sends an SMS message (MO message) from his mobile phone. The SMS contains the eBook Code sent to the Short-code number.

Phase 2: Payment Scheme using P-SMS

In this phase, the payment process will be performed. Merchant will send the transaction detail to the Telco and eP, also the Receipt message (MT) to Telco, then Telco will charge the buyer and forward the Receipt to the buyer. The payment scheme as depicted in Figure 3 consists of the following steps:

i.   The SMS message from the buyer will be transmitted to the MC.
ii.   The short-code will be used by the MC to identify the corresponding recipient (Merchant).
iii. MC will forward the SMS message to the corresponding Merchant.
iv.   Merchant upon receiving the SMS message; will process the request and respond back with the Receipt message.
v.   Merchant sends the Receipt message to the buyer through the Telco.
vi.   The transaction is recorded by the Merchant once the Receipt message is sent out to the buyer.
vii. Merchant sends the transaction detail (buyer's phone number and eBook Code) to the eP.
viii. eP will record the buyer's phone number and eBook Code to the corresponding entry in the database.
ix.   Telco upon receiving the Receipt message will validate the buyer's account to determine the account status. For the prepaid user; Telco will

check if the user has sufficient balance (if valid proceed to step xi, else proceed to step x).

x. The Receipt message will be discarded and the transaction ends.

xi. The Receipt message will be transmitted to the corresponding buyer and the charge is deducted from the buyer's prepaid amount. For the post-paid user, the charge is incurred in his monthly bill; the transaction will be recorded by the Telco.

xii. The buyer will receive the Receipt message from the Telco via SMS

Phase 3: Collecting Purchased eBook using Receipt System

In this phase, when a buyer has received the Receipt from Telco via SMS, he can then log on to eP web site,

enter the supplied password and download the eBook. The collecting purchased eBook phase as depicted in Figure 4 consists of the following steps:

i. The buyer visits the eP web site and he logins (A new user must register with the web site first).

ii. The buyer enters his mobile phone number to view purchased items.

iii. List of eBook purchased by the buyer will be displayed (the system will match the buyer's mobile phone number with the stored mobile phone number in the database).

iv. The buyer selects an eBook and keys in the password.

v. System will verify the password (if the password is valid proceed to step viii, else proceed to step vii).

vi. An error message will be displayed.

Figure 2. Phase 1 - Browsing eInfoC WAP site and making purchase

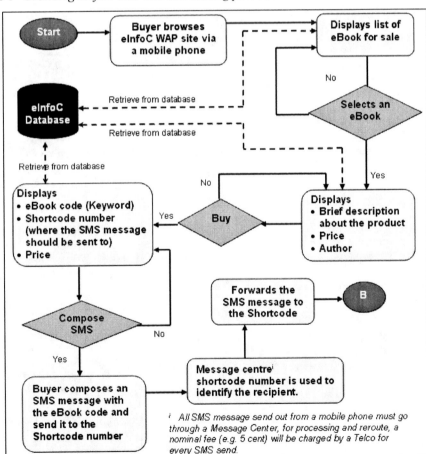

Figure 3. Phase 2 - Payment scheme transaction process

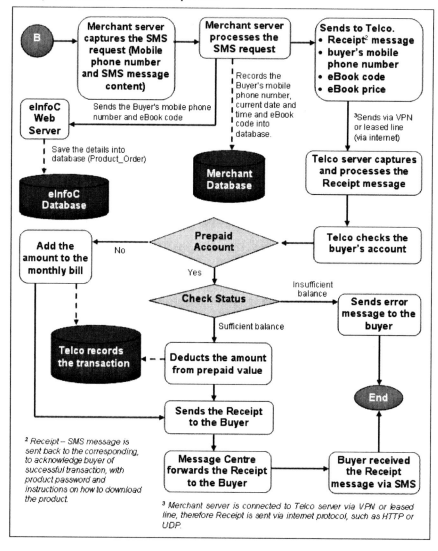

vii. The eBook will be downloaded to the buyer's computer.

viii. The system will enter the eBook Code and buyer's phone number to the *Delivered table* in the database, served as a remark that the eBook has been delivered to the corresponding buyer.

ix. The system will delete the eBook Code and buyer's phone number from the *ProductOrdered table*.

x. Repeat step v if the user has more than one eBook to be downloaded.

xi. Transaction ends when user has no more eBook to download.

DEMONSTRATING PROCESS FLOW THROUGH PROTOTYPING

In this phase, prototyping was utilized in order to demonstrate the process flow of buying eBook using mPayment:

a. WAP prototype for the first phase of the process flow (i.e. browsing of eP WAP site and make purchase)

b. P-SMS prototype for the second phase of the process flow

c. Web prototype for the third phase of the process flow (i.e. downloading of eBook)

Figure 4. Phase 3 - Collecting purchased eBook using receipt system

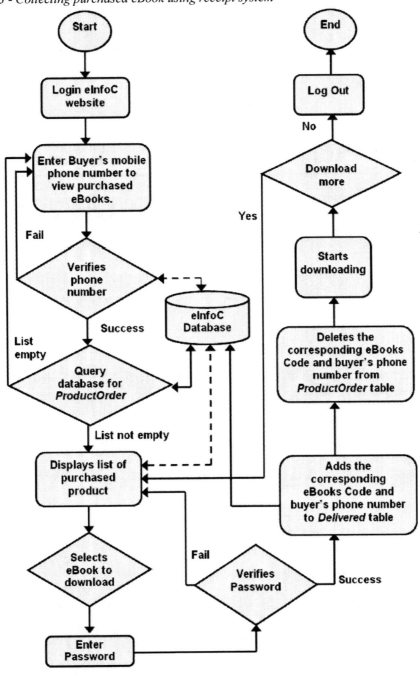

The eInfoC web site was used as the design basis since the flow is based on the eInfoC web site. Four design factors identified as the design guidelines for mobile application were followed (a) simple interface, (b) concise and short text, (c) keep data entry to a minimum, if possible use option list, and (d) use images sparingly. These resulted in four main screens used for browsing and purchasing at the WAP site:

Screen 1: The welcoming page for eInfoC WAP site. A brief description about the site will be displayed; a user needs to press the soft key labeled "List" to proceed to next page.

Figure 5. Descriptions of eBook

Figure 6. Purchase instructions

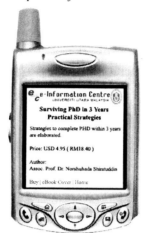

Figure 7. Phone number authentication page

Screen 2: The list of eBooks for sale will be retrieved from the database and displayed onto the mobile phone screen.

Screen 3: A buyer highlights eBook using the arrow key and presses the soft key labeled "Select" to view its description. The system retrieved the data from the database. A brief description about the items will be displayed along with the price and authors. See Figure 5.

Screen 4: User selects the "Buy" link to view buying instruction. An instruction on how to purchase, along with the product code, short-code number and product's price will be displayed. See Figure 6.

Then, a downloading facility was developed for the eInfoC web site. The objective of the download facility is to demonstrate the third phase of the process flow for collecting purchased eBooks using the Receipt system. The facility is a web-based application and requires a Microsoft Windows based web server to host the application and a web browser. This facility was developed using the ASP technology. Five main screens are involved in downloading the purchased item.

Figure 8. Entering password and downloading eBook

Screen 1: The buyer visits the eInfoC website at http://www.e-infoc.uum.edu.my/ and clicks the menu to download the eBook or enter directly the URL at http://www.e-infoc.uum.edu.my/ downloadWAP/login.asp.

Screen 2: The buyer enters his/her mobile phone number to view purchased items. See Figure 7.

Screen 3: A list of eBooks purchased by the buyer will be displayed (the system will match the buyer's mobile phone number with the stored mobile phone number in the database).

Screen 4: The buyer selects an eBook to download and keys in the password (as provided by the SMS. The password acts as a receipt). See Figure 8. The system will verify the password, if the password is valid it proceeds to the next step or else an error message will be displayed.

Screen 5: A successful transaction will allow a user to download the purchased eBook and it will be downloaded to the buyer's computer.

Acceptance of mPSMS

A survey was conducted in February 2006 to determine the degree of user acceptance of mPayment using mPSMS. A set of electronic questionnaire was developed asking participants, to provide their views on the items questioned. The items in the questionnaire were divided into six user acceptance categories or factors: Wireless Trust Environment, Perceived Usefulness, Perceived Ease of Use, Facilitating Conditions, Systems Complexity, and Social Influences (Lu, Yu & Yao, 2003).

A total of 48 mobile phone users participated in this study. These participants were allowed to test the mPSMS by browsing and buying eBooks from eInfoC. After the testing, the participants were required to fill up the electronic questionnaire. A five-point Likert scale was used, which are: 1-Completely disagree, 2-Disagree, 3-Unsure, 4-Agree and 5-Strongly agree. Based on the total number of items in each category (refer to Figure 9), the mean analysis was tabulated accordingly. The calculated means and standard deviations are: Wireless Trust Environment (4.03, s=.88), Perceived Usefulness (4.29, s=.79), Perceived Ease of Use (3.98, s=.89), Facilitating Conditions such as buying instructions, accessibility speed, access cost, and assistance (3.93, s=.84), Systems Complexity (3.76, s=.88), and Social Influences such as feeling proud, confidence and status (4.14, s=.75).

Overall findings indicate that mobile phone users are prepared to accept payment method via SMS such as proposed by this study (i.e. mPSMS). This is supported by the overall mean of users' acceptance factors which was found to be 4.02 ($p > 0.05$). Furthermore, respondents agree that it is more secured to buy via SMS because money is deducted from mobile phone prepaid card or paid after as compared to other payment methods such as deducting from bank account. In addition, they also agree to the fact that they feel secured when using mPSMS as they are not required to provide any personal information (mean = 4.20, s = .80).

Also, most agree that the design of the interface for the system is suitable for mobile devices (mean = 4.17, s =.79). Moreover, the downloading time of mPSMS is also acceptable and the transaction of SMS payment is executed successfully (mean = 3.80, s =.83).

CONCLUSION

In this project, P-SMS that employs profit sharing approach and electronic receipt system are proposed for the payment scheme in buying eBook. We called the system mPSMS. The use of SMS as the payment medium caters the demand of potential buyers especially in higher learning environments. eInfoC that was used as the case study in this project, can now offer the mPayment as one of the payment methods.

The deliverables of the project can be summed up as follows:

• Buyer's preference of mPayment modes in buying eBooks were identified. It was found that mPayment is the most preferred method compared to others such as mobile banking (mBanking) and electronic purse (ePurse).
• The models proposed clearly specify all the entities involved such as Telco, merchants, buyers, and eInfoC and how the data and transactions are flowing from one entity to another. The processes of browsing, buying, and downloading eBooks are also documented.
• Process flow model for mPayment was implemented successfully. The theoretical process flow that was designed based on the literature review and interview with representatives from

Figure 9. Contents of questionnaire

1. Wireless Trust Environment:
    a) mPSMS is secured because money is deducted from my mobile phone pre-paid card.
    b) Compared to payment such as deducting from my bank account, mPSMS is more secured when buying via SMS.
    c) I feel secured since I do not need to provide any personal information.

2. Perceived Usefulness:
    a) mPSMS speeds up the process of buying eBooks.
    b) It is very convenient for me to be able to browse eBooks via my mobile phone.
    c) It is very convenient for me to be able to buy eBooks via SMS payment method.
    d) mPSMS is not useful in buying eBooks.

3. Perceived Ease of Use:
    a) I found that mPSMS is easy to use when browsing and buying eBooks.
    b) I found that mPSMS is easy to learn when browsing and buying eBooks.
    c) The navigation system (going from one menu to another) is poor.
    d) Learning to use the system when buying eBooks takes little time.

4. Facilitating Conditions:
    a) The instructions provided when buying eBooks using the mobile technology is clear.
    b) The mobile device can get access to the system successfully.
    c) The cost of mobile Internet access is expensive in Malaysia.
    d) I am aware that buying via mobile devices is legal in Malaysia.
    e) I am aware that Malaysian government is encouraging the use of Wireless Internet Mobile Technology.

5. System Complexity
    a) The design of the interface for the system is suitable for mobile devices.
    b) The downloading (response) time is acceptable.
    c) The transaction of SMS payment was executed successfully.
    d) Small screen size of mobile devices affects the placements of displayed items.

6. Social Influences
    a) I feel proud of myself to be able to use mobile device to browse WAP sites (e.g. eInfoC).
    b) I feel proud of myself to be able to use mobile device to perform business transaction (e.g. buy using mPSMS payment system).
    c) I will definitely tell others to use mobile phones for browsing and buying WAP sites.

the merchants and banks was proven to be applicable.

- Six inter-related factors of technology acceptance for mPayment and their importance were identified. It is evident that any attempt to implement mPayment should take into account these six factors accordingly - Social influences, Wireless trust environment, Perceived usefulness, Perceived ease of use, System complexity, and Facilitating conditions.
- Prototype for browsing WAP site and making purchase was developed successfully. The prototype proved to be practicable and ready to be enhanced for a complete version of the eInfoC.
- Prototype for payment scheme transaction flow was developed effectively. This prototype is very important for related and future works as it shows that paying via mobile phones is convenient and practicable especially when buying eBook which involves only a small amount of money.
- Prototype for collecting purchased eBooks was developed successfully. This is another important outcome which shows that, once payment has been made via SMS; potential buyers can download easily the purchased materials.

Despite achieving the objectives, this study also has some limitations. First, although electronic contents in HLI consist of various types of materials such as eBooks, electronic journal (eJournal), electronic report (eReport), electronic magazine (eMagazine), and electronic proceeding (eProceeding), the proposed mPayment system was tested only on eBooks. Testing the payment scheme on other type of contents would further strengthen the findings of this project. Second, the mPayment process flow model was developed based on the assumption that a merchant will always be needed for the implementation. As such, a merchant, who provides the gateway to Telcos, is included as one of the entities in the process flow. However, the process flow can be improvised if the organization adopting the process flow model can deal directly with Telcos. Finally, no element of security was catered in this study. Extra measures to keep the mobile transactions secure and the financial information private should be of greatest concern (Blau, 2006). Song (2001) discussed the issues of mPayment and security in his article, and his study ought to be replicated to ensure transactions are secured.

REFERENCES

Adrian, B. (2002). Overview of the Mobile Payments Market 2002 Through 2007, *Gartner Research R-18-1818*, 22 November.

Blau, J. (2006). *PayPal goes mobile with payment service*. InfoWorld. Retrieved 7 Sept, 2006 from http://www.infoworld.com/article/06/04/06/77196_HNpaypalmobile_1.html?B-TO-C

Cellular news.com. (2005). *Mobile content market set to triple within a year*. Retrieved Jun 10, 2005 from http://www.cellular-news.com/search/index.php?term=malaysia

Cervera, A. (2002). *Analysis of J2ME for Developing Mobile Payment Systems*. IT University of Copenhagen. Retrieved 20 February, 2005 from http://www.microdevnet.com/articles/techtalk/mpayment?content_id=3734

Dahlström, E. (2001), *The common future of wallets and ATMs*, Mobile phones!, ePSO Newsletter Vol. 1.

Gross, S., Müller, R., Lampe, M., & Fleisch, E. (2004). Requirements and Technologies for Ubiquitous Payment. *Proceedings of Multikonferenz Wirtschaftsinformatik, Techniques and Applications for Mobile Commerce*, Essen, Germany.

Lu, J., Yu, C-S, & Yao, J. E. (2003). Technology acceptance model for wireless Internet. *Internet Research: Electronic Networking Applications and Policy*, 13, 206-222.

Lussanet, M. De (2001). *Mobile Payment's Slow Start*. Forrester Research, May.

Malte, K. (2001). *The Future of M-payment: Business Options and Policy Issues*. E-PSO Background Paper, No. 2, Institute for Prospective Technological Studies. Retrieved 10 Sept, 2005 from http://epso.intrasoft.lu/papers/Backgrnd-2.pdf

McKitterick, D., & Dowling, J. (2003). *State of the Art Review of Mobile Payment Technology*. Retrieved 25 January, 2005 from http://www.cs.tcd.ie/publications/tech-reports/reports.03/TCD-CS-2003-24.pdf

Mobile Payment Forum (2002). *Enabling Secure, Interoperable, and User-friendly Mobile Payments*. Mobile Payment Forum White Paper.

Norshuhada, S. (2005). E-Books in Higher Education: Technology, E-Marketing Prospects and Pricing Strategy. *Journal of Electronic Commerce in Organizations, 3*(2), 1-16.

Norshuhada, S., & Shahizan, H. (2005). Collaborative eBook Publishing and Marketing: Higher Institutions and E-Publishers. *International Journal of Book, 2,* 209-219.

Norshuhada, S., Shahizan, H., Syamsul Bahrin Z., & Sobihatun Nur, S. (2006). *E-Content Payment Methods: Process Flow Models and Technology Acceptance of mPayment and E-Purse.* Research report, Universiti Utara Malaysia, Malaysia.

Ondrus, J. (2003). *Mobile Payments: A Tool Kit For A Better Understanding Of The Market.* University of Lausanne. Retrieved 2 February, 2005 from http://www.hec.unil.ch/jondrus/files/papers/mpayment.pdf.

Rabussier, S. (2001). *E-Banking / M-Banking*, Oppenheimer Research. Retrieved 20 August 2005 from http://www.fininter.net/retail banking/Oppenheim E_Banking_eng.pdf

Rueangprat, S. (2003). *Mobile Bill Payment System.* Unpublished MSc Report. Universiti Utara Malaysia.

Song, X. J. (2005). *Mobile Payment and Security.* Telecom Software and Multimedia, Helsinki University of Technology.

KEY TERMS

Electronic Content: Content or services in electronic forms.

Mobile Banking: Wireless banking services.

Mobile Commerce: The extension of eCommerce from wired to wireless computers and telecommunications, and from fixed locations to anytime, anywhere, and anyone.

Mobile Payment: Any payment transactions involving the purchase of goods or services completed with wireless device such as a mobile phone, personal computer (wireless), or personal digital assistant (PDA).

Prototype: A working example of a concept.

WAP: A technology which provides a mechanism for displaying internet information on a mobile phone or any wireless device.

User Acceptance: A measure of technology acceptance.

Chapter XIII
Innovative Marketing Strategies for Wireless Broadband Services in the Sri Lankan Context

Dilupa Ranatunga
University of Colombo, Sri Lanka

Rasika Withanage
University of Wales, UK

Dinesh Arunatileka
Freelance, Sri Lanka

ABSTRACT

This chapter describes marketing strategies in concept for wireless broadband services in the Sri Lankan market. It also emphasizes different technologies offering fixed and mobile broadband services. Wi-Fi services which are mentioned here has been on offer for few years but actual marketing of such services are not actively done in Sri Lanka. Various marketing strategies that could be used to market this technology are also analyzed to gain an insight to all readers. In addition, a grid is provided to help readers to choose between different available technologies.

INTRODUCTION

This chapter describes innovative approaches of marketing Internet broadband services delivered by the wireless access technologies. The high speed broadband connectivity, through the Internet has resulted in a truly global market place, where people can find products and services they desire at one location. World Wide Web has become a global library and an information repository that is unprecedented in the history of mankind. The Internet is almost a representative of a doctor, lawyer, banker, government official – providing the users with a direct channel to government authorities, health services and local communities. Furthermore, the Internet is also becoming the entertainment channel of choice, offering the users an unparalleled selection of music, TV, video and news at our fingertips. The Internet will continue to develop as the place for information, communication, interaction and media consumption.

Broadband wireless sits at the confluence of two of the most remarkable growth stories of the telecommunications industry in recent years. Both wireless and broadband have enjoyed rapid mass-market adoption on their own right.

Wireless mobile services grew from 11 million subscribers worldwide in 1990 to more than two billion in 2006. During the same period, the Internet grew from being a curious academic tool to having about a billion users *(ITU. Telecommunications indicators, 2004)*. This exponential growth of the Internet is driving demand for higher-speed Internet-access services, leading to a parallel growth in broadband adoption. In less than a decade, broadband subscription worldwide has grown from virtually zero to over 250 million *(In-stat Report. Paxton. 2006)*.

However, to enjoy the complete benefits of the Internet, there is a need for high speed broadband connectivity. As a result, Internet broadband connectivity has become one of the most widespread communication developments ever and the growth in demand for high-speed Internet connections is said to continue. Today there are over 250 million broadband users: by 2012 this figure is forecast to grow to over 1.8 billion *(Strategy Analytics & Internal Ericsson)*.

Most people today experience broadband via a PC connected over a fixed line. However, for many of the broadband users expected to get online over the next few years, a fixed line is unlikely to be the choice. As per the Ovum report, wireless networks will be the primary broadband access method for the upcoming user categories (www.store.ovum.com).

Furthermore, once the users start depending on their broadband Internet connection that they want it wherever they may be. This means broadband cannot be limited only to a fixed connection at a physical address. People prefer a broadband that connects them to their services all of the time, whatever their device type or wherever their location. Figure 1 below compares the broadband markets of the world by region.

As per Figure 1, we can analyze Internet subscribers, based on their type of Internet connectivity.

Figure 2 depicts different connection types available for broadband access.

As per ITU statistics, Asia pacific region, having the highest number of internet subscribes as a region has a subscriber base in which almost twice the size of the internet subscribers in the American region. In Asia, substantial economic growth is common in

every country. Thus, a huge potential in increase of demand for broadband internet connectivity exists and expected in the future as well. However, Asian nations do not have fully deployed copper networks across their cities and villages. Therefore, in order to fulfill the demand for broadband connectivity, service providers have to identify alternative solutions rather than laying copper or fiber networks across the countries which is expensive as well as time consuming. As a result, service providers in Asia are looking for a speedy way to provide broadband connectivity without a huge capital outlay on network infrastructure. Wireless broadband technologies have proven that, they can play an immense role when providing broadband connectivity to regions which have no fully fledge copper networks *(ITU, Telecommunications indicators, 2004)*.

Wireless Broadband Technologies

Broadband wireless is about bringing the broadband experience to a wireless context, which offers users unique benefits and convenience. Benefits in the form of better coverage, higher speeds, more security and reliability are few of them. There are two fundamentally different types of broadband wireless services. The first type attempts to provide a set of services similar to that of the traditional fixed-line broadband but using wireless as the medium of transmission. This type, called *fixed wireless broadband,* can be thought of as a competitive alternative to DSL or cable modem. The second type of broadband wireless, called *mobile broadband,* offers the additional functionality of portability and mobility. Mobile broadband attempts to bring broadband applications to new user experience scenarios and hence can offer the end user a very different value proposition. Figure 3 predict the forecast of broadband growth.

According to Fgure 3, the future users projected would prefer to have the accessibility to the internet even while traveling. Thus to provide fully fledged mobile broadband connectivity, requires a massive improvements in mobile networks. Consequently when compared with fixed broadband solutions, mobile broadband solutions are costlier due to additional dimension of mobility. However, for domestic uses, people are more concerned about speed and the affordability rather than mobility, thus fixed solutions are more fitting for domestic users. Also fixed technology products are more mature than the mobile products that are in the market today.

Figure 1. Internet subscribers by region (Adapted from: ITU World Telecommunication/ICT Indicators Database)

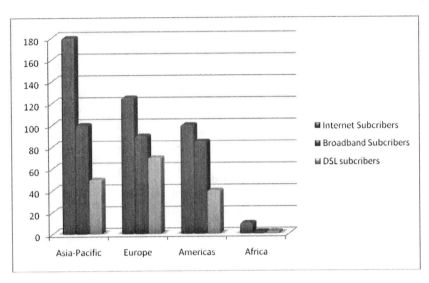

Subscriptions (Millions)

Figure 2. Internet connection type, Asia Pacific region

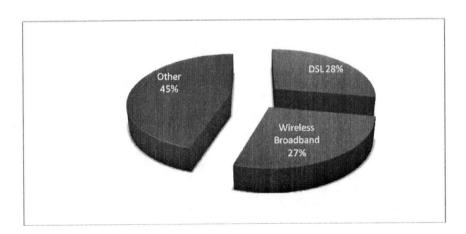

The constant growth of broadband market will enable new technologies to emerge, and it is difficult to predict which existing technologies will survive in the future. Described below is some technologies used currently for wireless broadband services.

WiMax

WiMax is short for *Worldwide Interoperability for Microwave Access*, and it also goes by the IEEE name 802.16. WiMax can provide broadband wireless access up to 50 km for fixed stations, and 5 - 15 km for mobile stations. WiMax is a fitting technology especially in countries like Sri Lanka where copper networks have not been fully developed. On the other hand, WiMax is a technology which is capable of providing enterprise wide connectivity for business, remote users to connect to corporate networks and to provide Internet connectivity at far greater ranges than current wireless

Figure 3. Forecasted broadband growth based on reported subscriptions (Adopted from: OVUM, Strategy Analytics & Internal Ericsson)

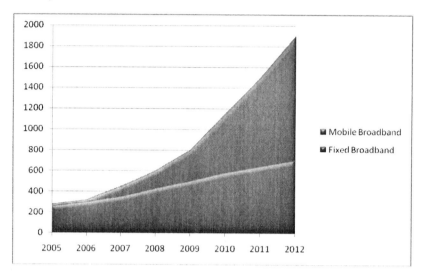

Subscriptions (Millions)

technologies allow.(*Understanding the fundamental of WiMax, 2007*)

Wi-Fi

Wi-Fi is short for wireless fidelity and is the term used generically when referring to any type of IEEE 802.11 networks, which is the current standard being used to provide wireless access today. A Wi-Fi hotspot is defined as any location in which IEEE 802.11 (wireless) technology both exists and is available for use by consumers. In some cases, the wireless access is free, and in others, wireless carriers charge for Wi-Fi usage. Generally, the most common usage of Wi-Fi technology is for laptop users to gain Internet access in locations such as airports, coffee shops, and so on, where Wi-Fi technology can be used to help consumers in their pursuit of work-based or recreational Internet usage.

HSDPA (High Speed Downlink Packet Access) / HSPA

High-Speed Downlink Packet Access (HSDPA) is a 3G (third generation) mobile telephony communications

protocol in the High-Speed Packet Access (HSPA) family, which allows networks based on Universal Mobile Telecommunications System (UMTS) to have higher data transfer speeds and capacity. Current HSDPA deployments support down-link speeds of 1.8, 3.6, 7.2 and 14.4 Mbps. Further speed increases are planned for the near future. The networks are then to be upgraded to Evolved HSPA, which provides speeds of 42 Mbps downlink in its first release. (*Basic Concepts of HSPA February 2007*)

Comparison between Wireless Broadband Solutions

Broadband technologies have their own advantages and disadvantages when compared. As a result the choice for a broadband solution has to be done through a comparison among available technologies. Before comparing technologies, the prospective users have to identify, why they require a broadband connection. Thereafter the user needs to identify traffic parameters for each of their applications using broadband technology. Table 1 tabulates this information.

Table 1 identifies the traffic parameters for each and every broadband wireless application. Subsequent to identifying traffic parameters, prospective broadband users can select best fitting technology for them, rather than choosing blindly. Table 2 gives depicts this picture.

There are a host of technologies competing to deliver commercial mobile broadband services. By far the most successful is HSPA (*Strategy Analytics, 2006)*. HSPA is a state-of-the art technology that provides mobile and wireless broadband services for the vast majority of the market, with unsurpassed performance and economies of scale.

Though it shows a tremendous performance in providing mobile broadband, still tariff rates are not that affordable for most users. When selecting a broadband technology, if the tariff rates are the primary concern, HSPA would not be the ideal solution. This technology is more appropriate for business people & frequent travelers, where they don't do heavy download.

Currently, many companies are closely examining WiMax for "last mile" connectivity. The resulting competition may bring lower pricing for both home and business customers or bring broadband access to places where it has been economically unavailable.

Among most of the wireless fixed broadband users, WiMax is a well-liked technology, because of the low prices and the ability to provide extensive coverage from a single base station.

The bandwidth and reach of WiMax make it suitable for the following potential applications:

- Connecting Wi-Fi hotspots with other parts of the Internet.
- Providing a wireless alternative to cable and DSL for last mile broadband access.
- Providing data and telecommunications services.

Having looked at the different technologies available for wireless broadband to be delivered to the customers, it is important to look at the strategies for market development. The next section explains a strategic marketing approach for wireless broadband technology.

Marketing of Wireless Broadband

Wireless Broadband Marketing is becoming competitive day by day due to the higher penetration in Internet Business Market. Internet Service Providers have developed various strategies to create personalized/ customized packages/Plans to fulfill the consumers'

needs while fitting into their valet. Let's look at the bases of Strategic Choice.

Bases of Strategic Choice

Corporate purpose and aspirations are based on four concepts

- Ownership
- Mission and strategic intent
- Scope and diversity
- The global dimension

Bases of SBU Strategy

- Achieving competitive advantage
- Price-based strategies
- Differentiation strategies
- Focus strategies

Enhancing SBU Strategy: Corporate Parenting

- Portfolio management
- Financial strategy
- The role of the corporate parent
- The parenting matrix

Based on the above choices, Strategies can be developed on the following routes as depicted in Figure 4.

The Strategy Clock: Bowman's Competitive Strategy Options

The 'Strategy Clock' is based upon the work of Cliff Bowman (C.Bowman and D. Faulkner 'Competitive and Corporate Strategy - Irwin - 1996). It's another suitable way to analyze a company's competitive position in comparison to the offerings of competitors. As with Porter's Generic Strategies, Bowman considers competitive advantage in relation to cost advantage or differentiation advantage. There are six core strategic options as depicted in figure 05.

The Strategy Clock

1. Low price/low added value, Likely to be segment specific

Table 1. Traffic parameters for broadband wireless applications (Adapted from Source: Understanding the fundamental of WiMax (Prentice Hall))

Parameter	Interactive Gaming	Voice	Streaming Media	Data	Video
Data rate	50-85 Kbps	4-64 Kbps	5-384 Kbps	0.01-100 Mbps	>1Mbps
Example applications	Interactive gaming	VoIP	Music, Video clips, Speech	Web browsing e-mail, Instant messaging, telnet, file downloads	IPTV, Peer- to- peer video sharing
Traffic flow	Real time	Real time Continues	Continues, Bursty	Non- real time, Bursty	Continues
Packet loss	Zero	<1%	<1% for Audio <2% for Video	Zero	$<10^{-8}$

2. Low price, Risk of price war and low margins/ need to be cost leader

3. Hybrid, Low cost base and reinvestment in, low price and differentiation

4. Differentiation, (a) Without price premium, Perceived added value by user, yielding market share benefits, (b) With price premium, Perceived added value sufficient to bear price premium

5. Focused differentiation, Perceived added value to a particular segment, warranting price premium

6. Increased price/standard, Higher margins if competitors do not, value, follow/risk of losing market share

7. Increased price/low value, Only feasible in monopoly situation

8. Low value/standard price, Loss of market share

Low Price Strategies

When considering Sri Lankan market place, by using a low price strategy, operators will be able offer raw internet facilities without any value addition to the consumers.

- ADSL/Broadband Internet, delivered through the copper network in Sri Lanka without virus protection or filtering
- Dial up internet offerings - Internet facility only

- Mobile internet offerings using WAP /GPRS & Edge technologies

Low Price Strategies Could Be Successful If

- The competitor is the *cost leader* ... but is this sustainable?
- All sources of cost advantages are exploited, developing competences in low cost management ... but the danger is a low (perceived) value service
- A competitor has cost advantage over competitors in a price sensitive markets segment ... but this may mean focusing on that market segment

Hybrid Strategies

Broadband products can be positioned and marketed using Hybrid strategies. Using Wireless technologies such as WiMax, HSPA, & 3G, Operators will be able to bundle voice & Data packages to the consumers in the market.

- Offering lower speed Broadband internet products (512Kb) to the home segment bundled with IP telephony facilities
- Offering own Web space facilities (15MB) with voice & data

Table 2. Technology wise analysis (Adapted from Source: Understanding the fundamental of WiMax (Prentice Hall))

Parameter	Fixed WiMax	Mobile WiMax	HSPA	Wi-Fi
Standard	IEEE 802.16-2004	IEEE 802.16e-2005	3GPP Release 6	IEEE 802.11 a/g/n
Peak down link data rate	9.4 Mbps in 3.5 MHz with 3:1 DL-to-UL ratio TDD; 6.1 Mbps with 1:1	46 Mbps[a] with 3:1 DL-to-UL ratio TDD; 32 Mbps with 1:1	14.4 Mbps using all 15 codes; 7.2Mbps with 10 codes	54 Mbps[b] shared using 802.11a/g;
Peak up link data rate	3.3 Mbps in 3.5 MHz using 3:1 DL-to-UL ratio; 6.5 Mbps with 1:1	7 Mbps in 10 MHz using 3:1 Dl-to-UL ratio; 4 Mbps using 1:1	1.4 Mbps initially; 5.8 Mbps later	
Bandwidth	3.5MHz and 7 MHz in 3.5GHz band; 10 MHz in 5.8 GHz band	3.5MHz, 7 MHz, 5 MHz, 10 MHz and 8.75 MHz initially	5 MHz	20 MHz for 802.11 a/g; 20/40 MHz for 802.11n
Duplexing	TDD, FDD	TDD initially	FDD	TDD
Frequency	3.5 GHZ and 5.8 GHz initially	2.3GHz,2.5 GHz and 3.5 GHz initially	800/900/1,800/1,900/2,100 MHz	2.4 GHz, 5GHz
Coverage	3-5 miles	<2 miles	1-3 miles	<100 ft indoors;
Mobility	Not applicable	Mid	High	Low

Figure 4. Development strategies

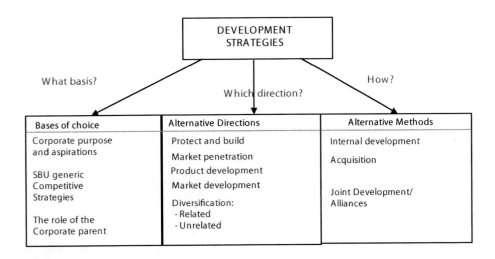

Figure 5. Bowman's competitive strategy options

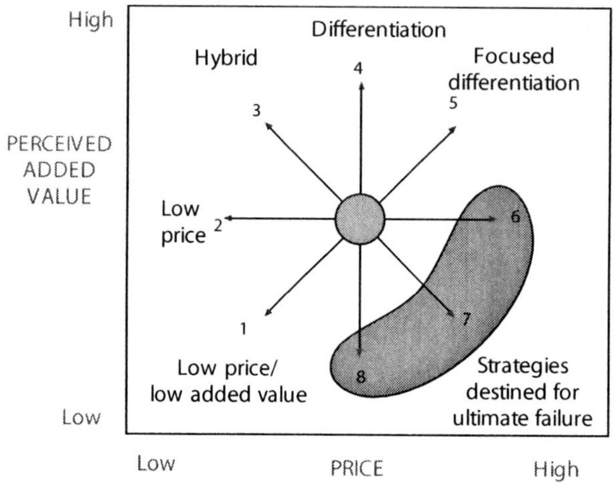

Source: C.Bowman and D.Faulkner. Competitive and Corporate Strategy, Irwin, 1996.

Differentiated Strategies

Some of the differentiated strategies would be to bundle few products and services as one offering and focus on SOHO & SME segments.

- Offering Data, Voice, PBX, Email, Web space as a one package
- Offering higher bandwidth products while customising as per individual requirements

The Success of Differentiation Strategies Depends On

- Clear identification of *who the customer* is
- Understanding *what is valued by the customer*
- Clear identification of *who the competitors* are and the value they offer
- Bases of differentiation which are *difficult to imitate*
- The recognition that bases of *differentiation may need to change*

Focused Differentiation Strategies

These strategies can be implemented by targeting a niche market. Products can be priced at a comparatively higher price. But the perceived value has to extremely higher.

- Audio conferencing facilities through IP telephony Broadsoft technology
- Managed services & Hosting services
- Lease lines

Focused Differentiation Scenario

- Global market developments increase the need for focus
- Clear definition of market segments in terms of customers needs is required
- Within a market segment choices of strategic direction relate to competitors within that segment
- Multi-focused strategies may be possible in some markets
- New ventures started through focus strategies may be difficult to grow
- Differences between segments may be eroded making bases of focus redundant

Selecting Rright Product for the Right Market

To portray alternative corporate growth strategies, Igor Ansoff presented a matrix that focused on the firm's present and potential products and markets (customers). By considering ways to grow via existing products and

Figure 6. Ansoff matrix

	Existing Products	New Products
Existing Markets	Market Penetration	Product Development
New Markets	Market Development	Diversification

Source: http://en.wikipedia.org/wiki/Product-Market_Growth_Matrix

new products, and in existing markets and new markets, there are four possible product-market combinations. Ansoff's matrix is shown in Figure 06.

Ansoff's Matrix Provides Four Different Growth Strategies

- Market Penetration - the firm seeks to achieve growth with existing products
  in their current market segments, aiming to increase its market share.
- Market Development - the firm seeks growth by targeting its existing products
  to new market segments.
- Product Development - the firms develops new products targeted to its existing
  market segments.
- Diversification - the firm grows by diversifying into new businesses by developing new products for new markets.

Selecting a Product-Market Growth Strategy

The market penetration strategy is the least risky since it leverages many of the firm's existing resources and capabilities. In a growing market, simply maintaining market share will result in growth, and there may exist opportunities to increase market share if competitors reach capacity limits. However, market penetration has limits, and once the market approaches saturation another strategy must be pursued if the firm is to continue to grow.

Penetration strategies

- Bundled offers
- Buy one get the second connection free offers
- More Wi-Fi hotspots – Train stations, Inside intercity trains, Central Bus stands, Parks, Public swimming pools,
- Kiosks – Near the school entrance

For parents, while they are waiting for children
For students, while they are waiting for school vans

Market development options include the pursuit of additional market segments or geographical regions. The development of new markets for the product may be a good strategy if the firm's core competencies are related more to the specific product than to its experience with a specific market segment. Because the firm is expanding into a new market, a market development strategy typically has more risk than a market penetration strategy.

Market development strategies

- Internet for farmers - To checkout the market price before selling
- Internet for Doctors - Consultation via video telephony
- Internet for patients - Pharmacies to have a online DOD where patients can
  discuss the problems online and get medicine from the pharmacy
- Internet for teachers - Rural schools can be given live feeds from a National
  school for exam tips seminars.

- Internet for Police - This will help them to find out more details, history of a suspected personal instantly

A product development strategy may be appropriate if the firm's strengths are related to its specific customers rather than to the specific product itself. In this situation, it can leverage its strengths by developing a new product targeted to its existing customers. Similar to the case of new market development, new product development carries more risk than simply attempting to increase market share.

Product development strategies

- Broadband packages for taxi drivers to be resell for the passengers
- Broadband packages for long distance busses
- Broadband packages/usage to be issued with the train/bus ticket

Diversification is the most risky of the four growth strategies since it requires both product and market development and may be outside the core competencies of the firm. In fact, this quadrant of the matrix has been referred to by some as the "suicide cell". However, diversification may be a reasonable choice if the high risk is compensated by the chance of a high rate of return. Other advantages of diversification include the potential to gain a foothold in an attractive industry and the reduction of overall business portfolio risk.

Diversification development strategies

- Internet to be delivered via Power cables to apartments
- Internet to be delivered via Power cables to all school and develop education

CONCLUSION AND RECOMMENDATIONS

The marketing strategies described herein are aimed to educate the prospective customers in Sri Lanka and also to suggest what strategies could be used to popularize wireless broadband technologies. The chapter also suggested a grid for prospective customers to choose between the many technologies to optimize the applications they are focusing on. The strategies suggested are partly on conceptual form and partly

what we have trialed with actual customers in the Sri Lankan market. However cultural values and demographics of the customers of most markets within Sri Lanka are generally similar therefore the trails could be extended to all the regional markets of Sri Lanka. We believe that the facts provided herein would help the customers to be more knowledgeable in their buying decision with regard to wireless broadband technologies.

REFERENCES

Andrews, J. (2007), *Fundamentals of WiMax: Understanding Broadband Wireless Networking*, Prentice Hall, USA.

Basic Concepts of HSPA (2007), Cost-efficient mobile/wireless broadband, Ericsson, p 8., February, 2007.

Gaskin, J.E.(2007), *Broadband Bible,* Wiley, Indiana.

ITU. Telecommunications indicators, www.itu.int/ITU-D/ict/statistics/, last accesses on 20th July, 2008

In-stat Report, *The broadband boom continues*, Paxton, March, 2006.

www.store.ovum.com, last accessed on 25th July, 2008.

AAKER, JENNIFER L. (1997), "Dimensions of Brand Personality", Journal of Marketing Research, 34 (August), 347-356.

Assael H., 1995, Consumer Behavior and Marketing Action, Cincinnati, South Western College Publishing

BALMER, JOHN M.T. AND EDMUND R. GRAY (2003), "Corporate Brands: What Are They

? What of Them?" European Journal of Marketing, 37 (7/8), 972-997.

KOTLER, PHILIP (2000), Marketing Management. The Millennium Edition, Upper Saddle River, Prentice Hall.

Stern L.W, El Ansary A.I., 1992, Marketing Channels, Englewood Cliffs (NJ), Prentice Hall

Wen Tong, "MIMO Will Power WiMax and Beyond", Presentation at Global WiMax Summit in China, Oct. 2006.

KEY TERMS

Broadband Technologies: Comparison between different broadband technologies

Broadband Technologies Used in Sri Lanka: Most popular broadband technologies available in Sri Lanka.

Innovative Marketing: Innovative marketing strategies used to promote broadband products.

Marketing Broadband Products: Marketing strategies of broadband products within South Asian markets.

Marketing Strategies: Strategies used to gain competitive edge to market broadband products.

Strategies for Developing Broadband Products: Methods to develop broadband products in order to capture the target markets.

Wireless Broadband: Definition of wireless broadband and its applications.

Chapter XIV

Extending Collaborative Business Model with Mobility and its Implementation in the Medical Tourism Industry

Amit Lingarchani
University of Technology, Sydney, Australia

ABSTRACT

This chapter discusses how to extend the collaborative business process model with mobility and how to implement such a model in the "Medical Tourism" industry. The implementation discussion in this chapter is based within the context of the booming Indian Medical Tourism industry that is growing rapidly with reported annual growth rate of up to 30% over past few years. The collaboration between various available services like lodging, transport, and hospital through separate domains, in order to provide a unified service to the potential client, is considered in this chapter. The resultant architecture can be considered as a Service-Oriented Architecture (SOA) which can provide immense value during implementation.

INTRODUCTION

Medical Tourism provides a cost effective private medical care in collaboration with the travel industry for patients needing medical treatment in a geographical region separate to where they reside. Medical Tourism (MT) is an integrated collaborative approach that derives services from both healthcare and travel/tourism domains. The reason for the growth of medical tourism is that there are cheaper and good quality medical services available in one region and there are patients waiting in a queue in another geographical region. The easier and sensible solution is for the patients waiting in a queue for a medical procedure to travel to another geographical region – resulting in what can be called Medical Tourism (MT). The market of Medical Tourism depends on awareness and application of significant issues such as social diversities, consumer benefits, branding of products, legal framework, infrastructure, target markets, the actual product and communication channels (Danell & Mugomba, 2007). The implementation of Medical

Tourism requires the bringing together of many different types of services under one roof. The technical model for such collaboration and its implementation is the Collaborative Business Model (CBM) that has been discussed in its core form by Ghanbary (2008).

Collaborative Business Model, as the name suggests, brings together separate business services and enables them to collaborate with each other in a technology neutral manner. There is a constant demand of services by business that are usually derived from disparate sources and which can satisfy multiple needs of the users. Usually, technical services, emanating out of technical applications, are executed under various technical domains and environment like .NET, and Java. Collaborative Business Model (CBM) helps in bringing these types of services by enabling them to "talk" or transact with each other and make them available and accessible.

Although different businesses may by physically at a great distance, their applications are now able to communicate and transact with each other over the Internet. The Collaborative Business Model brings this communication ability of various applications that also encompass the needs of the customers and their further dependencies. The needs of the customers to be able to perform their desired activities through a single portal and preferably through minimal clicks of the user interfaces is on the rise. Customers would prefer not to waste their money and time by searching through various service providers themselves and, instead, would want it all under one umbrella (or portal). This is where Collaborative Business Model (CBM) comes into picture.

The CBM has a great potential for direct application in the aforementioned Medical Tourism domain. A particular individual residing in one country wants to search for and utilize medical services which are cheaper and easily available in some other country. There are a lot of services that would be required by such an individual and which will be included in Medical Tourism. For example, this potential patient would require – apart from the actual medical procedure – numerous other services like flight service, taxi service, lodging and boarding service, insurance service, medical claim, medicines, special treatment, billing services, etc. All the above mentioned services are belonging to different businesses. Through the application of CBM, there is an opportunity to bring together all these required services together. The need for a web based solution that also includes a mobile element which can provide details of all types of services is imminent. The concept of Medical Tourism can thus be applied using CBM and it can be made online or mobile based so that we can achieve the best services at a cheaper rate and easily.

UNDERSTANDING THE COLLABORATIVE BUSINESS MODEL

According to Ghanbary (2008), CBM has the underlying technology of web services (WS). WS provide an easily modeled and implemented technology to bring together applications and services that belong to different organizations and on different technical platforms. A Web Service enables exposing a number of methods that provide the functionalities that can be used by one or more applications, regardless of operating systems, programming languages, and hardware platforms used to develop them.

As shown in Figure 1, Collaborative Business Model comprises the following elements:-

1. **XML:** XML (Extensible Markup Language) is used to exchange the data over the Internet. XML provides an easy tag-based suite of data and their descriptions that can be used extensively in order to retrieve and store the metadata.
2. **SOAP:** Simple Object Access Protocol. This protocol provides a wrapper on top of XML that then is used in order to make applications communicate with each other by accessing the required contents from one another. XML/SOAP helps to make the interaction between the various types of businesses.
3. **Web Service Description Language (WSDL):** WSDL is used to define know the services which are exposed by a web service. The Web Service Description Language helps to know the methods and ways of accessing the various services which would be made available through web.
4. **Universal Description, Discovery and Integration (UDDI):** It provides a standard mechanism to register and discover a web service. The web service provider registers the web service in the UDDI directory, which contains pointers to the Web Service and the WSDL document for the Web Service.. Thus UDDI is the component which helps to locate and reuse the web services (Lingarchani, 2007).

Figure 1. Collaborative business model (based on Iopsis Project Report) [3]

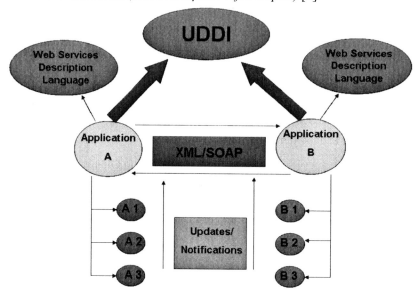

As shown in Figure 1, there are two applications, say Application A and Application B. These two applications have different types of services which are attached to them. These services should be used through different ways in order to satisfy various demands of the customers. Thus XML/SOAP, WSDL and UDDI together develop and make access of various services under one model which is Collaborative Business Model. UDDI is very useful as it helps for providing Enterprise Services, Web User Interface and Application Programming Interface Services. It also supports Authentication to some extent. Having discussed the concept of WS and its potential for transactions, we now have a look at medical tourism (MT).

MEDICAL TOURISM CONCEPT

Medical Tourism mostly includes traveling of patients to different countries for urgent or elective medical procedures. Today, medical tourism has developed as a worldwide industry. Medical tourism can be broadly defined as provision of cost-effective private medical care in collaboration with the tourism industry for patients needing surgical and other forms of specialized treatment. This process is being facilitated by the corporate sector involved in medical care as well as the tourism industry- both private and public.

Medical tourism is becoming a common form of vacationing. In earlier days, people used to travel for enjoyment but the reason most people go for a tour and travel is refreshment. Hence medical tourism mixes leisure, fun and relaxation together with wellness and healthcare.

The Medical Tourism Architecture inherits Service Oriented Architecture. It includes different services like transport service, hospital service, specialist treatments, bills payment, specialist treatment, mediclaims, insurance services, lodging service and even entertainment services like visiting historical places during leisure time after convalescing. These example services are shown in Figure 2. Furthermore, there can be many more additional demands of people like choosing treatment destination, providing the surgery and treatment in announced budget, providing more options for refreshment, etc which keep on increasing. Thus these needs are required to be merged in a collaborative manner in order to provide customer satisfaction. All these business services need to be electronically collaborating with each other and they need an understanding of both the technological as well as business models. The required service from each model is picked up and is made to interact with the other related applications.

All the above mentioned services are electronically made available through Web Services. These Web Services would be made to understand the different

Figure 2. Services offered – Medical tourism

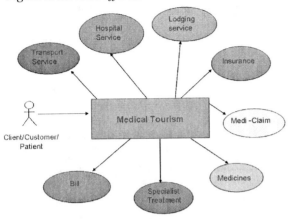

applications through SOAP protocol. WSDL would depict the meaning which is hidden behind every service. UDDI would make the different applications easily accessible.

For example, a hospital service would be including patient registration, consultation, doctors, wards (A.C. and Non A.C. Rooms), etc. These services under Hospital domain would be merged with Billing module which includes consultation fees, medicines bills, etc. Thus WSDL would understand the meaning of each service and would make an easy access of any service from anyone through UDDI.

REASONS OF MEDICAL TOURISM

Every person who undergoes a medical treatment will always think about various criteria that affect his or her decision making in the process. Typically, there are a number of characteristics that influence a person's decision to undertake Medical Tourism, especially with respect to the Indian region. Some of such characteristics are as follows:

1. **Savings:** Cost is always a big challenge for any individual. An individual would always be searching for a cost effective way for obtaining medical services. Medical claim might not cover the complete cost. Therefore, best and high quality services should be provided at a cheaper rate.
2. **Immediate service:** Services which are offered in cost effective way, if delayed, are going to be an area of disliking for users. A proper and

quick service should be provided without delay in appropriate time.

3. **Convenience:** The customers would always seek to enjoy services at ease. The chances are very rare when customers would like to roam and register the services which they want. The customers should be able to arrange for medical care from start to finish without roaming and searching for various facilities.
4. **Travel opportunities:** An opportunity to visit exotic destinations can be an additional attraction for most people. An outdoor attraction can lead to a relaxed and peaceful recovery for patients (Top 10 Reasons Why Medical Tourism is Popular, HealthBase).

FEATURES AND FACILITIES OF MEDICAL TOURISM

There are many countries from where people travel to India in order to get the benefits from their travels when it comes to medical treatments. Some of the notable regions from where this travel is taking place are countries like Oman, Nigeria, Kenya, Indonesia, Mauritius, US and UK. The main reason for taking medical services in India is that the services offered are relatively cheaper than in the countries of origin and are also immediately available than waiting in the queue.

Health holidays can, however, not only handle the medical situation but also enable people to relax and enjoy a change in their daily routine. This is true of not only the patient but also the family members to travel to help and support the patient. Medical Tourism helps people to enjoy new places and also avail medical treatment as well as orientation to improve their health. These facilities drag people from developed western countries to visit India and to enjoy the services offered here. Some additional attractions for the western region's travel to India is because the treatment can also be combined with the traditional yoga and ayurvedic treatments.

There are specific facilities which are provided to those people who want to take the services offered in India by coming here. Some of them are as follows:

1. **Medical registration:** The patients can register themselves in the hospitals before they start their actual treatment.

2. **Doctoral consultancy:** The patients who travel from abroad can consult specific surgeons, and doctors in order to take correct information and guidance before actual treatments start.

3. **Medical surgery:** The patients can undergo world class surgeries like Angio-Plasty, Angio-Graphy, Kidney Transplantation, Knee Replacement, etc at a very cheaper rate and also under hands of experienced surgeons (Wikipedia, Medical Tourism).

4. **Bi-Lingual personnel assistant:** This can be 24x7 service. Some people/ doctor assistants can be kept as translators who can help foreigners understand the local language. They can serve as translators.

5. **Doctors for day-to-day patient care:** This is also reflecting 24x7 service. Some doctors work in shifts in order to provide 24x7 help to patients who arrive and undergo treatment in India. Thus patients can get continuous service.

6. **Accommodation for family members:** Along with treatment services which are provided under medical roof in hospitals, accommodation services can also be provided to the patient's relatives. The relatives been not allowed to stay in hospitals can be provided with hotel and motel rooms till the patient completes the treatment.

7. **Tour and travel arrangements:** Complete arrangements can be made for tours of the whole family. The transport mode and its quality as well as the arrangement for the lodging and boarding can be made easily.

8. **Access to latest technology:** The technology and equipments used for medical surgery are latest and greatest. This helps patients to undergo an untiring surgery.

There are also some patients who would like to enjoy Indian services by sitting at their homes. For such scenario, a team of doctors is sent to specific countries with full facilities arrangement.

MOBILIZING MEDICAL TOURISM

The globalized world of today looks forward to mobilization of all kinds of services with the help of technology. This is also true in case of the field of medicine, wherein opportunities are arising on a regular basis to provide medical services to a global 'patient' base. However, more often than not, excellent hospital facilities are available at a fraction of a cost in developing countries, leading to patients from fully developed nations traveling across the globe to receive excellent medical treatment. The 'tours and travels' of patients for medical treatment comes to be known as medical tourism, as mentioned earlier in this chapter. However, now there is also an opportunity to develop the concept of medical tourism further by making it 'mobile enabled'. Technologies like Bluetooth, Wi-MAX, Wireless Local Area Network (WLAN) and WAP are providing increasingly rich opportunities for medical services to be mobilized. Here is a brief discussion on each of these mobile technologies, followed by how they relate to medical tourism.

Bluetooth is a short range service provider which cannot be used alone for providing all the services on mobile. Bluetooth needs to follow some protocols in order to work smoothly. These protocols can be made hand-set compatible. The biggest problem is the distance which needs to be traversed by data if Bluetooth is used for accessing the services between a central PC server and blue tooth enabled hand-set.

Wi- MAX stands for World Wide Interoperability for Microwave Access. The main advantages of the WiMAX standard are to enable the implementation of advanced radio features in a standardized approach, and provide people in a city with online access via their mobile device. Experiments are made to make it enable on notebook computers and PDA's but still it cannot be made compatible to hand-sets alone.

WLAN (Wireless Local Area Network) can be a good option for providing internet and intranet facilities. The wireless links would give a network connection to all users in the surrounding area, ranging from a single room to an entire campus. Even this alone cannot provide us with the complete access to services on individual's hand-set.

WAP stands for Wireless Application Protocol. WAP Architecture consists of a service called Short Message Service (SMS). This service if combined with above mentioned technology and its services can provide us with the complete access to various services of Medical Tourism.

WEB SERVICES BENEFITS

Web services can be made available on mobile. All the mobile web services work on specific workflows. The workflows add benefits to the web services in various ways. Following are the benefits which are gained of using workflow:-

1. Enables the exposure of a process oriented model to Web Service Interfaces

2. Provide a simplified interface to a set of interfaces as well as facilitate simplified packaging of a set of interfaces.

3. Web Services execution defined within Workflows can be better managed when compared to current Web Services Interfaces, especially when there exists inter-dependency.

4. Provides a clear usage model for a set of Web Services Interfaces.

5. Allows creation of composite services

6. Enabling more dynamic, semi automated composed processes (Rosemarie, 2002).

7. Enables specific design patterns depicting the best practices of using a set of Web Services Interfaces.

8. Allows Provisioning of an execution environment which can guarantee execution of the complex/composite service invocation with compensations.

WS CHOREOGRAPHY IN MT

Web Services Choreography is a specification by W3C defining a XML based business process modeling language which describes collaboration protocols (Rosemarie, 2002). Web Services Choreography provides a good environment for long running middleware infrastructure where there can be pre-defined set of operations that need to be performed over a period of time. This would simplify the client interactions with the Web Service Interfaces. It helps to monitor the status of the request and even manage the life cycle of the process.

Choreography based business processes can be initialized by sending a simple message with the content which will trigger the whole process. The rest of the interaction is handled by the choreography middleware.

The hand-set would connect to middleware architecture with help of WAP. Short Message Services (SMS) would be the prime mode of support to ask for the various services. SMS is very compatible for the initiation process of connecting to middle ware than GPRS because all the hand- sets might not be GPRS services enabled. Through SMS, we can send a list of query which would be reported as task in middleware.

In the middleware architecture, there would be a WAP server to which handset would get connected with SMS. This WAP server in turn would be connected to other servers which might be PC applications like Hospitals, Insurance, etc through GPRS. Thus the data can be exchanged between different application domains and the acknowledgements as well as data can be sent through SMS to a particular hand-set. The above mentioned process is shown in Figure 3 below.

Web Service Choreography Interface (WCSI) helps in bridging gap between web services and business process by providing a good understanding of how a web service can be used as a part of business process. WSCI provides an overall view of all the processes utilizing message exchange among interacting web services as well as describes the flow of messages exchanged by a Web service for a particular process. The business processes may be distributed among multiple organizations. Thus WSCI provides an effective solution to provide automated, application to application collaboration (Rosemarie, 2002).

RISKS IN MT

There are risks associated with Medical Tourism along with good features and facilities. These risks should be taken into consideration. Some of these risks are:

1. Insurance might not cover always the cost of additional treatments and surgeries needed due to overseas operation.

2. Legal systems might not be helping in getting full compensation in worst case.

3. Traveling soon after surgery can lead to serious complications like blood clots, swelling and infections.

4. An adequate follow-up care is required. It is required to be ensured that one gets healed properly and is healthy enough to travel home (Wikipedia, Medical Tourism Guide).

CHALLENGES IN MT

There are various challenges which are faced by Medical Tourism. These challenges can create a big impact on growth of Medical Tourism. Some of these challenges are as follows:

Figure 3. Web services choreography in MT

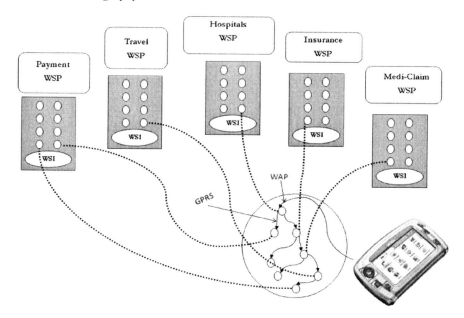

1. Lack of Support is a big challenge for Medical Tourism. There are chances that good physicians or surgeons might not be available 24 hours. It increases the pressure of work on available unreliable doctors.

2. The expectations of the customers are growing by leaps and bounds. The satisfaction of the ever growing demands of customers is another challenge which is faced by Medical Tourism.

3. Quality of services provided need to be according to customer satisfaction. Hence a constant improvement in services which are offered is required.

4. Duplication of data and services can lead to a great harm to the growth of medical tourism. There are many providers of same type of services which can confuse customers and hence can lead to inefficient and non reliable selection of services by customers.

5. Security is another big challenge. Security in sense of the data which is made available through mobile phones is of utmost importance.

6. Lower memory capacity is found to be a challenge in mobile phones as compared to desktop machines, which can hinder the execution of mobile applications on small hand-held devices

7. Authentication is another challenge wherein the identity of the user is confirmed by more than one source.

8. The medical tourism industry is new and evolving rapidly, hence there is limited information available on internet. As a result there are less potential clients who are using these services. There is a sort of uncertainty of full utilization of available services by the clients (Medical Insights International, 2007).

VALIDATION OF THE MOBILE MEDICAL TOURISM

The model for MT is in its initial phase. The only validation currently performed by the author is through experimentation. A set of WS were implemented in a collaborative model, and the services were made to communicate with each other through the common platform. Furthermore, the medical tourism WS model was made to 'talk' with an existing travel portal. However, further validation is ongoing at this moment and, with the help of additional sponsorship and sup-

Figure 4. Choreography Example (based on Alistair, 2005)

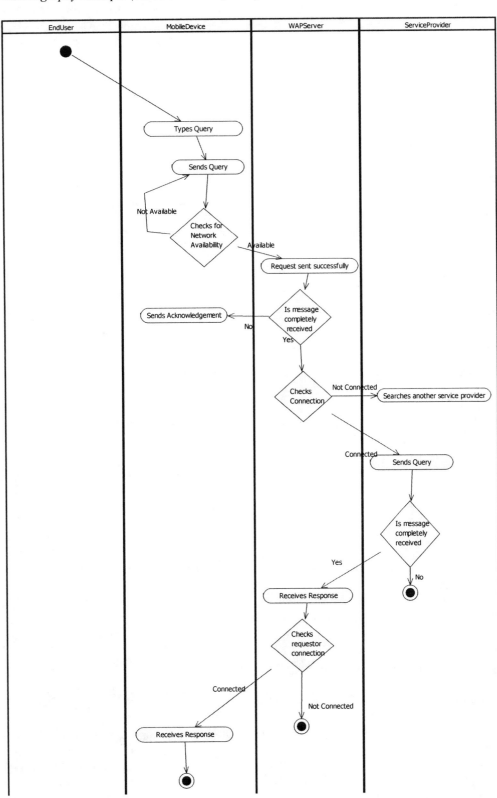

port from the industry, the model will be validated through action research.

FUTURE DIRECTIONS

Medical tourism is a way towards globalization of required services. The future of Medical Tourism is very bright. This is just an initial idea of implementing a model through paper. In one way, this model would bring ease of access to various needs in a secured way in real world. In another way, this model would reduce the effort required to provide all the services. Moreover, a good marketing and advertising strategy can bring a big fame to the concept of medical tourism.

In future, there is a high chance of outsourcing medical tourism concept. Information Technology can make this dream come true. Telemedicine is latest medical tourism concept which has started booming since few years. It involves treatment or monitoring patients remotely by 'telephone,' Web cam or video feed would be also used in those areas where physicians are scarce (Herrick, 2007). There is a high possibility of providing health insurance plans which include medical travel in future. Experiments are going on for providing international coverage by many health insurers.

Some institutions like World Medical Tourism Council can provide worldwide database that ranks medical professionals and matches them to patients. Incentives should be offered to patients who choose medical tourism in order to compensate inconvenience involved in the tour as well as accepting a perceived risk of going to other country and getting treated there (Imagining Medical Travel's Future, 2008).

CONCLUSION

Medical Tourism has the ability to bring various services together and utilize them to their best abilities through technologies of communications, such as the Internet. Moreover, with help of web service choreography, all types of applications are able to access the services that are offered by vendors that deal with only one aspects of the overall MT domain. The implementation of this concept of MT would provide the users with many different options and at a low price.

The main purpose of the chapter is to draw attention to the interaction of various web services and

their access on mobiles. The access of web services with help of Web Services Choreography can help to collaborate different businesses (Martins & Jones, 2005). Moreover, new services can also be added to the complete flow of services easily through Web Services Choreography Interface.

REFERENCES

(2007). *Medical Tourism – Healthcare in the Competitive Global Marketplace*, Medical Insights International, United States. Retrieved on 19 July 2008, from http://www.changemakers.net/en-us/node/1086

(2008, May 12). *Imagining Medical Travel's Future*. BridgeHealth International Incorporated, United States. Retrieved on 20 July 2008, from http://www.bridgehealthinternational.com/blog/2008/05/imagining-medical-travels-future/

Alistair, B. (2005, March). *A Critical Overview of Web Services Choreography Description Language*. Retrieved on 19 April, 2008, from www.bptrends.com

Danell, S., & Mugomba, C. (2007, January). *Medical Tourism and its Entrepreneurial Opportunities – A conceptual framework for entry into the industry.* Master Thesis, Goteborg University, Goteborg

Ghanbary, A. (2007). *IRMA Conference Paper.*

Ghanbary, A. (2008). *Collaborative Business Process Engineering (CBPE) Across Multiple Organizations.* PhD thesis, University of Western Sydney

Herrick, D. (2007, Nov). Medical Tourism: Global Competition in Health Care. *National Centre of Policy Analysis.* Retrieved on 18 July 2008, from http://www.ncpa.org/pub/st/st304/st304.pdf

Lingarchani, A. (2007). *Type Browser Extender.* Project Report, Gujarat University, Vadodara.

Martins, H., & Jones, M. (2005). Chapter V. Relevance of mobile computing in the field of medicine. *In Handbook of Research in Mobile Business: Technological, Methodological and Social perspectives, I,* B. Unhelkar (ed.). Hershey, PA, USA: IGI Global.

Rosemarie, G. (2002, June). *Web Services Choreography Interface (WSCI) Specifications Released to the Public.* Gamelan (developer.com). Retrieved on 20 July 2008, from http://www.developer.com/java/article.php/1379601

Top 10 Reasons Why Medical Tourism is Popular. (2008). HealthBase, Newton. Retrieved on 19 April 2008, from https://www.healthbase.com/hb/pages/Top-10-Reasons-Why-Medical-Tourism-is-Popular.jsp

Wikipedia. *Medical Tourism.* Retrieved from http://en.wikipedia.org/wiki/Medical_tourism)

Wikipedia. *Medical Tourism Guide.* Retrieved from http://medicaltourismguide.org/risks/

Chapter XV
Mobile Applications Development Methodology

Rok Rupnik
University of Ljubljana, Slovenia

ABSTRACT

The chapter introduces mobile applications development methodology. Mobile applications represent a new application model being introduced to information systems in the recent time. For that reason it represents a good challenge to expand research area of information systems development methodologies with research on mobile applications development methodology. The first part of the chapter introduces classical and a context-aware mobile application model. Based on that, the second part explores the role of mobile applications in information systems with the emphasis on showing the semantic contribution of the use of mobile applications in information systems. The core part of the chapter introduces mobile applications development methodology. The methodology is introduced through development phases and tasks which have to be performed within phases. The emphasis of methodology introduction is on phases of strategy and analysis.

INTRODUCTION

The information society is the society of ongoing progress and technological development. It is enabled by the technological development and progress achieved in the areas of information and telecommunication technology. The information society is enabled by technology, but it is far more than just a technology driven society. It is a complex and multidisciplinary society driven by knowledge, innovations and development. The information society is a service-oriented society in which the effectiveness of the individual

and the organisation as such depend on the ability to acquire the accurate information at the right time and react according to the information acquired.

The convergence between several technology sectors offers the opportunity for the emergence of new services. One of the most representative characteristics of the information society is the convergence between information and telecommunication technologies. Mobile applications are the consequence and the result of the convergence mentioned (Müller-Veerse 2000).

There are some characteristics of information society, which endorse the importance of mobile applications for the information society. Some of them are (Gams 1999; Rupnik 2003):

- *Metcalfe's law*, which defines the value of the network proportional to the square of the number of nodes connected to the network. Due to the fact that there are significantly more mobile devices than the number of computers connected to the Internet, mobile applications represent a high potential for services in the information society.
- *Employees are faced with the demand for higher productivity*. The ability to access information and use applications in the state of mobility will without doubt make a contribution to this area.
- *Ongoing emergence of jobs with direct or indirect demand for application use and information access*. Mobile applications will represent a contribution in this area as well.

Mobile applications therefore represent the consequence and the demand of information society (Rupnik 2001). Mobile applications are undisputedly worth full attention of information system science and information system managers.

MOBILE APPLICATIONS

A mobile application is a computer program running on a mobile device and presenting value to the mobile user. Mobile applications can offer information support in several areas. In our research we focus on business oriented mobile applications providing information support within the information systems to the users when they are mobile, i.e. not present in their traditional working environment. There are two groups of mobile users. The first group are mobile users spending more than a few working time away from their traditional working environment. According to their organizational roles granted they must be informed about unexpected and exceptional situations. On the other hand they also need the possibility of use of simple services and applications while being mobile. The second group are mobile users who belong to mobile workforce users doing their usual work in the state of mobility. We could say that the mobility represents their traditional working environment.

There are different types of mobile devices. The examples of mobile devices are: a Palm device, GSM

mobile phone and a notebook. In our research we focus on small devices like GSM mobile phone and Palm devices. Tarasewich, for example, also eliminated the notebook as a mobile device in his research (Tarasewich 2002). The reason for the elimination of the notebook as a mobile device is because it does not reflect the distinct characteristics and limitations of small mobile devices. The relationship between mobile device and mobile application will be discussed more in detail later on in this chapter.

The size is the most significant characteristic and limitation of mobile devices, because it determines other limitations of mobile devices. The most important of them are: battery power, limited storage capacity for the running of applications, low processing power, the size of display and uncomfortable input methods (Panis 2002; Dogac 2002; Ho 2003). The limitations of mobile devices are essential, because they determine the limitations of mobile applications. The limitations of mobile applications and mobility itself make the mobile application model distinct from other application models.

Mobile applications signify the connection of a mobile user with his organization and its information systems. Their scope is not to enable the same level of functionality as classical applications do, but to enable the use of applications and access to the important information and basic level of services in the state of mobility. The services they offer and the functionality they enable should be appropriate for mobility and the needs of a mobile user. We could say that they should offer mobility adapted and mobility suitable services. Mobile applications must provide a basic level of functionality, access to the important information and the possibility to be informed about exceptional, unexpected and other unusual situations happening within an organization he belongs to (Sacher 2001). In the following sub-sections we introduce two mobile application models.

LEVEL 2 (MOBILE APPLICATIONS): CLASSICAL MOBILE APPLICATION MODEL

The classical mobile application model is a basic mobile application model. It is a *pull* application model, which means that its main characteristic is that mobile application is run on the users' demand. The fact that the mobile user has run a mobile application indicates his current informational needs. The disadvantage of this application model is that mobile user can not be aware of what might be important at a particular moment, because he is not present in his traditional working environment. It assumes the perception of the mobile user: what information is essential at a particular moment, and accordingly which mobile application they should run in order to acquire that information or do an action.

We hold the opinion that the classical mobile application model is important, because the mobile user without any doubt needs the option to run the mobile application at a particular moment. But on the other hand it is obvious that in order to eliminate the before mentioned disadvantage we need another mobile application model which will enable the automatic triggering of mobile application based on condition. We see that the concept of mobility determines the triggering moment of mobile application to be the key issue.

LEVEL 2 (MOBILE APPLICATIONS): CONTEXT-AWARE MOBILE APPLICATION MODEL

The concept on which another mobile application model is based is called context. The context is a relatively new concept in the information systems area. Several authors have done research on the context (Schilit 1995; Brown 1997; Ryan 1998; Pascoe 1998; Dey 2000). Their definitions of context claim that the important aspects of context are: where and when you are, who you are with, and what resources are there nearby. They mostly cover physical and social component of the user's state.

In order to transform the context into an information system concept, its definition should give more emphasis to the informational component of the user's state, i.e. the user's informational needs. We believe that in order to become an information system concept, the context definition must be extended and cover the informational needs as well. The informational needs of a mobile user on the basic level are defined by the user's own perception about the information they need, which is supported by the classical mobile application model. On the other hand, the informational needs of a mobile user on advanced level are defined by informational needs of an information system in which the mobile user is an actor with one or more organizational roles granted. Organizational rules define the roles of a user within organizational system, and

the roles determine his current informational needs. According to these conclusions we define context as complete information on:

- The situation a mobile user is currently involved in. We define it as a context of situation which is defined by the user's location, social situation and physical environment.
- Informational needs of a mobile user which is determined by information systems' informational needs. We define it as a context of informational needs.
- Technical descriptions which carry the information about the places where the user is usually present at, the information about the technical characteristics of the users' mobile device and the information on the current state of the wireless network. We define it as the context of technical descriptions. The context of technical descriptions signifies the relationship between mobile application and mobile device. We already mentioned that in our research we focus on small mobile devices. On the other hand our definition of the context of technical descriptions also covers notebook, because notebook only means different context of technical descriptions.

The definition of context that we propose and the introduction of a classical mobile application model has revealed the characteristics required from another mobile application model. The new mobile application model should move the focal point from an application being run by a mobile user on demand to application being triggered by an application server based on the condition which depends on current circumstances within the business system and its information system.

According to the above stated discussion we define context-aware mobile application in the following way: *a mobile application is context-aware if it uses the context for determination of triggering moment and the forming of contents. It uses the context to provide information to the user. The information is relevant to the user due to the context of informational needs, limited by the context of situation and affected by the context of technical descriptions.*

A context-aware mobile application model is based on the aforementioned definition of context-aware mobile applications. It eliminates the disadvantage of a classical mobile application model, because it enables the triggering moment of application to be determined by the context of informational needs and not only on the user's demand. It is important to point out that context aware mobile applications can also be run on demand, like classical mobile applications. In our research we focus on the context of informational needs, because we believe that it is the key component within context in case of business oriented mobile applications in information systems (Rupnik 2003).

LEVEL 2 (MOBILE APPLICATIONS): THE ROLE OF MOBILE APPLICATIONS IN INFORMATION SYSTEMS

The fundamental task of information systems is to provide information support for business processes in business systems and other organizations. The introduction of mobile applications to information systems enables the information support of business processes in the state of mobility that stimulated us to do research in this area. We focused on their contribution at information support, i.e. what is the added value of the use of mobile applications in the state of mobility.

Mobile applications represent a new application model being introduced to information systems. They will not become prevailing application model and they will definitely not cause the distinction of other application models. Mobile applications only represent a niche application model suitable for organization and business systems with the need of information broadcasting and the use of simple applications in the state of mobility (Smith 2002). The mobile applications represent the connection channel for mobile users and enable them to maintain communication with their traditional working environment, i.e. their business system and its information system (Sacher 2001).

In our research we focus on the context of informational needs, because we believe that it is the key component within context in case of business oriented mobile applications in information systems. For that reason the next part of the paper will focus on the context of informational needs.

Figure 1 presents the meta model of the process view of information support which represents the dynamical view of informational support of business processes provided by information systems. The meta model shows several kind of functionalities of mobile applications. They are grouped into direct and indirect information support. We describe direct information support as information support that enables the execution of a business function. Direct information support means providing the sufficient level of functionalities to execute business function in the state of mobility in the sufficient extent as in traditional working environment. Mobile user who needs direct information support is in most cases doing his normal job while being mobile. An example would be employee delivering beverages or insurance agent selling insurance packages.

Through indirect information support mobile applications enable the mobile users to be informed about the execution of business functions, to control their execution and to confirm conditions. Mobile user who needs indirect information is usually not doing his normal job while being mobile. He simply must be involved in business processes according to organizational roles granted and therefore either control business processes or view summarized data regarding business process, either be informed about events or confirm decisions. An example would be manager visiting international conference being informed about important indicators of results of his company. We estimate that there will be considerably more mobile applications providing indirect information support than applications providing direct information support.

Meta model implicitly also presents the organizational component of process view of information support, because it shows organizational roles and emphasizes the fact that only some organizational roles allow mobile users, i.e. the use of applications in the state of mobility.

We believe that information systems need the following types of mobile applications (RokPHD 2002):

- **Messaging systems:** enable information broadcasting for the mobile users. Messaging systems can work as a classical application model and as context-aware application model. Classical model messaging enables context-unaware messaging, which means sending situation-unaware and informational needs un-aware messages. Context-aware model messaging enables messages with contents and triggering moment to be dependant on context. Example of context-aware messaging mobile application is application which sends message to managers when total day income is less than 10.000 Euro. We believe that context-aware messaging represents higher value to a mobile user,

- **Mobile transaction application systems:** typical classical application model with high value for business systems with mobile workforce with the need for transaction oriented information support. Example is mobile application supporting mobile worker delivering beverages,
- **Mobile decision support and controlling systems:** probably the most wanted mobile applications which will enable managers and decision makers to access important information about business processes (Sharaf 2002). Classical model applications enable access to that information at a running moment of application. Example is mobile application which

enables the viewing of all important parameters for a certain department. On the other hand context-aware model applications enable triggering of application when important parameter of a business process has changed or has crossed a certain value. Example is mobile application which enables the viewing of all important parameters for a certain department when one of those parameters has changed or crossed a certain value.

MOBILE APPLICATIONS DEVELOPMENT METHODOLOGY

Mobile applications represent a new application model being introduced to information systems. For that

Figure 1. Meta model of the process view of information support

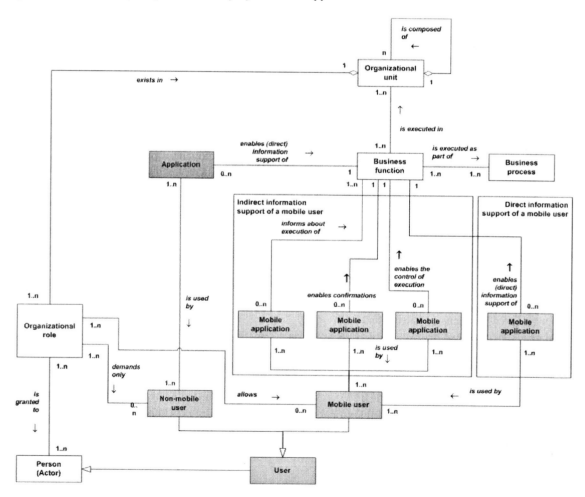

reason we put considerable emphasize in our research on mobile applications development methodology. Research was initiated with the following dilemmas:

- Do mobile applications call for changes in fundamental concepts of information systems?
- Do existing information systems development methodologies support/enable the development of mobile applications?
- Are the existing approaches, methods and modeling techniques sufficient in order to model context-awareness?

The objective of our research is find answers to the dilemmas mentioned through making a mobile application development methodology. The first version of methodology is already completed. Now it is being used on projects and based on the experience gained on projects methodology will be improved and enhanced.

We introduce our mobile applications development methodology in the following subchapters. After introducing related work we first introduce the concept of supportive application. Then we introduce four development phases: strategy, analysis, design and implementation. We introduce development phases through introducing tasks and methodological issues specific to mobile application development. Therefore we only introduce context modeling. At the end we present conclusions and future directions.

LEVEL 2 (MOBILE APPLICATIONS DEVELOPMENT METHODOLOGY): RELATED WORK

Several authors have discussed the area of mobile applications and mobile applications development methodologies (Karunanithi 2000; Tarasewich 2002; Abrahamsson 2004; Varshney 2003). Majority of them argue that mobile applications demand changes in information systems development methodologies, but they do not present any detailed or even rough directions for changes needed.

Hars has stated that the information systems research area often does not react fast enough to the information technology achievements and novelties. The purpose of his paper was not to discuss mobile applications development methodologies, but despite of that paper is important for our research because of the author's statement that information systems development methodologies must adapt to the changes and novelties in the area of information technologies (Hars 2000).

Karunanithi has stated that developers must know whether application they develop is going to be a mobile application or not. He believes that information systems development methodologies must adapt in order to support the development of mobile applications (Karunanithi 2000).

Tarasewich argues that the development of mobile applications represents a bigger challenge than the development of other kinds of applications. He points out the context-awareness and the fact that mobile applications are needed mostly in dynamic environments. He also states that information systems development methodologies must change in order to support the development of mobile applications (Tarasewich 2002). In his newer paper author discusses several issues for designing mobile applications, but he does not touch mobile application development methodologies (Tarasewich 2004).

Varshney makes an overview of challenges and research problems for the area of mobile information systems in his paper (Varshney 2003). He does not cover mobile application development methodology explicitly, but he addresses some research problems which are important for the area of mobile application development: *Design of mobile applications and services* and *Introduction of Mobile technologies in business and organizations.*

Abrahamsson introduces mobile application development approach called Mobile-D which is based on Extreme Programming (Abrahamsson 2004). Author discusses technical issues of mobile devices and some experiences with using the approach, but he does not introduce the methodological issues of approach.

LEVEL 2 (MOBILE APPLICATIONS DEVELOPMENT METHODOLOGY): MOBILE APPLICATION AND ITS SUPPORTIVE APPLICATION

Mobile application is in many cases intended to extend the functionalities of an existing classical non-mobile application. Let us for example consider classical application supporting delivery of beverages. Company decides to implement mobile application for mobile workers delivering beverages in order to enable the monitoring of delivery and broadcasting changes of delivery and delivery cancellations to workers. In such case we say that mobile application represents an additional application channel to existing application.

Mobile application provides value to a mobile user through providing mobility adapted and mobility suitable services. In order to implement those services there are several functionalities needed. Some of those functionalities are dedicated to a mobile user and they are implemented in mobile application. But there are also other functionalities needed to facilitate functionalities of mobile applications. On one hand there are administrative functionalities like maintenance of code tables. It would be irrational to implement administrative functionalities in mobile application. On the other hand there are process supportive functionalities like creating data for mobile application and monitoring data transformed by mobile application. Let us again consider mobile application for a mobile worker delivering beverages. On the administrative functionalities side there is maintenance of items (sales products) needed. On the process supportive functionalities side there are among other things at least two functionalities needed: order entry and monitoring of order delivery.

Administrative and process supportive functionalities must according to our methodology implemented in classical, non-mobile, typically web application. We say that supportive application has administrative and process supportive role. There are three possibilities concerning administrative and process supportive functionalities:

- **Existing application approach**: all administrative and process supportive functionalities are implemented in existing application. It means that the development process of mobile applications includes the upgrade of existing application. In this case existing application overtakes administrative and process supportive role.
- **New application approach**: there is no existing application and all functionalities are implemented in supportive application. It means that the development of mobile application includes the development of supportive application. In this case supportive application overtakes administrative and process supportive role.
- **Combined approach**: administrative and process supportive functionalities are distributed over existing application and supportive application. This approach is used in cases when

we either don't want or can not implement all functionalities in existing application. In this case the development of mobile application includes the upgrade of existing application and development of supportive application.

LEVEL 2 (MOBILE APPLICATIONS DEVELOPMENT METHODOLOGY): STRATEGY

We believe that the introduction of mobile applications to information systems should be performed through mobile application strategic planning, i.e. strategy phase. The reason for that is the fact that mobile applications are typically not independent from other applications in information systems. In most cases they represent additional application channel to one or more existing applications within information systems. The dependency is reflected through services and/or databases of existing applications which are used by mobile applications. For that reason it is very important to identify functionalities of existing application systems within information system and their data when defining functionalities of mobile applications. The main objective of strategy phase is to define mobile applications which will be fully integrated in information system.

The process of mobile application strategic planning has two tasks. The first task is called *Define the needs for information support for the mobile users*. The purpose of the task is to seek out business processes and organizational roles with the need for information support in the state of mobility. The aim is to identify mobile applications needed and functionalities they must provide to the mobile users. The deliverable of the task is *Model of the use of mobile applications*.

Two techniques can be used for the model of the use of mobile applications. Mobile application strategic planning can be performed as a part of information system strategic planning. In that case the model of the use of mobile applications can implicitly be present in business process model. It means that the model of the use of mobile applications becomes a part of business process model. eEpc diagramming technique is usually used for business process modelling (Krisper 2004).

An example of eEpc diagram representing business process model and implicitly showing the model of the use of mobile applications is shown below (Figure

2). It shows mobile applications used by the grantee's of organizational roles at business functions. We introduced four new symbols showing four mobile applications types of functionality. Type of functionality represents the general purpose, general functionality of mobile application. We believe that there are the following four types of functionalities:

- **Information broadcasting:** Mobile application broadcasts information to mobile users. As a rule these are context-aware mobile applications, because the information broadcasted based on condition in cases of unusual situations brings higher value added to the mobile user.
- **Confirming:** Mobile application broadcasts information and demands confirmation. It can either be the confirmation of a decision, the confirmation of default value presented, etc. Confirming functionality is more natural for context-aware mobile applications, but can also be present in classical mobile applications.
- **Viewing:** Mobile application enables the viewing of information. Viewing functionality is more natural for classical mobile applications, but can also be present in context-aware mobile applications.
- **Application running:** General functionality which covers either all other functionalities not covered by other three types of functionalities, either the mixture of introduced types of functionalities.

The model in the Figure 2 also shows that some mobile applications are not necessarily linked to any of business functions, because they cover either business processes as a whole or either organization as a whole.

Alternative technique for eEpc diagramming is simple technique using tables. Tables are used in cases when mobile application strategic planning is not performed as a part of information system strategic planning or if we do not decide to do business process modelling. Semantically both techniques provide the same information.

The example shows that context-aware mobile application can also be run on demand, i.e. used as classical mobile application. In the row where organizational roles are described for each role the type of use of mobile application is also shown. Mobile application can be used for the execution of a business function, in some cases actors must be informed either about the changes or the results of activities. When using the eEPC diagramming technique the same information is presented as the property of a connection between business function and organizational role.

The second task is called *Define supportive application and the dependency on existing applications.* The purpose of the task is to extend the previous deliverable by defining the functionalities of supportive application and to seek out the dependency of mobile application and supportive application on existing applications in the information system. The aim is to detect the existing data and services on which mobile application and its supportive application can rely. The deliverable of the task is *Model of mobile applications and supportive applications.*

The model of use of mobile applications and supportive applications extends the information provided by the model of the use of mobile applications. It extends it by providing information about the functionalities of supporting applications and the distribution of functionalities between supportive applications and existing applications in information system.

An example of the model is shown below (Figure 3). The model uses simple diagramming technique using different symbols for three types of applications: mobile application, supportive application and existing classical application. On the other hand the same symbol is used for all three types of applications for showing use cases which represent functionalities. Arrows show the data dependencies between existing classical application and mobile application with its supportive application. Lines ending with filled circle show that mobile application with its supportive application use API of existing classical application. The diagramming technique proposed is very simple and easy to understand in order to enable easier communication with the customer. Instead of it UML component and deployment diagrams can be used.

LEVEL 2 (MOBILE APPLICATIONS DEVELOPMENT METHODOLOGY): ANALYSIS

The analysis is mostly based on existing development methodologies concepts. On the other hand the analysis introduces context modeling as new modeling concept. Analysis phase is divided into two logical parts: mobile application part and supportive application part. There are six tasks in the analysis phase which will be introduced in the following part of the paper.

Figure 2. Example of eEpc diagram showing the model of the use of mobile applications

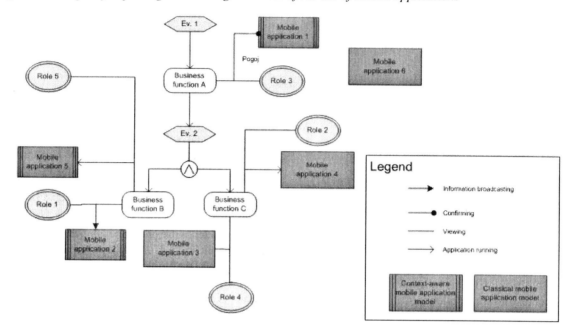

Create conceptual data model is performed in case of combined approach and new application approach. It is a classical analysis task which is in case of mobile application development not different from classical development methodologies. Special characteristic in case of mobile application development is more attention needed for status attributes and status entities. For example: in case of mobile application supporting mobile worker delivering beverages there might be some extra statuses needed for tracing delivery status. Depending on development approach used two diagramming techniques can be used for model creation: entity relationship diagrams or class diagrams. The deliverable of the task is *Conceptual data model.*

Upgrade conceptual data model of existing application is performed in case of existing application approach and combined approach. The aim of the task is to upgrade data model according to the changes and new functional needs defined for existing application within the task *Upgrade Functional Model of Existing Application.* There might be new entities or new attributes needed to support new functionalities. The deliverable of the task is *Upgraded conceptual data model.*

Upgrade functional model of existing application is performed in case of existing application approach and combined approach as well. The aim of the task

is to define new business functions needed to support functionalities of mobile application. New business functions defined cover administrative and process supportive functionalities. The input for the task is t*he model of mobile applications and supportive applications* from the strategy phase. The deliverable of the task is *Upgraded functional model of existing application.*

Create functional model of supportive application is performed in case of combined approach and new application approach. The aim of the task is to define business functions needed to support functionalities of mobile application. In this case business functions which are the responsibility of new application defined. Business functions defined, cover in this case administrative and process supportive functionalities as well. The input for the task is t*he model of mobile applications and supportive applications* from the strategy phase. Depending on development approach used, two diagramming techniques can be used for model creation: use case diagrams or functional decomposition diagrams. The deliverable of the task is *Functional model of supportive application.*

Create functional model of mobile application is performed in any approach used. The aim of the task is to define business functions and functionalities for a mobile application. Depending on development approach used two diagramming techniques can be used

Table 1. Example of the model of the use of mobile applications using tables technique

Short name of MA	MA01
Full name of MA	Mobile application for workers delivering beverages
Business function or business process	Delivering of beverages
The purpose of MA	Enables the information support of a mobile worker delivering beverages with the emphasize on the broadcasting of changes for a particular invoice
Functionalities of MA	• Mobile worker can view the delivery invoices which he must complete • Mobile worker can change the delivery status of the delivery after he delivered the goods • Mobile worker gets information in case if anything about the delivery changes (for example customer cancels a part of the delivery). The information can broadcasted as a message or as form popup.
Application model	Context-aware
Type of functionality	Information broadcasting and Application running
Organizational roles	Worker/Executing – Mobile application Worker/Must be informed about the change – Mobile application Supervisor/Executing – Supportive application
Condition	Something about the delivery invoice changes
Remarks	Mobile application can be split into two mobile applications: • context-aware mobile application for information broadcasting about delivery invoice changes • classical mobile application supporting the first and the second functionality declared above

for model creation: use case diagrams or functional decomposition diagrams. Inputs for the task are: *the model of mobile applications and supportive applications* and *the model of the use of mobile applications* from the strategy phase. The deliverable of the task is *Functional model of mobile application.*

Create context model is performed in case of context aware mobile application development. The aim of the task is to define conditions for the triggering of mobile application and conditions for forming of contents. In many cases context model is created as part of functional model of mobile application where descriptions are used to define context. This way, context requirements are defined as part of functional requirements. The deliverable of the task is *Context model.*

LEVEL 2 (MOBILE APPLICATIONS DEVELOPMENT METHODOLOGY): DESIGN AND IMPLEMENTATION

There are no special tasks and methodological elements in the design phase in mobile application development

methodology according to web application development methodology. *Context model* is input deliverable for modules design not only for mobile application module design, but for new supportive application and existing application module design as well. This is the consequence of process supportive role of supportive application. For example: with the mobile application supporting the delivery of beverages, the supportive application is the one which actually initiates the information broadcasting to the mobile worker if the order changes or if the order is cancelled.

Implementation phase for mobile applications development can be supported by two major development platforms: .NET and J2ME. They both enable the development of classical and context-aware mobile applications. In our opinion they will both remain key development platform and no one is going to prevail over another. In case of mobile applications development there is often a problem of on-line and off-line work which has to be implemented. The problem is that mobile device can not always be connected to the wireless network and therefore, off-line mode must be supported. Hence, local database and synchronization must be implemented.

Figure 3. Example of the model of mobile applications and supportive applications

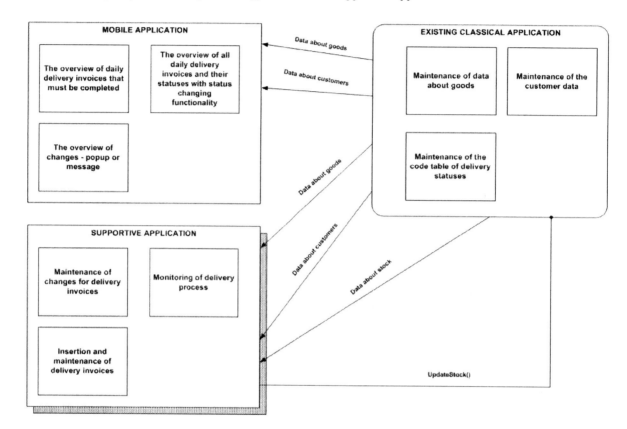

LEVEL 2 (MOBILE APPLICATIONS DEVELOPMENT METHODOLOGY): EXPERIENCES WITH THE METHODOLOGY

Methodology has been used on some projects in the last year. Both platforms .NET and J2ME were used on projects. One of the projects was mobile application supporting the delivery of beverages. We constantly change and improve it through experience gained on projects. On of the recent changes was the elimination of *Create context design model* task and *Context design model* deliverable. That deliverable was the only difference according to the web application development methodology. We eliminated it because the experience revealed that it is not necessary to have extra model for context in the design phase. Context can simply be designed through methods like other functional requirements.

CONCLUSION AND FUTURE DIRECTION

The research done so far in the area of mobile application development methodology and some test development projects revealed the importance of strategic planning of mobile applications. Mobile applications must be introduced to information phases through strategic planning, i.e. strategy development phase. The research also revealed that analysis phase demands tasks unique to mobile application development, e.g. context model creation. The important result of research is also that design phase and implementation phase do not require tasks and methodological changes unique to mobile application development. We plan to further improve and develop methodology through research on context modeling and additional test projects.

Figure 4. Analysis phase tasks

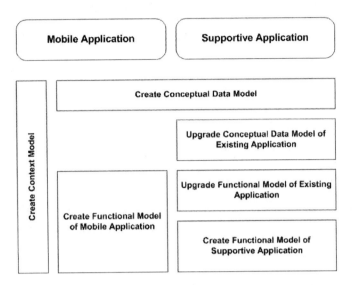

REFERENCES

Abrahamsson, P., Hanhineva, A., Hulkko, H., Ihme, T., Jaalinoja, J., Korkala, M., Koskela, J., Kvllonen, P., & Salo, O. (2004). Mobile-D: An Agile Approach for Mobile Application Development. *In Proceedings of 19th Annual ACM Conference on Object-Oriented Programming, Systems, Languages, and Applications,* p. 174-175

Brown, P. J., Bovey J. D., & Chen, X. (1997). Context-aware applications: From the laboratory to the marketplace. *IEEE Personal Communications, 4*(5), 58-64.

Dey, A. K. (2000). Providing architectural support for building context-aware applications, Phd. Thesis, Georgia Institute of Technology.

Dogac, A., Laleci, G., Kabak, Y., Kurt, G., & Acar, A. (n/d). A platform for semantically enriched mobile services. *In Proceedings of the First International conference on Mobile Business,* pdf, Greece, Athens

Gams, M. (1999). Information Society Promotes Intelligent Systems. *In Proceedings of the International Conference Information Society,* 1, Slovenia, Ljubljana.

Hars, A., Sawy, O.A.E., Gosain, S., Hirt, S., Im, I., Kang, D., Lee, Z., & Raven, A. (2000). Reengineering IS Research and Its Intellectual Infrastructure for the Electronic Economy. *Journal of Organizational Computing and Electronic Commerce, 10(2),* 67-83.

Ho, S. Y., & Kwok, S. H. (2003). The Attraction of Personalized Service for Users in Mobile Commerce: An Empirical Study. *ACM SIGecom Exchanges, 3*(4), 10-18.

Karunanithi, K., Haneef, K., Cordioli, B., & Umar A. (2000). In R. Jain (ed.) Building Flexible Mobile Applications for Next Generation Enterprises. In *Proceedings of Academia/Industry Working Conference on Research Challenges,* p.127-132

Krisper, M. et. al. (2004). *Information strategic planning methodology,* University of Ljubljana.

Müller-Veerse, F. (2000). *Mobile Commerce Report,* Research report, Durlacher Research.

Panis, S., Morphis, N., Felt, E., Reufenheuser, B., Bohm, A., Nitz, J., & Saarlo, P. (2002). Mobile commerce scenarios and related business models. *In Proceedings of the First International conference on Mobile Business,* pdf, Greece, Athens

Pascoe, J. (1998). Adding generic contextual capabilities to wearable computers. In *Proceedings of the 2nd IEEE International Symposium on Wearable Computers,* p. 92, PA, Pittsburg.

Rupnik, R. (2002). *Context-aware Mobile Application Model and the Role of Mobile Applications in Information Systems*. PhD Theses, University of Ljubljana

Rupnik, R. & Krisper, M. (2001). Mobile applications: The consequence and the demand of information society. In *Proceedings of the International Conference Information Society 2001*, 9, Slovenia, Ljubljana.

Rupnik, R., & Krisper, M. (2003). The Role of Mobile Applications in Information Systems. In *Proceedings of the 2nd International Conference on Mobile Business 2003*, Vienna, Austria.

Ryan, N., Pascoe, J., & Morse, D. (1998). Enhanced reality fieldwork: The context-aware archaeological assistant. In *Computer applications and quantitative methods in archeology*, Oxford press.

Sacher, H. (2001). *Uncovering the wireless interaction paradigm*, [available from: www.baychi.org, last accessed July 2002].

Schilit, B. N., Adams, N. I., & Want, R. (1994). Context-aware computing applications. In *Proceedings of the 1st International Workshop on Mobile Computing Systems and Applications*, p. 85, CA, Santa Cruz.

Sharaf, M. A., & Chrysanthis, P. K. (2002). Facilitating Mobile Decision Making. In *Proceedings of WMC conference*, p.45, USA, Atlanta

Smith, H. A., Kulatilaka, N., & Venkatramen, N. (2002). Developments in IS Practice III: Riding the Wave: Extracting Value From Mobile Technology. *Communications of the Association for Information Systems*, http://cais.aisnet.org

Tarasewich, P. (2004). Designing Mobile Commerce Applications. *Communications of the ACM, 46*(12), 57-60.

Tarasewich, P., R.C. Nickerson and M. Warkentin (2002). Issues in Mobile e-Commerce. *Communications of the Association for Information Systems*, http://cais.aisnet.org.

Varshney, U. (2003). Wireless I: Mobile and Wireless Information Systems: Applications, Networks, and Research Problems. *Communications of the Association for Information Systems*, http://cais.aisnet.org

Chapter XVI
Real Time Decision Making and Mobile Technologies

Keith Sherringham
IMS Corp, Australia

Bhuvan Unhelkar
MethodScience.com & University of Western Sydney, Australia

ABSTRACT

For business decision making to occur, data needs to be converted to information, then to knowledge and rapidly to wisdom. Whilst Information Communication Technology (ICT) solutions facilitate business decision making, ICT has not always been effective in providing the critical "data to wisdom" conversion necessary for real-time decision making on any device anywhere anytime. This lack of effectiveness in real-time decision making has been further hampered by a dependence upon location and time. Mobile technologies provide an opportunity to enhance business decision making by freeing users from complex information management requirements and enabling real-time decision making on any device anywhere anytime. This chapter discusses the role of mobile technologies in real time decision making.

INTRODUCTION

As society exits the industrial age and enters the knowledge era, society suffers from data overload, information is lacking, knowledge is scarce and wisdom is wanting (Balthazard, & Cook 2004). Instead of having the right information, presented at the right time in the right way to make decisions, society is epitomised by people spending large amounts of time trawling and sifting through data to try and find what is needed to make decisions (Adair 2007). This practice of searching and sifting through data

in an effort to find information poses a huge in-built inefficiency with higher costs and un-assured service delivery. Advances in mobile technology are likely to create further challenges to these searches and sorts as they bring in additional dimensions of location-independence and personalization.

The need for the rendering of information in context, as part of work-flow, to any device anywhere anytime to enable real time decision making is the goal of many organisations. The mobile enablement of business, as discussed by Sherringham and Unhelkar (2008a) in a separate chapter in this book, is expected to further drive the demand for real time decision making services (Ghanbary 2006). The emergence of real time decision making, the elements required to achieve that process and the implications of mobile technologies in real time decision making are discussed in this chapter.

DATA – WISDOM VALUE STACK

A record in a database, a marketing video or a company's financial report are all data. Data only becomes information when it is analysed, understood and needed. With the application of experience and skills information becomes knowledge and when such knowledge is applied at the right time in the right way, knowledge becomes wisdom (power/profit). This data to wisdom conversion is illustrated in Figure 1.

The familiar example is a hall porter, who by putting a favourite wine in a hotel room collects a reward. The hall porter takes the data elements (arrival at that hotel, to the appropriate room, at that correct time and with the wine) and because the elements are required and understood they are information. Context is given to the information (managing the relationships between pieces of information and used with work-flow) to achieve knowledge, which is then applied at the right time in the right way to realise a profit (Ghanbary and Arunatileka 2006).

The business imperative of the data – wisdom conversion has been widely noted, e.g. Macmanus et al. (2005), but the significance of the value stack

Figure 1. Data – Wisdom value-stack

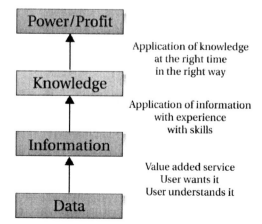

lies in the importance of providing *context* through managing relationships between pieces of information and by the integration of information with work-flow. Within mobile business, the significance of location provides additional context to the information.

Resolution of the data – knowledge conversion allows the right information to be presented at the right time in the right way to the right audience, providing two advantages. Firstly, the need for users to have advanced information management skills to complete the most rudimentary of tasks is reduced. Secondly, the difficulty of managing information on the small screen of current mobile devices is removed. Resolution of the data – knowledge conversion to service both business and mobile business will allow mobility to realise its true significance through the provision of real time decision making (Raton 2006) and provide business with a major competitive advantage (Ekionea 2005).

ELEMENTS OF REAL TIME DECISION MAKING

With real time decision making, our favourite restaurants can bid in real time to achieve our patronage on any device anywhere anytime. The information needed to take the best route home is supplied dynamically as the road is traversed and everything that is needed to make a foreign exchange trade is rendered to any device anywhere anytime for decision and execution (Gupta 2006).

The key elements of real time decision making are summarised in Figure 2 and are discussed as follows.

Consolidated Repository – Information for real time decision making is accessed from virtual consolidated repositories that combine spatial data, database data, transactional data and documents (including images). To stop the duplication of effort, information is single sourced from virtual consolidated repositories. Within these repositories, content is separated from presentation and from mechanism of delivery. Archiving, backup, recovery and version control, are all performed on the repositories on behalf of the user, freeing up both the end user and the end-device (Sherringham 2005).

The benefits of distributed computing power shall continue within the mobile computing environment but unlike the desktop environment where data were trapped locally, consolidated data storage ensures that data are single sourced and that data are not stored for extended periods of time on the end device (Sherringham 2008). To effectively support mobile computing, large centralised databases shall be replaced with virtual consolidated contextual information bases (Yang and Wang 2006).

Information Relationships – To achieve knowledge and to make decisions, different pieces of information often need to be drawn together, i.e. the relationships between elements of information need to be provided to give context. Information relationships are managed using a metadata framework that provides all of the supporting details to give context and by linking it to steps in a work-flow. A metadata framework includes classification schema, versioning details, role based access, security and privileges, as well as device specific information and spatial needs.

Use of metadata to manage information relationships is critical in the data to knowledge conversion and is a prerequisite to the provision of more sophisticated mobile business services.

Work-flow – By defining and integrating information to process, knowledge can be presented in context for real time decision making (Ekione and Abou-Zeid 2005). The user is taken through a series of recipes (process and information combined in sequence - recipes) to realise the required outcomes. The combination of information relationships and work-flow together provide context and allows the conversion of data into information and to knowledge. The challenge is the development and maintenance of the standard recipes by audience and of the virtual consolidated contextual information bases.

When providing mobile business services and products, it is ease of use that influences user acceptance and product adoption. The use of clearly defined recipes to guide the user to the assured outcome is part of the mobile business solution.

Unified search – Search shall be unified across all data types and tightly integrated with work-flow. Search harnesses the information relationships to provide context and uses role-based access and other usability information to provide focused results. The effectiveness of a search capability is a pivotal tool to the provision of services on mobile devices.

Artificial intelligence – Work-flow, search and information relationships are all expected to merge into one layer that is artificial intelligence. It is the presence of artificial intelligence that will liberate the end user and empower mobile business.

Security – As part of the overall security issue, a metadata framework facilitates the security provision and management because of the application of user access rights to the specific information elements.

Messaging – Real time decision making requires a unified messaging environment to combine voice, data, text, images and video. To guarantee service delivery the messaging environment needs to be architected around the FedEx model, where the quality of hand-off, the message, the delivery and storage of the message are all separated and utility infrastructure underpins the message processing.

Supporting the messaging environment are the device and asset management functionality and capability, including locational information. Tagging of messages for application specific processing or archiving for compliance shall also be part of the messaging environment.

Presentation – With a resolution of the information to be provided, the provision of context and work-flow, the remaining element is the presentation to the end of device. The interface will consist of a series of intuitive icons that provide the user with the required business functionality. Invoking an icon changes the interface to reflect the task on-hand with the work-flow embedded. The ability to customise and personalise the

Figure 2. Elements of real time decision making

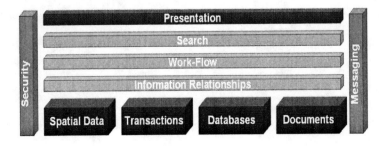

interface would also exist, together with an integrated search (Sherringham and Unhelkar 2008b).

ICT INDUSTRY TRENDS AND REAL TIME DECISION MAKING

Involving telecommunications companies, hardware and software suppliers, content providers and consulting services, real time decision making on any device anywhere anytime is an emerging trillion dollar business opportunity that will underpin business operations. The emergence of real time decision making from the evolving use of the Internet is shown in Figure 3.

Brochureware remains a major use of the Internet and will transition to mobile devices. Although the Internet is increasingly being used to support transaction processing, many opportunities for development still exist because the transaction processing capability is still in its infancy and advanced and complex transaction processing is currently not well supported. Basic transaction processing is starting to be seen on mobile devices but complex transaction processing requires some significant changes in business processes and resolution of security and authentication before a wide adoption on mobile devices occurs.

The emergence and growth of collaboration is the focus for much of the ICT industry and is increasingly providing other business opportunities. Collaboration includes Web 2.0, with social networking, business networking and the need for entertainment. The greater use of the Internet for messaging and the convergence of telecommunications with the computer are also aspects of the collaboration stage in the evolution of the Internet

and mobile business. Whilst mobile devices will play a significant role within collaboration, the maturity of business processes and of management frameworks remains an issue for business collaboration.

The natural extension of collaboration is real time decision making. Effective collaboration requires that the right information be shared with participants so that informed decisions can be made and then executed. With the provision of information in context linked to work-flow, real time decision making promises to add significantly to business capabilities.

Whilst many business talk about collaboration and the provision of collaboration services, the value lies in real time decision making because of its higher value and range of opportunities. Compared with the Internet wave that swept through society when Web sites and the Internet came to the fore, the changes seen in society as a result of real time decision making will transform humanity. Strategically aligning both business and ICT now to support and adopt real time decision making is required.

Real time decision making brings together some key and innovative technologies (Table I) whilst providing a unified approach to software development, enterprise architecture, business process and information management (Alag 2006).

Iconic interface – Currently, an iconic interface is the most effective approach for providing a common and intuitive interface on the small screen of a mobile device through to the more spatial screen real estate of the plasma television set. Iconic interfaces are increasingly used for many features of applications with the display automatically changing to reflect those most relevant features to the needs of the user, e.g. Apple's I-phone and the latest release of Microsoft

Figure 3. Evolution of the Internet and the emergence of real time decision making

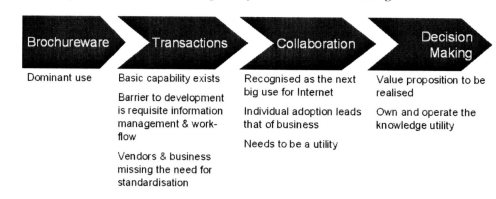

Brochureware	Transactions	Collaboration	Decision Making
Dominant use	Basic capability exists	Recognised as the next big use for Internet	Value proposition to be realised
	Barrier to development is requisite information management & work-flow	Individual adoption leads that of business	Own and operate the knowledge utility
	Vendors & business missing the need for standardisation	Needs to be a utility	

Table I. Summary of ICT trends impacting upon real time decision making

Trend	Description	Opportunity
Iconic interface	Iconic interface of business functionality that includes work-flow that changes to meet user need. Spans both the desktop and mobile devices.	Control the framework that manages the interface and control access to the rest.
Features to functionality	Move away from feature rich software used by few people to functionality driven applications used by many people across all devices.	The software of the future is development of functionality driven software, including work-flow, as object of functionality, delivered as required to any device.
Application consolidation	Focus is not on application specific software but bringing together objects of functionality. The killer applications that standardised the desktop will be replaced by integration of elements of functionality rendered on any device.	Standardisation and dominance over mobile computing, desktop computing and enterprise computing shall come from standardised seamless integration of elements of functionality.
Sound practice	Return to consolidated data storage and work-flow; separation of content from presentation and mechanism of delivery and use of smart end device with the load being taken by the server.	Position now and implement best practices in future developments ready to support mobile computing.
Software as a Service (SaaS)	Real time decision making is a natural extension of SaaS; with only those services required being rendered as needed.	Real time decision making on mobile devices will drive the definition of new SaaS opportunities.
End device & operating system	In the emerging mobile market, the de-facto standard for hardware and end device operating system are still to be realised.	Own the operating system of the mobile device and define the standards for the end device.
Data storage	Increasing demand for consolidated data storage is required to support mobile business.	Standardise and become the market leader in the development and provision of global virtual consolidated databases that Google has already started.
Consolidated contextual information bases	The advances required are in information in context integrated with work-flow – contextual information bases. These will be virtual consolidated information bases.	The software to support consolidate contextual information bases requires a new generation of database software that will underpin access from millions of users on mobile devices.
Context based searching	Google became a billion dollar company searching data in an effort to find information. Searching in context is the evolving opportunity.	Realsie the value in searching and managing knowledge. Realise the knowledge utility.

Office. The ability to personalise the interface and to be independent of location are extra features to be seen within mobile devices.

Features to functionality - Whilst the trend for more and more features to be supplied within software applications that are used by fewer people is still strongly present, this trend is set to change because of the need for a functionally driven iconic interface on mobile devices. An iconic interface that includes work-flow and which changes to reflect the functionality required by a user to achieve an outcome, removes the user from the need for intimate knowledge of feature

driven software. The successful software of the future delivers functionality and NOT features.

Application consolidation - The use of an iconic interface that invokes functionality instead of features creates a blurring in the need for distinct killer applications because it is about bringing elements of functionality together to meet a need. The focus will no longer be on launching an application to complete a task but it is about conducting a task and bringing together the functionality necessary to achieve the required outcomes. Whilst Microsoft's use of Outlook as a master application to drive desktop functionality is another step in the seamless integration of applications, this approach is still evolving.

Microsoft PowerPoint allowed people to be a presenter. Microsoft Word allowed people to be a typist and Microsoft Excel allowed people to be accountants. It was Microsoft's close linking of killer applications with its operating system that allowed for standardisation of the desktop environment and led to market dominance. In the world of real time decision making and mobile devices, it is the seamless integration of elements of functionality that shall lead to standardisation and dominance over mobile computing, desktop computing and enterprise computing (Armstrong 2006).

Return of sound practices – In the mainframe environment, the end device was dumb and everything was done centrally on a mainframe. The introduction of the PC realsied the benefits of distributed computing power and of an intelligent end device but also some bad trends occurred. Firstly, the end device was burdened with more and more applications which has caused update and coordination problems. Secondly the benefits of consolidated data storage and work-flow were lost. Furthermore, content was no longer separated from presentation and mechanism of delivery.

Through real time decision making and the demands from mobile business, some of the best practices can be returned to ICT (Kaliszewski 2006). To work effectively, the end device (mobile device) will be smart but it cannot become overloaded like the desktop PC. The bulk of the work will be done at the server end with results only being displayed on the mobile device and the prompt for the next stage of the process. The mobile end device remains simple and easily managed.

Using mobile devices to access contextual information from consolidated contextual information bases means that the benefits of consolidated data storage linked to work-flow shall be seen within mobile business. The separation of content from presentation and mechanism of delivery sees the return of another good practice and a requisite for real time decision making is implemented. In addition, real time decision making requires that the business logic and processing rules (Lucas 2005) be stored in contextual databases and not in the source code – a return to good coding practices.

Software as a Service (SaaS) – The provision of Software as a Service is in its infancy and the mobile opportunities for SaaS are still to be realised. Much of SaaS is still very application specific and there

have been concerns about the quality and applicability of code supplied with SaaS. Real time decision making and the elements of business functionality in the interface is a natural extension to current SaaS. Mobile business will provide many new opportunities for SaaS.

End device and operating system – Like any other market, the evolution of the desktop environment led to a highly diversified market with many players in hardware, software and killer applications. As the market evolved and matured, standards came into effect and it is this standardisation which drove the consolidation and the creation of market dominance by a few key players.

Within the emerging mobile business market, the de-facto standard for hardware, both server and end device, is still to be defined. The operating system, for both the server and end device, is also in need of standardisation. Market dominance comes with being the de-facto standard. The opportunities that come from standardisation in the mobile market are more extensive because of the convergence of the mobile phone with the laptop computer, with television, with the gaming console and with the music and video player.

Whilst the PC environment was characterised by an integration of killer applications with an operating system that led to standardisation, the mobile business environment is different. Within the mobile business environment, there is a decline in the importance of killer applications but a greater significance in elements of business functionality. Close integration of elements of business functionality through an iconic interface with the mobile device operating system is the path to standardisation and market dominance for software vendors.

Data storage – The demand for data storage capability is set to rapidly increase. It is not so much in the storage of transaction data and documents that will further significantly pressure data storage but it is the growth in imaging for work-flow, results for simulation, images from surveillance and services for entertainment. The storage will not be on the end device but on the server in global virtual consolidated databases (Raisinghani 2006).

Consolidated contextual information bases – Real time decision making and mobile business depends upon the use of contextual information bases to underpin its operation. These databases shall function along distributed lines and shall be viewed as one virtual global consolidated information base.

The database software to support consolidated contextual information bases requires a new generation of object orientated databases. Whether it is a user on a mobile device or a wireless napkin holder, these consolidated contextual information bases will service millions of devices.

Context based searching – Contextual based searching is key to the operation of real time decision making. The leading search capabilities present currently are not only data type specific, e.g. documents or transaction data, but because of the lack of context and work-flow, the searching is not contextual. Development of contextual based searching provides any given business with an unprecedented business opportunity and control over mobile business globally.

Artificial intelligence – Contextual based searching, the management of information relationships and linking to work-flow are necessary for real time decision making but the challenge is the sheer volume of data that currently exists, plus that which will evolve going forward. It is simply not possible for humans to classify and context this volume of information by audience; nor meet the dynamic nature of information and the evolving needs. Artificial intelligence shall be used.

Contextual based searching, the management of information relationships (metadata) and work-flow shall all merge to form a layer of artificial intelligence (Figure 2). The existing use of pattern matching and predictive capabilities in artificial intelligence shall be expanded upon to include perceptive and awareness capabilities. Artificial intelligence shall initially come to the fore in error and exception handling for routine transaction processing because the majority of information accessed in business is as part of routine transaction processing and it is standardised transaction processing that underpins business operations (Moonis 2006). The potential applications of artificial intelligence within mobile are almost limitless and with artificial intelligence present on all hand held devices, all fixed devices (napkin holders, fridges, PCs and TVs), the market opportunity is unprecedented.

FUTURE DIRECTION

Even though real time decision making is still emerging and there is much work to be done to see its full realisation, some future trends are already starting to be identified. Real time decision making is an emerging trillion dollar industry that will evolve over the next 10-years and collaboration between key players is how the opportunity will be realised. Whilst a unified approach may currently be absent from the industry, the business opportunity is too great for the collaboration not to occur.

Whilst the demands of mobility shall be the major driver in realising real time decision making on any device anywhere anytime, it is the telecommunications network that underpins real time decision making. Major telecommunications companies like Verizon and British Telecom are deploying fibre optic networks to support not only an integrated communications environment but also the whole scale future transmission of data. Whilst the mobile dominates the last step to the end user, the bulk of data traffic movement shall remain the fibre optic backbones. The future shall see an operating system layered on the routers and fibre optics of the telecommunication network to form one global virtual mainframe to support real time decision making.

Whilst the emergence of artificial intelligence is the critical layer in the solution that supports real time decision making (Figure 2), at least one more layer is to still to be developed, that of voice. Gone will be the days of data entry and management through a keyboard, voice shall be the key mechanism. Other bio-recognition solutions are also expected to be developed.

The ICT industry has seen standardisation of the operating system and of application. Standardisation has occurred at the desktop and is being seen at the enterprise level. Whilst standardisation of the mobile device is still to be realised, the real opportunity is standardisation of the marketplace. Business operates in market places, e.g. banks and standards to operate globally, and the opportunity to standardise the marketplace ICT awaits (the emergence of marketplace computing).

Access to information shall become a consumer right in the knowledge era. In the knowledge era, information shall underpin society and like power and water, the Internet and knowledge will be a utility. Of all the utilities (gas, water or electricity), and of all the infrastructures (roads, ports, rail or communications), the knowledge utility will be the most demanding and the most valuable.

CONCLUSION

Living in the knowledge era provides many opportunities and rewards to the individual, to business and to society. For humanity to realise its true potential in the knowledge era, users need to be freed from the need for advanced information skills and empowered by real time decision making on any device anywhere anytime. Information in context, sourced from virtual consolidated contextual information bases and integrated with work-flow for delivery through a common interface across devices is what is required. Artificial intelligence is how contextual based searching is achieved and how the relationships between information managed to give context.

Real time decision making is a trillion dollar business opportunity that is set to evolve over the next 10-years and to become the de-facto industry standard. Whilst the demands of mobility shall drive the evolution of real time decision making, it is the benefits derived in routine business transaction processing that will be the initial incentive for realisation. Beyond this, however, lies the moral responsibility for realising real time decision making for the betterment of humanity because knowledge is freedom and knowledge is the liberator from poverty and tyranny.

REFERENCES

Adair, J. E. (2007). *Decision making & problem solving strategies 2nd edition*, Philadelphia: Kogan Page

Alag H. S. (2006). Business Process Mobility. In Unhelkar B. (Ed.), *Handbook of Research in Mobile Business: Technical, Methodological and Social Perspectives*. Hershey, PA, USA: IGI Global

Armstrong, M. (2006). *A handbook of management techniques: a comprehensive guide to achieving managerial excellence and improved decision making*, Rev. 3rd ed. London: Kogan Page

Balthazard, P. A., & Cook, R. A. (2004). Organizational Culture and Knowledge Management Success: Assessing the Behaviour-Performance Continuum. *Paper presented at the Proceeding of the 37th Hawaii International Conference on System Sciences*, Hawaii, USA.

Ekionea, J. B., & Abou-Zeid, E. (2005). Knowledge Management and Sustained Competitive Advantage: A Resource-Based Analysis. *Paper presented at the IRMA Conference*, SanDiego, USA.

Ghanbary. A. (2006). Evaluation of mobile technologies in the context of their applications, limitations and transformation. In Unhelkar B. (Ed.), Chapter 42 of book: *Handbook of Research in Mobile Business: Technical, Methodological and Social Perspectives*. Hershey, PA, USA: IGI Global

Ghanbary, A., & Arunatileka, D. (2006). Enhancing Customer Relationship Management through Mobile Personnel Knowledge Management (MPKM). *Proceedings of IBIMA International Conference*. IBIMA 2006. Bonn, Germany. 19-21 June.

Gupta, J. N. D. (2006). *Intelligent Decision-making Support Systems Foundations, Applications and Challenges*. London: Springer-Verlag London Limited

Kaliszewski, I. (2006). *Soft computing for complex multiple criteria decision making*. New York, NY: Springer

Lucas, H. C. (2005) *Information technology: strategic decision making for managers*. Hoboken, NJ: Wiley

Macmanus, D. J., Snyder, C. A., & Wilson, L. T. (2005). The Knowledge Management Imperative. *Paper presented at the IRMA Conference 2005*, San Diego, USA.

Moonis, A. (2006) Advances in Applied Artificial Intelligence. *Proceedings of 19th International Conference on Industrial, Engineering and Other Applications of Applied Intelligent Systems*, IEA/AIE 2006, Annecy, France, June 27-30. Berlin Heidelberg: Springer-Verlag GmbH.

Raisinghani, M. S. (2006). M-Business: A Global Perspective. In Unhelkar B. (Ed.), Chapter 31 of book: *Handbook of Research in Mobile Business: Technical, Methodological and Social Perspectives*. Hershey, PA, USA: IGI Global.

Raton, B. (2006). *Autonomous mobile robots: sensing, control, decision-making, and applications*. FL: CRC/Taylor & Francis

Sherringham, K. (2005). Cookbook for Market Dominance and Shareholder Value: Standardising the Roles of Knowledge Workers. Athena Press: London. (p. 90).

Sherringham, K. (2008). Catching the Mobility Wave Information Age April-May 2008 (p. 5).

Sherringham, K., & Unhelkar, B. (2008a). Elements for the Mobile Enablement of Business. In (Unhelkar et al. 2008) Handbook of Research in Mobile Business: Technical, Methodological and Social Perspectives – 2nd Edition, IGI Global.

Sherringham, K., & Unhelkar, B. (2008b). Business Driven Enterprise Architecture and Applications to Support Mobile Business. In (Unhelkar et al. 2008) Handbook of Research in Mobile Business: Technical, Methodological and Social Perspectives. 2nd Edition, IGI Global

Yang C. C., & Wang, F. L. (2006). Information Delivery for Mobile Business: Architecture for Accessing Large Documents through Mobile Devices. In Unhelkar B. (Ed.), Chapter 18 of book: *Handbook of Research in Mobile Business: Technical, Methodological and Social Perspectives.* Hershey, PA, USA: IGI Global.

KEY TERMS

Activity Objects: A series of objects invoked from a standard iconic interface that provide business functionality because they contain the necessary content, images, business logic, processing rules, work-flow and presentation rules.

Contextual Search: Searching of information in context so that useful results are obtained.

FedEx Model: A model for the operation of a unified messaging environment based on the proven principles to move messages (parcels) around the world by leading logistics companies.

Information Bases: The next generation of databases but instead of storing data, information is stored in context.

Information Relationships: The associations between elements of information to provide context and convert information to knowledge.

Knowledge Utility: Like power and water, knowledge shall become a utility infrastructure that underpins humanity.

Marketplace Computing: Standardised computing (tightly integrated hardware and software) operating at the marketplace level to allow businesses to interact effectively in a marketplace. Business currently standardises at the enterprise level but to operate effectively, standardisation shall be at the marketplace level.

Real Time Decision Making: The provision of information in context and integrated with work-flow in real time to any device anywhere anytime is needed so that decisions can be made.

Chapter XVII
Channel Optimization for On Field Sales Force by Integration of Business Software on Mobile Platforms

Rishi Kalra
Symbiosis International University, India

Amit Nanchahal
Symbiosis International University, India

ABSTRACT

Marketing and sales channels are a significant lifeline for the sales force of a business. Sales professionals work on the concept of creating and widening channels that are then fed by the supply chain and distribution network of the businesses. Sales teams are constantly pushed to meet customer expectations while generating revenue for the company. As companies grow, these pressures increase. Sales teams are now looking at Mobile Sales Force Automation technologies to handle the ever increasing customer demands. Companies want to keep costs low, increase productivity and efficiency through mobile devices for the much needed edge on the field. This chapter is based on literature review of channel optimization as well as mobile software platforms and challenges faced by the sales force. This chapter discusses the need for integrating business software on mobile platforms that will optimize and enhance the performance of sales processes.

INTRODUCTION

The concept of the mobile enterprise is growing[a] in today's corporate world taking interest in tools supporting enterprise mobility for their sales force. These mobile enterprise solutions promise efficiency and productivity gains resulting from the sales function optimization. The change in mindset towards mobile applications in business has created a strong opportunity for companies to extend their core data and applications through smart phones, cell phones, and personal digital assistants (PDAs). This extension of the business process applications results in creation of location independent links between the office (or a centralized location) with an increasingly dispersed workforce – notably the sales force which is continuously on the move.

The reason why companies are looking at incorporating such small handheld devices in their business processes is because by increased usage of mobile phones, PDAs and laptops, the company can keep in constant touch with its staff and managers who are spending more and more time away from the corporate network. These devices also provide vital access to these staff for email and the Internet. Istart Technology research found that:

- 27% of e-mail requires immediate action[b]
- 40% of the workforce is mobile
- 60% of senior management time is spent away from the desk[c]

Sales force management is the art of managing sales team on the field that enable an organization to generate revenue by selling their products to customers and increase customer satisfaction.

Companies are spending huge resources on their sales force and incorporating the new systems and applications into their operations management that help automate business processes. These applications are combined with the existing CRM functions in the organization which help enhancing the selling tactics of the on field sales force across industries by providing up to date information helping them win in the global business battlefield.

On field sales force for any company is concerned with all the stages of the sales process, starting from contact management, sales forecasting, recording sales, product solution details, integration of the various departments companywide.

A sales force personnel on the field requires constant communication with the home office for sales leads, invoicing, inventory[d] tracking, order fulfillment, and other supporting information. Recent advances in wireless technology field staff had to make do with laptops that required a physical connection and voice-based mobile phones neither providing the added value of mobility.

A new breed of user friendly Internet capable applications on smart phones and mobile devices are freeing the traditional sales force from their desks and allowing them to be incredibly effective. Sales personnel now have access to the same information and tools as their peers back at the office. This chapter discusses the various aspects in the channel for sales in an organization and the intervention of mobile devices to increase productivity.[e]

CHANNEL OPTIMIZATION CHALLENGE

Distribution channel is the structure that the company uses to reach its products/services to customers through intermediaries at the right place, at the right time with special consideration for profit and effectiveness. As shown in *Figure 1* products of a company may be passed from one intermediary channel member to another after keeping a certain margin for their services. The optimization of the distribution channel poses a challenge to organizations with different entities trying to transfer the product title and risk to the next successive channel member. The coordination and smooth working for optimum output for the company is the job of the sales team.

Distribution channels basically provide three functions: *information flow* (outward information about the supplier's offering and inward flow about customers' needs), *logistics* to get the supplier's product to the end customer, and *value-added services* that augment the supplier's product (local selling, financing, customization, after-sales parts and service, etc.). When improved alternatives for providing these functions evolve or when customer expectations rise, the failure of existing channels to respond prevents the supplier from adequately satisfying the customer. *Figure 2* describes the flow from the manufacturer to the retail point in Fast moving consumer goods category.

The shortcomings in a distribution channel are shown below:

- Excessive time taken for order processing due to lack of proper and effective communication between order procuring and order processing. [f]

- Inefficient forecasting techniques as calculated using past data rather than current on field inputs from sales force.

- Insufficient information supplied by sales personnel to retailers while pushing for sales; due to incomplete product knowledge and changing product lines.

- Increased threat of cannibalization and market fragmentation by inefficient order tracking and stock management techniques.

Figure 1. Distribution channel for a packaged goods industry

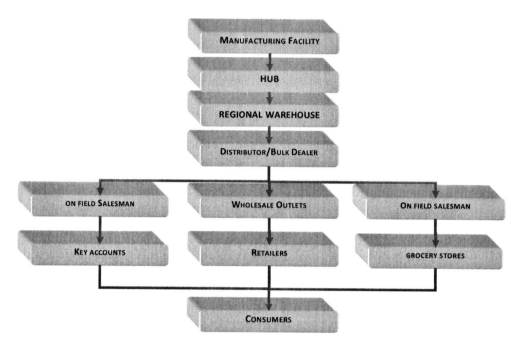

Reference: Report by Rishi Kalra on "Entry Stratefy for Haats/Shandies as a distribution channel in Orissa" at ITC Ltd Vizag Branch in June 2007.

- Demographically heterogeneous consumers with changing habits, behavior and wants which are ineffectively monitored and stored by the sales force.
- Declining margins due to price erosion and increased costs due to excessive paperwork for completing the sales process leading to lost sales time.

Sales team for a company requires a lot of data support from the office or central location to close a deal or sell the company's products to demanding clients. The systems available now as shown in *Figure 3* incorporated on mobile devices enable the sales person to re-quote proposals, negotiate prices, manage orders and constantly update product knowledge on the move. Today the requirements from the sales force are more demanding and focused on monitoring all new business opportunities in the area, client reviews, marketing activities, competitor analysis and strategies for business development.

The various roles of a sales person are:[g]

- **Generate Sales:** Pre sales call planning, prospecting, presentations, entertain, closing sales, arrange delivery, collect payment.
- **Provide Service:** Technical consulting / solution formulation, arrange & oversee installation, train users, testing & monitoring.
- **Territory management:** Gather & analyze industry data – on customers & competitors, map distribution coverage, forecast.
- **Professional development:** Take part in sales meetings, trade shows, update product knowledge, upgrade skills, changing sales plan.
- **Other services:** Train new sales persons, counseling juniors, prepare manuals, and represent company in sponsored civic/social events.

The shortcomings of the **on field sales force** are mentioned below:[h]

- *Figure 4* shows the various challenges faced by the on field sales force.
- Faster decision making required at the time of sales, access to information about price, product and stock to help close the sale on the spot.
- Need to remain as one point of contact for the company and the customer.

Figure 2. Physical flow of goods in a distribution channel

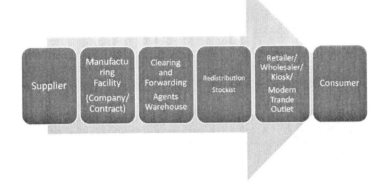

Figure 3. Process flow followed by sales force

- Inefficiently addressing customer requirements and problems during interactions due to lack of proper negotiation and problem solving support on field.
- Challenge in identifying new sales opportunities at existing client accounts and at noncustomer, or whitespace, for companies due to lack of access to market data and current trends.
- Improper communication for receiving scheduled alerts about sales performance leading to inefficient planning and managing sales activity.
- Lack of access to customer/channel partner requirements and payment track record to manage the clients better on field.

- Inefficient use of field time[i]: A manual system requires a lot of time for data capture leading to lower efficiency. Moreover, loss of time is the most important edge against competition; increased efficiency allows sales force more time to generate sales.
- Possibility of human error: There are multiple jobs being performed by the sales force personnel while on the field which require manual data entry or estimation. Human error is critical when the decisions are made by the sales force for stock, sales forecasting, order due date, recording sales, and competition benchmarking.
- Lack of effective coordination during preparation of sales proposal due to improper flow of information between the various departments and the central database to on field agents making sales.
- Inefficient monitoring and coordination of channel partners and sales force personnel on the field due to dispersed data.

The goal of Small Handheld Devices (SHD) is to streamline the entire sales process by integrating business software on the mobile devices to make businesses function efficiently, improve customer interaction, increase customer satisfaction, and save time.

Key research findings of mobile device management leader Mformation Technologies, Inc:[j]

- US enterprises reported more than half of managers using company-supplied mobile devices and nearly one-third of staff, with 56 percent reported increased usage among managers and 60 percent reporting increases in staff usage.[k]

Figure 4. Challenges with the existing sales process system

- Mobile email, Internet and calendar applications are already pervasive, with more than 90 percent of companies using them, and businesses are set to significantly increase the use of new mobile applications such as sales force applications and company file share systems.
- 81 percent of respondents reported significant productivity increases from current mobile investments, with more than one-third of these reported increase higher than 20 percent.
- Four-fifths of CIOs interviewed look for improved management of mobile devices, applications, and data to accelerate the productivity trend, and more than 8 out of 10 US CIOs believe the mobile operator should take the lead in providing these device management services.

The major benefits of **Small Handheld Devices** for the on field sales force are:

- Data capture process optimization by pre drafted e-forms instead of manual filling of sales orders, reports, activity reports, and/or call sheets by on field sales people[l].
- Seamless information transmission from field to the central location rather than printing out reports and taking them to the sales manager.[m]
- Efficient response to client queries by use of hand held devices rather than waiting for paper based product inventory data and sales prospect lists resulting in long-lasting, profitable customer relationships.

- Ease of data entry mechanisms improve sales staff morale by reducing the amount of record keeping and/or increase the rate of closing.
- Sales staff can be easily trained with product information and sales technique training using SHD tools faster and more efficiently.
- Better communication and co-operation between sales personnel facilitates successful team selling.
- More and better qualified sales leads could be automatically generated by the software.
- This technology increases the sales person's ratio of selling time to non-selling time. Non-selling time includes activities like report writing, travel time, internal meetings, training, and seminars.
- Mobile technology providing instant access to information, applications, and services anytime and anywhere. This saves a lot of time most important business commodity.
- Improved supply chain efficiency by integrating various levels of corporate activity[n]
- Digital catalogue of products (including pictures) with sales representatives at all times.
- Orders placed by sales representatives can be automatically assigned to the sales representative that placed the order, thus streamlining the commission calculations and incentives.
- Improves cash flow by accelerating payments from customers – increasing efficiency of gathering data needed to create and deliver invoices customers.

186

Table 1.

Sales Process	Challenges	SHD Optimizations
Contact Management	1. Inefficient classification of contacts on the field 2. Cumbersome to develop new contacts from prospects with improper data capturing. 3. Difficult to remember old transactions with the contacts.	1. Efficient classification using the central database and parameters 2. Ease of recording data from prospects 3. Complete access to all transactions with the contact and customization of solution.
Order Management	1. Increased lead time in order processing due to time lag in information flow 2. Inefficient cumbersome order booking 3. Human error in recording data leading to incorrect demand estimation 4. Lack of real time access to client orders	1. Faster delivery due to reduced lead time 2. Effortless order capture 3. Increased accuracy in order processing 4. Access to past data of client orders and delivery dates.
Sales Forecasting	1. Micro level knowledge and view of the sales in the region. 2. Outdated information about targets of the served region	1. Integrated timely sales forecast generation from on field sales force (hourly, daily etc) 2. Coordinated updating of data from all mobile devices providing a holistic view of the database to sales force.
Recording Sales	1. Sales recorded manually on sale books and transferred to the database at the end of the day. 2. Human errors while recording data due to time constraints	1. Directly transferred to the database on a periodic basis synchronizing with the central database. 2. Less chances of human error due to efficient data entry mechanisms.
Charting Proposals	1. No data available from past interactions 2. Lack of access to latest sales data (product details, pricing, schemes, etc) available to field agents for preparing proposal.	1. Quicker access to past client interactions. 2. Access to latest sales data from the central database to give the client the most competitive quote.
Negotiation and Re-quote	1. Inefficient support on the field from the office during negotiations. 2. Decision making postponed till approved from higher authorities thus delaying the sales cycle,	1. Instant access to relevant sales data on the move. 2. Decision making and approval process streamlined.

- Since the data is collected in an electronic format the chances of errors are considerably reduced. These devices reduce human error by instructing the user with logic structure-based informational questions.
- Due to the compact form factor it can easily carried by the field work force. Handheld devices also score over notebooks as they are lightweight and fit easily into pockets. An SHD can provide quick, convenient, discreet Internet access.

MOBILE PLATFORMS REVIEW

With any new technology/solution, it is important to match requirements` with the benefits and limitations of the solution. The operating system determines a phone's features, performance, and security, providing APIs for add-on applications and technical hooks to manage it all. Decision makers face a tough choice when weighing which mobile platform or operating system to deploy to mobilize the workforce. There's BlackBerry, Windows Mobile, Palm OS, Symbian, Linux and J2ME.

Blackberry

BlackBerry offers the best combination of mobile phone, server software, push e-mail, and security from a single vendor. It integrates well with other platforms, it works with several carriers, and it can be deployed globally for the sales force which is on move.

It is easy to manage, has a longer than usual battery life, and has a small form-factor with an easy-to-use keyboard. BlackBerry is good for access to some of the simpler applications, such as contact list, time management, and field force applications. It's a good device for doing e-mail, but it would be a bad choice if what you're looking for is a way to deploy business-critical applications to mobile workers.

Windows Mobile

Windows Mobile comes in two flavors. A smart phone edition is good for wireless e-mail, calendaring, and voice notes. A Pocket PC edition adds mobile versions of Word, Excel, PowerPoint, and Outlook. Palm's Treo 700w, with the full functionality of the Pocket PC edition, is a better choice for sales force professionals.

The main draw of the Windows Mobile operating system is its maker Microsoft. For a Windows or Microsoft shop, it's a wise decision, since it's fairly easy to add into the mix if a company has an affinity to other Windows applications, like Word and Excel. Windows Mobile also actively syncs to the Exchange and SQL servers. This augurs very well for use by the sales force.

Mobile sales force solutions for Windows Mobile are available from companies like SAP, Siebel, PeopleSoft, and Salesforce.com as well as other leading solution providers.

Palm OS

Palm OS is the most sensibly laid out and easy-to-use operating system on a smartphone today. This might suit the business requirement of some sales force implementations. Palm brings an open approach to business with two enterprise-ready, non-proprietary operating systems: classic Palm OS platform and the familiar Windows Mobile platform. Both platforms deliver secure mobile email, Palm's ease of use, access to thousands of industry-specific enterprise applications, and the ability to build custom applications using your existing development resources. The Palm OS does not allow for multitasking, which many enterprises could find a great hindrance. For example, if a user is working in an application and the phone rings, the application has to be closed down in order to take the call.

Symbian

Symbian° is one of the most widely used platforms. Its plug-in architecture makes it easier for manufacturers to add technology of their own which hastens delivery of new and in-demand features. Although Symbian is feature rich, it doesn't integrate well with corporate back-end systems such as VPN connections and other enterprise-oriented tools. These devices work well for many traveling professionals, managers, knowledge workers and sales teams, but enterprise IT departments may find Symbian OS devices to be too expensive and too feature rich for verticalized field-force applications. Symbian has a strong feature set and is relatively easy to use. Its main stumbling blocks are the limited number of Symbian devices and its lack of support for CDMA. However, Symbian will start making its way to mobile workforces, even if it can't conquer the enterprise market.

Linux

Mobile Linux is not really a mobile operating system, but a kernel that can be a central part of any number of different operating systems. Mobile Linux cannot really be weighed against other mobile operating systems like Palm OS and Windows Mobile, simply because there are many flavors of Linux. Linux has an advantage over other mobile operating systems: a far-reaching community of developers ready to write smartphone applications. One can say things like 'Palm OS has an intuitive user interface' or 'Windows Mobile requires a more powerful processor,' but these generalizations can't be made about mobile Linux because it can have many different user interfaces depending on the distribution.

J2ME

J2ME is also not an operating system, it is a platform. The main selling point for J2ME is that it's lightweight and has a simple methodology for designing applications. Because it is lightweight, it requires very little storage. There are a few key applications that perform well in a J2ME environment, namely those from SAP AG, Oracle Corp. and IBM. What holds Java back is similar to what keeps Linux from infiltrating the enterprise as a viable mobile platform. The issue is there's no single party in charge of Java. In a company with a deployment of several different devices, that could create issues, since applications written to Java would have to be tested and tweaked for each, creating more work and potentially introducing performance issues if it is not tweaked just right.

Google's Android Mobile Platform

Google's Android Mobile platform is the latest mobile platform on the block. This open-source development platform is built on the Linux kernel, and it includes an operating system (OS), middleware stack and a number of mobile applications. Enterprises will benefit from Android because the availability of open-source code for the entire software stack will allow the existing army of Linux developers to create special-purpose applications that will run on a variety of mobile devices. If Android makes it into phones designed specifically for the enterprise, those products will have to include technology from the likes of Sybase, Intellisync or another such company to enable security features like remote data wipe functionality and forced password changes.

BUSINESS SOFTWARE INTEGRATION

The heart of the SHD device is its software and companies want employees on the field to get a feel of familiar applications they are trained to use on their mobile devices. Applications being developed in the SHD space depend upon the companies' requirements. There are industry-specific applications being developed; for instance, applications for an FMCG sales force, for insurance agents, the police, the military, and for e-governance. However, the applications have to be simple and effective. A salesman capturing information during a sales call has to complete all information, then and there, in a short span of time. Hence it is very important for the applications to be simple and effective.

SHDs have proved to be a boon for the sales force of many organizations. Prior to having a handheld device the sales force had to depend on manual, paper-based systems. It used to take a month to compile data collected from different sources such as dealers, distributors etc. Software loaded in the SHD enable each member of the SF to maintain, store and feed information, and then transfer the same to central location. There are several protocols that sales people

have to meet in different set-ups when they contact a distributor or retailer during their visits. They have to get information about products based on re-launch, regular purchase and different schemes. A salesperson does not spend much time with each channel partner and the challenge of recording all the parameters is automated and this has reduced the time required.

We'll understand the business software integration through an example from Insurance industry[p]. Gathering assets through partnerships and affiliations is critical for insurers to increase revenue. Third-party distribution continues to dominate the distribution of insurance products. Sales personnel spend most of their workday in the field in prospecting the customers. These sales personnel come back to home office periodically to update the office records which in turn would trigger the processing cycle. This often induces delay in the policy processing and increases the chances of data related errors. These work customs compel insurance carriers to seek cost-effective ways to deliver "anytime, anywhere" interactions between sales personnel, their home office, and their clients.

Mobile solutions[q] are being adopted in areas of new business acquisition and claims processing. It can improve day-to-day service levels for sales field force as it thwarts the need for duplicate data recording. Mobility lessens the need for multiple local offices in the same city which are frequently established for convenience of sales personnel[r]. Instead of sales personnel shuttling between local offices and client they can assess the insurability on site and immediately communicate with the carrier.

Exhibit illustrates a typical new business acquisition process flow using mobile devices to move data and information from the field to the home office of the agent. By instantly notifying underwriting[s] office of a new customer application and assigning them the case dynamically, Insurance[t] companies could expedite new policy processing. Through secure mobile environment, carriers can transmit applicant's demographics information, health information and other key details. The sales personnel can accept the business in real time, thereby improving the continuity between the sales activities and underwriting office.

As the sales agent can collect detailed information on the spot, it often improves the accuracy of data and transactions. Mobile technology streamlines new business acquisition; increasing productivity in the process and reducing the potential for delayed policy processing and causing discontent among newly acquired customers. Both life and P&C carriers need to examine how a business process will work with handheld devices and then optimize these processes. Companies will have to do this optimization in perspective of the mobile wireless existing infrastructure available with the company and in the country, and how much is the company willing to spend on new mobile devices and wireless networks.

VALIDATION CASE

To illustrate the effectiveness of Mobile handheld devices in Sales-force management the following case has been chosen.

In a typical Consumer packaged goods company the sales force of the distributor typically perform the functions of Order Capture, Order Entry, Business Development and transfer of promotions designed by the company to the dealer. A typical day of the sales force is spent visiting outlets making calls, booking orders manually, collection of pending claims, checking display efficiency. After covering his beat the sales person returns to the office to make the order entry for

the day and plan the dispatch for the next morning. In addition to this he prepares invoices to be handed out to the retailers once Pros are dispatched. Since there is a time lag of 7-10 days between the dispatch and payment of the invoice the sales person also needs to keep a track of pending claims which is currently done manually and then fed into the system. If we analyze the current system there are gaps in terms of: duplication of effort when the order entry is done both at the dealer's premises and the office, manual entry of figures which can be mishandled. Moreover additional effort needs to be undertaken in terms of preparing statement claims, interpreting these and analysis of the offtake levels is adhoc.

Let us consider a scenario when handheld devices are used by the organization. The sales-force of the organization is equipped with portable devices. The first capability of the device is towards enhancing the order booking process. The device can either be 'always on' – permanently connected to office servers wirelessly – allowing users to dispatch their orders real-time. Or it can connect and synchronize at various times during the day – sending orders and receiving

Figure 5. Architecture for a possible mobile sales force application

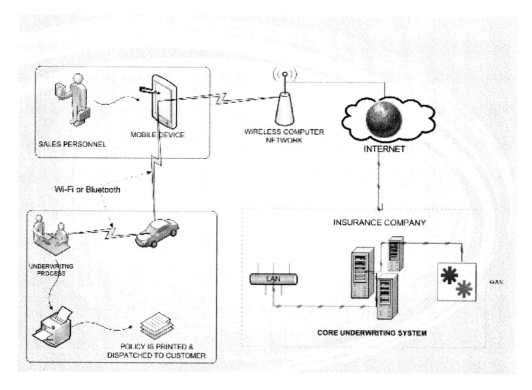

relevant sales information and emails etc. The order process will in many ways mimic what was once done with paper orders, however, instead of faxing them in or delivering them to the office by hand, the orders are sent wirelessly. The suite of tools & information available in a mobile sales application include sales orders, customer sales history, corporate email, (typically synchronized with Microsoft Outlook or Lotus Notes), sales opportunities and promotions, often with the ability to record proposals and quotes, and marketing information like special trade promotions relevant to that particular customer. These modules contain potentially useful information about past promotions, their effectiveness with the customer and various options which may be customized to the buying pattern of the concerned customer.

This means the order dispatch process begins almost as soon as the order is taken, and it also means office bound order entry staff don't have to re-key orders (and potentially make mistakes while doing so) which ultimately means less credits and more satisfied customers. This is a significant improvement over the manual process where in the sales person had to replicate the effort in order booking and order entry which doubled the time required and the risk of inaccurate entries. Moreover when linked with the database maintained at the distributor/stockist premises reports related to the claims pending, off-take levels, success of promotional schemes can be tracked and used seamlessly by the company to make decisions. Another application is the automatic replenishment of stocks at the distributor level once the stocks reach a certain level. This helps in seamlessly integrating information across the supply chain and improving efficiency of channel partners and the manufacturing organization

This apart one major benefit is better utilization of a sales rep's time. The new operation enables the sales representative to undertake more calls, enhance the value of each order and gather competitive intelligence with the saved time.

We attempt to evaluate the benefit of investing in mobile technology. Let us assume the hypothetical example of a team of 20 sales reps, making an average of eight sales calls a day. Assuming that a sales person spends 15 minute per outlet visited to transfer the order information into an order sheet and this plus the travel time spent in driving to the office premises at the end of the day would amount to two hours wasted in a day. Even if the additional time generated by using as mobile

application allowed the sales representative to make an additional sales call each day, or an additional $40 profit per sales (including the additional profits made due to better service) call made, this would amount to a staggering additional profit of $41,600 made in a year by the team. Add to this the additional benefits of better reporting, information synergies which help in designing strategies by the company and the reduced chances of stock unavailability at the distributor premises and the application brings excellent value. Assuming an investment of $800 per mobile device and the additional cost of altering the IT infrastructure the fixed one time cost would amount to $20000; thus illustrating the profitability of the technology.

CONCLUSION

An integral part of any mobile device system trying to automate the company's processes is company-wide integration among different departments. If the systems aren't adopted and properly integrated to all departments, there might be a lack of communication which could result in different departments contacting the same customer for the same purpose. In order to mitigate this risk, sales force mobile devices must be fully integrated and kept up to date from all departments that deal with customer service management. The applications that are transferred or made mobile ready should be chosen such that they provide the most relevant, effective and up to date information to the on field sales force rather than over burdening the sales team member with other administrative tasks.

Some of the applications available for the mobile devices are:

- There is a growing breadth of specialist applications on or coming to the market which enable fast efficient interface with your customers.
- These include specialist Sales Force Automation, Field Service Automation, Job dispatch and Tracking, Mobile Sales Force Management, Easy Order Software and Transport and Logistics Management. These applications all ensure delivery of a higher customer service level or increase the efficiency of the remote team your company has on the ground.
- To attain a sustainable advantage over competition, as the geographical boundaries become redundant, it is medium like telecommunication which will define the rules of the game.

191

REFERENCES

Author, Cynthia Saccocia & Author, Bob Egan(2006). Handheld device trends in the US Insurance Industry: TowerGroup Inc.Microsoft (2006). *Mobile Field Sales.* Redmond, WA: Microsoft Corporation

Frost and Sullivan report on mobile business on www.allbusiness.com, 7 Feb. 2007 Retrieved on 4th January 2008.

http://www.expresscomputeronline.com/20021223/indtrend1.shtml, pricing and applications will drive PDA growth retrieved 7th January 2008.

IDC (2006). Enterprise mobility - Not a packaged solution. Network Magazine India. Retrieved January 16, 2008, from http://www.networkmagazineindia.com/200601/index.shtml

Informal telephonic survey carried out in companies in India like Cognizant and ITC Ltd.

Jennifer O'Brien (2007). Evolving to a mobile enterprise platform. ARN. Retrieved January 16, 2008, from http://www.arnnet.com.au/index.php/id;346556794;pp;1

LOMA (2006), Supporting the Insurer's Distribution Systems. Chapter 7, LOMA-290: Life Office Management Association, USA

LOMA (2006), The process of underwriting, Chapter 8, LOMA-290: Life Office Management Association, USA

Mobile Business Application Usage to Surge by 2009, Driving Need for Device Management, Business wire, Monday, July 23 2007 retrieved on 6th January 2008.

Mobile Business Application Usage to Surge by 2009, Driving Need for Device Management, publication: Business Wire, Date: Monday, July 23 2007 retrieved on 13th January 2008.

Mobile Business solution overview retrieved from www.istart.com on 19th Jan 2008.

Mobile business solutions from http://www.istart.co.nz/index/HM20/PC0/PV22447 Retrieved on 7th January 2008

Nokia, *The Symbian platform (2000). Finland*: Nokia Group

Retrieved from http://www.istart.co.nz/mobile-business.htm on 19th Jan 2008

Rohit Prakash (2006). *PDA Applicability for the Sales Field Force. Marico, India.*

Sales Force Automation Software, retrieved from http://www.stylusinc.com/Common/Scenarios/pda.php on 18th January 2008.

Sales on the move, David McNickel investigates the inherent power of today's mobile sales applications, September 2006 retrieved on 7th January 2008.

Slide presentation on the sales force by Professor of marketing Mr Abhijit Ranade, SIBM, pune.

Smartphones add to mobile productivity, by Abhinav Singh, 2001 Business Publications Division (BPD) of the Indian Express Newspapers

TCS (2007). *Handheld Solution on Symbian Platform*: Tata Consultancy Services

KEY TERMS

Claim Processing: The process of obtaining all the information necessary to determine the appropriate amount to pay on a given claim. Process of determining an insurance company's liability for each claim.

New Business Acquisition: The risk evaluation an MCO performs when it first issues coverage to a group.

Underwriting: Assessing and classifying the degree of risk represented by a proposed insured

ENDNOTES

[1]   Retrieved from http://www.istart.co.nz/mobile-business.htm on 19th Jan 2008

[2]   Frost and Sullivan report on mobile business on www.allbusiness.com, 7 Feb. 2007 Retrieved on 4th January 2008.

[3]   Mobile Business solution overview retrieved from www.istart.com on 19th Jan 2008.

[4]   Sales on the move, David McNickel investigates the inherent power of today's mobile sales applications, September 2006 retrieved on 7th January 2008.

[5]   Slide presentation on the sales force by Professor of marketing Mr Abhijit Ranade, SIBM, pune.

[6]   Mobile Business Application Usage to Surge by

2009, Driving Need for Device Management, Business wire, Monday, July 23 2007 retrieved on 6th January 2008.

[7] Rohit Prakash (2006). PDA Applicability for the Sales Field Force. Marico, India.

[8] Mobile Business Application Usage to Surge by 2009, Driving Need for Device Management, publication: Business Wire, Date: Monday, July 23 2007 retrieved on 13th January 2008.

[9] Smartphones add to mobile productivity, by Abhinav Singh, 2001 Business Publications Division (BPD) of the Indian Express Newspapers

[10] TCS (2007). Handheld Solution on Symbian Platform: Tata Consultancy Services

[11] http://www.expresscomputeronline.com/20021223/indtrend1.shtml, pricing and applications will drive PDA growth retrieved 7th January 2008.

[12] Sales Force Automation Software, retrieved from http://www.stylusinc.com/Common/Scenarios/pda.php on 18th January 2008.

[13] Nokia, The Symbian platform (2000). Finland: Nokia Group

[14] Author, Cynthia Saccocia & Author, Bob Egan(2006). Handheld device trends in the US Insurance Industry: TowerGroup Inc.Microsoft (2006). Mobile Field Sales. Redmond, WA: Microsoft Corporation

[15] Jennifer O'Brien (2007). Evolving to a mobile enterprise platform. ARN. Retrieved January 16, 2008, from http://www.arnnet.com.au/index.php/id;346556794;pp;1

[16] IDC (2006). Enterprise mobility - Not a packaged solution. Network Magazine India. Retrieved January 16, 2008, from http://www.network-magazineindia.com/200601/index.shtml

[17] LOMA (2006), The process of underwriting, Chapter 8, LOMA-290: Life Office Management Association, USA

[18] LOMA (2006), Supporting the Insurer's Distribution Systems. Chapter 7, LOMA-290: Life Office Management Association, USA

Chapter XVIII
A Composite Software Framework Approach for Mobile Application Development

Mohammed Maharmeh
University of Western Sydney, Australia

Bhuvan Unhelkar
MethodScience.com & University of Western Sydney, Australia

ABSTRACT

This chapter presents the use of Composite Application Software Development Process Framework (CASDPF) for Mobile Applications Development. This framework for software development, as its name suggests, is made up of the waterfall, iterative, and agile approaches to software development. There is a need to apply such a framework in developing mobile applications. The chapter explains and provides details on what comprises a CASDPF and how it can be used to develop a mobile application.

INTRODUCTION

The increasing use of mobile technology in business provides people and organization with flexibility to access information remotely at anytime and from anywhere. For example, people who were earlier reliant on a form of a desktop computer in an office or a laptop in a hotel room (Mark et al., 2001) are now able to access that information independent of even these locations. The development of mobile applications is considered challenging and complicated due to the specific demand and technical constraints of the environments. These constraints relate to the nature of mobile devices, security requirements and wireless networks. Thus, there is a need to have a proper and formal software development process framework to

model and construct a mobile application. The composite process framework described in this chapter combines the business rules and processes that are involved in mobile application development. This chapter proposes the use of a Composite Process Framework that comprises elements of each of the process lifecycles concurrently from software processes such as Waterfall, Iterative-Incremental or Agile, to enable developers of mobile applications to create models as well as adopt the good points in the application software development methods. A composite software development process framework, as envisaged here, retains the flexible aspects of the agile development approach and, at the same time, facilitates exchange of information between project stakeholders (such as business users, developers and testers) during the project life-cycle. Therefore, the CASDPF increases the chance of project success.

The aim of this chapter is to provide an insight on the background of software development processes, and the potential use of a composite application software development process framework for development of mobile applications. The chapter is organized as follows. The next section provides a background about software development processes, it followed by another section that highlights the definition of a composite software development process framework. Next it provides details of using the composite framework for mobile applications development and finally the conclusion and future direction.

SOFTWARE DEVELOPMENT PROCESSES BACKGROUND

Software development methodology or process is the application of best-practice business analysis and project management techniques to facilitate exchange of project information and knowledge between the project stakeholders (business users, developers, and testers), to shorten the development Life-cycle, and deliver the product on time and within the budget. Depending on the client's, project's or department's needs, a combination of one or more of proven methodologies and/or emerging standards (i.e. Waterfall approach (Royce, 1970), Rapid Application Development – RAD (Martin,1991), Spiral (Boehm, 1988), Rational Unified Process – RUP (Kruchten, 2000), or Agile approach - eXtreme Programming (XP) (Beck, 1999) could be used during the System Development Life-Cycle (SDLC) process.

The process itself can be made of a reusable 'process-components'; and a process-component can be defined as a collection of activities, tasks, roles, and deliverables in a process. Unhelkar (2003) has described the process components that can be used in three modelling spaces (Problem space, Solution space and Design space). According to Unhelkar (2003), the architecture of a process-component is made up of three major parts:

- **Deliverable:** What is produced at the end of a process, such as a suite of UML diagrams, programs, databases or quality checks.
- **Activity Task:** This is the step-by-step guide to how a particular process component is created.

- **Role:** That represents the person who is carrying out the activities and tasks.

A high-ceremony process provides the necessary guidelines (such as Deliverables, Activities, and Roles) within a project that will help in defining and controlling the project. This high-ceremony development process requires that every step of the development to be defined and followed in details, which make it relatively inflexible.

A low-ceremony process does not require any pre-definition of deliverables, activities and roles, which make it more flexible to adopt rapid changes, but lack for scalability and project control. The CASDPF achieves a balance between flexibility and rigour when using it for developing a mobile application.

COMPOSITE SOFTWARE DEVELOPMENT PROCESS FRAMEWORK

Overview

The Composite Software Development Process Framework is a standard procedure for adopting a combination of software development approaches in a single project within an organisation in such a way that could resolve some of the issues and problems associated with the implementation of these processes in software development projects.

Composite Process Conceptual Model

The Composite approach shown in Figure 1 below splits the project into a set of increments; each increment consists of a set of project life-cycle phases. For each increment, it attempts to bring the best aspects of available software development processes (Waterfall, Iterative and Agile) together that can be used to manage application software development. In this iterative incremental approach, development of increments goes throughout circles, a careful consideration required during the planning and execution of increments to ensure that it goes across the project life-cycle phases.

Composite Process Details

The "Composite" framework consists of three layers as shown in figure 1 that uses a composition of two or more processes, which are "Waterfall approach and Iterative approach" or "Waterfall approach, Iterative and Agile approach". The composite approach divides the project into phases, each phase or group of phases could use different approach.

For example, the Waterfall approach could be used to take care of planning large scale project management that includes dealing with project initiation, definition, analysis, design, coding, testing, deployment, and project closure.

The Iterative-incremental approach could be used to take care of analysis, design, coding and testing of every increment of the project. Finally, the flexibility aspect of agile approach, results in utilising this approach within each iteration of the project.

Advantages of the Composite Framework

The composite approach maximise the advantages of each of the participating approaches, by incorporating more than one approach together, and amalgamate the advantages from each of these approaches. The

composite approach allows one to choose a model that would be made up of the right combination of high and low ceremony aspects.

The composite approach provides organizations with the following benefits:

- It is a disciplined approach that provides the project manager with full control over the project
- It increases the process efficiency by creating an instance of the process at the project level.
- It provides a reference model to be used by organizations
- It provides a better process control at all levels of the project
- It provides the necessary planning, control and tracking that is required for large projects.
- It provides better management to risks by allowing the areas of risks to be controlled and explored.
- It maximises the user input by involving the user in the whole process

Limitations of the Composite Process

The main limitations of the composite approach are its attempts to minimize the advantages of each of the

Figure 1. Composite process framework conceptual model

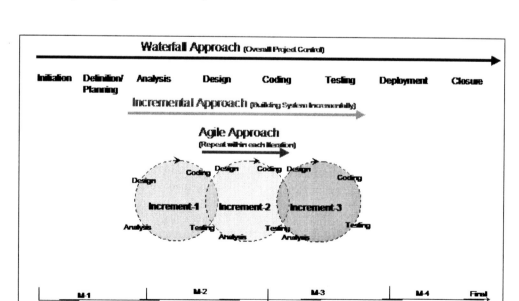

participating approaches. In addition to, the complexity it adds to project management.

Suitability of Composite Approach to Mobile Application Development

The composite approach is very suitable for large and very large mobile application development projects with multiple releases. The composite framework allows each release to use the most appropriate approach for different development phases.

MOBILE APPLICATIONS DEVELOPMENT

The design and implementation of mobile applications is complex as it needs to support different mobile devices such as: Mobile phones, Smart phones and PDAs (Personal Digital Assistants), anywhere and at anytime via a mobile telecommunication network as a delivery channel of electronic services for the customer. Therefore, the mobile application development should cover the following two main components:

Mobile service as stated by Alahuhta, et al (2006), refers to the use of mobile device such as Mobile phones, PDAs and Mobile network, while the service can be a delivery of information (such as news and tickets) or entertainment content (like video clips, ring-tones, and images), or a controlled operation (such as a remote control for controlling heating, etc.).

Mobile Application as stated by Alahuhta et al (2006), refers to the program code that is executed on the mobile device. This mobile application might use networking capabilities that makes it part of the mobile service. The mobile application may be a stand-alone application such as single-player games, calculators and clocks in mobile devices.

The development of large complex systems such as mobile application will involve technical and project management issues that are important and that should be handled right from the beginning to ensure the success of the project. These issues will have impact on the business process as well as software development processes.

TAILORING OF COMPOSITE PROCESS FRAMEWORK FOR MOBILE APPLICATION DEVELOPMENT

The Mobile applications are usually made up of objects and components. Therefore, these mobile applications will be developed in an Object Oriented development environment. The composite framework will be tailored to support the Mobile Application development process. The development of mobile application components will be performed iteratively, meaning that the development tasks might be repeated in a number of iterations during the actual development, incrementally, meaning that small pieces of the mobile application deliverables will be created and delivered at different times possibly every few weeks and integrated as they are completed, in parallel, meaning that project team will work concurrently on several deliverables or products of the system. This IIP (Iterative, Incremental, Parallel) development life-cycle that is supported by the Composite framework will help the project team return to earlier parts of the life-cycle in order to improve what has been created based on the knowledge gained in earlier phases.

Mobile application development as any other standard applications will go through the following development phases:

- **Project initiation:** This is a high level phase, where the initiative is initiated and approved to become a development project, the project steering committee is established and a project manager is nominated.
- **Project planning:** In this phase the estimation of time and cost is carried to produce a project budget and project plan.
- **Analysis:** In this phase analysis and engineering of gathered requirements is conducted to produce a detailed business requirements document and business model .
- **Design:** In this phase, the design of the over whole solution is constructed that include user interfaces, object model, class diagrams, business flows and database model.
- **Coding:** In this phase, the development team is involved to develop the product components and other related deliverables.
- **Testing:** This phase includes the creation of testing plans, test designs and test cases as well

as assigning resources needed to carry out these tasks and testing architecture that describes the testing iterations and types of testing.

- **Deployment:** This phase includes the creation of deployment plan, and deployment of the system components into target environment.
- **Post implementation (closure):** This phase include all activities related to assessing and solving any post implementation issues and project closure that includes hand over of final system from development team into production support team.

Based on the tasks performed in every phase of the project life-cycle, we can see that Waterfall approach is best for project initiation, project planning and post implementation phases as it gives the project manager full control over the project life-cycle. The Iterative approach is the best during the analysis, design, and coding phases since it gives the project team more flexibility to address evolving system requirements and to iterate within these phases to ensure a comprehensive analysis and design has been done. The use of Agile approach is better during the deployment and testing phases since it helps produce incremental small software releases within a short iterative development cycles.

The lightweight iterative agile development processes are suitable for mobile applications development for the following reasons:

- Mobile applications need to get to the market fast as their lifespan is expected to be short, according to Gartner, the lifespan of mobile solutions may be as short as 18 months, including development (Jonas, 2004).
- The development of corporate mobile applications usually changes working processes, that have social implications in the working environment. The only way to tackle these implications is to adopt a collaborative, iterative and evolutionary approach to developing mobile applications (Jonas, 2004).

The incorporation of different types of processes (Waterfall, Iterative-incremental, and agile) as a composite framework, and the amalgamation of the advantages of each of those approaches benefits the mobile application development with a sufficient planning, risk reduction and more user participation during the development process.

FUTURE DIRECTION

The creation of a composite application software development framework is still in its early stage and further research is required to tailor the final composite framework to suit development of different types of applications that include mobile applications.

CONCLUSION

When developing a mobile application, Waterfall approach is best to use during the project initiation, planning and post implementation phases as it gives the project manager full control over the project life-cycle. The Iterative approach is better to use during the analysis, design, and coding phases since it gives the project team more flexibility to address evolving system requirements and to iterate within these phases to ensure a comprehensive analysis and design has been done. The use of agile approach is better during the deployment and testing phases since it helps produce incremental small software releases within a short iterative development cycles.

REFERENCES

Alahuhta, P., Lothman, H., Helaakoski, H., Koskela, A., & Roning, J. (2007). *Experiences in developing mobile applications using the Apricot Agent Platform.* London: Springer-Verlag.

Beck, K. (1999). Extreme Programming Explained: Embrace Change. Reading MA: Addison-Wesley Pub Co.

Boehm, B. (1998, May). *A Spiral Model of Software Development and Enhancement.* IEEE.

Jonas, N. (2004). Allow for Mobile Application Development's Growing Pains. *In Strategic Planning, SPA-21-4442.* Gartner Inc. (p. 7).

Kruchten, P. (2000). The Rational Unified Process: An Introduction. NY: Addison Wesley; 1st edition.

Mark, P., Kenton, O., Abigail, S., Barry, B., & Richard, H. (2001). Dealing with mobility: Understanding access anytime, anywhere. *ACM, 8.*

Martin, J. (1991). *Rapid Application Development.* Macmillan Coll.

Royce, W. W. (1970). *Managing the Development of Large-Scale Software: Concepts and Techniques Proceedings*. Wescon.

Unhelkar, B. (2003). *Process Quality Assurance for UML-Based Projects*. Boston, MA: Addison-Wesley.

KEY TERMS

Composite Framework: Composition of multiple process models.

Incremental Development: A development of various parts of the project at different times and deliver the system in different increments

Iterative Process: A process of repeating a project development operations.

Methodology: A set of procedures and rules that can be applied within a discipline.

RAD: Rapid Application Development.

RUP: Rational Unified Process.

SDLC: System Development Life-Cycle.

UML: Unified Modeling Language.

Chapter XIX
Mobile Devices and Mobile Applications:
Key Future Trends

Carol Charsky
TWU, School of Management, USA

Mahesh Raisinghani
TWU, School of Management, USA

ABSTRACT

Mobile devices are comprised of a multitude of various applications and operating systems that have significantly impacted the way people interact with each other as they go about their lives in this growing global economy. Today, businesses and organizations are facing new challenges in defining strategies, visions, and business processes in an effort to support the up and coming mobile market of devices and applications. In addition, companies are confronted with the need to monitor their critical business practices and processes throughout the organization in an effort to keep the competitive advantage in the growing mobile technology market. Since many company funds are limited with their IT budgets, organizations will need to prioritize its goals to determine how deeply committed they are to keep a vision on the future through the mobile market. This chapter will show how mobile devices with all of its various software and hardware devices can move an organization's strategy into showing how it is important for companies to invest in this growing technology. Some of the more commonly known devices, operating systems, and critical applications will be identified. Finally, a conclusion will be drawn on the future of the mobile technology environment

INTRODUCTION

Mobile devices and the various mobile applications are shaping the future of how people communicate, work, travel and perform daily tasks in a constant changing global economy. People are being impacted in their jobs, at home and even when they don't even realize it. Major manufactures of mobile devices and mobile operating system have stood up and have taken notice for the demand of mobile devices. This technology is the driving force for the future. Technologies for wireless communications are a viable and growing market with new demands for speed and abilities to interact with applications on back systems at corporate offices. Mobile based servers will bring new services and technology to the future of mobile computing.

IMPACT OF MOBILE DEVICES ON PEOPLE

People have become accustomed to changes in their environment as new generations of technology touch their everyday lives. This shift in technology is causing people to see the world through new views and paradigms (Singh, 2003). We see these paradigm shifts in phases such as when our parents went from listening to radio to watching television. We have seen the shift in the paradigm when our generation went from stand-alone personal computers to retrieving information off the Internet (Singh, 2003). The latest shift in paradigm is the explosive developments of the mobile devices and the applications. These developments are constantly being expanded upon to further the use of mobile devices in everyday personal needs and strategic business processes. People today are reeling from the benefits of mobile devices through increased productivity. The people benefiting the most are the mobile workers, especially the executives, middle management managers and salespeople who are not bound by a desk or specific work locations (Cozza, 2005). Mobile devices are giving added levels of service to people through better customer support and improved customer care that in turn has increased the company return on investment (Cozza, 2005). Employees have access their email, contacts, corporate data and up to date meeting schedules. This invaluable asset information is shaping the corporate employee of today.

The impact of mobile devices has created new experiences for people in a way that stretches beyond the individual. Corporations are feeling the impact of the added availability of mobile devices, as their employees are able to stay abreast of hour-by-hour changes in the company daily business. Corporate IT staffs responsible for supporting mobile devices are impacted by their own set of challenges in their daily work. Many companies have been forced to increase staffing positions specifically to support the mobile infrastructure. Companies are coming to understand that staffing requirements are changing as they look at the total cost of ownership in supplying mobile devices to employees (Cozza, 2005). IT staffing personal affected by deployment of these devices are responsible for maintaining the hardware, licensing agreements and the profiles associated with each device. Mobile devices can even impact people who don't actually have their own mobile device. Companies must follow a strict security policy in securing the access and use of mobile devices to all employees. Otherwise data can and will be compromised.

MOBILE DEVICES AND MOBILE OS IMPACT ON THE ENVIRONMENT

People today can't help but get involved with mobile devices on today's market. These devices are small data-centric handheld computers (Cozza, 2005). They are about one pound or less in weight. People are incorporating them into their everyday life. People today use cell phones for talking but are also starting to use the cell phone for (SMS) messages, sending pictures and graphics (Singh, 2003). Personal Digital Assistant also called the PDA is another device that is growing on corporate America. It offers the individual the ability to view high-resolution graphics, handwriting recognition, and point-and-click pen to make it easier to navigate around the device (Singh, 2003). These devices are starting to impact the contents of corporate data. People today can now access corporate data and downloaded to their mobile device. Mobile devices are expanded the tools and reach of the corporate employees access to corporate data. Employees changing the way they function in their daily jobs. Yet another important mobile device impacting our lives is the pocket pc. It is a fully powered pc. It may not have the same abilities as a workstation in the office, but it does increase the efficiency of the corporate employee by giving them workstation like applications to manipulate the corporate data locally on their mobile device. The range of the market strength is limited in the mobile device market. Currently only a limited a few vendors are able to make headway. Some of the vendors with devices that are known for impacting the environment are Dell, HP, Nokia, Palm and RIM (Cozza, 2005). The vendors that make mobile device operating systems impacting the environment today are Microsoft Windows Mobile, Palm OS, RIM OS and Symbian OS (Cozza, 2005).

MOBILE APPLICATIONS IN THE ENVIRONMENT

People today are thirsting more and more for new and creative mobile applications. The highest impact of mobile applications to date has been surrounded around short message service (SMS) and ring tones (Gartner, 2006). In the near future, the impact of mobile applications will appear to be at its strongest in mobile messaging applications, like e-mail service and instant messaging, which is gaining ground with the younger generation (Gartner, 2006). But not all mobile applications impacting people today will show signs of continued influence. Such mobile applications are full-track music downloads and gaming (Gartner, 2006). Applications that are showing promise on impacting the future include mobile banking and payment applications (Gartner, 2006). But there are many other applications that will continue to bare themselves in the mobile market place. Many of them will not last. They will just fade by the wayside. Some of the up and coming applications that will show an impact on mobile applications is Microsoft .NET. It hasn't impacted the mobile market with any great impact as of yet, but it will bring applications to mobile devices to support a strong Microsoft consumer oriented market. Users today are asking for and demanding local information and navigational aids to assist them in their everyday lives (Gartner, 2006). Applications have impacted people's lives to the extent that location-based services will be a necessary for most carriers to carry in their inventory of mobile applications (Gartner, 2006). A chart below helps to identify some of the mobile applications that will show their visibility and effectiveness to influence people.

MOBILE COMMUNICATIONS AND REGULATIONS

People today have not felt much of an impact by mobile regulations. But many state, regional and federal levels are close to passing regulations that ensure data protection and security regulations are in place (Gold, 2006). As the market for mobile devices will continue to expand in the coming years, states such as California, have passed and will continue to pass regulations. The state of California passed a Civil Code Section 1798.8 in 2002 specifically in regards to mobile technology (Heard, 2004). The California law, went into affect in 2003 and focused on data privacy within organizations that brought a new standard for companies. Companies in California will know need to understand the importance and impact of electronically stored information that could include mobile devices. As these mobile devices continue to grow in popularity, the communications side that supports mobile devices is also growing with the increased demand for services. Many people have become hooked on the use of mobile communications such as Bluetooth communications that they

Figure 1.

Benefit   **Years to mainstream adoption**

	less than 2 years	2 to 5 years	5 to 10 years	more than 10 years
transformational			VoIP WWAN	
high	Mobile Search Presence on Mobile	Location-Based Services Mobile E-Mail		
moderate	Mobile Gaming Push-to-talk Over Cellular Ring Tone and Logo Downloads Mobile Video on Demand	Mobile Banking Mobile Blogging Mobile Gambling Mobile Payment Full-Track Music Streaming and Downloading Wireless Instant Messaging	Mobile TV Broadcasting Mobile TV Streaming	
low	Multimedia Messaging Service Wireless Video Calling	Push-to-Talk	VoIP Over WLAN	

As of June 2006

Source: Gartner (June 2006)

Figure 2.

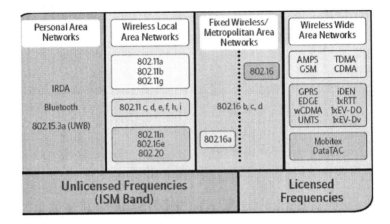

use with their mobile devices. Bluetooth offers users the ability to move about hands free. It is growing in popularity even though it is designed for short range and is referred to as personal-area network technology (Cozza, 2005). It is impacting people's lives as it gives people the ability to be hands free from their mobile device to perform other tasks. Most mobile devices use a long-range wireless communication. This impacts the users ability to have long ranges of communication channels. Some of the standardized communication technology that is driving future use is the WLAN/802.11,GSM, GPRS, CDMA, GPS and EDGE (Cozza, 2005).

WORK ENVIRONMENT AND MOBILE DEVICES

The main users of mobile devices are corporate professionals (Cozza, 2005). But the use of these devices goes way beyond the corporate office. These devices are also used in conjunction with people's personal lives. It is a trend that is not showing any signs of slowing down. Many office workers have intertwined their mobile devices into all aspects of their lives. Many corporate office's are seeing these mobile devices as a way to change company specific applications to enhance employees productivity and improved corporate standing (Cozza, 2005). Even some CRM vendors such as SAP, Siebel and PeopleSoft have put smaller versions of their software on mobile

devices to improve company goals (Cozza, 2005). Companies see the need to use mobile devices in the global market place as an edge for competitiveness. Even simple everyday applications are being added to mobile devices to encourage people to become more productive. Some of the applications are Adobe PDF, Microsoft word, Excel and PowerPoint presentations (Cozza, 2005). Mobile devices today have over run any corporate considerations not to implement a mobile deployment strategy in organizations. The simple fact is everyone is requesting and getting mobile devices in the corporate offices today (CBR, 2003). The age of wireless technology is here and is seen as cool cutting edge technology to all age groups (CBR, 2003). Gartner even projected that all office professionals will have several mobile devices, as many as three at one time (CBR, 2003). Employees today are doing less in the office and more on the road and at home. It is estimated that as much as 50% of jobs are mobile (Singh, 2003). Mobile devices are becoming an ever-increasing key to successful business transactions. The (ROI) Return On Investment in any company will show better teamwork and a stronger competitive company (Singh, 2003).

THE FUTURE OF MOBILE DEVICES

The future of mobile devices is going to be fueled by developing countries (Best, 2006). Many people that can't afford cars, good jobs and other items that we take for granted are making room for a cell phone. Mobile devices will probably turn into the only computer

Figure 3.

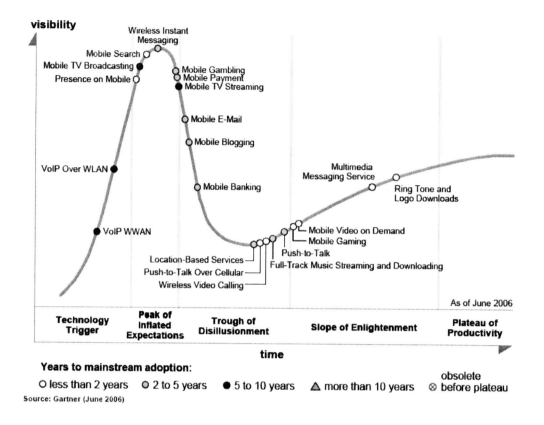

some people many ever purchase (Best, 2006). Mobile devices will be the social connection for many, just as they have buddy lists today, the mobile device will give them that plus more (Best, 2006). Today, the biggest demand in mobile devices is for connectivity. People expect and demand to be able to browse the Internet, check on email using a Varity of portable devices. Notebooks and pocket PCs have features such as WiFi and Ethernet connections. Today people can walk into Panara Bread or Star Bucks for a cup of coffee and a bit to eat while working over the Internet using the restaurants hot spot. People are moving forward with technology and wireless mobile devices. They need it and expect it to be there now and in the future.

REAL WORLD CASE STUDIES

A major greetings card company had problems in their ability to communicate with their staff and clients in the field. The staff members fell into two basic categories, the merchandiser and the business manager.

The merchandiser worked mainly at the client's stores, managed inventory, updated order history and took care of other products. The business manger worked at the office and set up promotions, managed the customers from the corporate view and kept track of time sheets. The problem the greeting card company was facing was the inability to keep up-to-date views on customers inventory and new orders. Another problem, orders had to be manually typed into the system at the corporate office before any orders would be processed. This caused not only a delay but also incurred extra overhead in labor to type the orders into the computer. The company was suffering with limited access to data, lack of managerial awareness of client activities in the field and time spent on getting orders into the system (Macmillan, 2005). The solution was to implement mobile applications to support the key business areas lacking proper attention (Macmillan, 2005). So the greeting card company decided to give handheld PDAs to the merchandisers and tablet PCs to the business managers (Macmillan, 2005). The company was able to lower wage costs, cut back on photocopying, had fewer service and reporting errors, took stock inventory at a much quicker pace, saved on user training and was able to supply better customer service (Macmillan, 2005).

Chesterfield County Police Department had a system with GPS/GIS/AVL to send dispatch units to incidents (Vining, 2005). But the county found as the years went on growth in the county caused problems for the emergency dispatchers getting emergency-responses to the sites in an efficient manner (Vining, 2005). The county found that a new road was being constructed on a daily basis that interfered with their existing AVL system (Vining, 2005). The county also had other problems with building expansion in industrial facilities like chemical plants (Vining, 2005). But with bandwidth latency and poor GPS tunneling the county had to find a better solution to properly manage the growing population of 280,00 Chesterfield county residents (Vining, 2005). The counties solution was to incorporate an 800 MHz radio communications system with a new AVL system. This system allowed CAD, mobile message switch equipment, GPS receivers, mobile data terminals, and advanced tactical mapping software to bring Chesterfield County quicker response times and increased safety for law enforcement officers (Vining, 2005). These real world examples illustrate how mobile devices can and will continue to improve the way we conduct business in everyday life.

REFERENCES

Best, J. (2006). *Qualcomm confident of bright future for mobiles.* Retrieved July 01, 2006 from http://news.znet.co.uk/communications/3ggprs/0,39020339,39278577,00.htm

Bitpipe. (2006). *CIO's Guide to Wireless in the Enterprise.* Retrieved July 01, 2006 from http://www.bitpipe.com/detail/RES/1148307822_406.html

CBR (2003*). On being mobile.* Retrieved July 02, 2006 from http://www.cbronline.com/article_cbr.asp?guid=CDF79049-ADAD-484D-995C- EB-149D1AD693

Cozza R. (2005). *PDAs: Overview.* Retrieved July 01, 2006 from Gartner.

Gold, J. (2006). *Compliance in the mobile enterprise.* Retrieved July 01, 2006 from http://searchmobile-computing.techtarget.com/generic/0,295582,sid40_gci1191893,00.html

Heard, B. (2004). *Dealing with mobility, data privacy regulations and civil code section 1798.8.* Retrieved July 01, 2006 from http://searchmobilecomputing.techtarget.com/generic/0,295582,sid40_gci1049279,00.html

MacMillan, D. (2005). *How Mobile Sales Automation Helped Australian Card Company.* Retrieved July 13, 2006 from Gartner.

Shen, S., Pittet, S., Milanesi, C., Ingelbrecht, N., Hart, T. J., Nguyen, T. H., Desai, K., Liew, E., Basso, M., Redman, P., & Siddall, D. (2006). *Hype Cycle for Consumer Mobile Applications, 2006.* Retrieved July 05, 2006 from Gartner.

Singh, H. (2003). *Leveraging Mobile and Wireless Internet.* Retrieved July 02, 2006 from http://www.learningcircuits.org/2003/sep2003/singh.htm

Vining, J. (2005). *A Virginia County Learns Lessons in Auto Vehicle Locator Technology Implementation.* Retrieved July 13, 2006 from Gartner.

Chapter XX
Strategic Approach to Globalization with Mobile Business

Walied Askarzai
Melbourne Institute of Technology, Australia

Bhuvan Unhelkar
MethodScience.com & University of Western Sydney, Australia

ABSTRACT

This chapter discusses the importance of strategic approach to the phenomenon of globalization with mobile business. Globalization is the exclusion of geographical boundaries when conducting business, considering that, in today's business world the concept of the dynamic aspect of the globalization is inevitable. Advances in information and communications technologies have helped globalization to evolve rapidly, providing the opportunity for local businesses to operate internationally. A mobile business also can exploit the opportunity of globalization. This chapter also examines how a mobile business can approach globalization strategically. Further more this chapter explains that a semi-mobilized business can become fully mobilized in order to operate more efficiently and effectively.

INTRODUCTION

Globalization is playing an important role in the business world today. The effects of globalization upon businesses are mounting and most unlikely that any business will be immune from the influence of globalization. Globalization has been growing at a rapid rate, particularly in recent years. The businesses should welcome the globalization as an opportunity to expand their global operation. Approaching globalization requires strategic plan in order to acquire sustainable competitive advantage in short term as

well as long term. Mobile businesses also need to be a part of strategic global market. This chapter consists of three sections. In the first section the concept of globalization is defined from a general perspective since there are different perspectives formed on the notion of globalization. The key element in the second section is strategy and the importance of strategic approach. Section three examines the position of mobile businesses in the context of globalization. This section also addresses the transition of semi mobilized business to fully mobile business as part of global strategy. Semi mobilized Business is a business that its operation is in some measure mobilized and partially traditional.

AN OVERVIEW OF GLOBALIZATION

Globalization is the exclusion of geographical boundaries when conducting business and, in today's business world, it is dynamic and inescapable. Globalization gathers the world economies for the purpose of trade and culture removing the trade barriers such as language and cultural barriers (Roll, 2001). Based on the World Bank (1995) report on world development, globalization is unavoidable. The phenomenon of globalization is the dominant and the most controversial concept. Businesses have no alternative but to face this phenomenon nevertheless they have to approach it strategically and secure a place for themselves in the global market.

There are many literatures on the concept of globalization delineating different perspectives of globalization. George and Wilding (2002) argue that there are five perspectives on globalization, technological enthusiasts, Marxian pessimists, pluralists, skeptic internationalists, and a political approach. These perspectives can fall into two categories pessimistic view and optimistic view.

"Globalization itself is neither good nor bad. It has the power to do enormous good-but for many, it seems closer to unmitigated disaster." (Stiglitz (2002) the economic noble price winner)

Optimistic spectators argue that globalization is an opportunity for any type of business any where around the world. As an example a mobile business can expand its operation globally acquiring new customers increasing its global market share.

The pessimistic viewers perceive globalization as a threat to small business survival due to intense competition forces as an example a small mobile business has to fight the forces of globalization in order to retrieve its operation.

Hibbert (2005) suggests that the driving forces for globalization are global economy, global politics, global work, global culture, global trade, global loan, global investment, global bodies, global business, global language, global communication, and global competition. Figure1 below portrays these driving forces.

Globalization is a result of the following causes. Each cause is briefly explained here.

- Labor movements across the borders. Post World War II there has been major labor movement across the globe for the purpose of better employment opportunities, higher income, job flexibility, and shortages of labour in more developed countries.
- Increase in traveling technology with lower costs. The rapid increase in speed of traveling around the globe with lower cost encouraged people to travel more and discover more places.
- Transition of international companies to multinational operation. Most of the world known companies recently transformed to multinational and recently to global companies such as giant food chain restaurant of McDonalds and KFC.
- Migration, most of the countries around the world are facing the political instability which resulted in intense migration for the purpose of a secure life.

Figure 1. The driving forces of globalization

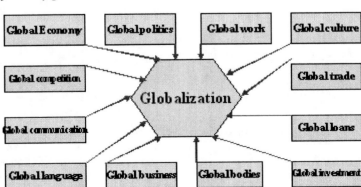

- Advances in technology, the advance in the technology post World War II facilitated advances in telecommunication, trade (i.e. increase in export and import), increase in production, and increase in world GDP. Developing economies increased their share of global output from $42.4 trillion in 1995 to $61.3 trillion in 2005, an increase of 39% to 46%. (World Bank, 2007)
- The internet, the internet is a bank of information, a marketing tool, and a communication device that over the past decade served as a main connectivity device for global village. There is perhaps no longer expression of the development of the information economy that the advent of the Internet-a technology that has undergone rapid growth since the mid 1990s (Turner, 2000)
- Free trade policies resulted in increase in export an import. World exports increased from 295,621 in 1950 to 5,817,080 in1998. (Hibbert, 2005).
- The IT revolution. Globalization has been growing at a rapid rate, particularly in recent years as a result of intense revolution in information technology. Mobile technology is the next wave of IT revolution, extending IT into wireless medium, there for providing 24/7 flexibility in communication, collaboration of a business functions and facilitating information sharing.
- Increase in foreign investment. Foreign direct investment in 1990 was under $50 billion in 2005 it was over $250 billion. (World Bank 2007).
- International bodies. The international bodies such as UN, IMF, World Bank, and WTO came into existence post World War II for the purpose of a better world and harmony.

MOBILE BUSINESSES IN GLOBALIZATION CONTEXT

Mobile businesses have a profound place in global era. Global business can be defined as all the economic activities that are global in scope and operation, and structured that is similar to the structure of a mobile business. The operation is flexible, collaborative, anywhere, at anytime, Mobile business aligns the operation of a global business with its objectives and it can be used as a strategy to reach the objectives of a global business.

Post World War II businesses around the world evolved from operating in domestic market to inter-

national market to multinational market, and now global market, therefore there are four phase into the evolution of businesses. Figure 2 below portrays this evolution processes.

More importantly is to note that Mobility is the future operation of global business because the structure of a mobile business aligns with the operation of a global business. Mobility facilitates freedom to collaborate the functions of a business across the borders regardless of the time zone differences. Location and time are no longer hurdles to the operation of businesses whishing to expand its operation globally. It is also clear that Mobility suits the operation of international businesses and multinational businesses. Mobility is the driven force for virtual business and global business. It facilitates virtual interaction.

Phase 1: Operating in domestic market. The operation of a business is limited to only one country or one local area. The operation is limited in geographical aspect. This type of business can also benefit by encompassing its operation to mobility.

Phase 2: Operating in international market. An international business is a business that operates more that one country. The international businesses also can utilize mobility in their operation to create values and reduce the cost of operation.

Phase 3: Operating in multinational market. A multinational business is a business that is operating in at least more than 10 countries. Multinational businesses can integrate mobility into their operation creating efficiency, speedy operation and adding value to their business.

Phase 4: Operating in global market. A global business is a business that virtually operates in every corner of the world. Global businesses can integrate mobility into their operation creating efficiency, speedy operation and adding value to their business by becoming fully mobilized.

Turner (2000) argues that information technology is the fundamental reason for change in global business. The evolution of business is the result of evolution in information technology and globalization. Arguably, there is correlation between information technology and globalization. The internet with its information superhighway is a good example of this correlation. Global market is relied on the function of internet because the transition from a physical market place to a no-physical market place is only possible by the use of internet and other information technology applications such as mobility. Mobile business is a holistic set of tools that can be used in the operation of a global

Figure 2. The evolution of a business

business. Mobility is the necessity attribute of a global business having the intention to compete globally.

IMPORTANCE OF STRATEGIC APPROACH AND AN OVERVIEW OF STRATEGIC APPROACH

Strategy is a set of plan(s) subject to objectives, competitors, and customers. According to Harvard Business Review (1991), the need for the strategic sound is no longer a luxury but a necessity. A company's strategy consists of the combination of competitive moves and business approaches that managers employ to please customers, compete successfully, and achieve organizational objectives (Thompson and Strickland, 2003).

The choice of the strategy is subject to the objectives of the business and the nature of the mobile business. Mobile businesses have to have specific strategies to reach sustainable competitive advantage. In order to develop an edge over competitors, companies in general need to create a sustainable competitive advantage based on increased operational effectiveness and adequate strategic positioning (Porter 1996).

As the 21st century unfolds, many companies throughout the world are intent on transforming theme selves into global business powerhouses via major investments in global e-business, e-commerce, and other IT initiatives.

Adler (1990) argues that, in today's business world, international experience has become critically important. Companies can no longer get away with operating loosely connected groups of businesses that happen to be located around the world, but must strategically integrate their activities.

Porter suggests that strategy is all about competition and how to compete with business rivals. He argues that competitive strategy can support a business to differentiate itself from rivals in term of production process, marketing and customer's perspective (Porter, 1996). The differentiation of a mobile business must deliberately chose strategy(s) in order to acquire competitive advantage.

Living in globalization era businesses must implement transitional strategies to combat the global competition. According to Adler (1990), Global competition has forced executives to recognize that they must think differently about management. As a global company, the only way to succeed is to develop an effective global human resource management system with personnel capable of designing and implementing translational business strategies.

HOW TO APPROACH GLOBALIZATION STRATEGICALLY

Roll (2001) suggests the following methods (strategies) to expand internationally, the methodologies can be useful for expanding multinational and global.

- *Skim strategy*: the aim is low investment cost by importing the product through foreign agents to distribute the product. For example a mobile business operating in Australia aiming low investment can export its product to other countries and sell there via distributing agencies. The production process takes place within Australia.
- *Penetration strategy*: the aim is to build plants and building in the host countries which requires high investment cost. For example a mobile business can open plants in countries other than country of origin.
- *Dump strategy*: when a company for some reason is unable to sell its surplus therefore it has no option but to sell the product at a lower cost in a host country.
- *Explore strategy*: starts with a small quantity of product been exported to host countries and

then continue exporting based on the outcome of the export.

Thompson and Strickland (2003) suggest the following strategies for entering and competing in foreign markets depending on the nature of the business.

- *Export strategy*: the production takes place in country of origin and then exported to host countries. This strategy is initial step in expanding into sales into foreign markets. This strategy is most suitable for those businesses intending to expand their market share internationally, since the cost of investment is low compare to other strategies such as opining a plant in foreign country.
- *Licensing Strategies*: this strategy supports a business that has a valuable technology (comparative advantage technology) and wants to license other business(s) to use the particular technology and generate income.
- *Franchising Strategies*: franchising works the same way as licensing however it is more suitable to service and retailing enterprises.
- *Global strategy*: A combination of export, licensing and franchising strategies aiming to expand market share into global market.

A mobile business can chose numerous strategies based on its nature, country of origin, and its objectives. The correct strategy facilitates the organization to find the most suitable approach to mobile business in global market. The positive view of strategy is concerned with the firm's actual strategy and how it comes to be. The normative view, on the other hand, is concerned with what the firm's strategy should be (Burgelman, Maidique and Wheelwright, 1996).

The systematic approach can add value to a mobile business. Mobile business need to enter the global market strategically and systematically. This strategic and systematic approach consists of five stages. Figure 3 below portrays the five stages involved in strategic and systematic approach. Applying these five stages in strategic and systematic formulation is crucial for a mobile business desiring to be global business.

The task of analyzing, setting objectives, formulating strategy, implementing strategy and evaluating strategy are the important and interrelated elements of strategic approach. The following strategic application tool and the above strategies are no prescription

to a mobile business. A mobile business intends to approach globalization strategically can use the above strategies as menus, and the strategic application tool as an enabler to approach globalization.

- Analyse environmental factor. Analyse environmental factor includes analyzing internal and external environment. The information from this analysis will enable the business to set objectives according to the environmental requirement.
- Setting objectives and the success criteria. Objectives can be a dependent variable to success criteria. For any particular mobile business going global there is always a cost involves which can be an investment. The most important criterion therefore is return on that investment. Objectives are subject to the nature of mobile business, its strategy, and time availability.
- Formulating strategy (s). During this stage the mobile business requires to set up its vision that is what the business wants to achieve in future. A mobile business should utilize a specific strategy which is suitable to its operation and supports the process of fulfilling its objectives. Next the mobile business has to have a mission statement-that is the reason for the existence of the business. Taking the vision and mission into consideration a mobile business would be able to formulate a strategy that is subject to its objectives.
- Implementing strategy (s). This stage is the translation of the formulated strategy from last stage into action.
- Evaluating the strategy (s) against the success criteria. Evaluation is vital in any plan to determine whether the plan achieved the objectives of the project. It is the evaluation of the project against the selected criteria that really examines the success of the project. The evaluation allows room for any necessary amends that may be required.

The advantages of strategic approach to globalization consist of:

- Encompass a guideline on how to reach the objectives. The process of strategic approach consists of five stages that will enable a mobile business to fulfil its objectives.

Figure 3. Strategic approach application tool

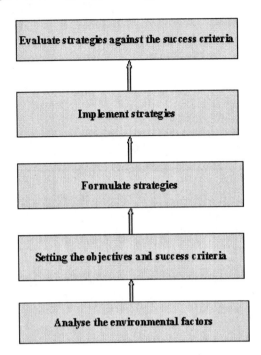

- Becoming aware of the opportunities and threats facing the business. Stage one of strategic approach facilitates the opportunity for a mobile business to outline the opportunities and threats in context of globalization.
- Promoting increase in market share. For a mobile business having the objective to operate globally-strategic approach will support the process of increase in market share both in domestic market and global market.
- Increase in productivity. Strategic approach aims lower cost, cost effectiveness, and in long term economies of scale. Therefore eventually a mobile business will be enabling to increase its production.
- Economies of scale. To cope with dynamic and volatile global economy economies of scale is the survival mechanism for a mobile business. The term economies of scale refer to decrease in cost of production when production is increased as a result of advancement in technology or any other production element.
- Combating the forces of globalization. A mobile business approaching globalization strategically will be enabling to combat the forces of globalization such as intense competition.

- Sustainable competitive advantage. Economies of scale are an enabler for a mobile business to reach sustainable competitive advantage in long term. A mobile business experiencing competitive advantage will add value to its product.

TRANSITION OF SEMI MOBILIZED BUSINESS TO FULLY MOBILIZED BUSINESS AS PART OF GLOBAL STRATEGY

Mobile technology is the next wave of information technology, extending information technology into a wireless medium. Mobile technology extends computing and the |Internet into wireless medium, and provides greater flexibility in communication, collaboration, and information sharing. (Hong Sheng, Fiona Fui-Hoon Nah, Keng Siau, 2005).

Mobile technology is the crucial element of a business's future operation based on two reasons. First reason is that a business in the future needs to be wireless in order to survive in global market as well as be part of global market. The second reason is that mobile technology is the next wave of information technology hence it is an indicator that a business's future is mobile technology.

A semi mobile business is a type of business that operates partially mobile and partially traditional. A semi mobile business can approach globalization strategically by becoming fully mobilized. Mobile technology can be used as a strategic tool for a semi mobile business to operate internationally, multinational, and globally. A semi mobile business incorporating mobile technology fully in its operation can manage to enhance its production, be part of a global market, and improve sales and marketing strategies. Kalakota and Robinson (2001), suggest that the mobile business industry is a very promising industry which is emerging thanks to the appearance of wireless data networks enabling the convergence of the Internet, e-business and the wireless world. Camponovo, Debetaz, and Pigneur (2004), argue that Mobility enhances productivity by adding flexibility to traditional work routines so that they can be done at the right time regardless of location. Essentially, mobility makes it easier to Manage a business.

Mobility can be the next step in the natural evolution of doing business. The role of mobility will become stronger in the next decade or so.

Taking into consideration that wireless technology is emerging in many businesses, then there is hypnotises that the world is transiting to the mobile world. A semi mobile business focusing on becoming fully mobile business can take the advantage to position itself in a better place in m-world. Figure 4 below portrays some of the advantages of mobile business. These advantages highlights how a semi mobile business can be benefited by operating fully mobile as part of its strategic approach to globalization.

Supports People Management: A fully mobile business supports the management of people. For example a manager can be in touch with his/her staff at any time-any where hence mobility makes it simple for the management to manage people.

Supports production process: Managing staff any where-at any time speeds the process of production leading to increase in production, hence mobility provides support for the production process.

Provides flexibility: Mobility increases flexibility. For example an employee does not have to worry about the imbalance in between work and life. Mobility can help the employees to build a balance between life and work.

Provides collaboration: Mobility provides collaboration between different elements of a business. For example a sales person on the field can order the stock directly from suppliers.

Non-physical structure: The most elegant advantage of mobility is that a business can operate from anywhere at any time. The physical element of a business is no longer a hurdle to the operation of an international, multinational and global business.

Suits a global business: A global business can be defined as all the economic activities that are global in scope and operation. Mobility best suits the operation of a global business because mobility razes obstruct to global business such as time, place, and space.

CONCLUSION

This chapter highlighted that globalization is dynamic and unavoidable. Globalization is caused by many factors the most important factor of all is revolution in information technology in the past two decade. The operation of a mobile business is flexible, collaborative, anywhere, at anytime, Mobile business aligns the operation of a global business with its objectives and it can be used as a strategy to reach the objectives of a global business. Therefore mobile business has a profound place in the era of globalization.

Businesses worldwide are under intense forces of globalization such as increase in competition. A Mobile business is also under threat from forces of globalization. A mobile business has to combat forces of globalization strategically. Approaching globalization strategically will support the process of combating the dynamic and volatile forces of globalization. Strategy is a set of plan(s) subject to objectives, competitors, and customers. Today as never before, the need for sound strategies is no longer a luxury but a necessity for a mobile business. The strategic approach consists of four stages, setting objectives, formulating strategies, implementation, and evaluation. Mobility facilitates freedom to collaborate the functions of a business across the borders regardless of the time zone differences. A semi mobilized business should become fully mobilized in order to approach globalization strategically. The benefits of mobility for a semi mobile business are flexibility, increase in production, speed, collaboration, and be a part of global market.

REFERENCES

Adler, N. J. (1990). *Globalization and Human Resource Management: Strategic International Human Resource Development*. Simon Fraser University.

Figure 4. Advantages of a mobile business

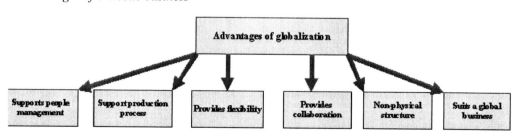

Birch, C. (2001). *Successful E-Business strategy*. Sydney: Pearson Education.

Burgelman, R. A., Maidique, M. A., & Wheelwright, S. C. (1996). *Strategic Management of Technology and Innovation*, 2nd edition. Boston: Irwin.

Camponovo, G., Debetaz, S., & Pigneur, Y. (2004). *A comparative analysis of published scenarios for M-Business*. Lausanne: The University of Lausanne.

Downing, D. (2007). *Global Business*. Oxford: Heinemann Library.

Garrett, G. (2000). *The Causes of Globalization*. New York: Yale University

George, V., & Wilding, P. (2002). *Globalization and Human Welfare*. London: Palgrave.

Haig, M. (2002). *How Come You Don't Have An E-Strategy*. London: Kogan Page Limited.

Hartel, C. E. J., Fujimoto, Y., Strybosch, V. E., & Fitzpatrick, K. (2007). *Human Resource Management*. Sydney: Pearson.

Hibbert, A. (2005). *Globalization*. Oxford: Heinemann Library.

Kalakota, R., & Robinson, M. (2001). *M-Business: The race to mobility*. New York: McGraw Hill.

Mobile Technology. Linclon: Department of Management, University of Nebraska.

Montgomery, C. A., & Porter, M. E. (1991). *Strategy-Seeking and Securing Competitive Advantage*. Boston: Harvard Business Review.

Morath, P. (2001). *Survival at E-Speed*. London: McGraw Hill.

Nickols, F. (2000). *Strategy: Definitions and Meaning*. Distance Consulting.

O'Brien, J. A. (2004). *Management Information Systems*, 6th edition. New York: McGraw Hill.

Porter, M. E. (1986). *Competitive Strategy*. New York: Harvard Business Review.

Porter, M. E. (1996). *What is strategy?* New York: Harvard Business Review.

Roll, G. (2001). *Global Business*. Victoria: Warringal Publication.

Sheng, H., Fui-Hoon Nah, F., & Siau, K. (2005). *Strategic Implications of Mobile Technology*. Lincoln: University of Nebraska.

Siegel, D. (1999). *Business strategies in the Age of the E-Customer*. USA: John Wiley & Sons, Inc.

Stiglitz, J. E. (2002). *Globalization and its Discontents*. London: Hardcover.

Thompson Jr., A. A., & Strickland III, A. J. (2003). *Strategic Management*, 13th edition. New York: McGraw Hill.

Turner, C. (2002). *The information E-Conomy*, 2nd edition. London: Kogan Page Limited.

World Bank. (1995). *World Development Report 1995*, (New York, Oxford University Press).

World Bank. (2007). *World Development Indicators*. World Bank Publication.

Chapter XXI

Business Driven Enterprise Architecture and Applications to Support Mobile Business

Keith Sherringham
IMS Corp, Australia

Bhuvan Unhelkar
MethodScience.com & University of Western Sydney, Australia

ABSTRACT

Information Communication Technology (ICT) needs to provide the knowledge worker with an integrated support system of information management and work-flow. This challenge, however, is further exacerbated in mobile business wherein the knowledge work is not identified with a particular location. Information systems need to be analyzed and modeled, keeping the location-independence of the users in mind. A Model Driven Architecture (MDA) approach, aligned with Object-Orientated Design principles, and driven dynamically as the user interacts, has immense potential to deliver solutions for the systems used by the knowledge worker. An MDA approach provides a unified approach to solutions architecture, information management, and business integration. At the enterprise level, the desktop, the mobile device and at the emerging marketplace level, the evolving need for real-time decision making on any device, anywhere, anytime, to support mobile business is providing a framework for aligning ICT to business. Further details are presented in this chapter together with some of the challenges and opportunities to be seen within mobile business.

INTRODUCTION

Enterprise architecture, application development and requirements gathering have all faced a common problem, that of the business environment being highly dynamic and continuously evolving. An application that worked is often quickly in need of revision and an existing infrastructure readily looses its performance advantage because business needs are continually changing. Although the demands of mobile business are adding another level of complexity to application development and enterprise architecture, the mobile enablement of business (Sherringham and Unhelkar 2008a) provides a convergence of events to realign Information Communication Technology (ICT) as the assembly line for knowledge workers.

Further recognition of ICT as a utility infrastructure and all of the utility principles underpinning design, operation and management of ICT can also be realised in the mobile enablement of business. The significance of a business focused approach, driven by how the customer interacts, will also be championed during the alignment of ICT to meet mobile business (Lan and Unhelkar 2005). Using the demands of mobility, this chapter discusses the alignment of enterprise architecture and application development to meet current and future needs and how the resulting need for real time decision making will shape some key trends in the ICT industry.

ROLE OF KNOWLEDGE MANAGEMENT IN MOBILE BUSINESS

Through the application of proven business principles, business has standardised catering, cleaning, farming, minerals extraction and manufacturing. The last great challenge is the standardisation of knowledge workers to lower costs and assure guaranteed service deliver (Sherringham 2005). This need for standardisation and the resolution of information management and work-flow becomes more pressing when the needs of mobile business are considered (Sherringham 2008).

This situation portrayed in Figure 1 often occurs in organisations, where a Customer contacts a Service Representative who is faced with querying multiple disparate backend systems to find the required information to respond to the Customer's request. The Service Representative may not find what they want, so they have a discussion with a co-worker who tries to do the same thing and who may bring in another co-worker. In the mean-time, the Customer gets frustrated and approaches another Service Representative who goes through the same process. Add to this the duplication between Internet and Intranet, disparate Web sites and the sending of e-mails that are not coherently managed and an in built hidden cost with a failure to guarantee service delivery is seen.

Incumbent within the desktop environment and within many enterprise architectures is the isolation of data in disparate silos with a resulting duplication

of effort. A scarcity of context for the information and a lacking of integration with work-flow further increases hidden costs because of the time spent trying to find information. The demand by customers for mobile business services and because of the constraints imposed by mobile devices, a redefinition of enterprise architectures and an optimisation of the desktop environment shall result.[a]

The small screen size inherent in current mobile devices means that if mobile business services are to be provided and accepted by the user, all of the information management currently required will need to have occurred before delivery to the mobile device. Mobile business will drive the implementation of real time decision making. Instead of users searching and sifting through information, the right information is presented at the right time in the right way to allow decisions to be made, e.g. our favourite restaurants bid in real time to achieve our patronage on any device anywhere anytime (Sherringham and Unhelkar 2008b).

The demand for real time decision making from mobile business is expected to be one of the main drivers for the provision of mobile business services, resolution of information management and for the realignment of ICT to support business needs.

ALIGNMENT DRIVERS FOR ICT WITHIN MOBILE BUSINESS

Having the correct enterprise architecture is an enterprise's key business system, information / data, application, technology strategy and it impacts on their business processes and users (Cummins, 2002). Through defining the ICT necessary to support knowledge workers as an assembly line for knowledge workers and by addressing the issue of integration of information with work-flow (driven by how the customer interacts), the necessary elements of enterprise architecture can be readily defined and the necessary integration required determined. This assembly line approach leverages the modelling capabilities of Model Driven Architecture to develop platform independent models and solutions (McGovern et al. 2004).

In addition to assembly techniques, there are several other principles that have been have been standard engineering practices for many years which can be brought to ICT, applications and enterprise architecture to support mobile business and align information management with work-flow:

Figure 1. Hidden costs of knowledge management present in the enterprise

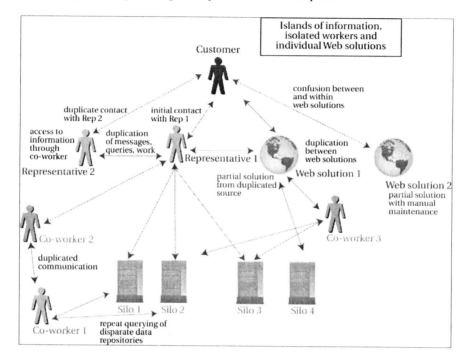

- **Market maturity:** The maturity of the market in which mobile business is occurring
- **Business dynamics:** How a business responds to the forces of markets, customers, suppliers and legislation.
- **Business maturity:** The maturity of a business in the application of ICT.
- **Utility infrastructure:** ICT as a utility infrastructure for mobile business.

Market maturity – As mobile business offerings are brought to market, businesses will operate in an emerging market (size, share or offering). In such emerging markets there are few standards and the market is highly dynamic. Solutions need to be rapidly developed and quickly changed to support growth and product diversification. As markets mature, product diversification is required, specialist needs arise and standards start to develop. Change becomes less prevalent and the focus moves to assured delivery and scalable growth.

In highly mature markets, standards dominate, e.g. ATMs or air-craft. Government compliance is stringent and only a few players can effectively compete. In mature markets, utility infrastructure is the order of the day. A different level of enterprise architecture

is required to operate in all of these markets and to supporting evolving mobile business.

Business dynamics – Even within a market and its sector and segment, business needs are dynamic and are not uniform. Business is driven by market forces, government legislation, customer demand and costs (Figure 2) and although a lot of commonality of function exists across business, different types of business and different areas of business have differing needs.

Markets are often highly dynamic and where business is heavily impacted by market trends, the need for dynamic real time information and fast updates prevail. Mobile business offerings that support dynamic markets are often high volume in nature with a strong focus on supporting real time updates.

Legislative changes are often slow but regularly have a significant impact, e.g. Sarbanes Oxley Act (Bowersox et al. 2007). Less dynamic and more considered solutions with extensive audit capabilities are required to support legislative needs. The ability to record mobile business transactions and reconstruct events impact upon the solution design considerations.

Customers are highly dynamic and are often very demanding. New customers are added regularly to

Figure 2. Business factors impacting enterprise architecture and solution design in mobile business

Figure 3. Progressive approach to business maturity and application sophistication

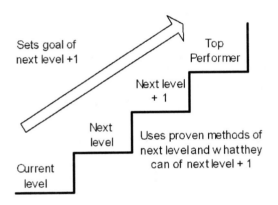

systems and products are quickly shipped in response to demand. Rapid and frequent updates are required to ensure currency of information to service customers. Mobile business solutions that support customers often require sustained and frequent network connectivity with user authentication and transaction validation.

Standing orders and long term contracts are often in place with suppliers and much of the supply process is automated. The ability to place a routine order from a mobile device and to track delivery requires connectivity to the network but frequent updates are not required.

Business maturity – Within an organisation, different areas of business are at different levels in

their respective markets, in their mobile business enablement and in their ability to apply ICT to business. This diversity is a powerful tool for business growth, enterprise architecture alignment and in application development because it provides an upgrade path for application sophistication, business maturity and mobile enablement. By looking at the next level of performance up from current operations, the goal of achieving that level of performance and operation can be set and achieved without the need to reinvent the wheel. Successive levels of performance can be progressively realised (Figure 3).

Utility infrastructure – With ICT being an assembly line for knowledge workers and its critical role within business and mobile business, ICT plays the role of a utility infrastructure with the following principles included within its design:

- **Redundancy:** Surplus capacity is included and protected and available to readily scale.
- **Fail-over:** Include self-initiation and self-configuration should fail-over occur.
- **Load bearing capacity:** Capability to bear load throughout all parts of the solution.
- **Multiple layers of safeguard:** Assumes failure will occur, single points of failure are avoided and are not aligned.
- **Simple:** Solutions are kept simple and are highly standardised and modularised.

The following design considerations are also catered for within utility infrastructure and will be required to support mobile business:

- **Accommodates change:** Change is the norm and are designed to accommodate through automatic configuration.
- **Achieve scalability:** If it can not be automated, it is not scalable.
- **Best of breed:** Best of breed is brought together to provide an assembly line for the processing of jobs.
- **Form an emergent behaviour:** Standardised components do what they do best and the resulting emergent behaviour delivers an industrial strength utility solution.

All of these principles impact upon the enterprise architecture, the design of applications and the ability to provide mobile business services.

USER INTERACTION AND REAL TIME DECISION MAKING TO ALIGN ICT FOR MOBILE BUSINESS

With a strong business focus inherent to the design and application of ICT and a recognition of the drivers impacting design, a methodology for delivering a scalable Service Orientated Architecture (Soley et al. 2000) that meets current and future mobile business needs can be established Figure 4.

The process starts with a common interface that crosses platforms and devices and which incorporates work-flow to provide context. Such an interface can be readily designed and applied by users at all levels of business. Using the visual elements of the interface to drive requirements and process definition, non-technical resources can conceptualise the required business functionality and with clarity of vision comes a well defined scope and a clear expectation.

The user interface of Apple's I-phone marks an evolution in the type of interface that is required for supporting mobile business and real time decision making on any device anywhere any time. The interface is clean, simple and uses self-explanatory icons that when invoked, provide the required functionality. The extension of the Apple I-phone approach is to build in the required work-flow to conduct business into the interface. Rather than having icons launching software applications (the desktop) or control elements (adjust volume on an I-phone), they launch objects of business functionality, e.g. pay an account.

An iconic interface has other advantages including the use of icons is intuitive and spans languages; the interface can be readily customised to reflect branding and personal preferences; and the interface presents a common environment across different devices and operating systems. One other advantage that becomes more significant to mobile business is that an end user defined and process driven iconic interface would also eliminate the need for specific applications because it is about presenting the required elements of functionality only irrespective of where it resides within a software application suite.

An interface consisting of a series of icons that invoke business functionality can be created in real time to reflect specific needs i.e. the interface automatically refreshes to reflect the changing activities being undertaken by a user. The interface would also include the supporting elements to complete an activity, i.e. seamless interface into searching and messaging, whilst connecting to other tasks without the need for cumbersome menu driven navigation. The interface embeds business logic and supports standardised processes.

Whether the icon is on a desktop PC or a mobile device, clicking an icon would invoke the appropriate activity object that delivers the required business functionality, e.g. those for a sales process (Figure 5A). As its name implies and to be discussed subsequently, an activity object is an object of business functionality that when invoked, implements the task required off it. An activity object contains images, data, processing rules and business logic necessary to complete the purpose it has been created for.

Invoking one activity object would implement the other activity objects required for the process. Using the sales process example, objects for prospecting, product details, account details, contact details, events management and financials could all be included. Activating the account object (Figure 5B) would initiate a series of other objects, e.g. credit management, service management, account update, company and contact details, account creation and update, and guarantees and warranties. An object hierarchy exists and this extends from the interface through the hierarchy into the event specific details and finally, the underlying code.

This activity object approach allows common objects of functionality to be established, e.g. banking. A hierarchy of activity objects exists to reflect standardised processes and these activity objects are drawn together and presented as required. These activity objects can be included in multiple processes and accessed from within and across enterprises on any device.

Any activity object (Figure 5C) is made of the following:

- **Content:** The content that an activity object needs to use and process. Content shall be for both the activity objects themselves and their functionality.
- **Images:** The images that an activity object needs to use and process. Images are for both the activity object itself and for its functionality.
- **Business logic:** This is the actual business logic an activity object uses for completion of its processing task.
- **Processing rules:** These are the rules that define how an activity object operates, i.e. what information, images and business logic an activity object needs to process.

Figure 4. ICT to support mobile business solutions

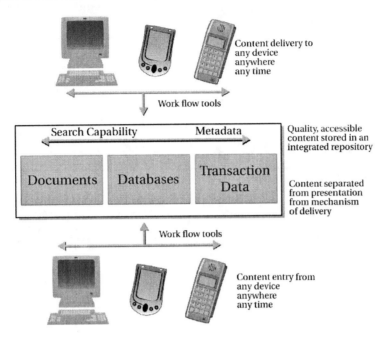

Figure 5. Definition of activity objects: A) Sales object, B) object hierarchy, C) object structure

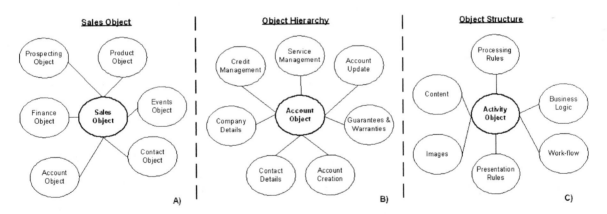

- **Work-flow:** This is the work-flow in which an activity object resides, i.e. the context of the activity object. This allows users to work their way through a process to the required outcome.
- **Presentation rules:** The rules that go to create or make an activity object, i.e. what information, images and business logic an activity object needs to function and how the activity object functions.

Supporting the activity objets is a series of virtual contextual information bases that allow the activity objects to function.

- **Information databases:** Information that provides the required knowledge within an activity object.
- **Information relationship databases:** Manage informational relationships that transforms information to knowledge.

- **Rule processing databases:** Providing the rules for work-flow, business logic and processing of the information, i.e. a recipe compiler.
- **Activity object databases:** Database for the configurable rules, images, etc. for the activity objects that flow through into the interface.
- **Exceptions databases:** Details on how to handle exceptions for a given activity object in a given circumstance.
- **Messaging databases:** Handling the rendering of information to multiple devices irrespective of location and time. This includes device configuration and management information.

This simple approach of defining activity objects from the user interface into the enterprise architecture has many advantages including:

- Solutions are driven by the end user as the customer interacts – gain their buy in and support.
- The required information and businesses processes are readily determined.
- The solutions required to support operation are defined.
- The required enterprise architecture and applications are determined.
- Simply rendering activity objects to an end device with all of the required elements ready for implementation has many advantages to the implementation of mobile business.

The use of activity objects has the following impacts:

- **Seamless iconic interface:** The interface is a series of icons managed within one coherent framework which invoke functionality. The interface encapsulates the required work-flow which integrates and refreshes as required. Such an interface works on any device (desktop or mobile) providing ready business functionality, intuitive use and ease of training.
- **Business driven functionality:** The activity objects and their hierarchy can be readily defined and reflect business operations. The activity objects drive outcomes and can be integrated to support many business operations. A single set of activity objects can be determined and used on both mobile devices and the desktop.
- **Definition of work-flow:** Business process and the information required at each step are defined

as the customer interacts to realise the outcome. Contrast this with the current practice of designing processes around feature driven software. This functional approach is well suited to mobile devices because of their small screen size.

- **Clear requirements:** Many development projects suffer because requirements are not clearly defined. By defining the required processes and objects necessary to deliver outcomes, requirements are clearly defined. In contrast with many ICT projects, mobile business services can now be brought to market on time and to budget.
- **Application development:** Application development changes from feature driven and a series of specialised applications to a series of activity objects that are linked together within a common framework as required. Developers no longer code applications, they code object functionality which are brought together to deliver outcomes as required by the user.
- **Standardised activity objects:** Elements of business functionality are common across many areas of business operation and types of business. When using activity objects, banking functionality is no longer tied to accounting and financial applications; elements of banking functionality become available as needed. This use of activity objects allows for standardised elements to be developed and delivered across business, markets and devices.
- **Resolution of information:** An iconic interface traps work-flow, processes are defined and the steps required to deliver outcomes are also clearly specified. By definition the information required at each step is also determined. This approach defines the information required and the context necessary for its application, i.e. it resolves the information management problem.
- **Information sharing:** Activity objects are ideal for sharing information between other objects or for interfacing with other applications and mobile devices because they contain the required information, business rule and processing rules necessary to function. In addition, activity objects can address the error handling and exception handling. These self contained objects can be readily used and shared between mobile devices.
- **Resolution of the ICT assembly line:** Whether it is insurance premiums, foreign exchange trades or answering customer queries for product, business is about routine transaction process-

ing and having the right information presented at the right time in the right way, i.e. ICT is the assembly line for knowledge workers. The activity object approach defines the knowledge worker assembly line across the desktop and mobile devices.

- **Definition of Service Orientated Architecture:** From a definition of the knowledge worker assembly line comes a resolution of the ICT required to support the assembly line, both hardware and software. How ICT is to be deployed and operated is also determined, i.e. a Service Orientated Architecture is defined that is driven as the customer interacts.

MOBILITY, ACTIVITY OBJECTS AND MODEL DRIVEN ARCHITECTURE

The Model Driven Architecture approach and the use of activity objects comes to the fore when it comes to mobile computing and the demand for mobile services (Lee et al. 2004). Many incumbent solutions with their inefficiency in accessing information and an absence of the unification of information with work-flow, become almost ineffective in servicing mobile devices. Cumbersome interfaces that do not deliver outcomes can not be used on mobile devices because of their screen size. Unlike the desktop PC, the storing of data locally on an end device is no longer an option. Complex business applications rich in features that people rarely use are not easily transferred to mobile devices (Paavilainen 2001).

Simplicity, with clear interfaces that deliver outcomes is what works on the mobile device. The need for effective and efficient mobile interfaces shall in turn impact upon the incumbents in the desktop environment and create both a common interface across devices and an optimised supporting infrastructure.

Other areas where the application of mobility leverages model driven architecture include:

- **Information Relationships:** To be effective, information needs to be delivered in context for decision making. Context is given by managing the relationships between information through a metadata framework that integrates with work-flow.
- **Work-flow:** Activity objects include their own work-flow and business logic but their strength

comes in the combining of standard activity objects together to provide a consolidated work-flow.

- **Messaging environment:** Mobility requires a unified messaging environment combining voice, data, text, images and video. To guarantee service delivery the messaging environment needs to be architected around the FedEx model, where the quality of hand-off, the message and the delivery and storage of the message are all separated and utility infrastructure used. A business model driven architecture approach services the needs of a unified messaging environment.
- **Error and exception handling:** Effective and efficient transaction processing is all about how the errors and exceptions are managed. Whilst addressing the quality of hand-off issues is part of the solution, having dedicated processes to mange errors and exceptions is also required. Specific objects to handle errors and exceptions can be defined and called in sequence until the issues are resolved.
- **Hand-off:** Integration of information, integration between systems, integration of context and work-flow all rely on an effective quality of hand-off between different elements. Self contained objects with all of the required elements provide an effective solution for ensuring a quality of hand-off.
- **Security:** The topic of security is complex and is the subject of much concern and extensive discussion (Nand 2006). An object approach helps to facilitate the security because the necessary role-based access and functionality is included within the object. Additional security features and capabilities can be included as elements within the objects.

Mobility and the demand for mobile services is what will drive the development of object orientated solutions that shall manifest on both the desktop and in the enterprise. Delivering objects of functionality to a mobile device, as required with all of the necessary information, business logic and work-flow has several advantages:

- Across platform – A common interface with standard user driven functionality can be delivered across devices and platforms. This provides the end user with what they need irrespective of which device they use and location in which they operate, i.e. "my desk where I want it and how I want it".

- Consolidated information-bases – With the creation of virtual consolidated information-bases, information can be single sourced. Information is no longer trapped on the end device and all of the archiving and backup are conducted at the server.
- Smart end devices – The benefits of distributed computing power are realised without all of the complexities inherent to the desktop environment. The end device is a smart device. The benefits of lower cost, ease of use and better asset management are transparent.
- Information management simplification – The inefficiency of the desktop environment and the need for advanced information management skills to manage versions, locations, formats and applications is not sustainable on the mobile device. Information presented at the right time in the right way to any device anywhere anytime is required. The optimisation necessary for mobility shall also drive changes in the desktop environment.
- Defines ICT required – A business focused model driven architecture approach helps determine the business need, is driven by the business process, the information required is identified and integrated to work-flow. At this point the ICT solution necessary to support a business and how it should be deployed is transparent.
- Responsive to business need – Business is very dynamic and one of the existing challenges is trying to define requirements against a rapidly changing business environment. An object approach allows those objects required to be combined in real time to meet business needs. Since standardised objects can be used defined and applied across many processes and areas of business, application development becomes much more responsive to dynamic business needs.

FUTURE DIRECTIONS

Real time decision making and activity objects have many uses within both mobility and in the wider enterprise business application of ICT. One of the evolving needs is in the application of gaming solu-tions to business training, education and simulation. Gaming is one of the fastest growing services of mobile computing and whilst gaming offers many market opportunities in its own right, it is the wider business use from mobile devices that are to be realised. Flight simulators and their use has been widely applied to train and skill staff and to provide experience in handling difficult situations. The next level is to assist in business decision making through simulation and what-if scenarios. Strong visual presentation and a rich immersive and interactive experience to provide scenarios and identify issues and outcomes is a major area where model driven architecture and activity objects shall be used. The simulation and modelling results shall be accessible from mobile devices as well as the desktop.

The provision of Software as a Service (SaaS) is in its infancy and the mobile opportunities for SaaS are still to be realised. Much of SaaS is still very application specific and there have been concerns about the quality and applicability of code supplied with SaaS. The activity object approach is the natural extension of SaaS; with only those activity objects required being rendered as a service.

The development of mobile computing will see a proliferation of solutions and services and an incredible diversity of offerings. As the market matures, standards shall come into play and consolidation shall be seen. Standardisation lower costs and guarantees service delivery and in turn this creates market dominance. Being the de-facto market standard is how a business gains market dominance. The software of the future is not feature rich applications but tightly integrated activity objects drawn together as needed to deliver outcomes. Being the de-facto standard for activity objects shall lead to standardisation of the desktop, at the enterprise, at the mobile device level and in turn, at the marketplace level (the emergence of marketplace computing).

CONCLUSION

Mobile business and the demand for real time decision making is a powerful driver for aligning ICT and applications to deliver the ICT infrastructure necessary for mobile business. The use of a standard iconic interface and activity objects that invoke business functionality provides an effective solution for delivering mobile business services, whilst resolving the information management and work-flow issue and aligning enterprise architecture and application development.

REFERENCES

Bowersox, D. J., Closs, D. J., & Cooper, M. B. (2007). *Supply Chain Logistics Management*, 2nd edition. McGraw-Hill Companies, Inc.: Irwin

Cummins, F. A. (2002). Enterprise Integration: An Architecture for Enterprise Application and Systems Integration. Canada: Willey Computing Publishing, John Wiley & Sons, Inc.

Lan, Y., & Unhelkar, B. (2005). *Global Enterprise Transitions: managing the process.* Hershey, PA: IGI Global.

Lee V., Schneider H., & Schell R. (2004). *Mobile Applications: Architecture, Design, and Development.* Hewlett-Packard Development Company L.P., publishing by Pearson Education as Prentice Hall Professional Technical Reference.

Paavilainen J. (2001). *Mobile business strategies: understanding the technologies and opportunities.* Wireless Press; Addison-Wesley in partnership with IT Press.

McGovern, J., Ambler, S. W., Stevens, M. E., Linn J., Sharan V., & Jo, E. K. (2004). Foreword by O. Sims. In *A Practical Guide to Enterprise Architecture.* Pearson Education, Inc.

Nand, S. (2006). Developing a Theory of Portable Public Key Infrastructure (PORTABLEPKI) for Mobile Business Security. In Unhelkar B. (Ed.), Chapter 27 of book: *Handbook of Research in Mobile Business: Technical, Methodological and Social Perspectives.*, Hershey, PA, USA: IGI Global.

Sherringham, K. (2005). Cookbook for Market Dominance and Shareholder Value: Standardising the Roles of Knowledge Workers. London: Athena Press. (p. 90).

Sherringham, K. (2008, Apirl/May). Catching the Mobility Wave Information Age. (p. 5).

Sherringham, K., & Unhelkar, B. (2008a). Elements for the Mobile Enablement of Business. In (Unhelkar et al. 2008) *Handbook of Research in Mobile Business: Technical, Methodological and Social Perspectives.* (pp. xxx –yyy).

Sherringham, K., & Unhelkar, B. (2008b). Real Time Decision Making and Mobile Technologies. In (Unhelkar et al. 2008) *Handbook of Research in Mobile Business: Technical, Methodological and Social Perspectives.* (pp. xxx –yyy).

Soley, R., & OMG Staff Strategy Group (2000). *Model Driven Architecture.* Object Management Group. White Paper.

KEY TERMS

Activity Objects: A series of objects invoked from a standard iconic interface that provide business functionality because they contain the necessary content, images, business logic, processing rules, work-flow and presentation rules.

FedEx Model: A model for the operation of a unified messaging environment based on the proven principles to move messages (parcels) around the world by leading logistics companies.

Information Bases: The next generation of databases but instead of storing data, information is stored in context.

Information Relationships: The associations between elements of information to provide context and convert information to knowledge.

Knowledge Worker Assembly Line: Knowledge workers take information and value-add to it to provide services. ICT needs to provide the right information at the right time in the right way for knowledge workers to effectively operate, i.e. ICT is the assembly line for knowledge workers.

Marketplace Computing: Standardised computing (tightly integrated hardware and software) operating at the marketplace level to allow businesses to interact effectively in a marketplace. Business currently standardises at the enterprise level but to operate effectively, standardisation shall be at the marketplace level.

Real Time Decision Making: The provision of information in context and integrated with work-flow in real time to any device anywhere anytime is needed so that decisions can be made.

ENDNOTE

[a] The introduction of the automatic telling machine (ATM) led many banks to redevelop their enterprise architectures and those that could not respond effectively were at a competitive disadvantage and in some selling off their retail operations.

Section II
Sociology and Culture

Chapter XXII
Composite Process–Personalization with Service–Oriented Architecture

Rajani Shankar Sadasivam
University of Alabama at Birmingham, USA

Murat M. Tanik
University of Alabama at Birmingham, USA

ABSTRACT

The integration of large systems remains problematic in spite of advances in composite services approaches, such as Web services and business process technologies. The next challenge in integration is composite process-personalization (CPP), which involves addressing the needs of the interaction worker. An interaction worker participates and drives business processes. As these workers increasingly perform their work from mobile devices, CPP becomes an important area of mobile research. In this chapter, an agent-based approach to composite services development is introduced, addressing the lack of CPP in integration. A case study is used to demonstrate the steps in the agent-based approach.

INTRODUCTION

Enterprise development approaches have continually evolved to meet the ever-changing demands of businesses. Business gurus in the fifties preached management dimensions of planning, organization, integration, and measurement. Consequently, in the sixties and seventies, advancements in mainframe computers and computer languages enabled businesses to implement systems addressing the different management dimensions. In the eighties, the focus was on information processing, and consequently, the rise of information processing tools in the late eighties and early nineties addressed these needs. In the nineties, the focus was on integration of business processes, which has lead to the rise of the service-oriented architecture and business process engineering in the early 2000s. The next challenge of enterprise development is the composite process-personalization (CPP) challenge (Sadasivam, 2007), which involves developing personalized, customized systems to address the needs of the interaction worker (Harrison-Broninski, 2005; Miller, 2005; Ramamoorthy, 2000).

An interaction worker participates and drives business processes (Harrison-Broninski, 2005). Business analysts, CEOs, market analysts, accountants, and researchers can all be categorized as interaction workers. Interaction worker processes are knowledge-intensive, that is, processes in which humans are involved in the decision-making processes (Ramamoorthy, 2000). The rich sets of applications that are available in handheld and mobile devices make it possible for interaction workers to conduct their business from these devices. Therefore, interaction workers are interacting with enterprise systems from their mobile devices increasingly. This option of working from mobile devices, in turn, implies that the processes should also adapt to the needs of the mobile worker. In (Liang & Wei, 2004), different examples of mobile applications for interaction workers are provided: time-critical services, location-aware and location-sensitive services, identity-enacted services, ubiquitous communications and content delivery services, business process streamlining, and mobile offices. The success of each of these applications depends on the ability of the enterprise processes to adapt to the needs of the mobile worker (Brezillon, 2003; Gutmann & Fox, 2002). As such, CPP becomes an important research area of mobile computing.

The knowledge-intensive nature of the interaction worker processes dictates that these processes constantly change (Harrison-Broninski, 2005). As a result, current process-oriented approaches of developing integrated systems in which the processes are specified during design time, using technologies such as Business Process Execution Language (BPEL), and cannot adapt to constant changes cannot work. Therefore, a critical need exists for flexible yet comprehensive approaches of representing business processes to accommodate the complex and flexible needs of interaction workers.

This chapter discusses the following: First, the notion of CPP is expanded and an example is used to show the lack of CPP in large systems integration. Process-oriented composite services development is leveraged to address the lack of CPP problems. A discussion of process-oriented composite services development is provided. An agent-based development approach is described to alleviate the problems of supporting CPP. A case study is used to outline the steps in the agent-based development approach and differentiate them from current approaches.

COMPOSITE PROCESS-PERSONALIZATION AND PROCESS GAP

Composite services technologies have evolved to address the many integration challenges of enterprises (Alesso & Smith, 2005; Juric, Mathew, & Sarang, 2004; Newcomer & Lomow, 2005; Pasley, 2005). The advances in Web services and business process technologies, in particular, have enabled us to develop enterprises by composing services quickly and effectively (Leymann, Roller, & Schmidt, 2002; Sadasivam, Sundar, Tanik, Jololian, & Tanju, 2007; Stone, 2004; Tsai, 2005; van der Aalst, Aldred, Dumas, & ter Hofstede, 2004; Yeh, Pearlson, & Kozmetsky, 2000). In spite of these technological advances, a process gap occurs in most integration efforts (Fingar, 2006; Gleghorn, 2005; Khoshafian, 2007; Vojdani, 2003; Yeh, Pearlson, & Kozmetsky, 2000). The process gap occurs when the implemented system delivers a process that does not meet the needs of the users. The complex needs of the interaction worker (Harrison-Broninski, 2005) and the use of mobile devices only compounds the problem of process gap.

The lack of CPP support causes the process gap problem. Reflect on Ramamoorthy's interaction model (RIM) of enterprises (Ramamoorthy, 2000). RIM describes three types of enterprise interactions (Ramamoorthy, 2000): 1) Mechanistic interactions among service processes, 2) interactions between service processes and individuals, and 3) interactions between service processes and teams. RIM implies that the scope of the integration problem is more than just the integration of mechanistic processes. It encompasses the integration of processes with human interactions. However, our Web service and business process technologies are only suitable for integration of mechanistic processes (Harrison-Broninski, 2005). They are not capable of handling processes with human interaction. We refer to this integration challenge as the CPP challenge (Sadasivam, Sundar, Tanik, Jololian, & Tanju, 2007).

Consider the following example of an interaction worker in a firm that deals with stock quotes. Assume that one of the specific tasks of the worker is to obtain some data from the Yahoo finance portal (Yahoo Inc., 2007); perform a few transformations on a spreadsheet, such as sorting and drawing customized charts with

Figure 1. Sample workflow described in the problem scenario

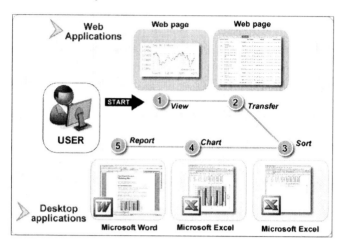

the data; and, finally, generate personalized reports. The employee uses Microsoft Excel to do the transformations such as sorting, and uses the charting feature of Microsoft Excel to draw the charts. He also uses Microsoft Word to generate the reports. As depicted in Figure 1, it is apparent that this process is highly cumbersome, requiring the user to switch back and forth between four to five different applications that are both Web- and desktop-based. This particular case highlights three issues that the user confronts:

- The user switches between one Web application to another, for example, from the market summary to recent quotes.
- The user switches between one desktop application to another, for example, from Microsoft Excel to Microsoft Word.
- The user switches from Web-based application to another desktop application or vice versa, for example, from the market summary to Microsoft Excel.

In such highly interactive scenarios, the interaction worker prefers or needs certain tools for accessing data and accomplishing tasks. In this example, as in most integration efforts, the integration scope is restricted only to the data needs of the user. For example, the Yahoo finance portal provides access to market quotes. However, the user tools are not seamlessly integrated with the data, which leaves the user to transfer the data between the tools. This process can be time-intensive and error-prone, resulting in a poor user experience that implies the lack of CPP.

The disruption effect of lack of CPP support can be seen in the confusion caused by the divergence of integration technologies used in enterprises. Two groups of technologies have been developed to address the integration of enterprise processes. One is the BPM technologies group that address the automation of mechanistic processes (Elzinga, Horak, Chung-Yee, & Bruner, 1995; Havey, 2005). Another is the groupware technologies group, including knowledge management tools, collaborative systems, and content management systems, that address the integration needs of human participants in a process (Desouza, Awazu, & Baloh, 2006). The divergence of technologies, instead of solving the problem, have caused greater confusion in enterprises (Fingar, 2005; Harrison-Broninski, 2005).

Figure 2. Integration confusion in enterprises

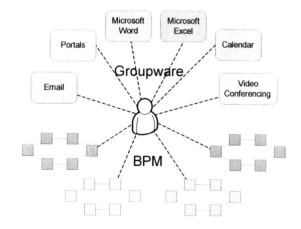

The reason is that these two groups of technologies exist in function silos, which implies that they do not integrate well with each other leading to a lack of integrated information to the user. The ineffective use of collaborative technologies results in collaboration that occurs out of context of enterprise processes, resulting in the inefficient operation of enterprises (Harrison-Broninski, 2005). Figure 2 depicts the integration confusion in enterprises.

PROCESS-ORIENTED COMPOSITE SERVICES

Our approach to CPP leverages process-oriented composite services development. Composite services development can be defined as a large systems development approach in which the focus is on specifying, discovering, selecting, and integrating services. A service in this context refers to the resources that perform work to satisfy the needs of the large system (Ramamoorthy, 2000).

Process-oriented development of composite services is an approach emphasizing the use of processes throughout the composite services life cycle. Processes will guide the composition of services. There are several advantages of this approach. Composite services provide standards and powerful tools for composition of services (Leymann, Roller, & Schmidt, 2002; Stone, 2004; van der Aalst, Aldred, Dumas, & ter Hofstede, 2004). Second, we know that enterprises are organized as processes (Delcambre & Tanik, 1998; Fingar, Kumar, & Sharma, 2000; Harrison-Broninski, 2005; Juric, Mathew, & Sarang, 2004). This implies that a process-oriented approach provides a natural and systematic approach for modeling and developing composite services

Since the term "process" has been used with different connotations (Coalition, 1999; Delcambre & Tanik, 1998; Elzinga, Horak, Chung-Yee, & Bruner, 1995; Humphrey, 1989; Tanik & Chan, 1991), the use of the term process is clarified before describing process-oriented development of composite services. A process is considered to be made up of the semantic and syntactic elements of composite services. The semantic elements capture the tasks of users and the resources needed to perform the task. The syntactic elements provide the structure for the process. The definition of tasks and resources are based on Coffman and Denning's task system model (Coffman & Denning, 1973). A task constitutes the unit of compositional activity in a process. The task is specified in terms of its external behavior, such as the input it requires, the output it generates, its action or function, and its execution time. Resources are any (not necessarily physical) device, which is used by tasks. For example, the tasks of a process could use multiples resources, such as a service, software, or a human activity.

Every composite services development starts with identifying that a "service need" exists. A service need refers to something that the user requires. The user can be an individual or an enterprise. Once the existence of a need is identified, the first step in composite services development is to analyze and decompose the need into a set of processes. The second step is to discover and select the services necessary to realize the composite services workflow. The third step is to integrate and compose the selected services to form the composite services. Composition analysis and monitoring is required to verify and validate the formation of composite services. Therefore, the life cycle of process-oriented composite services is as follows:

- Process modeling, in which the focus is on the development of abstract processes followed by deriving the executable processes from the abstract processes.
- Process composition, in which the focus is on the composition of the executable processes to develop composite services.
- Process analysis and optimization, in which the focus is on the analysis and optimization of the performance of the composite service. Process analysis can also be performed in the process modeling stage. In this case, process enactment would be used to simulate the data for analysis (Delcambre, 1994).

Figure 3 shows the life cycle of process-oriented composite services. The dashed line in the figure indicates the feedback loop in the life cycle. The feedback is achieved by process analysis and optimization.

The following steps describe the engineering activity of developing composite services (Figure 4). The process modeling stage starts with the development of abstract process models. Abstract process models should provide support for the semantic and syntactic aspects of an enterprise. The abstract process models provide a good model for process enactment and analysis. The development of the abstract processes starts with a high-level model with few details. The abstract process development continues until models with suf-

Figure 3. Composite services development using process-oriented composite services

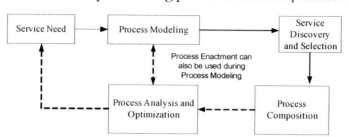

Figure 4. Engineering activity for composite services development

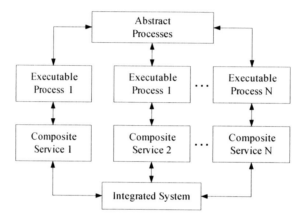

ficient details are reached from which it is possible to generate an executable process. The abstract process models are then transformed to executable process models for composition. The executable processes provide an executable representation of the process for composing services. The executable processes must be directly composable on a composition engine and can represent processes that are either mechanistic, that are devoid of any human interaction, or supporting human activities. The above steps imply that a systematic application of process engineering techniques that can effectively capture the semantic and syntactic aspects of the enterprise becomes an important component of composite services development.

ISSUES IN SUPPORTING COMPOSITE PROCESS-PERSONALIZATION

There are two issues in providing CPP in process-oriented composite services development. First, there is a need for an approach to compose tools-as-services

(TAS), which enables the tools to be seamlessly integrated with the data. In the TAS approach, an application and its functions (tools) could be used the way Web services are used (Sadasivam, Sundar, Tanik, Jololian, & Tanju, 2007; Sadasivam, Sundar, Tanik, & Tanju, 2006). An example of TAS is provided in (Jololian, 2003; Jololian, Kurfess, & Tanik, 2003), which shows the spell-check feature of Word exposed as a service. The TAS approach is a three-step process. In the first step, the desired tools would be componentized using service descriptions and placed in a repository, such as the UDDI. This step is analogous to publishing a Web service. The second step involves the use of an application that searches for tools in the registry based on their service descriptions. This process is similar to service discovery. As a third step, an aggregator application such as the SOD or a portal can then use the invoked tool, thereby delivering the invoked tool's functionality in a completely different application interface. The TAS approach is not addressed in this chapter. The TAS approach in discussed in detail in (Sadasivam, 2007; Sadasivam, Sundar, Tanik, Jololian, & Tanju, 2007; Sadasivam, Sundar, Tanik, & Tanju, 2006; Sundar, 2007).

The second issue is addressed in this chapter. There is a need for an approach to comprehensively capture, configure, and manage the semantics of user needs in composite services development. First, the need of the user has to be captured. Second, the captured need has to be represented and configured in a machine actable way for the composition engine. Third, the configured need has to be managed to incorporate the changes that arises in the user needs.

The semantics of the user needs come from the problem domain, that is, the semantics describe the user tasks and the resources needed for those tasks. The difficulties in capturing, configuring, and managing the semantics exist because of multiple reasons, such as lack of understanding of the problem domain by the developer, lack of understanding of the scope of the integration problem, use of ad hoc approaches, and the lack of technology support as discussed in (Harrison-Broninski, 2005).

Consider the steps in process-oriented composite services development. In the first step, process models that consist of both the abstract and executable process models are developed. Abstract process modeling starts with a high-level model of the enterprise with minimum details. Models with increasing levels of semantics follow this high-level model. Each stage of the abstract process modeling can be associated with process analysis to improve the model. Once a model of sufficient detail is realized, the model is transformed to an executable process model such as BPEL to develop composite services.

The problem of supporting CPP occurs at three stages because of loss of semantics of user needs. First, the loss of semantics occurs at the abstract process modeling stage because the semantics captured by abstract process models might not be as comprehensive as needed.

Second, there is loss of semantics during the transformation from abstract process models to executable process models. This is because executable process modeling technologies are inadequate in their support to configure and manage the captured semantics. Harrison-Broninski describes this limitation in his book (Harrison-Broninski, 2005), showing that executable process technologies were designed to help technicians build automated process execution engines capable of orchestrating distributed computing resources of various kinds. Harrison-Broninski further observes that the current work on executable process technologies is driving it downwards towards programming rather than upwards, which makes it more difficult to configure and manage semantics. It is important that the executable process technologies be driven downwards towards programming to support the efficient composition of services. It follows that there must be a mechanism to support the executable processes with semantics to develop composite services with CPP.

Third, there is loss of semantics because of the continuous changes in the knowledge-intensive processes of the interaction worker. These changes to the interaction worker processes happen because of multiple reasons. For instance, the worker might have changed the process to reflect his new understanding of the work to be accomplished. The process might also change because the worker has moved from one location to another, or switched between desktop to a mobile device. Therefore, if the changes are not reflected in the process, then the system delivers a process different from the needs of the worker.

AN AGENT-BASED APPROACH FOR COMPOSITE PROCESS-PERSONALIZATION

An agent-based approach is developed to address the problem of supporting CPP (Figure 5). The approach is based on process-oriented composite services development. It consists of a process modeling, process composition, and process analysis stage. The process modeling is enhanced by the use of the agent-based approach for supporting the configuring and managing of semantics of user needs.

In the abstract modeling stage as depicted in Figure 5, every user's need is decomposed as tasks and resources. To address the capture problem, a systematic approach, such as the task system model is used to model the different tasks and resources. Each task is associated with the CPP resource semantics (Sadasivam, 2007), which identify the different types of resources. The CPP resource semantics were identified based on published literature on supporting interaction workers (Sadasivam, 2007). The six types of CPP resource semantics are Knowledge Semantic (KS), Rules Semantic (RUS), Roles Semantic (ROS), Users-Profile Semantic (UPS), Infrastructure Semantic (INS), and Communication Semantic (COS). Their role in providing CPP is defined as follows:

- KS answers specific questions required to address a task.

Figure 5. Agent-based approach for composite process-personalization

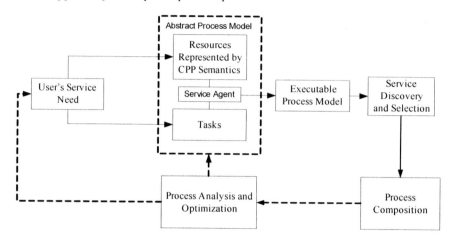

- RUS provides specific conditions required to perform a task.
- ROS provides a representation of the group of users interacting with a task and their access permissions.
- UPS provides a representation of the users associated with a task and their preferences.
- INS provides a representation of the mechanistic resources and tools that are needed to perform a task.
- COS provides a representation of the input and output messages that are involved in performing a task.

The service-agent modeling approach (Sadasivam, 2007) is used for configuring and managing the semantics of user needs and developing composite services with CPP. The service-agent combines two concepts, services, and agents. The services concept provides the abstraction for the modeling of different types of resources. The agents concept provides support for configuring and managing semantics to address the CPP needs of users. The service-agent can be used to represent mechanistic and people resources.

Once the abstract process model is completed, the service-agent is then used to generate the executable process models dynamically for composition. The advantage of linking resources to tasks using service-agents and the CPP semantics is that is that the semantics are systematically derived from the abstract process models, represented in a machine actable way,

and mapped to the executable process models. As the user needs changes, the CPP semantics can be modified to represent the change. The service-agent then modifies its behavior, which alters the characteristics of the delivered process.

The concept map, depicted in Figure 6, shows the linking of the tasks to the resources using the service-agent. The concept map can be described as follows: A task can have multiple service-agents. The service-agents can be of two types, mechanistic or people. Mechanistic service-agents are abstractions of composable resources, such as services, methods, and programs. People service-agents are abstractions of human activity. Every task requires input messages for operation and generates output messages. The input and output messages are types of INS. The input messages are required or provided by service-agents. For instance, input messages are required to invoke mechanistic resources, such as Web services. Input messages can also be provided by a service-agent to trigger a task. A service-agent may require knowledge for performing a task. Knowledge answers the specific needs of service-agents to perform a task. Rules specify the conditions necessary to carry out a task. The concept map also shows that a people service-agent can be accessed by certain roles of users that are specified by ROS. Each role can have a set of users specified by UPS. Users can use certain tools, a type of INS, to perform their tasks. Users can also have history, a type of KS, which can be used to tailor their interaction with the process. The representa-

Figure 6. Concept map for task representation for composite process-personalization

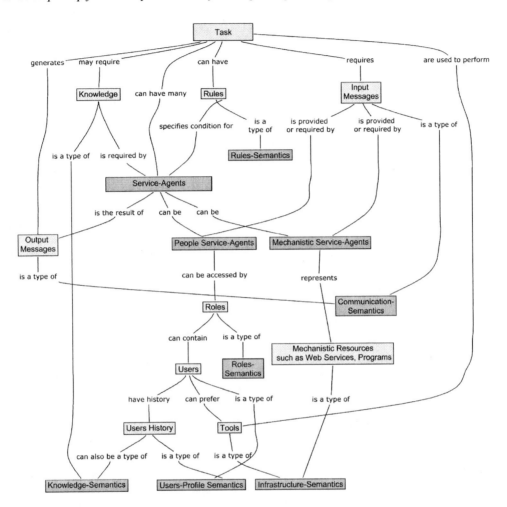

Figure 7. Weather composite services example

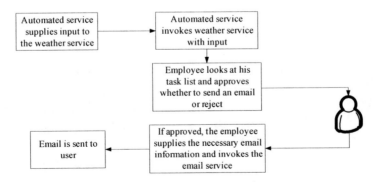

Figure 8. Task system model of the weather composite service

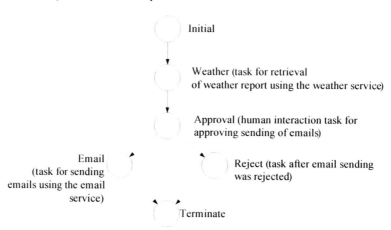

tion of the tasks of a process using the relationships described in the concept map is demonstrated in the case study examples.

CASE STUDY: WEATHER COMPOSITE SERVICES

The case study is a weather composite services (WCS) example. The example includes an approval task, a human activity, to indicate whether the WCS should email users with the weather report. The WCS is depicted in Figure 7.

After identifying the tasks and resources of the WCS, first, a BPEL implementation is shown. Next, the steps to implement the WCS using the agent-based approach are shown. The two implementations are used to demonstrate the support of the agent-based model to dynamically configure and manage the semantics of user needs.

The WCS example is also used to show a conceptual mapping between the service-agent and CPP semantics and a popular process-oriented development technology BPEL. The mapping outlines a strategy for developing process-oriented composite services with CPP using current technology.

The task system model (Coffman & Denning, 1973) is used to represent the abstract process model of the WCS. Figure 8 depicts the task system model of the WCS. The WCS task system can be represented as $C_{WCS} = (\tau, <*)$, where τ is the set of tasks and $<*$ is the precedence relation on τ The set of tasks is

$$\tau_{WCS} = \{\text{Weather}, \text{Approval}, \text{Email}, \text{Reject}\}.$$
(1)

The weather task involves invoking the weather service, supplying the necessary parameters, and receiving the report. The approval task represents the process of an employee looking at the weather report and verifying whether to send an email to another user or reject the email. The email task represents the process of invoking the email service, supplying the necessary information, and sending the email. The reject task represents the process of choosing not to send an email to the user. For the purpose of this example, the reject task is considered as an empty task with no resources. The task system $C_{WCS} = (\tau, <*)$ can be defined as

$$C_{WCS} = \{(Weather, Approval), (Approval, Email), (Approval, Reject)\}$$

The resource types of the task system model can be defined as

$$\rho_{WCS} \equiv \{ RT_{weatherservice}, RT_{automatedservice}, RT_{weatherparameters}, RT_{weatherreport},$$
$$RT_{employeeknowledge}, RT_{employeerole}, RT_{approvalresponse}, RT_{emailservice}, RT_{desktop},$$
$$RT_{mobile}, RT_{employee}, RT_{emailrules}, RT_{approvalportal}, RT_{emailmessage}, RT_{emailresponse} \}.$$

Table 1 provides the description of each resource of the WCS. Table 2 provides the input and output resources for each task.

Table 1. Resources for the weather composite services task system model

Resource	Description
$RT_{weatherservice}$	Indicates the weather services used for the task.
$RT_{automatedservice}$	Indicates the automated service that invokes the weather service.
$RT_{weatherparameters}$	Indicates the input parameters of the weather service. The parameters could be stored in a database or configuration file and retrieved by the automated service when needed.
$RT_{weatherreport}$	The output of the weather report that is an XML document.
$RT_{employee}$	The employee performing the approval task.
$RT_{employeerole}$	Indicates the role of the employee performing the task.
$RT_{employeeknowledge}$	The employee's knowledge that plays a part in the approval task.
$RT_{approvalportal}$	The portal with which the user performs the approval process.
RT_{mobile}	Indicates if the user is using a mobile device and the tools used to interact with the process.
$RT_{desktop}$	Indicates if the user is using a desktop device and the tools used to interact with the process.
$RT_{emailrules}$	The email rules dictate the minimum condition on which the emails should be sent.
$RT_{approvalresponse}$	The employee's response indicating whether an email should be sent or not.
$RT_{emailmessage}$	The message of the emails sent to the user.
$RT_{emailservice}$	The email service that is used to send emails.
$RT_{emailresponse}$	The confirmation response of the email service.

Implementation of the Weather Composite Services using BPEL

The WCS is implemented using Intalio's business process management system (BPMS) (Intalio, 2007). The Intalio system uses Business Process Modeling Notation (BPMN) (OMG, 2006) constructs to derive the BPEL executable process. Figure 12 show the WCS implemented using the Intalio BPMN designer.

BPMN separates the different participants of a process using the pools indicated in Figure 9 with large, rectangular boxes. Figure 9 shows that there are five participants in the WCS: The automated service

Table 2. Input/output sets for the weather composite services task system model

Tasks	Input set I_T	Output Set O_T
Weather	$RT_{weatherservice}$, $RT_{automatedservice}$, $RT_{weatherparameters}$	$RT_{weatherreport}$
Approval	$RT_{employee}$, $RT_{employeeknowledge}$, $RT_{approvalresponse}$, $RT_{emailrules}$, $RT_{weatherreport}$ $RT_{approvalportal}$, $RT_{emailmessage}$, $RT_{employeerole}$, $RT_{desktop}$, RT_{mobile}	$RT_{emailmessage}$, $RT_{weatherreport}$, $RT_{approvalresponse}$
Email	$RT_{emailmessage}$, $RT_{emailservice}$, $RT_{weatherreport}$	$RT_{emailresponse}$

indicated by the "Interface" pool, the processes flow indicated by the "Process" pool, the "User" pool, the "WeatherService" pool, and the "EmailService" pool. Therefore, the different service-agents can be mapped to the BPMN pools. The tasks in BPMN are represented as small, rectangular boxes with curved edges. A gateway is represented as a diamond-shaped box with a cross. A gateway determines traditional decisions, as well as the forking, merging, and joining of paths. An if-loop in programming is a type of gateway. BPMN defines four attributes to describe user tasks: The "Performers" attribute describes the human resources assigned to the task, which could be a user or a group of users. The "InMessage" attribute specifies the input messages for the task. The "Out-Message" attribute specifies the output messages for the task. The "Implementation" attribute describes the technologies that are used to perform the task.

The Intalio BPMS system has partial support for the semantics of human activity, which is based on the implementation of the BPEL4People specification (Endpoints et al., 2007). For instance, the pool that encloses the human activity, the user pool in this example, is associated with the employee role.

Figure 10 depicts a portion of the relevant syntax of the derived BPEL from the BPMN model. The human

activity and the mechanistic services in the process are modeled as partner links in the BPEL model. We can also see that XForms are used to implement

$RT_{approvalportal}$. Xforms (Dubinko, 2003) provides an XML-based approach for developing the Web-

based approval portal. The user role $RT_{employeerole}$ has been integrated using the NIST role-based access control (Ferraiolo, Kuhn, Chandramouli, & Barkley, 2007). The Intalio BPMS system provides support

for handling human interaction. $RT_{emailrules}$ has been supported through the use of a gateway in the BPMN model, which is represented as <bpel:if> and <bpel:else> in the derived BPEL code.

There are two drawbacks with this approach of implementing WCS. First, the resource semantics are integrated at design time. Therefore, as the user needs changes, the processes cannot adapt to the needs of the user. Second, there is only partial support for the semantics of the user needs. Therefore, the other resources are integrated in an ad-hoc manner. If these semantics are to be modified over time, other mechanisms have to be built into the system and cannot happen systematically.

Figure 9. BPMN model of the weather composite services

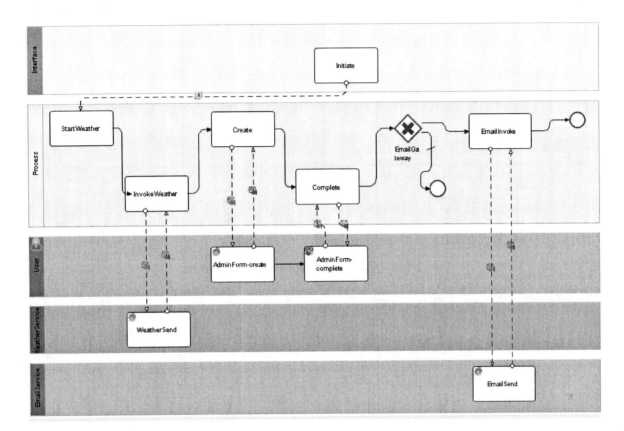

Implementation of the Weather Composite Services using the Agent-Based Approach

In the agent-based approach, after the tasks and resources are identified, there are three steps to generating the executable processes for composition. First, the resources are classified and represented according to the CPP semantics. Second, the service-agent model is used to link the resources to each task. Third, the executable process model is generated dynamically for composition from the service-agent-based description of the tasks.

Table 3 shows the classification of the WCS resources based on the six types of semantics: KS, ROS, RUS, UPS, INS, and COS. From Table 3, the four service-agents of the WCS are identified: $RT_{SA\_weatherservice}$, $RT_{SA\_automatedservice}$, $RT_{SA\_emailservice}$, and $RT_{SA\_employee}$ he service-agents $RT_{SA\_weatherservice}$, $RT_{SA\_automatedservice}$, and $RT_{SA\_emailservice}$ represent mechanistic resources.

The WCS example also includes a human interaction activity, which is the task of approving or rejecting the sending of emails. The task is carried out by an employee $RT_{employee}$ of a certain role $RT_{employee\,role}$ in the enterprise. The service-agent $RT_{SA\,employee}$ represents the human activity. The input and outputs sets are reclassified based on the identified service-agents and the classification of the resources according to the semantics. The reclassified input and output sets of the WCS are shown in Table 4.

The concept maps for the WCS tasks are depicted in Figure 11 of the weather task, Figure 12 of the approval task, and Figure 13 of the email task. The concept maps show the representation of each task with the CPP semantics and also articulate the relationship of the CPP semantics to the service-agents.

We also show a conceptual mapping between the implementation of the WCS and the service-agent-based approach. The mapping can be used as a potential implementation strategy for developing composite services enhanced with CPP. As discussed,

Figure 10. BPEL code for the BPMN model of the weather composite services

```
<bpel:partnerLinks >
       <bpel:partnerLink name ="wFmagic_v0TFUGzDEdy8_fgUbrSKpgPlkVar"
partnerLinkType ="diag:WFmagic_v0TFUGzDEdy8_fgUbrSKpg" initializePartnerRole ="false"
myRole="Process_for_UserForThePortTypexformProcess " partnerRole ="User_for_ProcessForXformPort " />
           ...
  </bpel:partnerLinks >

  <xform:userOwner />
  <xform:roleOwner >examples\employee </xform:roleOwner >
  <xform:claimAction>
   <xform:user></xform:user>
   <xform:role></xform:role>
  </xform:claimAction>
  <xform:revokeAction>
   <xform:user>  </xform:user>
   <xform:role></xform:role>
  </xform:revokeAction>

       ...

  <xform:formUrl>oxf://PhDDemoCWS/AdminForm /AdminForm .xform</xform:formUrl>

   <xform:userProcessCompleteSOAPAction >http://example .com/AdminForm /AdminForm/xform/Process/
notifyTaskCompletion</xform:userProcessCompleteSOAPAction >
  <xform:isChainedBefore >
  </xform:isChainedBefore >

   <xform:userProcessEndpoint >http://localhost:8080 /ode /processes /PhDDemoCWS/CompositeProcess /XWS/
Process/User/Process_for_UserForThePortTypexformProcessPort </xform:userProcessEndpoint >
   <xform:userProcessNamespaceURI>http://example .com/AdminForm /AdminForm /xform </
xform:userProcessNamespaceURI>
```

Table 3. Semantic-dimension-based classification of the weather composite services

Semantics	Resources
KS	$RT_{employeeknowledge}$
RUS	$RT_{emailrules}$
ROS	$RT_{employeerole}$
UPS	$RT_{SA\_employee}$
INS	$RT_{SA\_weatherservice}$, $RT_{SA\_automatedservice}$, $RT_{SA\_emailservice}$, $RT_{desktop}$, RT_{mobile}
COS	$RT_{weatherparameters}$, $RT_{weatherreport}$, $RT_{emailmessage}$, $RT_{emailresponse}$

Table 4. Reclassified iinput/output sets for the weather composite services task system model

Tasks	Input set I_T			Output Set O_T
	Service-Agents	COS	Associated Semantics	COS
Weather	$RT_{SA\_automatedservice}$, $RT_{SA\_weatherservice}$	$RT_{weatherparameters}$	NA	$RT_{weatherreport}$
Approval	$RT_{SA\_employee}$	$RT_{weatherreport}$, $RT_{approvalresponse}$, $RT_{emailmessage}$	$RT_{employeeknowledge}$, $RT_{employee}$, $RT_{employeerole}$, $RT_{emailrules}$, $RT_{approvalportal}$, $RT_{weatherreport}$, $RT_{desktop}$, RT_{mobile} ,	$RT_{emailmessage}$, $RT_{weatherreport}$, $RT_{approvalresponse}$
Email	$RT_{SA\_emailservice}$	$RT_{emailmessage}$, $RT_{weatherreport}$	NA	$RT_{emailresponse}$

the WCS is implemented using Intalio's BPMS, which uses BPMN constructs to derive the BPEL executable process. Therefore, the mapping to the BPEL processes is achieved in two steps: first, by mapping the service-agents to the BPMN constructs, and second, by deriving the BPEL processes from the BPMN model.

In the BPMN implementation, the different participants of a process are separated using the pools "Interface" pool, "User" pool, "WeatherService" pool, and the "EmailService" pool. Therefore, the different service-agents can be mapped to the BPMN pools.

$RT_{SA\_weatherservice}$ would be mapped to the "WeatherService" pool, $RT_{SA\_automatedservice}$ would be mapped to the "WeatherService" pool, $RT_{SA\_emailservice}$ would be mapped to the "EmailService" pool, and $RT_{SA\_employee}$ would be mapped to the "User" pool. The other resource semantics would be then incorporated as properties of the agent, which are supported by an agent system.

CONCLUSION AND FUTURE DIRECTIONS

Development of large systems with a composite service approach is important because we can leverage the rich set of composite services tools, technologies, and approaches (Mandell & McIlraith, 2003; Petrie & Bussler, 2003). The rich set of composite services tools, technologies, and approaches come from the industrial and academic track, which are complementary to each other (Petrie & Bussler, 2003). For instance, the industrial track of composite services research, such as Web services and business process technologies has provided several sophisticated tools and standards for developing composite services. The academic track has developed agent-based approaches, such as Semantic Web services (OWL-S) for automated discovery and composition. However, despite these advances, the integration and development of large systems remain problematic (Fingar, 2006; Gleghorn,

Figure 11. Concept map of weather task in the weather composite services

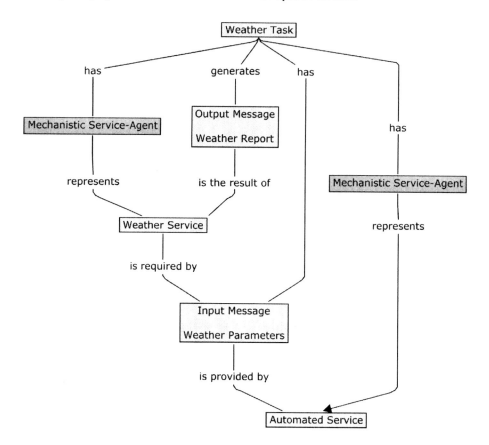

2005; Khoshafian, 2007; Vojdani, 2003), which we have defined as the CPP challenge.

The reasons for the integration problems are that we have difficulties in capturing, configuring, and managing the semantics of user needs. As discussed, these problems exist because of multiple reasons, such as lack of understanding of the problem domain by the developer, lack of understanding of the scope of the integration problem, use of ad hoc approaches, and the lack of technology support.

An agent approach is introduced in this chapter to address the problems of supporting CPP. It introduces two new concepts. First, is the use of the CPP semantics to support the capture of the resources of a task. Second, is the use of the service-agent model to configure and mange the resources in a dynamic manner. A case study was used to outline the steps of developing composite services with CPP. The case study also showed a conceptual mapping to BPEL, which outlines potential implementation approach.

This agent-based approach and CPP incorporates a broad area of research for developing a systematic approach for CPP. Several research opportunities exist in this area of CPP. First, six types of semantics of CPP were identified in this chapter. While several approaches can be used for representing the semantics in machine-accessible form, continued research is required to find effective ways of identifying, organizing, and representing the semantics of CPP.

As technology, such as mobile technology improves our interaction with processes also changes. Continued research is required on human interaction with processes to take advantage of technological advancements in composite services development with CPP. One of the issues for mobile researchers would be to identify ways in which the needs of mobile users, such as localization can be mapped to the CPP semantics.

Another research area is the TAS model, which provides enhanced integration of processes. Integration

Figure 12. Concept map of approval task in the weather composite services

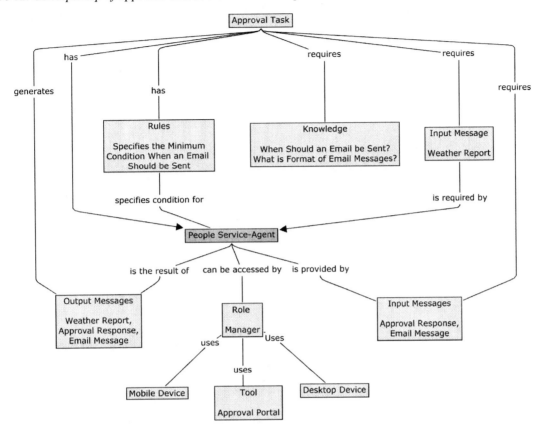

of the TAS model with composite services requires that several issues be addressed, such as data transparency between the tools and availability of tools in a service form (Sadasivam, Sundar, Tanik, Jololian, & Tanju, 2007; Sadasivam, Sundar, Tanik, & Tanju, 2006). Research is required to identify effective ways of composing desktop and mobile applications as TAS.

ACKNOWLEDGMENT

We thank Gayathri Sundar, Master thesis student at the Department of Electrical and Computer Engineering, for her contributions to the development of TAS and CPP. We acknowledge the contributions of Dr. Murat N. Tanju, Accounting and Information Sciences at UAB, for his critical evaluation of our work. We thank Dr. Leon Jololian, Computer Science Department at the New Jersey City University, for his advice, which represented an invaluable contribution to this work. We also thank the Division of Continuing Medical Education for their support of the authors' work. The authors acknowledge the immense contributions of Dr. Chittoor V. Ramamoorthy, Professor Emeritus at the Electrical Engineering and Computer Sciences Department at UC Berkeley, whose seminal work on service enterprise forms the basis for this chapter. Finally, we thank Dr. Unhelkar for his support and patience through the writing process.

REFERENCES

Alesso, H. P., & Smith, C. F. (2005). *Developing Semantic Web Services*. Natick, MA: A. K. Peters.

Brezillon, P. (2003). Focusing on context in human-centered computing. *Intelligent Systems, 18*(3), 62-66.

Figure 13. Concept map of email task in the weather composite services

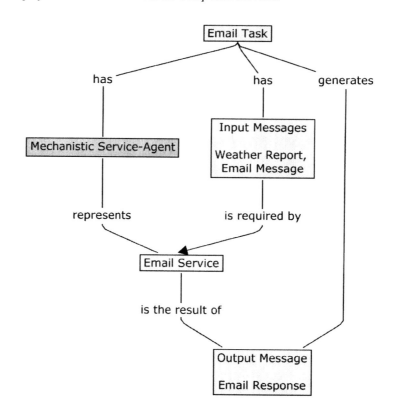

Coalition, T. W. M. (1999). *Terminology & glossary (Issues 3.0)* (No. WFMC-TC-1011). Winchester, UK: Workflow Management Coalition.

Coffman, E. G., & Denning, P. J. (1973). *Operating Systems Theory*. Englewood Cliffs, NJ: Prentice Hall.

Delcambre, S. (1994). *A software process modeling framework as a basis for process analysis and improvement*. Unpublished Ph.D. dissertation, Southern Methodist Univ., Dallas, TX.

Delcambre, S., & Tanik, M. M. (1998). Using task system templates to support process description and evolution. *Journal of Systems Integration, 8*(1), 83-111.

Desouza, K. C., Awazu, Y., & Baloh, P. (2006). Managing knowledge in global software development efforts: issues and practices. *IEEE Software, 23*(5), 30-37.

Dubinko, M. (2003). *XForms Essentials* (1st ed.). Farnham: O'Reilly.

Elzinga, D. J., Horak, T., Chung-Yee, L., & Bruner, C. (1995). Business process management: survey and methodology. *IEEE Transactions on Engineering Management, 42*(2), 119-128.

Endpoints, A., Adobe, BEA, IBM, Oracle, SAP, et al. (2007, Jun.). WS-BPEL extension for people. Retrieved September 15, 2007, from http://www.ibm.com/developerworks/webservices/library/specification/ws-bpel4people/

Ferraiolo, D. F., Kuhn, R., Chandramouli, R., & Barkley, J. (2007). NIST role based access control. Retrieved September 25, 2007, from http://www.bpcommunity.org/2005/08/01/bpm-the-next-generation/ http://csrc.nist.gov/rbac/

Fingar, P. (2005, Aug.). *Business process management: the next generation (a preliminary draft of a book chapter on extreme competition)*. Retrieved Aug., 2007, from http://www.bpcommunity.org/2005/08/01/bpm-the-next-generation/

Fingar, P. (2006). *Extreme Competition: Innovation and the Great 21st Century Business Reformation* (1st ed.). Tampa, FL: Meghan-Kiffer Press.

Fingar, P., Kumar, H., & Sharma, T. (2000). *Enterprise E-Commerce: The Software Component Breakthrough for Business-to-Business Commerce*. Tampa, FL: Meghan-Kiffer.

Gleghorn, R. (2005). Enterprise application integration: a manager's perspective. *IT Professional, 7*(6), 17-23.

Gutmann, J. S., & Fox, D. (2002). An experimental comparison of localization methods continued. *Paper presented at the Intelligent Robots and System, 2002. IEEE/RSJ Int. Conf.*

Harrison-Broninski, K. (2005). *Human Interactions: The Heart and Soul of Business Process Management*. Tampa, FL: Meghan-Kiffer Press.

Havey, M. (2005). *Essential Business Process Modeling*. Sebastopol, CA: O'Reilly.

Humphrey, W. S. (1989). *Managing the Software Process*. Reading, MA: Addison-Wesley.

Intalio. (2007, Feb.). *Intalio company and platform overview*. Retrieved September 15, 2007, from http://bpms.intalio.com/images/stories/start/intalio_overview.pdf

Jololian, L. K. (2003, June 12-16). Towards semantic integration of components using a service-based architecture. *Paper presented at the Integrated Design and Process Technology*, IDPT, Beijing, China.

Jololian, L. K., Kurfess, F. J., & Tanik, M. M. (2003). Data, function, and control as elements of component integration. *Paper presented at the Integrated Design and Process Technology*, IDPT, Austin, TX.

Juric, M. B., Mathew, B., & Sarang, P. (2004). *Business Process Execution Language for Web Services: BPEL and BPEL4WS*: Packt Publishing.

Khoshafian, S. (2007). *Service Oriented Enterprises*. Boca Raton, FL: Auerbach Publications, Taylor & Francis Group.

Leymann, F., Roller, D., & Schmidt, M.-T. (2002). Web services and business process management. *IBM Systems Journal, 41*(2).

Liang, T. P., & Wei, C. P. (2004). Introduction to the special issue: Mobile commerce applications. *International Journal of Electronic Commerce, 8*(3), 7-17.

Mandell, D. J., & McIlraith, S. A. (2003). *Adapting BPEL4WS for the semantic Web: The bottom-up approach to Web service interoperation*. Paper presented at the 2nd Int. Semantic Web Conf., Sanibel Island, FL.

Miller, J. (2005). The user experience [Internet]. *IEEE Internet Computing, 9*(5), 90-92.

Newcomer, E., & Lomow, G. (2005). *Understanding SOA with Web Services*. Upper Saddle River, NJ: Addison-Wesley.

OMG. (2006, Feb.). *Business process modeling specification: OMG final adopted specification*. Retrieved Aug., 2007, from http://www.bpmn.org/Documents/OMG%20Final%20Adopted%20BPMN%201-0%20Spec%2006-02-01.pdf

Pasley, J. (2005). How BPEL and SOA are changing Web services development. *IEEE Internet Comput., 9*(3), 60-67.

Petrie, C., & Bussler, C. (2003). Service agents and virtual enterprises. *IEEE Internet Comput., 7*(4), 68-78.

Ramamoorthy, C. V. (2000). A study of the service industry - functions, features, and control. *ICICE Transactions Comm., E83-B*(5), 885-903.

Sadasivam, R. S. (2007). *An architecture framework for composite services with process-personalization* Unpublished Ph.D. dissertation, Univ. of Alabama at Birmingham, Birmingham, AL.

Sadasivam, R. S., Sundar, G., Tanik, M. M., Jololian, L., & Tanju, M. N. (2007, June 3-8). A process personalization model for enabling biological research. *Paper presented at the Int. Design and Process Technology*, Antalya, Turkey.

Sadasivam, R. S., Sundar, G., Tanik, M. M., & Tanju, M. N. (2006). *Process personalization framework for service-driven enterprises*. Paper presented at the IEEE SouthEastCon, Memphis, TN.

Stone, A. (2004). Demanding Internet enterprise. *IEEE Internet Computing, 8*(3), 13-14.

Sundar, G. (2007). *Design of a service-oriented dashboard*. Unpublished M.S. thesis, Univ. of Alabama at Birmingham, Birmingham, AL.

Tanik, M. M., & Chan, E. S. (1991). *Fundamentals of Computing for Software Engineers*: Van Nostrand Reinhold.

Tsai, W. T. (2005, Oct 20-21). Service-oriented system engineering: a new paradigm. *Paper presented at the IEEE Int. Workshop on Service-Oriented Syst. Eng.*

van der Aalst, W. M. P., Aldred, L., Dumas, M., & ter Hofstede, A. H. M. (2004). Design and implementation of the YAWL system. In *Advanced Inform. Syst. Eng.* (pp. 142-159).

Vojdani, A. F. (2003). Tools for real-time business integration and collaboration. *IEEE Transactions on Power Systems, 18*(2), 555-562.

Yahoo Inc. (2007). Finance portal. from http://finance.yahoo.com/

Yeh, R. T.-Y., Pearlson, K., & Kozmetsky, G. (2000). *Zero Time: Providing Instant Customer Value – Every Time, All the Time*. New York: Wiley.

Chapter XXIII
Cultural Impacts on the Spread of Mobile Commerce:
An International Comparison

Ralf Wagner
University of Kassel, Germany

Martin Klaus
University of Kassel, Germany

ABSTRACT

Culture predefines the framework of needs, beliefs, and norms in most decisions humans make in their lives. However, the impact of culture often tends to be neglected in the investigation into adaptation of mobile business technologies. This chapter aims to address that lacuna by highlighting cultural differences and their consequences for the diffusion of mobile technologies in business and society, as well as its acceptance in mobile direct marketing and mobile commerce. We achieve our objective in the following four steps:

- *Highlight the impact of culture on the adoption and acceptance of mobile technologies,*
- *Introduce measures for the assessment of cultures by means of quantitative indices (e.g., Schwartz values, the Hofstede dimensions),*
- *Correlat the assessment of culture with mobile activities in selected societies, and*
- *Discuss implications for the introduction of innovative mobile commerce services.*

INTRODUCTION

Culture constitutes the framework of references related to all buying decisions. In this respect, culture defines

- Buyers' needs,
- Buyers' perception of appropriateness of offers, and
- Acceptability of innovative technologies and services.

The cultural framing of vendors and customers impacts on all types of businesses, but it tends to be critical in m-commerce applications because these are frequently new to customers. Therefore, m-commerce services contradict the conception that technical innovations are culture free and might be successfully introduced to markets neglecting cultural differences (Pressey & Selassie, 2002). Both the technology acceptance model and the m-banking acceptance model (Luarn & Lin, 2005) do not take into consideration cultural differences. Particularly communication and the benefits to (prospective) customers of new products or services need to be aligned with the customers' cultural background.

Building on Rokeach (1973) and Hofstede (1994), we propose:

Definition 1 (culture): *Culture consists of a knowledge reservoir common to all members of a group that distinguishes them from other people in other cultures.*

This knowledge reservoir embraces explicit and implicit rules learned by the members of the culture in order to adopt their behavior to meet the expectations and standards of their society. Clearly, the benefits and advantages associated with mobile commerce activities differ in the light of cultural differences. For instance, from the perspective of Western cultures, Keen and Mackintosh (2001) argue that the key value proposition is the creation of choice or new freedoms for customers. Naturally, freedom is one of the most important values of the authors' home culture, the US, but it is of minor importance in other cultures in countries such as India. Consequently, culture turns out to be relevant for conducting mobile commerce activities for three main reasons:

1.   The value propositions (e.g., prestige or self enhancement) associated with mobile services and related devices depend on aims and desires predefined by one's culture.
2.   The acceptance of products and services by customers differs substantially across cultures.
3.   Similarly, mobile technologies employed by vendors, as well as the usage of marketing techniques to establish and maintain customer relationships, differ in respect to national markets.

Despite similar technological conditions, remarkable differences in the usage of cellular devices are observed in various studies (Fraunholz & Unnithan 2004; Kim et al. 2004; Mobinet 2005). Mahatanankoon, Wen and Lim (2005) claim that the factors that influence consumers' attitudes and value perceptions of m-commerce are understood only fragmentarily. This chapter aims to provide some empirical evidence on the relation between culture and the usage of mobile services in different countries.

The remainder of this chapter is structured as follows: In the next section, we introduce the concepts for quantifying culture discussed in psychology, sociology und marketing. The dimensions grasped by these concepts are linked to m-commerce activities by highlighting their relevance. Subsequently, we present empirical results from an investigation of Hofstede's cultural dimensions and the mobile activities in six countries.

The chapter concludes with a discussion on the implications for further research.

BACKGROUND: CONCEPTS FOR QUANTIFYING CULTURE

Mobile device functions are embedded in networks, and consequently their usage should not be considered in isolation. Patterns of usage are collective rather than individual phenomena, and are therefore influenced strongly both by individuals' predispositions and usage circumstances and by culture. Therefore, a cross-cultural investigative approach of m-commerce acceptance is likely to provide both academic insights as well as advice for practitioners to improve their m-commerce activities. Working out cultural differences in a tangible manner is an obvious approach for this purpose. A quantification of culture according to definition 1 is essential to derive sound results which are superior to conceptual considerations and anecdotal evidence. In this section, different approaches to address this challenge, as discussed in the sociology, management and marketing related literatures, are introduced and related to mobile commerce activities.

Culture, according to definition 1, is neither observed nor measured directly. Instead, indicators, grasping particular aspects of the knowledge reservoir, are considered in these approaches. With respect to m-commerce activities, important aspects for quantifying culture are values, or beliefs. In line with Schwartz and Bilsky (1987), we propose:

Definition 2 (values): *Values are beliefs about some desirable end state that transcends specific situations and guides the selection of behavior shared by the members of a culture.*

Humans develop a set of values that guides them through the decisions they make in their lives. These values are formed by social interaction with other individuals. Mobile devices support these interactions in:

- The relations of consumers with one another,
- Communication of organizations to their customers (consumers or other organizations) and,
- Communication of organizations to make up networks, for instance the management of joint ventures.

Since humans tend to seek contacts with others with a value system similar to their own, values tend to be stable over time. However, individuals may shift their value priorities in the course of time because of new acquaintances or other occurrences communicated by the mass media. The extent to which people share a value system is a function of individual, social and cultural forces.

In order to provide an assessment of individuals' cultural framing, we propose several concepts. Next, we provide a brief overview of the most prominent concepts for the appraisal of culture and their link to mobile commerce activities.

The Rokeach Value Survey

The Rokeach Value Survey (RVS) is a survey instrument introduced by Rokeach (1969) to operationalize the value concept (it has also been used for measuring personal and social values). The RVS is characterized by two different kinds of values:

- *Instrumental values* apply to many different countries and are socially desirable.
- *Terminal values* refer to idealized end states of existence or lifestyles.

Table 1 depicts the relation of values selected from Rokeach (1973) to mobile commerce activities.

Clearly, the value of being broadminded is the antagonism to being dogmatic in the sense of Rokeach (1973), and dogmatists may refuse to use modern mobile devices for various reasons. For example, mobile devices are judged by dogmatists in Eastern cultures as symbols of Westernization, and the notion of being reachable at any time, night or day, as conflicting with their religious beliefs, although in reality, we find

Table 1. Interpretation of the Rokeach values in the context of mobile commerce

Rokeach Values	Interpretation with respect to mobile commerce
Instrumental values	
Broadminded	Owning and using mobile devices demonstrates openness to new technologies, functions and services.
Independent	Mobile communication and data exchange enable a higher degree of independence.
Responsible	Individuals become accessible, regardless of time and location.
Self-Control	Control of own information exchange, regardless of context or location. .
Terminal values	
A comfortable life	Cellular phones make one's life easier by providing telephony and information gathering as well as processing and storing services.
An exciting life	Many innovative services, directly (e.g., games) or indirectly (e.g., dating services), are designed to add new thrill to consumers' lives.
Freedom	Mobile devices might be used to work around communication limitation by employers, governments or families.
Pleasure	By recording and playing sounds and movies, the mobile devices provide pleasure to their owners.
Social recognition	Phones and more sophisticated devices such as PDAs are recognized to symbolize one's social status within a society.

Muslim clericalists using mobile phones. Relating mobile commerce services to one of the recipients' value priorities provides ample reasons for subscribing to m-commerce services.

Nevertheless, the RVS provides researchers with a well-established framework to derive culture-related hypotheses in empirical studies concerned with attitudes toward and acceptance of mobile services (e.g., Oh & Xu, 2003; Lin & Shih, 2008).

Kahle's List of Values

The List of Values (LOV) scales were developed by Kahle (1983) to make up special and isolated values which are highly connected to direct marketing applications (Beatty, Kahle, Homer & Misra, 1985). The list is composed of nine consumer values which are related to differences in consumption behavior: (1) self-fulfillment, (2) sense of belonging, (3) security, (4) fun and enjoyment in life, (5) excitement (6) being well respected, (7) warm relationships with others, (8) sense of accomplishment (9) and self-respect. In comparison with the RVS depicted in Table 1, this list appears to be more comprehensive, but covers all aspects with relevance to mobile business.

From Table 2, it is clear that the LOV scales directly fit the needs of both academic and commercial studies of mobile business. Interestingly, the LOV has been found to provide an explanation of consumers' adoption of innovations (Daghfous, Petrof, & Pons, 1999). Moreover, Haghirian, Madlberger, & Inoue (2008) attribute differences in the perception of mobile advertising to this conceptualization of culture.

Hall's Cultural Dimensions

Hall (1977) follows an anthropological approach of cultural dimensions. Accordingly, culture is the

Table 2. LOV constructs, explanations, and relations to mobile commerce

List of Values	Explanation	Relation to mobile commerce
Self-fulfillment	Includes desirable goals for individuals and if/how they are reached.	Due to location-independence, m-commerce provides ability to fulfill needs instantaneously.
Sense of belonging	How individuals belong to their culture, family, community, country, etc.	Due to personalization, provides a sense of identity with and belonging to desired community.
Security	Degree of protection granted by a community to individual members.	Ability to call for help, advice or assistance from members of the culture.
Fun and enjoyment in life	Elements make people "feel good" and raise their quality of life.	Contact with others, music, movies, etc. are transmitted on mobile devices.
Excitement	Various kinds of stimulation that are perceived positively.	Games or dating services aim to add new thrills to consumers' lives.
Being well respected	Attributing good faith and competence to a person by the person himself as well as others.	Mobile devices serve as status symbols and utility to demonstrate immediate problem-solving competence.
	Association of individuals with each other.	
Warm relationships with others	Cultivating a close and trusting relationship in social interactions.	Using mobile services to maintain and strengthen interpersonal relationships.
Sense of accomplishment	Extent of approving individuals' ambitions.	Location- and time-independence provide immense sense of timely accomplishments (e.g., academic results being made available anywhere).
Self respect	To be proud of yourself and confident with whom you are.	No direct relation to m-commerce

human built environment of space, time and communication. This approach leads to four dimensions listed in Table 3.

Most prominent of Hall's work is the "classic pattern", which refers to the distinction of "low-context" cultures from "high-context" cultures. In the realm of mobile advertising, in high-context cultures, the information content of advertisements should be lower than in low-context cultures (Al-Olayan & Karande, 2000; Cyr, Head, & Ivanov, 2005). For future m-commerce applications, the distinction in polychrome and monochrome time orientation is likely to become an important criterion for practitioners aiming to identify target segments. Bell, Compeau and Olivera (2005) argue that individuals with polychrome time orientation are more likely to adopt new mobile services allowing for interaction in a multi-tasking manner.

The Trompenaars Databank

The approach of Trompenaars and Hampden-Turner (1998) is based on a dataset consisting of surveys conducted with more than 11,000 employees from 46 countries worldwide. The basic assumption is that the culture of any country becomes salient in dealing with the following three main problems: employees' attitude toward their fellow men, time and the environment. The *interpersonal problem* is again divided into another five contradiction pairs which characterize cultural behavior:

1. *Universalism* versus *particularism*
2. *Individualism* versus *collectivism*
3. *Neutral* versus *emotional*
4. *Specific* versus *diffuse*
5. *Achievement* versus *ascription*

The acquaintance with *orientation in time* is distinguished by consecutive and sequential, respectively, synchrony or polychrome dichotomy. Additionally, the culture's orientation toward the past, the present and the future and the relationship of the three to one another is proposed to assess the cultural framing of individuals. Considering the *attitude toward the environment*, a rather fatalistic attitude can be distinguished from an autonomous, more self-directed approach.

Although the control of the environment distinguishes the Trompenaars dimensions substantially from other concepts, the use of this concept is scarce with respect to the domain of m-commerce.

The Schwartz Value Survey

The Schwartz Value Survey (SVS) is based on a survey of over 60,000 individuals in 63 countries worldwide. In this approach, the responses are characterized by ten motivational values and seven cultural-level dimensions. Each of these dimensions is a composite index of a set of values which varies according to the culture. Therefore, this approach allows the inclusion of values which turn out to be meaningful in only a

Table 3. Hall's cultural dimensions, explanations, and relations to mobile commerce

Dimension	Explanation	Relation to mobile commerce
Context orientation	Within an interaction, a certain amount of information is transferred in the context of interaction rather than the explicit.	Mobile devices enable personalization and the virtual imagination in the context of interactions.
Space-/Room orientation	The quality of actions and interactions differs with respect to location, e.g., private versus public.	Depending on whether a person is in a cinema hall, sports venue, or in a hospital, mobile devices can add location as well as context related information.
Time orientation	In cultures with monochrome time understanding, time is seen as linear. In cultures with polychrome time perception, time is seen as circular.	Connection to others whenever you want – as it is possible to communicate irrespective of time, and the recipient can decide when to receive the information. In monochrome time societies, consumers are likely to cue their tasks rather than processing them in parallel.
Information speed	This means the speed at which information is coded and can be decoded in a communication situation.	Information exchange is in real time while speaking or very fast by sending e-mails, SMS, MMS, etc.

few cultures, but sustains the comparableness of nations by a unified set of dimensions. Specifically, it distinguishes between cultures and types of media consumption behavior better than the traditional dichotomy of individualism and collectivism (Schwartz, 1994). The ten individual-level dimensions and their link to m-commerce are outlined in Table 5.

These values are not generally uncorrelated. The extent of correlation has been found to vary with respect to culture. In addition to the motivational values depicted in Table 5, seven dimensions for describing national cultures have been proposed: affective autonomy, conservatism, egalitarianism, harmony, hierarchy, intellectual autonomy, and mastery. The typology motivational values depicted in Table 5 are frequently used in international comparisons of consumer behavior. Interestingly, Guzmán-Obando Gonzalez, de la Rosa, Ruiz, & Castan (2006) utilize this conceptualization of culture to make up a recommender system that considers the cultural differences explicitly and concisely.

A subset of the values depicted in Table 5, hedonic needs, or the need for stimulation and social innovativeness, are clearly reflected in the measurement of innovativeness by Roehrich (2004). With regard to the value of self-direction, the autonomy in innovative decisions has also been considered as a relevant dimension. These dimensions have been found to have a significant positive impact on the degree of perceived usefulness of the mobile Internet (Lee, Kim & Chung, 2002) and individuals' attitude toward the usage of wireless application protocol (WAP) services (Hung, Ku, & Chang, 2003).

The Hofstede Dimensions

These dimensions originate from the study on how cultural values influence business behavior, organizations and CEOs in the time span 1967 to 1973. The initial study was restricted to employees of IBM in 70 countries. In subsequent studies, the results have been validated with other respondents, including airline pilots, students, civil service managers, consumers and "elites". Hofstede (1980, 1994) first developed a model that identified four main value dimensions to assess cultural differences. Later, a fifth dimension, the long-term orientation, was added after recognizing that Asian cultures with a strong link to Confucian philosophy acted differently from Western cultures. Table 6 depicts the five Hofstede cultural dimensions and their relation to mobile commerce.

Kim et al. (2004) attribute the tendency of Japanese respondents to regard the mobile Internet with some misgivings in terms of contribution to e-commerce to the high UAI level in Japan. Interestingly, although their comparison of Korean, Hong Kong and Japanese respondents is based on Hofstede's dimensions, they highlight another result: Japanese users prefer to communicate via e-mail rather than phone calls. The authors explain this by "meiwaku", which means a strong sense of inhibition about being a nuisance in public. This perfectly fits the dimension of conformity in the framework of the SWS, but is not captured by the Hofstede dimensions. Nevertheless, Hofstede's operationalization of culture is most frequently referred to in investigations of the impact of culture on the adoption and acceptance of mobile services. For instance, Kim et al. (2004) found consumers from Hong Kong and Korea strongly opposed to paying additional fees for m-commerce services because of their higher scores in the collectivism dimension. Other m-commerce related studies relying on the Hofstede cultural dimensions are Lee, Y., Kim, J., Lee, I., and Kim, H. (2002), Urbaczewski, Wells, Sarker and Koivisto (2002), Ford, Connelly and Meister (2003) and Van Biljon (2006).

Hofstede (2008) provides us with a list of the five values for 74 examined countries (the fifth value is only available for 23 countries) and also depicts each of them in a figure, exemplified in Figure 1 for the US.

From the figure it is clear that the PDI is below the world average in North America, which indicates greater equality across societal levels. The IDV of 91 in the US is by far above the world average of 43. It is evident, therefore, that US citizens are more individualistic and have relatively loose bounds with others. MAS is only slightly above the world average, but the second highest dimension of the US. The value symbolizes a higher degree of gender differentiation of roles. The low score for UAI indicates that this culture has fewer rules and also a greater tolerance for a diversity of ideas. The additional dimension of *long-term orientation* is the lowest of all scores for the US and also lowers than the average world value of 45. It is interpreted as societies' belief in meeting its obligations and tends to reflect an appreciation of cultural traditions. The Hofstede dimensions are not uncorrelated and are subject to an inner-organizational culture bias due to the sampling of IBM employees. McSweeney (2002) provides a recent compilation of further critics. However, the study by Denison (1996) reveals a "striking set of similarities" to other

Table 4. The relation of the Trompenaars interpersonal problem dimensions and m-commerce services

The Trompenaars Dimensions	Relation to mobile commerce
Interpersonal problem	Mobile devices might assist the settlement of conflicts and help to overcome misunderstandings by enabling access to relevant data regardless of the time and location of individuals. Additionally, mobile devices allow for interaction as a substitute for face-to-face communications. Moreover, mobile services might support individuals to make up or maintain their relations to other individuals.
Universalism versus particularism	Mobile services particularly can help consumers in universalistic cultures to overcome the limits of their society without violating any rules.
Individualism versus collectivisme	Mobility enables to maintain the connection to the community in communitaristic cultures and provides individuals with opportunities to re-assure their decisions.
Neutral versus emotional	At first glance, interactions via mobile devices have been neural due to their digital nature. Modern devices and services aim to add the emotional elements (prominent examples are individualized ring tones or wallpapers).
Specific versus diffuse	Particularly in Western cultures, business relations are frequently described in terms of a goal-orientated interaction that is limited to the activities needed to reach the goal. In Asian cultures, diffuse relationships are not only preferred, but necessary before business relationships are set up. Mobile services may assist to strengthen these diffuse relationships.
Achievement versus ascription	In achievement-focusing cultures, mobile service providers should emphasize the functional values offered by their services. In contrast, in ascription-oriented societies, the prestige and brand essence should be communicated. Additionally, referring to other users assigned to the mobile services network is likely to increase its valuation of the services offered.
Orientation in time	In addition to the opportunities outlined in Table 3, mobile services allow the retrieval of information on the past, present and most interestingly – highly profitable – on the future (e.g., horoscopes, local weather forecasts, etc.).
Attitudes toward the environment	Mobile services give control to the user of the mobile device, e.g., parents may localize their children, spouses each other, etc., but in another sense, they can be used to control other technical equipment, e.g., domestic central heating, other mobile devices.

quantifications of culture: the underlying dimensional constructs are very similar. Since Hofstede's four dimensions of culture served as consistent starting points in prior cross-cultural studies, e.g., Urbaczewski et al. (2002) and Kim et al. (2004), we use these dimensions in the subsequent section to analyze and compare countries by different data from their mobile communication market like phone penetration or SMS sending in a specific time period.

Relation between Cultural Dimensions and Characteristics of Mobile Technology in Six Countries

The impact of culture on the exposure to mobile technologies will be demonstrated with the Hofstede value dimensions and collected data for mobile technologies. The data obtained from the OECD (2006) dataset cover the total number of outgoing minutes for 2004

and 2005. The dataset comprises data on SMS sending, mobile phone penetration and phone subscriber penetration in China, France, Germany, Japan, the United Kingdom and the United States.

The total number of minutes individuals phoned in different countries in 2004 are correlated to the four cultural dimensions. The correlation coefficients are shown in Figure 2.

It is evident from the figure that the UAI is negatively correlated to the number of minutes people call in a year. The results are in line with those reported by Kim et al. (2004) for Japanese consumers. However, the results are unexpected, because individuals in cultures with high scores for UAI could reduce their perceived uncertainty by confirming information, reporting information to related individuals, and acknowledging their whereabouts and activities. One explanation for this is the lack of durability in comparison to other media (e.g., letters or fax), the related credibility and

Table 5. Schwartz motivational values and their impact on m-commerce

Schwartz Values	Relation to mobile commerce
Power	The ownership of mobile devices and the subscription to particular services symbolizes social status and prestige as well as the control of other individuals or resources.
Achievement	The familiarity with and usage of mobile services demonstrate a desirable competence with respect to social standards.
Hedonism	Mobile devices facilitate a variety of self-gratification applications, e.g., games.
Stimulation	Modern mobile devices consolidate communication technologies with entertainment, e.g., music.
Self-direction	The user gains independence by means of reachability and access to different resources stored on the device or accessible via the mobile device.
Universalism	Mobile services may support individuals in their ambition to understand others, interact fairly und increase the welfare of societies.
Benevolence	Mobile devices enable a closer contact with people in frequent interaction, particularly family and friends.
Tradition	Yet, mobile devices are an element of any society's history. However, mobile devices enable the members of societies to develop their traditions in modern formats, e.g., access to religious texts or prayers, regardless of the individual's place and local time.
Conformity	In business life, most individuals are expected to be reachable during business hours and beyond. In contrast, the usage of any mobile services might violate social norms, e.g., the usage of mobile devices during religious ceremonies or in places of cultural interest.
Security	The perception of safety and harmony as well as the stability of relationships can be increased by mobile services.

the lower level of trust in the information received. Another explanation is the uncertainty of the costs incurred by the use of mobile devices – the tariffs for the usage of mobile services are made up of at least two components: a basic fee and a charge for the call. The extent of the latter frequently depends on the service provider of the other user, the local time or day, and so on. Experiments by Estelami (1999) indicate that even 25% of a group of marketing students, who were provided with all the necessary data and trained in calculating the costs, failed to work out the costs with perfect accuracy. The majority of users of mobile devices are not trained in calculating these costs, are rarely provided with the necessary data, and, most important, lack the motivation to work it out. Therefore, it is a reasonable strategy to reduce uncertainty by avoiding calls using the mobile phone.

A second remarkable result depicted in Figure 2 is the high positive correlation between the IDV and the called minutes per year. This result shows that people in individualistic societies phone a lot more than those in collectivistic societies. Societies with loose ties among individuals, who primarily look after themselves and their immediate family, and disregard communities, are more egoistic and career oriented. They use the phone more often to stay in contact with other like-minded individuals and to power their career. This result is in line with previous results by Kim et al. (2004).

For a further investigation, the Hofstede dimensions are correlated with the penetration of mobile contract subscriber numbers (OECD, 2006), mobile phone penetration and the average number of SMS messages sent per inhabitant each month. The results are shown in Figure 3.

Akin to the calling minutes, the proportion of mobile contract subscribers, mobile phone penetration and SMS-usage are positively related to the dimension of individualism. Therefore, we argue that the cultures with high individualism scores provide good

Table 6. Overview of Hofstede dimensions explained and in the context of mobile commerce

Hofstede Dimensions	Relation to mobile commerce
Power distance (PDI):	This dimension reflects the need to have mobile devices in order to maintain control over other individuals as well as other resources. Since this dimension captures the accepted degree of inequality, it also reflects the acceptance and appropriateness of very high-priced devices and services.
Individualism (IDV):	Mobile devices enable vendors to contact their customers individually, in contrast to mass media advertising. However, in individualistic cultures, the benefits of maintaining the connection to a group by using mobile services are likely to be less esteemed.
Masculinity (MAS):	The metaphor of masculinity refers to assertiveness, performance, success and competition. Mobile services and the related devices are frequently associated (and promoted) with these attributes.
Uncertainty avoidance (UAI):	Mobile devices and services aim to support users in structuring their situations and provide access to information to reduce the perceived uncertainty.
Long-term orientation:	Users of mobile devices get their services instantly. Therefore they need not plan or wait.

Figure 1. Example of the Hofstede cultural dimensions for the US

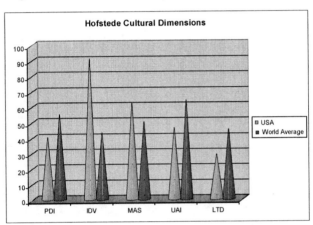

Figure 3. Correlation between the Hofstede dimensions and mobile phone characteristics (contract subscriber, phone penetration and SMS) (BNA, 2006; BD, 2006)

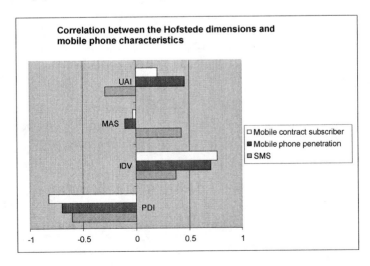

preconditions for mobile phone activities.

Contrarily, the PDI again has a clear negative impact. A rationale for the negative correlation with the extent of text messaging is given by Sarker and Wells (2003). In high PDI cultures, the sending of SMS messages is more likely to be considered unsuitable for formal communication. In the interaction of individuals of different status – an employee with his work supervisor, for example – it might even be perceived as a serious offense. The same argumentation might hold for the negative correlation of UAI and text messaging. Clearly, the UAI is positively related to the mobile phone penetration, although it is shown to be negatively related to the calling minutes in Figure 2.

Harris Rettie, & Kwan (2005) argue that high PDI in a culture is associated with acceptance of one's lot in life and being more relaxed and fun-loving. Because of the hedonic value associated with mobile devices, a positive correlation between the proportion of mobile phone subscribers and mobile phone penetration is expected, but nor supported by the data. This point clearly calls for further research.

The positive correlation of MAS and text messaging contradicts prior conjecture: Straub Keil, & Brenner (1997) argued that individuals in cultures with a high score of masculinity rely on rich media to improve their assertiveness in social interactions. The richness of media is qualified by (1) the capacity for immediate feedback, (2) the capacity to transmit multiple cues such as voice inflections or gestures, (3) the variety of language, and (4) the capacity of the medium to have a personal focus (Daft, Lengel, & Trevino, 1987). Since SMS do not meet the second and the third criteria, the richness is low, which limits assertiveness in social interactions.

Culture not only impacts on individuals, by means of determining need and desires, but it also affects a society's progress in building a digital interaction infrastructure (Ho, Kauffman, & Liang, 2007). This progress is quantified by the country's national e-readiness:

Definition 3 (e-readiness): *E-readiness refers to a country's ability to benefit from the electronic advantages as an engine of economic growth and human development.*

E-readiness has several components, including telecommunications infrastructure, human resources, and a legal and policy framework. This assessment is not restricted to m-commerce, but serves as a suitable proxy for the quality of technical, economic and legal condition for successful m-commerce activities (Ferguson & Yen, 2006).

The data on e-readiness are taken from the EIU (2006). E-readiness is quantified by scores from 1 to 10 comprising the following categories: connectivity, business environment, consumer and business adoption, legal and policy environment, social and cultural environment and supporting e-services. In addition to the e-readiness in 2005, the cell phone penetration in Italy, Germany, the UK, France, Spain, Japan, South Korea, the US and China is depicted in Figure 4.

It is clear from the figure that the European countries under consideration have a similar phone penetration, between 70% and 80%, and their e-readiness scores are also quite similar, oscillating between 70% and 85% (standardized in the range from 0 to 100 for comparability). However, in Asia, and especially in the US, the results strongly disband. Clearly, in the US, the use of the mobile phone falls short behind e-readiness.

Considering the correlations between the Hofstede dimensions and e-readiness in Figure 5, their similarity is striking. This seems reasonable because in a national culture with a high e-readiness score, the people are prepared for different kinds of modern technologies, and are therefore likely to invest individually in mobile phones.

A high UAI is associated with increased e-readiness and mobile phone penetration. Notably, Gong, Li and Stump (2007) hypothesized a negative impact of UAI on Internet use and access, but failed to support this hypothesis with their data. Consequently, we suppose that people aim to maintain an opportunity for staying in contact with one another via mobile phone and use more modern technology like the mobile Internet.

IDV is positively related to the ubiquitous spread of mobile phones and e-readiness. This result fits the findings of Lee, Choi, Kim, and Hong (2007), which highlight the fact that people in individualistic countries benefit from a higher perceived enjoyment and usefulness of mobile applications. This result and the negative impact of PDI are in line with the results by Gong et al. (2007). The impact of masculinity is relatively small, a finding that fits the observation of Hofstede (1994), who deems that the MAS dimension deploys a lower impact than the other three dimensions.

Figure 4. Comparison of the penetration of cellular phones and e-readiness scores (OECD, 2006; EIU, 2007)

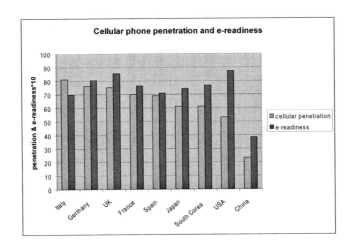

Figure 5. Correlations of the Hofstede dimensions and mobile phone penetration and e-readings (OECD, 2006; EIU, 2007)

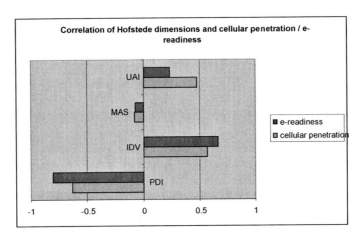

Implications for Further Research

The contribution of this chapter aims to shift attention from technical aspects and isolated consideration of technology diffusion to the cultural frames of the use of mobile devices.

Yet, most researchers take identical needs and desires of the users for granted when investigating m-commerce service adoption or designing innovative business models using mobile services. The results outlined in this chapter are reason enough to change this misleading point of view. In the marketing related literature, there is an ongoing debate on the necessity and the limits of standardization. The empirical results of this chapter call for an adaptation of m-commerce services with respect to the cultural predisposition of the users. A detailed investigation is just emerging in the realm of m-commerce.

Most of the results presented in the current chapter are in line with prior conjecture, some of which is conflicting. Particularly the relation of UAI and e-readiness and the relation between MAS and text messaging should be explored in more detail, not only for the cultures under consideration, but also for other cultures.

In this study, we have demonstrated the quantification of culture by means of Hostede's dimensions, just one approach among a few similar ones, which has been shown to provide a valid assessment of quantifying culture. Clearly, an investigation using other quantification methods would be an avenue for further research. All the approaches discussed in this chapter, however, are taken from related social sciences, but not developed to foster research on mobile or more broadly defined digital research. Consequently, design and validation of scales for a quantitative assessment of culture appear to be the more challenging endeavor.

Implications for Practice

The lack of cultural fit is likely to become a common argument for explaining the failure of m-commerce business models as it is rarely taken into account in the planning of an m-commerce business strategy. Practitioners from all domains of m-commerce should be urged to take advantage of adapting their offers to the cultural expectations of their target users. The data analysis in this chapter results in two rules of thumb:

1. Users in cultures with low PDI and UAI are more likely to adopt m-commerce services. Vendors should target these markets first, when introducing or re-launching their services. Moreover, e-readiness is higher in these cultures. Consequently, the technical infrastructure will support the diffusion of innovative services.
2. Cultures with high IDV scores are suited to the introduction of voice-related services, and entertainment opportunities in general.

If practitioners investigate the manner in which the population of a country uses mobile technology, they will run their business more successfully both from a short- and a long-term perspective. Mobile technology applications like SMS, MMS, WAP, mobile e-mail and even more accruing new services like "Mapion Pointing" or "Point & Find", which use GPRS to locate the user and UMTS for a very fast data transfer, encourage acceptance, which has turned out to depend on the cultural predisposition of the user. From the technical perspective, users of mobile devices can be reached any time and anywhere. Moreover, this might be achieved on many levels, with text content, music, pictures or even movies, but attention paid to these services and

their acceptance differs significantly with respect to their cultural embedding. On the contextual level and formal configuration of any communication, mobile users need to feel culturally engaged with the vendors. The metaphor, "clash of cultures", gains importance for all m-commerce services, which are elements of particular societies' "modern way of life", if these societies and their values are disapproved of by other relevant target groups.

CONCLUSION

This chapter highlights the importance of culture for the acceptance of m-commerce offers by correlating the adoption of different services to Hofstede's cultural dimensions. The reasons for varying adoption rates have turned out to be critical to the success of m-commerce business models, and call for a reliable quantification of the relevant dimensions of culture. Clearly, m-commerce vendors are well advised not to standardize their offers or their communication to and with their customers. The challenge of adapting to the cultural needs appears to be more daunting than the somewhat milder challenge of adapting to the stationary Internet. In the latter case, the alignment of languages and symbols provides a sufficient level of customization. In m-commerce, the different usages of mobile devices open or lock communication channels. Moreover, the culture determines the appropriateness of the interaction gestalts with respect to the users' situational contexts.

REFERENCES

Al-Olayan, F. S., & Karande, K. (2000). A content analysis of magazine advertisements from the United States and the Arab world. *Journal of Advertising, 29*(3), 69-82.

BD (2006). *Business Digital*. Retrieved February 27, 2007, from http://www.itu.int/osg/spu/publications/digitalife/docs/digital.life-chapter3.pdf.

Beatty, S. E., Kahle, L. R., Homer, P., & Misra, S. (1985). Alternative measurement approaches to consumer values: List of Values and the Rokeach Value Survey. *Psychology and Marketing, 2*(3), 181-200.

Bell, C. S., Compeau, D. R., & Olivera, F. (2005). Understanding the social implications of technological multitasking: A conceptual model. *Proceedings of the Fourth Annual Workshop on HCI Research in MIS*, 80-84.

BNA (2006). *Bundesnetzagentur Jahresbericht.* Retrieved December 21., 2007, from http://www.bundesnetzagentur.de/media/archive/9009.pdf.

Cyr, D., Head, M., & Ivanov, A. (2005). Website design and mobility: Culture, gender, and age comparisons. *Proceedings of the Fourth Annual Workshop on HCI Research in MIS*, 20-24.

Daft, R. L., Lengel, R. H., & Trevino, L. K. (1987). Message equivocality, media selection, and manager performance: Implications for information systems. *MIS Quarterly, 11*(3), 355-366.

Daghfous, N., Petrof, J. V., & Pons, F. (1999). Values and adoption of innovations: a cross-cultural study. *Journal of Consumer Marketing, 16*(4), 314-331.

Denison, D. R. (1996). What is the difference between organizational culture and organizational climate? A native's point of view on a decade of paradigm wars. *The Academy of Management Review, 21*(3), 619-654.

EIU (2006). The 2006 E-Readiness rankings. Economist Intelligence Unit Retrieved, February 27, 2007, from http://graphics.eiu.com/files/ad_pdfs/2007Ereadiness_Ranking_WP.pdf.

Estelami, H. (1999). The computational effect of price endings in multidimensional price advertising. *Jornal of Product and Brand Management, 8*(3), 244-256.

Ferguson, C. W., & Yen, D. C. (2006). A regional approach to e-commerce global expansion. *International Journal of Electronic Business, 4*(1), 99-114.

Ford, D. P., Connelly, C. E., & Meister, D. B. (2003). Information systems research and Hofstede's culture's consequences: An uneasy and incomplete partnership. *IEEE Transactions on Engineering Management, 50*(1), 8-25.

Fraunholz, B., & Unnithan, C. (2004). Critical Success Factors in Mobile Communications: A Comparative Roadmap for Germany and India. International *Journal of Mobile Communication, 2*(1), 87-101.

Gong, W., Li, Z. G., & Stump, R. L. (2007): Global internet use and access: Cultural considerations. *Asia Pacific Journal of Marketing and Logistics, 19*(1), 57-74.

Guzmán-Obando, J., Gonzalez, G., de la Rosa, J. L., Ruiz, R. U., & Castan, J. A. (2006). Modelling the human values scale from consumers transactional data bases. *Computing, Proceedings of 15th CIC, IEEE Computer Society*, Mexico, 86-91.

Haghirian, P., Madlberger, M., & Inoue, A. (2008). Mobile advertising in different stages of development: A cross-country comparison of consumer attitudes. *Hawaii International Conference on System Sciences*, 48-56.

Hall, E. T. (1977). *Beyond Culture.* New York.

Hall, E. T., & Hall, M. R. (1990). *Understanding Cultural Differences.* Yarmouth.

Harris, P., Rettie, R., & Kwan, C.C. (2005). Adoption and usage of m-commerce: a cross-cultural comparison of Hong Kong and the United Kingdom. *Journal of Electronic Commerce Research, 6*(3), 210-24.

Ho, S.-C., Kauffman, R. J., & Liang, T.-P. (2007). A growth theory perspective on B2C e-commerce growth in Europe: An exploratory study. *Electronic Commerce Research and Applications, 6*(3), 237-259.

Hofstede, G. (1980). *Culture's Consequences: International Differences in Work-Related Values.* Beverly Hills CA: Sage.

Hofstede, G. (1994). Management scientists are human. *Management Science, 40*(1), 4-13.

Hofstede, G. (2008). Geert Hofstede™ Cultural Dimensions. Found at http://www.geert-hofstede.com.

Hung, S. Y., Ku, C. Y., & Chang, C. M. (2003). Critical factors of WAP services adoption: An empirical study. *Electronic Commerce Research and Applications, 2*(1), 42-60.

Kahle, L. (1983). *Social Values and Social Change: Adaptation to Life in America.* New York: Praeger Publishers.

Keen, P. & Macintosh, R. (2001). *The Freedom Economy: Gaining the M-commerce Edge in the Area of the Wireless Internet.* Berkely: Osborne & McGraw-Hill.

Kim, J., Lee, I., Lee, Y., Choi, B., Hong, S. J., Yan Tam, K., Naruse, K., & Maeda, Y. (2004). Exploring the mobile Internet businesses from a user perspective: A cross-national study in Hong Kong, Japan and

Korea. *International Journal of Mobile Communications, 2*(1), 1-21.

Lee, Y., Kim, J., Lee, I., & Kim, H. (2002). A Cross-cultural study on the value structure of mobile Internet usage: Comparison between Korea and Japan. *Journal of Electronic Commerce Research, 3*(4), 227-239.

Lee, I., Choi, B., Kim, J., & Hong S.J. (2007). Culture-technology fit: Effects of cultural characteristics on the post-adoption beliefs of mobile Internet users. *International Journal of Electronic Commerce, 11*(4), 11-51.

Lee, W. J., Kim, T. U., & Chung, J. Y. (2002). User acceptance of the mobile Internet. *Proceedings of the First International Conference on Mobile Business, Mobiforum*, Athens, Greece.

Li, H., Edwards S. M., & Lee J.-H. (2002). Measuring the intrusiveness of advertisements: Scale development and validation. *Journal of Advertising, 31*(2), 37-47.

Lin, Y. M., & Shih, D. H. (2008). Deconstructing mobile commerce service with continuance intention. *International Journal of Mobile Communications, 6*(1), 67-87.

Luarn, P., & Lin, H. H. (2005). Toward an understanding of the behavioral intention to use mobile banking. *Computers in Human Behavior, 21*(6), 873-891.

Mahatanankoon, P., Wen, H. J., & Lim, B. (2005). Consumer-based m-commerce: exploring consumer perception of mobile applications. *Computer Standards & Interfaces, 27*(4), 347-357.

McSweeney, B. (2002). Hofstede's model of national cultural differences and their consequences: A triumph of faith – a failure of analysis. *Human Relations, 55*(1), 89-118.

Mobinet (2005). *Mobinet 2005: An A.T Kearney/University of Cambridge study.* Retrieved February 27, 2007, from www.atkearney.com/shared_res/pdf/Mobinet_2005_Detailed_Results.pdf.

OECD (2006). *Mobile commerce DSTI/CP(2006/7) final.* Retrieved October 17, 2007, from http://www.oecd.org/dataoecd/22/52/38077227.pdf.

Oh, L. B. & Xu, H. (2003). Effects of multimedia on mobile consumer behavior: An empirical study of location-aware advertising. *Twenty-Fourth International Conference on Information Systems*, 679-691.

Pollay, R. W. (1983). Measuring the cultural values manifest in advertising. *Current Issues and Research in Advertising, 6*(1), 71-92.

Pressey, A. D., & Selassie, H. G. (2002). Are cultural differences overrated? Examining the influence of national culture on international buyer-seller relationships. *Journal of Consumer Behaviour, 2*(4), 354-368.

Roehrich, G. (2004). Consumer Innovativeness: Concepts and measurements. *Journal of Business Research, 57*(6), 671-77.

Rokeach, M. (1969). The role of values. *Public Opinion Research, 32*(4), 547-559.

Rokeach, M. (1973). *The Nature of Human Values.* New York.

Sarker, S. & Wells, J. D. (2003). Understanding mobile handheld device use and adoption. *Communications of the ACM, 46*(12), 35-40.

Schwartz, S. H., & Bilsky, W. (1987). Toward a universal psychological structure of human values. *Journal of Personality and Social Psychology, 53*(3), 550-562.

Schwartz, S. H. (1992). The universal content and structure of values: Theoretical advances and empirical tests in 20 countries. In Zanna, M.P. (ed.), *Advances in Experimental Social Psychology, 25*, San Diego: Academic Press, 1-62.

Schwartz, S. H. (1994). Beyond Individualism-Collectivism: New Cultural Dimensions of Values. In Uichol K., Kagitcibasi, C., Triandis, H. C, and Yoon, G. (eds.), *Individualism and Collectivism*, Newbury Park, Sage, 85-119.

Straub, D., Keil, M., & Brenner, W. (1997). Testing the technology acceptance model across cultures: A three country study. *Information & Management, 33*(1), 1-11.

Trompenaars, F., & Hampden-Turner, C. (1998). *Riding the Waves of Culture: Understanding Diversity in Global Business* (2nd ed.). New York: McGraw Hill.

Urbaczewski, A., Wells, J., Sarker, S., & Koivisto, M. (2002). Exploring cultural differences as a means for understanding the global mobile Internet: a theoretical basis and program of research. *Proceedings of the 35th Annual Hawaii International Conference on System Sciences*, 654-663.

Van Biljon, J. A. (2006). *A model for representing the motivational and cultural factors that influence the mobile phone usage variety.* Doctoral theses, University of South Africa, http://etd.unisa.ac.za/ETD-db/theses/available/etd-09062007-131207/unrestricted/thesis.pdf

Wehmeyer, K. (2007). Mobile ad intrusiveness: The effects of message type and situation. *In Proceedings of the 20th Bled eConference*, Slovenia.

KEY TERMS

High-Context Cultures: Societies where relationships of individuals are long lasting and qualified by means of individuals' status. Individuals in high-context cultures are used to understanding implicit communication.

Individualism: The extent to which people are expected to stand up for themselves and consider their own well-being in any decisions. Dimension for quantifying culture with Hofstede's framework.

Instrumental Values: Beliefs about some desirable end state that transcends specific situations, which apply to many different countries and are socially desirable.

Long-Term Orientation: The extent to which the individual considers future impacts of their decisions. Dimension for quantifying culture with Hofstede's framework.

Low-Context Cultures: Societies where the relations between individuals are formed by rules and where communication has to be explicit.

Masculinity: The extent to which competitiveness, assertiveness, ambition, and the accumulation of wealth and material possessions are considered to be desirable within a society. Dimension for quantifying culture with Hofstede's framework.

Media Richness: Theoretical framework for qualifying communications with respect to social cues (e.g., gestures or moods) that are conveyed in the course of interactions by using particular media. (This is also known as Information Richness)

Meiwaku: The Japanese term describing the strong sense of inhibition about being a nuisance in public in this culture.

Power Distance: The extent to which an unequal assignment of control people and resources is accepted by the individuals of a society. Dimension for quantifying culture with Hofstede's framework.

Uncertainty Avoidance: Extent to which individuals attempt to cope with anxiety by minimizing uncertainty. Dimension for quantifying culture with Hofstede's framework.

Terminal Values: Beliefs about some desirable end state that transcends specific situations which refer to idealized end states of existence or lifestyles.

Chapter XXIV
The Mobile Services Market:
An Exploratory Analysis of Mobile Phone Usage by French Consumers

Călin Gurău
Montpellier Business School, France

ABSTRACT

This paper presents the situation of the mobile services market in France, based on a survey conducted in the city of Montpellier, in November- December 2006. After a presentation of the existing research background related with mobile services, the article presents the research objectives and the research methodology applied to collect primary data for this project. The results of statistical data analysis are then presented and discussed, allowing an identification of the main consumer segments in terms of characteristics, attitudes and behaviours. The paper ends with a summary of the findings, and with suggestions for future research.

INTRODUCTION

The mobile phone technology provides users with a telephone connection any place, anytime. The main innovation that has facilitated mass adoption and use of mobile phones is the cellular approach in transmitting a radio signal (Layton, Brain, & Tyson, 2005). The introduction of digital technology (2G) has increased even further the number of communication channels. Finally, the current 3G technology represents the latest trend in mobile phones standards, offering increased bandwidth and information transfer rates to accommodate Web-based applications and phone-based audio and video files.

The use of mobile phones beyond the standard voice and data, and its use to access Internet applications, presents a number of challenges. Some of these challenges are related to the specific interface of mobile phones, and others with the existing Web protocols adapted for mobile networks. The screens of mobile phones are small and have a lower resolution in comparison with PC or laptop screens/monitors. Furthermore, the Wireless Application Protocol (WAP) does not always work efficiently on wireless devices with small screens as it also depends on mobile technology's bandwidth (such as GSM or CDMA) for access to information and services (Yeo, & Huang, 2003). There are also challenges related to connections with the Web navigation and site structure, and with the input methods available for mobile phone users (Buchanan, Farrant, Jones, Thimbleby, Marsden, & Pazzani, 2001).

While mobile services provide opportunities for quick diffusion and diversification to the business, there are not many studies presenting the mobile market structure and evolution. This chapter attempts to present the situation of the mobile services market particularly with respect to France. The material in this chapter is based on a survey conducted in the city of Montpellier, in December 2006. After a presentation of the existing research background related with mobile services, the study presents the research objectives and the research methodology applied to collect primary data for this project. The results of statistical data analysis are then presented and discussed, allowing an identification of the main consumer segments in terms of characteristics, attitudes and behaviours. The chapter ends with a summary of the findings, and with suggestions for future research.

BACKGROUND: THE DEVELOPMENT OF MOBILE SERVICES MARKET

A specific characteristic of mobile-business is that a person using mobile services can conduct business anywhere, even when out of office, travelling between places, or visiting a different location (Kristofferson, & Ljungberg, 2000).

The technological features of 3G mobile phones permit the transmission as well as downloading of multimedia files. This facility has increased the range of mobile services that can be offered to consumers. In addition to the classical voice-based communication and SMS, the new mobile services add the MMS –Multimedia Message Service, and increase the web browsing capabilities.

Mobile communication technology is also used by enterprises – either to send adverts to individual mobile phone users (Spurgeon, 2005), or to use the mobile phone as a communication tool for the highly mobile employees/entrepreneurs (Donner, 2005). New business models have been already introduced in order to increase the effectiveness of specific mobile phone services.

These new areas of applications have triggered an interest among researchers regarding the consumer

profiles and how these profiles affect the evolution of the market for mobile services. Some researchers investigated the adaptation of advertising techniques to the interactive characteristics of the new communication tools (Spurgeon, 2005) while others investigated consumers' profile and their willingness to adopt and use various mobile services (Donner, 2005; Leppäniemi, & Karjaluoto, 2005; Mort, & Drennan, 2005; Suoranta, & Mattila, 2004), or the importance of mobile marketing in the promotion mix of companies (Karjaluoto, Leppäniemi, & Salo, 2004).

A consumer survey conducted by Jarvenpaa and Lang (2005) has identified a series of paradoxes perceived by consumers in their use of mobile phones, which provide possible explanation about the fears/concerns of the general public regarding the mobile technology. Mort and Drennan (2005) have attempted to identify and define the profile of various consumer segments, in relation to their propensity to adopt and use mobile phone technology. The gender of consumers seems to make a significant difference in the adoption of use of some mobile services: males usually express higher intensions to use m-services than females, but no statistically significant influence was found regarding age. Malhotra and Segars (2005) have focused on the pattern of wireless web adoption in the US, while Xiaoni and Prybutok (2005) investigated the specificities of the Chinese market, in comparison with US and Europe.

Despite the increased interest in understanding the mobile service market, until now the research was limited and fragmented, both in terms of geographical areas – there is more data for some countries that for others, and of research objectives – the research is rather heterogeneous, addressing specific elements of mobile service usage.

The present chapter attempts to provide a clear picture of the use of mobile services in France. proposing an analysis of the market based on gender and age categories. With the exception of official statistics (ARCEP, 2005) and professional studies (TNS Sofres, 2005), until now the academic research of the French mobile market is scarce.

Research Methodology

In order to identify and describe the profile of the French market for mobile services, the following research objectives have been defined in this project:

1. To identify the popularity and the frequency of use of various mobile services.
2. To understand the context in which the mobile phones are used in France.
3. To analyse the attitude of customers towards mobile advertising.
4. To identify the main fears of the French consumers in relation to mobile technology.

All these research objectives were investigated from the perspective of two independent variables: the gender and the age of respondents.

The data was collected during November-December 2006, by applying a questionnaire to randomly selected individuals, in the city of Montpellier, France. 238 respondents have provided information about their use of mobile phones and their attitudes toward mobile technology, from which 205 (86.1%) have indicated that they use mobile phone services, while 33 (13.9%) declared that they do not own or use mobile phones.

The collected data has been analysed using the SPSS software of statistical analysis. The Chi Square test has been applied to all cross tabulations in order to verify the influence of gender and age on the behaviour and attitudes of respondents.

Presentation and Analysis of Data

The General Situation of the Mobile Phone Market in France

The statistical indicators provided by the official French Authority for the Regulation of Electronic Communications and Post (ARCEP) indicate that the penetration rate of mobile phones in France was 75.1% of the population in September 2005, presenting a 5% increase from September 2004. However, the penetration rate is different from one administrative region to another, showing discrepancies such as 55.6% in Auvergne, and 107.6% in Paris-Ile de France. The region in which the survey was realised – Languedoc-Rousillon is closest to the national rate of penetration, with 74%, which reinforces the representativeness of the study.

In France there are at present three major metropolitan mobile network operators: Orange France, which controls 47.3% of the market; S F P with 35.8% of the market and Bouygues Telecom with 16.9% of the market (Le Journal du Net, 2005).

The gender of respondents appears to have no significant influence on their propensity to own and use a mobile phone: 86.9% of the male respondents and 85.4% of the female respondents have indicated that they use a mobile phone.

The system adopted for mobile phone use – subscription or cards – is slightly different for the two genders: the male respondents seem to prefer the subscription in a larger proportion than female respondents (85.1% in comparison with 82.1%), while for the card system the preference is more significant for female respondents (21.4% in comparison with 14.9%).

Table 1 presents the use frequency of various mobile services used by the respondents. The percentages are based on 206 answers for the SMS and MMS, and on 204 responses for the Internet service. These percentages indicate the proportion of male and female respondents that adopt a certain frequency of use for various mobile services. Although the gender has no statistically significant relationship with the frequency of use, a few differences can however be outlined. A larger proportion of female respondents declared they use frequently the SMS service than the male respondents, but for the other two services the male respondents show a higher intensity of use. Overall, the SMS is clearly the most popular mobile service, while a large proportion of respondents indicated that they rarely use mobile phones to access the Internet. The reason for this preference is probably the specific problems of mobile phone-based Internet access systems: small display, poor screen resolution and browsing difficulties.

Table 2 shows the context in which mobile devices are used by the genders. The Chi Square test demonstrates that there is a statistically significant relationship between gender and the context of using mobile phones, to a level of $p = 0.025$ (see Table 2). The male respondents are more inclined to use the mobile phones for work (8.3% in comparison with only 2.9% female users), or both for work and for personal needs (20.2% in comparison with only 9.8% female users).

The majority of mobile phone users perceived mobile advertising as having none or little importance, and the distribution of responses on the two genders is almost similar, although the males seem to be more inclined than females to take into account mobile adverts (See Table 3). This demonstrates that the market for mobile advertising is still in development in France, the customers not being ready to accept

Table 1. Cross tabulation between the gender of respondents and the use frequency of mobile services

	Rarely	Sometimes	Frequently
SMS			
Male	6.4%	23.4%	52.1%
Female	8.9%	14.3%	62.5%
MMS			
Male	16%	10.6%	11.7%
Female	15.2%	10.7%	7.2%
Internet			
Male	60.2%	18.3%	18.3%
Female	72.1%	14.4%	10.8%

and to take into account this specific use of mobile communication.

The fears expressed by the respondents in relation to mobile technology show some important differences between the two genders, as shown in Table 4. A relatively large percentage of female respondents indicated that they fear 'too much publicity' (7.9% in comparison with only 7.6% of male respondents). On the other hand, the males are slightly more concerned than the female about the threat of viruses (15.8% of males in comparison with 9.6% of females).

The age of respondents has a strong statistical influence on the propensity to own and use a mobile phone (to a level of p < 0.0001). The percentage of respondents owning a mobile phone has a tendency to decrease with the increase of respondents' age: 94.2% of people less than 21 years old, 96.7% of people between 21 and 35 years old, 85.7% of people between 36 and 50 years old, 75% of people between 51 and 70 years old, and only 40% of people older than 70 years own and use a mobile phone.

The access to mobile phone services is influenced by the age of respondents (see Table 5). Although in all age categories there is a clear predominance of people that prefer to subscribe to regular mobile services, there is an increase of percentage of people who prefer to buy mobile phone cards as the category of age increases, although the trend is not linear.

The data displayed in Table 6 demonstrates that the age of respondents influences the frequency of use of various mobile services. This influence is confirmed by the Chi square test for the use of SMS

(to a level of p < 0.0001) and for the use of MMS (to a level of p = 0.004). The use of SMS is extremely frequent among young people (79.3% of teenagers and 73.6% of the respondents aged between 20 and 35 years old use SMS frequently). The adult and old people have a much lower propensity to use mobile services no respondents above 50 years old use MMS or Mobile Internet.

These results demonstrate that the age of respondents influences the frequency of use of various mobile services. This influence is confirmed by the Chi square test for the use of SMS (to a level of p < 0.0001) and for the use of MMS (to a level of p = 0.004). The use of SMS is extremely frequent among young people (79.3% of teenagers and 73.6% of the respondents aged between 20 and 35 years old use SMS frequently). The adult and old people have a much lower propensity to use mobile services no respondents above 50 years old use MMS or Mobile Internet.

Table 7 shows that a majority of respondents from each age category prefer to use mobile phones for personal communication. However, the use of the mobile phone for professional purposes shows some significant differences. An important proportion of people between 21 and 70 year old use the mobile phone in professional or both in professional and personal contexts. This tendency shows the gradual penetration of the mobile phone in the modern day working environment, where it provides mobility and facility of access. However, considering the results, we can conclude that the use of mobile phones for professional purposes is still not very developed in France.

As already indicated in Table 3, many respondents feel that mobile advertising is not an important facility. However, Table 8 indicates two interesting results: a relatively large proportion of old respondents (above 50 years old) indicate some interest in mobile advertising. This can be a sign that mobile advertising can provide an increased convenience and therefore attractiveness especially for aged people. This trend can also indicate that the vendors are getting aware of this cross-section of the market and therefore providing appropriate adverts that target this market. Unfortunately, however, the small number of responses that indicate this trend does not permit yet a generalisation of results, more research being necessary to confirm this phenomenon.

Among the major fears related with mobile technology expressed by respondents from different categories of age, the one with largest percentages of answers was 'too much publicity' (see Table 9). Cost also seems to

Table 2. Cross tabulation between the gender of respondents and the context of using mobile phone services

Use context / Gender	Male		Female		Total	
	N	%	N	%	N	%
Professional	7	8.3	3	2.9	10	5.4
Personal	60	71.4	89	87.3	149	80.1
Both	17	20.2	10	9.8	27	14.5
Total	84	100	102	100	186	100

Chi square = 7.386   **p = 0.025**

Table 3. Cross tabulation between the gender of respondents and the perceived importance of mobile advertising

Importance / Gender	Male		Female		Total	
	N	%	N	%	N	%
None	50	64.1	62	66	112	65.1
Little	21	26.9	27	28.6	48	27.9
Some	7	9	4	4.3	11	6.4
A lot	0	0	1	1.1	1	0.6
Total	78	100	94	100	172	100

Table 4. Cross tabulation between the gender of respondents and the main fears linked with the use of mobile phones

Fears / Gender	Male		Female		Total	
	N	%	N	%	N	%
Too much publicity	28	7.6	44	37.9	72	33.2
Less freedom	10	9.9	12	10.3	22	10.1
Viruses	16	15.8	11	9.6	27	12.4
Cost	36	35.6	39	33.6	75	34.6
Dependence	11	10.9	10	8.6	21	9.7
Total	101	100	116	100	217	100

Table 5. The percentage of respondents from different categories of age who choose subscription or card mobile phone systems

	Subscription	Card
Less than 20 years	86.6%	17.1%
20-35 years	86.2%	13.8%
36-50 years	80%	23.3%
51-70 years	78.6%	21.4%
More than 70 years	62.5%	37.5%

represent a matter of concern for an significant percentage of customers as well. 'Less freedom' is especially emphasised by mature and older people, while the fear of dependence is expressed predominantly by teenagers and old people (51-70 year old).

CONCLUSION

The results of the survey demonstrate some interesting tendencies, which can provide useful information for mobile phone operators. These tendencies, highlighted in this chapter can help the reader understand the present structure of the mobile service market in France. The young people are obviously the predominant users of additional mobile services (SMS, MMS and mobile Internet), however the use of MMS and mobile Internet is still comparatively low with SMS usage.

This is in line with the tendency showed by some statistical reports, in relation to the slow development of the SMS in France: until 2003, France was on the last place among West European Economies (Netherlands, Germany, Spain, Italy, Portugal, Finland,

Sweden, United Kingdom) in terms of monthly SMS usage per customer (ART, 2004). However, in the last couple of years the use of SMS usage has shown a quick development, with an increase from 2003 to 2004 of 27.6%. The French market of MMS and Mobile Internet services can, therefore, be interpreted as still in a developing stage.

Another important tendency demonstrated in this chapter is the use of mobile services for professional purposes, a practice that is becoming increasingly spreading in France. However, the mobile networks operators might do more to promote the development of this trend, by introducing specific services for professionals and creating attractive offers for enterprises.

Finally, the mobile advertising is still relatively neglected in France, most respondents not showing any interest in this mobile commercial service. This trend can also be reversed by a more creative use of mobile phone services by the specialised enterprises. Indeed it is not enough just to launch the adverts used on the Internet, television or radio on the mobile phones networks. These adverts and their delivery to customers must be specifically adapted to the features of mobile

Table 6. Cross tabulation between the age of respondents and the use frequency of mobile services

	Rarely	Sometimes	Frequently
SMS	Chi Square =	110.827 p < 0.0001	
Less than 20 years	2.4%	11%	79.3%
20-35 years	5.2%	15.5%	73.6%
36-50 years	20%	40%	20%
51-70 years	14.3%	25%	10.7%
More than 70 years	12.5%	12.5%	0
MMS	Chi Square =	34.663 p = 0.004	
Less than 20 years	19.5%	17.1%	12.2%
20-35 years	19%	8.6%	13.7%
36-50 years	10%	10%	3.3%
51-70 years	7.1%	0	0
More than 70 years	0	0	0
Internet	Chi Square =	25.729 p = 0.175	
Less than 20 years	61%	13.4%	23.2%
20-35 years	56.9%	20.7%	17.2%
36-50 years	75.9%	20.7%	0
51-70 years	82.5%	14.8%	0
More than 70 years	100%	0	0

Table 7. Cross tabulation between the age of respondents and the context of using of mobile phone services

Context / Age	< 20		21-35		36-50		51-70		70 <		Total	
	N	%	N	%	N	%	N	%	N	%	N	%
Professional	1	1.3	4	7.4	3	12	2	8.3	0	0	10	5.4
Personal	69	90.8	38	70.4	17	68	18	75	7	100	149	80.1
Both	9	7.9	12	22.2	5	20	4	16.7	0	0	27	14.5
Total	76	100	54	100	25	100	24	100	7	100	186	100

Table 8. Cross tabulation between the age of respondents and the perceived importance of mobile advertising

Importance / Age	< 20		21-35		36-50		51-70		70 <		Total	
	N	%	N	%	N	%	N	%	N	%	N	%
None	42	56.8	38	74.5	12	63.2	15	71.4	5	71.4	112	65.1
Little	26	35.1	11	21.5	7	36.8	3	14.3	1	14.3	48	27.9
Some	6	8.1	1	2	0	0	3	14.3	1	14.3	11	6.4
A lot	0	0	1	2	0	0	0	0	0	0	1	0.6
Total	74	100	51	100	19	100	21	100	7	100	186	100

communication. On the other hand, the avoidance of mobile adverts might be related with negative customer perceptions – as it is shown by the answers indicated the main fears linked to the mobile technology, which has to be challenged and change if mobile advertising is ever to be successful in France.

This study attempted to provide a picture of the main mobile phone services in France and of the customers' behaviur in relation to gender and age categories. This chapter has a number of research limitations determined by the research methodology adopted. The sample is relatively small in comparison with the size and the variability of the French population. Although the penetration rate of the Languedoc-Rousillon region, in which the survey was applied matches the mean penetration rate of mobile phones in France, the results of this study cannot be generalised to the entire population of France. In fact, the

Table 9. Cross tabulation between the age of respondents and the main fears linked with the use of mobile phones

Fears / Age	< 20		21-35		36-50		51-70		70 <		Total	
	N	%	N	%	N	%	N	%	N	%	N	%
Too much publicity	27	32.5	21	36.8	12	38.7	6	20	6	37.5	72	33.2
Less freedom	5	6	3	5.3	5	16.1	7	23.3	2	12.5	22	10.1
Viruses	8	9.6	7	12.3	5	16.1	5	16.7	2	12.5	27	12.4
Cost	32	38.6	21	36.8	8	25.8	8	26.7	6	37.5	75	34.6
Dependence	11	13.3	5	8.8	1	3.2	4	13.3	0	0	21	9.7
Total	83	100	57	100	31	100	30	100	16	100	217	100

important differences in mobile phones penetration among various administrative regions indicate the need for future research in order to discover the causes of these discrepancies. On the other hand, the independent variables used to investigate the profile of consumers are limited to only two dimensions: age and gender. More demographic variables should be measured in relation to consumers' attitudes and behaviours towards mobile services – such as revenue, level of education, socio-professional category - in order to understand the structure and the dynamics of the mobile services market in France.

REFERENCES

ARCEP (2005). The Mobile Market Survey 2005. http://www.art-telecom.fr [accessed January 2006].

ART (2004). Les SMS. http://www.art-telecom.fr [accessed January 2006].

Buchanan, G., Farrant, S., Jones, M., Thimbleby, H., Marsden, G., & Pazzani, M. (2001). *Improving Mobile Internet Usability*. http://www10.org/cdrom/papers/230/ [accessed December 2005].

Donner, J. (2004). Microentrepreneurs and mobiles: An Exploration of the uses of mobile phones by small business owners in Rwanda. *Information Technologies & International Development, 2*(1), 1-21.

Jarvenpaa, S. L., & Lang, K. R. (2005). Managing the paradoxes of mobile technology. *Information Systems Management, 22*(4), 7-23.

Karjaluoto, H., Leppäniemi, M., & Salo, J. (2004). The role of mobile marketing in companies' promotion mix. Empirical evidence from Finland. *Journal of International Business and Economics, 2*(1), 111-116.

Kristoffersen, S., & Ljungberg, F. (2000). Mobility: From Stationary to Mobile Work. In K. Braa, C. Sorenson, & B. Dahlbom (Eds.), *Planet Internet*, 137-156, Studentlitteratur, Lund.

Layton, J., Brain, M., & Tyson, J. (2005). *How Cell Phones Work*. http://electronics.howstuffworks.com/cell-phone.htm [accessed December 2005].

Le Journal du Net (2005). *France: Les operateurs mobiles*. http://www.journaldunet.col/cc/05_mobile:mobile_marche_fr.shtml [accessed January 2006].

Leppäniemi, M., & Karjaluoto, H. (2005). Factors influencing consumer willingness to accept mobile advertising. A conceptual model. *International Journal of Mobile Communications, 3*(3), 197-213.

Looney, C. A., Jessup, L. M., & Valacich, J. S. (2004). Emerging Business Models for mobile brokerage services. *Communications of the ACM, 47*(6), 71-77.

Malhotra, A., & Segars, A. H. (2005). Investigating wireless web adoption patterns in the US. *Communications of the ACM, 48*(10), 105-110.

Mort, G. S., & Drennan, J. (2005). Marketing M-Services: Establising a usage benefit typology related to mobile user characteristics. *Journal of Database Marketing & Customer Strategy Management, 12*(4), 327-341.

Spurgeon, C. (2005). Losers and Lovers: Mobile Phone Services Advertising and the New Media Consumer/Producer. *Journal of Interactive Advertising, 5*(2), http://jiad.org/vol5/no2/spurgeon [accessed January 2006].

Suoranta, M., & Mattila, M. (2004). Mobile banking and consumer behaviour: New insights into the diffusion pattern. *Journal of Financial Services Marketing, 8*(4), 354-366.

TNS Sofres (2005). *Observatoire societal du téléphonie mobile*. http://www.tns-sofres.com/etudes/pol/031105_telmobiles.htm [accessed January 2006].

Xiaoni Z., & Prybutok, V.R. (2005). How the mobile communication markets differ in China, the US, and Europe. *Communications of the ACM, 48*(3), 111-114.

Yeo, J., & Huang, W. (2003). Mobile E-Commerce Outlook. *International Journal of Information Technology & Decision Making, 2*(2), 313-332.

KEY TERMS

2G Technology: 2nd-generation technology represents digital wireless technology standards, which, in comparison with analog wireless standards(1G), permit an increase data transmission capacity.

3G Technology: 3G represents the third generation of mobile communications technology, which offers increased bandwidth, permitting the quick transfer of large data files.

MMS (Multimedia Messaging Service): A communications technology developed by 3GPP (Third Generation Partnership Project) that allows users to exchange multimedia communications between capable mobile phones and other devices.

Mobile Advertising: Direct and personalized advertising transmitted through wireless devices.

Mobile Internet: The possibility to access the World Wide Web through a wireless device, such as a cellular telephone or personal digital assistant (PDA).

Mobile Marketing: The application of marketing operations using mobile wireless devices.

SMS: A feature available on modern mobile phones that allow users to send and receive short text messages.

WAP (Wireless Application Protocol): A set of communication protocols that standardise the use of various wireless devices for Internet access.

Chapter XXV
Mobile Direct Marketing

Ralf Wagner
University of Kassel, Germany

Martin Klaus
University of Kassel, Germany

ABSTRACT

The role of mobile terminals such as mobile telephones, or PDAs, is shifting from gadgetry to serious platforms for direct marketing actions. The ubiquitous use of these devices offers companies a perfect medium through which to promote their products and services in a personalized and interactive way. Since mobile phone users are rarely without their mobile phones, mobile electronic devices provide marketers with almost permanent contact opportunities to introduce their products directly to potential clients. Although potential customers are attracted by the promotion of appealing technologies and sophisticated products and services via mobile communication, the intended impact of this direct marketing approach is often thwarted as it is seen by some as invasive and an infringement of privacy. This chapter outlines the opportunities and challenges of mobile technology applications for direct marketing and relates mobile technologies to a scheme of tasks for successful direct marketing. The chapter concludes by highlighting examples to demonstrate ways of conducting successful mobile direct marketing.

INTRODUCTION

Direct marketing activities, by means of communication via mobile devices, can be used either as a self-contained measures or they can be integrated in comprehensive campaigns utilizing several communication channels. In contrast to classic marketing activities, mobile direct marketing benefits from frequent and exclusive attention from the recipients. Early direct marketing applications using mobile devices, listed by Yunos, Gao, and Shim (2003), comprised simple functions providing local entertainment information, stock quotes, dining and restaurant reservation ser-

vices, and wireless couponing (transmitting coupons to the mobile devices). Although vendors' mobile marketing efforts are increasing worldwide, the greater part of their impact is not overwhelming. Currently, the full potential of mobile direct marketing cannot be achieved, as technical, legal, and psychological barriers have yet to be overcome. Indeed, overcoming these barriers is critical for all activities because the exclusive attention of recipients entails an increased likelihood of reactance behavior on the part of the recipients if they feel annoyed by this marketing approach (Li, Edwards, & Lee, 2002; Wehmeyer, 2007). Clearly, to provoke a positive response, the measures need to fit directly with the interests and preferences of the recipients.

In order to guide the development of innovative mobile direct marketing, this chapter is structured as follows: The next section gives an assessment of the relevance of mobile devices for direct marketing purposes, provides a definition of mobile direct marketing and outlines its features. Subsequently, a comparison is made between mobile devices and classic channels of marketing communication. The different services which have turned out to be relevant for direct marketing are outlined and the distinction between push and pull campaigns is introduced. The psychological theories that have been found to explain aspects of users' acceptance of mobile direct marketing measures are briefly summarized in the subsequent section. Building upon these criteria, a four-stage scheme of implementing successful mobile direct marketing campaigns has been derived and this scheme is illustrated with two empirical examples. The last section focuses on the current trends which might affect and shape the future of mobile direct marketing, and draws some final conclusions.

BACKGROUND

Both direct and mobile marketing are becoming more important in terms of marketing budgets (Barwise & Farley, 2005), a tendency which is supported by the increasing popularity of mobile devices. In June 2007, the number of mobile telephone contracts worldwide exceeded the three billion mark, a figure that had trebled since 2001 (EITO 2007). Statistically, almost half the people in the world will be mobile connected by the end of the year. Phenomenally, in some industrial countries like Italy, Sweden and Germany, the number of mobile phones outstrips the number of inhabitants. However, in these countries, mobile services in general have not taken off as expected; their popularity is still restricted to narrow segments of users (Åkesson & Ihlström, 2007). Thus, direct marketing contents have to find and establish their way to the mobile respondents.

The purpose of direct marketing is to establish a relationship with a customer in order to initiate an immediate and measurable response (Kraft, Hesse, Höfling, Peters, & Rinas, 2007; Wagner & Meißner, forthcoming). According to the Mobile Marketing Association (2004), mobile marketing is the use of any mobile medium as a communication and enter-

tainment channel between a brand and an end-user. Mobile marketing is the only personal channel enabling spontaneous, direct, interactive, and targeted communications at any time and anywhere.

Consolidating these two definitions, we refer to mobile direct marketing as follows:

Definition 1 (Mobile Direct Marketing): Mobile Direct Marketing (MDM) is the usage of digital mobile devices to communicate with (potential) customers in a personalized and individual way, anytime and anywhere, in order to stimulate an immediate and measurable response.

From a users' perspective, this way of marketing communication differs from conventional marketing mass communication as well as marketing on the WWW with respect to (Facchetti, Rangone, Renga, & Savoldelli, 2005):

- **Accessibility:** Mobile devices accompany the users most of the day.
- **Personalization:** Mobile devices are usually used by only one identified individual.
- **Location awareness:** Mobile devices are connected in geographic call to a wider telephony network and/or via Bluetooth© to a local area network. This enables a track-down to a user's physical location.

These features give rise to scepticism on the part of many customers toward mobile marketing measures because they increase feelings of intrusiveness perceived by the recipients.

From a technical perspective, mobile devices provide advantages in comparison to e-marketing on the WWW:

- **No booting:** The system is usually in sleep mode (on standby) and immediately available, if needed.
- **No installation or configuration of applications:** The Java standard enables the execution of all programs, regardless of the technical sophistication of the mobile devices.
- **No media change needed:** The recipients might react or interact using the mobile device, if they wish.

However, mobile devices also incur some technical disadvantages:

- The display screens are small and could cause inconsistent formatting as well as color distortion.
- The user frequently has no full keyboard and, consequently, is likely to refuse to complete detailed ordering forms, and so on.
- Depending on the transmission protocol and the capacity of the service provider, the download might be slow. Moreover, the memory and processor power are lower than the capacity of fully equipped personal computers.

Nevertheless, MDM provides vendors with increasing opportunities for a variety of marketing activities. Table 1 provides a comparison of competing channels with respect to the features found to be relevant for marketing communication (modified from Facchetti et al., 2005).

From Table 1, it is obvious that mobile devices are the channel that combines most of the desirable features. Thus, a shift in marketing budgets from e-marketing using the WWW to MDM is likely, but clearly e-marketing will – similar paper-based mails – remain a substantial element of integrated marketing concepts. The suitability of mobile devices for direct marketing originates from the alignment of personal interests with location awareness. Thus, MDM constitutes an alternative to classic marketing using mass media as well as electronic marketing. In the next section, the authors outline the different services and their relevance for MDM.

RELEVACE OF MOBILE SERVICES FOR DIRECT MARKETING

The definition above of MDM is non-technical with respect to ways of establishing customer contacts. Technical improvements like GSM (Global Systems for Mobile Communication), WAP (Wireless Application Protocol), GPRS (General Packet Radio Service) and UMTS (Universal Mobile Telecommunications System) provide marketers with the basis for transmitting innovative MDM communication. The user localization is conducted by GPS (Global Positioning System) or COO (Cell of Origin), or a combination of both (Giaglis, Kourouthanassis, & Tsamakos, 2002). Recipients might walk into a store or mall and be given an advertisement specifically targeted at their location. Another scope is the payment with mobile phones via tickets or vouchers. Table 2 provides an overview of services for establishing and maintaining customer contacts using mobile devices.

1. **Mobile Messaging:** This includes using SMS (Short Messaging Service), MMS (Multimedia Messaging Service), and EMS (Enhanced Messaging Service) to make up a communication process. The main disadvantages of SMS lie in its limited content size and the small screen display of many devices, particularly mobile phones. The MMS aims to overcome this limitation, but this service is more costly (with respect to both transmission fees and product costs) and has not yet gained popularity with recipients, except in Japan and South Korea. There, measures are

Table 1. Profiles of direct marketing communication channels

Marketing channels/ Marketing features	TV	Radio	Press	Billboard	Mailing*	Internet	Mobile
Appeal, Communication	●	◕	◕	◕	●	◕	◓
Interactivity	⊘	⊗	⊘	⊗	⊗	●	●
Timeliness	⊗	◓	◕	◓	◓	○	●
Personalization	◓	○	◓	○	●	●	●
Context sensitivity	◓	◓	○	⊗	⊗	◓	●

Legend: High = ● ; Average = ◕ ; Low = ◓ ; None = ⊗ ; * = paper-based mail

Table 2. MDM services and their popularity

Type of Services	Explication	Relation to MDM	Control of (Inter)action
Mobile Messaging	Sending text, pictures, movies, or sounds	Customer acquisition, relationship retention	Vendor
Mobile Browsing	Mobile Internet services	Opportunity for searching offers and contacting vendors for the customers. Information gathering, comparing offers, agreeing to contracts, etc.	Customer
Mobile Voice	Direct Call, voice recognition	Broadening dialogue, providing further information as well as technical support.	both equally
Enriched services	Special entertainment, use of new technologies (e.g., mobile DVBT-TV)	Customer detection, information gathering to make up interest profiles. Providing incentives for customers to engage in interaction.	Vendor

regarded as being dominated by the vendor, because even in the case where the customer sends the SMS/MMS/EMS (for instance to participate in a raffle), the vendor is known to vet the content of the message.

2. **Mobile Browser:** This includes WAP (Wireless Application Protocol), i-MODE (Internet portal for mobile devices), and PDA (Personal Digital Assistant) to deliver Internet information and data on mobile devices. The mobile browser extends the message-based communication process, but it is still cumbersome to use with ordinary mobile phones. Although the customer is restricted to the content prepared by the vendor, the user dominates by managing the navigation process by predefining the flow of content sifting through in the course of traversing the pages. Furthermore, a clever user might well outsmart the design by using search engines, thus restricting the vendor's influence, and the competing vendor is just one click away. Interestingly, already 92% of Japanese owners of mobile devices, but only 70% of European owners of mobile devices use this service on a regular basis. It is even less popular in Latin America.

3. **Mobile Voice:** This service stems from the initial function of mobile phones. The services take the form of dialogues, used, for example in competition promotions, where customers have to make a call in order to win a prize, order hotlines, and information hotlines. Closely related are voting facilities, where the target group is actively involved with polls by phone. When interaction takes place with humans, vendors and customers have equal impact on the dialogue. This changes when customers interact with answering machines, as the customers' options are inevitably limited by the menu prompting.

4. **Enriched Mobile Marketing Services:** These services differ from those above in that they are they are context sensitive. The context of the recipient might be defined with respect to the time of contact, the activities recently conducted by the user, the interests of the user, or the current location of the user or any combinations of these criteria. These services, particularly those that are time- and location-based, make use of the full potential of mobile direct marketing. At a simple level of the scale, retailers might advertise special offers to customers passing the outlets (Salo & Tähtinen, 2005), but mostly, these precise actions depend on sophisticated intermediary services which:

- Syndicate the users data,
- Control the stream of marketing measures, and
- Provide mobile payment services.

Clearly, these services amalgamate all the advantages of MDM applications to urge the recipients to respond to any offers. Similar to conventional marketing, in MDM, pull and push strategies, outlined in the next section, are used to involve the consumers in special offers or promotions.

PUSH AND PULL STRATEGIES OF MDM

Frequently, vendors utilize additional media, such as coupons or tags (Quick Response Codes, Semacodes) in showcases to promote their mobile marketing campaigns. This marketing approach aims at stimulating consumers' interest and therefore "pull" MDM elements out of the mobile net.

Definition 2 (Pull Elements of MDM): Pull elements of MDM campaigns, according to definition 1, stimulate a response on the part of the recipient to make a request. These elements can be either digital, which can be transmitted to mobile devices, or non-digital, such as coupons giving codes to dial for free gifts.

Conversely, vendors can use mobile devices to make contact and to push the recipient to respond to the initial contact.

Definition 3 (Push Elements of MDM): Push elements of MDM campaigns, according to definition 1, are transmitted with the authorization of the recipient in order to create mutual benefit by providing context sensitive information and response opportunities to the recipients.

Both push and pull MDM strategies have to provide a substantial benefit to the user, the value added, in order to intrigue. If they fail to do this, the user will refuse to respond in the intended way. In the pull strategy, the consumer initiates the digital interaction by means of his mobile device. In the pull strategy, the vendor grasps the nettle, but this requires the permission of the recipient. In direct marketing, two procedures of managing permission are established. The opt-out procedure is appropriate if the vendors are authorized to establish the initial contact unless the recipient denies this. Since an uninvited contact on a mobile device can be considered by some as profound annoyance, national laws frequently require vendors to offer an explicit opt-in option. Table 3 depicts profiles of push and pull MDM measures with respect to the value added, the degree of interactivity, the enabling technology and localization of the user. Additionally, the relevant markets are differentiated with respect to the customer category: organizational customers in a business-to-business (B2B) context have preferences and needs very different from those of private customers (B2C).

Clearly, the two extremes, high-level language and SMS are appropriate for MDM in B2B markets. In these markets, the number of customers usually significantly undercuts the number of customers in B2C markets. This reduces the efforts of high-level language interaction, which might be justified by the higher sales volume per customer. However, examples exist where high-level iterations are not necessary, and where SMS interactions are appropriate: for instance, financial information services offer SMS-based alert services to their organizational clients.

The second row of Table 3 distinguishes four different types of incentives for motivating the recipients to grant this permission. Proving a monetary gratification is one option (e.g., misteradgood.de), but as low amounts are not likely to attract affluent consumers, alternative types of value added are more appropriate for the majority of applications. Technically, the user can subscribe to such services on the mobile net, the WWW or simply by activating the Bluetooth ports of their mobile devices in *Micro area networks* to grant vendors authorization. Vendors can then respond by sending direct marketing media, such as digital coupons to recipients in a very limited area: a mall, for example, or a retail outlet (Salo & Tähtinen, 2005), or the immediate vicinity of an outdoor billboard. Permission is granted by activating the Bluetooth function of the mobile device in combination with indoor billboards at the entrances of the vendors' outlets, malls and other commercial centers. This procedure benefits from time and location awareness.

If a vendor aims to establish a contact with a large number of new customers, who were not involved with offers of this vendor before, a push-strategy may be chosen. Clearly, from the table, the recipients' opt-in is frequently obtained via a conventional channel. In most countries, the national laws stipulate an opt-in procedure also known as *permission marketing*, which means the recipient of the message has consented to receive it (Facchetti et al., 2005). Table 4 provides an overview of the current situation regarding legal procedures in different countries.

Clearly, in conflict with the rules of the European Union (Directive on Privacy and Electronic Communications 2002/58/EC), as well as the rules of the European Free Trade Association (Standing Committee of the EFTA States Ref. 1073426), some of the member countries have not enacted the opt-in legislation. In the US, the CAN-SPAM Act of 2003 applies, and, for instance, Australia's marketers have had to fit their measures to the "Act" since 2003.

Table 3. Profiles of push MDM and pull MDM (modified from Wehmeyer, 2007)

Initiation	Push		Pull	
value added	information	entertainment	raffle	monetary incentive
opt-in	conventional	electronic	mobile	none
degree of interactivity	dialogue	reaction		none
enabling technology	high-level language	WAP	MMS	SMS
positioning	mobile network dependent tech.	specialized positioning system	manual	none
prevailing relevant market	B2B	B2C	B2C	B2B and B2C

To assess the data in Table 4, one should keep in mind that Japan, South Korea and West European Countries are leading the MDM initiative, because it was in these countries that the third-generation (3G) cellular infrastructure – enabling the rich-media mobile marketing services – was established first (OECD, 2006). Thus, obtaining respondents' opt-in is one of the central issues in MDM as the opt-in procedure applies in the most relevant markets.

SINGLE RESPONESE, MULTIPLE RESPONSE, AND VIRAL MARKETING

For both strategy types – pull MDM and push MDM – the decision has to be made as to whether the campaign aims at a single response (mostly a monetary transaction) or a multi-response (establishing an ongoing customer vendor relationship). The former is the mobile version of the traditional marketing approach comprising discrete transactions for each buying situation (see Coviello, Brodie, Danaher, & Johnston, 2002 for a distinction of traditional and modern marketing approaches). According to this approach, no data storage (e.g., the purchase history or preferences already recognized) is needed, because in every purchase situation, all customers are treated like new customers. Consequently, the focus of the vendors relying on this approach is on the identification of mobile users who might be interested, and getting them involved by push MDM measures. The single response approach is appropriate in countries with restrictive privacy protection legislation and in markets where the respondents are anxious to preserve their data privacy.

The latter multiple response measures lead to the modern relationship-centred marketing approaches. Here, the vendors aim to establish a resilient long-term relationship with their customers, which is supported by a mutual commitment of resources. The customers devote time, attention, and data, in addition to the monetary transaction, and benefit from customized products and services. Fast data processing capacity and sophisticated privacy protection are essential, particularly in MDM data storage, to avoid recipient reactance behavior (Mahatanankoon, Wen, & Lim, 2005). If these measures are conducted properly, they are likely to result in superior customer satisfaction and loyalty, not to mention above average national industry profits (Brodie, Winklhofer, Coviello, & Johnston, 2007). The pull approach is frequently used to simulate an initial response by the prospective customers to subscribe to a service, for instance, either free or chargeable. A straightforward development of the multi-response approach is the concept of viral marketing. This concept is mostly related to activities via the WWW, where vendors encourage the recipients of marketing measures to forward messages or even whole digital marketing measures to others (Helm, 2000). As in the spread of viruses, the diffusion of marketing communication within a population is supported by exponential growth of "infectors". This procedure has naturally been adopted in MDM.

Definition 4 (Viral MDM): Digital MDM elements offering additional value by means of information or entertainment for the recipients are passed to members of the recipients' social networks by using local area network interfaces of mobile devices.

This procedure offers several benefits:

- **No authorization is needed:** Since the recipients are forwarding the digital contents, the originating vendor does not need authorization.
- **Increased appreciation:** The elements are regarded as gadgets (e.g., ring tones or games) rather than marketing communications.
- **Undermining the discrimination of advertising:** Since short, self-produced films, for example, recorded using the camera of modern mobile phones, are in the same digital formats and distributed using the same interfaces, advertising becomes a regular part of the content of social network communities.
- **Avoiding transmission costs:** The local area networks, as well as personal area networks, typically do not involve any services of the telephone network provider. Consequently, the mobile network provider does not charge fees for distributing the gadgets.

In contrast to conventional word-of-mouth communication, the position of the sender with social sphere is not so important, because the quality of the digital gadget and the value added might compensate for a lower persuasive power of an individual. Thus, viral MDM does not depend on the engagement of opinion leaders, but can consider recipients as "customer salesmen".

In the next section, a framework derived form the psychology literature is outlined to explain the acceptance of or reactance toward MDM. This framework is used to derive a scheme of tasks that have to be tackled for successful MDM.

A SCHEME OF TASKS FOR SUCCESSFUL MDM

From a psychological perspective, several competing theories explaining the acceptance of innovative marketing and related phenomena of reactance toward marketing measures, are discussed in the literature. The most prominent of these are the Reactance Theory by Brehm (1966), the Theory of Planned Behavior (TPB) by Ajzen (1985), Technology Acceptance Model (TAM) by Davis (1989), and the decomposed TPB by Taylor and Todd (1995).

With respect to MDM, we define reactance precisely:

Definition 5 (Reactance toward MDM): Reactance toward MDM is the repudiation of MDM measures and the antagonism toward all (re)actions intended by MDM measures because of the subjective perception of any relevant restrictions of the enjoyed freedom of the recipients.

Reactance arises from recipients classifying the MDM measures as spam, or even worse, as nuisance. The spam problem is more serious in mobile marketing than in e-marketing of conventional direct marketing, because mobile devices frequently attract the exclusive attention of the recipients and force them to interrupt

Table 4. The status of opt-in in different countries (data from Stratil & Weissenburger, 2002 and EuroCauce, 2007)

Countries where "Opt-in" legislation has been enacted.	Austria, Denmark, Finland, Germany, Greece, Hungary, Italy , Japan, Norway, Poland, Slovenia, South Korea, Spain, USA.
Countries where "Opt-in" legislation is under consideration.	Belgium, Estonia, France, Russia, Sweden.
Countries where "Opt-in" legislation has not been enacted.	Albania, Armenia, Azerbaijan, Bosnia & Herzegovina, Belarus, Bulgaria, Croatia, Cyprus, Czech Republic, Georgia, Iceland, Ireland, Israel, Latvia, Liechtenstein, Lithuania, Luxembourg, Macedonia, Malta, Moldova, Netherlands, Portugal, Romania, Slovakia, Switzerland, Turkey, Ukraine, United Kingdom, Serbia and Montenegro.

their activities. Clearly, such a restriction of recipients' sovereignty of time and attention is unlikely to lead to intended marketing success. This problem arises from the deficit in assessing the recipients' current situation. Measures which might be welcome in a situation where a recipient is waiting for something, will be considered as annoyance in situations where the recipient is busy. This directly links to the TPB, which emphasizes the link of attitudes to behavior. A positive attitude toward MDM measures increases the likelihood of the intended reaction on the part of the recipient. Creating a positive attitude is achieved mainly by offering entertainment or information in a manner whereby using this channel increases the perceived self efficiency of the recipient.

From the TPB viewpoint, it is known that MDM measures need to fit the actual context (time, location, and interests) of the recipients to avoid the boomerang effect of reactance. Clearly, the pull approach is advantageous. In the light of empirical studies of the TAM and the decomposed TPB (e.g., Pagani, 2004; Hung & Chang, 2005; Scharl, Dickinger & Murphy, 2005), the perceived ease of use and the perceived usefulness are critical determinants for the success of MDM measures.

The conceptual implications of the psychological foundations are summarized in Figure 1.

The left-hand side of the figure lists the design features of MDM, which have been found to have significant impact on the latent level of beliefs. Their relation to latent constructs, in the center of the figure, are assessed using the psychometric measurement techniques (confirmatory factor analysis), but this is restricted to (market) research investigations and not feasible for a permanent control of MDM. In the decomposed TPB, the set of beliefs is split into components, which are largely consistent with the TAM, except the compatibility is added. Moreover, in the decomposed TPB, social norms are considered explicitly. These make up the peer influence as well as the superior influence. All latent impacts are depicted in the center pillar of the figure. These need to be taken into account by the vendors in order to increase the users' acceptance and to reduce reactance of the recipients. On the right-hand side of the figure, the different kinds of MDM success are listed. Needless to say, the success assessment, which is needed to control and coordinate all MDM activities, should fit the aims of the MDM campaign.

According to the components of MDM success depicted in Figure 1, the following steps need to be accomplished:

In the next section, this process is illustrated using two successful examples of MDM marketing.

EXAMPLES FOR SUCCESSFUL MOBILE MARKETING

Example 1: Coca Cola in Austria

Coca Cola is a prominent example of frequently bought packaged goods, for which the classic transaction marketing approach is said to be most relevant (Coviello et al., 2002). Consequently, the brand is in danger of suffering from low customer retention and high exchangeability. Moreover, fierce competition is likely to impact on prices and, therefore, reduce profits for manufactures and retailers. To overcome these challenges, the brand Coca Cola aimed to maintain its position in Europe as a quality leader in the majority of retail outlets und in all lifestyle-related pubs and discothèques, as well as cinemas. The brand's positioning is maintained by accentuating fun, light-heartedness, and youthfulness in mass-media communication. Additionally, a broad range of lifestyle-related events were sponsored, or even created, by the agencies engaged in the marketing of this brand. In June 2001, Coca Cola was one of the first companies to accomplish an MDM campaign and achieve success.

According to the scheme depicted in Table 5, the goal of this campaign was to get closer to the customers and remain in their minds as symbol of a hot lifestyle. The target recipients were "young people of all ages" aiming to distinguish themselves from others by exploiting the full potential of their modern mobile devices. For the three-month duration of the campaign, the customers could register via SMS with an alpha-numeric code printed inside the cap of the bottles for a lottery which raffled 380 prizes every day.

According to the goals of the campaign, the success was measured by the number of consumers who became involved in the measures.

To define the content-related issues to reach the customer, Coca Cola needed to understand what the interests of these young consumers were and what caught their attention. Initially, measures were not customized. The interaction was restricted to 160 symbols available in SMS interaction, and there was no opportunity for the customers to acknowledge their interests in different kinds of winnings. Clearly, this has changed since. The modern version of these codes in the bottle are "Coke Coins", which reduce the price and give gadgets offered by the Coca Cola Company webpage.

The technical implementation was done by simply using a database comprising users' data. The users were notified by SMS whether or not they had won one of the prizes.

To establish the recipients' recognition, the company made daily contact with their customers by sending SMS messages. To avoid reactance, they implemented a Coke-to-consumer interaction, which ensured an answer within a maximum of 15 seconds, informing them if they had won or not. The opt-in of the customers is provided by initially sending the code. In the first response, they were asked if they would like to be informed about further promotions by Coca Cola. With the "code in the bottle", the Coca Cola Company convinced consumers to opt-in and assigned the control to them, which resulted in a positive impact. Since the members of the target group were eager to enhance their social recognition by participating in the campaign, no special infringements had to be taken into account.

The company directed the customers' interests by promoting the campaign on TV and radio, at point-of-sale events and, of course, on the label of the bottle itself. Thus, according to definition 2, this measure is a pull MDM measure.

The assessment of success at the end of the campaign turned out to be positive. Out of 2,484,458 participants, 97% responded by mobile phone and 3% over the Internet, and in the end, there were 802,375 happy lottery winners. The number of interactions between the consumers and the Coca Cola Company exceeded 7,200,000 SMS messages sent back and forth. This response overshot expectations fivefold.

Example 2: Mona Lisa Smile

To promote this movie, a viral MDM marketing campaign was organized. Similar to the Coca Cola campaign outlined above, the respondents were invited to participate in a lottery, but in order to do so, they needed to make up groups of four members.

The aim of this campaign was not only to attract potential movie-goers to this movie, but also to encourage them to discuss the movie with their friends afterwards. This is an example of viral MDM according to definition 4.

The campaign was launched prior to the first showing of the movie in the cinemas and targeted female movie enthusiasts in the age range of 14-25 years. The target group was selected from a database "B!Direct", which comprises individuals who have agreed to receive marketing measures on their mobile devices. The campaign was designed as push MDM according

Figure 1. Making up the MDM success (modified from Balasubrmanian, Peterson, & Jarvenpaa, 2002; Pagani, 2004 and Scharl et al., 2005)

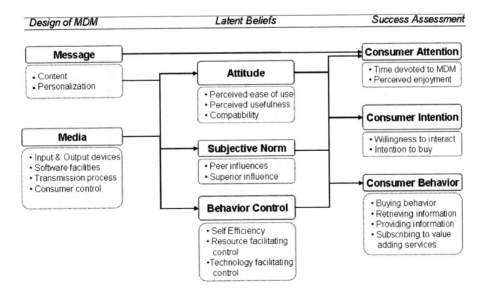

Table 5. Task scheme for successful MDM

1	**Definition of goals**
1.1 1.2 1.3 1.4	List the objectives that should be achieved. Define one or more groups of recipients with relevance for achieving the goals. Commit the time period in which the goal should be achieved. Predefine metrics for a success assessment.
2	**Definition of content-related issues**
2.1 2.2 2.3	Identify interests and select topics. Decide on the extent of desirable customizing. Choose the technological features for implementation.
3	**Setting up the recipients' recognition process to avoid reactance and increase acceptance**
3.1 3.2 3.3	Evaluate subjective norms prevailing in the target group(s) and check for infringements. Define arguments to change the recipients' attitudes positively and establish ways to communicate these (off- or online). Explicate the recipients' opportunities of behavior control, particularly the individual self efficiency.
4	**Controlling of the campaign**
4.1 4.2 4.3	Define routines for success assessment. Identify parameters for adjustment. Evaluate the expiration date regularly.

to definition 3. The initial invitation to participate was sent as an SMS linked to a landing page on the Web, specifically designed for display on mobile devices. On this page, the recipients were informed about the opportunity to invite their friends to participate in the lottery. The success of the campaign was assessed by the number of responses and the number of groups participating in the lottery.

With respect to the content-related issues, the vendor already catered for the interests of the respondents in the definition of the target group. Similar to the first example, the messages had not been customized for individual respondents. However, the campaign achieved a response rate of 4.25% of all SMS messages sent out. Of the respondents, 28.22% subscribed to a newsletter, thus enabling a continuing customer relationship. An additional 5% response was created by the viral effect of inviting friends (data from Holland & Bammel, 2006).

These effects appear to be moderate but reasonable. The viral element of the campaign is particularly low because initially, respondents had to provide the phone numbers of their friends in order to participate in the lottery, a requirement that is likely to cause reactance and reduce rather than enforce positive attitudes.

FUTURE DIRECTION

Several trends related to MDM are emerging in the contemporary usage of mobile devices.

- *Integrating mobile devices in conventional retail transactions.* The personalization of mobile devices enables the payment for goods, similar to the credit card method: the amount invoiced is added to the telephone operator's bill. This feature becomes relevant for serving customers without a credit card (minors, members of low income groups, etc.) or individuals under obligation to provide their credit card details for particular purposes.
- *Yield management for services vendors.* An increasing number of services providers adopt flexible pricing strategies to assimilate to the actual use of capacity. Because of location awareness, MDM becomes an excellent channel for communicating special offers to a selected set of customers living close to the vendor's location. For instance, restaurants and cinemas might optimize their client attendances by offering special deals to selected recipients only.
- *Tagging.* An increasing number of products are tagged with a two-dimensional barcode

(e.g., Semacodes), which can be recognized by mobile devices. These codes enable the retrieval of further information related to the product, as well as activating an order process if the item is for sale. Using this highly innovative method, consumers may even place orders immediately for goods shown on billboards.

- *Retrieving best prices in bargaining situations.* Nowadays, many consumers are familiar with price comparison platforms (e.g., bestprice.com, priceline.com or geizhals.at). These platforms also offer mobile interfaces, which enable consumers to retrieve the best prices by using their mobile devices in arbitrary bargaining situations when, for example, they are in a retail outlet.

- *Compensating for weak social status of communicators.* In the classic concept of viral marketing, the status of a communicator (e.g., opinion leaders or technical experts) has been argued to be important for the coverage of measures. The value offered by MDM gadgets (e.g., information or entertainment) might compensate for a lower status of the communicator, because the customer will welcome and distribute the gadgets with respect to the values offered and not with reference to the communicator. A prominent example of this phenomenon is the "Moorhuhn" game, which was created to support a whiskey brand, but then became the most popular online game in Germany.

CONCLUSION

The contribution of this chapter outlines the opportunities and challenges of mobile devices for direct marketing applications. Both are related to a high level of personalization, a high level of accessibility and the location awareness of mobile devices. These features facilitate a close interaction with recipients, and ultimate benefits from their virtually exclusive attention. Clearly, this implies the danger of increased intrusiveness perceived by the recipients if the marketing measures do not fit their interests and needs. Building upon results from psychological research, mainly the Reactance Theory, Theory of Planned Behavior and the Technology Acceptance Model, we derived a four-stage scheme for successful mobile direct marketing. This scheme is aimed at supporting vendors to overcome the current gap between the opportunities provided by modern mobile technologies and actual consumer

behavior. A comparison of mobile devices with classic marketing media lends support to the proposition that mobile direct marketing will become more accepted by many consumers and, therefore, become more relevant for all vendors striving to establish enduring relationships with their customers.

REFERENCES

Ajzen, I. (1985). From intensions to actions: A theory of planned behaviour. In J. Kuhl, and J. Beckmann (Eds.), *In action control: From cognition to behavior* (11-39). New York: Springer.

Åkesson M., & Ihlström, E. C. (2007). The vision of ubiquitous media services: How close are we? *In Proceedings of HCI International*. Bejing.

Balasubramanian S., Peterson R. A., & Jarvenpaa S. L. (2002). Exploring the implications of m-commerce for markets and marketing. *Journal of the Academy of Marketing Science, 30*(4), 348-361.

Barwise, P., & Farley, J. U. (2005). The state of interactive marketing in seven countries: Interactive marketing comes of age. *Journal of Interactive Marketing, 19*(3), 67-80.

Brehm, J. W. (1966). *A Theory of Psychological Reactance*. New York: Academic Press.

Brodie R. J., Winklhofer H., Coviello N. E., & Johnston W. J. (2007). Is E-Marketing coming of age? An examination of the penetration of e-marketing and firm performance. *Journal of Interactive Marketing, 21*(1), 2-21.

Coviello, N. E., Brodie, R. J., Danaher, P. J., & Johnston, W. J. (2002). How firms relate to their markets: An empirical examination of contemporary marketing practices. *Journal of Marketing, 66*(3), 33-46.

Davis, F. D. (1989). Perceived usefulness, perceived ease of use, and user acceptance of information technology. *MIS Quarterly, 13*(3), 319-340.

EC (2002). Directive 2002/58/EC of the European parliament and of the council of oktober 1995 concerning the processing of personal data and the protection of privacy in the electronic communications sector. *Official Journal of the European Communities,* (L) 201/37.

EFTA (2007). EEA EFTA position on the proposal for a directive of the European Parliament and of the council amending directive 89/552/EC; Television without frontiers directive (TVWF Directive). Geneva.

EITO (2007). *European Information Technology Observatory*. Frankfurt: EITO EEIG.

EuroCauce (2007). *Opt-in versus opt-out*. Retrieved October 12, 2007, from http://www.euro.cauce.org/en/optinvsoptout.html.

Facchetti, A., Rangone, A., Renga, F. M., & Savoldelli, A. (2005). Mobile marketing: An analysis of key success factors and the European value chain. *International Journal of Management and Decision Making*, 6(1), 65-80.

Giaglis, G. M., Kourouthanassis, P., & Tsamakos, A. (2002). Towards a classification framework for mobile location services. In Mennecke, B. E. & Strader, T. J. (Eds.), *Mobile Commerce: Technology, Theory, and Applications*. Hershey: Idea Group Publishing.

Helm, S. (2000). Viral Marketing: Establishing Customer Relationships by 'Word-of-mouse. *Electronic Commerce and Marketing*, 10(3), 158 – 161.

Holland, H., & Bammel K. (2006). *Mobile Marketing*. Munich: Vahlen.

Hung S.-Y., & Chang C.-M. (2005). User acceptance of WAP services: Test of competing theories. *Computer Standards & Interfaces*, 27, 359-370.

Krafft, M., Hesse, J., Höfling, J., Peters, K., & Rinas, D. (2007). *International Direct Marketing Principles, Best Practices, Marketing Facts*. New York, Springer.

Li, H., Edwards S. M., & Lee J.-H. (2002). Measuring the Intrusiveness of advertisements: Scale development and validation. *Journal of Advertising*, 31(2), 37-47.

Mahatanankoon, P., Wen, H. J., & Lim, B. (2005). Consumer-based m-commerce: exploring consumer perception of mobile applications. *Computer Standards & Interfaces*, 27(4), 347-357.

Mobile Marketing Association (2004). *What is Mobile Marketing?* Retrieved September 2, 2007, from http://www.mmaglobal.com.

OECD (2006). *Mobile commerce DSTI/CP(2006/7) final*. Retrieved October 17, 2007, from http://www.oecd.org/dataoecd/22/52/38077227.pdf .

Pagani, M. (2004). Determinants of adoption of third generation mobile multimedia services. *Journal of Interactive Marketing*, 18(3), 46-59.

Salo, J., & Tähtinen, J. (2005). Retailer use of permission-based mobile advertising. In Clarke III, I & Flaherty, TB (eds.), *Advances in Electronic Marketing*. Hershey, PA: Idea Publishing Group.

Scharl A., Dickinger A., & Murphy J. (2005). Diffusion and success factors of mobile marketing. *Electronic Commerce Research and Applications*, 4, 159-173.

Spam Act (2003). No. 129, 2003, 01.07.2005. Retrieved September 30, 2007, from

http://www.comlaw.gov.au/comlaw/legislation/act-compilation1.nsf/0/

DED153276FD7C6F9CA2570260013908A/$file/SpamAct03WD02.pdf.

Stratil A., & Weissenburger, E.-M. (2002), *Telekommunikationsgesetz* (telecommunication law). Vienna: Manz. Taylor, S., & Todd, P. A. (1995). Understanding information technology usage: A test of competing models. *Information Systems Research*, 6(2), 144-176.

Wagner, R., & Meißner M. (forthcoming). Multimedia for direct marketing. In Pagani, M. (Ed.): *Encyclopaedia of Multimedia Technology and Networking* (2nd Edition). Hershey: Idea Publishing.

Wehmeyer, K. (2007). Mobile ad intrusiveness: The effects of message type and situation. *In Proceedings of the 20th Bled eConference (June 4-6, 2007)*, Slovenia. Yunos, H. M., Gao, J., & Shim, S. (2003). Wireless advertising. *IEEE Computer*, 36(5), 30-37.

KEY TERMS

Opt-In Procedure: The consumer enables direct marketing communication by subscribing in a list or sending a query that he is willing to receive advertisements via e-mail, SMS, etc. For an increasing number of countries, the opt-in is required for direct marketing measures with high perceived intrusiveness by law.

Opt-Out Procedure: Consumers who are not interested in particular marketing measures, or in direct marketing measures in general, can subscribe to a list, which is checked by commercial address brokers.

Permission Marketing: Consumers provide their explicit permission to the contractor to receive advertisements. Most common are newsletters and catalogues, but also phone calls and mobile marketing measures.

Pull Marketing: Focuses the communication channel on the buying public who demand the products from the retailers. This way, the products are pulled through the channel of distribution.

Push Marketing: Focuses the communication channel on retailers to cause them to list the offered products and services and, thus, make them available to the customers. This way, the products and services are pushed through the channel of distribution.

Technology Acceptance Model (TAM): The TAM was initially proposed by Davis (1989). It comprises two beliefs, the *perceived utilities* and the *perceived ease of application*, which determine attitudes to adopt new technologies. The attitude toward adoption will decide about the adopter's positive or negative behavior in the future concerning new technology.

Value Added/Perceived Usefulness: Describes the utility for the customers provided by mobile direct marketing measures, e.g., games, pictures or ring tones.

Viral Marketing: Is the technique to animate and motivate the customer to recommend products voluntarily to others. For example, catching ideas for a product or its advertisement becomes like a "virus" that spreads in an epidemic manner.

Chapter XXVI
Mobile Commerce Adoption in Spain:
The Influence of Consumer Attitudes and ICT Usage Behaviour

Joaquin Aldas-Manzano
University of Valencia, Spain

Carla Ruiz-Mafe
University of Valencia, Spain

Silvia Sanz-Blas
University of Valencia, Spain

ABSTRACT

The chapter aims to present an in-depth study of the factors influencing mobile commerce adoption. The authors analyze the influence of Mobile use experience, ICT ownership, Mobile affinity and Mobile Commerce compatibility in the m-commerce adoption decision. After identifying the key drivers of Mobile shopping adoption, the second part of the chapter presents an empirical study of the Spanish market. Results based on a sample of 470 Mobile users show that Mobile affinity, ICT ownership, and m-shopping compatibility are positive key drivers of M-shopping adoption. Mobile use experience has no significant influence on m-shopping adoption. This chapter will give managers and students insight into the Mobile Commerce industry and the different factors that influence m-commerce adoption. In addition, these factors can be applied to the specific context of the Spanish market.

INTRODUCTION

Information and Computer Technologies (ICTs) are currently experiencing spectacular growth, especially as they enter our homes. People are becoming increasingly familiar with the use of Internet and also the new mobile terminals such as personal data assistants.

With the rapid development of modern wireless communication technology, coupled with the increasingly high penetration rate of Internet, M-commerce is becoming increasingly important for firms and consumers (Nysveen, Pedersen and Thorbjorsen, 2007; Wu and Wang, 2005; Yang, 2005). According to Wireless Week (2004) there were 94.9 million M-

Commerce users worldwide in 2003 and the segment is expected to grow to 1.67 billion by 2008. Global income from M-Commerce was $6.86 billion in 2003 and is expected to reach $554.37 billion in 2008 (Wireless Week, 2004).

Unctad (2002) defines M-commerce as the buying and selling of goods and services using wireless hand-held devices such as mobile telephones or personal data assistants (PDAs). Such transactions include mobile banking, investing, shopping and services. This chapter accordingly defines M-shopper as "the consumer who buys goods and services by using mobile access to computer-mediated networks with the help of an electronic device".

A Mobile service is an activity or series of intangible activities that occur when mobile consumers interact with service providers. There are various categories of Mobile services (Rao and Troshani, 2007): (i) mobile content and information services (map and location-based services, news, personalization and entertainment content downloads) that make information available to mobile users; (ii) messaging services (SMS), multimedia messaging services (MMS) and email that enable the exchange of text and multimedia information; (iii) transaction-based services that enable transactions such as mobile banking.

The increased mobile usage in recent years is a clear example of the growth of mobile services as it offers significant opportunities as independent sales channel – deserving special attention from researchers. While published work on M-commerce applications and technologies and the different mobile operators and their services is becoming more abundant and representative, there is a lack of sufficient literature on the profile of users who buy products/services through the different mobile operators and on the analysis of the factors which most influence M-commerce patronage.

Insufficient user acceptance has long been an obstacle to the successful adoption of information technologies. As the future commercial success of Mobile technologies and applications depends to some extent on whether current Mobile users also use this medium for product purchases, it becomes crucial for managers to analyze which variables determine M-commerce adoption in order to assign resources effectively to obtain competitive advantages.

Previous research into Mobile Commerce has mainly focused on its adoption in the context of high E-commerce adoption rates regions such as Norway or Finland (Nysveen et al., 2007; Skog, 2002) and to a lesser extent in developing regions such as Taiwan (Wu and Wang, 2004; Luarn and Lin, 2004). This study offers an insight into Mobile Commerce adoption in Spain, which has not previously been investigated.

The chapter aims to present an in-depth study of the factors influencing Mobile Commerce adoption. The chapter's specific goals are to:

i.   provide a holistic view of factors influencing Mobile Commerce adoption
ii.   identify consumer segments more likely to adopt Mobile Commerce services
iii. analyse the impact of the consumer psychological attitudes and ICT usage behaviour that encourage and discourage customers to adopt Mobile Commerce
iv.   provide empirical research on the Spanish market that analyses the influence of Mobile use experience, ICT ownership, Mobile affinity and Mobile Commerce compatibility, in the M-Commerce adoption decision

BACKGROUND: KEY DRIVERS OF MOBILE COMMERCE ADOPTION

Past research has identified a number of behavioural and attitudinal factors predetermining Mobile Commerce adoption by consumers. This section shows a description of the impact of ICT ownership, Mobile use experience, M-commerce Compatibility and Mobile affinity on Mobile Commerce adoption.

ICT Ownership

The literature review shows that distance shoppers enjoy using direct shopping media (Park and Kim, 2003), are more innovative than non distance shoppers (Donthu and García, 1999) and often use other technologies as well (Eastlick and Lotz, 1999).

Rogers (1995) argues that "the adoption of one new technology may trigger the adoption of several others in a cluster which consists of one or more distinguishable elements of technology that are perceived as being interrelated". The technology cluster concept has been used to examine the adoption of videotext (Etteman, 1984), cable television (La Rose and Atkin, 1992), E-Commerce (Eastin, 2002) and M-Commerce (Yang, 2005). This concept posits that consumers are likely to adopt a technology offering the same functions as those already adopted.

M-commerce is a technology developed from computer and communication technologies (Yang, 2005). Therefore it is to be expected than consumers who adopt similar technologies like PDAs, laptop computers or GPRS mobile phone, should be more likely to adopt M-commerce.

Mobile Use Experience

An influential factor in consumer attitude to distance shopping is exposure to technology. Previous studies show that as exposure to technologies increases, so does the likelihood of developing favourable attitudes to distance shopping channels (Yoon, Cropp and Cameron, 2002).

Distance shoppers modify their behaviour and responses to marketing actions as their experience of the new environments increases (Dahlen, 2002). For example, expert Internet shoppers surf more rapidly, their sessions are shorter, they visit a very small number of particular websites and enjoy their surfing experience more than novice shoppers (Csikszentmihaly, 1997). Another example is of teleshopping, wherein it has been shown that teleshoppers watch significantly more television than non teleshoppers and have greater teleshopping genre exposure (Eastlick and Lotz, 1999; Grant et al., 1999). Bigné, Ruiz and Sanz (2007) found that length of Mobile use influences positively both on frequency of M-commerce and M-commerce future intention.

Therefore, it is to be expected that Mobile use experience influences positively M-commerce adoption.

Mobile Affinity

Media affinity has been conceptualised as the importance of a medium in the lives of the individuals (Perse, 1986; Rubin, 1977). Media affinity has been utilized to assess the attitudes of individuals towards a medium and its content. There is evidence that the closer an individual's relationship with a medium, the greater the probability of purchase based on the content observed (Ball-Rokeach, 1985). Previous studies have found a positive, significant association between affinity and levels of televiewing (Rubin, 1977; Rubin and Perse, 1988; Perse, 1986). It has also been found that this variable is one of the most significant predictors for certain medium relations such as dependency, parasocial interaction or cultivation effects (Perse, 1986). Bigné, Ruiz and Sanz (2007) found that there is a positive correlation between Mobile affinity and

M-commerce patronage. This leads us to suggest that Mobile affinity has a favourable influence on M-commerce adoption.

Compatibility

Innovation diffusion literature suggests that the following perceived innovation attributes have an impact on the rate of innovation diffusion: relative advantage, compatibility, complexity, divisibility (trialability) and communicability. These characteristics are used to explain the user adoption and decision making process. Results from previous studies found that compatibility, complexity and relative advantage are the most important predictors of innovation adoption (Agarwal and Prasa, 1998; Wu and Wang, 2005).

Compatibility has been defined as "the degree to which an innovation is consistent with adopters' behaviour patterns, life-styles and values" (Holak and Lehmann, 1990). Research by Wu and Wang (2005) found that Mobile Commerce compatibility had a positive and strong influence on behavioural intention to M-commerce. Therefore, it is to be expected that M-commerce compatibility influences M-commerce adoption decision.

THE CASE OF SPANISH MOBILE USERS

After identifying the key drivers of M-commerce adoption, the second part of the chapter presents an empirical study of the Spanish market.

At present, the Spanish mobile market has a penetration rate of 91.63% with 39.4 million mobile subscribers (CMT, 2006). Spain has four mobile operators: *Orange, Movistar, Vodafone* and *Yoigo*. With more than 18 million subscribers and a 48% market share, Telefónica MoviStar dominates the Spanish market. Around 60% of Spanish end-users are prepaid users, but the trend is downward as the result of improved contract conditions to gain user loyalty.

The conceptual model of Mobile Commerce adoption which is contrasted with the Spanish market (see Figure 1) is an outcome of the literature review presented above.

The quantitative analysis provides answers to the following research questions:

a. Are there 'more compatible' consumers with respect to M-commerce than others? Does that

Figure 1. Conceptual model

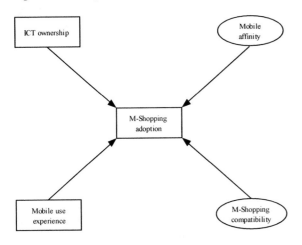

compatibility influence M-commerce adoption?

b.   Does the household degree of electronic devices ownership influence M-commerce for Spanish consumers?

c.   How does Mobile use experience influence M-commerce adoption?

d.   What are the effects of Mobile affinity on decision to purchase using the Mobile phone?

METHODOLOGY

The sample consisted in 470 mobile users selected on a convenience basis. This non-probabilistic sampling method is frequently used in this kind of studies (Harris et al., 2005; Lee et al., 2002). The fieldwork was developed in Spain from April to June 2006 and the sample included both M-shoppers and non M-shoppers. A questionnaire with close-ended questions was used for this study. Forms were delivered to and collected from volunteer participants over 14 years old.

Constructs and the other variables of the model are operationalised from existing measures developed in previous research. The measures have also been adapted and modified to fit the purposes of the present study.

A variable which captures the importance of a medium for the individual is affinity. A 5 item scale from previous studies was used to measure Mobile affinity (Perse, 1986; Bigné, Ruiz and Sanz, 2007) as shown in Table 1 (see below). Evaluation for each item ranged from 1 "totally disagree" to 5 "totally

agree". Respondents were also asked to indicate if they own 15 devices listed in Table 1 (Yang, 2005). ICT ownership was measured as the arithmetic sum of the number of devices owned by the respondent. Mobile use experience was measured following the same criteria used in other research work (Bigné et al., 2007) that use variables relating to seniority with media use to measure this concept. Mobile commerce compatibility was measured via a two item scale based on research by Wu and Wang (2005).

M-commerce adoption was determined by the response to the question "Have you ever purchased any product or service through the Mobile?" The answers were Yes or No.

Table 1 displays demographic and usage variables associated with the sample. Respondents were mainly young (69% below 30 years old) and well-educated (68.2% secondary level or above) Mobile users. Most of the respondents had never used their mobile to buy any kind of product or service (71.3%). A high percentage of the sample is composed of heavy-Mobile users (65.4% use the Mobile more than 3 times a day and 69.6% have over 3 years of Mobile use experience). Table 1 shows that Mobile users attach medium importance (affinity) to the Mobile and medium levels of M-commerce compatibility. Participants where asked whether they owned a list of ICTs, ranging from GRPS mobile phone, 3G mobile phone, VCD player, DVD player, MP3 player, Minidisc player, fax machine, CD walkman, CD-RW, MD placer, Digital camera, Laptop computer, Videogame playstation, Personal Digital Assistant and TDT . As to past adoption of technological innovations, DVD player (79.6%), VCD player (65.2%), digital camera (65%) and CD-RW were the devices with the highest adoption rate.

As Table 2 shows, rings (22.5%), logos (17.0%) and mp3 songs (16.8%) were the more frequently acquired services through the Mobile shopping channel. The mobile is also used to top up credit (12.1%) and send SMS to vote (9.6%) or take part in prize draws (8.9%). These are low cost products which considerably reduces the perceived purchase risk.

RESULTS

Reliability and Validity Assessment

The Mobile Affinity and M-commerce compatibility scales were analysed statistically, verifying their multidimensionality and compliance with the psycho-

Table 1. Profile of respondents

Measure	Items	% (N= 470)
Gender	Male	54.0
	Female	46.0
	Total	100.0
Education	Under Primary	2.5
	Primary	29.3
	Secondary	38.7
	University	29.5
	Total	100.0
Age	14-19	36.3
	20-29	32.7
	30-39	10.6
	40-49	9.3
	50-59	9.6
	60 and older	1.5
	Total	100.0
Patronage	M-Shoppers	28.7
	Non M-Shoppers	71.3
	Total	100.0
Frequency of mobile use	More than 10 times a day	16.8
	Between 5 & 10 times a day	24.6
	Between 3 & 4 times a day	24.0
	Between 1 & 2 times a day	18.7
	Several times a week	12.1
	Once a week	1.3
	Twice a month	1.5
	Less frequently	1.0
Length of mobile use	Less than 1 year	2.8
	Between 1 and 2 years	10.4
	Between 2 and 3 years	17.2
	Between 3 and 5 years	33.4
	Between 5 and 8 years	30.2
	Over 8 years	6.0

Table 1. continued

ICT ownership	GRPS mobile phone	41.0
	3G mobile phone	16.6
	VCD player	65.2
	DVD player	79.6
	MP3 player	49.0
	Minidisc player	12.8
	fax machine	16.1
	CD walkman	36.3
	CD-RW	58.0
	MD player	47.1
	Digital camera	65.0
	Laptop computer	30.1
	Videogame playstation	44.6
	Personal Digital Assistant	9.1
	TDT	27.6
Mobile affinity (Mean)	Using the Mobile is one of my main daily activities	2.72
	If the Mobile is down I really miss it	3.03
	The Mobile is important in my life	3.04
	I can't go for several days without using the Mobile	3.04
	I would be lost without the Mobile	2.66
M-commerce compatibility (Mean)	Using M-Commerce is compatible with the way I like shopping.	2.04
	Using M-Commerce fits with my lifestyle	2.14

metric properties established by the literature. Both scales were applied to Spanish Mobile users. To assess measurement reliability and validity, a confirmatory factor analysis (CFA) containing the two multi-item constructs in our framework (affinity and compatibility) was estimated with EQS 6.1 using the maximum likelihood method.

An initial CFA led to the deletion of 1 item of Mobile affinity based on non-significant or low loading estimates (below .50), patterns of residuals and Lagrange multiplier tests (Anderson and Gerbing, 1988). The results of the final CFA are reported in Table 3 and suggest that our final measurement model provides a good fit to the data on the basis of a number of fit statistics. As evidence of convergent validity the CFA results indicate that all items are significantly ($p<.01$) related to their hypothesized factors, and all the standardized loadings are higher than .60 (Bagozzi and Yi, 1988) and item-to-factor loading averages are higher than .70 (Hair, Anderson, Tatham and Black, 1998).

Table 3 also demonstrates the high internal consistency of the constructs. In each case, Cronbach's alpha exceeded Nunnally and Bernstein's (1994) recommendation of .70. Composite reliability represents the shared variance among a set of observed variables measuring an underlying construct (Fornell and Larcker, 1981). Generally, a composite reliability of at least .60 is considered desirable (Bagozzi and Yi, 1988). This requirement is met for every factor. Average variance extracted (AVE) was also calculated for each construct, resulting in AVEs greater than .50 (Fornell and Larcker, 1981). Evidence for discriminant validity of the measures was provided in two ways. First, none of the 95 per cent confidence intervals of the individual elements of the latent factor correlation

Table 2. Products and services purchased

Acquired products or services	Logos	17.0
	Rings	22.5
	Songs	16.8
	Videos	5.7
	Tickets	1.3
	Mobile credit for calls	12.1
	Vending products	0.8
	News	4.0
	SMS to vote in a TV program	9.6
	SMS to participate in a draw	8.9
	None	71.3

matrix [.32;.57] contained a value of 1.0 (Anderson and Gerbing, 1988). Second, the shared variance between pairs of constructs (.21) was always less than the corresponding AVE (Fornell and Larcker, 1981). On the basis of these criteria, we concluded that the measures in the study provided sufficient evidence of reliability, convergent and discriminant validity.

Model Testing

We tested the proposed conceptual model (Figure 2) using structural equation modelling. The empirical estimates for the main-effects model are shown in Figure 2. The results indicate that the data fit our conceptual model acceptably (S-Bχ2=43.90, df=20, p<.01; root mean square error of approximation [RMSEA]=.053; Non-Normed Fit Index [NNFI]=.963; Comparative Fit Index [CFI]=.980).

The SEM analysis reported in Figure 2 shows that Mobile affinity (β=.183; p<.01), ICT ownership (β=.123; p<.01) and M-commerce compatibility (β=.202; p<.01) are positive key drivers of M-commerce adoption. Mobile use experience (length of Mobile use) (β=-.078; p>.05) has no significant influence on M-commerce adoption.

Discussion of these results follows in the conclusion section.

CONCLUSION

This chapter gives managers and students insight into the Mobile Commerce industry and the different factors that influence M-Commerce adoption. These factors and their adaptability is discussed in the specific context of the Spanish market.

In terms of the academic contribution of this chapter, it should be noted that while in the literature there are descriptive studies on the evolution of M-commerce and its advantages and drawbacks, there are hardly any studies which propose purchase behaviour models for Mobile commerce.

The SEM analysis on the set of variables analysed has highlighted the fact that Mobile Affinity, M-commerce Compatibility and ICT ownership are key drivers of Mobile shopping adoption.

Mobile use experience does not influence M-commerce adoption. Looking at the profile of the respondents interviewed, we realize that 2/3 of the sample have been using mobile phones for more than 3 years. Therefore, we can conclude that the skills for Mobile use in the purchasing process are acquired when mobile

Table 3. Internal consistency and convergent validity of the theoretical construct measures

Variable	Indicator	Factor loading	Robust t-value	Loading average	Cronbach's alpha	Composite reliability	AVE
M-commerce compatibility	COMP1	.88**	20.42	.87	.87	.86	.76
	COMP2	.86**	20.99				
Mobile affinity	AFF1	.70**	18.85	.74	.83	.83	.55
	AFF2	.77**	21.65				
	AFF3	.77**	19.99				
	AFF5	.72**	17.26				

S-B χ^2 (df = 13) = 25.44 (p=0,02); NFI=.981; NNFI=.984; CFI=.990; RMSEA=.045

*Note: AVE=Average Variance Extracted **p<.01; *p<.05*

Figure 2. Final model

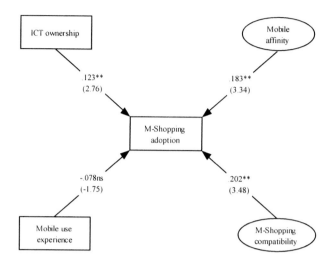

S-B Chi-Squared = 43.90 (p<.01; BBNNFI=.963; CFI=.980; IFI=.980; GFI=.979; AGFI=.953; RMSEA=.053

use begins and from that point on greater experience does not affect M-commerce adoption. This means that experience is not particularly suitable as a segmentation variable because, although segment construction is easy, the variable has little discriminatory capacity as most users have had a Mobile long enough to have acquired the skills necessary for m-shopping.

The influence of ICT ownership on M-commerce adoption suggest that as technology becomes more important in an individual's life, to the point where he owns a growing number of devices, his willingness to use the Mobile for shopping also increases. These findings are consistent with previous studies using the technology cluster concept that concludes "the adoption of new communication technologies is best predicted by the adoption of functionally similar technologies and user perception toward them" (Rogers, 1995; Yang, 2005). Therefore, individuals who belong to a technological cluster (consumers who adopted ICT devices in the past) perceive M-shopping as just another technology. These users seem to be more inclined towards trying to use all the features in a given device. In comparison to consumers that use the mobile mainly for simple services such as voice services and text messaging, ICT devices owners use the mobile as a ubiquitous platform with much more potential.

We have found that Mobile affinity has a direct and positive influence on the M-commerce adoption,

agreeing with findings of previous research focused both on television (Perse, 1986) and Mobile (Bigné et al., 2007). The more important mobile phones are in people's lives (affinity) the higher the probability of acquiring services through mobile phones. Therefore, the more important the mobile is in our daily lives, the more we will use it and the fewer obstacles we will find to use it for purposes other than mere communication. When something is important to us, we find out how it works and what other features it can offer us. We are always less afraid of what is familiar to us and that undoubtedly helps to reduce perceived M-shopping risk, mainly the financial and confidentiality risk (Wu and Wang, 2005).

The influence of life-style compatibility in general and the shopping method in particular on M-shopping is the most influential variable for M-commerce adoption. This result agrees with previous studies (Wu and Wang, 2005) and highlights the importance of psychological factors in M-commerce adoption.

This chapter can help managers to develop effective strategies to attract Mobile shoppers and, therefore, to gain competitive advantages.

The influence of ICT ownership on M-commerce adoption has important managerial implications. The segment of users who have adopted ICT devices in the past becomes a potentially profitable group. In addition, their patterns of exposure to the media appear to be foreseeable. Thus printed and online hardware and software magazines, technological blogs and forums become candidates for advertising investment by online shops offering M-commerce.

The increased performance and services offered by mobiles nowadays: full colour screens, MP3 players and integrated videos, loudspeakers, polyphonic ring tones, high speed Internet connectivity, etc., make these devices a perfect medium for reproducing all types of contents, offering the consumer a wide range of possibilities and consequently increasing mobile use and mobile affinity. Mobile operators are in the best position to profit from the implications of Mobile affinity on M-commerce adoption. The direct information on individual mobile use available to mobile companies provides them with an indicator of greater or lesser affinity, especially if that use includes data calls or multimedia messages. It would appear logical for the companies to have their own catalogue of logos, rings, songs, videos and own platforms for selling tickets to supply these greater affinity segments. An appropriate CRM system could substantially increase the profitability of each subscriber.

The influence of compatibility on M-commerce adoption presents more challenges than answers. This relationship may help us speculate on what lifestyles would be more compatible with M-commerce: individuals who are very involved with technology (shown by a higher level of device acquisition than others) and also for those who show dependency on the mobile telephone or at least have made it a central element in their life (affinity).

In terms of the limitations of this study, maybe the most important one is the sampling technique used. Lack of randomness in the sample limits the generalisability of our findings beyond our specific sample. However, the convenience sampling technique is being increasingly used in M-commerce research (Harris et al., 2005; Lee et al., 2002). Additionally, there are complementary aspects not included in the questionnaire which it could be relevant to analyse. Despite the importance of the behavioural and attitudinal variables analysed in Mobile shopping adoption, we have not analysed the antecedents of Mobile affinity and compatibility. For this reason, and bearing in mind the lack of research in this field, we are considering as a line of research, to propose and empirically test a general model of M-commerce behaviour that includes the antecedents of these attitudinal variables.

The consumer's cultural background is one of the aspects which can influence the creation of a favourable climate for developing and consolidating Mobile

shopping (Lee et al., 2002; Harris et al., 2005; Yang, 2005). For this reason, we consider that another interesting line of research would be to contrast the validity of the proposed behavioural model with samples of consumers from other cultures and compare the results obtained.

In this chapter we have noted that psychological variables have greater influence on the M-shopping decision (affinity and compatibility) than mere experience or possession of technology. Therefore, another future line of research would be to analyse the lifestyles of individuals who declare themselves most compatible with M-Commerce.

FUTURE DIRECTION

Four future trends can be observed in the current Mobile sector which are undoubtedly favoured by the introduction of the Mobile as a non-store channel.

Convergence with other Media

The Mobile in combination with other direct shopping media such as Internet or the television will optimise consumer convenience and offer a wider scope, in addition to overcoming some of the mobile's limitations as a shopping tool. Furthermore, media convergence in households is fast becoming a reality. 64% of users in Thailand and 26% of young people in the UK use the mobile to download music (Sense Worldwide, 2006), downloads of films and chapters from TV series can be seen on DVD and television, Ipods with music downloaded from Internet can connect to home sound systems and software companies market their products independently of the device receiving the content.

Market research (Gaptel, 2006) indicates that in 2010 the number of handsets providing television and data on the same screen will be over 50 million and 30% of mobile handsets will be used for broad band services (that is, for television and music consumption). Furthermore, there are over 4.5 million users in Spain with handsets capable of receiving television channels and in the United States, it is estimated that the number of subscribers to mobile television will increase from one million in 2005 to 30 million by 2010.

The new 3G and 4G handsets work on IP protocols making them a gateway to the Internet universe, permitting all types of transactions. The popularity of interactive services has generated new market niches as mobile handsets mean that people who could not afford a PC can adopt M-commerce, meaning youngest users particularly.

A trend to be taken into account is the growing tendency to integrate several devices in one. This is already happening with smartphones which include mobile telephone, PDA, GPS, mp3 and video. The mobile has a screen and an operational system which the individual finds familiar as it is very similar to the PC, and this undoubtedly facilitates its use for shopping.

Eliminating the Mobile's Limitations as a Marketing Channel

Limited and insufficient information is provided to Mobile Commerce users during the shopping process due to the constraints of mobile terminals, mobile networks and content.

Nowadays the major limitations of M-commerce are: small screens on wireless devices, limited processing power, modest memory, restricted power consumption, poor voice quality, low-speed data transmission, unproven security and limited bandwidth, which have the potential to offset ubiquity benefits. Due to "made-for–the medium" content, type and design may be required, the available technologies which determine screen size, display quality and process speeds should be taken into consideration (Rao and Troshani, 2007). To sum up, all these limitations need to be eliminated to favour M-commerce development.

The mobile phone market is reaching maturity in practically every country. Currently 8 out of 10 people have a mobile phone and the penetration rate is over 100% in some countries such as Sweden and Italy. Countries such as Japan, Korea or the EU are already in a more advanced phase of growth, leading towards the creation of new added value services.

Due to mobile services market saturation, mobile companies must focus their marketing strategies on incremental revenue per user (ARPU). Companies which use the Mobile as a shopping channel should be able to offer new, innovative services and contents with added value to improve consumers' affinity with the Mobile as this would allow consumers to maintain a relationship with the medium and increase the probability of purchase.

Thus, the Mobile phone has to be capable of satisfying the need for information, communication, entertainment, convenience and efficiency, in addition to becoming an alternative shopping channel (Bigné, Ruiz and Sanz, 2005).

The highly-personalized, context-aware, location sensitive, time-critical applications are the most promising applications in M-commerce. It is therefore the perfect medium for the consumer to receive instantaneous information in the form of short messages adapted to individual requirements.

Other applications include: i) digital cash (to enable mobile users to settle transactions requiring micropayments), ii) human-to-machine communications (to facilitate mobile users to communicate to stationary locations for access and security, iii) telemetry (to activate remote recording devices for sensing and measurement information), and iv) broadband-interactive multimedia communications and messaging anytime, anywhere.

Increased Security and Confidentiality

From the consumer perspective, the cost concern is one of the main barriers to adopt M-commerce. Moreover, a number of users are still alarmed about personal privacy and transaction security (Rao and Troshani, 2007; Wu and Wang, 2005).

4G systems with more security, higher speeds, higher capacity, lower costs, and more intelligent infrastructures and devices will help realize M-commerce applications. With improved wireless security and privacy through data encryption and with the wide deployment of 4G systems, it is anticipated that M-commerce will become the most dominant method of conducting business transactions.

REFERENCES

Agarwal, R., & Prasa, J. (1998). A conceptual and operational definition of personal innovativeness in the domain of information technology. *Information Systems, Research, 9*(2), 204-301.

Anderson, J. C. & Gerbing, D. W. (1988). Structural equation modelling in practice: A review and recommended two-step approach. *Psychological Bulletin, 103*, 411-423.

Bagozzi, R. P. & Yi, Y. (1988). On the evaluation of structural equations models. *Journal of the Academy of Marketing Science, 16*(1), 74-94.

Ball-Rokeach, S. J. (1985). The origins of individual media system dependency: A sociological framework. *Communication Research, 12*(4), 485-510.

Bigné, E., Ruiz, C., & Sanz, S. (2005). The Impact of Internet User Shopping Patterns and Demographics on Consumer Mobile Buying Behaviour. *Journal of Electronic Commerce Research, 6*(3), 193-209.

Bigné, E., Ruiz, C., & Sanz, S. (2007). Key Drivers of Mobile Commerce Adoption. An Exploratory Study of Spanish Mobile Users. *Journal of Theoretical and Applied Electronic Commerce Research, 2*(2), 48-60.

Csikszentmihalyi, M. (1997). *Finding Flow: The Psychology of Engagement with Everyday Life.* New York: Basic Books.

Dahlen, M. (2002). Learning the Web: Internet User Experience and Response to Web Marketing in Sweden. *Journal of Interactive Advertising, 3*(1). Retrieved June 5, 2004 from http://www.jiad.org/vol3/no1/dahlen/index.html.

Donthu, N., & Garcia, A. (1999). The Internet shopper. *Journal of Advertising Research, 39*(2), 52-58.

Eastlick, M., & Lotz, S. (1999). Profiling potential adopters and non-adopters of an interactive electronic shopping medium. *International Journal of Retail & Distribution Management, 27*(6), 209-223.

Eastin, M. (2002). Diffusion of E-Commerce: An analysis of the adoption of four E-commerce activities. *Telematics and Informatics, 19*, 251-267.

Etteman, J. (1984). Three phrases in the creation of information inequties: An empirical assessment of prototype videotext systems. *Journal of Broadcasting, 28*, 293-385.

Fornell, C., & Larcker, D.F., (1981). Evaluating structural equation models with unobservable variables and measurement error. *Journal of Marketing Research, 18*, 39-50.

Gaptel (2006). Contenidos digitales. *Nuevos modelos de distribución online.* Retrieved February 10, 2007 from http://observatorio.red.es/gaptel/

Grant, A. E., Guthrie, K. K., & Ball-Rokeach, S. J. (1991). Television shopping: A Media System Dependency perspective. *Communication Research, 18*(6), 773-798.

Hair, J. F., Anderson, R. E., Tatham, R. L. & Black, W. C., (1998). *Multivariate data analysis.* 5th ed. Englewood Cliffs, NJ: Prentice Hall.

Harris, P., Rettie, R., & Kwan, Ch. (2005). Adoption and usage of m-commerce: a cross-cultural comparison of Hong Kong and the United Kingdom. *Journal of Electronic Commerce Research, 6*(3), 210-224.

Holak, S. L., & Lehmann, D. R. (1990). Purchase Intentions and the Dimensions of Innovation: An Exploratory Model. *Journal of Product Innovation Management, 7*(1), 59-73.

Larose, R., & Atkin, D. (1992). Audio text and the reinvention of the telephone as mass medium. *Journalism Quarterly, 69*, 413-421.

Lee, Y., Kim, J., Lee, I., & Kim, H. (2002). A Cross-cultural Study on the Value tructure of Mobile Internet Usage: Comparison Between Korea and Japan. *Journal of Electronic Commerce Research, 3*(4), 227-239.

Luarn, P., & Lin, H. H. (2004). Toward and understanding of the behavioural intention to use mobile banking. *Computers in Human Behaviour.* Retrieved March 10, 2005, from http://www.elsevier.com.

Nysveen, H., Pedersen, P. E., & Thorbjørnsen, H. (2005). Intentions to use mobile services: antecedents and cross-service comparison. *Journal of the Academy of Marketing Science, 33*(3), 330-346.

Nunnally, J., & Bernstein, I. H.. (1994). *Psychometric Theory.* New York: McGraw-Hill.

Park, C., & Kim, Y. (2003). Identifying key factors affecting consumer purchase behaviour in an online shopping context. *International Journal of Retail and Distribution Management, 31*(1), 16-29.

Perse, E. M. (1986). Soap opera viewing patterns of college students and cultivation. *Journal of Broadcasting & Electronic Media, 30*(2), 175-193.

Rao, S., & Troshani, I. (2007). A conceptual framework and propositions for the acceptance of mobile services. *Journal of Theoretical and Applied Electronic Commerce Research, 2*(2), 61-73.

Rogers, E. (2005). *Diffusion of Innovations.* New York: The Free Press.

Rubin, A. M. (1977). Television usage, attitudes and viewing behaviours of children and adolescents. *Journal of Broadcasting, 21*, 355-369.

Rubin, A. M., & Perse, E. M. (1988). Audience activity and soap opera involvement. *Human Communication Research, 14*(2), 246-268.

Sense Worldwide (2006). *The Londown on the download. A research study commissioned jointly by MTV networks International and Verising, Inc.* Retrieved March 12, 2007 from http://www.senseworldwide.com.

Skog, B. (2002). Mobiles and the Norwegian teen: Identity, gender and class. In J. E. Katz & M. Aakus, (Ed.). *Perpetual Contact.* New York: Cambridge University Press.

Telecommunications Market Comission-CMT (2006). Annual report of the telecommunications market. Retrieved February 10, 2007 from http://www.cmt.es

Unctad (2002). E-Commerce and development report 2002. *Paper presented at United Nations Conference on Trade and Development,* New York.

Wireless Week (2004). Buying numbers. (p. 30).

Wu, J. H., & Wang, S. C. (2005). What drives mobile commerce? An empirical evaluation of the revised technology acceptance model. *Information & Management, 42*(5), 719-729.

Yang, K. C. (2005). Exploring factors affecting the adoption of mobile commerce in Singapore. *Telematics and Informatics, 22*(3), 257-277.

Yoon, D., Cropp, F., & Cameron, G. (2002). Building relationships with portal users: The interplay of motivation and relational factors. *Journal of Interactive Advertising, 3*(1). Retrieved September 11, 2003 from http://jiad.org/vol3/no1/yoon

KEY TERMS

4G: Fourth-Generation Communications System is a term used to describe the next step in wireless communications. A 4G system will be able to provide a comprehensive IP solution where voice, data and streamed multimedia can be given to users on an anytime, anywhere basis, and at higher data rates than previous generations

Compatibility: The degree to which an innovation is consistent with adopters' behaviour patterns, life-styles and values

Media Affinity: The importance of a medium in the lives of the individuals

Mobile Commerce: The buying and selling of goods and services using wireless hand-held devices such as mobile telephones or personal data assistants (PDAs)

Mobile Service: A mobile service is an activity o series of intangible activities that occur when mobile consumers interact with systems or service providers.

Mobile Shopper: The consumer who buys goods and services by using mobile access to computer-mediated networks with the help of an electronic device

Technologic Cluster: This concept posits that "the adoption of one new idea may trigger the adoption of several others in a cluster which consists of one or more distinguishable elements of technology that are perceived as being interrelated".

Chapter XXVII
Social Aspects of Mobile Technologies on Web Tourism Trend

Fernando Ferri
IRPPS-CNR, Rome, Italy

Patrizia Grifoni
IRPPS-CNR, Rome, Italy

Tiziana Guzzo
IRPPS-CNR, Rome, Italy

ABSTRACT

This chapter analyzes how the development and use of mobile and Web technologies are changing the way to search information, to plan, to buy, and to travel. The new technologies are changing several aspects of our life, such as the way in which people work, buy, learn, travel, and how they relate to each other, and so on. The tourist sector certainly represents one of the most dynamic markets, able to capture innovations and opportunities provided by the Web, in such a way that gets to be an out-and-out model of e-business. Internet access now is not restricted to personal computer. In fact the use of mobile devices is becoming increasingly important. The chapter's goal is to analyze social implications of Web applications and mobile devices and how they are improving the attitude of the customers both the fruition of tourism services and to development of sustainable tourism.

INTRODUCTION

The widespread use of Internet and Web technology in every aspect of our daily life has brought great change in the consumers habits in any field but mainly in the tourism sector. Every year, million of tourists approach to Internet in order to find tourist information: vacations, flights, guides, last minute, cruises, destinations and routes. This situation is changing the concept of tourism. In particular, tourism was defined by the World Tourism Organisation as "the activities of persons travelling to and staying in places outside their usual environment for not more than one consecutive year for leisure, holidays, business, health treatment, religion and other purposes".

A new concept of "intelligent tourism" is spreading, based on all those innovative technological solutions offered by Web that allows achieving information on cultural, artistic and other kinds of natural interest.

The Web imposes itself more and more as relevant reference and indispensable resource in the tourism sector both for customers and tourism companies, thanks to undisputed advantages such as:

- Speed for information exchange,
- Improvement of interaction among people located in different places,
- Improvement of information sharing, knowledge and services availability for all the users.

These above three aspects are very important because they are producing the markets globalisation and the spatial and of temporal boundaries break down. Moreover the information and knowledge production and sharing improves both quality development of social inclusion. Moreover, the success of the Web and mobile technologies in the tourism sector is given by very competitive prices, but also by the ability to differentiate the offer, by the improvement of possibility to reach the market niches and by proposing new services with a good usability degree. The user is not a passive subject and when s/he visits a business site s/he knows that s/he will not be able to find negative aspects of a choice. This has brought to the creation of virtual communities where users share their own travel experiences with other tourists and where the potential tourist consumer finds relevant information. The tourist seems in fact to prefer descriptions and testimonies of other people that have already visited that place.

In the next sections we introduce the passage from the old economy to the new economy in tourism sector, in particular we describe how the advent of e-commerce has marked the passage from traditional travel agencies to Internet. In succession we describe the different tools tourist used for Web and mobile and their social aspects. Finally we describe the new scenarios of tourism using the new technologies and how the mobile devices can develop the sustainable tourism, increasing both tourism demand and tourism supply.

FROM TRAVEL AGENCIES TO ONLINE TOURISM E-COMMERCE

The tourism initially involved an elite activity. In the last years it has been becoming a mass phenomenon shared by million of people all over the world, and it has been becoming one of most relevant economic sector of most countries. Data provided by World Tourism Council (1997), in fact talk of seven hundred million of arrivals of tourists all over the world. The tourism represents the 7% of the total occupied people and the 2% of global gross domestic product. It is a dynamic phenomenon, mutable and complex, it can be defined as a "social fact", it changes with transition of tendencies, of orientations, of necessities and needs of society.

In the past tourists had to go to the travel agencies, i.e. in the physicals commercial places where to plan and buy a travel. These agencies execute activities of reservation and selling of single tourism services or services packages confectioned by Tour Operators. This means that people, have to go to a physical place to use such services. The choice of the agency can be limited by the physical distance. Moreover services obtained depended by operators, by their personal skills and by their limited information.

When tourists visit different locations guidebook can be very useful. The paper guidebooks more frequency used by tourist in the old economy. Even if they are still now the principal tool used by travellers, because it is easy to consult and information is well structured, they have a lot of limits. Information in tourist paper guidebooks can be outdated because items written many years before could not be updated, hotels and other tourist activities could be ceased (Schwabe, 2005). Actually the new Web and mobile technologies can provide more timely and complete information than paper guidebooks. In fact user can obtain an updated answer to her/his question, more than a paper guidebook and improve the information quality and consequently the travel quality.

Thanks to technology innovation of the last thirty years, not only users have obtained several advantages but also the tourist companies. The most innovative ones in fact, can actually be able to redefine their own organization structure and relationship with partners, optimising the operating costs and improving the quality of services.

Information and Communication Technologies (ICT) have allowed tourism companies to increase their efficiency and their market value. In fact ICT offer the chance to share data-bases with other organizations and other customers' information resources and services. Besides ICT allow to optimize other internal functions, either lowering costs and by expanding services to offer (Poon, 1993).

In latest three decades the tourism sector has been characterized by three technological phases: Computer Reservation System in the 70s, Global Distribution System in the 80s and Internet Revolution since the second half of 90s. (Buhalis, 1998). The first two have allowed to create, to develop and to globalize availability of services by travel agencies, who have exclusive access to automatic booking systems. The last phase has allowed the customer to perform bookings by themselves, redefining the entire business tourism system, modifying the same tourism fruition and improving the tourist experience. (Stipanuk, 1993).

The first change registered in tourism market according to these technological evolutions is a great increase of e-commerce. On-line tourism is one of the most meaningful achievement cases of the e-commerce in the world. The tourism products in fact have ideal characteristics for e-commerce, they can be represented in Web site utilizing potentiality of multimedia and hyper-textual communication. Some studious, such as Werthner and Klein, assert in fact, that tourism is considered as one of more important field of application in the World Wide Web.

Some statistic data can help to understand the Internet impact on tourism sector. According to research of Eyefor Travel Research (2007), the tourism e-commerce field represents about the 30% of Web purchases. In 2005 the on-line booking represented the 33,6% of the worldwide tourism market, in 2006 the market quote of travel agencies is of 36,6%, it goes over with the 37,5% by on-line market. However the United States remains on the top of e-commerce for tourism services creating a gap with other countries.

In Figure 1 it is possible to see how the online market is very important and relevant respect to offline market. In Europe the off-line canal is traditionally the one preferred by consumers but it is loosing more and more market quote to vantage of on-line tourism, the online selling since 2002 to 2006 are increased constantly of 43% per annum. Data in the next table is showing the Internet relevance to improve relation between demand and supply operating on promotion and vending of tourism services to consumers. The trend of on-line tourism market (table 1), in fact, shows an yearly increase on-going ascent of 30% in 2006 respect to 2005. Among reasons of this increase there are different factors; first of all the raise of Internet utilise, then the coming of low cost companies and last the expansion of large band-width and of electronic credit card.

Analysing the European countries scenario of on-line travel market, United Kingdom is the best one with 34% thanks mainly to large presence of low-cost flight. In the

Figure 1. Value of tourism European market: Comparison online offline (Reference: Mele, 2007)

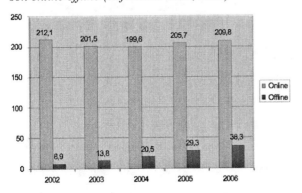

second position there is Germany with 20% of on-line travel market. On the bottom of it there is the Southern Europe, the reason of this gap is also due to socio-cultural factors. The UK consumers in fact, are used to buy everything on the Web, thanks to wide presence of large band-width and frequent usage of electronic credit card. In Southern Europe there is distrust to buy in Internet especially by people more traditionalists. There is a cultural distaste to use credit card because they fear to be deceived. Moreover, there is a short access to the large band-width. It's noticeable that the Web diffusion depends on structural and cultural factors linked to countries' policies and economies. In Figure 2 is represented the European scenario of on-line travel market 2006.

Regarding the service typologies the purchases more frequent on the Web in the European online market are occupied by: Air travel 56%, following booking hotel and travel packages 16%, train 8%, car renting 3% and finally car ferry 1%. Increasing also others segments as holiday houses and cruises. Another data about European scenario is about selling channel: in 2006 the direct sellers accounted for 69% of online sale and intermediaries the 31%. This is way low-coast companies sells flight tickets directly to consumers by their sites, avoiding intermediaries actions.

The new trend of tourism is also influenced by duration and kind of holiday. In particular short trips, especially in the weekend, are growing. The Online Travel Agencies (OTA) have understood (exploited) this tendency and created the Dynamic Packaging, that allow travellers to organize the travel about their needs.

As reported by travel weekly (www.travelweekly.co.uk) "Dynamic Packaging is the practice of selling holiday components separately rather than in a single package." OTA have to create the Dynamic Packaging to compete with the prices and flexibility offered by online retailers. In general, we can affirm that tourist behaviour shows the wish to adapt vacation to his/her own needs, adopting consequently travel solutions.

The business travel are the most purchased on Internet due to several advantages: convenience, best prices, speed and availability of tools to search travel and services, possibility to change default packages for personal needs, possibility to choice the hotel franchising, the renting society, possibility to read on one page all options about flight and so on.

After to have analysed the transition from offline to online market tourism, in the next section we will describe the new online tools for Web and mobile that improve the quality of tourism services fruition.

Table 1. Trend in European online travel market (Reference: Mele, 2007)

YEAR	TOURISM MARKET (SELLING)	ONLINE SELLING %	ONLINE % SELLING INCREASE
2002	221.036	4,04	77
2003	215.303	6,4	54
2004	220.094	9,3	48
2005	235.017	12,4	43
2006	247.16	15,5	30
2007	253.506	18,4	22
2008	259.723	21,1	17

NEW TOOLS FOR WEB AND MOBILE INTERACTION

New technologies in hand (at disposal) of tourists have deeply enhanced the tourism information quality. We know that Internet usage is still increasing dramatically, mainly through personal computers and mobile devices. So far, much of this growth has come from new Internet users. Another aspect to consider is that in the short to medium future, users will be accessing the Internet more frequently using a variety of other mobile devices for different purposes and some of these will be quite surprising.

Users can use advanced tools such as wikis, blog, personal spaces, mush-up and their own passage to mobile devices to organise their travels and relate to each others.

Wiki is a Web-based application that allows users to add content and also to edit content supporting collaborative writing, opening discussions, interaction and Web-authoring (Desitlets 2005). At the same time it also allows to delete every content of a new page or another

already written by others, to restore an old version, to avoid risks of damages by hackers or non-collaborative members. Thanks to wiki everybody can write everything about a place, a city or a country, and can read everything, or improve what is already written.

Wiki is the most important example of collaborative online community, and applied to a tourism site give to every traveller the chance to share their own experience and to collaborate with other members, activeness and loyalty to the site is guaranteed. The Web site www.wikitravel.org represents an example of a collaborative and updated online global travel guide.

Another kind of Web application important for tourism is represented by personal pages (that can be part of a social network). Technically they are more simple than wikis, in fact they only represent a page created and modified by only its owner. But their technical ease allows users to concentrate on their own contents, and besides they can also build their own buddy network by adding other user's personal pages to their "friend list". Every page becomes in this way an host joint to a bigger network, and every user can discover new paths by starting from the page of a friend. A personal space usually includes blogs: diaries of text or pictures in chronological order (such as Blogspot), personal pages where the contents are more static and includes every kind of multimedia items (such as MySpace) or every other thematic social content (list of Web links, list of news, musical tastes, and so on).

It is easy to understand that Internet promotes the making of thematic sub-network such as travel blogs. In the blog every author talks about her/his own favourite topics, and it's easy to quote other's news or opinions in this way; for example, a list of travel blogs links each

Figure 2. Geographic status of the European online travel market 2006 (Reference: Mele, 2007)

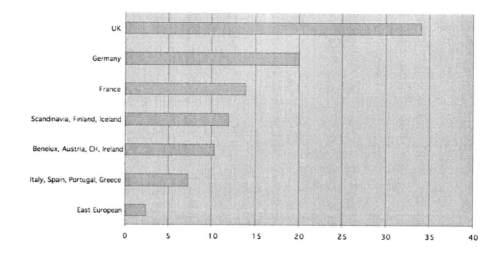

other to compose a thematic travel network. In fact, new Internet users do not utilize only one tool at time. They use a wide set of Web tools: they write their daily thoughts on a blog, post their best pictures on a photo blog, collect their favourite Web sites on social bookmarks, and so on.. Every kind of new Web application has one special feature that makes the difference among the infinite offer of Internet; however there is the necessity to do not neglect the role of the "pass the word" in the choices of potential tourists. After the vacation, contacts are kept by email and messenger, different opinions are compared on forum, suggestions before leaving are read online, the best offers and discounts are accessible everywhere and every time. In fact, the advanced tools do not swap tools such as emails or forums.

It is important to have an idea about how Internet users relate to wikis and blogs. (Fig. 3-4). About wikis, David White (2007) reports in his research, that most users not know what they are, but when talking about Wikipedia (the famous free encyclopaedia created and continually updated by its users) he reports that nearly the 80% have used it for study, work or simply for fun (see fig. 3). Instead about blogs, users have been asked about their own blogs, other blogs and institutional blogs. What emerged is that only the 20% write their own blog and nearly the 75% read other's blog to work, to study but the most of them is for fun; but if we talk about blogs run by institutions or company the percentage decrease to 45%.

We can easily see that blogs are more used than wikis for fun because they are easier to use and similar to personal diaries then more appropriated to socialise, they are more used by young target under 18 then from 18 to 34 years, less by adult public. Instead Wiky are more complex and reference target is heterogeneous, they are in fact more used for study and for work.

The question is: what does make new Web tools really powerful? This question find its answer in the fact that one of the main goals of Web operator is actually of giving to every content a real meaning; this is the goal of the semantic Web (also called Web 2.0). The simple text of any content over the Internet can always be misconceived by search engine and other Web applications; the goal of semantic Web is giving every object (a picture, a paper, a clip and also papers) a real meaning, and this is possible by linking one or more keywords to that particular object. In this way it is possible for every user to find e.g. pictures of a "puma" without obtaining sport wear brand "Puma" images. The same text, can now have two or more meanings! That's the reason of users' vitality for social networks and new collaborative Web tools, which represent the first step to give texts, pictures, video clip or every other object a real meaning. Moreover, tagging is a new emerging way to categorise, share and search information based on meaning of keywords that facilitate tourists in their choices.

Once contents of every kind are meaningful, becomes important accessing these information and the Web tool that helps user to do that is: RSS (Really Simple Syndication). RSS is a new file format used to communicate information by following a syntax. It is used to spread news, new blog posts and new multimedia object, and it is read by software (Web based or not and also called "aggregator"). Thanks to RSS provided by almost every kind of site, users can read news about their favourite site without visiting every single site. Users can also rearrange their own subscribed feeds to obtain thematic news, by adding labels or tags, the same kind of keywords we talked about Web 2.0. It is easy to understand that the use of RSS allows everybody to improve their own information needs, besides it represents a tool available by every kind of technological device, from a desktop computer or even a small cell phone or a palmtop.

This technology has several positive impacts also for tourism supply. Many companies have adopted RSS feeds in their Web sites to keep a communication with their customers and enhance their search engines optimisation. It is difficult keep update offers and purposes because they are short life. This technology is characterized as a demand-pull rather than a supply push model. (Sigala, 2007). Furthermore, information flows about travels, special offers or more interesting places are real time provided on computer's monitor by a special software (Web-based or not) called "aggregator".

We have already talked about sites that offer the chance to upload pictures, tagging them with keywords (giving these pictures a real meaning), organizing them by creating albums or slide-shows; but now the new scenario is about people, or travellers, who can take pictures with digital camera and/or smart phones and immediately send to these to online services. For travellers this means they can prove their skills and their travel experience; for all the other Internet users means to have the chance to find pictures from all over the world, especially when some special happening occurs. This new trend allows old media such as newspaper and television news to report flash news by showing images or video clip, taken from (respectively from Flickr or YouTube).

Another very important field on mobile devices applications for social activities (and consequently for tourists) are organizers and planning sites. They allow to set a calendar of events (to be shared with other users or customers) that can be subscribed, edited and shared. For example Google Calendar allows a hypothetic travel or service agency, to set a special calendar of event about new destinations, prices updates or happy-hour promotion. The users and customers can subscribe this particular

Figure 3. Different types of usage of wikis and wikipedia (Reference: White, 2007)

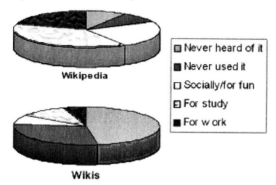

Figure 4. Different types of usage of blog (Reference: White, 2007)

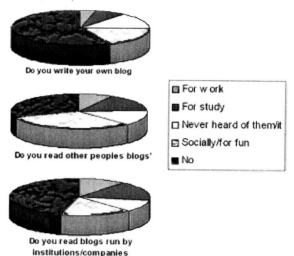

calendar, and they can even receive on their own cellular phones SMS reminders that advice about expiring offers or new item added in that particular moment. These mobile technologies make available tools to plan the complete travel and the localization of the places of interest. Among these technologies we find the Internet mapping: the digital interactive maps that supply information on the hotel proximity, restaurants, stores, services, monuments, situated historians, archaeological sites. It is also possible to know the territory classified in different topics (sport, well-being, wine and food, information on traffic, weather forecast). The customer can generate personalized itineraries, search useful services and visualize more specific information on places of interest.

Newer technologies also allow mixing different applications (usually Web-based applications) to each other, to obtain a completely new one with new different functions. These are called "mashups", and they represent the newest scenarios in new Web technologies. The most famous mashups are those regarding Google; the Mountain View company in fact, has built a global system of satellite maps covering the whole world, and thanks to GPS devices, users can add new information such as pictures, short videos or information of any kind, exactly relating to a place on the map. In this way tourists can share information of any kind, in a very simple and funny way. Tourists can create their own path by describing with words, by drawing the route on a digital map, by adding digital pictures relating to a special point on the map. So they can create thematic itinerary and share for other tourist, just as every other digital tool we previously described.

Almost every Web 2.0 site involves the chance to interact with the site itself and other users too. The whole Web based application (and so, also online tourism market) is going towards Web 2.0 and so called Mobile2.0, this means that collaboration among users and participation is fundamental for the content site. The future of the e-

commerce plays a very important role in the field of the collaboration and sharing: friendships, fellow traveller, socialization are carrying elements of each kind of travel. The main use of mobile devices by tourists is photo and video sharing whit others by personal blog or site.

Portable mp3 devices also give another chance for the tourists. In fact, they allow tourists to bring with them, in a very low weight, a large amount of video or audio files, such as thematic guides. Some operators have also started to provide their customers, with mp3 devices already filled by guides about the subject of the travel (a museum tour, a walk in the historical centre of a town, and so on).

The main reason that allows to tourism to benefit from the use of mobile technologies is the new services to travellers on the move. An example of this technology is the location – based Services.

The term *location-based services* (LBS) refers to information services that are accessible through a mobile handset and based on the current geographic location of the mobile device (Antikainen, H., 2006). The most commonly used is the satellite-based Global Positioning System (GPS). The conventional application areas of LBS include mapping, tracking, routing and logistic, electronic yellow pages, data collection and public safety (Beaulieu & Cooper 2001, Maguire 2001, Veijalainen et al. 2001, Zipf & Malaka 2001).

The primary functions of LBS for tourism are usually regarded as being the localization of persons, objects, and places, search of restaurants, shops, hotels, or points of interest in proximity and information about traveling conditions. Currently, mobile services facilitate the reservation of last-minute trips, rental cars, and hotels;

and they provide information about changes and delays of flights and trains, offer guides on restaurants, events, and sightseeing opportunities at the destination (Berger *et al.* 2003, Eriksson 2002).

In the last years mobile devices such as mobile phones with embedded camera, palmtop, notebook and last but not the least GPS systems, have enhanced the use and the production of personal sites and blogs. In fact they allow everybody to post, not only reviews of a new bed & breakfast but also the pictures of the rooms or a short movie showing the landscape.

This brings to birth of the mobile virtual communities. In the next section will be analyse the social aspect of virtual communities.

SOCIAL ASPECTS OF VIRTUAL TRAVEL COMMUNITY

All these new tools that we have described are changing the way of people to interact and to communicate among them. In fact, the users can use these tools and meet new people in a virtual community that is a virtual place where people can speak (textual chat), can meet (video chat), can discuss about different matters (newsgroup and forum), can play and can exhibit themselves (personal home page and free Web).

The first sociological definition of "virtual community" was given from Rheingold in 1993 where he defined the virtual communities as: "...social aggregation that emerge from the Net when enough people carry on those public discussions long enough, with sufficient human feeling, to form Webs of personal relationship in cyberspace. A virtual community is a group of people who may or may not meet one another face to face, and who exchange words and ideas through the mediation of computer bulletin boards and networks".

The first element of a virtual community is the absence of territorial boundaries due to its missing physical dimension; it changes for anyone the perspective to interact with other people according to their own needs and interests enhancing the real interaction and communication possibility. Whatever reason motivates a user to join network, sooner or later, s/he will need or curiosity to interact with other.

The advantage of Web is that it encourages humans to establish "weak" relationship with unknown people; this enables the communication also among persons that have different social characteristics. Moreover the on-line communication usually is uninhibited favouring sincerity in the discussion. The impact in the real social life is not decried but reinforced. The networks represent an aggregation form similar to society in which we live: weak and strong relationship, need comparison and exchange.

This form of social aggregation is not ground on politic, ethnic, linguistic, religious affiliation but volunteer cooperation between individuals that share the same interests, hobbies and goals.

It is easy to understand that Web community has become a term who involves any group of people who communicate online. These people can share different goals, interests or hedonistic pleasures. The term "online community" is also used to mean community network. One of the fields where all these concepts are successfully applied is the online travel community. This is a virtual community where backpackers, globetrotters, and other adventurers from all over the world to join together at different online platforms to exchange information, experiences, and plans in their favorite pursuit travel. In fact, in the travel and tourist industry, Internet encouraged more and more people to join into virtual communities to satisfy their needs, to fulfil their asking tips and suggestion before having a "real" travel.

Recently also travel organizations have realized the power of the new technologies for the core of their activity and the importance of virtual travel communities for their own marketing actions, by broadening their borders.

The travel and tourism virtual communities represent an ideal place without space and time, where people can meet experiences and different worlds. The travel is in its own nature delocalised in respect to point in which oneself is; for this reason it needs a strong communications and information exchange.

The travel experience is rich of emotional and relational contents that for this nature can be shared in the community. A person accesses a virtual community for different reasons: to search information and services, to contact different kind persons, to find partners to share experiences, amuse (oneself). All that is very compatible with tourism that is an "experience reality" and that needs of aggregation places.

Wang, Yu and Fesenmaier (2001) study, analysed needs of online tourists communities related to tourism organization marketing.

They have identified three main classes of needs: functional, social and psychological one. Functional needs include: transaction, information, entertainment, convenience and value. Social ones include: relationship, interactivity, trust, communication and escape among humans. Finally, psychological needs are include: identification, engagement, and sense of belonging, relatedness and creativity. In their work they pointed that since tourism is traditionally studied referring to geography location and space, it is noticeable that tourism-market organizations lack skill in how an online community can be used as a marketing tool. In fact, we cannot forget technological evolution about Internet since the last 15 years. They also predict growing of community concept as the Internet becomes more and more widespread with the new global economy. The network technology has allowed people to be more connected to each other.

People can obtain a lot benefits by joining themselves to the community depending on the different nature of communities and the various characteristics of community members (i.e. many people want to make efficient business transactions and interact with others people; many other rather want to have fun, meet fellow traveller and to express their own opinions; many other still want to develop a sense of belonging, to express their cultural and economic interests and establish relationships).

In 2004 Wang and Fesenmaier expanded their theory with a further study on modelling participation in an online travel community. In particular, were examined the relationship between members' needs and their level of participation in a virtual travel community. In their work they added to the user's needs identified in their previous papers, a hedonic need (including entertainment, enjoyment, amusement and fun). According to them, members participate in on line travel communities to satisfy four fundamental needs: functional needs, social needs, psychological needs and hedonic needs. In this latter work the authors also analyse the role of demographic differences in the behaving of tourism online consumer. It was hypothesized that users' needs in a VTC are not constant but can change with demographic characteristics such as gender, age, education and so on. For example female members usually attach more relevance to hedonic needs, while male members are more significant to membership duration. Other important results of their analysis are about differences according to different ages. For example they observed that groups who are aged 56 or more, versus young members are less attached to functional needs. The aged 20 or younger attribute greater importance than the older groups to social and psychological needs. Differences are also found between members with different education level and their respective needs.

All virtual travel communities have some common features. Communities mostly provide a warm, trusting, and supportive atmosphere. When members share information, they do it with great care and responsibility. They rely on each other more than they do on outdated travel guidebooks or on second-hand and static information from conventional travel literature. They also have to attract a lot of members and give them benefits and satisfactions to be successful. This aspect is very important for tourists because they need to solve a wide range of problems, starting from the pre-visit, the post-visit and of course the travel itself. Before the new technological and digital tools, the traveller could only trust a travel agency operator, but

now s/he can find help to choose her/his destination, to solve the most common problems during the planning of the travel (medical suggestions or documents needed), and obviously buying the cheapest flight rate; every question asked by the traveller finds an answer from a user already experienced in that way. But not only, virtual communities are also widely used by tourists to enhance their journey; in fact as seen before, mobile devices allow users to access the infinite Web without sitting in front of the computer at their home, and heavy guidebooks are now substituted by light mp3 reader or other mobile devices. Finally, tourism virtual communities are important after the travel itself, in fact if a traveller has made use of others' resources, it is now the time to contribute with his own by uploading pictures, writing a review or an itinerary, answering to other's questions, or by simply writing his personal blog to share with friends, but sooner or later someone will find his writing and they will find it useful.

Every user approach a community to search something for himself. This usually is the first step in a lot of other cases, and it is important because the user identifies himself with the community; after this first step her/his loyalty is guaranteed, and it is very easy that s/he will become also a content creator contributing to the growth of the community.

NEW SCENARIOS ABOUT TOURISM AND NEW TECHNOLOGIES

In the early section we analyse the technological and cultural changes trigged by Internet in the tourism fruition and the motivations that encourage the users to belong to a virtual community. All the different modalities used by tourists to plan, buy and do their own vacations, can be classified in off-line, on-line and mobile approach; we can represent them in a pyramid (fig. 5).

The bottom of pyramid is occupied by off line approach; they firstly appeared in chronological order and are the most used by people because they are largely widespread and accessible to the large part of the tourists. Moving upward we find the online technologies more powerful but less widespread and less accessible to users. On the top of the pyramid there are very advanced technological tools (such as mobile devices) but fewer diffused than the other, in fact the pyramid tightens.

It's easy to imagine that in the future this pyramid will probably completely reversed. The traditional paper guidebooks will probably be less utilized and available to tourists while online tools on advanced mobile devices will be largely accessible and commonly used.

The objects in the pyramid of Figure 5 are sorted to help us to simply keep in mind evolution of tourism tools. The basis of the pyramid contains "old economy tools" such as paper guidebook and travel agency. Indeed, they are the most common tools used by travellers, and are concrete objects based on an economy made of selling of products (the paper book itself) or services (travel agency). The next step is represented by the rising of the Web technology; in fact Internet has deeply changed everything, and of course economy too. Everything was concrete in the old economy has now become immaterial and "made of bits". People have Web pages to browse using a computer instead of such a book to read in several contexts. They contain forums, blogs, personal pages and wikis. Then, over the Web era, the top of the pyramid contains technological mobile devices. They are obviously the most advanced tools among the all previously described, and we also have to point that they have to be used jointly with the previous one. In fact, all Web applications will use mobile device so users will have access to information from any place and anytime.

In this way, what we have hypothesized about the future of this evolution (the previously described rotation bottom up) is already in progress, because mobile devices of every kind are used much more than other Web tools. This is causing tourism to benefit from use of mobile technologies about new services to travellers on the move.

Every new technology that we described, can be used to enhance tourist's experience, and they can also be a great chance for local administrations or local tourist promotion organizations to improve their tourism appeal and promotion between appropriate operators.

Mobile technologies give great opportunity to increase the value of territory and to develop sustainable tourism. The virtual community is in fact one of the most effective business models and provides great opportunities for both tourism organizations and customers. (Armstrong & Hagel, 1996).

Users more and more approach to mobile virtual communities to search new and unique contents, uncontaminated places, not commercials and far from mass-tourism. The new tools can allow promoting a sustainable tourism with respect of people and places.

People are searching more and more a high quality environment, but environmental resources on which tourism is based are limited. That's why it is very important to invest in a sustainable tourism. This kind of tourism is defined by the World Tourism Organisation as "tourism which meets the needs of the present tourists and host regions while protecting and enhancing opportunities for the future." A fundamental characteristic of sustainable tourism is that it creates safeguard and respect for the environment and local traditional culture. Moreover it recognizes the centrality of hospitality.

Tourism is a worldwide phenomenon that is very important for the socio-economic development of a lot of countries. It can contribute to the progress of a country but there is the risk it causes environmental degradation and loss of local cultural heritage.

Through digital mobile communication, the natural and cultural heritage that characterize the geographical area, could be communicated in an integrated way to tourist to guide him/her, also by geo-referenced information, toward their own fruition and knowledge with the other purpose, to contribute, through tourism, to the developing of minor tourist centres and their own neighbouring zones. The tourist communication can be made using a Personal Digital Assistant (PDA) or a Smart Phone and thanks to GPS system, it is so possible not only to localize the tourist on the territory, but also the cultural heritage of the location, by sending to users, on their wireless devices, the geo-referenced information with geographic route to reach that particular cultural heritage. The information sent to tourists can be personalized, integrated, complete, clear and multimedia: it can be communicated by text, but also map, video clip, 3D images and audio files.

Social innovations consist of tourists that can reach also places that are not necessarily promoted by tourist book guides or catalogues and they can be reached by messages concerning particular events at the particular time in that place.

Local administrations will have the opportunity, to promote and improve their own territory, to reinforce the sense of belonging and share memories and experiences. The promotion of these cultural aspects of a country will give the chance to have a positive impact on local economies and particularly on the tourism sector.

Promotion of a territory can produce added value to the economy of a place. To promote the local typical products, the local artisan products, to characterize thematic itineraries, fairs, that distinguish a country, is

Figure 5. Tourism technology evolution

very important to improve the productivity, to create new job and new opportunities and to stimulate the development and innovation. The promotion of a territory is an important moment in the economic development of a community.

Thanks to the use of virtual communities, moreover, local people can enter in contact with people from all over the world and can attract tourists interested in culture and nature of their country.

The use of mobile technologies for sustainable tourism will remove the risk of cultural marginality or isolation because they represent an opportunity for cultural exchange and a possibility to integrate local knowledge into social, economic and cultural development. The importance of natural and cultural safeguarding is confirmed by increased demand of tourism, that joints attention for nature with the interest for intangible culture.

The intangible culture refers to a set of non-physical characteristics, practices, representations, expressions and skills that characterizes cultures, people and places.

The protection and safeguarding of cultural tradition: social practices, typical products, performing arts, rituals and festive events, language, knowledge and practices concerning landscape, has played an important role in the cultural politics and programmes at all levels (local, regional, national, European and international) in recent years. Furthermore people's interest to knowledge and their research of tourism that improves these aspects will remove the risk that a large number of cultural traditions can be lost.

Mobile technologies in the tourism sector represent an important opportunity to improve the vitality of a community. Its bring economic, environmental, image benefits. For example it can stimulate performing of traditional events and festivals that otherwise could be lost. Moreover mobile technologies can stimulate the development of the tourism in marginal regions and can reduce emigration from local areas. They can improve job and earning perspectives of the local population and improve the quality of the tourism activities and the related skills. Moreover they can improve the quality of life of the local population due to the creation of facilities and services, upgraded infrastructure, health and transport improvement, restaurants, food, and so on.

CONCLUSION

In this chapter we explained how mobile technologies have modified tourism sector and how they became important for the tourists themselves and for the global economy.

We have provided a description of the main social implications of the Web technologies earlier, and mobile later. We have analysed how users approach tourism Web applications; they firstly use (for example) Internet to buy low cost flight or to plan trips, later they start writing their blog, sharing their pictures or reviewing their trips, and in this way they start contributing to build a virtual community that will be used by other users for advices to buy their tickets, to plan or share their trip or just for fun. That's why all this, is now called social network.

The next step we have analysed is the coming of mobile devices that have revolutionized the way that tourists enjoyed their experiences. In fact, it is obvious that Internet, as described above, helps tourists before and after their trips, but now, thanks to mobile devices, the high potential of Internet is brought straight to their hands to facilitate the fruition of tourism. Mobile technologies can improve accessibility, information and service provisioning and safety for both tourists and tourism resorts.

Then we have hypothesized a pyramid representing on the bottom the old economy of a travel agency or a paper guidebook, in the centre all the new economy tools belonging to the Internet world, and on the top the mobile devices. Anyway analysing the future scenario we have also described the rotation of the pyramid because in the near future mobile devices will be more accessed and utilised than old economy tools, and what was rarely diffused in the past, will be commonly used.

Finally we focused on the issue of sustainable tourism a new way to travel respecting environment and traditions, by merging information sharing and new technological devices.

Thanks mobile devices several small places and particular events far from commercial routes can be promoted by local administrations and discovered by tourist, contributing both sustainable tourism and development of small place's economy.

REFERENCES

Antikainen, H., Rusanen, J., Vartiainen, S., Myllyaho, M., Karvonen, J., Oivo, M., Similä, J. & Laine, K. (2006). Location-based Services as a Tool for Developing Tourism in Marginal Regions. *Nordia Geographical Publications, 35*(2), 39-50.

Armstrong, A., & J. Hagel (1996, May/ June). The Real Value of On-line Communities. *Harvard Business Review, 74*(3), 134-141.

Beaulieu, M. & Cooper, M. (2001). Wireless Internet Applications and Architecture. *Addison-Wesley.*

Berger, S., Lehmann, H., & Lehner, F.(2003). Location-based Services in the Tourist Industry. *Information Technology & Tourism, 5*(4), 243–256.

Buhalis D.(1998). Strategic Use of Information Technologies in the Tourist Industry. *Tourism Management, 19*(5).

Desilets, A., Paquet, S., & Vinson, N. (2005). Are wikis usable? *WikiSym Conference,* Oct 16-18, San Diego.

Eriksson, O.(2002). Location Based Destination Information for the Mobile Tourist. In Wöber K.W., Frew A. J., Hitz M. (eds.). *Information and Communication Technologies in Tourism.* Springer-Verlag.

Eyefor Travel Research. (2007). European Online Travel Market Report 2007.

Maguire, D.(2001). Mobile Geographic Services Come of Age: ESRI Dives into Wireless Markets. *GeoInformatics, 4*, March. 6–9.

Mele, M. (2007). Mercato turistico on line: è boom anche in Europa. http://www.ghnet.it/Article396.html

Poon, A. (1993). Tourism, Technology and Competitive Strategies, UK. *CAB International.* Wallingford, UK.

Rheingold, H.(1993). The Virtual Community: Homesteading on the Electronic Frontier. *Addison-Wesley* 57-58.

Schwabe, G., & Prestipino M. (2005). How tourism communities can change travel information quality. *13th European Conference on Information Systems (ECIS).*

Sigala, M. (2007). *Web 2.0 in the tourism industry: A new tourism generation and new E-Business models.* http://www.ba.aegean.gr/m.sigala.

Stipanuk, D. M. (1993). Tourism and Technology. Interactions and Implications. In *Tourism Management.*

Stockadale, R. (2006). Borovicka M., Developing an Online Business Community: A Travel Industry Case Study. *39th Hawaii Int Conference on System Sciences.*

Veijalainen, J., Virrantaus, K., Markkula, J., & Vagan, T. (2001). Developing GIS-Supported Location-Based Services. In Ozsu, T., Schek, H.-J. & Tanaka, K. (eds.), *Proc of the 2nd International Conf on Web Info Systems Eng* (WISE 2001), Kyoto. 3-6 Dec. (pp. 423–432).

Wang, Y., Yu, Q., & Fesenmaier, D. R. (2001). Defining the Virtual Tourist Community: Implications for Tourism Marketing. *Tourism Management, 23*(4), 407-17.

Wang, Y., & Fesenmaier, D. (2004). Modeling Participation in an Online Travel Community. *Journal of Travel Research, 42*(3).

Werthner, H., & Klein, S.(1999). *Information Technology and Tourism – A Challenging Relationship.* New York: Springer Verlag, Wien.

White, D. (2007). SPIRE Project – *Results and analysis of Web 2.0 services survey*, Version 1.0-2007. http://spire.conted.ox.ac.uk/trac_images/spire/SPIRESurvey.pdf.

World Tourism Organisation (WTO/OMT). (1997). International Tourism: A Global Perspective. *WTO Tourism Education and Training Series*, Madrid.

Zipf, A., & Malaka, R. (2001). Developing location based services for tourism – The service providers view. In Sheldon, P. J., Wöber, K. W. & Fesenmaier, D. R. (eds.): Information and Communication Technologies in Tourism, 83–92. *8th International Congress on Tourism and Communications Technologies in Tourism,* Montreal, Canada. Springer, 2001.

KEY TERMS

Mobile Interaction: The relation between users using mobile devices, it allows users to communicate and to access Web applications from any place.

Mobile Technologies: A parent category for mobile telephony, mobile computing, and miscellaneous portable electronic devices, systems, and networks.

Online Tourism: The purchases, the selling or the consultation about services tourism on Internet, both Web and mobile technologies.

Social Network: A community of people who share interests and activities, or who are interested in exploring the interests and activities of others. Each user create contents and uses others' contents.

Sustainable Tourism: A tourism which meets the needs of the present tourists and host regions while protecting and enhancing opportunities for the future.

Virtual Travel Community: A group of people that primarily interact via communication media such as forum, blog, chat room, instant messaging and that are interested in sharing information about tourism or travel.

Web Interaction: The relation between users and Web applications in order to search information about their own needs or for fun.

Chapter XXVIII
Sources of Trust and Consumers' Participation in Permission–Based Mobile Marketing

Heikki Karjaluoto
University of Oulu, Finland

Teemu Kautonen
University of Vaasa, Finland

ABSTRACT

The chapter investigates different sources of trust as factors affecting consumers' willingness to provide companies with personal information and the permission to use it in mobile marketing. The chapter develops a conceptual model, which is tested with data from a survey of 200 young Finnish consumers. The data were analyzed by means of structural equation modeling (LISREL8.7). The main source of trust affecting the consumers' decision to participate in mobile marketing is the company's media presence, rather than personal experiences or social influence. Hence, mobile marketers should focus on building a strong and positive media presence and image in order to gain consumers' permission for mobile marketing. Further, international research is required in order to investigate especially institutionally-based sources of trust in different regulatory and cultural environments.

INTRODUCTION

The development of mobile handsets and new mobile network technologies such as 3G and wireless local area networks (WLAN) opens up new opportunities to how to manage customer relationships. The literature on mobile marketing has mainly focused on consumer perceptions of mobile marketing (e.g., Barnes & Scornavacca, 2004; Bauer, Reichardt, Barnes, & Neumann, 2005; Dickinger, Haghirian, Murphy, & Scharl, 2004; Karjaluoto, & Alatalo, 2007; Lewis, 2001; Merisavo et al., 2007; Okazaki, 2004; Tsang, Ho, & Liang, 2004), and its effectiveness (e.g., Barwise & Strong, 2002; Kavassalis, Spyropoulou, Drossos, Mitrokostas, Gikas, & Hatzistamatiou, 2003; Nysveen, Pedersen, & Thorbjornsen, 2005). Emerging areas such as the role of mobile marketing in the integrated marketing communications mix (Karjaluoto, Leppäniemi, & Salo, 2004; Karjaluoto, Leppäniemi, Salo, Sinisalo & Li, 2006) and brand building (e.g., Rettie, Grandcolas, & Deakins, 2005; Sultan & Rohm, 2005) are receiving more and more attention in the literature (for a literature review see Leppäniemi, Sinisalo & Karjaluoto, 2006).

Most studies agree that mobile marketing, the most common current form of which is text messaging, will turn into an active direct marketing medium as part of the promotion mix. In other words, given the special features of the mobile medium including its personal nature and ubiquity, it works best in activating consumers to either purchase a product or react in some other way intended by the marketer right after the message has been received. The benefits of mobile marketing in CRM programs include a high rate of personalization, interactivity and a low cost of reaching large target audiences at the right time and in the right place (Anckar & D'Incau, 2002; Facchetti, Rangone, Renga, & Savoldelli, 2005).

Mobile marketing is in many countries subject to government regulation and it is thus permission-based (Barnes & Scornavacca, 2004; Barwise & Strong, 2002; Leppäniemi & Karjaluoto, 2005). Besides a prior permission to send multimedia or text messages, mobile marketing also requires the consumer to provide at least basic personal information to the marketer. In addition to the mobile phone number, this may include background and location information. The more companies can utilize various kinds of customer data, the more personalized and effective their mobile marketing messaging is likely to be (Yunos, Gao, & Shim, 2003). Moreover, data on customer preferences enables the companies to make their messages relevant to the customer, whereby the messages also become more welcomed by the customers (Ho & Kwok, 2003).

A relevant concern from the consumer perspective is how companies use these data. Previous studies have associated trust with the consumer's decision to provide personal information to marketers (Gordon & Schoenbachler, 2002; Shen & Siau, 2003). However, while there is an abundance of marketing and management literature on trust focusing on contexts such as business relationships (e.g., Ganesan & Hess, 1997; Sako, 1992; Zaheer, McEvily, & Perrone, 1998), organizational issues (e.g., Creed & Miles, 1996; Six, 2005) and electronic transactions in general (e.g., Ba, Whinston, & Zhang, 2003; McKnight & Chervany, 2002; Shen & Siau, 2003; Yang, Hung, Sung, & Farn, 2006), the literature on the role of trust in the particular context of mobile transactions is still at an early stage (e.g., Cheng & Yuan, 2004). However, according to a recent study (Greenville, 2005) one of the main reasons

explaining the slow uptake of mobile marketing is the lack of consumer trust. This U.K. based study found that companies are reluctant to adopt mobile marketing mostly because they fear that the consumers are reluctant to participate, as the consumers are expected to worry about the problems of e-mail spamming being paralleled on their mobiles.

Even though the trust literature is relatively consistent in attributing positive characteristics and effects to trust such as open communication, flexibility, reduction of transaction costs and enhancement of commitment (Ganesan & Hess, 1997; Sako, 1992; Zaheer, McEvily, & Perrone, 1998), there is considerable ambiguity as to what trust actually is (Kautonen, 2006) and how it should be operationalized (Sargeant & Lee, 2004). Trust is often treated as a multidimensional construct consisting of various dimensions such as benevolence and competence (Ganesan & Hess, 1997; Selnes & Grønhaug, 2000). These refer to the object of trust, that is, whether it is the ability or the intentions of the trustee that is being evaluated by the trustor. However, while the object and effects of trust have received considerable attention in management and marketing literature, fewer studies have investigated the antecedents or sources of trust (Bachmann, 2001; Welter & Kautonen, 2005; Zucker, 1986), especially in the context of new technologies in general and mobile marketing in particular. Understanding the sources of trust is a key question both for strengthening the effectiveness of specific mobile marketing campaigns, products and services, as well as developing the legitimacy of mobile marketing in general.

Against this backdrop, this chapter examines the role of different sources of trust on the customer's willingness to provide and allow the use of personal information in mobile marketing communication. Hence, this paper contributes to the understanding of the factors that affect the formation of trust in mobile marketing and more generally, and how these contribute to the customer's willingness to participate in permission-based mobile marketing. Moreover, it provides implications to mobile marketing practitioners as to where their trust-building efforts should be targeted.

The chapter is organized as follows. First, we develop a conceptual model, which describes different factors that may affect trust in the mobile marketing context. These are subsumed under the constructs of personal and institutionally based trust. The operationalization of these factors is also discussed in this section. Second, the method applied in the analysis is described and a test of the model is performed with empirical data consisting of 200 young Finnish consumers using LISREL8.7. Next, the results of the model test are analyzed, while the final section discusses the conclusions and implications for further research and mobile marketing practice.

BACKGROUND TO THE STUDY

This study was carried out as part of the research project FUMMAS (Future Mobile Marketing Solutions, www.fummas.fi) which aims to examine mobile marketing acceptance and use from the perspectives of both companies and consumers. The project aims at increasing knowledge on how the mobile channel can be effectively used as a part of an organization's marketing mix. The main objective of the project is to examine the suitability of various mobile technologies such as SMS, MMS, WAP-PUSH and JAVA into customer communications. The project duration is two years (2006-2008) and it is funded by the Finnish Funding Agency for Technology and Innovation and seven Finnish companies. Additionally, the project has cooperated closely with the leading global organization in mobile marketing, the Mobile Marketing Association (www.mmaglobal.com).

CONCEPTUAL MODEL: SOURCES OF CONSUMER TRUST IN THE MOBILE MARKETING CONTEXT

Trust is commonly defined as the trustor's expectation of such behavior from the trustee that is "beneficial or at least not detrimental" to the trustor's best interests (Gambetta, 1988, p. 217). This expectation is based on what Nooteboom (2002) defines as reflected trustworthiness, which refers to the trustor's assessment of the reasons why the trustee would behave in a trustworthy manner. This assessment, on the other hand, is based on the information that the trustor has about the trustee, the situation and the surrounding environment. Thus, information is a central concept in analyzing trust. Information in form of external stimuli becomes knowledge through interpretation, and it is this knowledge that the trustor uses as a foundation for his or her trusting behavior (see Kautonen, 2006; Koch, 1998). The interpretation of information

is based on the cognitive schemata of the individual, which act as filters for information and are a product of the individual's cumulative knowledge to date. This subjective "background knowledge" has been found to play an important role for trust (Alesina & LaFerrara, 2000; Nuissl, Schwarz, & Thomas, 2002). Since knowledge is both explicit and tacit, trust research must consider the fact that a large share of trust and trusting behavior is actually routine-based.

The sources of the information that affect an individual's assessment of trust can be analyzed in terms of two categories: personal trust and institutionally based trust (Zucker, 1986; Welter & Kautonen, 2005). These consist of a number of variables that we have included in the model presented in Figure 1 (codes used in the model are in parentheses where they are explained in text). Appendix 1 provides details on each variable and shows how they were operationalized in the empirical study.

Personal trust comprises two factors. The first one of them (EXP) concerns the customer's past experiences with the company (Sztompka, 1999; Yamagishi & Yamagishi, 1994). These are not limited to the particular context of mobile marketing, but they also accumulate in a more general sense as experiences for instance with the company's products and services. All of these experiences form the individual's perception of the company, including its perceived trustworthiness. The individual items in our operationalization of experience were developed based on concepts presented in a number of studies (Ba, 2000; Gefen, 2000; Gordon, & Schoenbachler, 2002; Keat & Mohan, 2004; Sztompka, 1999; Yamagishi & Yamagishi, 1994). Personal trust can also be based on information received from friends, family members, colleagues or other acquaintances in the customer's social network in form of narratives or recommendations (Welter & Kautonen, 2005). Thus, the second factor related to the general construct of personal trust is social influence (SOS) which was operationalized in this study through three items measuring different aspects of social influence derived and adapted from literature (Choudhury, McKnight, & Kacmar, 2002; Coleman, 1990; Sztompka, 1999).

Institutionally based trust refers to the wider institutional environment, including for example market, cultural and political institutions, civil societal organizations such as clubs and associations, and the media (Raiser, 1999; Sztompka, 1999; Zucker, 1986). Given its rather abstract nature, institutionally based trust in general can be assumed to be largely based

Figure 1. Conceptual model of the factors affecting the customer's willingness to participate in permission-based mobile marketing

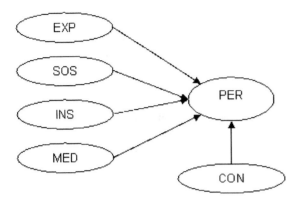

on tacit knowledge. In the context of the permission to use personal information in mobile marketing, we argue that the media and institutional regulation warrant particular attention.

Given the limited scope and amount of information available via personal experience and social networks, individuals also rely on the representations of the media, including news reporting and advertising (Shapiro, 1987). We propose that the company's media presence (MED) affects the way the consumer perceives the trustworthiness of the company and its mobile marketing communications. For example, continuous advertising and a general presence in major media communicates a certain seriousness and stability of the company and increases the consumer's familiarity with the company and its products, thereby constituting a source of trust (see e.g. Spence, 2002; Sztompka, 1999). The results of Li and Miniard's (2006) experimental study indicated that advertising enhanced a brand's perceived trustworthiness – even if the advertisements did not contain any overt trust claims.

The sources of institutional regulation (INS) that can provide safeguards against the misuse of customer information include governments, the European Union and trade associations such as the Mobile Marketing Association. For example, the European Union approved a new directive (Directive/58/EC) which established standards for the processing of personal data and the protection of privacy in the electronic communications sector (European Union, 2002).

However, customers need not only be informed about the rules, but they also have to be convinced that the rules are credibly enforced (see e.g., North, 1990) if these are to affect their decision-making. This may be difficult because in order for legal sanctions to be imposed, the misuse of customer data, or any other breach, must not only be noticed, but also credibly proven. The Mobile Marketing Association (2003) can provide a source of trust by establishing a universal Code of Conduct. However, in order for the Code of Conduct to influence the customers' decision-making, the association must establish its legitimacy and convince the customers of its value. Moreover, the criterion of credible enforcement may be difficult to achieve and communicate convincingly in the market. Media presence (MED) and institutional regulation (INS) were both measured with three items based on ideas presented by McKnight, Cummings, & Chervany (1998), Li and Miniard (2006), Sztompka (1999), and Zucker (1986).

Control is often considered a substitute for trust (Nooteboom, 2002; Blomqvist, Hurmelinna, & Seppänen, 2005; Vogt, 1997) and based on the study by Hoffman, Novak, & Peralta (1999) the feeling of lack of control may be a factor preventing consumers from participating in mobile marketing. In order to take these ideas into account, we added the customer's control (CON) over the number of mobile messages and the continuation/discontinuation of the mobile service into the model. The operationalization of these two items is based on the concepts presented in the aforementioned studies. Finally, the permission to send mobile marketing messages and use personal information is operationalized with three items adapted from Tsang, Ho, & Liang (2004) and Bauer et al. (2005).

METHOD

Data collection was carried out by means of a survey questionnaire in Finland in October 2005. The questionnaire was available on the Internet and it was also distributed as a paper version and as an email link at the campuses of two Finnish universities. Although the online questionnaire was available to anybody who speaks Finnish, the age distribution of the sample suggests that the majority of the respondents are students. A largely student-based sample suits a study of mobile marketing very well: this particular demographic group is in general more familiar with mobile services and uses them more than the population on average (Enpocket, 2004; Karjaluoto et al., 2005; Wilska, 2003). Hence, we could ensure that we have enough respondents in the sample that have experience from giving permission and personal information to mobile marketers.

The sample consists of 200 respondents. The gender distribution shows 59 percent female respondents, while most of the sample consists of 16-35 year olds. With respect to the respondents' experience of mobile marketing, 69 percent had received at least one marketing text message during the last month, and around 11 percent had received more than five marketing text messages. Additionally, close to 20 percent reported having received at least one marketing text message in the previous month from a source to whom they could not remember having given permission. In terms of participating in mobile marketing, 46 percent reported having ordered ring tones, screen savers or logos during the last month. Close to 20 percent had

responded to a mobile marketing message either by visiting a website, phoning or sending a text message. Around 34 percent of the respondents reported having participated in a lottery or having voted by using text messaging.

In addition to enquiring information as to the respondents' age, gender and their use of mobile services, the questionnaire featured a seven-point Likert scale based on the operationalization of the conceptual model as presented above. The variables as well as their averages and standard deviations are shown in Appendix 1. An explanation of the factors that determine the customers' willingness to participate in mobile marketing was constructed using structural equation modeling with LISREL8.7.

Figure 2. Standardized model 1: Factors affecting the customer's willingness to participate in permission-based mobile marketing

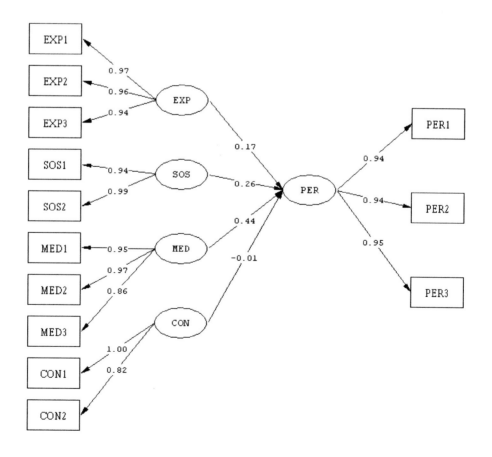

RESULTS

With all items included from the hypothesized model included, the fit of the model was poor and the solution had to be developed further. All the items relating to institutional regulation (INS) were dropped due to their weak loadings and strong cross-loadings with other variables. The resulting model categorized 13 items under five factors displayed in Figure 2. The goodness of fit statistics indicate that the proposed model provides a fairly good fit to the data (chi-square=98.49 with 55 degrees of freedom, p=0.00, GFI=0.99, CFI=1.00, RMSEA=0.069, NFI=0.99) (Browne & Cudek, 1993).

Table 1. Standardized model

Variable	Factor loading	t-value
EXP1	.97	79.77
EXP2	.96	53.04
EXP3	.94	41.09
SOS1	.94	40.84
SOS2	.99	37.37
SOS3	-	-
INS1	-	-
INS2	-	-
INS3	-	-
MED1	.95	62.20
MED2	.97	76.32
MED3	.86	25.98
CON1	1.00	26.54
CON2	.82	17.14
PER1	.94	-
PER2	.94	38.34
PER3	.95	48.15
Chi-square (df)	98.5(55), p=.00	
RMSEA	0.069	
GFI, CFI, NFI	0.99, 1.00, 0.99	
Paths to PER	**Path**	**t-value**
EXP	.17	1.26
SOS	.26	2.49
INS	-	-
MED	.44	5.16
CON	-.01	-.013

The high t-values of the items loading on the factors ranging from 17.14 to 79.77 confirmed good convergent validity among the items measuring the constructs (Table 1). Factor loadings of the items ranging from 0.82 to 0.99 were high, thus confirming model fit.

Moreover, convergent validity of the model was calculated by investigating the average variance extracted (AVE) of the constructs. Fornell and Larcker (1981) consider a model to have good convergent validity if AVE is higher than 0.5, indicating that at least 50 percent of measurement variance is captured by the construct. The average variance extracted of all the constructs in the model exceeded the cut-off criteria and ranged from 0.63 (CON) to 0.73 (EXP) indicating good convergent validity of the model. Discriminant validity of the model was assessed by using a cross-loading check that indicates that all items load higher on the construct they were intended to measure than on other constructs. Fornell and Larcker (1981) propose assessing discriminant validity by investigating whether average variance extracted for the items is greater than their shared variance, that is, to examine whether the square root of the AVE for a given construct is greater than the absolute value of the standardized correlation of the given construct with any other construct in the analysis. In the final model there were no large correlations between any latent constructs larger than the square root AVE of the constructs. On this basis it can be concluded that all constructs in the model measured different concepts and that the model has acceptable convergent and discriminant validity.

ANALYSIS OF THE MAIN RESULTS

The model proposes that media presence (MED) is the strongest indicator (path= .44, t=5.16) of whether a person is willing to give his or her personal information and a permission to send mobile marketing to a company. The influence of social networks (SOS) to permission was the other significant factor in the model (path= .26, t=2.49). Experience with the company's products and services, marketing campaigns and the duration of the customer relationship (EXP), as well as having control over the number and type of messages and the discontinuation of mobile marketing (CON), were both insignificant.

It is surprising that the factor media presence, a factor of the "institutionally based trust" category, is clearly stronger than the factors social influence and personal experience, factors in the "personal trust" category. This finding is in contrast to previous research (e.g., Sztompka, 1999; Welter & Kautonen, 2005), which tends to attribute personal trust a more important role than institutionally based trust. A possible explanation can be found by applying the concept of experience accumulation. In the context of business relationships, a strong determinant of trust is the length and depth of the relationship, or how well the partner is known (e.g., Kautonen & Welter, 2005). It is possible that a consumer perceives to "know" the media better than individual companies, and thus assigns more value to the company's appearance in the media – and media as a source of trust – than experiences with the company as such.

Another possible explanation relates to the early development phase of mobile marketing as an industry, and the possible low level of market legitimacy that it therefore enjoys among consumers. If consumers are not very much used to mobile marketing or using mobile services, they might not have much personal experience and therefore rely more on presentations of the company in the media and the experiences made by their social acquaintances. According to theory, personal experiences as the "strongest" source of trust (Sztompka, 1999) should start replacing the "weaker" impersonal sources as experiences accumulate. In other words, when people get more used to mobile marketing, they should place more weight on personal experiences as a source of trust. We tested this proposition by seeking correlations between the trust factors and a number of variables included in the survey which indicated how much the respondents had received mobile marketing and used mobile services. Positive correlations were found between trust factors and the active use of mobile services, such as responding to a marketing text message either by a text message, phone call or via the Internet, or participating in a television show for instance by voting via SMS. Interestingly, the strongest correlations were found between these variables and media presence. Therefore, more experience with mobile services does not seem to enhance the role of personal experiences as a source of trust, which underlines the importance of building and maintaining a strong media presence in the context of permission-based mobile marketing.

Two further results attract attention. First, why is social influence a more important source of trust than personal experience in the context of permission-based mobile marketing? Many studies have shown a strong relationship between social influence as a source of

trust and attitudes / intentions (for a review see Bailey, 2004). One possible reason for the importance of social influence in the context of the present study might be related to the mobile marketing medium, which is considered as an extremely social media especially among younger people. The mobile media allow people to connect with other people (see e.g. Haste, 2005) and with marketers in certain contexts such as sports events, shopping streets and concerts. Furthermore, as social networking in the mobile space has been found to be the most youth-driven category of mobile content (M-Metrics, 2006), perhaps in this context social influence simply is more important than own experiences.

Second, the insignificant role of the customer's control over the number and type of messages they receive, and the continuation/discontinuation of mobile services, contrasts previous research where control has been found to play a significant role in the context of business relations (e.g., Blomqvist, Hurmelinna, & Seppänen, 2005; Dyer, 1997). However, it is possible that trust may be a pre-requisite for control (see e.g., Nooteboom, 2002 for a related discussion in the context of business relations). That is, if customers do not trust the company, then they do not trust the company's promise to allow them to "control" the nature and duration of the permission in the first place. We tested this proposal with another structural equation model with the same constructs as in the previous model.

The results showed that personal experience (path=0.60, t=7.34) and media presence (path=0.34, t=4.12) strongly explain the role of control, which then explains the willingness to give permission (path=0.65, t=7.72). Social influence did not explain control in this model but had a strong relationship with permission (path=0.34, t=4.12). The goodness of fit indices for the second model were also acceptable (chi-square=137.5 with 58 degrees of freedom, p=0.00, GFI=0.99, CFI=0.99, RMSEA=0.091, NFI=0.98). Therefore, it appears that if the consumer does not have prior trust in the company, the company's promise to allow control is irrelevant.

DISCUSSION

This study set out to investigate how different sources of trust, subsumed under the categories of personal and institutionally based trust (Welter & Kautonen, 2005;

Zucker, 1986), affect the customer's willingness to provide companies with personal information and the permission to use it in mobile marketing. A conceptual model was constructed based on a literature review, and it was subsequently tested on data consisting of 200 young Finnish consumers using structural equation modeling with LISREL 8.7. Media presence (path= .44, t=5.16) and social influence (path= .26, t=2.49) emerged as the statistically significant factors that have an impact on whether the consumer is willing to participate in permission-based mobile marketing.

The main finding supports the initial proposal presented in the discussion of the conceptual model that a continuous presence in the media increases the general trustworthiness of a company. It seems to be easier for a customer to rely on a company to treat their personal data with appropriate care if the company is well-known. In addition to media presence, the social influence from individuals in the customer's social network appeared as a significant source of trust. This seems to be related to the social nature of the mobile medium especially among younger consumers, which our empirical study focused on. Further research is required to investigate the role of social influence across different age segments.

Interestingly, control over the number and type of messages, as well as the continuation/discontinuation of the mobile service, had no impact on a consumer's willingness to participate in permission-based mobile marketing. This rather interesting finding was examined in the second model that showed that prior trust in form of personal experiences and media presence is required for consumers to actually trust the company's promise to allow control. This supports Nooteboom's (2002) notion that trust can be a prerequisite for control.

The main limitation of this study relates to the sample obtained, which covers only one demographic segment even if it is one that is more acquainted with mobile services than the population on average. The second limitation relates to the newness of the topic and lack of prior studies looking at the factors that explain the willingness to participate in permission-based mobile marketing from a trust-based perspective. Therefore, future studies should develop and test the conceptual model with other data sets to validate the findings presented. Moreover, since the conceptual model involves elements from the social and institutional environment in which consumers live, the model should be examined with cross-country data. How do the roles played by the different sources of trust vary between different countries in the context of permission-based mobile marketing?

ACKNOWLEDGMENT

The financial support of the Finnish Funding Agency for Technology and Innovation is gratefully acknowledged.

REFERENCES

Alesina, A., & LaFerrara, E. (2000). The determinants of trust. *National Bureau of Economic Research Working Paper, 7621*.

Anckar, B., & D'Incau, D. (2002). Value-added services in mobile commerce: an analytical framework and empirical findings from a national consumer survey. *Proceedings of the 35th Hawaii International Conference on System Sciences* (HICSS-35), Hawaii, USA.

Ba, S. (2001). Establishing online trust through a community responsibility system. *Decision Support Systems, 31*(3), 323-336.

Ba, S., Whinston, A. B., & Zhang, H. (2003). Building trust in online auction markets through an economic incentive mechanism. *Decision Support Systems, 35*(3), 273-286.

Bachmann, R. (2001). Trust, power and control in trans-organizational relations. *Organization Studies, 22*(2), 337-365.

Bailey, A. A. (2004). The interplay of social influence and nature of fulfillment: Effects on consumer attitudes. *Psychology and Marketing, 21*(4), 263-278.

Barnes, S., & Scornavacca, E. (2004). Mobile marketing: The role of permission and acceptance. *International Journal of Mobile Communications, 2*(2), 128-139.

Barwise, P., & Strong, C. (2002). Permission-based mobile advertising. *Journal of Interactive Marketing, 16*(1), 14-24.

Bauer, H. H., Reichardt, T., Barnes, S. J., & Neumann, M. M. (2005). Driving consumer acceptance of mobile marketing: a theoretical framework and empirical study. *Journal of Electronic Commerce Research, 6*(3), 181-192.

Blomqvist, K., Hurmelinna, P., & Seppänen, R. (2005). Playing the collaboration game right: balancing trust and contracting. *Technovation, 25*(5), 497–504.

Browne, M. W., & Cudek, R. (1993). Alternative ways of assessing model fit. In K. A. Bollen and J. S. Long (Eds.), *Testing structural equation models* (pp. 136-162). Newbury Park, CA: Sage.

Cheng, C., & Yuan, S. (2003). Ontology-based personalized couple clustering for heterogeneous product recommendation in mobile marketing. *Expert Systems with Applications, 26*(4), 461-476.

Choudhury, V., McKnight, D. H., & Kacmar, C. (2002). The impact of initial consumer trust on intentions to transact with a Web site: A trust building model. *Journal of Strategic Information Systems, 11*(3/4), 297-323.

Coleman, J. S. (1990). *Foundations of social theory.* Cambridge, MA: Belknap Press.

Creed, D. W. E., & Miles, R. E. (1996). Trust in organizations: A conceptual framework linking organizational forms, managerial philosophies, and the opportunity costs of controls. In R. M. Kramer and T. R. Tyler (Eds.), *Trust in organizations: Frontiers of theory and research* (pp. 16-39). Thousand Oaks, CA: Sage.

Dickinger, A., Haghirian, P., Murphy, J., & Scharl, A. (2004). An investigation and conceptual model of SMS marketing. *Proceedings of the 37th International Conference on System Sciences* (HICSS-04), Hawaii, USA.

Dyer, J. H. (1997). Effective interfirm collaboration: how firms minimize transaction costs and maximize transaction value. *Strategic Management Journal, 18*(7), 535-556.

Enpocket (2004). *Enpocket mobile media monitor* (UK). Research Report (February).

European Union (2002). *2002/58/EC. Official Journal at OJ L201/37, 31*(2). Retrieved from http://europa.eu.int/information_society/topics/telecoms/regulatory/new_rf/index_en.htm

Facchetti, A., Rangone, A., Renga, F. M., & Savoldelli, A. (2005). Mobile marketing: an analysis of key success factors and the European value chain. *International Journal of Management and Decision Making, 6*(1), 65-80.

Fornell, C., & Larcker, D. (1981). Evaluating structural equation models with unobservable variables and measurement error. *Journal of Marketing Research, 18*(1), 39-50.

Gambetta, D. (1988). Can we trust trust? In D. Gambetta (Ed.), *Trust: Making and breaking cooperative relations* (pp. 213-237). Oxford: Basil Blackwell.

Ganesan, S., & Hess, R. (1997). Dimensions and levels of trust: implications for commitment to a relationship. *Marketing Letters, 8*(4), 439-448.

Gefen, D. (2000). E-commerce: The role of familiarity and trust. *Omega: The International Journal of Management Science, 28*(6), 725–737.

Gordon, G. L., & Schoenbachler, D. D. (2002). Trust and customer willingness to provide information in database-driven relationship marketing. *Journal of Interactive Marketing, 16*(3), 2-16.

Greenville, M. (2005). *Stats & research: big brands still won't use mobile.* 160Characters. Retrieved from http://www.160characters.org/news.php?action=view&nid=1647

Haste, H. (2005). Joined-up texting: mobile phones and young people. *Young Consumers, 6*(3), 56-67.

Ho, S. Y., & Kwok, S. H. (2003). The attraction of personalized service for users in mobile commerce: an empirical study. *ACM SIGecom Exchanges, 3*(4), 10-18.

Hoffman, D. L., Novak, T. P., & Peralta, M. (1999). Building consumer trust online. *Communications of the ACM, 42*(4), 80-85.

Karjaluoto, H., & Alatalo, T. (2007). Consumers' attitudes towards and intention to participate in mobile marketing. *International Journal of Services Technology and Management, 8(2/3),* 155-173.

Karjaluoto, H., Karvonen, J., Kesti, M., Koivumäki, T., Manninen, M., Pakola, J., Ristola, A., & Salo, J. (2005). Factors affecting consumer choice of mobile phones: two studies from Finland. *Journal of Euromarketing, 14*(3), 59-82.

Karjaluoto, H., Leppäniemi, M., & Salo, J. (2004). The role of mobile marketing in companies' promotion mix. Empirical evidence from Finland. *Journal of International Business and Economics, 2*(1), 111-116.

Karjaluoto, H., Leppäniemi, M., Salo, J., Sinisalo, J., & Li, F. (2006). The mobile network as a new medium for marketing communications. A case study from Finland. In B. Unhelkar (Ed.), *Handbook of research in mobile business: Technical, methodological and social perspectives, 2*, 708-718. Hershey: Idea-Group Reference.

Kautonen, T. (2006). Trust as a governance mechanism in inter-firm relations: conceptual considerations. *Evolutionary and Institutional Economics Review, 3*(1), 89-108.

Kautonen, T., & Welter, F. (2005). Trust in small-firm business networks in East and West Germany. In H.-H. Höhmann and F. Welter (Eds.), *Trust and entrepreneurship: A west-east perspective.* Cheltenham: Elgar.

Kavassalis, P., Spyropoulou, N., Drossos, D., Mitrokostas, E., Gikas, G., & Hatzistamatiou, A. (2003). Mobile permission marketing: framing the market inquiry. *International Journal of Electronic Commerce, 8*(1), 55-79.

Keat, T. K., & Mohan, A. (2004). Integration of TAM based electronic commerce models for trust. *The Journal of American Academy of Business, 5*(1/2), 404-410.

Koch, L. T. (1998). Kognitive Determinanten der Problementstehung und –behandlung im wirtschafts-politischen Prozeß. *Zeitschrift für Wirtschafts- und Sozialwissenschaften, 118*, 597-622.

Leppäniemi, M., & Karjaluoto, H. (2005). Factors influencing consumer willingness to accept mobile advertising. A conceptual model. *International Journal of Mobile Communications, 3*(3), 197-213.

Leppäniemi, M., Sinisalo, M., & Karjaluoto, H. (2006). A review of mobile marketing research. *International Journal of Mobile Marketing, 1*(1), 2-12.

Lewis, S. (2001). M-commerce: ads in the ether. *Asian Business, 37*(1), 31.

Li, F., & Miniard, P. W. (2006). On the potential for advertising to facilitate trust in the advertised brand. *Journal of Advertising, 35*(4), 101-112.

M:Metrics (2006). *Connected creators' go mobile.* Retrieved from http://www.marketwire.com/mw/release_html_b1?release_id=135275

McKnight, D. H., & Chervany, N. L. (2002). What trust means in E-Commerce customer relationships: An interdisciplinary conceptual typology. *International Journal of Electronic Commerce, 6*(2), 35-59.

McKnight, D. H., Cummings, L. L., & Chervany, N. L. (1998). Initial trust formation in new organizational relationships. *Academy of Management Review, 23*(3), 473-490.

Merisavo, M., Kajalo, S., Karjaluoto, H., Virtanen, V., Salmenkivi, S., Raulas, M., & Leppäniemi, M. (2007). *Journal of Interactive Advertising, 7(2).* Retrieved from

http://www.jiad.org/vol7/no2/merisavo/index.htm

Mobile Marketing Association (2003). *MMA releases code of conduct for mobile marketing.* Retrieved from http://mmaglobal.com/modules/news/ article.php?storyid=6

Nooteboom, B. (2002). *Trust: Forms, foundations, functions, failures and figures.* Cheltenham: Elgar.

North, D. C. (1990). *Institutions, institutional change and economic performance.* Cambridge: Cambridge University Press.

Nuissl, H., Schwarz, A., & Thomas, M. (2002). *Vertrauen – Kooperation – Netzwerkbildung: Unternehmerische Handlungsressourcen in prekären regionalen Kontexten.* Wiesbaden: Westdeutscher Verlag.

Nysveen, H., Pedersen P. E., & Thorbjornsen, H. (2005). Intentions to use mobile services: Antecedents and cross-service comparisons. *Journal of the Academy of Marketing Science, 33*(3), 330-346.

Okazaki, S. (2004). How do Japanese consumers perceive wireless advertising? A multivariate analysis. *International Journal of Advertising, 23*(4), 429-454.

Raiser, M. (1999). Trust in transition. European Bank for reconstruction and development. *Working Paper, 39.*

Rettie, R., Grandcolas, U., & Deakins, B. (2005). Text message advertising: Response rates and branding effects. *Journal of Targeting, Measurement and Analysis for Marketing, 13*(4), 304-312.

Sako, M. (1992). *Prices, quality and trust: Inter-firm relations in Britain and Japan.* Cambridge: Cambridge University Press.

Sargeant A., & Lee, S. (2004). Trust and relationship commitment in the United Kingdom voluntary sector: Determinants of donor behavior. *Psychology and Marketing, 21*(8), 613-635.

Selnes, F., & Grønhaug, K. (2000). Effects of supplier's reliability and benevolence in business marketing. *Journal of Business Research, 49*(3), 259-271.

Shapiro, S.P. (1987). The social control of impersonal trust. *Americal Journal of Sociology 93*(3), 623-658.

Shen, Z., & Siau, K. (2003). Building customer trust in mobile commerce. *Communications of the ACM, 46*(4), 91-94.

Six, F. (2005). *The trouble with trust: The dynamics of interpersonal trust building.* Cheltenham: Elgar.

Spence, M. (2002). Signaling in retrospect and the informational structure of markets. *American Economic Review, 92*(3), 434-459.

Sultan, F., & Rohm, A. (2005). The coming era of 'brand in the hand' marketing. *MIT Sloan Management Review, 47*(1), 83-90.

Sztompka, P. (1999). *Trust: A sociological theory.* Cambridge: Cambridge University Press.

Tsang, M. M., Ho, S.-C., & Liang, T.-P. (2004). Consumer attitudes toward mobile advertising: an empirical study. *International Journal of Electronic Commerce, 8*(3), 65-78.

Vogt, J. (1997). *Vertrauen und Kontrolle in Transaktionen: Eine institutionenökonomische Analyse.* Wiesbaden: Gabler.

Welter, F., & Kautonen, T. (2005). Trust, social networks and enterprise development: exploring evidence from East and West Germany. *International Entrepreneurship & Management Journal, 1*(3), 367-379.

Wilska, T.-A. (2003). Mobile phone use as part of young people's consumption styles. *Journal of Consumer Policy, 26*(4), 441-463.

Yang, S.-C., Hung, W.-C., Sung, K., & Farn, C.-K. (2006). Investigating initial trust toward E-Tailers from the elaboration likelihood model perspective. *Psychology and Marketing, 23*(5), 429-445.

Yamagishi, T., & Yamagishi, M. (1994). Trust and commitment in the United States and Japan. *Motivation and Emotion, 18*(2), 129-166.

Yunos, H. M., Gao, J. Z., & Shim, S. (2003). Wireless advertising's challenges and opportunities. *IEEE Computer, 36*(5), 30-37.

Zaheer, A., McEvily, B., & Perrone, V. (1998). Does trust matter? Exploring the effects of interorganizational and interpersonal trust on performance. *Organization Science, 9*(2), 141-158.

Zucker, L. G. (1986). Production of trust: Institutional sources of economic structure, 1840-1920. *Research in Organizational Behavior, 8*, 53-111.

KEY TERMS

Institutionally Based Trust: A dimension of perceived trust and consists of trust related to institutions and regulation.

Media Presence: Relates to an organization's general presence in major media.

Mobile Marketing: Can be defined as "the use of wireless media as an integrated content delivery and direct response vehicle within a cross-media or stand-alone marketing communications program" (Mobile Marketing Association). In general it means marketing on or with a mobile device. Current techniques include text and multimedia message campaigns, mobile web advertising such as banners and keywords, location-based advertising and various downloadable solutions on a mobile phone.

Permission-Based: In this context means that marketing messages received on mobile phones should be based on opt-in rules. In other words, marketers are not usually allowed to send any communications to mobile phones without the user's prior permission.

Personal Trust: A dimension of perceived trust and consists of personal experiences with an organization and social influences.

Sources of Trust: Refer to various antecedents of trust, i.e. sources from which information used as a basis of a trust decision is derived. These can be grouped into personal and institutionally based trust.

Trust is a multidimensional concept generally referring to a relationship of reliance. Trust is commonly defined as the trustor's expectation of such behavior from the trustee that is "beneficial or at least not detrimental" to the trustor's best interests.

APPENDIX A. MEANS AND STANDARD DEVIATIONS OF THE VARIABLES*

Variable	Mean	s.d.
EXP – Experience (alpha= .88)		
I am willing to give my personal information and permission to send mobile marketing to Company X, if		
EXP1. I have had good experiences with the company's products/services	4.68	1.67
EXP2. I have had good experiences with the company's previous direct marketing campaigns	4.34	1.74
EXP3. I have been a longstanding customer of the company	4.58	1.79
SOS – Social influence (alpha= .86)		
I am willing to give my personal information and permission to send mobile marketing to Company X, if		
SOS1. A person I am familiar with has recommended the company's mobile services	4.26	1.83
SOS2. My friends/family members have positive experiences of the company	4.34	1.79
SOS3. My friends/family members use mobile services	4.05	1.75
MED – Media presence (alpha= .86)		
I am willing to give my personal information and permission to send mobile marketing to Company X, if		
MED1. Mobile marketing is related to a TV or radio program / advertisement	3.26	1.73
MED2. Mobile marketing is related to a newspaper or magazine advertisement	3.13	1.57
MED3. I remember seeing the company's advertisements	3.24	1.71
INS – Institutional regulation (alpha= .93)		
I am willing to give my personal information and permission to send mobile marketing to Company X, if		
INS1. The company indicates that it adheres to the regulations and codes of best practice that govern mobile marketing	4.17	1.97
INS2. The company indicates that it uses customer information only for the purposes approved by the customer	4.67	1.95
INS3. The company clearly states to which purposes the data will be used	4.74	1.94
PER – Permission to send mobile marketing messages and use personal information (alpha= .91)		
Generally speaking,		
PER1. I am willing to give my mobile phone number to a company that practices mobile marketing	2.75	1.55
PER2. I am willing to provide my background information (e.g. gender, age) to a company practicing mobile marketing	2.96	1.61
PER3. I am willing to receive mobile marketing	2.89	1.64
CON – Control (alpha= .79)		
I am willing to give my personal information and permission to send mobile marketing to Company X, if		
CON1. I can easily control the number of messages that I receive	4.91	2.01
CON2. I can easily cancel the permission to send mobile marketing messages to me	5.63	1.97

*Note: Scale ranging from 1 (strongly disagree) to 7 (strongly agree). Translated from the Finnish original questionnaire.

Chapter XXIX
Social Impacts of Mobile Virtual Communities on Healthcare

Alessia D'Andrea
IRPPS-CNR, Rome, Italy

Fernando Ferri
IRPPS-CNR, Rome, Italy

Patrizia Grifoni
IRPPS-CNR, Rome, Italy

ABSTRACT

Mobile technologies, such as PDAs, pocket PCs and cell phones, are transforming interpersonal communications, making them independent from a fixed location and then "situated nowhere". The widespread diffusion of mobile technologies combined with the popularity of virtual communities is giving rise to the development of mobile virtual community. Mobile virtual community has the great potential to serve information needs. A relevant application's domain for mobile virtual communities is healthcare, where the need for information is deeply felt and has a long-term nature. Mobile virtual healthcare communities encourage information exchange between patients, between physicians, and between patients and physicians. The exchange of information can be used for detecting patients and physicians that have common objectives in order to establish interaction among them.

INTRODUCTION

Social relationships are a key component of human life. Whilst in earlier times communities were bound to the limitations of time and space, these restrictions are removed thanks the evolution brought by the Internet (Whitepaper, 2007). In the Web people organize themselves into virtual communities at the same manner they organise themselves in communities in the real word. A Virtual Community can be defined as an information source in which people share interests and information. It consists of tree elements;

- People interacting to satisfy their own needs or play special roles;
- A shared purpose, such as a need, an interest that provides the reason for belonging to the community.

- Communication systems and server architecture that support social interaction and promote a sense of been together.

The popularity of virtual communities, combined with the widespread diffusion of mobile technologies, such as PDA, pocket PC and cell phone, has given rise to the phenomenon of mobile virtual communities. Mobile virtual communities are considered to be the natural evolution of virtual communities. They can be seen as virtual communities to which mobile services are added. Using mobile technologies, users have an anytime-anywhere connection to their community. The use of mobile devices allows members of the community to communicate among them anywhere and anytime and not only if they are in the same physical place. In this way they can constantly have a connection with other members. The communication is both one-to-many and many-to-many. The participants of a mobile virtual community can exchange useful information by communicating and interacting with each other. Mobile virtual communities should be information rich and it should allow information available for many people because they improve and encourage social processes allowing interaction among colleagues, friends etc..

The aim of this chapter is to analyse the social impacts that mobile virtual communities have in the healthcare sector. Belonging to a mobile virtual healthcare community enables patients with diseases to interact in a virtual space with people that have the same experience. This interaction can allow the improvement of knowledge and the decreasing of problems. Moreover mobile virtual healthcare communities offer to physicians an opportunity to improve the awareness of patients' health conditions enhancing their satisfaction. They give the opportunity to increase the involvement of patients in their treatments improving access to health care information and communication possibilities between patients and physicians. The use of discussion forum gives physician the possibility to communicate with patients continuously allowing better information sharing. For patients with chronic illnesses, especially those in rural or outlying areas, consultation with an appropriate specialist can vastly improve the quality and outcome of their healthcare. Finally mobile virtual healthcare communities allow physicians to participate in continuous medical education at a time and location convenient for them, along with useful communication. The use of mobile virtual communities improves possibilities to maintain

communication and collaboration with colleagues investigating the same subjects. Here physicians aggregate observations from their daily practice and then challenge or collaborate each others' opinions, accelerating the emergence of trends and new insights on medications, treatments and devices. They can apply the collective knowledge to achieve better outcomes for your patients.

The chapter is organized as follow. After a short introduction, which deals with some issues of categorization and definition of virtual communities, the chapter proceeds to analyse mobile virtual communities. Then the chapter first proceeds to describe mobile virtual communities/communication in healthcare sector and then it analyses three kinds of relationship: between patients, between patient and physicians and between physicians.

VIRTUAL COMMUNITY: A MULTI-DISCIPLINARY CONCEPT

The term "virtual community" was even coined long before electronic communication in any form took place. It was a concern of many social theorists and scientists of the 19th and 20th centuries (Reinhard and Wolkinger, 2003). There are many definitions of virtual community that depend upon the perspective from which they are defined.

From the technology perspective virtual communities are defined according to the software supporting them like newsgroup, list server, bulletin board, Internet Relay Chat (IRC), or Multi-User Dungeon (MUD). These software technologies support the communication within the community, and help in creating the boundaries of the community.

From the sociology perspective virtual communities are defined based on the strength and type of relationship. Etzioni and Etzioni (1999) define a virtual community as "a Web of affect-laden relationships encompassing group of individuals (bonding) and commitment to a set of shared values, mores, meanings and a shared historical identity (culture)". Romm, Pliskin and Clarke (1997) define a virtual community "as a group of people who communicate with each other via electronic media, such as the Internet and share common interests unconstrained by their geographical location, physical interaction or ethnic origin". Ridings et al. (2002) define virtual Communities as "groups of people with common interests and practices that communicate regularly and for some duration in an organized way over the Internet through a common location or mechanism".

Ferguson,et al. (2004) define virtual Communities as "groups of people drawn together by an opportunity to share a sense of community with like-minded strangers having common interest".

On the contrary Balasubramanian and Mahajan (2001) take an economic perspective and define a virtual community "as an aggregation of people, who is rational utility-maximizes, who interact without physical collocation, in a social exchange process, with a shared objective".

In all of these definitions virtual communities are described as social entities comprised of individuals who share information or other bases for social interaction.

The notion of information refers to the possibility to access to specific information regarding areas of interest. The exchanging of a lot of information in a virtual community, allows users to discuss about different questions and problems by creating a global vision about them. Within virtual community individuals can give information (by posting conversations) or get information (browsing information by posting questions). These information resources are socially helpful because they allow people to easily establish contact among them. A virtual community can be used also to improve the knowledge-sharing process using the experiences of the participants. The most effective way for allowing knowledge-sharing is the conversation. It is through conversation that we learn how to learn together. In a virtual community conversations can occur using a shared space where people can interact, creating new knowledge and, mainly, sharing knowledge. Therefore, common functionalities, provided by virtual community and aimed at sharing resources within the community, contain discussion boards, that provide individuals with the ability to post and reply to messages in a common area, whiteboard, that allows individuals to brainstorm together, draw graphical objects into a shared window etc, video/audio conferencing, that allows making virtual face-to-face meeting, and shared notepad, that provides community's members with the ability for cooperative writing and documents. Other functionalities concern the scheduling of common events and activities, the organization and retrieval of knowledge and the broadcast of shared documents on the Web.

Whilst the notion of interaction refers to the search of relationship during which individuals can share,

with others, interests and experiences that can facilitate to overcome difficulties and to solve problems. Community is the process of bringing those who have interest in specific domain and remove interaction barriers, to build trust and relationships among the members of the community. In the created community each member develops his/her own identity in relation to the community (Bouras, Igglesis, Kapoulas, and Tsiatsos, 2005). The members' interactions over time help members in creating a network of trustees, composed of those who feel confident and comfortable with. This in return creates a reference source to ask for help when it's needed. An important factor in a community is the mutual engagement among community's members. Members whether joined the community voluntarily or were obliged to join and they can not be forced to contribute to it. Virtual community members should underline not only the content but also promote the social aspects as well if they wish to increase the success of their virtual community.

People have the need to be affiliated with others, because groups give individuals with a source of information and help in attaining goals and receiving social support. Social support plays a major role in influencing the well being of individuals. According to Turner, et al. (2001), the support received through virtual communities is perceived as helpful as support provided by real-world contact persons. Positive effects of online support are also mentioned by Gustafson and Maloney-Krichmar (2001). Both these studies report that members of online self-help groups superiorly cope with information about their disease due to the received support; furthermore, their emotional situation improves. A study conducted by Loader et al. (2002) identifies emotional as well as informational support as types of support provided by virtual relationships.

MOBILE VIRTUAL COMMUNITIES

Today we live in a mobile-devices-focused society. Mobile technologies, such as PDA, pocket PC and cell phone, transform interpersonal communications, which are independent from the fixed location, and result in the phenomenon of "situated nowhere," in which communication occurs everywhere. The ubiquitous form of communication allows people to micro-coordinate activities without prearranging an agreed-upon time and space. (Chih, 2007). Mobile technologies provide all the services that the traditional PC based Internet can offer. Even though the screen is smaller, it is not an obstacle. Everything is available on the Web, including its interactivity, can be available on mobile virtual communities. In order to analyse mobile virtual communities, it is useful to firstly illustrate mobile characteristics. Several studies specify mobile characteristics as classified by the chronology of their realization while others studies do not suggest any systematic order. On analysing the literature, we classify mobile characteristics into the following classes: location awareness, connectivity, ubiquity, identification and immediacy (Table 1).

Mobile technologies are very useful to support people communication and interaction. Using the standard functions of mobile technologies people can communicate with others by sending photos, videos, etc. from a mobile device equipped with Internet functions. The Internet presents new opportunities for one to many and many to many interactions, creating a proliferation of virtual community. The popularity of virtual communities, combined with the widespread diffusion of mobile technologies has given rise to the phenomenon of mobile virtual community (Figure 1).

Rheingold (2006) asserts that a mobile virtual community "is characterized by blending the features of virtual communities and mobile communication, which are characteristic of affinity-based and local-acquaintance-based social communication". More specifically, mobile virtual communities are known as a platform for many-to-many communication, a platform for coordinating activities in geographic space, and an arena for socializing.

Mobile technologies extend computing and Internet into the wireless medium, and provide flexibility in

Table 1. Mobile characteristics

Location Awareness	Connectivity	Ubiquity	Identification	Immediacy
Thanks to the wireless technology it is possible to determine the physical location of mobile terminals and at the same time that of the mobile users, as well as their movement as long as their devices are switched on.	Mobile technologies enable people to provide products and services that subscribers can use to connect to their mobile virtual communities. Anytime they want to share an experience, they do it at the push of a button.	On the traditional internet users need to set up a payment system like Paypal, or they need to submit credit card info etc. Instead on the mobile technologies users can handle any payments at the click of a button.	The use of mobile technologies help to improve security matters for example in closed community chat-rooms: mobile technologies can guarantee an identification of users by providing security mechanisms like identification by phone number, PIN or SIM-Card.	Immediacy allows instant action and reaction to arising demand. All mobile technologies are always on. By using mobile devices, people benefit from real-time information and communication services as e.g. SMS-Alerts.

Figure 1. Mobile virtual community application

Figure 2. Krebsgemeinschaft.de structure. ©2008 OSP Stuttgart. Used with permission.

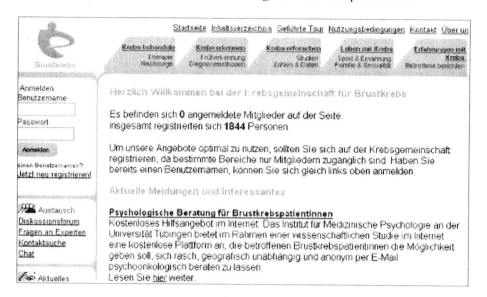

communication and information sharing. By using mobile technologies, people can get an anytime-anywhere connection to their community und benefit from real-time information and communication services (Siew, 2001) Anytime/anywhere computing remove time and space constraints enhancing capabilities for communication, coordination, collaboration, and knowledge exchange. Users of mobile technology can access to the Internet and mobile applications whenever the need arises, such as when "travelling, wandering, and visiting". Examples of mobile virtual communities are Myspace and Facebook.

MySpace is a social networking Website offering an interactive, user-submitted network of friends, blogs, personal profiles, groups, music, videos and photos. MySpace is the world's sixth most popular English-language Website and the sixth most popular Website in any language, and the third most popular Website in the United States, though it has topped the chart on various weeks. It has become an increasingly influential part of contemporary popular culture.

Facebook is a social networking Website that allows people to communicate with their friends and exchange information. In Facebook users can select to join one or more participating networks, such as a high school, workplace, or geographic region.

MySpace and Facebook redefine the notion of community and encourage friends, family, colleagues and strangers to interact and exchange information.

MOBILE VIRTUAL HEALTHCARE COMMUNITIES

In this section we introduce the mobile virtual community concept for healthcare sector. The literature indicates a virtual community in healthcare sector as "a group of people using telecommunication with the purposes of delivering health care and education, and/or providing support, covers a wide range of clinical specialties, technologies and stakeholders" (http://www.ncbi.nlm.nih.gov/pubmed/16406472)..In respect of this definition, we can describe mobile healthcare virtual community as "a group of people using mobile technologies with the purposes of delivering health care and education, and/or providing support, covers a wide range of clinical specialties and people with the same medical problems". An example of mobile virtual healthcare community is krebsgemeinschaft. de (see Figure 2).

Krebsgemeinschaft.de has the potential to serve ubiquitous needs (Leimeister & Krcmar, 2003). Such an omnipresent problem situation exists in healthcare when patients develop a need for information and interaction, which exceeds the offer of physicians. Several studies demonstrate that there are different kinds of health information that people exchange in krebsgemeinschaft.de (Table 2).

These kinds of information underline that usually patients want to become well informed about healthcare. Krebsgemeinschaft.de represents an unprecedented opportunity for patient self-education. This is due to the simplicity of use and to the fact that access and age barriers are rapidly disappearing and patients express their needs in using the krebsgemeinschaft.de to develop:

- Consumer-oriented health care models;
- The increase of health information;
- Actions that increase the possibility to access to best care.

For this reason patients see it as an important information source. This is particularly relevant for illness such as cancer. Also interaction and social support play a relevant role in positively influencing the well being of cancer patients (Leimeister & Krcmar, 2006). In krebsgemeinschaft.de people with particular health problems have the possibility to share information and potential solutions with other people; this can facilitate to overcome difficulties and to solve that problems. In order to analyse how people use medical information and how they interact on krebsgemeinschaft.de we carried out an interview

(Table 3). The interview is short and it was designed to be less intrusive as possible. Twenty people, members of the mobile virtual community, were involved in the interview. The interview aims to analyse the frequency of community connections, the average time of each connection and the motivations that stimulate users to join community. Moreover, the interview aims to identify the level of satisfaction that users achieve in belonging to the community.

The results of the interview underline that members are interested in using information provided by other members and disclose personal experiences within the community. They demonstrate trust that information provided by other members is trustworthy and correct. As proof of this, interviewed people indicated that they have based their real-life actions on information gathered in the community.

INTERACTIVE GROUP ACTIVITIES

The mobile virtual healthcare communities are formed by people organised according to three major groups of activities (Figure 3):

Table 2. Social aspects of krebsgemeinschaft.de

Category	Description	Dimensions	Examples
Exchange Information	Obtain information about: - a specific medical problem; - a certain medical treatment; - nutrition, diet, or nutritional supplements; - alternative medicines or treatments; - stress, depression, anxiety or mental health issues; - a particular hospital or physician; - experimental medicines or treatments; - vaccinations or immunizations.	Shared knowledge, collective experience, self-esteem, valued role	To get ideas
			To learn new medical information
			To share my knowledge
Interaction	Obtain emotional support	Motivation, skills, confidence, well being.	To get health advice
			To talk with people with similar health problems

Table 3. Interview

1) How many hours per week do you spend on the Internet for private use such as entertainment, gaming, e-mail?
2) How long have you been using the krebsgemeinschaft.de?
3) How many times a week do you connect on the community?
4) How would you describe your general health status?
5) Why did you decide to join this community?
6) How would you describe the community use?
7) How much sense of community do you feel among the members?
8) How important do you perceive your role in the community? Are you active or passive member?
9) Do you provide health information to the community?
10) How often do you write within the community?
11) Do you provide support to other members?
12) How much health information do you receive from the community?
13) Are you satisfied with this information?
14) How much support do you receive from the members?
15) Are you satisfied with this support?

Figure 3. Interactive group activities

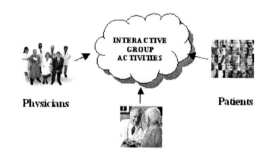

The first is a group of professionals who actively seeks each other and share authentic information. Professionals from one part of the world with expertise in one particular field can share their experience with people from other parts of the world. Interaction can be purely unilateral (e.g. expert review of pathology slides and X-rays of cancer patients), or it can be bilateral (e.g. group of intensivists discussing the practices at their institutes). These groups also provide a cheap, fast and reliable mode of sharing relevant information or knowledge for the clinicians who often find it difficult to spare enough time from their busy schedules to attend conferences or courses in order to keep themselves up to date. Not to mention the cost of these events.

The second is a group of people that share common health problems (e.g. cancer, infertility etc). Mobile virtual healthcare communities mainly provide infor-mation and mutual support for users. They provide information concerning treatments, health insurance or particular medical problems. Mobile virtual communities are socially helpful because they allow people to easily establish contact among them and to have a mutual knowledge that is much more sound. People with particular problems have the possibility to share their problems with other people or with physicians that can facilitate to overcome difficulties and to solve problems. Emotional support in mobile virtual healthcare communities benefits from the absence of traditional barriers to access and the possiblity to assure online anonymity thath can be helpful for those who have stigmatizing or embarrassing conditions.

Third are a group of professionals and a group of patients. Patients see mobile virtual healthcare communities as a convenient way to interact with physician who is important to them. With the continued increased development of Internet, mobile virtual communities can be a simple, valid, convenient and inexpensive mechanism for interact. They can support the health care distribution process by allowing written follow-up clues, test results, as well as, a means for patients to easily contact their physician. The evolution of patient-physician communication shows that mobile virtual communities have a relevant impact on the way in which patients and doctors interact. Mobile virtual communities allow patients and physicians to share opinions and medical information every time and everywhere. Mobile virtual communities offer to physicians an opportunity to improve the awareness of patient's health conditions and enhance their satisfaction.

THE RELATIONSHIP BETWEEN PHYSICIANS

Regarding the relationships between physicians, mobile virtual healthcare communities allow them to participate in continuous medical education at a time and location convenient for them, along with:

• Useful communication and collaboration
• Knowledge sharing.

The use of mobile virtual healthcare communities improves possibilities to maintain communication and collaboration between physicians. In a virtual space physicians aggregate observations from their daily practice and then challenge or collaborate each others' opinions, accelerating the emergence of trends and new insights on medications, treatments and devices (Ebner, Leimeister & Krcmar 2004). Technology is an essential requirement of any mobile virtual healthcare communities to ensure an effective and rapid communications among physicians, especially distant ones. Technology used in mobile virtual healthcare communities allows transmitting, extending, saving and managing knowledge shared among community members. The most common technologies used in mobile virtual healthcare communities are the asynchronous tools, such as discussion boards, that provide physicians with the ability to post and reply to messages in a common area, whiteboard, that allows physicians to brainstorm together, draw graphical objects into a shared window etc, video/audio conferencing, that allows making virtual face-to-face meeting, and shared notepad, that provides community's members with the ability to create a document together (Malkary, 2005). Other functionalities concern the scheduling of common events and activities, the organization and retrieval of knowledge and the broadcast of shared documents to the Web.

Although technology cannot completely substitute face-to-face interactions, mobile virtual healthcare communities can foster the growth of knowledge sharing between physicians. In this sense mobile virtual communities will supplement, not supplant, traditional communities (Table 4).

As Tab. 4 shows, virtual community supplements traditional community in creating a more dynamic environment oriented to innovation and knowledge sharing. In healthcare sector mobile virtual communities allow the enhancing of "meeting opportunities" between physicians. As consequence, emerge the increasing number of skills, competencies and "knowledge profiles" of each physician involved into the mobile virtual community. In this perspective, a mobile virtual community amplifies openness, interoperability, scalability, and extensibility of a traditional community. In the same time, this does not mean that in a mobile virtual community of creation face-to-face interactions are substituted by electronic communications. On the contrary, face-to-face interactions are enabled and supported by electronic communications that try to make easier, more immediate and less expensive the knowledge relations, amplifying their efficacy.

THE PATIENT-PATIENT RELATIONSHIP

Patients' demands for information often increase after a diagnosis of a disease or during medical treatment. Patients may seek information to help them make

Table 4. Traditional community vs mobile virtual community

	Traditional community	Mobile virtual community
Knowledge	Localized	Distributed
Boundaries	Fixed	Dynamics
Membership	Sometime forced	Volunteer and explicit
Feature	Oriented to consolidate the accumulated knowledge	Oriented to innovation and knowledge creation

sense of a diagnosis. Recent research on patients' information needs (Leimeister Arnold Y., Krcmar H. 2006) demonstrates a strong information interest in the following areas:

1. Side effects.
2. Explanation of disease and prognosis.
3. Treatment options and explanations of therapy.
4. Logistical issues (transportation, work, etc.).
5. Lifestyle issues (exercise, diet, sexuality, smoking).
6. Follow up/what happens after therapy finishes.
7. Support or self help groups, alternative medicine.

Besides demands for information, there is a desire to seek emotional support with other patients (Leimeister & Krcmar 2005). Several studies have identified five, interrelated forms of emotional support common to face-to-face and virtual mutual aid groups. These forms of emotional support help to reduce members isolation and empathy to enhance self-esteem and sustain hope. People join mobile virtual communities to experience a sense of community with others like themselves. To obtain this benefit, members must stay involved long enough to feel a sense of connection with other members. They are more likely to have this experience if they begin exchanging messages with other members. Researchers have found that when members write longer posts and ask questions, they are more likely to post again. There are various types of technologies used by patients to form and facilitate interactions within a mobile healthcare community. Some of these include:

- **E-mails:** the exchange of electronic messages between peers via e-mail is widespread. However, it is often a clumsy tool to be used to converse with other community members and it lacks security due to the high probability of deleting or misplacing mistakenly a document or a message.
- **Instant messaging:** exchanging messages simultaneously is a real-time approach used for immediate correspondence among individuals. Nevertheless, excessive instant messaging and/or many members participating in the same conversation can be annoying to users.

In addition, it takes extra effort to save these conversations.

- **Newsgroup:** represents a repository of messages posted by many users from different locations. It can be considered as a virtual space where physicians exchange ideas, discuss, communicate and even make friends.
- **Web conferencing:** refers to synchronous (live) meetings, Web seminars and applications sharing over the Web. In a Web conference participants can see whatever is on the presenter's screen, and simultaneously share applications (ex: spread sheet) and discuss matters of common concern.
- **Blogs:** is a cooperation environment that contains reverse chronologically order posts that are contained in a common Web page.
- **Wikis:** provide an effective virtual forum that allows physicians to add content and also to edit content supporting collaborative writing, opening discussions, interaction and Web-authoring. They also provide an asynchronous platform for virtual community, and with their capacity to archive different page versions can act as repositories, thereby enabling effective knowledge management. It is sure that the use of mobile virtual healthcare communities presents very clear advantages in different area (Table 5).

THE PATIENT-PHYSICIAN RELATIONSHIP

Mobile virtual communities are rapidly changing the physician-patient relationship. They allow patients and physicians to share opinions and medical information every time and everywhere. Moreover, they offer to physicians an opportunity to improve the awareness of patient's health conditions and enhance their satisfaction. They also give the opportunity to increase the involvement of patients in their treatments and they improve access to health care information and communication possibilities between patients and physicians. Through the use of mobile virtual communities physician have the possibility to communicate with patients continuously allowing better data collection. (Leimeister & Krcmar 2003). For patients with chronic illnesses, especially those in rural or outlying areas, consultation with an appropriate specialist can vastly improve the quality and outcome of their healthcare.

Table 5. Advantages of mobile virtual healthcare communities

Convenience	Access	Information sharing	Satisfaction	Efficiency
- advantages in time and space. People can interact at any time from anywhere; - mobile healthcare community is convenient for information that patients have to remember or to write down.	- mobile healthcare community facilitates the access to care for patients with physical disabilities or patients that live in a remote area.	- the opportunities for patients to use friendly medium to ask clarification after a face-to-face consultation; - the opportunities for patients to discuss the content of messages with friends or family to improve the care understanding	- traditional barriers of social differences, age, and non-familiarity dissolve in the informality of electronic communication; - free style of writing; - anonymity for patients; - speed of communication; - opportunities for groups that are difficult to reach by face-to-face contact.	- opportunities to improve the diffusion information on healthy behaviour to several people simultaneously; - cost savings.

Mobile virtual communities can be used by doctors to send instant messages to patients reminding them when they need to take their medication. This serves to eliminate certain administrative costs that are associated with hospitalisations that result from not taking the prescribed medication at the correct time. People and doctors could also have a mutual knowledge that is much more sound *and mobile technologies.*

There are many potential benefits for patients and physicians who communicate in mobile virtual communities:

- patients may feel more comfortable in addressing sensitive, complex or personal issues;
- mobile virtual communities can solve problems related to large distances or patients' disability;
- patients can influence physician prescribing decisions by presenting product information they find online.

Mobile virtual communities have the potential to educate health consumer, by giving information on health and health services, supporting patient choice, guaranteeing convenience, anonymity, and quantity of information (Kane & Sands, 1998).

For incorporating virtual consultations into routine medical practice it is necessary to proceed on the basis of secure evidence.

It is important to understand the following aspects related to the communication between physicians and patients: how the communication by mobile virtual communities can be integrated with other modes to communicate the patient and physician preferences in the use of mobile virtual communities and identify people that most likely can benefit from virtual communication.

However mobile virtual community does not have the capability to reproduce the traditional relationship because of the impossibility of the physical presence. In fact medical practice includes complex processes as diagnosis, treatment, prognosis and these processes require the presence of the patient for several activities. Therefore, in conclusion we can observe that mobile virtual communities can modify and integrate the traditional physician-patient relationship but, at the moment, cannot replace this relationship.

CONCLUSION

Mobile technologies represent a familiar part of the lives of many people today. They give virtual words a new character, with the simultaneosly information exchange. On the virtual space, mobile virtual communities are accessible by mobile devices. Mobile virtual communities have the great potential to serve ubiquitous information and communication needs.

This applies especially to the healthcare sector where the need for information and communication is deeply felt and of a long-term nature.

In this chapter we analysed the social impacts that mobile virtual healthcare communities have on relationships between: 1. patient and physician; 2. patients; and 3. physicians has been shown.

With respect to the first relationship the evolution of patient-physician communication shows that mobile virtual communities have a relevant impact on the way in which patients and physician interact. Mobile virtual communities allow patients and physicians to share opinions and medical information every time and everywhere and offer to physicians an opportunity to improve the awarness of patient's health conditions and enhance their satisfaction. They also give the opportunity to increase the involvement of patients in their treatments and they improve access to health care information and communication possibilities between patients and physicians. Through the use of mobile virtual healthcare communities physician have the possibility to communicate with patients continuously allowing better data collection. For patients with complicated cases or chronic illnesses, especially those in rural or outlying areas, consultation with an appropriate specialist can vastly improve the quality and outcome of their healthcare. Moreover mobile virtual communities can be used by doctors to send instant messages to patients reminding them when they need to take their medication. This serves to eliminate certain administrative costs that are associated with hospitalisations that result from not taking the prescribed medication at the correct time.

Concerning the patient-patient relationship, the use of mobile virtual communities enables patients with long-term chronic diseases to interact with people that have the same experience (Ferguson, 1998). This interaction can allow a decrease of the problem. Online anonymity can be helpful for those who feel embarrassment discussing their health conditions. Mobile virtual communities mainly provide information and mutual support for users. They provide information concerning treatments, health insurance or particular medical problems. Information shared between users includes reports on how the disease was contracted and how it affects daily life.

Regarding the relationships between physicians, mobile virtual communities allow them to participate in continuous medical education at a time and location convenient for them, along with useful communication. The use of mobile virtual communities improves pos-

sibilities to maintain communication and collaboration with colleagues investigating the same subjects. In a virtual space physicians aggregate observations from their daily practice and then challenge or collaborate each others' opinions, accelerating the emergence of trends and new insights on medications, treatments and devices. They can apply the collective knowledge to achieve better outcomes for your patients.

In sum on discussing the social impacts of mobile virtual communities on the traditional physician-patient relationship, patient-patient relationship and physician-physician relationship, we emphasize that they are transforming these relationships. One of the most important advantages of mobile virtual communities is that they promote the opportunity for users to interact with more people than in the past. Is it clear that these communities don't have the capability to reproduce the traditional relationship because of the impossibility of the physical presence. This is mainly valid for medical practice that includes complex processes such as diagnosis, treatment and prognosis. These processes require the presence of the patient for several activities. However the information exchange can be used for detecting patients and physicians that have common objectives and share common interests in order to establish communication and interaction among them.

REFERENCES

Bouras, C., Igglesis, V., Kapoulas, V., & Tsiatsos, T. (2005). A Web-based virtual community. *Int. J. Web Based Communities, 1*(2), 127–139.

Chih, H.L. (2007). Understanding the Design of Mobile Social Networking: The Example of EzMoBo in Taiwan. *Journal of media and culture, 10*(1).

Demiris, G. (2006, August). *The diffusion of virtual communities in healthcare: Concepts and challenges. Patient Education and Counseling, 62*(2), 178-188.

Ebner, W., Leimeister, J. M. & Krcmar, H. (2004). Trust in Virtual Healthcare Communities: Design and Implementation of Trust-Enabling Functionalities. *Journal Title: Hawaii International Conference on System Sciences 2004.*

Etzioni, A., & Etzioni, O. (1999). Face-to-face and computer-mediated communities, a comparative analysis. *The Informatio Society, 15* (4), 241-248.

Ferguson, D., Sairamesh, J., & Feldman, S. (2004). *Open Frameworks for Information Cities. Communications of the ACM, 47* (2), 45-49.

Ferguson, T. (1998). Digital doctoring-Opportunities and challenges in electronic patient-physician communication. *Journal of the American Medical Association, 280.*

Kane, B., & Sands, D. (1998). Guidelines for the clinical use of electronic mail with patients. Internet Working Group, Task Force on Guidelines for the use of Clinic-Patient Electronic Mail. *Journal of the American Medical Informatics Association.*

Leimeister, J. M., Arnold, Y., & Krcmar, H. (2006). Developing community-platforms for cancer patients-the COSMOS-project. *European journal of cancer care.*

Leimeister, J. M., & Krcmar, H. (2006). Designing and Implementing Virtual Patient Support Communities: A German Case Study. *The Internet and health care: Theory, research and practice,* M. Murero, & R.E. Rice, (eds.). Verlag: Lawrence Erlbaum Associates; Erscheinungsort. Mahwah: Erscheinungsjahr.

Leimeister, J. M., & Krcmar, H. (2003). Engineering Virtual Communities in Healthcare: The Case of www.krebsgemeinschaft.de. *Electronic Journal of Organizational Virtualness, 5,* 47-59. ISSN: 1422-9331.

Leimeister, J. M., & Krcmar, H. (2005). Patient-oriented Design of Online Support Communities Jan Marco, Helmut. *Proceedings of the 11th International Conference on Human-Computer Interaction (HCI International 2005).*

Loader, B., Muncer, S., Burrows, R., Pleace, N., & Nettleton, S. (2002). Medicine on the line? Computer-mediated social support and advice for people with diabetes. *International Journal of Social Welfare, 11,* 53-65.

Malkary G. (2005). Healthcare without Bounds: Mobile Computing for Physicians. *Journal Mobile Computing for Physicians.*

Reinhard, F., & Wolkinger, T. (2003). Customer integration with virtual communities: Case study: The online community of the largest regional newspaper in Austria. *Hawaii International Conference on System Sciences, January 6-9, 2003, Big Island, Hawaii.*

Rheingold, H. (2006). *Mobile Virtual Communities.* Retrieved from http://www.thefeaturearchives.com/topic/Culture/Mobile_Virtual_Communities.html

Ridings, C. M., Gefen, D., & Arinze, B. (2002). Some antecedents and effects of trust in virtual communities, *Journal of Strategic Information Systems, 11,* 271-295.

Romm, C., Pliskin, N., & Clarke, R. (1997).Virtual communities and society: toward an integrative three phase model. *International Journal of Information Management, 17*(4), 261-270.

Siew, T. P. (2001). Mobile Community Computing Applications (MOCCA). *SIMTech Technical Report (MIT/01/017/OSCA).*

Turner, J.W., Grube, J.A., & Meyers, J. (2001). Developing an Optimal Match within Online Communities: An Exploration of CMC Support Communities and Traditional Support. *Journal of Communication, 51,* 231-251.

KEY TERMS

Collaboration: A structured, recursive process where two or more people work together toward a common goal.

Electronic Communication: The assisted transmission of signals over a distance for the purpose of communication.

Healthcare: The prevention, treatment, and management of illness and the preservation of mental and physical well being through the services offered by the medical and allied health professions.

Mobile Services: A radiocommunication service between mobile and land stations, or between mobile stations.

Mobile Technologies: A combination of hardware, operating system, networking, and software.

Social Network: A social structure made of nodes that are tied by one or more specific types of interdependency, such as visions, idea, friends etc.

Virtual Communities: A group of people that primarily interact via communication media such Usenet rather than face to face.

Chapter XXX
Impact of Mobile Technologies and Gadgets on Adolescent's Interpersonal Relationships

Jigisha Gala
M.S. University of Baroda, India

Bhuvan Unhelkar
MethodScience.com & University of Western Sydney, Australia

ABSTRACT

This chapter discusses and depicts the wide range of changes induced in the lives of adolescents by the use of mobile gadgets, as viewed by a certain cross-section of the society–the adolescents themselves and the teachers of young adolescents. The various stakeholders who view the effect of mobility on adolescents include the parents, the teachers, peers and friends, and the young adolescents themselves. This chapter particularly focuses on the view of the adolescents and teachers on the effect of mobility on young emerging adults within the Indian context.

INTRODUCTION

This chapter describes the investigations into the effect of mobile gadgets on interpersonal relationships of adolescents in the Indian Context. The chapter is based on the research work carried out by the lead author in order to identify the various ways in which adolescents are affected by location- and time-independence. As a part of this study, it was discovered that there are various stakeholders who are affected by the use of mobility by adolescents – these stakeholders include not only the adolescents themselves but also their parents or guardians, the teachers and their peers or friends. In order to ascertain the full effect of mobility on adolescents it is important to study these four stakeholders, depicted in Figure 1.

BACKGROUND TO THIS RESEARCH

a. Mobility and Adolescents

The changes and effects of mobility on adolescents include the opportunities to develop intimate relationships, maintaining secrecy and privacy, satisfying the intrinsic needs of 'contact', and at the same time freeing them from physical proximity and spatial immobility associated with land-based communication techniques. Moreover these location-independent mobile technologies function as stress-busters, owing to the multi-functionalities they provide to their users. These are some of the interesting aspects of mobility

Figure 1. Adolescents and the various stakeholders for mobile influence

Various Stakeholders affected by Adolescent Mobility

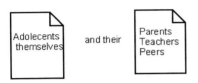

and adolescents described in this chapter. Furthermore, this chapter also delves into the issue of ever growing 'consumerism' that influences adolescents; this is so because mobile gadgets also serve a 'status symbol;' both - due to the status resulting from possessing a "cool" gadget and also due to the increasing opportunities for cross-gender interactions.

b. Indian Context

The use of mobile gadgets has increased at a remarkable rate in less than 5 years in India. The present chapter focuses on mobile telephony and its impact on adolescents' social networks and its dynamics. In the year January 2003, India had just 10 million mobile subscribers which increased to 28 million by the end of December 2003 (Ahmed, 2004). Various surveys across the globe indicate that youth are the most important drivers of mobile business (Macro, 2004) and this is also evident , as companies keep adding features such as 'cool' ring tones, screen savers etcetera that appeal to the youth. It would be interesting to understand the adoption of this relatively new technology by this characteristic life phase.

RESEARCH METHODOLOGY

The study is descriptive in nature and has adopted a quantitative survey method to compare the two groups under investigation. A survey was created by the lead author and administered to a group of adolescents and teachers from schools within Vadodara (erstwhile Baroda city) in India. The survey questions were based on ascertaining the views of the adolescents and teachers pertaining to mobile adolescents.

MOBILE ADOLESCENTS

c. Adolescence: A Life Phase

Adolescence is a transition phase from childhood to adulthood. 'Adolescence' as distinct life phase has been recognized in the west, after 1900's. The factors accounting for this recognition are segregation of young people from adult and children, establishment of school and passage of laws for prevention of child labor due to the industrial revolution (Grotevent, 2000).

In India 'adolescence' is a relatively new term because the process of transition from childhood to adulthood is gendered and class based in India (Saraswathi, 1999). For example, there is greater continuity between childhood and adulthood in traditional settings while in the contemporary Indian society for upper and middle class the discontinuity is greater. Upper class adolescents enjoy greater freedom due to less supervision of parents and have an easy access to material resources. They spend more time with peers as compared to adolescents belonging to other SES. Also child-adult continuity is more clearly evident in girls as the socialization to become good wives and mothers begins early in life. However, with globalization such distinctions seem to blur and 'adolescence' and 'emerging adults' as phases are widely becoming an Indian phenomenon.

Owing to the various physical, psychological and social changes taking place, adolescents have a great need to develop identity and intimacy (Erikson, 1968). There is also a shift in the attachment figures, when peers and opposite sex partner become more significant compared to parents (Fraley & Shaver, 2000; Furman & Simon 1998; Furman & Wehner, 1993). Therefore, there is a need for privacy and emancipation from parental supervision.

In this pursuit adolescents employ various strategies in guise of extreme fashions and styles, jargons and language that clearly distinguish them from the older generation (Morris, 1969). And this struggle for distinct tribal identity is an ancient biological need for the human species when we take an evolutionary perspective. Therefore we find that although friendships are the least institutionalized of all relationships, they nevertheless have their own customs and private cultures (Dornbusch, 1989).

Having talked about the most important developmental characteristics and needs of adolescents, we can now appreciate how this 'magic transmitter', which we call the cell phone, not only serves the basic social needs, but also creates new adjustments and dilemmas for the mobile users! No wonder this nascent technology has been equally welcome in all human societies and cultures in the past: that is, under all imaginable specific cultural or socio-economic conditions (Geser, 2004).

The present study specifically attempts to understand the most important factors that make mobile phones very widely accepted amongst the youth according to the adolecent'sadolescent's themselves and their teachers. This study includes the teacher's perception about the impact of cell phones on adolescents, because India like any other place, as a CIT (Communication and Information Technology) culture has transformed at a greater rate than the generational change. Hence, along with the adolescents views, adult understandings of adolescent's espousal of cell phones is a critical factor in mapping the cultural changes taking place in context of the youngsters' interpersonal relationships.

d. Mobile Adolescents and their Changing Social Worlds

Adolescence, as mentioned earlier has been described as a transition phase and hence is equated to the nomadic life. This group is preoccupied with seeking emancipation, establishing careers, finding mates and managing social lives and the cell phone offers a logical means to this end. In our modern nomadic lives, we have to face with two kinds of issues related to spatial distance; one is extreme and unavoidable spatial proximity with indifferent masses and on the other hand tolerate physical separation with loved ones e.g. crowded cities (Morris 1969; Gesar, 2004). Although landline phones have eliminated the need for face to face interactions, it nevertheless has reinforced fixed settlements. Wireless technology on the other hand has proven that there need not be any fundamental tradeoff between communication and mobility.

Studies with youth have revealed that adolescents usually start with a narrow concept of their need for mobile phones and gradually expand their use (Palen,Salzman & Youngs 2001, as in Geser, 2004). It is now being used for expressive communication rather than merely in case of emergencies or for sharing information (Ling, 2001).

Although Sociologists are of the view that mobile phones can no longer serve as "status –symbols" because today they are so common that both boys and girls, lower or middle class people use mobiles. Interestingly studies have revealed that adolescents who do not own a mobile phone, sometimes do feel let down in front of their peers (Foley, Holzman & Wearing, 2007; Campbell, 2005).

Mobile phones serve as personal fashion statements, help create micro –cultures amongst a group who share the meanings of specific language jargons, then there is a whole range of mobile etiquette and dilemmas associated with it. Other implication that it has on face to face interactions is that of suspension of interaction with people here and now, and they are helplessly waiting for an indefinite period of time till a call is ended. However, mobile phones make personal relationships very individualized because it frees them from unsolicited vigilance of adults.

INVESTIGATION QUESTIONS

The following questions were investigated in this study.

1. How important is cost of mobile gadgets, cards and transactions to adolescents?
2. How much importance do adolescents place on context in the use of mobile gadgets?
3. How important are mobile gadgets as a fashion accessory?
4. What is the significance of cell phones in meeting security and privacy needs?
5. How important is a mobile phone in establishing and maintaining social network?

DATA ANALYSIS

Sample

A total of 120 responses were received, of which there were 60 adolescents and 60 teachers as revealed in Figure 2. Since these were physically carried out surveys, all surveys were returned. The data was subsequently entered in an Excel spreadsheet, and analysis on the data was carried out. The following section presents graphs that show the comparison of adolescents' perception and teacher's perception pertaining to the most and least important factors affecting mobile usage amongst Indian adolescents. Most of the respondents reported that mobile phones

Figure 2. Distribution of sample

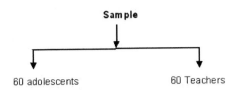

are more of a rule rather than an exception for the young adults today.

53 % of the teachers reported that maintaining social contact with peers is the most important factor affecting mobile usage of adolescents. Although 34 %, adolescents have also ranked peer contacts as one of the important factors, multifunctionalities of the mobile gadget are given the first priority by 39 % of adolescents. 45 % of the teachers have also reported that multifunctionality is one of the major factors affecting mobile usage amongst the youngsters. Therefore, there is a similarity between the adolescents' and teachers' perceptions; yet, there is a difference in emphasis. Also, both groups have laid equal emphasis regarding the costs per transaction as an important factor impacting mobile usage.

As presented in Figure 3, privacy has been given moderate importance and intriguingly teachers more than adolescent have ranked it higher in importance. This could be so as India being a 'high context'' culture focuses more on reinforcing social bonds. Nevertheless individual factors such as cognitive functions have also ranked high, indicating that the individual within the context is as important. Also interesting to note is that 'fashion' which is generally related to peer culture or peer pressure plays least important role among the Indian youngsters compared to their western counter parts.

Figure 4 depicts the factors that are ranked highest as the least important category affecting mobile usage. While costs per transactions are important, both groups (13 %) report that costs of handsets are least important factors impacting mobile usage. Also mobiles serving as tools for reinforcing intimacy and social signaling are not crucial factors. 25 % of adolescents compared to 9 % of the teachers felt that cognitive functions that mobile serve are also least important factors affecting mobile usage. Surprisingly again more adolescents (24%) than teachers (13%) reported that mobile phones for finding cross sex friends is least important. 11 % of both adolescents than teachers have reported that the privacy functions of the mobile phone are least important for adolescents!

Figure 3. Important factors impacting mobile usage

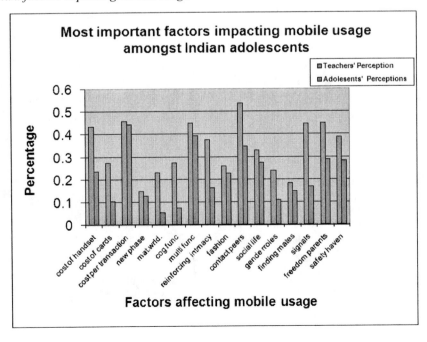

Figure 4. Least important factors impacting mobile usage

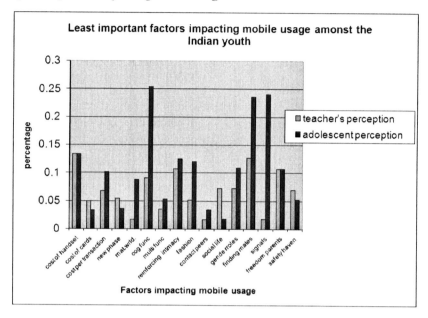

CONCLUSION AND FUTURE DIRECTION

All the six domains viz., cost, context, mobile usage, social, interpersonal and security factors influence mobile usage differently. Within these domains some factors are ranked highly important while others least important. For example, while multi functionality is an important factor affecting mobile use, within the same domain cognitive functions of mobile are not considered so important. Similarly while privacy is an important factor in the security domain while social signaling is not. Again while maintaining peer network is an important factor, maintaining intimacy and finding cross sex peers is not ranked very high.

As mentioned earlier, apart from adolescents and their teachers, it is important to study parents and peers views as they are also significantly affected by and in turn influence adolescent mobility. Further deeper investigations and more semi-structured and open ended responses can elicit various factors from the perspective of the respondents. For example, some adolescents mentioned the importance of mobile for professional networking, communicating more effectively and also mobility highly valued at times of emergency. Some of them also confessed about their addiction to mobile phones despite being concerned about unwanted calls and waste of time and money.

While some feel that spending money on mobiles is a good way of spending the pocket money. Therefore deeper investigations using a combination of survey and interview method may yield richer data giving better insight into responses of the respondents.

REFERENCES

Ahmed, Z. (2004, April). Youth drives India's mobile phone revolution. BBC news. *Retrieved February, 2007 from http://news.bbc.co.uk/2/hi/business/3585257. stm*

Campbell, M. (2005).The impact of the mobile phone on young people's social life. *Paper presented to the Social Change in the 21st Century Conference Centre for Social Change Research Queensland University of Technology.*

Dornbusch, S. M. (1989). The sociology of adolescence. *Annual Review of Sociology, 15,* 233-59.

Erikson, E. H. (1968). *Identity, youth and crisis.* New York: Norton.

Fraley, R. C., & Shaver, P. R. (2000). Adult romantic attachment: Theoretical developments, emerging controversies, and unanswered questions. *Review of General Psychology, 4(2),* 132-154.

Foley, C., Holzman, C., & Wearing, S. (2007). Moving beyond conspicuous leisure consumption: adolescent women, mobile phones and public space. *Liesure Studies 26*(2), 179-192.

Furman, W., & Simon, V. A. (1998). Cognitive Representations of Adolescent Romantic Relationships. In W. Furman, B. B. Brown, & C. Feiring (Eds.) *Contemporary Perspectives on Adolescent Romantic Relationships.* New York, NY: Cambridge University Press.

Furman, W., & Wehner, E. A. (1993). Romantic Views: Toward a Theory of Adolescent Romantic Relationships. In R. Montemayor, G.R. Adams, & G.P. Gullota (Ed.), *Advances in adolescent development: Volume 6, Relationships during adolescence* (pp. 168-195). Thousand Oaks, CA: Sage.

Gesar, H. (2004). Towards a sociological theory of mobile phones. *In sociology in Switzerland: Sociology of the mobile phone.* Online Publications. Zuerich, May 2004 (Release 3.0) http://socio.ch/mobile/t_geserl.pdf

Grotevant, H. D. (1998). Adolescent development in family contexts. In W. Damon (Series Ed.) & N. Eisenberg, (Vol. Ed.), *Handbook of Child Psychology: Vol.3. Social, emotional and personality development.* (5th ed., pp. 1097-1040) NY: John Wiley.

High context culture. (2007, November 24). *Wikipedia, The Free Encyclopedia. Retrieved 05:01, November 25, 2007, from http://en.wikipedia.org/w/index. php?title=High_context_culture&oldid=173392530*

Ling, R. 2001. *Adolescent girls and young adult men: The two subultures of mobile phone.* Kjeller, Telenol Researh and development 2001 (R&D report r 34/2001).

Macro (2004). *A report on study of mobile phone usage among teenagers and youth in Mumbai. Retrieved February 6, 2007, from http://www.newsnmuse.info/images/cellphonestudy.pdf*

Morris, D. (1969). *The Human Zoo.* NY: Kondansha America, Inc.

Saraswathi, T. S. (1999). Adult child continuity in India: Is adolescence a myth or an emerging reality. In T. S. Saraswathi. *Culture, socialization and Human development.* (pp 213-233). New Delhi: Sage.

KEY TERMS

Adolescents: Young individuals in the transition phase from childhood to adulthood in the age range of 16-19 years for this study.

High-Context Cultures: These cultures are relational, collectivist, intuitive, and contemplative and emphasize interpersonal relationships for example much of the Middle East, Asia, Africa, and South America.

Interpersonal Relationships: Establishing and maintaining social connections and associations which may range from casual friendships, professional contacts to intimate friendships and kinships.

Mobile Gadgets: Portable devices which confer mobility to the users through mobile technology which may include a combination of hardware, software, operating system and networking.

Mobility: Ability to send and receive communications anytime anywhere with the help of mobile technologies and gadgets.

Multi-Functionalities: Capable of serving more than one purpose.

Quantitative Survey: A formal, objective, systematic process in which numerical data is generated and utilized to obtain information about the topic under study using a survey questionnaire on a fairly large sample group.

ENDNOTE

[1]   **High-context cultures** (including much of the Middle East, Asia, Africa, and South America) are relational, collectivist, intuitive, and contemplative. This means that people in these cultures emphasize interpersonal relationships (High context … 2007)

Chapter XXXI
The Mobile Network as a New Medium for Marketing Communications:
A Case Study

Heikki Karjaluoto
University of Oulu, Finland

Matti Leppäniemi
University of Oulu, Finland

Jari Sall
University of Oulu, Finland

Jaako Sinisalo
University of Oulu, Finland

Feng Li
University of Newcastle upon Tyne, UK

ABSTRACT

This chapter discusses the mobile network as a new medium for marketing communications. It illustrates that the mobile medium, defined as two-way communications via mobile handsets, can be utilized in a company's promotion mix by initiating and maintaining relationships. First, by using the mobile medium companies can attract new customers by organizing SMS (short message service) -based competitions and lotteries. Second, the mobile medium can be used as a relationship building tool as companies can send information and discount coupons to existing customers' mobile devices or collect marketing research data. The authors explore these scenarios by presenting and analyzing a mobile marketing case from Finland. The chapter concludes by pondering different future avenues for the mobile medium in promotion mix.

INTRODUCTION

In the repercussion of the mobile hype around wireless access protocol (WAP), followed by the launch of third-generation (3G) networks/Universal Mobile Telecommunications System (UMTS), the debate over the role of the mobile medium in promoting goods and services has emerged as a topic of considerable magnitude that echoes across different academic disciplines. The burst of the telecommunications bubble in 2000 eventually led telecommunications companies and information technology firms to change their way of thinking, from a technology-driven viewpoint to a more user-oriented perspective. In Europe, only a few mobile services have prospered, while others like many WAP-based services have proved to be unpopular (e.g.,

Williams, 2003). In fact, only ring tone downloading, logo services, and Short Message Service (SMS) can to date be considered as successful mobile services. The reasons underlying the success of these services fundamentally lie with the strong market demand and easy-to-use technology. When thinking about future mobile services, the *Mobile Internet* is often seen as a messiah of the 3G. Third-generation mobile telephony protocols support higher data rates, measured in kbps (kilobits per second) or Mbps (megabits per second), intended for applications other than voice-centric (3GPP, 2005; Symbian Glossary, 2005). The underlying idea of the 3G/UMTS networks is that mobile phones are always connected to the best available network ranging from 2G GSM networks to EDGE (General Packet Radio Service), HSCSD (High-Speed Circuit-Switched Data) to WLAN (Wireless Local Area Network), and 3G networks. However, many companies operating in the telecommunications field are facing the same challenge when thinking about the right mobile services to the right mobile users. Recently, a project led by Nokia and a couple of other Finnish companies announced that television will find its way on mobile phone screens. Consumer acceptance of mobile TV services as well as the underlying technology will be tested and developed with 500 users in Finland (Nokia, 2005).

Since the future of mobile services is still unpredictable, this chapter will not speculate on new mobile services that might take off in the next few years. Instead, we will focus on technologies and applications that are already here and in use, which allow us to examine the utilization of text messaging (SMS) in managing customer relationships in the business-to-consumer markets. In this chapter, we will present a mobile marketing case in a Finnish general store that integrated mobile media in its marketing communications mix as shown in Figure 1.

BACKGROUND TO THE RESEARCH PROJECT

This research is based on a project called PEAR, Personalized Mobile Advertising Services (www.pear.fi), which aims at developing a multi-channel mobile marketing service system for planning, implementing, and analyzing mobile marketing that utilizes value-added features such as personalization, user grouping, presence, profile, and location information. The service system will be tested and developed with end

Figure 1. Mobile marketing campaign integrated with other marketing channels

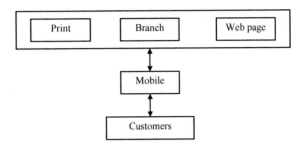

users in real-life settings. The results are expected to contribute to the invention of new customer-oriented service concepts and business models, which can open up potential new business opportunities in global markets. Mobile marketing is in this project defined as marketing communications sent to and received on smart phones, mobile phones, or personal digital assistants (PDAs).

The Campaign Logic

The basic idea of the advertising campaign was to redirect customers to the company's Web page and to get them to register on the company's electronic marketplace. The campaign was advertised in various media (print media, Web pages, and at the store). Advertisements contained instructions of how to participate in the lottery that offered a prize worth 200EUR for registered users. Users were requested to send a text message to a short number and receive a text message back from the company that contains a five-digit short code. The mobile marketing service system generated 100,000 different five-number digits so each participant received an individual code. With the use of this "lucky number"—the five-digit code—customers were able to register with the online shop and thus participate in the lottery.

INTEGRATING THE MOBILE MEDIUM INTO THE MARKETING COMMUNICATIONS MIX

Generally speaking, marketing communications refer to the promotion of both the organization and its offerings (Fill, 2002). The marketing communications mix, also called the promotional mix, comprises a set of tools that can be used in different combinations and in different degrees of intensity in order to communicate with a target audience. In recent years, the traditional way of thinking about how firms communicate with their customers has changed (e.g., Duncan & Moriarty, 1998; Kim, Han, & Schultz, 2004). With the help of new technologies, companies nowadays have a variety of digital channels allowing assorted ways to both send and receive information. Broadly speaking, we have been witnessing a change from mass communications to more direct and personal communications in which the messages are highly targeted and personalized. This has happened especially in digital communication channels (Kitchen & Schultz, 1999).

Mobile marketing (m-marketing) communications, defined as all forms of marketing, advertising, or sales promotion activities aimed at consumers (MMA, 2003), is one of the most modern digital channels in the promotion mix. Its role in advertising campaigns has not been studied widely, and relatively little is known of its role in the overall communications mix (Karjaluoto, Leppäniemi, & Salo, 2004). M-marketing can be either *push* based, which refers to communications such as SMS alerts sent to wireless devices requiring user permission, or *pull* based, which refers to information a user requests from a provider or advertiser (Barnes & Scornavacca, 2004; Carat Interactive, 2002). The mobile medium has to date mainly been used in promotions such as lotteries and various competitions (e.g., Pura, 2002). However, the market seems to be ready for more sophisticated two-way mobile marketing campaigns such as mobile customer relationship management (Finnish Direct Marketing Association, 2004), as customers are more and more using mobile data services such as text messaging and multimedia messaging in buying purposes and in providing feedback.

SPECIAL FEATURES OF THE MOBILE MARKETING MEDIUM

The mobile medium has some unique features that other direct marketing channels lack. In general terms, the mobile medium is favoured by marketers for its broad reach, low cost, and high retention rates (Clickatell, 2002). For mobile phones, several features are particularly relevant: the mobile phone is seen as an extremely personal, immediate, and interactive medium allowing marketers an effective way to reach customers in a fresh manner (Koranteng, 2001;

Peters, 2002). As a marketing communication channel, the mobile (especially text) messaging is seen as immediate, automated, reliable, personal, discreet, and customized, allowing an efficient way to reach markets directly and providing mobile phone users a direct call-to-action, which would be almost impossible via other channels (Barnes & Scornavacca, 2004; Clickatell, 2004; Leppäniemi & Karjaluoto, 2005). These special features are illustrated in Figure 2.

As mobile phones are extremely personal in nature, advertising to mobile devices has to be very discreet in the sense that unwanted messages are easily perceived as spam. Messaging services (e.g., SMS and MMS) can be considered a very reliable way to distribute information, not only due to the fact that messages almost always arrive in time, but also because the majority of consumers usually read all messages they receive. In relation to mobile marketing campaigns, studies reported that in over 90% of cases, respondents read mobile advertising messages they receive (Enpocket, 2003). Moreover, the mobile media can also be regarded as an interactive media. As Enpocket's (2003) study indicated, of 5,000 consumers participating in SMS campaigns, 15% of them responded to mobile marketing messages. Finally, mobile devices have the ability to identify the location of users through the use of various technologies such as network-based positioning (or remote positioning), accurate local area positioning techniques, and satellite positioning (Kumar & Stokkeland, 2003; Zeimpekis, Giaglis, & Lekakos, 2003). Location-based advertising (LBA) is based on the idea that in a certain location, and

Figure 2. Special features of mobile media

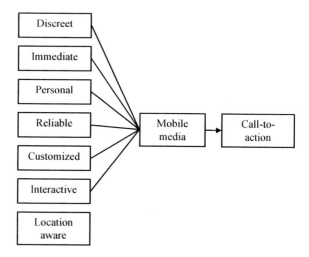

additionally at a certain time, consumers receive advertisements based on their location (Salo & Tähtinen, 2005; Tsang, Ho, & Liang, 2004). However, as the rules of protecting consumers' privacy, including the use of location-based information for marketing purposes, are becoming stricter, the development and diffusion of location-based advertising have many obstacles to overcome.

Research has shown that the primary role of mobile marketing in a company's promotion mix has to date been promoting call-to-action (e.g., Paananen, 2003; Clickatell, 2004; Karjaluoto et al., 2004). In providing a direct call-to-action, location awareness and time open up the possibility to personalize messages in the manner that provide straight call-to-action. For instance, if a consumer arrives at a store, he or she might receive a personalized advertisement from that store based on his or her profile. It is important to note that to receive the benefits, for instance a discount to the store, consumers need to be in a certain location.

CUSTOMER RELATIONSHIP MANAGEMENT WITH MOBILE PHONES

Over the past decade it has become increasingly difficult to differentiate from competitors in serving the general product needs of customers. Therefore, companies have had to shift their focus to customer orientation and to search for novel ways to create value to customers. As a result, customer relationship management (CRM) is currently gaining widespread popularity in several disciplines and industries (e.g., Ryals, 2003; Zablah, Bellenger, & Johnston, 2004). On the one hand, the objective of CRM is to build and maintain customer relationships, and on the other to provide value for customers. Despite the potential of traditional CRM to provide value for customers, customers are expecting more and more individual attention. From the viewpoint of marketing communications, new digital marketing channels such as the Internet and mobile phones are considered to be powerful new media to reach consumers by allowing personalization and interactivity of both the content and the context of the message (Heinonen & Strandvik, 2003; Kim et al., 2004). Furthermore, as mobile marketing can combine the capacities of both direct marketing and ever-present nature and power of mobile digital technology, this form of communica-

Figure 3. Dimensions of the initiation stage of m-CRM

tion is seen to provide synergy that will increase the potential of direct marketing (Mort & Drennan, 2002). Although electronic customer relationship management (e-CRM), defined broadly as CRM through the Internet, has received much attention among practitioners and academics (Bradshaw & Brash, 2001; Feinberg, Kadam, Hokama, & Kim, 2002; Fjermestad & Romano, 2003), the mobile medium as an element of CRM has gained far less attention.

Customer relationship management with mobile phones—in other words mobile customer relationship management (we use the term m-CRM)—can be defined as an ongoing process that provides seamless integration of every area of business that touches the customer, for the purpose of building and maintaining a profit-maximizing portfolio of customer relationships, by taking advantage of the mobile medium.

Because customer relationships evolve with distinct stages (Dwyer, Schurr, & Oh, 1987), companies should also interact with customers and manage relationships differently at each stage (Srivastava, Shervani, & Fahey, 1998). The CRM process outlines three key stages, namely the initiation, maintenance, and termination phases (Reinartz, Krafft, & Hoyer, 2004). In this study, it is implicitly assumed that m-CRM consists of these three stages as well. Because the main interest of this study is about how to redirect customers to the company's Web page and to get them register to the company's electronic marketplace, we focus primarily on the initiation stage.

USING MOBILE CRM IN INITIATING RELATIONSHIPS

Integrating the mobile medium as an element of CRM involves three key aspects: technology, implementation, and customers. This has been illustrated in Figure 3.

The first key aspect to consider during the initiation stage of m-CRM is the technology. The company has to decide whether to rent the hosting mobile marketing server or to acquire it. Then gateways have to be built to connect with the mobile operators whose customers are allowed to be contacted.

The implementation consists of two decisions: first, through what marketing medium that the customers are acquired; and second, how much it will cost customers to use the messaging service—that is, sending the SMS message.

Given the personal nature of mobile phones, customers are often unwilling to use the mobile medium for marketing purposes due to fears of unsolicited marketing messages or even spam. Therefore, the third aspect of the initiation stage comprises understanding customers; to discover what are the key factors that lure the customer to use the mobile medium; and in this case, to redirect them to the company's electronic marketplace.

CASE STUDY

The central idea of the case study was to analyze the role of mobile media in generating traffic to company A's e-commerce Web page. Moreover, we wanted to investigate the company's (an ironmonger store) consumer responses to mobile marketing. The marketing campaign began at the end of November 2004 with a full-page advertisement in local newspaper. The newspaper advertisement contained instructions on how to participate in the SMS lottery. Consumers were asked to send a simple text message to a five-digit short number code. Immediately after sending the message, the mobile service system generated a four-digit code that the consumer received on his or her phone. This code was then entered on the company's Web site. After entering the code to the Web site, consumers were guided to the registration page and asked to fill in the registration form. In case a registered person is participating in the campaign, they are guided to update their registration information. All registered consumers would be entered into a drawing for a digital video camera. The logic of the campaign is illustrated in Figure 4.

MAIN RESULTS

Altogether 232 consumers took part in the lottery during the period from November 24 to December 20, 2004. The newspaper advertisement on November 24, 2004, generated approximately 100 new registered

Figure 4. Marketing communications mix in company A's case

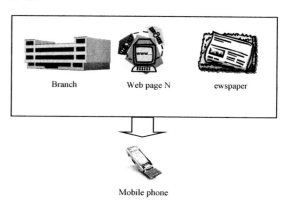

customers in two days. After the newspaper advertisement, the company's Web site was, practically speaking, the only advertising channel for the lottery. The amount of new registrations per day varied from a few to around 10, with a final number of 232 registered consumers. Of these, only five were existing customers of the case company's online store. There were 47 female (20.3%) and 185 men (79.7%) in the sample. Approximately 33% of the participants were between ages 36 and 49, 22% were between 26 and 35, and 12% were between 50 and 64. The remaining categories had less than 11% of responses per category. With respect to careers, most respondents were blue-collar workers (34%), followed by white-collar workers (24%); 13% belonged to top or middle management and 11% to lower management, and students were 15%. Additionally, the registration form inquired about respondents' areas of interests. A total of 118 respondents reported interest in electronics and photography, followed by computers, leisure time, and motor vehicles. Of the total 21 interest areas, pets (26 responses), toys (29 responses), and watches and jewelry (30 responses) were considered least interesting.

CONSUMER WILLINGNESS TO RECEIVE DIRECT MARKETING

The registration form finally inquired about respondents' willingness to receive digital marketing communications from the company either via SMS or e-mail. While most respondents wanted to opt out of text messaging service (73%), the majority opted in to e-mail marketing (67%). This finding might relate to the fact that the case in question was relating to online commerce, and thus respondents regarded the e-mail channel as more suitable for them to receive marketing communication. In addition, approximately 24% of the respondents opted out of both marketing communication channels.

We next compared willingness to receive SMS and e-mail marketing with demographic variables with the use of a series of chi-square analyses. In respect of gender, 25% of males welcomed SMS marketing from the company, whereas the corresponding number for females was 34%. Concerning willingness to receive e-mail marketing, around 70% of males and 55% of females opted in to e-mail marketing. However, the difference between genders was neither statistically significant for SMS (chi-square=1.612, p=0.204) nor for e-mail (chi-square=3.510, p=0.061), although in e-mail it was relatively close to significant (p<0.05 level). With regard to respondents' age and willingness to receive digital marketing communications, a statistically significant difference was found in welcoming e-mail marketing (chi-square=15.725, p=0.008). This finding indicates that the younger age categories were not so willing to receive e-mail marketing compared to the older ones. Age category 26 to 35 most eagerly welcomed e-mail marketing (86% opted in), followed by age group 36 to 49 (70% opted in), and age group 50 to 64 (64% opted in). Approximately 50% of those under 18 opted in to e-mail marketing, as the corresponding number for age group 19 to 25 was 48%. No relationship was found between age and willingness to receive SMS communications (chi-square=4.752, p=0.451).

In terms of careers and willingness to receive marketing communications, no differences were found with the original classification of professions. However, after recoding the profession variable into a two-class variable, in which 1 was equal to blue-collar worker and 2 equal to white-collar worker, a statistically significant difference was found between profession and willingness to receive SMS communications (chi-square=5.520, p=0.019). It seems that blue-collar workers more eagerly welcomed SMS communications (33% opted in) than white-collar workers (15% opted in). No differences were found between profession and willingness to receive e-mail marketing (chi-square=0.236, p=0.627).

Finally, there is some evidence that respondents' place of residence has an impact on willingness to receive both SMS and e-mail marketing. The place of residence variable was divided into three categories, in which one was equal to "I live within ten-mile radius of the company's physical store," two was equal to "I live within a hundred-mile radius from the company's physical branch," and three was equal to "I live elsewhere in Finland." Interestingly, with respect to willingness to receive SMS marketing, most respondents living elsewhere in Finland did not want to receive SMS marketing (80% opted out). A total of 71% living near the store opted out of SMS marketing, and 65% of those living in a hundred-mile radius opted out. The difference between groups was close to statistical significance (chi-square=5.664, p=0.059). Moreover, those living the farthest away from the store were most willing to welcome e-mail marketing (75% opted in), followed by those living within a hundred-mile radius (60% opted in), and those living near the store (54% opted in). The chi-square value (chi-square=6.860, p=0.032) indicates a statistically significant relationship between place of residence and willingness to receive e-mail marketing. On this basis, it seems that the further a person lives, the more likely he or she is to opt in to e-mail marketing. However, in regard to SMS marketing, there is no linear relationship between location and willingness to receive SMS marketing.

To conclude, our results indicate that blue-collar workers are more willing to receive SMS marketing from the case company than white-collar workers. This fresh finding should be interpreted in light of the empirical case setting, which might indicate that blue-collar workers are not in general so familiar with e-mailing as white-collar workers, and thus they regard the SMS channel as more suitable for them in receiving marketing communications. However, validation of further work is needed. Moreover, with regard to welcoming e-mail marketing, it seems that age groups 26-35, 36-49, and 50-64 offer the most potential for e-mail marketing campaigns, as more than 50% of them welcomed e-mail marketing. Furthermore, it seems that age itself has no influence on willingness to receive SMS marketing communications. Finally, our results showed that place of residence has an impact on willingness to receive e-mail marketing. The further a person lives from the physical store, the more likely he or she was to opt in to e-mail marketing communication.

CONCLUSION AND FUTURE DIRECTIONS

This chapter responds to the call for research on the use of mobile media in the marketing communications mix by investigating its specific features and role in integrated marketing communication mix and by describing the use of mobile media in amassing mobile marketing customer database. Our objective was to discuss the ways to integrate the mobile medium into the promotion mix of companies. By using a single case study from the retail sector, we showed that by combining the mobile medium and e-commerce store, it is possible to build a customer database in an efficient and cost-effective manner. Although our empirical case mainly contributes to the discussion of how to initiate customer relationships, it also gives some insights into the maintenance process of relationships by asking respondents about their digital channel preferences.

In light of the main results, several conclusions can be drawn. First of all, with relatively small promotional activity, the case company gained close to 250 new registered customers to their online store mainly by the use of a newspaper advertisement and online advertising on the company's own Web site. As most respondents opted in to e-mail marketing (67%), and most opted out of SMS marketing (73%), in the next stage of relationship building, the e-mail channel might be the right avenue to continue. However, some specific customer segments (blue-collar workers especially) welcomed SMS marketing. This finding should be interpreted as: those customers who opted in to SMS channel either do not use e-mail or for other reasons want marketing communications via SMS. By giving customers a choice, it is supposedly also contributing to the overall customer satisfaction and thus driving those registered potential customers into purchasing online customers as well.

This study has some limitations that present opportunities for further research. First, the study is among the first ones examining the use of a mobile device as a marketing communication channel, and thus the results obtained should be considered tentative. Second, we study only one retailer and its marketing communication, and despite the fact that its communication mix is in line with other companies operating in the same field nationwide, it would be valuable to scrutinize other retailers as well. In sum, we assume that these limitations do not endanger the reliability and validity of the findings, yet they do place bounds on the conclusions and implications that can be drawn from the study.

While mobile marketing is today almost entirely SMS based, the diffusion of MMS-enabled phones will presumably shape the industry in the future (Paananen, 2003; Barwise & Strong, 2002). Also the mushroom of devices with larger screens will guide mobile marketers to new avenues (Yonos, Gao, & Shim, 2003). These should be taken into consideration when planning future studies. Furthermore, a natural extension of our study would be the investigation of the role of mobile media in the marketing communications mix with other retailers. By doing so we might get valuable insights into how companies nationwide use, or plan to use, mobiles as a media in marketing communications.

REFERENCES

3GPP. (2005). *Terms & abbreviations*. Retrieved March 17, 2005, from http://www.3 gpp.org

Barnes, S., & Scornavacca, E., (2004). Mobile marketing: the role of permission and acceptance. *International Journal of Mobile Communications, 2*(2), 128-139.

Barwise, P., & Strong, C. (2002). Permission-based mobile advertising. *Journal of Interactive Marketing, 16*(1), 14-24.

Bradshaw, D., & Brash, C. (2001). Managing customer relationships in the e-business world: How to personalize computer relationships for increased profitability. *International Journal of Retail & Distribution Management, 29*(12), 520-529.

Carat Interactive. (2002). The future of wireless marketing. *Research Report.* Retrieved from http://www.mmaglobal.com/resources/Wireless_WhitePaper.pdf

Clickatell. (2004). Business mobility guide. *Research Report.* Retrieved from http://www.clickatell.com

Duncan, T., & Moriarty, S. E. (1998). A communication-based marketing model for managing relationships. *Journal of Marketing, 62*(2), 1-13.

Dwyer, R., Schurr, P., & Oh, S. (1987). Developing buyer-seller relations. *Journal of Marketing, 51*(2), 11-28.

Enpocket. (2003, February). The response performance of SMS advertising. *Research Report, 3*. Retrieved from http://www. enpocket.com

Feinberg, R. A., Kadam, R., Hokama, L., & Kim, I. (2002). The state of electronic customer relationship management in retailing. *International Journal of Retail & Distribution Management, 30*(10), 470-481.

Fill, C. (2002). *Marketing communications—Context, strategies and applications.* Englewood Cliffs, NJ: Prentice-Hall, Harlow.

Fjermestad, J., & Romano, N.C. (2003). Electronic customer relationship management. Revisiting the general principles of usability and resistance—An integrative implementation framework. *Business Process Management Journal, 9*(5), 572-591.

Heinonen, K., & Strandvik, T. (2003, May 22-23). Consumer responsiveness to mobile marketing. Paper presented at the *Proceedings of the Stockholm Mobility Roundtable*, Stockholm, Sweden.

Karjaluoto, H., Leppäniemi, M., & Salo, J. (2004). The role of mobile marketing in companies' promotion mix. Empirical evidence from Finland. *Journal of International Business and Economics, 2*(1), 111-116.

Kim, I., Han, D., & Schultz, D.E. (2004). Understanding the diffusion of integrated marketing communications. *Journal of Advertising Research, 44*(1), 31-45.

Kitchen, P., & Schultz, D. (1999). A multi-country comparison of the drive for IMC. *Journal of Advertising Research, 39*(1), 21-38.

Koranteng, J. (2001). ZAP! There's no escaping the mobile ad. *Ad Age Global, 1*(5), 9.

Kumar, S., & Stokkeland, J. (2003). Evolution of GPS technology and its subsequent use in commercial markets. *International Journal of Mobile Communications, 1*(½), 180-193.

Leppäniemi, M., & Karjaluoto, H. (2005). Factors influencing consumer willingness to accept mobile advertising. A conceptual model. *International Journal of Mobile Communications, 3*(3), 197-213.

MMA (Mobile Marketing Association). (2003). *MMA code for responsible mobile marketing.* Retrieved December 14, 2003, from www.mmaglobal.co.uk/

Mort, G., & Drennan, J. (2002). Mobile digital technology: Emerging issues for marketing. *Journal of*

Database Marketing and Customer Strategy Management, 10(1), 9-23.

Nokia. (2005). *Mobile TV pilot begins in Finland.* Retrieved March 17, 2005, from http://press.nokia.com/PR/200503/983665_5.html

Paananen, V. M. (2003, February 12). *European mobile marketing: Case Add2Phone.* Presentation at the NETS Seminar, Helsinki, Finland.

Peters, B. (2002, November 6). The future of wireless marketing. *Carat Interactive Study.* Retrieved from http://www.caratinter active.com/resources/articles.html

Pura, M. (2002). Case study: The role of mobile advertising in building a brand. In B. E. Mennecke & T. J. Strader (Eds.), *Mobile commerce: Technology, theory and applications* (pp. 291-308). Hershey, PA: Idea Group Publishing.

Reinartz, W., Krafft, M., & Hoyer, W. (2004). The customer relationship management process: Its measurement and impact on performance. *Journal of Marketing Research, 41*(3), 293-305.

Ryals, L. (2003). Making customers pay: Measuring and managing customer risk and return. *Journal of Strategic Marketing, 11*(3), 165-175.

Salo, J., & Tähtinen, J. (2005). Retailer use of permission-based mobile advertising. In I. Clarke, III, & T. B. Flaherty (Eds.), *Advances in electronic marketing* (pp. 139-155). Hershey, PA: Idea Group Publishing Group.

Srivastava, R., Shervani, T., & Fahey, L. (1998). Marketing based assets and shareholder value: A framework for analysis. *Journal of Marketing, 62*(1), 2-18.

Symbian Glossary. (2005). Retrieved March 17, 2005, from http://www.symbian.com/technology/glossary.html

Tsang, M. M., Ho, S.-C., & Liang, T.-P. (2004). Consumer attitudes toward mobile advertising: An empirical study. *International Journal of Electronic Commerce, 8*(3), 65-78.

Williams, C. (2003, March 17). Can GPRS get back on track? *Lucent Technologies: 3G Solutions for Operators, 12.* Retrieved from http://www.lucent.com/livelink/0900940 380033c60_Newsletter.pdf

Yonos, H. M., Gao, J. Z., & Shim, S. (2003). Wireless advertising's challenges and opportunities. *IEEE Computer, 36*(5), 30-37.

Zablah, A. R., Bellenger, D. N., & Johnston, W. J. (2004). An evaluation of divergent perspectives on customer relationship management: Towards a common understanding of an emerging phenomenon. *Industrial Marketing Management, 33*(6), 475-489.

Zeimpekis, V., Giaglis, G. M., & Lekakos, G. (2003). Towards a taxonomy of indoor and outdoor positioning techniques for mobile location-based applications. *ACM SIGecom Exchanges, 3*(4), 19-27.

Chapter XXXII
Successful Implementation of Emerging Communication Technologies in a Mobile–Intense Organization:
A Case Study of Sydney Airport

Keyurkumar J. Patel
Box Hill Institute, Australia

ABSTRACT

Wireless Technology is growing at a phenomenal rate. Of the many present challenges highlighted by the author, increased security is one of the main challenges for both developers and end users. This chapter presents this important security aspect of implementing a mobile solution in the context of Sydney International airport. After tackling initial challenges and issues faced during the implementation of wireless technology, this chapter demonstrates how security issues and wireless application were implemented at this mobile-intense airport organization. The decision to deploy and manage the wireless spectrum throughout the Airport campus meant that the wireless LAN had to share the medium with public users, tenants and aircraft communications on the same bandwidth. Therefore, this case study also demonstrates invaluable approach to protect unintended users from breach of existing security policies adopted by their corporate network. Authentication and data privacy challenges, as well as complete WLAN connectivity for tenants, public and corporate usage is presented in this case study.

INTRODUCTION

Sydney's International Airport forms the hub of aviation in the Pacific region. It is an 85-year-old site, approximately 8 kilometers from Sydney CBD. With 5 terminals with 34 international, 31 domestic, and 5 airfreight gates, it is the largest airport catering to 8.7 million international and 15.5 million domestic passengers per year (McCubben, 2003). As such, an acute need was felt to ensure a high level of timely and quality service to the entire infrastructure of the airport. Mobile technologies were considered as a crucial ingredient in provision of this service. This need continues to be corroborated worldwide; for

Figure 1. Typical wireless LAN topology

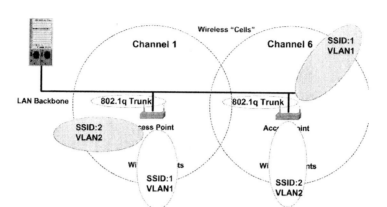

example, at the Airport Council International (ACI) World Assembly in Santiago in November 2000, the airport community expressed the importance of a wireless infrastructure at airports managed by the airport authority (Sydney Airport Corporation Limited, 2000). The following resolution was agreed upon:

Airport Operators should assert control over the use of Wireless Infrastructure at Airports, both inside and outside terminal buildings. Tenants, concessionaires and others should use a common infrastructure for wireless managed by the Airport Operator. In return for this exclusivity, Airport operators should constantly evaluate competing technologies, so as to maintain low costs, increased capacity and security in line with demand for the benefits of all tenants, concessionaires and others.

Meanwhile, in 1998, with the impending Sydney Olympics 2000, Sydney Airport Corporation Limited (SACL) was formed. SACL took it upon itself to embark on the challenge of becoming the sole provider of wireless infrastructure at the International Terminal and Airfield. Past experience indicated that business customers preferred to install their own networks, and wireless—still an evolving technology with no ratified security standards and ease of deployment—gave SACL a unique challenge. This chapter discusses in detail the successful deployment of mobile applications at the Sydney International Airport.

WLAN Architecture and Security Challenges

With a typical wireless LAN (WLAN; see Figure 1), transmitted data is broadcast over the air using radio

waves. With a WLAN, the boundary for SACL's network has moved and is now located in many airfield remote sites. In early 2001, SACL deployed some 120 access points within the International Terminal (Terminal 1) and at various sites on the airfield. Sydney Airport WLAN implementation in early 2001 deployed Cisco Aironet 350 Series Access Points. The IEEE 802.11b standard adopted uses the unlicensed 2.4x gigahertz frequency band, providing only three non-overlapping channels (1, 6, and 11) with data-rates of 1, 2, 5.5, and 11Mbps.

However, without stringent security measures in place, the wireless infrastructure is equivalent of putting Ethernet ports everywhere. Thus, SACL's wireless deployment challenge was to ensure that the implementation of the wireless network did not breach its existing security policies for the corporate network. SACL regards the wireless network infrastructure in much the same fashion as the Internet, an untrusted zone. Even with this view, SACL has still ensured that wireless network security protects Sydney Airport's wireless VLAN. The following outlines the type of wireless and network security utilized at Sydney Airport.

Network Architecture and Security Policy

An important decision when deploying a WLAN is how it will interface back into the corporate infrastructure. The Wireless LAN (WLAN) at Sydney Airport has been designed so that the WLAN infrastructure access is located outside the corporate firewalls (see Figure 2). This approach creates more administrative overhead, because of the need for configuration of the External access network, consisting of router access lists and firewall rules. Furthermore, Sydney Airport does not need to maintain multiple WAN (Wide Area Network) remote sites. This is due to the fact that SACL's WLAN network is not deployed in order to replace the wired LAN in the office and is a network not solely accessed by SACL users. All external access from the wireless network is via the Wireless Access Router (WAR). The WAR is a Cisco 3550 Router configured to perform access-list filtering on all traffic based on source and destination IP address, protocol, and port numbers (Cisco Systems, 2002).

Many regard wireless technology as insecure (Arbaugh, 2001). SACL regards the wireless infrastructure at Sydney Airport as an untrusted zone. There are only two ways that a SACL wireless client can gain access to data from SACL's corporate network. The first option is to install an application proxy server. The proxy server allows data to move from the wireless untrusted zone to a semi-trusted zone located in the De-Militarized Zone (DMZ) outside SACL's Corporate Network, Firewall 1. This application proxy server located in the semi-trusted zone accesses the corporate network or trusted zone via Firewall 1 on the clients' behalf. The second option and only way resources can be accessed directly from an untrusted to a trusted zone is via the use of a Virtual Private Network (VPN). A VPN is established between SACL's wireless client and the Cisco VPN concentrator connected in parallel to the PIX firewall located in the DMZ. Both of these methods are described in detail further on.

SACL Wireless Authentication

Originally, SACL only offered a Cisco Propriety Wireless Security solution of Light-weight Extensible Authentication Protocol (LEAP) for all tenants and concessionaires utilizing SACL's infrastructure. Cisco's LEAP utilizes a 128-bit dynamic Wireless Equivalent Privacy (WEP) key, along with radius username and password authentication (Geier, 2002). The WEP key is dynamically assigned from one of two Remote Authentication Dial-In User Service (RADIUS) servers (Cisco Secure ACS 2.6 or greater) when an authenticated user associates with an access point. This WEP key is again negotiated between the client and the RADIUS server after a pre-configured period set on the RADIUS server. At present this period is set at less than 10 minutes (see Figure 3).

The new firmware software introduced by Cisco for their access points supports the termination of 802.1q trunk. This allows a trunk to be provisioned between the access point and an Ethernet switch, the end result allowing users in a wireless VLAN cell to belong to different VLANs. With the use of different VLANs, user traffic is segmented per group (i.e., per VLAN) with the use of differentiated security policy per VLAN. The Service Set Identifier (SSID) is used to map the client to the wireless VLAN. RADIUS attributes passed in between the access point can also override this mapping if the users are not authorized for that SSID. Up to 16 wireless VLAN's can be supported on each access point.

Figure 2. Network architecture and security policy

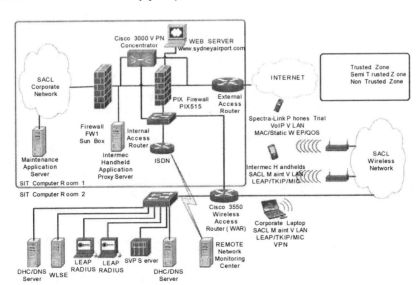

Figure 3. SACL wireless authentication—LEAP

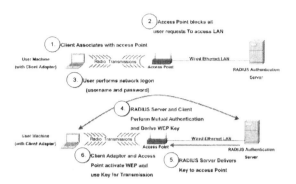

The introduction of wireless VLAN's allows the use of non-priority client cards, along with different security models. Although SACL believes that the Cisco LEAP solution is still the most secure and manageable solution presently available, when used in conjunction with Temporal Key Integrity Protocol (TKIP) and MIC, (TKIP and MIC security are explained in the next section), it is possible for a static WEP, Media Access Control (MAC), and or EAP security options to be used on a separate wireless VLAN. This enables the use of all vendors' 802.11b wireless clients adaptor and gives greater flexibility for products not yet supporting LEAP, such as most voice over IP wireless phones. At present SACL continues to use the LEAP solution with TKIP and MIC, as all their devices make use of Cisco client adapters.

Wireless Data Privacy Enhancements

While WLAN security that relies on Service Set Identifiers (SSIDs), open or shared-keys, static WEP keys, or MAC authentication is better than no security at all, it is not sufficient or truly manageable for the size of the Sydney Airport wireless network.

Sydney Airport, like all wireless network administrators, eagerly awaits the wireless IEEE 802.11i security standard that will allow vendor interoperability and still solve all known vulnerabilities of WEP (Stubblefield, 2002), the basic mechanism to date for interoperable security of Wireless 802.11b products. The IEEE 802.11i standards were published at the end of 2003. The Wi-Fi Alliance represented by many of the wireless vendors and in conjunction with the IEEE, has driven an effort to bring strongly enhanced, interoperable Wi-Fi security to market in the first quarter of 2003. The result of this effort is Wi-Fi Protected Access (WPA). Wi-Fi Protected Access is a specification of standards-based, interoperable security enhancements that strongly increase the level of data protection and access control for existing and future wireless LAN systems. Designed to run on existing hardware as a software upgrade, WPA is derived from and will be forward compatible with the upcoming IEEE 802.11i standard. One 802.11i component not required in WPA is Advanced Encryption Standard (AES) support. AES will replace 802.11's WEP initialization Vector RC4-based encryption under 802.11i specifications. Migrating to AES encryption, though, will require hardware changes, so this has been deferred by the Wi-Fi Alliance until the formal standard is in place to give vendors and customers some breathing room. The bad news is that 802.11i will require hardware changes regardless of whether WPA gets deployed over the next year or not.

Cisco has already been given WPA certification on the new IOS software available for both the 1100 and 1200 series Access Point range, with firmware for the 350 Series Access Points installed at Sydney Airport scheduled for the third quarter of 2005. Until the release Sydney Airport utilized Cisco's proprietary solution that features a subset of the 802.11i draft. As mentioned previously, Cisco has developed an 802.1X authentication type called EAP Cisco Wireless, or Cisco LEAP. Access points at Sydney Airport can be configured to support Cisco LEAP and all 802.1X authentication types, including EAP Transport Layer Security (EAP-TLS provides for certificate-based mutual authentication that relies on client-side and server-side digital certificates). With 802.1X authentication types such as LEAP and EAP-TLS, mutual authentication is implemented between the client and a RADIUS server. The credentials used for authentication, such as a log-on password, are never transmitted in the clear, or without encryption, over the wireless medium. Another benefit of 802.1X authentication is centralized management of WEP keys. Once mutual authentication has been successfully completed, the client and RADIUS server each derive the same WEP key, which will be used to encrypt all data exchanged. The result is per-user, per-session WEP keys. AP software running at the airport provides several enhancements to WEP keys that have formed part of the Wi-Fi Protected Access. These WEP enhancements include Cisco's pre-standard Temporal Key Integrity Protocol and support for Message Integrity Check (MIC).

When TKIP, also known as key-hashing support, is implemented on both the AP and all associated client devices, the transmitter of data hashes the base key with the IV (Initialization Vector of RC4 Key Scheduling Algorithm) to create a new key for each packet (Fluhrer, 2001). By ensuring that every packet is encrypted with a different key, key hashing removes the predictability that an eavesdropper relies on to determine the WEP key by exploiting IVs.

When MIC support is implemented on both the AP and all associated client devices, the transmitter of a packet adds a few bytes (the MIC) to the packet before encrypting and transmitting it. Upon receiving the packet, the recipient decrypts it and checks the MIC. If the MIC in the frame matches the calculated value (derived from the MIC function), the recipient accepts the packet; otherwise, the recipient discards the packet. Using MIC, packets that have been (maliciously) modified in transit are dropped. Attackers cannot use bit-flipping or active replay attacks to fool the network into authenticating them, because the MIC-enabled client and access points identify and reject altered packets.

Mobile Maintenance

The initial deployment of the wireless network within Terminal 1 and the airfield coincided with the Mobile Maintenance Project. The project utilized the wireless network to track and complete maintenance work in the field. Maintenance staff at Sydney Airport uses a Computerized Maintenance Management System (CMMS) known as MAXIMO (see Figure 5). The one limitation of MAXIMO was its inability to follow staff to the job. Previously "work orders" or job sheets were printed directly off the system and then taken into the field by the relevant trade staff or technician. Once the work was completed, the sheet was completed manually and the written data then entered in MAXIMO, either on return to the workshop or at the end of a shift. The mobile solution utilizing an industrialized handheld personal digital assistant (PDA) eliminates re-entry of data and has a positive follow-on effect in allowing more accurate reporting and a paperless system. With the limitation of VPN clients for PDAs at the time of delivery for the project, an application proxy server was installed within SACL's semi-trusted DMZ area to proxy wireless client requests to the MAXIMO application server. The PDA used was fitted with a Cisco Client Adaptor card and set up to use LEAP. The only changes from the initial installation are the upgrade of wireless client driver to utilize Cisco's

Figure 4. SACl wireless deployment (map © Sydway Publishing Pty. Ltd. Reproduced with permission)

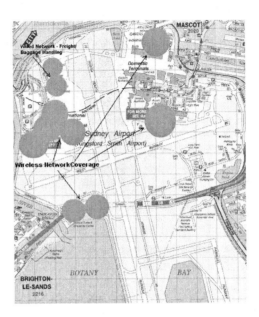

TKIP and MIC security enhancements configured on the access points.

Wireless VPN Remote Access Solution

In December 2002 SACL embarked on a corporate remote access solution. The solution enables SACL corporate users to access the corporate network with all desktop applications from broadband Internet access, corporate dialup, and wireless access. By placing the wireless infrastructure access outside the corporate firewalls, it allows SACL to best utilize its remote access VPN solution. The implemented solution integrates a Cisco VPN 3000 Concentrator, Microsoft 2000 Certificate Server, Microsoft VPN Client, USB Port Token, and Centralized remote PC firewall (ZoneLabs Integrity) to provide strong security, ease of use, and centralized management. The original goal was to utilize the Cisco VPN Client that allowed cooperative reinforcement with the remote PC firewall. The ZoneLabs VPN Enforcement feature ensures that the VPN users can only connect to and remain connected to the SACL network as long as the client is running a verified version of the ZoneLabs firewall agent and the client is enforcing the most up-to-date security policy.

The Cisco VPN client used was incompatible with a few of the corporate applications which required the client to have a virtual adaptor IP address in order to ftp data from a server back to the remote PC. Cisco released a VPN client that has a virtual adaptor which is still being piloted by SACL. In the interim period, SACL chose to utilize a Microsoft VPN client that does not provide cooperative reinforcement of the remote PCs. Remote PCs have utilized the Microsoft XP operating system to lock down the ZoneLabs application to ensure that the user cannot shutdown the firewall. As all the wireless users within SACL are utilizing Cisco wireless adaptors, the same Wireless VLAN utilizing LEAP is used. This will change in the near future, as the new laptops have inbuilt wireless adapters. As the VPN solution does not require the additional wireless security, as it is geared for broadband and hotspot users, another wireless VLAN will be created with a different security model. Figure 2 shows the present VPN establishment and logon process to the corporate network. Strong authentication is required to secure the VPN connections (see Figure 6). VPN users must have a computer with a valid SACL digital certificate, valid Windows account, or USB eToken with SmartUser certification to successfully establish a VPN connection. After the use of valid Digital Certificate for Internet Key Exchange (IKE) authentication, the Microsoft VPN uses Internet Protocol Security (IPSec) Encryption ESP (encapsulation protocol)—Layer Two Tunneling Protocol (L2TP)—Transport IPSec SA.

Wireless Voice Over IP Pilot

The third device that has been trialed by SACL across its wireless LAN is a pilot of wireless IP phones. During the last quarter of 2002 SACL, undertook a voice over IP trial. This pilot included the deployment of wireless handsets that ran over the terminal's live wireless network. The wireless IP handsets used were spectralink phones. These phones did not support LEAP, so a dedicated WLAN with static 128-bit WEP was set up across the international terminal. This wireless VLAN was also given the highest quality of service (QoS) on each access point to ensure phone calls would not drop out if a wireless access point was supporting multiple clients. Knowing the security vulnerabilities of static WEP, SACL combined MAC-level security on the wireless VLAN. MAC-level security on the Cisco access points can be centrally managed by the Cisco Secure ACS RADIUS Servers. This is performed by entering the MAC address of the phone as a user and password in the RADIUS server. While the security solution is not necessarily ideal, it was the only means available at the time of the pilot. Cisco's latest release of software for the 1100 and 1200 access points has a feature known as fast secure roaming. This feature allows EAP authentication to be used for Wireless Voice Over IP.

Tenant Wireless Connectivity

As the wireless infrastructure is a shared medium for both SACL and its tenants, it is necessary to establish

Figure 5. Computerized maintenance management system

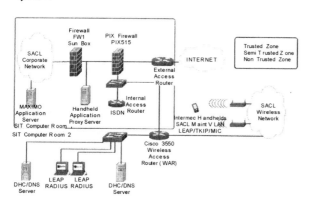

Figure 6. VPN authentication process

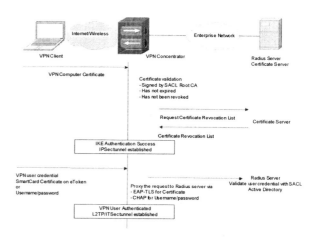

Figure 7. WLAN public Internet connectivity

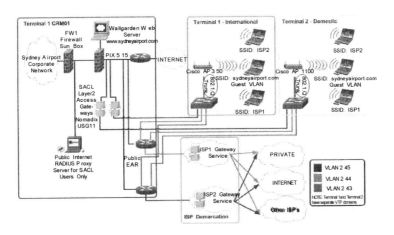

connections back into the tenants' own corporate network. Figure 8 shows how this connection is implemented, indicating demarcation points. A range of IP addresses is assigned to each tenant who will either hard code or utilize SACL's DHCP servers. Every tenant utilizing SACL's wireless infrastructure will be given a dedicated 100 Mbps UTP routed connection to the Wireless Access Router. Within the WAR, access-lists filtering on IP address, protocol, and port numbers are configured. It is advised that the 100 Mbps Ethernet port be connected to the tenants' network via their own firewall. The tenant is responsible for any additional security measures such as VPNs with their own wireless clients. The tenant is set up with their own Wireless VLAN that can be given a security policy that best meets their needs or device capabilities.

Until, the introduction of Wireless VLANs, there was only one option—to use Cisco client adaptors utilizing LEAP. This interoperability proved to be challenging, with one of the International Airline Lounges already entered into a commercial agreement with an ISP to provide wireless Internet access to their Frequent Flyer Members. As SACL could not control the public users' client adaptor card, an interim solution was put in place. Other tenants wanting to utilize symbol barcode scanning devices were told the warranty on the device would be void if they replaced the wireless adaptor with a Cisco Card. With the release of wireless VLANs, two organizations utilizing SACL's wireless network can now use symbol devices with symbol wireless client adaptors. Both are using static WEP with Symbols own VPN solution AirBEAM Safe.

Public Internet Connectivity

Sydney Airport deployed a public wireless network (see Figure 7) to allow high-speed Internet connectivity to public users. SACL is strategically well placed to target this market of mobile professionals. SACL has partnered with Internet service providers to offer their existing customers and new subscribers all the Internet services including e-mail, Web browsing, and connection back into their corporate networks via secure VPN. Like most hot spots, the wireless public LANs are set to open authentication with no WEP key encryption configured. The portal page login for the subscriber is made by opening an SSL-encrypted session hypertext transfer protocol over Secure Socket Layer (HTTPS). The difference between most hotspots is that Sydney Airport hosts three unencrypted wireless LANs on each of its access points. As Sydney Airport already had the wireless infrastructure installed, it made commercial sense to cater for multiple service providers instead of the usual "ISP-grabbing-real-estate" approach. The commercial model with each of the ISPs is based on revenue sharing of subscriber usage. The subscriber can be classified as retail and wholesale. A wholesale customer refers to a subscriber who is signed with a roaming partner of the ISP. To cater for multiple ISPs proved quite challenging. The technical challenges of routing users down different Internet service connections, government regulations on IP interception rules in Australia, and the airport not wanting to lawfully become an Internet service provider led to the decision of running multiple wireless VLANs. The latest 350 IOS firmware for

Figure 8. Total wireless connectivity diagram

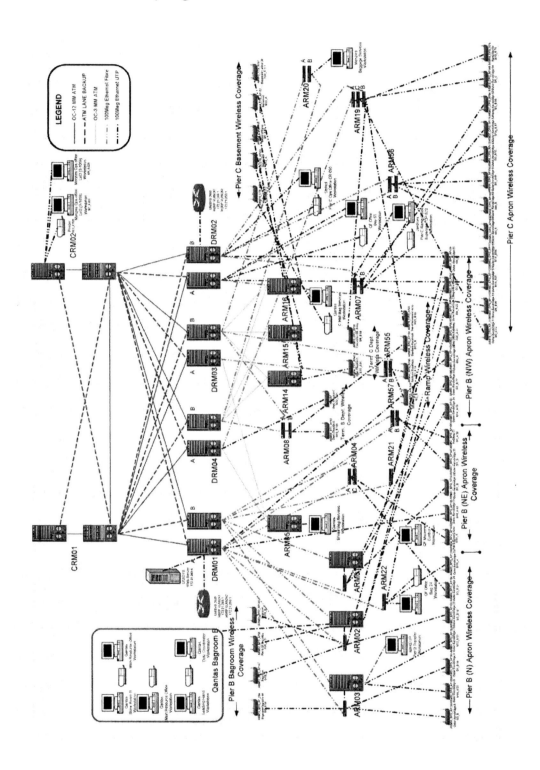

Cisco access points allows for multiple unencrypted VLANs. SACL therefore maintains control of the access point infrastructure and WLAN services on the airport site, being responsible for ensuring the WLAN technical capability of the network. Each ISP is provided with a non-broadcast unencrypted wireless LAN, with their nominated Wireless Network Name (SSID) as set up in their other hotspot sites. This WLAN will be connected to the ISP's gateway service infrastructure. The Internet service provider will ensure compliance with the relevant government regulations. This compliance will mean that they will solely be responsible for interception of all IP traffic pertaining to their WLAN on the airport site. The Internet service provider shall provide to SACL a non-repudiable system for reporting and auditing of the Sydney Airport hotspot site. The system shall be accessible to SACL in real time or close to it. Sydney Airport requires online data such as billing or RADIUS accounting records that detail each user's IP session time along with data byte usage.

CONCLUSION AND FUTURE DIRECTION

The security interoperability challenges are being addressed by Wi-Fi Protected Access range of Wi-Fi products based on the upcoming IEEE802.11i standard. With the WPA and ultimately 802.11i standard implementation in place, the need for add-on solutions such as VPNs may be deemed unnecessary in some enterprise wireless LAN environments (Patel & McCubben, 2004a). Other future enhancements not referenced in this chapter include the upcoming release of 802.11g Wireless Access Points. 802.11g can ideally deliver 54 Mbps maximum data rate and offer an additional and compelling advantage—backward compatibility with 802.11b equipment. This means that 802.11b client cards will work with 802.11g access points, and 802.11g client cards will work with 802.11b access points. Because 802.11g and 802.11b operate in the same 2.4 GHz unlicensed band, migrating to 802.11g will be an affordable choice for Sydney Airport with existing 802.11b wireless infrastructures (see Figure 8).

One drawback is that 802.11b products cannot be "software upgraded" to 802.11g because 802.11g radios will use a different chipset than 802.11b in order to deliver the higher data rate (Patel & McCubben, 2004b). However, like Ethernet and Fast Ethernet, 802.11g products can be co-mingled with 802.11b products in the same network. Sydney Airport will continue to provide solutions to business needs by utilizing innovative and leading-edge technology. Future applications include Mobile Self-Service, Check-In Kiosks, RF Bag Tags, Wireless Point of Sale, Wireless Stock Take, Wireless VoIP, and the end-of-the-year government requirements for Baggage Reconciliation. To-date total wireless connectivity diagrams are shown in Figures 4 and 8. So far it is safe to say that the wireless technology will play an important part in the future of Sydney Airport's total journey experience.

REFERENCES

Arbaugh, W. A., Shankar, N., Justin Wan, Y.C. (2001). *Your 802.11 wireless network has no clothes.* Retrieved June 20, 2003, from http://www.cs.umd.edu/~waa/wireless.pdf

Cisco Systems. (2002). Retrieved June 20, 2002, from http://www.cisco.com/en/US/netsol/ns340/ns394/ns348/ns337/networking_ solutions_package.html

Fluhrer, S. R., Mantin, I., & Shamir, A. (2001). *Weaknesses in the key scheduling algorithm for RC4.* Retrieved November 11, 2001, from http://downloads.securityfocus.com/library/rc4_ksaproc.pdf

Geier, J. (2002). *802.11 security beyond WEP.* Retrieved July 12, 2002, from http://www.wi-fiplanet.com/tutorials/article.php/1377171

McCubben, S. (2003). *Trim document reference: M2003/06745.* Sydney: Sydney Airport Corporation Limited.

Patel, K. J., & McCubben, S. (2004a). Addressing wireless security issues during implementation of wireless applications in a highly mobile organization. In *Proceedings of the International Conference on Computing, Communications and Control Technologies* (Vol. 7, pp. 13-18).

Patel, K. J., & McCubben, S. (2004b). Implementation of wireless technology in a highly mobile organization: Challenges and issues. In *Proceedings of the 8th World Multi-Conference on Systemics, Cybernetics and Informatics* (Vol. 11, pp. 43-48).

Stubblefield, A., Ioannidis, D., & Rubin, A. (2001). *Fluhrer, Mantin, Shamir attack to break WEP.* Retrieved June 20, 2002, from http://www.isoc.org/isoc/conferences/ndss/02/proceedings/papers/stubbl.pdf

Sydney Airport Corporation Limited. (2000). Retrieved June 24, 2000, from http://www.sydeyairport.com

Section III
Technology, Networks and Security

Chapter XXXIII
ISI Cancellation in
4G Wireless Mobiles

Kumar Priyatam
BVB Collage of Engineering and Technology, India

R. M. Banakar
BVB Collage of Engineering and Technology, India

B. Shankaranand
National Institute of Technology, India

ABSTRACT

Physical layer issues of broadband wireless communication systems form the bottleneck in providing fast and reliable communication over wireless channel. Critical performance limiting challenges are time selective fading channels, frequency selective fading channels, noise, inter symbol interference (ISI), inter carrier interference, power, and bandwidth. Addressing these challenges of wireless broadband communication systems, one can provide faster data processing with lower computational complexity, higher data throughput, and improved performance in terms of bit error rate (BER). In this chapter an effective technique (SISO estimation) to handle interference cancellation is developed. ISI is caused by multi-path propagation. It can be reduced by using a channel equalizer which provides the receiver with the prior knowledge of the channel. Channel estimation is a technique to acquire behavior of the channel. Accuracy of the channel estimation improves the system performance. At BER of 10-4 SISO estimator provide an improvement of 2dB as compared with MMSE DFE estimator.

INTRODUCTION

Fourth Generation (4G) mobile systems are expected to provide global roaming across different types of wireless and mobile network. Communication may be from satellite to mobile networks and to Wireless Local Area Networks (WLANs). Main objective of 4G is to overcome the shortcomings and limitations of 3G systems prime amongst which is the issue of available bandwidth.

The term 4G is used broadly to include several types of broadband wireless access communication systems, including cellular telephone systems. One of the terms used to describe 4G is MAGIC—Mobile multimedia, Anytime anywhere, Global mobility support, Integrated wireless solution, and Customized personal service. The vision of 4G wireless/mobile systems are of broadband access, seamless global roaming and Internet/data/voice communication. The 4G system provide facilities to integrate terminals, networks and applications to satisfy the increasing user demands.

The 4G mobile networks are being developed with two main objectives. One of these objectives is to overcome the shortcomings and limitations of 3G, prime amongst is the issue of available bandwidth. 4G systems are expected to offer a speed of over 100 Mbps in stationary mode and an average of 20 Mbps for mobile stations reducing the downlink time of graphics and multimedia components by more than ten times compared to currently available 2 Mbps on 3G. The second main objective behind 4G development is to make good use of the achievements in the area of wireless technology. Currently 4G system is a research and development initiative based upon 3G, which is having trouble meeting its performance goals. The challenges for development of 4G systems depend upon the evolution of different underlying technologies, standards and deployment.

Presently there are various techniques to minimize ISI. To remove ISI equalizers are used. The prevailing methods are liner equalizer (LE), least-mean-square (LMS), Kalman estimation (KEST) and recursive-least-square (RLS), which concentrate on multipath channel and fading amplitudes. In the above mentioned methods the computational complexity is high and the delay time is not optimized for the BER of 10^{-6}. These methods operate on the present sample of data only. They do not consider the previous or next data sample to predict present data. The novel approach presented in this paper overcomes the above mentioned demerits. Performance improvement is observed by using this new approach.

Most commonly used equalizers are ML sequence estimation (MLSE) or MAP symbol estimation (MAPSE). An efficient implementation of the MLSE equalizer is the Viterbi Algorithm (VA), which is described in standard literature about coding [5]. A MAPSE equalizer is often based on the forward backward algorithm from Bahl et al. (BCJR) [6]. Compared to the original paper, Rabiner [7] provides a more tutorial introduction on the BCJR algorithm. Forney [8] applied the VA to MLSE for digital communication on ISI channels including an extensive analysis of its performance.

All known MAP/ML based methods suffer from high computational complexity with increasing channel length M and alphabet size q due to the exponential complexity $O(q^M)$ Furthermore , they can be applied directly only block wise, since a time reversed backward step is involved. Complex algorithms exist to overcome these using sliding window techniques such as "Turbo coding "applications [9].

The received data is segmented into frames and these frames are received over a time period specified by the window. The basic idea is to obtain a symbol estimating by filtering the received data (LE) or by filtering the past symbol decisions (DFE). Both the LE and DFE contain linear filters as basic functional elements. The DFE also contains nonlinearity, namely a hard decision element, to provide estimates of past symbols for feedback. To implement the linear filters, several structures such as transversal, cascade, parallel or lattice filter implementations are available. The associated parameter to set up the filters are obtained using the channel response h[n] cost criteria such as the zero forcing (ZF) or minimum mean squared error (MMSE) criterion. Receivers using LE and DFE approaches are inherently suboptimal in terms of error probability since they are designed using different cost criteria. Also, some inherent weakness such as constraint filter lengths, noise enhancement in ZF based solutions, or error propagation in DFE solutions limit the capabilities of pure LE or DFE approaches. None the less, they are widely used in practice since a broad knowledge about them is available and computational complexity is significantly smaller compared to optimal techniques introduced in the LF/DFE.

A number of standard texts [1,2] in the communication literature contain more information about LE and DFE approaches. A valuable review about LE/DFE system using ZF/MMSE criteria is available [3], together with probability of error analysis techniques. More advance LE/DFE techniques include fractionally spaced (FS) or state space (SS) LE or DFE approaches. Other than symbol spaced receivers, FS receivers sample the matched filter output at an integer multiple rate of the symbol rate T to decrease aliasing.

For digital communication, a common cost criterion is the bit error rate (BER) of the system, which does not necessarily coincide with equalization criteria. The optimum receiver with respect to minimization of the BER is a maximum a-posteriori probability (MAP) or maximum likelihood (ML) detector does not remove ISI, but tries to find the most likely channel input given the output symbols disrupted by noise, which is equal to minimizing the BER. Whereas a ML detector assumes the symbols to be equally likely to occur on any value of the symbol alphabet, a MAP detector employs knowledge about the occurrence probability as well. To obtain an ML/MAP equalizer, two key criteria can be applied. Find the most likely input sequence or find the most likely input symbol given a distorted channel output sequence. Accordingly, either the sequence error or the symbol error probability is minimized using an ML/MAP equalizer.

CHANNELS

Typical for radio communication is that transmission between a transmitter and a receiver takes place via many different propagation paths. The energy arrives at the receiver by way of the direct wave alone or in combination with the ground reflected wave and the many random scattering rays. The sum of these rays is called the scattered wave. Propagation of the signal is affected by free space attenuation, reflection from the surface of the earth and various objects and shadowing. Shadowing is attenuation of the direct wave caused by roadside trees, buildings, hills and mountains. Its effect strongly depends on the type of surrounding buildings and vegetation as well as the signal frequency. Shadowing attenuation increases with increasing the frequency. These factors in the nature and in the signal cause random variations in the local mean of the received signal strength, which is called slow fading. The scattered wave results from various reflections from the surrounding terrain. The different components in the scattered wave have traveled different paths in a randomly manner. Therefore, they vary randomly in amplitude and phase and cause large variations in signal amplitude within

a relatively small area. The signal variations due to multipath propagation occur at a much faster rate than the variations caused by shadowing. Therefore, these variations are called fast fading.

A wide range of experiments [3] have showed that the statistical character of the signal variations strongly depends on the type of environment in which the mobile receiver is located. Therefore, different types of environments can be distinguished according to the propagation wave into urban, suburban and rural, and open areas. In open areas there are essentially no obstacles on the direct path, and the received signal consists of the direct wave interfered with the scattered wave. The received signal statistics can be described by the Rician distribution [3]. In urban areas the direct line between the base station and the mobile station is almost completely obstructed by large buildings. Therefore, the numbers of reflected signals are large and the envelope of the scattered signal follows Rayleigh distribution [3]. In mobile communication, the propagation is generally dominated by shadow loss and multipath reflections. Hence, the model used in our chain is a Rayleigh model because we assume that there is no direct wave.

MODEL OF SISO EQUALIZER

An iterative receiver algorithm processes the received data by at least two distinct processing blocks (equalizer and decoder), interacting with each other in both directions. The blocks will process the same set of received data several times until a termination or convergence criterion is matched. Fig. I such a scheme for joint equalization decoding is depicted. The data

Figure 1. Data transmission using iterative approach

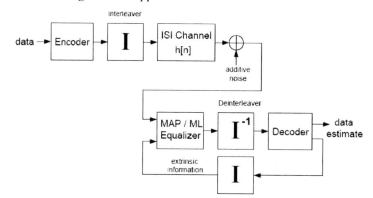

transmission system is split into an outer and inner layer. As layer is considered to be a pair of processing devices working on the same set of data or code system symbols, where one component is located within the transmitter block should equal the output of the corresponding receiver block. Fig. 1 the inner layer is the channel equalizer pair. The outer layer is the coding scheme consisting of encoder and decoder.

Between the two layers of processing stages required by an iterative scheme we install an interleaver (I) and de-interleaver (I^{-1}). Assuming block wise data transmission the interleaver shuffles the code symbols of the encoder output with in the given block length. The de-interleaver reverses this step such that the decoder reads the code symbols in the same ordering in which the encoder sent them. The feedback information from the decoder in interleaved to provide the correct code symbol ordering within the channel equalizer layer.

All receiver blocks are assumed to output soft information. One block of received data is repeatedly equalized and decoded using feedback from the decoder until applying a convergence criterion stops the iterative receiving process. After termination the decoder finally outputs estimates of the data to be transmitted. An essential requirement for such iterative systems is that only the extrinsic information [10] is passed between the processing blocks. Similar to other feedback systems (DFE, the iterative scheme is sensitive to error propagation). This problem can be carefully choosing the output information of the processing blocks.

The principle of turbo principle which was derived originally for two coding layers turbo coding for data transmission on an additive white Gaussian noise (AWGN) channel without ISI. Replacing the inner layer with the channel equalizer pair, the turbo coding turns into turbo equalization. A considerable amount of research has been done in this area, yielding systems with remarkable BER performance [10-13].

As for as the non-iterative solutions, the ML/MAP suffer from the high computational load for load channels or convolutional codes with high memory order. The situation is worsened since the equalization and decoding steps are performed several times for each block of data. Even with sophisticated algorithms or suboptimal solutions, the inherent exponential complexity of the ML/MAP techniques limits their range of possible applications. Wang and Poor [4] proposed a possible way out to overcome this problem. As part of the code division multiple access (CDMA) literature,

a receiver has been outlined for multiuser data transmission over an ISI channel. An iterative scheme is introduced based of turbo equalization using an LE to remove ISI and MAPSE decoding. The MAP equalizer is thus replaced with LE whose filter parameters are updated for every output symbol of the equalizer. An efficient implementation of the algorithms yields an O (N^{2}MK) complexity of the LE given the equalizer filter length N, channel length M and number of users K. Binary symbols b$_i$ taken from the alphabet {0,1}. The symbol b$_i$ is assumed to be independent and equally likely to take on values of 0 and 1. The data symbol

rate is $\frac{1}{T_B}$. After transmission, equalization and decoding the final estimates b$_i$ ∈ {0,1} of the data are provided by the receiver. The coding layer shown in Fig. 2 is a convolutional code with an encoder providing the code symbols c$_n$ and a decode using the BCJR algorithm

for MAPSE. The code symbol rate is $\frac{1}{T_c}$ yielding the rate R of the code:

$$R \cong \frac{Tc}{T_B}, \qquad 0 \le R \le 1 \qquad (1)$$

Thus chosen alphabet are {1,-1}. Both the signaling constellation and the code symbol alphabet were chosen for simplicity of the derivation. The direct implementation of the BCJR algorithm requires block wise processing of the data symbols b$_i$. The transmission and receiving tasks are therefore applied to data blocks of length L$_B$. Given the code rate R and the signaling scheme, the length L$_C$ of a block of code symbols, and the length

Lx of a block of channel input symbols x$_n$ we have

$$L_c = L_X - \frac{L_B}{R} \qquad (2)$$

In the sequel, we represent blocks of data in column vector from and use the notation $b_{\le i,j\ge} \cong [b_i b_{i+1}...b_j]^T$. The symbols x$_n$ are transmitted over the ISI channel with sinc pulse response h[n] as defined in equation (3).

$$h[n] = \sum_{k=-M_1}^{+M_2} h_e(nT)\delta[n-k]$$
$$= \sum_{k=-M_1}^{+M_2} h_{k,n}\delta[n-k] \qquad (3)$$

Figure 2. Iterative equalization using priors

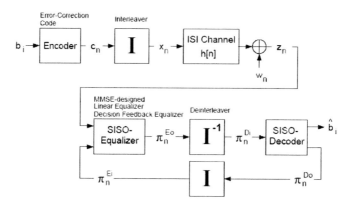

Receiver noise introduced in the analog system is modeled in the equivalent discrete time representation as AWGN with zero mean. This model is realistic if the noise added in the electronics and the channel noise is white and the receiver filter is an ideal low pass filter. Accordingly the noise samples w_n are real valued, independent, identically distributed (i.i.d) and drawn from the distribution

$f_w(x) = N(0, \sigma_w^2)$ With

$$N(\mu, \sigma^2) \cong \frac{1}{\sqrt{2\pi}\sigma} \exp(-\frac{(x-\mu)^2}{2\sigma^2}) \qquad (4)$$

The symbols z_n are input to the receiver consisting of two soft in soft out (SISO) devices, an equalizer and a convolutional decoder. Both devise interact via soft information that represents prior information over the data symbols. Unlike the turbo equalization schemes [17-19], where the soft information represents log-likelihood ratios, the priors used here are probability measures, ranging from 0 to 1.The SISO equalizer has access to the priors π_n^{Ei}

$$\pi_n^{Ei} \cong \Pr\{x_n = -1\} \qquad (5)$$

The output of the equalizer is the prior π_n^{E0}. Ideally a MAP equalizer provides the conditioned probability

$$\Pi_n^{MAP} \cong \Pr\{x_n = -1 \mid z_{<1,Lx>}, \pi_{<1,n-1>}^{Ei}, \pi_{<n+1,Lx>}^{Ei}\} \qquad (6)$$

Since Lx symbols x_n are sent, the SISO equalizer receives a sequence of length Lx, i.e the block $z_{<1,Lx>}$. Observes that π_n^{MAP-E0} does not dependent on the input prior π_n^{Ei} with the same index n. The true output prior π_n^{Eo} though still a probability measure can thus just approximate the quantity π_n^{MAP-E0}. The decoder receives the input prior's π_n^{Di}, defined as $\pi_n^{Di} \cong \Pr\{c_n = -1\}$, equal π_n^{Eo} after accounting for the de-interleaver. The decider produces π_n^{Do} and the data estimates b_i.

$$\pi_n^{Do} \cong \Pr\{c_n = -1 \mid \pi_{<1,n-1>}^{Di}, \pi_{<1,Lc>}^{Di}\}$$
$$\hat{b}_i = \arg\max_{k \in \{0,1\}} \Pr\{b_i = k \mid \pi_{<1,Lc>}^{Di}\} \qquad (7)$$

Hence the decoder is a SISO device, too, which is well behaved with respect to the output prior's π_n^{Do}. The definitions for π_n^{Ei} and π_n^{Di} imply that both equalizer and decoder assume no knowledge of the origin of the input priors. They are considered to be correct statistics about the occurrence of the symbol values -1 and 1, respectively, for a specific sample x_n or c_n.

SISO Equalizer with a Linear Equalizer as Estimator

Given the solution to compute the estimate $\hat{x}_n$ in Equation

$$c_n = (\sigma_w^2 I_N + HD_n H^H)^{-1} s \qquad (8)$$

the time varying matrix that appears through its inverse in the formula for updating the parameter set $\mathbf{c}_n$ is

$$\mathbf{R}_n \triangleq \sigma_w^2 \mathbf{I}_N + \mathbf{H}\mathbf{D}_n\mathbf{H}^H .$$

With the quantities (see Equation 9.)

We rewrite Equation (8) and include Equation as (see Equation 10).

A low complexity approach for computing π_n^{Eo} can be obtained by exploiting the inherent structural properties of the quantities in Equation (10). The main idea is to express the vector $\mathbf{c}_{n+1}$ at time step n+1, which is computed as $\mathbf{R}_{n+1}^{-1}\mathbf{s}$, as a function of $\mathbf{c}_n$ and the inverse $\mathbf{R}_n^{-1}$. To do this, the following partitioning scheme is introduced (see Equation 11 and 12).

Where $\mathbf{R}_i$, $\widetilde{\mathbf{R}}_i$, $i \in \{O,N\}$, are $(N-1)\times(N-1)$ matrices, $\mathbf{c}_i$, $\mathbf{s}_i$, $\mathbf{r}_i$, $\widetilde{\mathbf{r}}_i$ are length (N−1) column vectors, and c_i, s_i, r_i, $\widetilde{r}_i$ are scalars. The subscript $_O$ denotes quantities at the "old" time step n and $_N$ at the "new" time step n+1. The derivation of the low complexity algorithm arises from noting that the sub matrices $\widetilde{\mathbf{R}}_O$ and $\widetilde{\mathbf{R}}_N$ are identical. This can be verified easily from

the definition of $\mathbf{R}_n$ in Equation (10). Now a similar partitioning scheme for the inverses of $\mathbf{R}_n$ and $\mathbf{R}_{n+1}$ is introduced

$$R_n^{-1} \triangleq A_n \triangleq \begin{bmatrix} A_O & \mathbf{a}_O \\ \mathbf{b}_O^H & a_O \end{bmatrix},$$

The components of $\mathbf{A}_n$ are expressed in terms of components of $\mathbf{R}_n$ by solving

$$R_{n+1}^{-1} \triangleq A_{n+1} \triangleq \begin{bmatrix} a_N & \mathbf{a}_N^H \\ b_N & A_N \end{bmatrix},$$

(13)

$$\begin{bmatrix} R_O & \mathbf{r}_O \\ \mathbf{r}_O^H & r_O \end{bmatrix}\begin{bmatrix} A_O & \mathbf{a}_O \\ \mathbf{b}_O^H & a_O \end{bmatrix} = \begin{bmatrix} I_{N-1} & 0_{N-1}^H \\ 0_{N-1} & 1 \end{bmatrix},$$

(14)

The quantities $\mathbf{A}_O$, $\mathbf{a}_O$, $\mathbf{b}_O$, and α_O of the inverse matrix $\mathbf{A}_n$ are

Equation 9.

$$t_n^1 \triangleq 4\,\pi_n^{Ei}\,(1-\pi_n^{Ei}),$$

$$\mathbf{t}_n^1 \triangleq [t_{n+M1+N1}^1 \quad t_{n+M1+N1-1}^1 \quad t_{n-M2-N2}^1]^T$$

$$t_n^2 \triangleq 1-2\pi_n^{Ei},$$

Equation 10.

$$\pi_n^{EO} = \tfrac{1}{2}\left(1-\tanh\left(\cdot\frac{x_n}{1-c_n^H s}\right)\right)$$

$$\mathbf{R}_n = \sigma_w^2\,\mathbf{I}_N + \mathbf{H}diag(\mathbf{t}_n^1)\,\mathbf{H}^H + (1-t_n^1)\mathbf{s}\mathbf{s}^H,$$

$$\mathbf{c}_n = \mathbf{R}_n^{-1}\mathbf{s},$$

$$\hat{x}_n = \mathbf{c}_n^H(\mathbf{z}_n - \mathbf{H}\,t_n^2 + t_n^2\mathbf{s}),$$

$$\pi_n^{Eo} = \frac{1}{2}\left(1-\tanh\left(\frac{\hat{x}_n}{1-c_n^H s}\right)\right).$$

Equation 11.

$$\mathbf{c}_n \triangleq \begin{bmatrix} \mathbf{c}_O \\ c_O \end{bmatrix},\quad \mathbf{c}_{n+1} \triangleq \begin{bmatrix} \mathbf{c}_N \\ c_N \end{bmatrix},$$

$$\mathbf{s} \triangleq \begin{bmatrix} \mathbf{s}_O \\ s_O \end{bmatrix},\quad \mathbf{s} \triangleq \begin{bmatrix} \mathbf{s}_N \\ s_N \end{bmatrix}$$

$$\mathbf{R}_n \triangleq \begin{bmatrix} R_O & \mathbf{r}_O \\ \mathbf{r}_O^H & r_O \end{bmatrix}$$

Equation 12.

$$\triangleq \begin{bmatrix} \widetilde{R}_O & \widetilde{\mathbf{r}}_O \\ \widetilde{\mathbf{r}}_O^H & \widetilde{r}_O \end{bmatrix} + \left(-\,t_n^1\right)\begin{bmatrix} S_O S_O^H & S_O S_O^* \\ S_O S_O^H & S_O S_O^* \end{bmatrix}$$

$$R_{n+1} \triangleq \begin{bmatrix} r_N & \mathbf{r}_N^H \\ \mathbf{r}_N & R_N \end{bmatrix}$$

$$\triangleq \begin{bmatrix} \widetilde{r}_N & \widetilde{\mathbf{r}}_N^H \\ \widetilde{\mathbf{r}}_N & \widetilde{R}_N \end{bmatrix} + \left(-\,t_{n+1}^1\right)\begin{bmatrix} S_N S_N^* & S_N S_N^H \\ S_N S_N^* & S_N S_N^H \end{bmatrix}$$

359

$$\mathbf{A}_O = \left(\mathbf{R}_O - \frac{\mathbf{r}_O \mathbf{r}_O^H}{ro} \right)^{-1}, \mathbf{a}_O = -\frac{1}{ro} \mathbf{A}_O \mathbf{r}_O, \quad \mathbf{b}_O = \mathbf{a}_O,$$

$$\alpha_O = \frac{1}{ro} \left(1 - \mathbf{r}_O^H \mathbf{a}o \right). \tag{15}$$

It can be seen that the inverse of $\mathbf{R}_n$ is also Hermitian, since α_O is a real number, $\mathbf{b}_O = \mathbf{a}_O$ and $\mathbf{A}_O = \mathbf{A}_O^H$. The inverse $\mathbf{A}_n$ is required to compute $\mathbf{c}_n$ and is therefore stored and updated at every time step n. To obtain $\mathbf{c}_{n+1}$, the matrix $\mathbf{A}_{n+1}$ is required. We will derive a time-recursive update algorithm to compute $\widetilde{\mathbf{R}}_O^{-1}$ from $\mathbf{A}_n$ and then $\mathbf{A}_{n+1}$ from $\widetilde{\mathbf{R}}_N^{-1}$ based on the identity $\widetilde{\mathbf{R}}_O = \widetilde{\mathbf{R}}_N$. Altering the first line in Equation (15) gives

$$\mathbf{R}_O^{-1} = \left(\mathbf{A}_O^{-1} + \frac{\mathbf{r}_O \mathbf{r}_O^H}{ro} \right)^{-1}$$

$$= \mathbf{A}_O - \mathbf{A}_O \mathbf{r}_O \left(ro + \mathbf{r}_O^H \mathbf{A}o \mathbf{r}o \right)^{-1} \mathbf{r}_O^H \mathbf{A}_O,$$

using the matrix inversion lemma. This result can be simplified using again Equation (15) to (see Equation 16).

The matrix $\mathbf{R}_O$ is the sum of ( ) and an outer vector product as shown in Equation (12).

Applying the matrix inversion lemma again yields (see Equation 17).

The equation yielding $\mathbf{c}_n$ in Equation (10) can be written using the partitioning schemes Equations (11) and (13) (see Equation 18).

Using Equation (16), we write ( ) in Equation (17) in terms of $\mathbf{c}_O$, $\mathbf{c}_O$, and $\mathbf{a}_O$ and obtain an efficient scheme to compute

$$\widetilde{R}_O^{-1} : v_O \triangleq$$

$$R_O^{-1} s_O = c_O - \frac{\mathbf{a}_O \mathbf{a}_O^H s_O}{a_O} - \mathbf{a}_O s_O = c_O - \frac{c_O}{a_O} \mathbf{a}_O,$$

$$\widetilde{R}_O^{-1} = R_O^{-1} + \frac{v_O v_O^H}{\frac{1}{1-t_n^1} - s_O^H v_O} = R_O^{-1} + \frac{(1-t_n^1) v_O v_O^H}{1 - (1-t_n^1) v_O s_O^H}$$

$$\tag{19}$$

Equation 16.

$$\mathbf{R}_O^{-1} = \mathbf{A}_O - \frac{\mathbf{a}o \mathbf{a}_O^H}{ao}.$$

Equation 17.

$$\widetilde{R}_O^{-1} = \left(R_O - (1 - t_n^1) s_O s_O^{-H} \right)^{-1}$$

$$= R_O^{-1} + \frac{R_O^{-1} s_O s_O^H R_O^{-1}}{\frac{1}{1-t_n^1} - s_O^H R_O^{-1} s_O}$$

Equation 18.

$$\begin{bmatrix} c_O \\ c_O \end{bmatrix} = \begin{bmatrix} \mathbf{a}_O & \mathbf{a}_O \\ \mathbf{a}_O^H & \mathbf{a}_O \end{bmatrix} \begin{bmatrix} s_O \\ s_O \end{bmatrix},$$

where the vector $\mathbf{v}_O$ was introduced to simplify notation. The chain $\mathbf{A}_n \rightarrow R_O^{-1} \rightarrow \widetilde{R}_O^{-1}$ is now reversed to compute the corresponding quantities at time step n+1, $\widetilde{R}_N^{-1} \rightarrow R_O^{-1} \rightarrow \mathbf{A}_{n+1}$. The partitioning for $\mathbf{R}_{n+1}$ in Equation (12) gives an equation for $\mathbf{R}_N^{-1}$ similar to Equation (17):

$$v_N \triangleq \widetilde{R}_N^{-1} \mathbf{s}_N,$$

$$R_N^{-1} = (\widetilde{R}_N^{-1} + (1 - t_{n+1}^1) s_N s_N^H)^{-1} = \widetilde{R}_N^{-1} - \frac{\widetilde{R}_N^{-1} s_N s_N^H \widetilde{R}_N^{-1}}{\frac{1}{1-t_{n+1}^1} + \widetilde{R}_N^{-1} s_N s_N^H}$$

$$\tag{20}$$

The vector $\mathbf{v}_N$ was introduced to simplify notation, but also functions as intermediate quantity to compute $\mathbf{c}_{n+1}$ later. The derivation of each of the components of $\mathbf{A}_n$ is given in Equations (13),(14),and (15). With the partitioning for $\mathbf{R}_{n+1}$ and $\mathbf{A}_{n+1}$ in Equation (13), similar expressions for the components of $\mathbf{A}_{n+1}$ can be derived:

$$A_N = \left(R_N - \frac{r_N r_N'^H}{r_N} \right)^{-1} = R_N^{-1} - \frac{R_N^{-1} r_N r_N'^H R_N^{-1}}{-r_N + r_N r_N'^H R_N^{-1}},$$

$$\mathbf{a}_N = b_N = -\frac{1}{r_N} A_N r_N, a_N = \frac{1}{r_N} \left(1 - \mathbf{a}_N r_N'^H \right)$$

We alter the ordering of the equations to

$$r_N' \underset{=}{\Delta} R_N^{-1} \mathbf{r}_N,$$

$$a_N = \frac{1}{r_N - r_N'^H r_N'}, \mathbf{a}_N = -a_N r_N', A_N = R_N^{-1} + a_N r_N' r_N'^H, \tag{21}$$

in order to optimize the computation by using the quantity r_N' and already computed components of $\mathbf{A}_{n+1}$. The parameter vector $\mathbf{c}_{n+1}$ for time step n+1 is computed using the partitioning in Eq. (11) similar to Equation (18)

$$\begin{bmatrix} c_N \\ \mathbf{c}_N \end{bmatrix} = \begin{bmatrix} a_N & \mathbf{a}_N^H \\ \mathbf{a}_O^H & A_O \end{bmatrix} \begin{bmatrix} s_N \\ \mathbf{s}_N \end{bmatrix}. \tag{22}$$

However, the required matrix-vector product $\mathbf{A}_{N*}$ $\mathbf{s}_N$ need not be computed, since the related quantity $\mathbf{v}_N$ is already available through Equation (20). Using $\mathbf{v}_N$ together with Equations (20),(21),and (22) gives equations for c_N and $\mathbf{c}_N$:

$$c_N = a_N s_N + \mathbf{a}_N^H \mathbf{s}_N = a_N \left(s_N - r_N'^H \mathbf{s}_N \right)$$

$$\mathbf{c}_N = \left(\tilde{R}_N^{-1} - \frac{\mathbf{v}_N \mathbf{v}_N^H}{\frac{1}{1 - t_{n+1}^1} + \mathbf{v}_N \mathbf{s}_N^H} + a_N r_N'^H r_N' \right) \mathbf{s}_N + \mathbf{a}_N s_N$$

$$= \mathbf{v}_N - \frac{\mathbf{v}_N \mathbf{v}_N^H \mathbf{s}_N}{\frac{1}{1 - t_{n+1}^1} + \mathbf{v}_N \mathbf{s}_N^H} + a_N^0 (s_N r_N'^H r_N' - s_N r_N')$$

$$= \frac{\mathbf{v}_N}{1 + (1 - t_{n+1}^1) \mathbf{v}_N \mathbf{s}_N^H} - c_N r_N'. \tag{23}$$

Finally, the quantities $\mathbf{r}_N$ and r_N are derived, as they are required in Equation (21). Using the definition of $\mathbf{r}_N$ and r_N in Equation (12) and the definition of $\mathbf{R}_{n+1}$ in Equation (10) gives

$$\begin{bmatrix} r_N \\ \mathbf{r}_N \end{bmatrix} = \begin{bmatrix} \sigma_\omega^2 \\ 0_{N-1} \end{bmatrix} + H diag(t_{n+1}^1) H^H \begin{bmatrix} 1 \\ 0_{N-1} \end{bmatrix} + (1 - t_{n+1}^1) ss_N^*. \tag{24}$$

Once the parameter set $\mathbf{c}_{n+1}$ is obtained, the SISO equalizer output π_{n+1}^{Eo} is computed using Equation (10). For the introduced time-recursive update procedure an initial condition is required. One approach is to perform one ordinary matrix inversion yielding $\mathbf{A}_1$ at the starting time step. Within a sequence of blocks to be processed, the matrix $\mathbf{A}_1$ is obtained with the update procedure using the matrix $\mathbf{A}_{Lx}$ from the last block (of length L_x).The matrix-vector multiplication $H\ t_{n+1}^2$ in Equation (10) is the convolution of the sequence of the t_n^2 with the channel response h[n]. Hence, it can be implemented with O(M).complexity. The quantity $H diag(t_{n+1}^1) H^H \begin{bmatrix} 0_{1 \times (N-1)} \end{bmatrix}$ in Equation (24) is obtained by first computing $diag(t_{n+1}^1) H^H \begin{bmatrix} 0_{1 \times (N-1)} \end{bmatrix}$ and then multiplying with $\mathbf{H}$, which is an order O(M²) scheme. Overall, the most demanding operations are four outer vector products and two matrix-vector products per update yielding a O(N²+M²) complexity per time step n given the estimator filter length N and channel length M.

SISO Equalizer with a Decision Feedback Equalizer as Estimator

The derivation of an exact low complexity recursive update for a SISO equalizer using an MMSE-DFE as estimator is closely related to the MMSE-LE approach. Taken from Eq. $\hat{x}_n = c_n^{fH} z_n + c_n^{bH} x_n^d + d_n$, the time-varying matrix appears as an inverse is now

$$\mathbf{R}_n \underset{=}{\Delta} \sigma_\omega^2 \mathbf{I}_{Nf} + H \tilde{D}_n^{ff} H^H.$$

We redefine the quantities t_n^1, t_n^2 and introduce t_n^3:

$$t_n^1 \triangleq \left[t_{n+Nf-1}^1 \; t_{n+Nf-2}^1 \cdots \; t_{n+1}^1 \right]^T,$$

$$t_n^2 \triangleq \left[t_{n+Nf-1}^2 \; t_{n+Nf-2}^2 \cdots \; t_{n-N_b}^2 \right]^T,$$

constraints in Equation $N_2^f = M_1$,

$$N_{min} = N^b = M - 1, \; N_1^f = N^f - M_1 - 1$$

(25a)

were applied. Equation $\hat{x}_n = c_n^{fH} z_n + c_n^{bH} x_n^d + d_n$ is rewritten including equation

$$\pi_n^{Eo=} \frac{1}{2} \left(1 - \tanh\left(\frac{\hat{x}_n}{1 - \mathbf{c}_n^H \mathbf{s}} \right) \right) \text{ to}$$

$$\mathbf{R}_n = \sigma_\omega^2 \mathbf{I}_{N^f} + \tilde{\mathbf{H}} diag \, (t_n^1) \tilde{\mathbf{H}}^H + \mathbf{s}\mathbf{s}^H, \mathbf{c}_n^f = \mathbf{R}_n^{-1}\mathbf{s}, \mathbf{c}_n^b = -\mathbf{I}^{fb}\mathbf{H}^H\mathbf{c}_n^f,$$

$$\hat{x}_n = \mathbf{c}_n^{fH} (\mathbf{z}_n - \mathbf{H}t_n^2 + t_n^2\mathbf{s}) + \mathbf{c}_n^{bH} (\mathbf{x}_n^d - t_n^3), \pi_n^{Eo} = \frac{1}{2} (1 - \tanh(\frac{\hat{x}_n}{1 - \mathbf{c}_n^{fH}\mathbf{s}})),$$

(26)

where $\tilde{\mathbf{H}}$ is the $N^f \times (N^f - 1)$ submatrix taken from the upper left corner of $\mathbf{H}$. The partitioning scheme for the MMSE-DFE solution is as follows:

$$\mathbf{c}_n^f \triangleq \begin{bmatrix} c_o \\ c_o \end{bmatrix}, \mathbf{c}_{n+1}^f \triangleq \begin{bmatrix} c_N \\ c_N \end{bmatrix}, \mathbf{s} \triangleq \begin{bmatrix} s_O \\ s_O \end{bmatrix}, \mathbf{s} \triangleq \begin{bmatrix} s_N \\ s_N \end{bmatrix},$$

$$\mathbf{R}_n \triangleq \begin{bmatrix} R_O & r_O \\ r_O^H & r_O \end{bmatrix} \triangleq \begin{bmatrix} \tilde{R}_O & \tilde{r}_O \\ \tilde{r}_O^H & \tilde{r}_O \end{bmatrix} + \begin{bmatrix} s_O s_O^H & s_O s_O^* \\ s_O s_O^H & s_O s_O \end{bmatrix}$$

$$R_{n+1} \triangleq \begin{bmatrix} r_N & r_N^H \\ r_N & r_N \end{bmatrix} \triangleq \begin{bmatrix} \tilde{r}_N & \tilde{r}_N^H \\ \tilde{r}_N & \tilde{r}_N \end{bmatrix} + \left(- t_{n+1}^1 \right) \begin{bmatrix} s_N s_N^* & s_N s_N^H \\ s_N s_N^* & s_N s_N^H \end{bmatrix}$$

(27)

where $R_i, \tilde{R}_i, i \in \{O,N\}$, are $(N^f - 1) \times N^f - 1)$ matrices, $c_i, s_i, r_i, \tilde{r}_i$ are length $(N^f - 1)$ column vectors and, $c_i, s_i, r_i, \tilde{r}_i$ are scalars. The definition and the parti-

tioning for the inverses of $\mathbf{R}_n$ and $\mathbf{R}_{n+1}$ are identical to Equation (13):

$$\mathbf{R}_n^{-1} \triangleq \mathbf{A}_n \triangleq \begin{bmatrix} A_O & a_O \\ a_O^H & a_O \end{bmatrix}, \; \mathbf{R}_{n+1}^{-1} \triangleq \mathbf{A}_{n+1} \triangleq \begin{bmatrix} a_N & a_N^H \\ a_N & A_N \end{bmatrix},$$

where we already incorporated the fact that $\mathbf{A}_n$ and $\mathbf{A}_{n+1}$ are Hermitian. Using the similarity of the partitioning scheme to Equation (11), we can apply the same steps for computing $\mathbf{A}_{n+1}$ and $\mathbf{c}_{n+1}$ from $\mathbf{A}_n$ and $\mathbf{c}_n$ to the MMSE-DFE solution. Here we compute $\mathbf{A}_{n+1}$ and c_{n+1}^f from $\mathbf{A}_n$ and c_n^f using Equations (13) to (23). The first step is to obtain the matrix $\tilde{\mathbf{R}}_O^{-1}$ based on the chain $A_n \to \mathbf{R}_O^{-1} \to \tilde{\mathbf{R}}_O^{-1}$ (Equations (15)-(19)):

$$\mathbf{v}_O \triangleq c_O - \frac{c_O}{a_O} a_O, \quad \tilde{\mathbf{R}}_O^{-1} = A_O - \frac{a_O a_O^H}{a_O} + \frac{\mathbf{v}_O \mathbf{v}_O^H}{1 - s_O^H \mathbf{v}_O},$$

With the identity of $\mathbf{R}_O^{-1}$ and $\tilde{\mathbf{R}}_N$, we apply the second step $\tilde{\mathbf{R}}_N^{-1} \to \mathbf{R}_N^{-1} \to A_{n+1}$ yielding the components $\mathbf{A}_N$, $\mathbf{a}_N$, and α_N of $\mathbf{A}_{n+1}$ (Equations (20)-(21)):

$$\mathbf{v}_N \triangleq \tilde{\mathbf{R}}_N^{-1} - \frac{(1 - t_{n+1}^1)\mathbf{v}_N \mathbf{v}_N^H}{1 + (1 - t_{n+1}^1)\mathbf{v}_N \mathbf{s}_N^H},$$

$$r_N' \triangleq \mathbf{R}_N^{-1} r_N, a_N = \frac{1}{r_N - r_N^H r_N'}, \mathbf{a}_N = -a_N r_N', \mathbf{A}_N = \mathbf{R}_N^{-1} + r_N' r_N'^H a_N$$

(28)

The estimator filter parameters:

$$c_{n+1}^f = [c_N c_N^T]^T \text{ and } c_{n+1}^b$$

are given as

$$c_N = a_N s_N + \mathbf{a}_N^H s_N, \mathbf{c}_N = \frac{\mathbf{v}_N}{1 + (1 - t_{n+1}^1) s_N^H \mathbf{v}_N} - c_N r_N', c_{n+1}^b = -\mathbf{I}^{fb} \mathbf{H}^H c_{n+1}^f,$$

(29)

The quantities $\mathbf{r}_N$ and $\mathbf{r}_N$, required in Equation (3.20), are as follows:

$$\begin{bmatrix} r_N \\ r_N \end{bmatrix} = \begin{bmatrix} \sigma_\omega^2 \\ 0_{Nf-1} \end{bmatrix} + \widetilde{H} diag(t_{n+1}^1)\widetilde{H}^H \begin{bmatrix} 1 \\ 0_{Nf-1} \end{bmatrix} + (1-t_{n+1}^1)ss_N^* \tag{30}$$

Finally, the SISO equalizer output $\pi_{n+1}^{E_0}$ is computed using Equation (26). As initialization, we could compute A1 either directly or using A_{L_x} from the last block. The matrix-vector multiplication Ht_{n+1}^2 in Equation (18) can be realized using a filter with impulse response h[n]. The expression $\widetilde{H}diag(t_{n+1}^1)\widetilde{H}^H[1 \quad 0_{1\times(N^f-1)}]^T$ in Equation (30) is computed by solving from right to left yielding a $O(M^2)$ complexity. The matrix vector product $-I^{fb}H^H c_{n+1}^f$, yielding the parameter vector c_{n+1}^b, has order $O(K^{nob} \cdot M)$, Which is equal to the $O(M^2)$ due to equation (25a).

ALGORITHM

SISO Equalizer Implementation with a MMSE-DFE as Estimator Given Initial Input Priors

Input:

- incoming data from the channel, $Z_{<1,L_x>}$
- initial input prior information about sent
- data

$$X_n : \pi^{Ei}_{<1,Lx>} = \begin{bmatrix} \frac{1}{2} \cdots \frac{1}{2} \end{bmatrix}^T$$

- channel characteristics: h[n], M_1, M_2 Where M is channel length and N is filter length

$$h[n] = \sum_{k=-M1}^{+M2} h_c(nT)\delta[n-k] = \sum_{k=M1}^{+M2} h_{k,n}\delta[n-k],$$

- Noise characteristics: σ_w^2
- Initialization:

$$c^f[n] = \sum_{k=-N^f}^{+N_1^f} c_{k,n}^f d[n-k] \quad c^b[n] = \sum_{k=1}^{+N^b} c_{k,n}^b d[n-k]$$

- set up N^f Equation above,

$$N_2^f = M_1, \ N^b = M-1, \ N_1^f = N^f - M_1 - 1,$$

- define quantities

$$\bar{C}^f \leftarrow \left(\sigma^2 I_{N^f} + H \begin{bmatrix} 1_{N \ XN^f} & 0_{N^f \ XN^b} \\ 0_{N^b \ XN^f} & 1_{N \ XN^b} \end{bmatrix} H^H \right)^{-1} s$$

where $I^{fb} \cong D_n^{bb-1} D^{fbH} - [0_{N^b XN^f} \ I_{N^b}]$,

- initialize Z_n for $(1 - N_2^f) \leq n < 1$ and $L_x < n \leq (L_x+N_1^f)$
  X_n^d for $(1- N^b) \leq n < 1$
  FOR n = 1 TO L_x DO
  Compute prior: obtain Z_n

$$\Pi_n^{Eo} \leftarrow \frac{1}{2}\left(1 - \tanh\left(\frac{1}{1-C^{fH}s} \bar{C}^{fH} Z_n + C^{b\bar{H}} X_n^d \right) \right)$$

Output:

- Prior information about sent data X_n: $\pi^{Eo}_{<1,Lx>}$

RESULTS

The larger the frame size, bigger the S-window. Therefore, it will produce larger distance by using an inter-leaver. The correlation between the two adjacent bits will become smaller. Hence the decoder gives better performance. The simulation results verified this conclusion. However, since Turbo code is a block code, it causes time delay before getting the complete decoding output. Increasing the frame size also increases the delay time. Fig. 3 shows the BER's of Turbo code under static channel with the code rate=1/3, iteration=3, frame size L =1024 bits. When the code rate is decreased, more bits have to be punctured. The bandwidth requirement is also decreased. However, some information is lost. This means that the performance of the Turbo code will also degrade in general. Fig. 3 shows the effects of the punctuation on BER. The higher the code rate the lower the BER. In the simulation, decode iteration=5, frame size=1024, uncorrelated AWGN environment

Figure 3. Frame size effect and effects of puncturing on BER

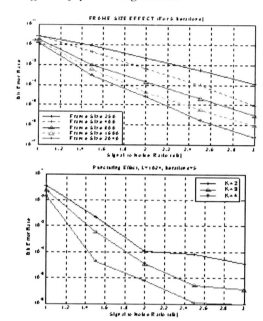

Figure 4. Performace of the MMSE DFE,MMSE LE and SISO estimators

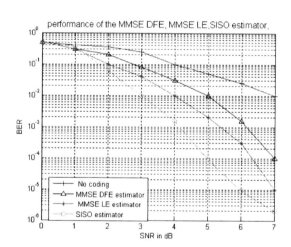

applied. The three curves are corresponding to code rate=1/2, 1/3, and 1/4 respectively.

$$SNR = 10 \log_{10} \frac{Ez}{NoR}$$

The BER curves are plotted along the signal to noise ratio(SNR) for the received symbol z_n per data bits b_i given the code rate R , the unit energy constraint, the symbol alphabet {+1,-1} for the symbol x_n. We implemented a MAP detector as SISO equalizer. A good reference is an efficient noniterative data transmission system. In particular, the Turbo equalizer system is run in a separate setup for one iteration with and without interleaving. The ultimate goal of a data transmission system using a ISI channel is the complete removal of the channel influence.

To show the performance degradation due to ISI, we included the BER curve of an ISI free coded data transmission system only an encoder and a decoder are used and the only obstacle is the receiver noise. For the experiment block length of 1024 were transmitted yielding 10^{-6} symbols x_n to be transmitted over the channel. All the iterative systems performed 5 iterations. The noniterative system without interleaving shows the worst performance. By including interleaving the coding gain is improved enormous. The implemented MAP detector as equalizer and the Map decoder are optimal in terms of the BER. By iterative MAP detection and MAP decoding the coding gain is improved by 4dB at 10^{-3} BER is achieved. Thus it provides ISI free coded transmission at low BERs

Figure 5. Illustration of coverage area with and with out SISO estimator

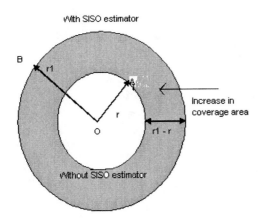

and can compensate for the degradation caused by the ISI channel. Within the SNR range from 2dB to 6dB the iterative system improves the BER performance during several iterations. Within this SNR range, the convergence test is most difficult. The receiver must decide whether to keep iterating in the hope for the priors π_n^{Do} to become more reliable, which is assumed to correspond to a declining BER.

It is depicted that 12dB is the minimum SNR for an AWGN channel used in practice for reconstruction of the original information. Using the experimental data from Fig. 4, it is clearly analyzed that in SISO estimator the coverage range can increased. Fig. 5 illustrates coverage area with and without SISO estimator. Consider a transmitter station located at point O which has a transmitter power of K watts. Without SISO estimator if the receiver is placed within radius r (point A), the signal can be comfortably received when the signal strength is 12 dB. Once the receiver moves in the zone greater than radius r the signal strength is reduced and faithful reconstruction of the signal is not possible without the SISO estimator. Hence once the signal strength decreases below 12 dB it is not possible to retrieve the information.

With the SISO estimator it is found experimentally that with signal strength of 5 dB the received data will be correct. Hence even if the receiver is placed at a radius r1 (point B) there is no degradation in the received signal. Observing that $r_1 > r$ it is concluded that the coverage area is increased by a factor of (r1-r). It is possible to reconstruct the original signal at lower dB (5dB against 12 dB) because the estimator is capable to predict the correct information for BER of 10^{-4}. The increase in coverage area is illustrated in the Fig. 5.

The MMSE estimator is suffered from estimation error at high SNR. But the SISO estimator approach to channel estimation is robust over a range of SNR and independent of correcting the correlating of the received signals.

CONCLUSION

In this chapter, the simulation results show that Turbo code is a powerful error correcting coding technique in low SNR environments. It has achieved near Shannon capacity. A trade-off between the BER and the number of iterations is to be made. e.g., more iteration will get lower BER, but the decoding delay is also longer. Although the Turbo code with larger frame size has better performance, the output delay is longer. The higher coding rate needs more bandwidth.

A coded data transmission system was introduced using an iterative algorithm in the receiver, which performs joint equalization and decoding. The iterative receiver consists of a SISO equalizer and SISO decoder. For the SISO equalizer, efficient exact and suboptimal implementation yielding O (N^2+M^2) and O $(N+M)$ complexity, respectively, per received symbol were discussed. The proposed system performing iterative equalization using priors was shown to perform well compared to establish approaches and to be feasible due to the low computational complexity.

REFERENCES

Bahl, L., Cocke, J., Jelinke, F., & Raviv, J. (1974). Optimal decoding of linear codes minimizing symbol error rate. *IEEE Transactions on Information Theory,* 284-287.

Bauch, G., & Frnz, V. (1998). A comparison of soft in/ soft algorithms for turbo detection. In *Proceedings on International Conference on Telecommunications,* 259-263.

Benedetto, S., Dsalar, D., Mondorsi, G., & Pollara, F. (1999). Algorithm or contain decoding of turbo codes. *IEEE Electronic Letters, 32*(4), *314-315.*

Berrou, C., Glavieux, A., & Thitimajshima, P. (1993). Near Shannon limit error-correcting coding and decoding: Turbo-Codes (1). In *Proc. IEEE Global Telecomm. Conference, Geneva, Switzerland,* 1064-1071.

Berrou, C., & Glavieux, A. (1996). Near optimum error correcting coding and decoding: Turbo codes. *IEEE Transactions n Communications, 4*(10), 261-1271.

Douillard, C., et al. (1995). Iterative correction of inter symbol interference: Turbo equalization. *European Trans. on Telecomm., 6,* 507-511.

Douillard, C., Jezequel, M., Berrou, C., Picart & Glavieux, A. (1995). Iterative correction of inter symbol interference: Turbo equalization. *European Transactions on Telecommunications, 6*(5), 507-511.

Forey, G. D. (1972). Maximum likelihood sequence estimation of digital sequences in presence of inter symbol interference. *IEEE Transactions on information Theory, 18,* (3), 363-378.

Gerstacker, W. H., & Schober, R. (2002). Equalization concepts for EDGE. *IEEE Transactions on Wireless Communications, I*(1),190- 199.

Glavieux, A., & Labat, I. (2001). Turbo equalization: adaptive equalization and channel decoding jointly optimized. *IEEE Journal on Sel. Areas in Comm., 19*(9), 1744-1752.

Glavieux, A., Laot, C., & Labat, J. (1997). Turbo equalization over a frequency selective channel. *In Proc. Int. Symposium on Turbo codes & related topics, Brest, France,* 96-102.

Hagenauer, J. (1997). The turbo principle: Tutorial introduction and state of art a *International symposium on Turbo codes,* September 1997, 1-11.

Hagenauer, J., & Höher, P. (1989). A Viterbi algorithm with soft-decision outputs and its applications. *In Proc. IEEE Global Telecomm. Conference, Dallas,* 1680-1686.

Hagenauer, J., & Höher, P. (1989). A Viterbi algorithm with soft-decision outputs and its applications. *In Proc. IEEE Global Telecomm. Conference, Dallas,* 1680-1686.

Haykin, S. (1994). *Communication systems,* 3rd Edition. Canada.

Lin, S., & Costelloo Jr., J. (1983). *Error Control Coding.* Englewood cliffs, New Prentice Hall.

Proakis J. G., & Salehi, M. (1994). *Communication systems Engineering.* New Jersey; Prentice Hall.

Rabiner, L. R. (1998). A Tutorial on Hide Markov Models and Selected Application Speech Recognition. *In Proceedings of the IEEE, 77*(2), 257-286.

Smee J. E., & Beaulieu, N.C. (1995). New methods for evaluating equalizer error rate performance. *In IEEE Proceedings on the 45th Vehicular Tech,* 87-91.

Tuchler, M., Koetter, R., & Singer, A. (2002). Turbo equalization: Principles and new results. *IEEE Trans. on Comm., 50*(5), 754-767.

Vogelbruch, E., & Ha, S. (2003). Turbo Equalization based on optimized Soft ISI Cancellation. *In Proc. IEEE Global Telecomm. Conference, San Francisco,* 1736-1740.

Wang, X., & Poor, H.V. (1998). Turbo multiuser detection and equalization for a coded CDMA in multipath channels. *In IEEE International Conference on Universal personal Communications, 2,* 1123-1127.

Chapter XXXIV
RFID and Supply Chain Visibility

Sumeet Gupta
Shri Sankaracarya Institute of Management and Technology, India

Miti Garg
The Logistics Institute – Asia Pacific, Singapore

Heng Xu
The Pennsylvania State University, USA

Mark Goh
NUS Business School, The Logistics Institute – Asia Pacific, Singapore

ABSTRACT

Supply chains have become increasingly complex and interdependent in the globalization era. Regulatory authorities are demanding stricter customer compliance, and customers are demanding real-time data for better decision making. At the same time, customer demand is becoming more erratic thus the need for enhanced supply chain coordination with an objective to enhance overall customer value. Radio Frequency Identification RFID, an enabler of supply chain visibility, has the potential to provide customers with large amounts of information at any point in the movement of goods through the supply chain. This technology complements the barcode technology. However, with the acceptance of RFID technology, several managerial and technical issues arise. The focus of this chapter is to thus discuss the relevance of RFID technology for enabling supply chain visibility and adoption related issues.

INTRODUCTION

Increasing efficiency and cost reduction have been the primary value creating strategies for traditional supply chains (Kalakota and Robinson 2002). However, today's supply chains are much more complex, inter-twined and messy primarily due to increasing globalization. Uneven demand, more frequent and shorter order-to-shipment times, and stricter customer compliance requirements are the key parameters that influence today's supply chains. As a result, companies are re-examining their business processes from a business-to-business (B2B) commerce perspective in an effort to be more effective and efficient. The value for today's supply chain lies in the flexibility in procurement, execution, and visibility across the entire supply chain as well as in managing reverse logistics. Supply chain design must accommodate requests by fickle customers who change their mind after the order is placed so that the company retains control of the manufacturing and fulfillment processes.

Improving flexibility entails improving supply chain coordination for which new tools are required (Kalakota and Robinson 2002). While the Internet has been a primary enabler of many supply chain coordination activities, mobile applications such as mobile phones are beginning to play a central role in enabling *real-time* supply chains. Most traditional supply chain applications have been hindered by the inability to obtain real-time data on attributes such as accurate customer demand and the ability to track assets in transit. Customers want real-time order status information and demand greater visibility into the supply chain execution processes. They increasingly expect to be able to find out the location and status of their orders whenever, and from wherever, they want. To better monitor and optimize asset utilization, they need visibility into the pipeline inventory, inventory at rest (inside a factory or distribution center), and a real-time view of their assets. Customers also want immediate notification in case of the failure to meet the standards outlined in the company's delivery terms and service agreements by supply chain performance. Supply chain visibility requires the technological ability to match a unique customer transaction with the customer's products as these products flow through the supply chain. This matching process is often done manually or through visual inspection which increases the potential for error. The utopia is to have technologies that, using either a customer serial number or pallet, enable the tracking of products from the original product components to the product's receipt by the customer. As a result, companies are investing more in real-time asset tracking. These investments help companies achieve inventory reductions, eliminate sources of order fulfillment variance, reduce leakage, and hence fewer returns.

SUPPLY CHAIN VISIBILITY ENABLERS

A range of technologies, such as barcodes, biometrics, machine vision, magnetic stripe, optical card readers, voice recognition, and smart cards have been developed for automated data collection to augment Enterprise Resource Planning (ERP) (Gupta 2000). Barcodes are already widely used to improve supply chain efficiency especially in quick checkouts at supermarket counters. Since its adoption thirty years ago, it has enabled the creation of important new applications ranging from tracking customer buying habits to managing inventory. The U.S. Postal Service uses bar-coding as a way of identifying product shipments and to gain greater visibility into a product's physical location and status as it moves through the chain. The barcode is an excellent example of the power a single technological innovation can have in changing core business processes.

However, bar-code technology alone is insufficient for handling changing customer demand towards greater supply chain visibility. Radio Frequency Identification (RFID) technology, which permits tagging and tracking of physical goods, is considered a significant improvement over the conventional barcode, which needs to be read by scanners in a line-of-sight fashion and can be stripped away if the paper product labels get ripped or damaged (Angeles 2005). RFID can also facilitate inter-organizational E-Commerce initiatives such as continuous replenishment or vendor-managed inventory (Smaros and Holmstrom, 2000).

HOW DOES RFID WORK?

The RFID value chain involves three parts: tags, readers and enterprise integration software that power these systems. The data generated by the application software can interface with other systems, such as, ERP, Supply Chain Management (SCM) and Customer Relationship Management (CRM), used in an enterprise (Figure 1).

There are three types of RFID tags: active, passive and semi-passive. When most people talk about RFID, they talk about passive tags. In passive tags radio frequency is sent from a transmitter to a chip or card. Passive tags do not have power cell and it uses the transmitted signal to power itself long enough to respond with a coded identifier. This numeric identifier really carries no information other than a unique number, but keyed against a database that associates that number with other data, the RFID tag's identifier can evoke all information in the database keyed to that number. An active tag has its own internal power source and can store as well as send even more detailed information. Active tags are traceable over a much longer distance than passive tags which work within a specific range of one meter (Curtin et

Figure 1. RFID integration with enterprise wide systems

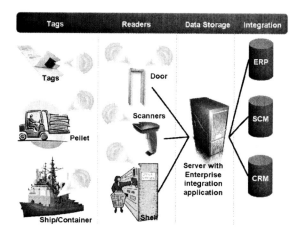

al. 2005). Semi-passive tags use both battery and the waves sent out by the reader to power themselves. Typically, active and semi-passive tags are used for higher-value goods, while passive tags are used for lower-value goods.

IMPORTANCE OF RFID TOWARDS SUPPLY CHAIN VISIBILITY

RFID is considered a technology initiative in enabling supply chain visibility. One of the big benefits of RFID technology is that it streamlines the movement of goods through a supply chain. Several major buyers and retailers have come to recognize the potential usefulness of RFID technology as a way of tracking physical goods across the supply chain, which has led them to mandate its adoption to their trading partners (Bacheldor and Sullivan 2004). There are four scenarios for RFID implementation ranging from applying this technology to a discrete process to using it for inter-organizational synchronization (Fontanella 2004). Here, we briefly explore these scenarios.

a.   Improving inter-organizational logistics

Inter-organizational (both inbound and outbound) logistics form a major and critical operation of any supply chain firm. In general, the procurement process of any firm demands matching of goods from the supplier with a prearranged purchase order either visually or via barcode to ensure that the shipment is as expected. The manual operation of scanning the

barcode, however, takes more time and is inefficient. By labeling the goods with an RFID chip, the contents of the shipping container can be automatically verified upon receipt thus saving time and effort as compared to the manual scanning of a barcode. Not only physical goods but also fork lifts and even the vehicle operators can be tagged to ensure that they are available and in position when needed thus streamlining the operations further. RFID can help in gaining further efficiencies when linked to the enterprise wide Electronic Data Interchange (EDI) system, which would help in efficiently managing containers.

b.   Improving efficiency of internal operations

The ability of RFID to streamline the movement of goods through a supply chain has attracted the attention of various retailers (E.g., Walmart, Best Buy, Tesco, Carrefour), airlines (e.g., Delta) and logistics service providers (Curtin et al. 2005). The process of storing and retrieving items from a large warehouse is a laborious task. However, the use of RFID can streamline the whole process whereby the products can be placed and retrieved in the warehouse automatically. Walmart was among the leaders to reap the benefits of RFID through automated warehousing. Walmart had earlier announced mandatory adoption of RFID to its largest 100 suppliers on shipped items at the pallet level by January 2005 (Roberti 2003). Walmart could save over US$8 billion annually using RFID by reducing the labor costs of scanning items, reduction in out-of-stock items, improvement in the supply chain, and reduced item theft (Haley 2003).

Several airlines have started reaping the benefits of RFID through reducing economic losses due to misdirected baggage. Delta Airlines, for example, handles 70 million pieces of luggage every year and spends about tens of millions of dollars on locating misdirected luggage. It believes that tremendous returns on investment can be generated by using RFID which would accelerate immediate identification of lost luggage (Brewin 2004). RFID systems are also used in airport baggage handling systems. For instance, at the San Francisco International Airport, RFID tags are affixed to passenger bags. The tags are then used to move the bags through a labyrinth of conveyor belts and security checkpoints. Another application of RFID tags is in libraries, where the tags are affixed to books (de Souza, Goh and Wong 2007). Patrons insert their library cards into a self check-out kiosk and then scan the books, which updates the library records and deactivates the RFID tag.

c.   Improving consumer marketing

Opportunities abound in improving personalized marketing using RFID tags. Fusaro (2004), for example, demonstrates the potential interest of clothing retailers to tag products that will be sold and subsequently worn by customers. Most retail stores provide customers with frequent customer perks cards. By tagging these cards with RFID tags, retailers can obtain useful data about the customer purchase behavior, albeit requiring powerful data mining techniques to elicit useful information for decision making. By tagging individual items, retailers can obtain dynamic data on the customer's usage of particular products in a store, consumer attraction to promotional flyers and so on which can then be used for personalized marketing to the customer.

d.   Improving customer service

After-sales service can be improved by retrieving the data regarding purchase date, warranty status, potential abuse, and diagnostic details from the RFID tags placed on the products when sold.

Although promising, RFID poses potential challenges for mass commercialization as there are a variety of obstacles in realizing the return on investment on RFID. We discuss some of the technical and managerial issues that prevent or hinder widespread adoption of RFID.

TECHNICAL ISSUES

RFID readers communicate with tags using inductive coupling. The coiled antenna of the reader creates a magnetic field with the tag's antenna, which subsequently draws energy from this field and uses this to send back waves to the reader. These waves are transformed into digital information representing the Electronic Product Code (EPC). The "read range" of the tag depends on both the reader's power and the frequency used to communicate (Angeles 2005). The major technical issues are related to collision and seamless signal detection of RFID tags by readers.

a.   Collision issues

Collision refers to the signal interference that occurs while detecting signals using RFID tag readers. When there is more than one reader, signals from one reader can interfere with signals from another reader when their physical coverage overlaps. Collision can also occur when readers are reading many chips in the same field, whereby there may be interference from other chips. The Auto-ID Center at Massachusetts Institute of Technology (MIT) has addressed this problem by making the readers ask tags to respond only if their first digits match the digits communicated by the reader. The reader keeps querying the tags until such time when one and only one tag responds, which is the desired condition.

b.   International agreements on standard UHF frequency

The use of radio waves is regulated by the governments around the world. Different governments have assigned different uses for the various parts of the spectrum. Most countries have adopted 13.56 MHz for the high RFID systems. However, Europe and the US currently utilize 869 MHz and 915 MHz for UHF respectively. With the exception of the special ISM (i.e., industrial, scientific, and medical) bands there is no part of the spectrum available everywhere in the world. Because of the lack of a unified standard frequency tags tag operating at a certain frequency in one country may not be readable in another country where the same spectrum is used for a different purpose. As today's supply chains span global boundaries, there is a need for a unified international standard for RFID tags. The Auto-ID Center at MIT have designed reference specifications for "agile readers" that can read chips at different frequencies. This will enable firms to use only one reader in situations where multiple frequencies are involved and save them the cost of having separate readers for each frequency (Angeles 2005).

b.   Signal detection issues

Although RFID technology is constantly improving, it is limited by the inability of the signals to pass through certain materials including human and animal tissue, liquids, metals, and other types of packaging materials. Moreover, the presence of other tags in close proximity hampers the accurate reading of the signal by RFID signal detectors. For example, if a forklift driver passes by a shelf tag about three times to fix the placement of a pallet, it is not certain if the reader will record three separate pallets or recognize that one pallet information as one and the same. Another issue is the distance at which the tags are read. The greater the distance, greater is the size of the antenna required on the transmitting tag which increases the size and cost of the tag. Further, the accurate reading of tag is hindered by the speed with which the item passes the reader.

MANAGERIAL ISSUES

a.   Technology standard and network effect

The widespread adoption of RFID has been limited due to the fact that the standards for RFID technology have not yet been developed completely although vendors and users are beginning to cooperate with standards development bodies and one another to evolve RFID standards to ensure adoption (Edwards 2003). The lack of widespread adoption prevents network externalities. Most firms follow early adopters. If the technology is not widely adopted, then the investment in such technology becomes risky.

Moreover, the vendors supplying reader and tags can take advantage of network externalities as the tag reader and tags are complementary goods. By pricing tag readers artificially low, the vendor can increase the demand for tags. This is particularly true in the absence of a technology standard whereby a vendor can sell tags that can only be read by its tag reader.

Widespread use of RFID will increase its value to other entities in the network. However, one problem that arises is its potential detection by competition. Competitive or negative externalities may exist when a major buyer introduces a technology to a set of users who do not communicate with each other (Grover and Segars 1999; Riggins and Mukhopadhyay 1999). In such a case, firms would be tempted to develop proprietary tags that could only be detected by the firm and the network in which it allows other firms to access its RFID tags.

b.   Business process redesign

Since, business process redesign has become common and more frequent as technology is evolving very fast. The adoption of RFID raises major critical issues related to business process redesign. Challenges arise regarding the readiness and capabilities of suppliers in buyer-supplier relationships as evidenced by Walmart's attempts to mandate RFID adoption (e.g., Sullivan 2005). Full realization of the value of RFID requires wide adoption among trading partners that often will require mandates of subsidies necessary to encourage full adoption. The ownership of equipment and data, plus the equitable distribution of technology benefits further complicates the inter-organizational adoption of the technology.

An important element of realizing value from RFID technology is its integration with the firm's operations. The cost associated with such systems integration efforts are huge and time consuming. Since RFID is an emerging technology, most observers expect that the standards associated with it will migrate over the course of the next few years, as the support for different technological capabilities improves. In the meanwhile, the process redesign may cause unrest among employees. If applied improperly, firms may lose substantial business or in some cases go bust.

c.   Return on investment

The investment in RFID consists of the cost of the tag, tag readers and related equipment, an integration software and hardware that integrates tag data with the enterprise wide EDI, ERP, CRM or SCM solutions. One important issue preventing the widespread adoption of RFID tags is in the unit cost. The direct effect of the high cost of RFID tag is on the Return on Inventory (ROI) generated by the use of RFID. Currently, an RFID tag costs about US$0.50 when purchased in volumes of a million tags or more. In most cases, these tags have an effective read range of less than 20 feet. To make RFID tags cheaper is easily recognized as a chicken-and-egg technology adoption and diffusion game. In order to make tags cheaper, it will be necessary for market demand to dramatically increase, creating additional volume-based manufacturing results. However, for demand to materialize, RFID tags will need to be cheaper and more effective that they currently are.

Firms may have to overlook short-term ROI from RFID technology. According to Fontanella (2004), firms that adopt a more simplified and focused approach to RFID incurs much less risk in implementation and still create tangible value and capabilities that differentiate them significantly from competitors.

d.   Privacy issues

Customer privacy issue has been a main bugbear for the widespread adoption of RFID in retailing. While after sales service can be considerably improved by tagging goods with RFID tags, considerable anxiety is generated in the minds of the individuals who worry that mobile units may scan people's homes from the neighborhood street and determine what items are inside their homes. While the concepts and issues of privacy are not new, RFID technology introduces new complexity to the landscape of privacy considerations. RFID technology creates data fusion opportunities across applications to identify personal identity and classify individuals in ways that increase the privacy risk. Consumer groups are pressing for legislation to ensure that tags are appropriately deactivated at the time of sale to ensure that firms are not tracking the use of after-sale items or tracking the movements of people with live tags still on the person (CASPIAN 2003). In addition, the National Institute of Standards and Technology (NIST 2007) in the U.S. issued the *Guidelines for Securing Radio Frequency Identification (RFID) Systems*, which detailed how to address the issues on privacy protection and trans-border flows of personal data (NIST 2007).

e.   Data management issues

The use of RFID technology will lead to a sharp increase in the incoming volume of product data, primarily because the data will now be incoming in the real time rather than in a batch mode. Firms that have tracked pallets and cases with RFID tags report at least a 30 percent increase in data that needed to be processed (Angeles 2005). In dealing with voluminous data, there is the issue of redesigning product/item master file data structures so that they are consistent across the firm and its value chain participants (RFID Journal, 2003). The level of granularity for data collection also needs to be determined. Goods that may need to be recalled such as fresh produce, perishables, or high-value items such as luxury designer goods may require a more detailed record of their movements through the purchase experience. Moreover, a firm must have appropriate capability to interpret the real time data being transmitted through RFID tags.

FUTURE OF RFID

RFID technology promises to offer near-perfect information visibility throughout the supply chain across different industries. Several firms have benefitted in one way or another by implementing RFID. However, the technical and managerial issues arising out of the use of RFID limit its global adoption on a single platform. A number of issues may arise in its adoption in fast developing countries like India and China, thereby raising the need to closely study the feasibility of RFID adoption in these countries. The major question for many RFID adopters is the ROI in RFID. However, it is clear that as the technology and technology standards improve, RFID would change the rules of business.

REFERENCES

Angeles, R. (2005). RFID Technologies: Supply-Chain Applications and Implementation Issues. *Information Systems Management*, 22(1), 51-65.

Bacheldor, B. and Sullivan, L. (2004). Target wants suppliers to use RFID. *InternetWeek*, February 24.

Brewin, B. "Delta Begins Second RFID Bag Tag Test." April 1, 2004. Available online at www.computerworld.com/mobiletopics/mobile/technology/story/0,10801,91826,00.html. Retrieved September 9, 2007.

CASPIAN (Consumers against Supermarket Privacy Invasion and Numbering) (2003). Position Statement on the Use of RFID on Consumer Products." Electronic Frontier Foundation, November 13. Available online at www.eff.org/Privacy/Surveillance/RFID/rfid_position_statement.php. Retrieved September 9, 2007.

Curtin, J. Kayffman, R.J. and Riggins, F.J. (2005). Making the 'Most' out of RFID Technology: A Research agenda for the study of the adoption, use and impacts of RFID. Available online at: http://misrc.umn.edu/workingpapers/fullpapers/2005/0522_103005.pdf. Retrieved September 9, 2007.

De Souza R., Goh, M. and Wong, T.W. (2007). RFID in Singapore. In Banks, J., Hanny, D., Pachano, M.A. and Thompson, L.G. (eds.) RFID Applied, Wiley, Hoboken: New Jersey, pp. 415-422.

Edwards, J. "Tag, You're It." *CIO Magazine*, February 15, 2003. Available on the Internet at www.cio.com/archive/021503/et_article.html. Retrieved February 6, 2005.

Fontanella, J. (2004). Finding the ROI in RFID," *Supply Chain Management Review*, 8 (1), 13-14.

Fusaro, R.A. (2004). None of Our Business? *Harvard*

Business Review, December, 33-44.

Grover, V. and Segars, A. (1999). Introduction to the Special Issue: Electronic Commerce and Market Transformation. *International Journal of Electronic Commerce*, 3(4), 3.

Gupta, A. (2000). Enterprise resource planning: The emerging organizational value systems. *Industrial Management & Data Systems*, 100(3), 114–118.

Haley, C.C. (2003). Are You Ready for RFID? *Wireless Internet.com—the Source for WiFi Business and Technology*, November 13, Available online at www.wi-fiplanet.com/columns/article.php/3109501. Retreived September 9, 2007.

Kalakota, R. and Robinson, M. (2002). M-Business: The Race to Mobility, New York: McGraw-Hill.

NIST (National Institute of Standards and Technology) (2007). Guidelines for Securing Radio Frequency Identification RFID Systems: Recommendations of the National Institute of Standards and Technology, National Institute of Standards and Technology, April 2007. http://csrc.nist.gov/publications/nistpubs/800-98/SP800-98_RFID-2007.pdf

RFID Journal (2003). March 31, Part 9: RFID and IT challenge.

Riggins, F.J. and Mukhopadhyay, T. (1994). Interdependent benefits from interorganizational systems: Opportunities for business partner reengineering. *Journal of Management Information Systems*, 11(2), 37-57.

Smaros, J. and Holmstrom, J. (2000). Viewpoint: reaching the consumer through grocery VMI. *International Journal of Retail & Distribution Management*, 28(2), 55–61.

Sullivan, L. (2005) RFID: The Plot Thickens. *Information Week*, January 3, 2005.

KEY TERMS

Barcode: A barcode (also bar code) is a machine-readable representation of information (usually dark ink on a light background to create high and low reflectance which is converted to 1s and 0s). Originally, barcodes stored data in the widths and spacings of printed parallel lines, but today they also come in patterns of dots, concentric circles, and text codes hidden within images.

Customer Relationship Management: Customer relationship management (CRM) is a broad term that covers concepts used by companies to manage their relationships with customers, including the capture, storage and analysis of customer, vendor, partner, and internal process information.

E-Commerce: Electronic commerce, commonly known as e-commerce or eCommerce, consists of the buying and selling of products or services over electronic systems such as the Internet and other computer networks.

Enterprise Resource Planning: Enterprise Resource Planning (ERP) system integrates all data and processes of an organization into a unified system using multiple components of computer software and hardware and a unified database to store data for the various system modules.

Inductive Coupling: Inductive coupling refers to the transfer of energy from one circuit component to another through a shared magnetic field. A change in current flow through one device induces current flow in the other device.

Network Effect: A network effect is a characteristic that causes a good or service to have a value to a potential customer which depends on the number of other customers who own the good or are users of the service. In other words, the number of prior adopters is a term in the value available to the next adopter.

Supply Chain Management: Supply chain management (SCM) is the process of efficiently planning, implementing, and controlling the operations of the supply chain. It spans all movement and storage of raw materials, work-in-process inventory, and finished goods from point-of-origin to point-of-consumption

Supply Chain Visibility: Supply chain visibility refers to customer's ability to monitor their inventory in motion and at rest, optimize asset utilization, track and trace the status of their orders whenever, and from wherever, they want. In other words, the whole supply chain is visible to the customers.

Chapter XXXV
Cell Broadcasting Opportunities of Modern Mobile Communications and Its Usage in Emergency Warning Facilities

Ioannis P. Chochliouros
Hellenic Telecommunications Organization S.A. (OTE), Greece

Anastasia S. Spiliopoulou
Hellenic Telecommunications Organization S.A. (OTE), Greece

George Agapiou
Hellenic Telecommunications Organization S.A. (OTE), Greece

Nikolaos Lazaridis
M.D. Ph.D., Greece

ABSTRACT

In the scope of the present chapter, the authors evaluate several potential opportunities from the suggested use of cell broadcasting systems in mobile communications and its specific usage mainly in emergency warning facilities, at the global level. Cell Broadcasting (CB) is a cellular-based public notification system, existing in the vast majority of all modern mobile infrastructures, worldwide. It can instantly (within a brief timeframe of some seconds) broadcast a cell phone text alert or message to a large number of people (independently of their network operators) specific to a geographical area, covered either by a single cell or by the entire (regional or national) network. Thus, CB technology enables governmental and other appropriate authorities/entities to securely transmit emergency alerts of natural or manmade disasters to the cellular phones of the subscribers in specific areas. Simultaneously, it can offer multiple extra advantages for further market offerings and development. This chapter discusses the challenge imposed by the fast development of the corresponding cellular facilities and, after providing some fundamental technical informative background, it focuses on the advantages offered due to CB with an overview of the current European and international market. The chapter then analyzes options for further evolution in several sectors (political issues, technical matters, and regulatory perspectives). CB is a strong, viable, and immediate communications solution, which can be put in place to better alert citizens.

INTRODUCTION

In modern societies, the assurance of an appropriate level of fundamental communications facilities and/or any other appropriate means towards realizing this aim can be considered as a major duty and a high priority of public authorities in the scope of their activities. The challenge becomes greater for state, regional and local authorities (and for the appropriate response teams) when there is a strong need for immediate, efficient and "wide" warning of (and/or communication with) citizens in emergency cases during times of crisis. Consequently, there is a necessity for developing high quality communication techniques and infrastructures to fulfil this prerequisite.

After numerous recent natural disasters (floods, forest fires, hurricanes (like hurricanes Katrina and Rita in the US and the 2004 tsunami in Asia), earthquakes, landslides, etc.) and several cases of accidents (chemical and industrial accidents, nuclear emergencies, transport accidents, technological disasters, etc.) a lot of effort has been spent on developing ways people could be timely informed in emergency cases. In the same scope, the increased criminal and/or terrorist events in the international scenery have also imposed the necessity for immediate notification/warning of the public in cases of attacks and for civil protection. Specific strategic initiatives have been deployed, worldwide, (for example see: European Commission, 1999) to efficiently deal with various kinds of disasters.

The current effort intends to examine possible benefits, for both users and (market) operators, of mobile networks' potential usage in emergency situations. The fast deployment of mobile infrastructures (and of related facilities) has been performed at the global level: More specifically, the Western European and some Asian markets have reached a very high level of mobile usage penetration. The same is true for the American market when considering moderate- to high-level spending customers. However, this does not necessarily mean that the growth in number of subscriptions will end, since there is still a large untapped subscriber potential in new markets as well as emerging applications (Ericsson, 2006).

Currently, mobile applications comprise a "basic" feature of our every-day life, in multiple societies. Recent studies have demonstrated that there are more than 2 billion mobile phones in use all over the world, of which 1.5 billion are GSM (Global System for Mobile Communications) phones, representing the well-known "second generation" mobile system. Due to their extended penetration and under appropriate circumstances, mobile devices could be considered as "proper" means in public warning systems. More specifically, as millions of people (not only in the European Union (EU) but internationally) are existing users of GSM amenities (European Commission, 2001) such systems can provide a remarkable prospect for the growth of civil protection-oriented facilities, dealing with crisis management on hazardous events, and thus providing immediate and reliable notification to the public.

In parallel, we provide some fundamental information about the existing GSM system/infrastructure, while explain how it operates and on how it could be further deployed. Since the main advantage of cellular networks is the provision of ubiquitous connectivity along with the localization and a broadcasting option in their packets, fast and direct warning of people in emergency situations (of various nature) can be achieved.

Cellular communication networks/systems are still developing very rapidly, and apart from their commercial benefits they are able to provide significant advantages to benefit civilians, governments, homeland security and crisis management. These systems can save lives by informing the people located in a certain area immediately. Furthermore they can prevent from accidents, help in traffic problems (e.g. by informing about traffic jams) and be used as a new way of advertisement, promoting new business applications (Watson, 1993; European Commission, 2003).

BACKGROUND: FUNDAMENTAL ARCHITECTURAL ISSUES OF CELLULAR NETWORKS

During the last decade of the 20th century and following to requirements imposed by the extreme international revolutionary progress of cellular telephony, ETSI (European Telecommunications Standards Institute) has described "GSM" as a *European digital cellular model of telephony offering high voice quality, call privacy and increased network security*" (ETSI, 1993). Then, an additional feature has been introduced and incorporated, called as "*Cell Broadcast*"; currently, all GSM phones and base stations have this specific feature latent within them, though sometimes it is not "enabled" in the actual network. Before it usage there were other methods of fast informing (Redl, Weber, & Oliphant, 1995).

Modern cellular systems consist of mobile units communicating among themselves via radio network by using dedicated non-wireless lines to an infra-structure of switching equipment, interconnecting the diverse parts and allowing access to the fixed Public Switched Telephone Network-PSTN (Chochliouros & Spiliopoulou, 2005). Several functions are needed for a GSM network to operate. The main "sub-systems" of the core GSM structure are listed as follows:

- The Base Station sub-System (known as BSS): It deals with the transmission between mobile stations and the NSS (as described below) by checking and managing radio links. It provides radio coverage in certain (pre-defined) areas, commonly known as the "cells", and it contains the hardware for communication with the ex-isting mobile stations. Operationally, the BSS is implemented by the Base Station Controller (BSC) and the Base Transceiver Station (BTS). A BSS can control multiple BTSs and can serve several cells. The essential parts of a BSS are: (i) the BSC, i.e. a selective switching centre, responsible for the wireless part of the mobile network and; (ii) the BTS which is used as a "connection" between the mobile phone and the rest of the network.
- The Network Switching sub-System (known as NSS): It consists of MSC (Mobile Switching Centre) which is a telecommunication switch or exchange within specific network architecture, capable of interworking with location databases, HLR (Home Location Register is the database storing all subscriber data and it is an essential part in the roaming process). In addition, there is the VLR (Visitor Location Register), i.e. a database acting as an operational unit where subscribers' data are stored; it changes every time a subscriber is located in a certain area, covered by a specific VLR of a MSC and AUC (Authentication Center). The latter is a protected database using algorithms for identity certifica-tion, as well as a kind of phone call cryptography for secure communication (Mouly & Pautet, 1992; ETSI, 1999b).
- EIR (Equipment Identity Register) is a database used for security purposes, i.e. to prevent a mobile phone from unauthorized access.
- The Operating Services sub-System (OSS) is the part responsible for network maintenance.

Its basic functionality is to supervise network operations, by incorporating intelligent error detection mechanisms, and to inform operator of any probable malfunctions.

Figure 1 depicts the "links" between the above parts and/or related functional modules.

SMS SERVICES IN CELLULAR ENVIRONMENTS

Mobile phones are simple to use and their most sig-nificant benefit is mobility-portability. Thus, anyone can be reached when being in the coverage area of an appropriately operating network. However, apart from performing phone calls, mobile handsets also provide the possibility of sending and receiving written messages, either from similar terminals or from other devices (ETSI, 1999a). These messages are widely known as "*Short Message Service Point-to-Point*" (SMS-PP). They have been described in the GSM Recommendation 03.40 (ETSI, 1992) and can be up to 160 strings (when a string is represented by a 7-bit word, according to the 7-bit GSM alphabet). There are actually two types of messages: mobile originated and mobile terminated. In the former case, messages are sent from the mobile station to the mobile centre. In the latter case, the service centre sends them to the mobile station. Mobile terminated messages can be sent from the SMS Center to one or more dedicated phone numbers or can be sent to a complete cell (i.e. BSC or MSC). These are called as "cell broadcasted messages" (SMS-CB) and have been detailed in the context of the GSM Recommendation 03.41 (ETSI, 1991). These compose the basic issue to deal with, in the continuity of the present work. In fact, as these messages are not extensively used in all instances of the actual modern marketplace (with the excep-tion of some advertising purposes), it is remarkably interesting to examine how they could be used as a convenient "*information system*" in emergency cases and how such this could be implemented in existing GSM infrastructures.

CELL BROADCASTING ACTIVITIES

Message broadcasting (or data broadcast) is an in-novative and challenging technique intending to the improvement of the bandwidth utilization and the potential maximization of system's capacity, as "messages" can be received by numerous mobile users by only one transmission. Such an operation significantly reduces power consumption in mobile communications, as users are not obliged to send requests to the broadcast center (3GPP, 2002; Raissi-Dehkordi & Baras, 2002). A very interesting type of message broadcasting is *Cell Broadcasting* (CB), which is an existing and fully established function of most modern digital mobile phone systems (including both GSM and UMTS (Universal Mobile Telecommunications System)). As it has already been mentioned previously, the scope of the present approach is mainly focused upon the evaluation of "GSM"-based issues, as the relevant systems are widely deployed both in Europe and internationally. It should be expected that the related situation will get even more complex, if taking into account the expected development (and/or the exploitation) of the enhanced third generation-3G (and further) mobile systems (i.e. 3G+, 3G++, UMTS). In particular, it should be expected that 3G cell broadcast messages will be much more capable, so different cell data will be needed for the "multimedia" and "plain text" future versions of messages (3GPP, 2006).

Indeed, existing CB features permit text messages to be broadcast to all mobile handsets found in a given geographical area (Cell Broadcast Forum, 2002b; 3GPP 2006), ranging from the specific one covered by a single radio cell to whole regional territory or even the entire country. Nevertheless, only those handsets that have CB-channels activated will immediately receive messages, at "real time". The basic CB's advantage is that sending a message to millions of handsets is only a matter of some seconds. As CB operates by targeting

particular cells, no awareness of mobile phone numbers is needed, contrasting to bulk SMS. Furthermore, CB imposes no remarkable extra load on the entire network functioning activity: in fact, a cell broadcast to every subscriber on the system is equivalent to sending an SMS message to a single phone. This implies a "prerequisite" for proper functionality and performance, as network loading (and/or overloading) states can lead to severe problematic situations in emergency cases, especially when network usage is likely to be very high and SMS messages can be delayed for hours or days or even lost altogether.

CB technology allows messages (of up to 15 pages of 93 characters each) to be distributed to all mobile stations within a geographical region. It is a service comparable to the videotext. Cell broadcasted messages (SMS-CB) are sent point-to-area (whereas SMS are sent point-to-point) and so they suggest an efficient method for delivering of data to a large number of users in cellular networks. In particular, one SMS-CB can reach a significant number of subscribers in just a few seconds, without the originator knowing who has finally received these messages. A new message can be transmitted every two seconds and terminal users can decide whether to accept or reject it (Cell Broadcast Forum, 2002a). Thus, CB becomes an almost "ideal" solution for delivering local or regional information which is "suited" to all the people in the "area", rather than just one or a few people (DHI Group, 2005). Notable examples can include not only hazard (or security) warnings but other information as well, such as local weather conditions, tourist and cultural information, parking and traffic information, flight or bus delays, cinema programs, etc. In this context, CB can become a consistent and reliable location-specific,

Figure 1. Basic architecture of GSM networks

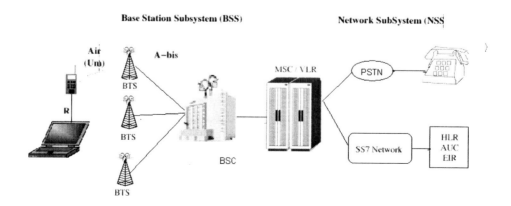

source of information, especially for "people on the move" (including those visiting other countries).

Both gained experience and current approaches in the sector suggest that are three main reasons for using CB in emergency cases (Cell Broadcast Forum, 2005): The first is that CB already exists in most network infrastructure and mobile equipment deployed in the marketplace, so it does not require any extra activity nor additional investment. Secondly, it does not cause traffic load, which can be a vital feature during a disaster situation (when load spikes tend to "crash" networks). The final core advantage is the high scalability because of the independence of system performance to the number of terminals and the provisioning of "equivalent" quality of service to every connected user.

Some recent experimental works demonstrated that message broadcasting can only be attained over a single channel (for example: ETSI, 2004; Jiun-Long & Ming-Syan, 2004). CB messages can be sent only by an operator and not by a single user. These messages are originated in an "entity" called as the "CBE" (Cell Broadcast Entity), and there they are formatted and split into pages (or messages) of 82 octets. Every broadcast network can have one or more CBEs that can be connected to one or more BSCs. Most of the mobile handsets offered in the market are able to support reception of such messages. The end-user has only to activate it on the mobile phone, choose to receive the messages of his interest and block the rest.

SMS-CBs are received only when the mobile station stands in the "idle" mode of operation and, *more specifically*, when message is characterized by the following features:

- It is based on one-way system (this explains why no acknowledgment is sent by the mobile handset);
- It is sent by control channels in a "limited" area, defined by the originator of the message with the same service quality options;
- It is only mobile-terminated;
- The CB Message is sent continuously and it is repeated so as to be received by users moving through a group of cells;
- The maximum number of characters in each SMS-CB depends on the coding group. (The maximum length can vary from 40 to 93 characters).
- A given message can be repeatedly received, although the user has already seen it. To avoid

this, the network provides a serial number to each message. Consequently, if a specific message with the same message identifier and serial number has been received earlier, then the mobile station ignores it. If the information contained is updated, then the network gives the message a new serial number to be considered as "new" and to be received by the mobile station.

CB messages are stored in the BSC, in the *Cell Broadcast Message File* (CBFILE). The broadcast area can be as small as one cell or as large as the whole Public Land Mobile Network-PLMN (ETSI, 2002). In theory, a message takes 1.88 seconds to be transmitted. This implicates that in two minutes time about 64 SMS-CBs can be sent. As previously mentioned, every message can only have up to 15 pages, but 60 different active messages per cell can be defined. The maximum storage capacity is 1,280 cell broadcast message pages. The BSC has the ability to store the 80 most recent broadcast counters of CB messages per cell (www.cellbroadcastforum.org). For an efficient management of CB messages, the responsible entity is the *Cell Broadcast Centre* (CBC) which operates as a server for all CBE clients. It takes care of the administration of all SMS-CB messages it receives from the CBEs and realizes communication to the GSM network. The GSM network itself takes care of delivering the SMS-CB messages to the mobile terminals.

The relevant transmission protocol, however, is based primary on the simple hardware functions and cannot be used to deliver high volume traffic (such as video). Moreover, it can only be developed within an environment where no conflicts exist between the (broadcasted) messages and where communication exists between CBE, CBC and BSC (Datta et *al.*, 1999).

ESSENTIAL ADVANTAGES FROM CB ACTIVITIES

CB usage in emergency warning cases implicates several advantages for licensed market players (i.e. network operators, content providers and service/application providers) corresponding not only in their social sector activities but in other areas as well (Cell Broadcast Forum, 2002a; 2005). Some indicative benefits can be listed as follows:

Development and Growth of Location-Based "Push" Services

SMS-CB offers the ability to discriminate the "push" messages (i.e. those oriented to the end-user), depending on the location. Messages can be widely broadcast to areas as small as one single radio cell, as big as the entire network and any cluster of areas in between (Van Oosterom et al., 2005).

Performing an Efficient "Trade-Off" between SMS and CB

Whenever textual messages are to be forwarded (or "pushed") to a great number of end-users, this "*one-to-many*" technology is much more efficient than the basic "*one-to-one*" SMS. This can have an effect on the cost structure of such services, and makes network dimensioning easier. (In the scope of an ordinary "average" network it would take 100 SMS with the same content approximately 30 seconds to get to its destination, whereas in a network with a CB-message transmission path of 30 seconds, all end-users (even 5,000,000) in that network (tuned in to a CB-channel) are able to receive the message in real-time).

CB Messages Provoke SMS, WAP (Wireless Application Protocol) and Voice Traffic

End-users connected to operating cellular networks can receive various textual (or other) messages. However, in several cases a customer enlisted to a service may be susceptible to unwanted communications/notifications, and reception of SMS messages may appear troubling. In the case of CB, channel commercials could have the form triggers for SMS, WAP or voice services. It is quite clear that extreme advertising and/or promotion may have negative results for the consumers' behaviour and this practically "kill" the media: dependent on the objective and the nature of services requested by each category of customers, the telecommunications operator could promote, however, specific events or services. The cell broadcast alert causes the cellular phone to sound a ring and to display a warning message on the screen. The message is relayed with greater efficiency than a two-way call or a SMS text message, without overloading the underlying network.

Achievement of Real-Time Communication

The time to broadcast a message over a CB channel is non-sensitive to the number of subscribers who will finally receive the corresponding ("push") message. In a typical network case, a CB message can be sent in up-to 30 seconds, to reach all connected handsets. Furthermore, the bandwidth needed to carry the message is non-sensitive to peak hours (i.e. the bandwidth is independent of the amount of handset users actually reading the message). In addition, CB does not use the signalling network for carrying messages, like SMS does.

Achievement of a Variety of Multi-Language "Push" Services:

On one single CB channel, message broadcasting can be realized in various languages. As, in usual cases, handsets are sensitive to the (pre-)selected language, only messages in that language will be displayed on the screen. This provides an attractive opportunity not only for multi-lingual countries but for services dedicated to roamers (to make them loyal to a network) as well.

Provision of Emergency Location Based Information Services

In case of local emergencies (e.g. chemical air pollution, fires, fluids, hurricanes or for the support of civil and citizen protection), the governmental (or other) authorities desire to immediately broadcast (early) warning messages to the end-users, present in a specific area. Thus, citizens on the move (together with those having direct access to the media such as radio, TV, Internet) can be reached and informed (by emergency alert) about severe natural or manmade disasters, in order to react properly. CB's advantage is that it allows sending messages without having to know the phone numbers of the users found in the region.

In addition, CB is "geo-specific", i.e. messages can be directed at only those citizens in an area requiring notification. For example, government disaster managers can avoid panic and road jamming by notifying priority neighbourhoods of an emergency evacuation while reassuring unaffected those neighbourhoods that they are safer to stay in their homes, reducing gridlock (Klein, 2007).

SMS-CB has the Ability to Broadcast Binary Messages

Next to broadcast of text-messages, binary data can be also be transmitted. This option implicates that for these cases where CB is used as a bearer, encryption/decryption opportunities for subscribed services are possible, together with machine-to-machine communication. The gradual 3G penetration will further offer opportunities even for specific streaming video broadcasting (ETSI, 2006a).

Implementation and Realization of Conceptual Opt-In and Opt-out Features:

Several trends in privacy protection regulation are already translated into some (EU and international) regulations or even domestic laws in the global scenery. Fast Internet's expansion makes theses rules appear more necessary and become more acute (i.e. as for anti-spamming cases). Thus, specific concepts relevant to "push" services targeted at mobile handset users that require the previous agreement (or the permission) of the end-user have to become clear. As for this case, both "Opt-In" (the case where customer wants to access) and "Opt-Out" (the case where the customer wants to step out) are exiting conceptual features of current CB technology. As a result, content providers will only reach those users that voluntarily switch on to a CB service. This advantage allows for promising mobile marketing campaigns to be targeted at just the "right" mobile community.

Messages Stream is not Stored

A characteristic feature of a CB message is that it is only displayed. In principle, no information is stored, neither in the SIM (Subscriber Identity Module) nor in the handset (unless the user desires to archive the message). Consequently, CB messages could be seen as form of "streaming content". Instead of with SMS no inboxes will ever overflow, just because the message never reaches any inbox.

Developing Opportunities for Making Users Educational to Text Messaging

Users in emerging markets, who are mainly using their mobile phones for voice calls, have to be educated in the use of data services. Providing messages on CB channels that are free of charge can make the user familiar with textual presentation and treatment on the mobile phone.

Moreover, CB can offer many supplementary advantages as for emergency notification of the public. Some among these benefits are summarized as following:

i.   Guarantee for an adequate system capacity, as there is no practical "limit" to the number of mobile handsets, able to be alerted at the same time. In fact, the load imposed on the cellular network is insignificant, which constitutes an essential consideration for dealing with an emergency situation; (ii) Guarantee for sufficient local, regional and national geographical coverage, as almost every citizen will have access to the relevant notification messages; (iii) Avoidance of any extra equipment or facility purchasing, as the existing GSM market handsets (in almost their majority) can be accessible at all times; (iv) Opportunity for the provision of multiple (and occasionally distinctive) alert types, dedicated for specific purposes, and; (v) Establishment of a significant business case, as CB is cheap to be implemented. There is no extra cost to individual subscribers and CB can work with all concerned parties to make emergency alerts a viable proposition. CB is already resident in most network infrastructure and in most cellular phones, so there is no need to build any towers, lay any cable, write any software, or replace terminals. Thus, market players in certain areas would be interested in sending customers (and potential customers) information about special offers and attractions such as sales, offers, extended opening times, etc. Shopping centers, exhibition halls, airports and sports stadiums are some among the kinds of location that could be targeted for CB-based services.

THE CURRENT STATE OF THE EUROPEAN AND THE INTERNATIONAL CB MARKET

In the past, various methods have been used for warning citizens of emergency cases, without being, however, able to guarantee efficiency and proper functionality. As a response, modern solutions have begun to emerge in the international markets, challenging the old business models and providing new ways to interact with users. In this scope, CB is gradually promoted by the industry sector (or it is even suggested as "mandatory" for cellular operational networks), to be considered as a fully efficient means for achieving broadcasting of public emergency alerts. Such an approach can create the impetus needed for the wholesale rollout of commercial CB services as well (Sandin & Escofet, 2003). More specifically, some networks already have cell broadcast capability implemented (i.e. they have a CBC), but they have lacked an effective use for it. Emergency alert notification using cell broadcasting is a "high visibility" application which has minimal impact on the other parts of the network. CB's ability to convey information to a huge number of subscribers at once without overstretching network capacity makes it a practical and a very useful tool. In its basic form, CB is relatively cheap, simple to deploy and requires little bandwidth to broadcast messages (FCC, 2004).

Under certain circumstances (more of technically-oriented nature and less of regulatory- and/or business- oriented nature), existing cellular networks can offer the CB facility free of charge "for the public good", although they could also gain commercial benefits in a number of ways: (i) In particular, there is always opportunity to "gain" new subscribers as people who do not currently have a mobile device may well be tempted to obtain one, following the publicity that would generated by an emergency notification system; (ii) Increased traffic in retail outlets - As the cell broadcast facility needs to be activated on each appropriate mobile device this suggests an opportunity to encourage customers into retail outlets to have this facility switched on and outlines new market challenges; (iii) The entire effort contributes to the promotion of further 3G penetration as the related 3G cell broadcast messages can offer access to multimedia content, thus suggesting users a reason for upgrading their equipment; In such a way, end-users may be encouraged to use their devices for accessing websites for informative reasons and for other applications; (iv) Subscription of cell broadcast channels

- Whilst emergency messages should always be free to the subscriber once the cell broadcast infrastructure is in place, "paid for" information could be provided such as continual weather updates. Alternatively, these services could be provided "free of charge", as a network loyalty incentive.

Public safety is traditionally regarded as a national "priority" for many countries, (especially for the EU Member States, as discussed in (ETSI, 2006b)). On the other hand, the number of natural disasters has been increased during the last 35 years, with an exponential growth observed during the last five years, in parallel with major climate and weather changes (as demonstrated by various information sources collected from the International Disaster Database (http://www.em-dat.net)). However, as for the European environment, current emergencies remain almost the same as the last decade, as not many European countries extensively use early warning systems. There are two main reasons explaining the case: The first one is that cellular mobile operators have not considered the option that they could generate extra profit with a one-directional broadcast service offered in the marketplace; the second reason is the fact that Europe does not belong to countries of low human development (according to the United Nations' approach), which are the ones that suffered more from natural disasters. However, it is nowadays clear that CB is a useful service and, under specific conditions it can be profitable. Thus, several countries have already used it.

In fact, CB is now working successfully in Asia, Europe, and the Mediterranean region. Due to its effectiveness, the United Nations, its International Telecommunications Union, and other international governing bodies are already developing global harmonization standards for emergency cell broadcast warnings. The World Health Organization is planning to use it for pandemic alerts.

In Europe, the Dutch government has already started to use cell broadcast as an emergency warning system (http://cell-broadcast.blogspot.com/2005/08/cell-broadcast-in-europe.html). The proposed technology allows the authorities to send text messages to mobile phone users, found in a specific area. Major market operators participate in the initiative which is considered as the first "multi-operator warning system" in the world. The governments of Belgium and Germany have declared that they intend to adopt the suggested system in order to use it in times of a national emergency case (www.publictechnology.net). Within the same context, the European Commission is currently developing a Global Disaster Alert and Co-ordination System (GDACS) (http://www.gdacs.org) in collaboration with the UN to provide early warning and relief coordination in future disasters. The system is expected to send out an alert to emergency services by SMS and e-mail within 30 minutes and there are potential opportunities for CB inclusion. In addition, the European Commission has adopted other measures on reinforcing disaster and crisis responses in third countries (European Commission, 2005) by introducing specific CB-based options for public alert purposes. As GSM Cell Broadcast is an existing capability on most GSM networks, it could realize an important role in this regard, in parallel with the possibility of sending alerts in a multi-lingual society. In the same scope, standardization activities have been initiated in European standardization bodies, in order to come to a more "harmonised" implementation (Chochliouros & Spiliopoulou, 2003) and market adoption.

The most remarkable example of successful use of CB technology took place by the government of Hong Kong during the SARS crisis in 2003. With the assistance of six mobile operators, it has been succeeded coverage 90% of the population. In North America the technology is available by many operators, but still not offered to the subscribers. In China, the Ministry of Civil Affairs announced preliminary research in January 2006, to test an SMS-based warning system in the Gansu, Anhui and Hunan regions. There is hope that this system will overcome delays in providing relief efforts that has occurred in the past.

FUTURE DIRECTION AND CONCLUSION

Cell Broadcast technology provides for 64,000 broadcast channels so that diverse types of message (severe weather, terrorist attacks, natural disasters, missing child etc.) can be broadcast on different channels among the numerous available ones. However, every subscriber will not necessarily receive all channels (and hence all messages sent). Channels can be activated either from the handset (by the user himself) or remotely by the network operator. Ideally, certain channels have to be allocated for certain message types and these need to be standardised globally, so that travellers would receive alerts wherever they happen to be. In order to make emergency notification by cell broadcasting a "real fact", several issues need be

elucidated, mainly of political and technical nature, as discussed below:

Political Issues

In the framework of liberalized and competitive economies there may be some "scepticism" about the efficiency (and the affordability) of warning systems proposed to become applicable in the marketplace, especially if these measures imply extra investments for market players, with no "obvious" economic benefit for their business promotion. As a consequence, many corporations are seeking public funding to develop sophisticated solutions for providing better emergency management tools, while capability to communicate an emergency alert is already available. To this aim, relief from an obsolete tax or provision of corporate tax credits to encourage deployment of the relevant facility could provide adequate incentives for the industry to offer this public safety benefit within a reasonable timeframe.

Due to the growth of mobile telephone users, cell broadcast is a decisive way to communicate with citizens in cases of emergency. Cell broadcast is a cheap and effective way of alerting the vast majority of the population in the event of a natural or a man-made disaster. Simultaneously, CB can provide assistance in crime reduction and detection if used in cases of child abduction and for similar incidents.

There are numerous challenges demanding more efficient and increased responses to deal with various emergency cases. For example, recent world events have led to a rising fear of terrorist threats on the part of the general public, while there is a general perception that our weather is getting more erratic and extreme. In response to the above characteristic cases, any contribution offered by cell broadcasting (i.e. the ability to reach millions of people within minutes) implicates an extreme "responsibility" for the providers of the relevant facility (both network operators and service providers) as the public will desire to have faith and trust in the reliability of the received messages (as severe decisions can be made on the basis of the transmitted and received information). Thus, governmental authorities have to provide the appropriate assurance that exact steps have been performed to make sure that only "bona-fide" and authoritative sources of information (e.g. civil protection authorities, the police or law enforcement authorities, fire services, environmental or meteorological services, etc.) are allowed to initiate broadcasts.

In addition, specific requirements have to become applicable for network operators; for the latter, their aim is not to have the responsibility for any kind of information/data which turns out to be inaccurate, as priority is the protection of the good functionality and the reputation of their networks, with the interests of their subscribers (by ensuring that messages are timely, pertinent and not seen as a nuisance).

Technical Issues

Competition in the electronic communications markets implicates that various network operators can cover the same area. In several instances there is no co-ordination of cell planning between such competing actors and as a result, cell layouts and cell identities of different networks may "differ" to a significant degree. In addition, due to changes in cell coverage and capacity, the size and "layout" of cells covering a particular geographic area can be highly dynamic issue. Thus, it is necessary to support interoperable market solutions especially in the context of suitable interconnection agreements, to provide guarantee for further effective usage of the underlying infrastructures. The corresponding challenge becomes more significant as existing networks have a hierarchical cell structure with "overlapping" patterns of cells of different sizes, umbrella cells, macro-cells, overlaid cells, micro-cells and pico-cells as well as up to 8 layers of sub-band structure in different frequency bands. The situation will get even more complex with the introduction of more advanced mobile applications (*like 3G GPRS, CDMA2000 and UMTS*) and necessitates appropriate procedures.

To make cell broadcast emergency notification a viable proposition the user will need a simple, intuitive graphical interface which will allow him to define a geographical area, create the message and send it to the appropriate cells on all relevant networks (http://www.cell-alert.co.uk/, www.cell-alert.com). Such an interface must communicate with the (possibly numerous) cell broadcast centres belonging to the different networks, with all underlying complexity hidden from the user.

Regulatory Issues

Correlated to the earlier issues, some regulatory and standardization matters have to be examined and resolved. For instance, there is an urgent need for a harmonized channel identification scheme to make it practical for travelers and tourists, while further improvements to standards are required to make sure that mobile devices give priority to emergency messages (i.e. messages must be authentic and follow national policy). In any case, national sovereignty must be respected and national systems must fully integrate results or experience from similar international efforts. In addition, it is necessary to promote a harmonized approach to language codes for the corresponding uses.

Cell Broadcast will increase revenues for SMS, MMS (Multimedia Message Service), WAP and IVR (Interactive Voice Response) services. From the operator customer loyalty perspective, offering CB information, in cooperation with governmental authorities, will help customers receiving the right information, on the right moment, on the right location, from a reliable source, via their mobile handsets.

In order to reach citizens with an important warning (or advisory) message, it is necessary to use a method that will be intrusive and all pervasive. With the current development of cellular network infrastructure, interoperability levels are multiple and in most cases sufficient. Cell Broadcasting is a very powerful tool for the initial warning, it is pervasive throughout society and the fact that it rings the phones bell means that it is intrusive.

REFERENCES

3rd Generation Partnership Project - 3GPP (2002). *TS 23.041 V3.5.0 (2002-06); Technical Specification Group Terminals; Technical realization of Cell Broadcast Service (CBS); (Release 1999).* Sophia-Antipolis, France: 3GPP.

3rd Generation Partnership Project - 3GPP (2006). *TS 23.041 V7.0.0 (2006-03); Technical Specification Group Terminals; Technical realization of Cell Broadcast Service (CBS); Release 7.* Sophia-Antipolis, France: 3GPP.

Cell Broadcast Forum-CBF (2002a). *CBF-PUB(02)2R2.1: Handset Requirements Specification.* Berne, Switzerland: CBF.

Cell Broadcast Forum-CBF (2002b). *CBF-PUB(02)3R2.1: Advantages and Services using Cell Broadcast.* Berne, Switzerland: CBF.

Cell Broadcast Forum-CBF (2005). *CBF-PUB(05)02RO.2: Cell Broadcast in Public Warning Systems*. Berne, Switzerland: CBF.

Chochliouros, I. P., & Spiliopoulou, A. S. (2003). European Standardization Activities: An Enabling Factor for the Competitive Development of the Information Society Technologies Market. *The Journal of The Communications Network (TCN), 2*(1), 62-68.

Chochliouros, I. P., & Spiliopoulou, A. S. (2005). Visions for the completion of the European Successful Migration to 3G Systems and Services - Current and Future Options for Technology Evolution, Business Opportunities, Market Development and Regulatory Challenges. In M. Pagani (Ed.), *Mobile and Wireless Systems beyond 3G: Managing new Business Opportunities*. Hershey, PA: Idea Group Inc.

Datta, A., VanderMeer, D. E., Celik, A., & Kumar, V. (1999). Broadcast protocols to support efficient retrieval from databases by mobile users. *ACM Transactions on Database Systems (TODS), 24(1),* 1-79.

DHI Group (2005). *Cell broadcasting for dissemination of flood warnings; Press release, 01 June 2005*. Hørsholm, Denmark: DHI Water & Environment (DHI). Retrieved on April 11, 2007 from http://www.dhigroup.com/News/NewsArchive/2005/CellBroadcasting.aspx

Ericsson (2006). *GSM & WCDMA Seamless Network. White Paper - March 2006 (284 23-3011Uen RevC)*. Retrieved on September 11, 2007, from http://www.calcomwebsite.com/default.asp?id=2695

European Commission (1999). *Vade-mecum of Civil Protection in the European Union*. Brussels, Belgium: European Commission.

European Commission (2001). *Communication on The Introduction of Third Generation Mobile Communications in the European Union: State of Play and the Way Forward, [COM(2001) 141 final, 20.03.2001]*. Brussels, Belgium: European Commission.

European Commission (2003). *Communication on Towards the Full Roll-Out of Third Generation Mobile Communications [COM(2002) 301 final, 11.06.2002]*. Brussels, Belgium: European Commission.

European Commission (2005). *Communication on Reinforcing EU Disaster and Crisis Response in third countries [COM(2005) 153 final, 20.04.2005]*. Brussels, Belgium: European Commission.

European Telecommunications Standards Institute-ETSI (1991). *GSM 03.41 V3.3.0-1 (Jan-1991): Technical Realization of the Short Message Service - Cell Broadcast*. Sophia-Antipolis, France: ETSI.

European Telecommunications Standards Institute-ETSI (1992). *GSM 03.40 V3.5.0 (Feb-1992): Technical Realization of the Short Message Service - Point to Point*. Sophia-Antipolis, France: ETSI.

European Telecommunications Standards Institute-ETSI (1993). *ETR 107 (Oct-1993): European digital cellular telecommunication system (Phase 2); Example protocol stacks for interconnecting Cell Broadcast Centre (CBC) and Mobile-services Switching Centre (MSC);(GSM 03.49)*. Sophia-Antipolis, France: ETSI.

European Telecommunications Standards Institute-ETSI (1999a). *ETS 300 559 ed.4 (1999-06); Digital cellular telecommunications system (Phase 2) (GSM); Point-to-Point (PP) Short Message Service (SMS) support on mobile radio interface (GSM 04.11)*. Sophia-Antipolis, France: ETSI.

European Telecommunications Standards Institute-ETSI (1999b). *TR 101 635 V7.0.0 (1999-08): Digital cellular telecommunications system (Phase 2+) (GSM); Example protocol stacks for interconnecting Service Centre(s) (SC) and Mobile-services Switching Centre(s) (MSC) (GSM 03.47 version 7.0.0 Release 1998)*. Sophia-Antipolis, France: ETSI.

European Telecommunications Standards Institute-ETSI (2002). *TS 122 003 V4.3.0. (2002-03): Digital cellular telecommunications system (Phase 2+) (GSM); Universal Mobile Telecommunications System (UMTS); Circuit Teleservices supported by a Public Land Mobile Network (PLMN) (3GPP TS 22.003 version 4.3.0 Release 4)*. Sophia-Antipolis, France: ETSI.

European Telecommunications Standards Institute-ETSI (2004). *TR 125 925 V3.5.0 (2004-12); Universal Mobile Telecommunications System (UMTS); Radio Interface for Broadcast/Multicast Services (3GPP TR 25.925 version 3.5.0 Release 1999)*. Sophia-Antipolis, France: ETSI.

European Telecommunications Standards Institute-ETSI (2006a). *TS 125 324 V7.1.0 (2006-06): Universal Mobile Telecommunications System (UMTS); Broadcast/Multicast Control (BMC) (3GPP TS 25.324 version 7.1.0 Release 7)*. Sophia-Antipolis, France: ETSI

European Telecommunications Standards Institute-ETSI (2006b). *ETSI TS 102 182 V1.2.1 (2006-12): Emergency Communications (EMTEL); Requirements for Communication from Authorities/Organizations to individuals, groups or the general public during emergencies.* Sophia-Antipolis, France: ETSI

Federal Communications Commission - FCC (2004). *FCC-04-189A1: "Review of the Emergency Alert System", EB Docket No. 04-296.* Federal Communications Commission, US.

Jiun-Long, H., & Ming-Syan C., (2004). Dependent Data Broadcasting for Unordered Queries in a Multiple Channel Mobile. *IEEE Transactions on Knowledge and Data Engineering, 16*(9), 1143-1156.

Klein, P. (2007). *Cell Broadcast Technology for Emergency Alert Notifications. A White Paper.* Houston, US: CellCast Technologies. Retrieved on October 06, 2007, from www.fcc.gov/pshs/cmsaac/docs/pdf/CellCastComment070307.pdf

Mouly, M., & Pautet, M.-B., (1992). *The GSM system for mobile communication.* Palaisau, France: M. Mouly.

Raissi-Dehkordi, M., & Baras, J. S. (2002). *Broadcast scheduling in information delivery systems - Technical Report.* Institute for Systems Research, University of Maryland at College Park.

Redl, S. M., Weber, M. K., & Oliphant, M. W. (1995). *An introduction to GSM.* Norwood, MA: Artech House.

Sandin, J., & Escofet, J. (2003). *Cell Broadcast: New interactive services could finally unlock CB revenue potential.* Mobile location Analyst, March 2003: Baskerville. Retrieved on April 14, 2007 from http://www.baskerville.telecoms.com/z/mla/mla0303.pdf.

Van Oosterom, P., Zlatanova, S., & Fendel, E. M (Eds.) (2005). *Geo-information for Disaster Management.* Berlin, Germany: Springer.

Watson, C. (1993). *Radio equipment for GSM Cellular Radio Systems.* In Balston, D. M., & Macario, R. C. V. (Eds.). Boston: Artech House.

KEY TERMS

Cell Broadcast Centre (CBC): It is the core of the Cell Broadcast System and acts as a server for all CBE clients. It is responsible for the administration of all SMS-CB messages it receives from the CBEs and realizes the communication towards the GSM network. The GSM network itself takes care of delivering the SMS-CB messages to the mobile terminals.

Cell Broadcast Channel (CBCH): This channel is a feature of the GSM system. It is a downlink only channel and is intended to be used for broadcast information. It is mapped into the second subslot of the Standalone Dedicated Control Channel.

Cell Broadcast Entity (CBE): It is a multi-user front-end that allows the definition and control of SMS-CB messages. A CBE can be located at the site of a content provider.

Cell Broadcast Forum (CBF): It is a non-profit Industry Association that supports the world standard for cell broadcast wireless information and telephony services on digital mobile phones and other wireless terminals. Its primary goal is to bring together companies from all segments of the wireless industry value chain to ensure product interoperability and growth of wireless market (http://www.cellbroadcastforum.org).

Cell Broadcast Message (SMS-CB): It is textual or binary message that is used for delivering information to all mobile phone users that are located in a certain geographical area.

Cell Broadcasting (CB): A mobile technology feature defined by the ETSI's GSM committee and is part of the GSM standard. Allows a text or binary message to be defined and distributed to all mobile terminals connected to a set of cells in a certain geographical area.

Global System for Mobile Communications (GSM): It is the dominant 2G digital mobile phone standard for most of the world. It determines the way in which mobile phones communicate with the land-based network of towers. It operates in the 900MHz and 1.8GHz bands in Europe and the 1.9GHz PCS band in the U.S. Based on a circuit-switched system that divides each 200 kHz channel into eight 25 kHz time slots, GSM defines the entire cellular system, not just the TDMA air interface. It is a fast-growing communications technology, there were more than 250 million GSM users early in 2000. By mid-2004, the one billionth GSM customers were connected.

Home Location Register (HLR): It is the main database of subscriber information for a mobile network. Every subscriber is allocated to a HLR which is an integral component of code division multiple access (CDMA), time division multiple access (TDMA), and Global System for Mobile Communications (GSM) networks.

Short Message Service (SMS): It is a well known service, available on all mobile phones and on most other mobile devices and allows users exchange text messages.

Chapter XXXVI
Mobility for Secure Multi-Factor "Out of Band" Authentication

Matthew Tatham
Alacrity Technologies, Australia

Arsi Honkanen
Alacrity Technologies, Australia

ABSTRACT

Securing data is a key concern for individuals and organisations throughout the world, especially within information and communications infrastructure. With the help of highly sensitive data such as individual account information, criminals can carry out a variety of fraudulent activities; most notably financial fraud, which can be carried out through a multitude of channels. The increasing utilization of technologies, devices, and processes has further exacerbated these risks to organisations. This chapter identifies and describes the issues surrounding the secure authentication of individuals attempting to access or transact with organisations using online networks. This chapter then explains how to secure access to sensitive data through the use of multi-factor out-of-band authentication.

INTRODUCTION

Security is of major concern to organisations across the globe. As Nand (2006) stated, issues of security are a particularly significant and critical success factor in mobile business. This is the case since, although wireless connectivity offers portability and hence mobility - it adds to the risk of unauthorised access to the system and data disclosure. Guarding access to sensitive data, particularly in large government organisations and financial institutions, is becoming increasingly important to the overall security strategy for organisations. According to Dunn (2006):

"Global crime is now one of the three big issues facing the world, the other two being political violence and climate change. Of course, if you were sitting in an air-conditioned office insulated by layers of security guards, this might not have dawned on you. But it will, one day."

The flexibility and cost effective nature of the Internet, as a vehicle for communicating as well as processing data has allowed organisations and individuals to consider utilising the Internet more than ever before. Utilisation of this method for processing data has also created opportunities for a hacker (who would be interested in gaining unauthorised access to the network). This issue underscores the importance of securely authenticating legal users of the networks who are attempting to gain access to funds or data.

The risks to the use of the Internet has understandably affected consumer confidence resulting, for many, in a negative perception of this important channel of communication. Society has begun to place pressure on organisations to implement stronger controls to prevent hackers from gaining access to sensitive data. Organisations are required to take responsibility for the protection of customer and employee information.

This chapter discusses practical implementation of stronger security for online authentication activities. The chapter aims to share market research and personal experiences of the authors to assist security managers in examining their current authentication practices as part of an extensive security strategy.

The information in this chapter has been broken down into three distinct segments. The first section of the chapter analyses online banking fraud; cardholder not present (CNP) fraud and data theft; the current tools and methods used by hackers; and the impact this has on organisations and individuals around the world. The second section identifies the various types of authentication solutions available, and the different paths that can be utilised to authenticate an individual for an online transaction. The third section describes the way in which mobility can improve the level of security in the authentication space by utilising a mobile application named Closed Loop Environment for Wireless (CLEW®).

This chapter is written using a combination of the researchers' experiences, along with surveys and statistics used around the world to measure the current state of online fraud and the subsequent effect this type of fraud has on society as a whole. This chapter draws a bridge between mobility and secure authentication through a combination of technologies. Most noteworthy is the use of the mobile device to empower individuals and organisations across the world to prevent unauthorised persons from gaining access to their restricted data.

GROWTH IN ONLINE FRAUD

Fraud, as mentioned in the introduction, is a big challenge in online transactions. However, increasingly it is being combated with the implementation of new controls, such as chip and PIN (Personal Identification Number) for cardholder present transactions. For transactions that utilise the Internet, such as online banking and CNP transactions however, fraud still remains a major concern. There have been a number of articles published regarding the threat of online fraud and the impact this has on society. For example, a BBC article in January, 2007 - "Bank loses $1.1m to online fraud", and the article by Easier Finance "Cyber fraud hitting online retailers hard".

Overall, the cost of online fraud is difficult to determine. This section attempts to analyse some of the hard costs associated with online fraud to consumers, merchants and financial institutions.

Consider, for example, online fraud in Australia. Figures from the Australian Institute of Criminology in 2005 suggest that the total cost of fraud for 2005 in Australia was AU$5 billion. Westpac Banking Corporation (2006) publicly stated that online fraud equates to 6.5% of the total fraud figure. Once these figures were combined, it was determined that, conservatively, the cost of online fraud to Australians is currently AU$325 million, annually.

In the United Kingdom (UK), the UK Payments Association (APACS) stated that online banking fraud increased from £23.2m in 2005 to £33.5m in 2006. This is an increase of 44% year-on-year, and has been driven by an increase in phishing incidents, which went up from 1,713 in 2005 to 14,156 in 2006.

Of the £600 million attributed to credit card fraud for the year 2006 in the UK, £212.6 million was related to CNP transactions. Once again this is recognised as conservative, and CNP fraud is estimated to be increasing at approximately 16% per annum. The introduction of new technologies has reduced all other types of credit card fraud; however CNP fraud is now rising significantly as the fraudsters have moved their attention to the Internet.

In the United States (US), online fraud is still a major issue. The cybercrime forums gird a criminal economy that robs US businesses of $67.2 billion per year, according to a Federal Bureau of Investigations (FBI) projection. Consumer Reports notes that over the past two years US consumers lost more than $8 billion to viruses, spyware and online fraud schemes.

The problem of online fraud is set to increase, with continued use of the current authentication processes. Most authentication processes use the same path for both authentication and the transaction. This use of the same path allows fraudsters to have access to vital information through Trojans and key-logging programs that sit inside many personal computers.

GROWTH IN DATA THEFT

Online and unauthorised access also leads to data theft. While data theft is not a new crime, it has increased over recent years, and has become a topic of consumer interest. Systems that are secured in an inadequate manner such as single factor authentication security, easily guessed passwords, unencrypted data provide hackers with an easy path to an organisation's confidential data. The methods of discarding access codes and other personal identification information by personnel is also a major problem for organisations.

Data breaches have resulted in a billion dollar cost to society. In one case Kerber, and Staff (2007) point out that, in the US, TJX, Cos had costs of US$256 million, resulting from the largest computer data breach in corporate history. In this instance, thieves stole more than US$45 million customer credit and debit card numbers.

REASONS FOR CONCERN

There are a variety of factors which have an adverse effect on organisations and consumer confidence when transacting online. Hackers and their ability to steal vital information using methods such as phishing and pharming are driving the need for enhanced levels of authentication for consumers.

Phishing

Phishing is the most common way used by Internet criminals to infect an individuals computer to access confidential information. Phishing is a practice that involves an Internet criminal attempting to send emails pretending to be a genuine company. This is an attempt to trick an individual into disclosing confidential information at a fake website that is operated by the Internet criminal. These emails usually ask the individual to update or verify a username or password to confidential information through a web link contained in the email. Any information that is entered into this fake website is utilised by the criminals to conduct fraudulent activities.

Phishing exercises also allow hackers to pass on Trojan programs to conduct key logging exercises which is explained later in this chapter.

Keizer claimed, through a recently released survey that phishing scams in the US cost nearly $1 billion in 2005.

Gartner conducted a poll in May 2005 consisting of approximately 5,000 US Internet users and found that not only have phishing attacks risen, but are set to grow at a rapid rate.

"A lot of people -- analysts mostly -- thought that phishing was just a bunch of noise in the system, and that after 2004, it would slow down," said Avivah Litan (2005), a research director with Gartner. "That hasn't happened."

Instead, during the 12 months preceding May 2005, 73 million American adults who use the Internet said that they "definitely" received or "thought they received" an average of more than 50 phishing e-mails during this period. That number, said Litan, was 28 percent higher than the previous year, when 57 million Americans reported that they had been the target of phishing scams.

Trojans

Trojans are a computer virus that can be downloaded onto a computer without a user recognising that is has occurred. The virus can be picked up by selecting a web link in an email which can take users to a malicious website where the virus is installed into the individual's computer. The virus is capable of carrying out a number of criminal activities but is commonly used by Internet criminals for installing key logging software. This allows the criminal to capture any keystrokes that are entered into a computer's keyboard. Certain Trojans aim to capture passwords entered at certain Internet sites or take screen shots of Internet sites that individuals visit. These programs allow criminals to intercept and compromise confidential activities.

Phishing Email Reports and Phishing Site Trends for June 2007

The Anti-Phishing Working Group (APWG) is an industry association focusing on eliminating identity theft and fraud that results from phishing and email spoofing.

APWG received 28,888 unique phishing reports in June, 2007, which was an increase of over 5,000 reports from May, 2007. This information was received by the APWG from the public, its members and its research partners.

Figure 1 indicates June had a 23% increase in phishing reports from May 2007.

Figure 1. Phishing reports received June '06 – June '07

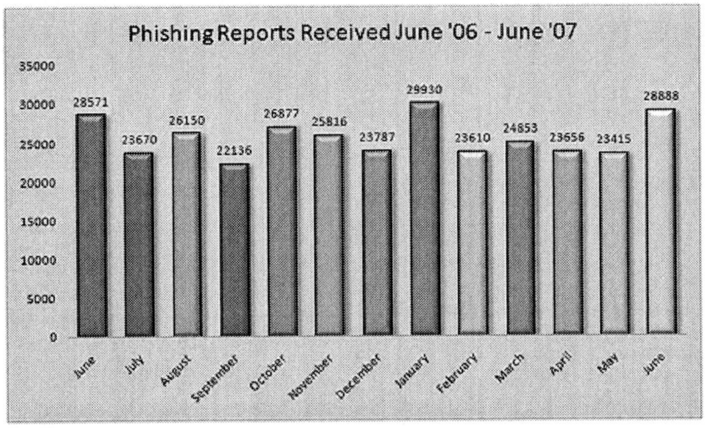

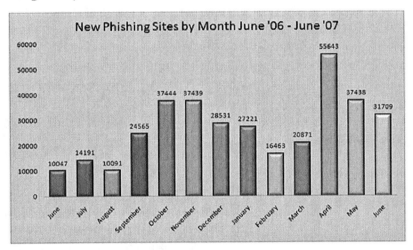

Figure 2. New phishing sites by month June '06 – June '07

Figure 2 indicates that new phishing sites reached a record high at 55,643 in April, 2007. The number of new phishing sites for June, 2007 was down 75% from the April record.

Consumer Impact

A survey carried out late in 2006 by RSA, the security division of EMC, suggested that online customers are concerned with the current state of online fraud.

Consumer trust in transacting online is falling, with 52% of respondents stating they are less likely to sign up for online banking as a result of the threat of fraud, here are some further statistics:

- 38% of consumers knew what phishing was;
- 29% were aware of the term but did not know what it means;
- 33% were unaware of the term; and,
- 52% were less likely to sign up for or use online banking due to the threat of phishing.

Customer Identification Measures

More than half of customers surveyed would like tougher measures to be deployed.

- 69% would prefer stronger identification than the standard username and password; and,
- 91% would be willing to use a new, tougher method.

Even though the RSA used a small sample of 1,678 adults from eight countries it is clear that the public is concerned about online fraud, it also states that 9 out of 10 individuals surveyed would be willing to use a tougher security measure if it was implemented!

According to Lacy (2006), 41% are purchasing less online in 2006 than in 2004. This drop in online activities in 2006 from 2004 was because of identity theft. In 2005 identity theft cost consumers US$680 billion.

AUTHENTICATION SOLUTIONS

Organisations in a variety of sectors must protect themselves, their customers, and their staff from fraud-sters-both internally and externally. Organisations must identify their security needs and analyse all the solutions available in the marketplace. They must then incorporate a solution that not only protects sensitive data but also meets the needs of a mobile society.

There are three forms of authentication that may be used in an authentication strategy, which are discussed below. These include single-factor, two-factor or multi-factor authentication.

Single-Factor Authentication

Single-factor authentication is the traditional authentication process that requires a username and password before granting access to the user.

Single-factor authentication relies on the diligence of the user, who needs to strengthen this inherently weak form of authentication. Creating a strong password, that is, choosing a password that cannot be easily guessed, preventing unauthorised access. If an organisation requires a high level of security, it is advisable to implement more complex authentication and security systems.

Two-Factor Authentication

Two-factor authentication solutions deliver another method of identification on top of single factor username and password. This may be a product, such as a hardware token or SMS PIN system. Once a user enters their username and password, they are asked to enter a code into the PC, which is generated by the token or SMS system. Once this code is entered they will be given access to the data or be able to success-fully complete a transaction. Although this is stronger than single-factor authentication, these authentication solutions can still be hacked because they do not use true out-of-band authentication. This process will be discussed later in this chapter.

Multi-Factor Authentication

Technically, multi-factor authentication utilises multiple levels of security to authenticate or identify a user before an online transaction of any type can occur.

Multi-factor authentication can incorporate various layers of authentication solutions implemented in conjunction with one another, such as user name and password with a token and a biometric finger scanner. It may also be a single solution that delivers multiple layers of security.

TRANSACTION AUTHENTICATION PATHS

Out-of-Band Authentication

One of the major issues facing organisations is the amount of virus programs that circulate on PCs, which individuals utilise to access sensitive data. A Trojan or key logging program in an individual's PC can allow a fraudster to compromise a transaction or gain access to highly sensitive data. This virus may be in a dormant state within the PC and thus the user may be unaware that there is a virus on their PC when they attempt to complete a transaction or access sensitive data.

Organisations can do little to prevent virus programs being installed on PCs. Therefore the key question is, how do we prevent fraudsters from gaining access to unauthorised information?

Organisations must address the issue of protecting themselves, personnel and their customers from fraud by authenticating the person (not the device) for each online transaction. The process that can ameliorate the risk in online transactions is called out-of-band authentication. Out-of-band authentication uses a different path for authentication to the transaction itself, preventing the hacker from entering and compromising an online transaction.

Single factor and two-factor authentication solutions, like tokens, are based around authenticating the device-(not the person). This allows hackers to intercept and phish valuable details using the trojans and key logging software discussed allowing unauthorised access to sensitive information.

The following diagrams indicate the two types of authentication paths. The first (Figure 3) depicts an in-band transaction; the second (Figure 4) is an out-of-band transaction. In Figure 3, a user is attempting to access information or conduct a transaction on a PC which is compromised by a trojan or key logging program. The user is attempting to use two-factor authentication systems that do NOT use a true out-of-band method of authentication. This allows a hacker to intercept and compromise the activity using the virus program.

Similar to Figure 3, Figure 4 depicts the process of an individual who is attempting to access information or conduct a transaction on a user's PC which is compromised by a trojan or key logging program. In the out-of-band authentication process, the individual is attempting to use a single product with multiple layers of security (multi-factor authentication).

This product utilises the individual's mobile device to authenticate the activity. It uses a true out-of-band method of authentication, as nothing is entered back into the PC. This prevents the hacker from intercepting and compromising the activity, and it subsequently makes the virus program on the PC obsolete.

AUTHENTICATION THROUGH MOBILITY

Mobility allows access to information through communication tools, regardless of an individual's location. A new communications platform which uses a combination of technologies, including the Internet and mobile devices, can allow society to conduct transactions securely and conveniently.

Closed Loop Environment for Wireless (CLEW®) combines the Internet and mobile devices to enable organisation's to send time-critical information to an interested individual/s and enables those recipients to intelligently interact and respond to that information in a secure fashion. CLEW provides organisations with an additional communications channel tailored to mobile device users. CLEW allows real-time interaction in a secure environment. CLEW utilises a combination of protocols and technologies to solve a range of current communications and authentication issues.

CLEW offers a range of products in the communications and authentication space, but this chapter will only describe the authentication element.

CLEW is a secure, real-time, out-of-band, multi-factor authentication system, that can dramatically reduce fraudulent activity in the areas identified in this chapter.

Unlike current two-factor authentication systems, CLEW addresses the issue of protecting the organisation, employees and customers from identity fraud. CLEW does this by authenticating the person (not the device) attempting to access information or transact online using true "out-of-band" authentication.

CLEW is easily integrated and initiated by an organisation's backend operating systems, allowing organisations to minimise the chance of manual errors.

CLEW Process for Authentication

The CLEW system sends a secure alert that is created from the organisation's backend systems to authorised users before they can access the network. The user will then receive the alert on their Internet connectable mobile device, after securely entering a session via a login and password. Additional methods of security can be incorporated if requested by the organisation.

The user then responds to the information and, if they are trying to transact online, they will approve the alert. If the user is not trying to transact, they will decline the request which will restrict access to the hacker.

Figure 5 depicts a generic example of a CNP authentication case utilising the Internet as the purchase channel. An online customer utilises a browser to carry out a purchase at a merchant's Internet store using a secure connection.

The merchant's software passes the request to the bank's web server. The bank's diagnostic software then examines the customer's request against the customer's profile. If the bank's diagnostic software deems the transaction to require authentication via the CLEW system, the CLEW system will send an alert to the credit card holder with a link to the CLEW server. When the credit card holder receives the alert, they select the link and read the transaction details. The individual then makes the decision to approve or reject the transaction. The CLEW system then forwards the customer's response into the bank's central management system, which again updates the merchant software about the transaction result. Finally, approval or rejection of the transaction is displayed on the customer's mobile device, effectively completing the transaction.

Figure 3. Single path of authentication

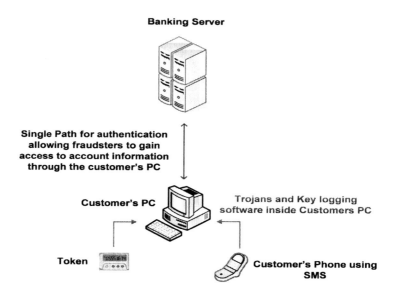

Figure 4. Out-of-band authentication

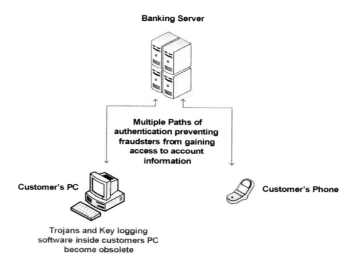

The process for online banking authorisation in Figure 6 and secure access control in Figure 7 are basically identical. In Figure 6, the account holder utilises the bank's data centre online. In Figure 7, an employee accesses the organisation's central management system. In Figure 6 and 7, the CLEW process itself is identical to Figure 5.

CLEW technology uses SSL platform security in its communication between the application and the mobile user. The technology includes several security features for stronger security in session management and authentication control. These features prevent attacks such as session hijacking, eavesdropping and phishing from occurring. CLEW has the intelligence to detect hijackings and prevent intruders from entering the system, even if user credentials have been stolen. CLEW uses some of the strongest possible cryptographic techniques available, such as one-time padlock to secure session management.

Figure 5. CLEW for cardholder not present (CNP) authentication

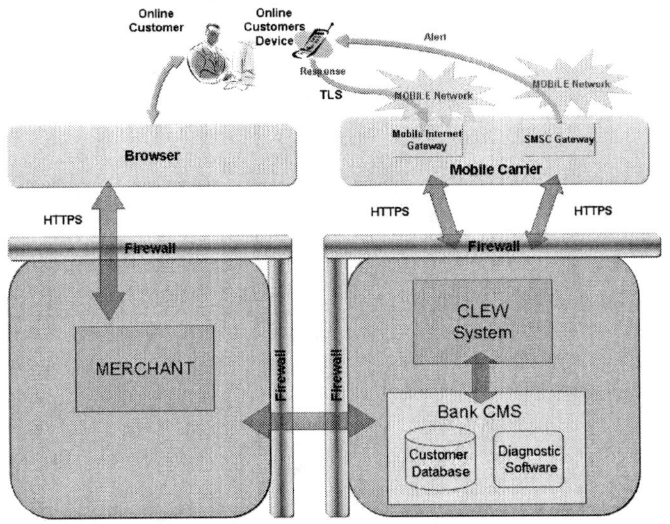

Figure 6. CLEW for online banking authentication

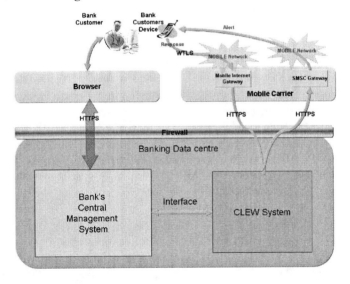

Technological Aspects

The CLEW technology is universal in nature and can be utilised by organisations for a number of purposes in almost any industry. CLEW does not require any software to be installed onto mobile handsets. The only requirement is that the device utilised has Internet connectivity.

The CLEW authentication process is secure, and can easily be encrypted further with platform-level security protocols, such as HTTPS. CLEW does not only operate with truly packet-based GPRS or 3G networks, but also with CSD-enabled GSM networks.

CLEW's low technical requirements mean that it can be readily used in more than a billion current

Figure 7. CLEW for secure access control

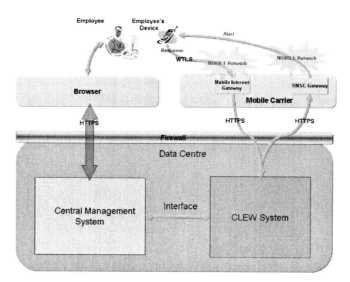

mobile handsets. CLEW is compatible with 90% of Nokia handsets of which there are over 1 billion worldwide. This figure indicates CLEW is truly a global product.

CLEW streamlines business processes and improves the flow and security aspects of the authentication process. This translates to further operational and capital efficiency. The operational outcomes are due to the fact that CLEW is a "lean" tool, which can reduce waste and lead to more efficient business processes. It can also increase the level of co-ordination of activities within enterprises.

Summary of CLEW

CLEW demonstrates the power of mobility as a solution to the authentication issues damaging society throughout the world. CLEW's greatest advantage lies in its simplicity and out-of-band aspect.

CLEW is not threatened by the security vulnerabilities that plague in-band authentication solutions. CLEW also decreases the issues associated with end-user errors, which can otherwise be easily exploited by hackers using an in-band method of authentication.

CLEW utilises a combination of factors, such as something you have (mobile device) and something you know (password), along with the out-of-band aspect. Thus, it is a simple yet too complicated for

hackers to compromise. By carrying out authentication in a mobile environment, organisations remove the threat of fraud.

CLEW presents numerous benefits from a technical, operational and financial perspective. CLEW's technical benefits lead to operational benefits, which in turn transpires into financial and strategic benefits.

Organisations applying the CLEW solution for authentication can be confident that, by using true mobility, their systems will be securely protected.

CONCLUSION

Information and statistics regarding the current state of Internet fraud suggest it is a problem that will not be going away in the near future. In fact, the problem is expected to escalate as hackers develop more innovative and sophisticated systems to gain unauthorised access to sensitive data.

The Internet is seen by many as the transaction channel for the future, as it is a flexible way for personnel to gain access to sensitive data, and it is a cost effective method for society to conduct banking activities. Financial institutions, in particular, have taken significant steps to promote this channel specifically for online banking and implement secure authentication solutions. However, the solutions that have been implemented are only stop gap measures, and the institutions have freely admitted this.

The current methods are not strong enough to prevent hackers from gaining access to sensitive information and never will be. Organisations must strengthen their authentication offerings and implement true multi-factor, out-of-band authentication systems which will meet society's requirement for mobility.

Before implementing a solution, all institutions must carry out a strict evaluation of the technology available for securing online activities based around their exact needs and requirements.

Institutions worldwide must act on the information presented in this chapter and take the necessary steps to provide customers and personnel with stronger levels of authentication. This should be achieved utilising true mobility and out-of-band authentication to prevent fraudsters from gaining access to sensitive information.

REFERENCES

Acohido, B., & Swartz, J. (2006). Cybercrime Flourishes in Online Hacker Forums. *USA Today* [ONLINE] Available: http://www.usatoday.com/tech/news/computersecurity/infotheft/2006-10-11-cybercrime-hacker-forums_x.htm

Anti-Phishing Working Group (2007). Phishing Activity Trends, Report for the Month of June, 2007. Anti-Phishing Working Group [ONLINE] Available: http://www.antiphishing.org/reports/apwg_report_june_2007.pdf

Arnold, B. (2005). Caslon Analytics Identity Crime. *Caslon Analytics* [ONLINE] Available: http://www.caslon.com.au/idtheftprofile.htm

Bank Safe Online (2007). *Phishing Explained. What is Phishing?* [ONLINE] Available: http://www.bank-safeonline.org.uk/phishing_explained.html

Enter Here bank safe online

BBC News (2007). Bank Loses $1.1m to Online Fraud [ONLINE] Available: http://news.bbc.co.uk/1/hi/business/6279561.stm

Dunn *J. E. (2006).* HSBC fires shot at two-factor authentication. Turn up the hearing aid. Is this banker being serious? *Techworld.* [ONLINE] Available: http://www.techworld.com/security/features/index.cfm?featureid=2825

Keizer, G. (2005). Phishing Costs Nearly $1 Billion. *Channel Web Network* [ONLINE] Available: http://www.crn.com/it-channel/164902685

Kerber, R., & Staff, G. (2007). Cost of data breach at TJX soars to $256m; Suits, computer fix add to expenses. *The Boston Globe.* [Online] Available: http://www.boston.com/business/globe/articles/2007/08/15/cost_of_data_breach_at_tjx_soars_to_256m/

Lacy, S. (2006). Symatec's New Target: Consumers. *Business Week* [ONLINE] Available: http://www.businessweek.com/technology/content/feb2006/tc20060216_135983.htm?campaign_id=rss_tech

Nand, S. (2006). Developing a Theory of Portable Public Key Infrastructure (PORTABLEPKI) for Mobile Business Security. In Unhelkar B. (Ed.), Chapter 27 of book: *Handbook of Research in Mobile Business: Technical, Methodological and Social Perspectives.* IGI Global, Hershey, PA, USA, 2006.

RSA Security Press Release (2007). RSA Announces Findings of Annual Consumer Online Fraud Survey [ONLINE] Available: http://www.itsecurity.com/press-releases/press-release-rsa-online-fraud-survey-012507/

The UK Payments Association (2006). Card Fraud Losses Continue to Fall. The UK Payments Association [ONLINE] Available: http://www.apacs.org.uk/media_centre/press/07_14_03.html

Westpac Banking Corporation (2006). Westpac Welcomes Collaboration in the Fight against Fraud. Westpac Banking Corporation [ONLINE] Available: http://www.westpac.com.au/Internet/publish.nsf/Content/WIMCMR+Archive+media+release+11+Nov+2006

KEY TERMS

Authentication: This is the act of establishing or confirming something is authentic or true.

Cardholder not Present Fraud: A thief has obtained an individuals credit or debit card details and attempts a transaction on the card utilising a payment method that does not require the thief to be present e.g. Internet or the telephone.

CLEW: Closed Loop Environment for Wireless technology allows organisations to communicate time-critical information to individuals securely using the Internet and mobile devices.

Date Theft: Word used to describe when information has been stolen or copied from an individual or an organisation in an illegal manner. This may include information like passwords, confidential company documents, credit card information or other personal information.

Merchant: Function as professionals who operate in the chain between the producer and the end user.

Online Fraud: A crime that is performed using the Internet channel to carry out illegal transactions.

Out-of-Band: A communication activity that occurs using a different path to the established communications method or channel. This is a more secure method of communication for financial type activities.

Single Path: Sending data within the same band, on the same channel.

Chapter XXXVII
Asynchronous Communication Protocol for Multiple Transactions in Mobile Architecture for a Mobile Agent System

Anand Kuppuswami
Dialog Information Technology, Australia

ABSTRACT

Mobile agents and framework built on mobile agents have been the key research area for the past few years. The major impedances like latency factor, abrupt disconnection in service, and minimal processing power, were solved in the mobile agent paradigm. Also, with the advent of intelligent framework of mobile agents, mobile agents were empowered with decision making powers and were able to roam the network in search of the best service provider. This further increased the efficiency of the system and reduced the system outage time. Although the system projected itself as the ideal solution to the real-world problems, it could not be implemented in commercial applications. This is attributed to the lack of sessions in the mobile agent's environment. Predominantly in the mobile agents paradigm architecture was still the client-server architecture. In this chapter the framework has been extended to incorporate transaction capabilities to the mobile agents. This would enable them to perform a full transaction and complete a workflow. We present the scenario of Customer Relationship Management (CRM) where the framework could be put to use.

INTRODUCTION

There has been a tremendous growth in the usage of mobile technologies for the past few years. Previously the mobile technologies were seen as an extended form of Internet and Intranet applications, but with

the number of mobile handsets crossing the billionth mark, mobile environment have become an independent area of work. They offer several advantages like dynamic connectivity, smaller gadgets and information processing power irrespective of place and time Gray (1996). Although they seem to be a promising technology, their certain inherent qualities like low memory and latency factor restricts their usage to many real world applications (Jipping, 2002). Remote Procedure Call (RPC) provided by Java (Birrell, 1984), Network Command Language (NCL) (Meandzija, 1986), Remote Evaluation (REV) (Stamos, 1990) and SUPRA-RPC (Stoyenko, 1994) offered various techniques wherein the inherent short comings of mobile technologies could be bypassed. But all of the approaches lack a crucial feature: Coordination between various application nodes.

The novel approach of transportable programs (Gray, 1995; Cybenko, 1994) offers a promising solution for various issues raised. Transportable agents or Mobile agents, as they are called now, are autonomous programs that can migrate from one machine to another machine in the network. By migrating to the machine having the resource, the agents have the advantage of working on site where the resource is present and also use the processor's power. This eliminates all the middleware that is required for transporting the data to the client's site. Mobile agent's paradigm provides an effective solution to the problem of low latency, poor interface and bad network conditions (Gray, 1996). The middleware and the communication control mechanism form the major workload in client-server architecture and by eliminating them we can build a better working environment and increase the efficiency of the system. This is so because the code as well as the state of code in execution is migrated to another machine for resuming its execution. This also eliminates the interface required for service access. The fact that there is no need for permanent connection makes it very suitable to the mobile environment. The ad hoc client-server model is overridden by the peer-peer model which matures into grid computing, where the machines can act as client or server depending on the environment. The programmer is swayed away from traditional multi-tier architecture to grid computing (Lauvset, 2001). Majority of the mobile agents architecture present in the literature lacked the feature of intelligence embedded into the mobile agents. The system designed by Cabri and Kendall (Cabri, 2002; Kendall, 1998) and Anand (Anand 2005) had agents roaming autonomously and making intelligent decisions. They could navigate and collaborate with other agents with minimal human intervention. They also learn and adapt to the environment. A detailed review of various mobile agents present is presented in the work by Anand (Anand 2005)

The typical architecture of mobile agents service would be a client server one. In the typical Internet based applications, a new request would be generated and submitted to the server through the TCPIP and the server would respond to the request with a valid response. In both the channels data would be transported and requires the channel to be active till the end of response receipt. This would be fine applications requesting small amount of data and applications having very low latency factor. In some cases even though the amount of data transmitted would be low, their might be a huge number of requests to the server. There would be a load balancer which parses the request to the server with the minimum load. This typically reflects the commercial application of large multinational companies. The applications like Enterprise Resource Planning (ERP), Customer Relationship Management (CRM) are some applications which have a low data demand but very high number of requests involved. In such applications, the channel has to remain active till the response is received from the server for each request. This puts an unnecessary load on the network usage and increases the response time and average waiting period. Mobile Agent's technology seems to be the perfect answer to the issues raised.

Although the Mobile Agent's technology offers various advantages, and offers a promising solution, they still cannot be implemented as they do not have the concept of Sessions in them. Most of the commercial applications are based around some workflows which involves multiple requests and responses between the service requester and service consumer. If the nature of communication remains stateless as now, for each request and response a large amount of redundant data would be flowing through. Typical large applications would involve multiple servers which further increases the amount of redundant data. In case of heterogeneous application we would have to avail the service of Asynchronous Message Queues to perform the operation. We present a solution to the various issues raised with the proposal of introducing SessionState into the Mobile Agents framework and show how this could be implemented for CRM application.

SYSTEM ARCHITECTURE

The general architecture of the system is as shown in Figure 1 and the involved steps are described below. The client can be a PC connected to the network or a

Figure 1. System functioning

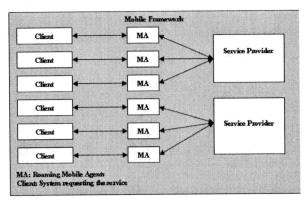

Figure 2. Mobile agent's state machine diagram

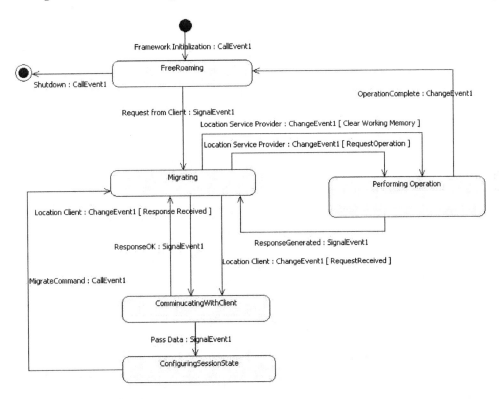

mobile device connected through the wireless connectivity protocol. In the insurance sector a client doing a claim through his mobile device would be the example of the wireless scenario. The client requests the mobile agent to perform certain operation. The MA migrates to the mobile device, collects serialized object created by the client and creates a new configuration file with a unique GUID. The GUID value is stored in mobile device for further reference. MA carries the configuration file and migrates to the service provider location. MA transfers the configuration file to the service provider location and starts performing the requested operation. Once the operation is completed successfully, it migrates back to the mobile device with the response and verifies if the client is happy with the response. If the client is satisfied with the response, the MA

Figure 3. Business entities class diagram

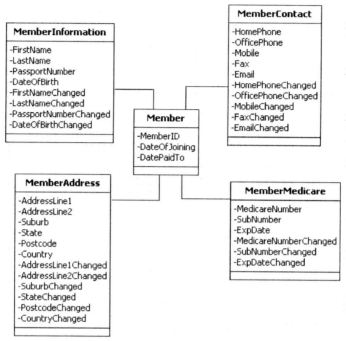

migrates to the service provider location and purges the configuration file and clears the working memory and starts roaming freely in the mobile environment. In between this process if any error is thrown by the service provider, MA communicates that to the client. Client rectifies the error and creates the objects that were changed and set the PropertyChanged Flag for the corresponding attribute. MA migrates back to the service provider with the new object, opens the existing configuration file corresponding to the GUID it has, and changes the values of the attributes which have the PropertyChanged Flag value of "Y". It then performs the operation again with the new data. This process continues till the operation is successful or the client aborts. The overall system functioning would be as shown in Figure 1. The different states of the MA are shown in the Figure 2.

IMPLEMENTATION AND UML MODELS

Let us start applying the SessionState to the mobile agents for "Add New Member" workflow for CRM

in a Health Insurance Sector. Typically this workflow would involve various tasks like gathering of information, generating request, validating request, data persistence and generating response. Assuming the application has been developed following standard patterns and practices, the gathering of information would be happening in the presentation layer in the form of Customer Service Operator's (CSR) keying the data. Initial validation of typo errors would also happen in this layer. Then the request would be generated and passed on to the server. The validation of data would be happening at the business logic layer. Errors at various stages may be raised which is then communicated back to the client. The client goes thorough the error messages and takes further action as required. Let us assume that the date of birth was in the future and this is unacceptable by the business logic. In this case the data is rectified, new request is generated and passed on to the server. Next let us say that there is already a record in the system with the given details. In that case either the add member workflow should be aborted or proceeded based on the CSR's judgement. This process continues till the new member is created or the CSR cancels the workflow.

With the introduction of Mobile Agents, the process would change as follows. Instead of a series of request and response happening over the channel, the MA would gather all the respective data, create appropriate objects, migrate to the server and execute itself and return back with the response. If there is ever going to be only one set of request and response for each operation, then a normal Client Server architecture would be no different to the MA paradigm as the amount of data transmitted would be similar. But this would drastically change when there are a series of request and response between the client and server creating a conversation like scenario. In that case the MA migrating between the server and client location with the whole object would be unnecessary. This could be avoided if the MA knows which transaction it is currently executing. This could be saved in the SessionState configuration file and be stored in the server location. Only the messages would be transferred back and forth in the channel. It may also include data depending on the situation. With the capability of having SessionState, the new process would be as follows.

The data is keyed in by CSR and the Create New Member action is initiated. The presentation layer rectifies the typo errors without the intervention of server. The business logic layer constructs the respective objects. The objects would be serializable to conform to the SOAP standards. Let us assume that based on the data keyed in the objects for the classes shown in the Figure 3 are created.

All these information is attached to the SessionState configuration file `SessionStateID.ssc`. The SessionStateID would be an unique 32 character long system generated string which would identify the transaction. This file is attached to the MA for further processing. MA then migrates to the server with the file and executes the process. While executing there might be various errors raised. Depending on the nature of error actions are taken correspondingly. We can broadly classify the errors into 3 main categories.

Data Error

This could have been raised because of some inconsistent data. This could be like invalid date of birth, invalid postcode or invalid Medicare number. Let us take the case of invalid Medicare number. As there is no way to rectify this error automatically, the MA has to get back to the client with the list of errors for further assistance. The client rectifies the error and builds the

new object. In this new object the properties that was changed is identified with the PropertyChanged flag set to "Y". Client then hands it over to the MA. MA migrates back to the server, reads the SessionState file with its SessionStateID. It reads the new object and locates all the properties that has been changed and then assigns them to the SessionState file. In this case the client would have given 4 objects, 3 of them unchanged and the MemberMedicare object's property MedicareNumber changed. So the MA reads the property MemberMedicareChanged and checks if it has a value of "Y. Then it changes that property in the residing SessionState file. Once this process is over it re-executes itself. This process continues till all the data errors are rectified.

Business Logic Error

In case of business logic error, the course of action would be more complicated. Let us assume that the server returned an error stating that another member with exactly same information is already present in the system. The MA returns to the client with the error code. The CSR would need to use his judgement to decide wether a new member needs to be created with similar information, cancel the operation or identify that it is in fact the same member details which are present in the system and then update the details instead of creating them. In case of cancelling the workflow, the MA deletes the SessionState file, resets itself and gets ready for the next request. If the CSR opts to create another member with the details provided, the MA overrides the server message and creates the new member. If the CSR identified the member as an existing one, then the MA changes its persistence to an Update method instead of Create. This would need reading few more identity columns from the database for data consistency. All this would be handled by the MA.

Communication Error

These errors would be generally related to physical breaks in the communication channel. This could be attributed to various factors like an abrupt loss connection, unauthorized access to the resources and outage of resources. These errors cannot be fixed by either MA or by the CSR. So these errors are logged and sent to the respective authorities for further action.

CONCLUSION AND FUTURE WORK

A mobile agent's framework has been proposed in this paper that is built on the framework already built. With the introduction of sessions in mobile agents, we have introduced the workflow concept into the mobile agent paradigm. This makes its commercial implementation viable. This has been applied to the CRM application in the health insurance sector for its verification. There are a few factors like multi-session variables which still need to be addressed. Also as the security protocols and channels are very crucial in commercial applications we need extensions to the existing protocols for mobile agent's architecture.

REFERENCES

Birrell, A. D., & Nelson, B. J. (1984). Implementing remote procedure calls. *ACM Trans. Comput. Syst.,* 2(1), 39-59.

Cabri, G., Leonardi, L., & Zambonelli, F. (2002). Engineering Mobile Agent Applications via Context-Dependent Coordination. *IEEE Trans. Softw. Eng.,* 28(11), 1039--1055.

Cybenko, G., Gray, R. S., Wu, Y., & Khrabrov, A. (1994). *Information Architecture and Agents.*

Gray, R. S. (1995). Agent Tcl: A transportable agent system. *Proceedings of the CIKM Workshop on Intelligent Information Agents, Fourth International Conference on Information and Knowledge Management (CIKM 95)*, Baltimore, Maryland, December 1995.

Gray, R. S., Kotz, D., Nog, S., Rus, D., & Cybenko, G. (Eds.). (1996). *Mobile agents for mobile computing.* Dartmouth College.

Jipping, M. J. (2002). *Symbian OS Communications Programming.* John Wiley & Sons, Ltd.

Kendall, E. A., Krishna, P. V. M., Pathak, C. V., & Suresh, C. B. (1998). Patterns of intelligent and mobile agents. *In AGENTS '98: Proceedings of the second international conference on Autonomous agents* (pp. 92--99): ACM Press.

Lauvset, K. J. (2001). Separating Mobility from Mobile Agents. *In HOTOS '01: Proceedings of the Eighth Workshop on Hot Topics in Operating Systems* (pp. 173): IEEE Computer Society.

Meandzija, B. (1986). A formal method for composing a network command language. *IEEE Trans. Softw. Eng., 12*(8), 861-865.

Stamos, J. W., & Gifford, D. K. (1990). Remote evaluation. *ACM Trans. Program. Lang. Syst., 12*(4), 537-564.

Stoyenko, A. D. (1994). SUPRA-RPC: SUbprogram PaRAmeters in remote procedure calls. *Softw. Pract. Exper., 24*(1), 27-49.

Chapter XXXVIII
Reliable Computing in Heterogeneous Networks:
A Review Report

R. B. Patel
M. M. Engineering College, India

Vijay Athavale
JIET, Jind, Haryana, India

ABSTRACT

Mobile computing extends the horizons of conventional computing model to a ubiquitous computing environment that serves users at anytime, anywhere. Most distributed applications and services were designed with the assumption that the terminals were powerful, stationary, and connected to fixed networks. One of the biggest challenges in future application development is device heterogeneity. In the future, users expect to see a rich variety of computing devices that can run applications. These devices have different capabilities in processors, memory, networking, screen sizes, input methods, and software libraries. We also expect that future users are likely to own many types of devices. Depending on users changing situations and environments, they may choose to switch from one type of device, to another that brings the best combination of application functionality and device mobility. Applications, middleware, and systems can be measured in a variety of dimensions, including usability, distributability, integration, conformance to standards, extensibility, internationalizability, manageability, performance, portability, scalability reliability-fault tolerance, and security. The authors call these pervasive attributes, since they can apply to the system as a whole, not just to the system's components. Mobility brings additional uncertainties, as well as opportunities to provide new services and supplementary information to users in the locations where they find themselves. In general, most application software, operating systems, and network frameworks are intended for more conventional environments, and so the mobile, wireless user has great difficulty exploiting the computational framework as fully as he/she might. There is an emerging consensus among researchers that a new architecture and dynamic framework is an appropriate way to address above problems. This report presents a prototype for secure and reliable computing that will address above issues and can both assist developers to build multi-platform applications that can run on heterogeneous devices and allow a user to move/migrate a running application among heterogeneous devices might be among different networks.

INTRODUCTION

Mobile computing is a rapidly emerging research and development area. There exists a plethora of application scenarios where wireless access to heterogeneous information sources would be of great value. Law enforcement, access to medical information from an ambulance, off shore drilling (Sumatra, Goa, Chennai, etc.) scientific fieldwork, and emergency crisis management such as natural disaster-Tsunami, Sea Storm, agriculture, bushfire control, mass disasters, wildlife monitoring, for instance, the crisis management involved during a hurricane event like tsunami. Before, during, and after a hurricane hits a region, the crisis management personnel need fast and reliable access to a wide range of information sources [18]. There has been a considerable research effort going on around the world in this respect.

Mobile computing is associated with mobility of hardware, data and software in computer applications. Mobile computing has become possible with convergence of mobile communications and computer technologies, which include mobile phones, personal digital assistants (PDA), handheld and portable computers, and pervasive networks, such as GSM [21] or wireless local area networks (WLAN), wireless wide area networks and wireless ATMs [21]. The increasing miniaturization of virtually all system components is making mobile computing a reality [1, 2]. Mobile computing - the use of a portable computer capable of wireless networking - is already revolutionizing the way we use computers.

Mobile Computing System is subdivided into Nomadic systems and Ad Hoc systems. Nomadic systems are those containing a core fixed network and some mobile nodes, which are usually just leave in the network: cellular networks are typical examples of systems with this topology. Ad Hoc systems have a much decentralized structure where no fixed core exists and where each node may be mobile. In both cases the type of network links is wireless. Devices change their location continuously, with different frequency depending on the applications.

The components of mobile computing infrastructure are illustrated in Figure 1. The architectural model consists of two distinct sets of entities: mobile hosts (MH) and fixed hosts (FH). Some of the FHs, called mobile support stations (MSS) [12] or Base Host (BH) [16] have a wireless interface to communicate with MHs. Mobile hosts can connect to any other FH where it can register as a visitor. This node is called the visitor

base node (VBN). The VBN routes all transactions, messages and communication calls to and from the MH to its appropriate BH.

The layered conceptual architecture of mobile computing systems is illustrated in figure 2. The bottom layer of Figure 2 involves a larger computer network or a geographical area controlled by a corresponding BH is called its zone of influence. FHs and communication links between them constitute the static or the fixed network, and can be considered to be the trusted part of the infrastructure. Thus, the general architecture for the network with MHs is a two tier structure: powerful and reliable fixed network with mobile support stations and a large number of MHs, which are roaming within and across multiple heterogeneous networks and are connected by slow and often unreliable wireless links. Wireless communication services can be grouped into relatively distinct groups [11, 14]. The grouping is done with respect to the scale of mobility and communication modes and is summarized in Table 1. The middle layer of Figure 2 involves system level support for mobile computing environment. This support includes database management systems (DBMS), distributed operating systems, algorithms and models that enable mobility in distributed computations across heterogeneous computing environments. Changes and enhancements to operating systems, as well as other system level additions are discussed in [12, 3]. The major issues typically involved here, include disconnection management, file system design, concurrency, query processing, transparent delegation of tasks and responsibilities, data replication, and transaction models.

Support for disconnected operations is very important for mobile computing systems as the moving host can frequently disconnect from the network while dropping out of the coverage areas. Unlike traditional distributed systems, this should not be treated as a failure. Implicit support via the OS, or explicit support embedded in the application should enable continued processing on a local file system. Such disconnected processing can also be based on advance caching [39], when the application is mobility aware and downloads enough data to survive between two successive connection/disconnection cycles.

The challenges in developing software infrastructure for mobile computing environment are quite different from those involved in the design of stationary distributed networked systems [2]. The top layer of the figure 3 is deals with such type software infrastructure. The implications of host mobility on

Figure 1. Mobile computing environment

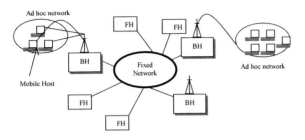

Figure 2. Layered view of mobile computing system

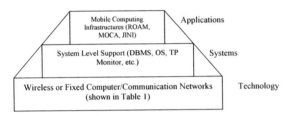

distributed computations are quite significant. Mobility brings about a new style of computing. It affects both fixed and wireless networks. On the fixed network, mobile users can establish a connection from different locations. Wireless connection enables virtually unrestricted mobility and connectivity from any location within the radio coverage. Today's mobile computing devices are only an intermediate stage in this evolution, but the vision of mobile computing [4] has become realistic to the extent that big software companies and popular magazines are initiating to talk about it, often coining their own terms, but basically describing similar ideas.

The success of mobile computing today is hampered by many debilitating factors. These include slow networks, wasteful protocols, frequent disconnections, weak terminals, immature IP access to networks, security and privacy, poorly optimized Operating Systems (OS) [5] for mobile applications, content conversions from wired to wireless networks, and among others.

Users in mobile computing environments can be mobile and have computing sessions distributed over a range of devices. The software framework's role with respect to users should be to maintain knowledge of their context and to manage tasks related to their mobility. There are two different notions of mobility.

The first, **mobile computation** has to do with virtual mobility (mobile code [15]). The second, **mobile computing** has to do with physical mobility (mobile hardware). These two fields are today almost disconnected, the first dominated by a software community and the second dominated by a hardware community. However, the borders between virtual and physical mobility are fuzzy and eventually we have to treat all kinds of mobility in a uniform way.

Virtual mobility: The agent can move by propagating over the network, but can also move by being physically transported with the mobile devices from one location to another [16]. When an agent moves it may have to undergo through security checks (e.g., byte code verification) when it crosses administrative domains [17]. When the agent move through mobile devices it may have to undergo through security checks (e.g., virus detection) when the mobile device is physically allowed inside a new administrative domain. Do we need two completely separate security frameworks for these two cases, or can we somehow find a common principle? A plausible security policy for a given domain would be that a physical barrier (a building door) should provide the same security guarantees as a virtual barrier (a firewall).

Physical Mobility: Software exists that allows remote control of a computer, by bringing the screen of a remote computer on a local screen. The providers of such software may claim that this is just as good as moving the computer physically, e.g., to access its local data. Moreover, if the remote computer has a network connection, this is also equivalent to stringing wire from the remote location, since the remote network is now locally accessible. For example, using remote control over a phone line to connect from home to work where a high-bandwidth Internet connection is available is almost as good as having a high-bandwidth Internet connection brought into the home.

Mobility also raises another major issue of discovery of software components- Service discovery protocols enable finding and using networked services without any previous knowledge of their specific location. Some Service Discovery Protocols (SDP) are Jini [35], SLP [9], UPnP [10] and Salutation [11], SOAP [41], etc.

With the advent of both mobility and wireless networking, SDPs are taking on a major role in networked environments, and are the source of a major heterogeneity issue across middleware. Furthermore, once services are discovered, applications need to use the same interaction protocol to allow unanticipated connections and interactions with them. Consequently, a second heterogeneity issue appears among mobile computing infrastructures. Mobile computing infrastructures for the networked home environment must overcome two heterogeneity issues to provide interoperability, i.e., (i) heterogeneity of service discovery protocols, and (ii) heterogeneity of interaction protocols between services. Interoperability is also difficult between devices made by different manufacturers, as they can

implement differently a standardized protocol. Thus, user can discover and use the environment resources and export the resources carrying to the environment [40]. We feel that a large portion of the community in both research and industry is still using RPC (or its newer implementation like ROI, RMI) even when it is harmful. For example, UpnP, Easyliving and others have recently devised SOAP [41], based on RPC semantics, for home automation. Likewise, even notable mobile agent systems like Ajanta [42]

Table 1. Wireless connectivity technologies

Technology	Costs	Advantages	Disadvantages
On-premises wireless messaging (e.g., by using messaging pagers, PDAs)	• Low fixed cost for simple, shrink-wrapped applications and devices • Low operating cost	✓ Shrink-wrapped applications do not require IT support ✓ Easy, fast implementation for shrink-wrapped applications	➢ Small data display area ➢ Range limited to few hundred feet ➢ Custom applications may require additional support ➢ Signals can be intercepted, posing security risk
Wireless Local Area Network (WLAN)	• Low to high capital cost, depending on complexity of network and data rate • Low to moderate operating cost depending on stability of software	✓ Medium to high data rates ✓ User interface similar to landline Local Area Network (LAN); little additional end-user training is needed ✓ Eliminates need for wiring in older buildings or where impractical. ✓ Can be combined with landline LAN to network mobile devices on a large campus	➢ New technology for most IT departments; another support burden ➢ More expensive than landline LAN for equivalent data rates ➢ Not supported by most handheld devices ➢ Very short range ➢ Signals can be intercepted, posing security risk unless appropriate security measures are used
2.5G, 3G wireless devices (e.g., 2.5 generation cell phones)	• No fixed costs except for mobile devices (usually phones) • High operating costs (per-minute connection charges)	✓ Cell network supported by the vendor, usually the Internet service provider (ISP) ✓ Wide area coverage in metropolitan areas ✓ Fast implementation	➢ Not widely implemented in U.S. ➢ Low data rate except for newest technology in test markets ➢ Coverage usually does not include rural areas ➢ Small data display area ➢ Poor Wireless Access Protocol (WAP) security
Broadband wireless	• Moderate fixed costs for receivers • Operating costs depend on ISP service level	✓ Network supported by vendor (ISP) ✓ High data rate may compete with T1 speeds ✓ Potential low cost alternative to T1 in metropolitan markets	➢ Currently available in only a few markets ➢ Requires fixed point receiver for speeds greater than 384 Kbps ➢ Coverage does not include rural areas ➢ Security concerns are identical to those of Internet

continued on following page

Table 1. continued

Satellite	• Low to high fixed costs for receivers, depending on the application • Low operating cost per data rate	✓ Network supported by the vendor (ISP) ✓ At present, easier and faster to get than DSL in many markets, especially rural ones ✓ Medium to high download data rate; can be much better than T3 in dedicated applications	➤ Upload data rate equivalent to dial-up ➤ Off-the-shelf commercial offerings more expensive than cable or DSL with slower data rates ➤ High speed, high capacity applications require custom engineering; difficult and expensive to implement ➤ Signal can be intercepted, potentially compromising security
Free Space Optics	• Low to high fixed costs for receivers, depending on the application • Low operating cost per data rate	✓ Medium to high data rate; can be much better than T3 ✓ Prices will be competitive with broadband wireless ✓ Signal may be received at much greater distance than broadband wireless	➤ In prototype stage ➤ Coverage is unlikely to include rural areas in the near future ➤ Reliability can be degraded by several environmental conditions, reducing data rate as distance increases ➤ Requires fixed point receiver; appropriate only for data replication and synchronization ➤ Signal cannot be intercepted without detection, providing security no other media can match

solely rely on java-RMI for agent interaction. More astonishingly, distributed Event architectures of even the mainstream systems like CORBA [20] and Jini [35] have been implemented on top of RPC (RMI), which, although alleviates the applications from RPC semantics, leads to an inefficient implementation at the system level.

Research has picked up on this topic about a decade earlier and today many groups spend considerable amounts of sweat and funding on the investigation of various aspects of mobile computing. Often the first step towards research in this field is choosing or establishing a hardware and/or software infrastructure with which prototype scenarios can be developed and tested. These infrastructures or frameworks then provide the basis for building mobile computing applications as distributed interactive systems. They provide abstractions for networking, sensors or data, as well as formalisms and models for the specification of such systems. So under the highly variable computing environment conditions that characterize mobile platforms, it is believed that existing traditional distributed computing systems are not capable of providing adequate support for the wireless mobile computing environment. Here we identified the needs of mobile computing infrastructure that must be incorporated to provide the reliable computing in heterogeneous computing environment. These are categorized as **functional** and **non-functional** needs. Scalability, heterogeneity, fault-tolerance, openness and security are some examples of **non-functional** requirements that need to be addressed when implementing a computing infrastructure that can suit the needs of different mobile applications. **Functional** requirements must be addressed in order to enable communication between the mobile application that knows nothing about the network infrastructure and the network itself. Requirements such as event notification, logging, addressing, discovery, and context-awareness are inherently related to the functionality of the computing infrastructure. The brief overview of non-functional requirements of mobile computing infrastructure is shown in Table 2.

Requirements of Mobile Computing Infrastructure (MCI)

Event Notification: the ability to deliver messages to one or more recipients. Event notification systems are often also called publish-subscribe systems. In nomadic networks the event notification functionality is usually taken care of by the core fixed infrastructure, while the mobile devices simply receive the events. In ad hoc network, the solutions need to be more decentralized as the nodes have roughly the same kind of roles. Each node has an event notification component. Typically publish/subscribe (P/S) systems contain information providers and information consumers. The information providers publish events to the information consumers and information consumers subscribe to particular categories of event. The P/S middleware ensures the delivery of published events to all interested subscribers.

Mobility and location awareness: the ability to roam or move from location to location is an essential component for these kinds of systems. In terms of MCI, the mobility is the ability to recognize a new environment and adapt to it.

Addressing: this component recognizes the different devices around in order to be able to communicate with them.

Service discovery: the ability to identify new services and, possibly protocols. This is an essential component of the MCSI, which also relate to the ability of relocating.

Code Updater: the ability to dynamically change the protocol and the code of the running applications or of the MCI itself in order to adapt to context.

Distributed Task Scheduler: It is responsible for allocating task on different hosts according to their specific capabilities and energy status.

High-level components: This set of components exploits the previously mentioned components to offer high-level functionalities to applications.

- *Local data storage:* this component controls the access to the local data, providing abstractions (e.g., SQL-like) for data retrieval.
- *(Distributed) event notification:* it implements a distributed event notification service, allowing sensors to subscribe to interested events and to publish event notifications. If present, it may leverage off content-based routing as provide by multi-hop routing component, otherwise it may employ different strategies.
- *(Distributed) query:* it exposes a query-based interface to retrieve data on remote hosts.
- *Code and state relocation:* while code updater provides primitives for replacing running code on the host, this component takes care of all the issues concerning a distributed reprogramming of the network such as deployment, global consistency, etc.
- *Code Updater:* It provides mechanisms for replacing the code running on the sensor, ranging from a single application routine to the entire operating system. It supports both weak (only code is transferred) and strong (the state and the program counter are transferred too) mobility.

Cryptographic System: This block contains the standard functions for cryptography such as data encryption, decryption and hashing.

Cross-layer Communication: Its goal is two-fold: it exposes the hardware status (battery level, sensors characteristics, etc.) to the application or other components and it allows the application to specify the desired QoS in terms of sensing rate and accuracy, reliability and network management. It spans both the local and distributed level.

Multi-hop routing: It provides multi-hop point-to-point and multipoint style of communication. In particular, in the case of multipoint communications, the set of receivers may be identified by the specific subject of the message (multicast or subject-based routing), by its content (content-based routing) or by the receivers' physical location (Geo cast).

There is a great demand for designing a new integrated software framework that can support above requirements of MCI imposed by mobility. In this research report we present an agenda for future software infrastructure of mobile computing society. In addition, we summarize current state of art in field of mobile computing software that includes limitations, left issues in existing software mobile computing infrastructure. Finally, we outline a practical roadmap to the next generation reliable mobile computing infrastructure.

LITERATURE: A REVIEW

In [19] authors described the design of a platform that is implemented using ANSAware platform to support collaborative multimedia applications in a mobile environment. The platform provides a programming interface compatible with emerging open systems standards and includes services for processing multimedia information. It also provides feedback to applications and users on the state of their communications framework - an important requirement in mobile environments. The services provided by the platform have been used to develop a collaborative multimedia application designed to support a specific class of mobile worker, i.e., field engineers. But platform and application works over a specific range of wireless network types, poor utilization of bandwidth and QoS. It works with a limited range of wireless communications technologies.

In [23, 24] author developed the CRAS (Client Representative Agent Server) architecture together with a location and query management strategy. Each client or MH has an associated representative which lies on the fixed network. The connection between MH and representative is wireless. The CORBA ORB is used as the means of communication between the different components which is again a heavy weight middleware that restrict the mobility and this architecture needs to be extended in a variety of ways to accommodate the components needed to allow transparent access to distributed information sources and to take changes in the way mobile computing is handled and also proposed another architectural model which allow the support of architectural model [25] which allows the support to mobile users in accessing heterogeneous information sources. But this model also relies heavily on the usage of CORBA middleware.

The MobiWare [22] offers a CORBA based middleware toolkit for mobile services providing alternatives to existing network architectures, this toolkit installed on PCs with wireless local area network (WLAN), radio access nodes for WLAN with inter-working to IP/ATM and servers with content/services. On this infrastructure Mobiware overlay three layers, from link to transport, which is used to transport signalling, management and media traffic. This complex and fully controllable mobile infrastructure provided the needed QoS service to the application. However, this approach again deviates widely from existing standards in the area due to it's close dependency to the mobile network elements, the concept is considered to impractical for industrialisation. One needs more flexibility and architecture less dependent of the mobile infrastructure.

In [28] author proposed the application-aware adaptation that supports a collaborative relationship between application and system. However, the prototypal

system is only based on network-aware application. It also raises the question on how to structure systems that can support pervasive applications [34]. Many other systems that provide an adaptive behavior to mobile applications were also analyzed in [28, 31, 37].

In [7, 8] author presented Aura system, core part of this system is a task manager called prism which tries to minimize the distraction of the user in the following four cases: the user moves to another environment; the environment changes; the task changes; and the context changes. The prism has the following components available and communicates with them: One or more context observer, with possibly varying degrees of sophistication, an environment manager as gateway to environment and file access, and several service suppliers. Furthermore, the prism can also communicate with other prisms to allow the seamless relocation of the user and its tasks to another environment. Aura uses a task-centered approach with platform-independent description and migration of the tasks. It supports Java, C/C++, LISP, etc. languages and TCP/IP network protocol. It is implemented on Linux, Windows and but it is suitable only for suspend/resume of user tasks as a logical unit, both on a single machine as well as across different locations.

In [6] author proposed an infrastructure for a campus-wide network that uses a central server for all components except data acquisition and user interaction, in order to ease administration and to minimize requirements placed on mobile devices. Additionally, centralization provides limited freedom to organize (server-side) components according to extensibility concerns. Sensors and display devices communicate with the server using SOAP. The server is a web server running PHP, backed by an SQL database. The architecture contains five layers. At the top is the device layer, where mobile devices connect to the ActiveCampus server. Next is the environment proxy that abstracts raw sensor data. A situation modeling layer aggregates context from several sensors, whereas an entity modeling layer refines context over time. At the bottom is the data layer, which handles persistent storage. Data regarding entities (users, buildings, etc.) is stored in a normal form in the database. For example, each user has a unique numeric identifier. All other information (name, picture) is associated with that identifier. Similarly, all position information is represented in a normal Cartesian form. Services are decoupled from another using introspection: each service has a method that returns whether the service may be invoked upon a certain entity. Thus, for

Table 2. Non-functional requirements of MCI

REQUIREMENT	DESCRIPTION
Heterogeneity	Components written in different programming languages, running on different operating systems, executing on different hardware platforms should be able to communicate using a middleware platform. Generally, in a distributed system, heterogeneity is almost unavoidable, as different components may require different implementation technologies.
Openness	The capability to extend and modify the system, for example, with respect to changed functional requirements. Adding new services or re-implementing existing ones should be possible within an open distributed system.
Scalability	The ability of the system to accommodate a higher load at some time in the future. A system's load can be measured using many different parameters, such as the maximum number of concurrent users, the number of transactions executed in a time unit, etc.
Failure handling	The ability to recover from faults without halting the whole system. Faults happen when software or hardware components fail to complete their delegated actions/methods, but still any distributed component must continue to operate even if other components they rely on have failed.
Security	Security mechanisms, such as authentication, authorization, and accounting (AAA) functions may an important part of the middleware in order to intelligently control access to computer and network resources, enforcing policies, auditing network/user usage, etc.
Performance	Performance can constitute a requirement of the MCI in various situations. For example, a MCSI used for a real-time distributed application should export functions with a minimal, as possible, execution time, whereas a memory-limited device would require optimization of the memory usage of the MCI.
Adaptability	Changes in applications' and users' requirements or changes within the network may require the presence of adaptation mechanisms within the MCSI. For example, a different transport protocol should be chosen by the MCI when a mobile device enters a network supporting a different transport protocol than the one offered by the current network hosting the device.
Feasibility	Constraints of available resources may limit the feasibility of performing certain tasks or offering certain services in a given system/network environment. Mechanisms should be provided to ensure that a function, task or a service is feasible to be provided in a given system/network instance.

example, a buddy service can easily be integrated with an e-mail service, so that users can send mail to buddies they were chatting with. The ActiveCampus system has been experimentally deployed in a large environment. It uses HTTP, SOAP network protocol with Client/server paradigm and it is especially suitable for wide-area mobile computing applications but only on window CE platform.

In [29] authors describes a dynamic service reconfiguration model where the proxy is composed of a chain of service objects called Mobilets (pronounced as mo-be-lets), which can be deployed onto the network actively. This model offers flexibility because the chain of Mobilets can be dynamically reconfigured to adapt

to the vigorous changes in the characteristics of the wireless environment, without interrupting the service provision for other MHs. Furthermore, Mobilets can also be migrated to a new proxy server when the MH moves to a different network domain. We have realized the dynamic service reconfiguration model by crafting its design into a programmable framework that forms the baseline architecture of the WebPADS system.

In [26] authors presented the challenges, design, and implementation of the ROAM system. The ROAM system is a seamless application framework for building seamless applications that can migrate at runtime across heterogeneous devices. It provides adaptation strategies at the component level, including dynamic instantiation, offloading computation and transformation. In ROAM with the existing SGUI toolkit it is difficult to customize a device-independent representation for a particular device. When the developers change the device-independent model at a later time, they may also have to update transformation rules that are affected by the change. There is no secure fault tolerance support for seamless application migration for real time applications such as video conferencing. For example, a user may want to migrate a video conferencing from a mobile phone to a car navigation system when he/she is entering a car. This places a real time constraint on migration latency and there is no way to make sure that the interruption time is minimized during application migration. The system need the support of repository to save execution state of the service where a user can save a ROAM application on one device and restore it at a later time on any device so that application migration cannot be suspended. And this should be extended to each user level such that every user can save and restore application execution state individually without affecting other users.

In [27] work deals with re-configurable control functions and protocols for supporting mobile computing applications in heterogeneous wireless systems like cellular networks and WLANs (Wireless Local Area Networks). The control functions are implemented in a software module named- re-configurable access module for mobile computing applications (RAMON), placed in mobile and/or base stations. RAMON operates on abstract models of the main communication functions of wireless systems (e.g., transmission over the radio channel, coding end error recovery, capacity sharing and packet scheduling, handover, congestion control, etc.). But it does not providing fault tolerance and security to communication channel.

MOCA [36] is similar to Jini [35], aims to provide a dynamic service environment; however, it focuses on satisfying the requirements of mobile computing environments. MOCA provides dynamic service discovery, limited forms of adaptation to changes caused by mobility, such as disconnection from the mobile network, support for device heterogeneity, and location-transparent access to services. The framework consists of two components that reside on the mobile device: the service registry, which is a repository of information about available services, and a set of core services that provide local file caching, file loading and application management. Its model of locating both service discovery and essential services on the mobile

device was designed with disconnected operation in mind. Unfortunately, this model places considerable resource demands on the mobile device, rendering the framework unsuitable for extremely resource-poor devices. Jini and MOCA address service provision within relatively small service environments and ignore scalability.

Existing most of the infrastructures are not fulfilling the complete need of mobile computing environments as a single entity. But research work within software infrastructure solutions is best effort, but these are sufficient for a particular domain like enterprise domain. In other domains, such as mobile and grid computing, these systems are not meeting the all the needs of above said environment. When the characteristics of the environment vary over time, the existing platforms are not able to well discover and adapt to these changes in-line with the QoS needs to the application. Adaptation may require changes in the platform, such as protocol stack, media coding and error protection scheme. Comparative study of the some of the existing software infrastructures is given in Table 3. Providing solutions to the development of Software that are adaptive to the rich context raises a number of challenging issues relevant to all phases of software development. And, although useful approaches have emerged since the early 2000s, open problems remain to be addressed and solutions need be integrated into a comprehensive development platform, possibly aimed at a specific application domain and/or computing infrastructure. Hence, there is a need of integrated software infrastructure, which can provide the reliable computing in the heterogeneous environments. In that direction, the following presents an overview of the research that we will undertake focuses on assisting the development of reliable and adaptable software services in mobile computing environment.

RESEARCH CHALLENGES

Mobile computing represents a shift in the distributed systems paradigm. The potential of decoupled & disconnected operation, location-dependent computation & communication and powerful portable computing devices gives rise to opportunities for new patterns of distributed computation which requires a revised view of distributed systems. However, factors such as weak network connectivity, energy constraints, and mobility itself raise new concerns regarding the security, reliability and even correctness of a mobile computing system. When it is required to shift applications from one mobile device to another in heterogeneous network then the task application must be adaptive and reliable or computing system should provide reliability to the application. If we consider reliability for an application in heterogeneous network [38] several requirements arise which are as under:

1. Dynamic reconfiguration is thus required and can be achieved by adding a new behavior or changing an existing one at system runtime. Dynamic changes in system behavior and operating context at runtime can trigger re-evaluation and reallocation of resources. Framework supporting dynamic reconfiguration needs to detect changes in available resources and either reallocate resources, or notify the application to adapt to the changes.

2. Adaptivity is also part of the new requirements that allows applications to run efficiently and predictably under a broader range of conditions. Through adaptation a system can adapt its behavior instead of providing a uniform interface in all situations. The framework needs to monitor the resource supply/demand, compute adaptation decisions, and notify applications about changes.

3. Asynchronous interaction tackles the problems of high latency and disconnected operations that can arise with other interaction models. A client using asynchronous communication primitives issues a request and continues operating and then collects the result at any appropriate time. The client and server components do not need to be running concurrently to communicate with each other. A client may issue a request for a service, disconnect from the network, and collect the result later on. This type of interaction style reduces the network bandwidth consumption, achieves decoupling of client and server, and elevates system scalability.

4. Context–awareness [31] is an important requirement to build an effective and efficient adaptive system. The context of a mobile unit is usually determined by its current location, which in turn defines the environment where the computation associated with the unit is performed. The context may include device characteristics, user's activities, services, as well as other resources of the system. Context-awareness is used by several systems; however, few systems sense execution context other than location. The system performance can be increased when execution context is disclosed to the upper layer that assists middleware in making the right decision.

5. Lightweight middleware needs to be considered when constructing software framework for mobile computing. Current middleware platforms like CORBA are too heavy to run on devices with limited resources. By default, they contain a wide range of optional features and all possible functionalities, many of which will be unused by most applications. For example, invoking a method on a remote object involves only client side functionality and either Dynamic or Static Invocation Interface. Most of the existing ORB implementations provide either a single or two separate libraries for the client and server sides that contains all functionality. This forces the client program to be glued with the entire functionality without having a choice to select a specific subset of this functionality.

These requirements raise the various issues that are as under:

a. If a mobile application needs information on the current status for internal logic adaptation, how does the framework convey such information? It is desirable for the framework to expose a set of generic interface for status subscription and query.

b. The mobile application needs to specify the requirements for framework services, such as the type of service (ToS), and the quality of service (QoS). Again, a comprehensive set of abstracted interface needs to identify for negotiating the required framework services.

c. How mobile framework knows under what situation should it carry out adaptation? What are the combinations of parameters for framework services that should be chosen to best adapt to the current status [29, 30], while fulfilling the requirements of the mobile application?

d. Data Management issues–where to keep the data, when to transmit it, whether to use caching and where in the network, how to optimize data placement, pull/push approach, transactional services, location-independent queries and how the network recognize the stage of disconnection of mobile applications. Another issue is which applications can be implemented and used effectively regarding the often-narrow bandwidth, limited computing power, small memory and battery capacity and other resources of the terminals?

To address the issues and requirements discussed above, we have identified several components that can provide support reliable computing wireless mobile environment:

- A transparent view of the user's dynamically changing computing and communication environment.
- A stack of protocols needs to be integrated in it to support mobile computing and computation. The protocols support interoperation between many kinds of frameworks (e.g. wire-line, wireless).
- Ability to deal with unpredictability of user behavior, network capability and computing platforms.
- A fault tolerance mechanism for providing reliability to the opened channels between two communicating parties (viz., client-server, server-server or client-client).
- Scaling regarding the heterogeneity, address space, quality of service (QoS), bandwidth, geographical dimensions, number of users, etc.
- Integrated and ad-hoc access to services.
- Maximum independence between the network and the application from both the user's viewpoint as well as from the development viewpoint.
- Ability to match the nature of what is transmitted to the bandwidth availability (i.e., compression, approximation, partial information, etc).
- Cooperation among system elements such as sensors, actuators, devices, networks, operating system, files system, middleware, services and applications.

Thus, Software in the future will need to cope with variability, as software systems get deployed on an increasingly large diversity of computing platforms. Software will have to be usable in various environments, due to tremendous evolution in information and communication technologies. Heterogeneity of the underlying communication and computing infrastructure, mobility and continuously evolving requirements demand new software paradigms that span the entire life-cycle from development to deployment and execution. Software must be developed in a way that facilitates both its deployment over heterogeneous networks of heterogeneous nodes, and its interaction with end users, their environment and/or other existing systems, depending on the application domain. Moreover, Software should be reliable and meet the user's performance requirements and needs. Thus, there is need of a secure and reliable mobile computing infrastructure for reliable computing in heterogeneous environments.

PROPOSED SYSTEM ARCHITECTURE

In this research we take up problems identified in the previous section and propose a prototype known as "Platform for Device and Computation Management (PDCM)". The proposed architecture of this system is shown in Figure 3. In this system it is assumed that mobile computing system consists any number of MHs connected through one or more BH (called Mobile Service Stations (MSSs)) also known as servers, over some wireless network like infrared. MH will often be disconnected for prolonged period of time due to the low power of battery or unreachable of signal but they will also frequently reallocate between different BHs at different time. Mobile computing environment no longer requires users to maintain a fixed and universally known position in the network and enables unrestricted mobility of the MHs. There may be any numbers of BHs, which communicate through the existing wireless Ad-hoc network infrastructure. It is suggested that there should be a BH in between Internet and other network for providing mobility to the heterogeneous mobile device among heterogeneous networks.

PDCM system will serves users at anytime, anywhere. It is the integration of independent modules, and the synergy provided by a well established, unified baseline architecture that promotes the development of efficient, secure and fault tolerance mobile computing applications. PDCM consists of the manager modules and the Kernel. The Kernel is the basic utility module, which lies below the manager modules and is responsible for driving the PDCM, by ensuring proper co-ordination between the various managers and making them work in tandem.

The secure communication pipe provides a hosting facility to the carrier agent which regularly monitors requests issued by the Kernel of the local host or from remote to receive the request, to transfer requests to/from other PDCMs. Various manager modules help to perform functions like- execution to mobile code, communication, mobility, name services, adaptation, fault tolerance, etc.

Architecture is described as below: when any MH want to communicate with some BH for the fulfilling of the requirement for some required resources (viz., data file) which may be available on that BH. To make this type of communication user friendly User Interface (UI) is provided which run on the server machine and enables the mobile applications to communicate with the BH. UI is platform independent and adapts variety of MHs displays. To establish the communication link among the MHs and BHs UI calls the Communication Manager (CM), which manages the data exchange between the different components of the PDCM. Usually,

the MHs use different types of network connections to access the necessary information. The major task of CM is to decide which network component will perform desired task efficiently at lower cost. CM also supports the adaptivity of the system in case of bandwidth fluctuation.

Mobility Manager (MM) performs two types of task Location Management (LM) and Handoff Management (HM) of MHs. LM and HM modules manage the two type of roaming for mobile hosts (MHs) in wireless system: intra-system (intra-domain) and intersystem (inter-domain) roaming. Intra-system roaming refers to moving between different cells of the same system. Intra-system mobility management techniques are based on similar network interfaces and protocols. Inter-system roaming refers to moving

Table 3. Comparison of the mobile computing infrastructures

Sr. No.	Infrastructure	Characteristics	Limitations
1.	Platform to support collaborative multimedia applications in a mobile environment	1. Implemented using ANSAware platform to support collaborative multimedia applications in a mobile environment. 2. Platform provides a programming interface compatible with emerging open systems standards. 3. Also provides feedback to applications and users on the state of their communications framework. 4. Used to develop a collaborative multimedia application designed to support a specific class of mobile worker, i.e., field engineers.	1. Platform and application works over a specific range of wireless network types, poor utilization of bandwidth and QoS. 2. Designed specifically for multimedia applications in mobile computing environment, not a generic one.
2.	CRAS	1. Client Representative Agent Server architecture together with a location and query management strategy. 2. Each client or MH has an associated representative which lies on the fixed network. 3. The CORBA ORB is used as the means of communication between the different components, which is a heavy weight middleware that restrict the mobility.	1. This architecture needs to be extended in a variety of ways to accommodate the components needed to allow transparent access to distributed information sources and to take changes in the way mobile computing is handled and also proposed another architectural model which allow the support of architectural model [25] which allows the support to mobile users in accessing heterogeneous information sources. But this model also relies heavily on the usage of CORBA middleware.
3	MOCA, Jini	1. Aims to provide a dynamic service environment. 2. MOCA provides dynamic service discovery, limited forms of adaptation to changes caused by mobility, such as disconnection from the mobile network, support for device heterogeneity, and location-transparent access to services. 3. The framework consists of two components that reside on the mobile device: the service registry, which is a repository of information about available services, and a set of core services that provide local file caching, file loading and application management.	1. This model places considerable resource demands on the mobile device, rendering the framework unsuitable for extremely resource-poor devices. 2. Jini [35] and MOCA address service provision within relatively small service environments and ignore scalability.

continued on following page

Table 3. continued

| 4. | ROAM | 1. Seamless application framework.
2. Assist developers to built multi platform applications that can run on heterogeneous devices.
3. Allow a user to move/migrate a running application among heterogeneous devices.
4. It provides adaptation strategies at the component level, including dynamic instantiation, offloading computation and transformation.
5. Based on the partitioning of an application into components. | 1. In ROAM with the existing SGUI toolkit it is difficult to customize a device-independent representation for a particular device.
2. When the developers change the device-independent model at a later time, they also have to update transformation rules that are affected by the change and transformation rules are application specific it means application during migration has to be suspended.
3. System rune on different system with different JVM, there is a great need of a system, which is adaptable to the available JVM.
4. Not applicable for the real time applications because the run time migration latency is in seconds.
5. At design time, developers must have to make the decision on how to partition an application in to separate components. It is very complex job.
6. Roam system requires developers to provide execution state transformation logic for some components.
7. Security is provided only for unauthorized applications not for the system itself
8. There is no secure fault tolerance support for seamless application migration for real time applications such as video conferencing. |
| 5. | RAMON | 1. Deals with re-configurable control functions and protocols for supporting mobile computing applications in heterogeneous wireless systems like cellular networks and WLANs (Wireless Local Area Networks).
2. Operates on abstract models of the main communication functions of wireless systems (e.g., transmission over the radio channel, coding end error recovery, capacity sharing and packet scheduling, handover, congestion control, etc.). | 1. It does not providing fault tolerance and security to communication channel.
2. Based on TCP/IP protocol suit.
3. Functionality are not separated, they are integrated in a single module that is not safe for fault tolerance and security. |

between different backbones, protocols, technologies, or service providers. Based on intra- or inter-system roaming, the corresponding LM and HM modules can be further classified into intra- and inter-system location module and handoff module (IILM and IIHM): LM enables the system to track the locations of MHs between consecutive communications. It includes two major tasks. The first is location registration/location update, where the MH periodically informs the system to update relevant location databases with its up to date location information. The second is call delivery, where the system determines the current location of the MH based on the information available at the system databases when a communication for the MH is initiated. For inter-system roaming, the design of LM techniques has the following objectives: (1) Reduction of latency of service delivery. (2) Quality of service (QoS) guarantees in different systems. (3) When the service areas of heterogeneous wireless networks are fully overlapped:(a) through which networks an MH should perform location registrations. (b) In which networks and how the up-to-date user location information should be stored. (c) How the exact location of an MH would be determined within a specific time constraint. General architecture of MM comprises of Mobile Client Managing Agent (MCMA), Virtual Single Account Agent (VSAA) and Secure Mobility Gateway Agent (SMGA) which are discussed next.

The MCMA is mainly responsible for creating and maintaining a mobile IPsec tunnel between the user's system and the corporate network over the best available wireless network. It interacts directly with, and controls, the available wireless, interfaces and Modems.

The VSAA provides several functions. It stores every authentication credential used to access wireless networks and the intranet. It also serves as a back-end authentication server for the SMGA and provides an

Figure 3. Architecture of PDCM

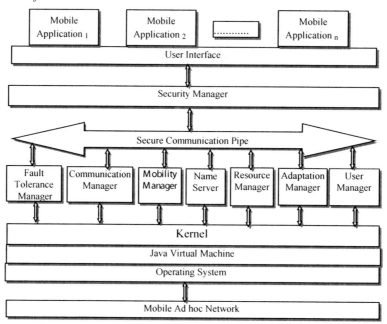

interface for system administrators to manage each user's access rights and authentication credentials. It also provides authentication-credential-updating services to the MCMAs. The VSAA stores access credentials in a VSAA record, which contains a user's single sign on VSAA certificate, an intranet profile, a cellular profile, and several WLAN profiles. Multiple profiles are needed because we assume the user will need to use various networks that can be managed by different entities, and that will typically have different configuration parameters. The intranet profile contains the user's authentication credential for accessing the corporate intranet; the cellular profile contains the commands and parameters needed to establish a cellular data connection. A WLAN profile contains configuration parameters, access parameters, and an authentication credential.

The SMGA is a special IPsec gateway deployed between the public Internet and the corporate intranet. It authenticates a user's system with the VSAA's help, tracks the system's location with the MCMA's help, and relays IP packets between the Mobile device and other IP nodes. The IP packets transmitted between the SMGA and the Mobile device's current location are encrypted and encapsulated.

The HM keeps MH connection active when it moves from one access point to another. The handoff process can be intra or inter-system. Intra-system handoff is the handoff in homogeneous networks. The need for intra-system handoff (or horizontal handoff) arises when the signal strength of the serving BH deteriorates below a certain threshold value. The need for inter-system handoff (or vertical handoff) between heterogeneous networks may arise in the following scenarios: (1) When a user is moving out of the serving network and will enter another overlaying network shortly. (2) When a MH is connected to a particular network, but chooses to be handed-off to the underlying network for its future service needs. (3) When distributing the overall network load among different systems are needed. At this level Resource Manager (RM) manages the resources of the system (viz., system memory used by MH, files, etc.), and also controls the admission of mobile applications that subscribe the services. Main duties include: authentication, Type of Services (ToS) and QoS negotiation, service subscription and un-subscription. To simplify the functionalities RM is subdivided into two another modules Resource Allocator (RA) and Replication Controller (RC). RA allocates and controls the resources for newly subscribed services. Resources are allocated fairly among mobile applications, at the same time fulfilling individual application's requirement. RC keeps the global state of the distributed resources consistent among all local resources based on a given coherence strategy. We have assumed n number of mobile application (MHs), and the coordination among all the applications are managed by a User Manager (UM), which collaborates with Name Server (NS) because names are symbolic ways of referring to objects across a network. Names are detached from their corresponding objects: one may possess a name without having immediate access to any object of that name. To enable mobility and disconnected operation, all objects across a wireless network should be denoted by unique names. Name Server manages the process of naming and identification. During this process there is very much risk of security and inconsistency of the data due disconnection and security. Security, trust and privacy must be addressed from the very beginning of system design and on all levels such as hardware, operating system, protocols, and architecture. So the Security Manager (SM) is provided which has the duties of (1) Protecting BH against unauthorized modifications, (2) Program validation/verification (what an uploaded/downloaded piece of software really does), Trust modeling, (3) How fragments of information can be efficiently shared in a controlled manner, Key/certificate management, and (4) Implications of ad-hoc communities (what can be done without trusted servers). Fault Tolerance Manager (FTM) is implemented for recovering the loss of information during disconnection while performing the mobile computations. It also provides fault tolerance to the communication channels on failure. The execution environment for both public architecture services (one set of services that are shared among all mobile application) and application specific architecture services (each mobile application has its own set of services) is provided by the core module of the architecture, which is known as kernel with the help of different managers running just above.

CONCLUSION

To achieve the secure and fault tolerance mobile computing, it is redundant and inefficient for mobile applications to maintain the required resource availability independently. It is also not appropriate for application developers to check the status of all related applications exactly. Instead, a more generalized and abstracted description of the current application would be adequate for a mobile application to work effectively. Another problem is how mobile applications utilize the underlying system service to adapt to the current status of the system. This is a challenging task for application developers since mobile applications have to implement their own adaptation mechanism to the system level. It is also necessary to exploit optimal application performance. However, adaptation mechanisms by mobile applications usually suffers from the problem of unfairness to other applications, in contrast, adaptation by the operating system focuses more on the overall system performance, while neglecting the needs of individual applications. Hence, the adaptation task is best coordinated by a Adaptation Manager in the PDCM that is able to cater for individual application's need on a fair ground, while maintaining optimal system performance. This will be achieved by the PDCM that sits in between the mobile application and the operating environments.

REFERENCES

Alonso, R., & Korth, H. F. (1993). Database System Issues in Nomadic Computing. *Proceedings of ACM SIGMOD Conference on Management of Data, 22*. 388-392.

Angin, O., Campbell, A., Kouvanis, M., & Liao, R. (1998). The Mobiware Toolkit: programmable support for adaptive mobile networking. *IEEE Personal Communications Magazine, Special Issue on Adapting to Network and Client Variability, 5*(4).

Banavar, G. et al. (2000). Challenges: An Application Model for Pervasive Computing, In Proceedings of MOBICOM 2000: The 6 Annual International Conference on Mobile Computing and Networking, August 6-11, Boston, MA USA, (pp. 266-274).

Beck, J., Gefflaut, A., & Islam, N. (1999, August). *MOCA: A Service Framework for Mobile Computing Devices. Proceedings International Workshop on Data Engineering for Wireless and Mobile Access.*

Bettstetter, C., & Renner, C. (2000). A comparison of service discovery protocols and implementation of the service location protocol. *In Proceedings of the 6th EUNICE Open European Summer School: Innovative Internet Applications.*

Box, D. et al. (n/d). *Simple Object Access Protocol 1.1.* http://www.w3.org/TR/SOAP

Brewer, E. A., Katz, R. H., Chawathe, Y., Gribble, S. D., Hodes, T., Nguyen, G., Stemm, M., Henderson,

T., Amir, E., Balakrishnan, H., Fox, A., Padmanabhan, V. N., & Seshan, S. (1998, October). *A Network Architecture for Heterogeneous Mobile Computing IEEE Personal Communications 5(5).*

Cardelli, L. (1999, August). Mobility and Security. *In Proceedings of the NATO Advanced Study Institute on Foundations of Secure Computation,* (pp. 3-37), Marktoberdorf, Germany.

Chen, G. & Kotz, D. (2000). *A Survey of Context-aware Mobile Computing Research.* Technical Report TR2000-381, Dartmouth Computer Science.

Chiasserini, C-F., Cuomo, F., Piacentini, L., Rossi, M., Tinirello, I., & Vacirca, F. (2004). Architectures and protocols for mobile computing applications: a reconfigurable approach, *Computer Networks, 44,* 545–567.

Chu, H., Song, H., Wong, C., Kurakake, S., & Katagiri M. (2004). ROAM, a seamless application framework. The Journal of Systems and Software, *69*(3), 209–226.

Chuang, S. N., A.T.S. Chan, J. Cao, Ronnie Cheung, Actively Deployable Mobile Services for Adaptive Web Access, IEEE Internet Computing, 8(2): 26-33, March/April 2004.

Chuang, S. N., Chan, A.T.S., Cao, J., & Cheung, R. (2003, May). Dynamic Service Reconfiguration for Wireless Web Access. *In Proceedings of the Twelve International World Wide Web Conference,* Budapest, Hungary, (pp. 58-67).

Chung, H., & Cho, H. (1998). Data caching with incremental update propagation in mobile computing environments. *Australian Computer Journal.*

Davies, N., Gordon, S., Blair, K., & Cheverst, A. (1996). Friday, Supporting collaborative applications in a heterogeneous mobile environment. *Computer Communications, 19,* 346-358.

Elwazer, M., & Zaslavsky, A. (1997, April). Infrastructure support for mobile information systems in Australia. *In Proceedings of Pacific-Asia Conference on Information Systems (PACIS'97),* Brisbane.

Forman, G. H., & Zahorjan, J. (1994). The Challenges of Mobile Computing. *IEEE Computer, 17*(4), 38-47.

Griswold, W. G., Boyer, R., Brown, S. W., & Truong, T. W. (2003). A component architecture for an extensible, highly integrated context-aware computing infrastructure. *In Proceedings of the International Conference on Software Engineering,* (pp. 363–372), Portland, Oregon.

Haahr, M., Cunningham, R., & Cahill, V. (199). Supporting CORBA Applications in a Mobile Environment. *In Proceedings of Mobicom'99,* Seattle, WA, August 15-20.

Hodes, T., Katz, R. H., Servan-Schreiber, E., & Rowe, L. A. (1997, September). Composable Ad-Hoc Mobile Services for Universal Interaction. *Third ACM Mobicom Conference,* Budapest, Hungary.

Imielinski, T., & Badrinath, B. R. (1994). Mobile Wireless Computing: Challenges in Data Management. *Comms. of the ACM, 37,* 18-29.

Imielinski, T., & Korth, *H. F.* (1996). Introduction to Mobile Computing. *Mobile Computing,* 1-43. Kluwer Academic Publishers.

Kunz, T., & Black, J. P. (1999). An Architecture for Adaptive Mobile Applications. *In Proceedings of Wireless '99, Calgary, Canada.*

Lawton, G. (1999, February). Vendors battle over mobile-OS Market. *IEEE Computer,* 13- 15.

Noble, B. (2000, February). System Support for Mobile Adaptive Applications. *IEEE Personal Computer Systems,* 44-49.

Patel, R. B. & Garg, K. (2003). Providing Security and Robustness to Mobile Agents on Open Networks. *In Proceedings of 6th International Conference on Business Information Systems (BIS 2003),* Colorado, Spring, USA, June 4-6, 2003, pp. 66-74. (Received Best Paper Award).

Patel, R. B. (2004). Design and Implementation of a Secure Mobile Agent Platform for Distributed Computing. PhD thesis, Department of Electronics and Computer Engineering, IIT Roorkee, India.

Patel, R., Nikos, B., Mastorakis, K. S. (2005, November). A Platform for Device and Computation Management. *WSEAS Transactions on Circuits and Systems, 4*(11), 1742-1751.

Pissinou, N., Makki, K., Hong, M., Ji, L., & Komar, A. (1997). An Agent Based Mobile System. *In Proceed-*

ings of 16th International Conference On Conceptual Modeling, Los Angels, CA, pp. 361–374, Springer, New York.

Pissinou, N., Makki, K., & Konig-Ries, B. (2003). Mobile users in heterogeneous environments with middleware platform. *Computer Communications, 26,* 700–707.

Pissinou, N., Hossain, M. & Makki, K. (1998). On the Design of a Location and Query Management Strategy for Mobile and Wireless Environments. *Computer Communications Journal, 22,* 651–699.

Salutation Consortium. (1998). White paper: Salutation Architecture.

Satyanarayanan, M. (1996, February). Mobile Information Access. *IEEE Personal Communications, 3*(1), 26-33.

Sousa, J. & Garlan, D. (2002, August). *Aura: an Architectural Framework for User Mobility in Ubiquitous Computing Environments.* Software Architecture System Design, Development and Maintenance (Proceedings of the 3rd Working IEEE/IFIP Conference on Software Architecture). Bosch, Gentleman and Kuusela (Eds.), Kluwer Academic Publishers, pp 29-43.

Sousa, J. P., & Garlan, D. (2003, August). *The Aura Software Architecture: an Infrastructure for Ubiquitous Computing.* Technical Report CMU-CS-03-183, School of Computer Science, Carnegie Mellon University, Pittsburg, PA 15213-3890, August 2003.

Tripathi, A., Karnik, N., Vora, M., Ahmed, T., & Singh, R. (2000). Mobile Agent Programming in Ajanta. *In Proceedings of the 19th International Conference on Distributed Computing Systems (ICDCS '99)*

Universal Plug and Play Forum. Universal Plug And Play Device Architecture.

Wahlster, W. (2000). Verbmobil: Foundations of Speech-to-Speech Translation. Springer, Berlin.

Waldo, J., (2002). *Technology Architectural Overview.* White Paper, Sun Microsystems: available at http://wwws.sun.com/software/**jini**/whitepapers/architecture.html, 2002.

Weiserm, M. (1991). The computer for the 21st century. *Scientific American, 3*(265), 94–104.

Wi-Fi, Cellular, and Wired Networks Merging To Form Pervasive Networks in Homes and Offices, Says INSIGHT Research, available at http://www.prweb.com/releases/2004/12/prwebxml190056.php

Yeo, L. H., & Zaslavsky (1994, June). Submission of Transactions from Mobile Computers in a Cooperative Multidatabase Processing Environment. *Proceedings of IEEE/CS 14th International Conference on Distributed Computing Systems*, Poland, (pp. 372-379).

Chapter XXXIX
Mobility in IP Networks

Sanjay Jasola
Wawasan Open University, Malaysia

Ramesh C. Sharma
Indira Gandhi National Open University, India

ABSTRACT

With the ever increasing use of portable and hand held devices for voice and data transfer, there is a growing expectation to access information anytime, anywhere. Today there are different technologies providing access to voice, data, and video. These need to be converged in all Internet protocol (IP) based network. Next generation telecom networks will be having convergence of voice and data traffic and use of IP based mobility solutions. Mobile IP is a TCP/IP-based protocol that has been standardized by the IETF (Internet Engineering Task Force) for supporting mobility. Mobile IP is part of both IPv4 and IPv6 standards. Mobile IP works at network layer (layer 3), influencing the routing of packets and can easily handle mobility among different media. This chapter discusses different technical operations involved in Mobile IPv4 and Mobile IPv6 and compares them.

INTRODUCTION

Wireless mobile devices are encountered almost everywhere i.e. at home, at work, on the road. These are being used to access the Internet and to provide data services in general. This leads to a growing expectation of the users to be able to access information anytime anywhere. Open, flexible architectures that can be adapted quickly to changes in communications standards or customer demands are being developed by the standards organization like IEEE and IETF. Separate networks that transmit voice, data, and video are converging into pipelines that are capable of delivering all three. The term "mobile" refers to connectivity and automatically maintenance of one

or more Internet applications of the user despite the change of user's point of attachment. TCP/IP protocol (Transmission Control Protocol/Internet Protocol) is playing an increasingly important role in the mobility. Generic scenario of IP mobility is that when an IP node moves to a new network, it has to change its IP address to reflect the new point of attachment. Every time a mobile node moves to a new network, a solution to infrequent roaming is to change the IP address as seen by the transport and the application layers. This solution can not be used for mobility in general. This is because the IP address is known to the next higher layer in the protocol architecture. When a TCP connection is set up, TCP entity on each side of the connection knows the IP address of correspondent node. When a TCP segment is handed down to IP layer for delivery, TCP provides IP address. IP layer creates an IP datagram with that IP address in IP header and sends the datagram to the data link layer. If this IP address is changed, then the correlation is lost and the sessions need to be restarted. Mobile IP depends on giving the mobile node two IP addresses and managing the correlation between a changing IP address called care-of address and static home address. Transport and application layers keep using the home address, allowing them to remain ignorant of any mobility taking place.

The rest of the paper is organized as follows. In section 2, the different operations involved in Mobile IPv4 have been explained. In section 3, features of Mobile IPv6 for supporting mobility in IPv6 based networks are discussed. The features of Mobile IPv4 and Mobile IPv6 are compared in section 4. The future directions are discussed in section 5. Finally section 6 summarizes the conclusions.

MOBILE IPV4

Mobile IP (Perkins, 1997) was originally defined for IPv4 through IETF request for comment (RFC) 2002 and finally through RFC 3344 (Perkins, 2002). The mobility support for IPv4 is an add-on, and the vast majority of IPv4 nodes do not support Mobile IP. Mobile IP for IPv4 is comprised of following four components, mobile node (MN), home agent (HA), foreign agent (FA) and correspondent node (CN) as shown in figure 1.

A MN is a node, for example, a PDA, a laptop computer, or a data-ready cellular phone. A mobile node is assigned to a particular network, known as its

home network. A HA is a router on the home network of the MN that maintains an association between the home IP address of the MN and its *care-of address* (CoA), which is the current location of the MN on a foreign or visited network. A CN is a node which is communicating with the mobile node. A FA is a router on foreign network that assists the MN in informing its current CoA to HA. IP address of MN on its home network is known as home address and it is static. The address of home agent is known as HA address. While a mobile node is attached to some foreign link away from home, it is also addressable at one or more care-of addresses. The mobile node can acquire its care-of address through conventional IPv4 mechanism. Mobile IP includes four basic capabilities to support mobility operations which are agent discovery, registration, tunneling and de-registration.

Agent Discovery

During agent discovery phase, HAs and FAs advertise their presence on their network by periodically multicasting or broadcasting messages called *agent advertisements.* MN uses discovery procedure to identify prospective home agents and foreign agents. Any home agent can also offer its services as a foreign agent for the mobile nodes that are visiting its area. The discovery process in Mobile IP is similar to router advertisement process defined in ICMP (Internet Control Message Protocol) (Perkins, 1998). Accordingly, agent discovery makes use of extended ICMP router discovery protocol (EIRDP). The extended router advertisement and router solicitation messages are known as agent advertisement and agent solicitation messages (Stallings, 2001). The *agent advertisement extension* follows the ICMP router advertisement fields and consists of the fields which indicate the CoA supported by this agent on the network, type of tunneling supported and lifetime, in seconds, to accept a registration request from a MN.

Mobile node listens to advertisements of the FA and HA and determines if it is connected to its home link or a foreign link. MN compares the network portion of the received IP address with the network portion of its own home address. If these network portions do not match, then the MN is on a foreign network. Because handoff from one network to another occurs at the physical layer, a transition from the home network to a foreign network can occur at any time without notification to the network layer. Thus, agent discovery for a MN is an ongoing process that lists one or more

Figure 1. General scenario of data transfer in Mobile IPv4

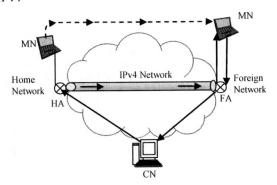

Figure 2. Agent discovery and registration processes in Mobile IPv4

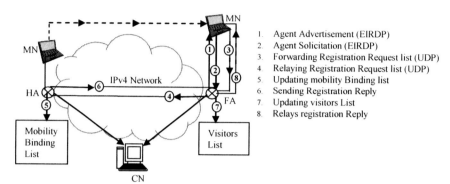

1. Agent Advertisement (EIRDP)
2. Agent Solicitation (EIRDP)
3. Forwarding Registration Request list (UDP)
4. Relaying Registration Request list (UDP)
5. Updating mobility Binding list
6. Sending Registration Reply
7. Updating visitors List
8. Relays registration Reply

available CoAs and informs MN about the special features provided by FA. If a MN determines that it is connected to a foreign link, it acquires a CoA. Two types of CoA exist, foreign agent CoA and co-located CoA. A co-located CoA is an IP address temporarily assigned to the interface of MN by the mobile node itself or through dynamic host configuration protocol (DHCP). A co-located CoA represents the current position of MN on the foreign network and can be used by only one MN at a time.

Instead of waiting for agent advertisements, MN can also send an *agent solicitation.* This solicitation forces any agents on the link to immediately send an agent advertisement. If advertisements are no longer detectable from a foreign agent that previously had offered a CoA to the MN, The MN presumes that foreign agent is no longer within the range of the MN's network interface (Campbell & Gomez, 2001). The agent discovery and registration processes are shown in figure 2.

Registration

The registration process communicates between an application on MN and other application in the home agent, hence uses a transport-level protocol. Registration is a simple request and response transaction, so u*ser datagram protocol* (UDP) is used. R*egistration request message* and r*egistration reply message are two messages* carried in UDP segments. A MN uses an authenticated registration procedure to inform its HA of its CoA. Registration process ensures that registration request is actually sent by agent rather than an attacker seeking to impersonate actual user. After receiving a care-of address, the MN registers

this CoA with its HA through exchange of messages. The *registration request message* consists of fields for lifetime, home address, CoA and address of HA. It also contains the *identification field which is a* 64-bit number generated by the MN, used for matching registration requests to registration replies and for security purposes.

The MN forwards a registration request message with CoA, its permanent home address and its HA address to FA which in turn relays this registration request to HA. The home agent checks the validity of the registration request, which includes authentication of the MN. If the registration request is valid, it updates the mobility binding list by associating the CoA of the MN with its home address. To send the packets of a local host on home network to MN, local host will compare its network ID with that of MN and realizes that it is on same network so will not route its packets but directly send them to MN through layer 2. The local host will use address resolution protocol (ARP) to get the data link layer address of MN. Local host searches its ARP cache and if it finds media access control (MAC) address of MN, it will use this address. As the MN is not present in its home network, the packets will never reach MN. When there is no ARP entry in cache, local host sends an ARP request to get MAC address of MN. Home agent sets up a proxy ARP. Proxy ARP is a technique in which HA answers ARP requests intended for MN and provides its MAC address to local host which wants to communicate with MN. Because of the movement of MN to a foreign area, the ARP entries of local hosts corresponding to MN will not be valid. Hence, HA sends gratuitous ARP to all local hosts on home network to refresh their ARP cache which associates the

Figure 3. IP within IP encapsulation

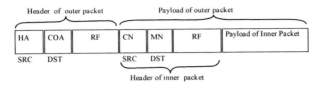

data link layer address of HA with the IP address of mobile node. The home agent then sends a registration reply to the foreign agent. HA returns the 64 bit identification value and life time of registration along with address of HA and home address of MN. If the registration reply is valid, FA adds MN to its visitor list and relays the reply to the MN. This process is shown in figure 2.

The HA must be certain that registration was originated by the MN and not some other malicious node pretending to be the MN. Mobile IP is designed to resist two types of attacks (Lass et al, 2000 ; Perkins, 2000). In the first case, a node may pretend to be a foreign agent and sends a registration request to a home agent so as to divert traffic intended for a MN to itself. In second case, a malicious agent may replay old registration messages, effectively cutting the MN from the network. The technique that is used to protect against such attacks involves the use of message authentication and the use of the identification field of the registration request and reply messages. Registration request and reply messages use authentication extension for message authentication among home agent, foreign agent and mobile node. The default authentication algorithm uses keyed message-digest algorithm 5 (MD5) to produce a 128 bits message digest. The message digest is generated by placing identification field of registration message between shared secret keys. The authentication extension protects the identification field, which protects from above two types of attacks.

Tunneling

Tunneling is used to forward IP packets from a home address to a CoA. Being a layer 3 protocol, Mobile IP deals routing of packets to mobile users. Mobile IP offers a tunneling based solution. Different types of tunneling used are IP-within-IP encapsulation (Perkins, 1998), minimum encapsulation (Perkins,

1996) and GRE tunneling (Farinacci et al, 2000). The traffic destined for the MN is forwarded in a triangular manner. When the CN sends a packet to the MN, HA intercepts packets using proxy ARP and then encapsulates packets. When an IP packet is put inside other IP packet, this process is known as encapsulation. These encapsulated packets are then tunneled to the care-of address of the MN on the foreign network. After receiving packets from the HA, FA decapsulates these packets and forwards them locally to the MN. However, packets sent by MN are routed directly to CN with source as home address. This will cause packets to be dropped by ingress filtering as routers discard packets which contain the source address that is topologically incorrect.

In the IP-within-IP encapsulation approach, the inner original IP header is unchanged except that *time to live* (TTL) is decremented by 1. The outer header is a full IP header. Two fields viz. version number and the type of service are same for inner and outer header. These are copied from the inner header to outer header. RF refers to the remaining fields of the IP header. In the inner IP header, source address refers to host that is sending original packet, and destination address is the home address of the intended recipient. In the outer IP header, the source and destination addresses refer to the entry and exit points of the tunnel i.e. home agent, and the care-of address for the intended destination. The format of IP-within-IP encapsulation is shown in figure 3.

Minimal encapsulation results in less overhead and can be used if the MN, home agent, and foreign agent all agree to do so by exchanging agent advertisement and registration messages with M bit set to 1. With minimal encapsulation, the new header is inserted between the original IP header and the original IP payload. The processing for minimal encapsulation is as follows. The home agent prepares the encapsulated packet with the specified format. This packet is now suitable for tunneling and is delivered across the Inter-

Figure 4. General scenario of Mobile IPv6

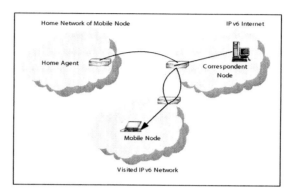

net to the care-of address. At the care-of address, the fields in the minimal forwarding header are restored to the original IP header and the forwarding header is removed from the packet. Total length field in the IP header is decremented by the size of the minimal forwarding header (8 or 12) and the header checksum field is recomputed.

Deregistration

When MN powers down or determines that it is re-connected to its home link, it deregisters by sending a registration request with the lifetime set to zero. The HA then reclaims the MN. There is no need for deregistering with the foreign agent as registration automatically expires when lifetime becomes zero.

Extension to Mobile IPv4

Many enhancements have been proposed to Mobile IPv4 to counter some of the identified problems, which include triangular routing, ingress filtering and multiple home agents. These are explained briefly below.

Triangular routing: All packets sent to the MN are routed through its home agent, causing increased load on the home network and higher latency. This problem could be solved with route optimization extension (M ho et al., 1998), which is explained in section 3.2.

Ingress filtering: A denial of service (DOS) attack is characterized by an explicit attempt by attackers to prevent legitimate users of a service from using that service. In order to consume bandwidth and resources,

attackers flood the victim with as many packets as possible in a short span of time. In order to prolong the effectiveness of the attack, they spoof source IP addresses to make tracing and stopping of DOS difficult. Spoofing is a method of sending a packet with a forged source IP address. To avoid DOS attacks, border routers incorporate ingress filtering (Ferguson & Senie, 1998). In this method, routers allow a packet only when its source address field is consistent with its origin. In Mobile IPv4, the MNs that are away from home, i.e., in a foreign link, use their home address as the source IP address for sending packets to CN. The routers incorporating ingress filtering will not permit the packets sent by MN with their home address as the source IP address to CN, so Mobile IPv4 was updated to include reverse tunneling (Montenegro, 2001). In reverse tunneling, all packets travel via home network in both directions. This step wastes more bandwidth and adds latency.

Multiple home agents: Single home agent model is simple and easy to configure, but once HA breaks down, MN becomes unreachable. **It is, therefore,** advantageous to have multiple HAs. If one home agent fails, there are other home agents who can route packets for the MN.

MOBILE IPv6

Mobile IPv6 is a protocol developed in the Mobile IP working group of the IETF and it carries forward the work done in Mobile IPv4. Basic purpose of Mobile IPv6 (Johnson & Perkins, 2004) is to provide a functionality for handling the terminal, or node mobility between IPv6 subnets. For IPv6, the mobility support has been included since inception so it is expected that all IPv6 nodes will have minimal mobile IP support. In Mobile IPv6, all the elements like HA, MN, CN are present except foreign agent. While a MN is attached to some foreign link away from home, it is also addressable at one or more CoAs. As long as the MN stays in this location, packets addressed to this care-of address will be routed to the mobile node. Figure 4 shows the general scenario of Mobile IPv6.

While away from home, MN registers its primary CoA with home agent by sending a binding message. Mobility header is used by MN, CN and home agents in all messaging related to creation and management of bindings. Mobile IPv6 provides support for multiple home agents, and reconfiguration of home network. In these cases, MN may not know the IP address of its own HA and even the home subnet prefixes may change over time. A mechanism known as dynamic home agent address discovery allows a MN to dynamically discover the IP address of a HA on its home link, even when the MN is away from home. MNs can also learn new information about home subnet prefixes through prefix discovery mechanism. Mobile IPv6 also introduces four new ICMP (Conta & Deering, 1998) message types, two for use in the dynamic home agent address discovery mechanism, and two for renumbering and mobile configuration mechanisms. Home agent address discovery reply and home agent address discovery request are two new ICMP message types used for home agent address discovery. Mobile prefix solicitation and mobile prefix advertisement message types are used for network renumbering and address configuration on the MN.

Tunneling is avoided in Mobile IPv6 as much as possible. Though the first few packets of every session are still tunneled via the home agent, MN also sends binding updates to every CN. Mobile IPv6 defines a new routing header variant, viz. the type 2 routing header. It allows the packets to be routed directly from a CN to CoA of MN. This type 2 routing header enables firewalls to apply different rule to source routed packets than to Mobile IPv6. When routing packets directly to MN, CN sets destination address in IPv6 header to CoA of MN. Similarly, MN sets source address in the IPv6 header to its current CoA. MN adds a new IPv6 home address destination option to carry its home address. The inclusion of home address in these packets makes use of CoA transparent above the network layer.

Movement Detection

Movement detection is used to detect L3 (layer 3) handovers. Because of mobility of a node, change of point of attachment from one to another, is called handover. MN can determine its current location by listening to the router advertisement. In the absence of router advertisements, MN might be unaware of L3 handover that occurred. So indications from link-layer are used. MN uses neighbor un-reachability to find out that default router is no longer bi-directionally reachable. Once MN has detected an L3 handover, it will perform duplicate address detection on its link-local address, selects a new default router as a consequence of router discovery and then performs prefix discovery with the new router to form new CoA. To obtain a CoA, the MN can use either stateful (Dromes, 2003) or stateless (Thomson & Narten, 1998) address auto-configuration. In the first situation, the MN obtains a CoA from a DHCPv6 server. In case of stateless auto-configuration, the MN extracts the network prefixes from the router advertisements and adds a unique interface identifier to form a CoA.

Location Update

Binding messages are used to update the location of mobile node. While away from home, a MN registers its primary CoA with a router on its home link, requesting this router to function as the home agent for the MN. The MN performs this binding registration by sending a binding update (BU) message to HA. BU is used to

Figure 5. Binding management in MIPv6

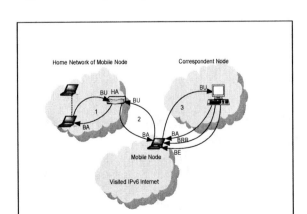

inform the HA and any active CN of current (new) binding. It consists of new CoA, the home address and a binding lifetime. Each IPv6 node is required to understand BU message, enabling the packets destined to MN to be efficiently routed without going through the HA. Initially a new CN knows only home address, but when MN receives packets routed via HA, it can send a BU to the new CN. When MN moves back to its home link, it will notify the home agent to delete the binding. HA replies to MN by returning a binding acknowledgement (BA) message that is used to acknowledge receipt of a BU, if an acknowledgement was requested in BU. MN can provide information about their current location to CNs. If CN wants to know CoA of MN, it can send a binding refresh request (BRR) to MN, which does not necessarily have to respond to the request by sending a BU. A BRR is used to request MN to re-establish its binding with CN. This message is typically used when the cached binding is in active use but the lifetime of binding is close to expiration. Binding error (BE) is used by CN to signal an error related to mobility, such as an inappropriate attempt to use home address destination option without an existing binding. All the above cases have been shown as 1, 2 and 3 in figure 5.

The binding messages are sent using the mobility header, which is shown in figure 6. Payload proto field identifies header type immediately followed by mobility header. Header length represents the length of mobility header. MH type defines whether it is a BU, BA and BRR etc. All these are implemented as IPv6 destination options, allowing them to be either piggybacked with any IPv6 packet being destined to a desired destination, or sent separately with no upper layer payload. Checksum contains the checksum for mobility header. Message data field contains data specific to indicated mobility header type. IP Security is applied to BU and BA. IPsec authentication header (AH) (Kent & Atkinson, 1998) is required for authentication. Encapsulating security payload (ESP) (Kent & Atkinson, 1998) can also be used together with AH, if encryption is desired. No authentication is required for binding refresh request.

Data Communication in Mobile IPv6

There are two possible modes of communication between MN and CN. The first mode, bi-directional tunneling, does not require Mobile IPv6 support from CN and is available even if the MN has not registered its current binding with CN. It is shown in figure 7.

Packets from CN are routed to HA and then tunneled to MN. Packets to CN are reversed tunneled from MN to HA and then routed normally from home network to CN. In this mode, HA uses proxy neighbor discovery to intercept any IPv6 packets addressed to the home address of MN on home link. Each intercepted packet is tunneled to the primary CoA of MN. This tunneling is performed using IPv6 encapsulation (Sanmateu et al, 2002).

The second mode known as route optimization, requires MN to register its current binding at CN. Packets from CN can be routed directly to CoA of MN. When sending a packet to any IPv6 destination, CN checks its cached bindings for an entry for the packet's destination address. If a cached binding for this destination address is found, node uses type 2 routing header to route packets to the MN by way of CoA indicated in this binding. When packets are routed directly to the CoA of MN, it allows shortest communication path to be used. It also eliminates congestion at the home agent of MN. In addition, the impact of any possible failure of HA or networks on the path to or from it, is reduced.

Extensions to Mobile IPv6

Fast Handovers for Mobile IPv6: Any change from one point of attachment to another of a node because of its mobility, is called handover or handoff. Fast handover mechanism for Mobile IPv6 (Koodli, 2005) focuses on reducing lengthy address resolution time when entering a foreign domain. It describes two different types of handover mechanisms. These are tunnel based and anticipated handover. Tunnel based handover relies on L2 trigger and anticipated handover is solely based on L3 information.

Hierarchical Mobile IPv6: In Mobile IPv6, every movement of MN introduces rather long registration latency. Hierarchical schemes separate mobility management into micro and macro mobility. The handoff operations regarding latency and signaling overheads can be optimized in micro-mobility. Hierarchical mobile IPv6 (Soliman et al, 2005) introduces a new entity called mobility anchor point (MAP). It allows a MN to send only one binding update to MAP to register its new CoA after movement within a local MAP domain. HMIPv6 allows MN to register locally in a domain and then minimizes the amount of signaling to HA and MN.

QoS: It is essential to provide proper quality of service (QoS) forwarding treatment to packets sent by

Figure 6. Mobility header

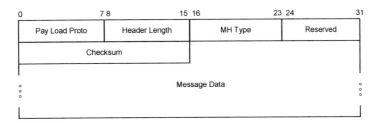

or destined to MN as they propagate along different routes in the network due to node mobility (Manner et al, 2002). There are two main architectures supported by IETF for ensuring QoS in IP based networks. These are integrated service (IntServ) architecture (Braden, Clark & Shenker, 1994) and differentiated service (DiffServ) architecture (Blake et al, 1998). The applications need to state their requirements, either ahead of time in some sort of service request functions, or on the fly by means of fields in the IP packet header. In case of IntServ, the former approach is chosen whereas the later approach is chosen in DiffServ. The IntServ architecture provides a kind of circuit switched service in packet switched network. IntServ architecture is characterized by resource reservation. An application requiring QoS must first set up paths and reserve resources. The Resource ReSerVation Protocol (RSVP) (Braden et al, 1997) is a signaling protocol for setting up paths and reserving resources. RSVP has been chosen as a signaling protocol for IntServ. Although IntServ has made significant progress towards providing QoS, it is widely considered too heavyweight to scale across Internet. DiffServ architecture addresses the issue of scalability by defining QoS mechanism that operates on aggregates of flows with similar QoS requirements. The DiffServ architecture achieves its scaling properties by offering hop-by-hop differentiated treatment of packets.

MOBILE IPv4 VS MOBILE IPV6

Mobile IP provides mobility support in both the versions of IP. In IPv4, it is Mobile IPv4 and in IPv6 it is Mobile IPv6. Mobile IPv6 protocol has the advantages of being developed from the experiences gained from development of Mobile IPv4 and features supported by IPv6. Mobile IPv4 uses a separate UDP for registrations. In Mobile IPv6, mobility features are built as header extensions which allows IPv6 packets to contain the extra protocol information to deal with issues such as QoS and prioritization. In mobile IP, extensible headers are used to make each packet contain both the permanent and the care-of address, satisfying both higher-level protocols and Internet routers. Major differences between Mobile IPv4 and Mobile IPv6 are given below.

In Mobile IPv6, foreign agents are not required as in Mobile IPv4. Route optimization is a fundamental part of the protocol and it can operate securely even without pre-arranged security associations. It is also possible for allowing route optimization to coexist efficiently with routers that perform ingress filtering. Mobile IPv6 can handle the mobility management in multi-access network e.g. a network with wideband code division multiple access (WCDMA) and wireless local area network (WLAN) coverage using multi-mode mobile terminals supporting both technologies. Mobile IPv6 uses neighbour discovery of IPv6 so it is decoupled from any particular link layer and improves robustness. Mobile IPv4 uses ARP. In Mobile IPv6, the movement detection mechanism provides bidirectional confirmation of the ability of mobile node to communicate with its default router in its current location. In Mobile IPv6, most packets sent to MN are sent using an IPv6 routing header rather than IP encapsulation, reducing amount of overhead compared to Mobile IPv4. The advantage of using dynamic home agent address discovery mechanism in Mobile IPv6 is that it returns single reply whereas in Mobile IPv4 broadcast returns separate replies from each home agent.

Figure 7. Data communication using bidirectional tunneling in Mobile IPv 6

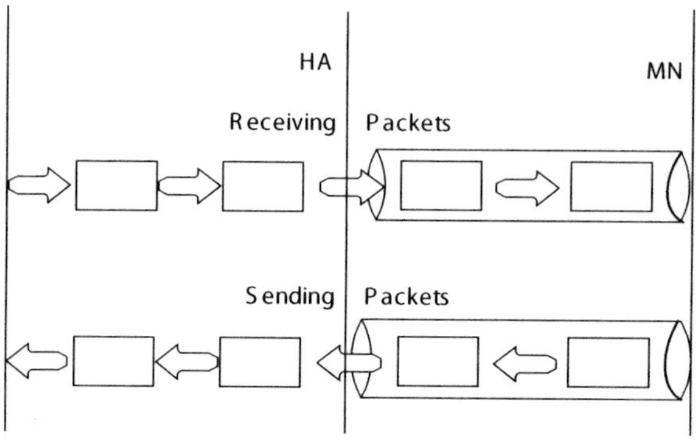

FUTURE DIRECTION

IPv4 has proved to be a robust, easy to implement and interoperable protocol suite. It has passed the test of scaling from an internetwork to Internet which is a global utility today. Although IPv4 has not changed since RFC 791 was published in 1981, but the exponential growth of the Internet has resulted in inadequacy of the IPv4 addresses. As a result of this, network address translator (NAT) has been used to plan multiple private addresses to a single public IP address. Under such developments, IPv6 provides a significant backbone for next generation networking technology. Some of the benefits offered by IPv6 include lower network administration costs, protection of company assets via unified security model, investment protection by phased transition and deployment of new applications. Another advancement is in the form of 128 bit addresses of IPv6 (IPv4 has 32 bit addresses). This results in a very large increase in the number of IP addresses available, facilitates end-to-end connectivity, auto-configuration of IP addresses on IPv6-enabled devices, offering a solid security framework for Internet communication in the form of IPSEC. But a word of caution is also in place as the switchover from IPv4 to IPv6 would take some time as the applications, hosts, routers and DNS to support the IPv6 will take time to fully convert to IPv6-nodes only. Till then IPv6 and IPv4 would coexist.

CONCLUSION

Mobile IP is a layer 3 protocol, which enables a mobile node to use its home IP address despite its movement in a foreign area. Mobile IP works by maintaining two IP addresses per host i.e. a fixed home address and a dynamic care of address. In this paper, the operations of Mobile IPv4 and Mobile IPv6 protocols are reviewed and compared. In the both versions of Mobile IP, three major operations are performed. These are movement detection, location update and data communication. Agent advertisements are used to detect the movement of the node. Registration process is used for location update. In case of Mobile IPv4, UDP based registration messages are used. Mobility header based bindings are used for location update in Mobile IPv6. The tunnels are used for data communication in Mobile IPv4. In Mobile IPv6, more efficient method of data communication called route optimization is used. Mobile IP enables transparent routing of IP packets to mobile node during its movement. Mobile IP is most useful in environments where a wireless technology is utilized. This includes cellular environment as well as wireless LAN situations that may require mobility. Mobile IP is still used rarely, partly because there is little need for it and partly because present implementations waste bandwidth and requires at least two precious IP addresses per user. However, Mobile IP is expected to become more important as wireless networks and IPv6 become ubiquitous.

REFERENCES

Blake S. et al, (1998). *An Architecture for Differentiated Services*, RFC 2475, IETF.

Braden R. et al, (1997). Resource ReSerVation Protocol (RSVP) – Version 1, *Functional Specification*, IETF, RFC 2205, September.

Braden, R., Clark, D., & Shenker, S. (1994). *Integrated Services in the Internet Architecture: An Overview*, IETF, RFC 1633.

Campbell, A. T., & Gomez, J. (2001). IP micro-mobility protocols. *ACM SIGMOBILE Mobile Computer and Communication Review (MC2R) 4*(4), 45-54.

Conta, A., & Deering, S. (1998). *Internet Control Message Protocol (ICMPv6) for the Internet protocol version 6 (ipv6) specification.* RFC 2463, IETF.

Dromes, R. (2003). *Dynamic Host Configuration Protocol for IPv6,* RFC 3315, IETF.

Farinacci D. et al, (2000). *Generic Routing Encapsulation*, RFC 2784, IETF.

Ferguson, P., & Senie, D. (1998). *Network Ingress Filtering: Defeating Denial of Service Attacks which employs IP source address spoofing*, RFC 2267, IETF.

Johnson, D., & Perkins, C. (2004). Mobility Support in IPv6, RFC 3775, IETF.

Kent, S., & Atkinson, R. (1998). *IP Authentication Header.* RFC 2402, IETF.

Kent, S., & Atkinson, R. (1998). *IP Encapsulating Security Payload* (ESP), RFC 2406.

Koodli, R. (2005). *Fast Handovers for Mobile IPv6*, RFC 4068, IETF.

Lass S. G. et al, (2000). *Mobile IP Authentication, Authorization and Accounting Requirements*, RFC 2977, IETF.

M ho J.S. et al., (1998). Mobility Management in Current and Future Communication networks. *IEEE Network, 12*, 39-49.

Manner J. et al, (2002). Evaluation of mobility and quality of service interaction. *Computer Networks, 38*, 137-163.

Montenegro, G. (2001). *Reverse Tunneling for Mobile IP*, RFC 3024, IETF.

Perkins, C. (1996). *Minimal Encapsulation within IP*. RFC 2004, IETF.

Perkins, C. (1997). Mobile IP. *IEEE Communication magazine, 35*, 84-99.

Perkins, C. (1998). *Mobile IP: Design Principles and Practice.* Prentice Hall PTR

Perkins, C. (1998). Mobile Networking through Mobile IP. *IEEE Internet Computing*, January.

Perkins, C. (2000). *Mobile IPv4 Challenge/Response Extensions*, RFC 3012, IETF.

Perkins, C. (2002). *IP Mobility Support for IPv4*, RFC 3344, IETF.

Sanmateu A. M. et al, (2002). Seamless mobility across IP networks using Mobile IP. *Computer Networks, 41*(5), 181-190.

Soliman H. et al, (2005). *Hierarchical Mobile IPv6 mobility management*, RFC 4140, IETF.

Stallings, W. (2001). *Mobile IP, The Internet Protocol Journal*, Cisco Systems.

Thomson, S. & Narten, T. (1998). *IPv6 Stateless Address Auto-configuration.* RFC 2462, IETF.

KEY TERMS

Mobile IP: An IP enhancement that forwards e-mail and other data to moving users.

TCP/IP: A communications protocol to internetwork dissimilar systems.

Tunneling: Carrying a protocol from another networking system within an IP packet.

Chapter XL
Role of Mobile Technologies in an Environmentally Responsible Business Strategy

Bharti Trivedi
DDU Nadiad, India

Bhuvan Unhelkar
MethodScience.com & University of Western Sydney, Australia

ABSTRACT

This chapter aims to investigate and expand the role of mobile technologies in an Environmentally Responsible Business Strategy (ERBS). An ERBS with mobile technologies can help organizations achieve socially responsible goals of reducing green house emissions, reducing physical movement of men and materials, and recycling materials, to name a few. Organizations are electronically collaborating globally through the medium of the Internet and by employing service-oriented architectures. This electronic collaboration amongst large numbers of globally spread businesses creates a collaborative business "ecosystem" that is also virtual. Virtual collaborations between businesses create further challenges for environmentally responsible strategies as they make it difficult to identify the precise contributors to green house emissions and pollutions. This chapter delves deeper into the role of mobile technologies in creating and enhancing what can be considered as Environmental Intelligence (EI) – extending business intelligence with mobility for a "Green" enterprise.

INTRODUCTION

This chapter discusses the effect of mobility on a collaborative business ecosystem. Previously, before the advent of the Internet connectivity, business implied physical commercial transactions between entities that were in close proximity with each other. This business understanding was particularly true before

the advent of the ability of the Internet-based services to enable electronic-commerce and, more recently, mobile commerce. Today, however, communication network structures and the corresponding concepts of business collaboration (Ghanbary and Unhelkar, 2009) are perceived as effective means to cope with the challenges of 21st century business transactions and growth. This business growth today is characterized as global and competitive (Gothlich, 2003). The globalization of business organizations is achieved by the communication revolution that is based on the use of computers, their peripherals (such as monitors, printers, storage devices) and strong, standardized and reliable networking and communications systems. Information and Communications Technologies (ICT) play a vital role in the development of any collaborative system. However, this phenomenal and ever increasing use of networks and computers also puts increasing demands on energy consumption. Computers and other IT infrastructure consume significant amounts of electrical energy, placing a heavy burden on the electric grid and contribute to greenhouse gas emissions. Greenhouse gas emission is creating an imbalance in our environmental equilibrium. In addition, computers pose severe environmental problems both during manufacture and at disposal. (Unhelkar and Dickens, 2008)

However, most studies related to green house gases and the strategies to reduce their emissions and effect on the environment are focused on the 'hardware' aspect of ICT. There is a significant need to study, understand and change the 'process' aspect of ICT in business. This process aspect of ICT in business comprises 'how' we use the people, processes and technologies of business which can reduce the carbon footprints. The need to persuade the business activities of an organization, including the way in which its people and technologies and employed and its processes are carried out from an eco-friendly viewpoint is vital. However, creation of such eco-friendly business processes can succeed only when it's a part of the overall environmentally responsible business strategy. Mobile communications integrated in the business strategy can help to attain an environmentally responsible strategy. Mobile devices require less power and generate less heat than full workstations or PC's , their cooling cost is also less than the PC's, so the company enjoys the benefits of powering a small unit,. Using mobile devices instead of conventional PCs would lower energy consumption by 51 percent and reduce CO2 emissions, concludes a recent study by the Fraunhofer Institute (www.windowsfordevices.com). Mobile capabilities not only can improve the style of the business by automating process and promoting more reliable connections but also will be a step ahead towards green environment. The business-specific applications can be developed for the mobile devices and solutions that target improvements in areas including email and Internet access, automation of paper-based processes, training and

professional development, asset management, employee safety, inventory management, collaboration and security. This will result to an Environmentally Responsible Business Strategy (ERBS).

This chapter discusses and incorporates the use of mobility in the overall greenhouse gas emission, which is creating an imbalance in our environmental equilibrium of an organization.

SIGNIFICANT FACTORS IN THE CREATION AND IMPLEMENTATION OF AN ERBS

Mobility is increasingly playing a vital role in the development of environmentally intelligent (EI) systems. Mobility helps to strengthen the social as well as business relations and also have positive environmental aspects.

Mobility infrastructure planning is an increasingly crucial aspect of environmental planning, essential to boost regional economies and social relations, as well as critical for environmental impacts involved. Structuring inherently complex issues and problems is a major challenge of mobility planning. Today, therefore, a major issue is the setting up of system architectures that take into account the impacts of the mobility system on environmental and social quality (Borri, Camarda and Liddo, 2005). Mobile devices and their applications are no longer a mystery for any one. Now a days the corporate world believes in virtual or mobile employment strategy where workers need not be present at the company offices. The employees have an access to the crucial business intelligent information system and according the authorities analyze, plan the finance and make strategies.

Dial up connectivity and wireless access have empowered most (Business Intelligence) BI users to access, analyze, and share information if they are sitting at their desks or to access data from their home.

The need of the business community for mobile Business intelligence is obvious, and if business personnel are not physically moving from one place to another and are not using any vehicle then we can say that network mobility is a one successful step in going green. Mobile business intelligence plays a vital role to attain an ERBS as location independently strategic business objectives can be met without any physical movement. Therefore, ICT must have its own set of mobile BI capabilities to maintain and sustain the

Figure 1. Significant Factors in the creation and implementation of an ERBS

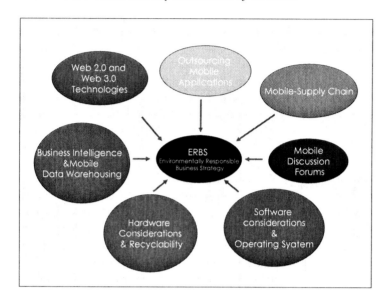

overall environment (Imhoff ,2005). Figure 1 shows significant factors which help in the creation and implementation of an ERBS.

Business Intelligence (BI) and Mobile Data warehousing (DW) : Business Intelligence (BI) can be thought of as a bunch of applications and techniques to collect, store , process , analyze and access the data to achieve fast and better business decisions. Decision support system (DSS), online analytical processing (OLAP), statistical analysis, forecasting, data mining are mainly used tools in BI. An ERBS combined with BI can result in a centrally driven architecture that integrates with an enterprise's operation. This centrally driven architecture of data organization will help to reduce the number of data centers, and reduced number of data centers is directly proportional to reduction in the consumption of the electrical energy.

Business Intelligence plays a very significant role in Decision Support System. Strategic decisions on data integration with the help of data warehousing, an operational data store, multiple data marts, metadata repository, Online analytical processing (OLAP) can help the company to make better decisions with best utilization of the resources (Enterprise own resources as well as outsourced resources) (Moss , 2006). Mobility enhances the data sharing among the business collaboration and thus enables location independent data sharing. Once the data set is retrieved, the logical and physical designs should be modeled and reviewed

in such a way that the access time becomes less and also the data which is extracted very often should be stored in cache data repository to minimize the data retrieval time. (Slebodnick,2006) To access data using mobile devices web must be considered as a platform so that database as well as web services can be accessed through the mobile device. Using optimal search techniques will reduce the burden on the mobile networks. Data warehouse on the web can make the data available anywhere, anytime monitoring the carbon emissions by reducing the paper use and minimizing the walled offices. Thus this strategy will implemented in the corporate business ecosystem will result in an ERBS.

Software concepts (Operating System design): Computers are an integral part of any business and they emit CO_2 while working, so there should be environmental sensors and intelligent control to monitor remote computing system. A wireless control is preferable to generate an alert in response to the occurrence of a monitored event. Mobile device management solutions can support various devices in different operating systems. The mobile devices supported by mobile device management can be used for asset management, marketing, outsourcing, security and information distribution and other business collaborative activities location independently. This can ensure performance and availability of the corporate system by real time access of the enterprise. The integration of the operating system on the mobile devices provides real time access of the enterprise; enable the managers of the enterprise to take better decisions, increase customer service and satisfaction and thus increases business productivity and profitability. This leads to an ERBS as the execution of the corporate activities will be handled by the mobile gadgets which emits less CO_2 as compared to desktop computers as discussed in the previous section of this chapter, it also reduces the unnecessary movement of men and material and result in green computing.

Hardware Considerations: Desktop computers and its peripherals are manufactured with many toxic materials such as lead, cadmium, zinc etc. Hardware companies who manufacture computers have to think in the direction to make a computer which help to reduce environmental impacts. Energy use is an important issue for computer manufacturers. Rising energy prices, concerns about energy security and increasing pressure from society to reduce greenhouse gas (GHG) emissions related to fossil fuels, have heightened the demand for energy efficiency and renewable energy sources. (Unhelkar and Dickens, 2008). The huge demand of power and it's extraction from hydrocarbons (ex: coal) lead to accumulation of carbon dioxide and green house gases which in turn lead to the dramatic increase in our Earth's temperature, and is threatening life on the long term(Fares 8, 2008). Mobile computers such as notebooks, sub notebooks, and palmtops require low weight, low power consumption, and good interactive performance (Douglis, Cáceres, Kaashoek, Krishnan, Li, Marsh, Tauber, 1994). *Mobile Computing* technology is helping schools, businesses and organizations worldwide dramatically reduce carbon emissions by cutting energy consumption up to 90 percent. With more than 500,000 virtual PC seats deployed in 70 countries, *mobile computing* has cut electricity consumption by 88 million kilowatts per year, compared with the same number of PCs. This represents a reduction of 55,000 metric tons of carbon emissions into the atmosphere

In addition to the electricity reduction, the computing through the mobile devices using virtualization also greatly reduces the amount of e-waste that piles up in landfills every year. According to the Environmental Impact Assessment Review (July 2005), between 1994 and 2003, PC disposal resulted in 718,000 tons of lead, 287 tons of mercury, and 1,363 tons of cadmium being placed in landfills. As PC penetration continues to increase worldwide, the e-waste problem will only get worse. Fortunately, the mobile devices are smaller, lighter and contain far fewer electronic parts compared to a PC. In fact, mobile gadgets reduce e-waste by 98% because they weigh less than a typical PC. (www.hardwarezone.com)

Green Mobile

Mobility promotes green IT and adds environmental intelligence to a collaborative business ecosystem and that is why Green mobiles are also required to be designed and manufactured so that they can give something back to the environment. Firstly, mobile companies should encourage user to keep their current phone rather than upgrade when they switch to them. The line rental of green mobiles should be cheaper than that of current mobiles available such as Orange, Vodafone, T-mobile and O2. **Now there is a need to go mobile with green technology. Recently** Green Mobiles are set to be the first to introduce the new "Sunflower Phone" to the UK. It's a totally biodegradable phone that has a built-in seed that will grow once the phone is planted in the ground.

The Nokia 3110 Evolve uses what Nokia is touting as a 'bio-cover', the casing is composed of 50% recycled material and packaging made from 60% recycled material. Nokia has announced a new eco-friendly mobile phone at an event in Amsterdam. The phone, 3110 Evolve, is said to be made out of bio-sourced materials, which means the material is fifty percent renewable. The Nokia phone 3110 will use a high efficiency charger, which saves energy. (www.hp.com)

Discussion forums through blogs on Mobile Devices: *Green Blogs* are one of the free form of exchange of information and ideas globally. The advantage of green blogs is to enable interaction without use of physical paper such as journals or magazines, and at the same time the discussion is current. However, there can be issues related to unedited material that has not been reviewed. There are geographical limits on the world of green blogs as well as the community behind the green blogs is relatively narrow. *Green blogs* are attracting more readers than just most *environmentally oriented print magazines*. The free form of information exchange between the readers can become an important part of public dialog on environmental matters. (www.iprimus.com.au). Communication with blogs on mobile will enable a user to exchange ideas about the enterprise , give new suggestions, give feedback and share the new concepts of the business anywhere, anytime. *Green Broadband* programme is one more initiative taken by broadband providers for Green IT. Green Broadband program allows broadband customers to minimize the greenhouse impact of their internet usage. Some companies are offering Green Broadband to new or existing customers for less than a dollar per month extra on green broadband plans which encourages the customers and the company to do more plantations so that the trees soak up greenhouse emissions. (Information Age,2007)

Use of Web 2.0 and Web 3.0 Technology in Mobile Devices: Web 2.0 and Web 3.0 are the new trends in the communication technologies which are preparing a virtual world wide communications network that goes beyond the basic task of communication (Unhelkar and Trivedi, 2009) . The characteristics of these technologies are rich user experience, user participation, dynamic content, web standards and scalability (Best, 2006). The mobile platforms using these web services will increase the user communication, help the user to get incremental updates about the data, facilitate the user to provide feedback to the service provider or the enterprise at any given instance of time and place. This will improve the functional capabilities of an organization in the real time .Using the web services provided by Web 2.0 and further Web 3.0 technologies, users *or executives will be able to execute all their services when roaming as well as from their home networks (Jaokar ,2005). Implementation of Web 2.0 technologies on the mobile devices will reduce the energy use as mobile gadgets consume less energy than desktop computers as well as virtualizes the server resources leading to a sustainable and environment friendly system.*

M-Supply Chain Management: The use and application of IT will continue to require significant investments in energy generation for their operations (Sarkis and park, 2008). *Energy efficiency and carbon neutrality* are likely to become growing factors as a source of business ecosystem. Mobile - SCM (Supply chain management) enables business transactions to be location independent, reduces unnecessary inventory and transportation of material. The Internet has already had a tremendous impact on the field of supply chain management. SCM with Internet successfully lower costs, add value to the businesses as well enable location independence and thus helps the environment go green. The mobile flow of information can further create more sourcing opportunities for raw materials; combining the long term effects such as reduction in stocks and the holding costs. The emerging standards like Web Services (XML, SOAP, UDDI, and WSDL)

on mobile gadgets can simplify information exchange and business processes within the enterprise and between supply chain partners; Mobile device -enabled supply chain helps companies

- Reduce unnecessary inventory
- Increase in working capital
- Reduce administrative overhead
- Decrease the number of hands that touch goods on their way to the end customer
- Eliminate obsolete business processes
- Help in cost-cutting and revenue-producing benefits
- Speed up production and responsiveness to consumers
- Garner higher profit margins on finished goods

As Internet diffusion and mobile phone penetration continue their explosive increase, SCM design must accommodate the accompanying change in customer preferences and expectations as well. Adding web and mobile functionality to its ERP solutions to enable Internet ordering for its customers, web-based call centre support, and membership in B2B (Business to Business) Web exchanges will benefit a corporate with better environmentally sound approaches like vendor assessment, total quality management, lean supply and collaborative supply strategies by the analysis of relevant consumer attitudes, legislation and concepts in environmentally-sound management (life-cycle analysis, waste management, recycling, product procurement, etc.).

Mobile Supply Chain Management (MSCM) can encompasses many strategic issues such as number, location, and size of warehouses, and distribution centers and facilities; partnerships with suppliers, distributors, and customers; product design impact; and technology infrastructure. Tactical processes such as demand planning, forecasting, sourcing, production, third-party logistics, scheduling, inventory and transportation can be handled by the mobile devices supported by mobile ERP's.

Most applications of wireless technologies today involve the use of Radio Frequency Identification (RFID) devices for material handling in distribution warehouses, moving inventory, cycle counting, shipping and receiving, and direct store delivery programs.

Typical requirements for wireless in supply chain logistics management are mobile dispatch, mobile order tracking, package tracking, instant messaging, on-the-spot mobile printers, exception alerts, virtual real-time vehicle tracking, DoT reporting, fuel tax reporting, yard management, cross docking, converged voice, data, GPS, route and vehicle information and integration to various data collection devices, eg barcode, RFID, electronic signatures.

Improving efficiency and accuracy in logistics and material handling using the mobile technology leads to better demand management. AMR Research revealed that companies that excel at demand forecasting have 15% less inventory, 17% stronger order fulfillment, and 35% shorter cash-to-cash cycle times than typical companies. (Subramanyam, 2008).

Outsourcing Mobile Applications: Outsourcing in business helps to lower firm cost , conserves energy and make more efficient use of manpower , money and other resources as well as technology. Using mobility for product design and manufacturing will be a collaborative step for ERBS. Outsourcing using mobility solutions can ensure the user that enterprise applications will be accessible to the organization on an anywhere, anytime basis. This will result in an increase in productivity, customer satisfaction and employee satisfaction. The organization can also benefit from reduced response time. (www.outsource2india.com) Outsourcing mobile applications can include functions such as voice and data management, and bring in new users and extend them technical support. Outsourcing in this sector can better manage mobile services and reduce costs, and also provide enhanced service to customers. (Redman, 2005) Users can potentially manage those mobile services better and reduce costs. If there are several hundred mobile users of an enterprise, and it costs $100-$200 per year to support each user, but outsourcing that support would cost $60-200 per user, then there's a potential gap where an enterprise can save some money by outsourcing. (Parizo, 2005) Companies can also provide better service to their users, and maybe even provide more services because costs are lower. Plus it lets the organization to focus on key issues and take advantage of personnel strength, which is focusing on IT. Thus outsourcing mobile applications not only saves money but also effectively saves energy by providing the services to the user without actual transportation.

CONCLUSION AND FUTURE DIRECTIONS

This chapter outlines an overall strategic approach to environmentally responsible business strategies (ERBS) together with mobile technologies. Different applications of the mobile technologies aim to build on and expand Environmental Intelligence are discussed. Incorporation of mobile and communication technologies in collaborative business ecosystem can add Environmental Intelligence to the current Business Intelligence. This chapter has focused on the concept of applying mobility and mobile technology tools to business applications so that they will directly and indirectly benefit the environment. This chapter argues for strategic incorporation of environmental considerations in the reduction of the green house gas emissions. Such strategic incorporation of mobility in environmental consideration is termed "Environmental Intelligence" (EI). The corporate sector is still in infant stage with respect to EI, but with the increasing business awareness of the adverse effect of business activities on the environment it is mandatory to enforce the organization's software systems to be environmentally intelligent. This chapter has suggested some techniques such as recycling the hardware, using the operating systems which are able to monitor the hardware so that there is less CO_2 emission in the environment. Providing green Broadband for the data communication and using green mobiles can be way to start with. Data bank is growing vigorously with the expansion of the businesses that is why handling database in such a manner that we can get a solution to our query in the most optimal time is required, data rescheduling is required so that data which is used frequently by the users is kept in a data cache and other data can be handled separately.

This chapter has suggested many ways in which mobility can be applied at different phases of business to reduce greenhouse gas emissions. Green Broadband is a very effective way to use Internet. Saving environment and going green is essential to save our earth but it may be expensive. New measures, rules should be set by the Government, Business organizations and society to move toward Green IT. Techniques which are EI like green broadband, green mobile, green blogs, m-SCM etc as discussed in this chapter should be incorporated in all collaborative business enterprises to go Green.

REFERENCES

Best, D. (2006). Web 2.0 Next Big Thing or Next Big Internet Bubble? *Lecture Web Information Systems.* Techni Sche Universiteit Eindhoven.

Borri, D., Camarda, D., & Liddo, De , A. (2005, September 22). Mobility in Environmental Planning: An Integrated Multi-agent Approach. *Cooperative Design, Visualization, and Engineering, 3675.* Heidelberg: Springer Berlin. Retrieved Jan 2, 2008, from http://www.springerlink.com/content/8r09mvbfq42glv26/

Dicum, G. (2006 March 22). Green Blogs: The Green revolution moves online. Retrieved Jan 10, 2008 from http://www.sfgate.com/cgi-bin/article.cgi

Douglis, F., Cáceres, R., Kaashoek, M. F. , Krishnan, P., Li, K., Marsh, B., & Tauber, J. (1994). Storage Alternatives for Mobile Computers. *Operating Systems Design and Implementation.*

Gothlich, S. E. (2003). From Loosely coupled system to Collaborative Business Ecosystem. Retrieved Jan 7, 2008 from http://www.wiso.uni-kiel.de/bwlinstitute/controlling

Ghanbary & Unhelkar, B. (2005). Handbook of Research on Mobile Business -2

ICT gets Its green House in Order. (2007 October). Information Staff. Information Age. Retrieved Jan10, 2008 from http://www.infoage.idg.com.au

Imhoff, C. (2005, July 12). Business Intelligence Environments: The Need for Mobility, *Business intelligence network^{TM}.* Retrieved Jan 2, 2008 from http://www.b-eye-network.in/view-articles/1128

Introducing Australia's first green broadband. Retrieved Jan 10, 2008 from http://www.primus.com.au/PrimusWeb/HomeSolutions/Green+Broadband/)

IIMM Newsletter – Vadodara Chapter (October, 2007)

Jaokar, A. (2005). Mobile Web 2.0: Web 2.0 and its impact on the mobility and digital convergence. Retreived Dec 25, 2005.

Moss, L. T. (2006 August). Data Strategy: Survival Guide for the Information Age. *Cutter IT Journal.*

Parizo, E. B. (2005). The case for mobile outsourcing. *News Editor.* SearchMobileComputing.com

Rao, M. (n/d). Internet –enabled Supply Chain Management ushers in a new wave of "C-Commerce" for collaborative business. *Second Annual European Logistics Summit in Brussels.* Retrieved Feb 3, 2008 from http://www.techsparks.com/Internet-enabled-supply-chain-management.html.

Redman, P. (n/d). *Mobile Outsourcing a good option.* Retrieved Feb24, 2008 From http://www.blogsource.org/

Sarkis, J., & Park, J. (n/d). Understanding the Linkages between IT, Global Supply Chains , and the Environment. *Cutter IT Journal, 21*(2).

Slebodnick, J. (August ,2006). Bridging the canyon: Introducing Business-Oriented Practices to an Environmental data project. *Cutter IT Journal.*

Subramanyam, R. (2008). *Mobilizing Supply Chain Management - Dataquest.* Retrieved February 11, 2008.

Unhelkar, B., & Dickens (2008). Lessons in implementing Environmentally Responsible Green Business strategies with ICT. *Cutter IT Journal.*

Unhelkar, B., and Trivedi, B. (Due 2009). *Extending and Applying Web 2.0 and Beyond for Environmental Intelligence, Handbook of Research on Web 2.0, 3.0 and X.0: Technologies, Business, and Social Applications,* S. Murugesan (ed.). Hershey, PA, USA: IGI Global.

www.iprimus.com.au

www.hp.com

www.hardwarezone.com

http://www.compareindia.com

www.outsource2india.com

www.windowsfordevices.com

KEY TERMS

Collaborative Business Ecosystem: A business ecosystem where enterprise developments are multidisciplinary in nature such as social, environmental, economical and organizational.

Environmental Intelligence (EI): An intelligent use of business tools and technologies which can lead an enterprise to a green enterprise.

Environmentally Responsible Business Strategy (ERBS): A business approach that incorporates environmental factors in it.

Green IT: The study and practice of using computing (IT) resources efficiently.

Mobile Business Intelligence: Aims at use of mobile applications and mobile devices in a business organization resulting in reductions in operating costs, emissions and energy usage and thus reduction in energy consumption.

Chapter XLI
Mobile Technologies Extending ERP Systems

Dirk Werth
Institute for Information Systems at German Research Centre for Artificial Intelligence, Germany

Paul Makuch
Institute for Information Systems at German Research Centre for Artificial Intelligence, Germany

ABSTRACT

Nowadays the majority of enterprises use Enterprise Resource Planning (ERP) software to improve their business processes. Simultaneously, mobile technologies which can be used within ERP have gained further importance. This is because ERP, together with mobile technologies, offers a wide spectrum of synergies and both have a significant impact on enterprise efficiency. The improvement possibilities in ERP due to mobility range from sales activities, over logistic processes, up to effects on the human resource management.

INTRODUCTION

Enterprise Resource Planning (ERP) systems have become the IT backbone of most enterprises. Several publications, articles and surveys mention that almost 70-80% of Fortune-1000 enterprises use ERP systems to improve their business processes. ERP systems have changed the way enterprises conduct their business as many functionalities, which only a few years ago had be done manually, now are automatically provided by the system.

Similar to the Internet, technologies have largely grown in the last years. E.g. mobile phones have become a standard communication device in most countries. In the near future mobility and flexibility will be a key issue that will enable organizations to withstand competition in an environment characterized by in-

creasing cost pressures. Using mobile technologies for commercial purposes is one option that can certainly make business processes more efficient. This chapter discusses mobile business has opened new opportunities in ERP systems. Furthermore, we also discusses various other business processes that are influenced by mobile technologies (e.g. buying train tickets via the mobile phone). However, it should be noted that the influence of mobile technologies is not limited to consumer interactions. Also, established applications can be enriched by mobile technology resulting in new or improved functionalities. This chapter explores the impact of mobile technology on ERP systems and demonstrate some use cases where such technology can significantly improve ERP functionality.

ERP SYSTEMS

Enterprise Resource Planning Software offers a spectrum of activities which support enterprises to organize important business processes by providing multimodular software applications. ERP systems have evolved in the middle of the 1990s from manufacturing resource planning (MRPII) systems. Such systems aim to plan and steer the output generation within an enterprise. They comprise of all logistic activities, from the purchase planning and execution through the manufacturing planning, steering and supervision to the sales and after-sales activities. MRPII systems mainly cover the logistical view of the enterprise. Extending MRPII systems by human resource management and by financial management has resulted in ERP systems, that aim to cover all activities and business processes within an enterprise. Nowadays every business transaction can be monitored, analyzed and evaluated.

The performance properties of ERP systems are:

- **Branch neutrality:** ERP software is normally not aligned to a specific branch
- **Operating efficiency:** the special emphasis is placed on efficiency, not on technology
- **Modularity:** There are enclosed areas of activity within the software, called modules
- **Integration:** All business activities as an aggregate are continuously supported
- **Standard software:** ERP systems are not designed for individual purpose. In fact they are sold on an anonymous market, but of course they can be customized, i.e. adapted to fit customer needs.

ERP systems differ from each other in their complexity, range of functions and procurement costs. First it depends on the branch the enterprise operates using ERP technology. With an ascending number of suppliers or products, more modern warehouse systems or new distributions channels, the complexity of such a system increases. Second, the size of the enterprise including their whole network matters. Small and medium sized businesses don't need the same range of functions like a world wide operating multinational company. This certainly has an influence on the price of the software solutions, e.g. small sized businesses can install standard versions, whereas concerns need specially developed additional modules.

Third, the number of users working with the ERP system plays an important role. The more accounts work simultaneously, the more powerful hardware is needed to guarantee an unproblematic process. Last, the technological base used to realize an ERP system, especially the database and the programming language, is a key factor determining the complexity and the range of functions.

In the future, ERP systems will be increasingly standardized. Therefore the flexibility and mobility of user interfaces will play a more and more important role in order to generate additional advantages.

MOBILE TECHNOLOGY

Mobile technology is newer than ERP systems. The first technological achievements covered the mobile speech transmission using analog mobile phones. At the end of the 1990s, the technology has broadened by two streams: On the one side the digitalization of mobile technology, on the other side the inclusion of text and data services. Besides, the mostly used service is the short massage service (SMS), originally developed for usage in the global systems for mobile communications (GSM). Today, several kinds of mobile devices are available on the market. It ranges from simple GSM mobile phones, over ultramodern personal digital assistants (PDA) connected via the universal mobile telecommunications standard (UMTS), up to radio frequency identification (RFID) tags which can simplify warehouse processes.

By using portable terminals and mobile data transfer technology, users establish a connection to wireless firm-owned network services. They are locally and temporally independent and always available. As a result they are able to make transactions from almost every place on the earth. Additionally, portable terminals are easier to operate and have a shorter boot time than locally installed user interfaces due to the fact that decentralized devices normally only include the essential range of functions. As far as security is concerned the software or the hardware normally includes personal identification processes, e.g. a subscriber identity module (SIM) card or password protection. This is necessary to ensure that third parties are not able to enter the network and see or manipulate enterprise information. As each network user has its own mobile device and the corresponding account, personalization possibilities are nearly unlimited, i.e. it is possible to define different views and accesses to the central database. Personalization allows users to work more effective because everyone is allowed to individually determine its preferred properties. This also leads to more cost-effectiveness. In addition, the costs for mobile devices like PDAs are continuously decreasing and far away from comparable notebook prices. In terms of realizing saving potentials the localizability aspect probably plays the most important role. For example RFID tags allow enterprises to improve their logistic activities (see point "Logistic improvements").

In the next sections we will discuss potential advantages by presenting a use case to each improvement field.

SALES IMPROVEMENT, COST REDUCTION

Sales can be increased by using mobile technology in order to extend the functionality of ERP systems. In order to get a better idea of the improvement potentials we take a look at the example of the "traveling salesman". His main fields of activity are customer acquisition, providing information to customer, product sales and their ordering and after-sale activities. These tasks are normally supported by the ERP system, e.g. new customers have to be set up with their individual customer number. All customer orders, including their content, volume and value are registered and can be tracked up on the basis of a voucher. With a mobile device this information can be entered or accessed wherever the salesman, respectively the customer is located. Furthermore, constantly updated price lists can be presented and products can be ordered online, including such special services like delivery time determination. This allows both to increase customer satisfaction and business efficiency. On the one side the enterprise is able to respond fluidly to changing conditions in customer demand as the salesman is always directly linked to the development and purchase department via mobile technology. Thus production can be flexibly adapted and it is not necessary to estimate potential sales figures, i.e. the risk of wasted production capabilities as a result of non-saleable goods is significantly reduced. On the other side the complexity of the ERP system is decoupled. Only the functions needed for salesman's activities are supported by the mobile device, unnecessary and complex features of the system are removed, respectively not available. By

embedding automatic synchronize and update functions the employee spends a minimum of its working time on administrating the ERP system.

LOGISTICS IMPROVEMENT

With regard to cost efficiency ERP supported enterprise warehouse systems gain in importance. In the near future the new generation of the radio frequency identification (RFID) standard will help to save expenses. The RFID concept is based on contactless data transmission by electromagnetic alternating fields [Hertel J., Zentes J., Schramm-Klein, H. (2005)]. Special RFID tags serve as data volumes and allow the reading, processing and changing of chip contained information. The main application possibilities are quiet varied [ECR-D-A-CH (2003); Füßler (2004)]:

- **Production:** After production goods are individually equipped with an RDIF tag which allows identifying their position at every step of the supply chain.
- **Stocks monitoring:** RFID technology allows to trace the receipts of goods, the warehouse process itself, and outgoing goods. As periodically recurring inventory processes always retain a lot of employees, mobile devices in correspondence with the RFID technology can help to make counting operations more efficient, i.e. easier and faster. All stocks can be counted by scanning the RFID tags with a mobile scanner unit, e.g. a modern PDA extended by a radio frequency receiver. Especially with regard to homogeneous stocks, documentation operations can be accelerated.
- **After sales activities:** Even after the selling process, the RFID tags remain on the products and can be used for automatic replenishment, reclamation or exchange procedures and after-sales disposal activities.

Due to relatively high costs of the needed transponder technology RFID was only used in big business logistics, e.g. in container handling facilities. As costs of the obligatory hardware are decreasing the usage of the technology becomes more and more efficient for other purposes. Point-of-Sales will use RFID in order to accelerate sale activities or to reduce consignment and personnel costs. E.g. a supermarket can save costs by providing fully automatic cash desks. It is not necessary to scan each product a consumer wants to buy, not even a visual contact has to be established, as several RFID data carriers can be ascertained within one single read operation. All goods within the customer's shopping carriage are identified by driving through a scanner unit.

HUMAN RESOURCE IMPROVEMENT

In this section we discuss improvement potentials for human resources (HR) by looking at the accounting of travel expenses. ERP systems also support automatic note of expenses. If an employee comes back from a business travel and wants its travelling expenses to be reimbursed, the system only needs the payment vouchers, the employee number and the release signal for clearing the payment. With mobile technology this operation can be accelerated once again. Contemporary to the prepayment of the employee, the vouchers can be digitally submitted to the office, the system validates the sums and pays the bill, e.g. paying bus and train ticket via mobile phone. Since April 2007 there is a pilot project with twelve participating German cities, providing such a service to their citizens. The system is nationally standardized and was developed by member firms and groups of the Association of German Transport Companies (VDV), Siemens IT Solutions and Services, DVB LogPay and the Frauenhofer-Institut IVI Dresden. After completing a one-time registration and selecting a preferred payment method, users receive a text message containing a Java application element that is used for ordering the tickets. The mobile phone screen allows the user to enter the type and value of the ticket, whereby single tickets and day passes are available. After the payment process the mobile phone owner receives an on-screen confirmation serving as a receipt, e.g. for ticket inspection [Soft32 (2007)]. This could be extended by directly sending a voucher to the company's ERP system. Obviously this development reduces personnel cost and saves administration time because no paper documentation is needed.

CONCLUSION

This chapter explored new ways of enriching standardized ERP systems with modern mobile technology.

Mobile components or devices enable enterprises to make their business processes more efficient. Via wireless networks employees are permanently linked to the ERP system, are able to work online and can use the saved time for more productive activities.

The cases we presented above give a general overview of possible new business opportunities if ERP systems are used in connection with mobile devices. They will have a significant influence on future activities within an enterprise. With increasing technological performance of mobile devices the structure of an ERP system will be changing from a centralized main system into a network consisting of independently operating and interlinked mobile devices. The discussion in this chapter can be further enhanced by subjecting it to research validation that is currently outside the scope of this chapter.

REFERENCES

ECR D-A-CH (2003). *RFID – Optimierung der Value Chain*. Köln.

Füßler, A. (2004). Auswirkungen der RFID-Technologie auf die Gestaltung der Versorgungskette. In J. Zentes, H. Biesiada, H. Schramm-Klein (Hrsg.), *Performance-Leadership im Handel*. Frankfurt a.M., (pp. 137-155).

Hertel J., Zentes J., & Schramm-Klein, H. (2005). Supply Chain Management und Warenwirtschaftssysteme im Handel. Heidelberg: Springer (pp.207-210).

Soft32 (2007). http://news.soft32.com/bus-and-train-tickets-via-mobile-phone-in-munster-germany_5232.html.

KEY TERMS

Business Process: A target-oriented, logical sequence of activities which can be performed by multiple collaborating organisational units by using information and communication technologies. This system of functions makes a substantial contribution to the generation of added value.

Enterprise Resource Planning (ERP) Systems: Integrated packages of standardized software applications supporting the resource planning of an enterprise. Financial, logistical and human resource related business processes can be improved by using an ERP system.

Mobile Business: Describes the initiation and the entire support, execution and maintenance of business transaction between business partners by the use of wireless electronic network communication technology and mobile devices.

Mobile Business Processes: Integrate mobile solutions into classic business processes. Mobile work leads to new collaborative opportunities, improves the enterprise workflow and enables the transaction of digital business processes.

Mobile ERP: Solutions extend traditional ERP systems by location-independently collecting and exchanging data via mobile devices and wireless transfer mechanisms. Standardized interfaces allow a direct and steady connection to the ERP hardware and lead to more flexible and efficient business processes within an enterprise.

Radio Frequency Identification (RFID) System: Allows contactless data transmission by electromagnetic alternating fields and is often used for automatic identification and data acquisition.

Sensory ERP: A concept for next generation ERP systems. It enables the ERP system to automatically acquire data and supervise enterprise states and events by using sensors (e.g. RFID tags and gates, GPS tracker, etc.). Interfacing between the physical world and the ERP system is no longer performed through human workers, but this data is collected by sensors that directly assess the physical states and that are part of the real world itself. By this, the error rate significantly decreases and business processes become more efficient.

Chapter XLII
Techniques for Exploiting Mobility in Wireless Sensor Networks

Ataul Bari
University of Windsor, Canada

Arunita Jaekel
University of Windsor, Canada

ABSTRACT

A sensor network consists of tiny, low-powered and multifunctional sensor devices and is able to perform complex tasks through the collaborative efforts of a large number of sensor nodes that are densely deployed within the sensing field. Maintaining connectivity and maximizing the network lifetime are among the critical considerations in designing sensor networks and its protocols. Conservation of limited energy reserves at each sensor node is one of the greatest challenges in a sensor network. It has been suggested that mobility of some nodes/entities in a sensor network can be exploited to improve network performance in a number of areas, including coverage, lifetime, connectivityy, and fault-tolerance. In this context, techniques for effectively utilizing the unique capabilities of mobile nodes have been attracting increasing research attention in the past few years. In this chapter, the authors focus on some of the new and innovative techniques that have been recently proposed to handle a number of important problems in this field. It also presents a number of open problems and some developing trends and directions for future work in this emerging research area.

INTRODUCTION

A *sensor network* is an interconnection of tiny, lightweight, energy-constrained devices, known as *sensor nodes*, and is usually deployed to monitor some kind of physical phenomena from the territory of its deployment. For example, a sensor network may be deployed to monitor the humidity or the temperature of a certain region, or it may be deployed to detect the presence or absence of some objects, as well as the movement of objects within the area being monitored. Recent technological advances in the field of micro-electro-mechanical systems (MEMS) have made the development of such tiny, low-cost, low-powered and multi-functional sensor devices technically and economically feasible (Akyildiz, 2002; Chong, 2003). These nodes are usually equipped with a sensing unit, a processing unit, a memory unit and a RF unit that is used for wireless data communication.

The data generated by each sensor is required to be sent to a central point, known as *Base Station (BS)* (also referred to as *sink* or *access point*). The base station is not power constrained and its location may or may not be fixed. A general layout of a sensor network, including the sensor nodes and a base station, is shown in Figure 1. Some researchers have also proposed the deployment of multiple sinks within a sensor network.

The nodes in a sensor network are deployed inside or very close to the phenomenon being monitored, in order to carry out the sensing task effectively. The placement of sensor nodes in a network can be pre-determined (e.g. the deployment of a sensor network in a factory or in the body of a human, an animal or a robot) or random (e.g. the deployment of nodes by dropping them from a helicopter/airplane or delivering them in an artillery shell or in a missile) (Akyildiz, 2002; Chong, 2003). All data from the sensor nodes must eventually be collected at the base station(s) or sink(s). The collected data may be aggregated and forwarded to the user, possibly using the Internet, where it can be further analyzed to extract useful information.

Although the capability of an individual sensor node is limited, a sensor network is able to perform bigger tasks through the collaborative efforts of a large number of sensor nodes (hundreds or even thousands) that are densely deployed within the sensing field (Ak-kaya, 2005; Akyildiz, 2002; Chong, 2003). There is a wide range of applications, for both military and civil purposes, where the use of sensor networks can be very useful that include medical, industrial, military, and environmental fields. For example, sensor networks can be used for target and/or movement detection, which is extremely important for military/battlefield applications as well as habitat monitoring and health monitoring.

In sensor networks, all data flow from the sensor nodes towards the base station(s). The transmission power dissipated by a source node to transmit each bit of data to a destination node increases significantly with the distance between the source and the destination (Akyildiz, 2002; Chong, 2003; Duarte-Melo, 2002; Gupta, 2003, Heinzelman, 2000). As a result, the use of multi-hop paths has been proposed for conserving

energy, in both *flat architectures* (where all sensor nodes are treated equally and each are responsible to send/route data towards the sink) and *hierarchical architectures* (where sensor nodes are partitioned into clusters and one node takes responsibility of being the cluster head of a cluster (Bari, 2006). Each sensor sends data to the respective cluster head, which sends/routes data towards the sink). In the multi-hop routing scheme, nodes located further away from the base station use some intermediate nodes to forward the data to the base station. In such a data-gathering model, it is possible that some nodes (close to the base station) are required to relay more data, which they have received from the neighboring nodes, compared to other nodes. Therefore, these nodes may dissipate energy at higher rates than the nodes which are not relaying (or relaying very little) data from other nodes. This uneven energy dissipation among the nodes may lead to the faster *death* of some nodes in the network due to the complete depletion of the batteries of these nodes, assuming that initial energy provisioning for all nodes are equal. Such unbalanced energy dissipation has an undesirable effect on the functionality of the sensor networks, as the inoperative node(s) will not be able to perform either sensing or routing. This can cause the entire network to prematurely lose its usefulness, even though many other nodes in the networks still retain power. Therefore, a careful load distribution scheme can be effective to prolong the useful lifetime of the network (Bari, 2007).

Role of Mobility in Addressing Sensor Network Design Challenges

Sensor networks pose many challenges in design, operation and maintenance in each layer of the networking protocol stack. Some important issues in the design of sensor networks include:

- *Network deployment in ad hoc manner:* The nodes in sensor networks, which are deployed in remote areas, need to self-configure and self-organize themselves so that they can form the networks.
- *Unattended operation with limited battery power:* Replacing or recharging batteries in sensor networks is usually not feasible, either physically or economically, so that, in many cases, the lifetime of a sensor network expires as soon as *critical* node(s) run out of battery power (Heinzelman, 2000).

Figure 1. A general layout of sensor network

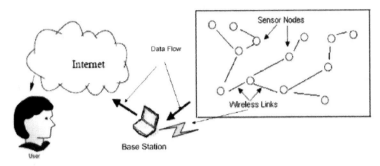

- *Changes in network condition:* Sensor networks need to be adaptive to node failure(s), node mobility and link failures.
- *Scalability:* As the size of networks may vary from one application to another, the protocols need to be scalable to accommodate a large number of nodes.
- *Connectivity:* The system needs to ensure that all the nodes are connected even in the event of failures.
- *Coverage:* As each sensor node can only cover a limited physical area around its vicinity, the entire area to be monitored needs to be covered by the nodes in the sensor network.
- *Quality of Service:* There may be a trade-off between the quality of the result and the conservation of energy.

Mobility in wireless environment is usually considered as a part of the 'problem' as handling the mobility requires additional overhead, but for sensor networks, it has been seen as 'blessing' by many researchers. It is possible to enhance network performance in a number of the above mentioned areas by enabling network nodes with movement capabilities or/and deploying some special mobile entities within the network. Mobile nodes/entities can be used to improve network connectivity in sparse networks, as well as to increase network lifetime by shifting the traffic from heavily loaded nodes and reducing transmission distances between distantly located source-destination node pairs. A number of important applications exploit node mobility to detect and eliminate coverage holes (areas not covered by any sensing node) and respond to failures by relocating mobile nodes. Mobility can also be conveniently used for the purpose of efficient deployment of a network as well as dynamic re-con-

figuration of the network. In the following sections, we will outline how mobile elements can be effectively utilized in a sensor network to address design challenges in key areas such as network connectivity, lifetime, coverage, fault-tolerance and quality of service. We will also highlight recent advances and new techniques used in each area.

EXPLOITING MOBILITY TO IMPROVE NETWORK LIFETIME AND CONNECTIVITY

The sensor network architectures that exploit mobility for the purpose of improved lifetime and connectivity broadly falls into one of the two approaches, *mobile observer* based approaches and *mobile sink* based approaches. In the mobile observer (or data collector) based approaches, some special mobile entities are deployed into the network whose sole purpose is to move around and collect data from the sensor nodes within the network. Data are buffered in sensor nodes until they can be downloaded, usually in single hop, to a mobile observer. On the other hand, in mobile sink based approaches, sinks are capable of movement and sensor nodes relay data to the mobile sinks with little or no buffering (Ekici, 2006). Hybrids of these two approaches are also available.

Mobile Observer Based Approaches

In sparse sensor networks the nodes are distributed in large areas and data are collected from various distant points in the network. A network with sensors placed along a road to collect traffic data is one example of such a network. As this kind of data is highly correlated, a small number of sensors can be used to handle the task. However, such sparseness may cause connectivity problems due to the increased distance between nodes. On the other hand, providing the network with a large number of extra nodes to relay data, or providing sensor nodes with long range communication capabilities may not be very cost effective and hence, not practical. Long range communication will also shorten the lifetime of the network due to the high energy dissipation by the widely separated nodes. To address this problem, the use of some mobile entities, referred to as Data MULEs (Mobile Ubiquitous LAN Extensions) (also as *Mobile Element* (ME) or *Mobile Observer*) in sensor networks have been proposed (Shah, 2003). A sensor network with MULEs may be seen as a three tiered network (Jain, 2006) where,

- Sensor nodes constitute the bottom tier;
- Sinks (or access points) constitute the top tier, and
- MULEs are positioned at the middle tier.

In this architecture, the nodes at the top and bottom layers are typically considered to be static. The MULEs, lie in the middle layer, are mobile and are responsible for ferrying data from the sensors to the access points. As compared to the sensor nodes, MULEs are provided with larger buffers and renewable power supply. A sensor node transmits data to a MULE, but can do so only when a MULE is present within its specified communication range. The sensor node must buffer its data until there is an available MULE within its transmission range. The use of MULES can significantly reduce energy dissipation, since each sensor node has to transmit only over a short distance. The critical issues for this type of approach are to determine

i. The sensor buffer size,
ii. The trajectory of the MULEs, and
iii. The interval between the consecutive visits to a sensor node by a MULE.

Depending on the application and network configuration, the trajectory of the MULE may be *random, predictable* or *controlled.* All these approaches can be exploited to sustain network capabilities. In a heterogeneous network, the data generation rates as well as buffering capabilities of different sensor nodes, in a given network, may vary widely. This means that some nodes need to offload their data more frequently than others, requiring more frequent visits from the mobile observer (or data-collectors). Effective *scheduling* of mobile elements is needed to handle such requirements. In the following sections, we will discuss a number of ways these issues can be addressed.

Exploiting Random Mobility of the Mobile Observer

In a sensor network with random mobility of the mobile observers, the path taken by the MULEs is not repetitive, not determined beforehand and also cannot be predicted accurately. The example in (Shah, 2003) shows that random mobility can be useful in a sensor network where sensor nodes, capable of buffering data, are sparsely distributed. In this model, the MULES move randomly within the network and pick-up data from the sensor nodes, when they enter the direct communication rage of the sensor nodes. The performance of the network, using random mobility, typically depends on a number of parameters including:

- Buffer size in the sensor nodes,
- Average amount of data generated by the sensor nodes,
- Number of mobile nodes available for transferring data,
- Average time interval between visits to a sensor node, and
- Number of sensors and access points.

For a specified rate of successful data transmission, the buffer capacity on each MULE can be traded-off with the number of MULES. In (Jain, 2006) a queuing theory based mathematical model, analyzing the performance and trade-offs of the three-tier architecture, has been proposed and a number of benefits and the limitations have been identified. The benefits include:

- *Energy savings:* Less transmit energy dissipation by the sensor nodes due to the requirement of only short range transmission. Also, for the multi-hop communication, the loads on the sensor nodes are distributed.
- *Reduced routing overhead:* In this type of networks, sensors do not have the burden of implementing complex routing protocols.
- *Graceful degradation of performance:* Failure of a mobile element resulted in little increase in the latency.

- *Simplicity and Scalability:* No network reconfiguration or synchronization is necessary for the MULE architecture hence the network scales easily with any additional deployment of sensor nodes.

The Limitations include *latency* and *Best-effort delivery.*

- *Latency:* Due to the architecture, high latency is inherent in this type of networks.
- *Best-effort delivery:* Data delivery can not be guaranteed, because a MULE may not always be able to reach a sensor (access point) to pick (deliver) data, or may fail after collecting data from a sensor.

Another practical application of a network with random mobility is found in (Juang, 2002), where the sensor network (called *ZebraNet*) is deployed to monitor wile life. The sensor nodes are attached to the collars of the animals being monitored, which cause the mobility pattern to be random, though characterized by three major components, *grazing, graze-walking* and *fast moving.* An additional degree of flexibility is introduced by allowing the base station to move, if desired. Experimental results show that *history based* routing protocols are more appropriate for such applications compared to *flooding.* In history based protocols, instead of transmitting data to every neighbour, a node selects the target nodes based on the pattern of the previous communication. This leads to lower overall energy dissipation, since much less redundant data needs to be processed by each node.

Exploiting Predictable and Controlled Mobility of the Mobile Observer

Instead of random movements, if the route and timeline of the mobile data collectors is known beforehand, this information can be exploited to gain significant improvements in network performance (Chakrabarti, 2003). *Predictable mobile observers* (PMO) use the same path repeatedly, and their trajectory is known to the sensors. Examples of such observers include public transportation vehicles such as buses, shuttles and trains. In PMO-based networks, sensors can predict the time at which the data transfer will take place, and sleep until that time, which saves energy. In (Chakrabarti, 2003), a queuing formulation modelling a PMO-based network with randomly placed

sensors shows that considerable power saving can be achieved using predictable mobility, compared to networks with static observers. Specialized *observer-driven communication protocol*s that let the sensors to sleep, until they are awakened by an observer in their immediate vicinity, can be used to further reduce energy consumption.

The effect of introducing controlled mobile components into an embedded network infrastructure has been studied by Kansal (2004). Network lifetime is improved by introducing a single mobile router, whose sole purpose is to collect data, into a network of static devices embedded in the field. In this model, nodes located close to the path of the mobile router transmit data directly to it, when the router appears within the node's transmission range. However, sensors located farther away use a multi-hop path to relay data to the nodes closest to the mobile node. In addition to increased lifetime, such a model can be used to improve data fidelity, increase data rates and reduce latency as well as to handle disconnected and sparse networks. The single mobile node model is extended in (Jea, 2005) to include multiple mobile elements, for the purpose of data collection in sensor networks. In this model, multiple mobile elements travel in parallel straight paths and collect data from the sensor nodes. This approach provides scalability and load balancing, in terms of the number of sensor nodes that are to be visited by each mobile element.

Scheduling of Mobile Elements

There are a number of applications where sensors may generate different amounts of data due to different sampling rates, so buffers of different nodes may be filled at different times, e.g. a network where sensors monitor pollution in large cities (Somasundara, 2004). In this scenario, nodes located in the industrial areas may need to sample the environment more than the nodes in the residential areas, and require more frequent visits by the mobile element, to prevent sensor node buffer overflows. For applications where the mobility of the data collector can be controlled, the scheduling problem can be formulated as an optimization problem. The scheduling algorithms attempt to calculate the trajectories of the mobile elements and minimize the data loss due to buffer overflows (Somasundara, 2004). Optimal ILP formulations for the problem have been shown to be NP-complete, and quickly become computationally intractable. A number of heuristic algorithms have also been proposed for scheduling mobile nodes and are briefly outlined below.

1. *Earliest Deadline First* (EDF): In EDF, the mobile element visits a sensor node that has the earliest buffer overflow deadline.
2. *EDF with k-lookahead*: This is a variation of the EDF algorithm, which considers all possible permutations of the *k*-earliest buffer overflow deadline nodes and chooses a sequence of nodes to visit such that none of the *k* nodes exceed their buffer overflow deadlines.
3. *Minimum Weighted Sum First* (MWSF): In MWSF approach, weights are assigned for visiting each node, based on the buffer overflow deadlines and cost, and the mobile element visits the node having the minimum weighted sum.

A comparative study of the three algorithms found that *Minimum Weighted Sum First* algorithm performed better than the others, with less computational overhead.

Partitioning Based Scheduling (PBS) is another scheduling heuristic that can be used to compute the ME trajectory (Gu, 2005). The focus in this approach is the reduction of data loss due to sensor buffer overflow. The whole scheduling problem is solved in two parts, *partitioning* and *scheduling*. First, nodes are partitioned into a number of groups based on their locations and data generation rates. In the next phase, a node visiting schedule that minimizes the movement of ME is generated within a group. The path to be taken by the ME is computed by combining the solutions of the groups. The ME then visits each node with a frequency that is sufficient to prevent the sensor buffer overflow. This approach is able to reduce the minimum speed required by the ME to prevent data loss, and also provide predictability between the inter-visit times. If the ME has to move slower than minimum required speed, the algorithm attempts to minimize the data loss due to sensor buffer overflow.

The scheduling algorithms discussed so far treat all messages equally with respect to latency. But latency restrictions may not be met in certain cases where urgent messages need to be delivered to the ME within a certain deadline. In Gu (2006), the abovementioned scheduling algorithms are extended to take into account different latency requirements. In this *Differentiated Message Delivery* (DMD) model, a collection of both regular and urgent messages are considered. A heuristic algorithm called *Multihop Route to Mobile Element* (MRME) is used to deliver urgent messages to the ME within a maximum al-lowable time delay, by forwarding such messages to some neighbouring node that is visited by the ME with higher frequency.

Mobile Sink (MS) Based Approaches

As mentioned earlier, in a sensor network, data flow from the sensor nodes to the sink(s). In many sensor networks the position(s) of the sink(s) is(are) usually fixed. In multi-hop data communication model, the sensor nodes located around the vicinity of the base station(s) are likely to deplete their energy (and "die") sooner, compared to the other sensor nodes in the network. This is because these nodes are burdened with relaying the data that they receive from the neighbouring nodes, which uses them as an intermediate hop for forwarding data to the base station(s). The MS based approaches attempts to change the location of the base station(s), mainly by computing suitable MS trajectories, so that the energy dissipation by all nodes is evenly distributed.

In Gandham (2003), the deployment of multiple mobile base stations is exploited to prolong the lifetime of the sensor network. The lifetime of the network is split into equal periods of time, called *rounds* during which, the base stations remain stationary. At the end of a round, each base station's location is recomputed, using an ILP, and the base stations are relocated to the recomputed locations at the beginning of each round. A flow-based routing protocol is used to ensure energy efficient routing during each round. This approach can be used to

i.   Minimize the total energy consumption of all sensors or
ii. Minimize the maximum energy consumption of any sensor node.

The first objective typically increases the amount of data collected and the second objective results in increased lifetime. The use of multiple mobile base stations has been shown to increase the network lifetime significantly.

Data dissemination (Kim, 2003) in the presence of mobile sinks can be seen as consisting of three parts, namely,

i.   Dissemination tree (d-tree) construction,
ii. Data dissemination, and
iii. Linkage (to mobile sinks) maintenance.

A distributed self-organizing protocol, called *Scalable Energy-efficient Asynchronous Dissemination* protocol (SEAD), which saves energy at each of the three levels is presented in Kim (2003). The approach takes into consideration the distance and the traffic rate between nodes while creating a near optimal dissemination tree. Data from the tree is collected at specific sensor nodes, called access nodes, which deliver the data to the sink. Mobile base station(s) can also be used for load balancing among the nodes in a sensor network (Luo, 2005). The objective is to extend the network lifetime, which is constrained by the energy depletion of some nodes (*hot spot* nodes) located near the fixed base station(s). An analytical model describing the communication load shows that the lifetime can be improved if the fixed sinks are replaced by a mobile sink, even when the movement of the mobile sinks is arbitrary. For circular sensor networks (sensors are deployed in a circular area), the best strategy for a mobile sink is to follow the periphery of the network. Further improvements can be achieved if a suitable routing strategy is coupled with sink mobility. A heuristic algorithm that considers the joint problem of mobility and routing is also available in (Luo, 2005), which demonstrates that a combination of circular routes and short paths achieves better results in terms of improved lifetime. In this approach, the MS moves along a circular trajectory and the sensor node, located inside the trajectory, communicates with the MS using the shortest path. Nodes located outside the trajectory use paths composed of circular arcs and straight lines to forward their data towards the center of the trajectory. In this way, otherwise unused transmission capabilities of the nodes located at the periphery of the network are utilized to extend the lifetime of the network.

A linear optimization model, enforcing balanced energy consumption constraints, has been proposed in (Wang, 2005). The proposed linear programming formulation addresses the joint problem of sink mobility and the sojourn time at each point in the network such that the lifetime of the network is maximized. The problem of shortened lifetime of a multi-hop network due to large energy dissipation by the nodes located closer to the sinks has been addressed using a gradient-based routing approach with restricted flooding in Fodor (2007). In this approach, each node maintains a list of its neighbour and sends data to the neighbor that is in the right direction for data to travel to the sink. As the sinks move, the protocol makes a trade-off between optimal routing and signaling overhead (number of messages that need to be exchanged to find routes).

MOBILITY FOR IMPROVED COVERAGE AND TO HANDLE FAILURE

In addition to improving network lifetime and connectivity, node mobility can be effectively used for filling *coverage hole(s)* in the sensing area. A coverage hole in a sensor network is defined as the area within the network that is not covered by any sensor node, resulting in lack of monitoring of that area. Controllable mobility of nodes is used to optimize the network monitoring capabilities (Cao, 2005), for both sensing and routing purposes. Node mobility is also exploited to provide fault tolerance by relocating sensors in the event of failure. The solution algorithms for exploiting node mobility must consider a number of factors such as the connectivity of the network, the energy consumption (for both communication and movement) as well as the desired network lifetime. A number of approaches have been proposed, including:

- *Mobility assisted sensing*: deals with relocation of redundant mobile nodes. Proposed solution has to find the redundant nodes and redeploy them to appropriate locations.
- *Mobility assisted data dissemination (routing)*: deals with exploiting sensor mobility to improve network communications.
- *Integrated mobility management for sensing and routing*: deals with manipulation of the movement by defining utility functions that optimize the network capability, by taking into consideration the requirements of all missions.

In a sensor network with static nodes, the coverage is fixed after the initial deployment of the network. However, in a network where sensor modes are mobile, an area currently uncovered may get covered when a mobile sensor node enters into the vicinity and a covered area may get uncovered when all nodes, currently monitoring the area, leave the vicinity. Area coverage over a time interval is the fraction of geographical area covered by one or more sensors, during a given interval of time. On a randomly deployed sensor network with random mobility of the sensor nodes, the area coverage over a time interval is shown to be larger, compared to a similar network with stationary nodes (Liu, 2005). The mobile sensors are also able to detect a target (or intruder) that may remain undetected by a static sensor network.

An interesting work on energy harvesting in distributed sensor networks is presented in (Laibowitz, 2005). The network contains *parasitically actuated nodes* that can decide when to engagement with or disengage from mobile hosts to harvest mobility and navigational intelligence. In this model, the nodes themselves are not capable of movement, and hence relieved from the cost associated with self mobility due to increased node size and power consumption. However, like parasites, they can attach (embed) themselves selectively to (within) some mobile host. As the mobile host (e.g., a human, animal or moving vehicle) is expected to be aware of navigational intelligence in its own environment, parasitic nodes are further relieved from performing these duties and left with only to decide upon whether a host can take them to the target location.

EXPLOITING MOBILITY FOR EFFICIENT DEPLOYMENT

A distributed approach to coordinating the movement of sensor nodes may be necessary in many applications. Depending on the application, different objectives are of importance, such as coverage, time for deployment, communication range, moving distance and scalability. In Wang (2004), a distributed approach to the self-deployment of sensor nodes is presented, where the holes are first discovered using Voronoi diagrams, then target locations for the sensor node to move into, to fix the coverage hole(s) are computed. Three movement-assisted methods are proposed - i) *vector* (VEC), ii) *Voronoi* (VOR) and iii) *minimax*. In VEC, closely located sensors are pushed away from one another, motivated by the property of electro-magnetic particles where an expelling force pushes away particles that are very close. The VOR is a *pull-based* approach where a sensor pulls itself to the furthest Voronoi vertex upon the detection of a coverage hole. The *minimax* method picks a target location within the Voronoi polygon such that the distance to the furthest Voronoi vertex is minimized.

A method for the deployment of multiple sinks in *heterogeneous* sensor networks, using only local information about the nodes, is available in (Vincze, 2007). An algorithm, referred to as *1-hop algorithm*,

was used that iteratively determines the position of each sink, starting from a given initial deployment. Each sink calculates a vector based on the positions of its neighbors, as well as other nodes that communicate with it indirectly. If the resultant vector is above a specified threshold, the sink moves towards the direction given by the resultant vector, otherwise, it does not move. The process repeats until no sink moves. The approach was shown to be effective under various environments such networks with heterogeneous sensor density, or with obstacles in the sensing area.

An electrostatic model, for dynamically positioning multiple sinks has been proposed in (Vincze, 2006). In an electrostatic field, two similarly charged particles repulse each other and oppositely charged particles attract each other. In the proposed model, sinks are assigned *positive* charge, nodes having higher than average residual energy are assigned a negative charge, and nodes having lower than average residual energy are assigned a positive charge. This causes energy depleted nodes to be pushed away from the sinks and stronger nodes to be drawn closer to the sinks. As nodes located close to the sinks become depleted (by the burden of forwarding data from the other nodes), they are shoved away from the sinks, and the nodes having more residual energy are drawn closer to the sinks. This allows the load to be distributed within the network.

In summary, the mobility of the sensor devices can be used to extend the sensor network application space, especially for distributed sensor networks. This is due to the inherent need for context-dependent deployment, for relocation and recovery (of nodes), as well the ability to provide coverage to a larger area (Laibowitz, 2005). Communication devices on mobile platforms can also address the coverage, connectivity and lifetime problems of sensor networks. For example, a mobile node may move into an unmonitored area and start monitoring (improved coverage), or isolated entities in a network may exchange information using mobile devices (improved connectivity), or a mobile device may be used for information exchange so as to reduce the transmission distance for some energy-depleted node (improved lifetime). Mobility can also be exploited for the efficient deployment of the network.

CONCLUSION

Unlike many other types of networks, mobility can be viewed as 'beneficial' in the context of wireless sensor networks. Mobility of network elements can be exploited in many dimensions including extended lifetime, improved connectivity, coverage and efficient deployment of the network. Mobility has already been shown to help maintain the networks within an acceptable performance level for a longer period of time, and enhance the capabilities of a sensor network. However, there are a many interesting open problems and design challenges that need to be addressed for effective utilization and application of mobile sensor networks in the future. These include deciding upon the optimal number of mobile entities and their trajectories; proper scheduling of the mobile elements as well as buffer sizes for both mobile and stationary nodes; determining appropriate design objectives and possible trade-off among conflicting objectives such as quality of service and cost. The exploitation of mobility in sensor networks is a novel and emerging field of research. The full potential and possible limitations of this approach are yet to be understood clearly. However, the recent research suggests a promising direction that can be explored in the coming days.

REFERENCES

Akkaya, K., & Younis, M. (2005). A survey on routing protocols for wireless sensor networks. *IEEE Transactions On Mobile Computing, 3*(3), 325–349.

Akyildiz, I. F., Su, W., Sankarasubramaniam & Cayirci, E. (2002). Wireless sensor networks: A survey. *Computer Networks, 38,* 393–422.

Al-Karaki J. N., & Kamal, A. E. (2004). Routing techniques in wireless sensor networks: A Survey. *IEEE Wireless Communications, 11*(6), 6-28.

Bari, A., Jaekel, A., & Bandyopadhyay, S. (2006). Optimal Load Balanced Clustering in Two-Tiered Sensor Networks. *In the proceedings of Third IEEE/CreateNet International Workshop on Broadband Advanced Sensor Networks (BASENETS).*

Bari, A., Jaekel, A., & Bandyopadhyay, S. (2007). Integrated Clustering and Routing Strategies for Large Scale Sensor Networks. *IFIP International Federation for Information Processing, NETWORKING 2007, LNCS 4479,* 143–154. Springer.

Cao, G., Kesidis, G., La Porta, T., Yao, B., & Phoha, S. (2005). Purposeful Mobility in Tactical Sensor Networks. *Sensor Network Operations.* IEEE Press.

Chakrabarti, A., Sabharwal, A., & Aazhang, B. (2003). Using Predictable Observer Mobility for Power Efficient Design of Sensor Networks. *Proceedings of the second International Workshop on Information Processing in Sensor Networks (IPSN).*

Chong, C.-Y., & Kumar, S. P. (2003). Sensor Networks: Evolution, Opportunities, and Challenges. *Proceedings of the IEEE, 91*(8), 1247–1256.

Duarte-Melo, E. J., & Liu, M. (2002). Analysis of energy consumption and lifetime of heterogeneous wireless sensor networks. *IEEE Global Telecommunications Conference, 1,* 21–25. IEEE.

Ekici, E., Gu, Y., & Bozdag, D. (2006). Mobility-Based Communication in Wireless Sensor Networks. *IEEE Communications Magazine, 44*(6), 56-62. IEEE.

Fodor, K., & Vidács, A. (2007). Efficient Routing to Mobile Sinks in Wireless Sensor Networks. *2nd International Workshop on Performance Control in Wireless Sensor Networks (PWSN).* ACM.

Gandham, S. R., Dawande, M., Prakash, R., & Venkatesan, S. (2003). Energy Efficient Schemes for Wireless Sensor Networks With Multiple Mobile Base Stations. *GLOBECOM,* 377–381. IEEE.

Gu, Y., Bozdag, D., Ekici, E., Ozguner, F., & Chang-Gun Lee, C. G. (2005). Partitioning-Based Mobile Element Scheduling in Wireless Sensor Networks. *Proceedings of the IEEE ComSoc Conference Sensor and Ad Hoc Communication and Network.*

Gu, Y., Bozdag, D., & Ekici, E. (2006). Mobile Element Based Differentiated Message Delivery in Wireless Sensor Networks. *Proceedings of the IEEE International. Symposium World of Wireless, Mobile and Multimedia Networks.*

Gupta, G., & Younis, M. (2003). Load-balanced clustering of wireless sensor networks. *IEEE International Conference on Communication, 3,* 1848–1852. IEEE.

Heinzelman, W., Chandrakasan, A., & Balakrishnan, H. (2000). Energy efficient communication protocol for wireless micro-sensor networks. *The 33rd Annual Hawaii International Conference on System Sciences (HICSS-33),* (pp. 3005–3014). IEEE Computer Society.

Jain, S., Shah, R., Brunette, W., Borriello, G., & Roy, S. (2006). Exploiting Mobility for Energy Efficient Data Collection in Sensor Networks. *Mobile Networks and Applications, 11*(3), 327-339. ACM.

Jea, D., Somasundara, A. A., & Srivastava, M. B. (2005). Multiple Controlled Mobile Elements (Data Mules) for Data Collection. *In Sensor Networks Proceedings of the Distributed Computing in Sensor Systems, LNCS, 3560*, 244-257. Springer.

Juang, P., Oki, H., Wang, Y., Martonosi, M., Peh, L., & Rubenstein, D. (2002). Energy-efficient computing for wildlife tracking: Design tradeoffs and early experiences with zebranet. In *Architectural Support for Programming Languages and Operating Systems (ASPLOS)*. ACM.

Kansal, A., Somasundara, A. A., Jea, D. D., Srivastava M. B., & Estrin, D. (2004). Intelligent Fluid Infrastructure for Embedded Networks. *Proceedings of the 2nd international conference on Mobile systems, applications, and services,* ACM.

Kim, H. S., Abdelzaher, T. F., & Kwon, W. H. (2003). Minimum energy asynchronous dissemination to mobile sinks in wireless sensor networks. *Proceedings of the First International Conference on Embedded Networked Sensor Systems, SenSys 2003*, (pp. 193–204).

Laibowitz, M., & Paradiso, J. A. (2005). Parasitic Mobility for Pervasive Sensor Networks *PERVASIVE, LNCS 3468*, 255-278. Springer.

Liu, B., Brass, P., Dousse, O., Nain, P., & Towsley, D. (2005). Mobility improves coverage of sensor networks. *Proceedings of the 6th ACM international symposium on Mobile ad hoc networking and computing.* (pp. 300-308). ACM.

Luo, L., & Hubaux, J.-P. (2005). Joint Mobility and Routing for Lifetime Elongation in Wireless Sensor Networks. *Proceedings of the INFOCOM.* IEEE.

Shah, R. C., Roy, S., Jain, S., & Brunette, W. (2003). Data mules: Modeling a Three-Tier Architecture For Sparse Sensor Networks. *Proceedings of the IEEE Workshop. Sensor Network Protocols and Applications.* IEEE.

Somasundara, A. A., Ramamoorthy, A., & Srivastava, M. B. (2004). Mobile Element Scheduling for Efficient Data Collection in Wireless Sensor Networks with Dynamic Deadlines. *Proceedings of the 25th*

IEEE International Real-Time Systems Symposium (RTSS'04) (pp. 296–305).

Vincze, Z., Fodor, K., Vida, R., & Vidács, A. (2007). Electrostatic Modelling of Multiple Mobile Sinks in Wireless Sensor Networks IFIP Networking Workshop on Performance Control in Wireless Sensor Networks, (pp. 30-37)

Vincze, Z., Vida, R., & Vidács, A. (2007). On the Efficiency of Local Information-based Sink Deployment in Heterogeneous Environments. *2nd International Workshop on Performance Control in Wireless Sensor Networks (PWSN)*. ACM.

Wang, G., Cao G., & La Porta, T. (2004) Movement-Assisted Sensor Deployment. *Proceedings of the INFOCOM, 4* (pp. 2469-2479). IEEE.

Wang, Z. M., Basagni, *S.*, Melachrinoudis, E., & Petrioli, C. (2005). Exploiting Sink Mobility for Maximizing Sensor Networks Lifetime. *Proceedings of the 38th Hawaii International Conference on System Sciences.* IEEE.

KEY TERMS

Base Station: The data generated by the sensor nodes in a sensor network is collected to one or more central points, known as Base Station(s). A base station is also referred to as access point or sink.

Coverage Hole: A coverage hole in a sensor network can be defined as the area within the network that is not covered by any sensor node, resulting in lack of monitoring of that area.

Flat Sensor Network Architectures: In a sensor network with flat architecture, all sensor nodes are treated equally and each are responsible to send/route data towards the sink.

Hierarchical Sensor Network Architectures: In a sensor networks with hierarchical architecture, sensor nodes are partitioned into clusters and one node takes responsibility of being the cluster head of a cluster. Each sensor sends data to the respective cluster head, which is responsible to send/route data towards the sink

Multi-Hop Routing Scheme: In the multi-hop routing scheme, nodes located further away from the base station use some intermediate nodes to forward the data to the base station.

Mobile Observer (mobile data collector): A mobile observer is a special mobile entity that can be deployed into a sensor network, whose sole purpose is to move around and collect data from the sensor nodes within the network. Data are buffered in sensor nodes until they can be downloaded into a mobile observer.

Mobile Sink: In a sensor network with mobile sink, sinks are capable of movement and sensor nodes relay data to the mobile sinks with little or no buffering.

Wireless Sensor Networks (WSN): A sensor network is an interconnection of tiny, lightweight, energy-constrained devices, known as sensor nodes. These nodes are usually equipped with a sensing unit, a processing unit, a memory unit and a RF unit that is used for wireless data communication.

Chapter XLIII
Independent Component Analysis Algorithms in Wireless Communication Systems

Sargam Parmar
Ganpat University, India

Bhuvan Unhelkar
MethodScience.com & University of Western Sydney

ABSTRACT

In commercial cellular networks, like the systems based on direct sequence code division multiple access (DSCD-MA), many types of interferences can appear, starting from multi-user interference inside each sector in a cell to interoperator interference. Also unintentional jamming can be present due to co-existing systems at the same band, whereas intentional jamming arises mainly in military applications. Independent Component Analysis (ICA) use as an advanced pre-processing tool for blind suppression of interfering signals in direct sequence spread spectrum communication systems utilizing antenna arrays. The role of ICA is to provide an interference-mitigated signal to the conventional detection. Several ICA algorithms exist for performing Blind Source Separation (BSS). ICA has been used to extract interference signals, but very less literature is available on the performance, that is, how does it behave in communication environment? This needs an evaluation of its performance in communication environment. This chapter evaluates the performance of some major ICA algorithms like Bell and Sejnowski's infomax algorithm, Cardoso's Joint Approximate Diagonalization of Eigen matrices (JADE), Pearson-ICA, and Comon's algorithm in a communication blind source separation problem. Independent signals representing Sub-Gaussian, Super-Gaussian, and mix users, are generated and then mixed linearly to simulate communication signals. Separation performance of ICA algorithms is measured by performance index.

INTRODUCTION

Wireless communication networks and systems that are used for example, by mobile phone users, have an essential challenge in division of this common transmission medium among several users. A primary goal of communication system is to enable each user of the system to communicate reliably despite the fact that the other users occupy the same resources, possibly simultaneously. As the number of users in the system grows, it becomes necessary to improve the efficiency of these common communication resources. Various communication systems based on CDMA (Code Division Multiple Access) techniques have become popular, because they offer several advantages over the more traditional FDMA and TDMA schemes based on the use of nonoverlapping frequency or time slots assigned to each user. The capacity of CDMA based communication system is larger, and it degrades gradually with increasing number of simultaneous users who can be asynchronous. CDMA systems require more advanced signal processing methods, and correct reception of CDMA signals is more difficult because of several disturbing phenomena such as multipath propagation, possibly fading channels, various types of interferences, time delays, and different powers of users.

The most important use of a spread spectrum communication system is that of interference mitigation. In fact, a spread spectrum communication system has an inherent temporal interference mitigation capability. At times, however, the interference can be too strong, or the requirements for the link quality are more stringent, so that additional interference mitigation is needed. In a cellular network the interference originating from the neighboring cells, called inter-cell interference, is one of the reasons for the need for additional interference mitigation capability in a receiver. Independent Component Analysis (ICA) use as an advanced preprocessing tool for blind suppression of interfering jammer signals in direct sequence spread spectrum communication systems utilizing antenna arrays. The role of ICA is to provide a jammer-mitigated signal to the conventional detection.

Jutten and H'erault provided one of the first significant approaches to the problem of blind separation of instantaneous linear mixtures. Since then, many different approaches have been attempted by numerous researches using neural networks, artificial learning, higher order statistics, minimum mutual information, beam-forming and adaptive noise cancellation, each claiming various degrees of success. Attempts have to been made to compare the various algorithms for their convergence speed, computational load and accuracy. Several ICA algorithms exist for performing Blind Source Separation (BSS).

This chapter evaluates the performance of some major ICA algorithms like Bell and Sejnowski's infomax algorithm, Cardoso's joint approximate diagonalization of Eigen matrices (JADE), Pearson-ICA and Comon's algorithm in a blind source separation problem. The main aim of this chapter is to determine accuracy of the algorithms by measuring performance index. Performance index versus number of Super-Gaussian, sub-Gaussian and mix users have been considered for comparison.

ICA ALGORITHMS

Consider the classical ICA model with instantaneous mixing

$$x = As + n \tag{1}$$

where the sources $s = [s_1, s_2, ..., s_n]^T$ are mutually independent random variables and A_{nxn} is an unknown invertible mixing matrix and noise $n = [n_1, n_2, ..., n_n]^T$. The goal is to find only from observations, x, a matrix W such that the output

$$y = Wx \tag{2}$$

is an estimate of the possible scaled and permutated source vectors.

Several algorithms exits for blind source separation. This chapter describes the performance of some major ICA algorithms. This section presents a brief description of the respective approaches of the compared ICA algorithms.

JADE Algorithm

The JADE algorithm relies on second and fourth-order cumulants to separate the sources. SOS is used to obtain a whitening matrix Z from the sample covariances. To reduce the computational load, only the n most significant eigen pairs of fourth order cumulants obtained from the whitened process are joint diagonalized by unitary matrix U. The separated matrix can be estimated as $U^\dagger Z$, where $\dagger$ represents pseudo inverse. The JADE contrast function is the sum of squared fourth order cross cumulants

$$\Phi^{\text{JADE(Y)}} = \sum_{ijkl \neq iikl} (\mathbf{Q}_{ijlk})^2 \qquad (3)$$

As this algorithm uses cross-cumulants, there is no need to go for gradient descent and hence there is no chance of divergence. Also there is no problem of updating the weights and tuning the parameters as in Bell and Sejnowski's infomax algorithm.

Bell and Sejnowski's Algorithm

Bell and Sejnowski have developed an unsupervised learning algorithm (Infomax algorithm) based on entropy maximization in a single layer feed-forward neural network. The main idea is that maximizing the joint entropy $\mathbf{H}(y)$ of the outputs of a neural processor can approximately minimize the mutual information among the output components. It is proved that infomax is equivalent to maximum likelihood. The joint entropy of n variables, $y_1, y_2, \ldots y_n$, which are the outputs of the neural network, may be written as:

$$\mathbf{H}(y_{1, \ldots}y_n) = \mathbf{H}(y_1) + \ldots + \mathbf{H}(y_n) - \mathbf{I}(y_{1, \ldots}y_n) \qquad (4)$$

If the nonlinear transfer function of a neural network matches the probability density function of the inputs, and the joint entropy $\mathbf{H}(y_{1, \ldots}y_n)$ of the outputs is maximized, the mutual information $\mathbf{I}(y_{1, \ldots}y_n)$ among the outputs is then minimized. The output signals are assumed to be independent. The learning rule for a single layer feed-forward neural network to implement the separation is

$$\Delta \mathbf{W} \ \alpha \ \ [\mathbf{W}^T]^{-1} + (1-2y)\mathbf{x}^T \qquad (5)$$

$$\Delta \mathbf{w}_0 \alpha \ (1-2y) \qquad (6)$$

where $y = f(u)$, $u = \mathbf{W}\mathbf{x} + \mathbf{w}_o$ and $f(u)$ is a sigmoid contrast function.

Usually $f(u) = 1 + e^{-(u-1)}$ or $f(u) = tanh(u)$. Here $\mathbf{W}$ is the weight matrix and $\mathbf{w}_o$ is the bias vector.

Comon's Algorithm

A specific contrast function is proposed, based on minimization of mutual information between the components at the output of separator (which is directly

related to Kullback-Leibler divergence between the output vector probability density function (pdf) and it's pdf if it was made of independent components). After some manipulations on the Edgeworth expansion of the source joint pdf, the contrast function simplifies into sum of the output squared rth-order marginal cumulants and for $r = 4$ it becomes output squared kurtosis:

$$\Psi_4 (\mathbf{Q}) \ = \ \sum_{i=1}^{q} (\mathbf{k}^s_{iiii})^2 \qquad (7)$$

Pearson-ICA Algorithm

This algorithm combines two well known techniques for Independent component analysis (ICA): fixed non-linear contrast functions and maximum likelihood approach. The Pearson system is a parametric family of distributions that may be used to model a wide class of source distributions. The pearson system is defined by the differential equation

$$f(x) = (x- a)f(x)/b_0 + b_1x + b_2x^2 \qquad (8)$$

where $a;$ $b_0;$ b_1 and b_2 are the parameters of the distribution. In the maximum likelihood approach to ICA the score function $\varphi(\mathbf{y}_k)$ of hypothesized source distribution is used as a contrast. The score function of the Pearson system is easily solved from equation (8). The parameters $a;$ $b_0;$ b_1 and b_2 may be estimated by the method of moments. In this paper, for experiment used fixed point algorithm and hyperbolic tangent contrast $\varphi(y)$ = $tanh(2y)$ for both clearly sub-gaussian and clearly super-gaussian sources. The boundaries between contrasts are chosen by experiments. The procedure for the Pearson-ICA may be given as follows:

Repeat until convergence

1. Calculate the third and fourth sample moments α_3 and α_4 for current data $\mathbf{y}_k = \mathbf{W}_k\mathbf{x}$ and select the Pearson system or fixed *(tanh)* contrast.
2. If the Pearson system was selected estimate parameters of the distribution by method of moments.
3. Calculate scores $\varphi(\mathbf{y}_k)$ for the Pearson system or fixed contrast.
4. Calculate the demixing matrix $\mathbf{W}_{k+1}$ using algorithm (4).

$$\mathbf{W}_{k+1} = \mathbf{W}_k + \mathbf{D}(E\{\ \varphi(\mathbf{y})\ \mathbf{y}_T\} - diag(E\{\ \varphi(\mathbf{y}_i)\ \mathbf{y}_i\}))\mathbf{W}_k \qquad (9)$$

Figure 1. No of sug-Gaussian input users

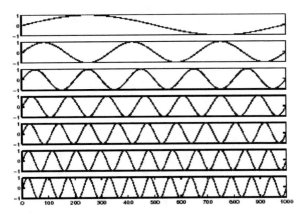

Figure 2. Performance index as a function of number of sub-Gaussian users

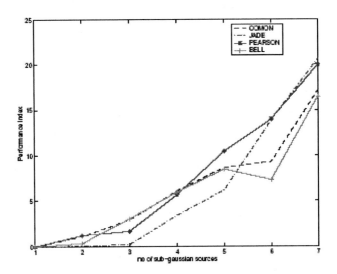

where $\mathbf{D}=diag\left(1/(E\{\varphi(y_i)y_i\}-E\{\varphi'(y_i)\})\right)$ since both moment estimators for parameters and score function are simple rational functions, the Pearson-ICA is computationally fast.

EXPERIMENT SETUP

As the number of users in the communication system grows, it becomes necessary to improve the efficiency of common communication resources. Independent Component Analysis (ICA) use as an advanced pre-processing tool for blind suppression of interfering signals in direct sequence spread spectrum communication systems utilizing antenna arrays. The role of ICA is to provide a mitigated signal to the conventional detection. As the number of users in the communication system grows, it becomes necessary to measure the performance of these ICA algorithms.

Figure 3. Number of super-Gaussian input users

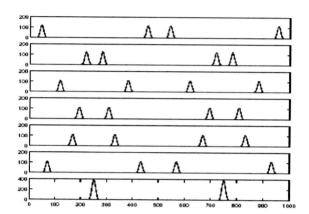

Figure 4. Performance index as a function of number of super-Gaussian users

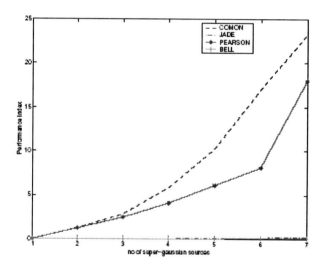

Users Generation

Simulations have been done using artificially generated data to observed different users in communication systems. In the first setup all users were sub-Gaussian. In another experimental setup super-Gaussian users were taken. Finally, simulations were done with mixed users (sub-Gaussian and Super-Gaussian and Gaussian). These users are linearly mixed and separations are carried out by different ICA algorithms.

Linear Mixing

In a linear, isotropic medium use a mixing matrix since this approximates the fading. Set the mixing coefficient randomly between input users and fixed for all practical.

Performance Evaluation

To quantify the higher order performance of the demixing use the performance index, *PI*. This is a measure

Figure 5. No of mix input sources

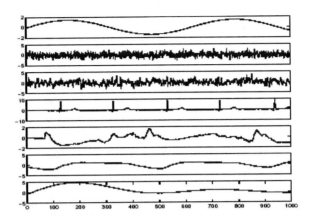

Figure 6. Performance Index as a function of number of mix users

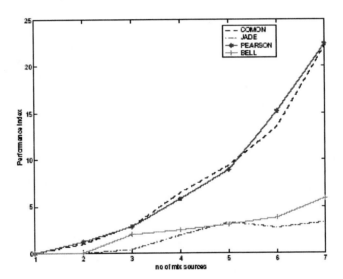

on the global system matrix **P=WA** suitable for the degeneracy conditions **W** = **A**$^{-1}$ and is calculated

$$PI = \sum_{i=1}^{n} \{ \left(\sum_{k=1}^{n} |p_{ik}|^2 / max_j |p_{ij}|^2 - 1 \right) + \left(\sum_{k=1}^{n} |p_{ki}|^2 / max_j |p_{ji}|^2 - 1 \right) \}$$

(10)

where p_{ij} is the $(i, j)^{th}$ element of the global system matrix **P**=**WA** and $max_{}p_{ij}$ represents the maximum value among the elements in the ith row vector of **P**, $max_{}p_{ij}$ does the maximum value among the elements in the

i^{th} column vector of **P**. When perfect user separation is carried out, the performance index *PI* is zero.

EXPERIMENTAL RESULTS AND DISCUSSION

In the first setup all users were sub-Gaussian (sine waves with different frequencies) Fig 1.

Mixing matrix was randomly generated and fixed for all practical. The results have been plotted in Fig. 2.

461

The results indicate that as the number of user increases, performance of all algorithms degrades. In another experimental setup, simulations were done with all super-Gaussian users Fig 3.

The result of super-Gaussian users is given in Fig. 4.

Again, JADE and Bell algorithms give good results (Ideal results Performance Index zero). Finally, mixed users (sub-Gaussian and super-Gaussian and Gaussian) were taken for simulation Fig 5.

The plot of Performance Index vs. Number of users is given in Fig. 6.

It is evident that the performance of the algorithms badly degrades for the mixed users, but JADE and Bell least affected.

CONCLUSION

This chapter calculates the performance of the JADE, Bell, Pearson-ICA and Comon's ICA algorithms in BSS problem. Using simulated independent sub-Gaussian, super-Gaussian and mix users. The results of super-Gaussian users show JADE and Bell algorithms gives good results (Ideal results Performance Index zero). For sub-Gaussian and mix users all algorithms are able to extract the users but with different Performance index. Even for high value of Performance index, qualities of separated users are quite satisfactory for all algorithms. These results are useful for selecting the ICA algorithms for particular applications where users are only sub- Gaussian, super-Gaussian and mix users, to mitigate various interference problems in wireless communication systems.

REFERENCES

Bell, A., & Sejnowski, T. (1995). An information maximization approach to blind source separation and blind deconvolution. *Neural Computing, 7*, 1129-1159.

Cardos, J. F. (1997). *Statistical principles of source separation*, 1837-1844.

Cardoso, J. F. (n/d). Higher order contrasts for independent component analysis. *Neural computation, 11*(1), 157-192.

Cardoso, J. F., & Souloumiac, A. (1993). Blind beamforming for non-gaussian signals. *In Proc. IEEE*, 362-370.

Comon, P. (1996, July). Contrasts for multichannel blind deconvolution. *IEEE Signal Processing Lett., 3*, 209-211.

Comon, P. (1994, April). Independent component analysis, a new concept? *Signal processing, 36(Special Issue Higher Order Statistics)*, 287-314.

Jutten, C., & Herault, J. (1991). Blind separation of sources part I: An adaptive algorithm based on neuromimatic architecture. *Signal Processing, 24*, 1-10.

Karvanen, J., Erriksson, J., & Koivunen, V. (2000). Pearson system based method for Blind Separation. *Proceedings of Second International Workshop on Independent Component Analysis and Blind Signal Separation*. Helsinki. (pp. 585-590).

Parmar, S. D., & Sahambi, J. S. A Comparative Survey on removal of MECG artifacts from FECG using ICA algorithms. *Proceeding of International Conference on Intelligent Sensing and Imformation Processing-2004, Chennai-India*, ICISIP-2004. (pp. 88-91).

Ristaniemi, T. K., Raju, J., Karhunen, & Oja, E. (2002). Jammer cancellation in DS-CDMA array systems: Pre and post switching of ICA and RAKE. *In Proc. of the 2002 IEEE Int. Symposium on Neural Networks for Signal Processing (NNSP 2002)*, (pp. 495-504), Martingy, Switzerland, September 04 - 06.

Ristaniemi, T., Raju, K., & Karhunen, J. (2002). Jammer mitigation in DSCDMA array system using independent component analysis. *In Proc. of the 2002 IEEE Int. Conference on Communications (ICC 2002)*, New York, USA, April 28 - May 02, 2002.

Seungjin, C., Chichocki, A., & Amari, S. (2000). Flexible independent component analysis. *Journal of VLSI Signal Processing*. Boston: Kluwer Academic Publishers.

KEY TERMS

s_i: i[th] source signal

x_i: i[th] sensor output

n_i: i[th] noise signal

s: Source signal vector

x: Sensor signal vector

n: Noise vector

y: Separator output vector

q: Number of sources

p: Number of observation

A: Mixing matrix

W: Demixing matrix

PCA: Principal Component Analysis

ICA: Independent Component Analysis

pdf: Probability density function

BSS: Blind Source Separation

TDMA: Time Division Multiple Access

ISI: Inter-Symbol Interference

MAI: Multiple Access Interference

CDMA: Code Division Multiple Access

Chapter XLIV
A Case Study in the Installation of Wi–Fi Networks in a Chemical Manufacturing Unit in India

Bhargav Bhatt
Ultra InfoTech, India

ABSTRACT

This chapter describes a case study in installation of a Wi-Fi network in a chemical manufacturing company. This project, carried out in India, was meant to connect the various dispersed manufacturing units of the organization as well as its administrative offices. Initial studies indicated that a physical network was not appropriate due to the local corrosive chemical environment; Ultra InfoTech was invited to install Wi-Fi network within the complex. This chapter reports on how the project progressed, the lessons learnt and the way to approach this kind of work in future in terms of wireless networking.

INTRODUCTION

This chapter describes the installation of a Wi-Fi network in a chemical manufacturing company in India and the lessons learnt in the process of that installation. This practical experience of Wi-Fi network installation begins with the need to and advantage of having such a network in the first place. Subsequently, the organization – a chemical plant - in which this installation is carried out, is described. This discussion is then followed by the various options available to the organization in terms of putting together a network for its computers. Later, this case study takes the readers through the actual process of Wi-Fi installation at a chemical plant in India. The advantages, limitations, risks, and suggestions on how to handle the risks are also provided.

MOBILE TECHNOLOGIES AND NETWORK

Mobility plays a significant role in almost all aspects of today's life style whether it is a business or personal. This is so, because of the location-independence offered by the mobile networks (Unni and Harmon, 2005). For commercial establishments, increasingly, mobility is becoming mandatory irrespective of nature of commerce being carried out. Out of the many different aspects of mobility as discussed by (Unhelkar, 2008), networks form a vital and often deciding aspect of mobile usage in practice.

There are many different types of mobile networks that can be grouped into two: the short range and the long range networks. Kuppuswami (2005) has discussed these mobile networks in greater detail than others with respect to their capabilities to connect varied devices by mapping them to neural networks using wireless technologies. In the context of this chapter, the types of networks that are discussed are LAN (Local Area Network), WAN (Wide Area Network), MAN (Metropolitan area network) and RFID (Radio Frequency Identification). The reason for discussing these networks is that they provide some of the options that need to be considered while deciding type of network to be used for environment such as a chemical manufacturing plant.

LAN

Local area network (LAN), generally which is a group of computers and associated devices that share a common communication line or wireless link. Typically, this is a network where connected devices share the resources of a single processor or server or share resources of each other within a small geographical area. Usually, the server has applications and data storage that are shared in common by multiple computer users. A local area network may serve as few as two or three users (e.g., in a home network) or as many as thousands of users (for example, in an FDDI network). Major local area network technologies that are discussed below are usually used in setting up a LAN in an organization.

Ethernet

Ethernet is the most widely installed local area network technology that has been specified in a standard called IEEE 802.3 (http://standards.ieee.org/getieee802/802.3.html). An Ethernet LAN typically uses coaxial cable or special grades of twisted pair of wires. Ethernet is used in wireless LAN also. The most common Ethernet systems are called 10BASE-T which provides transmission speeds up to 10 Mbps. Devices are connected to the cable and compete for access using a Carrier Sense Multiple Access with Collision Detection (CSMA/CD) protocol. Fast Ethernet or 100BASE-T provides transmission speeds up to 100 Mbps and is generally used for LAN backbone systems, supporting nodes with 10BASE-T cards. Gigabit Ethernet provides an even higher level of backbone support at 1000 Mbps. However, it should be noted that these speeds are reflecting those of the local hardware rather than the network speeds across the Internet. Furthermore, in the context of a corro-

sive environment such as the shop floor of a chemical manufacturing plant, it is important to note that these physically connected networks need to be protected as well as maintained in a preventative manner.

Token Ring

A Token Ring network is a LAN in which all computers are connected in a ring or star method and a bit or token-passing scheme is used to prevent collision of data between two computers that want to send messages at the same time. The Token Ring protocol is the second most widely used protocol in LANs after Ethernet Networks. However, token ring networks usually have the challenge of a missed token and thereby loss of data packet.

FDDI

FDDI (Fiber Distributed Data Interface) is a set of ANSI and ISO standards (www.ansi.com) for data transmission on fiber optic lines in a LAN which can be extended in range up to 200 km. This protocol is based on the Token Ring protocol. FDDI LAN is used when the area to be covered is larger and number of users to be supported are more. Many times the FDDI is used as a backbone of a wide area network (WAN).

WAN

The term Wide Area Network (WAN) usually refers to a network which covers a large geographical area, which uses communications circuits to connect the intermediate nodes. A major factor impacting WAN design and performance is a requirement that they lease communications circuits from telephone companies or other communications carriers. Transmission rates are typically 2 Mbps, 34 Mbps, 45 Mbps, 155 Mbps, and 625 Mbps (or sometimes considerably more).

Numerous WANs have been constructed, including public packet networks, large corporate networks, military networks, banking networks, stock brokerage networks, and airline reservation networks. Some WANs are very extensive, spanning the globe, but most do not provide true global coverage.

MAN

Metropolitan area network (MAN) is a network that interconnects users with computer resources in a geographic area or region larger than that covered by even a large local area network (LAN) but smaller than the area covered by a wide area network (WAN). The term is applied to the interconnection of networks in a city into a single larger network (which may then also offer efficient connection to a wide area network). It is also used to mean the interconnection of several local area networks by bridging them with backbone lines. The latter usage is also sometimes referred to as a campus network.

RFID

RFID (radio frequency identification) is a technology that incorporates the use of electromagnetic or electrostatic coupling in the radio frequency (RF) portion of the electromagnetic spectrum to uniquely identify an object, animal, or a person. RFID is coming into increasing use in industry as an alternative to the barcode. The advantage of RFID is that it does not require direct contact or line-of-sight scanning. An RFID system consists of three components: an antenna; transceiver (often combined into one reader); and a transponder (the tag). The antenna uses radio frequency waves to transmit a signal that activates the transponder. When activated, the tag transmits data back to the antenna. The data is used to notify a programmable logic controller that an action should occur. The action could be as simple as raising an access gate or as complicated as interfacing with a database to carry out a monetary transaction. Low-frequency RFID systems (30 KHz to 500 KHz) have short transmission ranges (generally less than six feet). High-frequency RFID systems (850 MHz to 950 MHz and 2.4 GHz to 2.5 GHz) offer longer transmission ranges (more than 90 feet). In general, the higher the frequency, the more expensive the system is. RFID is sometimes called dedicated short range communication (DSRC).

Infrared

Infrared Data Communication is a simple example of short range wireless network. The most important characteristics of IrDA Communication consist of range, angle and modulation. The Standard range of two devices in an infrared line of sight network is 1 m with low-power to low power is 0.2 m and Standard to low power: 0.3 m.

Infrared Communication is very agile and is interrupted by various factors including angle, distance, noise and heat. Light waves also form an interruption pattern in Infrared Communication. Infrared Communication works on a few layers which constitute the complete Infrared Communication Protocol for Data Transfer and Communication between IrDA devices.

Having discussed and considered the various types of networks, the team at Ultra Infotech started focusing its attention on the wireless LAN (WLAN). The opportunity to consider the coexistence of WLAN and WWAN as discussed by Shuaib and Boulmalf (2006) was also considered by the team. Furthermore, as mentioned earlier, this wireless networking provided many advantages in the chemical manufacturing setup. There were basically three different types of WiFi networks as discussed by Bhattar *et al*, (2006) that were in contention for our client.

- Wide area networks that the cellular carriers create,
- Wireless local area networks, that you create, and
- Personal area networks, that creates themselves.

Wide Area Networks

Wide Area Networks, as mentioned earlier in this chapter, include the networks provided by the cell phone carriers. Originally providing cellular voice services, the carriers added data services as well, at first by overlaying digital data services on top of the early analogue voice services, and later by building out brand new generation voice-plus-data networks. Wireless data services are available just about everywhere you can use a voice cell phone today. However, the network carriers usually determine where to provide coverage based on their business strategy, and they also control Quality of Service (QoS). Usually, large organizations with bulk buying power partner with the network carriers that results in extra network resources being made available in the corporate tower. Thus, there are repercussions of the size and bulk of business being carried out with the network operator on the networking strategies within the organization.

Where would you use WANs? You would use WANs when reach is the most important aspect of your solution, and speed is less important. Reach is important if you are providing wireless solutions to the public at large, for example, or you want to give your employees wireless access to your corporate data, whether they are in the office, across town, out of town, or (in some cases) in other countries.

Wireless Local Area Networks

Wireless LANs are networks set up to provide wireless connectivity within a finite coverage area. Typical coverage areas might be a hospital, a university, the airport, or a plant. They usually have a well-known audience in mind, for example health care providers, students, or field maintenance staff. WLANS are used when high data-transfer rate is the most important aspect of the solution, and reach is restricted. For example, in this case of a manufacturing plant having administrative and local sale-cum-marketing offices in the same campus, internet connectivity is one of other important requirement of a network.

Wireless LANS work in an unregulated part of the spectrum, so anyone can create their own wireless LAN, say in their home or office. In principle, you have complete control over where coverage is provided. In practice, coverage spills over into the street outside exposing you to a particular range of vulnerabilities.

Wireless LANs have their own share of terminology, including:

- 802.11 - this is the network technology used in wireless LANs. In fact, it is a family of technologies such as 802.11a. 802.11b, etc., differing in speed and other attributes
- WiFi - a common name for the early 802.11b standard.

In addition to creating your own private WLAN, some organizations and some carriers are providing high speed WLAN internet access to the public at certain locations like airports in India. These locations are called hotspots, and for a price you can browse the internet at speeds about 20 times greater than you could get over your cell phone.

Personal Area Networks

These are networks that provide wireless connectivity over distances of up to 10m or so. At first this seems ridiculously small, but this range allows a computer to be connected wirelessly to a nearby printer, or a cell phone's hands-free headset to be connected wirelessly to the cell phone. The most talked about technology is called Bluetooth.

Personal Area Networks are a bit different than WANs and WLANs in one important respect. In the WAN and WLAN cases, networks are set up first, the selecting which devices to use. In the Personal Area Network case, there is no independent pre-existing network. The participating devices establish an ad-hoc network when they are within range, and the network is dissolved when the devices pass out of range.

PAN technologies add value to other wireless technologies, although they wouldn't be the primary driver for a wireless business solution. For example, a wireless LAN in this type of manufacturing plant may allow a QC person to see properties of a chemical being manufactured on a handheld device. If a QC person's handheld was also Bluetooth enabled, he could walk to within range of the nearest Bluetooth enabled printer and print the chart of properties of chemical being manufactured.

The discussion thus far has covered the most logical approach to wireless networking. The following discussion is on the chemical plant where this network is to be installed.

CHEMICAL PLANT: BACKGROUND AND CHALLENGE

The project described here deals with the installation of a wireless network in a chemical manufacturing complex. The wireless communications technologies and networks described thus far in this chapter are now applied in this practical situation. This chemical manufacturing complex is located in the Western region of India and is spread in an area of around 120,000 square meters. This complex comprises of various sections that deal with sourcing of materials, undertaking chemical processes, storing the output and distributing the product. Furthermore, there are supporting resource management, accounting and payroll functions as well. There was a need to computerize these sections under one network so to make the operations more accurate, faster & reliable. There was also a need to connect these various dispersed manufacturing units, as well as the administrative offices through a network. Ultra InfoTech, as a consultant and networking service provider of the company, reviewed customer requirements and feasibility of different types of networks for this project. Initial studies

Figure 1. Chemical manufacturing plant: Location map

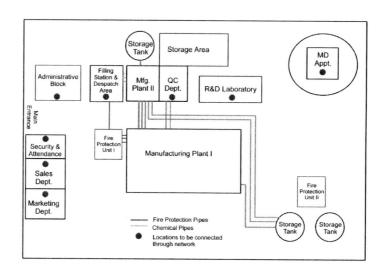

Figure 2. Chemical manufacturing plant: Wi-fi network plan

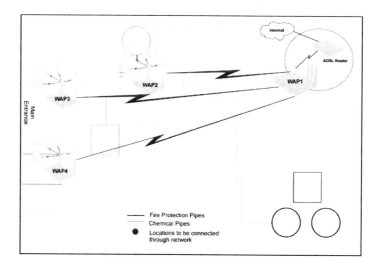

indicated that a physical network was not appropriate due to the local industrial environment. This industrial environment included corrosive physical/chemical environment; physical cabling was virtually deemed impossible due to the fact that the factory already exists, and it was highly risky to dig through the existing chemical plant in order to lay the cables. Alternatively, the passing of physical overhead cables was equally risky. Thus, ultimately, we arrived at a conclusion that

Wi-Fi network was the best solution. Ultra InfoTech was then further invited to complete the installation for a Chemical Manufacturing Company. Figure 1 shows the physical layout of the organization and the needs for connectivity between them.

According to the study carried out at the location of the plant a network was required to be setup for different departments. These departments started from security at the main entrance, through to administrative department, purchase & stores department, chemical manufacturing plants, Research & Development Laboratory, QC Laboratory & manufactured goods dispatch department. As mentioned earlier, and obvious from the Figure 1, laying underground cables was difficult or next to impossible as most of the area is sensitive area and is prone to chemical hazards from the manufacturing activities of the company. The Wi-Fi network would facilitate easier installation, usage and maintenance.

INSTALLATION OF WI-FI NETWORK IN CHEMICAL PLANT

This section describes the process of installing the network. Firstly the purpose of the network itself is studied in order to ascertain where it will be used. Shanmugavel & Gomathy (2006) have discussed the use of fuzzy logic in scheduling and using mobile ad-hoc networks. During a similar study of the current environment, it is discovered that the network is meant primarily to connect the PCs (personal computer) of the organization. The PCs themselves are studied for their need to share documents and files and also their need to connect to the Internet. There is also a pressing need for the production department of the chemical factory to communicate with the quality control department in almost a real-time basis. The data relates to the properties of the chemicals manufactured, which in turn would be used by the quality control department to determine whether the batch is to be approved or not.

The most appropriate mechanism to connect these PCs through the Wi-Fi network is the MIMO (Multiple-In Multiple-Out) technology. This MIMO technology is used to connect the Wireless Access Points and has been discussed by Gilbert, *et al.* (2005). A total of 4 such connection points were identified. Furthermore, the reason for using WAP device with MIMO technology is its greater performance as compared with conventional routers. The MIMO technology provides consistent network connectivity & higher throughput under challenging circumstances. For example, if one of the multiple networking WAP devices fails then also the network is available through alternate route.

Figure 2 describes how the specific Wi-Fi network is planned and installed at the site of the chemical factory. The main WAP (Wireless Access Point 1) is setup at managing director's (MD's) Office. Three

other WAP devices, i.e. WAP1, WAP2 & WAP3 are connected to the WAP1 located at MD's office. Thus the network is established between the four locations in the plant. The 3 WAP devices (WAP1, WAP2 & WAP3) form a network within its coverage area and, in-turn; connect all PCs within its range of working. All 4 WAP devices are further equipped with multiple antennas that are used for specific purposes. One of two antennas of each of three WAP devices communicates with the main WAP device at MD's office. The second antenna of these three WAP devices communicates with PCs of each network. This connectivity leaves the door open for further expansion and creation of a sub-network for a particular location within the factory. As also mentioned earlier, one of the requirements of this Wi-Fi network is that it should provide the PCs with connectivity to the Internet. This connectivity to the Internet is provided by means of an ADSL router. This ADSL router is connected to the main WAP device (WAP1) from where it takes the PCs on to the external Internet.

LESSONS LEARNT IN THE WI-FI INSTALLATION

The lessons learnt through this Wi-Fi installation in practice are as follows:

- The decision to use WAP together with MIMO turned out to be a good decision despite the fact that the cost of this solution is higher than the conventional device. This is so, because of the redundancy offered by MIMO-based network.
- The power consumption of the MIMO-based solution is also higher; however, in the situation of a chemical factory environment, this additional power consumption is considered a worthwhile investment that pays off in terms of reliability of the network.
- The security of the Wi-Fi network requires checking at the WAP1 for external access; however, the internal network with WAP1-2-3 does not face much security problem. Security between the production and the quality assurance department is also not a big problem as the network is accessible only within the range of the factory and not accessible external to the factory.
- Unwanted use of resources of Wi-Fi Network
- The challenge of collision between Wi-Fi network & other digital devices like cordless phones,

Bluetooth or even the machinery being used in plant is an important consideration. However, the Wi-Fi network is tuned in such a way as to ensure no collision or conflict between the external devices.

FUTURE DIRECTION

The future of Wi-Fi network installations is significant. This is so because Wi-Fi networks provide excellent opportunities for connectivity with minimal overheads and risks. Following are the additional features that are likely to be implemented in the chemical factory using the network that has already been installed:

- The ease of access to data and reports is to be used for printing of records from manufacturing plant to head office & vice-e-versa.
- Track dispatch / order status.
- Track trucks carrying dispatched goods.
- Monitor manufacturing process or output of a plant from administrative office located at different location.
- Can have conference of sales or support teams at manufacturing plant & administrative plant.
- Ability to connect the local manufacturing plant with the corporate head office located in a different city.

CONCLUSION

This chapter describes the installation of a Wi-Fi network within a chemical manufacturing plant. The chapter described the process, as well as the advantages and limitations of using such Wi-Fi network.

ACKNOWLEDGMENT

The author would like to acknowledge the discussions and original thoughts of Mr. Prashant Limbachiya on the Wi-Fi networks and their value to this project.

REFERENCES

Bhattar, R., K. R. Ramkrishna, Dasgupta K. S., 2006, "Review of Wireless Technologies and Generations", Chapter 11 in *Handbook of Research in Mobile Business: Technical, Methodological and Social perspectives,* (Ed. B. Unhelkar), IGI Global, Hershey, PA, USA

Gilbert J. M., Choi Won-Joon, Sun Qinfang 2005, "MIMO Technology for Advanced Wireless Local Area Networks ", A paper presented at "Annual ACM IEEE Design Automation Conference, Anaheim, California, USA"

Islam, M.M., and Murshed, M., Mobility Support Resource Management for Mobile Networks, Chapter 24, p332, in *Handbook of Research in Mobile Business: Technical, Methodological and Social perspectives,* (Ed. B. Unhelkar), IGI Global, Hershey, PA, USA.

Kuppuswami, A., 2006,"A Neural Network-Based Mobile Architecture for Mobile Agents", Chapter 20 in *Handbook of Research in Mobile Business: Technical, Methodological and Social perspectives,* (Ed. B. Unhelkar), IGI Global, Hershey, PA, USA

Pauraj A., Nabar R., & Gore D., 2003 Introduction to Space-Time Wireless Communications. Chapter 3 in *Introduction to space-time wireless communications* Cambridge University Press, Cambridge, 2003

Shanmugavel S. & Gomathy C., 2006,"A Novel Fuzzy Scheduler for Mobile Ad Hoc Networks", Chapter 22 in *Handbook of Research in Mobile Business: Technical, Methodological and Social perspectives,* (Ed. B. Unhelkar), IGI Global, Hershey, PA, USA.

Shuaib, K., and Boulmalf, M., 2006, Co-Existence of WLAN and WPAN Communication Systems, Chapter 23 in *Handbook of Research in Mobile Business: Technical, Methodological and Social perspectives,* (Ed. B. Unhelkar), IGI Global, Hershey, PA, USA.

Unni, R., Harmon, R., "Location-Based Services: Opportunities and Challenges", Chapter 2 in *Handbook of Research in Mobile Business: Technical, Methodological and Social perspectives,* (Ed. B. Unhelkar), IGI Global, Hershey, PA, USA

Unhelkar, B., 2008, *Mobile Enterprise Architecture,* Cutter Executive Report, USA

www.ultrainfotech.net referenced in July, 2008

http://portal.acm.org/citation.cfm?id=1065689 referenced in July, 2008 for MIMO Technology

http://www.dlink.in/Upload/UploadCaseStudies/icici_infotech_installs_d.htm referenced in July, 2008 for installation of a Wi-Fi Network at corporate level.

http://www.linksys.com/servlet/Satellite?c=L_Product_C1&childpagename=US%2FLayout&cid=1115416936433&pagename=Linksys%2FCommon%2FVisitorWrapper&lid=3643303676N03, referenced in July, 2008 for available models of wireless access point device (WAP).

KEY TERMS

FDDI: Fiber Distributed Data Interface.

IEEE 802.3: IEEE Standard for Information Technology.

MIMO: Multiple In Multiple Out.

Wi-Fi Installation: Installation of Wireless Network.

Wireless Networking: Network of PCs and other equipments through wireless devices.

WLAN: Wireless Local Area Network.

Chapter XLV
Social Context for Mobile Computing Device Adoption and Diffusion:
A Proposed Research Model and Key Research Issues

Andrew P. Ciganek
University of Wisconsin – Milwaukee, USA

K. Ramamurthy
University of Wisconsin – Milwaukee, USA

ABSTRACT

The purpose of this chapter is to explore and suggest how perceptions of the social context of an organization moderate the usage of an innovative technology. We propose a research model that is strongly grounded in theory and offer a number of associated propositions that can be used to investigate adoption and diffusion of mobile computing devices for business-to-business (B2B) interactions (including transactions and other informational exchanges). Mobile computing devices for B2B are treated as a technological innovation. An extension of existing adoption and diffusion models by considering the social contextual factors is necessary and appropriate in light of the fact that various aspects of the social context have been generally cited to be important in the introduction of new technologies. In particular, a micro-level analysis of this phenomenon for the introduction of new technologies is not common. Since the technological innovation that is considered here is very much in its nascent stages there may not as yet be a large body of users in a B2B context. Therefore, this provides a rich opportunity to conduct academic research. We expect this chapter to sow the seeds for extensive empirical research in the future.

INTRODUCTION

What causes individuals to adopt new information technologies (ITs)? How much influence do the perceptions of the social context of an organization have on the acceptance of new ITs? These questions are significant because systems that are not utilized will not result in expected efficiency and effectiveness gains (Agarwal & Prasad, 1999), and will end up as unproductive use of organizational resources. Academic research consequently has focused on the determinants of computer technology acceptance and utilization among users. Some of this research comes from the literature on adoption and diffusion of innovations (DOI), where an individual's perceptions about an innovation's attributes (e.g., compatibility, complexity, relative advantage, trialability, visibility) are posited to influence adoption behavior (Moore & Benbasat, 1991; Rogers, 2003). Another stream of research stems from the technology acceptance model (TAM), which has become widely accepted among IS researchers because of its parsimony and empirical support (Agarwal & Prasad, 1999; Davis, 1989; Davis, Bagozzi, & Warshaw, 1989; Hu, Chau, Sheng, & Tam, 1999; Jackson, Chow, & Leitch, 1997; Mathieson, 1991; Taylor & Todd, 1995; Venkatesh, 1999, 2000; Venkatesh & Davis, 1996, 2000; Venkatesh & Morris, 2000).

Individual differences indeed are believed to be very relevant to information system (IS) success (Zmud, 1979). Nelson (1990) also acknowledged the importance of individual differences in affecting the acceptance of new technologies. A variety of research has investigated differences in the perceptions of individuals when using TAM (Harrison & Rainer, 1992; Jackson et al., 1997; Venkatesh, 1999, 2000; Venkatesh & Morris, 2000); however, the perceptions and influences of the social context of an organization have not been widely examined in the literature. Hartwick and Barki (1994) suggest that it is imperative to examine the acceptance of new technologies with different user populations in different organizational contexts.

Although mobile computing devices have existed for several years, strategic applications of this technology are still in their infancy. Mobile computing devices (in the context of business-to-business—B2B) is treated as a technology innovation in this chapter due to their newness and short history. An investigation into the usage of mobile computing devices within a B2B context, which we define as two or more entities engaged within a business relationship, is of value because of its increasing popularity (March, Hevner, & Ram, 2000). As an emergent phenomenon, relatively modest academic literature has examined the nature of adoption and use of this technology. Mobile computing devices, which have been described as both ubiquitous (March et al., 2000) and nomadic (Lyytinen & Yoo, 2002a, 2002b), offer a stark difference from traditional, static computing environments. A good characterization of these differences is provided in Satyanarayanan (1996). New technology innovations typically require changes in users' existing operating procedures, knowledge bases, or organizational relationships (Van de Ven, 1986). Such innovations may even require users to develop new ways of classifying, examining, and understanding problems. The domain of mobile computing devices has the potential to become the dominant paradigm for future computing applications (March et al., 2000), and topics of such contemporary interest are recommended to be pursued in IS research (Benbasat & Zmud, 1999; Lyytinen, 1999).

The primary objective of this chapter is to examine whether and how perceptions of the social context of an organization moderate the adoption, use, and infusion[1] of mobile computing devices for B2B transactions. We extend TAM to include individuals' perceptions of the social context of their organization, which incorporates aspects of both culture and climate research as recommended in the literature (Denison, 1996; Moran & Volkwein, 1992). Aspects of the social context of an organization are suggested as having a significant role in the introduction of new technologies (Boudreau, Loch, Robey, & Straub, 1998; Denison & Mishra, 1995; Legler & Reischl, 2003; Orlikowski, 1993; Zammuto & O'Connor, 1992), particularly with the introduction of mobile computing devices (Jessup & Robey, 2002; Sarker & Wells, 2003). Only a handful of studies in the past have specifically looked at the micro-level connections of these relationships (Straub, 1994); unfortunately, even this has not been within a mobile computing context. We argue that an organization's social context will have a significant moderating effect on the perceptions of employees considering adoption and use of mobile computing applications for B2B purposes.

The chapter proceeds as follows: the next section presents the background research in the domains (adoption and diffusion of technology innovations within the context of TAM, DOI, and social context) underlying this research. This will be followed by the presentation and discussion of our proposed model and accompanying propositions. A brief discussion of the types of B2B application domains that are relevant to mobile-computing and would be of (future) interest to our investigation is then presented, accompanied by one methodological approach to how such research can be conducted. This chapter concludes with some potential implications for research and practice, limitations of the book chapter, and potential future directions.

Figure 1. Technology acceptance model (Adapted from Davis, Bagozzi, & Warshaw, 1989)

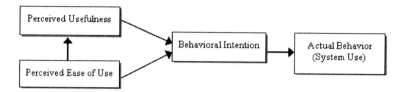

BACKGROUND RESEARCH

In this section, we first discuss the extant research connected with the technology acceptance model followed by research related to social context.

Technology Acceptance Model

The technology acceptance model proposed by Davis (1989) has its roots in the theory of reasoned action (TRA) of Fishbein and Ajzen (1975). As earlier alluded to, it is one of the most widely used models of IT acceptance. This model accounts for the psychological factors that influence user acceptance, adoption, and usage behavior of new IT (Davis, 1989; Davis et al., 1989; Hu et al., 1999; Mathieson, 1991; Taylor & Todd, 1995). The TAM model is displayed in Figure 1.

As is fairly well known in the IT literature, TAM specifies two beliefs—*perceived usefulness* (PU) and *perceived ease of use* (PEOU)—to be determinants of IT usage. It incorporates behavioral intention as a mediating variable in the model, which is important for both substantive and sensible reasons. In terms of substantive reasons, the formation of an intention to carry out a behavior is thought to be a necessary precursor to actual behavior (Fishbein & Ajzen, 1975). In terms of sensible reasons, the inclusion of intention is found to increase the predictive power of models such as TAM and TRA, relative to models that do not include intention (Fishbein & Ajzen, 1975). Perceived usefulness is defined as "the degree to which a person believes that using a particular system would enhance her/his job performance"; perceived ease of use is defined as "the degree to which a person believes that using a particular system would be free of effort" (Davis, 1989, p. 320).

The TAM model and other subsequent IT models of acceptance have largely ignored the influence that continued usage has on the acceptance of an IT. For example, Karahanna, Straub, and Chervany (1999) found differences in the determinants of attitudes between potential adopters and actual users of an IT. In particular, they found that perceived usefulness continued to play an important role in the attitudes of IT users, while ease of use ceased to be important over time. Consequently, the relationship between actual/demonstrated usefulness and continued use is added by us to the original TAM model. Once the actual/realized usefulness of an IT is confirmed by a potential adopter, it is likely to continue to play a significant role in the overall infusion of the technology.

Based upon conceptual and empirical similarities across eight prominent models in the user acceptance literature, Venkatesh, Morris, Davis, and Davis (2003) developed a unified theory of individual acceptance of technology (the unified theory of acceptance and use of technology, or UTAUT). The UTAUT theorizes four constructs as having a significant role as direct determinants of acceptance and usage behavior: performance expectancy (subsuming perceived usefulness), effort expectancy (subsuming perceived ease of use), social influence, and facilitating conditions. In addition, it considers four moderators—age, gender, voluntariness of use, and experience of the users to influence the relationship between the four direct antecedents and intentions to use (and in the case of facilitating conditions on actual use behavior). Although the UTAUT model explains a significant amount of variance in the intention to adopt an IT, the model lacks the parsimony and empirical replication of the TAM model. In this light, the modified TAM model that we propose may be considered a viable and prudent alternative to the UTAUT model. An empirical comparison between these two models is, of course, necessary.

Recent research employing the TAM model had identified individual differences as a major external variable (Agarwal & Prasad, 1999; Jackson et al., 1997; Venkatesh, 2000; Venkatesh & Morris, 2000). Individual differences are any forms of dissimilarity across people, including differences in perceptions and behavior (Agarwal & Prasad, 1999). For example, Agarwal and Prasad (1999) found that an individual's role (provider or user) with regard to a technology innovation, level of education, and previous experiences with similar technology were significantly related to their beliefs about the ease of use of a technology innovation. Agarwal and Prasad also found a significant relationship between an individual's participation in training and their beliefs about the usefulness of a technology innovation. Jackson et al. (1997) examined variables such as situational involvement, intrinsic involvement, and prior use of IT by users, and Venkatesh (2000) considered individual specific variables such as beliefs about computers and computer usage, and beliefs shaped by experiences with the technology in the traditional TAM. Both these studies found significant relationships among these individual differences and TAM constructs. Further, Venkatesh and Morris (2000) argue from their findings that "men are more driven by instrumental factors (i.e., perceived usefulness) while women are more motivated by process (perceived ease of use) and social (subjective norm) factors" (p. 129). Thus, while the various above-noted research studies have investigated the differences in the perceptions of individuals using TAM as the underlying theoretical basis, as noted earlier, perceptions of the social context of an organization is not common in the literature. Most of these refinements to TAM and findings are accommodated in the earlier-noted overarching UTAUT model proposed by Venkatesh et al. (2003).

Social Context of an Organization and Innovativeness

As noted in the introduction, although the social context of an organization has been suggested as having a significant role in the introduction of new technologies (Boudreau et al., 1998; Denison & Mishra, 1995; Legler & Reischl, 2003; Orlikowski, 1993; Zammuto & O'Connor, 1992), particularly with the introduction of mobile computing devices (Jessup & Robey, 2002; Sarker & Wells, 2003), it has not been widely examined in the literature. In this chapter we extend the TAM to incorporate an individual's perceptions of the social context of their organization. The perceptions of the social context are of value to consider since they are likely to be fairly stable in the mind of the potential adopter and less subject to change than other perceived factors or the underlying technological innovation. As recommended in the literature, we examine the social context of an organization to incorporate aspects of both culture and climate (Denison, 1996; Moran &

Volkwein, 1992). We take the stand that a study of organizational culture and organizational climate actually examine the same phenomenon—namely, the creation and influence of social contexts in organizations—but from different perspectives (Denison, 1996). Following the recommendation of prior research, we examine the broader social context in order to improve our understanding of the organizational phenomenon (Astley & Van de Ven, 1983; Denison, 1996; Moran & Volkwein, 1992; Pfeffer, 1982).

Organizational climate can be described as the shared perceptions of organizational members who are exposed to the same organizational structure (Schneider, 1990). Zmud (1982) suggests that it is not the structure of the organization that triggers innovation; rather, innovation emerges from the organizational climate within which members recognize the desirability of innovation, and within which opportunities for innovation arise and efforts toward innovation are supported. As summarized in Schneider (1990) and in Moran and Volkwein (1992), a number of different conceptualizations of organizational climate have been suggested over the years. Pareek (1987) advanced the idea that climate and culture can only be discussed in terms of how it is perceived and felt by individual members/employees of the organization, which is a perspective that is supported in the literature (Legler & Reischl, 2003). Thus, we are interested in capturing the perceptions of individuals within organizations. Since the unit of analysis (during empirical evaluation) in this chapter is the individual employees within organizations, appropriate measures of examining social context can be derived from psychological climate literature.

Rather than focusing on how the psychological climate of an organization gets formed and can be influenced (certainly important), of interest in this chapter is how the prevailing climate of an organization moderates the relationship between individuals' perceptions of an innovation's usefulness and ease of use, and their intentions to adopt and use the innovation. Psychological climate is a multi-dimensional construct that can be conceptualized and operationalized at the individual level (Glick, 1985; Legler & Reischl, 2003). In an attempt to integrate several different measures of psychological climate, Koys and DeCotiis (1991) derived eight summary dimensions—*autonomy, cohesiveness, fairness, innovation, pressure, recognition, support,* and *trust.* A brief definition/description of each of these dimensions is provided in Table 1.

In the next section, while presenting our research model and associated propositions, we will discuss how each of these dimensions would be expected to moderate the relationship between an individual's perceptions (of an innovation) and behavioral intention (to adopt and use it). Briefly, however, we will take a couple of these climate dimensions (*support* and *autonomy*) and discuss the relevance of these dimensions of organizational climate for the adoption of technological innovations.

Senior management's attitude toward change (consequential to the introduction of technology innovations) and thus the extent of their *support* impacts the adoption of these technology innovations (Damanpour, 1991). Senior management teams may be very conservative, preferring the status quo and using current or time-tested methods innovating only when they are seriously challenged by their competition or by shifting consumer preferences (Miller & Friesen, 1982). By contrast, they may be risk prone, actually encouraging and actively supporting the use of innovative techniques to move the organization forward, usually trying to obtain a competitive advantage by routinely making dramatic innovative changes and taking the inherent risks associated with those innovations (Litwin & Stringer, 1968). The potentially disruptive

features typically associated with the adoption of (radical) innovations require an organizational context where managers encourage individual members of the organization to take (prudent levels of) risk, support adoption of technology innovations, and be supportive of changes in their organizations (Dewar & Dutton, 1986). Organizations should be wary, however, that a follower approach taken by employees may promote a "mindless" environment resulting in undesirable levels of risk-taking, which can cause significant problems (Swanson & Ramiller, 2004).

Organizational context/climate also reflects the extent of focus on autonomy/empowerment vs. control of its members. An organic organization as contrasted with mechanistic organization is typically associated with open and free-flowing communication, sharing of necessary information and knowledge, flexibility, and absence of rigid rules and regulations; such an organization context is usually positively related to innovation (Aiken & Hage, 1971; Kimberly & Evanisko, 1981). Furthermore, an organizational climate that is geared toward and has built-in expectation of high levels of achievement and high standards of excellence nurtures a vibrant base of challenges posed to its members who have the freedom to apply innovative technologies, techniques, and procedures

Table 1. Dimensions of psychological climate (Adapted from Koys & DeCotiis, 1991)

Dimension Name	Definition
Autonomy	Employee's perception of their own sovereignty with respect to work procedures, goals and priorities.
Cohesion	Employee's perception of sharing and togetherness within their organization.
Trust	Employee's perception of freedom to communicate openly with members at higher organizational levels about sensitive or personal issues with the expectation that the integrity of such communications will not be violated.
Pressure	Employee's perception that time demands are incongruent with respect to task completion and performance standards.
Support	Employee's perception of the tolerance of their behavior by superiors, including the willingness to let employees learn from their mistakes without fear of reprisal.
Recognition	Employee's perception that their contributions to their organization are acknowledged.
Fairness	Employees' perception that their organization's practices are equitable and non-arbitrary.
Innovation	Employee's perception that change and originality are encouraged and valued within their organization, including risk-taking in domains where the individual may have little to no prior experience.

to effectively accomplish the tasks (Rosenthal & Crain, 1963). Such an organizational context will be more prone to encouraging its members to adopt technology innovations to accomplish high levels of performance.

RESEARCH MODEL AND TENTATIVE PROPOSITIONS

Based on the foregoing brief discussion of the extant research, we extend the standard TAM model with social context dimensions as shown in Figure 2.

Traditional TAM Propositions

An individual's intention to adopt/use technology is driven by his or her perceptions of the usefulness of the technology (Davis et al., 1989). This contention, as noted in the background research section, has been supported extensively in previous research (Agarwal & Prasad, 1999; Davis et al., 1989; Hu et al., 1999; Jackson et al., 1997; Venkatesh, 1999, 2000; Venkatesh & Davis, 2000; Venkatesh & Davis, 1996; Venkatesh & Morris, 2000). A primary reason why individuals would intend to adopt/use mobile computing devices for B2B transactions is that they believe that this technology will provide them the flexibility to perform their job and enable their job performance enhancement (Davis, 2002; Intel, 2003). Furthermore, following the findings of Karahanna et al. (1999), the perceived usefulness of an IT influences the attitudes of both potential adopters and users of an IT. However, we contend that when an IT has demonstrated its usefulness over time, it is

Figure 2. Research model

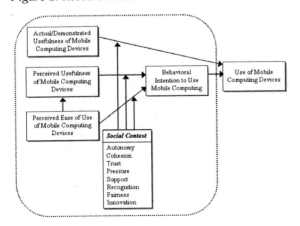

likely to play a significant role in the overall infusion of the technology. Therefore, we propose:

- **Proposition 1:** Perceived usefulness will have a positive effect on organizational members' intention to adopt/use mobile computing devices for B2B transactions.
- **Proposition 2:** Actual/demonstrated usefulness will have a positive effect on organizational members' continued usage of mobile computing devices for B2B transactions.

As noted earlier, the second major determinant of behavioral intentions in the TAM model, *perceived ease of use,* has been observed to have both a (somewhat weak) direct influence on behavioral intention as well as a (strong) indirect influence through its effect on perceived usefulness (Davis, 1989; Davis et al., 1989; Hu et al., 1999; Jackson et al., 1997). This is understandable since a person who believes that a technology innovation is (relatively) easy to understand and use, and is less demanding of efforts, would likely believe that using such a technology is also more useful. While perceived ease of use may trigger users' intention to adopt/use the innovation (mobile computing devices for B2B), it is unlikely to play a key role in the spread/infusion since users would likely become more familiar with all the features of the innovation and gain significant expertise with time following the initial use. Hence, we propose the two following propositions:

- **Proposition 3a:** Perceived ease of use will have a positive effect on organizational members' intention to adopt/use mobile computing devices for B2B transactions.
- **Proposition 3b:** Perceived ease of use will positively influence organizational members' perceptions of the usefulness of mobile computing devices for B2B transactions.

Extended TAM Propositions

One of the key objectives of this chapter is to examine what role, if any, social context plays in the link between individuals' perceptions of usefulness/ease of use and behavioral intentions of the TAM model. We pointed out that social context, when conceptualized in terms of climate/culture, is a multi-dimensional construct composed of eight dimensions (Koys & DeCotiis, 1991). Since there has been no attempt to examine this additional set of dimensions within the context of TAM, many of the arguments and much of the rationale that we provide in the rest of this section while developing the propositions are likely to be tentative.

Autonomy

At one end of the spectrum, an organization can be extremely control and compliance oriented (*mechanistic* organizational context) in formulating, administering, and closely monitoring and enforcing a set of policies and procedures that guide employee work activities. At the opposite end of the spectrum, an organization can be performance and achievement oriented (*organic* organizational context) by empowering their employees to determine their task priorities and schedule, providing them the autonomy to make use of any and all techniques, tools, and technologies that they deem best for getting the work done, and being flexible with respect to adherence on the standard policies and procedures. Thus, organizations where the members perceive greater *autonomy* and flexibility being provided to them in making decisions and choices on their task-related activities are likely to more quickly exploit (any) opportunity that technology innovations offer. While this is fairly obvious when the technology is perceived to be useful and easy to use, even in instances where such perceptions (of ease of use and usefulness) may not be completely true, the organizational members may still be more willing to make informed decisions that they are responsible and accountable for (Aiken & Hage, 1971; Kimberly & Evanisko, 1981). To become better informed, they may actively seek out knowledge from various pockets of the (internal) organization as well as from external sources (e.g., consultants, vendors, trade literature, etc.). Therefore:

- **Proposition 4a:** The relationship between employees' perceptions (of usefulness and ease of use of the technology) and their intentions to adopt/use mobile computing devices for B2B transactions will be stronger in organizational contexts that provide greater autonomy to their employees.
- **Proposition 4b:** The relationship between the actual/demonstrated usefulness and continued usage of mobile computing devices for B2B transactions will be stronger in organizational

contexts that provide greater autonomy to their employees.

Cohesion

As would be noted from the brief description provided in Table 1, *cohesion* refers to an organizational context/climate that fosters a sense of sharing, caring, accommodation, and togetherness among the members/employees (Koys & DeCotiis, 1991). Communication, sharing, and exchange of information and knowledge amongst the members is bound to be much more open in such a context. Employees would more willingly share their experiences and support one another when attempting to make decisions on complex and unknown topic areas (e.g., relevance and mastery of new technologies). It is, therefore, reasonable to expect that potential adopters of new technology innovations (mobile computing devices) would be more willing and prepared to assume any challenges posed by the new technology environment in view of the potential support that they can expect from their colleagues in their work environment. Therefore, we propose the following:

- **Proposition 5a:** The relationship between employees' perceptions (of usefulness and ease of use of the technology) and their intentions to adopt/use mobile computing devices for B2B transactions will be stronger in organizational contexts that foster a greater sense of cohesion/cohesiveness among their employees.
- **Proposition 5b:** The relationship between the actual/demonstrated usefulness and continued usage of mobile computing devices for B2B transactions will be stronger in organizational contexts that foster a greater sense of cohesion/cohesiveness among their employees.

Trust

The third dimension of organizational climate, *trust*, refers to the extent to which employees within the organization can openly communicate with their superiors, seek their guidance and expertise, and be confident that the integrity of sensitive information will not be compromised (Koys & DeCotiis, 1991). It is easy to visualize that such expectations of trust work in both directions—from subordinate to superiors and vice versa. Trust also involves an expectation of confidence in the goodwill of others in the organizational context/environment, as well as the prospects for continuity of the relationship entered into (Hart & Saunders, 1997). It is normal to expect that in these trusting organizational contexts, employees will be more prepared to share their difficulties and concerns (work related and even personal), propose potential technology-based solutions, and seek approval/guidance/advice from their superiors and peers. This can be quite important as in the case of introduction of mobile computing devices where the work arrangements and workflows are bound to be disrupted and changed quite radically (e.g., employees may not have to be always present on site and could increasingly work from off-site locations, at home, or on the move). Trust is a significant determinant of a stable relationship (Mayer, Davis, & Schoorman, 1995; McKnight, Choudhury, & Kacmar, 2002). Therefore, we propose:

- **Proposition 6a:** The relationship between employees' perceptions (of usefulness and ease of use of the technology) and their intentions to adopt/use mobile computing devices for B2B transactions will be stronger in organizational contexts that promote and reinforce trust between employees and the organization.
- **Proposition 6b:** The relationship between the actual/demonstrated usefulness and continued usage of mobile computing devices for B2B transactions will be stronger in organizational contexts that promote and reinforce trust between employees and the organization.

Pressure

The fourth dimension of organizational climate, *pressure*, refers to the fact that the work context may not provide adequate time for the employees to accomplish their task-related activities and achieve the required standards of performance and goals (Koys & DeCotiis, 1991). Typically, it would be reflective of a situation of significant stress, perhaps hasty decisions and actions resulting in suboptimal results, and generally chaos. However, such a stressful environment may also be one that could spur the organizational members to creatively look for (technologically) innovative solutions to alleviate the difficulties and infuse some order. To the extent that the performance of tasks is not geographically constrained (e.g., assembly-line work in automotive manufacturing, patrons being serviced in a restaurant or a bank), it is possible that mobile computing devices may indeed alleviate the

time pressure that is so rampant in the work context. For example, employees may become skillful in time management through the convenience of mobile computing devices in coordinating work and personal tasks (Davis, 2002; Intel, 2003). Therefore, surprising and counter-intuitive as it might sound, we propose:

- **Proposition 7a:** The relationship between employees' perceptions (of usefulness and ease of use of the technology) and their intentions to adopt/use mobile computing devices for B2B transactions is likely to be stronger in organizational contexts that reflect one of (time) pressure for employees to accomplish their task and realize the set performance standards.
- **Proposition 7b:** The relationship between the actual/demonstrated usefulness and continued usage of mobile computing devices for B2B transactions is likely to be stronger in organizational contexts that reflect one of (time) pressure for employees to accomplish their task and realize the set performance standards.

Support

The fifth dimension of organizational climate, *support*, reflects an organizational context that is tolerant of errors and mistakes that employees may commit, and is supportive of them as long as they learn from these (Koys & DeCotiis, 1991). An environment that is permissive and lets its members learn from mistakes without fear of punishment and reprisal could engender deep-rooted learning, a "can-do" attitude to problem solving, and (reasonable) risk-taking orientation (Litwin & Stringer, 1968). As noted earlier, management's attitude toward change (often triggered by the introduction of technology innovations) and thus the extent of their support impacts the adoption and successful implementation of these technology innovations (Damanpour, 1991; Sanders & Courtney, 1985). The potentially disruptive features typically associated with the adoption of (radical technology) innovations require an organization context where managers encourage individual members of the organization to take (prudent levels of) risk, support adoption of technology innovations, and be supportive of changes in their organizations (Dewar & Dutton, 1986). Supportive organizational context is also conducive to successful IT implementation (Ramamurthy, Premkumar, & Crum, 1999). Caron, Jarvenpaa, and Stoddard (1994) chronicle how CIGNA Corporation, due to its supportive and tolerance-for-failure environment, facilitated significant learning to accrue in the context of major disruptive and radical changes triggered by business process reengineering projects. Therefore, we propose:

- **Proposition 8a:** The relationship between employees' perceptions (of usefulness and ease of use of the technology) and their intentions to adopt/use mobile computing devices for B2B transactions is likely to be stronger in organizational contexts that are tolerant and supportive of employees in accomplishing their work.
- **Proposition 8b:** The relationship between the actual/demonstrated usefulness and continued usage of mobile computing devices for B2B transactions is likely to be stronger in organizational contexts that are tolerant and supportive of employees in accomplishing their work.

Recognition

The sixth dimension of organizational climate, *recognition*, reflects an organizational context where employee achievements and accomplishments are acknowledged and recognized (Koys & DeCotiis, 1991). *Human relations management* and *job enrichment* literature (Hackman & Oldham, 1980) points out that intrinsic rewards (e.g., employee-of-the-month recognition) at times are more important than extrinsic rewards (e.g., salary raises, promotion). Extrinsic and intrinsic motivation literature has also been used significantly to explain adoption and use of innovations (Davis, Bagozzi, & Warshaw, 1992). Resource-based theory also acknowledges the vital role human assets/resources play in contemporary hyper-competitive external environments where progressive organizations strive to keep their employees satisfied and thus retain top talent. It is, therefore, natural to expect that organizations should strive to create a climate that spurs their employees to constantly look out for creative solutions (including new technology innovations) that foster excellence in achievement. Obviously, this is unlikely when such efforts and accomplishments go unrecognized. Thus, we would propose:

- **Proposition 9a:** The relationship between employees' perceptions (of usefulness and ease of use of the technology) and their intentions to adopt/use mobile computing devices for B2B transactions is likely to be stronger in organi-

zational contexts that are open to acknowledge and recognize the accomplishments of their employees.
- **Proposition 9b:** The relationship between the actual/demonstrated usefulness and continued usage of mobile computing devices for B2B transactions is likely to be stronger in organizational contexts that are open to acknowledge and recognize the accomplishments of their employees.

Fairness

The seventh dimension of organizational climate, *fairness*, reflects an organizational context where employees believe in equitable and non-arbitrary treatment (Koys & DeCotiis, 1991). This reinforces the notion that hard, sincere, and smart work pays off. Individuals that believe an inequity exists, for example, are likely to resent and resist organizational changes (Joshi, 1989, 1991). Clearly an organization that does not design its workplace context with work/job assignments that are perceived to be fair and rewards that are perceived to be equitable for similar accomplishments would trigger significant discontent and distrust. Such an environment is hardly likely to evoke any voluntary or enthusiastic response to work-related organizational challenges, including searching for new technology innovations. Therefore, we would propose:

- **Proposition 10a:** The relationship between employees' perceptions (of usefulness and ease of use of the technology) and their intentions to adopt/use mobile computing devices for B2B transactions is likely to be stronger in organizational contexts that are deemed to be fair in the treatment of their employees.
- **Proposition 10b:** The relationship between the actual/demonstrated usefulness and continued usage of mobile computing devices for B2B transactions is likely to be stronger in organizational contexts that are deemed to be fair in the treatment of their employees.

Innovation

The last (eighth) dimension of organizational climate, *innovation*, reflects an organizational context where employees believe change from status-quo can be good, that originality is valued, and risk taking will be encouraged (Koys & DeCotiis, 1991). As noted earlier, management's attitude toward change (often triggered by the introduction of technology innovations) impacts the adoption of these technology innovations (Damanpour, 1991). Some senior management teams may have conservative attitudes toward innovation and associated risk, preferring the status quo and using current or time-tested methods; such organizations innovate only when they are seriously challenged by their competition or by shifting consumer preferences (Miller & Friesen, 1982). By contrast, other senior management teams may be risk prone, actually encouraging and actively supporting the use of innovative techniques to move the organization forward. Such organizations usually try to obtain a competitive advantage by routinely making dramatic innovative changes and taking the inherent risks associated with those innovations. The potentially disruptive features typically associated with the adoption of (radical technology) innovations require an organization context where managers encourage individual members of the organization to take prudent levels of risk, support adoption of technology innovations, and be supportive of changes in their organizations (Dewar & Dutton, 1986). Thus, we would propose:

- **Proposition 11a:** The relationship between employees' perceptions (of usefulness and ease of use of the technology) and their intentions to adopt/use mobile computing devices for B2B transactions is likely to be stronger in progressive/innovative organizational contexts.
- **Proposition 11b:** The relationship between the actual/demonstrated usefulness and continued usage of mobile computing devices for B2B transactions is likely to be stronger in progressive/innovative organizational contexts.

B2B APPLICATION DOMAIN AND SUGGESTED RESEARCH METHODOLOGY

Some of the broad domains of B2B application areas that are relevant for mobile-computing and of interest to us for this research would be inventory management, customer relationship and service management, sales force automation, product locating and purchasing, dispatching and diagnosis support to, say, technicians in remote locations, mobile shop-floor quality control systems, as well as those applications and transactions

in supply chain management (SCM) that facilitate the integration of business processes along the supply chain (Rao & Minakakis, 2003; Turban, King, Lee, & Viehland, 2004; Varshney & Vetter, 2001). An example of B2B transactions in the SCM context includes data transmission from one business partner to another through the typical enterprise resource planning (ERP) interactions. Other scenarios may involve the ability to continue working on projects while in transit or the ubiquitous access to documents via "hot spots" or wireless network access (Intel, 2003). Consequently, in light of the fact that a number of application domains have preexisted the Internet, the choice of application areas could be either Internet or non-Internet based.

As noted before, mobile computing is still in a very early stage of its evolution and use within organizations in a B2B context. Although a large-scale field survey would be required to test the research model that we presented, such an approach may not be appropriate in this context due to the exploratory nature of the inquiry proposed here. Therefore, the research methodology that we suggest and propose that researchers use at this stage is a combination of both qualitative and quantitative research for data collection. Rather than a large national random sample, we propose a purposive convenience-based sample of a few (say, 8-12) large and medium-sized corporations with almost equal composition of manufacturing and service sectors. Furthermore, based on secondary information and personal contacts, we would prefer that researchers select an equal mix of corporations that do not (yet) use and those that currently use mobile computing so that we can capture their "intention" and subsequently their "continued use." Although the "social context" or "climate" prevailing within each of these organizations may be a "given reality" at least at a point in time, as observed in most past research, it is the interpretations of this social context/climate that would drive individual actions, especially when the intended/actual behavior (in this case, adoption and use of mobile computing) is not mandatory (Moran & Volkwein, 1992). Thus, in-depth interviews coupled with a questionnaire survey from a number of focal members (about 20 to 25), sampled from multiple functional areas (that are amenable for use of mobile computing devices such as sales and marketing, purchasing, and operations) within participant organizations, should be used to capture individual perceptions of the mobile computing devices and their organization's social context. As argued above, since the rate of diffusion for mobile computing devices for B2B transactions is still relatively small, a convenient sampling approach among organizations that have and have yet to adopt these technologies is appropriate. To ensure relevance and reasonable generalizability of the study findings of the convenience-based sampling suggested by us, participants from each organization should be chosen randomly. A number of statistical techniques such as logistic regression (for the "intention to adopt" stage) and structural equation modeling or hierarchical moderated regression analysis (for the "infusion" stage) would be candidates for data analyses.

CONCLUSION

In this chapter we incorporated the social context of an organization into TAM and proposed an extended model to investigate adoption/use of mobile computing devices for B2B transactions as a technological innovation. We believe that such an extension is appropriate because aspects of social context have in general been found significant with the introduction of new technologies. In particular, a micro-level analysis of this phenomenon for the introduction of new technologies is rare. Since the unit of analysis of this chapter is individual employees, we utilized dimensions of psychological climate to represent the social context of an organization. The primary objective of this chapter was to posit how perceptions of the social context of an organization would moderate the intention to adopt/use and infusion of a technology innovation.

A key feature of this study is that we examined an information technology that has the potential of becoming a dominant paradigm and platform for future computing applications. As we noted, although mobile computing devices have existed for several years, their use for business-to-business transactions or operating context has not been adequately or systematically explored in academic research. We drew upon theories from the diffusion of innovation, information systems, and organizational behavior literature, among others, to develop our research model and the associated 10 propositions. The model we proposed could serve as a foundation for one stream of IS research that integrates social context of an organization into TAM to examine the vital role of mobile computing devices in electronic commerce.

IMPLICATIONS, LIMITATIONS, AND FUTURE RESEARCH DIRECTIONS

Since the empirical segment of this research has not yet been conducted, we can only conjecture several potential research contributions for researchers and practitioners. One implication that this work has for future research is the exploration of how the social context of an organization may influence the acceptance and spread of an information technology innovation. The social context of an organization has not been applied to TAM, and an extension focusing on the micro-level aspects of the social context have not been widely examined in the literature. By explicitly investigating the social context of an organization, this study extends the innovation adoption and TAM literature base. Our model may be considered a viable and prudent alternative to the UTAUT model. Utilizing a (valid and popular base) model and measures that have become widely accepted among IS researchers allows for researchers in future research to replicate our study and examine other factors of interest. This chapter also addresses the need to explore technology that is close to the "leading edge" (Lyytinen, 1999, p. 26), which is recommended for maintaining the relevance of IS research (Benbasat & Zmud, 1999; Lyytinen, 1999; Orlikowski & Iacono, 2001). Obviously, considerable care and precautions (in the design of the study, operationalization, and evaluation of the measurement properties) will be needed in translating the theoretical model proposed in this chapter into a large-scale empirical investigation that can establish validity and reliability of its results.

The potential implication that this work has for IS practice is that it identifies a number of contextual factors that may influence the acceptance of a technological innovation that an organization wishes to introduce. Mobile computing devices can enhance employee productivity by granting them flexibility in work location and time management (Intel, 2003). Organizations that covet such gains in productivity are likely cognizant of the investments typically at stake when implementing IT innovations. Given that aspects of the social context of an organization are suggested as having a significant role in the introduction of mobile computing devices (Jessup & Robey, 2002; Sarker & Wells, 2003), it is desirable to understand the influence that the social context of an organization plays. Moran and Volkwein (1992) state that focusing on the micro-level aspect of the social context is appealing because it is relatively accessible, more malleable, and the appropriate level to target short-term interventions aimed at producing positive organizational change. This study helps to uncover several future opportunities for organizations since mobile computing devices have the potential to become the dominant paradigm for future computing applications (March et al., 2000; Sarker & Wells, 2003).

Although this chapter offers several potential contributions, several limitations exist. The social context of an organization is operationalized through psychological climate dimensions. The definition of social context that we adopted takes a much broader view than focusing on the individual incorporating traditions from research in the organizational culture literature as well. We feel that it is appropriate to use the social context of the organization to begin the integration of culture and climate literature. It is our opinion that the psychological climate research is the most appropriate theory to support the research model, which presents opportunities in future work to examine other aspects of the social context of an organization that may be influential in the acceptance of a technological innovation. Another limitation of this study (when an empirical investigation is conducted) is that it may obtain retrospective accounts/information from (current) users of mobile computing devices. Retrospective accounts are an issue because individuals may not be able to accurately recall the past. It would be necessary to consider preventive measures on this front to ensure validity and reliability of the results.

REFERENCES

Agarwal, R., & Prasad, J. (1999). Are individual differences germane to the acceptance of new information technologies? *Decision Sciences, 30*(2), 361-391.

Aiken, M., & Hage, J. (1971). The organic organization and innovation. *Sociology, 5*, 63-82.

Astley, W., & Van de Ven, A. (1983). Central perspectives and debates in organizational theory. *Administrative Science Quarterly, 28*, 245-273.

Benbasat, I., & Zmud, R. W. (1999). Empirical research in information systems: The practice of relevance. *MIS Quarterly, 23*(1), 3-16.

Boudreau, M., Loch, K., Robey, D., & Straub, D. (1998). Going global: Using information technology to advance the competitiveness of the virtual transnational organization. *Academy of Management Executive, 12*(4), 120-128.

Caron, J., Jarvenpaa, S., & Stoddard, D. (1994). Business reengineering at CIGNA Corporation: Experiences and lessons learned from the first five years. *MIS Quarterly, 18*(3), 233-250.

Damanpour, F. (1991). Organizational innovation: A meta-analysis of effects of determinants and moderators. *Academy of Management Journal, 34*, 555-590.

Davis, F. (1989). Perceived usefulness, perceived ease of use, and user acceptance of information technology. *MIS Quarterly, 13*(3), 319-340.

Davis, F., Bagozzi, R., & Warshaw, P. (1989). User acceptance of computer technology: A comparison of two theoretical models. *Management Science, 35*(8), 982-1003.

Davis, F., Bagozzi, R., & Warshaw, P. (1992). Extrinsic and intrinsic motivation to use computers in the workplace. *Journal of Applied Social Psychology, 22*, 1111-1132.

Davis, G. (2002). Anytime/anyplace computing and the future of knowledge work. *Communications of the ACM, 45*(12), 67-73.

Denison, D. (1996). What is the difference between organizational culture and organizational climate? *Academy of Management Review, 21*(3), 619-654.

Denison, D., & Mishra, A. (1995). Toward a theory of organizational culture and effectiveness. *Organization Science, 6*(2), 204-223.

Dewar, R., & Dutton, J. (1986). The adoption of radical and incremental innovation: An empirical analysis. *Management Science, 23*, 1422-1433.

Fishbein, M., & Ajzen, I. (1975). *Belief, attitude, intention, and behavior: An introduction to theory and research.* Reading, MA: Addison-Wesley.

Glick, W. (1985). Conceptualizing and measuring organizational and psychological climate: Pitfalls in multilevel research. *Academy of Management Review, 10*(3), 601-616.

Hackman, J., & Oldham, G. (1980). *Work redesign.* Reading, MA: Addison-Wesley.

Harrison, A., & Rainer, R. (1992). The influence of individual differences on skill in end-user computing. *Journal of Management Information Systems, 9*(1), 93-111.

Hart, P., & Saunders, C. (1997). Power and trust: Critical factors in the adoption and use of electronic data interchange. *Organization Science, 8*(1), 23-42.

Hartwick, J., & Barki, H. (1994). Explaining the role of user participation in information system use. *Management Science, 40*(4), 440-465.

Hu, P., Chau, P., Sheng, O., & Tam, K. (1999). Examining the Technology Acceptance Model using physician acceptance of telemedicine technology. *Journal of Management Information Systems, 16*(2), 91-112.

Intel. (2003). *Effects of wireless mobile technology on employee productivity.* Intel Information Technology White Paper (pp. 1-20), USA.

Jackson, C., Chow, S., & Leitch, R. (1997). Toward an understanding of the behavioral intention to use an information system. *Decision Sciences, 28*(2), 357-389.

Jessup, L., & Robey, D. (2002). The relevance of social issues in ubiquitous computing environments. *Communications of the ACM, 45*(12), 88-91.

Joshi, K. (1989). The measurement of fairness or equity perceptions of management information systems users. *MIS Quarterly, 13*(3), 343-358.

Joshi, K. (1991). A model of users' perspective on change: The case of information systems technology implementation. *MIS Quarterly, 15*(2), 229-242.

Karahanna, E., Straub, D., & Chervany, N. (1999). Information technology adoption across time: A cross-sectional comparison of pre-adoption and post-adoption beliefs. *MIS Quarterly, 23*(2), 183-213.

Kimberly, J., & Evanisko, M. (1981). Organizational innovation: The influence of individual, organizational and contextual factors on hospital adoption of technological and administrative innovations. *Academy of Management Journal, 24*, 689-713.

Koys, D., & DeCotiis, T. (1991). Inductive measures of psychological climate. *Human Relations, 44*(3), 265-283.

Legler, R., & Reischl, T. (2003). The relationship of key factors in the process of collaboration. *The Journal of Applied Behavioral Science, 39*(1), 53-72.

Litwin, G., & Stringer, R. (1968). *Motivation and organizational climate.* Boston: Harvard University Press.

Lyytinen, K. (1999). Empirical research in information systems: On the relevance of practice in thinking of IS research. *MIS Quarterly, 23*(1), 25-28.

Lyytinen, K., & Yoo, Y. (2002a). Issues and challenges in ubiquitous computing. *Communications of the ACM, 45*(12), 63-65.

Lyytinen, K., & Yoo, Y. (2002b). Research commentary: The next wave of nomadic computing. *Information Systems Research, 13*(4), 377-388.

March, S., Hevner, A., & Ram, S. (2000). Research commentary: An agenda for information technology research in heterogeneous and distributed environments. *Information Systems Research, 11*(4), 327-341.

Mathieson, K. (1991). Predicting user intentions: Comparing the Technology Acceptance Model with the Theory of Planned Behavior. *Information Systems Research, 2*(3), 173-191.

Mayer, R., Davis, J., & Schoorman, F. (1995). An integrative model of organizational trust. *Academy of Management Review, 20*(3), 709-734.

McKnight, D., Choudhury, V., & Kacmar, C. (2002). Developing and validating trust measures for e-commerce: An integrative typology. *Information Systems Research, 13*(3), 334-359.

Miller, D., & Friesen, P. (1982). Innovation in conservative and entrepreneurial firms: Two modes of strategic momentum. *Strategic Management Journal, 3*, 1-25.

Moore, G., & Benbasat, I. (1991). Development of an instrument to measure the perceptions of adopting an information technology innovation. *Information Systems Research, 2*(3), 192-222.

Moran, E., & Volkwein, J. (1992). The cultural approach to the formation of organizational climate. *Human Relations, 45*, 19-47.

Nelson, D. (1990). Individual adjustment to information-driven technologies: A critical review. *MIS Quarterly, 14*(1), 79-98.

Orlikowski, W. (1993). Learning from notes: Organizational issues in groupware implementation. *The Information Society, 9*, 223-250.

Orlikowski, W., & Iacono, C. (2001). Research commentary: Desperately seeking the "IT" in IT research—A call to theorizing the IT artifact. *Information Systems Research, 12*(2), 121-134.

Pareek, U. (1987). *Motivating organizational roles.* New Delhi, India: Oxford and IBH.

Pfeffer, J. (1982). *Organizations and organizational theory.* Boston: Pitman.

Ramamurthy, K., Premkumar, G., & Crum, M. (1999). Organizational and inter-organizational determinants of the EDI diffusion: A causal model. *Journal of Organizational Computing and Electronic Commerce, 9*(4), 253-285.

Rao, B., & Minakakis, L. (2003). Evolution of mobile location-based services. *Communications of the ACM, 46*(12), 61-65.

Rogers, E. (2003). *Diffusion of innovations* (5ᵗʰ ed.). New York: The Free Press.

Rosenthal, D., & Crain, R. (1963). Executive leadership and community innovation: The fluoridation experience. *Urban Affairs Quarterly, 1,* 39-57.

Sanders, L., & Courtney , J. (1985). A field study of organizational factors influencing DSS success. *MIS Quarterly, 9*(1), 77-93.

Sarker, S., & Wells, J. (2003). Understanding mobile handheld device use and adoption. *Communications of the ACM, 46*(12), 35-40.

Satyanarayanan, M. (1996). Fundamental challenges in mobile computing. *Proceedings of the ACM Symposium—Principles of Distributed Computing,* Philadelphia.

Schneider, B. (Ed.). (1990). *Organizational climate and culture.* San Francisco: Jossey-Bass.

Straub, D. (1994). The effect of culture on IT diffusion: E-mail & fax in Japan and the U.S. *Information Systems Research, 5*(1), 23-47.

Swanson, E. B., & Ramiller, N. C. (2004). Innovating mindfully with information technology. *MIS Quarterly, 28*(4), 553-583.

Taylor, S., & Todd, P. (1995). Understanding information technology usage: A test of competing models. *Information Systems Research, 6*(2), 144-176.

Turban, E., King, D., Lee, J., & Viehland, D. (2004). *Electronic commerce: A managerial perspective.* Upper Saddle River, NJ: Prentice-Hall.

Van de Ven, A. (1986). Central problems in the management of innovation. *Management Science, 32,* 590-607.

Varshney, U., & Vetter, R. (2001). A framework for the emerging m-commerce applications. *Proceedings of the 34ᵗʰ Hawaii International Conference on Systems Sciences.*

Venkatesh, V. (1999). Creation of favorable user perceptions: Exploring the role of intrinsic motivation. *MIS Quarterly, 23*(2), 239-260.

Venkatesh, V. (2000). Determinants of perceived ease of use: Integrating control, intrinsic motivation, and emotion into the Technology Acceptance Model. *Information Systems Research, 11*(4), 342-365.

Venkatesh, V., & Davis, F. (2000). A theoretical extension of the Technology Acceptance Model: Four longitudinal field studies. *Management Science, 46*(2), 186-204.

Venkatesh, V., & Davis, F. D. (1996). A model of the antecedents of perceived ease of use: development and test. *Decision Sciences, 27*(3), 451-481.

Venkatesh, V., & Morris, M. (2000). Why don't men ever stop to ask for directions? Gender, social influence, and their role in technology acceptance and usage behavior. *MIS Quarterly, 24*(1), 115-139.

Venkatesh, V., Morris, M. G., Davis, G. B., & Davis, F. D. (2003). User acceptance of information technology: Toward a unified view. *MIS Quarterly, 27*(3), 425-478.

Zammuto, R., & O'Connor, E. (1992). Gaining advanced manufacturing technologies' benefits: The roles of organization design and culture. *Academy of Management Review, 17*(4), 701-728.

Zmud, R. (1979). Individual differences and MIS success: A review of the empirical literature. *Management Science, 25*(10), 966-979.

Zmud, R. (1982). Diffusion of modern software practices: Influence of centralization and formalization. *Management Science, 28,* 1421-1431.

ENDNOTE

[1]   We use the term *infusion* to refer to diffusion and spread of the innovation within an organization's internal environment.

Chapter XLVI
Extending Enterprise Architecture with Mobility

Ming-Chien (Mindy) Wu
University of Western Sydney, Australia

Bhuvan Unhelkar
MethodScience.com & University of Western Sydney, Australia

ABSTRACT

The Enterprise Architecture (EA) brings together various business processes, technologies, standards, systems, and IT infrastructure of the organization. This chapter considers extending the EA with mobility so that it would facilitate easier implementation of applications that overcomes the boundaries of time and location. This extension of EA with mobility will result in a comprehensive Mobility Enterprise Architecture (M-EA) that will provide the business with advantages of real-time business processes, reduced costs, increased client satisfaction, and better control. This chapter outlines the M-EA framework, which is based on the literature review, initial modeling, and a case study carried out by the lead authors. Later, the framework is validated by another case study carried out at international software development organization. Further validation of the model is envisaged through action research in multinational organizations.

INTRODUCTION

A carefully thought out and implemented Enterprise Architecture (EA) provides the business with competitive advantage by opening up opportunities to streamline processes, reduce costs, increase customer satisfaction and enable thorough strategic planning (Lan and Unhelkar, 2005). Businesses can further advance these benefits by extending the EA with strategic incorporation of Mobile Technologies (MT) - including wireless networks and handheld devices – into their business plans. This is so because of the phenomenal impact of the "time and location" independence provided by mobile Technologies (Unhelkar, 2006; Barnes, 2002). Furthermore, mobility extends the ability of the organization to create dynamic interconnections, in real time, between various parts of its information networks. This ability to dynamically interconnect various parts of its data and information through mobility results in "correlations" that provide new insights to the organization's decision makers and enhance their decision making. Thus, a Mobile Enterprise Architecture (M-EA), through location-independence, provides greater opportunities for business information systems to create these dynamic correlations, resulting in greater business advantage than information exchanges over land-based Internet and other communication mechanisms. Thus, the objective of this chapter is to outline a comprehensive framework for incorporation of mobile technologies in an organization's Enterprise Architecture that would provide it with competitive advantage. This framework is based on the literature review and initial modeling carried out by the lead author at the Mobile Internet Research and Applications Group (MIRAG) at the University of Western Sydney. Later, the framework is validated by case studies and action research in multinational organizations. Initial findings suggests an "all encompassing" approach to MEA in business that considers the business processes as well as the social aspects of mobile technologies, is likely to ensure greater success, as against a pure technical approach.

BACKGROUND TO RESEARCH

Information Technology (IT) growth is substantiated by the large number of infrastructures and products have been showing up in the market with ever-increasing frequency (Ramakrishnan et. al., 2006). However, in order to increase the ability of the enterprise to serve its customers and deal with its business partners in today's dynamic business environment, there is a need to integrate these products and services through a common EA (Linthicum, 2000). While EA has successfully managed to integrate these various technologies used by the enterprises (such as Internet-based application, reusable components, security and database components), enterprises are now seeking to capitalize on the MT. This has resulted in a need to further extend and integrate mobility into the EA. MT is a significant emerging technology that has the potential to influence various organizational applications (Unhelkar, 2005), in additional, impact EA as they are technologies without wires with the ability to communicate through a multiplicity of hand-held devices. The advantage of mobility comes from its ability to overcome "time and location" boundaries that would enable enterprises to operate effectively real-time respond to the ever-increasing changes on this competitive marketplace. The need, therefore, to have a comprehensive EA that would enable delivery of services to the "location independent" market has grown. Along with that need is the need to have a

formal process to incorporate and extend the EA with mobility. This chapter outlines the process of enabling such extension and incorporation of mobility in EA.

ENTERPRISE ARCHITECTURE OVERVIEW

Enterprise Architecture Background

In order to increase liveliness in today's dynamic business environment, enterprise needs to integrate their business processes, systems, databases, human resources, infrastructures and technologies together. This integration of various aspects of an enterprise results in what is known as Enterprise Architecture (EA). Kamogawa and Okada (2004) state that EA should integrate these various systems such as Supply Chain Management (SCM) system, Customer Relationship Management (CRM) system, and Enterprise Resource Planning (ERP) system. The overall EA comprises software systems that may have been created using different programming languages, databases, and may be operating on different technology platforms. Ross et. al. (2006) and Cook (1996) all state EA allows integration and coordination across whole enterprise, including internal and external enterprise. So, in Fig. 1 this research extends the original idea to integrate not only IS, but also the people, data, processes, applications, platforms, and middleware all should be integrated into EA. This integration makes EA could provide best solution of internal enterprise. Additionally, applications of other businesses, which are external enterprise users, include the customers, partners, suppliers, or all members in a supply chain should be enabling to see a unified view of the EA as well. This internal and external enterprise architecture integration is the blueprint solution for different generation information systems that already exist and / or future applications coordination.

Enterprise Architecture Definition

Enterprise Architecture represents the enterprise's key business system, information/ data, application, technology strategies and their impact on business processes also the users. META Group Inc. (2006) and VITA (2006) both demonstrate that EA consists of four key components, which are: Enterprise Business Architecture (EBA), Enterprise Information

Architecture (EIA), Enterprise Solution Architecture (ESA), and Enterprise Technology Architecture (ETA). Enterprise Business Architecture (EBA) defines the enterprise business model, process cycles and timing; also shows what functions should be integrated into the system. Enterprise Information Architecture (EIA) focuses on the data along with the corresponding data models that should be integrated into the system. Enterprise Solution Architecture (ESA), also referred to as an application selection which is the collection of information systems supporting EBA, which also helps the user to easily understand and use the interface and components. Enterprise Technology Architecture (ETA) is a consistent set of Information Communication Technology standards and selection of technology device, which uses technology infrastructures to support EBA, EIA, and ESA.

EBA focus on the integration of business information systems and how the business processes run. EIS considers on data storage, ESA focus on supporting people to easy understand and use, and ETA collects the technology devices, applications, middleware, platforms, and standards to support all the others. Based on it, EA (Figure 2) in this research has been defined as a structure of integrating business processes with IT supported, by providing a visualization enterprise solution of the relationships among the *System, Process, People, and Data* in an organization.

Enterprise Architecture Framework

The critical success factor of structured and implemented EA is having a best practice approach by using an architecture framework. The framework provides a method of organizing architecture documents, dividing them into manageable parts and defining cross linkages between them. One popular reference architecture on which an EA can be based is the Zachman framework. Zachman (1987) created the Zachman Framework which has been described by many authors as basis for their work. (see EAF work by Finkelstein (2006), for example). This framework provides a formal and highly structured way to define the concepts of an enterprise. The 6 x 6 table of the framework provides a classification model based on what (data), how (process), where, who (people), when and why – which then crosses with the distinct model of planner, owner, designer (system), builder (technology), implementer, and worker. The strong point on this framework is that it provides everyone in the enterprise and enterprise architect group a clear picture of how the enterprise is operating including its people, processes and technologies.

There are also several frameworks from government agencies, such as The Open Group Architecture Framework (TOGAF) (US), Department of Defense Architecture Framework (DOGAF) (US), Federal Enterprise Architecture Framework (FEAF) (US), and Ministry of Defense Architecture Framework (MODAF) (UK). These frameworks have influenced each other. The TOGAF framework (The Open Group website, 2007) is quite popular amongst these frameworks. TOGAF considers and provides a development method on the construction of the EA. It includes two parts of the architecture framework, TOGAF Architecture Development Method (ADM) and TOGAF

Figure 1. EA integrates several generations of EIS (Extended from Kamogawa and Okada, 2004)

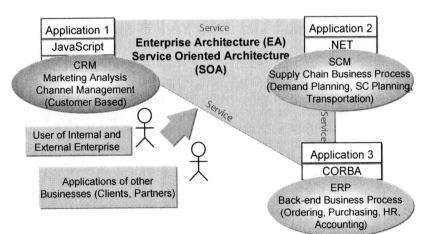

Figure 2. Enterprise architecture - Core structure

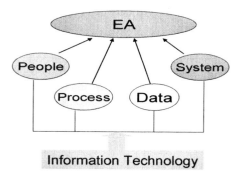

Enterprise Continuum. The Continuum describes as a series of "current" and "target", another set of terms for these are "as-is", "to-be", and the ADM is a "migration plan" to show the clearly process from current different generations of EIS to the Enterprise target dream architecture.

MOBILE TECHNOLOGIES OVERVIEW

Mobile Technologies Background

"Mobile Technology" is usually used to describe modern wireless connections such as those in cellular networks and wireless broadband Internet. Wireless technologies encompass communication that is achieved without land-based or wired mechanisms. In modern usage, wireless is a method of communication that uses low-powered radio waves to transmit data between the mobile terminals (Shuaib and Boulmalf, 2006; Hammer and Champy, 2001). The terminals, such as mobile phones, I-Pods, Personal Digital Assistants (PDA), Global Positioning System (GPS), watches, email-only devices, handheld computers, and "wearable" technology, are carried by individuals and are far more "personal" than mere desktop PCs. A wide range of MT comprise "3G" mobile network, Mobile satellite networks, Bluetooth, Wireless Local Area Network (WLAN), Wi-Max and Radio Frequency Identification (RFID).

Leading Edge of Mobile Technologies

- **3G Mobile Network**
- *Application:* mobile phone device
- *Characteristics:* Higher transmission rate, popular used and high marketing acceptance

The development of the third Generation -related technologies has overcome the limitation of the previous generation of mobile technologies by allowing higher transmission rates and more complex e-commerce interactions (Ramakrishnan et. al., 2006). According to "The Nielsen/NetRatings Australian Internet and Technology Report 2004-2005" (Film Victoria Australia, 2006), MMS usage in Australia has grown by 21% in the past years, mobile phones have already been popularly used. People utilize mobile phones for communication, working, banking, and shopping has been affecting all features of daily life in the real world.

- **Mobile Satellite**
- *Application:* GPS device and Internet phone (Voice over IP- VoIP)
- *Characteristics:* Space technology-Direction finding and map reading

Olla (2005) declared that integrating space technology into mobile communications offers two main advantages. The first advantage is in providing access to voice and data service anywhere in the world – of which the current popular application is Internet phone (Voice over IP - VoIP). The second advantage is exact positioning of useful location sensitive information used for direction-finding and map-reading based services - the current popular application is GPS. These applications are becoming commonplace; with Fitch (2004) pointing out that the technique for interfacing satellite links to global networks is well developed.

- **Bluetooth**
- *Application:* Bluetooth device, Bluetooth earphone
- *Characteristics:* Transfer data between a computer, server and one or more other mobile device "synchronously"

Buttery and Sago (2004) describe the Bluetooth application as being built into more and more mobile telephones, allowing some very interesting Mobility Commerce opportunities to be created. As people currently carry mobile phones equipped with Bluetooth technology, this technology can be used for making payments and related services through simple downloads on their mobile devices. Retailers might also be able to provide samples of products to download via a Bluetooth link located close to the actual item, potentially resulting in better customer service and an enriched shopping experience. Since Bluetooth technology is a radio transmission, it doesn't need line-of-sight with another Bluetooth-enabled device to communicate (Scheniderman, 2002). Once Bluetooth technology is in place, one can envisage consumers walking around and giving out messages wirelessly via Bluetooth in order to buy items from vending machines, or buying low value tickets, or even making small value 'cashless' purchases such as newspapers.

- **Wi-Max**
- *Characteristics:* Wireless online in urban by using mobile devices or computers.

WiMax Forum (2006) mentioned that the purpose of WiMax is to ensure that broadband wireless radios manufactured for customer use interoperate from retailer to retailer. The main advantages of the WiMax standard are to enable the implementation of advanced radio features in a standardized approach, and provide people in a city with online access via their mobile devices or computers.

- **Wireless Local Area Network (WLAN)**
- *Characteristics:* Wireless link PC or mobile device network connection in particular surrounding area

Currently, laptop, computers and some PDA devices can be attached to a Wireless Local Area Network (WLAN) using a Compact Flash (CF) or a Personal Computer Memory Card International Association (PCMCIA) card. In future, PDAs and mobile phones might support multiple network technologies. WLAN is expected to continue to be an important form of connection in many business areas. The market is expected to grow as the benefits of WLAN are recognized (Burness et. al., 2004).

- **Radio frequency identification (RFID)**
- *Application:* RFID tag, and reader

- *Characteristics:* Product tracking and controlling by system (automatically update from the RFID tag location through RFID reader to the system)

Radio frequency identification (RFID) is an emerging technology that has been increasingly used in logistics and SCM in recent years. RFID technology can help SCM system to identify, sort, and control the product and information flow all through a supply chain. Today RFID is a standard technology that uses radio waves to automatically identify people or objects. There are several methods of identification, the most common of which use RFID tags and readers (Kou et. al., 2006).

APPLYING MOBILITY TO ENTERPRISE ARCHITECTURE

Information Technology and Enterprise Architecture

EA represents a technology-business philosophy that provides the basis for cooperation between various systems of the organization that could be inside or outside the organizational boundary. EA also facilitates ability to share data and information with business partners by enabling their applications to 'talk' with each other. Cummins (2002) identifies that general characteristics of the EA integration are: distributed computing, component-based applications, event-driven processes, loose coupling of business functions, decision support information, workflow management, Internet access, and personalization of interfaces. The infrastructure spans across various technical among EA architectures, which includes database, applications, devices, middleware, network, platform, security, enterprise service bus, hosting, Local Area Network, Internet connection, operation system, servers, systems management and so on (Pulkkinen, 2006). There are numerous technologies that can be used for enterprise application integration, such as bus/hub, application connectivity, data format and transformation, integration modules, support for transactions, enterprise portal, web service, and also Service-Oriented Architecture (SOA) (Finkelstein, 2006).

Gap between Enterprise Architecture and Mobility-Enterprise Architecture

Umar (2005) states that the Next Generation Enterprises (NGEs) will rely on automation, mobility, real-time business activity monitoring, agility, and self-service over widely distributed operations to conduct business. Many organizations would like to build their entire systems by using the today's emerging technologies of which MT is a crucial part. Undoubtedly, MT can integrate in EA to provide the enterprise to have M-service and M-store. The enterprise can provide 24 hours, 7 days, globalization service and any product enquire or technical support to the customers. Inter-organizational integrates all process between extended enterprises, such as supply chain and customer relations systems. MT help to upgrade the traditional supply chain to Mobility Supply Chain Management (M-SCM), traditional CRM to Mobility Customer Relationship Management (M-CRM) (Lee, 2006) and trading procurement to Mobility procurement (M-procurement). This research looks at these extensions and integrations in greater brief detail considering capabilities of MT; moreover, these kinds of extensions and integrations will also bring EA to Mobility - Enterprise Architecture (*M-EA*).

The time and location independence of mobility open up tremendous opportunities for organizations to offer integrated services to their clients and partners. *M-EA* brings about not only internal integration but through extension, also offers much more efficiency to its external suppliers, customers and other trading partners over the Internet. Thus, *M-EA* will connect existing and new systems to enable collaborative operation within the entire organization in real-time – providing access among systems on production planning and control, inbound and outbound logistics,

material flows, monitoring functions, and performance measurements (Rolstadas and Andersen, 2000). However, EA with mobility has the challenges of security, privacy, computing power and usability. Our project aims to identify these challenges, understand and document them, and work out strategies to handle them, resulting in successful EA with mobility. An integrated EA with mobility will provide immense benefits to organizations in extending their business IS to beyond the organization's boundaries.

The literature review conducted as part of this study provides a better understanding of the problem. This problem is the gap between IT and IT supported and integrated with MT. This simple figure provides a visualization of the *M-EA* integrating *System, Process, People, and Data* in an organization in a manner that enables easy incorporation of Mobile Technologies in its business processes. As MT integrates into EA, business processes and IS will have to be reengineered. Following on from the changes to the systems and processes, people also need to know how to use the system to operate the process. As well as the data need to be changed to be adopted the new system functions. Therefore, the new *M-EA* model will have to handle these four aspects of an EA as they have a major impact on the way an organization functions.

Applying Mobile Technology to Enterprise Architecture

Mobile technology is very user centric and personalized. For example, the mobile phone is classified as a necessary gadget for most individuals in the 21st century. The uses of mobile devices are very popular specifically with the application of 3G Mobile network technology. Mobile network technology provides better service and real-time response communication

Figure 3. Gap from EA to M-EA

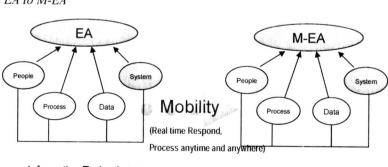

between business and consumer of EA. Some mobile devices have started to provide with Bluetooth device from last two years. Bluetooth technology is synchronization between a personal computer (PC) server and one or more other mobile terminals (Shuaib and Boulmalf, 2006); Synchronization has been particularly successful in cooperative applications, providing access to EA. WiMax can help EA integration much more effectively and update unanimity between all retailers of enterprise. The general intra-organizational *M-EA* application integration can use WLAN technology to provide all the employees to access the enterprise system anytime, anywhere. VoIP technology helps EA to extend the globalization business and also overcome the purchase timing problems though different countries. In addition, Hurster et. al. (2006) pointed out that GPS devices and RFID tags and readers have already used on SCM systems to improve delivery service and tracking production location. RFID Technology helps highly location-based tracking, reduces the cost and human-mistake risks, also improves the effectively and efficiency of EA (Schilhavy and Salam, 2006). Consideration of these

six MT is important in the exercise to integrate EA – particularly as the technologies self as well as their applications are maturing rapidly (Ghanbary, 2006).

Figure 4 shows the integration of mobile technology into enterprise technology architecture by describing it as "Mobile Enterprise Technology Architecture". The lower part of the Figure 4 demonstrates how the application service and information/data storage go through the enterprise bus or middleware cooperation. This transfer is a basis to help business processes orchestration reengineering. Moreover, the new processes are the basis of integration different generation of enterprise information systems. The most popular four enterprise information systems are SCM system, CRM system, ERP system, and financial (FI) system cooperation within enterprise architecture. RFID technology could specifically support the SCM system to help tracking the location of the materials and products. This underside section includes the M-EA business process, system, and data structure. People can hold various mobile devices through mobility server and access web service to connect to Internet portal, including web and mobile

Figure 4. Mobile enterprise technology architecture

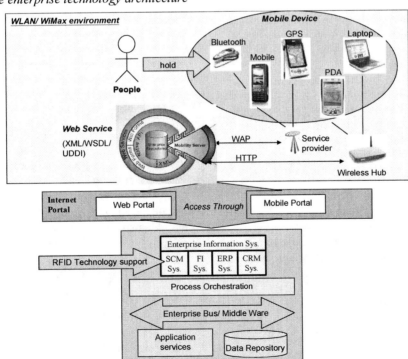

Table 1. M-EA migration plan table

	Current state "as-is"	Desired Target state "To-be"
Description	Key factors	Reserve assessment indicator
Analysis	Assessment indicator result	Target M-EA opportunities
Design	Construct current EA	Construct Target M-EA
Implementation plan	Target M-EA opportunities result	Target M-EA implementation plan

portal to run those business process, system and access through data base, The technologies of Web Services build on top of eXtensible Markup Language (XML), Web Services Description Language (WSDL) and Universal Description, Discovery and Integration (UDDI), provide an excellent basis for integrating the applications of the enterprise – particularly when they are on separate platforms. There is a need, however, to provide wireless glue to EA as outlined here. This would result in strategic incorporation of apply MT into EA starts on an enterprise repository which is a comprehensive system containing all applications and the enterprise model. People can reach the system using the Internet though the native API/ XML, web forms, and web service. They can use their mobile, some with Bluetooth headphone, GPS, PDA, portable computer (laptop) though service provider (WAP), or wireless Hub (HTTP) to connect with enterprise repositories to access the enterprise information systems.

The implementation of *M-EA* should use "Current" and "Target", "As-is" and "To-be" framework to identify the clearly process migration plan from current different generation EIS to the Enterprise target dream architecture - *M-EA*. The manner in which this IT and mobile technology incorporation takes place successfully is studied here through the framework outlined in the *migration plan table*. Table 1 is a migration table plan which lists information system lifecycles including description, analysis, design, and implementation plan (Irani et. al., 2003) of current state of enterprise, and desired target state *M-EA* of enterprise. Firstly, go through people, process, system, and data migration after applying mobile technology integration to have four *M-EA* migration plan tables. Then combine and cooperation these four

tables to have the M-EA migration plan to look down the blueprint of whole structure.

Firstly, the research team looks through the enterprise current enterprise information systems to understand the key factors of each aspect, and fill into the description section. Then making the platform and interoperability diagrams from existing enterprise information systems to show the reserve assessment indicator for target state. Follow by, the research team sets up a meeting with enterprise team to show diagrams and analysis those assessment indicator results and make the analysis documents of which IT and MT infrastructures could be extended with current EA as target M-EA opportunities. After the meeting, the research team will construct the current EA diagrams, also the target *M-EA* diagram to show how the MT integration to new *M-EA* can be matched the enterprise expected extension. Moreover, these diagrams will have be modified through the enterprise meeting to decide which MT application opportunities they would like to integrate into their M-EA and how the implementation processes will be considered. All of the diagrams and documents will be analysis the critical success point to enter into the migration plan table of each aspect, and then combine them into the comprehensive *M-EA* migration plan table.

VALIDATION OF M-EA MODEL (CASE STUDY AND ACTION RESEARCH)

Firstly, this research starts on constructing initial *M-EA* structure to investigate and analysis the changes at 5 aspects, which are data, process, people, system, and technology from Case Studies. This initial *M-EA* model provides the implementation details of enterprise need to change their architecture before they use mobile technology application. Enterprise can have a perspective view of what Business Process Reengineering (BPR) and Mobile-transformation preparation need to be done first before they integrate *M-EA*.

Secondly, this initial *M-EA* model would be implemented and validated by doing Action Research study in chosen organization. The business processes reengineering, practical issues, benefits, challenges and limitation will be identified, documented and discussed with MIRAG and implementation team during and after implementation. Follow by modifying the model from those results to reduce the challenges and keep benefits to the comprehensive *M-EA* model. Building on the work reported by Spewak (1992), this *M-EA* implementation planning project will based on the following steps: preliminary enterprise analysis and modeling -> analysis of current systems and technology architecture -> architecture extension plan for data and applications -> extension plan for Mobility in the overall EA -> implementation migration plan -> transition to implementation -> testing and validation -> release. The major steps of Action Research in this project are based on Oosthuizen's (2000) description of a typical action research circle: action -> results -> reflection -> plan.)

Following are the specific steps envisage in action research of this *M-EA* model validation to comprehensive model from these points onwards:

1. From case study to construct a draft *M-EA* model
2. Undertake comprehensive interviews to further identify and document the current business process and IS of chosen action research organization
3. Undertake detailed analysis of the current business process and IS need to be disparate or integrated. (How are the company's core business processes related to each other? What information drives these core processes? How must this information be integrated?)
4. Determine the current EA and whether it enables information flow.
5. Integrate mobility into the EA of the organization. (What technical capabilities should be standardized companywide to support IT and MT efficiencies and facilitate process standardization and integration?)
6. Consider the information sharing privacy and security condition apply.
7. Implementation *M-EA* model to enterprise.
8. Identify and document the key factors influencing the construction and collaborating mobility into the EA of these organizations.
9. Identify and document the key organizational benefits and challenges of implementing *M-EA* model to enterprise.
10. Modify the model of *M-EA* from discussing, present and obtain feedback from the research groups.
11. Bring the update version model go back action research organization to the first step.

However, security has to be given due consideration when the enterprise considered implement *M-EA*. The increased mobile computing power of handheld devices introduces new security threats. The security threats would be in the form of loss of confidentiality, loss of integrity and loss of availability. Password protection is included in most handheld devices as a countermeasure (Guizani & Raju, 2005). Furthermore, network and application security measures also need to be considered when using mobile technologies. Having risk identification and risk planning measures could help to overcome some risks (Ghosh, 2001). A possible solution is to build security measures into mobile platforms and applications themselves. Base on above, security is the important part that has not been considered in this research. CLEW (Closed Loop Environment for Wireless) is a new mobile-based technology designed by a company called Alacrity Technology based in Canberra, Australia (http://www.alacritytech.com.au/). This technology improves the security of using mobile technology, and this company- Alacrity is the first action research company of this research project, aims to improve *M-EA* security. CLEW technology is introduced as an Intelligent Mobile Internet Interaction (Tatham, 2006). CLEW is more secure than SMS message, and also records the replies from the receiver. Messages sent out by CLEW to recipients are authenticated by the recipients by signing off with a password. Therefore, it is much more secure than SMS, and also if the recipient does not sign off, the backend systems of CLEW can send out messages to other pre-agreed people in a list agreed upon with the organization until it schedules the required number of personnel.

CONCLUSION AND FUTURE DIRECTION

This chapter outlines the importance of *M-EA* model as a means of identifying integration challenges and providing that integration between various applications and technologies within the enterprise. Moreover, this chapter also provides an overview of EA, MT and applications of *M-EA*. This research argued that MT needs to be integrated with the overall EA and the business processes of the enterprise. Such integrated would result in *M-EA*, it has been identified that would enable the enterprise to conduct business across the location and time boundaries. Thus, an integrated *M-EA* is a powerful tool to help manage the enterprise' operation.

This research envisages continuing effort in the future to enable the researcher to validate the *M-EA* model. This research currently undertakes case studies and action research in various organizations in practice that will enable validation of the initial *M-EA* model. The initial action research suggests enterprises can benefit with the help of *M-EA* through its step-by-step framework for extending and integrating the existing EA. Furthermore, the key factors influencing the construction and collaboration of mobility into the EA of these organizations; and also the key organizational benefits and challenges of implementing *M-EA* model to enterprise are also been focused on in nearly future.

REFERENCES

Barnes, S. J. (2002). The mobile commerce value chain: analysis and future development. *International Journal of Information Management, 22*(2), 91-108.

Burness, L., Higgins, D., Sago, A., & Thorpe, P. (2004). Wireless LANs – present and future. *Mobile and wireless communications: Key technologies and future application*. British Telecommunications Plc.: The IEE.

Buttery, S., & Sago, A. (2004). Future application of Bluetooth. *Mobile and wireless communications: Key technologies and future application*. British Telecommunications Plc: The IEE.

Cook M. A. (1996). *Building Enterprise Information Architectures- Reengineering Information Systems*. Prentice-Hall, Inc.

Finkelstein. C. (2006) *Enterprise Architecture for Integration: rapid delivery methods and technologies*. U.S.A.: Artech House.

Cummins F. A. (2002). *Enterprise Integration: An Architecture for Enterprise Application and Systems Integration*. Canada: Willey Computing Publishing, John Wiley & Sons, Inc.

Film Victoria Australia (2006). iSH MEDIA. Digital Sanbox Seminar Film Victoria, June 2006. [online]. Available: http://film.vic.gov.au/resources/documents/S2_speaker_Kylie_Robertson_powerpoint.pdf

Finkelstein, C. (2006). *Enterprise Architecture for Integration – Rapid delivery methods and technologies*. Artech House: Boston Lonton.

Fitch, M. (2004). The use of satellite for multimedia communications. *Mobile and wireless communications: Key technologies and future application*. British Telecommunications Plc: The IEE.

Ghanbary, A. (2006). Evaluation of mobile technologies in the context of their applications, limitations and transformation. In Unhelkar B. (Ed.), *Handbook of Research in Mobile Business: Technical, Methodological and Social Perspectives.*.Hershey, PA, USA: IGI Global.

Ghosh, A. K. (2001). *Security and Privacy for E-Business*. New York: John Wiley & Sons

Guizani, M., & Raju, A. (2005). Wireless Networks and Communications Security. In Y. Xiao, J. Li and Y. Pan (Eds.), *Security and Routing in Wireless Networks, 3*, 320. New York: Nova Science Publishers, Inc.

Hammer, M., & Champy, J. (2001). *Reengineering the Corporation: A manifesto for business revolution*. London: Nicholas Brealey.

Hurster, W., Fuychtuller, H., & Fischer, T. (2006). Mobile Batch Tracking- a breakthrough in supply chain management. In Unhelkar B. (Ed.), *Handbook of Research in Mobile Business: Technical, Methodological and Social Perspectives.*, Hershey, PA, USA: IGI Global.

Irani, Z., Themistocleous, M., & Love, P. E. D. (2003). The impact of enterprise application integration on information system lifecycles. *Information & Management 41*, 177-187. Elsevier Science.

Kamogawa, T., & Okada, H. (2004). Issues of E-Business implementation from Enterprise Architecture viewpoint. *Proceedings of the 2004 International Symposium on Applications and the Internet Workshops* (SAINTW'04), 2004 IEEE.

Kou, D., Zhao, K., Tao, Y., & Kou, W. (2006). RFID Technologies and Applications. In W. Kou and Y. Yesha (Eds.), *Enabling Technologies for wireless E-Business.* Berlin Heidelberg: Springer-Verlag. (pp 89-108).

Lan, Y., & Unhelkar, B. (2005). *Global Enterprise Transitions: managing the process.* Hershey, PA: IGI Golbal.

Lee, C. (2006). Mobile CRM: Reaching, acquiring, and retaining mobile consumers. In Unhelkar B. (Ed.), *Handbook of Research in Mobile Business: Technical, Methodological and Social Perspectives.* Hershey, PA, USA: IGI Global.

Linthicum, D. S. (2000). *Enterprise application integration.* Addison- Wesley information technology series.

META Group, Inc. (2006) Adaptive Enterprise Architecture. META Group, Inc., CT-USA, 2004. – Bittler. R. S. private presentation to UWS Advanced enterprise Information Management Systems (AeIMS) Research Group on 13/11/2006

Olla, P. (2005). *Incorporating commercial space technology into mobile services: Developing innovative business models.* Hershey, PA, USA: Idea Group Inc.

Oosthuizen, M. (2000). Action research. In K. Williamson (Ed.), 2000: *Research methods for students and professionals: information management and systems.* Centre for information systems: Charles Sturt University. (pp. 141-158).

Pulkkinen, M. (2006). Systemic Management of Architectural Decisions in Enterprise Architecture Planning. Four Dimensions and Three Abstraction Levels. *Proceedings of the 39th Hawaii International Conference on System Sciences – 2006 IEEE.*

Ramakrisham, K. R., Bhattar, R. K., Dasgupta, K. S., & Palsule, V. S. (2006). Review of Wireless Technologies and Generations. In Unhelkar B. (Ed.), *Handbook of Research in Mobile Business: Technical, Methodological and Social Perspectives.*, Hershey, PA, USA: IGI Global.

Rolstadas & Andersen, B. (2000) *Enterprise Modeling- Improving global industrial competitiveness.* Kluwer Academic publishers.

Ross, W. J., Weill, P., & Robertson, D. C. (2006). *Enterprise Architecture as Strategy- creating a foundation for business execution.* Boston, MA: Harvard Business School Press.

Scheniderman, R. (2002). *The Mobile Technology Question and Answer Book.* Amacom: American Management Association.

Schilhavy, R., & Salam, A. F. (2006). Emerging mobile technology and supply chain integration: Using RFID to streamline the integrated supply chain. In Unhelkar B. (Ed.), *Handbook of Research in Mobile Business: Technical, Methodological and Social Perspectives.* Hershey, PA, USA: IGI Global.

Shuaib, K., & Boulmalf, M. (2006). Co-Existence of WLAN and WPAN Communication Systems. In Unhelkar B. (Ed.), *Handbook of Research in Mobile Business: Technical, Methodological and Social Perspectives*, Hershey, PA, USA: IGI Global.

Spewak, S. H., & Hill, S. C. (1992). *Enterprise Architecture Planning: Developing a Bluepoint for data, applications, and technology.* A Wiley-QED publication, John Wiley & Sons, Inc.

Tatham, A. (2006). *How CLEW could authenticate credit cards to avoid credit card fraud.* In U. AEIMS research Group (Ed.) (pp. Technical Presentation). Sydney: Alacrity.

Umar. (2005). IT Infrastructure to Enable Next Generation Enterprises. *Information Systems Frontiers, 7(3).* ISSN:1387-3326.

Unhelkar, B. (2005, August). Transitioning to a Mobile Enterprise: A Three-Dimensional Framework. *Cutter IT journal, 18*(8). Cutter Information LLC.

Unhelkar, B. (Ed.), (2006). *Handbook of Research in Mobile Business: Technical, Methodological and Social Perspectives.* Hershey, PA, USA: IGI Global.

U.S. Department of Defense Technical Architecture. TOGAF Architecture. The Open Group [Online]. Available: http://www.theopengroup.org

Virginia Information Technologies Agency (2006). *Enterprise Definitions and Models. Commonwealth of Virginia* [Online]. Available: http://www.vita.virginia.gov/cots/ea/modelAndArchitecture/index.cfm

WiMax Forum, (2006). WiMax Forum - Frequency Ask Question, [online]. Available: http://www.wimaxforum.org/technology/faq, WiMax Forum, WiMax Forum

Zachman, J. A. (1987). Zachman Framework. *The Zachman institute for framework advancement* [Online]. Available: http://www.zifa.com/

KEY TERMS

Enterprise Architecture (EA): A structure of integrating business processes with IT supported, by providing a visualization enterprise solution of the relationships among the System, Process, People, and Data in an organization.

Mobile Enterprise Architecture (M-EA): A structure of integrating business processes with Information Technology that are supported and integrated with MT. It integrates business Systems, Processes, People, and Data in an organization in a manner that enables easy incorporation of Mobile Technologies in its business processes.

Mobile Technologies (MT): Used to describe modern wireless connections such as those in cellular networks and wireless broadband Internet, also encompass communication that is achieved without land-based or wired mechanisms

Service-Oriented Architecture (SOA): Using of services to support the business and user requirements, one kind of modern today enterprise architecture.

Chapter XLVII
Extending Enterprise Application Integration (EAI) with Mobile and Web Services Technologies

Abbass Ghanbary
MethodScience.com & University of Western Sydney, Australia

Bhuvan Unhelkar
MethodScience.com & University of Western Sydney, Australia

ABSTRACT

Web Services (WS) technologies, generally built around the ubiquitous Extensible Markup Language (XML), have provided many opportunities for integrating enterprise applications. However, XML/Simple Object Access Protocol (SOAP), together with Web Services Definition Language (WSDL) and Universal Description Discovery and Integration (UDDI), form a comprehensive suite of WS technologies that have the potential to transcend beyond mere application integration within an organization, and to provide capabilities of integrating processes across multiple organizations. Currently, the WS paradigm is driven through parameters however; the paradigm shift that can result in true collaborative business requires us to consider the business paradigm in terms of policies-processes-standards. This chapter, based on experimental research carried out by the authors, demonstrates how the technologies of WS open up the doors to collaborative Enterprise Architecture Integration (EAI) and Service Oriented Architecture (SOA) resulting in Business Integration (BI). The chapter also provide a quantitative investigation based on organization's adaptation to mobile and Web Services technologies.

INTRODUCTION

This chapter describes how WS can be used in order to align and integrate business processes of organizations (internal and external processes) to satisfy the needs of Enterprise Architecture (EA). Thus far, the concept of Business Integration (BI) has been mainly focused on integrating the business processes internal to an organization; however this chapter is an investigation to identify how the organizations can extend this integration with those business processes belonging to other enterprises and how they adapt mobile and

Web Services technologies in order to integrate with those business processes.

According to Finkelsteing (2006) Enterprise Architecture (EA) builds on business knowledge and allows business specialist experts to apply their respective knowledge to determine the most effective technology and process solutions for the business.

Information and Communication Technology (ICT) architectures have not paid enough attention to integration of the services in the past. Service Oriented Architecture (SOA) is an architecture that makes the services of a system to interact and perform a task supporting a request. SOA is classified as sub-architecture of Enterprise Architecture.

Based on Barry (2003), a Service Oriented Architecture (SOA) is a part of an EA and can be viewed as "sub-architecture" of an Enterprise Architecture. SOA existed before the advent of Web Services. Technologies such as Common Object Request Broker (CORBA) and Distributed Component Object Model (DCOM) afforded the opportunity to create SOA. Web Services is ideal technology for developing sophisticated architecture.

The Open Group Architecture Framework (TOGAF) is a critical architecture for the effective and safe construction of business and information systems. TOGAF provides the TOGAF Architecture Development Method (ADM). TOGAF ADM is a comprehensive, detailed, industry standard method for developing Enterprise Architectures Integration (EAI), and related information, application, and technology architectures that address the needs of business, technology, and data systems (http://www.integrationconsortium.org).

Based on Chase (2006), originally designed as a way to develop the technology architecture for an organization, TOGAF has evolved into a methodology for analysing the overall business architecture. The first part of TOGAF is a methodology for developing the architecture design, which is called the Architecture Development Method (ADM). It has the following nine basic phases:

- **Preliminary phase: Framework and principles.** Get everyone on board with the plan.
- **Phase A: Architecture vision.** Define your scope and vision and map your overall strategy.
- **Phase B: Business architecture.** Describe your current and target business architectures and determine the gap between them.

- **Phase C: Information system architectures.** Develop target architectures for your data and applications.
- **Phase D: Technology architecture.** Create the overall target architecture that you will implement in future phases.
- **Phase E: Opportunities and solutions.** Develop the overall strategy, determining what you will buy, build or reuse, and how you will implement the architecture described in phase D.
- **Phase F: Migration planning.** Prioritize projects and develop the migration plan.
- **Phase G: Implementation governance.** Determine how you will provide oversight to the implementation.
- **Phase H: Architecture change management.** Monitor the running system for necessary changes and determine whether to start a new cycle, looping back to the preliminary phase.

These phases provide a standardised way of analysing the enterprise and planning and managing the actual implementation. The Service Oriented Architecture is considered in **Phase D: Technology architecture** where the TOGAF defines the services and their relationship with each other and define how the services could be invoked by different requesters.

Service Oriented Architecture (SOA) describes how the service could be invoked and how the service attributes are implemented. The concepts of SOA and TOGAF relate to each other when Technology Architecture is invoked by different requesters. TOGAF contains two reference models that can be used in this way: a platform-centric Technical Reference Model that focuses on the services and structure of the underlying platform necessary to support the use and reuse of applications, and an Integrated Information Infrastructure Reference Model that focuses on the applications space, and addresses the need for interoperability, and for enabling secure flow of information where and when it is needed (http://www.ebizq.net).

The highly competitive nature of the current business environment creates tremendous pressure for organizations to collaborate. It is essential for companies to understand rapidly changing business circumstances. The rapidly changing environment encourages the enterprises to integrate their business functions into a system that efficiently utilises ICT.

The chapter proposes a theoretical model as the recommended implementation of the integration that requires a substantial amount of time and financial commitment. The supplemental technologies of SOA, EAI and TOGAF automate the integration process with the collaborative environment of the business processes of multiple organizations.

LITRATURE REVIEW

The increase in the demand of the management of the Information and Communication Technology (ICT) has caused the research to focus their efforts on integrating of business processes and data. The term Enterprise Integration (or System Integration) reflects the capability to integrate a variety of different system functionalities.

Traditionally, information systems were implemented to support specific functional areas. However, the advancement of information technology enables new forms of organizations and facilitates their business processes to collaborate even when these organizations are not necessarily known to each other. As organizations become more complex and diverse in the collaborative context, it becomes nearly impossible for them to implement their collaborative business concepts without enterprise integration.

New technology seems to suggest that mobile services will be the greatest opportunity for businesses to develop richer and more profitable relationships with individual customers by giving them what they actually want (Falcone and Garito, 2006)

According to Jostad, et al, (2005) the demand for flexible, efficient and user-friendly collaborative services is becoming more and more urgent as competition in the current market oriented arena is becoming more intense. Enterprises have to be more dynamic in terms of collaboration with partners and even competitors. The Service Oriented Architecture is a promising computing paradigm offering solutions that are extendible, flexible and compatible with legacy systems. This chapter proposes and investigates the use of SOA in the construction of collaborations across multiple organizations.

Harrison and Taylor (2005) define an SOA that builds on the concept of a service. It is a collection of services capable of interacting in three ways, commonly referred to as 'publish, find and bind'. In other words, a service must be able to make its interface available to other services (publish), other services must be capable of discovering the interface (find), and finally services must be able to connect to one another to exchange messages (bind). The loose coupling of

an SOA is achieved firstly through the separation of data exchange from the software agents involved in the exchange, and secondly through the discrete nature of the service.

The biggest challenge may be the behaviour of the users to adapt to the developed system. According to Chen, et al, (2006) the consumer of a service is not required to have a detailed knowledge of implementation, implementation language, or execution platform of the service. The only concern of the consumer is how a service can be invoked according to the service interface.

Change management and transformation of an organization can be very difficult and sensitive issues. Conversely, it can be argued that behavioural integration is critical to the success of enterprise integration. The technical integration can be a success but if the organization is not going to internalise the enterprise system, the entire project is a failure. As such, to achieve the maximum benefit and impact from enterprise integration, we need to have both successful technical and behavioural integration (http://delivery.acm.org).

The successful architecture confirms that business requirements and information technology design are captured in models. The modelling technique of abstraction to separate business concerns from technology concerns (what the business system needs to do, versus its underlying computing platform) is also an important aspect of the success of the architecture.

The following issues also could be classified as the critical factor for the success of the Service Oriented and Enterprise Architecture:

- To capture business requirements.
- Platform-Independent Model (PIM) by promoting designing a business solution prior to selecting how it will be deployed.
- The Platform-Specific Model (PSM) adds to the PIM the details of a specific computing platform on which the business solution will be deployed.
- Transformations (mappings) are performed on these models to progress from a higher level of abstraction to a lower level of abstraction.
- All of this activity is based on internationally accepted standards.

Businesses that aim to support mobile workers and enhance process effectiveness will need to consider extending their process and systems beyond the workplace (Alag, 2006). According to Godbole, (2006) Mobile Commerce is best suited where the consumer is driven by a "sense of urgency" when they need to have their goods and services immediately for upcoming functions and events.

Every organization on the planet consisting of more than one person has already realised that their information technology infrastructure is effectively a distributed computing system. To integrate information assets and use information effectively, it must be accessible across the department, across the company, across the world and more importantly across the service- or supply-chain from the supplier, to one's own organization, to one's customers. This means that CPUs must be intimately linked to the networks of the world and be capable of freely passing and receiving information, not hidden behind glass and cooling ducts or the complexities of the software that drives them. www.omg.org/docs/omg/03-06-01.pdf

UNDERSTANDING SOA AND WEB SERVICES

Service-Oriented Architecture is architecture based on internal and external processes of an organization. Web Services technology is the most appropriate technology to develop SOA. Curbera, et al, (2003) states that Web Services provide generic coordination mechanisms that can be extended for specific protocols and Ghanbary (2006) extends this expression by stating that WS represent the applications that organizations publish/locate on unknown and disparate platforms. According to Unhelkar & Deshpande (2004), Web Services based technologies enable applications to "talk" with one another even across organizational firewalls, resulting in an opportunity for a cluster or group of organizations to simultaneously transition to Web-based entities.

Barry (2003) clearly states that the use of Web Services appears to be the missing puzzle piece in creating a complete picture of a service oriented architecture work. The statement given by Barry (2003) identifies the importance of universal adoption of Web Services by software vendors.

Figure 1 illustrates the importance of the adoption of the Web Service by internal as well as the external architecture. The following is the explanation of the functionality of the Web Services that could create successful service oriented architecture.

XML/SOAP AND SOA

Extensible Mark-up Language (XML) is a simple, very flexible text format derived from SGML (ISO 8879). Originally designed to meet the challenges of large-scale electronic publishing, XML is also playing an increasingly important role in the exchange

Figure 1. Internal and external impacts of WS

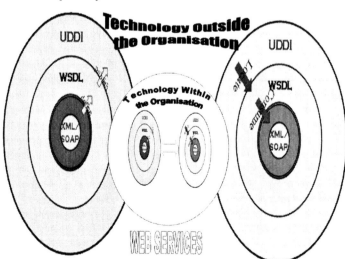

of a wide variety of data on the Web and elsewhere (http://www.w3.org/XML/).

XML schemas associated with SOAP message payloads often need to be designed with some of the more advanced features of the XML Schema Definition Language. Specifically, the use of extensible or redefined schemas may be required when building documents that represent multiple data contexts. See Exhibit A.

WSDL AND SOA

WSDL is an XML format for describing network services as a set of endpoints operating on messages containing either document-oriented or procedure-oriented information. The operations and messages are described abstractly, and then bound to a concrete network protocol and message format to define an endpoint. Related concrete endpoints are combined into abstract endpoints services (http://www.w3.org/TR/wsdl). See Exhibit B.

Exhibit A.

```
<collection>
  <description>Examples of code</description>
  <code id="VB">
    <title>Visual Basic code example</title>
    <codeExample>
      Private Sub Form1_Paint()
        Print "Hello World!"
      End Sub
    </codeExample>
  </code>
  <code id="Java">
    <title>Java code example</title>
    <codeExample>
      public class Hello
      {
        public static void main(String[] args)
        {
          System.out.println("Hello, World!");
        }
      }
    </codeExample>
  </code>
  <code id="COBOL">
    <title>COBOL code example</title>
    <codeExample>
        IDENTIFICATION DIVISION.
        PROGRAM-ID. Hello-World.
        *
        ENVIRONMENT DIVISION.
        *
        DATA DIVISION.
        *
        PROCEDURE DIVISION.
        PARA-1.
            DISPLAY "Hello, world!".
        *
            STOP RUN.
    </codeExample>
  </code>
</collection>
```

Exhibit B.

```
<businessEntity
   businessKey="uddi:4589150-5F12-9K45-H048-337910DA52F94">
   <name>ExampleCode Pty Ltd</name>
   <description>For all your example code needs</description>
   <contacts>
      <phone>612-9055-0047</phone>
      <email>info@examplecode.com</email>
   </contacts>
   <businessServices>
      <businessService
         serviceKey="uddi:8181F24-1A42-7850-3664-36599DA515K04"
         businessKey="uddi:35894A5-8745-95FD-0571-9161K577D2604">
         <name>ExampleCode Server</name>
         <description>ExampleCode.com's example code server</description>
         <bindingTemplates>
            <bindingTemplate
               bindingKey="uddi:2549842-F148-9758-24G7-2584D8789A5F5"
               serviceKey="uddi:8181F24-1A42-7850-3664-36599DA515K04">
               <accessPoint URLType="http">
                  http://www.examplecode.com/code
               </accessPoint>
               <tModelInstanceDetails>
                  <tModelInstanceInfo
                     tModelKey="uddi:5791FG2-3460-4G97-2771-1495GJ443925"/>
                  </tModelInstanceInfo>
               </tModelInstanceDetails>
            </bindingTemplate>
         </bindingTemplates>
      </businessService>
   </businessServices>
</businessEntity>
```

WSDL is extensible to allow description of endpoints and their messages regardless of what message formats or network protocols are used to communicate. Web Service Definition Language SOA starts with the design of a service. Building software services start with the definition of what the service is and what the service does. SOA provides a standardised means of building software services that can be accessed, shared, and reused across a network. While SOA is a well-established concept, it has become increasingly popular with the emergence of Web Services. The starting point in developing SOA services is the Web Services Description Language (WSDL).

UDDI AND SOA

Universal Description, Discovery and Integration (UDDI) specifications define a registry service for Web services and for other electronic and non-electronic services. A UDDI registry service is a Web service that manages information about service providers, service implementations, and service metadata. Service providers can use UDDI to advertise the services they offer. Service consumers can use UDDI to discover services that suit their requirements and to obtain the service metadata needed to consume those services (http://www.uddi.org/faqs.html).

Universal Description, Discovery, and Integration (UDDI) discover the prospective requester from the directory that is also an integral part of an organization. This specification allows for the creation of standardised service description registries both within and outside of organization boundaries. UDDI provides the potential for Web services to be registered in a central location, from where they can be discovered by service requestors. Hence SOA services should be accessed, shared, and reused across a network. The UDDI directory provides the channels of access across the network.

THE USE OF SOA IN COLLABORATIVE ORGANIZATIONS

One of the key challenges in modern day business is the pressing need to integrate their wide and varied software systems and applications. Furthermore, large organizations such as banks and insurance companies have vast amount of data that is embedded in their legacy systems. They have a need to expose those data and the corresponding applications in a 'unified' view to the customer on the Internet - resulting in what is known as 'business integration'. However, as a result of this integration, and technical ability of applications to transact over the Internet, businesses are now readily able to offer and consume 'services' across the Internet. Currently, there is a limited of literature on modelling and managing the challenges emanating from collaboration between varied businesses and applications.

Based on Pasley (2005), service interoperability is paramount. Although researchers have proposed various middleware technologies to achieve SOA, Web services standards better satisfy the universal interoperability needs. In order for multiple organizations to collaborate many challenges were identified as such: technological, methodological and social factors resulting rational interactions between businesses. The good architecture takes place when the services of different applications have the capability to communicate. The previous statement leads us to the concept of Service Oriented Application departing beyond the boundary of standard communications framework.

According to Erl (2004) an SOA is a design model with a deeply rooted concept of encapsulating application logic within services that interact via a common communication protocol. When Web Services are used to establish this communication framework, they basically represent a web-based implementation of Service Oriented Architecture. Business process integration is part of enterprise integration solutions, which is why coordination services for business activities are utilised exclusively for the management of long running business activities.

Based on Chung (2005), Web Services integration enables a dynamic e-business model that fosters collaboration with heterogeneous business services and opens the door for new business opportunities. A service-oriented architecture (SOA) is an application framework that takes everyday business applications and breaks them down into individual business functions and processes, called services.

Figure 2. The role oF SOA in collaborative organizations

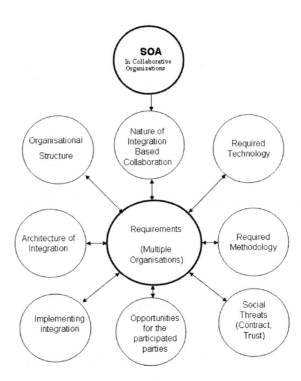

Figure 2 will clearly explain how Service Oriented Architecture will impact the requirements of collaborative Organizations.

The above Figure 2 shows the importance of SOA in developing the applications of Collaborative Organizations. The technology and the architectural aspects of this integration based on collaboration have also been demonstrated. The requirements of collaborations as far as the multiple organizations are the required technology, required methodology, social threats, how to implement the integration, how to architect the integration and investigate the structural changes to the organization after the integration.

ADAPTING MOBILE AND WEB SERVICES TECHNOLOGIES

The interoperation amongst multiple organizations needs a technology to support the collaboration across their business process especially when the participated organization are not necessarily known to each other, and have never collaborated previously.

According to Barry (2003) the main driving forces for adopting Web Services are classified as interoperable network applications, emerging industry-wide standards, easier exchange of data, reduced developing time, reduced maintain costs, availability of external services and availability of training and tools.

The main restraining forces are also classified as different semantics in data source, semantic translation effect on operation systems for up-to-moment data request, standards evolving not fixed and mergers and acquisition.

Based on our survey, we asked 60 different organizations in the Sydney metropolitan area to inform us about their ideas about the adoption of the Web Services from technical, methodological and social issues. The following Figures present the result of the survey which was already approved by the Ethics committees. The 43% of the organization amounting 26, were medium sized and 57% amounting 34, were large sized organizations. According to the ABS report, the organizations with the number of 10-200 employees are classified as medium size and the organization with the number of more than 200 employees are classified as the large size organizations (Trevin, 2001). Figure 3 illustrate the demographic of the organization based on their organizational size.

The organizations span across different industries, as listed in table below.

The Organization Category

This section is related to the category of the participated organization. The study identifies the importance of the organization's category as to reach different industries in order to evaluate the general technological adaptation in different organization. Table 1 demonstrate the organizational categories in which responded to the distributed survey.

The majority of the participants are from the Information Technology sector of the industry. The Government departments, education and banking are following in order. The study is able to proceed hence the distribution of the questionnaire has been correctly allocated and the study can evaluate the result achieved based on the different category of the organizations.

The Position of the Participant in the Organization

This part is related to the position of the individuals in the organization who has actually responded to the questions. This section is also very important since the research can understand the role of the respondent and their decision making power to change the technology of the organization. The positions of the respondent are presented in Table 2.

The participants who held the general management positions in their organizations formed the 21.7% while marketing manager and senior management holds 13.3% of the respondents. The remaining of 48.3% of the respondents holds the key role positions in their organizations. These people are the decision makers in the organizations.

MOBILE TECHNOLOGY INFORMATION

This section of the chapter demonstrates the result of the survey in regards to the respondents general thought about mobility in business.

Importance of the Mobility in the Organization

This section is evaluating the use of mobile technology (use of mobile devices) in the daily activities of the business. The query further investigates whether the organizations are already using mobile technology, or

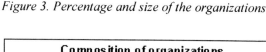

Figure 3. Percentage and size of the organizations

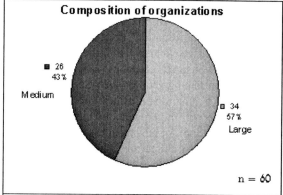

are planning to use it in the near future. The responses are detailed in Figure 4.

A substantial 87% (63% already using, and 23% that plan to use in the near future) of the organizations responded in the affirmative to this question, which verifies the fact that the key personnel in the selected sample are very much aware of the value of mobility and mobile technology for their organizations. Thirteen per cent of the respondents said that they do not have a plan to use mobile technology in the near future.

Used Mobile Devices in the Organization

The question is to identify what kind of the devices are in use in order to gain an insight into the current use of mobile technology in the organizations. The responses for this question are listed in Figure 5.

The main issue to consider in this section is that the organizations can use different devices in order to proceed with their daily business activities. The survey identified that 40% of the organizations are currently using mobile devices while 30% of the respondent use mobile enabled laptops. The Figure 6 clearly demonstrates that organizations have realised that they need to take advantage of mobile technologies.

The Scenario in Which Mobile Devices are Used

The respondents were queried about the use of these devices in their business activities. In this section of the

Table 1. The category of the organizations

Organizations Categories	Number	Percentage
Information Technology	20	33.3%
Government Departments	14	23.3%
Education and Training	7	11.7%
Banking, Finance and Insurance	7	11.7%
Professional Services (Legal and Accounting)	5	8.3%
Retailing	3	5%
Health and Community Services	2	3.3%
Utility Services and Equipment	1	1.7%
Manufacturing and Processing	1	1.7%
Total	60	100%

Table 2. The position of the respondent in the organization

Position	Number	Percentage
General Management	13	21.7%
Marketing Manager	8	13.3%
Senior Management	8	13.3%
Systems Analyst/Programmer	8	13.3%
IT/MIS Manager	6	10%
Technical Support	6	10%
Executive Manager	5	8.3%
Sales Officer	4	6.7%
Customer Care	2	3.3%
Total	60	100%

Figure 4. The use of mobile technology in the organizations

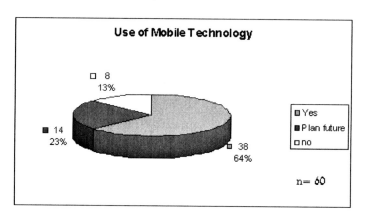

Figure 5. Type of mobile devices in organizations

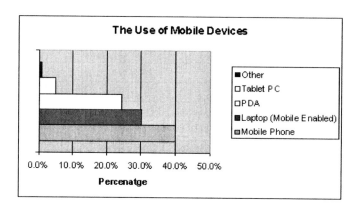

research is identifying the reason for the use of mobile devices in order to identify the use of this technology in the collaborative environment. The Figure 6 depicts the typical reasons for the mobile devices in the daily business activates.

Figure 6 presents the result by stating that the majority of participants believe that the use of mobility has increased the performance of their business activities enabling them to have greater access to the employee, as well as being accessible by their customers. The use of mobile devices has created flexibility, availability and better access.

Questions 7, 8, 9, 12, 21, 22 and 23 have been designed to rate the answers on different method of evaluation. The legends are as followings:

VSA – Very Strongly Agree
SA – Strongly Agree
Ag - Agree
DA – Disagree
SD - Strongly Disagree
VSD – Very Strongly Disagree

Based on these ratings, the following results are extracted from the survey of organizations. In the followings the letter P stands for the Point as it was presented in the survey called Point number.

Current Application of Mobile Technology

The question asked whether there are any new applications and areas in which mobile technology

Figure 6. Typical reason for the use of mobile devices

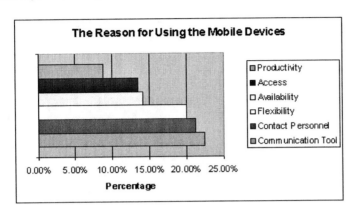

could be included in the daily business activities of the organization, under four propositions, as listed in Table 3.

1. Mobile technology as a special technology improve efficiency in customer meetings. 78.7% of the respondents either agreed or strongly agreed with this proposition.
2. Mobile technology has been used as a special tool to advertise in a captured market. 70.4% of the respondents agreed with this proposition.
3. Mobile technology as a tool has enabled people to contact with the office for employees engaged in official travel. 63.8% agreed to this proposition.
4. Mobile technology has enabled the business to track goods in transit. About 70.5% of the responses agreed with this proposition.

The result achieved states that the mobile technology is a major technology which could improve their business activities. Therefore, this technology could also facilitate this research to enter the new proposed collaborative environment.

Advantages of Mobile Technology

The question establishes the advantage of using mobile technology in organizations. Whilst the question queried the availability of applications of mobile technologies that can be included in the organization, the objective of next question is to re-emphasise this

question in an alternate way, by probing the advantages of using mobile technology, rather than directly asking about new applications. The results of this question are listed in Table 4.

1. Mobile technology as a special technology is very cost efficient. 72.7% of the respondents either agreed or strongly agreed with this proposition.
2. Mobile technology has been connecting people while out of the office. 93.8% of the respondents agreed with this proposition.
3. Mobile technology has been improving the business productivity. 71% of the respondents agreed with this proposition.
4. Mobile technology has enabled employees to be more flexible hence they can work disregard of their location and time. 72.3% agreed to this proposition.
5. Mobile technology has created better access method for the customer to contact the organization. 85.4 % of the responses agreed with this proposition.

Advantage of Mobile Technology for the Business

The question asked about other factors that would enhance the demand in introducing or using mobile technology in the organization. Four propositions were

Table 3. New applications/areas for use of mobile technology

New Applications	TOTAL	VSA	SA	AG		SD	VSD
1- Special Technology-Improve Efficiencies	47	6	15	16	8	1	1
PERCENTAGE	100	13	32	34	17	2	2
2-Advertise in Captured Markets	44	2	9	20	8	2	3
PERCENTAGE	100	5	20	45	18	5	7
3-Contacting Office (Any where/Any time)	47	13	15	12	3	1	3
PERCENTAGE	100	28	32	26	6	2	6
4-Track Goods in Transit	51	8	12	16	8	3	4
PERCENTAGE	100	16	24	31	16	6	8

presented to the respondents to choose from. Table 5 lists the results for the question.

1. Employees demand and show interest in using the mobile technology. 75% of the respondents either agreed or strongly agreed with this proposition.
2. Customer demand and show interest in using the mobile technology. 74% of the respondents either agreed or strongly agreed with this proposition.
3. Supply chain sector is more interested and show interest in using the mobile technology. 66.7% of the respondents either agreed or strongly agreed with this proposition.
4. Social-Psychological factors are influencing the people to use the mobile technology. 66% of the respondents either agreed or strongly agreed with this proposition.

Improvement Caused by Mobile Technology

The question investigated the perceived value of mobile technology in the daily activities of the organization. This section allows the respondents to select more than one choice. The survey results are listed in Figure 7.

The most important benefit of using the mobile devices as predicted has been classified as the availability to be contactable at any time, and anywhere. A fact revealed by this question is that cost savings are not the main driver for organizations to use mobile technology.

Problem/Difficulties of Mobile Technology

The question investigated the anticipated problems, difficulties and complaints the respondents may have when using the existing mobile gadgets. The results are listed in Figure 8.

The results state that the most important difficulty is the small screen while the limited applications, battery life span and complicity of mobile devices are classified as the remaining problem of mobile devices.

Disadvantages of Mobile Technology

The question investigated the disadvantages of using mobile technologies, as perceived by the respondents. The results are listed in Table 6.

1. Queried whether the cost of establishment of mobile applications is a concern for the organization. 74% of the respondents either agreed or strongly agreed with this proposition.
2. Queried the recurring cost of using mobile technology as a major tool. 83% of the respondents agreed with this proposition.
3. Queried whether technical drawbacks, which are inherent in current mobile technologies, are a factor considered as a disadvantage by organizations. 93% of the respondents agreed with this view.
4. Queried legal and privacy concerns using mobile technology. Around 80% of the respondents showed concern about the legal and privacy issues with regard to mobile technology.

Table 4. Main advantages of mobile technology for oganizations

Mobile Advantages		TOTAL	VSA	SA	AG		SD	VSD
1- Cost Saving		44	8	8	16	10	1	1
	PERCENTAGE	100	18	18	36	23	2	2
2-Connect Employees		48	21	15	9	3	0	0
	PERCENTAGE	100	44	31	19	6	0	0
3- Improve Productivity		55	13	26	10	6	0	0
	PERCENTAGE	100	24	47	18	11	0	0
4-Flexibility of Employees		47	7	10	17	12	1	0
	PERCENTAGE	100	15	21	36	26	2	0
5- Better Access for Customers		48	10	13	18	6	0	1
	PERCENTAGE	100	21	27	38	13	0	2

Table 5. Factors influencing the use of mobile technology in an organization

Factors Influencing Mobility		TOTAL	VSA	SA	AG	DA	SD	VSD
1- Mobility Demand by Employees		52	7	12	20	13	0	0
	PERCENTAGE	100	13	23	38	25	0	0
2- Mobility Demand by Customers		50	4	12	21	12	0	1
	PERCENTAGE	100	8	24	42	24	0	2
3- Mobility Demand by Supply Chain		48	3	12	17	12	3	1
	PERCENTAGE	100	6	25	35	25	6	2
4- Mobility Demand by Social-Psych Factor		47	4	8	19	14	1	1
	PERCENTAGE	100	9	17	40	30	2	2

5. Queried with adoption and training issues in an organization with regard to mobile technology. 78% of respondents in the selected sample agreed that such issues are a concern for their organizations.

WEB SERVICES TECHNOLOGY

The following questions help the research to evaluate the participant's opinion in order to adapt Web Services technology from technical, methodological and social prospective.

Technical Drawbacks of Adaptation Web Services

The question investigated the adaptation to WS technology from the technical perspective presented in Figure 9.

1. Queried whether the unfamiliar concept of the Web Services technology is the great concern for the organizations in order to adapt web Services. About 70% of the respondents either agreed or strongly agreed with this proposition.
2. Queried whether the limitation of the Web Services is important. 65% of the respondents agreed with this proposition.

Figure 7. Mobile technology advantages to business activities

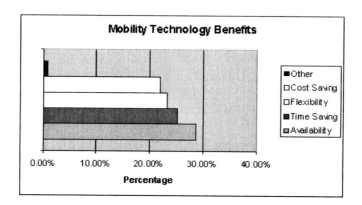

Figure 8. Problems faced by organizations using the mobile gadgets

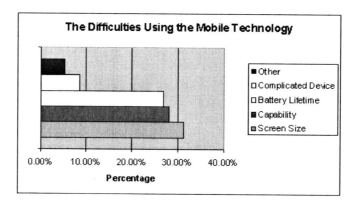

3. Queried whether the ambiguity of the Web Services is the major concern (What it is and what it does). 70% of the respondents agreed with this view.

4. Queried whether the participants understand how WS could facilitate collaboration. Almost 80% of the participants agreed with this proposition.

Methodological Drawbacks of Adaptation Web Services

The question investigated the adaptation to WS technology from the Methodological perspective presented in Figure 10.

1. Queried whether the impact on WS on existing business process is the main concern while adapting the WS. About 64.9% of the respon-

dents either agreed or strongly agreed with this proposition.

2. Queried whether the training of the employees is the main concern. 61.5% of the respondents agreed with this proposition.

3. The concept of the competition while collaborating (how can you collaborate with your competitor). 86.6% of the respondents agreed with this view.

4. The focus will shift to technology rather than process. Almost 80% of the participants agreed with this proposition.

5. How to manage the change when adapting the WS technology. Almost 75% agreed with the proposition.

Table 6. The Recognised disadvantages of mobile technology

Disadvantages of Mobile Technology	TOTAL	VSA	SA	AG	DA	SD	VSD
1- Establishment Cost of Applications	56	6	15	20	11	2	2
PERCENTAGE	100	11	27	36	20	4	4
2-Recruitment Cost of Mobility	54	5	16	24	6	2	1
PERCENTAGE	100	9	30	44	11	4	2
3- Technical Drawback	57	12	16	25	2	2	0
PERCENTAGE	100	21	28	44	4	4	0
4-Legal and Privacy Issues	56	9	12	24	9	1	1
PERCENTAGE	100	16	21	43	16	2	2
5- Training and Adaptation Issues	55	5	24	14	9	1	2
PERCENTAGE	100	9	44	25	16	2	4

Figure 9. The technical issues adapting the Web services

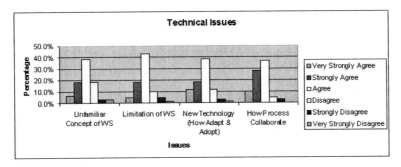

Social Drawbacks of Adaptation Web Services

The question investigated the adaptation to WS technology from the social perspective presented in Figure 11.

1. Evaluate the adaptation rate by customer and the employees. About 60% of the respondents either agreed or strongly agreed with this proposition.
2. How the competitor react to change. 75% of the respondents agreed with this proposition.
3. How the technology provide support in order to trust the competitor. Almost 75% of the respondents agreed with this view.
4. What happens to the organizations already in line of collaboration? Almost 65% of the participants agreed with this proposition.
5. The legal issues involved in collaboration (Government and the internal policies). Almost 65% of the participant agreed with the proposition.

ANALYSES OF THE DATA

This section describes the further analyses the overall assessment of the survey in regards to the adaptation of Mobile and Web Services technology as far as these technology are aiding the collaborative organizations.

Mobile Technology Information (Evaluation)

The mobility appears to be an important technology for the businesses to precede their daily activities. 63% of the organizations are already using their mobile devices

Figure 10. The methodological issues adapting the Web services

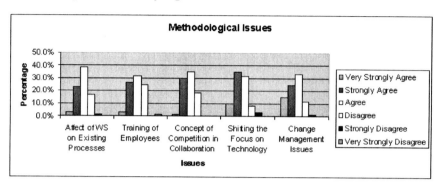

to run their ordinary activities while 23% has stated that they are planning to adapt it in the near future. The total of 87% of the organizations recognises the importance of the mobile technology while currently the majority of these people mainly use their mobile phones and mobile enabled laptops.

The respondents defined that mobility is a great communication tool, make it easier to find and locate personnel, create more flexibility and increases the general productivity. The major advantage of mobile technology is providing availability to people disregards of their location and time. The study revealed that the accessibility is one of the greatest advantage of the collaborative organizations therefore the advantage of the mobility (Anywhere – Anytime) could provide benefit to collaborative organizations.

The survey has also investigated the current and potential application of mobility, advantages and disadvantages of mobility and the improvements caused by mobility to provide a better understanding of this technology.

Interestingly, the survey identified the cost of mobility is not classified as a big disadvantage in comparison to the benefit it provides. All these disadvantages and drawbacks seem to be due to the fact that the technology is new and still evolving. When there is more commercialisation of the technology, applications will become cheaper and recurring costs will be less. The decreasing cost of technology while the capabilities are improving rapidly is highlighted in (Roth, 1998).

Web Services Technology (Evaluation)

The interoperation amongst multiple organizations needs a technology to support the collaboration across their business process especially when the participated organization are not necessarily known to each other, and have never collaborated previously.

According to Barry (2003) the main driving forces for adopting Web Services are classified as interoperable network applications, emerging industry-wide standards, easier exchange of data, reduced developing time, reduced maintain costs, availability of external services and availability of training and tools.

The main restraining forces are also classified as different semantics in data source, semantic translation effect on operation systems for up-to-moment data request, standards evolving not fixed and mergers and acquisition.

Based on our survey, all the issues identified by the research such as unfamiliarity concepts of Web Services, limitation of Web Services, how to adapt the new technology and how the processes collaborate are classified as the major concerns of the organization in order to adopt Web Services. Only the minority of 10% of the participants very strongly agree to understanding how Web Services could help the collaboration while close to 30% of the participants had the same concern with ticking the strongly agree box. The research has concluded that the organization knowledge in regard to the technical issues of WS is very limited. This lack of knowledge could be classified as the major drawback in adaptation of Web Services. More work is required to educate enterprises in regards to the

Figure 11. The social issues adapting the Web services

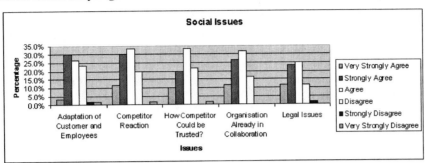

capability and functionality of Web Services from technical point of view.

Based on the result of the survey, all the issues identified by the study such as impact of Web Services on existing processes, training of the employees, concept of competition in collaboration, shifting the focus of technology and the concept of change management has been classified as important concepts. Almost 40% of the participants agree with these issues while close to 30% strongly agree. Close to 20% of the respondents classify the concepts of change management as their greatest concern for adopting WS technology for their organization. However, about 20% and 30% of these organizations disagree that the affect of WS on existing business processes and training the employees as a great importance. There is no doubt that the methodological issues play an important role in adopting Web Services technology.

Based on the survey, the customer/competitor reaction and the impact on the organizations that already in collaboration are classified by the participants as a strongly agree point. Almost similar number is attracting the very strongly agree comments however up to 35% of all participants classify all the issues identified by the study as the major drawback for adaptation of WS by organizations.

The research concludes that technical, methodological and social factors identified by this study are to impose the adaptation and adoption of new technology by organizations. The business opportunities resulting from WS have seen these technologies being rapidly adopted across the world. For example, an IDC Report in 2003 revealed that 30% of Australian organizations are already using web services – although a large number of these organization's applications are behind the corporate firewall. Another survey conducted by

CSC found 105 of Australia's largest organizations are already using web services or planning to do so (Mackenzie, 2003).

In general, the issues of incompatible technology, competition, licensing agreement (legal issues) and mistrust are also classified as additional major concern while adopting the new technology to be discussed later in the thesis.

The research concludes that technical, methodological and social factors identified by this study are to impose the adoption of new technology by organizations. In general, the issues of incompatible technology, competition, licensing agreement (legal issues) and mistrust are also classified as additional major concern while adopting the new technology.

CONCLUSION AND DIRECTION

Service Oriented Architecture and Web Services were introduced in this chapter extending the mentioned architecture and technologies that support the Collaborative Business Process Engineering. The technical, methodological and social factors in order to adopt Web Services technologies by organizations were also investigated. This chapter has also described a survey carried out in the Sydney metropolitan area in large and medium-sized organisations, in order to assess the organisations' concerns, readiness for and adaptability to emerging technologies of Mobile and Web Services technologies. The final result of the survey has revealed (in fact within the selected sample) that the key personnel of the organisations agree with the major concerns identified by the study and queried in the survey. The above 60% rate has been the result achieved for every individual question. The chapter has presented pictorial illustrations of the achieved results and the analyses provided of the collected data are also discussed.

REFERENCES

http://www.ebizq.net/hot_topics/soa/features/5857. html?&pp=1. Downloaded: 12/10/2006

Alag, H. (2006). *Business Process Mobility.* In B. Unhelkar (Ed.), *Handbook Resources of Mobile Business.* Hershey, PA, USA: IGI Global. USA.

Barry, D. K. (2003). *Web Services and Service-Oriented Architecture. The savvy Manager's Guide.* USA: Morgan Kaufmann Publishers. ISBN: 1-55860-906-7

Chase, N. (2006, February 14*). Introducing the open Group Architecture Framework, Understanding TOGAf and IT Architecture in today's World.* http://www-128.ibm.com/developerworks/ibm/library/artogaf1/ Accessed: 3/04/2007

Chen, X., Wenteng, C., Turner, S. J., & Wang, Y. (2006). SOAr-DSGrid: Service-Oriented Architecture for Distributed Simulation on the Grid. *Proceedings of the 20th Workshop on Principles of Advanced and Distributed Simulation.* ISBN ~ ISSN:1087-4097 , 0-7695-2587-3

Chung, J. Y. (2005). An Industry View on Service-Oriented Architecture and Web Services. *Proceedings of the 2005 IEEE International Workshop on Service-Oriented System Engineering (SOSE'05)* 0-7695-2438-9/05 © 2005 IEEE.

Curbera, F., Khalaf, R., Mukhi, N., Tai, S., & Weerawarana, S. (2003, October). The Next Step in Web Services. *Communications of the ACM, 46*(10).

Erl, T. (2004). *Service-Oriented Architecture. A Field Guide to Integrating XML and Web Services.* Pearson Education, Inc. ISBN: 0-13-142898-5

Falcone, F., & Garito, M. (2006). *Mobile Strategy Roadmap.* In B. Unhelkar (Ed.), *Handbook Resources of Mobile Business.* Herhsey, PA USA: Idea Group. ISBN: 1591408172

Finkelsteing, C. (2006). *Enterprise Architecture for Integration. Rapid Delivery Methods and Technology.*

British Library Catalogue in Publication Data. ISBN: 1-58053-713-8

Godbole, N. (2006). *Relating Mobile Computing to Mobile Commerce.* In B. Unhelkar (Ed.), *Handbook Resources of Mobile Business.* Herhsey, PA USA: Idea Group.. ISBN: 1591408172

Ghanbary, A. (2006). Collaborative Business Process Engineering across Multiple Organizations. A Doctoral Consortium. *Proceedings of ACIS 2006.* Australia: Adelaide.

Jostad, I., Dustdar, S., & Thanh, D. V. (2005). A Service Oriented Architecture Framework for Collaborative Services. *Proceedings of the 14th IEEE International Workshops on Enabling Technologies: Infrastructure for Collaborative Enterprise.* ISBN ~ ISSN:1524-4547 , 0-7695-2362-5

Harrison, A., & Taylor, J. I. (2005). WSPeer - An Interface to Web Service Hosting and Invocation. *Proceedings of the 19th IEEE International Parallel and Distributed Processing Symposium (IPDPS'05).* ISBN: 1530-2075/05

Miller, J., & Mukerji, J. (2003). *Model Driven Architecture (MDA) Guide Version 1.0.1.* http://www.omg.org/docs/omg/03-06-01.pdf. Downloaded: 5/10/06

Pasley, J. (2005, May/June). How BPEL and SOA are changing Web services development. *Internet Computing, IEEE, 9*(3), 60-67. Digital Object Identifier 10.1109/MIC.2005.56

The open Group Integration Consortium. http://www.integrationconsortium.org/docs/W054final.pdf. Downloaded: 5/10/2006.

The ACM Digital Library. http://delivery.acm.org/10.1145/610000/606273/p54-lee.html?key1=606273&key2=4006199511&coll=GUIDE&dl=portal,ACM&CFID=11111111&CFTOKEN=2222222#lead-in. Downloaded: 5/10/2006.

Unhelkar, B., & Deshpande, Y. (2004). Evolving from Web Engineering to Web Services: A Comparative study in the context of Business Utilization of the Internet. *Proceedings of ADCOM 2004, 12th International Conference on Advanced Computing and Communications,* Ahmedabad, India, 15-18 December

UDDI.org. http://www.uddi.org/faqs.html. Downloaded: 12/10/2006

W3Consortium. http://www.w3.org/TR/wsdl. Downloaded; 12/10/2006

W3Consortium. http://www.w3.org/XML/. Downloaded: 12/10/2006

Chapter XLVIII
Increasing the Performability of Wireless Web Services

Wenbing Zhao
Cleveland State University, USA

ABSTRACT

Wireless Web services are becoming a reality, if they have not already. The unique characteristics of the mobile devices and wireless communication medium, such as limited computing power, limited network bandwidth, limited battery life, unpredictable online time, mobility, and so forth,, imply that the infrastructure for wireless Web services will be very different from its wired counterpart. This chapter discusses the challenges and the state-of-the-art solutions to ensure highly performable wireless Web services. In particular, this chapter's focus is on three technical issues: optimization of the wireless Web services messaging protocol, caching, and fault tolerance. Finally, limitations of the current approaches and an outline of future research directions on wireless Web services are also discussed.

INTRODUCTION

With the evolution of the Internet technology, e-commerce, e-healthcare, and e-government services have become ubiquitous over the wired computer networks. There are obvious advantages in extending such services to mobile device users that connect to the Internet wirelessly. The possibility of conducting transactions reliably over wireless links also opens the door for business owners to offer additional services catering to mobiles customers specifically. Furthermore, the Web services technology, due to its strength in loose-coupling, extensibility, and interoperability, has also been gaining momentum to become the dominating enabling technology for the next generation of e-services, including those offered wirelessly to mobile devices (Ellis & Young, 2003). Thus, a case can be made for the merging and extending Web services with mobile technologies.

The Web services technology essentially transforms the Web from a publishing medium to a programmable platform. This transformation greatly improves the degree of automation of Web-based transactions, and makes it easy to compose value-added services by integrating existing services. However, great care is needed to extend the Web services technology, which was primarily designed to run on powerful stationary computers over wired networks, to mobile devices over wireless networks. This is so because of the aforementioned limitations of the operating environment, such as limited computing power, limited network bandwidth, limited battery life of mobile devices, unpredictable mobile user online time, and mobility. In this chapter, I introduce the background, challenges, and state-of-the-art solutions to enable the offering and consuming of Web services from mobile devices over wireless networks. I focus particularly on how to improve the performability of the wireless Web services. (Performability is an umbrella term referring to the runtime performance, availability, reliability and security of a service.) Business owners should strive to offer highly performable wireless Web services to succeed in this domain.

BACKGROUND

The Web Services Concept

There is no universal definition of the term Web services and its interpretation varies dramatically. On one end, it refers to any services offered over the World Wide Web. On the other end, only the services enabled by the Web services technology are referred to as Web services. In this chapter, I use the latter interpretation. The Web services technology refers to the set of standards that enable automated machine-to-machine interactions over the Web. The corner stones of the Web services technology include eXtensible Markup Language (XML) (Bray et al., 2006), HyperText Transfer Protocol (HTTP), Simple Object Access Protocol (SOAP) (Gudgin et al., 2007), and Web Services Description Language (WSDL) (Christensen et al., 2001).

XML is designed to facilitate self-contained, structured data representation and transfer over the Internet. XML is extensible because it allows users to define their own tags. The extensibility of XML makes it the essential building block for Web services. HTTP is an application-level protocol following the client-server interaction model. HTTP is designed to share and access Web resources (i.e., hypertext objects). However, HTTP is a stateless protocol in that it does not keep track of the state across different HTTP requests. The design of HTTP not only removes unnecessary complexity, it ensures high degree of scalability as well. As the name suggests, SOAP was originally designed to conduct remote procedure calls over the Web. It has evolved to become the main communication protocol to exchange XML documents. Like many public-domain application-level protocols, such as SMTP, a SOAP message contains a SOAP Envelop and a SOAP Body. A SOAP message often contains an optional SOAP Header element, and a Fault element if an error is encountered by the sender of the SOAP message. WSDL is an XML-based language used to describe Web services. For each Web service, the corresponding WSDL document specifies the available operations, the messages involved with the operations, and a set of endpoints to reach the Web service. Due to the use of XML, WSDL is also extensible. In particular, it allows the binding of multiple different communication protocols and message formats.

To enable dynamic services publishing and discovery, a Universal Description, Discovery and Integration (UDDI) (Clement et al., 2004) service could be used. UDDI provides the standard way for Web services providers to describe their services, and the consumers to search and discover the available services. However, the experiments of offering global-scale public-domain UDDI registries were not successful, as evidenced by the shutdown of once well-known UDDI registries provided IBM, Microsoft and SAP (Krill, 2005). One reason for this failure is perhaps due to the current business requirement, *i.e.*, inter-enterprise transactions can rarely take place before the relevant legal documents are signed by the companies involved in the transactions. There are also unresolved questions related to ownership, responsibility and enforceability of transactions occurring through UDDI. Nevertheless, UDDI has been gaining momentum to be used as a Web services registry *within* each enterprise. Thus, from an architecture point of view, the Web services platform consists of the Web services providers, the Web services consumers, and the UDDI registries that broker the providers and the consumers, as shown in Figure 1.

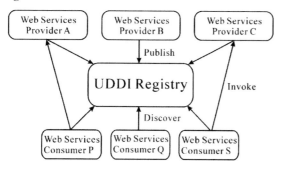

Figure 1. The Web services architecture

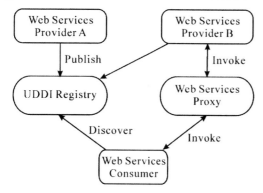

Figure 2. The wireless Web services architecture

Wireless Web Services Architecture

The general Web services architecture is not appropriate in the wireless environment when the mobile devices are acting as the Web services consumers. This is so primarily because of the limitation of the mobile devices such as limited processing power and battery life of the mobile devices, and the limited bandwidth and the unreliable links between the mobile devices and their Internet service providers. As such, the proxy-server based approach has been proposed (Hadjiefthymiades & Merakos, 2003), as illustrated in Figure 2.

The Web services proxy component (can be deployed at both the client and the server side) plays an import role in increasing the performability of wireless Web services. The proxy has the following functionalities:

1. It caches the results of the read-only queries so that the mobile users can get these results faster.

2. It temporarily logs results from all Web services invocations to cope with unreliable connections to the mobile users. When they reconnect to the proxy server, the logged results are sent back to the mobile users, without involving the Web services providers.

3. The proxy could offer enhanced transport protocols that are more suitable for wireless communication than those offered by the original Web services provider.

However, the proxy server has the obvious drawback of single-point of failure. In the following chapter, I present the strategies that could be employed to provide high availability to the proxy server.

INCREASING THE PERFORMABILITY OF WIRELESS WEB SERVICES

In this section, I discuss the current state-of-the-art techniques in building highly performable wireless Web services. I focus on the following three aspects: (1) techniques to optimize the messaging protocol to reduce the cost of wireless communication; (2) techniques to cope with limited bandwidth and unreliable connectivity; and (3) techniques to ensure reliable messaging and high availability of Web services.

SOAP Protocol Optimization

Straightforward use of the SOAP protocol for wireless communication is problematic because of two issues: (1) SOAP encodes the data in ASCII text and in a self-contained manner, which means the message is often several times longer than the original data in binary form; (2) SOAP usually runs on top of HTTP and in turn on top of TCP (often referred to as SOAP-over-HTTP). For short and periodically generated messages, this incurs unnecessary high latency and transmission overhead. For long documents, the use of TCP over wireless medium poses another problem. TCP assumes that a message loss is due to congestion, and therefore, throttles its sending rate. In wireless communication environment, this often is not the case because of the relatively high transmission error rate of the wireless medium.

There are two possible approaches to address the first issue. One approach is to compress the SOAP document, or to use alternative SOAP encoding so that the bandwidth usage is significantly reduced. The other approach is to use alternative SOAP-over-transport-protocol bindings to avoid the additional overhead introduced by HTTP. Obviously, the two approaches can be combined and used together to achieve the best result.

In the first approach, a number of mechanisms have been proposed. The mechanism can be as simple as using some general purpose compression algorithm, such as Jzlib. Surprisingly, Jzlib performs quite well in reducing the SOAP message size in most of cases, as reported by Apte, Deutsch, and Jain (2005). Besides using general purpose compression algorithm, several XML-aware encoding mechanisms have been proposed, such as differential encoding (Werner, Buschmann, & fischer, 2004) and WSDL-aware encoding (Apte, Deutsch, & Jain, 2005). Differential encoding attempts to reduce the SOAP message size by speculating the message content, deploying the speculated messages at both the sender and the receiver prior to the runtime, and sending only the differences between the actual message and the speculated message. The WSDL-aware encoding attempts to reduce the information needed to be included in the message. In the best cases, these schemes can reduce the message by a factor of 10 or more. An example of the second approach is the SOAP-over-TCP binding. This binding has been provided in Apache Axis and Microsoft Web Services Enhancement (WSE) 2.0. However, there does not seem to have standardization process on this binding. For small SOAP documents, SOAP-over-TCP can reduce the message sizes significantly, and therefore, achieve much shorter response time and higher throughput. For example, Phan, Tari and Bertok (2006) reported that the message transmitted over the wire is reduced from about 700 bytes to below 500 bytes for the echoDouble request, and the corresponding response time is reduced from about 270 ms to about 170 ms.

To partially address the second issue, the UDP protocol has been considered as the transport protocol, and a SOAP-over-UDP binding has been proposed as a Web Services Standard (Combs et al., 2004). The SOAP-over-UDP binding caters to certain types of applications that do not require the reliability provided by TCP, and/or need multicast. For example, the SOAP-over-UDP binding is a very good match for the WS-Discovery services. The use of UDP protocol not only avoids the overhead associated with TCP and HTTP, it further eliminates the connection establishment phase. Consequently, applications using SOAP-over-UDP exhibit the best performance in terms of response time and throughput, as reported in (Phan, Tari & Bertok, 2006).

Caching

Caching has been a classical technique to increase distributed systems performance. A cache (proxy) server is often positioned at or adjacent to the client and is used to cache the responses to the requests issued by the client. If a future request asking for the same object that has already been cached, the cached object will be returned immediately to the client without the need to send the request to the origin server. One of the main concerns of caching is cache consistency. To maintain strong cache consistency, it often requires application protocol support. It is beneficial to know which operations' results are cacheable and for how long, and what operations would invalidate a cached object. For example, HTTP has built-in support for caching. Unfortunately, the Web services platform lacks explicit support for caching. This makes caching for Web services particularly challenging.

First, to enable caching of a response object, a cache key of the corresponding request must be constructed so that when a future request is issued, the cache database can be searched for possible cached response object. Unlike HTTP, which enables the use of the URL as the cache key, SOAP does not offer a similar construct to be used as the cache key. The best scenario is when the SOAP request does not contain any parameter, in which case, the HTTP URL and the SOAPAction field together can be used as the cache key (assuming that the SOAP+HTTP binding is used for Web services communication). In general, however, the caching manager must understand the syntax of the SOAP request and build the cache key by parsing the XML request document and including the relevant elements in the cache key. Constructing the cache key by hashing the entire SOAP XML request document is not an option because each SOAP message contains a unique message identifier element.

Second, WSDL, which specifies the set of operations offered by a Web service, does not provide construct to indicate if an operation is cacheable and whether the invocation of an operation will invalidate the cached response objects of another operation. This requires the Web services provider to supply additional metadata information to enable effective caching at the client side. Before such metadata information is standardized, the caching cannot be interoperable across different Web services (Terry & Ramasubramanian 2003; Elbashir & Deters, 2005).

Third, unlike HTML page rendering, which is fairly inexpensive, SOAP response objects are in the form of XML documents, which are computationally expensive to parse. Even if the response objects are cached, their parsing and conversion to native objects format might be time-consuming. Takase and Tatsubori (2004) proposed to cache the parsed results instead of the raw XML document to improve performance. This may be particularly necessary for mobile clients, which have limited computing power and battery life.

For mobile devices, the caching technique can be extended to partially address the unstable connectivity problem. Terry and Ramasubramanian (2003) proposed to use caching together with playback to increase the perceived availability of the Web services. The main idea is that both the requests and the responses are cached at the client. If a response object is found in the cache database for a newly issued request for a cacheable operation, the response object is returned immediately. If a request is for an update operation, such request must be sent to the server, or played back when the connectivity to the server is restored to ensure the consistency between the server and the client. Furthermore, when the client issues an update operation on certain object, any cached object from a previous query must be invalidated, again, for the purpose of cache consistency.

Recently, Liu and Deters (2007) proposed a dual-caching strategy to further enhance the performability of wireless Web services. According to the dual-caching strategy, caching is performed at both the client side and the server side. Caching at the server side helps ameliorate the unstable connectivity problem perceived at the server side. When the server is ready to send a response to the client, the connection to the client might be broken. In the case, the existence of the server-side cache can be used to store the response until the connectivity is restored. The server-side cache manager can also handle duplicate requests by retrieving and sending the corresponding response objects to their clients.

Reliable Messaging

Caching can be used to reduce the bandwidth usage and the average response latency, and it can partially offset the problems caused by temporary disconnections. However, it does not guarantee reliable messaging between the client and the server, and the exactly-once execution semantics for all service requests, which is essential for many business transactions. Recognizing this need, a Web Services Reliable Messaging (WS-ReliableMessaging) Specification (Davis et al., 2007) has been proposed by a group of companies including IBM and Microsoft, and it has recently been ratified by OASIS.

The WS-ReliableMessaging Specification describes a reliable messaging (RM) protocol between two endpoints, termed as RM source (RMS) and RM destination (RMD). The core concept introduced in WS-ReliableMessaging is sequence. A sequence is a unidirectional reliable channel between the RMS and the RMD, as illustrated in Figure 3. At the beginning of a reliable conversation between the two endpoints, a unique sequence (identified by a unique sequence ID) must first be created (through the create-sequence request and response). The sequence is terminated when the conversation is over (through the terminate-sequence request and response). Each message sent over the sequence is assigned unique message number. The message number starts at 1 and is incremented by 1 for each subsequent message. The reliability of the messaging is achieved by the retransmission and positive acknowledgement mechanisms. At the RMS, a message sent is buffered and retransmitted until the corresponding acknowledgement from the RMD is received, or until a predefined retransmission limit has been exceeded. For efficiency reason, the RMD might not send acknowledgement immediately upon receiving an application message, and the acknowledgements for multiple messages can be piggybacked with another application message in the response sequence, or be aggregated in a single explicit acknowledgement message.

Because it is quite common for two endpoints to engage in two-way communications, the RMS can include an Offer element in its create-sequence request to avoid an explicit new sequence establishment step for the traffic in the reverse direction. Furthermore, WS-ReliableMessaging defines a set of delivery assurances, including AtMostOnce, atLeastOnce, ExactlyOnce, and InOrder. The meaning of these assurances are self-explanatory. The InOrder assurance can be used together with any of the first three assurances. The strongest assurance is ExactlyOnce combined with InOrder delivery.

The WS-ReliableMessaging Specification has been widely supported and there exist many imple-

Figure 3. WS-ReliableMessaging introduces the sequence construct to provide a unidirectional reliable messaging channel between an RMS and RMD. The sequence is implemented by the sending- and receiving-side message buffering, sequencing, and retransmission mechanisms.

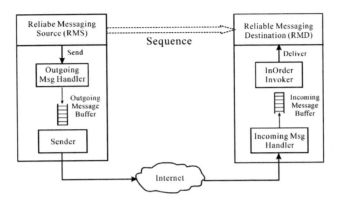

mentations, including both open-source projects and commercial products.

To improve the WS-ReliableMessaging performance over wireless networks, Lee and Fox (2004) proposed to introduce negative acknowledgement, in addition to the positive acknowledge mechanism for message reliability. They argue that the pure positive acknowledgement mechanism takes more bandwidth than their approach.

Fault Tolerance and High Availability

By integrating the WS-ReliableMessaging mechanisms and transaction processing at the RMD, exactly-once delivery of messages can be guaranteed, even in case of process crash failures and network message losses. However, WS-ReliableMessaging does not contribute to the high availability of Web services. To achieve high availability, the Web services must be replicated so that the failure of one of the replicas will not bring down the entire Web service. There are two common replication styles, namely, active replication and passive replication [Powell, 1991].

Active replication. All replicas accept and process the same set of requests, and generate the same set of responses in the same order. For active replication, the replicas are often modeled as state machines. Each request would cause the replicas to transit from one state to another. For active replication, the replicas must be deterministic or rendered deterministic, *i.e.*, given the same set of requests in the same order,

every replica must go through the same sequence of state transitions.

Passive replication. Only one replica (the primary) executes in response to the client's requests. Passive replication has two variations: warm passive replication and cold passive replication. In warm passive replication, the primary periodically checkpoints its state at the other replicas (backups). In cold passive replication, the backups are not launched until the primary is detected to have failed. It is the responsibility of the fault tolerance infrastructure to retrieve checkpoints from the primary and log them. Contrary to the common belief that passive replication does not require replica determinism because only one replica executes the requests at a time. One should not forget that the primary can fail. If the primary fails, a backup replica must step up to become the new primary. If there exist replica nondeterminism, the only way to guarantee a correct failover (without running a distributed consensus algorithm to determine the nondeterministic values) is to use systematic checkpointing, *i.e.*, the primary must checkpoint its state on the sending of every response and it must ensure the client receiving the response and the backup replicas receiving the checkpoint in a single atomic step. Systematic checkpointing, however, is often too expensive to be useful in practice.

There are two common approaches to replication. One is to use a group communication system that guarantees all the replicas in the same process group to receive the same set of messages in the same total order within the virtual synchrony model (Birman & van Renesse, 1994). The alternative approach is to use consensus algorithms. The message total ordering problem in itself is a consensus problem.

There exist many consensus algorithms that ensure the safety property without any synchrony assumption, *i.e.*, if some correct replicas agree on the total ordering of messages, all correct replicas eventually agree on the same ordering. Synchrony is required only for liveness, i.e., the system may not be able to make progress towards the consensus if the system is purely asynchronous. On the contrary, the group communication system depends on the use of an unreliable failure detector. Consequently, some replicas that are mistakenly removed from the membership might decide on some different ordering from that of the other replicas.

Due to this consideration, I choose to use a variation of the Paxos algorithm (Lamport, 2001), a well-known efficient consensus algorithm, to provide fault tolerance for Web services. The consensus algorithm contains two operation modes: (1) during normal operation and (2) during view changes when the primary fails, as shown in Figure 4. The detailed elaboration of the algorithm is omitted.

Implementation. Our fault tolerance framework for Web services is built on top of an open source library (called Sandesha2) that implements the WS-ReliableMessaging specification. I aim to provide backward compatibility to WS-ReliableMessaging while guarantee high availability. The architecture of the fault tolerance framework is shown in Figure 5.

The Total Order Invoker component is responsible to deliver requests to the replicated Web service in a total order. At each replica, the Total Order Invoker polls the replication engine for the next application request to be delivered, then it fetches the application message from the In Msg Queue, which stores all incoming application requests.

The Sender component is responsible to send messages to their destinations through point-to-point or multicast channels. On the server side, the multicast functionality is used only by the primary, and by a backup for the checkpoint messages. To perform the multicast, multiple threads are launched to concurrently send the same message to different destinations using Axis2. Each thread is responsible to send the message to a distinct destination point-to-point. The In handler in Sandesha2 is augmented to handle the control messages used by the replication algorithm. All incoming messages are placed in the In Msg Queue after preliminary processing, and before they are delivered to the Web service by the Total Order Invoker.

The Out handler performs preliminary processing on all outgoing messages. All outgoing messages are placed in the Out Msg Queue before they are sent out by the Sender component. The sending of the replication control messages is carried out using the normal Axis2 interface, which means such messages will be treated as application messages by the Sandesha2 mechanisms, except that some messages are multicast by the Sender component. The Sender knows what messages to be multicast by examining

Figure 4. The consensus algorithm used to coordinate the replicas for strong consistency. (a) Normal operation mode. (b) View change mode.

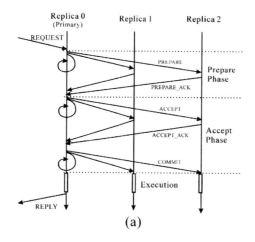

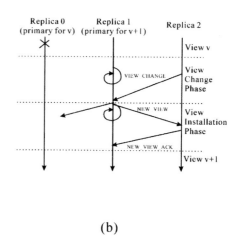

(a)   (b)

Figure 5. The architecture of the fault tolerance framework for Web services

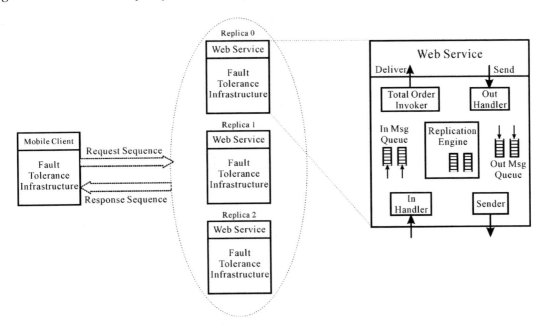

the SOAP action property included in each message. If a multicast is needed, the Replication Engine is consulted to obtain the multicast destinations.

The Replication Engine is the core addition to the *Sandesha2* framework. This component drives the execution of the replication algorithm. The Replication Engine uses its own storage to log the replication control messages, and the checkpoints. The client-side architecture is similar except that the application replies are not totally ordered (they are FIFO ordered within each sequence according to WS-ReliableMessaging, however). The Replication Engine simply keeps the server-side configuration information so that the Sender knows where to multicast the application requests.

Performance Evaluation. I evaluated our framework on a testbed consisting 5 Dell SC440 servers (runs the server replicas) and one Compaq laptop (runs the client) connected to the servers via 802.11g network. Each SC440 server is equipped with a 2.8GHz dual-core processor and 1GB RAM, running SuSE 10.2 Linux. The laptop runs Ubuntu 6.0.4 Linux. A simple echo test application is used to characterize the runtime overhead. The client sends a request to the replicated Web service and waits for the corresponding reply within a loop without any "think" time between two consecutive calls. The request (and the reply) contains an XML document with varying number of elements, encoded using AXIOM (AXis Object Model). At the replicated Web service, the request is parsed and a nearly identical reply XML document is returned to the client. In each run, 1000 samples are obtained. The end-to-end latency for the echo operation is measured at the client. In our experiment, I vary the number of replicas, the request sizes in terms of the number of elements in each request.

Figure 6 shows the end-to-end latency of the echo operation for replication degrees of 1 to 5. When there is only a single replica, our framework rolls back to the Sandesha2 implementation without incurring any additional overhead, which is why the latency is significantly smaller than other scenarios. The latency incurred by our replication algorithm for three-way replication ranges from 60 ms for short requests to about 100 ms for large requests. This is quite an acceptable penalty on the performance considering the high availability benefit from the fault tolerance infrastructure.

FUTURE DIRECTION

Perhaps the most prominent concern for wide-spread adoption of wireless Web services is the high cost of

Figure 6. End-to-end latency measurement results for the fault tolerant test Web service application over a wireless network

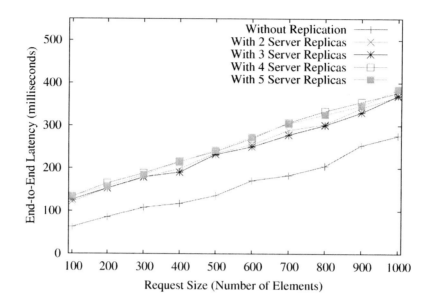

constructing/parsing SOAP XML documents and transmitting them over the wireless medium. This is particularly a problem if multimedia contents are involved, which will certainly be a trend into future mobile business transactions. Recently, the World Wide Web Consortium published three recommendations aiming to provide more efficient message packaging and less bandwidth usage, including XML-binary Optimized Packaging (XOP) (Gudgin et al., 2005a), SOAP Message Transmission Optimization Mechanism (MTOM) (Gudgin et al., 2005b), and Resource Representation SOAP Header Block (RRSHB) (Karmarkar et al., 2005). However, more research and empirical data are needed to establish their benefits.

It is envisaged that with mobile devices becoming more and more powerful and the wireless network bandwidth becoming bigger and cheaper, peer-to-peer wireless Web services interaction will become pervasive in the near future. Many ad-hoc wireless communication protocols have been proposed to enable such interactions. It will be interesting to study the new issues, both business and technical sides, for Web services transactions under this new environment.

Last, but not the least, one cannot ignore the security and privacy issues for Internet-based communications, wired or not. Such issues have often

been considered orthogonal to the other performability issues discussed in this chapter. However, there is a strong need to investigate the challenges and possible solutions on providing an integrated performability guarantee for all aspects of wireless Web services, including runtime performance, availability, reliability, security and privacy.

CONCLUSION

This chapter introduced the Web services technology and its applications to mobile business transactions. In particular, I focused on the issues that might affect the performability of wireless Web services. I surveyed the state of the art strategies on enhancing the performability of wireless Web services from a number of perspectives, including the optimization of wireless Web services messaging, the use of caching to alleviate the unstable connectivity problem, reliable messaging and fault tolerance. I also included the current research results on building highly available Web services, and provided an outline for future research and development for using wireless Web services to conduct mobile businesses.

REFERENCES

Apte, N., Deutsch, K., & Jain, R. (2005). Wireless SOAP: Optimizations for Mobile Wireless Web Services. *Paper presented at the International World Wide Web Conference*, Chiba, Japan.

Birman, K., & van Renesse, R. (1994). *Reliable Distributed Computing with the Isis Toolkit*. Los Alamitos, CA: IEEE Computer Society Press.

Bray, T., Paoli, J., Sperberg-McQueen, C. M., Maler, E., Yergeau, F., & Cowan, J. (Eds.). (2006). *XML 1.1 (Second Edition)*: World Wide Web Consortium.

Christensen, E., Curbera, F., Meredith, G., & Weerawarana, S. (2001). *Web Services Description Language (WSDL) 1.1*: World Wide Web Consortium.

Clement, L., Hately, A., Riegen, C. v., & Rogers, T. (Eds.). (2004). *UDDI Version 3.0.2*: OASIS.

Combs, H., Gudgin, M., Justice, J., Kakivaya, G., Lindsey, D., Orchard, D., et al. (2004). SOAP-over-UDP.

Davis, D., Karmarkar, A., Pilz, G., S.Winkler, & Yalcinalp, U. (2007). *Web Services Reliable Messaging (WS-ReliableMessaging), Version 1.1*: OASIS.

Elbashir, K., & Deters, R. (2005, July). Transparent caching for nomadic WS clients. *Paper presented at the IEEE International Conference on Web Services*, Orlando, FL.

Ellis, J., & Young, M. (Eds.). (2003). *J2ME Web Services 1.0*. Sun Microsystems, Inc.

Gudgin, M., Hadley, M., Mendelsohn, N., Moreau, J.-J., Nielsen, H. F., Karmarkar, A., et al. (Eds.). (2007). *SOAP Version 1.2*. World Wide Web Consortium.

Gudgin, M., Mendelsohn, N., Nottingham, M., & Ruellan, H. (Eds.). (2005). *SOAP Message Transmission Optimization Mechanism*. World Wide Web Consortium.

Gudgin, M., Mendelsohn, N., Nottingham, M., & Ruellan, H. (Eds.). (2005). *XML-binary Optimized Packaging*. World Wide Web Consortium.

Hadjiefthymiades, S., & Merakos, L. (2003). Proxies + Path Prediction: Improving Web Service Provision in Wireless–Mobile Communications. *Mobile Networks and Applications, 8*, 389-399.

Karmarkar, A., Gudgin, M., & Lafon, Y. (Eds.). (2005). *Resource Representation SOAP Header Block*. World Wide Web Consortium.

Krill, P. (2005). *Microsoft, IBM, SAP discontinue UDDI registry effort*. Retrieved from http://www.infoworld.com/article/05/12/16/HNuddishut_1.html

Lamport, L. (2001). Paxos made simple. *ACM SIGACT News, 32*(4), 51-58.

Lee, S., & Fox, G. (2004). Wireless reliable messaging protocol for Web services (WS-WRM). *Paper presented at the IEEE International Conference on Web Services*.

Lee, S., & Fox, G. (2004). Wireless Reliable Messaging Protocol for Web Services (WS –WRM). *Paper presented at the IEEE International Conference on Web Services*, San Diego, CA.

Li, L., Niu, C., Zheng, H., & Wei, J. (2006). An Adaptive Caching Mechanism for Web Services. *Paper presented at the The Sixth International Conference on Quality Software*, Beijing, China.

Liu, X., & Deters, R. (2007). An efficient dual caching strategy for web service-enabled PDAs. *Paper presented at the Proceedings of the 2007 ACM symposium on Applied computing*, Seoul, Korea.

Phan, K. A., Tari, Z., & Bertok, P. (2006). A Benchmark on SOAP's Transport Protocols Performance For Mobile Applications. *Paper presented at the ACM Symposium on Applied Computing*, Dijon, France.

Pilioura, T., Hadjiefthymiades, S., Tsalgatidou, A., & Spanoudakis, M. (2007). Using Web Services for supporting the users of wireless devices. *Decision Support Systems, 43*, 77-94.

Powell, D. (Ed.). (1991). *Delta-4: A Generic Architecture for Dependable Distributed Computing*. Berlin, Germany: Springer-Verlag.

Takase, T., & Tatsubori, M. (2004). Efficient Web services response caching by selecting optimal data representation. *Paper presented at the 24th International Conference on Distributed Computing Systems*, Tokyo, Japan.

Terry, D., & Ramasubramanian, V. (2003). Caching XML Web Services for Mobility. *Queue, 1*(3), 70-78.

Werner, C., Buschmann, C., & Fischer, S. (2004). Compressing SOAP Messages by using Differential Encoding. *Paper presented at the IEEE International Conference on Web Services*, San Diego, CA.

KEY TERMS

Caching: It has been a classical technique to increase distributed systems performance. A cache (proxy) server is often positioned at or adjacent to the client and is used to cache the responses to the requests issued by the client. If a future request asking for the same object that has already been cached, the cached object will be returned immediately to the client without the need to send the request to the origin server. One of the main concerns of caching is cache consistency.

Consensus Algorithm: A consensus algorithm ensures a group of entities to decide on the same value. In the context of replication, the safety property of a consensus algorithm ensures that if some correct replicas agree on the ordering of messaging, all correct replicas eventually agree on the same ordering. The liveness property refers to the capability that the group of replicas can make progress towards the consensus in a reasonable amount of time. Synchrony is needed for any system to achieve liveness.

Group Communication: A group communication system guarantees all the replicas in the same process group to receive the same set of messages in the same total order within the virtual synchrony model. The group communication system depends on the use of an unreliable failure detector.

Performability: It is an umbrella term referring to the runtime performance, availability, reliability and security of a service.

SOAP: SOAP stands for Simple Object Access Protocol. It was originally designed to conduct remote procedure calls over the Web. It has evolved to become the main communication protocol to exchange XML documents. A SOAP message contains a SOAP Envelop and a SOAP Body. A SOAP message often contains an optional SOAP Header element, and a Fault element if an error is encountered by the sender of the SOAP message.

UDDI: UDDI stands for Universal Description, Discovery and Integration. UDDI provides the standard way for Web services providers to describe their services, and the consumers to search and discover the available services.

Web Services: Electronic services enabled by the Web services technology. The Web services technology refers to the set of standards that enable automated machine-to-machine interactions over the Web. The core standards include XML, HTTP, SOAP, WSDL and UDDI.

WSDL: WSDL stands for Web Services Description Language. It is an XML-based language used to describe Web services. For each Web service, the corresponding WSDL document specifies the available operations, the messages involved with the operations, and a set of endpoints to reach the Web service. Due to the use of XML, WSDL is also extensible. In particular, it allows the binding of multiple different communication protocols and message formats.

WS-ReliableMessaging: It is short for the Web Services Reliable Messaging Specification. The specification describes a reliable messaging (RM) protocol between two endpoints, termed as RM source (RMS) and RM destination (RMD). The core concept introduced in WS-ReliableMessaging is sequence. A sequence is a unidirectional reliable channel between the RMS and the RMD. At the beginning of a reliable conversation between the two endpoints, a unique sequence must first be created. The sequence is terminated when the conversation is over. Each message in a sequence is assigned a message number. The message number starts at 1 and is incremented by 1 for each subsequent message. The reliability of the messaging is achieved by the retransmission and positive acknowledgement mechanisms.

XML: XML stands for eXtensible Markup Lanuage. It is designed to facilitate self-contained, structured data representation and transfer over the Internet. It is extensible because it allows users to define their own tags.

Chapter XLIX
Investigation into the Impact of Integration of Mobile Technology Applications into Enterprise Architecture

David Curtis
MethodScience, Australia

Ming-Chien (Mindy) Wu
University of Western Sydney, Australia

ABSTRACT

Enterprise Architecture (EA) is a role or function that primarily ensures the Information Technology strategy and implementation within an organization is correctly aligned with its business strategy and objectives. An EA function focuses on the collection and analysis of information including software applications, business processes, business information (data), technology, and governance (people). The result of this analysis delivers the technology strategy and the roadmap required to support what the organization is trying to achieve. Mobile Technology (MT) integration into the EA function creates the opportunities to deliver and respond to rapidly growing organizations that require immense flexibility from a technology perspective. This is so because mobility can overcome the boundaries of time and location in the dealings of the organization. The result of this extension is the creation of a Mobility Enterprise Architecture (M-EA) model, which will provide the organization with advantages of real-time business processing, better customer and end-user services, and the addition of increased control across the entire organization. This chapter brings together the experience of an Enterprise Architect with a Ph.D research candidate to investigate the M-EA model and its implementation. The chapter includes an overview of EA and M-EA models and also includes investigations of the advantages; limitations and blueprint overcome those challenges of M-EA implementation.

INTRODUCTION

The Enterprise Architecture (EA) model provides sound foundation for an enterprise's business applications. An EA provides the alignment of a business's strategic objectives with the Information Technology Strategy that supports it. Rapidly growing organisations needs to construct their EA, which is a structure of the required business processes, data, technologies, systems, people and governance of the organization, to deliver this alignment.

The extending of EA with mobility is designed to create opportunities to overcome the boundaries of time and location in the dealings of the organization. Thus, the research project reported herein is based on the idea of constructing a Mobility Enterprise Architecture (M-EA) model. The selected methodology for this research is a qualitative research method. These qualitative methods include: Constructive method, Case Studies by interviews, and Action Research. Literature Review is used to understand MT and the current frameworks for building EA; it results in the construction of the initial M-EA model based on this understanding.

The case studies by the interview method are able to help in creating a complete M-EA implementation framework and also provide an understanding of the potential benefits and challenges of implementing M-EA. These implementation challenges are aimed to be further be discussed by the researchers in order to provide the approach to implementing M-EA along with overcoming the challenges to such implementations. Finally, the Action Research studies described here are the future of this work. They will be concluded by visits to companies to study their M-EA implementations and thereby validating the results. This extension of EA with mobility through this research project will result in a comprehensive M-EA which will provide the business with advantages of real-time business processes, reduced costs, increased client satisfaction, and better control over business and its processes.

This chapter incorporates the experience of an Enterprise Architect in a large Insurance company together with the researcher whose focus is the construction and implementation of M-EA. The framework extending the organization's Enterprise Architecture with mobility is outlined and discussed in the chapter. The potential advantages of M-EA, implementation challenges, practical issues and limitations are analysed from the comments from the interviewees who were interviewed as a part of the case study interviews for this project. The chapter concludes with recommendations on how to overcome these challenges to organisations that would like to implement the M-EA model.

ENTERPRISE ARCHITECTURE (EA) OVERVIEW

The world of Information Technology Enterprise Architecture is still a relatively new discipline. This is so mainly because it is only in the recent past that the importance of Strategic IT planning has been considered similar to and with equal importance as the other strategic business planning functions within the organization. The Enterprise Architecture (EA) function within an organisation ensures that the IT Architecture is aligned with the Business Strategic goals and objectives, and more importantly, remains aligned (McGovern et. al., 2004).

This is an important differentiator to more project or system based objectives because whilst individual applications evolve typically to address a "point in time" business issue or opportunity, the EA seeks to address the more holistic organisational level requirements and business alignment objectives on an ongoing basis. A key output of the EA programme is the Target State Model. One of the important aspects of the Target State Model is that it helps guide the subsequent work that is carried out and is also used to identify and cost the opportunities in which the organization should invest to achieve its IT objectives.

An EA programme typically contains a number of streams:

- Business Strategic Objectives baseline capture
- Current Technology baseline capture
- Target State creation
- Opportunity analysis and identification
- Technology governance review

Furthermore, if the organisational structure is deemed to require changes to better support the target state then the model may also include staffing and resource models necessary to improve internal governance or delivery capabilities.

Figure 1 below provides an overview of a typical process flow of activities within an EA programme:

There are numerous EA Frameworks used to guide organizations in the creation of an Enterprise Model and Figure 1 provides an example of the process steps that can be used to deliver a model. It should be noted that a strategic architecture programme is cyclical or continuous in nature rather than project delineated with a specific start and finish. The purpose of utilizing this cyclical nature is to ensure that the organization's IT framework remains in alignment with its overall objectives which may be evolving along with the company. The process in Figure 1 is divided into 3 distinct processes – Business Model definition, IT Architecture definition and Implementation definition.

The Business Model is focused on defining the core processes to be supported by IT. The IT Architecture model defines the data, applications and processes required to support the business model focusing on the current and target states. The Implementation model focuses on defining the specific projects and activities that will be undertaken to change the current environment to achieve the overall target state.

Organization Strategic Goals and Objectives

The initial stage of an Enterprise Application Architecture is the development of a clear understanding of the direction of the organisation, its goals, principals and objectives. This understanding is used during the business services discovery work to identify what application services will be required to support the business objectives.

The work can be visualised as a layered process progressively getting deeper as outputs of the layer above are defined to support the layer directly beneath. This is depicted visually in Figure 2.

The Business Services discovery, shown in Figure 2, helps define the Business Processes that are needed to support the organization. These are defined in business terminology, such as "Create Order" or "Send Notification". A business service wraps an overall capability that is logical to an organization, e.g. completion of the process delivers some perceived value to the organisation. Once Business Services have been defined these can then be used to discover the Information Services (or subjects) that need to made available.

The Information Services layer, shown in Figure 2, focuses on the data necessary to deliver the identified Business Services. This type of service is normally focused around data subjects. Subjects such as client, order, credit rating and supplier represent information subjects. Once Information Services are defined the next stage of work involves identifying how and where this data can be delivered, via defined Application Services. An application service is the layer which is concerned with technology. Information needs are required to be mapped to where those needs can be sourced from in the organization. These information needs can be sourced from either existing silos of

Figure 1. EA process overview

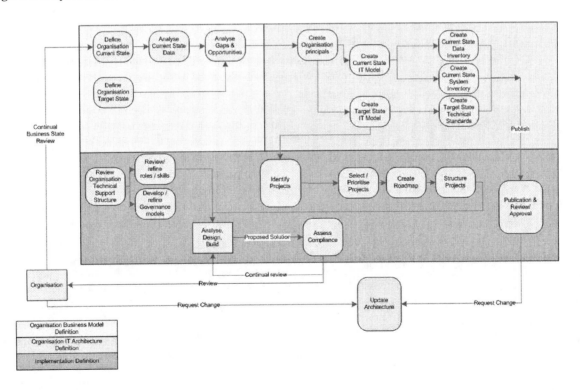

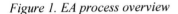

Figure 2. EA design layers

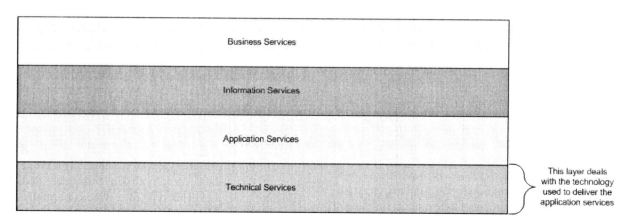

data and information or there may be a need to create new paths to new information. Depending on the environment this can include retrieval of data from existing services as well as identifying gaps where new application services need to be created. Additionally dependent on the nature of the data it may be further necessary to interact with 3rd parties to source the data that is required.

Some examples of an Application Service that satisfy a required Business Service would be functions that return information such as "all outstanding orders" or "display client credit limit" or perhaps "show parts on back order". The key aspects of understanding the Application Services is that it begins to identify where the information will be retrieved from and specific processing undertaken.

Application Services

The capture of an organization's strategic goals and objectives is a crucial part of the discovery work. The discovery activities are undertaken as a way of gaining the required information in the subject areas above. Sometimes this is also described as a business modelling, business engineering or business analysis exercise. Without this information recorded and understood it is impossible to create a future state architecture that is in alignment with the direction a business wants to move in. Part of this set of activities is the identification of the internal groups and external parties (the architecture touch points) which the EA must support. Focusing on the touch points is vital because the nature of the interactions between internal

organizational and external 3rd parties must be well understood before the correct mapping and alignment can be implemented. The key to understanding these interactions is that from an architectural perspective they typically manifest themselves in a future state architecture in the form of an interface of some description. This includes as an example:

- Programmatic interfaces (such as application services, e.g. API's)
- B2B interfaces (for example between 3rd parties such as XML gateways)

A distinction that can and should be made is the difference between the nature of an interface and the underlying technology support. Understanding the differences between a required interface and the technology support are important for a number of reasons but primarily because it ensures a level of abstraction between the nature of the information being sent or received and the technology used to handle that interaction.

Mobility and the Technology Baseline

A key output of the IT Architecture Definition is a Technology Baseline. As well as delivering a current state I.T. analysis for an organization part of this stage of work is to additionally map the future state (Umar, 2005). The future state will be needed to deliver the services required to support the business processes.

Often a working assumption about a Target Model (technical) is that, with the exception of noted constraints such as existing systems or infrastructure, there is a high degree of control over both design and implementation. Indeed one of the key concepts of an EA is that it is used as a reference guide to drive specific IT programmes to be delivered and in the ongoing decision making in an IT context.

Changing operational environments on a global scale are challenging the way in which the scope and approach to EA must be considered. Additionally as wireless technology and channels begin to mature the ability to control all aspects of the EA model are beginning to become more limited in nature (Paavilainen, 2001). Examples of the catalyst for this change include:

- The maturing capabilities of mobile devices and networks. Mobile capabilities have expanded incredibly in just the past decade as have the reliability of networks and reach that support it, e.g. mobile devices and networks are now treated like "common infrastructure"
- Social expectation. Related to the point above people expect to be provided with capabilities (and convenience) that were not available even 5 years ago

- Sheer volume of individuals that utilize mobile technology. E.g. a market large enough to justify the investment required to support it. This includes emerging Countries where mobile technology may become the de-facto standard in place of other, more costly, fixed infrastructure equivalents

The changes in capabilities described above culminate with significant changes in the way that interactions will occur within and external to an Enterprise and to some extent guarantees that mobile channels will need to be catered for within the Technology Baseline.

Figure 3 provides, at a high level, an example of the types of party interactions that might be present in the definition of a Business Architecture.

A key point about Figure 3 is that it doesn't identify the physical geography associated with the interactions. Whilst many of the interactions can clearly be identified as internal to the organization other such as those linked to the Customer, Sales Rep or Supplier and Distribution channel could be external (Olla, 2005). Historically, these interactions by necessity would have been handled in a manual way. However,

Figure 3. Business interactions

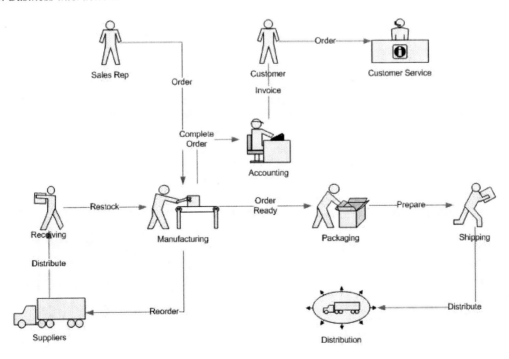

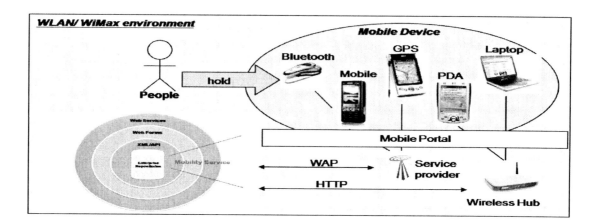

because of the rapidly maturing mobile infrastructure model these interactions continue to change as they become independent of the location. In this way the support of mobile capabilities within the scope of an EA will become more prevalent in the future.

MOBILE ENTERPRISE ARCHITECTURE (M-EA) OVERVIEW

The proper implementation of Enterprise Architecture (EA) provides the organization with competitive advantages. These advantages occur due to the creation of opportunities to streamline business processes, reduce costs, increase customer satisfaction and enable thorough strategic planning (Lan and Unhelkar, 2005). The modern organisation can further benefit by extending EA with strategic incorporation of Mobile Technologies (MT) including wireless networks and handheld devices. This is so because of the phenomenal impact of the "time and location" independence provided by MT (Barnes, 2002). However, mobile business resulting from adoption of MT should not be a mere repetition of electronic commerce on the mobile devices; rather, mobile business should adopt strategic use of mobility that would result in fundamental reengineering of the business processes.

M-EA Model

There are numerous approaches, technologies and their associated functions that can be used for Enterprise Application Integration (EAI). EAI can be considered as a part of the overall EA and it would be made up

of technologies such as wireless hub, application connectivity, data format and transformation, integration modules, support for transactions, enterprise portal, and web service (as described by Finkelstein, 2006). Most importantly however, the technologies comprising Web Services including eXtensible Mark-up Language (XML), Web Services Description Language (WSDL) and Universal Description, Discovery and Integration (UDDI), provide an excellent basis for integrating the applications of the enterprise – particularly when they are represented in separate and, more often than not, heterogeneous platforms. There is a need, however, to provide glue to EA based on MT as outlined here. This glue would result in strategic incorporation of MT in the enterprise.

There is also a pressing need to consider the penetration of mobile devices in both developing and developed societies that provide immense opportunities for an integrated business to offer wide and varied services. Mobile phone devices are most popular today and have high marketing acceptance (Canalys, 2007). Mobile network technology provides real-time communication between business and consumer of EA. Technology, such as Bluetooth, is now used in many mobile device functions and processes. Bluetooth technology enables easy synchronization between a personal computer (PC) server and one or more wireless devices (Buttery and Sago, 2004). This synchronization has been particularly successful in cooperative applications and providing access to M-EA. Another technology, Global Positioning System (GPS) devices and Radio Frequency Identification (RFID) tags and readers are already used in Supply Chain Management (SCM) systems to improve delivery service and tracking production location (Hurster, Fuychtuller,

Figure 5. M-EA implementation framework

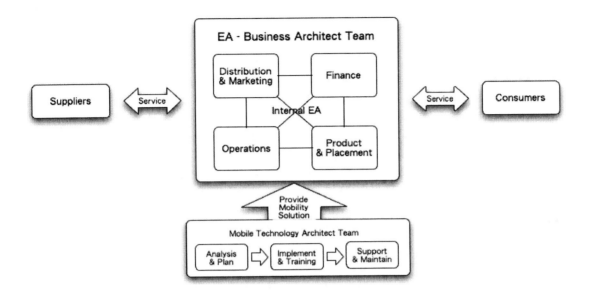

and Fischer, 2006). These two technologies improve location-based tracking, reduce the cost risk associated with human mistakes and also improve the efficiency and effectiveness of M-EA.

The initial M-EA model, as outlined in Figure 4, shows how mobile devices access the enterprise repository through web services. The enterprise repository is a comprehensive enterprise system containing all applications, business processes, business rules, and the enterprise model. In the WLAN or WiMax environment, people can hold various mobile devices to reach the enterprise information system including its repository using the Internet though the native API/XML, web forms and via web services anywhere, anytime. Once we integrate the mobile server into this EA model, we find that users (people) can utilise technology including mobile phones, some with Bluetooth headphone, Personal Digital Assistants (PDA), GPS, portable computer (notebook) to connect mobile portal though service provider (WAP), or wireless Hub (HTTP), or Simple Object Access Protocol (SOAP) to connect with enterprise repositories.

The web service publishes details of what it provides, the information to send, and what to expect in return in a registry (which may be public or private) (Krafzig et. al., 2005). These functions use the WSDL standards, and the directory itself follows the UDDI

standard. The customer finds out details of the service using the same two core standards (WSDL & UDDI), and then calls, or binds, to the service using SOAP.

M-EA Implementation Framework

At the "case study by interview" stage of this research project, we have conducted interviews of experienced Enterprise Architects, Business Analysts, Chief Information Officer's (CIO) and IT executives to help us construct this M-EA implementation framework. The experiences of these experts indicates that in order to reach a clear vision of M-EA and to build the many services that support M-EA, enterprises need to understand the human, system, process, and technology aspects of the M-EA. Thus, creating the centre of excellence or similar cross-functional group to provide resources and guidance, to serve as a repository for best-practice information, and to operate tools that support the M-EA implementation is the critical factor for success.

This framework of an M-EA implementation (see Figure 5) is outlined here based on output from numerous interviewees. The framework for implementation, shown in Figure 5, is divided into two cross-service architect teams: the first team is the Business Architects team, whose responsibility is to analyse the business systems, processes, information, and people structure of the M-EA; the second team is the Mobile Technology Architects team, whose responsibility is to support the creation of mobile technology solutions that meet the requirements from the Business Architects Team. The primary goal for these two teams is to understand how people work, who owns what responsibilities, and which interdependencies link business processes and technology resources.

Based on expert advice and discussions with another EA, the team of Business architects in the framework is further divided into 6 groups and it covers internal and hybrid organizations. The teams within the internal organization have 4 groups which are Distribution and Marketing groups, Financial groups, Operations groups and Product and Placement groups. Team of hybrid organization has 2 groups, SCM and CRM groups. The goal for the business team is to discuss and agree on the business elements of an application. The architects of all groups in a business team have to determine their department direction, describe the core business processes, define the department services, declare the application requests, priorities features and most importantly to meet the users and services requirements within the business strategy and support the department's objectives.

One CIO interviewee pointed out that Mobile Technology architects team should be divided into 3 groups, which are the Analysis and Planning group, Implementation and Training group and the Support and Maintain group. After the Business Architects team has documented the requirements for business processing, the Mobile Technology team formulates how to implement this technology to maximize the effectiveness of the business process implementation and provide a better services. The goal for mobile technology team is to discuss and agree on how to manage the technological underpinnings and support to the business.

The architects of the Analysis and Planning group initially analyse the expertise staff of new mobile technology and the adapted infrastructure. The architects should investigate the technical complexity of implementing the new mobile technology. The IT Executive manager interviewee provided some questions that need to be addressed in this stage including:

- Could the chosen mobile technology integration of M-EA support hardware, software and database software within the current support structure or not?

- Does the organisation have the right skills and expertise to implement or outsourcing is required?
- If outsourcing, how will this knowledge will be transferred to the support and maintain group internally?

Answering all the aforementioned questions after investigation from the architects, the analysis team helps understand how the M-EA utilizes the original enterprise information systems, servers, database and infrastructure. This can then be followed by making plans for implementation and getting corresponding funding to do so. Needless to say, the architects have to make available to the organization options for their transition plans.

Once the final implementation plan is completed, the documents and the work are passed to the Implementation and Training team. The implementation team follows the plan and also provides service and mobility solution to business architect team. The training of M-EA needs to be organized, so that is decided who should attend the training class, how to hold the class, and also the real-life practice training period support. Therefore, the help desk, desktop support, production support, systems team, computer operators, also support and maintain architect group should training during the implementation period. The support team and maintain team should have the mobile technology support outline or handbook from training group if the implementation project is outsourcing. Finally, once the M-EA is successfully implemented, the support and maintenance team should be able to fix and respond all the problems for EA Business architect team.

INVESTIGATION INTO THE IMPACT OF M-EA

This section outlines the results of M-EA advantages and challenges from the interview transcripts. Additionally, this section also indicates the blueprint and the current approach of overcoming those challenges from discussing and analysis in MIRAG.

Advantages of M-EA

The advantages of M-EA could be good assuming that the investigation of this mobile technology area was justified as a genuine opportunity within the Business Strategy and could support the company objectives. Following are list major three benefits of M-EA:

- M-EA allows people anywhere anytime access to applications

Mobile technology can have a positive impact on EA by enabling people access to conduct business anywhere and anytime. It enables access to information by linking the organization's systems to portable devices. Mobility could allow people to carry smaller devices and have more effective communication (Alag, 2006). It provides the enterprise with a far greater level of data mobility and potential productivity. Thus, in properly treating any external infrastructure and services that form part of an organization's mobile solution. Additionally, in many instances global organizations will leverage third party communications infrastructure and associated services as part of their overall mobility solution set as well (Rolstadas and Andersen, 2000).

- M-EA facilitates faster information flow

MT (mainly mobile phones and home wireless networks) have almost become ubiquitous and thus a mode of interaction that cannot be ignored by organisations which currently (or plan to) provide services via the internet. An increased reliance on mobile phones as compared to fixed line phones is noticeable. MT provide a newly evolving mode of interaction with corporate and enterprise systems. EA with integrated MT allows for the organization to provide services via any mode and thus design systems with just the business functionality in mind (Saha (Ed.), 2007). MT then becomes part of the infrastructure concerned with delivery of the information. Mobility is very useful on information flow fast when you enter the cooperation between internal departments to make faster easier to access external parties- customers or suppliers (Yang and Wang, 2006). If rules or policies change, the information flow fast to enterprise, thus, makes EA to respond to those changes easier and fast.

- Combination service provided through M-EA

Using MT facilitates the delivery of additional access channels that makes sense to have in a mobile context, e.g. service requests, payments and information/reminder channels. Better mobile processes become standard and accepted by all users (Qiu (Ed), 2007). A number of resource requests for travel, accommodation and for equipment (e.g. laptops, mobile) could be submitted using a mobile platform as it may be the natural choice of convenience. Infosys has an internal MT interest group. The modern mobile phone market caters for a wide variety of customer tastes and lifestyles. People can use smart phones and PDA which are very handy in terms of end user response and ease of use from the application point of view to access this combination service.

Limitations of M-EA

There are a number of limitations that need to be considered as part of an M-EA implementation.

- Security issues

It is important to incorporate the security concerns associated with mobility solutions into any related EA activity. Data security and non-repudiation (especially for financial transactions); Targeting only those applications which can be deployed with sufficient usability, security, it may not be safe to push customer or financial data to mobile handsets (Nand, 2006). Additionally this will vary greatly by type of handset or device. Multi-factor authentication, encryption, etc would need to be treated alongside the core mobile infrastructure.

- No single standard for mobile technologies

MT are still immature and are improving at a great rate (Ghanbary, 2006). Additionally there are a lot of competing standards. There is still considerable effort required to standardise technologies for interoperability. Additionally there are a range of protocols in use including GSM, Edge, 3G as well as the older CDMA.

- Mobile Device Form Factor

MT involves a different presentation mechanism to the currently well established ones such as via desktop computing for the Internet and Telephone. As with each presentation channel, the mode of communication along with the limitations of the devices used for the purpose pose the greatest challenges. E.g. size of display, communication infrastructure required authentication and authorization mechanisms, small screen and keyboards limiting the overall usability etc. Ease of use for the staff needing to operate the devices, overcome through thorough and regular training.

• Device Trust

It has taken a great deal of time to convince the public in general of the relative security of the Internet and it use in delivering financial transactions. This trust has yet to be reached in devices used in the Mobile space. This is especially true of financial transactions.

• Cost of M-EA implementation

Some of the challenges relate particularly to user perception of the real value of this area. At present a large extent MT are still seen as unnecessary "toys" as opposed to value channels to be supported/ utilized. The primary way to overcome this, in the context of an EA program, is to be very sure that the inclusion of this technology is both cost/value justified and is a key enabler in helping the business reach its desired strategic objectives. E.g. this must be measurable/ quantifiable. Also the cost of the internet usage on these devices is concern by customers as well.

Overcoming the Limitations of M-EA

MT are finally realizing some of their potential (lower operating costs for the consumer, better interfaces, and better integration) which makes the ability to carry out some functions more ergonomic now than in the past 3-4 years.

One example of reducing the problems with using MT is to use the web browsing capabilities of current mobile phones along with a redesigned web interface suited to a significantly smaller screen size as well as limitations of the communication infrastructure. This has the need for each application to have custom presentation mechanisms and relies on the user to decide and select the appropriate one. Even if the mobile phones are handy enough to use, hundreds of millions of people are not going to replace the full screen, mouse and keyboard experience with staring at a little screen. This is more conventional than adoption of things, but can be catered with time.

The other method is to use new mobile interfacing tools that adjust the information transfer based on the parameters of the device used in the communication. E.g. a mobile device with a large colour screen can display more information and use colours to distinguish the type of information. On a smaller monochrome screen, less information is displayed and a small number of grayscales are used to show the different types of information. A mobile phone with no web access would request information via SMS and the response would be optimised to cater to the limitations of the SMS technology.

By the way, security has to be given due consideration when the enterprise wants to implement M-EA into their company. The increased mobile computing power of handheld devices introduces new security threats. The security threats would be in the form of loss of confidentiality, integrity and availability. Password protection is included in most handheld devices as a counter measure. Data security, overcome by on-going encryption and secure connections. Furthermore, network and application security measures also need to be considered when extending enterprise architecture with mobility. Having risk identification and risk planning measures could help to overcome some risks. A possible solution is to build security measures into mobile platforms and applications themselves.

Blueprint of Overcoming M-EA Challenges

A key aspect is having a clear idea of the scope of use and capabilities of MT available today. One area of risk is the sheer size of the market for mobile devices and capabilities. This makes supporting this a potentially very complex and risky proposition. Especially in an EA environment, the internal capabilities are under the complete control of the organization.

There are several MT that have been standardised around the world and there is still a difficulty in achieving a ubiquitous standard technology that could be used for people travelling. This also brings with it many risks when new technologies are introduced and are completely new in the market, this creates confusion in the marketplace as consumers attempt to understand and choose from what is available.

Also, the hardware and software that these technologies are built on may be difficult to get in-depth knowledge about which may lead organizations to limit or stop their use. Thus, in an ever changing world wherein we get to see new technologies being introduced everyday, it may be difficult to just keep pace with it all let alone overcome the challenges it brings with it. But, in keeping with tradition following the right processes, having the right people and having the right technology may be the key to overcome any challenges new technologies may bring with it.

CONCLUSION AND FUTURE DIRECTION

This chapter provides an overview of EA, and how it migrates to M-EA. We argued that MT needs to be integrated within the overall EA model and the business processes of the enterprise. Such integration would result in an M-EA that would enable enterprise to conduct their business cross over the location and time boundaries. Thus, an M-EA is a powerful tool to incorporate, manage and develop the enterprise' processes. Moreover, this chapter outlined the importance of M-EA model as the means to identify and provide for the integration advantages and challenges between various applications and technologies within the enterprise. This chapter also indicated the current overcome and blueprint overcome approve to those limitations of M-EA.

Further validation of M-EA is the future direction of this research. The research team is currently undertaking validate the outlined M-EA model, as also the action research study being undertaken with our industrial partner. This action research study indicates that enterprises can benefit with the help of M-EA through its step-by-step framework for extending and integrating the existing EA with mobility and security. Furthermore, after completing the action research studies, the critical success factors that lead to implementation of M-EA will be investigated and summarized. This will result in immense practical validating of the key organizational benefits and challenges in implementing the M-EA model.

REFERENCES

Alag, H. S. (2006).Business Process Mobility. In B. Unhelkar (Ed.), *Handbook of Research in Mobile Business: Technical, Methodological and Social Perspectives.* Hershey, PA: IGI Global.

Barnes, S. J. (2002). The mobile commerce value chain: Analysis and future development. *International Journal of Information Management, 22*(2), 91-108.

Buttery, S., & Sago, A. (2004). Future application of Bluetooth. *Mobile and wireless communications: key technologies and future application.* British Telecommunications Plc: The IEE.

Canalys research release (2007/083). *Worldwide mobile navigation device market more than doubles– Garmin and TomTom neck and neck as global leaders in Q2 2007.* Canalys. com. Retrieved Dec 31, 2007, from http://www. canalys.com/pr/2007/r2007083.htm

Finkelstein, C. (2006). *Enterprise Architecture for Integration: Rapid delivery methods and technologies.* U.S.A.: Artech House.

Ghanbary, A. (2006). Evaluation of mobile technologies in the context of their applications, limitations and transformation. In B. Unhelkar (Ed.), *Handbook of Research in Mobile Business: Technical, Methodological and Social Perspectives.* Hershey, PA: IGI Global.

Hurster, W., Fuychtuller, H., & Fischer, T. (2006). Mobile Batch Tracking - A breakthrough in supply chain management. In B. Unhelkar (Ed.), *Handbook of Research in Mobile Business: Technical, Methodological and Social Perspectives.* Hershey, PA: IGI Global.

Krafzig, D., Banke, K., & Slama, D. (2005). *Enterprise SOA: Service-Oriented Architecture Best Practices.* Pearson Education, Inc.

Lan, Y. & Unhelkar, B. *Global Enterprise Transitions: Managing the process.* Hershey, PA: IGI Global.

McGovern, J., Ambler, S. W., Stevens, M. E., Linn, J., Sharan, V., Jo, E. K. (2004). Foreword by O. Sims. *A Practical Guide to Enterprise Architecture.* Pearson Education, Inc.

Nand, S. (2006). Developing a Theory of Portable Public Key Infrastructure (PORTABLEPKI) for Mobile Business Security. In B. Unhelkar (Ed.), *Handbook of Research in Mobile Business: Technical, Methodological and Social Perspectives.* Hershey, PA: IGI Global.

Olla, P. (2005). *Incorporating commercial space technology into mobile services: developing innovative business models.* Hershey, PA: Idea Group.

Paavilainen, J. (2001). *Mobile business strategies: understanding the technologies and opportunities.*

Wireless press; Addison-Wesley in partnership with IT Press.

Rolstadas, A., & Andersen, B. (2000). *Enterprise Modeling-Improving global industrial competitiveness.* Kluwer Academic publishers.

Qiu, R. G. (Ed) (2007). *Enterprise Service Computing: From Concept to Deployment.* Hershey, PA: Idea Group.

Saha, P. (Ed.) (2007). *Handbook of Enterprise Systems Architecture in Practice.* Hershey, London, Melbourne, Singapore: IGI Global

Umar, A. (2005, July). IT Infrastructure to Enable Next Generation Enterprises. *Information Systems Frontiers, 7*(3).

Yang, C. C., & Wang, F. L. (2006). Information Delivery for Mobile Business: Architecture for Accessing Large Documents through Mobile Devices In B. Unhelkar (Ed.), *Handbook of Research in Mobile Business: Technical, Methodological and Social Perspectives.* Hershey, PA: IGI Global.

KEY TERMS

Enterprise Architecture (EA): A strategic Information Technology model that provides a visualisation of the relationships between Processes, Data, People and Systems in an organisation and which acts as a guide in the implementation of technology to support the business goals and strategy.

Mobile Enterprise Architecture (M-EA): A structure of integrating business processes with Information Technology that are supported and integrated with MT. It integrates business Systems, Processes, People, and Data in an organization in a manner that enables easy incorporation of Mobile Technologies in its business processes.

Mobile Technologies (MT): Used to describe modern wireless connections such as those in cellular networks and wireless broadband Internet, also encompass communication that is achieved without land-based or wired mechanisms.

Chapter L
Security in Mobile Ad Hoc Networks

Ekata Mehul
Gujarat University, India

Vikram Limaye
India

ABSTRACT

Securing a "Wireless Ad Hoc Network" (WAHN) is a major concern of network administrators. This is particularly so in case of the wireless networks due to their unique characteristics that varies from the traditional networks. For example, WAHN are vulnerable to internal as well as external attacks relatively easily, as compared with traditional networks, because of their ability to be accessible from anywhere within their range. Many solutions have been proposed in this area and they are also being continuously improved. Most of these solutions involve encryption; secure routing, quality of service, and so forth. However, each of these solutions is designed to operate in a particular situation; and it may fail to work successfully in other scenarios. This particular research work offers an alternate to improving the trustworthiness of the neighbourhood and securing the routing procedure. This security is achieved by dynamically computing the trust in neighbours and selecting the most secure route from the available ones for the data transfer. There is also a provision to detect the compromised node and virtually removing it from the network.

INTRODUCTION

Securing a "Wireless Ad Hoc Network" (WAHN) is a major concern of network administrators due to their unique characteristics that varies from the traditional networks. This chapter proposes a scheme of calculating trustworthiness of the network neighbourhood and securing its routing process. In last few years, the popularity of wireless network has grown to an enormous extent. Features like spaghetti free networks, mobility, ease of use and accessibility, are the major reasons for the increased use of wireless networks. Wireless Networks provides flexible data communication system, which uses wireless media such as radio frequency technology to transmit and receive data over the air.

Wireless networks offer the following advantages over the traditional wired networks:

1. **Mobility:** It provides real time access to the mobile users – anytime, anywhere. This mobility supports productivity and service opportunities, which were not possible with wired networks.

2. **Installation and Speed of Simplicity:** Wireless systems can be installed rapidly and easily, it eliminates the need of the cables as well.

3. **Reach of the Network:** We can connect and extend our network to places, which can not be wired.

4. **Flexibility:** Wireless networks are more flexible and easily adapt system and configuration changes.

5. **Reduced cost of ownership:** Apart from the initial investment, overall installation and life cycle costs are very less than that of wired networks.

6. **Scalability:** Wireless systems can be configured in various topologies depending on required applications and installations. It ranges from peer-to-peer network for a small number of users to large infrastructure networks to enable roaming over a broad area.

Wireless networks are telephone or computer networks that use radio as their carrier or physical layer [3]. These radio waves simply perform the function of delivering energy to a remote receiver. The data is modulated on the radio carrier so that it can be accurately extracted at the other end. Multiple radio carriers with different frequencies can exist in the same space at the same time without interfering with each other. The receiver tunes into one of the radio waves to receive the data at the intended frequency.

Wireless LAN technology makes it possible for two or more computer to communicate using standard network protocols without network cables [4]. Computers are connected using Multiple Network Access points. A single access point covers large area. All wired and wireless computers can access the Internet through single software access point.

There are some limitations of the wireless networks, which sometimes override the above-mentioned advantages, are as follows: [14]

1. **Limited Bandwidth:** Wireless communications requires radio spectrum, which is very less and not able to support unlimited available wireless applications. The bandwidth is scares and hence, it is expensive.

2. **Coverage Problems:** Radio signals are attenuated and reflected by the obstacles. At higher frequencies, due to diffraction and reflections, coverage problems increases.

3. **Hostile Radio Channel:** Because of the coverage and obstacle problems, it is difficult to achieve

the quality of the radio signals. As a result efficient mechanism like error corrections systems, interleavers, equalisers and adaptive antennas are required to overcome such difficulties.

4. **Inadequate Battery Power:** Generally, small and lightweight portable devices are preferred in mobile wireless communication. Thus, the power consumption is an issue and the battery technology has not evolved at the pace of semiconductor technology. [14] This forces users to have low power transmitters and less powerful computational devices.

Mobile Ad Hoc Networks

MANET – Mobile Ad Hoc Networking is a new concept in a wireless communication world, where the networks are formed and destroyed on the fly without any centralized control. It is an autonomous system of mobile routers connected by wireless links.

In MANET, nodes are in transition and pose a dynamic network topology where a node can join and leave the network at any point of time. Due to limited transmission range, hop-by-hop data communication is required, where a data packet reaches its destination after travelling several nodes in between. Thus, each intermediate node acts as a router.

Security Issues in Mobile Ad Hoc Networks

Security is vital in Ad Hoc Networks. Securing the Ad Hoc Networks starts from the neighbour verification in the local community also termed as a cluster – collection of wireless nodes in a particular group. Mobility and limited range of bandwidth makes it difficult to detect the malicious activity in a self-organised network [1]. The security issues involve the activities like node authentication, key management, trust establishment, secure routing protocols and handling the node misbehaviour and traffic analysis.

Security Goals

Security is the utmost concern for ad hoc networks, especially for the security-sensitive applications [13]. Following attributes are generally considered to secure an ad hoc network.

- **Availability:** Ensures the survivability of network services even in case denial of service attacks, which can be launched at any layer.

Figure 1. Wireless communication using access point

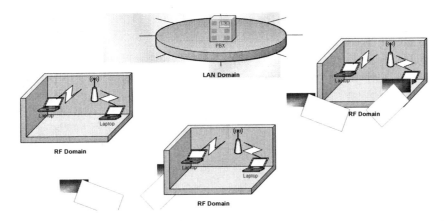

Figure 2. Mobile ad hoc network

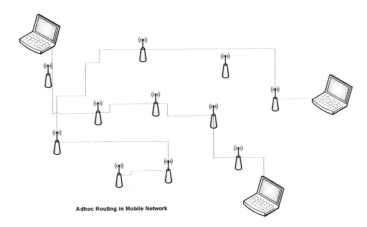

- **Confidentiality:** This property ensures that important data like, strategic or tactical military information is never disclosed to any unauthorised entities.
- **Integrity:** This feature guarantees that the message is not corrupted because of the radio propagation impairments or malicious attacks.
- **Authentication:** This ensures the authenticity of the communicating peer node. Unauthorized access can result into misuse of resources and information.
- **Non-repudiation:** This term helps in confirming that the origin of a message cannot deny having sent the message. This characteristic helps in detecting and isolating the compromised node.

Challenges

Ad hoc networks are vulnerable to a wide range of malicious attacks. There is a lack of centralised controlling mechanism, which makes it difficult to authenticate the participating nodes in the network. Thus, it is a complicated task to distinguish between trusted and non-trusted nodes. Such a system forces a co-operative nature of network operation.

A malevolent node, which appears to be legitimate, can disrupt the network by malicious activities like dropping the packets, changing the actual distance metric to the destination, announcing a routing update with a large sequence number (fresher update) or may also announce a failure of active link. It also fails the network by creating a links to the non-existing node.

i. Network layer is most susceptible to the attacks because of inherent link to link communication model. A malicious node can become a router and disrupt the normal network operations. The network layer is responsible for routing and packet forwarding. Routes from the source and destination are established and maintained by the routing protocols and intermediate nodes forward data packets. [1] A malicious node can cause misbehaviour in routing updates and packet forwarding activities. By spreading forged routing updates, entire traffic is diverted to the attacker or to some other node. [10] This leads to the idea of creating black hole, which routes all the packets to the particular node and discards them. A grey hole is an extension of black hole, which intentionally drops some packets by some probability e.g., forwarding of routing packets and not the data packets.

ii. An ad hoc network suffers from the low bandwidth constrained wireless links, which endanger the physical security issues.

iii. A mobile node without adequate protection is easy to manipulate and attack. In such cases, overhearing of the channels causes the problem like listening and modifying the flow of traffic.

iv. Another type of attack is the creation of a tunnel – a wormhole, in the network between two colluding malicious nodes linked through a private network. [10] Such kind of attack short-circuits the normal flow of routing messages creating a virtual vertex cut in the network that is controlled by the two colluding attackers.

v. A well planned fabricated attack by a malicious node – *rushing attack*, where a malicious node exploits the characteristics of Ad Hoc on Demand Distance Vector (AODV) Routing Protocol, which hold backs the duplicate packets at every node. Here an attacker rapidly spreads routing messages all through the network, suppressing the legitimate routing messages and the receiving nodes drop them as duplicate copies. In a same way, by fabricating a routing error message, an attacker can nullify an operational route to the destination.

vi. Most of the mobile nodes are having limited battery power. A malicious node can continually relay spurious data to a particular node, which will eventually drain off the battery power of that victim node by keeping that node busy. Alternatively, it can also jam the channel and forcing other contenders for back off repeatedly. Thus, it hijacks the network bandwidth so the network no longer operates correctly.

vii. A malicious node can spoof in the network by alerting its MAC or IP address, masquerades as another node, and alter the structure of the topology. Such an attack creates loops in the routing information collected by a node, causes partitioning of the network.

Thus, a node can schedule various types of passive, Denial of Service (DoS) attacks and disrupt the normal operation of the network. Since the network nodes operate in collaborative manner, there can be a trust relationship scheme implemented to resolve such problems.

BASIC INFORMATION

Let us focus on an Ad Hoc On Demand Distance Vector Routing Protocol (AODV). This protocol falls in the category of *"Reactive Routing Protocols"*, where a route is explored only if requested by a node. The trust level of the neighbour is computed depending on its activity in the network. A node selects and set up the communication path as per the trust value of its neighbour.

Ad Hoc On Demand Distance Vector Routing Protocol (AODV)

The ad hoc on demand distance vector routing protocol (AODV) is designed for mobile ad hoc networks. It is capable of unicast and multicast routing. It performs the route discovery if and only if demanded by a source node and maintains the route as long as they are needed. This protocol forms a group of trees to connect multicast group members, which uses a sequence number to confirm the freshness of the route and make them loop-free, self starting and scalable over the large numbers of the mobile nodes [6]. In this "pure on-demand route acquisition system", [7] nodes do not share routing tables but they only exchange the beacons to keep the path alive! This technique saves the memory and communication overhead. Local connectivity of the mobile node is established by local broadcasts known as "hello messages". There are several primary objectives of this protocol as follows [7].

- To broadcast discover packets only when requested.
- To differentiate local connectivity and general topology management
- To propagate the updates only to the local nodes who are affected.

In AODV, path discovery initiates with a route request from one of the nodes in the network. A source node sends out route request (RREQ) broadcast packet to its neighbours, which includes a known destination_sequence. A source_sequence and broadcase_id, uniquely identifies the RREQ. Each node maintains monotonically increasing sequence number and a new broadcase_id will be generated for a new RREQ.

The intermediate nodes receiving RREQ checks the routing table, if it finds the route to the destination with a greater sequence number then, it unicasts route reply (RREP) packet back to the neighbour from which it has received the RREQ packet, else it sets up the reverse path and rebroadcasts the RREQ with a hop_cnt incremented by one. To avoid traffic congestion, duplicate RREQ (with a previously received combination of source_sequence and broadcase_id) is silently dropped. In this manner, a request arrives at the destination and a source node is replied back with the path to the destination.

Trust in Wireless Ad Hoc Networks

Ad hoc networks are suitable for military or rescue operations where the environment is hostile and dynamic. In such an environment a node may become compromised and start to misbehave and disrupt the network. Nodes can form a trust level in their neighbour and work in a co-operative manner. Trust in incomplete, node does not consider another node completely trusted or completely bad. Trust can be represented in different levels and accordingly it helps in making the decisions like, selecting a route for electronic transactions, updating routing tables or sharing the information.

Current security trends provide the criteria to build certain level of trust in the network. For example, cryptographic algorithms for privacy and digital signatures, authentication protocols for providing authenticity and access control methods for managing authorisation. Nevertheless, these methods do not manage the general concept of "trustworthiness". For instance, a cryptographic algorithm is unable to say that, competent programmers have authored a piece of digitally signed code or a signed public-key certificate does not guarantee the owner's authenticity.

"Trust (or, symmetrically, distrust) is a particular level of the subjective probability with which an agent will perform a particular action, both before [user] can monitor such action (or independently of his capacity of ever to be able to monitor it) and in a context in which it affects [our] own action" [9]

We can make three points of the definition above.

- Trust is subjective.
- Trust is affected by actions that cannot be monitored.
- The level of trust depends on our own actions.

The network nodes must be able to manage trust relationships. Trust is a belief that the principal, when asked to perform an action, will act according to a predefined description, this implies that the principal will not attempt to harm the requester, regardless of how it carries out the request.

Trust has the following properties. [8]

Transitivity: Trust is not necessarily transitive, that is, if A trusts B and B trusts C, and A does not necessarily trust C.

Symmetry: Trust need not be symmetric, i.e. A trusts B does not imply that B trusts A.

Reflexivity: Trust is assumed to be reflexive, that is, a node trusts itself completely.

A trust level is requested by a "Requester" to the "Recommender", in reply a recommender send its own trust level in the requested node. Based on experience gained via hearing the channel and trust level received from the neighbour, a node calculates its own trust in a particular node for a specific entity. Ad hoc networks are based on *"trust your neighbour"* relationships. This relationship originate, develop and expire on the fly [10] A trust model can seclude an ad hoc network from the attacks to some extent and identify the routes with certain measure of confidence.

Trust: Definition and Assumptions

In general practise, by trust we mean, it is tested and proven to meet certain criteria. [10] However, that trust can be unreliable, because of following two reasons.

Figure 4. Route reply

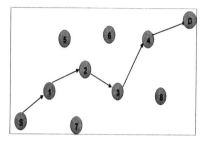

Figure 3. Route request

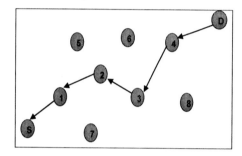

1. Failure of "Trusted System" designers to provide a concrete definition of "trust".
2. "Trusted" implies "nothing can go wrong", which confirms that, tests covered all eventualities. This is not always true and is difficult to guarantee – according to Bruce Scheier [11] "No amount of general beta testing will reveal a security flow and there's no test possible that can prove the absence of flaws"

Here, we are adopting the non-complete trust approach. None of the requestor will consider the direct value recommended by the recommender; instead, it will evaluate it against the other participating recommender's trust level and decide the final trust value of the target node. Rules of transitivity, symmetry and reflexivity are also applicable here.

Trust Relationships

Trust relationship exists between one-hop neighbours. Trust level non-symmetric and unidirectional. When one neighbour holds a belief about other, the same belief in the reverse direction need not exist at the same time. Mutual trust does exist between entities, but we represent them as two separate trust relationships, which can be manipulated independently.

Trust can be seen in two ways, viz.

1. Direct Trust Relationship and
2. Recommender Trust Relationship.

Each node maintains a database for its own use. Based on experience and recommendations, these values are changed in the database at any time. Depending on the behaviour of the direct (one-hop) neighbours, a node will calculate the trust value and will recommend the same in case of requested by any other node. For calculating the trust value of the remote node, a requester can demand recommendations from its neighbours.

TRUST MODELS AND DERIVATION

This model is based on the previous work represented by *Alfarez Abdul-Rahman* and *Stephen Halles* [12], which computes situational trust in agents based upon the general trust in the trusted node. Trust is generally calculated based on all the previous transactions and knowledge to weigh up the cost and benefits that a particular situation holds.

In the proposed model, trust is not calculated for any particular situation instead, it is computed based on a summery of behaviour of the node for a specific amount of period. A node observes its neighbour's activities in a passive mode and computes the trust level depending on their behaviour. In case of any malicious behaviour, a Single Intrusion Detection (SID) packet is broadcasted against compromised node and all the participating neighbours are informed about the malevolent activity performed. [1] Possible events that can be recorded to broadcast SID, are the measure and accuracy of: [10]

*   Frames received
*   Data packets forwarded
*   Control packets forwarded
*   Data packets received
*   Control packets received
*   Streams established
*   Data forwarded
*   Data received

Figure 5. Trust between network nodes

A node will calculate the trust level based on SID broadcasted by itself or other participating nodes and missing hello and acknowledgements during the communicaiton.

For one-hop neighbors, a node will calculate the trust level directly based on experience gained and in case of remote node, it will request the recommendations from its neighbors. A node will consider the recommendations based on its trust level in recommender.

Shortcomings of Existing Solution

There are several ambiguities in the existing solution. We have tried and cover those lapses by making some changes in the existing solution.

- The existing solution [12], computes the trust for a node in particular category. This may not be valid for all the situations. It is better to calculate global trust in some situations.
- Expiry timers are maintained for the recommendations. If the timer expires and the path is still active, again the original requester has to request for the trust value of the target. Thus, the process is duplicated even in case of unchanged trust value. This incurs more delays and waste of processing time and bandwidth.
- The recommender is simply passing on its trust value of target node to the requester and the original requestor computes the value on its own. There are chances of malicious recommendation from one of the recommender, lies in between the original requester and the target node.

In the proposed solution, we have tried to cover the above-mentioned flaws. Instead of a target node, calculating over all trust (without knowing neighbour's neighbour), a neighbour itself will calculate the percentage based trust and recommend it to the requester. This process continues until it reaches the original request node and thus, it helps in refining the trust value to the great extent and purifies (do not trust anyone completely) any recommendations from the malicious node.

PROPOSED METHODOLOGY FOR TRUST CALCULATION

Various solutions have been proposed to compute the trust level in ad hoc networks. Every solution has its own pros and cons and also designed and proposed by keeping particular situation in mind. Thus, it may or may not work in the other condition.

Ad hoc networks are based on *"trust your neighbour"* relationships. However, each node has to assure that, it is communicating with a trustworthy neighbour. This proposal offers a unique way of computing the trust level, direct and recommender trust level, in the network and reduces the communication overhead by limiting the size of packet containing trust level information.

1. **Direct Trust Value:** This is relevant to the direct trust relationships, where a mobile node in a range can scrutinize the activities of its neighbours and calculate the trust value on its own.
2. **Recommender Trust Value:** This is relevant to recommender trust relationship. In this case, trust value of out of range node is requested using RRQ (Recommendation Request).

Figure 6. Trust relationship in the network

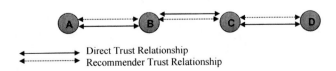

Figure 7. Broadcasting SID in the network

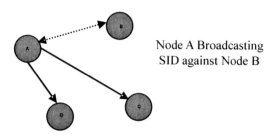

Node A Broadcasting
SID against Node B

Figure 8. Communication range

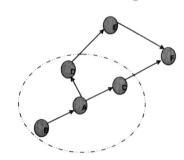

In Figure 8, node A can directly communicate with the node B, C and D, as all of them are in A's communication range. Node E and F are out of range of node A, but it can still reach these out of range nodes via D and C respectively. Thus, node C and D will relay the message for A, in case A wishes to communicate with node E and F.

Nodes mobility frequently causes topology change in the network. Such an activity may enforce recurrent connection loss and re-establishments. When a node C moves out of A's radio range, the link is broken, but still node A and C can communicate through node D, E and F.

Neighbour Monitoring

A node in a radio range of its neighbours can passively overhear the channel and ongoing activity at the other end. This is possible even if a node is not actively involved in a communication. Because of this unique characteristic of wireless networks, it is viable in ad hoc networks to monitor the neighbourhood activities and record any offences conducted. Each node constantly monitors the activity of its neighbours in terms of amount of successful data packets and

routing updates forwarded correctly. In case of any malicious activity, a node will broadcast SID (Single Intrusion Detection) against the malicious node. The affecting nodes (which are in a radio range of a malicious and SID originator node) will recompute the trust level of malicious nodes and update their trust level database.

Validating Single Intrusion Detection (SID)

A malicious activity by any node can be detected and other nodes are informed using Single Intrusion Detection (SID). It is quite likely that a malicious node may broadcast a false SID against a legitimate node or due to the unavoidable circumstances like poor radio connectivity, error in received packets, etc. a node may get detected as a compromised node by its neighbours and an SID may broadcasted against it. Thus, instead of blindly accepting the SID, following parameters are considered by a node receiving SID broadcast:

1. Trust level of a node, which is broadcasting SID against a compromised node.
2. If a compromised node is in a radio range, it will observe a compromised node for a certain period.
3. It will request other neighbours for their recommendations about the compromised node.
4. Depending on its conclusion, a node may recompute the trust level for either the compromised node or SID broadcasting node.

1. In the Figure 10, Node B, C, D and E are in the radio range of Node A, where as Node A, C, E and F are in the radio range of Node B.
2. Node B, broadcasts SID against Node C. All the nodes in the radio range of B except for node C, i.e. Node A, E and F will receive the SID message against C.

SID Evaluation Process

We will examine the SID evaluation process of A. The SID evaluation process will perform the following steps.

1. Node A will check the trust level of node B before further processing the SID message.

Figure 9. Topology change due to mobility of nodes

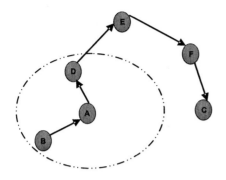

Figure 10. Node B broadcasting SID against node C

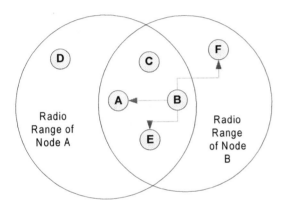

2.   Node A will compare and verify that a compromised node (here Node C), is in the radio range or not?

3.   If a compromised node is in a radio range, node A will observe its activities for a certain period of time and also request a trust level recommendation for a node C, from its other neighbours (here Node D and E). If a compromised node is not in a radio range of the SID receiver node, then in case of active communication with a compromised node, the SID receiver node will ask for the recommendations again.

4.   At this point there can be two possibilities.

i.   Node A may receive an approval of SID against node C, from its neighbours.

ii. Node A may receive a negative recommendation for the SID against C

Summary

1.   In case of first possibility, which conforms that node C is malicious, node A will recompute its trust in node C and update its neighbour trust level database

2.   In case of second event, node A will broadcast SID against node B and the process continues until a malicious node is found.

Note: We are not eliminating a malicious node from the network unless its trust level falls below a certain trust level threshold.

Requesting Trust for Secure Communication

Before commencing a communication a node will assure that, it is communicating with a legitimate node and the path is secure. For the purpose of data transfer, a node will check the trust level of the receiver. At this rule of direct or recommended trust applies. If a target node is in the radio range of the sender then it either will check its neighbour trust level database or may seek recommendation from other neighbours, eligible to recommend the trust level of the target node. In case of a remote node i.e. a target node is not in a communication radio range, the node will send RRQ – recommendation request message to its neighbours.

Since the node F is out of radio range of node A, in such case node A will broadcast RRQ message to its neighbours to know the trust level of node F. If node F is in a communication range of the neighbours of node A, receiving RRQ, they will reply back their trust in node F. In the figure below, node F is in a communication range of node C

and D, hence these node will recommend their trust in F, where as node B which is not in a radio range of node F will forward this RRQ to its neighbours (here node E).

As discussed earlier, node C, D and E will recommend their trust in node F. Since node B is not in a direct communication range of a node F, it will rebroadcast the RRQ message to its neighbours (here the node E). Since the node E has already received the RRQ for node F, it will discard the RRQ message from B. Thus, it will avoid packet duplication in the network.

Figure 11. RRQ message

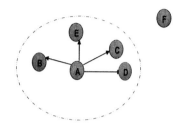

While broadcasting the RRQ message, each node will keep track of the node from which RRQ has received. This helps in case of change in trust level in future.

Trust Recommendation

Structure of the recommendation request (RRQ) message is almost same as the one used in [12].

In the above message, the RRQ does not contain Category and Expiry. We have not included these two parameters because we are not judging the trust of any node for a particular category. We are calculating the global trust, based on SID, hello beacons and acknowledgements. We have also not included the expiry time – during the ongoing communication, if the trust value of any active node is changed, the recommender will re-recommend the changed trust value to the requestor. This feature is based on the characteristic discussed earlier in which, a RRQ broadcasting node keeps track of the requester from whom the RRQ is received earlier. The Trust Recommendation message structure will be as:

Recommendation : : = Requestor_ID, Request_ID, Recommender_ID, Target_ID, Trust_Value

where,
Requestor_ID: represents identity of the requester
Request_ID : represents identity of the request
Target_ID: represents identity of the target

The RRQ and recommendation messages are fairly simple and straightforward. Trust id computed in a different manner, unlike the scheme proposed in [12], where trust from all the nodes in a particular path are computed at the requester end and recommendations from various paths are computed using Beth et al. In

this proposal, each node computes its own trust level and forward it to the requestor, this process continues until the original requestor computes the trust level for the targeted node.

Trust Computation

As discussed earlier, each node computes its own trust based on its observation or recommendations from its neighbours. Unlike the scheme proposed in [12], where an original requester node computes the trust level recommended by intermediate as well as final recommender, here every node computes the trust level based on its own trust in its neighbours and forwards the computed trust towards the original requester.

A node constantly observes the activities of the other nodes in its radio range and computes the trust level for each node. *In case of SID broadcast, the compromised node is not evicted out of the network immediately, rather trust level is computed and if it falls below certain threshold then only the node is expelled from the network.*

A node will compute the trust level of its neighbours based on SID (either broadcasted by it or other nodes), beacons and acknowledgements (during ongoing communication with a particular node). SID is broadcasted based on the events – Trust Model and Derivation. Trust level computation also depends on received / missing beacons and acknowledgements.

In above figure, node B and C is in the radio range of node A. Each parameter viz. SID, Beacon and Acknowledgement is rated on the scale of 0 to 5 where [12]

It computes the trust level as follows. Consider that node A is computing the trust level of node B. A node computing trust level, rates each of these events from 0 (zero) to 5 (five) based on its experience. This scheme proposed percentage based computation. It takes 60 % of SID, 20% Hello Beacons and 20% of Acknowledgements. In case of no data transfer there will not be any communication between two nodes and hence no acknowledgements, in this case it takes 60% of SID and 40% of Acknowledgements.

$$tv = 0.6 * sid + 0.2 * bcn + 0.2 * ack \qquad (1)$$

Here,

tv = Trust Value
sid = Single Intrusion Detection
bcn = Beacon
ack = Acknowledgement

Figure 12. Dropping duplicate RRQ

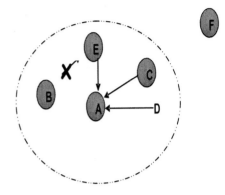

Figure 13. Network node computing trust level of its neighbours

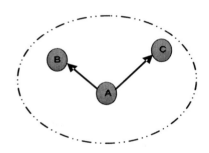

Lets assume that node A has gathered following details about node B after observing it for a particular period of time.

sid = 4, bcn = 3, ack = 2
tv = 0.6 * 4 + 0.2 * 3 + 0.2 * 2
= 3.4

Each node will use the above-described formula to compute its trust level in the neighbouring node. Even if it is recommending the trust level of its neighbours to the requestor, it will first calculate the trust level in above described manner and forward it to the recommendation requester node.

If a node (either intermediate or original RRQ generator) is seeking the trust level for a node, which is not in its radio range, it will broadcast RRQ to its neighbours.

In case of recommending the trust value of the target node, the recommender will calculate the trust using the equation (1) and forward it to the requester node. Upon receiving the recommendations from the neighbours, original requester will calculate the final trust value for the target node as follows.

Computing Trust Proportion of the Neighbor

$$S_r = \sum_{i=1}^{n} Ni \qquad (2)$$

where,

S_r = Sum of trust of neighbors (recommenders) of a requester
i = Neighbors of a requester
N = Trust value of i

Computing Trust Proportion between a Requester and a Recommender

$$T_{Rr(i)} = [100 * T_{r(i)}] / S_r \qquad (3)$$

Where,

$T_{Rr(i)}$ = Calculated trust proportion between a requester and a recommender

$T_{r(i)}$ = Trust recommended by a recommender

S_r = Sum of trust of neighbors (recommenders) of a requester

Computing the Final Trust Value of a Target

$$T_t = \sum_{i=1}^{n} T_{Rr(i)} \qquad (4)$$

Where,

T_t = Sum of trust proportion of neighbor nodes.

$T_{Rr(i)}$ = Calculated trust proportion between a requester and a recommender

The original RRQ requester node will calculate the trust level of a target node in above described manner. Firstly, it will calculate the total trust value of its neighbor and compute the individual trust proportion of each neighboring node based on it. At last, it will calculate the trust value for target node by adding the

Table 1. Trust value semantics

Value	Meaning	Description
0	Distrust	Completely Untrustworthy.
1	Ignorance	Can not make trust-related judgement about entity.
2	Minimal	Lowes possible trust.
3	Average	Mean trustworthiness. Most entities have this trust level
4	Good	More trustworthy than most entities
5	Complete	Completely trustworthy

recommended trust values based on the proportional trust in the recommender.

Algorithm to Compute the Trust in Ad Hoc Network

1. Check whether the target node is in the communication range or not. If it is not in a communication range then, broadcast RRQ in the vicinity.
2. Compute the trust percentage of each node against the sum of the trust of all the neighbours.
3. Consider the percentage of recommended trust value based previously computed trust level proportion of the neighbours.
4. Add the calculated recommendations from the neighbours and compute the final trust value of the target node.

Example:

In the scenario shown by Figure 14, node A wishes to communicate with node E. As a prerequisite for a secure communication, node A requests for a trust level for node E. Since E is not in a communication range of the node A, it will broadcast the RRQ message to its neighbors.

Node B, C and D can directly communicate with node A

Node A, C, D and E can directly communicate with node B

Node A, B and E can directly communicate with node C

Node A, B and E can directly communicate with node D

Node B, C and D can directly communicate with node E

As stated above, as a part of secure communication with node E, node A broadcasts RRQ to request. Here, node A and E is not in a direct communication link of each other. Neighbours of node A viz. node B, C and D, will receive the RRQ packets and fortunately, all of these nodes are in a direct radio communication rage of node E. All of these nodes have calculated the trust level of node E previously, using the equation (1).

Figure 14. Requesting trust level of out of range node

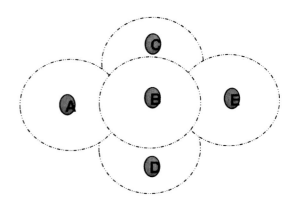

Figure 15. Transmitting fictitious recommendations

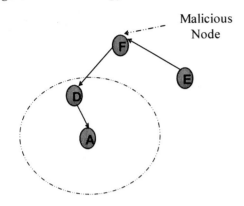

Malicious Node

A   B :   A,rrqA01,E
A   C :   A,rrqA01,E
A   D :   A,rrqA01,E

As a recommendation reply each node will send its own recommendation to node A – the requestor.

B   A :   A,rrqA01,B,E,2
C   A :   A,rrqA01,C,E,3
D   A :   A,rrqA01,D,E,2

Node A will calculate the trust level as follows. Initially,

- Node A trust node B value 1
- Node A trust node C value 3.5
- Node A trust node D value 5

Recommendations about node E from the neighbours of node A.

- Node B trust node E value 2
- Node C trust node E value 3
- Node D trust node E value 2

As per Equation (2)

Sr = 9.5

As per Equation (3)

$T_{Rr(B)} = 0.21$
$T_{Rr(C)} = 1.11$
$T_{Rr(D)} = 1.05$

Finally, Trust of Node A in a Target Node E according to the equation (4)

$T_t = 2.37$

The recommended proposal computes the global trust of the target node depending on its neighbour's recommendations and their trust levels. Each intermediate node computes the recommended trust value and forwards it to the requester. In this way, the original requester computes the final trust value of the target node.

ADVANTAGES OF THE PROPOSED SCHEME

As stated above, this scheme is proposed based on the idea described in [12]. The proposed scheme has significant variations and their benefits as follows.

1. The RRQ and recommendation reply messages are simple and do not contain unnecessary parameters and hence it reduces the overhead generated in the network.
2. Each node itself computes the proportional trust level of its neighbors and forwards it to the requester. Thus, there is no need of sending the list of intermediate recommenders in form of rec_path or rec_slip.
3. We do not calculate the trust for any specific category. We are calculating the global trust, based on SID, hello beacons and acknowledgements.
4. As stated earlier, in case of any change in the trust value of any active node, the recommender will re-recommend the changed trust value to the requestor, with the help of the forward path established previously. Hence, we do not maintain any Expiry Timer.
5. The original requester node calculates the trust level of target node in proportion with the trust level of his neighbourhood territory. The main reason behind having proportion based is to falsify any stale updates – recommendation during the intermediate trust level calculation. For example, even if node A has a trust value 5 for node D, still it takes only 53% of its recommendation. This is because node D might have

Scenario 1

Trust →	A in B	A in C	A in D	B in E	C in E	D in E	Final Trust for E
Trust Value	1	3.5	5	2	3	2	**2.37**
→	10.53	36.84	52.63	0.21	1.11	1.05	
	Percentage of Trust			Trust Proportion			

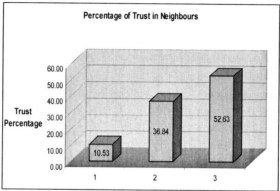

Percentage of Trust in A's Neighbours

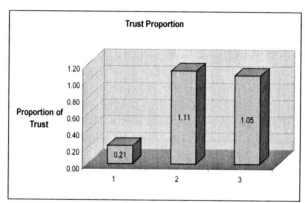

Calculated Recommended Trust Proportion by Node A

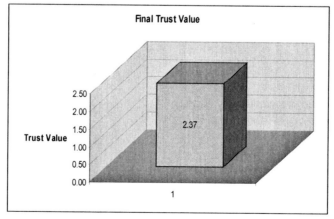

Final Trust Value of Node E, Calculated by Node A

Scenario 2

Trust →	A in B	A in C	A in D	B in E	C in E	D in E	Final Trust for E
Trust Value	1	3.5	5	5	3	2	**2.68**
→	10.53	36.84	52.63	0.53	1.11	1.05	
	Percentage of Trust			**Trust Proportion**			

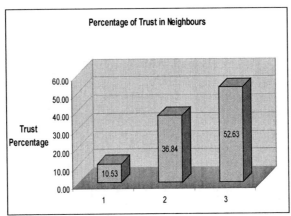

Percentage of Trust in A's Neighbours

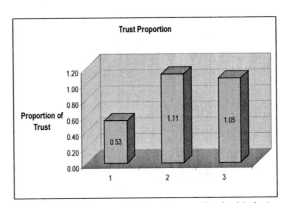

Calculated Recommended Trust Proportion by Node A

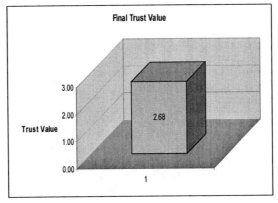

Final Trust Value of Node E, Calculated by Node A

Scenario 3

Trust →	A in B	A in C	A in D	B in E	C in E	D in E	Final Trust for E
Trust Value	1	3.5	5	2	3	5	**3.95**
→	10.53	36.84	52.63	0.53	1.11	2.63	
	Percentage of Trust			**Trust Proportion**			

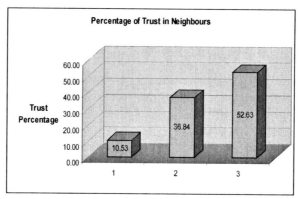

Percentage of Trust in A's Neighbours

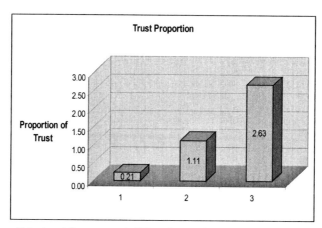

Calculated Recommended Trust Proportion by Node A

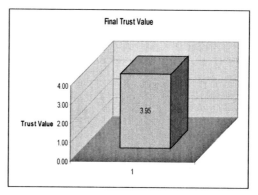

Final Trust Value of Node E, Calculated by Node A

received a recommendation from a malicious node, thus, we are judging the recommendation based on the trust proportion of a node in the neighbourhood and refining the trust level largely, which in turn helps in eradicating any major effects of malicious recommendations on a trust value.

In the above example, assuming that, if a node A has a trust value 4 for node D, then it would have considered 47% of its recommendation. Thus, this scheme takes a fair and proportion based recommendations from its neighbors rather than blindly trusting a neighbor with a higher trust.

Comparison of Above Scenarios

Initially in scenario 1 we have,

- Node A trust node B value 1
- Node A trust node C value 3.5
- Node A trust node D value 5

Recommendations about node E from the neighbours of node A.

- Node B trust node E value 2
- Node C trust node E value 3
- Node D trust node E value 2
- Using equations (2), (3) and (4) we get final trust value **2.37** for node E.

As stated earlier, while computing recommendations from various neighbours, we do not trust any node completely; rather we take percentage-based proportions of the recommended trust values. Thus, we implement fair and unbiased recommendation computation mechanism. We are considering recommended trust proportions based on the trust in neighbour. In above scenario node A trusts node D value 5, which is the highest of all, where as node A trusts node B value 1, which is the lowest. Thus, the node B's recommended value has very little significance over node D.

In scenario 2 node B recommends its trust value 5 for node E, still over all trust computed by node A has a little variance from **2.37** to **2.68**. This is because of the smaller trust proportion of recommended trust value by node B. On the contrary, in scenario 3, when a highly trusted node D changes its recommendation value from 2 to 5, over all trust value of node E also changed significantly from **2.37** to **3.95**.

The above description shows that we are considering recommended trust value based on a recommender's behaviour and trust level in the network. This feature allows us to nullify any malicious recommendations. Instead of trusting or prioritising any one node (generally, the highly trusted node), we consider some portion of the recommended values by all the neighbours.

CONCLUSION

The proposed system improves the existing system in various ways to ensure the non-detrimental networking operation.

- A global trust calculation based on overall behaviour helps in quantifying network node's trustworthiness in all-round manner.
- Proportion based trust calculation by each intermediate node helps nullify the recommendation from a malicious node.
- By adopting the above-mentioned techniques, this mechanism helps in selecting a secure communication path in a collaborative manner.
- Operation of the above protocol is fairly similar to that of AODV protocol in terms of informing the neighbours about the malicious activity or change in trust level. Thus, it can be easily employed with *reactive routing protocols.*

LIMITATIONS AND SHORTCOMINGS OF THE PROPOSED SCHEME

There are serveral shortcomings of the proposed scheme as follows:

- Since the proposed protocol is designed to prevent DoS attacks, it does not calculate the trust level in any perticular category, hence it may not help in selecting a route demanding a quality of service (higher bandwidth etc.)
- Each node computes its own trust level rather than simply forwding it to the requester, it may take more processing power and time to generate and forward its recommendation.
- I have ignored the memory requirements for storing reputations and behaviour of the recommen-

dation protocol (since it is not being implemented and tested in any kind of live environment)

FUTURE WORK

- Due to time and page limit constraints, I am not able to discuss on *"Battery Power Savining Option"*. As a future research, I would like work on a solution to save the battery power, which can be employed with the proposed turst computation scheme, based on the characteristics of collaborative operation and trust relationship in the network.
- Improvements in the proposed scheme to provide the Quality of Service (QoS) along with the secure and trustworthy communication.

REFERENCES

http://moment.cs.ucsb.edu/AODV/aodv.html#Description (Accessed on 16/05/06)

Abdul-Rahman, A., & Halles, S. (1997). A Distributed Trust Model. *New Security Paradigms Workshop, Proceedings of the 1997 workshop on New security paradigms.* (pp. 48-60).

Candolin, C., & Kari, H. H. (1997). Distributing Incomplete Trust in Wireless Ad Hoc Networks. *In Proceedings of the New Security Paradigms Workshop.* ACM

Diego, G. (2000). Can We Trust? In G, Diego (ed.) *Trust.*

Dykes, S. G. (n/d). *An Adaptive Ad Hoc Routing Network for Mobile Wireless Devices.* 10-9373. Texas: Southwest Research Institute

Making and Breaking Cooperative Relations (n/d). *Electronic edition.* Department of Sociology, University of Oxford. (pp. 213-237).

Perkins, C., Royer, E., Das, S., & Chakeres, I. (n/d). *Ad hoc On-Demand Distance Vector Routing (AODV).* Mobility Management and Networking (MOMENT) Laboratory, University of California, Santa Barbara.

Perkins, C., & Royer, E. (1999). Ad hoc on-demand distance vector routing. *In Proc. IEEE Workshop on Mobile Computing Systems and Applications.*

Pirzada, A. A., & McDonald, C. (n/d). Establishing Trust in Pure Ad-hoc Networks. *ACM International Conference Proceeding Series, 56; Proceedings of the 27th conference on Australasian Computer Science, 26,* 47-54.

Scheier, B. (1997, March). Why Cryptography is Harder than it Looks. *Information Security Bulletin, 2*(2), 31-36. Available at http://www.schneier.com/essay-037.html > (Accessed on 16/05/06).

Webb, W. *(n/d).* The Future of Wireless Communication. *Mobile Communication Series. Artechhouse Publishers.*

Wikipedia - The Free Encyclopaedia, http://en.wikipedia.org/wiki/Wireless_networks

Wireless Networking Q&A, Vicomsoft. (Accessed on 16/05/06), http://www.vicomsoft.com/knowledge/reference/wireless1.html#1

Wong, K. D., Kwon, T.-J., & Varma, V. (2004, March). Towards Commercialization of Ad Hoc Networks. *IEEE ICNSC 2004, Taipei, Taiwan,* (pp. 1207-1211).

Yang, H., Meng, X., Lu, S. (n/d). Self-organized network-layer security in mobile ad hoc networks. *Proceedings of the 3rd ACM workshop on Wireless Security.*

Zhou, L., & Hass, Z. J. (1999, November). Securing Ad Hoc Networks. *IEEE Network Magazine, 13(6),* 24-30.

Chapter LI
Data Warehousing and Decision Support in Mobile Wireless Patient Monitoring

Barin N. Nag
Department of Management, Towson University, USA

Mark Siegal
National Library of Medicine, USA

ABSTRACT

The recent advances in wireless communication technologies have made possible the development of wireless systems for monitoring the health and disease status of patients, in both in-patient hospital settings and outside. The volume of patient monitoring data requires Data Warehousing technologies for storage intended for analysis. The analysis is performed by Decision Support Systems (DSS) that provide clinical diagnoses and treatment methodology consistent with the urgency. The clinical DSS is critical in the analysis of a volume of data beyond the capabilities of a healthcare professional, and is effective in reducing workload, saving money, and providing better care for patients. This chapter also analyzes the technical aspects of the process.

INTRODUCTION

In recent years, the developments in wireless communication systems and technologies have made communication and data transfer capabilities ubiquitous and independent of location, with the possibility of transferring large amounts of data from a mobile location. The users and beneficiaries of this technology include consumers, businesses, and public services [Chaudhry *et al.* 2007]. The mobile technology includes cellular telephones, Internet systems with WiFi, and wireless radio communication.

One area in which wireless communication systems have been increasingly useful, although not as well known, is in clinical data systems and patient monitoring [Falas *et al.* 2003]. The wireless networks and technologies have allowed for a variety of systems for monitoring the health and disease status of patients, such as imaging test results and vital signs such as heart rate and blood pressure, both inside and outside of hospital settings [Koutkias *et al.* 2005]. These wireless patient monitoring systems provide a veritable deluge of data, and *Decision Support Systems* (DSS) are critical elements of processing and analyzing this data [Myers 2003]. Examples of these DSS for wireless patient monitoring include a system to let physicians diagnose a heart attack in the ambulance by sending electrocardiogram (ECG) data to the hospital, or children with diabetes using a cell phone as a glucose meter and disease monitor [Belazzi *et al.* 2003], and hospital patients that are free of wires but surrounded by automated warnings for their vital signs.

Three of the most common issues of clinical DSS for wireless patient monitoring are data management, data visualization, and data mining and artificial intelligence. After a statement of the background on the medical rationale and technical background for these systems, each of these types of DSS will be explored in turn.

MEDICAL RATIONALE

The rationale for DSS in wireless patient monitoring includes saving lives by faster diagnoses and treatments, faster turnaround and reduced workload for hospital staff saving money for hospitals, health insurance companies, and the patients [Eisenstein 2006]. The necessity of DSS arises because patient monitoring systems generate large volumes of data that is too much for the doctors and nurses to analyze [Abidi 2001].

DSSs are useful for managing, analyzing, and making decisions on large volumes of clinical data obtained from patient monitoring systems. For example, when patient monitoring is continuous, there is more data than can be analyzed by a health care professional [Falas *et al.* 2003]. The targeted users for these DSS consist of doctors and nurses, to aid in diagnoses and direct patient care, patients to facilitate self-maintenance of their conditions, hospital administrators in improving the ability to allocate hospital resources, and public health officials to use the abstracted data from these monitoring systems to provide high-level insights into public health matters [Nanningo & Abu-Hanna 2006].

Any disease or condition can use DSS for wireless patient monitoring, and a wide variety are seen in the literature and in practice. These systems are most useful for chronic diseases or acute attacks [Farmer *et al.* 2005]. These are the scenarios where the patient is at a recurring risk for health difficulties, and thus continual monitoring is preferable. These DSS are applicable to many medical situations, in the hospital, in transport, or elsewhere [Gouaux *et al.* 2003].

There are several important diseases and conditions that are prime targets for patient monitoring. One of the most common diseases in these systems is heart disease [Conforti *et al.* 2006]. Diabetes is one such disease that is common for patient monitoring using cellular networks [Farmer *et al.* 2005], in particular for regular glucose monitoring [Jun *et al.* 2006]. Another condition is sleep apnea, which is when a patient briefly stops breathing repeatedly in the night [Ishida *et al.* 2005]. Asthma is another example, because this common breathing illness leads to attacks that can be deadly if not treated [Ryan *et al.* 2005]. Other examples include wound maintenance care [Braun *et al.* 2005], dialysis [Nakamoto *et al.* 2003], urology [Liatsikos *et al.* 2004], and monitoring the health and safety status of the elderly [Lin *et al.* 2006].

TECHNICAL BACKGROUND OF WIRELESS PATIENT MONITORING

The timeline of patient monitoring reflects the development of technology. One of the earliest examples of transmitting patient data by telephone was in 1906 when Willem Einthoven used a telephone line to send an electrocardiogram (*ECG*) [Hofmann 1996]. When mobile cellular technology arrived, the new and convenient technology was the logical choice to transmit patient data. Although cellular technology began in the late 1940s, it was only in the mid 1980s when the 1G (*1st-generation*) cellular networks were deployed, and these networks began to see use for transmitting patient monitoring data [Shimuzu 1992]. Two-way radio telemetry was then being used to transmit ECGs from ambulances to hospitals [Pozen *et al.* 1977].

The equipment for the initial 1G or first-generation networks were bulky, and use was initially limited to vehicles, such as in patient monitoring during patient transport by ambulance to hospital. In the early days of mobile technology, a general concern about emergencies and disasters was disaster-related secondary communications traffic, *e.g.* individuals attempting to contact their friends and family might overwhelm the local cell preventing the use of the cellular networks for emergency-related transmission of patient data [Koehler 1990]. Since the mid-1990s, these various wireless technologies have become increasingly commonplace and advanced, and useful for clinical Decision Support Systems (*DSS*) [Stacey and McGregor 2007]. In modern times, common wireless technologies using DSS for remote patient monitoring, are cellular phone, satellite phone, WiFi, and Bluetooth. Each of these technologies are compared and described in more detail below.

Cellular Telephones

Cellular telephone technology is a system of mobile radio communication that is characterized by an extensive network of many low-power transmitters. The cells have a hexagonal geometry to allow for equal coverage with the antennas equidistant from each other [Stallings 2006]. Several cellular networks coexist throughout the United States and the rest of the world, and they are broadly categorized by first generation, second generation, and third generation, referred to as 1G, 2G, and 3G, respectively. While 1G cellular systems used analog signals and were low bandwidth, 2G and 3G networks are digital networks. These more recent networks provide higher bandwidth and capabilities for internet access and multimedia services.

Mobile telephone technology is used worldwide in metropolitan and rural areas, and is affordable, convenient, and widespread. Cell coverage is available almost everywhere, and is experiencing rapid growth. Some of the technical concerns with cellular telephone networks in general include quality of service, security, and compatibility between networks of different service providers. Quality-of-service issues include signal strength and fading. Fading in particular is a major technical concern with cellular communication, including multipath propagation. There is also some risk of environmental damage based on the growth of these networks [Scharnhorst 2006]. Cell phone networks are a useful existing network upon which to build telemedicine equipment for patient monitoring.

The advantages of cellular systems are their prevalence and widespread use. They are resources for transmitting patient data in transporting patients in an ambulance or in a *Medevac* helicopter. Data transmission would not be possible otherwise in transportation situations. Lives can be saved by the capability to transmit data with mobile systems. The fear that cellular telephone signals could interfere with other medical equipment being used in a hospital with dangerous effects has been shown to be largely unfounded [Ruskin 2006].

WiFi

Wireless Fidelity, or WiFi as it is more commonly known, is a type of wireless networking that has become extremely popular for wireless LANs [Yu and Chang 2005]. This includes the wireless Ethernet standard IEEE 802.11 and its variants 802.11g, 802.11n, etc. WiFi is used very commonly in home settings, with an increasing number of home users already having wireless WiFi routers at home for their internet access. Therefore, WiFi is useful for both patient monitoring in the home, as well as in hospitals [Smith *et al.* 2006].

The speeds can be significantly faster than cellular telephones, though not as fast as wired LANs. The cost tends to be lower than for cellular networks, especially because one is not charged for per-minute usage charges. The security is on par with that of cellular phone usage, as least with modern versions of the 802.11 standards. The range of transmission is on the order of 100 meters [Campbell & Durignon 2003]. The weakness of WiFi in comparison to cellular phones is that these are local networks [Park & Kim 2003]. WiFi has hotspots in individual areas, but not the widespread coverage offered by cellular telephone networks [Scanlon *et al.* 1996]. Thus, a WiFi connection may be used for a small area such as a house or a hospital for applications as for monitoring of implanted artificial hearts, but not for patient monitoring scenarios of patient transport in an ambulance or Medevac helicopter, or when a patient is traveling. WiFi can still be used locally in patient transport systems to minimize the use of wiring for the equipment used within the vehicle [Lin *et al.* 2004].

Bluetooth

As with WiFi technology, Bluetooth can also be quite effective for monitoring vital signs and similar biosignals in a hospital setting [Yu & Cheng 2005], and help the mobility of patients and healthcare providers [Bhatikar *et al.* 2002]. Bluetooth technology is also useful for creating a network between a wearable patient monitor during home care [Salamon *et al.* 2005]. These devices can connect to a computer located in the home and that then relay data across the Web to a centralized database, or directly to the physician. These technologies can allow for "plug and play" ability for setting the equipment up [Yao *et al.* 2005].

Bluetooth is a form of wireless connectivity that is specifically for much smaller ranges [Roth *et al.* 2002], on the order of 10 meters versus 100 meters for WiFi, and as compared to coverage nearly everywhere for cellular phones [Park & Kim 2003]. The range is thus even lower than WiFi and much lower than cellular phones. However, the cost is also lower. Security is higher in the sense that the range is smaller and thus there is a smaller area to be concerned about in terms of someone else listening into the data. Many of the analyses mentioned for WiFi are also applicable to Bluetooth, although there are also differences [Kim *et al.* 2005]. The limited range of Bluetooth means that it cannot be used for ambulatory or fully mobile environments.

CLINICAL DSS FOR WIRELESS PATIENT MONITORING

The area of DSS in Wireless Patient Monitoring has been the least explored. Using the Simon model of decision making, the four phases of decision making are implementation, choice, design, and intelligence. Within this framework, these three types of DSS most closely fall under the intelligence and implementation phases. However, these DSS can touch on all four areas of the Simon model, depending on the particular system in question [Herbert *et al.* 2006]. Decision support through data mining has been explored in [Rupnik *et al.* 2007]. Further data mining frameworks are analyzed in [Berzal *et al.* 2002]. A mobile clinical support system for pediatric emergencies is described in [Michaelowski 2003]. Some of the issues are discussed below.

Data Management

Data management can be defined as improving how wireless patient data is collected, transmitted, stored, and queried. Some examples include wireless transmission of ECGs from ambulances to the hospital, wearable devices to monitor chronic diseases such as diabetes while at home [Black *et al.* 2005], storing patient data automatically into databases or electronic health records [Celi *et al.* 2001], and automated alerts when vital signs go outside normal range [Stacey & McGregor 2007].

The core framework of DSS wireless patient monitoring requires only three components: a device to collect some form or forms of patient data, a wireless transmitter to send that data, and someone or something to receive that data. Any of the wireless networks can be used, with advantages and disadvantages for each. There are many types of patient data that can be monitored and transmitted over these networks. As mentioned above, ECG data for heart disease is a prime example. Another example is the vital signs, or basic measurements of heart rate, blood pressure, and

temperature, which are indicators for a wide range of illnesses, and for noting the trajectory of a patient's condition. The networks can be used for imaging data, *e.g.* X-ray scans and other radiological images. In fact, any type of biomedical signals can be used for patient monitoring over cellular telephone networks [Johnston *et al.* 2005]. In emergency circumstances, the time saved by transmitting data has the potential to save lives.

Visualization

Visualization refers to the graphical analyses of trends and outliers in patient data. A Dashboard for hospital administrators is one example of visualization, for these decision makers to observe status of each department. An example of visualization is showing scatterplots of blood glucose levels over time to diabetes patients [Bellazzi *et al.* 2002]. In a chronic illness it is highly useful to be able to see trends in the data over time. Another common use of visualization is in imaging test results, such as x-ray and MRI scans.

Data Mining and Artificial Intelligence

Data Mining (DM) refers to automated knowledge discovery from databases and device signals for decision support. Typically, methods of DM in clinical DSS are of Artificial Intelligence (AI), and not those of statistical analysis. Key examples of DM and AI include neural networks to suggest diagnoses and treatments for the doctor or nurse [Armstrong & Haston 1997], for patient self-monitoring systems [Biermann *et al.* 2003], or public health official searching for patterns in epidemiology through large quantities of disease patterns in the data from many patients [Saeed *et al.* 2002]. A mobile clinical support system using Palm PDAs is described in [Michaelowski *et al.* 2003].

Another important method, particularly for high-risk patients who have already suffered from heart attacks and heart disease in the past, is for the patient to wear a portable monitor at home throughout the day, with regular transmission of vital signs to the hospital for monitoring and automated analysis in a heart attack context [Bhatikar *et al.* 2003]. Heart disease is a particularly useful application for patient monitoring because heart failure can be detected in its early stages over a period of days or weeks prior to a specific heart failure event, and thus can be treated if detected early [Chaudhry *et al.* 2007].

AI systems are crucial for implanted organs such as artificial hearts or automated defibrillators [Okamoto *et al.* 1999]. Self-regulating computer programs are administered via a computerized device that is typically worn at the waist or sometimes is completely internal, and which communicates with the implanted organ via wireless signals such as Bluetooth [Eisenstein 2006]. These systems can themselves monitor the implants to make sure that everything is going acceptably [Nam *et al.* 2006], and if case of a problem call the doctor or health care environment for help [Mussivand *et al.* 1997]. Because these devices are directly and immediately responsible for sustaining the life of the patient, they must have local decision making capability in a time-critical situation [Nannings & Abu-Hanna 2006].

FUTURE DIRECTIONS AND CONCLUSION

However, much of the available literature suggests that these networks are still largely in the proof-of-concept phase, rather than being actively deployed. This is particularly true of the more advanced forms of these cellular network patient monitoring uses, such as realtime exchange of image-heavy data or other multimedia uses [Koch 2006]. Clinical trials and interventions are being used to test the effectiveness of patient monitoring systems.

One aspect of the future for these networks is the increased proliferation and penetration of these installations using the currently available systems [Rubel *et al.* 2004]. With the advent of 2G and 3G networks, the technology is available, inexpensive, and widespread. Further, with time patients and healthcare providers become more used to the technologies used. At the same time the monitoring equipment technology is improving, with reduced cost, compact size, and greater precision in data acquisition. Some devices could be miniaturized to the point that they are embedded in "smart clothing" [Lymberis & Olson 2003].

Wireless communication has innovative uses in clinical DSS for patient monitoring, especially for chronic disease and acute attacks. Particular areas of DSS in which this is the case are data management, visualization, and data mining and artificial intelligence.

These wireless networks are ever more commonplace and reliable, and progressively less expensive. These factors make wireless networks a prime target for DSS transmission of patient monitoring data. The usage of cellular and other networks is likely to only increase as time goes on, due to lowering costs and improved data rates and further miniaturization of equipment. In view of the improved treatment provided by mobile data transmission and automated decision making, and their life-saving characteristics, it is evident that these technologies will see increasing use.

REFERENCES

Abidi, S. S. (2001). An intelligent tele-healthcare environment offering person-centric and wellness-maintenance services. *Journal of Medical Systems, 25*(3), 147-65.

Armstrong, I. J, & Haston, W.S. (1997). Medical decision support for remote general practitioners using telemedicine. *Journal of Telemedicine and Telecare, 3*(1), 27-34.

Bellazzi, R., Larizza, C., Montani, S., Riva, A., Stefanelli, M., & d'Annunzio, G. (2002). A telemedicine support for diabetes management: The T-IDDM project. *Computer Methods and Programs in Biomedicine, 69*(2), 147-61.

Berzal, F., Blanco, I., Cubero, J-C., & Marin, N. (2002). Component-based Data Mining Frameworks. *Communications of the ACM, 45*(12), 97-100.

Bhatikar, S. R., Mahajan, R. L., & DeGroff, C. (2002). A novel paradigm for telemedicine using the personal bio-monitor. *Biomedical Sciences Instrumentation, 38*, 59-70.

Biermann, E., Rihl, J., Schenker, M., & Standl, E. (2003). Semi-automatic generation of medical tele-expert opinion for primary care physician. *Methods of Information in Medicine, 42*(3), 212-219.

Black, L., McMeel, C., McTear, M., Black, N., Harper, R., & Lemon, M. (2005). Implementing autonomy in a diabetes management system. *Journal of Telemedicine and Telecare, 11*(1), 6-8.

Braun, R. P., Vecchietti, J. L., Thomas, L., Prins, C., French, L. E., & Gewirtzman, A. J. (2005). Telemedical wound care using a new generation of mobile telephones: a feasibility study. *Archives of Dermatology, 141*(2), 254-258.

Campbell, R. J., & Durigon, L. M. (2003). Wireless Communication in Health Care: Who Will Win the

Right to Send Data Boldly Where No Data Has Gone Before? *Health Care Manager, 22*(3), 233-240.

Celi, L. A., Hassan, E., Marquardt, C., Breslow, M., & Rosenfeld, B. (2001). The eICU: It's not just telemedicine. *Critical Care Medicine, 29*(8), 183-189.

Chaudhry, S. I., Phillips, C. O., Stewart, S. S., Riegel, B., Mattera, J. A., & Jerant, A. F. (2007). Telemonitoring for patients with chronic heart failure: a systematic review. *Journal of Cardiac Failure, 13*(1), 56-62.

Choi, J., Park, J. W., Min, J. C., & Min, B. G. (2005). An intelligent remote monitoring system for artificial heart. *IEEE Transactions on Information Technology in Biomedicine, 9*(4), 564-573.

Conforti, D., Costanzo, D., Perticone, F., Parati, G., Kawecka-Jaszcz, K., & Marsh, A. (2006). HEART-FAID: A knowledge based platform of services for supporting medical-clinical management of heart failure within elderly population. *Studies in Health Technology and Informatics, 121*, 108-125.

Eisenstein, E. L. (2006). Conducting an economic analysis to assess the electrocardiogram's value. *Journal of Electrocardiology, 39*(2), 241-247.

Falas, T., Papadopoulos, G., & Stafylopatis, A. (2003). A review of decision support systems in telecare. *Journal of Medical Systems, 27*(4), 347-356.

Farmer, A., Gibson, O.J., Tarassenko, L., & Neil, A. (2005). A systematic review of telemedicine interventions to support blood glucose self-monitoring in diabetes. *Diabetic Medicine, 22*(10), 1372-1378.

Gouaux, F., Chautemps, L. S., Fayn, J., Adami, S., Arzi, M., Assanelli, D. (2003). Pervasive self-care solutions in telecardiology: Typical use cases from the EPI-MEDICS project. *Studies in Health Technology and Informatics, 95*, 119-24.

Hebert, M.A., Korabek, B., & Scott, R.E. (2006). Moving research into practice: A decision framework for integrating home telehealth into chronic illness care. *International Journal of Medical Informatics, 75*(12), 786-94.

Hofmann, B. (1996). A multiparameter, PC-based telemetry unit for biomedical signals. *Journal of Telemedicine and Telecare, 2*(3), 143-7.

Ishida, R., Yonezawa, Y., Maki, H., Ogawa, H., Ninomiya, I., & Sada, K. (2005). A wearable, mobile phone-based respiration monitoring system for sleep apnea syndrome detection. *Biomedical Sciences Instrumentation, 41*, 289-93.

Johnston, W.K., Patel, B.N., Low, R.K., & Das, S. (2005). Wireless teleradiology for renal colic and renal trauma. *Journal of Endourology, 19*(1), 32-36.

Jun, B., Park, K., Kim, S., Park, M., Kim, K., & Lee, T. (2006). Miniatured blood glucose measurement module interfaced with cellular phone. *Studies in Health Technology and Informatics, 122*, 859.

Kim, D., Yoo, S.K., & Kim, S.H. (2005). Instant wireless transmission of radiological images using a personal digital assistant phone for emergency teleconsultation. *Journal of Telemedicine and Telecare 11* Suppl 2, S58-61.

Koch, S. (2006). Home telehealth--current state and future trends. *International Journal of Medical Informatics, 75*(8), 565-76.

Koehler, G.A. (1990). Cellular communication. *Emergency Medical Services, 19*(9), 13-14.

Koutkias, V.G., Chouvarda, I., & N. Maglaveras, N. (2005). A multiagent system enhancing home-care health services for chronic disease management. *IEEE Transactions on Information Technology in Biomedicine, 9*(4), 528-37.

Liatsikos, E.N., L. Gortzis, G. Nikiforidis, & G.A. Barbalias. (2004). Tele-diagnostic and therapeutic guidance in urology. *Journal of Endourology, 18*(7), 625-628.

Lin, C., Chiu, M., Hsiao, C., Lee, R., & Tsai, Y. (2006). Wireless health care service system for elderly with dementia. *IEEE Transactions on Information Technology in Biomedicine, 10*(4), 696-704.

Lin, Y., Jan, I., Ko, P.C., Chen, Y., Wong, J., & Jan, G. (2004). A wireless PDA-based physiological monitoring system for patient transport. *IEEE Transactions on Information Technology in Biomedicine, 8*(4), 439-447.

Lymberis, A., & Olsson, S. (2003). Intelligent biomedical clothing for personal health and disease management: state of the art and future vision. *Telemedicine Journal and e-Health, 9*(4), 379-386.

Michaelowski, W., Rubin, S., Slowinski, R., & Wilk, S. (2003). Mobile clinical support system for pediatric emergencies, *Decision Support Systems, 36*(2), 161-176.

Mussivand, T., A. Hum, A., Holmes, K.S., & Keon, W.J. (1997). Wireless monitoring and control for implantable rotary blood pumps. *Artificial Organs, 21*(7), 661-664.

Myers, M.B. (2003). Telemedicine: An Emerging Health Care Technology. *Health Care Manager, 22*(3), 219-223.

Nakamoto, H., A. Kawamoto, A., Tanabe, Y., Nakagawa, Y., Nishida, E., & Akiba, T. (2003). Telemedicine system using a cellular telephone for continuous ambulatory peritoneal dialysis patients. *Advances in Peritoneal Dialysis. Conference on Peritoneal Dialysis,19*, 124-129.

Nam, K.W., Chung, J., Choi, S.W., Sun, K., & Min, B.G. (2006). Wireless patient monitoring system for a moving-actuator type artificial heart. *The International Journal of Artificial Organs, 29*(10), 973-980.

Nannings, B., & Abu-Hanna, A. (2006). Characterizing Decision Support Telemedicine Systems. *Methods of Information in Medicine, 45*(5), 523-527.

Okamoto, E., M. Shimanaka, M., S. Suzuki, S., Baba, K., & Mitamura, Y. (1999). A remote monitoring system for patients with implantable ventricular assist devices with a personal handy phone system. *American Society for Artificial Internal Organs Journal, 45*(3), 194-198.

Park, D. G., & Kim, H. C. (2003). Comparative study of telecommunication methods for emergency telemedicine. *Journal of Telemedicine and Telecare, 9*(5), 300-303.

Pozen, M. W., D. D. Fried, D. D., Smith, S., Lindsay, L. V., & Voigt, G. C. (1977). The outcome of pre-hospital life-threatening arrhythmias in patients receiving electrocardiographic telemetry and therapeutic interventions. *American Journal of Public Health, 67*(6), 527-531.

Roth, H., Schwaibold, M., Moor, C., Schöchlin, J., & Bolz, A. (2002). Miniaturized module for the wireless transmission of measurements with Bluetooth. *Biomedizinische Technik, 47*, Suppl 1 Pt 2, 854-856.

Rubel, P., Fayn, J., Simon-Chautemps, L., Atoui, H., Ohlsson, M., & Telisson, D. (2004). New paradigms in telemedicine: ambient intelligence, wearable, pervasive and personalized. *Studies in Health Technology and Informatics, 108*, 123-132.

Rupnik, R., Kukar, M., & Krisper, M. (2007). Integrating Data Mining and Decision Support through Data Mining Based Decision Support System, *The Journal of Computer Information System, 47*(3), 89-97.

Ruskin, K.J. (2006). Communication devices in the operating room. *Current Opinion in Anaesthesiology, 19*(6), 655-659.

Ryan, D., W. Cobern, W., Wheeler, J., Price, D., & Tarassenko, L. (2005). Mobile phone technology in the management of asthma. *Journal of Telemedicine and Telecare, 11* Suppl 1, 43-46.

Saeed, M., Lieu, C., Raber, G., & Mark, R.G. (2002). MIMIC II: a massive temporal ICU patient database to support research in intelligent patient monitoring. *Computers in Cardiology, 29*, 641-644.

Salamon, D., Bei, A., Grigioni, M., Gianni, M., Liberti, M., & D'Inzeo, G. (2005). Indoor Telemedicine in Hospital: a PDA-based Flexible Solution for Wireless Monitoring and Database Integration. *Proceedings of Annual International Conference of the IEEE Engineering in Medicine and Biology Society. 1*, 386-389.

Scanlon, W.G., Evans, N.E., Crumley, G.C., & McCreesh, Z.M. (1996). Low-power radio telemetry: the potential for remote patient monitoring. *Journal of Telemedicine and Telecare, 2*(4), 185-191.

Scharnhorst, W., Hilty, L.M., & Jolliet, O. (2006). Life cycle assessment of second generation (2G) and third generation (3G) mobile phone networks. *Environment International, 32*(5), 656-675.

Shimizu, K. (1992). Telemedicine by mobile communication. *IEEE Engineering in Medicine and Biology Magazine, 18*(4), 32-44.

Smith, G.B., Prytherch, D.R., P. Schmidt, P., Featherstone, P.I., Knight, D., & Clements, G. (2006). Hospital-wide physiological surveillance-a new approach to the early identification and management of the sick patient. *Resuscitation, 71*(1), 19-28.

Stacey, M., & C. McGregor, C. (2007). Temporal abstraction in intelligent clinical data analysis: a survey. *Artificial Intelligence in Medicine, 39*(1), 1-24.

Stallings, W. (2006). *Data and Computer Communications*. Prentice Hall, Upper Saddle River, NJ.

Yao, J., Schmitz, R., & Warren, S. (2005). A wearable point-of-care system for home use that incorporates plug-and-play and wireless standards. *IEEE Transactions on Information Technology in Biomedicine, 9*(3), 363-371.

Yu, S., & Cheng, J. (2005). A Wireless Physiological Signal Monitoring System with Integrated Bluetooth and WiFi Technologies. *Proceedings of Annual International Conference of the IEEE Engineering in Medicine and Biology Society, 3*, 2203-6.

KEY TERMS

Artificial Intelligence (AI): Methods of simulating human intelligence in computing.

Clinical DSS: Decision Support Systems for clinical use.

Data Mining (DM): Searching (mining) for nuggets of information, usually using methods of AI.

Decision Support Systems (DSS): Systems to evaluate critical factors in support of decision making.

Mobile Data: Data generated by mobile wireless devices.

Patient Monitoring: Collecting real time patient clinical data.

Wireless Data: Data generated by mobile wireless devices (same as Mobile Data).

Section IV
Case Studies

Chapter LII
Case Studies in Mobile Business

Marco Garito
Digital Business, Italy

ABSTRACT

Th first part of this chapter deals with various mobile business applications and initiatives taken from real-life companies of which successfully implemented their go-to-market strategy in the wireless world. The structure of this chapter can be summarized into three main areas. At the beginning, the current market situation for mobile environment is described through highlighting how decreasing revenue is forcing companies to quickly innovate their offering to cope with highly intensive competition, justifying such an assumption with the flexible and open value chain. The second part is covering the Lateral Marketing approach in its main points under a theoretical point of view. Eventually, some examples of mobile applications and services are provided to reinforce the validity and need of Lateral Marketing to build reliable and durable growth.

INTRODUCTION

The saturated market of Mobile Business, companies are daily challenged to implement new ways to attract and maintain customers who have become more and more demanding and ready to change as soon as a novelty is placed on a shelf or promoted by media. The choice for business is between a traditional marketing approach which leads to a fast products and services turnover because they become obsolete and a completely new but risky approach such as the Lateral Marketing. This chapter describes how Lateral Marketing can be and has been implemented in companies around the world delivering stable and long lasting customer value.

MARKETING ENVIRONMENT: AN OVERVIEW

Mobile business is characterized by an extremely high number of brands, products and services, generating many parallel segments and niches which shorten the product/service life cycle: a decreasing ARPU (average revenue per user) hit seriously the sector, with many operators and carriers competing for very short run target (with the latest ring tone, wall paper, handset device, cover or accessory): this mean that when the item is broken, it is cheaper, faster and easier to replace it rather than repair it for tangible items, which impacts environment too and, if intangible, the deletion if the unwanted software is a matter of seconds.

Daily experience demonstrates that consumers and buyers are ready to try any new brand item they spot:

the effect is that every new product or service takes sales away from existing items on the shelf or cannibalize adjacent products of the same brands. Companies have created increasing number of segments and niches, causing a highly fragmented market.

The previous edition of this handbook (Unhelkar 2006) explained how and why it is possible to create a life style as an extension or "conceptual development" of brand to optimize profitability: Virgin is an example of a company who has been collecting holiday travels, mobile phones and retail shops, in their quest to anticipate consumer behavior (http://www. virgin.com).

Consumers are now more and more selective individuals regarding products and ads: novelty and outstanding effect can be the only way to catch their attention because markets are now more competitive: the number of advertising messages is increasing: recent research findings refer to approximately 1500 messages every day for every person (Kotler 2001) therefore it is paramount to think in a different way to promote new products and services.

VALUE CHAIN FOR TELECOMMUNICATION

The diagram below describes the value chain scenario for Telecommunication operators and carriers in terms of end-to-end flow from content creation to customer with the revenue source for each step indicated with curved lines.

It demonstrates that some entities might fall outside the traditional domain of telecommunication provider and, most importantly, some of those performing such activities are already in direct contact with customer: therefore there is a limited space for IT based only operators or new carriers as their development is both expensive and only a few of them can afford additional investment (and costs) after the not so rewarding bid for 3G licenses: the real challenge is to play outside the typical IT mindset and focus on new content and services to deliver. Software is already being sold as a service rather than a product via ASP (Application Service Provider) platforms, thus aggregating tools and services in some corporate areas such as Human Resources or Payroll (for example http://www.adp. com) and therefore the underneath business model is now based on different criteria.

THINKING TOPSIDE DOWN AND OUT OF THE BOX

New products and services in mobile business can be provided by splitting the marketing process in pieces and analyze it to understand which type of novelties can be created; we can therefore discriminate the market into the following categories: a person who needs something in a given moment in time: the solution of the concrete need and of the specific person or situation where a product or service can exist, constitutes a closed and comprehensive system identified as "category". While business define a market and create a space of

Figure 1. Value chain scenario for telecommunication

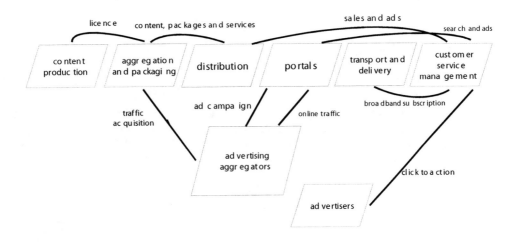

where company can compete, at the very same time it defines where company or business cannot be present (Kotler, 2001; Kotler, Trias de bes 2003). Marketers assume as fixed the element of a category as define a few lines above: it is a strong limitation that has been described in 70s in NLP research (Neuro-linguistic programming) where it is clearly defined the difference between "map" (i.e. where it is possible to go, what it is possible to do) and "territory" i.e. the hidden opportunities (Bandler, Grinder 1975)

The basic strategies through which product and service development happened in business can be identified as follows:

- Modulation: decrease or increase any basic characteristic of product or service
- Sizing: varying volume "only" without changing anything else
- Packaging: refers to the way a product or service is packaged, by modifying its perception of benefit, consumption or occasion
- Design based: product or services are the same but design or look is different.
- Innovation based: by adding some new ingredient in the feature of the basic product or service enabling variety creation
- Effort reduction: by reducing customer's effort and cost or risk involved in the purchase (Kotler 2001; Kotler, Trias de Bes 2003, De Bono 1970)

By opening categories, it is possible to design and execute a strategy to win over an overcrowded arena; the new market category is the most efficient way to compete in mature markets where micro-segmentation and an excess of brand do not leave enough room for new opportunities

LATERAL MARKETING

The traditional market approach develops within existing definitions: it is a logical sequence from a global perspective to a concrete one, specifically thought to create varieties; Lateral Marketing follows the opposite path, from a concrete dimension to a global one by reconstructing the existing scenario (Kotler 2001; Kotler, Trias de Bes 2003).

Lateral Marketing is based on reaching an expansion by approaching one or more needs, uses, targets or situation that have been eliminated during the process of market definition of a given product/service. Lateral marketing is a nevertheless a methodical process applicable to an existing product or service to eventually originate an innovation that can be a category, subcategory or market.

The step of lateral marketing can be summed up in the following points:

- Focus on one of the needs, use, target or situation: see figure 1 to identify this
- Lateral displacement, i.e. an "illogical" rethink of it that creates a gap
- Connection to fill this gap in a logical and workable way (Kotler 2001; Kotler, Trias de Bes 2003).

Once identified the focus, the lateral displacement intervenes: the challenge is to properly provide an answer to the stimulus originated by the gap as a consequence of lateral displacement and eventually find a logical connection.

This approach does not exclude the traditional vertical market, so the challenge is not to identify when one approach should be preferred to the other: the following table tries to provide an overview of the different scenarios

From a conceptual point of view, the acid test to discriminate lateral marketing from vertical marketing is the "gap": the absence of gap tells us that we are working within the same marketing categories (Kotler 2001; Kotler, Trias de Bes 2003).

From a practical point, the ways to get into lateral marketing can be:

- change it – invert it – combine it
- or, as Bob Eberle (1997) coined, the SCAMPER acronym, which stands for: substitute – combine – adapt – modify – put – eliminate (or reduce) – reorder (o invert)

It is possible to mention as example of this process, the "internet-cafe', places where people can use surf the web while drinking or eating or buying impulse shopping items in many cities and towns in the world. Mobile business gives us plenty of practical examples as to how mobile devices or services have been successfully used: mobile phones enabled to play music files or videos or provided with the capability of global positioning services (Kotler 2001; Kotler, Trias de Bes 2003, Michalko 2006).

The output of lateral market can be classified via these couple of identities:

Figure 2. Table of Vertical market and Lateral market characteristics

Vertical market	Lateral market
Newly created market or first stage of development process	Zero growth rate
When there is a need to convert potential customer into current customer; need to expand variety	Brand new market category creation; merging different business, reaching new targets
Low risk mindset	High risk mindset
Limited resources	More resources available or highly entrepreneurial attitude
Happy to have low but stable growth	Will to grow fast
Defensive strategy approach by creating new segments to make the markets less attractive	Aggressive approach disrupting current framework of competitors
Focus on current business	Redefine scoping of business and its mission

- same product with a new utility
- new product with a new utility
- same product with the same utility

The following diagram explains the process above described, regarding the internet café example

It is now introduced a collection of mobile business initiatives carried out by companies in different fields, of wireless technologies to validate the Lateral Marketing (LM) approach and show, through real life examples, how mobile business can advantage.

RADIO FREQUENCY IDENTIFICATION APPLICATIONS

RFID is a technique to retrieve and collect data, enabling automated identification to manage processes: its characteristics are a modifiable memory, and antenna and a given distance. The system has several advantages such as: flexibility, reliability, cost effectiveness and resistance; there are 4 set of frequencies: LF from 120/400 KHz, HF 13.56 MHz (the only one certified and recognized all over the world), UHF 860/980 MHz and Microwave 2.4/5.4 GHz. (Lahiri 2006)

The Municipality of Biella, (Italy) decided to use the RFID technology to protect its rhododendrons in some public parks: each plant was identified and mapped through GPS and data inserted into a transponder that has been buried (to avoid people to remove it). Person with a mobile device can read the story of each plant

Figure 3. Process of lateral marketing in Internet café

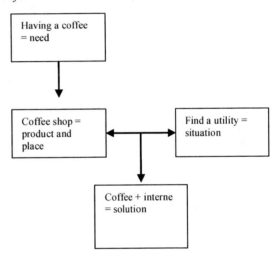

and at the same time the local government can fulfill environmental protection and give value to Public Park and visitors by adding a mobile technology, the Municipality created a more complete customer experience because visitors can get the data about the plant as much as they like and at the same time by making easier to protect their asset (the flowers) both financially and environmentally, have met their business and government objectives in terms of quality of services that local authorities are supposed to provide (Wireless Forum 2004)

The diagram below explains the innovative marketing process.

MOBILE PAYMENT

Companies can now use credit cards in a different way. This solution is available for retail and business customers and has been developed by a Banca Sella (http://www.sella.it) and Wind (http://www.wind.it) and provides secure, real time, cost effective wireless money transfer. Payments, transfers, deposits and withdrawals of money are executed by using credit card (Visa Electron) either pre paid or co branded and rechargeable, onto bank accounts or pre defined accounts.

For business environment, the solution fits into: corporate refunds, payment of incentives, other refunds, personal loans, retailers and e-government (for example m-ticketing and m-parking).

The company transfers real time a certain amount of money to its employee's special account that is linked with the credit card: therefore the company is not responsible to the bank, the balance can be used and filled up at any time. The employee can withdraw money everywhere at any time.

Each money transfer is notified by SMS: moreover the employee can recharge the card with his own money and have separate balance between personal money and company money. This system enables real time control of corporate expenses, before the money is actually spent and transferred to someone else's account) as the company knows who and when its money has been used: evidences and receipts will be lodged later by the employee, thus satisfying business controls and compliance regulations in place within the company.

The company can have its own bank account with a plafond (a capped amount of money) that is managed via web: at any time the company can transfer its money or recharge the credit card. Once the employee receives a SMS, he/she can use the balance everywhere. Cash flow details, transfers, refunds and any other operation are automatically and real time available. This solution is currently used for drivers (as the company does not know them, it is safe not to give them unlimited resources), sales force people, traveling workers.

The wireless solution has reordered a consolidated accounting process flow by providing a better visibility end-to-end and real time accuracy about sensitive information of disbursement (Wireless forum 2004).

The diagram below describes the lateral marketing process for mobile payment.

Mobile E-Health

A new mobility solution is keeping Northland district health nurses in touch – and helping to improve the health of residents in New Zealand. The local health service had to address the access to information and effectiveness of current processes used by district nurses when visiting patients in remote locations, nurses were able to access patient information, current schedules, and support for diagnosis and update the central system via i-mate Pocket PC supplied by Vodafone. Four key requirements of district nurses have been allocated to this initiative

1. Access to patient or medical data, either through existing databases, the web or colleagues via email or phone.
2. Capture patient data in the central database while on the road.
3. Schedule appointments or services for patients while on the road and access current schedules for appointments.
4. Enhanced safety and security through knowledge of nurses' whereabouts and advise nurses regularly of potential threats

Previously, patient information and data was captured on paper and scheduling appointments involving a paper diary. Diary information had to be transferred into official paper forms and sent through to base hospital via fax, mail or courier. This process was time and work intensive and, with multiple manual

Figure 4. Process of lateral marketing for RFID adoption in a park

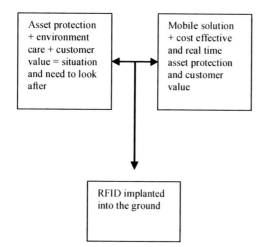

Figure 5. Process of lateral marketing for mobile payment

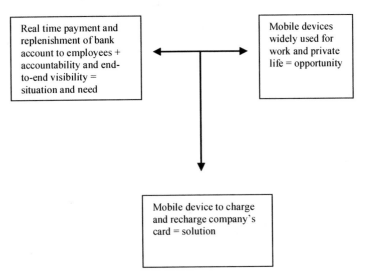

data entries, could result in inaccurate reporting. In addition, timely access to accurate information and support is crucial while nurses are in the district in a patient's home. Medical staff needs to make decisions based on a mix of the patient's past, current symptoms and other background healthcare knowledge. Remote environments mean nurses are far from data they would have access to in a hospital, where combining details from different sources make diagnosis more accurate. The technology solution is equally possible for other boards throughout the country, as the issues that nurses are facing are similar to those experienced in other regions. The new system streamlines current services and provides an easy-to-use integrated mobile tool for district nurses to minimize time spent on administrative tasks, enabling them to concentrate on caring for patients (http://www.nlh.co.nz ; http://www.istart. co.nz ; http://www.imate.com ; http://www.firstbase. co.nz ; http://www.vodafone.com).

Mobile solution changed the way medical staffs assess and take action upon patient's condition and the GPS capability of the system provides further benefit to healthcare organization as a whole and the diagram below describes and validates the process

MOBILE ADVERTISING

Response Ticketing wanted to find a totally integrated ticket sales solution that could complement their ex-

isting sales offices and online system. The company also needed a solution that could synchronize with its existing systems and easily be transported if clients – event hosts – needed to set up extra ticketing outlets at an event. The company sells tickets for events: the move was to enable purchasers to buy any time/any place, maximizing sales through giving customers the possibility to match and customize their preferences. The company is now providing event hosts with the technology and expertise to enable them to set up their own mobile ticketing outlets. Response ticketing clients can now quickly and easily start selling tickets from mobile outlets or combining fixed and mobile outlets. Customers only pay for the time spent transacting the data rather than paying to be online all the time. Speed is also a critical requirement for the mobile ticket points to be successful, allowing Response Ticketing to reassure its clients that, if necessary, the mobile ticketing application can quickly process queues of people and also make sure that the data is quickly integrated with other sales points. Where clients choose to administer a mobile ticketing outlet themselves, the company simply provides them with straight-forward training, deploys the system and then clients can start selling. The solution also helps to enhance clients' relationships with their sponsors because they can offer them the chance to get involved in the ticket sales process: a shortened value chain and faster time are typical effect of e-business transformation, enhanced in this case by mobile technology. Another advantage of the solution

Figure 6. Process of lateral marketing for mobile adoption in health service

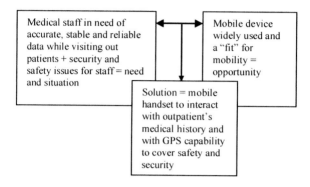

Figure 7. Process of lateral marketing for Mobile advertising solution

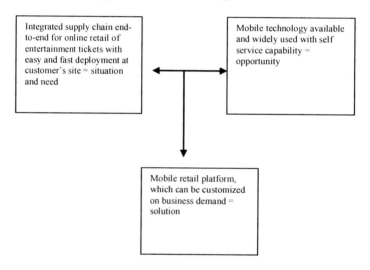

Figure 8. Process of lateral marketing for Mobile domain name

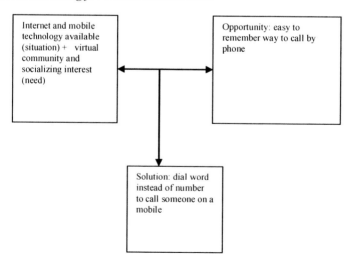

is that it's enhancing the level of customer service that Response Ticketing's clients can offer their customers. When people purchase tickets from mobile outlets, a full visual representation of the event's seating is displayed so that they can choose where they want to watch (http://www.istart.co.nz - http://www.telecom.co.nz – http://www.response.co.nz).

The described example demonstrates how it is possible to create customer value by adding mobile technology by combining infrastructure and content to have a unique sellable proposition.

MOBILE PERSONAL DOMAIN NAME

iTAGG (http://www.itagg.com) is a UK based company which enables to have a personal mobile domain name, a keyword on the short code 83248: any word is fine and mobile users can communicate by using a word instead of a number. iTAGGs come with a flexible set of facilities to help gather contact information, to distribute business details, to provide voting or subscription systems, to provide value-add information to your users, to provide a customer call-back service" (http://www.itagg.com) The possible applications encompass an SMS campaign data aggregation, an SMS marketing solution, workforce mobilization and so forth. If the mobile phone is WAP or color enabled, the user can access the map to get the right direction. The adoption of mobile technology combined with Location Based Services, can eventu-

ally split the market into two main segments: one for those using a regular phone (thus receiving a simple SMS) and those with advanced WAP or 3G devices who can enjoy an enhanced serviced, provided the fact that the SMS mode can be adopted as a default should the pub-goer be with an area not currently covered by 3G infrastructure.

M-GAMING

The same wireless technology has been used by Text-4Tips, another UK company – http://www.text4tips.net – to help beat the fruit machine: by sending a SMS with the word UNLOCK followed by the name of the machine to 83248, the caller will receive a message containing same clues about, to name a few, when to play and not to play, force the jackpot, which features pay more and less and so forth. This solution enables data capture and analysis by collecting the calls made by gamblers, regarding, for example, the most common or difficult or popular fruit machine type, the most attended venues where the machine is located, not to count peak and off peak game time. It is also possible to design and execute an entire CRM strategy.

CONCLUSION

The table below summarizes the Lateral Marketing cases so far analyzed through the SCAMPER lens

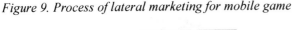

Figure 9. Process of lateral marketing for mobile game

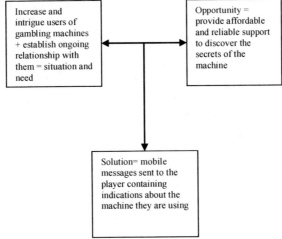

Figure 10. SCAMPER model against the case studies

Case study	S	C	A	M	P	E	R
RFID		X	X	X	X		
m-payment		X	X	X		X	X
e-health		X	X	X		X	
Mobile advertising		X	X	X			
Personal domain name		X	X	X	X		
M-gaming		X	X	X			
e-government	X	X	X			X	

Not each item of SCAMPER model applies to business in need of a revolutionary approach: marketer's task is to identify which is the best option to use in a timely manner to achieve the best result. Once again, execution is crucial. This chapter is just a suggestion of how to manage the challenge with a small portfolio of examples taken from business. The diagram explained at the beginning shows that value chain is extremely flexible (and vulnerable): it is marketer's task to identify the most appropriate entry gate and then by adopting the best possible technique, develop a breakthrough idea to implement in real business.

REFERENCES

Bundler, R., Grinder, J. (1975). *The structure of magic: A book about language and therapy.* Palo Alto Science and Behavior Book.

De Bono, E. (1970). *Lateral thinking.* London: Pelican.

Eberle, B. (1997). Scamper: Creative game and activities for imagination development. USA: Prufrock Press.

IBM Global Business Services (2007). A future in contention. IBM Institute for business value. IBM.

Kotler, P. (2001). Kotler on marketing. USA: Free Press.

Kotler, P., Tries de Bes, F. (2003). Lateral marketing New techniques for finding breakthrough ideas. USA: John Wiley.

Lahiri, S. (2006). *RFID Sourcebook.* USA: Pearson Plc.

Michalko, M. (2006). Cracking creativity. USA: Ten Speed Press.

Unhelkar, B. (2006). Handbook of research in mobile business. Hershey, PA: Idea Group.

Wireless Forum Fall (2004). Milan 24 November 2004 – speakers' notes.

WEB SITES

http://www.160characters.org

http://www.cgnz.com

http://www.firstbase.co.nz

http://www.healthfrontier.com

http://www.imate.com

http://www.inwind.it

http://www.istart.co.nz

http://www.itagg.com

http://www.nlh.co.nz

http://www.response.co.nz

http://www.sella.it

http://www.telecom.co.nz

http://www.text4tips.net

http://www.tim.it

http://www.vodafone.com

http://www.wilco-telephony.co.uk

http://www.wirelessforum.it

KEY TERMS

Bar Code: A machine-readable representation of information (usually dark ink on a light background to create high and low reflectance which is converted to 1s and 0s).

Lateral Marketing: New technique and marketing tools to find breakthrough ideas.

Location Based Services: Location Based Services (LBS) are information and entertainment services accessible with mobile devices through the mobile network and utilizing the ability to make use of the geographical position of the mobile device.

Mobile Advertising: Mobile advertising is a form of advertising via mobile (wireless) phones or other mobile devices. It is a subset of mobile marketing.

Mobile E-Health: Provision and supply of heath care via mobile device.

Mobile Payment: The collection of money from a consumer via a mobile device such as their mobile phone, SmartPhone, Personal Digital Assistant (PDA) or other such device.

Radio-Frequency Identification (RFID): An automatic identification method, relying on storing and remotely retrieving data using devices called RFID tags or transponders.

RFID Tag: An object that can be applied to or incorporated into a product, animal, or person for the purpose of identification using radio waves.

Chapter LIII
Secure Payment in Mobile Business:
A Case Study

Chitra Subramanian
Australia

ABSTRACT

Mobile commerce offers consumers the convenience and flexibility of mobile services anytime and at any place. Secured and private mobile business processes using a mobile gadget for payments are essential for the success of mobile commerce. Mobile payment is the process of two parties exchanging financial value using a mobile device in return for goods and services. This chapter is an analysis of the secure mobile payment services for real automated point of sale (PoS), which are frequently used in terminals such as vending machines.

INTRODUCTION

The term m-commerce (mobile commerce) is all about wireless e-commerce. Grosche& Knospe,(2002) as described, M-commerce is understood as use of mobile devices in order to do business on the Internet, either in the Business to Business (B2B) or Business to Consumer market (B2C).

The development of new mobile technologies and its increasing use day after day has created important commercial opportunities in the mobile commerce space. Mobile commerce that is now taking place in the market requires the introduction of mobile payment as a mechanism for completion of a transaction. The development of high speed mobile data networks that support the mobile devices have further created a new channel for commercial applications, where sophiscated mobile devices enable virtual exchange of payment information (S.Karnouskos, 2003). This chapter discusses the mechanism used in completing mobile transactions. Main contribution of this paper: a classification of mobile payment methods and a case study on the secure automatic mobile payment on vending machine.

BACKGROUND TO CASE STUDY

Mobile Payment (M-payment) is a critical component in m-commerce applications. According to the Wireless World Forum, M-payment on mobile devices will provide excellent business in coming years (Jerry Gao, 2005). Payment systems can be used by wireless based merchants, content provider, information and service providers to process and support payment transactions. Thus, the study of mobile payments is crucial to the success of mobile commerce. The discussion in this chapter, with respect of security in mobile payments, revolves around a case study. This case study illustrates two important factors which are essentials for a successful secure transaction and mobile payment systems involved currently. These factors are described in greater detail here.

Secure Transaction Essentials

Four properties are always considered essential for a secure transaction. These properties are authentication, confidentiality, integrity, and non-repudiation (Seema Nambiar, 2004). *Authentication* is concerned about verifying the identities of parties in a communication and confirming that they are who they claim to be. *Confidentiality* is about ensuring that only the sender and intended recipient of a message can read its content. *Integrity* is concerned about ensuring the content of the messages and transactions not being altered, whether accidentally or maliciously. *Non repudiation* is about providing mechanisms to guarantee that a party involved in a transaction cannot falsely claim later that she did not participate in that transaction (Seema Nambiar, 2004).

Major M-Payment Systems

Major M-payment Systems can be classified as:

- Account based Payment Systems
- Mobile Wallets
- Mobile Point of sale/service Payment Systems

Account Based Payment Systems

In account based payment systems, each customer is associated with a trusted third party (Chen, 2003). Transactions were either a post paid payment option or prepaid payment option. Here we can discuss about three types of account based payment systems.

- Mobile phone based payment systems - where customer can purchase goods or services through mobile phones. Example: Buying ringtones or subscribing for daily weather details.
- Smart card payment systems – where commuters, who could use a card to pay their fare at subway turnstile instead of standing in line to buy a token. People would hold the card--or phone or other device containing a card--within about 10 centimeters of a terminal, which would use wireless transmissions to send payment information.
- Credit card m-payment systems - where customers can make payments on mobile devices using their credit cards. A perfect example would be customers purchase goods from Ebay and pay via credit card.

Mobile Wallets

Mobile wallet is the most popular type of wireless transactions, which allows user to store the information while shopping with the mobile device. Secure Electronic Transactions (SET) technologies are already being used to provide secure transactions for merchants. MasterCard's using this technology for secure transactions.

Mobile Point of Sale/Service Payment Systems

Mobile PoS payment system that enables customers to purchase products on vending machines or at retail stores with their mobile phones. This payment system is planned to compliment existing credit card and smart card system for mobile users. At this time, there are two subdivisions of PoS payment systems (Jerry Gao, 2005).

a. Automated PoS payment systems, which are frequently used in terminals such as vending machines, photo booths and parking meters.
b. Attended PoS payment systems, which allow users to make payments with the assistance from a service party (Seema Nambiar, 2004). Example for Attended PoS system is ULTRA M-Pay system. This patented payment process is using voice to transfer the information necessary for the purchase. The data is transferred using customer's mobile phone (www.ultra.si).

The following diagram illustrates the Payment Process by ULTRA M-Pay System:

APPLYING SECURE PAYMENT ON VENDING MACHINE

The SEMOPS (Secure Mobile Payment Service) project that was to address effectively most of the challenges bundled with a mobile payment service, and develop an open, cross-border secure approach. The service concept is built on the credit push concept.

The project's aim is to combine the new payment solution with various forms of proven and state of the art mobile and wireless technology to achieve a high level of security, availability, user friendliness and interoperability.

The Transaction Procedure

Customers buying from a vending machine and making electronic payments for it, is practically making a payment to an unmanned PoS terminal. The vending machines are outfitted with an IrDA, Bluetooth or RFID, a kind of direct communication device that is capable of transferring the transaction details to the customer. When customers select a product and choose mobile payment, they receive the transaction details onto their mobile phones using the available direct communication channel. When payment is performed in the vending machine receives the authorization and provides the selected product (Gusev, 2003).

In Figure 2 one can easily distinguish the main players and components in a mobile payment scenario. Each user (customer or merchant) connects with his home bank/Mobile Network Operator (MNO) only. The banks can exchange messages between them via the Data Center (DC) (S.Karnouskos, 2003).

The merchant (in general any PoS/Automated Vending Machine) provides to the customer the necessary transaction details, which includes static and

Figure 1. Attended PoS payment system

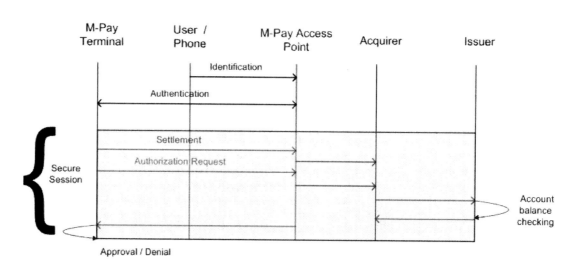

Figure 2. General Architecture of Mobile Payment Service – Vending Machine

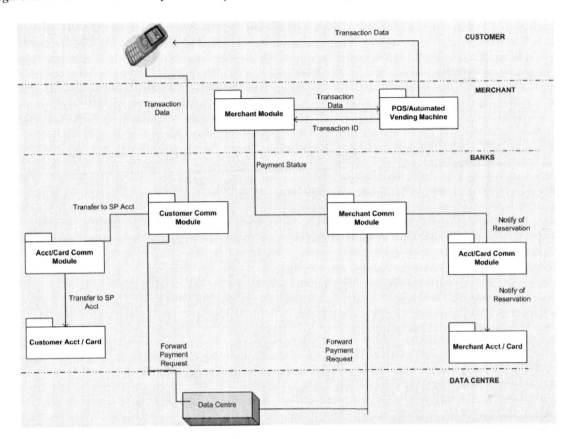

dynamic elements that identify the merchant and the individual transaction. During the whole payment process, the customer does not identify himself or herself to the merchant, nor does he/she provides any information about the bank being used or any other sensitive data. This characteristic covers the customer privacy of not letting his/her own details (S.Karnouskos, 2003).

The customer receives the transaction data from the merchant and combines it with information to identify and a standard format payment request is prepared. Then he selects the account manager, where the payment request is to be processed. This payment processor is the trusted partner of the customer – either his bank or his mobile network operator. When the payment request is ready for transfer, the customer checks its content, authorizes it (e.g. via PIN - Personal Identification Number) and sends the payment request to its account manager (S.Karnouskos, 2003).

The customer's account manager receives the payment request, identifies the customer and processes the payment request. Processing includes the verification of the availability of the necessary funds, and reservation of the required amount. When the processing is completed a payment notice is prepared by the account manager and is forwarded to the Data Center of the payment service, which forwards the message to the merchant trusted payment processor. The data center also handles the message delivery.

The merchant's payment processor receives the payment notice identifies the merchant and advises the merchant about the payment by forwarding the payment notice. The merchant can decide whether to approve or reject the transaction and confirms the transaction to payment processor.

When customer's payment processor receives the positive confirmation it initiates a regular bank transfer to merchant's bank. In case of successful money transfer, notifications will be sent to both merchant and customer by corresponding account managers. If upon rejection, the customer's payment processor releases the funds it has reserved for the purchase.

This aspect handles the major security concern of rollback credit at any time during transaction.

ADVANTAGES OF THE SECURED PAYMENT SYSTEM

One of the main advantages of the proposed system is the facility that it provides for the route management. The proposed system makes it possible for the vending machine operators to reduce their operational costs, as it provides inventory information, each time a mobile transaction takes place. The mobile payment offers customers additional value in terms of location free access (Laukkannen &Lauronan, 2005). Similarly, mobile payments provide consumer with ubiquitous purchase possibilities, timely access to financial assets of an alternative to cash payments. The users can, for example, pay for transportation tickets or car parking through vending machines remotely without the need to visit an ATM. (Begonha et al., 2002). Advantages of mobile payment compared with traditional payment instrument are thus likely to pertain to time and location independent purchase possibilities. The system designed in this project was constructed for micro payments in vending machines that have no connection to the vendor except for the connection supplied by the customers. The design was then used for analyzing the threats against the designed system and comparing it to an identical system where the connection is supplied by the seller in order to find out the effects on security when changing the communication channel (Ivarsson, 2008). The comparison shows that even though the designed system is more vulnerable, it is not a major difference and with low value payments, the mobile payment system can depend on the connection supplied by the user. The main advantage to security with this method is the protection against Denial of Service attacks and the protection against mass identity thefts as authentication is no longer done on the machine.

CONCLUSION

In this case study had examined security issues in mobile payment through vending machines perspective. The outcome of this paper is an empirically devised set of proportions which is suitable to serve as a basis for selection of appropriate indicators for further studies.

Security has been an issue of M-Payment development right from the start of this effort (Ivarsson, 2008). Current infrastructures considering the limitations and enhancements, offer a comfortable environment for secure m-payment transactions. The payment vendors will improve their solutions continually to keep up with the changing technological landscape. Successful payment methods will be those that can continue to meet the many requirements such as cost, technical requirement, particularly security.

REFERENCES

(n.d.). Retrieved from www.ultra.si.

Begonha, D. B., Hoffman, A., & Melin, P. (2002). M-payments; hang up, try again. *Credit Card Management, 15*(10), 40-44.

Chen, X. Z. (2003). Study of Mobile Payments System. *Proceedings of the IEEE International Conference on E-Commerce.*

Gusev, L. A. (2003). M-Payments. *25th Conferance Information Technology Interfaces.*

Ivarsson, S. (2008). *Mobile Payment with Customers controlled connection – can it be constructed to be sae enough?* Sweden.

Jean, E. v. A (n/d). Investigating Mobile Payment: Supporting technologies, methods and use. *Natural Sciences and Engineering Research Council of Canada and LIPSO.*

Jerry Gao, J. C. (2005). A Wireless Payment System. *Proceedings of the Second International on Embedded Software and Systems.*

Knospe, S.-G. (2002). Secure Mobile Commerce. *Electronics and Communiation Engineering Journal,* (pp. 228, 1-11).

Karnouskos, A. (2003). Secure Mobile Payment - Architecture and Business Model of SEMOPS. *EURESCOM Summit.* Heidelberg, Germany.

Laukkanen, T., & Lauronen, J. (2005). Consumer value creation in mobile banking services. *International Journal of Mobile Communications, 3*(4), 325-338.

Seema Nambiar, C.-T. (2004). Analysis of Payment Transaction Security in Mobile Commerce. *Proceedings of the IEEE International Conferance.*

KEY TERMS

Automated Vending Machine: Automated vending machines are outfitted with an IrDA, Bluetooth or RFID, a kind of direct communication device that is capable of transferring the transaction details to the customer.

Bluetooth: Bluetooth is a specification for the use of low-power radio communications to wirelessly link phones, computers and other network devices over short distances.

IR – Infrared (IR) Radiation: Electromagnetic radiation whose wavelength is longer than that of visible light, but shorter than that of terahertz radiation and microwaves.

Micro Payments: Micropayments are means for transferring very small amounts of money, in situations where collecting such small amounts of money with the usual payment systems is impractical, or very expensive, in terms of the amount of money being collected.

MNO: A mobile network operator (MNO), also known as wireless service provider, wireless carrier, or cellular company, is a telephone company that provides services for mobile phone subscribers.

Mobile Commerce - M-commerce (mobile commerce) is the buying and selling of goods and services through wireless handheld devices such as cellular telephone and personal digital assistants.

Mobile Payments - Mobile payment is payment using the mobile phone at the point-of-sale instead of using credit or debit cards.

Mobile Wallet: Mobile wallet is mobile phone that has functionality to supplant a conventional wallet and unlike mobile commerce, is a much more versatile application that includes elements of mobile transactions.

RFID (radio-frequency identification): An automatic identification method, relying on storing and remotely retrieving data using devices called RFID tags. RFID is a technology that incorporates the use of electromagnetic or electrostatic coupling in the radio frequency portion of the electromagnetic spectrum to uniquely identify an object.

Chapter LIV
Convergence in Mobile Internet with Service Oriented Architecture and Its Value to Business

Marco Garito
Digital Business, Italy

ABSTRACT

The word "convergence" refers to the combination of fixed and mobile communication, a situation where a private or business user can take advantage of being constantly connected and be able to retrieve applications and data by swapping device, with the limitations that a mobile device may have such as smaller screen and keyboard, reduced storage capability, and limited power provided by batteries. Convergence can also include imagining how mobile technology can be a component of everyday items and how data, applications, and services can be delivered via the network infrastructure. This chapter aims to cover RFID technology, Bar code and Service-Oriented Architecture (SOA): the first two technologies are dealt with in parallel to provide an overall view of advantages and disadvantages, while SOA will be part of a distinct discussion and analysis. Eventually, some practical examples of these discussed technologies are provided.

INTRODUCTION

RFID and Bar code are two emerging mobile technologies able to provide competitive strategic advantage to business when properly deployed and implemented. As extension of current fixed network infrastructure, the coordination with existing business processes, department and organizational structure are an essential part of rewarding implementation. The development of SOA environment can further enhance the capability and possible outcome of RFID and Bar code. The chapter outlines advantages and disadvantages for both of them, providing examples of how they co-exist and how they can create value.

RFID and Bar Code

Radio frequency identification (RFID) is one of the most interesting technologies today: its use impacts a large number of protagonists in private and business environment but it also raises simple and dramatic issues in legal, social and political affairs. RFID have histories back to 1930 and 1940, when the British Army, during WW2 pioneered RFID to identify their own aircraft returning home from bombing Europe. Early radar systems could spot an incoming airplane but not its type (Lahiri, 2006; Garfinkel, Rosenberg 2006; Ascential 2005)

RFID uses radio waves to detect physical items (both living and inanimate) and therefore the range of identifiable object includes everything and everywhere: RFID is an example of automatic identification technology through which an item is automatically detected and classified. Bar code, biometric, voice identification and optical character recognition systems are other example of automatic identification.

The RFID environment consists of a set of mandatory and optional components: Mandatory parts are: tag, reader, antenna controller. Sensor, actuator, host and software system and communication infrastructure are the optional parts. The table below describes the types and usage of RFID in different situations, according to their technical features

The advantages of RFID can be classified as follows (Lahiri, 2006; Garfinkel, Rosenberg 2006; Ascential 2005):

- RFID tag can be read without any physical contact between the tag and the reader
- The data of RFID can be rewritten several times with no diminishing quality or integrity
- A line of sight is not required for an RFID reader to read a tag
- The range can vary from few centimetres to some metres
- Storage capability of a tag is unlimited
- A reader can read different tags within its reach for a limited time

- A tag can be structured to perform unlimited duties
- The data quality is 100% guaranteed

RFID has its limitation that can be summarized as it follows

- RFID do not work well or not work at all with RF-opaque items or RF-absorbent items
- Surrounding conditions may affect performance
- There is a limit for how many tags can be read within a time slot
- Hardware set up may limit performance
- The technology is still immature

Bar code is a scheme representing textual information; the symbols are generally vertical lines, spaces, squares and dots: the bar code is probably the newest technology as the first patent was issued in 1949 and the first application of bar code technology was a rail car tracking system, implemented in 1960 (Lahiri, 2006; Garfinkel, Rosenberg 2006; Ascential 2005). The method encoding letters and numbers using these elements is defined as symbology, which has the following characteristics:

- Symbology with better encoding technique leads to error free and efficient encoding:
- Better character density can represent more information per unit physical area
- Better error checking capability enables data reading even in those cases where the some components are damaged or missing

Figure 1. Type and usage of RFID

Band	Frequency	Wavelength	Usage
Low frequency	125 – 134.s KHz	2.400 meters	Animal tags and keyless entry
High frequency	13,56 MHz	22 meters	As above
UHF (ultra high)	865.5-867 Europe 913 US 950-956 Japan	32.8 centimetres	Smart cards, logistic
ISM (industrial scientific and medical)	2.4 GHz	12.5 centimetres	items

It is possible to have three different categories of symbols: linear, with vertical lines with different spaces with the white spaces separating two adjacent lines, with an overall maximum number of 50 characters; two dimensional with high storage of data capacity, up to 3750 number of characters; Three dimensional which is a linear bar code integrated in a surface (Lahiri, 2006; Garfinkel, Rosenberg 2006; Ascential 2005)

Bar codes are read by scanners which flash a light through the bar code area: during this process, the scanner measures the intensity of the light reflected by the white and dark area of the bar code: the dark area absorbs light, the white area reflect back the light. The light pattern is captured and translated by a photodiode or photocell into an electric signal which is again converted into digital data, represented as ASCII characters. This same data has been incorporated within the bar code at the origin (Lahiri, 2006; Garfinkel, Rosenberg 2006; Ascential 2005).

The advantages are (Lahiri, 2006; Garfinkel, Rosenberg 2006; Ascential 2005):

- Rapid and accurate data collection;
- Increased operation efficiency;
- Reduced operation costs;

- The shortcomings are:
- Bar code can be easily damaged
- Reader efficiency can be affected by environment conditions
- Presence of obstacles does not allow the scanner to read the bar code
- Speeded items do not allow the scanner working properly

The following Table 2 summarizes advantages and disadvantages in RFID and Bar code all by listing specific and relevant characteristics, based on the considerations made above

However both RFID and Bar code are not immune of common disadvantages and the table below provides and overview

The situation described above enables to conclude that a replacement or take over of RFID technology against Bar code is unlikely to happen: RFID is still an immature and developing technology compared to a widely consolidated and used Bar code. It is possible to see many areas of improvement for both of them based on the analysis done so far and at the moment the logical conclusion is that RFID and Bar code can co-exist and many of the applications for RFID can be located out of the reach of current Bar code scenario

Figure 2. Comparison table between RFID and bar code

Characteristic	RFID	Bar code
Support for non static data	Data can be rewritten	Data is static
Line of sight	RFID does not need to see the tag but has to detect it	Bar code must be in sight
Operational distance	Longer range	Very close to scanner
Data capacity	Higher	Lower
Multiple reads	RFID reader can interact with several tag in a limited time	Not possible
Operational resistance	Higher resistance	Easily damaged
Multiple tasks	Possible	Not possible
Accuracy	Higher reliability	Lower reliability
Costs	Higher implementation cost	Low cost
Accuracy rate	No difference in same circumstances	No difference in some circumstances
Effect of material type	Opacity and reflection affect operation	Irrelevant
International restriction	Legal issues	Internationally used
Social issue	Privacy issue as reader can detect personal items	No issue
Maturity level of technology	Quite new	Mature and consolidated

Figure 3. Main disadvantages for RFID and bar code

Situation	RFID	Bar code
Presence of obstacles	Some objects as metals or water can prevent the RFID reader to properly work	If the bar code is covered by an item, the scanner cannot read the code
Presence of moisture	Water drops absorb energy so the item cannot be detected	Water drops can interfere with reader
Speed	If tag has not enough time to sync with the reader, the reading procedure is affected	Where scan reader is faster than the movement, the captured data is compromised
Location of RFID and Bar code on the item	External	external

where business needs require something else or other than Bar Code (Lahiri, 2006; Garfinkel, Rosenberg 2006; Ascential 2005).

RFID and Bar Code Application; An Example In Travel Industry

RFID and Bar Codes coexist though with mobile devices. In a joint initiative Finnair and Nokia have implemented a new initiative to manage ground-based staff: work assignment are directly transmitted via mobile so employees can directly tackle their job tasks and when they have finished, their mobile device can read the RFID tags located at each key point locations and this data is routed to the central management database. Again Finnair and TDC mobile are piloting a test to use mobile device to check in: the initiative is called "Mobile bar code boarding pass". After buying the ticket, passengers check in by mobile, on the internet or at the check-in desk and they receive a message with a 2-dimension bar code on their mobile phone; once at the airport, passengers retrieve the message and scan it for checking luggage, security screening and when boarding the aircraft: no further paper-based boarding card is needed (Toro, 2007)

RFID Applications Examples

Mobil introduced a "Speedpass" System in 1997 to fast track the payment to their petrol stations network: the system was later extended to convenience stores of Mobil. In 2001, the company augmented their Speedpass services to McDonald's, in 2004 Mobil entered an agreement with Stop & Shops stores to test whether or not Mobil's customers could buy their

grocery and food.: most likely, car drivers on the move do not have enough time, to dedicate to shopping task and the speed concept underneath demonstrates how mobile technology can enhance traditional shopping experience in everyday life (Lahiri 2006, Garfinkel and Rosenberg 2006).

Another example of RFID use can be retrieved in hospitals where three types of RFID can be identified: those to track people and items around the premises, those to safeguard use of medical equipment and those to assist medical staff in their daily job. Different situations but each of them can interact providing a unique view of hospital's environment. RFID can provide the needed granularity to properly asses moments, people or objects, even at home, when the need is to monitor the wellbeing of elderly people or children needing special care and attention (Lahiri 2006, Garfinkel, Rosenberg 2006)..

Still an example in retail industry, RFID and tag technology play an important role in asset protection in not food products: expensive items and items that can be easily hidden by shoplifters are protected by visible or invisible tags that must be removed at the check out points: in this case, RFID and Bar code technology can coexists because they cover two different needs. Once the tag has been removed (so the customer can pass through the exit grid without no alarm being activated), the same item can be scanned for payment process: eventually, the recording of the transaction is transferred to the back office enabling the marketing analysis described

Bar Code Applications Examples

The largest deployment of Bar code technology happened in retail industry: the major retail chains (Wal-

Mart in US, Tesco, Asda and M&S in UK for example, but list could continue) have recently adopted their stores with self check-out points or kiosk, enabling thus customer to scan their shopping products, pay by cash or credit/debit card, get a cash back and even utilize fidelity vouchers in view of current or future purchases.

This is also an extremely powerful way to capture data for marketing research and analysis because while scanning the product, the information is automatically transmitted to the central database which can thus calculate trends and attractiveness of the same product, the other products bought in combination with it and the success of a promotion campaign with real time information transmitted directly to the back office of the store chain to organize replenishment in a timely manner. Therefore, self service check-out kiosks is not just a way to reduce the number of cashiers and reduce the space.

The availability of complex and aggregated data about products in retail industry, within a bar code also play an important role in health and safety in food and many regulations around the world prescribe very specific and rigid rules for fresh and perishable food products. Each store can retrieve on daily basis the use by date food products and pull out each item from the regular shelf space or organize a dedicate space where these same items can be sold at a reduced price. This happens in many stores around London area: as the risk for the retail shop is to throw away food and therefore asset, it is a better off to try to sell as much as possible, even at a reduced price, relying on the fact that customers may be more tempted to buy items when their price is lower than usual for immediate consumption at home.

There are some though some concerns about privacy and more broadly pervasive computing because these are emerging technologies far from being stable yet: a tag reader can detect and collect information from any belongings, document or shop items bought elsewhere (the ringing alarm at the exit gate grids many people experience is an example). The main deployment of tagging and RFID is in retailer and supply chain environment therefore privacy is not an issue in such a circumstance; however when this technology is applied and attached to consumer good at item level.

It is now time to introduce the Service Oriented Architecture concept to analyze how wireless technologies can be deployed in a dynamic and user oriented way

Service Oriented Architecture (SOA)

Service oriented architecture can be defined as a method to conceive, implement and distribute business functions, data or applications, based on geography or across enterprise, enabling the reconfiguration of new business processed when necessary; there are some key points which must be taken into account (Sonic 2006; Cisco 2004 and 2005; Plumtree 2005, Sprott 2004, Symons 2005):

- SOA is based on WWW standards
- The services or, more precisely, the content of SOA allows business flexibility
- SOA can incorporate best practice to create design aimed to develop and enhance business processes
- SOA covers existing system (Sonic 2006; Cisco 2004 and 2005; Plumtree 2005, Sprott 2004, Symons 2005)

The combination of these characteristics demonstrates and confirm the fit between the RFID/Bar codes described below and the realization and distribution of services, applications or content through SOA: the difficulties and the challenges brought in by new technology development dictates to implement a model to facilitate the evolution of business process and supporting technology (Sonic 2006; Cisco 2005; Plumtree 2005, Ascential 2005). The table below provides a practical example about the moment in business development terms, in which mobile technologies can be adopted.

The key for a successful adoption and distribution of mobile technology based on SOA infrastructure is an evolving and continuous alignment between Business and Technology and the capability of IT to properly support Business to respond to competitive market and rapidly develop new solutions and at the same time change business models by gathering real time information through sensitive applications and services (Sonic 2006; Cisco 2005; Plumtree 2005, Symons 2005). The table 4 if properly understood and implemented, opens the door to the semantic web, where content and applications are exchanged, captured and analyzed real time, enabling thus to adopt and deliver sensitive answers to business needs. RFID and Bar code do this by capturing data from the end point and transferring it back to the source, at the opposite end, to eventually change the characteristics of the original data itself

It is now necessary to move onto the next step and possibly describe the IT and Business architecture Today's enterprises require a new IT strategy, one that will improve their ability to respond to competitive pressures and market demands.

From SOA to Service Oriented Network Architecture

The emerging solution takes advantage of a more flexible, adaptive, and feature-rich IT architecture: Service-Oriented Network Architecture. It helps enterprises evolve their existing infrastructure into an Intelligent Information Network (IIN) that supports new IT strategies, including service-oriented architecture (SOA), Web services, and virtualization and mobile. By integrating advanced capabilities enabled by intelligent networks, enterprises reduce complexity and management costs, enhance system resiliency and flexibility, and improve usage and efficiency of networked assets. It allows enterprises to use their network as a strategic asset that properly aligns IT resources with Business priorities. The result is lower total cost of ownership (TCO) and increased revenue, which over time enable organizations to shift an increasing proportion of their IT budgets toward strategic investment and business innovation (Sonic 2006; Cisco 2004 and 2005; Plumtree 2005, Sprott 2004, Symons 2005).

Service oriented networks architectures are based on a three-layer design

- Application layer: this layer includes all software used by end users within the enterprise for business purposes (such as enterprise resource plan-

Figure 4. Adoption of mobile technology

Maturity / business impact	Benefits	Scope	Success factors	People and organization success factors	Standards
Initial service **Functionality**	New functionality against current business scenario	R&D, pilot project, websites and portals	Standards and integration with existing environment	Developers team	XML, J2EE, .NET
Architected services **Cost efficiency**	IT cost reduction	Integrated applications	Messaging, database integration, versioning, security	IT architect group and SOA competency center – C level sponsorship	UDDI, XQuery
Business services **Responsiveness**	Business responsiveness and change business processes	Processes encompassing business units or enterprise	Reusability, easiness of modification, availability, process rules	Alignment IT and Business, SOA life cycle definition and governance	WS-BPEL Mobile technologies early stages
Collaborative services **Responsiveness**	Business responsiveness, collaboration with business and trading partners	Extranet and cross0enterprose	External services enablement, cross enterprise security,	Execs committee, event driven design skills. BU manager sponsorship	Rosetta, ebXML Mobile technologies enhanced
Measured business services **Transformation**	Transformation into real-time enterprise	Business unit or enterprise	Complex processes, system monitoring	Continuous measurement, CFO involvement	Convergence
Optimized business services **Optimization**	React and respond optimization	Business unit or enterprise	Event driven automation for optimization	Ongoing improvement, CEO sponsorship	Converged multiplatform

589

ning and customer relationship management) and software used for collaboration (for example, unified messaging and conferencing).

- Networked infrastructure layer: this layer interconnects devices at critical points in the network (campus, data center, network edge, metropolitan-area network [MAN], WAN, branch offices, and tele-worker locations) and facilitates transport of services and applications throughout the enterprise.
- Interactive services layer: this layer optimizes communications between applications and services in the application layer by taking advantage of intelligent network functions such as embedded security, identity, and quality-of-service (QoS) features.

The 7 OSI (Open System Interconnection) layers, described in Figure 5, provide the ground for understanding where the spoken mobile technologies can be successfully implemented (Simeneau 2005, White 2001). Since tags store information, which may include location data, not all intelligence need be held in corporate networks and enterprise systems. Exchange of information may be restricted to tags and readers may be processed by a local server via a LAN, or aggregated and passed on to a distribution centre.

Many organizations are starting with RFID pilots within the confines of their own environment, as localized internal deployments. The reason for this is simple: it restricts the scope to a manageable limit, allowing learning to occur in a controlled manner. But most organizations implement RFID to facilitate supply chain efficiencies, so extending RFID beyond the organization is inevitable. Even so, there are some small steps that an organization can take in venturing outside their own environment (Sonic 2006; Cisco 2005; Plumtree 2005, Brown, Wiggers 2005, Sprott 2005).

Creation of Value

The creation of value using RFID (as well as any other mobile technology) can be summed up by analyzing the Figure 6 below.

The circled areas describe the main development steps from an internally targeted phase (internal deployment) to a more complex extra-company connected enterprise encompassing many businesses: this evolutionary process implies two main issues:

- A growing sophistication of solutions and intensive use of the network infrastructure (vertical ax)
- An increasing density of the device which probably means a wider adoption of open source software to make easier the coding and connection between heterogeneous devices and systems, particularly when the need is to link enterprises (horizontal ax)

IT is still and enabler of efficiency and effectiveness (Sonic 2006; Cisco 2005; Plumtree 2005): as long as the development environment becomes more and more demanding, Business needs to step in and take the lead to properly support the roll out of the deployment by facilitating the required change in process and organizational structure and capturing inputs from the market and to translate into competitive advantage (Lahiri, 2006; Garfinkel, Rosenberg 2006; Ascential 2005) This means having a clear understanding of priorities and issues of RFID deployment and the table below describes them all based on the deployment phase, with the left side being the starting point

Over the years, computer systems and networks enabled the tracking of product across the supply chain to make sure that items departing from point A could get point B: in a retail environment, this is a crucial step to replenish shelves on time and based on customers' demand. The acid test is given by when the shopper decides which product to select off the shelf and when the shopper decide to buy it again after being satisfied by the product itself (Lahiri 2006, Garfinkel, Rosenberg 2006, Cisco 2004 Brown and Wiggers 2005).

The analysis carried out on previous paragraphs allow us to state the case for SOA as suitable vehicle for a relatively secure and fast deployment of the spoken mobile technologies: SOA and service oriented network architecture environment is a flexible enough infrastructure to host mobile devices which can now interact with other existing applications and systems, both in back end or front end side of the company's IT and Business structure.

The ever growing complexity and need of accurate and timely information about process and market data requires the availability of easy to use and portable devices. Mobile technology can be successfully implemented as extension of Supply Chain Management, Customer Relationship Management, business-to-employees for safety and security monitoring and the workflow of real time data and information may

Figure 5. OSI 7 layers

| 6. Presentation Protocol |
| 5. Session Protocol |
| 4. Transport Protocol |
| 3. Network Protocol |
| 2. Data Link |
| 1. Physical |

be transferred to Enterprise Resource Planning and Business Intelligence and more broadly to the whole organization and externally to Business Partners (Kalakota, Robinson 2000) and it is possible to understand how SOA environment can additionally enhance the capability with flexibility, speed of implementation, standardization of protocols and business practices, reducing the uncertainty of a relatively new wireless technology. From an end user point of view, this scenario can be considered as an example of MIMO (Multiple Inputs Multiple Output) where companies are able to capture and assess relevant business information about processed and markets for a wider and heterogeneous set of sources at the very same time (Lahiri, 2006; Garfinkel, Rosenberg 2006; Ascential 2005, Cisco 2004 and 2005, Sprott 2004)

Mobile Business, SOA and Semantic Web

Mobile technologies introduce advantages that cannot be obtained with fixed connectivity: these include localization and personalization. Previous paragraphs demonstrate this is valid for RFID and Bar codes because these allow the delivery of customized and customizable information and data to user both on locale or remote role (Coyle 2004; Sheshagiri, Sadeh, Gandon 2004)

The Semantic Web is an initiative supported by W3C aimed to support semantic meaning and context for internet resources: in such an environment, web services are an enabler for applications which can communicate with other automatically via the internet (both fixed and wireless) using standard internet protocol. It has been demonstrated and explained that such an opportunity also exists for RFID and Bar code and SOA can be the delivery platform for these protocols. (Coyle 2004; Sheshagiri, Sadeh,Gandon 2004)

Figure 6. Creation of Value by using RFID

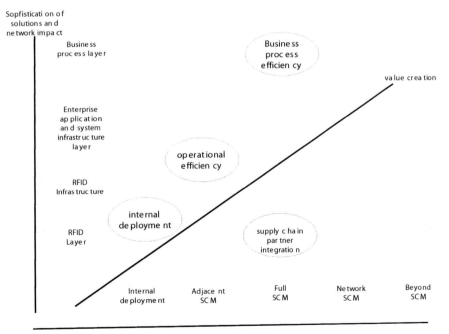

Figure 7. Understanding priorities in RFID

Business process layer	Planning improvement	Bottleneck identification and process redesign for RFID deployment	Increase of business information – need of network intelligence to cope	RFID is a commodity – competitive advantage based on event management
Enterprise applications and system infrastructure layer	Storage, capacity and device management planning	Identify the gaps – scalable infrastructure	Adapt quality-of-service with increasing usage of network and keep adequate level of voice and data quality	Data via RFID increases – properly quantify the consumption of network capacity
RFID network layer RFID layer	Standard selection and planning for mass deployment	Security	Device management as number increases	Universal standard for tag and reader

Internal deployment   Adjacent Supply Chain   Full Supply Chain   Supply Chain network   Beyond Supply Chain

All together these technologies open a completely new scenario for mobile computing, especially because device capability and sophistication is increasing and new enhanced devices reach the market at a fast pace. The wireless network therefore extend the richness and reach of the traditional web, which means that there is a need to add meaning to the data that's is generated and delivered; the broader scope of semantic web is hence to support the mapping of current and future system, protecting the universality of the web with the localized scenario. Once again, a scenario that fits with RFID and Bar code/ (Coyle 2004; Sheshagiri, Sadeh,Gandon 2004)

Mobile Semantic Web @ Work: MSpace

MSpace Mobile is a Semantic Web application enabling people explore the world around them by leveraging contexts that are meaningful to them in time, space and subject (Mulholland, Collins, Zdrahal 2005, Wilson, Russell, Smith, Owens and Schaefel 2005). People unfamiliar with any city, Sydney for example, may find their physical location to be the main context around which they wish all other requests to circulate (Mulholland, Collins and Zdrahal 2005, Wilson, Russell, Smith, Owens and Schaefel 2005).

Query like "which are main attractions at Circular Quay and Sydney CBD I'd like to see during the weekend within a walking distance from Sydney Tower" can be gathered in the "Selection" field of the diagram below, which contains the main parameters: Sydney, CBD and Circular Quay area, Sydney tower, weekend events"

The next step is provided by the "Organization" process which collects the available events on display during any given weekend: for example, the market at the Rocks area, a concert at Opera House and the Mardi' Gras Parade. With the "Exploration" step, it is possible, for example to view some pictures or the places, the map to get to each of them and the time-table for the events and eventually restart the loop to shortlist and schedule the visit according to user's own preferences.

Location Based Services and disseminated applications across multiple infrastructures and converging

Figure 8. Workflow for Mspace

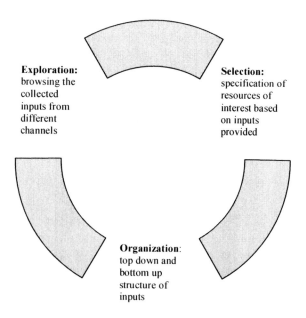

Exploration: browsing the collected inputs from different channels

Selection: specification of resources of interest based on inputs provided

Organization: top down and bottom up structure of inputs

fixed/mobile hubs and devices is another confirmation of the suitability of SOA and mobile semantic web as proper environment enabling and delivering enriching user experience: in a business-to-business standpoint, more relevant for this paper, the same comprehensive view of data and information can be achieved by integrating RFID and Bar codes and replacing the described tourist scenario with a proper business environment.

CONCLUSION

It has been demonstrated how mobile technology can successfully benefit the business when IT and Business align toward a clear understanding of targets and when companies are able to capitalize on market input. It has been proven, also, how innovative and "off the shelf" mind set can create real changing experience for customers and companies. It has also been demonstrated how a service oriented (network) architecture is one of the best hubs of business requirements and technology features to deliver applications and contents through mobile devices. This technology can deliver a unique view of processes, data and end standpoint in several environments

As the technology is still in its early stage, its potential is not well understood in each aspect and privacy is one of the most important. Once mobile applications are layered on network infrastructure with shared programs and features, they are part of the internet and exposed to its risk and threats.

REFERENCES

A new service oriented architecture (SOA) maturity model (2006). Sonic Software Corporation. http://www.sonicsoftware.com/solutions/service_oriented_architecture/soa_maturity_model/index.ssp

Brown, D., & Wiggers, E. (2005). Planning for proliferation. *The impact of RFID on the network*. http://newsroom.cisco.com/dlls/2005/Whitepaper_031105.pdf

Business overview of service oriented service network architecture (2005). Cisco Systems. http://www.cisco.com/en/US/netsol/ns477/networking_solutions_white_paper0900aecd803efff3.shtml

Cisco Internet Business Solution Group (2004). "2010" The retail roadmap for chief executives. Cisco Systems US. http://newsroom.cisco.com/dlls/2004/ts_011204.html

Cisco Systems (2005). *Business overview of service oriented network architecture. http://www.cisco.com/sona*

Coyle, F. (2004). *Mobile computing, web services and the Semantic Web: Opportunities for m-commerce.* Computer Science department, School of engineering, Southern Methodist University, Dallas, Texas.

Dubey, A, & Wagle, D. (2007). Delivering software as a service. *The McKinsey Quarterly.* http://www.mckinseyquarterly.com/article_abstract_visitor.aspx?ar=2006&L2=4&L3=43&srid=17&gp=0

Garfinkel, S., & Rosenberg, B. (2006). RFID. Applications, security and privacy. In S. Lahiri *RFID Sourcebook.* New Jersey: Pearson Education.

Kalakota, R., & Robinson, M. (2000). E-Business 2.0: Roadmap for Success. Addison Wesley.

Mulholland P., Collins, T., & Zdrahal, Z. (2005). Bletchley Park Text: Using mobile and semantic web technologies to support the post-visit use of online museum resources. UK: Knowledge Media Institute, The Open University.

Retail and consumer goods – RFID deployment (2005). Ascential Company – white paper, US. http://knowledgestorm.fastcompany.com/fastco/search/keyword/RFID+TAG/RFID+TAG

Strategic decision on SOA (2005). Plumtree Software Inc. LLP while paper US http://www.plumtree.com

Sheshagiri, M., Sadeh, N. M., & Gandon, F. (2004). *Using Semantic Web services for context aware mobile awareness.* Mobile Commerce laboratory, School of Computer Science, Carnegie Mellon University.

Simeneau P. (2005). *The OSI model: Understanding the seven layers of computer network.* Global Knowledge LLS.

Symons, C. (2005). *IT strategy maps. A tool for strategic alignment.* Forrester Research US. http://www.forrester.com/Research/Document/Excerpt/0,7211,38215,00.html

Sprott, D. (2004). *Service oriented architecture: An introduction for managers*. CBDI Forum, Ireland. http://www.cbdiforum.com/report_summary. php3?topic_id=20&report=709&order=member_ type&start_rec=0

Toro, R. (2007). *Bon voyage*. W3 IBM com corporate.

White, W. S. (2001). *Enabling eBusiness integrating technologies, architectures and applications*. Wiley.

Wilson, M., Russell, A., Smith, D. A., Owens, A., & Schaefel, M. C. (2005). *mSpace Mobile: A Mobile Application for the Semantic Web*. IAM Research Group School of Electronics and Computer Science University of Southampton.

KEY TERMS

Bar Code (also bar code): A machine-readable representation of information (usually dark ink on a light background to create high and low reflectance which is converted to 1s and 0s).

Open Systems Interconnection Basic Reference Model (OSI Reference Model or OSI Model): An abstract description for layered communications and computer network protocol design.

Radio-Frequency Identification (RFID): An automatic identification method, relying on storing and remotely retrieving data using devices called RFID tags or transponders.

Semantic Web: An evolving extension of the World Wide Web in which the semantics of information and services on the web is defined, making it possible for the web to understand and satisfy the requests of people and machines to use the web content.

Service-Oriented Architecture (SOA): A software architecture where functionality is grouped around business processes and packaged as interoperable services.

Service Oriented Network Architecture: Emerging technology based on network infrastructure particular set up which is similar to Service oriented architecture but based on a different approach.

Chapter LV
Balancing Business, Technology, and Global Expertise

N. Raghavendra Rao
SSN School of Management & Computer Applications, India

ABSTRACT

Recent changes in global economy have been focusing on the need for a proactive approach in the International Financial Services sector. Integrating business, the knowledge of experts, and emerging technologies are the basic components for proactive approach. The activities related to financial services are generally a complex process. The requirements for a global market need to be analyzed from various risks in business. Now organizations have to understand the value of sharing resources such as human centered assets, physical assets and the components of Information communication technology, to gain competitive advantage in virtual environment. The concept of virtual organization plays an important role in the present globalization scenario. All the virtual organizations will share the common resources for computing power and data across the globe. Grid and mobile computing concepts will be required to be integrated in the present global market.

INTRODUCTION

Financial deregulations and changes in foreign exchange controls in most countries are permitting large investors to increase their exposure to foreign capital. Financial services sector is making use of this opportunity. This has led to the belief financial assets that such as stocks and bonds are no more sheets of papers but have become digital documents. This has also made them to continue with their investment strategy in all the emerging markets also. Stock markets react on structured and unstructured information. The mix of unstructured information is more than the

structured. Here it is apt to quote the observation of Stephen H. Penman (2001): one thing professionals do have common: "They are in the business of advising expected returns. Since expected returns are made up of normal and abnormal components they can be broadly categorized as advising on normal returns to investments or abnormal return opportunities"(p.74). Investment consultants in financial services sector have realized the need for proactive approach in global financial markets. Integrating business knowledge of domain experts and emerging technologies are the basic components of proactive approach. The proactive approach is possible by making use of the services of global expertise forming global virtual teams. Their services can be made use through collaborative technologies. The elements of information and communication along with knowledge repositories can be considered as backbone of collaborative technologies. This chapter explains the concepts of collaborative technologies that would facilitate virtual enterprises to adopt proactive approach in their business. Further it relates the above concepts in the model GFSAG (Global Financial Services Advisory Group) discussed in Mobile Computing – An Enabler in International Financial Services (vide p.828 Hand book of Research in Mobile Business).

BUSINESS MODEL IN GLOBAL ENVIRONMENT

Concepts and Practice are generally divergent. The Challenge of developing effective business model by a global virtual organization is substantially greater than identifying relevant concepts in management and technology. GFSAG (Global Financial Services Advisory Group) is already a global virtual company. GFSAG has realized that in order to grow in global market, it is not just enough to be competitive but globally acceptable as a professional advisory group. This is very important and there is no easy route for this FIG-1 gives an overview of the concepts in the business model developed by GFSAG. Ensuing paragraphs in this chapter highlight the concepts that facilitated the development of the below model.

GFSAG MODEL

GFSAG (Global Financial Services Advisory Group) is a London based investment consultancy organization. GFSAG provides investment consultancy services in the areas of corporate securities, foreign exchange, metals and commodities. There are specific domain experts for each of the above areas of services. It is because of their technical and professional expertise they have made a good impact in the global financial sector. In the present fast moving global markets and fierce competition they have failed to produce results quickly. For this they need to accept proactive approach in their business activities. In this context they have formed a task force to identify the concepts related to business and ICT that would help them to implement their plan of action. The task force has recommended Grid computing and the advanced concepts of virtual reality to be used in the area of corporate securities. The task force has also identified the domain experts and ICT professionals to develop a model exclusively for advising in the area of corporate securities. The existing GFSAG model will be the base for development.

GLOBAL VIRTUAL TEAMS

Global virtual teams are those that spam time zones and geographical boundaries. A complete understanding of the role and technology have to be made very clear to global virtual teams in their respective activities. This team has to be familiar with technologies required

Figure 1. Overview of the concepts in the business model

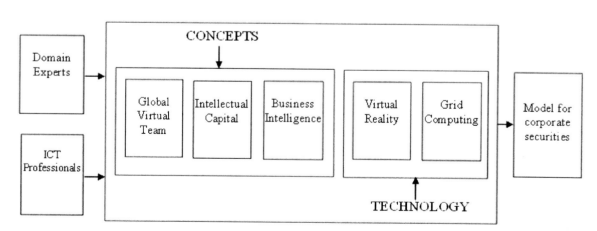

for their development work. It is required the team has to know the need for change and how the change will be affected by context as well as the nature of task assigned to them. Shared understanding among the members of the team would help them to improve their performance and to anticipate the behavior of others. The most promising communication media for developing shared understanding is through mobile communication. It would be opt to quote Arjun Raven (2003) on virtual teams "Virtual work groups have many of the same characteristics as face – to- face teams and cops, but have an important additional component : the members are typically dispersed over a broad geographical area, spanning countries and even continents and cultures. As a result they rely even more than collocated teams and communities do on collaborative technologies for their interactions" (p.299).

GLOBAL VIRTUAL TEAM FORMATION

Any development in this context means the patterns of change, growth or progression of a team to a more mature status. The team development process consists of three main elements 1. Selection of team members, 2. Development process and 3. Accomplishment of the task.

Selection of team members and development process results in accomplishment of the task. Fig.2 Global Development Team Frame provides the overview of these elements. Significance of virtual teams in the context of achieving a task is well described by Catherine Durnell Cramton and Kara L.Orvis (2003) "Teams are created in work settings in the hope of bringing the task of a pool of resources exceeding what any single individual could offer. The premise is that different members of the team offer unique information and expertise for the collaborative effort. As the result of the merging of these different resources of information a better product is produced" (P.214).

Selection of Team Members

In the selection process of the team talks about the individual characteristics and resources available to them. It also explains the team structure and level in the hierarchy as well as the nature of the team's work. The members and organization involvement and their perception are made explicit.

Development Process

The Process in global virtual team development can speed up the activities through interactions to accomplish its task. It is mainly on sharing knowledge with one another about their work contexts

Accomplishment of the Task

The team integrates people and contexts toward accomplishment of a task assigned to them. The team is expected to have the ability to sustain a common task focus and collaboration across multiple contexts. Mark Mass (1999) rightly states that in large software development projects, effective knowledge management (KM) must pay attention to the complex interrelationships between people, culture, strategy and technology. To this end, flexible cross functional networks and imaginative use of information systems often turn to be more appropriate than bureaucratize forms of organization (p.35).

Team Members at GFSAG

The members of the team formed specifically for developing a model exclusively for advising in the area of corporate securities are familiar with global development team frame. They are also aware that their business has become highly competitive and dominated by a set of aggressive global players. The concept of virtual reality can help them to follow proactive approach chosen by their organization.

VIRTUAL REALITY

Virtual Reality refers to the presentation of computer generated data made available in such a way that those who use it can perceive the information at their disposal. The ability to get real world perception interactively through computers explains interest associated with 3-D graphics virtual reality. One can master the concept of virtual reality through simulation. The way business model is being developed provides scope for the study of complex real world situations. It also helps to develop steps for simulation and studying complex business contexts.

Figure 2. Global development team frame

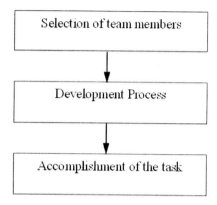

Selection of team members

Development Process

Accomplishment of the task

Virtual Reality at GFSAG

The vast world of data is already available in investment knowledge based system in GFSAG model. Complex ideas in respect of corporate securities in this model would be visualized by the team. Domain experts can experiment steadily and interact with other members of the team. Dimitris N Chrofas and Heinrich Steinmann (1995) rightly observe" Visualization addresses the ability to represent very large and small structures. The domain of visistraction is the graphical concentration of concepts and ideas"(p 49). Both require non numerical information. In the case of corporate securities, it has non numerical and numerical information. The concepts underlying numerical and non numerical information have similarities, but the methodology varies. While talking on these concepts, Dimitris N Chroafas and Heinrich Steinmann state "Given that many equations often can not be solved analytically, numerical methods have been developed that approximate the solution. One of the standard methods for achieving such an approximation is the Finite Elements Method (FFM) first used in structural mechanics but now extended into other fields – even banking. Solutions based on the Finite Elements Methods have embedded in them approaches of virtual reality" (P.50). Domain such as financial analysis has been becoming increasingly complex and requires the support of high technology that would help the process efficiently and effectively. Visualization is considered as a magnifying glass which provides to see what is in the simulated results. This is the reason the team at GFSAG has chosen the virtual reality concept.

Success of accomplishment of a task by global virtual team and success of its technology are inseparable. They are complementally dependent on the understanding of business and its trends as well as the competitive environment in which any global virtual team lives and operates. This is true in the case of global virtual team at GFSAG.

GRID COMPUTING

Grid Computing is an innovative extension of distributed computing technology for computing resources sharing among participants in a virtualized organization. In support of Grid Computing concept D.Janakiraman (2005) states "Clusters are formed by exploiting the existing computing resources on the network to work together as a single system. Thus they eliminate the need for super computers by providing better price performance ratio and fault tolerance as compared to the traditional main frames or computers" (p.231). Grid computing discipline provides immense computing power and distributed data sharing facilities. In today's pervasive world needing information anytime and anywhere, the explosive grid computing environments have proven to be so significant that are often referred to as being the world's single and most powerful computer solutions. While explaining the salient feature of grid computing Joshy, Joseph C and Craig Fellenstein (2004) say "Grid computing solutions are constructed using a variety of technologies and open standards. Grid computing in turn provides highly scalable, highly secure, and extremely high performance mechanisms for discovering and negotiating access to remote computing resources in a seamless manner. This makes it possible for the sharing of computer resources, on an unprecedented scale among an infinite numbers of geographically distributed groups" (p.5). Here it is apt to note the definition of grid made by Pawel Plaszczak and Richard Wellner, Jr (2006) "In 2002 Ian Foster proposed a three point test to restrict the definition. A system could be called a Grid if it: was decentralized, used open protocols and delivered non trivial QOS (Quality of Service)" (P.57).

The concept of grid computing facilitates managing business activities by global virtual organization. With the support of grid computing, virtual organizations are capable of forming of virtual task forces or groups to solve specific problems associated with their organizations. The dynamic collection of resources from heterogeneous providers based upon users needs are provided by virtual organizations through this concept. It also helps the management of resources including utilization and allocation to meet a budget and other economic criteria. It must be remembered that technology is providing the means to orient and position us in a way to make best possible use of systems, communications and software. One should know to exploit a situation that would help to implement new technology successfully.

GRID INFRASTRUCTURE

The Grid Infrastructure forms the core foundation for successful grid applications. This infrastructure is complex combination of a number of capabilities and resources identified for the specific problem and environment being addressed. There are four components in grid infrastructure. They are Security, Resource Management, Information Services and Data Management. They address several potentially complicated areas in many stages of implementation.

Security

It supports different types of computing resources hosted in differing security domains and heterogeneous platforms. Generally it addresses local security integration, security identity mapping, secure access / authentication and security federation.

Resource Management

Resource Management scenarios often include resource discovery, resource inventories, fault isolation, resource provisioning, resource monitoring, a variety of autonomic capabilities and service level management activities. The most interesting aspect of the resource management is the selection of the correct resource from grid resource pool based on the service level requirements. It facilitates user needs.

Information Services

Information Services provide valuable information such as resource availability, capacity and utilization just to name a few. Information services enable service providers to allocate efficiently resources for the variety of tasks assigned to users of grid computing infrastructure.

Data Management

Data forms are most important aspect in a grid computing system. This data may be input into the resource and the results from the resource on the execution of a specific task. If the infrastructure is not designed properly, the data movement in geographically distributed systems can cause scalability problems. Data movement in any grid computing environment requires absolutely secure data transfers both to and from the respective resources

MOBILE COMPUTING

The concept of Mobile Computing is to facilitate end users to have access to data, information or logical objects through a device in any network while one is on the move. It also enables the users to perform a task from anywhere using a computing device which has features mobile computing. Asoke K Talukder and Roopa R Yavagal (2005) point out that mobile computing is used in different contexts with different names. The most common names are 1.Mobile Computing, 2.Anywhere Any Time Information, 3.Virtual Home Environment, 4.Nomadic Computing, 5.Pervasive Computing, 6.Ubiquitous Computing 7.Global Service Portability, 8. Wearable Computers (PP 7-8)

Devices

The Convergence of Information and Technology is responsible for the production of new generation computers working on wireless technology. These devices can make concept of grid computing a workable solution in virtual organization scenario. While talking about mobile and wireless devices Jochen Schiller (2004) states "Even though many mobile and wireless devices are available, there will be many more in the future. There is no precise classification of such devices by size, shape, weight or computing power. Currently the mobile device range is sensors, embedded controllers, pager, mobile phones, personal digital assistant, pocket computer and notebook / Laptop" (PP 7-8).

COLLABORATIVE COMPUTING TECHNOLOGIES

Adding intelligence to the process of developing models or using existing models and to their management makes lots of sense because some models need considerable expertise. This happens only when people collaborate Communication primarily transmits information from the sender to a receiver, but collaboration is much deeper. While talking on group communication Ralf Steinmetz and Klara N Nashvstedt (2007) observe that Computer supported Cooperative work (CSCW) means that multiple activities among several users involved concurrently of activities distributed across several workstations or host systems and complex data and document management tasks (p..289). Collaboration implies people actively working together and collaborative computing support tools that build on communication methods. Charnell Havens and Dylan Hass (2001) rightly observe "Great accomplishments are most likely to occur in collaborative environments. The fundamental urge to organize and collaborate derives from people's innate sense that they can accomplish much more together than apart" (P.236).

BUSINESS INTELLIGENCE

Business rule systems, data profiling, information compliance, data quality, data warehouse and data mining are the basic components needed for the creation of business intelligence in an enterprise. Business analytics add an additional dimension to business intelligence. It is interesting to note the observation of Efraim Turban, Jay E. Aronson and Ting-Peng Liang (2006) on business intelligence "Models and solution methods are often buried so deep within the tools, however that the analyst need not get his or her hands dirty ". Typically, the terms are used interchangeably" (pp 249 – 250).

INTELLECTUAL CAPITAL

Intellectual Capital is not new. It has been there since the term "Customer is a king" was coined. Earlier days it was known as goodwill. Explosion of ICT has provided new tools with which we have built global economy. Many of these tools bring intangible benefits which never existed before, we are taking them for granted. Business enterprises can no longer function without them. Their ownership helps business enterprises to gain competitive advantage in the market. Therefore they are considered as an asset. Intellectual capital

Figure 3. Model for corporate securities

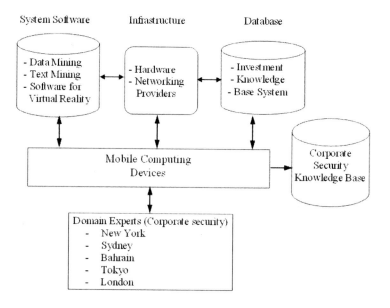

is the term given to combine the intangible assets of a business enterprise to function. Market assets and Intellectual property are the components of Intellectual Capital. While talking on knowledge creation in global context Stephen E;Little (2002) observes "The Speed of Technical and Infrastructure changes in business practice together with a new understanding of the centrality of intangible assets to wealth creation has brought the silicon valley paradigm of innovation to prominence" (p.369).

Market Assets

Brands, customer base, collaboration agreements and distribution channels are considered as market assets.

Human Centered Assets

Human centered assets comprise the collective expertise, creative and problem solving capabilities and managerial skills

Infrastructure Assets

Infrastructure assets are a wide range of assets which include business process, methodologies and IT system.

Intellectual Property Assets

Intellectual Property Assets are properties of the mind that belong to the business enterprise. They are protectable under law. These assets include patent, copyright, trademarks and trade secrets. It is interesting to note the observation of Manuluv Shahalia (2003) on intellectual property "Every local community has a certain knowledge base which has developed over a long period of time. This knowledge results from the use of resources. The use of resources results in products. Now within the given IP (Intellectual Property) regime there are two things that can lead to proprietary, patents and GIS (Geographical Indications) but only the latter prevails as the former protection requires absence of prior art/disclosure ; whereas in the latter we see that not only the product is safeguarded but its various derivatives as well as the method of production " (P.3).

MODEL FOR CORPORATE SECURITIES (MCS)

GFSAG Model discussed in Mobile computing – An Enabler in International financial services (vide page 828) is the base for Model for Corporate Securities. GFSAG Model talks about the activities such as Corporate Securities, Foreign Exchange, Metals, and Commodities. MCS confines itself with the activity relating to Corporate Securities. MCS has been developed by a Global Virtual Team formed by the task force at GFSAG. Sophisticated form of coordinated resource sharing has been provided to the developers of this model. FIG- 3 Model for corporate securities provides the overview of the system.

Features in the Model for Corporate Securities

Coordinated resource sharing includes any resources available within their organization including computing power, data, hardware, software and networking services. Model for corporate securities is being tested extensively in the areas such as 1. Continuously test for market opportunity, 2.Exploring portfolio alternatives, 3.Evaluation open pricing and 4.Interactively to present the results in graphs. Further it is being tested to identify fundamental financial attributes in respect of corporate security. The development team has been exploring information resources in the system for identifying patterns in new market segments. There is also focus on visual presentation and object orientation. The development team has been using extensively virtual reality concepts in solving complex problems related to corporate securities investment. Rearrangements of displays in a gallery walk through are being done with interaction among global virtual team. High technology with interdisciplinary characteristics is being explored by the development team.

Identification of Intellectual Capital at GFSAG

Professional and technical expertise in GFSAG's service to their global clients can be considered as market asset. Global Domain expert's knowledge in the development of the model for corporate securities is their human centered asset. IT infrastructure asset at GFSAG consists of Grid Computing, Virtual reality,

Mobile computing devices, Hardware and other related Software for the development of the above model. Collaborating the above assets through mobile computing has resulted in a model for corporate securities. This model is their Intellectual Property. Facilitating the business activities of their clients through their model can be considered as Business Intelligence. It is interesting to note the observation Adrian Buckley (2003) on usage of resources "One of the most important aspects of global financing strategy is to gain access to a broad range of fixed sources to lesson dependence on any one simple source" (P.460).

FUTURE DIRECTION

Once model for corporate securities is implemented after the testing, models for foreign exchange, commodities and metals will be tried. Though these activities come under financial services, the approach for each activity differs.

CONCLUSION

Model for securities has been jointly designed by domain experts in a global virtual team through a process of continuous exchange among members dispersed across the globe. This process helps generating alternative ideas by taking inputs from different sources and structuring through virtual reality application. Further it helps to structure the work flow by visualizing the various phases of development of a model. This type of approach in developing a model can increase the chances of successfully diffusing knowledge, technology and process. It will definitely provide scope for proactive approach with the help of intangible assets.

REFERENCES

Arjan (2003). Team or community of practice. In C. B. Gibson & S. G. Gibson (Eds.), *Virtual Team that work* (p. 299). San Francisco: Jossey.

Buckley, A. (2003). Financing the Multinational and Its Overseas Subsidiaries. *Multinational Finance*, 460. New Delhi Prentice Hall of India Pvt Ltd.

Chorafas, D. N., & Mann, H. S. (1995). The Concepts of cyberspace and Tele presence: Virtual Reality. *Practical Applications In Business and Industry* (pp. 49-50), New Jersey: Prentice Hall Ptr.

Cramton, C. D., & Orvis, K. L. (2003). Sharing in Virtual Teams, In C. B. Gibson & S. G. Gibson (Eds.), *Virtual Team that work* (p.214). San Francisco: Jossey.

Havens, C., & Mass, D. (2001). How Collaboration Fuels Knowledge. In J. W. Woods & J. A. Woods (Eds.), *The Knowledge Management year Book* (p. 236). Boston: Butterworth Heinemann.

Janakiraman, D. (2005). Introducing Mobility into Anonymous Remote Computing and Communication Model. *Grid Computing – A Research Monograph* (p. 31). New Delhi: Tata McGraw Hill Publishing Company Ltd.

Joseph, J., & Fellenste, C. (2004). *Introduction. Grid Computing* (p .5). Delhi: Pearson Education.

Little, S. E. (2002). Managing Knowledge In a Global Context. In S. E.Little, P. Quintas, & Timray (Eds.), *Managing Knowledge* (p. 369). London: Sage Publications.

Moss, M. (1999). Knowledge Management in a Software development Project. In H. Scarbrough & J. Swan (Eds.), *Case studies In Knowledge Management*. London: Institute of Personnel Development. Morgan Kaufmann.

Penman, S. H. (2001). Investment returns Valuation Models and Financial Statements. *Financial Statement Analysis and Security Valuation* (p. 74). New York: McGraw – Hill Irwin.

Plaszczak, P., & Wellner Jr., R. (2006). Business Meets Academia. *Grid Computing the Savvy Manager's Guide* (p. 50). San Francisco.

Schiller, J. (2004). *Introduction. Mobile Communications* (pp. 7-8). New Delhi: Pearson Education.

Shahalia, M. L. (2003). Geographical Indications & Environmental Law. In M. L. Shahalia (Ed.), *Perspectives In intellectual property Law* (p. 3). Delhi: Universal Law Publishing Co Pvt Ltd.

Steinmetz, R., & Nashrstedt, K. (2007). Group Communication Multimedia Systems (p. 289). New Delhi: Springer.

Talukder, A. K., & Yavalgal, R. R. (2005). Introduction. *Mobile Computing*. New Delhi: Tata McGraw Hill.

Turban, E., Aroson, J. E., & Liang, T. D. (2006). *Business Intelligence* (pp. 249-250). New Delhi: Pearson Education.

KEY TERMS

Nomadic Computing: The Computing environment moves along with the mobile user.

Pervasive Computing: This is a new dimension of personal computing that integrates mobile communication; Ubiquitous embedded computer systems, consumer electronics and the power of internet.

Ubiquitous Computing: Coined by Mark Weiser a "Disappearing" every place computing environment and nobody will notice its presence. User will be able to use both local and remote services.

Grid Computing: This involves the actual networking services and connections of a potentially unlimited number of ubiquitous computing devices within a "GRID".

Visibilization: This addresses the ability to represent very large and very small structures.

Visistraction: This is the graphical concretization of concepts and ideas.

Automatic Computing: The term "automatic" comes from an analogy to the automatic central nervous system in the human body, which adjusts too many situations automatically without any external help.

Chapter LVI
Improving Clinical Practice through Mobile Medical Informatics

Tagelsir Mohamed Gasmelseid
King Faisal University, Saudi Arabia

ABSTRACT

This chapter introduces the use of mobile medical informatics as a means for improving clinical practice in Sudan. It argues that mobile medical informatics, combined with new techniques for discovering patterns in complex clinical situations, offers a potentially more substantive approach to understanding the nature of information systems in a variety of contexts. Furthermore, the author hopes that understanding the underlying assumptions and theoretical constructs through the use of the Chaos Theory will not only inform researchers of a better design for studying information systems, but also assist in the understanding of intricate relationships between different factors.

INTRODUCTION

Healthcare organisations are undergoing major transformations to improve the quality of health services. While emphasis tends to be made (especially in developing countries) on the acquisition of improved medical technology, part of this transformation is directed towards the management and use of rapidly growing repositories of digital health data. However, the heterogeneity associated with such types of data (variety of formats, lack of data standardisation, mismatch between data and proprietary software architectures and interfaces, etc) call for addressing the problems of system and information integration. Medical and healthcare applications and services are becoming knowledge intensive. Therefore, advanced information systems' technology is essential to produce, coordinate, deliver, and share such information. The migration from static "medical" decision support systems technologies (a.k.a medical informatics technologies) towards a new breed of more malleable software tools allow the users of medical information systems to work with data and methods of analysis within the context of a "teleportal hospital". These medical information systems can remain efficient and effective by continuously adopting and incorporating the emerging mobile technologies. Mobile computing is going a long way in reshaping the context of healthcare provision and its efficiency. The growing physical mobility of patients mandates the use of mobile devices to access and provide health services at any time and any place. Example of such healthcare provisions range from car or sports-accidents through to research and cure of long-lasting diseases such as allergies, asthma, diabetes and cancer. The basic aim of this chapter is to investigate the potential of improving clinical practice in public hospitals in Sudan through the use of mobile medical informatics.

BACKGROUND

The health care sector in Sudan is being challenged by many organizational, institutional, technical and technological issues that endangered its ability to provide quality services (UNFPA website, UNCEF website, Ministry of Health website). Because public hospitals are competing with other government units for public funds, they failed to acquire appropriate medical technology and improve clinical practice through improved diagnosis and staff training and retention. The lack of a sound managing capacity has also reduced their ability to integrate backward (with community and rural hospitals) and coordinate forward (with educational institutions, industry and research community). The recent economic liberalization has also increased both the "financial" and "managerial" overheating of public hospitals who fail to run as self-sufficient units rather than "cost centers'. While the quality of the services provided by private clinics and hospitals (both inside and outside Sudan) tends to be high their paramountly high costs make them out of the reach of many patients.

The deterioration of the quality of health services and clinical practice due to the following:

1. The lack of financial resources on the side of public hospitals due to the fact that they compete for "limited" public funds with other institutions. Their failure to acquire funds has also been accompanied with a considerable difficulty in developing appropriate plans for the effective management of healthcare institutions at the primary and secondary health service provision spectrum. Such mis-management issue has resulted into a considerable failure to develop a matrix of priorities according to which tasks "especially at the two main entrants or gates of service provision for critically I and critically III patients": Accidents & Causality and Intensive Care Units (ICUs). Especially in public clinics

and hospitals the deterioration of service quality originates from the fact that there is a lack of medical supplies. Due to the privatization trends" patients are required to pay for basic inputs. Medical consultants, whose presence at this gate is paramountly important, are not prepared to be there because they are spending much time in their private clinics. Although the management of ICUs tends to scientific, there is a considerable difficulty regarding the development and adoption of the suitable management model. There are five ICU models: (a) open ICU model, (b) closed ICU model, (c) co-managed ICU model, (d) managed by an intensive model and (e) mixed model. Noticeably all ICUs across the country are managed using the open model and this reflects the fact that those clinics are not patient-centered to address patient service through innovative solutions. The acquisition of medical technology tend also to be affected by the inappropriate policy making where hospital decision makers tend to think and manage in medical orientations in a way that limits their ability to understand the determinants and processes of technology acquisition (including costs of technological infusion, diffusion, maintenance and training) that they fail to address the context of competition and market efficiency forms. Medical training of newly appointed medical staff (houseman-ship training programs) is negatively affected by economic trends that made specialists and consultants unavailable at attainable periods to train graduates as well as medical students. Moreover, clinical training of medical students has been negatively affected by the growing number of medical institutes and the mismatch between the number of patients, clinically-trainable beds, medical specialists and consultants (in different areas of expertise) and the number of students to be trained.

2. The lack of appropriate incident reporting systems, adverse drug events and order issuance and management protocols to address medical errors. It worth mentioning that this component depends upon intensive R&D and is fast moving.

The result of such issues is the deterioration of medication quality, error-inclusive clinical practice and the growing costs of health and medical services. Because the overall health sectors fails to develop and implement a maintainable financial and technical sustainability, patients continued to travel to other countries for further investigation and management. In addition to medication associated costs, patients continued to face additional travel, accommodation and misconduct costs. Costs of "mediation" and misconduct associated with abuse and payment policies (reserving even bodies till payment is made", unnecessary medication and operations and others are all examples.

MOBILITY IN HEALTHCARE

Mobile and wireless systems are gaining paramount importance and deployment in They have been widely used in medical informatics, e-business, e-learning, supply chain management, virtual enterprises (Jain et al 1999), information retrieval (Cabri, et al 2000), Internet-based auctions (Sandholm & Huai 2000), distributed network management (Du et al 2003), resource management and broadband intelligent networks (Chatzipapadopoulos et al 2000), telecommunication services, and mobile and wireless computing *(Keng Siau* et al, 2001). Their use in the healthcare system enhances operational and contextual functionality, improving the availability, accessibility and management of decentralized repositories of concurrent data (Gasmelseid, 2007d). Mobility allows different agents to move across different networks and perform tasks on behalf of their users or other agents, by accessing databases and updating files in a way that respects the dynamics of the processing environment and intervention mechanisms (Gasmelseid, 2007c).

The complexity exhibited in the healthcare industry is motivating the distribution of both the organisational structure and enabling information systems. The basic objective of such distributed environment is to build a network of complementary and integrated medical and health centres such as hospitals, laboratories, ambulatories, co-ordination centres, pharmacies, diagnosis centres and support units in accordance with diversity and imperativeness of services. Within this context, although each individual centre operates as an autonomous unit devoted to the delivery of a particular set of services, they are interacting to provide efficient prevention and care. According to Francesco Fedele (1995), the information systems supporting the individual centres must be structured as a federation of autonomous systems, individually optimised according to the specific characteristics of the involved units.

In parallel, the individual systems must be consistent with information and procedural standards, in order to permit the mutual interoperability to provide an effective and efficient support to the co-operation individually provided by each single unit.

Mobility is defined as the ability to "wirelessly" access all of the services that one would normally have in a fixed wired line environment such as a home or office, from anywhere. It includes terminal mobility (provided by wireless access), personal mobility (based on personal numbers), and service portability supported by the capabilities of intelligent networks. Especially in technology-intensive and information-rich distributed environments, mobile agents interact to gather information, route processing outcomes, update a database and read performance levels, among others. The efficiency of any mobile multi agent system is based on its capacity to achieve objectives and adapt to changing environments (Gasmelseid, 2007c).

Mobility in healthcare has been associated with the concepts of ubiquitous healthcare which extends the dimensions of web-based healthcare computation. It allows individuals to access and benefit from healthcare services through mobile computing devices. While such fully or semi automatic access of healthcare information and services assists in reducing operational complexity, it also turns healthcare institutions into effective learning organizations. Knowledge provided through mobile medical informatics includes clinical, personal, situational (environmental), and historical medical and health histories (relevant past diseases / operations / therapies mirrored upon current symptoms or already available diagnosis) indicators. Although under certain conditions, some of that knowledge may be captured from patients themselves through mobile devices, other knowledge may be accessed through distributed databases located any of the three at levels of the healthcare control process: federal, territorial and patient care centres such as hospitals, family doctors, medical specialists, pharmacy, and diagnostic centres. Because the maintenance of financial sustainability and competitive advantage (market efficiency forms, service differentiation, process efficiency, and improved patient relationship management) is looming very big in the healthcare system, mobile medical informatics offers an IT-enabled platform for continuous improvement.

The implementation of mobile medical informatics initiatives tend to be based on alternative technological, architectural, and infrastructure-based methodologies. This paper aims at using a mobile agent-enabled architecture to improve clinical practice through improved knowledge intensive cooperation among humans and intelligent software agents involved in producing, delivering, controlling, and consuming health services. The proposed technology proved to be useful also in improving operational efficiency through shared medical processes.

The importance and feasibility of using mobile multiagent systems stems from two main reasons:

1. The diversity and multi-dimensionality of the healthcare structure: The healthcare provision system in Sudan is spread over three levels each with different level of complexity. The federal level is concerned with the promotion of national health strategies. At the Territorial (state) level Epidemiological and coordination centres take the responsibility of epidemiological and planning activities. At the medical centres level, hospitals operate as the main providers of patient caring. Despite the fact that each hospital is composed of a set of specialized service-based units, they also interact consistently within the context of the overall functionality of the global structure. Mobility helps in improving the quality of healthcare services and medical practice through improved information provision and location-specific organizational and managerial control. It also maintains effective institutional (within each healthcare institution) and structural (across the three levels of health control) coordination.

2. The characteristics of software agents that make them good candidates to implement distributed management. Within the context of a distributed multiagent mobile medical information system, the entire structure can be populated with a wide range of software agents possessing different qualities and attributes. Based on such attributes they can be classified. An intelligent agent is as an autonomous, computational software entity that has access to one or more, heterogeneous and geographically distributed information sources, and which proactively acquires, mediates, and maintains relevant information on behalf of users or other agents (Gasmelseid, 2007a). While autonomy remains a leading agency attribute other attributes like mobility, pro-activity, conviviality, among others are characterizing the use of multiple agents within the context of an integrated organizational structure. The

topology of agents is based on their attributes and user-specific functions. Therefore, the classification includes internet agents, information agents, interface agents, shopping agents, search agents etc. However, the autonomous behaviour of these agents is determined by their proactiveness, reactive and deliberative actions, and social interactions. In a multiagent system, agents jointly use knowledge and resources to solve problems in a context-dependent way (Gasmelseid, 2007b). Within the context of a distributed healthcare, software agents can provide assistance in different ways. For example, they can facilitate (vertical and horizontal) coordination, cooperation and interaction among different remote health and medical centres at the three levels of the healthcare system. While this will improve the effectiveness of communication it also enhances interaction among medical staff and patient mobility resulting from embedded orchestration of service and physical mobility and service accessibility enabled by the uniformity of service points.

The use of mobile agents allows the incorporation of a wide range of object oriented features necessary for information sharing, encapsulation and inheritance. This is because their conceptualization is based on the "articulation" of roles, players and relationships on the one hand and "drawing" road maps for system-wide critical success "technical" factors including security and authentication on the other hand. In addition to their roles as information gatherers, filters and learners, multi agent systems support various phases of decision making and problem solving by serving as "problem analyzers and solvers" and are engaged in "implementation", "monitoring" and "negotiation" (Gasmelseid, 2006).

When multi agent systems are used, the problem-solving tasks of each functional unit becomes populated by a number of heterogeneous intelligent agents with diverse goals and capabilities (Lottaz, et al, 2000; Luo, et al, 2001; McMullen, 2001; Ulieru, et al, 2000; Wu, 2001). The system simplifies problem-solving by dividing the necessary knowledge into subunits, associating an intelligent independent agent to each subunit, and coordinating the agents' activity. Multi-agent systems offer a new dimension for coordination and negotiation by incorporating autonomous agents into the problem-solving process and improving coordination of different functional unit defined tasks,

Figure 1. A work-centered analysis

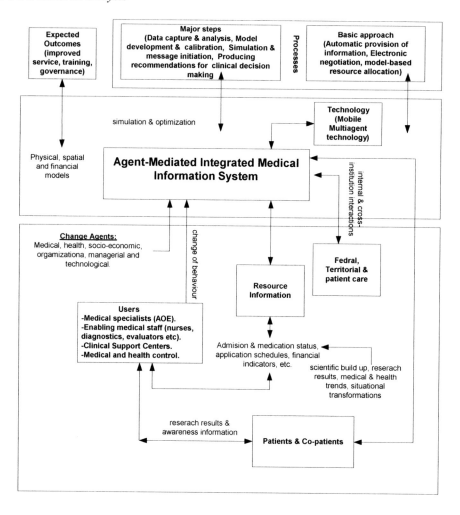

independent of both the user and the functional units under control (Byung & Sadeh, 2004).

IMPROVING CLINICAL PRACTICE THROUGH MOBILE MEDICAL INFORMATICS

Epidemiologic techniques are suited to complications and major transfusion errors that occur with reasonable frequency rather than rare ones. The conceptualization of medical errors is based on the taxonomy provided by Reason (1990; 1997; 2000) who classified errors into active error (occurs at the point of human interface with a complex system) and latent error (represents failures of system design). Medical errors

are also associated with the lack or inappropriateness of existing patient safety practices (mainly Quality improvement practices) that increases the probability of adverse events within the health care system across a range of conditions or procedures. The use of mobile agent-mediated medical informatics to improve clinical practice in Sudan can be conceptualized using the work centred analysis shown in Figure 1 below.

Work centred analysis is usually based on the identification of "users", "major steps", "basic approach", and "technology". The basic aim beyond the use of such kind of analysis as a methodological tool is to ensure the incorporation of an integrated distributed hospital environment. Therefore, emphasis tend to be made maintaining coordination between medical centres and units at the interface between inpatient and outpatient settings; promoting performance improvement and decreasing the number of diagnostic errors of omission. As shown in figure 2 below, the distributed environment of the system is based on building effective interfaces among the different medical areas of expertise in accordance with their shared functionalities and rule based integration and reasoning of acquired information.

The functionality of mobile information systems in clinical fields is contingent upon its operational capacity to provide clinical support as well as the "optimality" of the operating environment surrounding it as shown in figure 3 below.

The contribution of such agent mediated mobile medical information system in the Sudanese context can be outlined below:

Universality of Patient Data and Records

The question of managing and using patient's medical data looms very big in Sudan. Especially for kidney failure and dialysis patients their mobility is growing over the last couple of years due to the lack of reliable medical services in remote trajectories and/or their inability to meet the growing medication costs. Their migration to the capital originates from their interest to benefit from the financial support provided by social funds and the concentration of qualified medical staff. Under many conditions, when they move from one city to the other they miss to bring with them their medical history. Also the same applies for referred cases where the information provided by different hospitals lacks standardization in a way that make it difficult

Figure 2. system based interaction

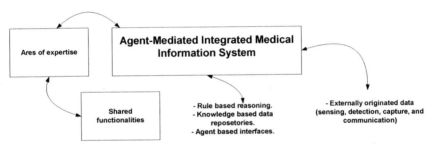

Figure 3. System enabling environment

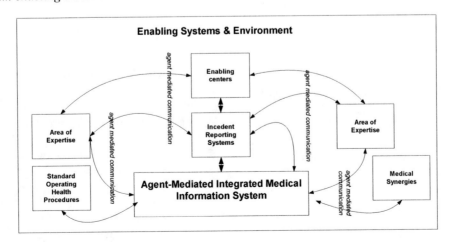

for different medical specialists to use them as valid entities in their operational databases.

The use of mobile multiagent systems provides an opportunity for reducing such complexity through the following:

1. Patients' data can be maintained by the first-to-see medical specialist in his hospital's data warehouse or knowledge base. Records of different patients are kept updated every time the patient visits his/her medical specialist. To facilitate information access patients' data can be stored on smart cards and updated frequently. Upon referring patients to another medical specialist or center, patient's data can be accessed from the smart card and updated accordingly by keeping original data unchanged. Because of the unprecedented technological developments witnessed in the medical field, mobile software agents can room and move across the internet or shared WANs to access the database of the originating medical center or specialist to retrieve necessary data. The advantage of this process are the following:

a. Originating medical center or specialist will be informed about the recent developments in his patient's health record and accordingly he/she can intervene at any point of time because of his access to the resulting real time information.

b. Access can be given to a third party for a second opinion about the medical status of the patient as well as the suitability of medical management practices. This process is supported by the possibility of sharing diagnosis data such as MRI and other ultra sound images and the outstanding interface qualities of software agent systems.

2. Due to such integrated counseling medication errors as well as adverse drug events will be minimized within a context of shared "responsibility". Because the process enables the update of incident reporting systems in different medical canters it assists in developing reasonable medical and clinical synergies.

Physician Order Entry Validation and Endorsement

A review of major studies of adverse medical events and medication errors led to estimations that in the

USA between 44,000 to 98,000 people die in hospitals each year as a result of medical errors. The solutions available range from electronic patient records, order processing, clinical documentation and reporting for nursing and physicians, to computerized physician order entry in combination with rules-based decision support and electronic medication dispensing and administration solutions (Baldauf-Sobez, et al, 2003).

Incorporating the Computerized Physician Order Entry (CPOE) into the backbone of the entire agent-mediated mobile information system allows both patients and healthcare institutions to gain some benefits (Mekhjian et al, 2002) such as: significant reduction in medication turn-around times, improvement in result reporting times, eliminated all physician and nursing transcription errors, and medication dispensing.

Patient Hospitalization and Recovery-Oriented Support

Geriatric

Hospitals address the risks of hospitalization and provide inpatient care for elders suffering from multiple co-morbidities by focusing on their special needs and geriatric syndromes. The main strategy to be adopted is to provide care by Geriatric Evaluation and Management (GEM) Units equipped with multidisciplinary teams in pursuit of improved mortality and other clinically relevant outcomes. Alternatively, geriatric hospitalization can be provided through comprehensive geriatric consultation service. On the other hand, Acute Care of Elders (ACE) Units incorporate the GEM unit design with additional enhancements and admit patients with acute illnesses. ACE units often provide improved flooring and lighting, reorienting devices, and other environmental improvements such as common rooms for patient use (Palmer, 1994; 1998). Within the context of the ACE unit, the GEM unit concept was enhanced by the use of more nurse-initiated protocols and a greater number of environmental and design modifications to emphasize the early assessment of risk factors for iatrogenic complications and the prevention of functional decline (Landefeld, et al 1995).

The integrated agent mediated medical information system provide assistance in this regard by the development of a platform that helps in strengthening and supporting the incorporation the GEM unit into ACE units. Within this context, patients can use the components and symbols of the entire system to know directions, ask for help, get drug and nutrition information and call for assistance in case of falling etc.

Paediatric

Parents used to co-patient heir children in hospitals sometimes for long periods of time. While emphasis tends to be made on clinical management, paediatric inpatients can be supported by a paediatric smart room in which patients and their co-patients (mainly parents) spend sometime entertainment time. The room can also benefit from the entire integrated system and include system-based smart toys, medication-based smart screens, as well as physical and digital tools. In addition to creating a home environment that assists in recovery, such rooms also provide some confidence for parents regarding the health status of their children. Since it operates through the backbone of the entire integrated system, it can provide useful feedback about the recovery progress of paediatric inpatients.

Medical Training

The integrated counseling environment constitutes an outstanding training environment for medical parishioners. Because of the growing number of medical and health-related students and graduates both on-study and houseman-ship training is challenged by the inability of public medical and health institutions to develop a conducive learning and training environment. Such an integrated system-based counseling environment provides an environment through which good practices can be shared.

FUTURE DIRECTION

The incorporation of agent-mediated mobile medical informatics to improve clinical practice in Sudan (as well as in other developing countries) calls for paradigm shifts in the following directions:

a. Institutional knowledge-oriented direction: The use of mobile medical informatics not only affects medical and clinical practice but also dictates new axioms for resources sharing, medical accountability (before institutions and patients). Because the majority of healthcare institutions are public establishments their ability to benefit from the use of mobile medical informatics ne-

cessitate the conversion of such establishments into learning organizations capable of managing technology intensive acquisitions. There is also a growing need for some degree of organizational flexibility to allow for automating some of the core clinical processes, widening the hand-eye dexterity of physicians to a wider domain of consultation and enriching all knowledge bases across the federated medical centers and applications. The use of mobile medical informatics also demands careful restructuring of hospitals to orchestrate processes throughout modified and innovative "value chains" rather than "chains of command".

b. Technology-oriented direction: The implementation of innovative agent-mediated mobile medical informatics requires more appreciation of the importance of changing technological orientations of users. While the installation of technological solutions is directly and inexorably linked to "functional" processes, it is also contingent upon the planning paradigms used to ensure system-function match. This direction emphasizes the role to be played by systems analysts in articulating roles, processes and relationships in a useful value-chain-related format that promotes informed utilization and minimize the impact of dysfunctional change agents that move the whole situation into disarray due to the "blind" jump to technological platforms. Based on the above mentioned directions, further research can be directed towards the following critical success factors:

1. Intelligent systems development and assessment with more emphasis on bridging methodological gaps associated with agent oriented software engineering when such systems are reduced to medical applications. While different agent oriented theories and methodologies are being developed and used, little has been done to address and re-engineer them to fit different domains of applications with varying degrees of functional complexity.

2. Orchestrating the qualities of agents with the core value adding medical processes and allowing rooms for both concurrent processing and flexibility of technological platforms in order to enable the incorporation of technological (and medical) developments and inventions.

CONCLUSION

The decreasing efficiency and lack of quality healthcare services in many developing countries motivates patients to consider alternative mediation and hospitalization scenarios. While public healthcare institutions are being challenged by the lack of funds and public service standard operating procedures, private ones are challenged by the growing operational costs associated with the acquisition of advanced medical equipments and specialists. The marathon of private healthcare institutions originates from the need to improve competitive edges within the healthcare system. However, the dysfunctional side effects of such race-for-competitiveness game ranged from high medication and hospitalization costs in Sudan (compared to other countries) to the institutional intension to find escape gates to avoid regulatory controls and quality assurance practices. If managed properly, the use of agent mediated mobile medical informatics provides a wide range of organizational, institutional and process-oriented functionalities that significantly contribute to improving clinical practice.

REFERENCES

Baldauf-Sobez, W., Bergstrom, W. M., Meisner, M. K., Ahmad, A., & Häggström, M. (2003). How Siemens' Computerized Physician Order Entry Helps Prevent the Human Error. *Electromedica* , *71*(1), 1-9.

Byung, K., & Sadeh, N. (2004). Applying case-based reasoning and multi-agent intelligent system to context-aware comparative shopping. *Decision Support Systems, 37*(2) 199-213.

Cabri, G., Leonardi, L., & Zambonelli, F. (2000). Mobile agent coordination models for internet applications. *IEEE Computer*, *33*(2), 82–89.

Chatzipapadopoulos, F., Perdikeas, M., & Venieris, L. (2000). Mobile agent and CORBA technologies in the broadband intelligent network. *IEEE Communication Magazine, 38*(6), 116–124.

Datta, A. & Thomas, H. (1993). The cube data model: A conceptual model and algebra for on-line analytical processing in data warehouses. *Decision Support Systems 27*(3), 289-301.

Du, T., Li, E., & Chang, A. (2003). Mobile agents in distributed network management. *Communications of the ACM, 46*(7), 127–132.

Fedele, F. (1995). Healthcare and Distributed Systems Technology. Retrieved December 23, from: www.ansa.co.uk/ANSATech/95/ansaworks-95/hltcare.pdf

Gasmelseid, T (2007c). Engineering Multi Agent Systems. *Encyclopedia of Information Security and Ethics.* Information Science Reference, Idea Group Publishing, USA. ISBN-10: 159140987X, EAN: 9781591409878.

Gasmelseid, T. (2006). "A Multi Agent Negotiation Framework in Resource Bounded Environments". *Proceedings of the international conference on information and communication technologies: from theory to practice.* Damascus Syria, 24-28 April, 2006. Also in Information and Communication Technologies, 2006. ICTTA '06. 2(1), 465-470, ISBN: 0-7803-9521-2. Retrieved from http://ieeexplore.ieee.org/xpl/freeabs_all.jsp?tp=&arnumber=1684414&isnumber =35470.

Gasmelseid, T. (2007a). A Multi agent Service Oriented Modelling of e-government Initiatives. *International Journal of Electronic Government Research, 3*(3), 87-105.

Gasmelseid, T. (2007b). From Operational Dash Boards to EBusiness: Multiagent Formulation of Electronic Contracts. *International Journal of E-Business Research, 3*(3): 77-97.

Goodhue D. L. & Thompso, R. L. (1995). Task-technology fit and individual-performance, *MIS Quarterly, 19*(2), 213-236.

Goodhue, D. L. (1995). Understanding user evaluations of information systems, *Management Science, 41*(12), 1827-1844.

Jain, A., Aparicio, M., & Singh, M. (1999). Agents for process coherence in virtual enterprises. *Communications of the ACM, 42*(3), 62-69.

Keng, S., Ee-Peng, L., & Zixing, S., (2001). Mobile commerce: Promises, challenges, and research agenda, *Journal of Database Management, 12(3), 4-10.*

Kirn, S. (n/d). *Ubiquitous Healthcare: The OnkoNet Mobile Agents Architecture.* Retrieved December 1, 2007 from: http://www.citeseer.

Koutsoukis, N.-S., Mitra, G., & Lucas, C. (1999). Adapting on-line analytical processing for decision modeling: the interaction of information and decision technologies. *Decision Support Systems, 26*(1), 1 - 30.

Landefeld, C. S, Palmer, R. M, Kresevic, D. M, Fortinsky, R. H, & Kowal, J. (1995). A randomized trial of care in a hospital medical unit especially designed to improve the functional outcomes of acutely ill older patients. *New England Journal of Medicine,* (332),1338-1344.

Lottaz, C., Smith, C., Robert-Nicoud, Y. & Faltings, B. V. (2000). Constraint-based support for negotiation in collaborative design. *Artificial Intelligence in Engineering 14*(3) 261–280.

Luo, X., Zhang, C. ,& Leung, H. F. (2001). Information sharing between heterogeneous uncertain reasoning models in a multi-agent environment: a case study. *International Journal of Approximate Reasoning, 27*(1), 27–59.

McMullen, P. R. (2001). An ant colony optimization approach to addressing a JIT sequencing problem with multiple objectives. *Artificial Intelligence in Engineering 15*(3), 309–317.

Mekhjian, H. S., Kumar, R. R., Kuehn, L., Bentley, T. D., Teater, P., Thomas, A., Payne, B., Ahmad, A. (2002). Immediate Benefits Realized Following Implementation of Physician Order Entry at an Academic Medical Center. *Journal of American Medical Information Association,* (9), 529-532.

Ministry of Health, Sudan. http://www.fmoh.gov.sd

Monica, C., hiarini T., Remblay, A., Robert F., Uller, A., Donald, B., Erndt, B., & James, S. (2006). Doing more with more information: Changing healthcare planning with OLAP tools. *Decision Support Systems,* doi:10.1016/j.dss.2006.02.008.

Münch, E. (2002). Teleportal-Klinik. Internal presentation, TU Ilmenau.

Palmer R.M, Landefeld C.S, Kresevic D, & Kowal J. (1994). A medical unit for the acute care of the elderly. *Journal of the American Geriatric Society,* (42), 545-552.

Palmer, R. M., Counsell, S., & Landefeld, C. S. (1998). Clinical intervention trials: The ACE unit. *Clinical Geriatric Medicine,* (14), 831-849.

Reason J. (2000). Human error: models and management. *British Medical Journal,* (320), 768-770.

Reason, J. T. (1990). *Human Error.* New York: Cambridge University Press.

Reason, J. T. (1997) *Managing the Risks of Organizational Accidents.* Ashgate Publishing.

Sandholm, T., & Huai, Q. (2000). Nomad: mobile agent system for an internet-based auction house. *IEEE Internet Computing, 4*(2), 80–86.

Sheth, A. P., & Larson, J. A. (1990). Federated Database Management Systems for Managing Distributed, Heterogeneous, and Autonomous Databases. *ACM Computing Surveys, 22*(3), 1183-236.

Ulieru, M. D., Norrie, R., Kremer, & Shen, W. (2000). A multi-resolution collaborative architecture for web-centric global manufacturing. *Information Sciences, 127*(1–2), 3–21.

UNFPA website: http://www.unfpa.org

Unicef website: http://www.unicef.org

Wu, D. J. (2001). Software agents for knowledge management: Coordination in multi-agent supply chains and auctions. *Expert Systems with Applications, 20*(1) 51-64.

KEY TERMS

Clinical Practice: The activities undertaken by medical staff at the different medical areas of expertise and specialization (such as surgery, pediatrics, etc) within the organizational domains of health-related organizations and prevailing professional medical codes of ethics.

Healthcare Control Levels: Reflect both the organizational and institutional dimensions of the healthcare system which varies from country to another. Especially in developing countries where public healthcare institutions play a significant role, three control levels tend to be used: federal, territorial and local. The efficiency of such levels is affected by the existing decision making context and technological platforms.

ICU Models: The key organizational characterization used for the description, coordination, and re-engineering (if necessary) of medical processes undertaken by medical (and supporting) personnel in the intensive care unit.

Medical Informatics: A term widely used to describe the use of information systems (mainly decision support systems) in medical processes and interactions. The basic aim is to improve operational efficiency of medical and health centers, enhance clinical practice and the quality of medical care and promote good practices.

Mobile Agents: Are software programs that use their "mobility" qualities to room across networks in order to access information and carry out tasks for their own processes, on behalf of their owners and/or other agents.

Multiagent Systems: A cluster of (homogenous or heterogeneous) software agents possessing diverse agency qualities and attributes orchestrated in an organization structure-alike context to share resources and achieve objectives within a predefined (center-specific) or universal (internet-based) processing environment.

Users: All stakeholders and partners who are in direct (main and subordinate) interaction with the provision of health care services (such as physicians, pharmacists, etc) (a.k.a affecters), third party partners (such as suppliers) (a.k.a facilitators) and patients who are directly affected by the quality of medical and clinical processes (a.k.a affected).

Chapter LVII
Traffic Management System (TMS) using WiMAX

Ishan Bhalla
University of Technology, Sydney, Australia

Kamlesh Chaudhary
University of Technology, Sydney, Australia

ABSTRACT

Mobile WiMAX has gained extensive support in the industry. Demand on wireless Internet bandwidth is increasing. Mobile WiMAX, also called WirelessMAN (Wireless Metropolitan Area Networks.), is Wi-Fi (Wireless Fidelity) of the Metro. Mobile WiMAX will offer wireless internet experience within the city as Wi-Fi offers within your office or home. Imagine making VoIP (Voice over Internet Protocol) calls from home and continuing to talk as you travel to work in the train or travel in the car on a freeway. Mobile WiMAX can make that happen. In this chapter the authors would describe what is Mobile WiMAX, how it can be combined with GPS (Global Positioning System) for Traffic Management, solve traffic related offences and help in providing a clear way for PSV's (Public safety vehicles) like fire brigades and ambulances.

WHAT IS MOBILE WIMAX

IEEE (**Institute of Electrical and Electronics Engineers**, Inc) defined 802.16 standard (known as WiMAX) for point to multipoint wireless broadband communication operating in 10-66GHz band. 802.16 need LOS (*Line of Sight*) to function. It underwent several enhancements. Finally, IEEE

802.16e-2005 (or *IEEE 802.16e*) popularly known as Mobile WiMAX, defined mobility extensions to IEEE 802.16 standard. IEEE 802.16e included capability for high data rate, quality of service, mobility etc.

Mobile WiMAX offers flexible network architecture for wireless broadband based on both fixed and mobile broadband networks using a common wide area broadband radio access technology (WiMax Forum 2006, 'A Technical Overview and Performance Evaluation')

The Mobile WiMAX certification program, managed by WiMAX Forum with 471 members from all across the industry, is helping in gaining acceptance of the technology all around the world. Recently it has also been ratified as a 3G standard by ITU (*International Telecommunication Union*).

WHY MOBILE WIMAX?

Mobile WiMAX is way ahead of other competing technologies in defining and adapting standards using efficient multiplexing techniques, advance antenna techniques, mobility features etc. Mobile WiMAX is coming close to 4G (*4th generation*) wireless broadband features (Santhi & Kumaran, 2006).

Key features and advantages of Mobile WiMAX technology, which make it the technology of choice for wireless internet connectivity and its suitability for TMS are:

- Physical Layer uses multiplexing technique OFDMA (*Orthogonal Frequency Division Multiple Access*). OFDMA offers better indoor coverage (*non Line of Sight capability*), higher capacity and throughput for Network companies. (Wimax Forum, 2006, 'The Best Personal Broadband Experience')
- Mobile WiMAX Network Architecture is based on all-IP (*Internet Protocol*) right from start (Iyer et al, 2007). Therefore,

it can offer end-to-end services using IP based QoS, session management security and mobility. (Santhi & Kumaran 2006).

- High Data rates of 63Mbps for downlink and 25Mbps for uplink in a 10 MHz channel are achieved because of MIMO (*Multiple Input, Multiple Output*) antenna techniques together with flexible sub-canalisation schemes, Advanced Coding and Modulation (WiMax Forum, 2006, 'A Technical Overview and Performance Evaluation, P10-11)
- Mobile WiMAX focused on QoS in MAC (*Medium Access Control*) Layer from the start. The WiMAX connection-oriented protocol is specified for each service flow and it can effectively support the end-to-end QoS control. (WiMax Forum, 2006, 'Mobile_WiMAX_Part2_Comparative_Analysis')
- Worldwide roaming and Interoperability: WiMAX Forum has setup a Network Working Group which is working on ways to make Roaming and interworking with other operators and technologies easier. It has recently defined interworking standards for 3GPP (*3rd Generation Partnership Project*), DSL (*Digital Subscriber Line*) etc. Mobile WiMAX equipments, complying with standards, are interoperable with other equipments in the same band (WiMax Forum, 2006, 'The Best Personal Broadband Experience', P2, 5,7)
- WiMAX supports both soft (with make-before-break links) and hard handoffs (with break-before-make links). Latencies less than 50 milliseconds is achieved that helps mobility. High-speed handoffs will be supported later on. (WiMax Forum, 2006, 'The Best Personal Broadband Experience', P7)
- Availability of Wi-Fi and WiMAX on a single chip (notebooks to have this built-in by early 2008), will increase popularity of WiMAX and will reduce the cost significantly for end-users. (WiMax Forum, 2006, 'The Best Personal Broadband Experience', P12)

- Power Saving: Mobile WiMAX supports two powersave modes the "Idle mode" and the "Sleep mode". Mobile devices (*phone, PDA* etc) attains 'Sleep mode' when it is inactive for brief period. In 'Sleep mode' the device is still in registered state. In case of inactivity for long periods the device attains 'Idle mode' where the device is de-registered. (Iyer Prakash, Nat Natarajan, Muthaiah Venkatachalam, Anand Bedekar, Eren Gonen, Kamran Etemad, Pouya Taaghol, 2007, P57)
- Security: Mobile WiMAX supports industry's best authentication Protocol EAP *(Extensible Authentication Protocol)* and strong encryption using AES (*Advanced Encryption Standard*). It also supports range of user credentials methods including SIM (*Subscriber Identity Module*), USIM (*Universal Subscriber Identity Module 3G equivalent of SIM*) cards, Smart Cards, Digital Certificates, and username/Password. (WiMax Forum, 2006, 'A Technical Overview and Performance Evaluation, P11)

Mobile WiMAX can be used for variety of innovative applications. This chapter will only cover how this technology can be used for TMS.

CURRENT TRAFFIC SITUATION

Vehicular traffic has seen a tremendous growth over the last few years. This has put an enormous strain on the road infrastructure resulting in traffic delays. Since GPS receivers have no/ limited live updates on traffic conditions, drivers do not get notified of alternative routes. Drivers also would not know of traffic accidents, road blocks or other traffic hazards like bush fires or flash flooding through their GPS receivers.

VISION: TRAFFIC MANAGEMENT SYSTEM (TMS)

TMS will receive live location information from each vehicle through a WiMAX network, calculate traffic congestion and advise individual users of the best routes to their destinations.

Key Components and Basic Construction of TMS

TMS will consist of 4 main components: a vehicle, a WiMAX network, TMS servers and External Sources.

A vehicle would require an onboard computer with a GPS receiver to calculate its position, speed and direction of travel. The onboard computer can be a low cost WiMAX capable computer (~$100 US) fitted with a GPSR (*Global Positioning System Receiver*) card such as the G12 GPS and WiMAX card like the MS120 from Beceem Communications (One Laptop Per Child, One Laptop Per Child, 17December 2007) *(*Navaids, *G12 Board*, Navaids, 20 August 2007).

Beceem Communications MS120 chipset consists of a high-performance baseband IC (MSB120) and an integrated RFIC (MSR120) for implementing a full-featured IEEE 802.16e/ WiMAX/WiBRO Wave 1 compliant mobile subscriber (MS) (Beceem, Chipsets MS 120, Beceem, 20 August 2007).

All vehicles will use a mobile WiMAX network providing end to end TCP (Transmission Control Protocol) support to communicate with TMS Servers.

TMS Servers will be a group of collaborating servers to run traffic management applications.

External Sources like Road Traffic Authority, police, weather bureau etc will provide information on road works, accidents, police chases, bush fires and any other traffic hazards that may affect traffic conditions.

Figure 1. TMS overview

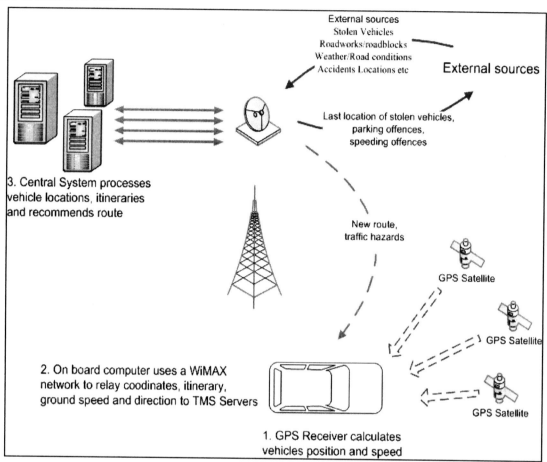

END TO END DATA FLOW

Data Gathering and Processing by TMS Servers

A vehicle would start its journey by registering its vehicle number and itinerary with TMS. During a vehicles journey TMS will be able to determine number of vehicles on a road section and compare it with already stored calibrated traffic data to calculate congestion. On the basis of received itineraries and updated data on traffic conditions TMS will be able to advise best routes to drivers with approximate travel time.

Other data that might affect recommendation of best routes by TMS will be road works from the Road Traffic Authority, bush fires from the Weather Bureau and countless other traffic hazards like accidents, police chases etc. Please refer to Figures 2, 3, and 4.

EXTENSION TO TMS

Once TMS is built authorities like Police, Road Traffic Authority and Weather Bureau can subscribe to TMS information. Police can then get the current locations of stolen vehicles. TMS will

Figure 2. End to end data flow

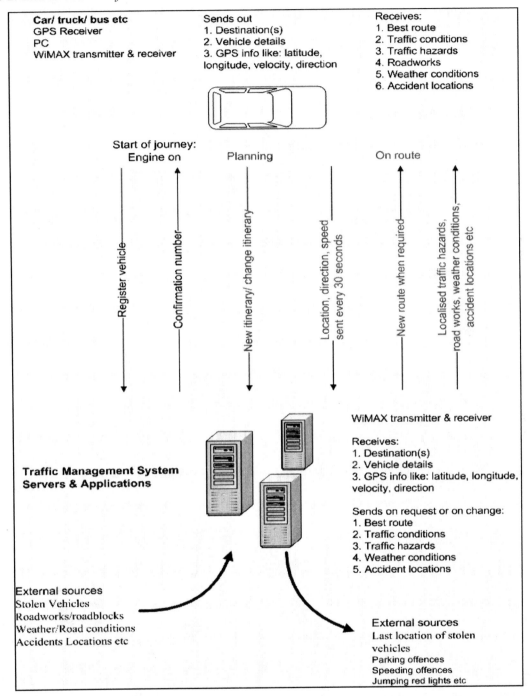

Figure 3. Basic traffic management cycle

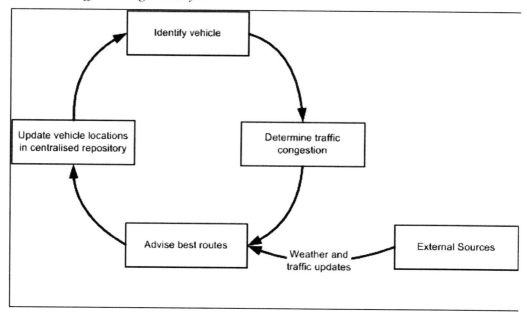

only require vehicle registration number to return the last position of a stolen vehicle. If TMS is fed with speed limits, it can also report speeding vehicles. If its databases stores parking zones, it can report improper parking.

If traffic lights are integrated into TMS, then ambulances and fire brigades can be given clearance to their destinations.

CHALLENGES

For TMS to determine routes accurately it will require to know about most of the vehicles on the road. So until majority of the vehicles are upgraded the system would not predict accurately.

Development of congestion calculation and route discovery software could be time consuming and expensive.

TMS needs a wireless solution with End to End IP support. Mobile WiMAX being in its infancy and not yet tested for major projects can

be substituted with alternate wireless network technology with End to End IP support for immediate implementation of TMS.

When TMS starts reporting on speeding vehicles it could create highly policed roads. Would society want such a system?

CONCLUSION AND FUTURE OF TMS

TMS will improve the road usage; reduce traffic offences like speeding and incorrect parking, help fire brigades and ambulances serve the community better by assisting them in getting to their destinations quicker.

TMS can be enhanced to develop parking applications that allow a user to pay only for the duration of park. TMS will know when a user parked and when he left. This is enough to generate an invoice.

TMS can also assist parents in keeping track of their vehicles when used by their children.

Figure 4. TMS flow chart for an overview of the route planning algorithm

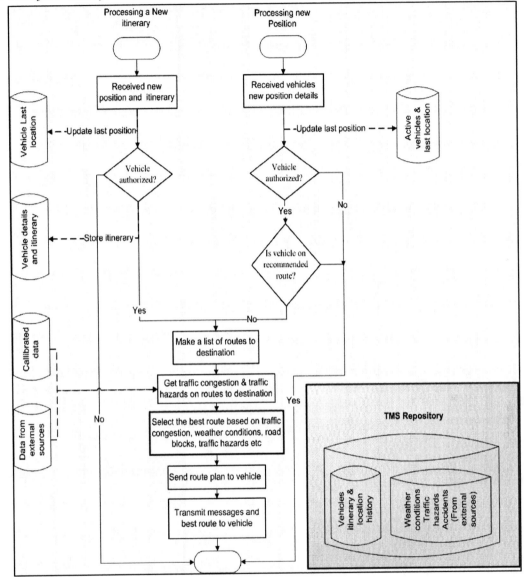

REFERENCES

Beceem (2007). *Chipsets MS 120*, Beceem. Retrieved 20 August 2007, from http://www.beceem.com/products/ms120.shtml

Kidman, A. (2007). Traffic channel to unjam those road hold-ups. *The Australian IT – Exec Tech*. Retrieved August 28, 2007, (p. 34).

Moonblink, *Tsunami MP.16 3500 Starter Kit - 3500-K00-AM0* (2007). Moonblink. Retrieved 6 September 2007, http://www.moonblinkwifi.com/pd_tsunami_mp16_starter.cfm

Navaids. (2007). *G12 Board*. Navaids. Retrieved 20 August 2007 http://www.navaids.com.au/images/G12BoardD.pdf

One Laptop Per Child. (2007). *One Laptop Per Child. Retrieved 17 December 2007* http://laptop.org/laptop/hardware/specs.shtml

Prakash, I., Natarajan, N., Venkatachalam, M., Bedekar, A., Gonen, E., Etemad, K., & Taaghol, P. (2007). *All-IP Network Architecture for Mobile WiMAX*. IEEE, *25*(29), 54-59. Retrieved August 28, 2007.

Santhi, K.R., & Kumaran, G. S.(2006). Migration to 4 G: Mobile IP based Solutions. *Proceedings of the Advanced International Conference on Telecommunications and International Conference on Internet and Web Applications and Services (AICT/ICIW 2006)*. IEEE & Computer Society, (p. 2), Kigali, Rwanda.

WiMAX Forum (May 2007). *A Comparative Analysis of Mobile WiMAX™ Deployment Alternatives in the Access Network*. WiMAX Forum, Retrieved 16 August 2007, from http://www.wimaxforum.org/technology/downloads/mobile_wimax_deployment_alternatives.pdf, Pages 12-13.

WiMAX Forum (2006). *Mobile WiMAX: The Best Personal Broadband Experience!* WiMAX Forum. Retrieved 16 August 2007, from http://www.intel.com/netcomms/technologies/wimax/Mobile_WiMAX_WP.pdf, Pages 5, 7-13.

WiMAX Forum (2006). *Mobile WiMAX – Part I: A Technical Overview and Performance Evaluation*. WiMAX Forum, Retrieved 16 August 2007, from http://www.intel.com/netcomms/technologies/wimax/WiMAX_Overviewv2.pdf, Pages 9-11.

KEY TERMS

4G: 4G refers to fourth generation mobile system which promises to offer high speed and IP based video service and global access.

AES: Advanced Encryption Standard - In cryptography, the Advanced Encryption Standard (AES), also known as Rijndael, is a block cipher adopted as an encryption standard by the U.S. government. It has been analyzed extensively and is now used worldwide, as was the case with its predecessor,[3] the Data Encryption Standard (DES).

EAP: Extensible Authentication Protocol - Extensible Authentication Protocol, or EAP, is a universal authentication framework frequently used in wireless networks and Point-to-Point connections.

GPS: The Global Positioning System (GPS) is the only fully functional Global Navigation Satellite System. The GPS uses a constellation of at least 24 (32 by March 2008) Medium Earth Orbit satellites that transmit precise microwave signals, that enable GPS receivers to determine their location, speed, direction, and time.

IEEE: Institute of Electrical and Electronic Engineers (read eye-triple-e) is an international non-profit, professional organization for the advancement of technology related to electricity. It has the most members of any technical professional organization in the world, with more than 365,000 members in around 150 countries.

ITU: International Telecommunication Union an international organization established to standardize and regulate international radio and telecommunications.

MIMO: Multiple Input, Multiple Output antenna techniques and refers to the technology where there are multiple antennas at the base station and multiple antennas at the mobile device. Typical usage of multiple antenna technology includes cellular phones with two antennas, laptops with two antennas (e.g. built in the left and right side of the screen), as well as CPE devices with multiple sprouting antennas.

Mobile WiMAX IEEE Standard 802.16e-2005: An amendment to 802.16-2004 and is often referred to in shortened form as 802.16e. It introduced support for mobility, amongst other things and is therefore also frequently called "mobile WiMAX".

OFDMA: Orthogonal Frequency Division Multiple Access is a multi-user version of the popular Orthogonal frequency-division multiplexing (OFDM) digital modulation scheme. Multiple access is achieved in OFDMA by assigning subsets of subcarriers to individual users. This allows simultaneous low data rate transmission from several users.

QoS: In the field of computer networking and other packet-switched telecommunication networks, the traffic engineering term quality of service (QoS) refers to resource reservation control mechanisms rather than the achieved service quality. Quality of service is the ability to provide different priority to different applications, users, or data flows, or to guarantee a certain level of performance to a data flow.

SIM: Subscriber Identity Module is part of a removable smart card ICC (Integrated Circuit Card), also known as SIM Cards, for mobile, telephony devices (such as computers) and mobile phones. SIM cards securely store the service-subscriber key (IMSI) used to identify a subscriber.

TCP: Transmission Control Protocol a transport protocol that is one of the core protocols of the Internet protocol suite.

WiMAX: The Worldwide Interoperability for Microwave Access is a telecommunications technology that provides wireless data in a variety of ways, from point-to-point links to full mobile cellular type access. It is based on the IEEE 802.16 standard.

WiMAX Forum: Non profit industry group steering global adoption and interoperability of WiMAX systems.

Chapter LVIII
Transformation of Business Processes of Export Companies to a Proposed Collaborative Environment with the Aid of Web Services and Mobile Technologies

Abbass Ghanbary
MethodScience.com & University of Western Sydney, Australia

Manish Desai
ImpexDocs, Australia

Bhuvan Unhelkar
MethodScience.com & University of Western Sydney, Australia

ABSTRACT

This chapter discusses the results of an action research project carried out at ImpexDocs in Sydney, Australia, by the lead author. The purpose of this action research was to investigate the business processes of companies involved in "EXPORTS" and to study how they collaborate with different service providers involved in exports from Australia. The report provides an insight in to understanding the applications of Collaborative Business Process Engineering (CBPE) in terms of improving the effectiveness and efficiency for all organizations involved in International Business, especially companies involved in exports and their associated service providers. The study demonstrates an understanding of the in-depth analyses of existing business processes, investigate the collaboration between the export companies system with other enterprises involved, investigate the existing channels of collaboration, investigate the common business processes threads through multiple application, investigate the applications that deal with external parties, and engineer collaborative processes across multiple organizations.

INTRODUCTION

This chapter outlines the key issues involved when the business processes and applications of the export companies integrate with those of associated service providers. A business process is a set of coordinated tasks and activities that guide the business in achieving its goals. Thus, a business process is an action taken in the course of conducting business. Whether manual or automated, all processes require input and generate output. Depending on the level of viewing and modeling, a process can be a single task or a complicated procedure made up of numerous phases, tasks and people - such as building a product (http://www.techweb.com/).

The technology of Web Services and mobile technologies (Emerging Technologies) have created the opportunities for businesses to integrate their applications and conduct business transactions irrespective of their technical platform and geographical boundaries. These advantages of Emerging Technologies (ET) adapted by organizations enable their business processes to interact on any platform by the aid of Web Services and at any location and time with the aid of Mobile Technologies. This chapter presents a collaborative business environment that enables integration of business processes across multiple organizations and applies it to an export organization. At the same, the proposed collaborative environment also has to face numerous challenges as such technical and methodological that needs to be studied and investigated as has been done in this chapter.

The chapter is classified in the following sections: a) abstract b) introduction c) literature on web services and mobile technologies d) literature of collaborative business e) description of the action research organization f) current collaborative environment g) proposed collaborative environment h) conclusions & future directions

WEB SERVICES AND MOBILE TECHNOLOGIES

The W3C (World Wide Web Consortium) has defined Web Services as a standard means of interoperating between different software applications, running on a variety of platforms and/or frameworks. Web Services can be understood through the Web services architecture that is, in fact, an *interoperability* architecture: it identifies those global elements of the global Web services network that are required in order to ensure interoperability between Web services (Booth, et al, 2004).

A Web Services (WS) is a delivery mechanism that can serve at the same time many different consumers on many multiple technological platforms. Web Services technology is an enabler to connect incompatible standalone systems to integrate a complex distributed system in a way that was not possible with previous technologies (Stacey & Unhelkar, 2004). WS are made up of the eXtensible Markup Langauge (XML), Web Services Description Language (WSDL) and the Universal Description and Discovery Integration (UDDI) stores both the technical information to build an application compatible with a Web services interface, as well as the information required to successfully bind to that interface at runtime. According to Unhelkar (2007), through the directory of the UDDI within the umbrella of WS, business can now register the services they are offering and allow the clients to search, locate and consume those services. The service properties within WS can be specified using a specific ontology (Leary & Salam & Singh, 2006)

Mobile technology has provided the organizations with a platform to access customers in special ways, reaching them through specific locations and otherwise providing a new value proposition (Unnithan, 2002). The correct application of mobile technologies into the business processes provides an opportunity for enterprises to gain advantages such as increased profits, satisfied customers and greater customer loyalty. These customer-related advantages will accrue only when the organization investigates its customer behaviour in the context of the mobile environment. Mobile Web Services (MWS) enable the creation of such environment. A MWS environment is capable of using Location Based Services and Global Positioning Services (GPS) which, as per Puustjarvi (2006) enable provision of location-specific services pertinent to their location.

The research has identified that such an extension is possible through the application of Web Services technologies. This statement also appears to be supported by Goethals and Vandenbulcke (2006), who mention that Web Services could be used for integrating system for collaboration even amongst unknown parties.

COLLABORATIVE ENVIRONMENT

Collaboration is an activity of a group of people, which is a virtual team that exchanges information among members (Yildiz, Marjanovic and Godart, 2006). Timmers (1991), and Fahey et al., (2001) have described collaboration as a group of individuals and/or organizations coming together for a specific purpose, such as a project or a task. Such collaborations provide the ability for businesses to share and leverage knowledge, and thereby increase the opportunity for their growth and development.

Based on Unhelkar (2007) Collaborations, through the communications medium of the Internet, provide a high level of freedom for customers – as businesses in such collaborations do not always control the actions of the customers. In fact, good collaborative businesses take the bold steps of facilitating collaborations between their customers. The collaboration amongst the business processes of organizations by the usage of the Internet is called Collaborative Commerce.

The Internet, especially combined with wireless technologies, has become more than just a communication media. Together, they form important business drivers for e-commerce (Electronic commerce) and m-commerce (mobile commerce) and, as such, have become integral features of the global economy (Godbole, 2006).

According to Chen, et al, (2007) Collaborative commerce (C-Commerce) is a set of technologies and business practices that allows companies to build stronger relationships with their trading partners through integrating complex and cross-enterprise processes governed by business logic and rules, as well as workflows.

A well thought out electronic commerce solution needs the following: gathering and analyzing the need of customers, anticipating purchasing automatically, cooperating with auto producing and configuring, tracking on-the-way materials and controlling inventory, and e-marketing and other services. In short, it should reflect 4C strategies: collaborative stock (C-stock), C-market, C-produce, and C-configure. The detailed interactive process carries out as: an automaker inquires associations of need management about demand (Li & Fan, 2005).

Traditional e-Collaboration plays strategic role in business direction and the proposed new business process (CBPE) is emerged from the traditional e-Collaboration looking beyond the boundaries of the internal processes to an organization. E-Collaboration is facilitated by Internet technology and is more than mere substitution of traditional collaboration.

DESCRIPTION OF THE ACTION RESEARCH ORGANIZATION

The study concentrated on the export companies and the organizations that the specific export organization (ImpexDocs) was collaborating with. For example, many organizations that need to link with the export companies are Banks, Insurance Companies, Chambers of Commerce, Customs and Quarantine authorities, permit issuing authorities, Freight Forwarders, Transporters, Stevedores, Packers and suppliers. The action research export organization, ImpexDocs, provides "Seamless Trade Solutions" to companies integrating their foreign trade business processes with software solutions. These solutions allow companies to automate and manage the complexity of their global trade, compliance and logistics processes. ImpexDocs provides software solutions and services that can be used by export companies dealing and their associated trade parties such as freight forwarders, bureaus, shipping lines (sea and air exports). The se software solutions includes export documentation, customs declaration, pre-receival advice and quarantine approval.

CURRENT COLLABORATIVE ENVIRONMENT

International trade is complex and difficult to manage. It involves a number of documents, permits, approvals and co-operation of trading partners and associated service providers as illustrated below to move goods and documents from the exporter to the importer. Figure 1 presents some of the partners involved in export supply chain process in the current collaborative environment.

The study identified that in the current environment, the export companies need to submit multiple application and contact each organization separately for each transaction. The other external parties such as Banks, Insurance Companies, Chambers of Commerce, Customs and Quarantine authorities, Other permit issuing authorities, Freight Forwarders, Transporters, Stevedores, Packers and suppliers can also collaborate with export companies while they need

Figure 1. Organizations involved in export supply chain

to use different channels of collaboration in order to collaborate with other organizations.

Most of the export documentation is currently paper-based which results in significant impediments to the efficiency of the overall export process. Some of these impediments are:

- Consignment data is faxed and re-keyed at many points along the supply chain
- There is a high volume of repeated, manual processing
- There is a high error rate in transport documentation
- There is a low first-time Letter of Credit matching with charges and cash flow implications
- Courier costs are high - particularly for regional exporters
- There are often long lead times on documentation, and
- Physical shipments are impeded by slow and inaccurate data transfer.

The compliance requirements of both the export and import countries involving differing terminology, documents and procedures makes the process time consuming, complex and prone to errors. It is clear that the export community needs a system to streamline the export logistics, documentation and compliance process which reduces this complexity. Reducing the time it takes to transform a customer order in to money in the bank offers strategic benefits to the company and creates more rewarding customer relationships.

There are several bottlenecks that are typical in conventional systems of order processing. Most of these have the potential to cause huge inefficiencies and significant costs within company finances.

From the arrival of the overseas order, all the way to document creation, processing, shipment and payment there are a number of manual touch points which can cause creation of incorrect shipments that may end up in the customer's hands, or misplaced orders resulting in business loss and customer dissatisfaction.

Figure 2. Conventional process flow

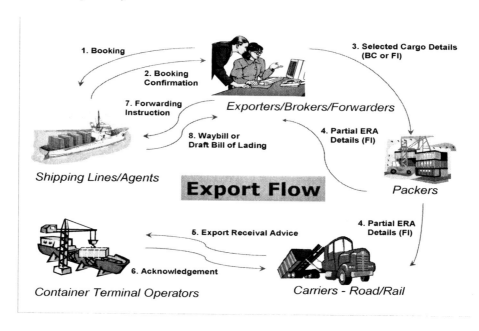

Figure 3. Proposed model of the organizations involved in export supply chain

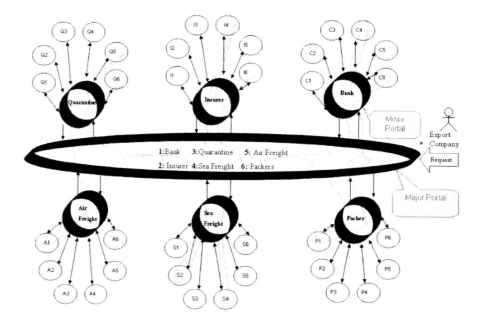

THE PROPOSED COLLABORATIVE ENVIRONMENT

The proposed model of CBPE enables all these organizations to collaborate with each other in the same channels on Collaborative Web Based System (CWBS). Export companies submit an application and the CWBS finds the suitable company capable of handling the request. When an individual company is unable to look after the requirements of the export companies, the CWBS distribute the request amongst different organizations. Figure 3, presents the proposed model of the CBPE for organizations involved in Export Supply Chain.

Asia-Pacific Economic Cooperation, or APEC, is the premier forum for facilitating economic growth, cooperation, trade and investment in the Asia-Pacific region. According to studies completed by the Asia Pacific Economic Cooperation (APEC) forum, the average international transaction involves 27-30 different parties, 40 documents, 200 data elements (30 of which are repeated at least 30 times) and the re-keying of 60-70% of all data at least once. Obtaining the necessary permits for import and export can take weeks in some cases.

Figure 3 depicts the proposed collaborative environment with only six of the organizations shown in Figure 1. Additional organizations could also be added in the system. As depicted in the Figure 3, the level 1 of the UDDI directory register the industry while the level 2 holds the registered businesses and their product and services. For example, the export company submits an application to Collaborative Web Based System (CWBS) requiring the deposit of US$1,000,000 to a company in US in an hour. At the same time the company needs a sea freighter capable of delivering 100 containers from Australia to US in the same day.

The CWBS deliver the application to the level one identifying the required industries. The CWBS will use any technology such as Web Services and Mobile technologies to deliver the published application to the parties in the level 2. The ticket will be logged, evaluated, allocated and the consultants will find the suitable package. After delivery of the package and testing the task is completed

Publishing the Service Required by Export Companies

The Business process Modeling Notation (BPMN) demonstrates the interaction amongst all parties involved in a step by step process. These descriptions will be further used to draw BPMN diagrams which will graphically present the chain of activities.

A standard BPMN will provide businesses with the capability of understanding their internal business procedures in a graphical notation and will give organizations the ability to communicate these procedures in a standard manner. Furthermore, the graphical notation will facilitate the understanding of the performance collaborations and business transactions between the organizations.

Publishing the consumable product/services on the proposed Collaborative Web Based System (CWBS) directory makes them available to the people who are capable of performing the requirement of the application (Banks, Insurance Companies, Chambers of Commerce, Customs and Quarantine authorities, other permit issuing authorities, Freight Forwarders, Transporters, Stevedores, Packers and suppliers.) but does not necessarily know the export company. By submitting a request to the directory they will be able to consume the request already published by the export company in the directory. Hence, some people are not necessarily in their office, the mobile applications could be included to the portal to deliver the request of the application to the person capable of handling the application requirements. This improves the service levels and enables a faster turnaround response. Based on Godbole (2006) Wireless operators are starting to work in a collaborative fashion to help promote benefits of mobility. The result is a new level of interoperability for both data and voice communication.

Proposed Use Cases

Registration in Proposed Collaborative Web Based System (CWBS)

See Exhibit A.

Place the Registration in the Directory

See Exhibit B.

Publish the Service Required by Export Companies

See Exhibit C.

Proposed BPMN

The following four figures, Figure 4, 5, 6 and 7 represent separate processes that deal with collaborations in an export environment. These are self explanatory processes that are modelled using the BPMN standard. The partitions are going left to right, and each partition represents a suite of activities.

Exhibit A.

Use Case:	Registration of Export Company
Actors:	Export Company, Collaborative Web Based System (CWBS),
Description:	Export Company is getting registered in the CWBS Please note that this is a generic use case. Different Export Companys could come in to register.
Pre-Condition:	Export Company is using Web Services. Export Company is willing to work through the CWBS
Post-Condition:	Export Company is upgraded to a Member
Type:	Complex
Normal Course of Events:	1. Export Company connects to the CWBS and requests to register in the Directory level 1 2. CWBS prompts the appropriate member registration form to the member 3. Export Company enters his details in the registration form (A1)(A2) 4. CWBS prompts that the registration form is to be submitted. 5. Export Company submits the registration form 6. CWBS registers Export Company sending a unique registration number 7. Member logs out of the CWBS.
Alternate Course of Events:	A1: Information entered is insufficient or incorrect. Export Company is asked to input correct member ID. A2: It is crucial for the Export Company to fill all details specifically identifying the relevant industry
References	• A Export Company is Export Company • After the registration process Export Company is a member.

Exhibit B.

Use Case:	Place the registration in the directory
Actors:	Collaborative Web Based System(CWBS), Directory level 1, Directory level 2, Administrator
Description:	When the CWBS place the registered members in the right place in order to locate and consume them.
Pre-Condition:	Registration has taken place
Post-Condition:	Directories communicates with each other
Type:	Very complex
Normal Course of Events:	1. CWBS identifies the relevant member area from the registration form (A1) 2. Directory level 1 will receive an identification number from that specific member 3. CWBS Register the member details of the member in Directory level 2. 4. Member details are stored in the database.
Alternate Course of Events:	A1: If the industry does not exist in the Directory level 2 the CWBS will inform the administrator for further direction.
References	This is an automated use case. Only instance of human actor involvement will occur when the specified industry is not available in CWBS.

Exhibit C.

Use Case:	Publish Request
Actors:	Export Company, Collaborative Web Based System CWBS, Directory level1 and Directory level 2
Description:	Export Company publishes the consumable application
Pre-Condition:	Export Company is Using Web Services
Post-Condition:	Export Company will receive a report that request is published ready to be consumed.
Type:	Very complex
Normal Course of Events:	1. CWBS accept the request and identify the members in need of such services (A1) 2. Directory level 1 checks Directory level 2 to identify the party capable in handling the requests 3. CWBS eliminates the options that are not meeting the environmental boundaries (geographical, budget, financial issues, etc.) 4. CWBS process the Export Company request and collaborate with selected members in need of such a request. 5. CWBS prompts a message to Export Company informing the outcome of the requested application.
Alternate Course of Events:	A1: If the industry does not exist the CWBS prompt a message denying the request. A2: If other industries should be involved in the request, the system will go through the process of locating them.
References	

CONCLUSION

This study was aimed at improving the existing business processes of export companies in Australia by making them collaborative business processes. While this study was a preliminary one that was aimed at modeling the collaborative business processes, we expect these collaborations to improve as there are further and rapid technological advances in the area of collaborative web services. We believe the action research carried out at ImpexDocs provided us with some valuable clues in the creation of collaborative web services in real life environment, in the context of an export organization. ImpexDocs plans to obtain further specific benefit by implementing some outcomes from this research. The graphical model of the proposed collaborative environment also provides basis for the organization to re-engineer its business processes that can help it to save time and money.

REFERENCES

Asia-Pacific Economic Co-operation Group. (2002). E-Commerce Exhibition Projects Program (ECEPP).

© Tradegate ECA – ECEPP ExportNet Final Report – May 2002.

Booth, D., Haas, H., McCabe, F., Newcomer, E., Champion, M., Ferris, E., & Orchard, D., (2004). *Web Services Architecture. World Wide Web Consortium.* http://www.w3.org/TR/ws-arch/. Accessed 5/03/2008, Accessed 5/03/2008

Chen, M., Zhang, D., & Zhou, L. (2007, March). Empowering collaborative commerce with Web services enabled business process management systems Source. *Decision Support Systems, 43*(2), 530-546. ISSN:0167-9236.

Fahey, L., Srivastava, R., Sharon, J. S., & Smith, D. E. (2001). Linking E-Business and operating processes: The role of knowledge management. *IBM Systems Journal Knowledge Management, 40(4).* http://www.research.ibm.com/journal/sj/404/fahey.html

Godbole, N. (2006). Relating Mobile Computing to Mobile Commerece. In B. Unhelkar (Ed.), *Mobile Business: Technological, Methodological and Social Perspectives.* New York: Idea Gruop Publishing. ISBN: 1591408172.

Figure 4. Proposed BPMN for the registration in CWBS

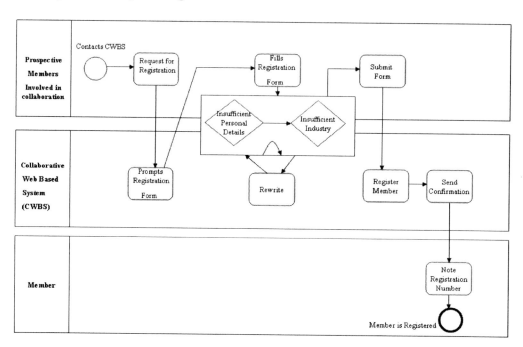

Figure 5. Proposed BPMN for placing the registration in the directory

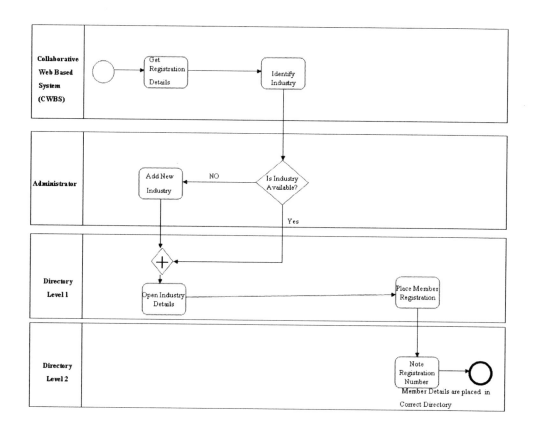

Figure 6. Proposed BPMN for publishing request

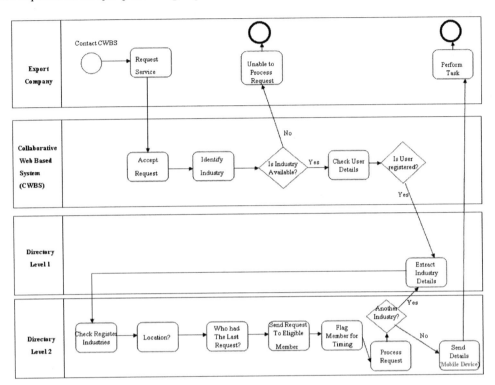

Goethals, F., & Vandenbulcke, J. (2006). Using Web Services in Business-to-Business Integration. In M. Fong (Ed.), *E-Collaborations and Virtual Organizations*. Herhsey, PA: Idea Group. ISBN: 1-59140-285-9

Leary, T., Salam, A. F., & Singh, R. (2006). Dynamic Matching of Supply and Demand in an M-Commerce Services Marketplace. In B. Unhelkar (Ed.), *Mobile Business: Technological, Methodological and Social Perspectives. New York: Idea Group Publishing*. ISBN: 1591408172.

Li, X., & Fan, H. (2005, August). Collaborative commerce architecture and process. *ACM International Conference Proceeding Series, 113. Proceedings of the 7th international conference on Electronic commerce.*(pp. 485-489). ISBN: 1-59593-112-0

Puustjarvi, J. (2006, January). Using Mobile Web Services in Electronic Auctions. *Proceedings of the 2nd IASTED international conference on Advances in computer science and technology ACST'06.*

Stacey, M., & Unhelkar, B. (2004). *Web Services in Implementation.* Paper presented at the 15th ACIS Conference, Hobart, Australia.

Timmers, P. (1999). *Electronic Commerce: Strategies and Models for Business –to- Business Trading.* New York: John Wiley & Sons.

Unhelkar, B. (2007). Beyond Business Integration – Management Challenges in Collaborative Business Processes. *ICFAI Journal.* India.

Unnithan, C. R., & Swatman, P. M. C. (2002*). On line Banking vs. Bricks and Mortar - or a hybrid model? A preliminery investigation of Australian and Indian banks.* Paper presented at the Seventh CollECTeR Conference, Melbourne, Australia.

Yildiz, U., Marjanovic, O., & Godart, C. (2006). Contact-Driven Cross-Organizational Business Process. *Full Proceedings of the 2nd International Conference on Information Management and Business (IMB 2006),* Sydney, Australia. ISBN: 1 74108122 X

Figure 7. Proposed BPMN for consumption of the published request

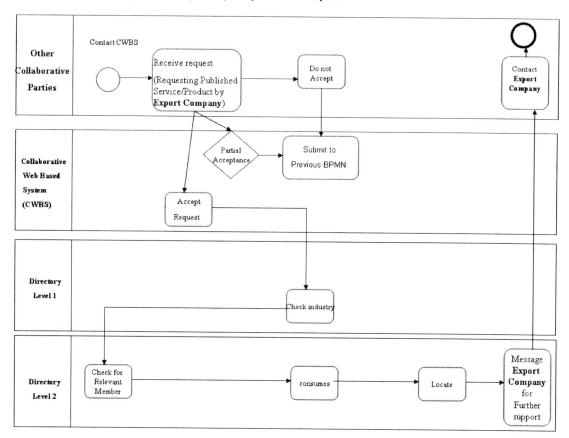

IMPEXDOCS

http://www.impexdocs.com.au/the_challenge/the_
challenge.html.Downloaded: 6/04/2007

Unified Business Media

http://www.techweb.com/encyclopedia/define-
term.jhtml?term=business+process. Downloaded:
26/04/2007

Asia-Pacific Economic Co-operation Group

http://www.apec.org/content/apec/apec_group.html.
Downloaded: 26/04/2007

E-Commerce Exhibition Projects Program (ECEPP)

"Diary of a Change Agent"

ExportNet Trials by SME Exporter Chains by Trade-
Gate ECA. Final Report May 2002.

About the Contributors

Joaquin Aldás-Manzano (PhD, business and economics, Universitat de València, Spain) is associate professor of marketing in the Department of Marketing, Faculty of Economics, Universitat de València and associate researcher of the Valencia Economics Research Institute (Ivie). His research interest is focused on advertising media planning, consumer behaviour and quantitative methods in marketing research and he has articles published in the *European Journal of Marketing, Journal of Product and Brand Management, Qualitative Marketing Research, European Journal of Innovation Management, Sex Roles, Equal Opportunities International* and in the best Spanish refereed journals. He has also presented numerous papers at AM, EMAC or AMS Conferences.

Rajeev Agrawal holds a BE in electronics engineering and an MTech in systems engineering. He has done his PhD in the area of wireless communication channels. His current areas of research are performance evaluation of wireless networks and ultrasound medical imaging. He has more than 10 publications in reputed international journal and conferences along with number of national conferences papers to his credit. He is also served / serving as one of the reviewer of *IEEE Communication* letters, *IEEE Trans. Parallel and Distributed Computing,* and *International Arab Journal of Information Technology.* He was also invited to serve on the technical program committee for NTMS'2007 (First International Conference on New Technologies, Mobility and Security) Paris - France. He is also a member of the EU-IndiaGrid community.

Dinesh Arunatileka obtained his Bachelor of Science special degree in computer science from the University of Colombo, Sri Lanka. He started his career as a management trainee but later moved in to IT solutions sales. He obtained his MBA form the University of Sri Jayewardenepura Sri Lanka and also moved into the telecommunication sector in Sri Lanka in sales and account management. He was serving as head of business development for a leading fixed Telecom Company in Sri Lanka when he left for his PhD to Sydney, Australia. In Sydney he was attached to the University of Western Sydney as a teaching fellow and followed his PhD in the area of mobile transformation of business processes. Upon completion of his PhD, Dinesh returned to Sri Lanka and is currently working as general manager marketing for a subsidiary of a leading Telecom Group in Sri Lanka. Dinesh has more than 10 research articles to his credit including two book chapters and has over 12 years experience in the ICT area.

Walied Askarzai (Bachelor of Economics, MBA) earned his bachelor's degree from the University of Western Sydney and his master's degree from theUniversity of Southern Cross. He has experience in teaching/tutoring introductory economics as well as other units in business management and commerce. He is currently a lecturer in human resource management and a tutor in economics and statistics at the Melbourne Institute of Technology. He is also a lecturer in business management and sales at Academies Australasia. He is teaching both the undergraduate and post graduate levels. He worked in private sector for three years prior to embarking upon an academic career. He has experience in teaching, tutoring, mentoring, management, business administration, customer service, and sales.

Tony Atkins is principal lecturer in applied computing in the Faculty of Computing, Engineering and Technology at Staffordshire University. He has an MSc in computing science, an MSc in process engineering and a

PhD in bioengineering. He is a chartered engineer in both computing and mineral and petroleum engineering and has taught and supervised PhD programmes in both disciplines in the UK, and at the University of Wollongong Australia and Virginia Polytechnic Institute and State University in the U.S. He is also a Churchill Fellowship in bioengineering and environmental engineering and has several patents in bioengineering and waste recycling with embedded real time systems covering the UK, EU, Australia and U.S. His main interests include mobile and RFID business technology in waste recycling in the construction industry, supply chain management (SCM) and mobile technological application to the ageing population. Other interests are in IT outsourcing and service management and knowledge management systems (KMS). He has published over 100 refereed publications consisting of journals, chapters in books, and conferences with his research students.

R.M.Banakar received a BE degree in electronics and communication engineering from Karnatak University, India in 1984 and an MTech in digital communication from Regional Engineering College, Surathkal, and Karnataka. She has several years experience in Indian Space Research Organization (ISRO). She completed her PhD in the area of low power application specific design methodology from IIT Delhi in 2004. Presently she is working as assistant professor, BVB Engineering College Hubli Karnataka. She is a member of ISTE, IETE, MIE and IEEE scientific and professional societies. Her current areas of research include SOC, VLSI architecture and WCDMA.

Ataul Bari obtained his BEngg degree in mechanical engineering from the University of Rajshahi (Engg. College), Bangladesh. He received his BCS[H] and MSc in computer science from the University of Windsor in 2004 and 2006 respectively. He is currently pursuing his PhD in the area of energy efficient protocols for wireless sensor networks. His other research interests include optical networks and bioinformatics.

Ishan Bhalla (BTech, MCAD) has over 10 years of professional experience in database, object oriented and application programming for various industries including: real estate, securities, defense, freight and logistics. He is a member of the Australian Computer Society and is currently pursuing his Master in Information Technology from the University of Technology, Sydney.

Bhargav Bhatt is in the development field for more than a decade. His company, Ultra InfoTech employs teams of planners, developers, administrators, designers & testers for different types of development projects starting from static Web sites to multi-layered database driven online applications, desktop softwares, servers & network planning & maintenance and real time streaming of audio-video for more than 5 years. Projects tools and technologies are developed under Bhargav Bhatt's guidance includes the most visited portal on Vadodara city, www.VadodaraYellowPages.net, www.RealestateVadodara.com, www.Vadodaramail.com, www.lampcentral.com www.TripCoordinator.com and many CRM and CMS systems which has a big potential for mobile communications.Bhargav supervises number of final year students of MCA, BCA, ME (IT), BE (IT) courses from reputed universities and educational institutes

Carol Charsky is a contractor for Customs and Border Protection in USA for 16 years working in the LAN Engineering Department.. She holds a bachelor's degree in information systems from George Mason University and a master's degree in e-commerce from University of Maryland University College.

Kamlesh Chaudhary (BE, pursuing master's degree in IT from University of Technology Sydney) has 25 year+ experience in application architecture, design, development and support. Kamlesh started his career in India as hardware engineer where he developed some microprocessor based system. He then moved to development of real-time on-line systems for mining and power industry. He has worked in India, Singapore and last 11 years he has been in Australia where he worked with IBM, Siemens etc. He has managed development and implementation of several business critical systems successfully.

Subramanian Chitra holds a bachelor's degree in computer science from University of Madras. She had worked as a faculty most of her professional tenure, and had also worked as a tutor in University of Western Sydney. She is currently applying for her PhD at the University of Western Sydney.

Ioannis P. Chochliouros is a telecommunications electrical engineer, graduated from the Polytechnic School of the Aristotle University of Thessaloniki, Greece, holding also a MSc and a PhD from the University Pierre et Marie Curie, Paris VI, France. He worked as a research and teaching assistant at the University Paris VI, in cooperation with other European countries. His practical experience as an engineer has been mainly in Telecommunications, as well as in various construction projects in Greece and the wider Balkan area. Since 1997 he has been working at the Competition Department and then as an engineer-consultant of the chief technical officer of OTE (Hellenic Telecoms S.A.), for regulatory and technical matters. He has been very strongly involved in major OTE's national and international business activities, as a specialist consultant for technical and regulatory affairs especially for the evaluation and adoption of innovative e-infrastructures and e-services. Author of more than 90 scientific and business works, he currently works as the head of the research programs section of the Labs & New Technologies Division. Under his supervision, the section has received several awards by the European Commission, for the successful realization of European research activities.

Dave Curtis is an enterprise architect, focusing on the strategic aspects of enterprise architecture. He relocated from the UK to Sydney, Australia in 2005 in order to take the up the Asia Pacific Enterprise Architecture role for a large insurance broker. Dave completed his formal IT training in the UK in the early 1990s. He spent a number of years as a systems analyst programmer developing and implementing systems across a range of industries including the manufacturing, insurance and financial services sectors. With a desire to move more towards systems design and architecture, Dave spent seven years in a consulting role as both a lead consultant and technical architect designing and delivering solution to customers in the energy, telecommunication and financial services sectors. Dave is a member of the Australian Computer Society (ACS) and is active in attending various forums, seminars and discussion groups. Additionally, Dave has also represented various groups in the past presenting at industry forums and workgroups on technology and design approaches.

Alessia D'Andrea received her degree in communication science at the University of Rome 'La Sapienza'. She is being a young researcher in social science at the Institute for Research on population and social politicies of the National Research Council of Italy. She is mainly interested in communication science, social science, virtual communities and health studies.

Tugrul U. Daim is an associate professor of engineering and technology management at Portland State University. He had worked at Intel Corporation managing technology planning, technology and product development before joining PSU. He is on the editorial board of *IEEE Transactions on Engineering Management, Technology Forecasting and Social Change*, and *International Journal of Innovation and Technology Management*. He is a program co chair of Portland International Conference on Management of Engineering and Technology Management (PICMET). He published articles in *Technology Forecasting and Social Change, Technovation, Technology in Society, Journal of High Technology Management Research*, and the *International Journal of Innovation and Technology Management*. He also authored three books of readings. He received funding from federal sources including NSF and DOE.

Manish Desai gained first hand experience in exporting and importing while working in trading companies in Singapore and United Kingdom through 5 years in international marketing. Manish is a qualified electronics engineer and has followed this up with MBA in international business. Manish then spent 8 years in IT working for companies such as IBM, Magnus, Woolworths before starting ImpexDocs. Manish is the driving force behind the ImpexDocs product suite and remains actively involved in the company to ensure that the business, service, and narketing objectives are met as the company grows.

Fernando Ferri received degrees in electronics engineering in 1990 and the PhD in medical informatics in 1993 from the University of Rome "La Sapienza". He is actually senior researcher at the National Research Council of Italy (2001-2007). From 1993 to 2000 he was professor of "Sistemi di Elaborazione" at the University of Macerata. From 1996 to 2001 he was researcher at the National Research Council of Italy. He is the author of more than 100 papers in international journals, books and conferences. His main methodological areas of interest are: human-computer interaction visual languages, visual interfaces, sketch-based interfaces, and multimodal interfaces, data and knowledge bases, geographic information systems. He was responsible of several projects funded by Italian Ministry of University and Research and European Commission.

Jigisha Gala is a PhD scholar in the Department of Human Development and Family Studies, Faculty of Home Science MS University of Vadodara. She is interested in studying interpersonal relationships and mental health issues pertaining to the adolescents and young adults. Her research during the master's program was pertaining to adolescent's coping responses to stressors. Apart from research, she is interested in reading and interacting with people.

Marco Garito has been working in marketing departments of IT companies both in Italy and UK and has been involved in marketing planning for internet business for fixed and mobile solutions: he is currently covering EMEA responsibilities for e-business infrastructure for channel marketing in IBM. He holds a bachelor's degree from University of Milan (Italy) and a master degree from University of Technology Sydney (Australia)

Miti Garg graduated with MSc (management) by research from the NUS Business School in 2006. She completed her undergraduate degree in architecture from the School of Planning and Architecture, N. Delhi, India. Her industry research experience includes working with the retail and leisure advisory team for Jones Lang LaSalle Ltd., Delhi, India. Her current research interests are in the field of global supply chain management, supply chain optimization and integration of multimodal transport networks. She is actively involved in industry as well as academic research and her work has been accepted for several reputed conferences including AOM, AIB and INFORMS and IMECS.

Tagelsir Mohamed Gasmelseid is an associate professor at the University of Medical Sciences and Technology (Sudan) and teaches in the filed of electronic and mobile business, e-banking, medical informatics, MIS and DSS. His research interests include multiagent systems, electronic governance, medical informatics, agent oriented software engineering, and agent based simulation. He published in some international journals and is currently acting as a member of the international editorial board of the international journal of *Electronic Business Research.*

Abbass Ghanbary (Bachelor of Applied Science, Honours, PhD) is a consultant and a post-doc researcher at the University of Western Sydney (UWS) in Australia. His specific research focus includes the issues and challenges in incorporating Web services in businesses integration and creating a model for collaborative business process engineering (CBPE). Abbass had earned a scholarship from University of Western Sydney to undertake his research. His investigation is mainly concentrated on the improvements of the Web services applications across multiple organizations. Abbass also teaches and tutors in UWS and he is a member of the emerging technologies sub-group with Advanced Enterprise Information Management Systems (AeIMS) and Mobile Internet Research and Applications Group (MIRAG) research groups at the University of Western Sydney. He is also a student member of Australian Computer Society (ACS) and is active in attending various forums, seminars and discussion groups.

Athula Ginige (BSc, Eng, First Class Honours; PhD, Cambridge) is professor of IT at University of Western Sydney. He is also the director of AeIMS research group. He graduated with BSc first class honours from University of Moratuwa, Sri Lanka. He obtained his PhD from the University of Cambridge. He is now a fellow of the Cambridge Commonwealth Society and a member of editorial board of the *International Journal of Web Engineering.* He has recently been appointed as editor-in-chief of the a new journal *The International Journal on Advances in ICT for Emerging Regions* (ICTer). Athula has extensive experience in assisting small and medium enterprises (SMEs) to enhance their business processes using ICT to become competitive in the market place. Athula has also made a significant contribution to the establishment of the new discipline area of "Web engineering". In the late 90's he published widely highlighting the need for a systematic engineering like approach to develop large complex web based information systems that can be easily maintained as well as evolved with changing business needs. He guest edited two special issues of *IEEE Multimedia on Web Engineering* which are now widely being acknowledged by the research community as having a significant impact in establishing the new discipline of Web engineering.

A former Colombo Plan scholar, Dr. **Mark Goh** holds a PhD from the University of Adelaide. In the National University of Singapore, he holds the appointments of director (industry research) at the Logistics Institute-Asia Pacific, a joint venture with Georgia Tech, USA, principal researcher at the Centre for Transportation Research, and was a program director of the Penn-State NUS Logistics Management Program. He also used to be director of supply chain solutions for Asia/Middle East with APL Logistics, crafting logistics engineering solutions for major MNCs in this part of the world. Dr. Goh was a board member of the Chartered Institute of Transport (Singapore), past chairman of the Academic Board of Examiners for the Singapore Institute of Purchasing and Materials Management, member of the advisory committee of the Transportation Resource Centre (NUS) and a past vice president of the Operations Research Society of Singapore, associate senior fellow of the Institute of South East Asian Studies. His other professional affiliations include membership of INFORMS, and the Academy of International Business. His biography appears in Who's Who in Asia and the Pacific Nations, Who's Who in the World, and Outstanding People of the 20th Century. He has held appointments as a visiting professor in business logistics strategy at Chulalongkorn University, Commonwealth Fellow to the UK, Citibank International Fellow to the U.S., visiting research fellow at UMIST, visiting scholar at Beijing University, visiting professor at Melbourne University, and adjunct professor at the University of South Australia. He is currently on the editorial boards of the *Journal of Supply Chain Management, Q3 Quarterly, Journal for Inventory Research*, and *Advances in Management Research*, and has served as an associate editor for the Asia Pacific *Journal of Operational Research*.

Patrizia Grifoni received the degrees in electronics engineering in 1990 from the University of Rome "La Sapienza". and is a researcher at the National Research Council of Italy. From 1994 to 2000 she was professor of "Elaborazione digitale delle immagini" at the University of Macerata. She is the author of more than 70 papers in international journals, books and conferences. Her scientific interests have evolved from query languages for statistical and geographic databases to the focal topics related to human-computer interaction, multimodal interaction, visual languages, visual interfaces, sketch-based interfaces and accessing Web information. She was responsible of several projects funded by Italian and international institutions.

Sumeet Gupta completed his PhD degree in information systems from National University of Singapore (2006). He was a recipient of President Graduate Fellowship award (2005). He graduated with MBA from NUS Business School, Singapore. His research interests are in logistics and supply chain intelligence and e-commerce (IT post-adoption, Internet shopping and virtual communities). His has published in various Tier 1 and Tier 2 journals such as *Decision Support Systems, Information Resource Management Journal, International Journal of Electronic Commerce, European Journal of Operations Research* and *OMEGA*. He has also presented his work in various Tier 1 and Tier2 conferences, namely, ICIS, AMCIS, ECIS, PACIS, POMS, AOM. He has worked on several supply chain intelligence projects with leading MNCs.

Călin Gurău is associate professor of marketing at GSCM - Montpellier Business School, France, since September 2004. His present research interests are focused on marketing strategies for high-technology firms and Internet marketing. He has published more than 30 papers in internationally refereed journals, such as *International Marketing Review, Journal of Consumer Marketing, Journal of Marketing Communications*, etc.

Tiziana Guzzo received the degrees in sociology in 2003 and the PhD in theory and social research at the University of Rome "La Sapienza". She is actually young researcher at the National Research Council of Italy. From 2005 to 2008 she was professor of Sociology at the University of Catanzaro. She is mainly interested in social change, new technologies, communication, virtual community, risk management, environment and tourism.

Robert Harmon is professor of marketing and technology management at Portland State. He has a joint appointment in the School of Business and the Maseeh College of Engineering and Computer Science. He earned a PhD in marketing from Arizona State University. He has over 20 years experience as a new products and technology marketing consultant. His research has appeared in publications such as the *Journal of Marketing Research, Journal of Marketing, Journal of Interactive Advertising, Technological Forecasting and Social Change, Journal of Advertising, Journal of Advertising Research, Journal of Interactive Advertising, Business and Society, IEEE Transactions on Engineering Management,* and *Decision Sciences.* He has received funding from the NSF and other numerous other sources.

Hahizan Hassan holds a PhD degree (information system) from the University of Newcastle upon Tyne; MA in IT from the University of Nottingham, and BSc from University of Manchester, UK. He is actively involved in Web studies, electronic government and knowledge management areas. Currently, he is the director of Industrial Placement Centre, Universiti Utara Malaysia. His latest national achievement is winning a governmental award in 2007 for the innovation of Student-Industrial Placement Online System which he headed.

Arsi Honkanen holds a master's degree in computer science and an MBA with specialisations in international business and technology. Arsi has over 10 years of software development and project management experience. He has been involved in the creation and implementation of new software innovations surrounding network management, mobile protocol software, GPS, mobile entertainment and network billing from a total of five companies including Nokia in Finland. Currently, at Alacrity, he plays the role of a technical architect for the underlying security architecture of CLEW, the product of Alacritytech.

Arunita Jaekel obtained her BEngg in electronics and telecommunications engineering from Jadavpur University, India. She received her MASc and PhD in electrical engineering from University of Windsor, Canada. She is currently a professor in the School of Computer Science at University of Windsor since. Her research interests include optical networks, survivable topology design and wireless sensor networks.

Sanjay Jasola is working as associate professor at School of Science and Technology, Wawasan Open University, Penang, Malaysia. He obtained his PhD in computer science from Jawaharlal Nehru University, New Delhi, India. The main focus of his thesis is on mobile IP communications. He has been the faculty of several engineering institutes in different capacities from lecture to associate professor in India. He has vast experience of teaching post graduate and graduate (MCA, BTech) students at several engineering colleges including visiting faculty to IIT Roorkee for MTech and MBA courses. His lectures on computer sciences are telecasted over Doordarshan and his several talks on IT related topics have been broadcasted on All India Radio. He has worked as deputy director at computer division of Indira Gandhi National Open University, New Delhi. A gold medal awardee by the Indira Gandhi National Open University for his contribution to the establishment of EDUSAT (the first educational television channel of India) as an innovation in open and distance learning, he has contributed a lot to the area of wireless networking, mobile communication, computer architecture and use of mobile and satellite technology in distance education. He is fellow of IETE, and life member of IE, CSI and ISTE in India.

Rishi Kalra is a final year student at Symbiosis Institute of Business Management, SIU Pune pursuing marketing as his major. A computer engineer with extensive training in UML-2, Rishi has worked on projects for Aphatek, UK and for Sarabhai Piramal pharmaceuticals on distribution channel automation in India. He has conceptualized a new distribution channel for ITC Ltd to reach untapped customers in rural India.

Teemu Kautonen is a research professor in entrepreneurship at the University of Vaasa, Finland. His current research focuses on trust in virtual environments, entrepreneurship and small business strategy and policy. Previous publications have appeared in the *Journal of Small Business and Enterprise Development, International Entrepreneurship & Management Journal, International Journal of Entrepreneurial Behaviour & Research* and *Evolutionary and Institutional Economics Review,* among others.

Heikki Karjaluoto is a research professor in electronic marketing at the University of Oulu, Finland. His research interests concern electronic business in general and mobile business and commerce in particular. Previous publications have appeared in the *Handbook of Research in Mobile Business, International Journal of Bank Marketing, Internet Research, International Journal of Retail & Distribution Management, International Journal of Mobile Marketing, Journal of Services Marketing,* among others.

Martin Klaus is a doctoral student at the SVI endowed chair of International Direct Marketing at the DMCC – Dialog Marketing Competence Center at the University of Kassel, Germany. Martin Klaus graduated from the Bielefeld University in September 2006. Since then, he has been a marketing research assistant while working on his doctoral thesis. His main research interests cover online and mobile marketing, social network analysis and communication strategies and methods via different media and in different cultures. He is also interested in environmental scanning, classification and data mining.

Priyatam kumar received the BE and MTech degree in electronics and communication from the Karnataka University Dharwad and National Institute of Technology Karnataka India in 1989 and 2004, respectively. He joined B.V.B College of Engineering and Technology Hubli Karnataka India 1989, where he was engaged in Teaching Antennas and Advanced Communication Systems. He is currently senior faculty and doing research in WCDMA and Mobile Communication. He is a member of the Institute of Electronics, Member of Indian Society of Technical teachers (MISTE).

Anand Kuppuswami completed his Bachelor of Engineering in electronics and communication from University of Madras. He started his research in the field of neural networks and mobile agents in 2000 and finished his MS from University of Western Sydney in 2002. He has worked on various commercial projects on Web services, CRM and asynchronous message queuing. He is currently working as a consultant at Dialog Information Technology at its Sydney office.

Amit Lingarchani has completed his bachelor's degree in computing from SVIT, Gujarat University, India. He served as a software engineer at VR Software Systems Pvt Ltd. He has hands on experience in object oriented analysis and design of software projects. He is currently pursuing his Master in Information Technology at UTS in Sydney, Australia.

Mohammed Maharmeh is a PhD candidate at the University of Western Sydney (UWS) and has more than 20 years of experience in project management, solutions architect and design, played different roles such as solutions architect, projects manager and systems analyst. Academically, Mohammed has earned his bachelor's and master's degrees in the field of computing and information technology. Mohammed currently is conducting a research in a creation of a composite application software development framework

Paul Makuch is a student in business administration at the Saarland University and in addition he works as student researcher at the Institute for Information Systems at the German Research Centre for Artificial Intelligence in Saarbruecken, Germany. His focus in research is on business process management, mobile business and enterprise resource planning systems.

Ioakim (Makis) Marmaridis is a technologist with a passion for solving real world problems through application of technology, innovative research and mentoring of others. Makis has over 10 years in the ICT industry architecting, creating, deploying or managing sophisticated platforms for ebusiness, elearning and collaboration. He also has extensive experience with Web-based systems and enterprise-level hosting platforms. Makis holds a Bachelor of Business in computing and information management with first class Honors and he is working towards his PhD. He is a Microsoft Certified Professional (MCP) since 2000, a full member of the Australian Computing Society (ACS) and a member of the IEEE. When he is not doing research or helping organisations through consulting he can be found blogging on his site at http://www.marmaridis.org/

Ekata Mehul is an assistant professor at the Babaria Institute of Technology (BIT), Gujarat University, in Vadodara, India where she also leads the faculty. She is also handling the Training and Placement Cell at the institute. She did her MTech in information and communication technology from Dhirubhai Ambani Institute of Technology (DAIICT). She has publications in the area of embedded systems, networking and compilers. She is also an executive member of various professional bodies like CSI, IETE, ISTE and ITForum.

Barin N. Nag is a professor at Towson University in Baltimore, MD. He has a PhD in business from the University of Maryland at College Park. He also has MTech and BTech degrees in electrical engineering from the University of Calcutta. He is a member of INFORMS and IEEE. He has over 50 publications in a number of journals including *European Journal of Operational Research, Decision Support Systems, Decision Sciences,* and *Journal of Management Information Systems.*

Amit Nanchahal is a senior business analyst with U.S.-based Cognizant Technology Solutions. An MBA in marketing from Symbiosis Institute of Business Management, India Amit also has an engineering degree in computer science. He has over 3 years of IT industry experience in consulting US Insurance clients. His interest areas are channel structure analysis, brand management, services marketing & B2B marketing.

Sargam Parmar is an assistant professor in the Electronics & communication Department at U.V.Patel College of Engineering, Kherva. Parmar has 10 years of teaching experience as a lecturer, senior lecture to assistant professor. Parmar did MTech in electronics & communication with specialization in signal processing in the year 2004 from Indian Institute of Technology-Guwahati (IIT-G). Parmar did BE in electronics & communication in 1997. Parmar published five research papers in national and international conferences and is a member of the Board of Studies, U.V.P.C.E- EC Department.

Jhoanna Rhodette Pedrasa is a PhD student at the University of New South Wales, Sydney working under Prof. Aruna Seneviratne at National ICT Australia. She earned her BS in computer engineering and an MS in electrical engineering from the University of the Philippines. Her research interest is in context aware systems and mobility management.

AK Hairul Nizam is a researcher of Staffordshire University currently completing his MRes in computing science. His research interest in mobile computing is due to the work experience in DST, national mobile company in Brunei, which broadened the areas of understanding in the socio-cultural trends of mobile phones.

Eranga Perera received a BSc degree in mathematics and computing with first class honors from the University of London. She received a master's degree in information science and a PhD in electrical and telecommunications engineering from the University of New South Wales. Her research interests are in mobile and wireless systems. She is currently working on two major projects - Ambient Networks project which is part of the European Union's Sixth Framework Program and the Context Aware Mobility Project linked with the 3 year Ericsson Umbrella programme.

Rok Rupnik, PhD, is an academic with experience and references in the area of research and projects in the industry. He has made PhD in the area of mobile applications, their role in information systems and mobile applications development methodology. He is a researcher and senior-lecturer at the Faculty of Computer and Information Science, University of Ljubljana. His main research areas and areas of projects for the industry include: information systems development methodologies, mobile applications development methodologies, information systems strategic planning, decision support systems and CRM. He is author or co-author of several papers in international journals and international conferences. In the last ten years he has been a project leader of several projects for the industry.

Mahesh S. Raisinghani is an associate professor in the Executive MBA program at the TWU School of Management. He is a Certified E-Commerce Consultant (CEC) and a Project Management Professional (PMP). Dr. Raisinghani was the recipient of TWU School of Management's 2005 Best Professor Award for the Most Innovative Teaching Methods; 2002 research award; 2001 King/Haggar Award for excellence in teaching, research and service; and a 1999 UD-GSM Presidential Award. His previous publications have appeared in I*EEE Transactions on Engineering Management, Information and Management, Journal of Global I.T. Management, Journal of E-Commerce Research, Information Strategy: An Executive's Journal, International Journal of E-Business Research, Journal of IT Cases and Applications, Information Resources and Management Journal, Journal of I.T. Theory and Applications, Enterprise Systems Journal, Journal of Computer Information Systems and Information Systems Management* among others. Dr. Raisinghani is included in the millennium edition of Who's Who in the World, Who's Who Among America's Teachers and Who's Who in Information Technology.

Dilupa Ranatunga obtained his first degree in Bachelor of Information and Communication Technology from University of Colombo School of Computing, Sri Lanka. He has organized many large scale projects to enhance the knowledge of Information Technology of school children in Sri Lanka. He was also instrumental in developing e-business strategies for several leading Sri Lankan companies. He started his career as a Systems Engineer in a multi national shipping company but later moved in to the telecommunication sector in Sri Lanka. Currently he is working for a Leading Telecom company in Sri Lanka.

N. Raghavendra Rao is a professor at SSN School of Management & Computer Applications, Chennai, India. Dr. Rao has a master's degree in commerce from Osmania University and a PhD in finance from the University of Poona. He has a rare distinction of having experience in the combined areas of IT and business applications. His rich experience in Industry is matched with a parallel academic experience in Management & IT in Business Schools. He has over two decades of experience in the development of application software related to manufacturing, service oriented organizations, financial institutions and business enterprises. He presents papers related to Information technology at conferences. He contributes articles on IT to main stream news papers and journals. His area of research interest is mobile computing and space technology.

Carla Ruiz-Mafé (PhD, Business and Economics, Universitat de València, Spain) is assistant professor in the Department of Marketing, Faculty of Economics, Universitat de València. Her primary research interests include e-commerce, mobile commerce, communication, interactive marketing and consumer behaviour and she has articles published in *Internet Research, Journal of Electronic Commerce Research, Journal of Consumer Marketing, Journal of Theoretical and Applied Electronic Commerce Research* and the best Spanish refereed Journals. She has also presented some papers at AM and EMAC Conferences.

Sobihatun Nur Ab Salam is a lecturer in the Multimedia Department, Faculty of Information Technology, Universiti Utara Malaysia and she holds a MSc and BSc degree in IT. She currently is pursuing her PhD in multimedia design.

Rajani Shankar Sadasivam is a systems analyst in the Division of Continuing Medical Education (CME) at the University of Alabama at Birmingham, Alabama. He is completing his PhD dissertation in the Department of Electrical and Computer Engineering. His research addresses issues in the development of a framework for composite service orchestration. Rajani received the Deans award for the most outstanding graduate student in the School of Engineering in 2004. He is an active member of IEEE, Tau Beta Pi honor society, and the Society for Design and Process Science.

Silvia Sanz-Blas (PhD, Business and Economics, Universitat de València, Spain) is associate professor in the Department of Marketing, Faculty of Economics, Universitat de València. Her primary research interests include communication, sales, e-commerce, interactive marketing and consumer behaviour she has articles published in *Internet Research, Journal of Electronic Commerce Research, Journal of Consumer Behaviour, Journal of Consumer Marketing, Journal of Vacation Marketing* and the best Spanish refereed Journals. She has also presented numerous papers at AM, AMS and EMAC Conferences.

Siti Mahfuzah Sarif is a lecturer at Cosmopoint College, Malaysia and she holds an MSc in IT, Universiti Utara Malaysia. She currently is pursuing her PhD in mobile application design.

Aruna Seneviratne is the director of the National ICT Australia, Australian Technology Park (ATP) Research Laboratory. He is also a professor of telecommunications in the School of Electrical and Telecommunication Engineering, University of New South Wales and where he holds the Mahanakorn Chair of Telecommunication. Professor Aruna Seneviratne has over 20 years of telecommunication and computer systems engineering experience. His research interests include mobile data communication systems, and in particular the development of mechanisms for managing the quality of service in wireless Internet environments.

Dr.B.Shankaranand received the BE in electronic and communication engineering from Mysore University India in 1973 and the MSc (Engg.) in microwave engineering from the Kerala, India in 1977. He completed his PhD at IIT Bombay in 1991. He joined National Institute of Technology Karnataka, India in 1979, where he has been engaged in teaching and research and development of broadband communication systems, focusing on communication applications, especially in satellite, optical and microwave applications. He is currently professor at NITK India. He is a member of Scientific and Professional Societies (ISTE, IETE, and MIE).

Ramesh Sharma holds a PhD in education in the area of educational technology and is currently working as regional director in Indira Gandhi National Open University (IGNOU). He has been a teacher trainer and has taught educational technology, educational research and statistics, educational measurement and evaluation, special education, psychodynamics of mental health courses. He had established a Centre of ICT in the College he was working. He is a member of many committees on implementation of technology in the Open University. His areas of specialization include staff development, on-line learning, student support services in open and distance learning, and teacher education. He is a member of advisory group meeting on Human Resources Development for the United Nations Conference on Trade and Development (UNCTAD). He is the co-editor of *Asian Journal of Distance Education* ISSN 1347-9008, (www.ASIANJDE.org). In addition to these, he is/has been on the editorial advisory board of several international journals as well as advisory board member and an author for the *Encyclopedia of Distance Learning* (four-volume set) released by IGI Global.

Keith Sherringham is a trusted advisor and consultant to many organizations in the Australian region. He is invited by the businesses to undertake diagnosis of their problems, provide appropriate prescription and thereby remedy the business problems. With over 15 years of experience, Keith has consulted to corporations, government and medium enterprises on business strategy, operation and management.

Norshuhada Shiratuddin holds a PhD (computer and information science) from the University of Strathclyde, Glasgow, Scotland; MSc in IT from the University of Nottingham, and BSc from UMIST, Manchester, UK. She is currently the deputy dean of research and postgraduate studies in the Faculty of Information Technology, Universiti Utara Malaysia. Her research interests include electronic books/multimedia design and development, Web publishing and mobile application development. She is actively publishing her works in international journals, proceedings, books and monographs, particularly research findings on digital content in education. She also has won many national and international research awards.

Mark Siegal is a program analyst at the National Library of Medicine in Bethesda, MD. He has a BS in communication from Cornell University and a certificate in epidemiology from Tufts University. His publications have appeared in *Molecular Nutrition, Nutrition and the MD*, and *Preventive Nutrition: A Comprehensive Guide for Health Professionals*.

Anastasia S. Spiliopoulou is a lawyer, LL.M., and member of the Athens Bar Association. She has an extended experience as a lawyer, while she has been involved in various research and business affairs. Her LL.M.'s postgraduated degree, from the Athens University Law School, has been taken place with specific emphasis given to the investigation of the multiple regulatory aspects related to the Internet (infrastructure, services, software, and content). During the latest years, she had a major participation in matters related to telecommunications & broadcasting policy, in Greece and abroad, within the framework of the Information Society. She has been involved in current research and business activities, as a specialist for e-commerce, electronic signatures, e-contracts, e-security and other information society applications. She is author or co-author of more than 70 recognised works in the international literature. She currently works as an OTE's (Hellenic Telecoms S.A.) lawyer for the Department of Regulatory Issues, of the General OTE's Directorate for Regulatory Affairs.

Murat M. Tanik is a professor in the Department of Electrical and Computer Engineering, University of Alabama at Birmingham, Alabama. He is the former president of the Society for Design and Process Science (www.sdpsnet.org). His research interests include component-oriented enterprise systems, component-oriented embedded software, service oriented architecture, and quantum information theory. His undergraduate is from METU, Turkey and he obtained his MS and PhD degrees in computer science from Texas A&M University

Matthew Tatham has over 5 years experience working as a manager and a supervisor in a variety of business environments including large multinationals and smaller more intricate organisations. Currently, he is managing the sales and marketing aspects of Alacrity. Matthew has an intimate knowledge of the mobile data space and specialises in security aspect of mobility – especially its relevance to business.

Amit Tiwary is practising business IT alignment consultant with 25 years of IT experience, and his management and technical portfolio includes project management, enterprise wide solution architecture using various standard frameworks, consulting on all aspects of methodology and process for software development, integration with legacy and other systems, Data conversion and loading from legacy systems to CRM based systems, initiating and conducting training programs, requirements modelling, system modelling, metrics, system development and testing. Amit has an executive MBA from Australia Graduate school of Management (AGSM part of University of NSW) and master's degree in IT from R.M.I.T. He has authored multiple papers in area of project management using metrics, collaboration between business, government and academics.

Bharti Trivedi (MSc, Comp. Sc.; PhD, candidate/researcher) is an IT consultant as well trainer on computer science combining more than 13 years of experience She has worked with leading private IT sectors and afterwards started her own consultancy in academic IT field. In addition, she is a senior visiting faculty at MS University, Vadodara, India. She is a life member of Computer Society of India (CSI) and member of (Indian institute of Material Management). She has published many articles in technical newsletters. She is member of board of studies at P.I.M.R Indore (College for Engineering and Management).

Ralf Wagner holds the SVI endowed chair of International Direct Marketing at the DMCC – Dialog Marketing Competence Center at the University of Kassel, Germany. Professor Wagner's research focuses on four domains: the impact of different cultures on marketing interactions, particularly the dialogue-oriented marketing measures; change in marketing concepts, where change in customers' value priorities, self concepts and media usage as well as technical developments are considered; competitive interactions and new opportunities for competitive intelligence enabled by digital information environments; and the development and adoption of new quantitative methods for empirical marketing research. Before joining the DMCC at the University of Kassel, Professor Wagner taught at the Bielefeld University, Germany. He is currently teaching at the Academy of National Economy in Moscow, University of Information Technology and Management in Rzeszow (Poland) and the International Business School at the University of Vilnius (Lithuania).

Mindy Wu (Master of IT, Information System Management) is undertaking her PhD level research at the University of Western Sydney (UWS), Australia. Her specific research focus includes the issues and challenges in extending the Enterprise Architecture with mobility and creating a model for Mobility Enterprise Architecture (M-EA). She is in the second year of her PhD studies starting from July of 2006. Mindy is a member of the emerging technologies sub-group with AeIMS and Mobile Internet Research and Applications Group (MIRAG) research groups at the University of Western Sydney. She is also a student member of Australian Computer Society (ACS) and is active in attending various forums, seminars and discussion groups.

Xu Heng is an assistant professor in the College of Information Sciences and Technology, The Pennsylvania State University. She received her PhD in information systems from the National University of Singapore (2005). She was a recipient of IBM PhD Fellowship (2004) and Singapore Millennium Postdoctoral Fellowship Award (2005-2006). She also won the Infocomm Development Authority Gold Medal and Prize (2006) for the best PhD dissertation in the School of Computing at the National University of Singapore. She has worked on managerial issues arising out of mobile commerce (location based systems) such as consumer privacy. Her research focus is on the convergence of information, technology and people with the overall goal of understanding the use and consequences of ubiquitous information environments. Her research projects have been dealing with privacy and security, human-computer interaction, and technology innovation adoption. She has also worked on managerial issues arising out of mobile commerce

Houman Younessi, PhD, is professor of science, engineering and management at the Rensselaer Polytechnic Institute – Hartford Graduate Campus where he also leads the faculty and is in charge of all academic programs. He is also the director of Rensselaer Initiative in Systems Engineering (RISE). Houman is an internationally renowned educator, practitioner, consultant and investigator. He is the inventor of the SBM (State Behavior Modeling) method and the co-inventor of the OPEN methodology and the new paradigm of recombinant programming. Houman earned his PhD in computer science in the area of software processes; this work has been further extended into many writings including a number of books and papers most of which deal with issues pertinent to the subject matter of the thesis to be examined. Furthermore, he has been a practitioner as well as a researcher in the broad area of business process, business engineering, information systems and software engineering (process) for over 20 years. He has examined numerous PhD and other higher degree theses during the course of his academic work. Dr. Younessi combines world class research based knowledge with recognized industry experience to bring forth innovations in research as well as in the classroom and to industry where his consultation is regularly sought by many leading organizations. A multi-disciplinarian, he has publications and expertise in many fields including software engineering, information systems, business and enterprise management and enterprise modeling and co-design, decision science, managerial economics and econometrics, and sustainable development. Dr. Younessi is regularly invited to speak at many prestigious venues.

Syamsul Bahrin Zaibon holds an MSc in multimedia & Internet computing from Loughborough University, UK and a BSc in IT, Universiti Utara Malaysia. He is a lecturer in Multimedia Department, Faculty of Information Technology, Universiti Utara Malaysia. His research interest is in Multimedia and Web design and development. He has also participated in many competitions and won a number of awards.

Wenbing Zhao received the PhD in electrical and computer engineering from the University of California, Santa Barbara, in 2002. Currently, he is an assistant professor in the Department of Electrical and Computer Engineering at Cleveland State University. His current research interests include distributed systems, computer networks, fault tolerance and security. Dr. Zhao has more than 40 academic publications.

Dirk Werth is head of the Business Integration Technologies group at the Institute for Information Systems at the German Research Centre for Artificial Intelligence in Saarbruecken, Germany. He was project manager and general project coordinator of several national and international R&D projects. Furthermore, he holds lectures on enterprise resource planning and business integration at Saarland University, Germany. His main research areas are collaborative business processes, business integration and enterprise resource management.

Rasika Withanage obtained his Higher National Diploma in management from the Association of Business Executives, UK. He started his career as a corporate sales manager and moved in to marketing communications and brand management. Recently, he obtained his MBA from the University of Wales, UK for the research of 'Creating value to brands by redefining brand rules in mobile phone industry in Sri Lanka'. Rasika gained experience by serving in the fields of Leisure, Banking, Media, PR, Advertising and Telecommunications for over a period of 12 years. Currently he is working as Manager, Brands Development and Management for Broadband Services and Fixed Wireless Telephony products In a Subsidiary of a Leading Telecom Group in Sri Lanka.

Index